BASIC HANDBOOK

OF

Child Psychiatry

VOLUME THREE

BASIC HANDBOOK
OF
Child Psychiatry

Joseph D. Noshpitz / Editor-in-Chief

VOLUME THREE

Therapeutic Interventions

SAUL I. HARRISON

EDITOR

Basic Books, Inc., Publishers / New York

To all those

who strive to ease the pain

and better the lives of troubled children

these books are dedicated

CONTENTS

PART A / Individual Therapies

PART B / Family and Group Therapies

Contents

Contents

CONTRIBUTORS

PHILIP BALCH, PH.D.
Associate Professor of Psychology, University of Arizona, Tucson, Arizona.

IRVING N. BERLIN, M.D.
Professor of Psychiatry and Pediatrics, Director, Division of Child and Adolescent Psychiatry and Children's Psychiatric Center, School of Medicine, University of Mexico, Albuquerque, New Mexico; Chairman, Task Force on Treatment and Education of the American Psychiatric Association.

NORMAN R. BERNSTEIN, M.D.
Professor of Psychiatry, University of Illinois, Chicago; Consultant to the Department of Plastic and Reconstructive Surgery at the University of Chicago, Chicago, Illinois.

BRUNO BETTELHEIM, PH.D.
Stella M. Rowley Distinguished Service Professor of Education, Psychology, and Psychiatry, University of Chicago; Director Emeritus of the Sonia Shankman Orthogenic School, University of Chicago, Chicago, Illinois.

GASTON E. BLOM, M.D.
Professor of Psychiatry and Elementary and Special Education, Michigan State University; Medical Coordinator, University Center for International Rehabilitation, Michigan State University, East Lansing, Michigan.

JUSTIN D. CALL, M.D.
Professor and Chief of Child and Adolescent Psychiatry Division, Department of Psychiatry and Human Behavior, School of Medicine, University of California, Irvine, California.

MAGDA CAMPBELL, M.D.
Associate Professor of Psychiatry, New York University Medical Center; Director, Children's

Psychopharmacology Unit, New York University Medical Center, New York, New York.

DONALD J. CAREK, M.D.
Chief, Youth Division, Department of Psychiatry and Behavioral Sciences, Medical University of South Carolina, Charleston, South Carolina.

JAMES P. COMER, M.D.
Professor of Psychiatry, Yale University Child Study Center, New Haven, Connecticut.

LLOYD O. ECKHARDT, M.D.
Assistant Professor of Child Psychiatry and Pediatrics, University of Colorado, Denver, Colorado.

RUDOLF EKSTEIN, PH.D.
Training and Supervising Analyst, Los Angeles Psychoanalytic Institute, Southern California Psychoanalytic Institute; Regular Guest Professor, University of Vienna, Vienna, Austria.

WILLIAM A. ELLIS, M.D.
Associate Clinical Professor of Psychiatry, Yale University Child Study Center and Health Services, New Haven, Connecticut.

NORBERT B. ENZER, M.D.
Professor and Chairman, Department of Psychiatry, Michigan State University, East Lansing, Michigan.

MAURICE FREEHILL, ED.D.
Professor and Chairman of Educational Psychology, University of Washington, Seattle, Washington.

ERNA FURMAN
Faculty, Cleveland Center for Research in Child Development; Assistant Clinical Professor, De-

partment of Psychiatry, Case Western Reserve School of Medicine, Cleveland, Ohio.

RICHARD A. GARDNER, M.D.
Associate Clinical Professor of Child Psychiatry, Columbia University, College of Physicians and Surgeons, New York; Faculty, William A. White Psychoanalytic Institute, New York, New York.

I. LEE GISLASON, M.D.
Assistant Adjunct Professor of Psychiatry and Human Behavior, University of California; Chief, Children's Psychiatric Outpatient Services, University of California, Irvine, California.

SAUL I. HARRISON, M.D.
Professor of Psychiatry, University of Michigan, Ann Arbor, Michigan.

IRENE JAKAB, PH.D., M.D.
Professor of Psychiatry, Western Psychiatric Institute and Clinic, University of Pittsburgh School of Medicine, Pittsburgh, Pennsylvania.

IRVIN A. KRAFT, M.D., P.A.
Clinical Professor of Mental Health, University of Texas School of Public Health, Houston; Clinical Professor of Psychiatry, Baylor College of Medicine, Houston, Texas.

THOMAS R. KRATOCHWILL, PH.D.
Associate Professor of Educational Psychology, University of Arizona, Tucson, Arizona.

STANLEY R. LESSER, M.D.
Associate Professor of Psychiatry, University of Toronto, Toronto; Senior Psychiatrist, Hospital for Sick Children, Toronto, Canada.

ALEXANDER R. LUCAS, M.D.
Head, Section of Child and Adolescent Psychiatry, Mayo Clinic; Professor of Psychiatry, Mayo Medical School, Rochester, Minnesota.

JOHN F. McDERMOTT, JR., M.D.
Professor and Chairman of Psychiatry, John A. Burns School of Medicine, University of Hawaii, Honolulu, Hawaii.

JAMES P. McGEE, PH.D.
Clinical Supervisor of Behavior Therapy, The Sheppard and Enoch Pratt Hospital, Towson, Maryland.

ROBERT J. MARSHALL, PH.D.
Private Practice, Northern Westchester Center for Psychotherapy, Yorktown Heights, New York, New York.

GILBERT C. MORRISON, PH.D., M.D.
Clinical Professor of Psychiatry and Child Psychiatry, College of Medicine, University of California, Irvine, California; Supervising and Training Psychoanalyst, Southern California Psychoanalytic Institute, Beverly Hills, California.

WILLIAM C. MORSE, M.D.
Professor of Educational Psychiatry and Psychology, School of Education, University of Michigan, Ann Arbor, Michigan.

JOSEPH D. NOSHPITZ, M.D.
Director of Education and Training, Department of Psychiatry, Children's Hospital—National Medical Center, Washington, D.C.

DORIS OLCH, PH.D.
Associate Professor of Educational Psychology, University of Washington, Seattle, Washington.

CECIL H. PATTERSON, PH.D.
Professor Emeritus of Educational Psychology (retired), University of Illinois, Champaign, Illinois.

ELVA ORLOW POZNANSKI, M.D.
Professor of Psychiatry, University of Illinois, Chicago, Illinois.

DANE G. PRUGH, M.D.
Professor of Psychiatry and Pediatrics, University of Colorado, Denver, Colorado.

MARK M. RAVLIN
Director, Behavioral Science Education Project, Washtenaw County Community Mental Health Center, Ann Arbor, Michigan.

DAVID E. REISER, M.D.
Director of Child Psychiatry, Granite Community Mental Health Center, Salt Lake City, Utah.

ALAN J. ROSENTHAL, M.D.
Director, Children's Health Council, Palo Alto; Clinical Associate Professor of Psychiatry, Stanford University Medical School, Stanford, California.

SUSANNAH RUBENSTEIN, M.A.
Associate in Research, Yale University Child Study Center, New Haven; Executive Administrative Assistant, Department of Mental Health, State of Connecticut, Hartford, Connecticut.

DONALD H. SAIDEL, PH.D.
Director, Adolescent Inpatient Service, The

Sheppard and Enoch Pratt Hospital, Towson, Maryland.

JACQUELYN SEEVAK SANDERS, PH.D.
Director, Sonia Schankman Orthogenic School, University of Chicago; Lecturer, Department of Education, University of Chicago, Chicago, Illinois.

JOHN E. SCHOWALTER, M.D.
Director of Training and Professor of Pediatrics and Psychiatry, Yale University Child Study Center, New Haven, Connecticut.

RENA SCHULMAN, M.S.
Associate Director, Jewish Board of Family and Children Services, New York, New York.

MOHAMMAD SHAFII, M.D.
Professor of Psychiatry and Director of Child Psychiatric Services, University of Louisville School of Medicine, Louisville, Kentucky.

LARRY B. SILVER, M.D.
Deputy Director, National Institute of Mental Health, Rockville, Maryland.

BERTRAM SLAFF, M.D.
Director, Adolescent Psychiatry Clinical Service, Mount Sinai Medical Center; Associate Clinical Professor of Psychiatry, Mount Sinai School of Medicine, City University of New York, New York, New York.

EDWARD SPERLING, M.D.
Associate Clinical Professor, Department of Psychiatry, Albert Einstein College of Medicine; Director, Child-Adolescent Division, Bronx Municipal Hospital Center, New York, New York.

LAWRENCE A. STONE, M.D.
Clinical Associate Professor of Psychiatry, Uni-

versity of Texas Health Science Center, San Antonio, Texas.

SUZANNE T. VAN AMERONGEN, PH.D., M.D.
Clinical Professor in Child Psychiatry, Boston University School of Medicine, Boston, Massachusetts; Supervising and Training Analyst, Boston Psychoanalytic Society Institute, Boston, Massachusetts.

JANE WALDRON, D.S.W.
Assistant Professor of Psychiatry, John A. Burns School of Medicine, University of Hawaii, Honolulu, Hawaii.

JACK C. WESTMAN, M.D.
Professor of Psychiatry, University of Wisconsin, Madison, Wisconsin.

RALPH J. WETZEL, PH.D.
Private Practice, Tucson, Arizona.

MARY FRENCH WHITESIDE, PH.D.
Assistant Professor of Psychology in the Psychiatry Department, University of Michigan Medical School, Ann Arbor; Faculty, Ann Arbor Center for the Family, Ann Arbor, Michigan.

DANIEL T. WILLIAMS, M.D.
Assistant Clinical Professor of Psychiatry, Columbia University, College of Physicians and Surgeons, New York; Director, Pediatric Neuropsychiatry Service, Columbia-Presbyterian Medical Center, New York, New York.

DAVID ZINN, M.D.
Director, Child and Adolescent Psychiatry, Psychosomatic and Psychiatric Institute, Michael Reese Medical Center, Chicago; Clinical Assistant Professor of Psychiatry, University of Chicago, Chicago, Illinois.

ACKNOWLEDGMENTS

The preparation of this volume was facilitated inestimably by the generous support provided by the University of Michigan's Department of Psychiatry. Particularly valuable was the stimulation and counsel offered by colleagues there as well as by those from around the country who collaborated in the preparation of the *Basic Handbook of Child Psychiatry*—notably Joseph D. Noshpitz, our co-editors, and the authors who contributed to this volume. Also appreciated was the secretarial assistance of Martha Fisch and Deborah Dettling Steinaway and the helpful and patient expertise extended by Herb Reich and his staff at Basic Books, which was of a rare quality.

Saul I. Harrison

PREFACE

Child psychiatry is now in its seventieth year. It has passed through an early phase of clinic practice, a later period of intense concern with inpatient care, and, most recently, a move into the universities. In the course of this evolution child psychiatry has advanced from a set of unique skills and techniques to an ever more complex scientific endeavor. It involves a basic science dimension, a wide array of specialized practices, and an increasingly intricate universe of research. Along with these have come an extensive literature, now international in scope, and an ever-widening impact on the cultural generally and on medicine and psychiatry in particular.

So rapidly has this growth proceeded that it has heretofore been difficult to find any single work that embraced the full complexity of the development of child psychiatry. The emphasis of most authors has been on specialized aspects of the field; only a few have attempted more comprehensive efforts in the form of textbooks, and some of these have tended to be rather brief surveys of major topics. As a result, teachers and residents in the many training programs and individual practitioners in the communities have long felt the need for an additional book—comprehensive in its scope—in which the array of topics would be sufficiently exhaustive and in which the study of each area would be examined in enough depth to satisfy student, scholar, and practitioner alike. It was the pressure to fill this need that brought forth the idea of the *Basic Handbook of Child Psychiatry*. The same sense of urgency led the more than 250 contributors and the six editors to commit time, energy, and industry to the accomplishment of this task. And it was in response to those pressures that the authors, editors, and publisher worked together for six years to produce these volumes. If their undertaking succeeds in its intent, the *Handbook* should provide a primary reference source for many of the questions and needs that arise within the discipline. It is with this hope that the *Basic Handbook* is presented.

The arrangement of materials in these volumes speaks for something of the logic of the discipline of child psychiatry. To begin with there is an account of the first basic science of the field, a detailing of *child development*. This is followed by a series of brief descriptions (the sort of statements that can be read quickly in connection with individual clinical cases) of different *varieties of child development*. Next comes a recounting of one of the major subdisciplines of child psychiatry, the *nature of assessment*, a section written in large part by Dr. Richard L. Cohen. These three topics comprise Volume I. The second volume is given over to the second basic science of child psychiatry, that of *child psychopathology*. Included here are studies of etiology and nosology and an account of the more important syndromes. Volume III follows, and treats another great subdiscipline, the field of *therapeutics*. The final volume, Volume IV, covers the field of *prevention* and contains a series of studies on the impact of current cultural issues on children and child psychiatry.

It should be noted that the *Handbook* is calculatedly eclectic. It is written by the working child psychiatrist as well as by the researcher and by other mental health professionals; a variety of views and opinions are therefore presented. Differences will be found among theories of development, techniques of assessment, modes of psychopathology, and approaches to treatment. No one will agree with them all—the editors certainly do not. Nonetheless they are all serious positions that demand respect if not accord. Such is the state of the art.

Grants from the Commonwealth Fund, the Maurice Falk Medical Fund, and the Grove Foundation supported the development of these volumes, and the funds are gratefully acknowledged.

Early on, Ginger Bausch lent the use of the offices of the American Academy of Child Psychiatry in Washington as a mailing address and a site to store *Handbook* materials, and Jeanne DeJarnette took on the coordination of the *Handbook* as an after-hours job. She acted as guardian angel, financial manager and factotum, kept track of documents, typed correspondence, maintained files, saw that people were informed about what was happening, and, all in all, made the enterprise work. Three years after it began, the central effort shifted from her capable hands to the secretarial staff of the Department of Child Psychiatry at the Children's Hospital National Medical Center. The Chairman of the Department was at that time Jerry Wiener, who gave a full measure of support to the demanding effort that the host of accumulated documents required. Later, Dr. James Egan took over the chairmanship and continued the pattern of unstinting support. Within the department, Mrs. Shirley Wells, ably backed up by Mrs. Penny Nolton, carried the brunt of the responsibilities, and it was she who brought the work to its final form. The sheer time involved was prodigious.

While this was going on in Washington, parallel efforts were being exerted in Pittsburgh by Dr. Cohen and his staff; in Ann Arbor by Dr. Harrison and his people: in Seattle and then in Davis, California, by Dr. Berlin and his associates; in Irvine by Dr. Call and his associates; and in San Antonio by Dr. Larry Stone, his wife Marnette, and others who worked with him. Indeed, when one ponders the amount of university assistance offered to the many authors, as well as the intensive and extensive efforts made by their staffs, it is no small contribution that the *Handbook* received from the academic world in its largest sense. The work entailed a truly massive effort, and it is impossible to list the names of the many, many people who helped it come to fruition.

For the publisher, the *Handbook* was shepherded through its labyrinthine way by the tireless efforts of Herb Reich, Behavioral Science Editor of Basic Books. This involved visits back and forth between Washington, D.C. and New York, endless attention to detail, and a sort of total immersion in the fullness of the effort needed to turn the mass of documents into a printable manuscript. Among the highly skilled staff at Basic Books who labored long hours over the thousands of pages that comprised the manuscript were Arthur Krystal, Kathi Lee, and Harry Lee who undertook the primary copyediting of the original material. Project editors Pamela Dailey and Debra Manette were responsible for final copyediting. Additionally, they cleaned up bibliographies, queried areas of uncertainty, and saw to it that scholarly rigor and clarity of expression prevailed throughout. Maureen Bischoff as editorial manager coordinated the publication work, and all played vital roles in the final outcome.

One final point remains. The original manuscript grew to such excessive proportions that it became necessary to cut out, cut down, and shorten materials. This distressing process was initiated by the publisher and then carried by the several editors, who trimmed and tightened until a shorter, more compact work emerged. In the course of editing, a number of papers were eliminated and several others were shortened. It caused both publisher and editors considerable pain to perform this task, yet it was vital to the actual production of the work. Both the editors and the publisher hope that the outcome will justify the surgery.

JOSEPH D. NOSHPITZ
Washington, D.C.
February 15, 1979

BASIC HANDBOOK

OF

Child Psychiatry

VOLUME THREE

1 / Child Psychiatric Treatment: Status and Prospects

Saul I. Harrison

Currently, the child psychiatric clinician's greatest challenge stems from the widespread demand for treatment. Consequently, more professional time and energy is devoted to therapeutic intervention than to all other child psychiatric clinical activities combined. In addition to these quantitative factors, therapeutic work tends to be the most intellectually demanding of all clinical activities. Inherent in this creative challenge for the clinician is treatment's tendency to be both the most rewarding thing he does and the most frustrating. Of course, this tendency is enhanced by the challenge to be therapeutically effective despite the relative immaturity and limited specificity of current treatment techniques.

In the history of medicine, when a multiplicity of treatments is available for a given condition, there tends to be a high correlation of limited effectiveness for all of them. In addition, whenever a truly definitive child psychiatric treatment has appeared in the past, such as the dietary measures for phenylketonuria, the responsibility for the administration of the treatment has been assigned to pediatricians. This is equally true for adult psychiatry and internal medicine, as exemplified by pellagra and central nervous system syphilis. Perhaps this is consistent with the fact that in both pediatrics and internal medicine the major intellectual challenge is posed by diagnostic work; indeed this tends to outweigh by far the relative simplicity of administering treatment. This will, perhaps, change for the mental health professions as well

if they should develop something resembling a broad-spectrum psychomycin or specific psychobiotics. This fantasy is not as utopian as it may appear; today it is altogether conceivable that physio-chemical genetics or therapy might someday ameliorate or even eliminate mental illness. However, it seems most unlikely that enzymes or other functional macromolecules could by themselves undo the effects of pathogenic experiences without a simultaneous process of unlearning and relearning akin to some of the psychosocial therapies. As Seymour Kety[32] speculated, "There may someday be a biochemistry or a biophysics of memory—but not of memories."

Clinical Specificity

None of the foregoing is intended to minimize the vital importance of diagnostic specificity in child psychiatric work (see volumes I and II). Unfortunately, child psychiatric diagnostic nomenclature is currently limited primarily to classifying clinical description. At best, it has minimal explanatory value regarding etiology or indications for treatment. In consequence, it is relatively simple to assign an appropriate diagnostic label. As the GAP report[22] noted, at our current level of knowledge, it is impossible to devise an ideal, universally useful nosological classificatory system encompassing syntheses of the clinical descriptive observations with psychodynamic, psychosocial, psychobiological, developmental, etiologic, prognostic, and therapeutic considerations. Despite this, clinicians need to match the individual child and his disturbance with specific therapeutic interventions. Irrespective of the orientation, training, and ideology of the clinician, such matching is the intended outcome of diagnostic assessment.

Compounding these limitations to the meaningfulness of diagnostic labels is the additional element of imprecision concerning just what it is about a given therapeutic intervention that is curative. This uncertainty is illustrated vividly by reviewing the history of different therapeutic methods and observing how numerous factors have alternately been lauded as the element essential for therapeutic effectiveness and then damned as useless. Early in this century, for instance, before the ascendancy of psychoanalysis, the most prominent factors within the psychological framework were suggestion, persuasive exhortation, and reassurance. Then, when psychoanalysis first appeared, beneficial results were thought to be a consequence of rediscovering a lost memory accompanied by the abreactive release of dammed-up emotions. Later developments in psychoanalytic thinking saw the emphasis shift to modification of superego standards, identification with the therapist, resolution of transference, increasing emotional discipline in the working through process, insight, the analysis of defenses, and expansion of ego functioning. Concurrently, there has been a similar waxing and waning of attention to learning-behavioral, social, biological, and other factors.

Although they are derived from different conceptual frameworks and expressed in markedly different languages, a considerable overlap exists between some of the aforementioned factors. It is inconceivable that all therapeutic progress with all patients can ever be the product of a unitary therapeutic factor; by the same token, it is highly unlikely that a single therapeutic element ever operates in isolation. Invariably, other influences are simultaneously at work. For instance, the therapeutic relationship itself, as such, inevitably gives rise to corrective emotional experiences. This may not have been explicitly designed by the therapist; indeed, it may be an accidental by-product of the clinician's empathic posture. Nonetheless it invariably exerts some influence.

Unfortunately, a tradition has grown up of mutual exclusivity of different therapeutic modalities. This has led to pseudopolarities of therapeutic approaches. Mental health training programs are all too frequently unidimensional. In a field burdened by ambiguity, the very process of learning tends to evoke discomfort and uncertainty. In turn, this encourages student clinicians to attempt to cope with their distress by jumping aboard what Halleck and Woods[23] designated a "bandwagon" therapy, a process that can readily turn into what Klagsbrun[33] labeled a "Garden of Eden" therapy. For the student there is now only one truth. Such an allegiance reduces the student clinician's anxiety, which is self-reinforcing, and often enjoys institutional support as well. Unfortunately, the search for an illusory certainty risks compromising the clinician's empathic sensitivity; as Adams[2] noted, it can result in forms of egocentrism on the part of both the clinician and the young patient which are remarkable for their similarity. This analogy is based on Piaget's[50] observation that as a consequence of the nature of the relationship between child and adult, the child's thinking tends to be isolated. The child is placed apart; while he believes he is sharing the point of view of the world at large, he actually remains shut off and isolated in his own viewpoint.

Varieties of Therapeutic Modalities

There are numerous modalities available to the therapist. There are the psychodynamically oriented intensive exploratory individual psychotherapies, supportive psychotherapies, brief time limited psychotherapies, family therapy, filial therapy, parent counseling and/or therapy, a variety of behavior therapies, various group therapies, a range of pharmacotherapeutic agents, milieu therapy, a multitude of psychoeducational approaches, special symptom-focused remediation such as tutoring or speech therapy, hypnotherapy, biofeedback, and on and on. To the extent that a clinician is committed to a specific value set, he is likely to combine only certain therapeutic modes while excluding others from this wide array of choices. It cannot be stressed too frequently that the use of these approaches singly or in combination should stem less from the clinician's preferences than from the assessment of the patient.

In an effort to enhance clarity of exposition, this volume on therapeutic intervention has been subdivided into separate chapters devoted to different modalities of therapy. This may well reflect an isolating tendency comparable to what Piaget has described for children. Although the artificiality of this organization inevitably cannot convey the multidimensionality of most therapeutic undertakings, it hopefully does reflect the currently prevailing preferences and expertise of most clinicians. This is a burgeoning field, and in outlining this volume, somewhere it was necessary to establish limits; certain developing approaches are therefore not represented—for example, primal scream, cosmic consciousness, acupuncture, TM, Zen, Erhard Seminars Training, and so on.

On one hand, the field of child psychiatric treatment may easily be perceived as a state of undisciplined chaos; on the other, however, any effort to bring order to it risks creating a form of tunnel vision. This would not serve the clinician well. As the following chapters show, the clinician must embrace a shifting pluralism which encompasses sociology, various types of psychology, genetics, biochemistry, physiology, and so on. Since these disciplines all employ different concepts and language, this demands multilingual thinking, at least to the extent of not automatically and routinely eliminating considerations from any of these perspectives. The problem is to avoid at the same time becoming a disorganized conceptual Tower of Babel. This volume is explicitly multidimensional. In the opening chapters, several authors describe a multitude of available therapeutic interventions. This is followed by a group of discussions which examine the special considerations required by certain developmental, psychopathological, and social factors regardless of the modality of treatment. Such a multiaxial approach inevitably includes discrepant meanings for identical language. For example, from the perspective of biological interventions, "environmental manipulation" includes psychotherapy. When the focus is on psychological interventions, however, psychotherapy and environmental manipulation are conceived of as two distinctly different processes.

A more common result of this conceptual-linguistic versatility is the tendency to obscure essential similarities and areas of overlap. What happens is that different words and phrases which mean the same actually sound quite different because of their derivation from different schools of thought. In 1946 this was highlighted vividly by Witmer's *Psychiatric Interviews with Children*[57] in which ten detailed child guidance cases are reported by nine psychotherapists, many of whom represented different schools of psychotherapy. Witmer noted that the differences between the allegedly discrepant theoretical frames of reference faded when applied in actual clinical practice. Observing that the several therapists responded sensitively to what was perceived as the child's needs, Witmer asserted that certain principles basic to all child psychotherapy overshadowed the influence of the therapist's theoretical inclination.

INTERRELATIONSHIP OF BEHAVIORAL AND PSYCHODYNAMIC THERAPIES

Perhaps we are currently observing something comparable in the process of developing. During the 1960s, there was a resurgence of interest and activity in behavioral techniques. This was accompanied by an emphasis on the differences between behavioral and psychodynamic approaches. Eysenck[13] underlined that treatment strategies which employed behavior explicitly should be distinguished from psychotherapy which employs psychological methods. A comparable segregationist attitude was as evident on the psychodynamic side, where similar efforts to demarcate boundaries permeated the literature and educational programs. There was active depreciation of treatment which focused on symptoms; it was assumed, inaccurately as it happened but nevertheless asserted dogmatically, that this could lead only to symptom substitution. Often enough there was a valid basis to this segregation; nevertheless too little attention was paid to the presence of psychological influences in even the most mechanistic behavioral techniques. The inevitable presence of behavioral influences in the "purest" psychological therapies was similarly ignored.

The exaggerated emphasis on this segregation has led to a tendency to neglect noteworthy integrationist efforts. In the 1950s, Mowrer[47] and Dollard and Miller,[12] as they endeavored to examine psychodynamic therapy from a learning-behavioral theory perspective, were able to document cross fertilization. More recently, there have been psychodynamically oriented discussions of children treated by behavioral therapy (e.g., Kessler,[31] Blom[8]). Feather (quoted in Aronson[4]) suggests that some of the effectiveness of systematic desensitization in behavior therapy may be a consequence of enhancing the patient's discrimination between fantasy and reality. Contrariwise, the effectiveness of interpretation in psychoanalysis and related therapies may in part be derived from its desensitizing effect. There have been additional efforts (not focused on work with children) to synthesize these apparently conflicting perspectives, and to do this without minimizing, demeaning, or sacrificing the essential richness of each point of view. Some of these attempts have been made by Alexander,[3] Brady,[10] Feather and Rhoads,[14] Lazarus,[36] Marks and Gelder,[45] Marmor,[46] and Sloane.[54] In fact, Marks[44] has noted that even the term "behavior therapy," which seems so amenable to description and classification when compared to many of the other psychotherapies, has lost much of its meaning. Today it denotes a number of different techniques, many of which Marks asserts have little in common with one another beyond "common lip-service to debatable, theoretical antecedents." In his view, there are more differences than similarities among desensitization, aversion, operant conditioning, modeling, covert sensitization, feedback control, and negative practice. Further, he observes that flooding or implosion is considered to be a behavior therapy, although it was originally conceived by Stampfl in psychodynamic terms; on the other hand, paradoxical intention, an allied technique, is thought of as a form of existential psychotherapy.

Probably the most vivid examples of integration of psychodynamic and behavioral approaches, even though they are not always explicitly conceptualized as such, are to be found in some of the chapters describing what could be designated as the environmental therapies (see chapters 14, 15, 16, 17, 18, 19, 20). Elsewhere, Noshpitz[49] noted what he referred to as a "ping-pong effect" in residential treatment. Behavioral change is initiated in the residential setting while its repercussions are explored concurrently in individual psychotherapeutic sessions so that the action in one arena, and the information stemming from it, augments and illuminates what transpires in the other arena. A case reported by McDermott, Fraiberg, and Harrison[40] vividly illustrates that what occurs in a residential milieu can enhance the understanding of the individual psychotherapist, and what transpires in the individual psychotherapeutic sessions can contribute to the formulation of behavioral management techniques for the milieu. Blom[8] summarized it succinctly by noting that change is "capable of being accomplished both from the inside out and the outside in."

Some years ago, the distinguished behavioral therapist Dr. Richard B. Stuart presented videotapes of his clinical work with one family to the predominantly psychodynamically oriented child psychiatry staff of the University of Michigan's Children's Psychiatric Hospital. What ensued illustrated the rich potential of these interrelationships as well as their complexity. Although two apparently opposing views of the same therapeutic endeavor will be described herein, it cannot be emphasized too strongly that the intent is not to underscore the correctness of one point of view by using the other as a straw man. The purpose is to illustrate that both perspectives can convey the impression of simultaneous validity and mutual incompatibility.

The author's recollection of *his perceptions* of that presentation were that Dr. Stuart began with charts quantifying the frequency of the use of reinforcers and the appearance of specific undesirable behaviors, both of which rapidly decreased. The audience was much impressed with the correlation between the intervention and the behavioral results, until they viewed the tapes.

Dr. Stuart had become acquainted with the family through the juvenile court, where several of the children had recent involvement because of minor delinquencies. All the manifest difficulties reportedly started shortly after the death of the father. In this home, he had been the nurturant, child-rearing, homemaking parent, whereas the mother was the breadwinnner. His death had been unanticipated and sudden, occurring while several of the children were at home and the mother at work. After his death, all the children experienced varying degrees of difficulty in school and in the community. These difficulties overwhelmed the mother, whose only means of dealing with her children was to have a male neighbor paddle them. Such physical measures had not been resorted to while the father was alive.

The taped therapeutic sessions were conducted with the family in their home. The first session began chaotically with what sounded like several of the children playing radios tuned loudly to different stations. Although this noise made it difficult to conceive of verbal communication, four-letter words were readily perceived, as simultaneous shouting and interrupting prevailed. Meanwhile, the mother sat quietly, apparently apathetic, disheveled, and overwhelmed.

Making himself heard above the din, Dr. Stuart asked the youngsters to turn off their radios. Then he asserted that he would be working with the family on a regular basis to help them overcome their difficulties. As he realized that his assistance might be required in the interim between the scheduled meetings, he gave the mother and the children telephone numbers where he could be reached twenty-four hours a day. He then tried to determine their concept of their difficulties; the children described this as insufficient money or items that money could purchase. Although finances were not a substantial problem, the therapist responded by using money as a reinforcer. The children were to be rewarded with coins for avoiding certain undesirable behaviors, such as interrupting, talking rudely and disrespectfully to one another, swearing, and forcing others to shout by playing the radio loudly. The rewards were accompanied by what appeared to be the therapist's approval, and he encouraged them to engage in interactions which could resolve some of the issues that were keeping them apart.

The videotapes of subsequent sessions confirmed the dramatic change in the children that had been demonstrated in the charts. The most striking change perceived by the audience, however, and one which had not been charted, was in the mother. She was now responsive to her children; she appeared alert and well groomed; and it was evident that she focused a great deal of attention on Dr. Stuart. He agreed that the change in the mother was striking, and he attributed it to two factors: (1) the mother learned (or relearned) some assertive strategies for child rearing, and (2) the diminution of the children's negative behaviors and the increase in their positive behaviors reduced the pressure under which the mother lived. These changes resulted from Dr. Stuart's employment of the three sets of skills which he conceptualized as necessary to effect therapeutic change.[55] The first of these were service delivery skills, which increased the client's readiness to accept constructive suggestions. The second requirement consisted of behavior change skills designed to alter focal behavior. The third essential was maintenance skills; there differed from those techniques needed to change the focal behavior in the first place. Instead, they were specifically designed to help the client anticipate and learn to deal with potential threats to the newly acquired changes. In the tape and vignettes just described, Dr. Stuart perceived the service delivery skills as including elements such as structuring the treatment environment and establishing a trustful relationship with the mother and the children. The behavior change skill included shaping constructive social interaction during the session and contracting for the predictable exchange of privileges and responsibilities between sessions. He summarized his view of the therapy illustrated on the tape as "an effort to first shape some level of effective management with the family and to model these techniques for the mother who is expected later to assume them herself."[55]

Without necessarily assuming that any of Stuart's observations or formulations were incorrect, the psychodynamically oriented clinicians in the au-dience perceived it from a markedly different perspective. They observed that the striking changes in the mother were neither charted, nor otherwise highlighted, nor were these alterations a consequence of any focal technology for promoting behavioral changes since none was directed toward her. These colleagues questioned whether there might not be a factor operating that was more potent than her reaction to the marked changes in her children's behavior. For example, to what extent could the changes in the mother be a response to the therapist's twenty-four-hour a day availability and to the sensitivity of his courtly and respectful demeanor toward her, even when she appeared apathetic? They reasoned that the children's negative behavior may well have been an effort to evoke a response from this seemingly indifferent, uncaring mother, who had initially sat impassive and apathetic while the children bombarded her with epithets. It was recalled that earlier, when the mother had first tried to cope with the children, she had enlisted the aid of an outside man. Could it be that the mother's new-found responsiveness was secondary to the therapist's graciously forceful participation with the family? More than that, when the mother responded to the therapist, had this then diminished the children's need for outlandish behavior? The audience was impressed also with Dr. Stuart's sensitive handling of interactions within the family; he had worked in the manner of a highly skilled family therapist. Thus, this psychodynamically oriented audience perceived the behavioral reinforcement that had been so rigorously quantified and precisely charted as a relatively minor therapeutic intervention. In response, it was pointed out that a psychiatric resident, who presumably possessed service delivery skills but lacked a mastery of focal technology designed to promote behavioral change, had previously attempted treatment without success. Nonetheless these questions persisted.

EVOLVING IDENTITY OF FAMILY THERAPY

It is unwise to render historical judgments about developments that are still in process. However, it does seem safe to say that over the course of its brief two decades of productively creative activity, significant aspects of family therapy have become increasingly segregationist. It has been striving for a special identity, one that is not just another modality that a clinician can add to his roster of therapeutic options. Thus, there have been declarations that family therapy is a distinctly unique perspective on the human condition. As such, it is asserted that family therapy is not conceptually interchangeable with other therapies. It goes further still and casts away the medical model, disease conceptions of emotional disturbance, and the individualistic and intrapsychic emphases in psychodynamic psychiatry. One may well question whether the vigorous maintenance of these increasingly impenetrable boundaries reflects insufficient distinction between the *study* of family processes and their *treatment*. (These topics are addressed in separate chapters in this handbook [see chapter 7 and volume II]). It is easy to envision that the investigation of families would be enhanced by segregation of research, in a manner analogous to a university's departmental structure, lending rigor and systematization to the area of study. On the other hand, therapy and the people seeking its help are different from departments; they are generally enriched by integration.

This segregationist trend appears to be gaining momentum. One of its unfortunate by-products is that some child-oriented clinicians are apparently becoming discouraged and are not benefiting from the fruitful productivity of the family therapy field. At the same time, there are encouraging indications. On an empirical level there is expanding integration of the systems-oriented transactional model with the developmental and psychodynamic models (e.g., Kramer[35]). McDermott and Char[39] point out that, on the one hand, systems theory appropriately suggests that the sum of the parts does not explain the whole; but on the other, the converse is also true: Knowledge of the whole family system does not necessarily entail understanding its parts—particularly those parts that are developing most rapidly. They recall that child psychiatry has struggled long and hard to establish that treating children's difficulties often requires more than counseling and treating parents. Malone[42] discusses the advantages of flexibly combining therapeutic work with individuals, family subsystems, and total families. In the course of this, he asserts that the "central concept involved is the inseparability of internal and external." This strikes a chord remarkably reminiscent of Blom's[8] observation about the interrelatability and interdependence of the behavioral and psychodynamic perspectives.

PHARMACOTHERAPY AND PSYCHOTHERAPY

The issue of combining multiple treatments that affect different aspects of the same difficulty in the same person is illustrated most vividly by the relationships between the psychotherapies and the pharmacotherapies. Over the past two decades their respective advocates have been characterized by considerable competitiveness, which has readily escalated into a mutually antagonistic exclusiveness. From a rational standpoint, prescribing medication should not preclude paying attention to intrapsychic and interpersonal factors, nor should the employment of psychotherapy necessarily preclude using medication or environmental intervention. Nevertheless, there has been a marked tendency for proponents of each treatment modality to view the other with suspicious concern and righteous indignation. This has frequently resulted in each behaving as if the other did not exist while ritualistically giving one another lip service. In fact, the choice of treatment method stemmed more from the clinician's education, orientation, skills, preferences, and so on, than it did from specific clinical indications and demonstrated effectiveness. The difficulty of building conceptual and empirical bridges between the two forms of treatment is illustrated by the discussions of the treatment of minimal brain dysfunction that follow in chapters 23, 37, and 38.

The accumulation of knowledge has exposed increasing numbers of physicians to the theory and practice of both psychotherapy and pharmacotherapy. With this, the competition between the two has been diminishing, and increasingly they are being judiciously employed together. Nevertheless, a scholarly GAP report[20] devoted to the paradoxes, problems, and progress in the interrelationships between pharmacotherapy and psychotherapy asserts (on pages 272 and 273) such physicians are unable to translate psychological conflict into cellular malfunction or biochemical dysfunction into behavioral difficulties. As a result, they often behave like "split-brain preparations." Thus, clinicians tend to be comfortable with either frame of reference when considered individually. Once faced with those complex therapeutic tasks which require the simultaneous use of both frames of reference, it becomes all too clear that there is a lack of any coherent integrating theory, or even of interrelating hypotheses, that combine what is known psychodynamically with what is known psychopharmacologically. Hence the reference to the split-brain preparation; such an experimental subject is capable of satisfactorily performing those tasks which have been learned with the one cerebral hemisphere, or with the other. When, however, it is faced with the kind of multifaceted challenges that require knowledge and skills from both hemispheres, not only does it fail to coordinate the two halves of the brain, but it may fall prey to a disabling onslaught of confused thinking and action.

Mandell[43] has labeled the need to forget psychodynamics selectively while prescribing psychotropic medication the "peek-a-boo" use of drugs. Hopefully, as a consequence of a growing number of promising contributions this will diminish in the future. Thus, in an investigation that represents a promising example of integration, Gittelman-Klein and Klein[19] studied imipramine's effect on youngsters with school refusal. From this they derived the concept that tricyclics reduce primary separation anxiety without affecting anticipatory anxiety.

Universal Seminal Concepts

There are certain seminal concepts integral to almost every therapeutic transaction. This is true even though any given concept is likely to be an integral part of a conceptual framework that is linked with a particular therapeutic strategy. This phenomenon makes it possible to relate truly different treatment modalities. For instance, the concept of operant reinforcement is an integral part of behavioral-learning theory; at the same time, it is hard to conceive of any therapeutic transaction to which this concept would not be applicable. Similarly, such psychoanalytic and/or psychodynamic concepts as transference and countertransference merit serious consideration in exclusively pharmacologic or behavioral therapeutic interactions. Indeed, it is likely that the operant reinforcements employed by the clinician, and how he or she elects to deal with the patient's transference reactions, are significant, if not central, in shaping the nature of every therapy.

Therapeutic Effectiveness

Assessing change and delineating the factors responsible for it represent one of the most challenging methodological issues in psychiatry. It is a particularly complex part of the investigations of the outcome of the psychotherapies (as has been discussed from different perspectives by Heinicke and Strassmann,[26] Levitt,[37] and Malan[41]). The reesearchers underscore the paucity of clinically meaningful, methodologically sound, rigorously executed investigations that publicly document the value of treatment. They point to the wide gap between these findings and the results reported by committed clinicians who are convinced of psychotherapy's value. Many of the chapters in this volume concern themselves with a particular treatment and contain information about investigations into its effectiveness. It is striking that the outcomes of different treatments (with the exception of pharmacological therapy) reveal insufficient differences on which to base discriminative employment. Thus far, objective studies make it appear that all the different things the convinced clinician does with enthusiasm prove to be equally effective (e.g., Frank[16]). Thus, it seems as if clinicians might as well employ those treatments they are persuaded that they do well and in which they have confidence. After all, comparative studies of the results of different therapies enabled Luborsky, Singer, and Luborsky[38] to conclude that like the dodo bird of Alice in Wonderland "everybody has won and all must have prizes." Given the therapist's competence, enthusiasm, and expectations, however, it is still possible that this apparent equality of effectiveness may be attributed to factors other than similarities inherent in all of the treatments, such as the helping relationship with the therapist. Most significantly, it might also have to do with the fact that there has been very little that is specific and discriminating in the prescription of different treatments for different disturbances. It seems clear that the choice of treatment stems far more from the therapeutic-professional system's institutional or personal preferences than from an assessment of the recipient's individual differences.

The critical tenor of this commentary should not be misconstrued; it is not advocated that professionals try to apply treatments for which they are ill prepared and not qualified. Rather, professionals are urged to be open and ready to consider a wide variety of treatments in the course of clinical diagnostic assessments. In this way they can maximize the possibility of matching the individual child and/or family and their disturbance with the most appropriate specific therapeutic intervention. This may mean that the evaluating professional may not be qualified to personally implement the recommended treatment, or combination of treatments, and will have to arrange for some other clinician(s) to administer it.

Selecting the Appropriate Treatment

To underscore the value of selective therapeutic discrimination based on diagnostic considerations, illustrative clinical syndromes and examples will be cited.

HYPERACTIVITY

Currently, perhaps the most prominent clinical symptom in children for which there is no standard unitary therapeutic approach is hyperactivity. The hyperactivity might represent a means for expressing or discharging anxiety resulting from an unconscious intrapsychic conflict over aggression. In such an instance some would recommend judicious time-limited use of antianxiety medication while instituting definitive counseling and/or exploratory psychotherapy, which is generally considered to be the treatment of choice at our current level of knowledge. On the other hand, if the hyperactivity is a consequence of minimal brain dysfunction, the clinician will endeavor to provide externally the controls that the youngster lacks internally. To do so may require a combination of stimulant medication and regulation of the child's life via supportive-suppressive, avoidant measures (such as helping the child learn to isolate himself from distressing stimuli).

These markedly different therapeutic approaches to a hyperactive youngster are not truly interchangeable. When the hyperactivity stems from underlying anxiety, regulating the child's life may indeed result in some diminution of the symptom; but this symptom relief is likely to be accomplished at the cost of inducing passivity as a means of handling the unconscious aggression. In other words, the inappropriate treatment might appear to be effective because it induces a new and unnecessary handicap that proves to be less troublesome to parents and teachers. On the other hand, when the hyperactivity is a consequence of organicity and the child is offered psychotherapeutic interpretations regarding underlying conflicts, these intepretations tend to be perceived as stimulating and may well cause the child to become excited and more hyperactive. In fact, this may be accentuated by the accuracy of the interpretations, because it is not the underlying psychological conflicts which are primarily pathogenic so much as the deficiency in internal controls.

The several foregoing therapeutic approaches to hyperactivity focus exclusively on the individual child. Despite the fact that the treatment may be both appropriate and effective, it may serve simultaneously to counterproductively reinforce a perpetuation of the hyperactivity! This occurs in those instances where a family's stability and well-being have come to depend on the hyperactive child behaving disruptively (and this is irrespective of the etiology of the hyperactivity). For instance, there are parents who never go out because they allegedly need to be with their children constantly in order to control difficulties created by the hyperactive child. In fact, this may be a way to avoid confronting painful marital difficulties. By tying themselves to the household, they are protected from being alone and they can maintain their marital alliance by perceiving the hyperactive child as a common "enemy" about whom they invariably agree. Siblings too can maintain their own sense of self-esteem by being able to rationalize all arguments and fights as caused solely by the obviously difficult hyperactive youngster. Such scapegoating may be identified by the clinical observation that one or both parents become depressed when treatment helps the youngster's behavior to improve. Another hint comes when the clinician tries to focus on the parents' attitudes and finds that his efforts are invariably sidetracked by the parents' soliciting counseling for complicated child-management problems. Again, a diagnostic family session may reveal siblings referring to the hyperactive youngster as "hyper-dummy" or by similar appellations that seem to be accepted casually by the entire family. In such situations, a family therapeutic approach would be indicated either as the sole treatment or in conjunction with one or several of the aforementioned modalities.

It should be emphasized that this discussion is not a comprehensive statement regarding the possible causes and treatment for hyperkinesis in children. Such an account would require review of the possible influences of allergies, intolerance of food additives, carbohydrate imbalance, insecticides, lead poisoning, fluorescent lighting, and so on (see volume II). Its intent is rather to be selectively illustrative of the general point about the selection of treatment methods.

LEARNING DISORDERS

Another common clinical problem is the child suffering from learning impairment. In planning intervention for such cases, it is of crucial importance to determine whether the academic difficulties are caused by developmental arrests, undefended regression, or psychological inhibitions. The treatment of choice for the child with developmental arrest is remedial education. But, with those children whose therapeutic need is for the reversal of regression or the exposure of intrapsychic conflicts to consciousness, such an approach may prove to be utterly futile, and can prove harmful as well. This type of therapeutic misapplication tends to occur as a consequence of failure to penetrate beyond the phenomenologic level in assessment. The youngster with reading retardation secondary to underlying emotional factors who does not respond to tutoring is likely to take this failure to be further evidence of his stupidity and hopelessness. Thus, regardless of how enthusiastically tutoring is pursued, if the therapeutic effort neglects the underlying cause, it may well reinforce the symptom. In addition, albeit unwittingly, such efforts may repeat a significant trauma.

CASE ILLUSTRATION

In his three years of schooling, eight-year-old John was unable even to begin to learn the alphabet. Intensive tutoring had been ineffective, and subsequent psychotherapy revealed that the tutoring had in fact increased his resistance to learning. During the course of psychotherapy, it emerged that John's sister, three years his senior, used to play school with him. This game had started when she was five and he was two. In the course of it, she played the role of the teacher, and John and some dolls were the pupils. His inability to learn the alphabet in this game prompted his five-year-old teacher to be abusively threatening and punitive. Harshly, she warned John repeatedly that he would never be permitted to attend school unless he learned. This frightening game and the warnings persisted until John's entry into school. Reconstruction in psychotherapy showed that John was sure he would dread and hate school. Unconsciously, he was determined not to learn, so that he would be denied entry into school. Only after uncovering and working through these experiences and their associated ideas, feelings, and attitudes was he able to dismiss them as inappropriate to his actual school situation and, for the first time, to benefit from tutoring. Until that point, he had unconsciously viewed tutoring as a punishment that reinforced his determination not to learn from it.[24]

SCHOOL REFUSAL

The GAP report on child psychiatric treatment planning[21] divided the goals of therapeutic intervention into the following five types. These are based on which aspect of the child's existence is identified as the principal target for change: (1) intrapsychic modification; (2) alteration of intrafamilial functioning; (3) alteration of peer-group interaction; (4) modification of the child's school or community adjustment; and (5) removal of the child for a period of time to an altogether different environment.

It was noted that in the course of therapeutic work with a family, at any given time the treatment plan usually tries to achieve at least two of the preceding goals. Five simplified hypothetical cases of school refusal are then cited to illustrate how diagnostic assessment leads directly to rational selection of therapeutic methods.

In the first case, diagnostic study revealed that the child's unwillingness to attend a school had to do with long standing and deeply rooted anxieties about separation from his mother . . . related to traumata in infancy. The therapeutic goal of intrapsychic change in the child dictated that the optimum intervention would be individual psychotherapy or psychoanalysis. . . .

In a second situation, the diagnostic study uncovered a family imbalance in which the parents used their child to avoid facing marital conflicts. The family shared an unconscious fear that some disaster would result if conflict was brought into the open. What the child perceived consciously as a fear of school was in fact his inability to move freely away from his parents into a school setting without anxiety about the outbreak of violence at home. Here the therapeutic task involved alteration of family functioning to relieve the intrafamilial pressure on the child; family therapy or couple therapy seemed the most appropriate way to accomplish that goal. . . .

A third case of school refusal occurred in a latency boy who had never known his father. Worse, he lacked a close relationship with any man to support the development of his masculine interests. His fears of school developed after he had become the scapegoat of his classmates. He was teased for avoiding rough sports and for trying to be "teacher's pet." In this situation, peer-group rejection precipitated regression in a vulnerable child. The therapeutic goal here might be to help this boy feel more secure with his peers and to counteract his tendency to take shelter with a protective maternal figure. With such a goal in mind, the clinical team might recommend activity group therapy or a Big Brother, as well as consultation with school personnel.

In the fourth case, diagnostic investigation revealed that the child had a specific reading disability and that his fear of school resulted from a problem with his teacher. His inattentiveness, hyperactivity, and poor performance—all symptoms of a mild dyslexia—had led to his becoming identified as the "bad child" in her class, and she had resorted to harsh punishments to deal with him. A first goal of treatment had to be modification of the school environment in a way that would both prevent further trauma and meet the child's needs. This might take the form of intensive work with his teacher or could involve transfer to a more sympathetic and specialized classroom situation. Simultaneously chemotherapy could be initiated. . .

In the fifth case, an adolescent boy came to professional attention because of his failure to attend school. The truant officer went to the home to investigate. When the mother mentioned casually that her son spent long periods locked up in his room and slept with knives under his pillow, he referred the boy for diagnostic evaluation. The boy was found to have been suffering from a paranoid psychotic reaction for months. The family had coped with the problem with massive denial; they simply ignored the boy's bizarre habits and gave up all attempts to set appropriate limits. Hospitalization seemed the only acceptable alternative, since this boy responded to his delusions of persecution by threats of violence and the family seemed completely unable to deal with him. After the boy was hospitalized, attempts were made to involve the family in casework.[21] [pp. 604–606]

Different Methods at Various Phases of Treatment

Subsequently the GAP report[21] noted that the treatment plan may incorporate a sequence of different goals; for example, in the third case of school refusal, the diagnostic assessment might conclude that

The boy could not enter a peer group without getting the other boys to attack him. Nor could he accept a positive relationship with a man until he had at least partially worked through his ambivalent feelings and distorted fantasies about men. Therefore, a relatively brief period of intensive individual psychotherapy which could focus on these intrapsychic problems should be recommended to prepare him for referral to a group or a Big Brother.[21] [p. 606]

Therapeutic intervention requires a capacity for effective problem solving in complex situations. The problem is usually multidimensional, of mixed etiology, with the unique idiosyncratic features of the individual and/or family always present. As a biopsychosocial synthesis, a person suffering disturbance in one aspect of the integrated human system often experiences it as being reflected in other parts of the system. Thus, the system manifesting the most disturbance is not necessarily the one where the basic problem resides. Similarly, the fact that a therapy directed to a particular system is effective does not necessarily constitute evidence that the primary difficulty is located there; for example, for a given hyperactive youngster the effectiveness of methylphenidate is not in itself proof of a chemical or organic etiology. Consequently, clinicians are inevitably faced with the interesting challenge of systemic interrelationships which demand multifaceted therapeutic modes.

CASE ILLUSTRATION

Eight-year-old Carol was displaying unsatisfactory academic progress and a lack of peer relationships. Both her third-grade teacher and the school psychologist urged her divorced mother to seek psychiatric help for her. Her unhappiness was evident in her demeanor and verbalization, as well as in her tendency to hang around school long after dismissal, seeking out male teachers and the male janitor. Although her mother had not perceived the difficulties, she nevertheless cooperated in a psychiatric evaluation. She accepted a recommendation for Carol to enter individual psychodynamically oriented exploratory psychotherapy (described in chapter 3). The goal of the work was to facilitate working through unresolved feelings about the parental divorce. The mother simultaneously participated in a combination of parent counseling and therapy (as described in chapter 8) designed to help her shaky self-concept and inconsistent parenting.

The same therapist saw Carol twice a week and the mother weekly for more than a year; both mother and daughter made considerable progress. Mother had always allowed others to dominate her, but she now stood up for what she believed to be right. She was evidently a far more effective person, with an enhanced self-concept as a parent. With the notable exception of peer relationships which were limited to her siblings or very young neighbor children, Carol's accomplishments were evident in all other areas.

At this point, the therapist elected to add focal family therapy to the therapeutic program. This added a third modality to the other two interrelated treatments; the rationale for this stemmed from the following: Carol's birth had been eagerly awaited by her parents. Her mother recalled with considerable warmth the closeness that she shared with Carol, her only daughter (the parents had three sons), as an infant; this was maintained until around age two when Carol's strides for autonomy assumed an oppositional negativistic flavor. This posed considerable difficulty for her parents, who proposed and implemented an unusual solution. They adopted a same-age sister for Carol, ostensibly to provide her with companionship. The clinical work with the mother suggested that their unconscious motivation was to bludgeon Carol back into being an obedient little baby by providing her with a model of correct behavior. Thus, when Carol was two and one-half, Charlene, who was also two and one-half, joined the family. Apparently spurred by her own need to establish herself in the family in the face of insecure feelings about adoption, Charlene readily assumed the assigned role of the model child. Over the years she developed into the perfect daughter as Carol, by contrast, appeared stupid and remained immature and vulnerable.

The individual therapeutic work illuminated the strong mutual identification between mother and biological daughter. The mother's inadequate self-concept stemmed substantially from perceiving herself as having always been a disappointment to her own father. The successful working through of this oedipal disappointment in therapy enabled mother to change her attitudes toward her daughter. Simultaneously, in her own work with the therapist, Carol dealt with competitive feelings for her sister. The family interaction, however, continued to encourage Carol to be the inadequate little girl, while Charlene kept the role of the capable model. In the face of these external familial factors, the therapist's efforts to resolve her intrapsychic internalized self-concept proved insufficient; Carol continued to maintain this "little" attitude. Charlene persisted in her successfully competitive attitude toward Carol. For instance, on those occasions when Carol would venture to bring a same-aged friend home, Charlene would work successfully to take the friend away from Carol.

The focal family therapy served to identify those external pressures on Carol and endeavored to make them family dystonic. To some extent this relieved Carol of the "identified patient" scapegoat role by making her shortcomings a family problem as well as her own. Simultaneously, an effort was made to take some of the pressure off Charlene's need to maintain her place in this family by being superior. During the family therapy, it became evident that Charlene's security within the family was vulnerable. This arose not only by virtue of her adopted status but also because of the extrusion of the divorced father, Charles, with whom Charlene shared other qualities besides the designed similarity in names.

HISTORICAL ROOTS

One of the consequences of the need for pluralism has been a phenomenal burgeoning of the number of available treatments. In 1966, Harrison and Carek[24] listed 70 psychotherapies found in the literature; and in 1975 the Research Task Force of the National Institute of Mental Health[51] conducted a similar review and tallied more than 130 therapies. Reviewing the quarter century of NIMH's active leadership in the field of mental health, the Task Force sketched a picture in the late 1940s and early 1950s in which psychoanalysis and its derivative psychodynamic therapies were the most developed forms of psychosocial treatment, behavior modification had not yet emerged from the laboratory, and the primary somatic treatments included electro-convulsive therapy, insulin coma, and lobotomy. Twenty-five years ago effective treatments were available for central nervous system syphilis and the psychosis accompanying pellagra; but for the most part the few psychopharmacological agents at hand then were typically employed to manage rather than to treat patients. The picture today is so different that one

of the words used by the Task Force is "revolutionized." It should be noted, however, that in its historical review, the Task Force did not distinguish between treatment of adults and children.

As surprising as it may seem, innovative therapeutic efforts with children have frequently served as the avant-garde cutting edge of pioneering therapeutic and conceptual advances. The early history of the development of many psychiatric treatment modalities is punctuated by accounts of therapeutic activities with children. This observation impresses many as inaccurate as well as surprising, because in the subsequent development of the treatment modality, child psychiatric work frequently has not sustained its leadership role. With the passage of time, psychiatric work with adults has tended to assume the lead, obscuring the earlier seminal child-psychiatric contribution.

For instance, currently the treatment of adult major mental disorders with psychotropic drugs appears far ahead of psychopharmacological treatment of children's disorders. It is thus all too easy to forget that pioneering work in clinical psychopharmacology, and the one that has withstood the test of time longest, was Charles Bradley's[9] introduction in 1937 of amphetamines for the treatment of disturbed children.

Similarly, modern community psychiatric activities, which are often faulted today for deemphasizing children's clinical needs, have significant conceptual and pragmatic roots in the child guidance clinic movement of the 1920s. At its inception, child guidance emphasized its preventive role, its community consultative responsibility, and outreach activities. In particular, it was the main site for the development of the mental health team approach.

Another outgrowth of these early child psychiatric tactics was the active involvement of the identified patient's family in the diagnostic and therapeutic work. Eventually, this led to the development of family therapy, again pioneered in the context of work with disturbed children, as exemplified by Ackerman's[1] seminal contributions. Again too, as McDermott and Char[39] remind us, the burgeoning family therapy field and its evolving systems orientation are often perceived today as neglecting the young children in the family.

Another example of the vanguard role played by treatment of children is afforded by the recent resurgence of behaviorism and its fruitful application to treatment techniques. This is rooted clinically in the pioneering demonstration by Mary Cover Jones[30] more than fifty years ago that an infant who had been conditioned to fear furry objects (similar to the demonstration four years earlier by Watson and Raynor[56] of the development of a phobia in the infant Albert) could be relieved of the fear by means of social imitation and direct reconditioning. The Mowrer pad technique of treating enuresis developed in the 1930s was one of the earliest and most enduring behavioral therapeutic techniques and technological devices.[48]

The development of the concept and practice of milieu therapy is vividly reviewed by Bettelheim and Sanders in chapter 14. This mode of treatment, which was defined and conceptualized as "therapeutic milieu" by Bettelheim and Sylvester[6, 7] in the late 1940s, represents a rare instance in which the fruitful adaptation of a method to adult psychiatry (e.g., Jones[29]) has not resulted in the work with children being overshadowed.

There are two notable exceptions to the generalization about work with children serving as the leading edge of innovative therapeutic developments. They are the nonpharmacological biological treatments and the development of psychoanalysis (and its historical antecedent and companion, hypnosis). Freud's pioneering work was with adults and older adolescents. To be sure, the seminal case report in 1909 of little Hans is responsible for ushering in the modern era of child psychotherapy; nonetheless, that case was really an example of filial therapy (see chapter 9). Freud asserted without equivocation that he was the adviser, that the young patient's father was the psychotherapist, and that the intimacy of the parent-child relationship was a vital prerequisite for the therapist.[18] The first reported attempt of direct psychoanalytic treatment of a child without the use of a parental intermediary was published in 1913. In that case history, Ferenczi[15] indicated that the psychoanalytic method, as then used with adults, could not be employed with his five-year-old patient, who rapidly became bored and wanted to return to his play. Eight years after Ferenczi's abortive effort, Hug-Hellmuth[28] reported the use of play in the treatment of emotionally disturbed children. The role of play in the development of modern child psychotherapy has been compared to the historical significance of hypnosis in facilitating the understanding of unconscious mental functioning in adult psychiatry. Child psychoanalysis has subsequently been elaborated in different directions under the fruitful leadership of Anna Freud[17] and Melanie Klein.[34]

Simultaneously, in the United States in the 1920s, under the aegis of the Commonwealth Fund and Clifford Beer's National Committee for Mental Hygiene, child guidance clinics sprang up. Their form was modeled on the foundation of William Healey's pioneering child psychiatric work at the juvenile court in Chicago and subsequently at the Judge Baker Clinic in Boston. Enriched by the psychoanalytic developments in Europe, the child guidance clinic movement contributed to enlarging and expanding the scope of psychotherapeutic efforts with children.

Qualities of the Clinician

It is inevitable that clinicians will be far more competent in some intervention modes than in others. With the passage of time it becomes increasingly difficult for individual clinicians to be so versatile that they are knowledgeable and expert in all the available types of child psychiatric treatment. As it is no longer easy to be "renaissance" therapists, it is incumbent on the practitioner to be alert to and to avoid the temptation to limit therapeutic recommendations to those modalities with which he is most familiar. The child psychiatrist is a psychosocially oriented human biologist with a specific skill in diagnostic assessment and multidimensional formulation of the problem. He must be prepared to prescribe a wide range of therapeutic interventions in a knowledgeable and selective fashion.

The hallmark of the professional is his trustworthiness, his sense of responsibility, and his grasp of realms of theory, their knowledge base, and their related technical modes. These include those methods which he may not personally have the skills to administer. In consequence, the professional may require the services of other mental health professionals or technicians for therapeutic intervention.

The ability to consider the broad range of possible treatment, and the readiness to do so, are prerequisites for a comprehensive diagnostic assessment. However, these do not have to be extended as far as the actual administration of the therapy. Indeed, in treating patients, it is often advantageous to tune out selectively those techniques judged to be inappropriate for the particular patient and/or family. Not only are many techniques contraindicated in a specific situation but endeavoring to keep the related ideas in mind would risk creating the aforementioned polyglot Tower of Babel confusion. Therefore, the initial diagnostic assessment and the ongoing reassessments during the course of therapy require the broadest gauged professional competence, but the actual administration of the treatment does not. Indeed, a limited focus may enhance the quality of the treatment.

It is evident that with the passage of time, other professionals and/or paraprofessionals are becoming more expert in specific delimited therapeutic skills. This tends to threaten those child psychiatrists who only recently were the most expert at everything and who surrounded themselves with an aura of clinical omnipotence. It has required adaptation to accept the fact that nurses and child-care workers may be far more expert in life-space interviewing, and that the paraprofessional inner-city resident is more gifted at talking down the drug overdosed, acutely psychotic adolescent from the same neighborhood. A variety of factors have enabled child psychiatrists to adjust to such situations; but would the same be true for such sophisticated and elitist techniques as psychoanalytic therapy?

Such demarcations of expertise are comfortably accepted by many child psychiatrists in other countries. Concern about it is primarily an American phenomenon and is often accompanied by a tendency of American psychiatry to think of psychiatry in other nations as inferior. There has been evidence of a diminution in this superior attitude; this may be associated with modification in the previously overwhelming influence of the psychodynamic point of view.

Other medical specialists have adapted to sharing health-care delivery with others who have greater expertise in well-defined limited areas. Consider the ophthalmologist vis-à-vis the optician, and increasingly, in relation to the optometrist. Another example is the orthopedist vis-à-vis the physical therapist and brace maker. Yet, the ophthalmologist, orthopedist, and others have retained exclusive expertise in what tends to be universally perceived as the most significant aspect of the activity. In child psychiatric work, however, diagnostic assessments, treatment planning, prescription, coordination, and ongoing reassessment have not always been considered the most esteemed aspects of the field.

This volume, which is dedicated to enhancing the clinician's familiarity with the broad range of available child psychiatric treatments, will not create instant experts. It is intended to help and encourage the mental health therapist to become a more complete clinician. The general physician must be familiar with insulin for diabetic coma and craniotomy for intracranial pathology in order to deal with the comatose patient; this is true even though he is not personally capable of administering all these forms of treatment. In a similar way, although the child psychiatrist should be familiar with the wide array of available treatment methods, he must recognize that he cannot be expert in them all. A little knowledge can be dangerous, if clinicians believe they have expertise in areas where they possess only a degree of familiarity. Professionals must expand their familiarity with a variety of intervention modes, if only to enhance their capacity to assess with greater precision where their expertise begins and ends. This broadening of horizons also helps clinicians achieve greater freedom from rigid adherence to any preferred theoretical model of human development and deviance, and should allow them to reach beyond integrally related therapeutic interventions to a broad-based approach. In the absence of such expanded knowledge, the clinician risks confining himself inappropriately to a limited therapeutic range which deals with only one aspect of the integrated psychobiosocial system.

Specialized Clinical Work with Children

The teaching of child-focused clinical skills has inherited a tradition of requiring training in clinical work with adults as preparation for work with children. Over the years, controversy has developed about the value of adult training as a prerequisite. In some quarters, an adult clinical background has come to be viewed not only as superfluous but also as educationally disadvantageous; it is felt to introduce too much that has to be unlearned. This view tends to accompany the opinion that work with children is not a subspecialty of an adult-oriented discipline; rather it represents an autonomous specialty in its own right. Simultaneously, distinct influences opposing this trend have emerged from some of the community mental health efforts. This approach seeks always to enhance the accessibility of mental health care. One of the means of bringing care geographically closer to the consumer is to decentralize and disperse specialized service delivery centers. If clinicians can function as all-purpose generalists, then the creation of a larger number of smaller but widely distributed satellite clinics is likely to be more feasible, both logistically and economically.

Unquestionably, prior experience in treating adults offers both potential advantages and possible handicaps in initial therapeutic work with children. In any case, there are unique forms of strain on the clinician working with children. At the outset, children typically do not seek help on their own initiative. Consequently, among the clinician's first tasks may be the stimulation of the child's interest and/or motivation. This may in turn be complicated by the fact that in the child's mind, the reasons for his referral may be contrary to his best interests. In fact, in his resistance to intervention, the child may in part be acting against what is viewed as the adults' hidden agenda for the child. Further, the adults' motivation may indeed be correlated with their insensitivity and/or anger toward the child. All of this makes it easy for the child to perceive the clinician as a punitive agent hired to get him to conform to some disagreeable requirement. In addition, children's naturally regressive behavioral and communicative modes require the clinician to think and act in ways alien to everyday adult roles. Even in the absence of a need for external controls, children's motoric orientation requires a degree of physical stamina on the part of the clinician that differs from that required in clinical work with adults. Also, the developmental appropriateness of certain primitive mechanisms such as denial and projection can complicate some therapeutic processes. Children's limited capacity for self-observation coupled with their readiness to externalize makes it difficult for them to conceive of problem resolution other than by changing the external environment. The therapist is dedicated to enhancing the child's opportunities and ability to change; this leads him to assume a perspective diametrically opposed to the child's. For instance, the passive masochistic boy who is the focus of peer teasing cannot conceive of modifying this by altering the way he handles his aggressive impulses. Instead, he wants the clinician or some other adult to control his tormentors; and his view may be reinforced by parental support.

Lest the foregoing make clinical work with children sound onerous, it should be emphasized that other factors more than counterbalance the points raised here. Among these are children's resiliency, their active maturational and developmental forces, their eagerness to learn, and their hunger for new experiences. These make clinical work with children an exciting, joyous, enriching challenge for those who have a ready capacity to communicate with them, and who understand, appreciate, and like them.

The Clinical Play Area

Since effective communication with children involves play, it entails architectural as well as personal considerations. Scott's[53] discussion of the structure, design, and furnishings of a playroom is organized within the context of child psychotherapy and child psychoanalysis; nevertheless it contains information that is useful for a wide variety of clinical intervention modes. He endorses Melanie Klein's suggestions that the clinical playroom contain a small number of simple, carefully selected toys so as to facilitate communication of the child's fantasy. This contrasts with Virginia Axline's recommendation that an exceedingly wide selection of playthings be available so as to increase the range of feelings that the child may express. Brody[11] sensitively attributes these divergences to the differences in their psychotherapeutic orientation. Axline's client-centered (Rogerian) orientation (see chapter 13) avoids interpretation, even of conscious ideas. The Kleinian psychoanalytic approach represents the other extreme, favoring rapid, direct interpretation of deep unconscious content (see chapters 2 and 25). Hence, their conflicting recommendations. Very likely, most psychotherapists tend to function somewhere between these two extremes and to modify their architectural and equipment preferences in keeping with their own professional and personal development. When inexperienced, clinicians have a tendency to derive a sense of security from having a wide variety of playthings available. With the acquisition of experience and the development of confidence in one's therapeutic ability, the clinician may regret the presence of competitive board games and model kits. They can lead to distraction from the clinical task, so the experienced clinician prefers to keep them in a drawer to be brought out only when especially indicated.

Obviously, individual considerations will be decisive. However, the following equipment can constitute a well-balanced playroom or play area that will enable children to communicate through play: multigenerational families of sturdy flexible dolls of various races; additional dolls representing special roles and feelings—policeman, doctor, soldier, and so on; dollhouse furnishings with or without a dollhouse; toy animals; puppets; paper; crayons; paints; blunt-edged scissors; clay or modeling dough; tools like rubber hammers; guns; rubber knives; cars; trucks; airplanes; and eating utensils. It is best to avoid mechanical toys because they break readily and thereby contribute to children's guilt feelings as well as to clutter. Although special equipment, such as genital dolls, amputation dolls, and see-through anatomically complete (usually except for genitalia) models have been employed, the unusual nature of such special equipment in the clinical setting risks making children wary and suspicious of the clinician's motives. Until the dolls children have in their homes include appropriate genitalia, the psychic content that these dolls are designed to elicit is more likely to become available with conventional dolls.

For those children who enter into a continuing relationship with a clinician, a special private drawer or box should be available. Thus, for each individual child there should be a storage place for items he has brought to the sessions or in which to set aside projects for future retrieval. Some assert that it is better not to make such arrangements; that unprotected possessions can evoke material about sibling rivalry, for example. Care should be taken, however, that this is not a rationalization for an architectural shortcoming or for insufficient respect for the child's autonomy and privacy. There are other means of facilitating expression of such feelings; and the architectural inadequacy can readily be overcome by the use of a stack of shoe boxes, labeled with each child's initials.

Chapter 25 includes a discussion of the utilization of play to enhance children's cooperation in treatment.

Clinician's Use of Self

Working with people's mental health differs from medical, surgical, and other helping professional undertakings. With the exception of parenthood,[5] there are few undertakings where the problems experienced by the provider of the help so closely resemble those of the patient or client. In other words, the range of emotional reactions within the therapist is likely to include some of the anxieties, depressions, regressions, and hostilities as well as the cannibalistic, murderous, and incestuous urges that are so central to the patient's difficulties. There is agreement that the clinician should differ from the patient by virtue of being less disturbed and by possessing a basic capacity for self-management. Nevertheless, there are many who believe that psychological vulnerabilities are overrepresented in people attracted to this work.

Indeed, there has been controversy regarding the relative advantages and disadvantages of such traits for clinical work. Some assert that psychological suffering is an essential ingredient in psychological-mindedness; while Holt and Luborsky's[27] study suggests that competence was correlated with psychological health and conventional adjustment.

Despite all the advances in psychopharmacology and in other therapeutic methods and techniques, the clinician's personality remains a most potent and important diagnostic and therapeutic instrument. Many psychiatric treatments are enhanced by a quality of spontaneity on the part of the therapist. Indeed, except in the biological and some of the behavioral therapies, the therapist has limited opportunity to calculate the extent of each therapeutic intervention. In consequence, once they have made some assessment of the situation and determined their approach, experienced therapists generally behave relatively spontaneously. These quasi "spontaneous" therapeutic interventions are then subjected to post-hoc scrutiny and critical review. Consequently, mental health work encompasses highly individualistic styles of practice requiring the clinician to achieve a considerable degree of self-understanding, self-realization, and self-actualization. These capacities, in turn, encourage the refinement of his sensitivity, empathy, and intuition. Such traits are central to the participant-observer combination of evocative listening and intervention that characterizes almost all diagnostic assessments and many of the therapeutic interventions of the mental health professional.

This use of self calls for a change in the detached approach model that characterizes traditional medical practice. During their formal education, many students have realized that to change may require substantial alterations in their previously adequate coping styles. This is one area in which educational programs frequently offer little help. In addition, using different clinical approaches tends to require further differentiation in use of self.

Many psychodynamically oriented approaches postulate that the patient changes via cognitive-affective reexperiencing the introjected past. This takes place in the course of a special kind of encounter with the therapist. To achieve this, the clinician is taught to keep personal reactions under control while observing his own internal processes. His goal is to discriminate between objective professional reactions, reactions stemming from his own past, and those reactions stimulated by the patient. Meanwhile, the patient is encouraged to look at himself, to explore the past, and to study its effect on the present. The result is a deep and powerful interaction that can approach aspects of the religious-magical contact between shaman and client. It places enormous demands on the therapist, who, in a sense, experiences the patient through himself as though the therapist were a part of the other's phenomenology.

In contrast, by virtue of incorporating a more naturalistic and scientific mode, the biologic and behavioral therapies do not burden the therapist with the same requirements. Indeed, they encourage the clinician to distance himself from the patient in an effort to maximize objectivity. Prediction and control of the problem are emphasized at the expense of understanding the patient's subjective experience.

On the other hand, a systems orientation, and the related social intervention modes such as family therapy, postulate that change stems from the therapist's affiliation with the family (or other social system). He uses his relationship to alter individual roles in the dysfunctional transactional processes of the family and in its total structural organization. In contrast to the psychodynamic, biologic, and behavioral modes, the systems-oriented clinician is usually taught not to guard against spontaneous personal responses. It is assumed that those responses will be system syntonic; even if they are not, however, they can serve as valuable exploratory probes. This intervention contributes to establishing an affiliation with the family and experiencing its pressures.

Thus, in the clinical illustration cited previously under "Different Methods at Various Phases of Treatment," for the same clinician to treat Carol with individual exploratory psychotherapy, to undertake a combination of parent counseling and personal psychotherapy with her mother, and to engage the entire family in focal family therapy requires a degree of dexterity in the clinician's use of self that may not be within the capacity of all. It is incumbent on clinicians to be cognizant of their capabilities and limitations in this regard.

Clinician's Personal Background

There is an irreducible minimum of educational and cognitive background that mental health clinicians share. This is enriched by the various differences between professional disciplines and by certain idiosyncratic individual factors. In contrast, there are no comparable irreducible similarities that apply to the clinician's relationship capacity and psychosocial background (including his sexual, racial, cultural, economic, and political value orientation, sensitivities, attitudes, and assumptions). Therefore, enhancing the clinicians noncognitive problem-solving abilities, his relationship capacities, his empathy, and his intuition have all too often been relegated to haphazard or sequestered parts of his professional development.

This entire book is written by adult authors for adult readers; they share in common the desire to understand and help children. To truly tune in with children, adults have to consider to what extent their own adulthood and childhood are interrelated aspects of a continuum and to what extent they are separate and polarized discontinuous stages. In other words, each clinician has to consider individually how, when, and why he views children as miniature adults, and adults as larger children, and the circumstances under which he·thinks of children and adults as distinctly different. How capable is he of appreciating the child who is impatient and cannot wait to become an adult, when, like most adults, he may look back with longing and nostalgia to his own childhood?

Albeit ambivalently, Americans like to think of this era as the century of the child, and of their families and society as child-centered; childhood itself is spoken of as the golden age. While this appears appropriate in comparison to past centuries, Adams[2] wisely reminds us that oppressed people typically accuse their oppressors of treating them like children. We have to consider carefully that, both collectively and individually, mental health professionals probably share what appears to be a pervasive though unconscious societal prejudice against children.[52] After all, there is no reason why adults should have any special immunity against feeling threatened by children, who frequently do not hesitate to be critical as they prepare themselves to replace the adults and send them out to pasture. More than that, adults who are intimately involved with children tend to find that psychological issues, which were presumably put to rest many years earlier, are now all too vividly reactivated.[5]

It is well known that some colleagues are attracted to work with children in part in an effort to allay anxiety by identifying with the aggressor; in effect they become surrogate parents. This motivation may be manifested by a tendency toward overidentification with the child along with a negative attitude toward the child's parents. Lack of awareness of the source of such motivations can lead into serious pitfalls. For example, the clinician may unintentionally add to the child's discomfort by accepting as literally true what is in fact an expression of hostile fantasies about parents; or he may enhance the child's pathological distortions by fostering projections onto the family. When children are temporarily separated from their family for residential treatment, false hopes may be engendered in the child by a clinician who presents himself as a knight in shining armor come to rescue the child from his "bad" parents. This encourages the child's allegiance to an elusive fantasy that works against resolution of conflicts and ultimate return to the family. One cannot prevent such problems by eradicating the clinician's motivations. Indeed, this type of attitude is probably inevitable; the only appropriate antidote is vigilant self-awareness, both for the individual and the clinical team. To know and accept oneself facilitates empathy and identification with the child while simultaneously allowing one to enjoy one's adult status. In the very nature of the work, many therapeutic interventions with children require that the clinician be an active participant—often at the child's level and following the child's lead—while simultaneously maintaining adult professional rapport with the situation. The clinician's familiarity with his own antiparent, antisibling, or whatever prejudice tends to contribute to resolution of this biased attitude. The resolution, in turn, should make it easier to work with the child's hate for the family without losing sight of the child's love for the family. Sensitive therapeutic attention to the totality of the child's feelings for and relationship with his family can play a powerful role in enabling the child to survive with his family. More than that, however, and of potentially greater significance, is the fact that helping the child maintain his loving attachment to the family will be a major support for the youngster's future capacity to love.

Therapeutic Differentiation

In the series of chapters that follow, descriptions of multiple therapeutic modalities are dedicated to a multidimensional pluralistic integration. However, it should not be denied that there are clinical situations in which a unitary approach is best. Thus, a careful clinical assessment may suggest that for a given case, an exclusive, rigidly adhered to therapeutic strategy is indicated for that particular youngster and/or family. Here, however, it is asserted that, by and large, children do not get better because a clinician has displayed an unvarying devotion to a particular technique with all patients—a devotion to which the mental health field seems to be exquisitely vulnerable. This unitary devotion is especially noticeable when a growing momentum of interest is building up around an exciting new therapeutic strategy. Some clinicians react to new developments by shutting their eyes to the new approaches and clinging tenaciously to what they have always done. At the same time, other clinicians may be readily persuaded to join the enthusiastic proponents of the new method who write and speak overzealously regarding the merits of exclusive use of that particular treatment. Such seems to have been the case with psychoanalysis in the 1940s and 1950s, whereas in the 1960s and 1970s, similar claims have been made for behavior therapy and family therapy.

There is much to be learned about how to prescribe treatment. The goal is specificity and therapeutic differentiation, and the method by which to achieve them are based on careful, meticulous diagnostic assessment. There is so much more to be learned about when nonspecific factors help; when the therapist's interest or charisma is all that is required; and when it is essential that children have the benefit of specific psychological, behavioral, physiologic, and/or environmental interventions. Perhaps the most important need is to learn when in fact there is nothing additional needed to enhance the child's developmental potential.

REFERENCES

1. ACKERMAN, N. W., *The Psychodynamics of Family Life*, Basic Books, New York, 1958.
2. ADAMS, P. L., *A Primer of Child Psychotherapy*, Little, Brown, Boston, 1974.
3. ALEXANDER, F., "The Dynamics of Therapy in the Light of Learning Theory," *American Journal of Psychiatry*, 120:440–448, 1963.

4. ARONSON, G., "Learning Theory and Psychoanalytic Theory," *Journal of the American Psychoanalytic Association*, 20:622–637, 1972.
5. BENEDEK, T., "Parenthood as a Developmental Phase," *Journal of the American Psychoanalytic Association*, 7:389–417, 1959.
6. BETTELHEIM, B., and SYLVESTER, E., "Milieu Therapy

—Indications and Illustrations," *The Psychoanalytic Review, 36*:54–67, 1949.

7. ———, "A Therapeutic Milieu," *The American Journal of Orthopsychiatry, 18*:191–206, 1948.

8. BLOM, G. E., "A Psychoanalytic Viewpoint of Behavior Modification in Clinical and Educational Settings," *Journal of the American Academy of Child Psychiatry, 11*:675–693, 1972.

9. BRADLEY, C., "The Behavior of Children Receiving Benzedrine," *American Journal of Psychiatry, 94(5)*:577–585, 1937.

10. BRADY, J. P., "Psychotherapy by a Combined Behavioral and Dynamic Approach," *Comprehensive Psychiatry, 9*:536–543, 1968.

11. BRODY, S., "Aims and Methods in Child Psychotherapy," *Journal of the American Academy of Child Psychiatry, 3*:385–412, 1964.

12. DOLLARD, J., and MILLER, N., *Personality and Psychotherapy*, McGraw-Hill, New York, 1950.

13. EYSENCK, H. J., *Behavior Therapy and the Neuroses: Readings and Modern Methods of Treatment Derived from Learning Theory*, Pergamon Press, London, 1960.

14. FEATHER, B. W., and RHOADS, J. M., "Psychodynamic Behavior Therapy," *Archives of General Psychiatry, 26*:496–511, 1972.

15. FERENCZI, S., "A Little Chanticleer," in Ferenczi, S., *Contributions of Psychoanalysis*, pp. 240–252, Robert Brunner, New York, 1950.

16. FRANK, J., *Persuasion and Healing*, Johns Hopkins University Press, Baltimore, 1961.

17. FREUD, A., *The Psychoanalytic Treatment of Children*, Imago, London, 1946.

18. FREUD, S., "Analysis of a Phobia in a Five-year-old Boy," in Strachey, J. (Ed.), *The Standard Edition of the Complete Psychological Works of Sigmund Freud*, vol. 10, pp. 1–49, Hogarth Press, London, 1955.

19. GITTELMAN-KLEIN, R., and KLEIN, D. F., "School Phobia: Diagnostic Considerations in the Light of Imipramine Effects," *Journal of Nervous and Mental Disease, 156*:199–215, 1973.

20. Group for the Advancement of Psychiatry, *Pharmacotherapy and Psychotherapy: Paradoxes, Problems and Progress*, vol. 9, Report no. 93, pp. 261–431, Group for the Advancement of Psychiatry, New York, 1975.

21. ———, *From Diagnosis to Treatment: An Approach to Treatment Planning for the Emotionally Disturbed Child*, vol. 8, Report no. 87, pp. 520–661, Group for the Advancement of Psychiatry, New York, 1973.

22. ———, *Psychopathological Disorders in Childhood: Theoretical Considerations and a Proposed Classification*, vol. 6, Report no. 62, pp. 173–343, Group for the Advancement of Psychiatry, New York, 1966.

23. HALLECK, S., and WOODS, S., "Emotional Problems of Psychiatric Residents," *Psychiatry, 25*:339–346, 1962.

24. HARRISON, S. I., "Individual Psychotherapy," in Freedman, A. M., Kaplan, H. I., and Sadock, B. J. (Eds.), *Comprehensive Textbook of Psychiatry—II*, pp. 2214–2228, Williams & Wilkins, Baltimore, 1975.

25. ———, and CAREK, D. J., *A Guide to Psychotherapy*, Little, Brown, Boston, 1966.

26. HEINICKE, C. M., and STASSMANN, L. H., "Toward More Effective Research on Child Psychotherapy," *Journal of the American Academy of Child Psychiatry, 14*:561–588, 1975.

27. HOLT, R., and LUBORSKY, L., *Personality Patterns of Psychiatrists: A Study in Methods of Selecting Residents*, Basic Books, New York, 1958.

28. HUG-HELLMUTH, H. V., "On the Technique of Child Analysis," *International Journal of Psychoanalysis, 2*:287–305, 1921.

29. JONES, M., *The Therapeutic Community*, Basic Books, New York, 1953.

30. JONES, M. C., "The Elimination of Children's Fears," *Journal of Experimental Psychology, 7*:382–390, 1924.

31. KESSLER, J. W., *Psychopathology of Childhood*, Prentice-Hall, Englewood Cliffs, N.J., 1966.

32. KETY, S. S., "The True Nature of a Book: An Allegory," *NIH Record*, June 7, 1960.

33. KLAGSBRUN, S., "In Search of an Identity," *Archives of General Psychiatry, 16*:286–289, 1967.

34. KLEIN, M., *The Psychoanalysis of Children*, Hogarth Press, London, 1932.

35. KRAMER, C. H., *Psychoanalytically Oriented Family Therapy: Ten Year Evolution in a Private Child Psychiatry Practice*, Monograph of the Family Institute of Chicago, 1968.

36. LAZARUS, A. A., "Behavior Therapy in Graded Structure," *International Psychiatric Clinics, 6*:134–143, 1969.

37. LEVITT, E. E., "Research on Psychotherapy with Children," in Bergin, A. E., and Garfield, S. L. (Eds.), *Handbook of Psychotherapy and Behavior Change: An Emperical Analysis*, pp. 474–494, John Wiley, New York, 1971.

38. LUBORSKY, L., SINGER, E., and LUBORSKY, L., "Comparative Studies of Psychotherapies," *Archives of General Psychiatry, 32*:995–1008, 1975.

39. McDERMOTT, J. F., and CHAR, W. F., "The Undeclared War Between Child and Family Therapy," *Journal of the American Academy of Child Psychiatry, 13*:422–436, 1974.

40. ———, FRAIBERG, S., and HARRISON, S. I., "Residential Treatment of Children: The Utilization of Transference Behavior," *Journal of the American Academy of Child Psychiatry, 7*:169–192, 1968.

41. MALAN, D. H., "The Outcome Problem in Psychotherapy Research," *Archives of General Psychiatry, 29*:719–729, 1973.

42. MALONE, C. A., "Observations on the Role of Family Therapy in Child Psychiatry Training," *Journal of the American Academy of Child Psychiatry, 13*:437–458, 1974.

43. MANDELL, A. J., "Dr. Hunter S. Thompson and a New Psychiatry," *Psychiatry Digest, 37(3)*:12–17, 1976.

44. MARKS, I. M., "The Future of the Psychotherapies," *British Journal of Psychiatry, 118*:69–73, 1971.

45. ———, and GELDER, M. G., "Common Ground Between Behavior Therapy and Psychodynamic Methods," *British Journal of Medical Psychology, 39*:11–23, 1966.

46. MARMOR, J., "Dynamic Psychotherapy and Behavior Therapy," *Archives of General Psychiatry, 24*:22–28, 1971.

47. MOWRER, O. H., *Learning Theory in Personality Dynamics*, Ronald Press, New York, 1950.

48. ———, and MOWRER, W., "Enuresis: A Method for Its Study and Treatment," *American Journal of Orthopsychiatry, 8*:436–459, 1938.

49. NOSHPITZ, J. D., "The Psychotherapist in Residential Treatment," in Mayer, M. F., and Blum, A. (Eds.), *Healing Through Living: Symposium on Residential Care*, pp. 158–175, Charles C Thomas, Springfield, Ill., 1971.

50. PIAGET, J., *The Moral Judgment of the Child*, Routledge and Kegan Paul, London, 1932.

51. Research Task Force of the National Institute of Mental Health, *Research in the Service of Mental Health*, National Institute of Mental Health, Rockville, Md., 1975.

52. REXFORD, E. N., "Children, Child Psychiatry, and Our Brave New World," *Archives of General Psychiatry, 20*:25–37, 1969.

53. SCOTT, W. C. M., "Differences Between the Playroom Used in Child Psychiatric Treatment and in Child Analysis," *Canadian Psychiatric Association Journal, 6*:281–285, 1961.

54. SLOANE, R. B., "The Converging Paths of Behavior Therapy and Psychotherapy," *International Journal of Psychiatry, 7*:493–503, 1969.

55. STUART, R. B., Personal communication, 1976.

56. WATSON, J. B., and RAYNOR, R., "Conditioned Emotional Reactions," *Journal of Experimental Psychology, 3*:1–14, 1920.

57. WITMER, H. L., *Psychiatric Interviews with Children*, Commonwealth Fund, New York, 1946.

PART A
Individual Therapies

2 / Psychoanalysis

Rudolf Ekstein

Description of the Method

Very early in the twentieth century, Sigmund Freud described and defined the particular psychotherapeutic procedure that he practiced as "psychoanalysis." It was an outgrowth of what was known as the "cathartic" method and was discussed by him and Joseph Breuer in their *Studies on Hysteria*.[16]

The task which the psychoanalytic method sought to perform may be formulated in different ways, although these ways are in a sense equivalent. It could be stated that the task of treatment is to remove all amnesias. When all gaps in memory have been filled in, and all the enigmatic products of mental life elucidated, the continuance, and even a renewal of the morbid condition, are made impossible. Or, the formula could be that when all repressions are undone the mental condition is then the same as one in which all amnesias have been removed. Another even more embracing formulation could say that the task is to make the unconscious accessible to consciousness by overcoming the resistances. But it must be remembered that an ideal condition such as this is not present even in normal functioning, and further, that it is rarely possible to carry the treatment to a point even approaching it. Health and sickness are, in a sense, separated only by a quantitative line of demarcation which must be determined in practice; similarly the aim of the treatment will be merely the practical recovery of the patient, the restoration of his ability to lead an active life, and of his capacity for enjoyment. Even in a treatment which is either incomplete or not totally successful considerable improvement in the patient's general mental condition may be achieved. The symptoms, while becoming less important to the patient, may continue to exist but without his feeling or meriting the label sick.[11]

This description of the method stems from an era in the emergence of psychoanalytic technique which did not yet differentiate between the phases of childhood, adolescence, and adulthood. Instead, the technique states the general principles of psychoanalytic treatment: the analysis of internalized, unconscious conflict including the task of overcoming resistances and of making the unconscious accessible to consciousness. In other words, the method seeks to bring the primary process under the control and mastery of the secondary process. At a later point, Freud discussed the place of transference; that is, the patient's reactions, thoughts, and feelings vis-à-vis the analyst which are repetitions of earlier states of conflict now projected onto the analyst. Freud then spoke about the transference neurosis as the recapitulation, or the repetition, of an earlier infantile neurosis. When the analytic treatment focused on the analysis of transference and resistance, it was inevitably led back to the exploration of this original infantile disturbance.

While child and adolescent analysis follows the general principles outlined earlier, workers in this realm have learned to take into account the unique differences between young children and adolescents in dealing with their life conflicts and tasks. This is particularly true in the area of the differences in ego and self-development, which require the use of special techniques. The basic *core technique* of analytical work with children and adolescents is an *interpretive* one. Interpretation of material must not be understood simply as offering explanations or giving intellectual insight or creating a new rationale for the suffering patient. Instead it must be seen as a process which integrates both the emotional and the intellectual functions. This integrating process allows the patient to work through these conflicts simultaneously on different levels. Left unresolved, such difficulties could lead to pathology, bring about a standstill in emotional and intellectual development, and result in an incapacity to deal with age-appropriate tasks. Ekstein[6] has suggested that the analyst's "twofold" activity, reflection and technical intervention, permits the patient both free association and self-observation. The analyst's interpretive actions may prevent him from reflecting sufficiently upon the effectiveness and validity of his interpretations. As he listens to his patient, he is constantly considering the meanings of the patient's communications, so that he could be regarded not only as a man of action (the interpretive act) but also as a man of reflection and, therefore, a man with a conscience. (It was Goethe who said that "the man of action has no conscience; the man of reflection has.") He, the analyst, must interpret, must act to help the patient change. As an interpreter who is busy developing a satisfactory methodology, he often has little time to acquire a conscience. This is one of the reasons the task of validation of psychoanalytic interpretations has created so many problems. A greater difficulty arises in work with children, since the communications of children do not follow the modes of adult personalities—that is, free association in the ordinary sense.

The child analyst is confronted with such completely different types of material as play, acting-out, and active demands for intervention, all of them requiring interpretive methods different from those used with adults. The interpretation allows the analyst to show the child or the adolescent the meaning of his play, his behavior, his verbalizations, his acting-out, and his place in the family or school. The subtle difference between an explanation and an attempt to see meaning in the material, along with the capacity to intervene at an appropriate emotional moment, distinguish the analyst's work from the mere attempt to "understand." The German language speaks of *Deutung* rather than interpretation, and thus Freud tried to convey the difference between mere explanation and effective interpretation at the appropriate moment when preconscious material is ready to be integrated with the conscious mind. In child and adolescent analysis, this requires that more consideration be given to levels of language, levels of maturation and development, levels of emotional expression, and to the subtleties of fantasy life on a conscious or unconscious level. It requires, too, that all these find expression in the analyst's empathic understanding of the young patient. One need only recall what an adolescent means when he suggests that he is either not understood or that he has found someone who understands him, who "digs" him. Frequently, merely identifying the conflict—he is afraid of his mother, he hates her, feels rejected by her, but at the same time yearns for her acceptance and her love—will not do. Interpretive work often takes entirely different forms.

OPPOSITION TO AND YEARNING FOR TREATMENT

An adolescent, sent by his mother to treatment, starts with the comment that he will not cooperate, he is only here because his mother sent him, and he is unwilling to talk about himself. The analyst does not press him but wonders whether perhaps his patient would prefer to use this time in some other way. The boy sees a chess set and wants to play. The game opens and after a little while the analyst observes that the patient overlooks all opportunities to attack his opponent's exposed queen. When the analyst suggests that the patient seems to be afraid of the queen, the boy angrily brings the game to an end.

Later material indicated that although the boy had indeed understood the interpretation, he had opposed it and only later on was he able to make use of it. At that time, the interpretation was brought to him on a metaphoric level within the context of the chess game, taking into account the patient's resistance and anger at his mother, while at the same time indicating his passive acceptance of the treatment situation and his eagerness to make some contact with the analyst. This interpretive act within the context of a game was not an explanation in the ordinary sense, even though it was derived from an understanding of psychoanalytic theory and technique. It was adjusted to the situation, allowing both participants to be aware of the youngster's struggle with libidinous and aggressive impulses. Examples later on in this chapter will permit a fuller appreciation of the nature of the interpretive process, that curious synthesis between act and reflection, affective and intellectual understanding.

History of the Development of Child Psychoanalysis

The first contribution on psychoanalysis, *Studies on Hysteria*, appeared in 1895, the year in which Anna Freud, perhaps the most important contributor and originator of child analysis, was born. Originally she was a teacher, as were many other early child analysts. In the early 1920s, a great deal of educational experimentation led to the development of psychoanalytic pedagogy. This experimentation was an attempt to influence the educational field and to avoid parents' and teachers' faults, a notion derived from adult analysis. Adult analysis very often gave the impression that the trauma of early childhood, the mistakes of the parents and educators, and the pressures of society led to adult neurosis and to mental illness.

The early 1920s, after World War I, were years which brought about social upheaval with an accompanying desire to review old methods and to renew society. It was in this atmosphere that those first pioneers, who were partly educators and partly therapists, did their work. For example, August Aichhorn, who wrote the classic *Wayward Youth*,[1] developed methods of remedial education for delinquents. Another pioneer of that time, Siegfried Bernfeld, studied adolescents. He influenced many modern educational methods for young people and is known to this day through his classic *Sisyphus, or the Limits of Education*.[2] An even earlier contributor to child analysis was H. von Hug-Hellmuth, whose original German version of her *A Study of the Mental Life of the Child* appeared as early as 1913.[17] In 1909 appeared Freud's classic *Little Hans*, the first analysis of a child via the child's father.[12]

These initial experiments had not yet developed a special technique for child analysis. They were the forerunners of the methods which were developed in the early 1920s. Reading Hug-Hellmuth's work today, one has the impression that she was a remedial educator who used knowledge gained from Freud to work with children, and perhaps with their parents, right in their homes, a method characteristic for many of these early educators. Shortly after World War I Bernfeld and Hoffer[3] experimented with youngsters who were war victims, as did Vera Schmidt[19] with kindergarten children in Soviet Russia at approximately the same time. Aichhorn himself tried to develop centers for children and adolescents who were war victims. While these attempts yielded a great deal of insight into the nature of the pathology of these youngsters and helped practitioners to find new tools, they were soon interrupted and discouraged by the powers that be. One could think of these precursors as the germinal seeds of later development.

Others of this early period were leading proponents of the new development: Berta and Steff Bornstein, Alice Balint, and, of course, Anna Freud and Melanie Klein. One might say, then, that child analysis has a history of approximately fifty years of constant development.

The first journal dedicated to these issues began about 1926 and was entitled "Zeitschrift für Psy-choanalytische Pädagogik" (*Journal for Psychoanalytic Pedagogy*); it ceased to exist at the time of the Nazi invasion in Austria. The title of this journal perhaps describes this early phase of child and adolescent analysis insofar as the struggle to differentiate between educational and therapeutic techniques was in full swing; only slowly did clearer definitions develop. The task of this journal was resumed in 1945 after World War II by *The Psychoanalytic Study of the Child*, which has since appeared regularly and with ever-improving quality.

Beginning in the early 1920s, two distinct schools of child psychoanalysis developed. One such school, associated with Anna Freud, originated in Vienna. It grew out of psychoanalytic pedagogy and never quite gave up its interest in nontherapeutic applications of analytical thinking, such as to education and the field of prevention. Anna Freud has given a number of accounts of the history of that school, and, in 1926, published her *Psycho-Analytical Treatment of Children*,[9] in which she discussed what alterations of the classical techniques of adult analysis had to be made in order to work with children, the necessity of substituting free association for free play, the importance of working with the parents and of selecting patients in special ways, and the nature of transference in child analysis—that is, transference reactions rather than transference neurosis—and examined the variations in technique necessitated by these differences. Hers was the first clear attempt to introduce notions of development as vital factors in determining technique.

Melanie Klein's school developed at approximately the same time in Berlin; it later led to the English School of Child Analysis. Her first main work, *The Psychoanalysis of Children*,[18] appeared in 1932. While Anna Freud's school stressed development (the analysis of the child's defenses and resistance and the special meaning of transference), Melanie Klein's school was concerned with the conflict between the life and death instincts, the function of projection and identification, and the preoedipal phases, particularly that of orality.

These two different developments, interrupted by and resumed after World War II, moved from central Europe to England and to the American continent. In England, the two schools exist side by side, continuing their work, but with comparatively little contact and little effort toward integration. The American scene is dominated by the training developed by Anna Freud and her collaborators; in different parts of South America, however, Melanie Klein's influence seems to outweigh that of Anna Freud.

Differences, such as the discussion concerning transference reactions only, rather than transference neuroses in childhood, are not quite as sharp as was true in earlier phases. In addition, the contributions in America to child and adolescent analysis which stem from the development of ego psychology has been considerable and valid. Perhaps it could be said that the English development put more stress on the theories of object relations. The recent *Handbook of Child Psychoanalysis*[20] offers a full discussion of these different trends.

Anna Freud has addressed the widening scope of child analysis, its use and its applications to therapeutic tasks, which in earlier years had not been tried; she indicates that the task of synthesis is a continuous one. Many old areas of disagreement will yield to integration, but new areas of experimentation will create new and, as yet, unanswered questions.

Rationale Underlying the Method

Psychoanalytic theory has been described and discussed in many volumes, and its history tells of its changes through its eighty years of existence. Perhaps it will suffice here to suggest that psychoanalysis which stem from the development of ego psychological concepts: the *dynamic point of view* asserts that in order to understand the interplay of psychological forces, they have to be studied in relation to direction and magnitude; the *economic point of view* suggests that psychological energy will have to be the decisive, quantitative factor which helps explain psychological phenomena; the *structural point of view* speaks about those mental structures which undergo only slow rates of changes and helps delineate personality in terms of a hierarchical order of functions; the *genetic point of view* requires that every structure be traced back through a preceding structure; and finally, the *adaptive point of view* explains psychological states of mind in terms of their interrelation with the external world.[5]

Freud's theories of personalities have included the theories of psychogenesis, the epigenetic ground plan of personality development. He has proposed a variety of models of the personality, such as the 1900 *topographic model* of the psychic apparatus and the 1923 model which is usually referred to as the *structural* or the *functional model*. The topographic model speaks about such levels of consciousness as the system conscious, the system preconscious, and the system unconscious. The structural model discusses the dynamic interplay between the *superego* (forces of conscience, incorporated parental imagos), the forces of the *id* (the drive system), and the forces of the *ego*, capable of perception, of motoric expression, of reality testing, etc. All these forces face the external world, *reality*, the interplay with the social fields, and so on. Pathology, symptom formation, and maladaptive functioning are explained through pathological interplay between the forces described, such as the power of the unconscious conflict over conscious capacity, or the struggle between instinctual drives and moral taboos as experienced by the superego, and so on. In order to apply these general concepts to child and adolescent analysis, one would need to follow the lines of *normal and pathological development* as described by Anna Freud and her coworkers[8] and to discuss the problems and tasks developing around the epigenetic scheme, the phases of the life cycle as discussed by Freud in his classic *Three Essays on the Theory of Sexuality*[15] and later elaborated by Erikson.[7] The different stages of psychosexual and psychosocial development, the different stages of ego development, and the different social tasks in an ever-changing society set the stage for internal and social conflict. *Pathology* is usually explained not as an external conflict but rather as an *internalized conflict* understood only in terms of the internal world of the child or the adolescent. It has often been suggested in the literature that in adult analysis it would be difficult to see the adult patient's suffering in any other but internal terms. But in the case of the child, one is often seduced into believing that environmental changes alone can redirect development in such a way that pathology can be dissolved. The rationale for child analysis and adolescent analysis implies that those cases requiring this technique must be understood primarily in terms of internalized conflict rather than in terms of social planning and manipulation.

Indications

PHOBIC REACTION: MOTHER'S OR CHILD'S?

A young child was brought by her mother for consultation. The mother wondered whether the child needed analysis because of what she considered to be severe phobic anxiety. The child had been attending kindergarten for a number of weeks but was unable to adjust. The mother had to stay there with her because the child could not separate. The child was seen in consultation and also in interaction with her mother. It became clear that the mother's anxiety was much stronger than the child's. The mother tried to follow the child into the interviewing room when it was evident that her presence was not needed. The child related fairly well to the interviewer and played and talked appropriately. Later during the interview, mother and child were seen together. The interplay between them made the clinician suggest to the mother that in order to separate herself, she should take the child to school and leave, even if there should be a few tears. He stated this suggestion quite strongly and told the mother that if this assessment of the child's strength proved to be incorrect, they could then discuss a treatment plan. After a few weeks, the mother called with great relief to tell him that the child had made a perfect adjustment to the school, and that the difficulties had very soon disappeared. That was the end of the mother's quest for child analysis.

In brief, one has to question whether a given symptom, such as the anxiety implicit in the child's request that the mother stay, is a situational one, the expression of a transitional conflict, or a lasting internalized conflict requiring therapeutic intervention. The intervention in this case was the use of the clinician's authority, which gave the anxious young mother the courage to trust the child and to leave her alone. The mother needed more help than did the child. How is one to assess the strength of the conflict, to assess whether it is an internal and lasting one or a transitional configuration? The clinical picture alone cannot be used but has to be related to maturational development.

Anna Freud's volume, *Normality and Pathology in Childhood*,[8] as well as her classic paper, "Indications for Child Analysis,"[10] provide the basic blueprint to help decide issues of this kind. The recommendation in the case was based on impressions and on a decision to wait and see whether or not the impression was correct. Diagnostic procedures, of course, usually have to be much more cautious, and the clinician has to assess developmental and maturational processes, the relation of ego development to the different instinctual phases, the parental situation, the school situation, and the intrapsychic as well as the interpersonal situation.

Analytic treatment will be decided upon if there is a perrmanent intrapsychic situation indicating lasting, internalized pathology. The parents' strength to support such treatment must also be assessed; are they capable of leaving the treatment situation intact? Can they collaborate? Do they themselves need help? The child's intelligence must be observed, along with his capacity for expression and observation on his particular level of achievement. In order to counteract the danger that the example given earlier permits a short and impressionistic approach, it should be strongly stated that in most cases thoroughness is indicated. In this respect, what Anna Freud wrote in 1945 still pertains:

At present our analytic knowledge about the developmental processes on the libido as well as on the ego side is still very incomplete. Besides, too little is known about the interactions between them, beyond the fact that a precocious ego is especially intolerant when coupled with the primitive pregenital component instincts. We are only slowly learning to distinguish the various characteristics that mark a neurotic disturbance as either transitory or as permanent, although this distinction is of extreme importance for our diagnoses. Not enough is known about the relation between the development of the purely intellectual factors and the other important functions of the ego, etc.

Until these gaps are filled by more clinical data from the psychoanalytic investigation of individual children, it will be necessary not to confine examinations to short cuts of any kind, helpful as they may be in furnishing additional data, but to adhere to the former, lengthy, laborious, and groping methods of individual approach.[10] [p. 149]

Complications, Disadvantages, or Side Effects

It is difficult to elaborate on complications, disadvantages, or side effects as the language belongs more to traditional medical treatment rather than to a method of psychological treatment. In effect, one is tempted to compare the disadvantage of a psychotherapeutic method with drug treatment or surgery. Psychotherapeutic methods do, however, offer special types of complications. The treatment may last for a long time; frequently it produces intensive dependency on the analyst; it is often accompanied by a powerful transference struggle, acting out, repercussions at home and in school or in the total social situation. The treatment is costly and temporarily may actually undermine (as a side effect) other influences in the process of social and psychological development. Much of what has already transpired in the life of the child or adolescent is replayed in the analytical situation, and conversely, much of what happens in therapy itself as the internal conflicts are worked through is also replayed at home or in school. The patient will frequently live out the expected and necessary regressions in school and at home, and, as the analysis unfolds, the initial fast recovery may later be accompanied by retreats, pleas to the parents for permission to discontinue treatment, and a playing off against each other of analyst and parents and such important adults in the child's life as teachers and others.

Occasionally, the patient may experience very serious regressions in the form of temporary experiences which seem to be on the borderline or psychotic side. These impose great strain on the patient himself, the analyst, and the parents and create obstacles which are not easily turned into opportunities.

Contraindications

There are numerous differing psychoanalytic techniques, and the answer to the issue of contraindication depends to some extent on the basic approach used. Anna Freud's school of thought, for example, has always assumed that only those children who have reached the level of verbal communication can be analyzed; it would therefore be contraindicated to treat a nonverbal infant. If such a child needs treatment, the kind of analytically oriented psychotherapy used would need to permit a collaborative approach with the parents, the inclusion of both the small child and the parents in the treatment situation, or simultaneous treatment of mother and child—but such treatment would not be called child analysis (see chapter 28). The Kleinian approach, on the other hand, has frequently suggested that much younger children can be treated by analysis, and the experiences of Melanie Klein and her coworkers have included younger children in very early phases of development. The school of Anna Freud has put more emphasis on developmental issues; in the earlier years, the children analyzed were usually of school age.

It is suggested that a child could not be treated analytically unless the parents were prepared to cooperate. This capacity for cooperation is said to depend on the educational level of the parents, their capability of insight, their own willingness to go into treatment, and their capacity and readiness to maintain the child's treatment. At the beginning of treatment, the child rarely has insight into his illness and is usually not motivated in the way that an adult patient would be. He has to be brought to the treatment and, during phases of resistance, has to be encouraged by the parents to come. This situation does not exist where the child has intense emotional suffering because, in such a situation, the child is self-motivated and not simply forced to attend by his parents.

The analytic literature is full of clinical examples where treatment of children had to be interrupted because the parents withdrew the child or moved to a different city or neighborhood; it is therefore suggested that the security of the social situation would be one of the necessary indications for treatment. The diagnostic range of children who need help is rather a wide one, and a good many of the conditions are beyond the neurotic range. Borderline and psychotic cases usually need the kind of variations of analytic technique which would make one suggest psychoanalytically oriented psychotherapy rather than child analysis. Again, it must be emphasized that approaches vary in their definitions of what constitutes child analysis and what constitutes analytic child therapy. Lack of space limits this discussion to the suggestion that a technique should be called child analysis only if it is basically oriented toward an interpretive approach and makes minimum use of such alternative interventions as remedial education, suggestions, or active use of environmental manipulation. Again, as suggested earlier, the two main schools of Anna Freud and Melanie Klein differ on that point. Those oriented to the Freudian technique emphasize collaboration with parents, while those following the suggestions of Melanie Klein usually underemphasize that point and think of a "pure" technique, unhampered by parental intervention or disturbance, as though it were possible to conduct child analysis in the same way that adult analysis is carried out.

Adolescents in a state of fierce rebellion against the adults in the parental and school worlds may not be ready and able to use an analyst. In the Anglo-Saxon culture, the adolescent's unwillingness to come to treatment is usually considered as a contraindication, and the issue of preparing the adolescent for treatment, perhaps by prior work with parents, is considered to be very important. In such Spanish-speaking cultures as South America or Mexico, the parents are frequently able to require the adolescent to come for treatment, and any apparent unwillingness he may manifest seems to be less of a contraindication than is true in North America.

Another contraindication that is usually described is a lack of ego strength; that is, the inability of the child to express his conflicts and to expose his inner world via play or word. Or it may take the form of acting-out that is not accompanied by self-observation, reality testing, and some form of inner controls. Whenever there is no capacity for inner controls and self-observations, the analyst is confronted with problems which do not allow the analytical process to develop. Temporarily, in both children and adolescents, this capacity for self-observation, for inner control and reality testing, will be undermined during certain phases of treatment. But these intermittent ruptures of the process are to be expected. Only in those cases where the degree of ego disruption makes such a treatment process impossible would one need to think of variations of technique.

Technique

As has been suggested earlier, the basic technique of the child analyst consists of observing the child's play and games in order to come to some understanding of his inner states of mind. The conflict situation can then be perceived, and, within the holding action of the transference, the child can be helped to understand himself via interpretive techniques. Some of the child's play activities seem to reflect his inner world, while others, consisting of interactions with the therapist, seem to be a replay of the child's social situation. This implies, of course, that his particular view of the social situation, with parents and school, with siblings and friends, is at the same time a special, indirect version of his inner world and his struggle with inner forces. Play activities may include toys, mechanical toys, dolls, puppets, games, stories, drawing and painting and smearing. It is, therefore, necessary for the child analyst to make available to the child materials of the kind described. Usually the play and game material provided will permit the child to project his inner world in a manner appropriate to his developmental stage. At times, the child may bring his own games and playthings from home, and at times, the play will consist of some form of interaction between child and therapist.

It may be useful to present vignettes to give an immediate sense of the techniques utilized in child analysis.

STRUGGLE ABOUT INNER AND OUTER CONTROLS

Michael, a five-year-old boy, is brought for treatment by his parents owing to lack of bowel and bladder control. An intensive struggle takes place between him and the parents, as well as the school authorities. He is the youngest of three children, and this struggle keeps him, in some special way, united with the mother, although the unity is one of struggle, anger, often hate, along with intensive experiences of rejection, provocation of hate, and sometimes outright temptation to brutal action by the parents. The parents feel they have reached the end of their endurance. They are also faced with the fact that nursery school and kindergarten authorities are un-

willing to cope with the boy, and he is in danger of losing the opportunity to go to school. He would defecate several times during the day, in school and at home; whatever methods the parents used to achieve the goals of toilet training failed. He had been forced to wash his pants, remove the feces, had been excluded from family outings, put into his room and sent to bed, and perhaps beaten at times.

The relationship of mother and child, the relationship between child and father, and the interaction between mother and father, are best described (albeit indirectly) through a number of the patient's play activities. These will also indicate what techniques were used to help the child cope with his social struggle and his inner conflicts.

He is actually a likable, charming little boy, and it should be of additional interest that no major eliminative accident ever happened during analytic sessions. It were as if the whole issue of toilet training was contained within the existing social situation. His perfect behavior in the treatment room seemed to be a kind of flight into health. Whatever references were made concerning his or the parents' reasons for coming to the treatment hour were angrily denied by the child. He would tell the analyst to "shut up," never to talk about it.

Once, when the therapist entered the waiting room to bring Michael to the consulting room, he was busily engaged with his mother. He sat in her lap, an eager love scene on both their parts, although mother had reported that this emotional relationship was frequently interrupted at home by her sense of rage and helplessness engendered by teachers' complaints and the ridicule of other children about the child's soiling. The child told the mother to close her eyes and to pretend that she was sleeping; he was playing "Sleeping Beauty" with her. He then kissed her and she was to open her eyes and speak to him, her beloved prince. He enjoyed the game immensely, and the analyst could not get him away from the waiting room. After a little while, the child told mother that she could close her eyes again, but instead of kissing her himself, he silently motioned the analyst to be the kissing prince who would awaken the sleeping beauty. The analyst interpreted to child and mother simultaneously that Michael wanted to share mother with others; with daddy, perhaps with his brothers, and certainly with the therapist. There was no need for competition; she should accept his expressions of love in the same way as she accepted his father's love. The child was to see how he tried to share mother and therapist at the same time in order to create a happy triangle, a kind of promise in the struggle for possession of the mother. His symptoms were his particular way of controlling the mother, of restoring the love, to be accepted by her, to be cleaned by her, to be taken care of by her. His violent objection to attending to himself was his way of saying that he did not want to grow up, that he wished to go back to a state where mother would consider him her little darling. The interpretations were directed to both mother and child in such a way that they stressed the positive, the struggle for love and acceptance, while at the same time, they were both helped to grow towards a less seductive situation, more age-appropriate for the child who was now, or should have been, at the height of the oedipal struggle, expressed by him through the struggle over toilet training.

Later he improved and sometimes had "weeks without incident." He developed a new game in the consulting room wherein he insisted that the analyst take the role of "Michael," who had problems. He was the "doctor" sitting behind the telephone with a prescription blank (his father was a physician) and would order the analyst in the role of "Michael" around. The patient would call "Michael's" parents and tell them to severely punish "him." He was to eat up what he made, to clean his own pants, not to go on vacation trips with the family. In the role of "Michael," the analyst retorted that he had tried all he could and could not get better by hate and punishment. "Michael" would only improve if he could understand himself, and he wanted the "doctor" to help him rather than to punish him; a doctor helps his patients and does not punish them. The patient in his "doctor" role then told the analyst that it was his method of treatment to punish "Michael," who was then ordered to go to sleep; he was not allowed to talk and had to "shut up" and close his eyes (as the patient had told his mother to do in the Sleeping Beauty scene in the waiting room) while the "doctor" was talking to the parents on the telephone.

Then the patient developed a new version. He went to the fireplace in the consulting room, opened the screen, and told the analyst that the lion would come out and would attack him if he would not behave. The analyst, in turn, would now say that he was so terribly afraid that he had just filled up his pants again; because he always did it when "Michael" thought he would lose his parents' love. He cannot help himself if he thought that his parents do not love him any more. "Michael" was also terribly afraid that the lion would eat him up and would bite him. The child in the role of the "doctor" comforted "Michael" and told him that the lion will come out but was a very nice lion. "Michael" could pet the lion, could love the lion, and could make the lion feel good. "Michael" was then a little happier and thought that perhaps he could do better if he was not afraid that the lion might bite him. (The analyst thought of the patient kissing his mother when she had her eyes closed—when she did not try to see what he had done.) But then "Michael" knew that suddenly the lion might jump at him and might bite him. The analyst said for "Michael" that he was afraid of the lion because he did not know whether the lion was really tame. Sometimes Michael felt he was the lion, and at times he perceived the analyst as lion.

The patient would then work out a method with the analyst by which it became clear that he was going back and forth between threat and punishment on the one hand, and overindulgence and love on the other. He played out the problem he had at home where he was, on the one hand, literally confronted with the maternal principle of indulgence and seduction, and on the other, by the paternal principle of severe punishment and overcontrol. The father and mother had severe disagreements about the upbringing of the child. The mother often felt that she had to protect him while the father attacked her for it. The father hoped he could help the child through

strictness but sometimes realized that he could not cope with his own rage at the boy's behavior and at the mother's "inconsistent behavior" toward the child.

The child, while struggling for autonomy against parental control, achieved but quasi-autonomy. The price for his capacity to resist, to defy, to not give in, was the symptom which he could not master. One might well say that he attempted to escape the slavery of commanding parents, but that he had not yet achieved freedom or genuine self-control. The quasi-oedipal struggle was carried out on the anal level, the persistent struggle about cleanliness, about self-control.

His attempt to help himself consisted of identifying with the aggressor. He tried to force his analyst to assume the role of the passive, helpless, dependent child who would be confronted by angry parents and would be exposed to indulgence, anger, and rage. The lion's double function was experienced both as threatening beast, devouring the helpless child, and as harmless pet who would treat him well. But as he played the lion out, the beast was unreliable and gave a good picture of the home situation.

Father and mother had endless struggles regarding what educational methods to pursue in order to cope with and help the child. They had also attempted various therapeutic measures and ideas before this particular analytic treatment started. Later, the issue of how to collaborate with such parents under these conditions will be discussed. In the child's therapy, however, the material was used to show the boy his inner problem indirectly. The reversal of roles, the projection of the childhood role on the analyst was accepted, but, while the analyst accepted the play and accepted the role that was given to him, he spoke through his role to the patient's ego and explained why he, in the role of patient, could not cope and could not be helped as long as he faced inconsistency and anxiety-arousing threats.

Slowly the situation changed. Michael learned to control himself and at the age of six suddenly explained to his parents that his birthday would also be a turnabout for him. From now on he would control himself. He managed quite well and had only rare soiling accidents. The parents, for their part, could cope with these, because they felt that the child was really trying, and that the therapy was effective.

As is often the case, at this point, the parents' resistance influenced the treatment. It was hard for them to understand that the most important progress would be made when the main symptom was under control, when the basic anxiety was about to yield, so that the child could be helped to see himself more completely and to have truer contact with his inner self. Instead, they wondered how much longer he should be in treatment; whether they could now stop. This behavior gives much reason to question whether these parents were merely interested in modifying the child's behavior rather than permitting true inner autonomy, and whether they cared about the emergence of a genuine and lasting new inner constellation as the product of emotional and mental growth.

During this period, the child's work with the analyst slowly moved into different areas. He wanted to do all kinds of productive things. He played gardener with the analyst. He wanted to build buildings, and he developed a play situation which did not consist of the expression of conflict, but more and more turned to productivity, to the solution of tasks rather than to the resolution of conflicts. The struggle between the id forces and the superego forces gave way to healthier ego activities, to issues of cooperation. One gained the impression that the child was now really ready to enter school; that he would not be caught in extreme conflict with parents and teachers; would not be shamed any longer by his classmates as he was when he was without self-control. Life with his brothers also became more bearable. Activities in the family became more useful. Whereas he had to be left at home in earlier months, he now participated in weekend activities. He had caught up with his true age.

The next vignette concerns analytical work with an adolescent.

DELINQUENCY OR PERFECTION

The patient was sixteen years of age when he came for treatment because of severe acting-out problems. He had been stealing, and, for this, he had been arrested and placed on probation. The true analytical phase of this treatment was preceded by a rather lengthy introductory phase, often a necessary step for acting-out youngsters. He was a child of divorce, living with his mother while his father, remarried, lived in another city. He was closely identified with his indulgent mother who constantly complained about the father, claiming that he did not do enough for the children, and made her live under substandard conditions when he himself was well-to-do. The father, on the other hand, felt that the mother was spoiling the children, that he actually did do a great deal for them, and that the young man should find a part-time job. A previous attempt at treatment had failed. On that occasion, the therapist had apparently overidentified with the mother and son. He had sought to help the child by trying to convince the father that the sixteen-year-old boy should have an expensive car in order to compete with his peers. This therapist had felt that the stealing symptom was caused by deprivation and would cease as soon as the father expressed his love with an expensive gift. After this experience and a police arrest, the boy started treatment with a psychoanalyst.

The initial phase of treatment has been described in another communication concerning the nature of the residual trauma.[4] After a cautious introductory period dealing with the reality situation and his probation, the boy settled down to analytical work. He literally withdrew to his room. At first he communicated very little about his life and tried to keep his mother and sister out of both his treatment and his life. As he took hold of the treatment situation and learned that he was allowed to reflect on whatever he wished, he started to worry about himself and to express considerable anxiety about his state of mind. He thought something dangerous had happened to him, since, while watching television, he had fallen in love with a television actress who played one of the officers on a spaceship. He found that he could not keep himself from thinking about her. He took photographs of her during the television show, would spin all kinds of fantasies around her, and developed the kind of play activity typical for this type of adolescent. At first, his play was in a very dangerous play space and involved him in delinquent activities in the real world. But now his acting-out became a kind of playing out, a weaving of his fantasies, his inner conflicts, his inner hopes and expectations around the television actress. Unlike the young boy described earlier, he would not use toys and weave his fantasies around the toy, the external object. Instead, he would entwine his fantasies around the fantasy borrowed from the television program. It is very frequently true that unlike younger children, adolescents do spin their fantasies from the stuff of heroes and heroines whom they discover in mythology or novel, in the movies, or on the television screen. After a while, he no longer followed the spaceship television script. In its place, he made up his own new spaceship fantasies which had for him great validity and would frequently be experienced with a great deal of anxiety and inner participation. No one, other than the analyst, knew about these fantasies. He developed his own television script specifically for the analytical treatment. The basic theme was an interesting one. He wanted to get to know the actress who played the officer on the spaceship. However, he did not want her to know he actually had two functions on the spaceship, each of them carried out in such a way that she could not know that each function was performed by one and the same person. He was the commander of the spaceship, an expert in spaceship technology, but he also was the lead singer of a small band of musicians who entertained the crew during leisure hours. It seemed as if the commander and the leader of the musical group were both playing for the young lady. The lady herself was described in such a fashion that it was difficult to know what she was thinking. She was friendly and somewhat accepting, but neutral, and never told much about herself, almost like an analyst. She would hardly smile, and even though she would not divulge much about her opinions and her preferences, he succeeded in getting involved with her. The involvement included the two projections of himself that he had created. Would she discover that he had two parts? He was terribly afraid that she would, and now the analytical work consisted of slowly working with him on the problem of who he really wanted to be, and whether he thought that she would prefer the commander over the musician or vice versa.

During his treatment, he spoke of the different expectations of father and mother. The distant father wanted him to study technology, while the mother was more impressed by his musical talents. Whom should he please? Should he be a commander or a musician?

The interpretive work of the analyst consisted of trying to help the boy to see whether he could possibly have his idol like both aspects of himself, or whether he should perhaps make up his mind who he really wanted to be, how he wanted to develop. What was going to be his future? In which direction did he want to grow? Would he succeed in high school? Would he study music or would he study engineering? Would he be willing to take a chance and ask himself whether the officer would prefer the one or the other part of himself? Would he finally permit her to recognize that he was both? As the therapy continued, his own television script—our private analytical show—progressed. Regardless of what he did to keep the two parts of himself separated, as he had to separate the loyalty he owed to his distant father from that which belonged to his mother, he suddenly discovered that she found out that he was both, and that she was willing to accept him for what he was. He did not have to hide one part from the other, as he had thought he must, to maintain his loyalty to each parent when he became embroiled in the family conflicts.

During the development of this script, he was able to bring into the psychoanalytic sessions conflicts of his own. Slowly, as he defined his problems vis-à-vis his parents, he realized that he must accept himself. The television actress could be considered in two ways: as a narcissistic expression of himself, or, as it were, a displacement for the analyst, a part of the transference paradigm. As all of this was worked through, the boy came to a point where he was unwilling to continue the script; he found his solution in self-acceptance and no longer felt the need to fantasize. The television show was over. He made friends in school. He won gymnastic competitions. He got his first girl friend, an achievement he had thought impossible in earlier months. He slowly worked toward college entrance, at which point the analytic treatment had to be interrupted.

The position of the parents vis-à-vis the treatment will be discussed in a later section of this chapter.

Frequency

Children and adolescents in analysis are seen as frequently as adults; that is, from four to five times per week. Perhaps during the ending phase, it may be possible to reduce this to three times a week. But it will usually be more profitable if the frequency of the treatment is carried out in the same way over long periods of time. The treatment may last many, many months; only in cases with less severe conditions, or with younger children, might the treatment last less than a year. At times optimum conditions cannot be created, and many analysts then prefer an analytically oriented psychotherapeutic program (see chapter 3), particularly in introductory phases, in the hope that such treatment, too, can bring some improvement. Occasionally a child or adolescent analysis cannot be completed, and it may be necessary to conduct it in rations, so to speak, in the form of inter-

mittent analysis. This is frequently the case when the child or adolescent comes to a phase where the intensity of resistance grows to such a level that the treatment cannot be continued. Sometimes a rest from analytical treatment is indicated to promote further growth. With the development of new growth phases, new conflicts arise, where the objective need for treatment may once again turn into the subjective need of the child. Most analysts conduct these sessions on a fifty- to sixty-minute basis and try to maintain continuity, although frequently some exceptions have to be made because of school vacations, summer camp, the absence of the analyst, and the like.

Preparation for the Child and Family

During the diagnostic phase of the treatment, it will be necessary to involve child or adolescent and the parents in the process so that they may be prepared not only in intellectual terms but also in terms of inner participation. In both cases described, the participation of the parents during the diagnostic situation was, of course, tremendously important. In both cases there was considerable parental friction. In the case of the young boy, the parents disagreed on educational methods and as well as in their views about what kind of therapy would be necessary. Frequently they would bring contradictory ideas as to the form the treatment should take. They were struggling with other treatment methods, and considerable time had to be spent to prepare them for the type of experience child analysis would offer.

In the adolescent's case, things were even more serious. The parents lived apart, and, frightened as they were by the stealing episodes and the arrest, they engaged in some form of mutual cooperation concerning the need for treatment. They saw the causes of the difficulty differently, however; the mother tried to influence each therapist to see things her way and to make greater demands on the father. The father viewed things in quite a different light, and, for a while during the diagnostic preparation, it was necessary to help them both to accept that the analyst would prefer to side with neither. In both cases, the parents respected the analyst as the decisive authority whose advice they wanted, but at the same time, against whom they fought. The specific transference reactions of parents to the therapist may become the most powerful stumbling block in the treatment. This reaction may often interrupt the treatment, but it can also be used in such a way that it can be turned into an opportunity for treatment as well as for direct or indirect help for the parents.

In all instances, the child's confidence must be gained so that a workable situation is possible. The child must expect that the analyst will respect his confidences and not carry information back to the parents unless so requested by the child. This requires a rather lengthy introductory phase, as was particularly necessary in the case of the adolescent. At first, he saw the analyst merely as someone to be used to intervene in his difficulties with the police or with his father. Only slowly could he allow himself to see the analyst as a helper for inner problems.

Economic Implications

Child and adolescent analysis is a very expensive mode of treatment. It may last years and puts a financial burden on the family which can be borne by very few people. Certain health insurance programs may cover this form of treatment, but, in many of the cases, the coverage runs out before the treatment is ended. It is hoped that this problem will change in the future as a result of accumulating evidence that despite its high individual cost, the relative infrequency of its usage has not made psychoanalytic coverage actuarially unsound in insurance programs for large populations. There is frequent expectation that psychoanalytic treatment for children should be less expensive than that for adults. The current rate for each session varies depending upon the community, the ability of the parents to pay, and the skill or prestige of the treating analyst. Some of the psychoanalytic training institutions offer treatment for reduced fees, and, from time to time, colleagues are able to undertake the analysis of a child at reduced fees. One wishes that this practice will grow, that the institutes can provide more funding for their clinic systems so that such treatment is available for children and adolescents. There is no question that treatment early in the life of a neurotic individual in need of such help will be much more successful than treatment later on in life. But the fact remains that today only a small group of people is able to sustain the expenses of this form of therapy.

Simultaneous Activities

One of the decisive differences between the analysis of adults and that of children, particularly adolescents, is the fact that while the adult can seek analytic treatment without involving the analyst in his reality situation (his environment), the child cannot. The child and the adolescent still depend on parents, emotionally, realistically, and, of course, financially. Therefore, frequently the analyst must find some way to collaborate with the parents without creating danger for the treatment situation itself. The young person must know and feel that within the analytical situation his communications to the analyst are safe and will be protected. The analyst will try not to tell. But nevertheless, the analyst, particularly in the case of very young children, needs information from the parents, and parents need help in sustaining the analytical situation as well as in dealing with very real problems in everyday life. There are differences in approach between different schools of child and adolescent analysis. Again, it seems clear from the literature that those who follow Anna Freud's way of thinking would be more inclined to work with parents in order to make the treatment more effective. They would not treat the parents, but they would try to use them for informaion, would sometimes try to give educational advice to the parents, explain certain emotional situations, or perhaps advise them to seek direct analytical treatment for themselves. The Kleinian literature usually describes much less involvement with parents. For example, it is taken for granted that the parents will bring the child to each session but would otherwise not participate, and that no particular communication will be necessary. One wonders which of these two methods will lead to more interruption of the child's analysis. To what degree is the collaboration with parents necessary? Or, to what degree may one simply leave it to chance whether or not the parents are ready and capable of supporting the treatment?

In the two cases presented here, it was indeed necessary to work with the parents. In the first case, both parents came frequently for direct advice. They wanted to know exactly what to do. Should they punish the child? Should they not take him on a trip? Should they do this or that? And they wanted concrete and explicit answers. Of course, the attempt was made to turn these questions into a therapeutic response so that the parents would be more aware of the meaning of their questions and would require less direct pre-scriptions. That proved easier with the mother than with the father. The father, a physician, really wanted prescriptions. For example, the analyst would be asked if a certain diet described in a recently published book would be desirable for this child; whether it would actually limit the symptom or completely cure it. The analyst could not deal with this question as if it were an expression of resistance to treatment or doubt of his work. Rather, he had to indicate that he did not know a great deal about dietary problems but had no objection if they wished to try it, as long as they continued to observe the child and introduce this new diet in a way that would not lead to new conflicts or new struggles of will. Thus while the analyst paid attention to issues of struggles of will, of control and autonomy, he left out any reference concerning his opinion about the effectiveness of the diet. He would be asked many similar questions. In particular, he avoided taking exception when they wished to discuss treatment methods, and a workable situation developed. He did not allow himself to be experienced as someone who would oppose them. It was necessary, from time to time, to have private sessions with the parents and to yield occasionally to interruptions of treatment, such as when they wanted to take the child on vacation. But none of these pressures was strong enough to endanger the treatment. The parents' curiosity into the nature of the sessions could not be fully satisfied, and he the analyst made remarks only when he knew that the child had made similar remarks, or when certain things became obvious in the waiting room as described earlier, or when, during the interplay, he knew that his remarks would be acceptable to the child and would not be experienced by him as exposure.

The child's mother had herself had long-term treatment and was able to be much more accepting of psychological thinking than the father, who already had doubts concerning the effectiveness of this form of treatment for his wife as well as for the child. But the comfortable personal relationship that existed between doctor and parents made it possible to continue the treatment.

The situation in the second example was much more complicated. The analyst did have some contact with both parents. The father, being far away, perceived the analyst as his delegate. The mother, everpresent and having to cope with the difficult boy, frequently wanted to intrude into the therapeutic situation. She tried to find out what the boy did alone in his room (when he pursued his

fantasy television love affair), or what actually happened in therapy. At certain crucial moments, she would try to get the analyst to intervene, but it was somehow possible, at least partly, for the analyst to get her on his side and to make her understand that the analytical process would only succeed if the sessions were protected from exposure.

It is a truism to say that he who works with children and adolescents frequently experiences parents as intrusive, as limiting the treatment opportunities, and as noncooperatve. By overidentifying with the child in the countertransference situation, the therapist frequently finds himself, as it were, fighting against the parents. He experiences them as opponents instead of understanding that they are really interested in cure and in help. To be sure, they seek it in their particular form, which perhaps originally contributed to the illness itself. But parents too need help, and perhaps one of the weakest aspects of working with young people lies in the fact that most professionals who work with children are more skillful with the young than they are with the parents.

In child guidance work or in a clinical setting where analysis with children is conducted, it is frequently possible to work in conjunction with a colleague, an analyst, a social worker, or a psychologist who can also work with the parents. This work with the parents may be independent therapeutic work, analysis, or psychotherapy. It may consist of what is sometimes called parent guidance, and it can focus on parenting rather than on the parents' internal stress. Sometimes the help may be more like marriage counseling. This broad issue is discussed in detail in chapter 8. Occasionally, other methods have been tried where the child, seen in child analytical or adolescent work or adolescent analysis, has also been included in simultaneous family therapy, group therapy, and the like (see chapters 7 and 10).

All these activities need special study; indeed each time an analyst considers introducing one of these supportive fringe activities, one may well ask: "Is this trip necessary?" It seems safe to say that additional supportive methods should be employed sparingly. They will be necessary during moments of crisis and when there is threat of interruption. They might be necessary when situations arise in which children or adolescents go through severe regressions during treatment, with clinical pictures suggestive of borderline states or psychotic experiences. Also, during the analysis of young children and adolescents, ways might frequently have to be found to cooperate with schools, teachers, social agencies, probation officers, lawyers, and so on. When necessary, these arrangements should be considered very carefully before they are introduced.

Follow Up Patterns

It is useful to arrange some form of follow up with parents and child, but specific rules cannot be given. After a few months or a year, some contact with the family may be desirable. This will be particularly necessary in those cases where termination of treatment is dictated by the social situation rather than at a time considered propitious by the analyst. For example, the young man in the second vignette was graduated from high school and went away to college. He lived elsewhere and started a new life away from his mother. He was on his own and exposed to the challenges and crisis situations that arise in college, including the drug situation that existed in the music-related part-time employment that he sought. The time limit for the analysis was not defined by an inherent evaluative process which indicated that everything had been worked out and that genuine solutions had been found. One rarely expects to find such a closing point, since one of the differences between the work with children and adolescents on the one hand, and adults on the other, is that the young people are in the midst of their development. Each new developmental phase brings a new task and a new crisis. The schoolchild who succeeds in finishing his analysis so that he is a success in school, may, toward puberty and early adolescence, regress once more and find himself in trouble with the next developmental crisis. From the point of view of research, it would be worthwhile to follow all these cases and see what happens over the next years. Some research is, in fact, conducted along such lines, but it is usually not possible or practical in individual practice.

Ordinarily, it would be natural to arrange a future meeting with parents and child and a way of communicating with each other after the treatment ends. The analyst might send an inquiry or place a telephone call a few months after the treatment ends. Occasionally he might have to resume the work at a later date. Intermittent child analysis and adolescent analysis is frequently indicated. Followup is desirable until one feels that the child is capable of coping with the tasks of growing up.

It is noteworthy that child guidance clinics with the facility to pursue such follow up systematically are usually known for their thorough diagnostic investigations at the beginning of treatment. Excellent workups and excellent diagnostic precision instruments are usually employed to establish the necessity for treatment and for the specific treatment to be utilized. Rarely are such workups done at the end of treatment. It would be desirable if, perhaps some six months after termination when things have settled, a new workup is initiated in the same way as the original workup. It should be just as thorough, and it should try to measure the results of treatment. It is interesting to observe how thorough one is before treatment is begun, as if hesitating to accept the new patient in the clinic. If one compares this with the fact that short descriptive statements are settled for at the end of treatment, one must ponder the meaning of the difference in the practice of evaluation at the beginning and at the end of treatment. It is self-protective for the professional and, of course, for the patient and parents, to be thorough in the beginning, but the same situation should prevail during and after the ending.

Relationships to Other Modalities of Treatment

While psychoanalysis is frequently seen as a treatment form in itself, and one that stands independent of other modalities, it must be realized that in many cases other modalities have to be used simultaneously and should be related to the method. Youngsters who cannot be kept at home but must live in institutions, foster homes, special schools, day-treatment centers, residential centers, and the like, fall within this category, as discussed in detail in chapters 14, 15, 17, and 18. In these cases, the analytical work must be related to the educational and remedial work and all the other therapeutic or educational agents (see chapters 19 and 20). In the literature, few attempts have been made to describe such collaboration between different specialists in the field. True, the great majority of patients treated in child analysis or adolescent analysis are less disturbed than the cases requiring these other supports referred to previously, but such patients would nevertheless benefit from treatment by the analytical method. In some severe cases, other psychiatric and medical conditions may also have to be dealt with, such as the use of drugs and many of the other psychiatric modalities described in the chapters to follow.

Generally speaking, the analyst tries to free himself from the danger of being overoriented toward environmental change. He wishes to focus on the internal problems, the necessary intrapsychic changes, and those therapeutic interventions which are directed toward intrapsychic change. He will therefore be less concerned about the relationship of his method to other modalities of treatment in order to keep the analytic instrument clean, as it were. Nonetheless, it is desirable that he learn that some of the treatment situations he will encounter may necessitate involving himself with the issues of collaboration and with studying the effect of different kinds of intervention.

One need be interested not only in other modalities of treatment but also in the carriers of these modalities. Sometimes these carriers of modalities, other treatment personnel or colleagues from different fields, are important in order to understand the progressive or regressive activity within the analysis itself. Sometimes, new figures of identification appear on the horizon, or displacement reactions appear that work either way. The child does not transfer only to the analyst his earlier stages of development, earlier expectations from and reaction to parental and educational figures; he will also go the other way around. The child and the adolescent will transfer feelings and thoughts about the therapist to people in his environment. Therefore, it is suggested that these relationships of the analytical method to other modalities include a consideration of the relationship of the child and the analytic situation to other relationships between child and the human carrier of a modality.

Therapeutic Results

Very few outcome studies have been made concerning long-range psychotherapeutic and psychoanalytic work. A number of studies have been carried out, usually dealing with adult analysis. Currently, new studies are underway which may provide clear evidence in quantitative terms about how useful the instrument of analysis is. Today's impressionistic studies, as reflected in published cases, incline one in a positive way. These individual studies offer hope in concrete terms that child analysis and adolescent analysis have come of age.

It seems that while there are many successful cases that enable the child or the adolescent to reach a point where he has acquired appropriate capacity to cope with other people and with life, a good many analytic treatment programs end by interruption and are, therefore, not conclusive. Even the interrupted cases described in the literature indicate that much has been done for the child, but the recovery is not complete and the indication is merely that the work has been advanced.

Child and adolescent analyses are the most powerful helping tools available to youngsters, but it must be stated also that so far they are perhaps most useful as learning and teaching devices, as research models (as the richest source of information about a youngster's inner functioning), and that they have not yet achieved the reliability one would wish them to have. What can and must be said about the results of child analytical treatment and adolescent analysis, most likely, can be said about most forms of child psychiatric treatment: The field is merely working in the beginning phase of its technical development. Therapists work with complex data. They cannot experiment with treatment situations as is possible with other disciplines. They deal with natural situations which differ from case to case, and they must always maintain the humanistic philosophy, the therapeutic responsibility, as they are worked with. Nevertheless, diagnostic studies are needed both at the beginning and at the end. Outcome must be studied, as well as the therapeutic processes with children, adolescents, and their parents. Such studies can be carried out in individual practice only to a very small degree, and, therefore, societal support is necessary for institutionalized research. A number of centers fulfill this obligation and should help move the field more and more away from impressionistic and intuitive methods to include those which utilize experimental testing, developing methods of verification, prediction, and comparison of results. A scientific clinical language must be developed which includes the analyst's theoretical assumptions but which also permits intersubjective studies, modes of verification, and comparisons. Psychoanalysts must learn increasingly to add scientific reflection to therapeutic action.

REFERENCES

1. AICHHORN, A., *Wayward Youth (Verwahrloste Jugend)*, International er Psychoanalytischer Verlag, Leipzig, 1925.

2. BERNFELD, S., *Sisyphus, or the Limits of Education*, University of California Press, Los Angeles, 1927.

3. ———, *Kinderheim Baumgarten*, Jüdischer Verlag, Berlin, 1921.

4. EKSTEIN, R., "Residual Trauma—Variations of and on a Theme," unpublished manuscript, 1975.

5. ———, "Psychoanalytic Theory: Sigmund Freud," in Burton, A. (Ed.), *Operational Theories of Personality*, pp. 20–64, Brunner/Mazel, New York, 1974.

6. ———, "The Nature of the Interpretive Process," in Ekstein, R., *Children of Time and Space, of Action and Impulse*, p. 125, Appleton-Century-Crofts, New York, 1966.

7. ERIKSON, E., *Childhood and Society*, Norton, New York, 1950.

8. FREUD, A., *Normality and Pathology in Childhood: Assessments of Development*, International Universities Press, New York, 1965.

9. ———, *The Psycho-Analytical Treatment of Children*, Imago Publication, London, 1946.

10. ———, "Indications for Child Analysis," in Eissler, R. S., et al. (Eds.), *The Psychoanalytic Study of the Child*, pp. 127–149, International Universities Press, New York, 1945.

11. FREUD, S., "The Ego and the Id," in Strachey, J. (Ed.), *The Standard Edition of the Complete Psychological Works of Sigmund Freud* (hereafter: *The Standard Edition*), vol. 19, pp. 12–66, Hogarth Press, London, 1961.

12. ———, "Little Hans," *The Standard Edition*, vol. 10, pp. 5–149, Hogarth Press, London, 1955.

13. ———, "Interpretation of Dreams," *The Standard Edition*, vol. 4, pp. 1–338, Hogarth Press, London, 1953.

14. ———, "Freud's Psychoanalytic Procedure," *The Standard Edition*, vol. 7, pp. 249–254, Hogarth Press, London, 1953.

15. ———, "Three Essays on the Theory of Sexuality," *The Standard Edition*, vol. 7, pp. 123–243, Hogarth Press, London, 1953.

16. ———, and BREUER, J., "Studies on Hysteria," *The Standard Edition*, vol. 2, pp. 1–305, Hogarth Press, London, 1955.

17. HUG-HELLMUTH, H., *A Study of the Mental Life of the Child*, Nervous and Mental Disease Publishing Company, Washington, D.C., 1919.

18. KLEIN, M., *The Psychoanalysis of Children*, Hogarth Press, London, 1932.

19. SCHMIDT, V., *Psychoanalytic Education in Soviet Russia*, Internationalier Psychoanalytischer Verlag, Leipzig, 1924.

20. WOLMAN, B. B. (Ed.), *Handbook of Child Psychoanalysis*, Van Nostrand Reinhold, New York, 1972.

---

3 / Individual Psychodynamically Oriented Therapy

Donald J. Carek

Historical Perspective

Rationally based child psychotherapy is indeed a twentieth-century discipline. It arises from a systematized conceptualization of children and their functioning, which in turn allows for an operational understanding of the psychotherapeutic process. In general, the development of psychotherapy has paralleled the evolvement of psychoanalytic theory.

Freud's treatment of little Hans,[10] though admittedly accomplished through the agency of the boy's father, ushered in the era of psychodynamic child psychotherapy. In the 1920s, Hermine von Hug-Hellmuth[16] initiated the analytic approach to children through the medium of play; this innovation introduced the utilization of play in the psychotherapy of children. Melanie Klein[18] and Anna Freud[9] contributed much to the further development of child psychoanalysis in which dynamic psychotherapy has its roots. Melanie Klein developed a therapeutic technique in which the child's free play was considered to be akin to the adult's free associations; ultimately, this was based on the view that a child's and an adult's personality structures are similar. In contrast, Anna Freud regarded the child's inevitable dependence on his parents as a critical differential factor; as she saw it, this state prevented the development of the same kind of transference neurosis in child analysis as normally occurred in psychoanalytic treatment of adults. She also viewed the child's free play as significantly different from adult free associations.

The Child Guidance Movement in the 1920s

helped widen the scope of child psychotherapy in the United States. Joseph Solomon[29] and David Levy[21] presented classic accounts of play therapy, and Frederick Allen[2] and Hyman Lippman[22] developed and deepened the understanding of child psychotherapy.

While the child psychotherapists of the 1970s identify closely with these earlier twentieth-century leaders, we share a heritage with the sprinkling of people who, over the previous several centuries, had developed an empathic and revolutionary way of looking at children. In the middle of the sixteenth century, Weyer is said to have handled his reported "fasting girl" with a sensitivity shared by few of his contemporaries and with an approach that did not become common to practitioners for another century and a half.[30] During the eighteenth century, Rousseau introduced into education the realization that the child was more than someone to be seen and not to be heard, that the child was an individual to be considered and respected in his own right.

In the late eighteenth century, Itard stands out with his breakthrough treatment of the "Wild Boy of Aveyron." This was a mute, severely retarded, feral, approximately eleven-year-old boy who in all likelihood had been abandoned by his parents at an early age. It is reported that Itard's adherence to the humanist tradition in the "psychotherapy" of children was continued by other alienists of the Bicetre and Salpetriere Hospital, such as Ferrus and Vosin.[30]

During this same time, Mesmer was practicing his novel treatment method, "animal magnetism." To account for his curative powers, he envisioned an invisible universal fluid which could be utilized in the service of mental healing. Today, his results would be attributed to empathy, suggestion, identification, and transference. A treatment account from one of Mesmer's disciples, D'Eslon, is of special interest. He took a troubled girl on his knees and began to treat her by talking to her about her doll.[30] By establishing rapport in this manner, he anticipated play as the everyday tool of the child psychotherapist.

The child psychotherapist's kinship with these forerunners is of more than mere historical interest. Awareness of this kinship should remind us of the true foundation of psychotherapy. Our twentieth-century based conceptualizations enhance a systematized approach to children; this, however, continues to rely upon the earlier empathic sensitivity that finally emerged and developed as a commonly shared attitude of those engaged in the care of troubled children.

Description

Dynamic child psychotherapy is a psychological means of helping children by developing a relationship between the child and his therapist. The ultimate aim is for the child to become freer within the experience, to gain a deeper awareness of himself and others, and to find a path to the reasonable expression of emotions. The psychotherapist engages the child as an active party in this experience of reflecting on himself and seeks to help the child bring himself naturally and spontaneously into this relationship. Many things besides the development of greater awareness do happen in psychotherapy. There is relief of suffering and other symptoms, removal of blocks to development, and improvement in target ego functions. Attainment of any of these goals may become an end in itself along the way, but ordinarily they constitute intermediate points in a process that culminates in greater awareness.

The rationale for psychotherapy is based on the realization that a child's development occurs within interpersonal relationships that afford him patterning experiences. In complex ways, the result of these interactions is the establishment of equilibrium among many personal and interpersonal forces. If any of these processes should go awry within the context of interpersonal relationships, problems ensue. Psychotherapy provides a relationship within which patterns can be reexamined and relived, where frozen formations can become unfixed, where psychological forces can then be channeled in more adaptive ways, and where, optimally, more realistic equilibria can be established. It is assumed that an expanded awareness of oneself and one's modes of relationship can be a powerful accompaniment of and, at times, the instigator of these psychological changes.

To emphasize awareness is not to make development of awareness the be-all and end-all of psychotherapy. To begin with, it must be remembered that awareness is a powerful tool, primarily when the child has "his house pretty much in order," that is, when he can function at a relatively independent level and has enough self-mastery so that he can effect conscious changes in his functioning as his awareness expands. Second, dynamic psychotherapy rests on the broad base of the child-therapist relationship within which a variety of things beneficial to the child do happen. In this connection, there are a number of therapeutic forces or principles at work; they are as follows:

1. There is the *relationship* itself. Joselyn[17] has written about surprising psychotherapeutic success that seems to result from the child's quick response to the interpersonal relationship with the therapist. Here the catalytic agent is the therapist's empathic response that helps the child enjoy fuller experiences. It might be argued that the child would do as well with a sensitive, intuitive person in the child's natural environment who was alerted to his needs. Since, however, the therapist carries the stamp of "healer," his professional identity enhances identification, transference, and suggestion. All these are important contributors to therapeutic success that might well be lacking in the child's relationship with a nonprofessional. The power of this relationship in itself needs to be appreciated; however, it merits being considered a psychotherapeutic relationship only to the extent that it provides a vehicle which allows the other therapeutic principles to become operative.

2. Almost all of child psychotherapy includes an element of a *corrective emotional experience*. As Alexander[1] observed, in approaching patients, the therapist is likely to counteract by chance, or by choice, some of the experiences that have warped the child. For example, the experience of approval in psychotherapy may counteract some prolonged exposure to unreasonable disapproval which the child has known; or his "receiving something" may help to counteract an earlier experience of emotional and/or material deprivation. The mere acceptance of the child as a person to be taken seriously, as a person allowed and even encouraged to experience a wide range of emotions without criticism, and as someone who can express himself more freely, inevitably carries the seed of a "corrective emotional experience."

3. *Catharsis* or *abreaction*, to the extent that it is a ventilation of pent-up affect, is a common ingredient of child psychotherapy. The troubled child ordinarily comes to therapy with developmental distortions or frank neurotic symptoms. These are compromise formations which reflect his ineffective attempts to cope with painful affects generated by various developmental and fortuitous crises in his life. Although the therapist recognizes, as did Anna Freud,[8] that catharsis alone is ordinarily not sufficient, at some point the child will certainly need to mobilize affect and express it—abreact, if you will. Ultimately, the child needs to experience affect in a fuller, nonconflicted manner and to learn to express it in a reasonable fashion.

4. There is no denying that *suggestion* or *persuasion* is a powerful factor permeating the whole process of therapy. This principle is operative from the very beginning of psychotherapy; it is effective to the extent that the child and his family are united in their hope to improve his personal functioning. The more the child, the family, and the therapist agree on the change for which to strive, and the more they share a "common assumptive world,"[7] that is, a similar sense of values about personal functioning, the greater is the influence of suggestion in psychotherapy.

During the course of therapy, the therapist is employing suggestion when he expresses even so simple a thought as his confidence in the child's ability to engage meaningfully in the work ("I'm sure you have the sense to reflect on your feelings and to talk about them here rather than lash out at your mother at home," and "I am sure you have the courage and the ability to talk about those painful feelings here."). Suggestion is basic to all supportive therapy and is operative in interpretive comments as well, especially when these comments are not right on target.

5. *Maturational pull* might be considered nature's boost to the therapist; that is, the gods are typically on his side and if the therapist wants to be successful, he had better be on theirs! Because of the pressure of growth, the child is naturally and spontaneously inclined toward more mature development; if unimpeded, he will move on progressively to more independent functioning. This inner, propelling force derives its momentum from innate, constitutional factors which are helped by the internalization of environmental expectations. Therefore, the psychotherapist's most effective tool is the child's natural developmental processes; indeed, to be successful, one need merely remove the impediments to this development.

6. If development of *awareness* is seen to be the ultimate goal of child psychotherapy, it is obviously a powerful healing principle. Indeed if the child is to be master of himself, he needs to come in touch with his internal functioning and to recognize those environmental influences that impinge on him. Conversely, he needs to be freed from neurotic constrictions and distortions that accentuate maladaptive behavior. More specifically, the aim is to have the child become aware of his affects and to experience an open and conflict-free encounter with them. From this pivotal point, the therapist can help the child understand the wellsprings of this affect (be their source the usual everyday interactions of childhood or the more troublesome neurotic conflicts), and he can point to coping devices in and out of therapy that offer the child more adaptive means for handling such affect.

Indications

The premium on the development of greater awareness or insight is realistic only when such awareness offers a handle by which a child can extricate himself from emotional turmoil. Yet, even if such a situation does not prevail, dynamically oriented psychotherapy lends itself to an enormous variety of conditions, to the management, at least in part, of most, if not all, childhood disorders. This is true because there are two faces to dynamic therapy, the intrapersonal and the interpersonal. Where intrapsychic conflict prevails, the development of awareness can be stressed. Where interpersonal conflict predominates, this therapy offers a child a relationship within which he can ventilate feelings and sort out realistically what he does and does not bring to the difficulties. When personality distortions prevail, the neurotic entanglements can be unraveled, and the therapist may serve as a model of identification for more adaptive ways of coping. With the psychotic child and his defects in personality skills, the relationship offers opportunity for him to develop more adequately through the supportive help of the therapist.

Thus it can be said that this psychotherapy has something to offer in all of the wide variety of childhood disorders. At the same time, there are practical limitations to the applicability of this mode of helping disturbed children. If the disorders are placed on a continuum so that at the near end are the ones most responsive to such therapy, and at the other end, the ones least responsive, one would start with the developmental crises and move on through the neurotic, psychotic, and personality disorders. It is safe to say that psychotherapy may be indicated when a child is experiencing emotional distress so great that it jeopardizes development, and when the usual supportive help of family and friends does not suffice.

A word of caution. While psychotherapy has much to offer to a wide variety of children in trouble, it is not "the amulet" with "unlimited, healing value."[17] At times—for example, with the neurotic child—dynamic psychotherapy alone may suffice. However, by itself it is often insufficient. Many a child is in need of a well-rounded rehabilitative program within which psychotherapy may be an integral part. For example, where impulsivity and marked egocentricity prevail and self-reflection is entirely foreign to the child, individual psychotherapy by itself may be futile. However, it might be an integral part of a more structured milieu program.

Complications or Side Effects

Providing the assessment of the appropriateness of psychotherapy is valid, in the hands of an empathic, sensitive, and skillful therapist individual psychotherapy is relatively free of major complications and side effects. This assumes that the therapist allows the child to proceed at his own pace and can help the child deal adequately with the feelings generated in therapy. As long as the therapist can convey a genuine interest in the child, can remain sensitive to him, and can allow the child to funnel feelings and conflicts into therapy for resolution, things hardly go wrong (which is not the equivalent of saying they necessarily go right). This awareness indeed ought to make the therapist humble about the power of his role in therapy. Yet one should not underestimate the discipline needed to be an empathic observer with whom the child can interact in this unusual fashion; that is, the child must find someone who listens, understands, and does not feel the need to come up quickly with solutions, pat answers, and unsolicited advice. In and of itself, this disciplined, humanistic stance affords much therapeutic potential; yet, there is far more the therapist can offer if he masters the craft. That is, he can help the therapeutic process focus more precisely upon the child and his particular needs.

A different situation prevails when the therapist's sensitivity is diminished or lacking; then the process becomes distorted. In this case the therapist, in a number of ways, is likely to add to, rather than help lighten, the child's burden. There is danger that the child may turn outside the therapy and act out in a self-defeating way those feelings and conflicts that could and should have been handled within it. When, under the guise of trying to understand, the therapist actually proceeds in a moralistic fashion, he may only burden a child further with guilt and anxiety. If he foists his own value system on the child, the therapist may place his patient in a precarious position—torn between the therapist and his parents.

The therapist who misperceives the child's difficulties exclusively in terms of intrapsychic, personal conflict and ignores the unreasonable external reality with which the child has to deal also puts an undue burden on the child. The therapist who derives vicarious gratification from the child's behavior can be destructive as he fosters aggressive or sexual acting out. For example, the therapist who has difficulty with authority figures may encourage the child to have unnecessary confrontations with parents or teachers.

What the therapist sees as change for the better, however, may look like a complication or an undesirable side effect to the parents. For example, they may want their inhibited, constricted child to come out of his shell; but when he becomes freer in psychotherapy, openly expresses his feelings, and begins to confront them directly with his grievances, they may have second thoughts. Or, however unrealistically, a family may see the child's problems as the cause of all its hurting. As he improves, however, and the focus shifts away from the identified patient, tensions among other family members may become pronounced. These complications can be avoided if the therapist is aware of the intrafamilial psychodynamics; he can then help the parents anticipate how their child's change in behavior may affect them or recommend additional therapeutic work for the parents or the entire family (see chapters 7 and 9).

When the focus is on his overt behavior and not on his needs and feelings, the child who enters therapy may be in a vulnerable position. That is, as his overt behavior improves and is no longer a cause of discomfort for other members of the family, he may be taken out of therapy. This can deprive him of other necessary opportunities to proceed to a level where he can function more independently, or even to work through anxieties associated with termination.

Contraindications

Dynamic individual psychotherapy should not be utilized for conditions that require much more than it can accomplish. Accordingly, an error in outpatient care is to address this approach to a child who is not able to benefit from such psychotherapy, who is unable to function within the community without very disruptive behavior. While the anxious or depressed youngster may settle down with therapy as he becomes more comfortable, the one with serious deficiencies in reality testing, impulse control, or object relationships may not reap such benefits. Such a child may not be able to make even the first step toward a meaningful relationship in which self-reflection and toleration of frustration are requisite for success.

The contraindications for dynamic individual psychotherapy may be fewer in the inpatient care of children where psychotherapy is part of an overall milieu treatment program and does not stand by itself. Even here, however, for the child whose personality disorder carries with it markedly maladaptive patterns of behavior, more might be gained with a program organized around Redl's "life space interviews."[28] That is, throughout the day the child may need to be confronted with his actions, have his behavior dealt with as it occurs, and have attempts made to provide patterning experiences that will engender more adaptive behavior.

Technique

To speak of technique may conjure up the image of a repertoire of gimmicks with which to approach a child. The therapist does not win the child's favor with an impressive display of tricks. What does happen in psychotherapy is in fact quite unspectacular. The process rests upon a relationship in which the child and the therapist are simply honest with each other, and in which the child can sense that the therapist is genuinely interested in him and his welfare. This is not to undervalue the therapist's ability to communicate with the child at his level and to draw from an empathic source in the wellsprings of his own childhood.[3] These are the innate talents that undoubtedly bring the child psychotherapist to choose his work. To speak of techniques is to talk of disciplining those talents, of developing the skill to direct capacity. An absence of those skills and capacities prohibits a meaningful discussion of technique.

Technique is not to be equated with stilted behavior or a hierarchy of ritualistic interventions. The psychotherapist must not become a cold, calculating deliberator who sticks to his "method" and loses his spontaneity with children. At the same time, technical maneuvers are part of a rational approach. That is, the therapist needs to rely on his knowledge of how the personality develops, how the hypothesized energies of the mind operate in the course of a child's adaptational maneuvers, and have a systematized understanding of the therapeutic process. Ideally, what he does or does not do in therapy follows from a practiced intuitive awareness at the moment under the guidance of his understanding of the child and the therapeutic process. That is, the therapist should act in accord with what he hears, sees, and feels at that moment in therapy and in accord with what he decides the child needs and/or what he believes will maintain the therapeutic process.

Unless he has some more objective criteria to guide him, the therapist may find himself rationalizing questionable behavior by asserting that he is acting according to what the child needs. It helps to organize the child's productions in terms of id, ego, and superego functioning and to think of being allied with the child's ego functions, more especially with his observing and reflecting. The therapist is not on the side of impulse gratification for itself or on the side of prohibition of impulses for itself; instead he stands for the kind of self-mastery in which the child is attentive to his own wishes and feelings and can gratify and express himself reasonably within the constrictions of a reality that he accurately perceives. With the inhibited child or the one with deficient superego functioning, the therapist may lean toward id or toward superego functioning; but he never directly encourages impulse gratification or censures the child. Always, he works through ego functioning. For example, the therapist may say, "Though you feel funny about getting angry at me, it would be good if you could feel angry and talk with me about it," rather than, "Now get angry and tell me off! It'll be good to get those feelings off your chest!" Or, "Too bad you don't feel bad about slugging him so impulsively," rather than, "You shouldn't go around slugging kids like that, it just isn't right to do it."

There are other ramifications to the therapist's allying himself with ego functioning. For example, whether and how he does this may influence the child's ability to engage in a "therapeutic alliance" with him, that is, to get involved in a "relatively nonneurotic, rational rapport" so as "to work purposefully in the treatment situation."[12] It has been noted that the child may have special difficulty if he does not come to the therapist of his own choice; it may then be easier for him to see the therapist as the enemy. Actually, when the therapist comes through as clearly allied with ego functioning and especially intent on observing, most children seem to be able to get involved readily in the business of psychotherapy. Many a child will become allied with the therapist more readily after he is helped to distinguish between the experience of feelings and wishes and their expression. His defensiveness may pale when he senses that he can experience anger freely, and that this experience is not expected to lead automatically into a temper outburst. For children, this simple-seeming discrimination is one of the most powerful clarifications; the subsequent conflict-free experience of feelings ordinarily makes it easy to cope with conscious and very real conflicts about how to express this anger at any given moment.

With an eye on ego functioning, it also behooves the therapist to be ingenious in keeping the child involved in their therapeutic alliance. To make the whole business too serious a matter may only stifle the child's spark. In contrast, a well-placed lightness may kindle his spontaneity and curiosity. As will be discussed later, play also lends itself to less threatening exploration and communication. Above and beyond that, there is room for the therapist to use himself in a manner that invites the child to join with him rather than be threatened. Most importantly, it is not tricks or gimmicks but the therapist's well-demonstrated curiosity about psychological matters, embodied in a tactful, inviting manner, that over the long haul helps the child maintain his involvement in the therapeutic venture.

When the therapist is actively aligned with ego functioning, the child senses that the therapist is not about to join any of the conflicting personal blocs the child may have established. The child may then join the therapist more readily in the task of observing and understanding. For example, when a child talks about how angry he is because everybody picks on him, the therapist need not get trapped into siding with the child or with his alleged foes. He can simply say, "I can well appreciate that you would get awfully mad feeling yourself picked on by all those kids." Even when quick to respond, "But I am picked on!" the child ordinarily perceives readily that the therapist is addressing his perceptions of the world. The ground is then set for the child to proceed on to an examination of what he perceives, the manner in which he perceives it, and what might heighten or distort his perceptions.

It is very difficult to tell the therapist what to do at any particular time in therapy. One can, however, categorize the variety of options that are available to him. Therapeutic interventions can be viewed on a continuum that ranges from those that will elicit a clearer picture of the child and his problems, to those that will help the child integrate and utilize the newly acquired information about himself.[14]

The simplest thing the therapist may do is to ask the child questions about what he says, or does, in order to get a clear picture of what the child presents, or to encourage spontaneity in the child. He may go on to clarify the picture further by recapitulation and reorganization of the child's productions so as to establish temporal sequence and logical order. After he has clarified the picture, he may be ready to confront the child, that is, aim to engage him in an active examination of the material at hand so the child can get at the implications of what he says and does. As the therapist confronts and asks the child to step back to take a look at the picture he has just drawn, the emphasis is still on the expressed or the implied feelings and motivations. That is, the therapist remains at the level of the material the child presents; he does not attempt to pursue new or deeper dimensions, for example, unexpressed motivations of which the child remains unaware.

When confrontation is established and the child acknowledges that he and the therapist are both tuned in to the same bit of reality, the therapist may seek an opportunity to interpret to the child something beyond his conscious awareness. Put in another sense, throughout the encounter the therapist tries to establish with the child the *what*, after which he may try to help him understand *why* he acted as he did, that is, understand what was taking place out of awareness and what were the unconscious motivations. It must be emphasized that the therapist should not try to get at the why and wherefore with a child before the two of them have agreed on what the child has said or done or on how he feels. When the therapist concentrates too much on unconscious motivation, he runs the risk of reducing psychotherapy to a pursuit that the child flees or to a series of intellectualized discussions that provide the child with an explanation rather than an experience.

While the content of the interpretation may be defense and affect, or impulse and conflict, it is material of which the child is not aware and of which he cannot readily become aware by his usual conscious effort. Meaningful interpretation is not a matter of plumbing the depths of the unconscious with utter abandon. It involves helping the child loosen many of the repressive forces and, only then, directing him to material of which he has had some difficulty becoming aware. Meaningful interpretation is ordinarily an assist to the child in his last step toward the development of awareness.

While the matter of interventions may sound abstruse, the therapist will find that if he closely follows the child's productions, he will move on naturally from one intervention to another. If he stays in tune with the child and deals with the material at hand, he will automatically encourage the progressive expansion of awareness. Experience teaches that it is wise to nudge but not to push. Furthermore, he does not have to reach for content so much as he needs to be in position to help the child unwrap it.

Next in line on this continuum of interventions lies education. It includes active attempts to expand or enhance personality functioning directly. This stands in contrast to the usual psychotherapeutic efforts. Educational intervention includes the imparting of new knowledge and directing the child to exercise certain personality functions such as impulse control and critical judgment. In the course of psychotherapy, it is helpful to aim to make the child more responsive to the usual educational forces afforded him by family and community; education itself should not become the goal of psychotherapy. However, the line between psychotherapy and education does become blurred, and education may play an important part in the process. For example, when further clarification of a problem might reveal that the child is indeed a victim of ignorance and not of emotional blocks or complexes, under these circumstances, education, rather than interpretation, might be indicated. Ordinarily, part of the task is to determine whether the child is uninformed because of his lack of exposure to knowledge or whether he has remained ignorant because of interferences with his assimilation of knowledge, for example, of sexual matters. Even when the child has indeed had a lack of exposure, it is usually wiser for the therapist not to don the hat of the educator too quickly. If he does, he will give up his role of therapist and forfeit his therapeutic advantage. He remains on surer footing if he reserves the bulk of his educative efforts in the sessions to teaching the child about the therapeutic process itself.

On the far end of the continuum, beyond education, are advising, counseling, and directing. Again, it is best for the therapist to advise, counsel, or direct the child primarily in matters pertinent to the therapeutic process itself. For example, during their session, he might curtail certain of the child's activities, be it assaultive behavior or "regression for the sake of regression," in order to keep the therapeutic process moving. He ought to intervene in this manner, however, only after it is obvious that he cannot activate the child's own reality testing and impulse control.

Each of these interventions is legitimate and valuable in its own right, and it is not reasonable to place a value judgment on any of them as such. Whether it is a "good" or "bad" intervention depends upon whether it maximizes therapeutic effectiveness. However, primary reliance on a given type of intervention is bound to shape the therapeutic process in one direction or another. For example, the more the therapist confines himself to confrontation and interpretation, the more he encourages the child to reflect on the influence of unconscious emotional complexes on his behavior. On the other hand, the more he leans toward education and counseling, the more he activates the child's conscious, volitional functioning. While both methods may enhance development, the former does it through the removal of emotional impediments, while the latter relies on patterning experiences. Ideally, the therapist emphasizes one method over the other on the basis of the child's needs rather than in response to his own biases. That is, the child with neurotic traits and neurotic conflicts may benefit more from emphasis on confrontation and interpretation, while the child with significant defects or deficiencies in personality skills may get more from interventions that foster patterning experiences.

The substance of interventions includes material from the child's behavior and productions in therapy and from what goes into the child-therapist relationship. In any event, the therapist needs to remain attuned to the child's level of awareness of the content; the therapist can start only with material of which the child is aware; that is, he must deal with manifest content before he can seek to opt for latent meanings. If the child cannot perceive the blatantly obvious, it would be pointless to expect him to be open to consideration of the hidden aspects of his behavior. For example, a child may deny that he is sad and angry, be unable even to acknowledge his obvious tearfulness, and cannot detect the sarcastic ring in his voice. In such a case it would be folly to expect him to be receptive to consideration of the underlying affect and its origins. Before he could have him reflect on his affect and its meaning, the therapist would need to deal first with the child's use of denial and his resultant lack of awareness. While the "action-oriented" child with behavior problems and the obsessional child may each isolate affect defensively in order to remain unaware of it, it also needs to be remembered that a child may be oblivious to affect because this is his style; he ordinarily just does not reflect on how he feels.

After the therapist deals with manifest content he can choose to consider defenses and resistances of which the child is relatively unaware. If he can bring the child to give up his defensiveness, he then sets the stage for a further development of manifest content. If he proceeds from manifest to latent content in this way, the therapist will find that he will move in step-wise fashion from overt behavior to affect by way of defenses and resistances until he finally arrives at impulse and conflict.

For example, with repeated confrontations of her pseudo-mature, grossly seductive and her very "silly" behavior, it was established with twelve-year-old Karen that she generally acted either as a much older girl or as a much younger girl. In turn, as she vacillated between these two behaviors in the sessions, the therapist pointed out how she thereby avoided her obvious anxiety at that given moment. Finally, it was interpreted to her how at the moment there seemed to be a real struggle in her between the part of her that wanted to grow up and the part of her that wanted to remain the little girl.

Another example is seen in the treatment of ten-year-old John, who interacted in essentially a sadomasochistic manner. Through numerous reviews with him of interactions in which he was involved, he was confronted with the fact that ordinarily in his relationships with others the end result was that either he was hurting the other person through physical or verbal attack or he was inviting a similar hurt against himself.

It was interpreted to him (and he agreed uneasily) that there was something pleasurable about either occurrence. Subsequent interpretations dealt with how this manner of dealing with people was related to his feelings of insecurity around others, especially since he was concerned about his physical appearance and his intelligence.

In his haste to get at "the heart of the matter," it is common for a therapist to err by dealing with impulses before dealing with the patient's defenses against these impulses. Rather than help the patient work through these defenses, he "plows through" these structures with "id interpretations." This does not help free up the child; instead, the therapist is likely to promote an "hypertrophy" of the defenses so that a greater resistance to awareness results. For example, if the child uses denial, he may now need to deny even more vehemently; if he "acts out," there may be an even greater flurry of such behavior to oppose the development of greater awareness.

Therapists often need to be reminded to accept the child's manifest content as significant in its own right and not merely something that masks "deeper" conflicts and impulses. Interpretations of "what you really think," or "what you really mean," or "how you *really* feel" make the therapist sound as though he were cynical enough to believe that the only reality is the hidden reality, and in the process he tunes children off! In contrast to this, if the therapist says, for example, "Even as you complain about how the other kids pick on you, you laugh as though maybe there were some fun in it for you," they may more likely proceed to consideration of the child's underlying sadomasochistic yearnings. That is, in the reflective tone of therapy, the therapist should acknowledge to the child that he is obviously unhappy with being picked on, but that it is also important for them to look at his unexplained laughter, to see whether it does not indicate other feelings about which he has been unaware.

The child's twofold relationship with the therapist also offers material for intervention. There are the "real" aspects, that is, how the child is dealing with him according to what the therapist gives of himself during the session. There are also the various transference elements, that is, reactions to the therapist that reflect the child's experiences with his parents and other important people in his life. These responses are not related primarily to what transpires between the two of them at the moment.

The more there is reliance on the therapeutic effectiveness of the relationship itself, the more the therapist will depend on the development and maintenance of a positive reaction to him. In order to keep things on the positive side, he will accordingly deal with negative transference reactions quickly. To the extent that therapy is of the "uncovering" variety, however, with an emphasis on the development of a more general awareness about self and about interaction with others, the therapist is advised to let transference reactions unfold more fully with their admixture of positive and negative elements. He will need to proceed especially slowly in the interpretation of transference reactions if he seeks development of a relative transference neurosis. It never will unfold if the child's transference distortions are corrected virtually as they manifest themselves.

To intervene is to be active. The question arises as to how active or how passive the therapist ought to be. To say categorically that the therapist should be either is unrealistic. Though some therapists may be likely to err on the side of being too passive, their strength lies in their ability to alternate between being passive and being active, moving from one stance to another as they interact with any given child over the course of therapy. There are times when the therapist can zero in very actively on problem areas and stimulate the child's ability to resolve a problem. There are times when

he needs to back off and be passive, because only this approach will allow the child to come out of himself. If the therapist actively pursues material at such a moment, the child will only retreat further into his defensive cocoon.

There are also guidelines according to which the therapist may decide *when* to intervene. Early in therapy, he may strive to create a therapeutic structure. The child finds himself involved in a totally novel experience, and it may be necessary to spell out the nature of therapy repeatedly. It is assumed that the therapist will have introduced the child to the whole idea of therapy and to their respective roles so that the youngster can realistically commit himself to a therapeutic alliance. Subsequently it may be important to remind a child and reassure him again and again that spontaneous behavior in sessions is not only acceptable but desirable.

Later in the course of therapy, it may be necessary to intervene to maintain some structure. The therapist may still have to remind the child that they come together to look at his behavior so that they might understand it more fully, and that the therapist is not there to give permission or to police. Or he may now act to maintain a therapeutic process in which there is reasonable equilibrium between regression and progression. Interventions that enhance regression involve all sorts of indications that the child is free to express himself, that the therapist does accept the child and his spontaneous behavior, for example, his talk and his play; that the inhibited, constricted child need not fear that he will elicit angry responses or criticisms. At other times, the therapist may need to intervene to curb regression when the child's assaultive, destructive, or continuously repetitious behavior allows for no therapeutic advantage. Whether to encourage or to curb regression, the therapist ought to intervene so as to call upon the child's ability to reflect and to act freely. When curbing regression is in order, he may need to take over more for the child and set limits or even to restrain him physically.

There are also times to encourage progression actively. The therapist might emphasize that the "big boy" or "big girl" way to cope with problems is to talk about them and to try to work out solutions rather than carry on and make a scene when frustrated. The aim here is to have the child step up a few notches in his development. Or there are interventions which provide the child assistance in any of the variety of his ego or superego functions in which he evidences some deficiency.

If the child cannot see things realistically, the therapist may regularly help him to assess reality, even while inviting the child to examine how his own denial and projection interfere with his ability to look at himself in his interactions with others. When impulse control is insufficient, the therapist can anticipate uncontrolled behavior and attempt to mobilize the child's own capacity to set limits. If that does not suffice, he might curtail certain activities or physically restrain the youngster when he does get beyond his own controls. To bolster superego functioning, the therapist may need to confront the child with the implications of his behavior and help him convert ego-syntonic behavior into ego-dystonic behavior, that is, help him feel uneasy about pleasurable behavior that is maladaptive. In such attempts, he ought not reprimand the child for his behavior; instead, he should confront him with a realistic assessment of it, for example, directly tell the older child that as he angrily pouts and sulks rather than talks about his distress that he is using the techniques of a much younger child to hide from his problems. There are also times to help the child "pat himself on the back" as his lopsided, severely punitive superego does not give him the "glow of virtue" when he does something "good" but makes him feel guilty when he does something "bad."

While intervening in the child's behavior, the therapist needs to be cautious that he does not virtually make the child identify with him in his style of behavior and means of coping. If there is any attempt to encourage identification, it ought to be primarily in the area of self-reflection and self-appraisal. Accordingly, the therapist might convey loudly and clearly that he approves of the child's self-reflection, of his frank, realistic appraisal of himself, and of the good feelings he experiences as a result of such diligent efforts.

In all these interventions (apart from physical restraint), the therapist conveys a message by words, but it is important to keep in mind the nonverbal accompaniments. He needs to be mindful of this especially when he questions the child about his behavior as an invitation to reflect on it, for his tone may convey a note of displeasure, especially when annoyance has in part prompted him to intervene. He should not fall back on the euphemistic "*why?*" This is really not so much an invitation to reflect as it is an ambiguous, covert demand that the child stop doing something.

While the nonverbal communication may actually carry the message, there is much to be said for dressing up the nonverbal in words. Many a child with characterological problems lives in a whirlwind of repeated nonverbal communications with ambiguous messages to which he remains oblivious. In the therapy of such a case, clear verbalizations may be especially important. A nonverbal intervention by itself—a shrug of the shoulders, a frown, a smile—is risky if the child can construe it to be a chastisement. It is even less desirable if the therapist uses it to express countertransference reactions that he finds difficult to handle. Verbalization may be especially important when physical restraint becomes necessary, as it may keep the transference and countertransference distortions to a minimum.

Discussion of physical restraint is in order, since, in therapy, it does become a controversial issue. It is an intervention not to be taken lightly, as it certainly may complicate the interaction between the child and the therapist, but there are impulsive children with whom anything short of physical restraint is to no avail. To be sure, at the moment, physical restraint does make the therapist a "real" person, and it does mitigate against his being a transference object. However, it is not every child who becomes so destructive or assaultive that physical restraint is necessary, and the one who does is probably not the one to benefit from therapy in which the emphasis is on the development of transference reactions or transference neurosis. Such a child needs to develop personality skills that will allow him to be the sort of neurotic who benefits from a relationship that permits emergence of transference. When a child can respond to nothing short of physical restraint, some therapists encourage termination of a session. However, this approach has its own complications. When the child is fighting against making a commitment to therapy, ending the hour may accomplish nothing. This is especially true when it helps maintain the child's fantasies of omnipotence. It is asserted that the child without a commitment to therapy perhaps should not be there to begin with, and there may well be something to this. There are some children of this sort, however, who do finally settle down and get very much involved in therapy. This can happen only after they get to realize that the therapist can get them under control in a nonpunitive manner, and that he can do it in a very open and direct fashion, without resorting to the unrealistic cajolement and bribery to which they have been exposed with other adults.

What about physical contact that conveys friendly overtures to the child? While a therapist might be naturally inclined to put his hand on a child's shoulder or to tousle his hair, he needs to consider what this approach means within the context of his relationship with the child. The extensive use of such physical overtures may smack of the overseer being "nice" to his underling; it can emphasize an inequality between the therapist and the child and can set the stage for a paternalistic approach. Nonetheless, there are times when comforting or affectionate physical contact is in order. The extremely frightened youngster may need a comforting hand, and the child especially deficient in his ability to develop a relationship may utilize close physical, but non-sexual, contact constructively. This happens in much the same way as an infant who builds a relationship on the foundation of repeated physical contacts.

The idea of friendly overtures to the child also brings up the whole matter of doing "nice" things for children in order to cement a firmer relationship with them. There may be the giving of candy or going out for treats to bring to the session, sending cards when on a trip, sending birthday greetings, or giving presents. Except in the case of children with serious defects in interpersonal relationships, ordinarily such overtures may be suspect, as more of a hindrance than a help. The main question is who benefits from them, the child or the therapist? To think that such overtures are necessary may reflect a demeaning attitude toward children. Children ordinarily can sense whether the therapist is a "nice" person without his having to go out of his way to be nice. Studied niceness may reflect a defensive paternalistic attitude, which too often in a child's everyday experiences with adults impedes, rather than facilitates, his spontaneous experience and his readiness to express a variety of feelings. How can the child, for example, get angry at someone who goes out of his way to be so nice!

There is much to be said for a matter-of-fact, businesslike approach to the task at hand. The emphasis should fall primarily on being an empathic listener who tunes in with the child as fully as is possible, who accepts him as he is, and with whom there is no question of a generation gap in communication. Childen ordinarily can step remarkably well into a relationship with such a therapist and get to work in a hurry. They may also be able to disengage in a hurry and get back quickly to the real world. This will happen if they are not entangled in the sticky, complicated relationships in which therapists unwittingly enmesh children if they worry unnecessarily about "establishing a relationship." The vast majority of children who come to the usual therapist are not so psychologically primitive that they need to be bribed and seduced.

The Role of Play in Therapy

The techniques outlined here are applicable to all of the interactions between the child and his therapist, including their involvement in play, which may be an intimate part of the psychotherapy of a child. Play is a spontaneous activity in which a child ordinarily engages comfortably. As such, it lends itself so well to use in therapy that it has assumed a central role in the development of modern-day mental health work with children.

Play occurs on various levels of interaction and understanding. It can be primarily a vehicle for the child's self-expression; thus, he may draw pictures that reflect his inner state, the flavor of his affect, the content of his preoccupations, and/or the nature of his inner conflicts. Play may also convey interpersonal messages to the therapist. These can be grasped through the content of drawings and puppet play, and by the manner and context in which the child engages in the activity. Ordinarily, in the course of psychotherapy with children, it may be helpful to afford the child an opportunity for play. The absolute need for this activity will vary according to the age of the child. That is, the therapist would be at a great disadvantage if he did not have playthings available for the child in the preschool and early-latency age groups, but the need for play may diminish with the older child.

In order to use play effectively in psychotherapy, the first need is for an appropriate setting. The therapist can have playthings available in his office, or he can arrange a separate playroom away from his office. If he elects to tell the patient that they will use the office for "talk" sessions and will use a playroom for "playing" sessions, he ought not convey a premium on talk. Some may unwittingly belittle the value of play in the therapy sessions by placing an undue emphasis on talk over play. Actually, the two together ordinarily prove to be the most productive.

An ideal arrangement for the child psychotherapist would include a separate playroom for the prelatency to early-latency children and a regular office setting without playthings for adolescent patients. For children between these two age groups, an office in which an area lends itself for play will suffice. The main consideration is that the play setting be suitable for the type of play anticipated. Play with water and clay, for example, obviously requires a more specialized setting than does the use of crayons, paper, and puppets. The therapist needs to anticipate and prepare for play therapy with the child. It will not work if the therapist has to hover anxiously and become more of a policeman than a therapist as he tries to keep the furnishings, or even the room, intact, let alone clean.

There are three types of playthings to consider. First are those that allow the child to express himself in a variety of ways. Paper, crayons, pencils, blackboard, and chalk allow one type of expression. Puppets, dolls, playhouse furnishings, cars, and trucks allow another type. For more regressive types of play, there is the second category of items that includes sand, water, fingerpaints, clay, and claylike materials. In the third category are a variety of board games and cards that may allow for just "getting things going" or for more clear-cut competitive interchange between the child and the therapist. The therapist should not strive for just a wide assortment of playthings; instead, he ought to select those he finds helpful and those he can comfortably let the child use in the particular setting.

The therapist can approach play along two general lines. First, he may elect to use "structured" or "directed" play,[13] whereby he leads the child to a given activity or to a prearranged setting of playthings and has him step in to carry out a theme. This approach may be helpful to get at particular conflicts. For example, the therapist may set the dolls as a family around a table and ask the child to tell him about the family and what they are doing. Formalized variations of such structured play include Newman and Stern's "age game,"[27] in which the child selects a certain age and behaves at that level, Gardner's "Mutual Storytelling Technique,"[11] and Marcus's costume play therapy.[24] Second, the therapist most commonly may opt for nondirective or unstructured play. Here, if the child elects to play, he spontaneously employs whatever playthings he chooses. This approach lends itself to expressive-exploratory psychotherapy in which the child can unfold himself in play at his own pace and in the manner that suits him best.

As an empathic observer, the therapist needs to appreciate the self-expressive and self-gratification aspects of the play. At the same time, he also must pay attention to what the child is attempting to communicate to him. All three aspects deserve consideration. In terms of self-expression, play does serve first as a form of catharsis and allows for the discharge of impulses and emotions. The element of catharsis may be especially important for an inhibited child; in his play he begins to free up a bit, and within the safe confines of the therapy session, he may even find it possible to tolerate some regression. This previously inhibited or overly controlled youngster may, at times, swing over to the adaptive style of the impulse-ridden child, and from this point forward, he may traverse a path similar to that followed by such an impulsive child. That is, from disorganized, markedly regressed play in which the discharge of drives is primary, there is a progression to more organized play that presently involves more advanced ego-functioning.

Second, play is a means by which the child unfolds his personality and displays the various levels of his functioning and his conflicts. Therefore, through play, the child can be helped to gain awareness of his coping and defensive maneuvers and to come to face that with which he struggles. As therapy proceeds, play can become a gauge by which to determine improvement in the child's functioning and the level of resolution of his conflicts.

The third element of play is communication, and it is the feature that spells the difference between play in the child's everyday life and play in therapy. As has been noted, in play, the child first of all communicates about himself. In addition, wittingly or unwittingly, he communicates much to the therapist, especially since the therapist's presence is bound to shape the nature of his play. In either event the child provides a great deal of information through his choice of play, through the manner in which he plays, and through the context of the play itself.

As in all of therapy, in play the therapist can be either a "real" person to the child or a "transference" figure. That is, if the therapist joins the child in play without specific attention to the manner in which he reciprocates to the child's wishes, he becomes the "real" person. If in the course of play, he does not satisfy the child's every whim, he will allow the child to communicate to him as a "transference" person. That is to say, the child will bring into the relationship feelings and attitudes he has toward other important persons in his life. The frustration, as it were, evokes the significant frustrations of the past whether they relate to weaning, toilet training, oedipal disappointment, or whatever. The child can gradually discover these as the play, and the interpretation of play, proceeds.

The first task may be to help the child become able to engage in play, because some children are so frightened of their feelings, or so afraid to lose control, that play in therapy may be much too threatening. One child may be inhibited because he is fearful of expressing himself in any form of play, while another may engage in car play or checkers but be much too defensive to project himself into puppet play. A third child may have difficulty when he goes to cards or board games, because he is unable to compete in any sort of reasonable fashion.

The therapist is well advised to be cautious about the use of competitive games. They can be an invaluable tool with which to build toward a meaningful relationship, especially if they help the child secure a comfortable position from which he can then proceed to express himself in a freer type of play. In this case the competitive elements may be unimportant, as playing a game may merely help the two participants through the initial awkwardness of getting to know each other. However, the patient can use games as a powerful resistance to the work, as a way of avoiding involvement in other play activity that will call for him to expose himself a bit more. The therapist may then need to decide whether these games have lost their usefulness and have in fact become an impediment to therapy.

When the development of awareness is the ultimate aim in therapy, communication becomes a vital aspect of the child's play. Regardless of the extent to which he decides to involve himself in the play, the therapist needs to be an acute observer of the child's behavior. An an observer, he can elect to be either a nonparticipant or a participant. Over the course of therapy he may very appropriately alternate between these two stances.

As a nonparticipant observer, the therapist does not get actively involved in a child's play. He needs to appreciate, however, that the child in his own mind may have the therapist pegged as an accomplice, critic, judge, adversary, or whatever his fancy dictates at the moment. As a nonparticipant observer, the therapist would obviously avoid any competitive games. If the child attempts to involve him in the play, the therapist may passively join in only to dramatize the script prepared by the child, or as a reporter who accompanies the child on his venture.

As a participant observer, the therapist can join the child in play on any of several levels. He may assume a role assigned to him by the child but write his own script, although primarily he should react to or elaborate on what the child presents.

This method lends itself to introduction of material from the "real life" experiences of the child, especially where the youngster is guarded about certain aspects of his life. Or the therapist might take the initiative in play. For example, he might make a "make-believe" phone call to the child with the aid of toy telephones. Or he may talk to a puppet who is assigned the role of being aware of the child, or whom he asks to communicate with the child. As the therapist initiates play in this fashion, he may help the child in several ways. By his own example he may encourage the child to regress and offer him an example of how it can be done. In any case, he may help him communicate more freely.

Last, the therapist can be a participant observer in a competitive game. There are several things to keep in mind about such games in therapy. The game should be age-appropriate, but it is also desirable that it be a type that will not require an inordinate amount of concentration, skill, or time. Games of chance that require little skill are most helpful as they do not demand the kind of total concentration that would block the therapist from being attentive to what else is going on in the session. Games are usually most productive if the therapist plays in a reasonably competitive fashion, availing himself of the usual opportunities to win. If he plays a keenly competitive game or if he "gives" the game to the child, he is likely to lose the opportunity to use it for therapeutic purposes. In games of skill, such as checkers, the therapist might reasonably give the child a handicap to make the contest more fair. However, it is not unusual to find that the child who has trouble with object relationships and is inordinately competitive will have problems both with winning and losing; such a child is likely to balk over handicaps. Board games may also pose other dilemmas. What about the child who cheats in a game? To reprimand him is hardly therapeutic, and to ignore the fact that he cheated is surely unrealistic. Ordinarily, it is helpful to take the position of observer, to confront the child with the obvious and to reflect with him on why he cheats. As Meeks[25] has pointed out, the possible reasons are manifold. For instance, one child may be looking for his therapist to be his "conscience" or a "policeman," while another child might be out to see whether the therapist is aligned with his superego or with his id. If the child persists in cheating in spite of these confrontations and explanations, the therapist may have no choice but to refuse to play that game; in effect, the road is closed for its reasonable use. If the child bends the rules in favor of the therapist, it is important to get at the meaning of this behavior. From the point of view of his mental health, he is scarcely better off if he takes what belongs to others than if he yields what is rightfully his.

The therapist may be in an even greater dilemma when a child constantly modifies the rules of the game, though not in order to win or to avoid losing. The therapist should hesitate to conclude that such elaborate modifications of rules is a sign of creativity; indeed, he is more likely to find it a manifestation of very prosaic resistance. More than likely, he and the child will be so preoccupied with the game and its modifications that they will have no time to pay attention to anything else in the session.

The whole array of interventions discussed previously are applicable to the content of play. The therapist can, however, approach the play material in two ways. First, he may approach the play productions strictly in terms of their displacements, that is, he talks to play characters, or about them and their actions, in a "make-believe" fashion. Second, he may proceed from the play into the child's real-life situation, using the play as a springboard into the child's "real" world. Ordinarily, it is wise to stay with the play world as much as possible and to make all interventions within the context of play, in the "make-believe" of play. When the child himself jumps from the "make-believe" to the "real" world, the therapist needs to decide whether to deal with the "real-life" events or to encourage the child to return to the play. He can do this more reasonably if he answers some questions for himself. Has the child retreated from the play into the real world because of his anxiety? Is further regression into fantasy at the moment desirable and therefore to be encouraged? Or is the step into reality a sign of progress? Would the advantage lie in discouraging further regression and fostering the reality work that the child now introduces?

In working with play, one of the more frequent technical errors is to return the child prematurely to real-life experiences. Either the therapist deals too quickly with the real-life situation to which the child has fled from the play or he actively seeks to bring the child prematurely out of play into confrontation with real-life issues. A therapist is most likely to make this error when he becomes engrossed with the symbolic elements of play. When the symbolism absorbs his attention, he may feel compelled to share his insights with the child. Unfortunately, in his haste, he may only drop wet blankets on the child's productions and offer, at best, intellectualized insights that do not expand the child's awareness.

When and where to set limits in play may also pose difficulties. Obviously it is necessary to stop destructive action before the child physically hurts himself and/or the therapist, or before he destroys everything in sight. Under less threatening circumstances, the therapist is in a position to decide more realistically if he looks at the child's play from the standpoint of ego functioning. First and foremost, the therapist wants the child to reflect on what is going on. If the child becomes so utterly involved in drive discharge that observation and reflection go by the board, it is reasonable to limit such play. When lack of impulse control or disturbed reality testing lead to extremes in play, it is appropriate to try to limit a child's play by activating his impulse control or his reality testing.

Above all, the therapist ought not to reduce his interaction with the patient to that of playmate. If he does, then therapy is reduced to nothing more than instinctual gratification for the patient, and yes, for the therapist. As playmate, the therapist may end up involved in endless games that lead nowhere; or he may blindly carry out whatever the child dictates, not taking into consideration what impact this form of participation has on the child. The submissive therapist playmate has been known to end up at the mercy of the child, securely tied to a chair or locked out of his office by his "playful" captor who fleeced him out of his keys.

Though in play he may assume an active or a passive role, a dependent one or one in which he is master, basically the therapist should maintain a realistically secure therapist-patient relationship. That is, regardless of the role he selects, he and the patient ought to be aware that he assumes this role by choice and that he has never really abandoned his *real* position in therapy. In contrast to this, the child may find it difficult to disentangle himself from a given role. These issues are discussed further in chapter 25.

Frequency and Intensity

The frequency and intensity of the therapy in which to engage a child will depend upon the goals that have been established based on an assessment of the child's needs and capacities. The therapist can think of therapy in terms of a relationship that will serve primarily to activate the child's personality skills. The mission will be to delineate his problem and to mobilize his ability to resolve it. With this in mind, the therapist might think of less frequent visits and a less intensive therapy relationship. Accordingly, if he expects therapy to continue over several months, he might think of one session per week. If he wants to make it a very circumscribed therapeutic arrangement, he might decide on two sessions a week for two to three weeks. If he wishes to establish a relationship that encourages the child to develop transference reactions and to examine neurotic distortions, the therapist might convene the sessions at shorter intervals and over an extended period of time.

A maximum of two sessions per week is usually optimal; with most therapists, it is questionable whether more frequent sessions are more productive. With the majority of children, one session per week proves to be optimal, and the children engage meaningfully at this frequency. This conclusion is based on material now available concerning children whose parents have been adamantly opposed to more than one session per week because of financial or time considerations. That is, these children have been found to make the kind of surprising gains that were originally thought possible only with more frequent sessions. However, a schedule of less than one session per week does not ordinarily lend itself to productive psychotherapy. It may be indicated only when the therapist tries to maintain a supportive relationship, for example, with a psychotic child, and the therapeutic experience is then built entirely on the use of relationship.

Preparation of Family and Child

It has been stated that in one way or another the therapist ought to inform the patient about the process of psychotherapy; this will help him become party to the transactions.[14] If there is to be more to therapy than the effects of transference and suggestion that are generated by what the child and his parents expect of the therapist, a fair amount of explanation is in order. First, the therapist should tell the child directly about the nature of his emotional disorder, spelling out something of the nature of the dynamic forces that lead to the emergence of his symptoms. Moreover, he should spell out what he hopes they will

accomplish in therapy, and how they will proceed in their efforts. For example, he might tell the depressed youngster that he sees his unhappiness as part of his difficulty in being free and open with his feelings, especially with anger. He can go on to explain that in therapy they will attempt to gain a better understanding of how the child functions and with what he struggles. The hope is that as he becomes more and more aware of himself, he will be able to be more free and open, more assertive in a reasonable way without a need to get himself so bottled up with feelings.

It is also important to tell the child what is expected of him in therapy. The therapist may explain as well that what they do in the session will be pretty much up to the child, be it talking together or using the playthings. He can further encourage the child to play freely and to talk about whatever comes to his mind in the sessions. The therapist can explain to him that from his play, and from what he says, they will get an idea of what sorts of things preoccupy him, what his struggles are, and why he has them. He should also assure the child of confidentiality, and let him know that he is not there to pick up information to report back to parents. He may explain to the child that he will try to help his parents with their questions, and to do this, he will fall back on his knowledge of the child and his family; but at no point will he report back to the parents what the child tells him. It is also wise to explain to the child that as the therapist he is not there to react, so he hopes that the child will be able to be free and open with him and not be fearful that he may elicit angry or hurtful responses.

A certain amount of preparation of the family is also in order. It is reasonable to explain to the parents the nature of their child's emotional disorder and the nature of the therapy. Ordinarily it is helpful to describe therapy to the parents as a process in which the child has an opportunity to develop a special relationship in which he and his therapist can examine what the child brings into a relationship and in which the child can learn to be more free and open with himself and with others. It usually is wise to spell out to the parents the nature of the confidentiality, namely, that the therapist will not report back to them what the child says and does in sessions. If he adds that their child is free to share with them whatever he wishes, it may be wise to encourage them not to prod their child for information but to let him decide if and what he wants to share with them.

It is understandable that parents may feel uneasy about having their child become so intimately involved with someone outside the family. The feeling is especially keen if they already lament the fact that he is not close to them. Therefore, it may be wise for the therapist to explain to the parents their child's confidential relationship with him over the long run will not draw him away from them. Instead, it will help him get to a point where he can be closer to them in an age-appropriate manner. To let the parents know that the therapist is mindful of the trust they place in him, that he will do nothing to violate this trust, and that he will do nothing to alienate their child from them may well go a long way to help the parents support their child's therapy.

It helps to invite the parents to call the therapist when they have questions or doubts. For questions that cannot be handled over the phone, he might mention that sometime in the near future it will be wise for all of them to meet to review matters. This is especially true when the child presents behavior problems on which the therapist might presently be able to shed some light. Further details can be found in chapter 8.

Goals and Stages of Therapy

Because it is so vitally important, yet so easy to gloss over, we will begin at the end with consideration of the termination of therapy. No one would argue that termination is in order when the originally established goal of psychotherapy has been reached, but the goal may have originally been stated in very vague terms—for example, the development of greater awareness of the self. When does the patient arrive at that point?

Ordinarily, it is not realistic for the therapist to try to talk children and parents into continued therapy. Nor will he find himself in that uncomfortable position if he keeps two things in mind. First, if he has formulated realistic expectations and goals, the child and his parents are less likely to be the ones to raise the possibility of termination. Second, under the usual circumstances, ultimately it is up to the child and his parents to decide on termination just as it was up to them to decide on entering therapy. Rather than sharpen his skills of persuasion, the therapist needs to develop guidelines by which he can decide when to recommend termination and according to which he can clarify issues with the child and his parents when they suggest ending therapy.

Since goals and termination go hand in hand,

in respect to the possibility of termination it is helpful to consider goals on two levels. The first goal may be to resolve the particular problem with which the child comes. The time necessary for this resolution constitutes the first stage of therapy, and with many children it involves a matter of weeks or, at most, a few months. At that point, the therapist can consider with the child what further needs to be done. Admittedly, there may be a number of children with whom such an approach is not appropriate. Their problems are long-standing and involve well-established neurotic patterns, so that from the very beginning, an extended period of intensive psychotherapy can be anticipated. Such a child may enter therapy at the second stage of therapy, which will be discussed presently. However, many a child comes with a recently erupted symptom such as school refusal, an emotionally determined somatic symptom, or a behavioral outburst of one variety or another. In the heat of the moment, as they feel compelled to do something and to do it quickly, the therapist, the child, and the parents may all commit themselves to more than will prove to be necessary. In the face of the child's evident emotional problems, and out of their feelings of helplessness and guilt, the parents may be ready to lend themselves to anything; but when he changes for the better, they will quickly have second thoughts.

After the child has settled down, the therapist too may find things to be different and that there is less of a feeling of urgency to do something. The initial assessment of the child's overall development will have given some indications as to whether more circumscribed problem-oriented therapy (see chapter 4) or therapy geared toward alteration of neurotic patterns (similar to that described in chapter 2) is necessary. Once the child's symptoms fade, however, the picture may change considerably. Originally, he may have seemed rigidly set in neurotic patterns; when relieved of some of the pressures of intolerable affect, however, he may prove able to cope very effectively with the usual situations of his life. Once he "returns to his old self," he and his family may feel quite differently about psychotherapy and about their earlier agreement. The converse can also occur—that is, as therapy proceeds, the therapist may find that he is into "more than he had bargained for," that more extensive work is necessary than he had originally anticipated. However, as a rule, therapists are more likely to see the pathology in a child's adaptation than the strengths. Accordingly, they are more inclined to overdiagnose and to overprescribe than the reverse.

The second goal in therapy involves helping the child unravel neurotic personality· patterns, alter maladaptive personality traits, and/or develop personality skills in which he is deficient. Such deficiencies contributed to the child's original symptoms and continue to leave him vulnerable. If the therapist is to proceed into this second stage, it may be wise for him to alert the child and his parents to the obvious fact that at this point, the rate of improvement is likely to change. In the first stage, the child is likely to have improved so rapidly that change was obvious. Once the neurotic reactions have cleared and the focus is turned to the neurotic patterns and troublesome personality traits, changes are likely to come about more slowly and less obviously. Before the therapist has the child proceed into this second stage, if the parents are flexible enough so that at least they will not foster these neurotic patterns, it might be wise to point out to the child and his parents that these neurotic patterns are problems that the family might want to try to modify on its own, without the aid of therapy. If the therapist recognizes that the parents accept or even encourage their child's neurotic patterns, however, he had better consider whether individual psychotherapy, at least by itself, offers much more for this child. Other approaches, such as family therapy (see chapter 7) or behavioral counseling (see chapter 11) may be advisable.

Once the second stage of therapy is entered, the therapist needs a separate set of guidelines by which to decide when to terminate. One indication appears when the child is so apathetic or negative about continuing that therapy comes to a standstill. If this continues over several weeks, the therapist should consider termination. These negative feelings may be covert and not easily brought to the child's attention, but they pose a significant obstacle to continued therapy. In such a case, there is specific need to consider the possibility of termination. The child may protest that he no longer needs therapy, and he may also flatly insist that he has no special feelings about therapy or about the therapist. If he continues in this vein, and he is convinced that he no longer needs help, he will divorce himself more and more from the therapy process.

If at this point the child is asymptomatic and evidences improved adjustment in his daily life, termination may well be in order. If the child's adjustment in everyday life is at best marginal, it may be wise to weather out the negative phase even though it seems interminable. In this second instance, the therapist is better able to deal with the protests as bona-fide resistance. Since there is an evident contradiction between the avowed and actual behavior, he is in a better position to enlist the child's ability to see it as such. When the child is doing well in his everyday life, it may be impossible to engage him in the exploration of his resistances to further involvement. At this point, to insist that he continue in therapy may in fact be unrealistic.

When a child improves initially, many therapists may hesitate to recommend termination. They fear that he is manifesting a "transference cure," that he has taken a "flight into health," that he has shown symptomatic improvement but still carries his old internal conflicts and vulnerabilities within. In fact, even though his overall adjustment improves, a child may indeed continue his conflicts unresolved. The therapist might be able to terminate more comfortably at a point short of conflict resolution if he recognizes therapy as primarily a catalytic action. It helps the child activate the whole process of self-reflection and its attendant potential for psychodynamic change. With this in mind, he may feel more secure about terminating therapy at a point where the child is well aware of his conflicts and struggles with them openly. Rather than aiming to alter or to eliminate troublesome personality traits, the therapist might think in terms of helping the child arrive at a point where he is aware of the vulnerabilities inherent in his traits. The child may then be in a position to modify them outside of therapy, for example, if his parents now are able to interact with him realistically and not so as to foster neurotic trends.

From all this, there emerges a general principle about when to terminate, which can be viewed from both a negative and a positive standpoint. First, termination can be considered whenever the therapist needs to choose between waiting it out with the patient and "smoking out" affect or conflicts through repeated confrontations. Thus, after the defenses and conflicts have been sufficiently highlighted on a number of occasions, the therapist may decide to terminate and to encourage the child and his parents to continue the introspection and confrontation that were begun in therapy. Second, termination would seem to be in order when the child arrives at a comfortable stance within his own life style and has developed an effective working awareness of assets and vulnerabilities contained in his way of coping.

The manner of terminating will vary from child

to child. There are times when it is wise to terminate with an air of finality, that is, with no promise for future therapy if the child should once again have difficulties, though of course the door is left open for future consultation. The therapist might proceed in this manner when the child has trouble facing the fact of termination, and avoids it, for example, because of the associated pain.

As a rule, it seems wise to terminate with the expressed idea that the child and his parents are free to contact the therapist in the future and to return for further therapy if he is again having difficulty. To terminate in this fashion does indeed carry the risk that the child will never face the reality of ending the therapeutic relationship; however, with most children, such termination does not pose a significant problem. Ending therapy can become a problem for the child who has suffered the loss of someone important in his life, especially if this has entailed a traumatic experience which he was never able to master. With such a child, termination does indeed become a much more critical experience and needs to be dealt with accordingly, with, for example, an air of finality.

The time needed to help the child disengage from his therapist and to tie together loose ends will depend upon the nature of the therapeutic relationship, the length of therapy, the intensity of the process, the child's typical therapeutic pace or rhythm, and whether the child harbors residues from traumatic experiences related to object loss. When therapy has gone on for only a matter of weeks or for a few months, termination over a course of two or three weeks may suffice. If the child has been in intensive therapy over a period of one or more years, it may be reasonable to plan on a month or two or more for termination. The main thing is that the therapist not proceed in a stereotyped fashion in deciding on length of time for termination. Though a child has been intensively involved in therapy over many, many months, he may also have begun to disengage himself for some time before he and the therapist actually begin to talk about termination. Here the child has already progressed well into the process, even before termination has been formalized, and the length of the formal termination stage might accordingly be unusually short.

Although there are situations in which there is need for the support of spacing sessions at greater intervals as part of termination, ordinarily it is wise to maintain the same weekly schedule that had been followed throughout up to the very end. If the child has shaky object relationships, grad-

uated separation from the therapist is in order. Ordinarily, however, such a change in the therapy schedule turns the remaining sessions into an unproductive holding operation.

In the final sessions it is usually helpful to have the child review what has been accomplished in therapy; this approach does help the reflective child consolidate his gains. There are children, however, who show remarkable changes in their adjustment, who are aware of change, but who have no idea of what might account for it.

During termination there may be a return of the symptoms and character styles which originally brought the child into therapy. This development is not uncommon among children who have been involved in intensive therapy over an extended period of time; it is not a common occurrence with children who are seen for shorter periods. When this phenomenon does occur, the symptoms are ordinarily of less intensity than they were originally and, as feelings about termination are resolved, they disappear. If neither of these characteristics is found, it would be wise not to dismiss prematurely the return of symptoms as evanescent phenomena generated by the heat of termination. However, even if there is a return of symptoms or an eruption of new symptoms at this time, the therapist should not hastily decide to postpone termination. The fact is that at this time, distress is to be anticipated; as it occurs, it can be handled like any turmoil that arises during the course of therapy. It is wise to consider postponement of the termination date only if resolution does not occur.

Patterns of Follow Up

If, at termination, the therapist encourages the child and his parents to call, and even to return if problems arise again, the therapist may thus foster dependency. To be sure, in this way, he does it very informally and not in a disruptive manner. Most parents seem to feel more comfortable about termination if they know that they can call the therapist if problems do arise again. This arrangement may also help the child and family consolidate gains that have been made in therapy; it may relieve them of the pressure of wondering if they can make it on their own.

Experience with this more casual approach to termination and follow up indicates that parents will occasionally call for advice. At times a parent or child will decide to return, either because a new problem has arisen or because the old problem reemerges. Some children return periodically. It is interesting that each time the process of psychotherapy seems to have remained dormant since the previous termination, and they have readily reactivated it. These patients are involved in a sequence that may be thought of as "interrupted long-term therapy." That is, upon his return, the child may continue where he left off at the time of his previous termination. Or, he may start at a slightly higher level as he has made some progress or consolidated some old gains since the last episode of formal psychotherapy. Once started, he may again continue to be involved for weeks or months, ultimately terminate at a higher level, or interrupt and subsequently return in the future. It would seem that much is yet to be learned from this group of children. Their closer study may help to tease out the element of "time" (i.e., repeated everyday experiences that capitalize on the confrontations of therapy) from the other ingredients of the therapeutic process. That is, in individual therapy, before things seem to fall in place and significant awareness emerges, there are often doldrums, periods in which nothing seems to be happening. It may be that these children who come episodically live through the relatively quiet time outside of therapy. They mull things over by themselves, at some level, and then return. It becomes the therapist's task to help them capitalize on their new readiness to be more obviously productive. During their episodic returns, such patients typically make considerable gains in the course of a short period of renewed formal therapy.

Economic Indications

Unless there is realistic attention to financial matters, psychotherapy may falter. Often enough, parents begin to feel that they are trading one set of problems for another. While overcommitment may seem to be the most likely danger, finances or the lack thereof can cloud clinical judgment. The therapist needs to be cautious on two counts. When money is lacking, he may too quickly settle for a program that is totally inadequate to meet the needs of the child. When finances are more than sufficient, he might err in recommending too much therapy. Private insurance coverage for the more self-sufficient and federally sponsored programs for the lower socioeconomic group do make reasonable psychotherapy available to a large segment of the population. There is no denying, however, that financially, families in the lower middle-income group may be caught in a real squeeze. In that group, psychotherapy for the troubled child may realistically be limited unless publicly sponsored clinics with sliding fee scales are available.

The fact that the parents are financially responsible may introduce some wrinkles. What happens if they become delinquent in their payments? As the therapist may not have much contact with them, it may be awkward to pursue the matter, and he will need to guard against feelings about the parents spilling over into his work with the child. What happens when the child is given responsibility to make it to sessions on his own but skips them? And this when he knows full well that the therapist has talked with his parents about charging for missed appointments? It may be unrealistic to let the child assume or retain such responsibility if it gives him opportunity to act out in that manner, or to expect the parents to be financially accountable when responsibility for their child's attendance is out of their hands.

Time may also be an important consideration. There is the time required for the parents to bring the child if he cannot come by himself. If the child is to have more than one session a week, the schedule could interfere with either his schoolwork or other activities, some of which may be very important to him as sources of pleasure. Moreover, they in themselves may be significant experiences which enhance his development. The overly zealous therapist needs to be reminded that the child and his family do not live by therapy alone.

Simultaneous Activities or Practices

To be effective for the child, psychotherapy must fall in line with many other factors in his life. Some of these are influenced by therapy, while others capitalize on, or sustain, the gains he derives from this experience. Foremost, the child in therapy ought not be burdened with unreasonable environmental pressures that can be, and ought to be, modified. There may be need to stabilize the child's environment, for example, when his future is undecided, when he is in a temporary foster home, or when he is the product of a broken home. When caught between contending parents, reasonable attempts should be made to establish his permanent residence. In the intact family, there are different pressures to be addressed. For example, there is the child who struggles with tensions generated by an alcoholic parent; if the pathological home situation is attended to, he may not be in need of therapy. Or, if the child is not allowed reasonable experience and expression of feelings, attention might more realistically be directed to remedying the home environment rather than to involving the child in therapy.

In most instances, it is not an either/or situation. That is, it is not alone the difficult set of circumstances which confronts the child, but his own rigidity that makes him become symptomatic. On the other hand, even while things need to be changed at home or at school, the child may also be in need of help to adapt in a more flexible manner. It is important that the therapist proceed in such a way that when a child is in therapy his outside experiences are not ignored. The aim both at home and at school is to have him enjoy a realistic structure in which reasonable, age-appropriate demands are placed on him. When the child is in an environment that is conducive to his development, the therapist can more securely deal with the child's neurotic complexes and study how they interfere with his attempts to cope reasonably with day-to-day stresses.

When the child is in therapy, his parents can, hopefully, help him capitalize on the gains he makes. The most prominent feature of therapy is really mobilization of affect, and the child needs the support of his environment to learn how to handle this affect in a more adaptive fashion. Accordingly, he will be in need primarily of models for identification. While the therapist may serve as one of these models, as a rule the really important ones will need to come from those who are responsible for him. Are the parents able to carry out this function, or do they first need some assistance of their own? In the extreme situation, placement of the child in a foster home or a residential treatment center may be necessary. This state of affairs prevails when the parents just cannot assume their role and are not likely to do so in the future (see chapters 8, 15, and 18).

One needs to make sure as well that the child will be able to sustain the skills he has activated in therapy. High on this list are the skills of self-reflection and more objective self-assessment. The therapist needs to study the family to see whether the child is in therapy in large part because the parents themselves lack these skills. If so, can these be mobilized in the parents with or without therapy? This is not to imply, however, that such skills are always lacking in the family of the disturbed child; the child may not have been able to respond to his parents' reasonable approach because of his own severely neurotic patterns.

It may be helpful for the therapist to have sessions with the parents to share thoughts and insights, and to synchronize their mutual efforts. This is discussed in detail in chapter 8. Sessions which include the child, his parents, and the therapist may be especially helpful. In this safe setting, the child may be able to confront his parents with grievances, and the parents may have an opportunity to identify with the therapist's ability to listen empathically and to discuss feelings less defensively. When the parents have found it difficult to confront their child realistically, the therapist may also have opportunity to help with that. Above all, such family sessions may further confirm to the child and his parents that the therapist is not about to drive wedges between them; instead he aims to help them interact more reasonably through more rational, and thus through more effective, communication. More details regarding family interviewing are available in chapter 7 and some of the challenges inherent in combining approaches are addressed in chapter 1.

Individual dynamic psychotherapy can be used as an adjunct to family therapy, group therapy, or a milieu treatment program in order to deal with the child's fantasy life and with other more strictly personal matters. Often such issues cannot be handled comfortably in a group setting where the focus is on interpersonal themes.

There are times when use of medication may be indicated in the course of a child's psychotherapy. The severely anxious child may be beside himself and unable to cope with his anxiety; his anxiety can severely disrupt both his sleep and his daytime activity. In such a case, a mild tranquilizer may be helpful. With greater understanding of the physiology of anxiety and depression, the adjunctive use of medication in psychotherapy may become even more important. Indeed, there may be times when the physiological imbalance becomes so pronounced that the child cannot mobilize psychological skills until the organic equilibrium is reestablished with the aid of medication. If the therapist prescribes the maximum intake of medication per day and leaves it to the child and his family to decide on how much medication he will actually take within these prescribed limits, the child and his family can still be made active participants in decisions about drug treatment. The entire range of psychopharmacological treatment is covered in chapter 23.

Therapeutic Results

Psychotherapists tend to vouch for the effectiveness of their efforts with anecdotal accounts of success; follow-up studies, however, are not of much help in settling the issue of outcome. Meltzoff and Kornreich[26] have reviewed the literature on psychotherapy in general. They conclude that controlled research has successfully demonstrated significantly more behavioral changes in treated patients than in untreated controls. They further conclude that the better the quality of the research, the more positive the results obtained. On the other hand, several follow-up studies of children seen in child guidance clinics give ambiguous answers. Zold and Speer[31] reported that six to twelve months after termination of treatment, parents reported that the deviance in their children's behavior had significantly decreased. In a five-year plus follow up of children, Levitt[20] and his coworkers, however, found no difference between the adjustment made by the treated and the untreated child patients. Cunningham[6] reported that of a group of children contacted five years after termination, 63 percent were found to be making satisfactory adjustment. Levitt[19] concluded that his survey of follow-up studies failed to support the hypothesis that treatment is effective. He cautioned, however, that his survey did not force the acceptance of a contrary hypothesis. He emphasized that because of the differences among the studies and the generally poor caliber of methodology analysis, this distinction is especially important. He recommended that a "cautious tongue-in-cheek attitude toward child psychotherapy" be maintained until additional evidence from well-planned studies becomes available.

There are obvious deficiencies in the studies found in the literature beyond the obvious methodological difficulties with controls, that is, what would have happened to the treated children if they had not had therapy. First, follow-up studies ordinarily lump together all children seen in a clinic without any breakdown according to the treatment modality in which the children were involved. The one exception is a study of a very limited number of children which sought to determine the differences in effectiveness between children seen once a week and those seen four times a week in psychoanalytic psychotherapy.[15] Second, there is too much emphasis on long-term follow up, as investigators become preoccupied with looking at children five to ten years later. Third, there is too much attention to overall adjustment rather than to resolution of problems for which the child came into treatment.

To be sure, there is a definite need for realistic follow up to determine the effectiveness of psycodynamic psychotherapy. However, several things need to be kept in mind in such a study. First, if effectiveness itself is to be studied, follow up should be done at a reasonable period of time, not too soon and not too long after termination. The reasons for not doing it too soon may be obvious. However, investigators ignore the fact that if they wait too long, the many other factors in the child's life, and his many new experiences, may overshadow and even modify bona-fide gains of the therapeutic experience. Ideally, follow up should best be done at a time when the gains derived from this psychotherapy can still be discerned. In that way, there is still a glimpse of what specific effects have been realized. It would seem that one year after termination would be a reasonable time for such a follow-up study. Second, follow up should concentrate on trying to determine how adequately the specific goals of psychotherapy were reached and what elements of the experience were therapeutic. Primarily, how well did therapy help the child resolve the problem for which help was sought? The "problem" needs to be reduced to the psychodynamic dysfunction that was manifested, and judgment of effectiveness ought to rest on how and how well therapy helped effect a change. It also needs to be remembered that in his overall adjustment, the child may have been plagued with other problems that realistically needed to be addressed by means other than psychotherapy.

Some investigators will not be satisfied that psychotherapy is effective unless the well-nigh impossible is accomplished. Unfortunately, in their tendency to emphasize major alterations of personality structure, while deemphasizing the value of helping the child through difficulties in development, psychotherapists have invited inordinately stringent criteria by which the effectiveness of their work is to be judged. At times there are some who expect that the child who has had psychotherapy should remain symptom-free for the rest of his life. It seems as though psychotherapy is supposed to reconstruct the child, so that he becomes invulnerable to emotional stress.

For the most part, emotional distress in children is akin to acute illness; much less frequently, it is like a chronic disability. As a child is repeatedly stressed with developmental crises, he reacts with psychological symptoms. Most of these are transitory and disappear as "normal" development proceeds. Other symptoms are more intense and reflect undue stress or inadequate ability to cope. In such instances, professional assistance becomes necessary. The psychotherapist who appreciates the process of development will find that he is called upon primarily to help the child through these crises.

In the ensuing work, he may also help the child effect some changes in personality functioning so that ultimately he becomes less vulnerable. In a small number of cases, he will find it necessary to have the child involved in more extensive therapeutic interaction with him; this is designed to effect some personality changes or to unfix neurotic complexes and neurotic patterns of behavior. In another small percentage, the therapist finds a need for more extensive rehabilitative programs of which psychotherapy may be but one part.

Many assume that careful follow-up studies will demonstrate that the current emphasis on length and intensity of psychotherapy is misplaced. Psychodynamic psychotherapy involves a process which can and should be tailored to the needs of the child. The child should be involved in this treatment at the level of his need; the subsequent effectiveness of the intervention ought to be judged on the basis of his response to that involvement. After careful study, Malan and coworkers[23] reported that even a single interview may effect significant psychodynamic changes in an adult. If such a finding is indeed confirmed by others, the child psychotherapist who thinks in terms of helping children in very specific ways may be even more encouraged. Ordinarily, we are dealing with a more responsive patient; that is, as part of his developmental flexibility, the child responds to the well-established therapeutic process much more than some may perceive due to their theoretical biases about what constitutes "real" change, and what is nothing more than a "flight into health."

Significance of Dynamic Psychotherapy

For many, individual psychodynamic psychotherapy represents the basic interventional modality and constitutes the prevailing framework of child psychiatry. Its principles are applicable in almost all child psychiatric interactions with children. Thus, to be well grounded in this approach is to have a firm grasp on many of the principles underlying any intervention with children. Once these principles are genuinely understood, the therapist has many options open to him. He is likely to find that other interventions—counseling, behavior modification, and the use of medication—can be utilized more effectively if used within the context of the guidelines provided by individual psychodynamic psychotherapy. If he does not fall back on this framework, he may engage in sterile, ritualistic practices whose effectiveness may be limited, and which may become mechanical moves in a dehumanized interaction. Psychodynamic psychotherapy offers a uniquely personal approach. It is grounded in an appreciation of the child as an entity unto himself; an individual person who is more than the product of his environment.

REFERENCES

1. ALEXANDER, F., *Psychoanalysis and Psychotherapy*, Norton, New York, 1956.
2. ALLEN, F. H., *Psychotherapy with Children*, Norton, New York, 1942.
3. ANTHONY, E. J., "Communicating Therapeutically with the Child," *Journal of the American Academy of Child Psychiatry*, 3(1):109–110, 1964.
4. BIBRING, E., "Psychoanalysis and Dynamic Psychotherapy, Similarity and Differences," *Journal of American Psychoanalytic Association*, 2(4):745–770, 1954.
5. CAREK, D. J., *Principles of Child Psychotherapy*, Charles C Thomas, Springfield, Ill., 1972.
6. CUNNINGHAM, J. M., WESTERMAN, H. H., and FISCHOFF, J., "A Follow-up Study of Children Seen in a Psychiatric Clinic for Children," *American Journal of Orthopsychiatry*, 26(3):602–611, 1956.

7. FRANK, J. D., *Persuasion and Healing*, Johns Hopkins Press, Baltimore, 1961.
8. FREUD, A., *Normality and Pathology in Childhood*, International Universities Press, New York, 1965.
9. ——, *The Psychoanalytic Treatment of Children*, International Universities Press, New York, 1946.
10. FREUD, S., "Analysis of a Phobia in a Five-Year-Old Boy," in Jones, E. (Ed.), *Collected Papers*, vol. 3, pp. 149–289, Basic Books, New York, 1959.
11. GARDNER, R. A., *Therapeutic Communication with Children*, Science House, New York, 1971.
12. GREENSON, R. R., *The Technique and Practice of Psychoanalysis*, vol. 1, International Universities Press, 1967.
13. HAMBIDGE, G. JR., "Structured Play Therapy," *American Journal of Orthopsychiatry*, 25(3):601–617, 1955.

14. HARRISON, S. I., and CAREK, D. J., *Guide to Psychotherapy*, Little, Brown, Boston, 1966.

15. HEINICKE, C. M., et al., "Frequency of Psychotherapeutic Session as a Factor Affecting the Child's Developmental Status," in Eissler, R. S., et al. (Eds.), *The Psychoanalytic Study of the Child*, vol. 20, pp. 42–98, International Universities Press, New York, 1965.

16. HUG-HELLMUTH, H. VON, "On the Technique of Child Analysis," *International Journal of Psychoanalysis*, 2:287–305, 1921.

17. JOSSELYN, I. M., "Child Psychiatric Clinics—Quo Vadimus?" *Journal of the American Academy of Child Psychiatry*, 3(4):721–734, 1964.

18. KLEIN, M., *The Psychoanalysis of Children*, Hogarth Press, London, 1959.

19. LEVITT, E. E., "The Results of Psychotherapy with Children," *Journal of Consulting Psychology, 21(3)*:189–196, 1957.

20. ———, BEISER, H. R., and ROBERTSON, R. E., "A Follow-up Evaluation of Cases Treated in a Community Child Guidance Clinic," *American Journal of Orthopsychiatry, 29(2)*:337–346, 1959.

21. LEVY, D. M., "Release Therapy," *American Journal of Orthopsychiatry, 9(4)*:713–736, 1939.

22. LIPPMAN, H. S., *Treatment of the Child in Emotional Conflict*, Blakiston, New York, 1961.

23. MALAN, D. H., et al., "Psychodynamic Changes in Untreated Neurotic Patients," *Archives of General Psychiatry, 32(1)*:110–126, 1957.

24. MARCUS, I. D., "Costume Play Therapy," *Journal of the American Academy of Child Psychiatry, 5(3)*:441–452, 1966.

25. MEEKS, J. E., "Children Who Cheat at Games," *Journal of the American Academy of Child Psychiatry*, 9:157–170, 1970.

26. MELTZOFF, J., and KORNREICH, M., *Research in Psychotherapy*, Atherton, New York, 1970.

27. NEWMAN, M. R., and STERN, E. M., *New Approaches in Child Guidance*, Scarecrow, Metuchen, N.J., 1970.

28. REDL, F., "A Strategy and Technique of the Life Space Interview," *American Journal of Orthopsychiatry, 29(1)*:1–18, 1959.

29. SOLOMON, J. C., "Play Technique," *American Journal of Orthopsychiatry, 18(3)*:402–413, 1948.

30. STONE, M. H., "Mesmer and His Followers: The Beginnings of Sympathetic Treatment of Childhood Emotional Disorders," *History of Childhood Quarterly, 1(4)*: 659–679, 1974.

31. ZOLD, A. C., and SPEER, D. C., "Follow-up Study of Child Guidance Clinic Patients by Means of the Behavior Problem Checklist," *Journal of Clinical Psychology, 27(4)*:519–524, 1971.

---

4 / Brief Focused Psychotherapy

Alan J. Rosenthal

Description of the Method

Describing brief psychotherapy requires nearly as many terms and definitions as there are practitioners who employ it. What is "brief"—two hours? a month? six months? And how does a month of brief therapy differ from six months? While these issues have significant theoretical, technical, and economic implications which will be discussed here, a number of elements are fundamental to this psychotherapeutic approach.

Duration. Brief psychotherapy is brief relative to more traditional, open-ended, dynamically oriented psychotherapy (see chapter 3) and psychoanalysis (see chapter 2). Actual duration may vary according to theoretical formulation; technique; patient or therapist preference; external time constraints, such as the departure of therapist or patient; limitations of insurance coverage; or clinic policies. Reports suggest that this therapeutic approach may be as brief as one visit of three hours[65] or as long as six months.[57] For most patients, the time limit itself may be set in advance or may be determined differentially according to the clinical situation. The essential feature, however, is that it is *time-limited* as opposed to open-ended.

Focus. In contrast to open-ended psychotherapy, the presence of a time limitation in brief psychotherapy requires that the therapist and patient focus on specific issues and develop particular goals consistent with the realities of time and psychopathology. While all psychotherapists should define goals and assess progress toward them, this is critical in brief psychotherapy.[61, 51]

Reality, "Here and Now" Orientation. Time-limited therapy does not allow lengthy excursions into the patient's past for detailed analysis of early conflicts. The patient's past is explored, but primarily to understand and relate it to present life situations. Brief therapy concentrates on present, "here and now" issues, both interpersonal and intrapsychic. This is not to say that brief therapy is limited to crisis intervention (see chapter 32) or symptom removal. It may focus on more chronic interpersonal and intrapsychic conflicts as well, but it does so with a present, reality-oriented approach.

Family-oriented Approach. Brief therapy with children, because of the child's obvious dependence on significant others for growth and development and for meeting physical and emotional needs, requires a family-oriented approach. Parents and other family members may become intensively involved in the brief therapy process, as much or even more than the child who is identified as the patient. Flexibility in involving other family members is a significant feature of this therapeutic approach and will be discussed later.

History of the Development
of the Method

The development of brief therapy, with adults as well as with children and families, has taken place in the shadow of a widespread bias among mental health professionals that the most valuable and preferred mode of treatment is long-term intensive psychotherapy without sufficient consideration of differential clinical indications. In consequence, other treatment modalities, including brief therapy, have been relegated to positions of second-class or inferior status. Actually, there is reason to believe that brief focused therapeutic approaches are as beneficial and effective as long-term, open-ended psychotherapy; moreover, they are useful for patients with a wide variety of clinical problems and sociocultural and educational backgrounds. Few patients are displeased with brief therapy approaches or feel it is a deficient or "second-class" therapy.[61, 51]

Brief psychotherapy itself was practiced by Freud and his followers, and has been encouraged by many psychoanalytic and psychiatric practitioners and writers—Breuer and Freud,[14] Rank,[60] Fenichel,[21] and Alexander,[2] to name only a few. In 1941, the Chicago Institute for Psychoanalysis examined the topic at a national scientific meeting on brief psychotherapy. It received further emphasis as emergency treatment, and brief therapy achieved importance in military psychiatry during World War II,[34] and as a result of Lindemann's development of crisis intervention techniques in the 1940s.[43] Since that time, the use of brief psychotherapy has continued to increase, particularly with adults. Numerous articles and volumes have been written about the topic,* and brief therapy

*See references 8, 42, 56, 66, and 77.

has become a more accepted treatment modality in general psychiatric practice.

Although practiced in community child guidance clinics for many years, therapy with children of relatively short duration was not originally identified as "brief therapy." From the reports of a number of early practitioners, it appears that at least some of the child psychotherapy they employed was relatively brief, that is, up to six months in duration. Witmer's[76] reports of several session-by-session case studies by different child therapists (Blanchard,[13] Rank,[59] and Allen[3]), in particular, describe cases treated within twenty sessions. Allen[4] examines a number of such cases in *Psychotherapy With Children*, published in 1942. Early reports by Solomon[68] and by Levy[41] describe play therapy methods that may be applied particularly well to brief therapy.

In addition, many community clinics and social service agencies have for years been confronted with large caseloads and long waiting lists. Inevitably, they long ago gravitated to this technique, and some have reported successful results.[5, 55] Labeled as such, brief psychotherapy with children and families has been used at least since 1949,[15] but while sporadic reports in the literature advocated its use in the following decade, it was not until the 1960s that reports of its success began to appear regularly.†

The now numerous accounts of brief therapy with children and families include a wide variety of approaches to treatment. Cytryn, Gilbert, and Eisenberg[19] utilized brief supportive therapy combined with drug therapy in treating children with behavior disorders. Shulman[65] reported success with "one-visit psychotherapy." A single consultation with parents and child, lasting three hours, was sufficient to handle most of the presenting complaints. Coddington[18] indicated that a majority of the children referred for emotional difficulties in a pediatric practice could be managed in a brief therapy setting. These and other studies have begun to focus on treatment techniques with this modality,[51, 61] types of problems best approached,[40, 62] and evaluation of treatment outcome and therapeutic results.§

Within the framework of community mental health there is increasing pressure for expanded treatment services to broader populations and for more help to larger numbers of emotionally disturbed children and families. As this process advances, reports of the use of brief therapy also increase. Indeed, a volume devoted entirely to

† See references 18, 19, 30, 33, 36, 40, 44, 65, and 69.
§ See references 30, 33, 36, 54, 55, 61, and 64.

brief therapy with children and their parents has recently been published.[10] This modality now appears to be developing a recognized position in child and family psychotherapeutic practice.

Rationale and Theoretical Basis

RATIONALE

Estimates of the amount of emotional disturbance in childhood and adolescence range from 10 percent to 20 percent of all children and youth.[28, 32, 71] Only 10 percent of those requiring psychotherapeutic intervention actually receive it.[1] It has become increasingly clear that the ranks of professionals are insufficient to meet the mental health needs of our children. Traditional treatment approaches cannot provide the necessary intervention, and a variety of alternate methods of delivering mental health care have been explored. Brief psychotherapy is one such method.

The community mental health movement has helped to bring mental health care to many segments of our child population. With the need and demand for services far exceeding the capacity to provide them, however, waiting lists in community clinics remain lengthy. Many children and families wait a long time for an opening for evaluation or treatment. Brief therapy is one way to deliver services more rapidly, decrease the waiting list, and provide intervention closer to the time of the actual request for service.

Community clinics often experience high dropout rates—that is, many patients leave therapy against advice after a few visits.[23, 25] Presumably many of these patients do not respond to traditional, insight-oriented, open-ended therapy. Many others, although they remain in treatment, do not improve with this therapeutic approach. Used as an alternative method with patients for whom traditional psychotherapy is inappropriate or ineffective, brief therapy has been shown to reduce dropout rates.[51] Moreover, it has allowed clinics to maintain on-going, though intermittent, therapeutic relationships with resistant patients.

Brief therapy also has an important role in programs of primary and secondary prevention. Exploring issues of child development, parent-child relationships, and parenting skills with individual or groups of families often uncovers potential, early, or relatively minor conflict areas.[7, 9, 72] These can then be approached within the context of a discussion group or of brief individual consultation. This may help to prevent development of more serious conflicts later.

THEORETICAL BASIS

For its technique, brief therapy draws upon a variety of psychological and behavioral schools of thought. A pragmatic approach, it utilizes effective interventions from widely diverse theoretical orientations.

Brief therapy relies heavily on the child's and family's motivation to change. At the time the family requests service, it is usually experiencing the maximum discomfort with a problem. Therapeutic intervention should then occur as soon as possible. While brief therapy is not synonymous with crisis intervention, its effects are based on elements of crisis theory (see chapter 32). The child's and family's greater motivation for change, and the greater fluidity of intrapsychic and interpersonal dynamics during times of crisis provide an opportunity for more rapidly effective psychotherapeutic interventions.[12, 72] Thus, brief therapy may be highly effective at times of stress when pressure to alter behavior, relationships, and maladaptive patterns is at a peak.

Brief therapy emphasizes the "self-healing" capacities of children and families.[9, 55] In the course of therapy, areas of conflict and pathological behaviors are explored and interpreted with a view toward change; at the same time, however, the family's psychological strengths receive significant attention and support.[9, 12, 61] Adaptive coping mechanisms are encouraged and developed, and family members learn to use these in response to present and future stress. Explicit responsibility for dealing with problems is placed upon the child and parents. As family members learn to cope with, and overcome, current conflicts, they are also guided in anticipating and successfully preventing or managing future conflicts. The therapist gives recognition to the family members' capacity to manage their own situation; he intervenes in a way which allows their psychological strengths to maintain the self-healing process. These elements are basic to the practice of brief psychotherapy.

Other theoretical principles of brief therapy also relate to its reality, here-and-now orientation. It is a directive process; the therapist actively intervenes in family members' relationships and behavior. Directive guidance can precipitate behavioral change, and it is well documented that persisting changes in affect, psychodynamics, and intrapsychic and interpersonal patterns can follow such brief therapeutic contacts.* Affective insights may occur after the brief therapy process and help to maintain the behavioral changes that began during the process itself. This does not imply that brief therapy will "cure" all present and future psychological distress. On the contrary, many families will experience additional stress as their development progresses, as children enter new developmental stages, as parents age, as economic, vocational and sociocultural shifts occur, as unforeseen tragedy strikes. These later periods of stress may require additional therapy, usually not as lengthy as the initial course. Again the focus would be to resolve the current issues and to guide the family back to independent functioning. Further, the need for additional brief therapy does not imply that the initial effort was a failure. Families vary in their abilities to cope with stress; following the initial course of brief therapy, many will require periodic "booster" sessions to manage later crises. The approach allows for therapeutic contact over an extended period of time and avoids the implication of failure for those requesting additional therapeutic assistance.

Brief therapy employs techniques from different theoretical positions. Intrapsychic conflicts of child and parents are explored and interpreted directly. It borrows from analytically oriented psychotherapy, behavior modification,[73, 75] communication theory, Gestalt therapy, marital and family therapy, educational approaches,[9] and others. Parent-child, marital, and other interpersonal relations are analyzed in detail. Directions are provided for improving communication, relationships, and feelings for the reduction of symptoms and for developing methods of reinforcing and maintaining improvement.

Indications

It is difficult to predict which children and families will do well in brief therapy. Many emotionally disturbed children and families are not responsive to traditional, long-term psychotherapy. This may ensue from particular educational, sociocultural, or attitudinal and personality characteristics; or because of particular types of psychopathology, for example, certain characterologic or conduct disorders. In such situations, a brief, directive therapeutic approach, with regular follow up, may be useful.

* See references 12, 31, 33, 35, 46, 55, 58, 72, and 77.

These, however, are indications by default. It has been argued that all children and families requesting treatment should initially receive brief therapy. Only after determining that this is demonstrably insufficient should there be a commitment to lengthier approaches.[9] Nevertheless, some situations do appear more appropriate than others to the briefer approaches. These situations may relate to the child and family, to the therapist, or to the external environment itself.

THE CHILD AND FAMILY

Prevention. The so-called "normal" problems of child and family development that may reveal themselves in the course of primary prevention services can usually be managed by brief therapy.[7, 9] Parent or child discussion groups or individual family consultations can provide the support, direction, and insight necessary for most families to cope with the situation successfully.[9] Secondary prevention programs, which emphasize the early identification of problems, may also uncover situations appropriate for brief therapy. The milder the presenting problems and the shorter their duration, the greater is the indication for brief therapy. In addition, prevention programs for target populations can identify potential or beginning conflicts which might be managed in a brief therapy setting. These could be addressed to mothers and infants at risk because of complications of pregnancy, prematurity,[16] birth trauma, deprivation, and others.

Acute Crises. As mentioned previously, family crises provide an opportunity for change; individuals are in distress, relationships and psychodynamic mechanisms are more fluid, and motivation for change is at its peak. Brief therapy is an appropriate approach during and following these crises.[12] Community programs may provide outreach services to target populations in crisis, such as families experiencing severe illness or death, divorcing families, and those experiencing other types of social or personal distress. Separation from or loss of a family member are particular indications for brief therapy.[38] Termination, with its related aspects of separation and loss, is a major issue in such a process. Because of this emphasis, brief therapy is especially useful to help the child and family cope with an experience of separation or loss.

Childhood Adjustment and Neurotic Problems. A wide variety of behavioral problems in childhood can be treated with brief therapy. This approach has been effective in cases of phobia, particularly school phobia;[36, 74] it has served with children who displayed depressive, withdrawn, aggressive, or regressive behavior; it has helped with delinquent, "hard-to-teach" children,[48] and with problems of drug abuse;[29] and it has been useful for families with parent-child conflicts[55] or with marital discord where a reasonable degree of family and environmental stability was present.[62] More severe symptomatology and more chronicity of child or parental problems have a less favorable prognosis with this modality.[9, 62]

More Severe Disturbances. Even with the more severe and chronic disturbances, brief therapy does have a certain utility. It may be appropriately used when the focus and goals of therapy are adequately circumscribed, and selected and pursued in a careful and realistic fashion. Families with a psychotic child, a significantly mentally retarded child, in which severe marital discord holds sway, parental psychopathology is present, or multiple problems are all active at once can nonetheless benefit from brief therapeutic interventions if the work is sharply focused on a specific area of difficulty or on a recent crisis situation.[6] In such cases, of course, continued care and therapeutic contact for the persistent difficulties are usually required. These families may receive ongoing care from a social service or child treatment center; the more intensive brief therapy would be reserved for them during times of particular stress or for specific focal issues.

Other Family Indications. Several other individual and family characteristics have been identified which are associated with a favorable prognosis in brief therapy.

1. *Motivation.* Motivation for change is a significant factor in successful brief therapy.[12, 61, 74] Motivation is often strong during an acute crisis. But whether the difficulties are acute or chronic, a strong desire for therapeutic change on the part of child or parent is in itself indication for brief therapy.
2. *Parental flexibility and capacity for change.* Regardless of their expressed motivation, the ability of parents to change their behavior and attitude is a critical factor in deciding on brief therapy. The presence of such flexibility is an indication for its use.[40]
3. *Developmental progression of child.* The child who moves through his developmental stages without *severe* blocks or fixations, who has a history of relatively stable early attachments, who relates reasonably well, and who displays no incapacitating handicap or illness has a more favorable prognosis in brief therapy.[40]
4. *Parental and family stability.* The presence of parental pathology and marital discord are not in themselves contraindications to the use of brief therapy. At the same time, some degree of

stability in parents and family structure is important for its use. A background of impending divorce or family dissolution, chronic ambiguity about the child's placement or living situation, or other factors indicating an uncertain or unstable family structure may not provide a sufficiently firm foundation on which to build psychotherapeutic change.[62] Of course, an acute situation of instability such as may occur in divorce, illness, or death may be a clear indication for this kind of intervention.

THE THERAPIST

In the use of this approach, a positive motivation on the part of the therapist for brief therapy is associated with a favorable outcome.[61, 62] A number of reports indicate that therapists who believe that only a brief period of time is necessary for treatment are successful in brief therapy.[24] There are many therapists who remain skeptical of the approach because of past training, experience, peer pressures, clinic policies, and so on. When they attempt to employ it, they are in general less successful. Low therapist motivation is associated with brief therapy failures and referrals for further treatment following the brief therapy period.[61]

Therapist style in conducting therapy is a further factor that contributes to success or failure. Therapists with inactive, nondirective, or relatively inflexible styles have less success with brief therapy. Therapeutic flexibility and an active, often directive, approach are associated with a more favorable treatment outcome.[9, 62] Given the need for therapeutic flexibility and for the ability to draw from a wide variety of psychological theories and techniques, therapists with experience are best suited for the practice of brief therapy.

THE ENVIRONMENT

Stability of the family's external environment is still another factor associated with successful brief therapy. Along with a predictable family structure, a reasonable degree of stability in the family's living situation, housing and neighborhood, economic situation, and social structure form the firm base upon which therapeutic change can occur.

Complications, Side Effects, Disadvantages

There are potential complications or disadvantages to brief therapy. These result from inexperience with the method, from absence of adequate supervision, or from errors in evaluation and development of therapeutic goals. Brief therapy is not an arbitrarily abbreviated form of traditional, long-term psychotherapy. It has a particular set of methods and techniques that are its own; inexperience with these principles, or failure to become familiar with them, may lead to therapeutic disappointment. Supervision or peer consultation will help to avoid a variety of pitfalls in the brief therapy process: errors in the assessment of family and therapist motivation; inadequate selection of treatment goals; poor management of the critical issues around termination; and/or failure to deal with transference and future planning. In addition, regular peer consultation provides stimulation and reinforcement for the therapist to continue the practice of brief therapy. Without such reinforcement, therapists frequently revert to more comfortable, less intense, open-ended therapy based on training and experience.

Rapid evaluation and setting realistic treatment goals are crucial to the brief therapy process. Errors in evaluation of the child and family may result in inappropriate goals, which will be beyond the capability of the child or family to achieve. Indeed, urging the family members toward goals beyond their capacity may push them into deeper difficulties or despair. With sufficient therapist preparation and experience, and with adequate consultation as the process continues, these potential complications can be avoided. Further, follow-up visits provide additional safeguards against these potential hazards.

Contraindications

Lester[40] identifies developmental retardation, an internalized and complicated neurotic structure, multiple phobias, and characterologic disorders as situations having an unfavorable prognosis in brief therapy with children and families; these disorders constitute a relative contraindication to its use.

Brief therapy should not be employed when there is small likelihood of achieving the therapeutic goals during the treatment period. Such unlikely situations may include: severe and chronic psychosis; significant mental retardation; the need for institutionalization; absence of early, stable attachments; lifelong severe characterologic problems; absence of any family or environmental stability; absence of family motivation; or absence of therapist motivation.[33, 61]

However, if limited and realistic therapeutic goals can be defined, then brief therapy may be useful, even in the face of these difficulties (with the exception of absence of motivation).[33]

Techniques

Time Limit. Basic to the practice of brief therapy is a specified period of time in which the formal work will go on. The time period may be similar for virtually all children and families selected for this approach,[62] or it may be individually determined depending on each family's problems and needs.[57] The existence of limited time causes a certain "therapeutic pressure,"[61] or expectation for improvement, on both therapist and family. If guided appropriately by the therapist—that is, not allowed to become excessive or demanding—this pressure appears to enhance the therapeutic process itself. Preset time limits in therapy have been associated with favorable treatment outcome, fewer patient dropouts, and greater patient motivation.[51]

The time limit itself must be specified explicitly with the family as treatment begins. Family members' cooperation and agreement to work on therapeutic issues within this time frame form the basis of the treatment contract.

Treatment Focus and Goals. As mentioned previously, brief therapy must be goal-oriented.[44, 51, 57, 61] Given a limited time period for therapy, rapid child and family evaluation and delineation of problem areas are essential. This evaluation should include both psychodynamic and behavioral formulations. On the basis of the findings, therapeutic goals are selected which become the focus of the therapy. It should be noted that rapid evaluation and goal selection require a considerable degree of experience on the part of the therapist. The inexperienced therapist may have difficulty with this procedure. At the very least, supervision and consultation should be available for the novice therapist during brief therapy and is often helpful for the more experienced therapist as well.

This selection process may involve "selecting out" therapeutic goals which are inappropriate. There may be aspects of family psychopathology which are unrelated to the presenting problems and which may be unsuitable for treatment in a brief therapy setting. Such psychopathology may be evident during the initial family evaluation; sometimes it is uncovered later in the therapy process. The therapist may have to avoid dealing with this psychopathology in order to focus efficiently on the selected treatment goals. Of course, such goals can and should be altered if other psychopathology becomes more prominent and pressing. In any event, if additional treatment is indicated parallel with or subsequent to the brief therapy, it should be clearly recommended.

Frank communication with the family at this point helps to enlist their cooperation and collaboration in the treatment process.[12] In language they can both accept and understand, family members are informed of the therapist's evaluation and the treatment focus or goals. Often the evaluation is consistent with the family's own view of its difficulties. This is particularly likely to be true when family motivation is high. Delineating the treatment goals then becomes a shared process, the beginning of a collaborative relationship between therapist and family. When the evaluation is inconsistent with the family's perceptions or attitudes, the therapist may first delineate formulations and treatment goals that he knows will be acceptable; at the same time, he may also propose, tactfully but directly and with sufficient explanation, additional formulations or treatment goals which he and the family may wish to pursue as therapy progresses. In our clinical experience, when such formulations are reasonably accurate, families either perceive them as sound or are willing to consider them further in therapy. A significant reluctance to consider important formulations may perhaps merely indicate resistance. However, it should also raise suspicions that the formulations themselves are wrong, or that the motivation for therapeutic change is questionable.

Formulations presented to the family by the therapist may be intrapsychic, interpersonal, communicational, behavioral, and/or symptomatic. Similarly, treatment goals may focus on any or several of these levels. Certainly a focus on presenting symptoms and "here-and-now" problems is essential. But an approach to the underlying psychopathology, either intrapsychic or interpersonal, is also appropriate and frequently very helpful. Treatment that addresses both symptoms and underlying psychopathology in the context of brief therapy can effect significant behavioral and attitudinal changes. Often it has lasting therapeutic benefit.[12, 33, 55, 77]

Rapport. The development of rapport or positive transference is an important feature of most psychotherapy, but it is critical for brief therapy.[57, 61, 64] With limited time, the collaborative work of therapist and family can occur only if there is an early establishment of rapport and a therapeutic alliance. The sharing of goals and a treatment focus is the beginning of the therapeutic alliance; maintaining this positive relationship is crucial to the process.

Therapist Activity. Active, often directive, interventions are characteristic of this work.[12, 61] Conveying formulations and setting treatment goals is an active process, and the therapist maintains this stance throughout.[9, 61] Therapist activity includes interpretations and confrontations, as well as support, advice, and direction.

The therapist utilizes his rapport with family members to urge them into active participation in the therapy process, both within and between therapy sessions. Family members are requested to undertake "homework assignments" related to their particular difficulties and treatment goals. Homework may involve family members consciously attempting to change a piece of behavior; structuring discussion of a conflictual issue; reading materials on child development,[22] temperament, and parent-child "fit,"[17, 72] family communication,[27] behavior modification,[11, 52, 53, 07] and parent-child relationships;[26, 63] restructuring tasks and activities at home to alter stereotypic patterns of behavior; or understanding activities to enhance parental and marital relationships.

Behavioral change may precede emotional and attitudinal change.* As motivated family members engage in new behaviors, the initial efforts may at first be somewhat structured and mechanical. As their hope and desire for further change is enhanced, however, the process, tends to become self-reinforcing. Therapy sessions are in part devoted to a review of the homework assignments, particularly the interpersonal encounters of family members, always relating them to treatment formulations and goals. Modifying difficult assignments so that they become more manageable, exploring affective levels in carrying out assignments, and reviewing successful assignments all serve to emphasize the responsibility family members must themselves take in the process.

In developing and assigning homework tasks, the therapist must assess the psychological strengths of the child and parents. His skill lies in helping them to utilize these strengths in coping with their difficulties. This emphasis on psychological strengths, coping mechanisms, and adaptive in-

---

* See references 12, 31, 33, 35, 46, 55, 58, 72, and 77.

teractions is basic. It further underlines the fact that therapeutic responsibility rests on the family members. This in turn enhances their independence and self-esteem, and fosters a "self-healing" process that can continue beyond the brief therapy period.

In the process of brief therapy, the therapist should:

1. Provide education and insight into the origins of, and factors maintaining psychopathology— intrapsychic, interpersonal, communicational, symptomatic, or environmental reinforcement.
2. Begin a process of therapeutic change through structured, assigned behavioral tasks for family members.
3. Gradually shift responsibility for maintaining and expanding behavioral change to the family, helping members to utilize psychological strengths and adaptive coping mechanisms, whether old or new.
4. Anticipate with the family potential pitfalls or future times of crisis.
5. Help plan adaptive responses based on the insights and new behaviors learned and practiced during the brief therapy period.

Various views have been expressed about a single therapist or cotherapists conducting this work. Our own preference is for a single therapist to conduct brief therapy; this is supported in the literature.[33] In contrast to cotherapists, the single therapist can more easily maintain a cohesive view and consistent approach in what he does and can avoid the often time-consuming collaborative conferences necessary for coordination. With this in mind, peer group consultation for the therapist becomes even more important.

Termination. Because of the time limitation, termination is a central issue throughout the brief therapy process.[44, 61] Work is begun on termination during the initial session, as the time limit is explained. Loss, or anticipated loss, is often a significant dynamic feature of the concerns or difficulties of any family; this is especially true for many of the families requesting psychotherapy. Termination in brief therapy is handled as a reality issue; where appropriate, however, it is also dealt with as a reliving of previous significant loss. Throughout the therapy period, the therapist reminds the family of the approaching termination and actively explores related feelings and behavior. Final sessions should include some review of the therapy, a summary of insights or knowledge gained, the identification of new attitudes or patterns of behavior developed, and consideration of the degree of progress in approaching the goals of treatment. Future difficulties should be antici-

pated with the family, with preparation for coping with potential crises.

Finally, brief therapy should not be viewed (nor perhaps should any psychotherapy) as marking the end of emotional upsets or crises in an individual's or a family's life. Hopefully, the family will be better able to handle crises after therapy, but it may require "booster" sessions to reinforce insights and behavior. Returning for further sessions does not necessarily imply a therapeutic failure, and the opportunity to return if additional family crises arise is an integral part of the process.[37, 61]

THERAPY STRUCTURE

1. Length and Frequency. While variations exist, brief therapy generally has a time limit of between two and six months;[57] three months is a commonly used period.[50, 62]

Frequency of therapy sessions is one to two hours per week. This includes sessions with the child, parents, or the entire family. For adequate evaluation, individual interviews with the child and each parent, as well as with the parents conjointly, are helpful. Following the evaluation, family members selected to be involved in further therapy sessions depend on the treatment focus and goals.

2. Family-oriented Approach. Both the specific goals and the particular family members to be involved in the therapeutic sessions require careful selection. All of this, of course, depends upon the case formulation. The focus of therapy may be on marital difficulties, in which case both parents would be involved in most sessions. If parent-child relationships and child management are the central issues, then parent and child would be involved, both individually and conjointly. The therapist must maintain a good deal of flexibility in providing therapeutic sessions for individual family members or appropriate combinations as the treatment goals dictate.

A family-oriented approach is usually maintained throughout. Family members, other than the child who was presented as the "identified patient," are seen as often or more often than the child himself.[9, 62] The issues addressed during therapy reflect this family orientation and usually consist of such topics as child-rearing practices, family communication, parent-child relationships, marital relationships, sibling rivalries, and the intrapsychic conflicts of child or parent which affect other family members.[61]

The following clinical vignettes illustrate some of these techniques:

CASE 1

Dennis was eleven years old. He and his parents presented themselves at the clinic because Dennis had run away from home and threatened to kill himself. This incident was precipitated by the parents' preparation for departing on a planned weekend vacation. Dennis and his seven-year-old sister were to remain at home with a relative. Initial interviews were conducted with Dennis individually and with his parents as a couple. The following historical and dynamic information emerged.

Separation had been a difficult issue in the history of this family. Neither parent had completely resolved the conflicts around separating from his and her own parents. When they met and married, they formed an almost inseparable bond themselves. Dennis's birth precipitated a severe crisis in the family as he literally came between his parents and interrupted their relationship. His father reacted with jealousy and resentment. His mother was torn between giving to her infant son and to her husband, with the result that she felt inadequate both as a mother and a wife. A period of stormy marital conflict ensued but gradually diminished as Dennis developed. Nevertheless, father's resentment and mother's feelings of inadequacy remained. The result was that his parents were unable to separate from Dennis during his first three years of life. Separation from mother was painful for Dennis as he entered nursery school, and again as he entered public school; however, the difficulties were not long-lasting. The family always took vacations together, and the parents seldom left Dennis or his sister.

On the rare occasions when they did leave the children, Dennis protested vehemently. His running away and suicide threat were the most severe of these reactions, and at this point his alarmed parents sought professional help.

The issue of separation was quickly identified by therapist and family as a central focus of therapy. During the ten-week brief therapy period, a number of treatment goals related to "separation" were delineated, and therapist and family attempted to approach these collaboratively. During individual and conjoint sessions with Dennis's parents, father's jealousy and resentments, and mother's feelings of inadequacy and ambivalence about separation were identified. On the basis of these discoveries, the parents resolved to redevelop their own identities, as well as to redefine their relationships within the marriage. They both began the pursuit of some individual interests. Mother entered an adult education class in which she had been interested for some time. The parents began to explore new activities as a couple, apart from their children. These included both recreation and discussion of conflictual areas between them. These activities were initially "homework assignments," carefully structured with the therapist's help. As the parents grew more comfortable with these "new" activities, the formal structuring and careful planning became less important for their continuation.

Dennis himself expressed ambivalent feelings about the issue of separation. He had strong urges to achieve more independence from the family and to have more to do with his peer group, but mother's previous difficulty in allowing him to develop more independence and self-sufficiency now led to many misgivings about his ability to relate to peers. Dennis had a strong interest in animals, and, after some discussion, his parents allowed him to join the school biology club. This involved after-school meetings and a number of evening and weekend field trips. With this beginning, Dennis established a few new friendships, one of which led him into two other peer activities, soccer and bicycling. These experiences led him to further such interactions and helped him to establish some greater independence.

The process of termination with this family regenerated their feelings of separation and loss. The therapist related these feelings to the central issues of the therapy; here was another and very immediate example of managing separation situations.

During the course of the therapy, an ever-increasing burden of responsibility had been placed on the family to discover and implement methods of handling their own concerns. The progress of therapy was now reviewed during the termination process. With this, the family began to perceive the degree of responsibility they had assumed. From this perspective they could see that their dependence and initial dismay at "losing" their therapist was an overreaction. Therapy was terminated as the parents had planned. They then took a week's vacation by themselves, without protest from or problems with the children.

At termination, the family members were symptom-free. They had acquired significant insights into the dynamic issues they faced and had developed a number of successful coping mechanisms with which to manage difficulties. At a follow-up appointment two months later, further therapeutic progress was evident. Dennis's independence and peer relationships had improved, and the parents were pleased with the continued development of their own relationship. About six months later, the family telephoned because of a minor crisis. Dennis had arranged to spend a month vacationing with a friend, but a few days before departure he became uncertain about leaving. After a fifteen-minute telephone consultation with the therapist, the family was able to discuss and resolve the situation themselves. They reviewed the separation issues, determined that they had themselves felt some ambivalence about the trip, and were then able to deal with their concerns. This resolved the issues, and Dennis left on the trip comfortably. After one week, Dennis called his parents long distance. He "wondered" if he should return home early. His parents assured him that all was well with them, and he was then able to finish the vacation successfully. The parents telephoned four months later to indicate continued progress in these areas. Although they realized that in the future circumstances involving separation might again generate problems, they felt they could recognize these as they arose and would be able to manage them satisfactorily.

CASE 2

Timmy was a five-year-old boy. His parents visited the clinic because of their concern about his "dressing up" in his three-year-old sister's clothing. Timmy had done this infrequently but intermittently over the past two years, usually in the privacy of his bedroom. Initially his parents tried to ignore it; then they became disapproving of this behavior, although they did not punish him for it. They requested an evaluation because of their concern about his sexual development.

During the initial evaluation, the parents were interviewed jointly, and Timmy was seen individually in a play diagnostic session. The therapist was impressed by a variety of evidence during the play session that Timmy's identifications and gender role were developing along masculine lines. At the same time, his play indicated a great deal of generalized aggressive and angry affect. On the basis of information from these evaluation interviews, a number of formulations and treatment goals were developed. These were reviewed with Timmy's parents at the next meeting.

The therapist informed the parents that Timmy appeared to be developing in a masculine way. However, another issue had impressed him, which they had not previously raised, an issue that might be related to the dressing up. Timmy seemed excessively angry and was displaying intense aggressive feelings and behavior. Both parents immediately confirmed this impression. They stated that there were indeed some minor concerns about his dressing up. But more often, still, they were quite disturbed by his very aggressive behavior with other children, particularly his sister and other girls.

The parents and therapist together formulated hypotheses about Timmy's behavior. Timmy's father was raised by controlling, dominating parents who inhibited his expressions of anger and assertiveness. He was determined that Timmy should be free to assert himself. Father regularly reinforced Timmy's aggressive and defiant behavior and often failed to set appropriate limits. For her part, Timmy's mother identified with her own rather perfectionistic mother. She tended to overcontrol Timmy and to level excessive demands and expectations. These often inconsistent parental messages contributed to Timmy's aggressive behavior toward others. To further complicate the situation, Timmy's younger sister was the "apple of father's eye." The boy's resentment, jealousy, and feelings of rivalry resulted in anger and aggressiveness on the one hand, and "dressing up to be like" his sister on the other. Several areas of conflict in the parents' relationship also emerged as their personality characteristics and manner of relating to each other were discussed.

Within the framework of these formulations, several treatment goals were identified: to help father develop more appropriate reinforcement and limit-setting for Timmy; to help mother relinquish some of her overcontrolling behavior and allow Timmy more autonomous choices within appropriate and consistent limits; to help both parents recognize Timmy's feelings and frustrations and relate to him with more warmth and empathy; to explore the parents' inconsistencies in child management as well as their relationship with each other, with a view toward beginning indicated therapeutic intervention.

The parents were assigned readings in parent-child communication and relationships, in child development, and in child management and behavior modification. They were helped to reinforce appropriate behavior at moments of particular difficulty for Timmy and the family—at dinnertime, bedtime, and while playing with his sister. Consistent limits and patterns of reinforcement helped mother to avoid overcontrol and father to avoid encouraging Timmy's defiance and aggressiveness. At the same time, the parents began to communicate and to relate more positively with Timmy, recognizing and accepting his anger and frustration. Instead of being taken up with continual parent-child conflicts, their time with him began to be more enjoyable.

As the parents applied appropriate reinforcements and began to meet Timmy's emotional needs for acceptance and autonomy, his defiance and aggressiveness decreased significantly. He became more active with his peer group, which also promoted improvement. Moreover, the difficult experience of altering their behavior in these ways forced both parents to examine their own personal styles of relating with the children and with each other. In several ways, mother's overcontrol and father's inhibition and tendency toward passive-aggressiveness (including subtly encouraging his son's defiance) resulted in significant stress in their marriage. The parents began to face these issues during the brief therapy period; after it was over, they entered couple therapy elsewhere to improve their marital relationship.

During the nine weeks of brief therapy, most of the sessions involved the parents, both individually and as a couple. However, several hours were spent with Timmy in play therapy, exploring his feelings of anger, aggressiveness, and jealousy. With some directive guidance and suggestions, Timmy began to discover alternative means for expressing his angry feelings. He had the opportunity to develop these further as his parents altered their approach with him in terms of relating and reinforcement. Timmy's parents were enthusiastic about the changes in the family. They were themselves reinforced to continue to work on and maintain them. Follow-up telephone calls indicated that Timmy's improvement persisted and that the parents had made progress in a brief course of marital couple therapy. About two months after the brief therapy, Timmy once again experimented with "dressing up." Since his other needs were being met, however, he soon lost interest in this. There have been no further reports of this activity.

CASE 3

Sara, seven years old, and her parents were referred to the clinic by her school teachers because of her disruptive behavior. Although quite petite, Sara virtually terrorized others in her class with rage outbursts involving screaming, throwing books, and overturning desks. She was regularly sent to the principal's office and her mother would be called to take her home. Her rages seemed to be associated with academic frustrations and with any requirement to follow teachers' directions. Intellectually, she was highly capable; academically, however, she was performing well below her potential. Sara also had great difficulties in relating to other children; her controlling behavior alienated most of her peers.

Sara was an only child, and her parents had had difficulties with her for several years. Her school problems, in fact, had existed since nursery school. Her father, a lawyer, was a strict disciplinarian who expected and demanded high levels of adultlike behavior from his intelligent, somewhat precocious daughter. Her mother, a former schoolteacher, tended to ignore any misbehavior by Sara until it reached an intolerable level. She then overreacted with screaming rages, often throwing and breaking plates and utensils. During a play diagnostic session, Sara related well to the therapist. However, she was both manipulative and controlling, and had difficulty conforming even to limits of time and space. During the evaluation sessions with the parents, each of them displayed evidence of significant individual psychopathology. Sara's father was often bothered by obsessive-compulsive symptoms and tended to have mildly paranoid thoughts. Her mother was significantly depressed and felt overwhelmed in her daily life.

In attempting to develop formulations and treatment goals with the parents, the therapist pointed out several obvious relationships between the parents' behavior, their expectations of Sara, the inconsistencies in handling her, and Sara's disruptive and manipulative school behavior. The parents were willing to acknowledge these relationships but were quite resistant to any further examination of their own personality characteristics or interpersonal relations. They tended to see the situation largely as Sara's problems and requested help to change her behavior. The therapist agreed that therapy with Sara was indicated and that he would be willing to begin with this, but also explicitly stated his belief that parent-child interactions and parental personality characteristics contributed to the situation. He urged regular sessions with the parents to "coordinate" the treatment approach and to explore further the parent-child interactions. The parents agreed to this and therapy began.

Sara was seen in play therapy once a week for the twelve-week brief therapy period. Sara's father had three individual sessions, her mother had six sessions, and the couple was seen jointly for the final two sessions. Although father's resistance remained high, in the individual sessions he was able to accept that his excessive expectations of Sara contributed to her frustration, her anger at being unable to accomplish goals immediately, her fears of failure, and her consequent resistance to direction as well as her need to control others. With support, father was able to reduce some of his demands on Sara and to tolerate a less than perfect performance from her. The fact that he did alter some of his behavior in this way clearly helped in Sara's gradual improvement. At the same time, he remained resistant to additional therapy and refused further individual appointments. Sara's mother, on the other hand, seemed to welcome the opportunity for individual therapy sessions. She readily accepted therapeutic intervention for her depression and was eager for guidance to improve her relationship with her daughter. Readings in parent-child communication and in child management helped her to develop more appropriate approaches in relating to Sara, both in general interactions and in limit setting. Increased confidence in these areas encouraged her to begin to communicate more openly with her husband about their relationship, as well as about their handling of Sara's difficulties. Her husband responded well to her attempts to communicate, and their relationship began to develop more openness and warmth. The final two sessions of the brief therapy included additional support and guidance for their therapeutic progress.

Play therapy for Sara consisted of gradual attempts to challenge her need for total control and help her to accept appropriate limits more comfortably. Her positive relationship with the therapist helped support her through these difficult changes. In the therapy sessions, her anxiety at giving up her controlling behavior and accepting limits began to decrease. With simultaneous support by her parents and teachers, this attitude began to generalize to home and school as well. The therapist consulted with Sara's teachers once at school and twice by telephone to help them provide appropriate therapeutic approaches. As these changes developed, Sara began to improve academically and to tolerate more sharing relationships with her peer group. This, in turn, further reinforced the changes she, her parents, and her teachers were making. Follow-up visits were scheduled every six to eight weeks for six months, and several further telephone consultations were held with her teachers. While her course was uneven, she continued to show improvement as her school and peer relationships improved. It is anticipated that Sara's parents will continue to require periodic help as further issues in her development and in their own relationship arise.

Preparation for the Child
and Family

Clinical experience indicates that children and families readily accept brief therapy. In fact, this approach results in fewer dropouts from therapy.[51] Offering therapy immediately after the family applies for service, when motivation is high, is an important factor. Once the evaluation is complete and the decision made that brief therapy is indicated, the family should be informed of the time limit, the particular treatment goals, and the need for collaboration between therapist and family during the therapy process. The family must understand the responsibility it will be asked to assume during the therapy—attempting behavior changes, completing homework assignments, and confronting issues that may be uncomfortable or even painful. At the same time, the fact that serious difficulties and specific treatment goals can be approached in a three-month period with intensive work casts an optimistic and hopeful tone over the therapy and may further enhance motivation. It must be explained, of course, that problems will not disappear or "be cured" in a three-month period. But family members may gain insights into the difficulties and develop the coping mechanisms to handle them themselves in the future.

Economic Implications

The economics of brief therapy may be viewed from the family's point of view and from the therapist's standpoint. For the family, the point of therapy termination is known from the outset; families can then plan for the financial requirements and adjust to the time involved. They may return for follow-up visits as needed but usually without the uncertainty of an open-ended commitment of money and time.

Viewed by the therapist, brief therapy is an efficient, as well as effective, approach. Treatment goals must be explicitly and clearly specified. The time limit exerts its "therapeutic pressure" toward achieving these goals. The family is given direct responsibility for change within the therapy and afterward. Family members in a sense become "therapist" for each other to maintain and expand gains made during the brief therapy process.[38]

In addition, such an approach allows for the extension of therapeutic services. More families may be seen in therapy, waiting lists may be reduced, and waiting periods for therapy diminished. The chances are that the more widespread practice of brief therapy would not in itself solve the problem of the many untreated emotionally disturbed children and families; it would, however, provide an additional approach to extend help to more people.

Simultaneous Activities

During the brief therapy process, there are other things the therapist can do to stimulate therapeutic change during treatment and to maintain it following termination. For example, the use of appropriate medication for the treatment of hyperkinesis, anxiety, and other symptoms may enhance the therapeutic process.[19] The use of medication is covered in detail in chapter 23; it is often a valuable adjunct in the practice of brief therapy.

Other simultaneous activities often involve some form of "environmental manipulation." They may involve brief consultations by telephone or visits with supportive individuals significant in the child's and family's life—pediatricians, clergy, close relatives, associates, welfare workers, and so on. Schoolteachers or counselors may be valuable allies in supporting the therapeutic work by class and school activities.[9] With the family's approval, anyone who is sufficiently involved in the family's life to provide ongoing support for therapeutic change may be included in the therapeutic process.

Depending on the specific therapeutic goals, still other activities during and following brief therapy may be indicated. Structured peer group activities for the child, outside-the-home activities for the single parent or the marital couple, and prescribed total family activities may help to support and maintain therapeutic change that began during the brief therapy period.

Follow Up

After termination, follow-up appointments may be scheduled for several reasons. Obviously, two to three months of therapy will not fully resolve the difficulties that many children and families face. The opportunity for follow-up visits becomes important if further crises in the family arise, or if some aspects of the changes made during therapy require further management. Often one to three further visits, several months following the brief therapy, are sufficient to accomplish this.

Follow-up visits may also be used as "checkup" appointments to assure that therapeutic changes are continuing. Family members often require structured guidance in maintaining behavior change, at least for a period of time until these changes become internalized. One or two follow-up "checks" may provide this guidance, prevent therapeutic deterioration, and stimulate further therapeutic movement. These follow-up appointments are useful as well in evaluating the longer term benefits of the therapy. Occasional appointments or at least some telephone or mail contact with the family over a year or longer following therapy may satisfy any or all of these indications for follow up.

Relation to Other Therapy

The use of brief therapy with children and families does not preclude their later involvement in more traditional long-term psychotherapy, nor in any other type of treatment. At times, in fact, a course of brief therapy will stimulate a family member's desire to enter longer-term therapy for further personal insight, change, and growth.

Following the brief therapy period, the question of need for further therapy for child and family is a complicated one. Many feelings are generated by termination, both within the therapist and the family members. Feelings of loss, sadness, abandonment, guilt, or dependence, a return of symptoms, or other phenomena may influence therapist or family to press for further therapy. It is of critical importance that this decision be made on the basis of therapeutic need, rather than because of transference or countertransference issues. In such instances, peer group consultation for the therapist can help clarify the issues involved and aid the therapist in making the clinically best decision. If further therapy is indicated, it is of course possible to contract for a further period of brief therapy, again with specific goals and treatment focus.

Evaluation of Therapeutic Results

The evaluation of treatment outcome in psychotherapy presents numerous methodological difficulties. Works which review psychotherapy outcome studies repeatedly point out their limitations and inadequacies.[47, 70] Relatively few studies exist of the therapeutic results of brief therapy with children and their families; those that do have numerous methodological problems. While partially limited by lack of adequate controls, by global or general assessment criteria, or by inadequate follow up, a number of studies do provide some information about efficacy and results.

Maher and Katkovsky[45] reported improvement in nervousness, fighting, and destructive behavior among children and parents receiving three hours or less of semidirective therapy. When compared with an untreated control group, other symptoms or behavioral difficulties were not improved. Coddington's experience in pediatric practice indicated that the majority of cases referred to him for psychotherapy could be successfully managed by a brief, direct type of psychotherapy.[18] Brief family therapy by Kaffman was reported successful in 75 percent of twenty-nine cases treated.[33] Success was based on the disappearance of the presenting symptoms or problems. Kaffman suggests that brief therapy is indicated when motivation is high, when emotional conflict has not been internalized, and when a positive relationship can be developed with the therapist.

School phobia has been successfully treated with brief treatment according to a number of reports.[36, 48, 74] Success is measured by the child's prompt return to school. Success rates of 80 percent to 90 percent in this condition are not unusual, provided that treatment is initiated early, that is, while symptoms are acute and family motivation is high.

Other studies of treatment outcome in brief psychotherapy with children report success rates of 70 percent to 80 percent. Hare[30] was able to achieve a 72 percent improvement rate with unselected cases in a child guidance clinic. Shaw, Blumenfeld, and Senf,[64] Eisenberg, Connors, and Sharped,[20] Nebl,[49] and Lessing and Shilling[39] report similar results and indicate that improvement is maintained in most treated children during follow-up periods. In studies by Phillips[54] and Phillips and Johnston,[55] children and their parents treated with brief therapy have even higher improvement rates than those treated with conventional long-term therapy.

Our own studies,[61, 62] as well as those mentioned, suggest that brief therapy with children and their parents is as effective as long-term psychotherapy when measured by improvement of presenting symptoms and ongoing conflicts. Further, they indicate that beneficial results are sustained during follow up periods of one to two years. The success rates, however, are achieved under particular conditions. These studies emphasize the structure of brief therapy with children and the factors leading to its success. Among the factors cited repeatedly in these reports are family motivation, acuteness of problems, therapist motivation, some measure of family stability, clearly defined time limits, therapeutic goals and focus of treatment, working intensively with parents as well as children, and supporting healthy psychological mechanisms in the family to enable the development of successful coping for the future.

While more methodologically sophisticated outcome studies are needed to evaluate brief therapy with children, numerous preliminary reports provide suggestive evidence of its efficacy and beneficial results. Given proper patient selection, appropriate therapist motivation and style, and careful structure of the brief therapy process, this approach holds promise for reaching a great many emotionally disturbed children and families.

Conclusion

As issues in community mental health and health-care delivery have achieved prominence, brief focused therapy with children and families has emerged as a useful and beneficial approach in psychotherapeutic practice. For many therapists, brief therapy requires a new orientation.[9] As described here, it requires an intensive and pragmatic approach, utilizing theory and active techniques from numerous, and often diverse, areas of psychology and psychotherapy. Consequently, brief therapy offers difficulties or complications that may not be encountered in long-term, open-ended psychotherapy. Rather than a "second-class" approach to be practiced by the inexperienced, brief therapy is the treatment of choice for many patients, and its intensity and complexities are best handled by the more experienced clinician who has the opportunity for regular peer consultation.

Brief therapy recognizes the family's health, psychological strengths, capabilities, and responsibility for maintaining and continuing therapeutic progress during and following the therapy process. Its successful practice requires a specific kind of "set"[61, 62] or orientation by both therapist and family. The elements of this set must include:

- therapist motivation
- family motivation
- "therapeutic pressure" of time-limited structure
- collaborative effort in defining the therapeutic focus and working toward specific treatment goals
- encouraging family responsibility for therapeutic progress
- "here-and-now," reality orientation
- rapidly developed therapeutic alliance
- termination as a central issue of therapy
- flexible, family-oriented approach
- therapist activity in directing and structuring the therapy, and developing adaptive family coping mechanisms
- follow-up contacts and the opportunity to return if further stress or family crises arise

While brief therapy is not a panacea for the emotional ills of children and families, it clearly offers the promise of an effective, as well as efficient, psychotherapeutic approach for many of our emotionally disturbed. With continued recognition and acceptance by child and family psychotherapists, brief therapy will provide relief for many more of the large number of emotionally disturbed families in our society.

REFERENCES

1. ALDERTON, H. R., "The Therapeutic Paradox," *Canadian Psychiatric Association Journal, 14(3)*:287–293, 1969.
2. ALEXANDER, F., "Principles and Techniques of Briefer Psychotherapeutic Procedures," *Proceedings of the Association for Research in Nervous and Mental Diseases, 31*:16–36, 1951.
3. ALLEN, F. H., "Case 8, Betty Ann Meyer," in Witmer, H. L. (Ed.), *Psychiatric Interviews With Children*, pp. 259–331, Harvard University Press, Cambridge, 1946.
4. ——, *Psychotherapy With Children*, Norton, New York, 1942.
5. ALPERN, E., "Short Clinical Services for Children in a Child Guidance Clinic," *American Journal of Orthopsychiatry, 26(2)*:314–325, 1956.
6. ARGLES, P., and MACKENZIE, M., "Crisis Intervention with a Multi-Problem Family: A Case Study," *Journal of Child Psychology and Psychiatry, 11(3)*:187–195, 1970.
7. AUGENBRAUN, B., REID, H. L., and FRIEDMAN, D. B., "Brief Intervention as a Preventive Force in Disorders of Early Childhood," *American Journal of Orthopsychiatry, 37(4)*:697–702, 1967.
8. BARTEN, H. H. (Ed.), *Brief Therapies*, Behavioral Publications, New York, 1971.
9. BARTEN, H. H., and BARTEN, S. S., "Introduction," in Barten, H. H., and Barten, S. S. (Eds.), *Children and*

Their Parents in Brief Therapy, pp. 1–20, Behavioral Publications, New York, 1973.
10. ——— (Eds.), *Children and Their Parents in Brief Therapy*, Behavioral Publications, New York, 1973.
11. BECKER, W. C., *Parents are Teachers—A Child Management Program*, Research Press, Champaign, Ill., 1971.
12. BERLIN, I. N., "Crisis Intervention and Short-Term Therapy: An Approach in a Child Psychiatric Clinic," *Journal of the American Academy of Child Psychiatry, 9(4)*:595–606, 1970.
13. BLANCHARD, P., "Case 1, Tommy Nolan," in Witmer, H. L. (Ed.), *Psychiatric Interviews With Children*, pp. 59–92, Harvard University Press, Cambridge, 1946.
14. BREUER, J., and FREUD, S., *Studies on Hysteria*, Basic Books, New York (published in German, 1895), 1957.
15. BRUCH, H., "Brief Psychotherapy in a Pediatric Clinic," *Quarterly Journal of Child Behavior, 1(1)*:2–8, 1949.
16. CAPLAN, G., MASON, E. A., and KAPLAN, D. M., "Four Studies of Crisis in Parents of Prematures," *Community Mental Health Journal, 1(2)*:149–161, 1965.
17. CHESS, S., THOMAS, A., and BIRCH, H. G., *Your Child Is a Person*, Parallax Publishing Co., New York, 1965.
18. CODDINGTON, R. D., "The Use of Brief Psycho-

therapy in a Pediatric Practice," *Journal of Pediatrics,* 60(2):259–265, 1962.

19. CYTRYN, L., GILBERT, A., and EISENBERG, L., "The Effectiveness of Tranquilizing Drugs Plus Supportive Psychotherapy in Treating Behavior Disorders of Children: A Double-Blind Study of 80 Outpatients," *American Journal of Orthopsychiatry, 30(1):*113–128, 1960.

20. EISENBERG, L., CONNERS, C. K., and SHARPED, L., "A Controlled Study of the Differential Application of Outpatient Psychiatric Treatment for Children," *Japanese Journal of Child Psychiatry, 6(1):*1–8, 1965.

21. FENICHEL, O., "Brief Psychotherapy," in Fenichel, H., and Rapaport, D. (Eds.), *The Collected Papers of Otto Fenichel,* pp. 142–178, Norton, New York, 1954.

22. FRAIBERG, S. H., *The Magic Years,* Scribner, New York, 1959.

23. FRANK, J., et al., "Why Patients Leave Psychotherapy," *A.M.A. Archives of Neurology and Psychiatry, 77(3):*283–299, 1957.

24. FRANK, J. D., *Persuasion and Healing,* Johns Hopkins Press, Baltimore, 1961.

25. FREEDMAN, N., et al., "Dropout from Outpatient Psychiatric Treatment," *A.M.A. Archives of Neurology and Psychiatry, 80(11):*657–666, 1958.

26. GINOT, H. G., *Between Parent and Child,* Macmillan, New York, 1965.

27. GORDON, T., *Parent Effectiveness Training,* Wyden, New York, 1970.

28. GORMAN, M., "An Action Program for the Mental Health of our Children," Paper presented at the San Francisco Mental Health Association Meeting, San Francisco, June 25, 1969.

29. GOTTSCHALK, L. A., et al., "The Laguna Beach Experiment as a Community Approach to Family Counseling for Drug Abuse Problems in Youth," *Comprehensive Psychiatry, 11(3):*226–234, 1970.

30. HARE, M. K., "Shortened Treatment in a Child Guidance Clinic: Results in 119 Cases," *British Journal of Psychiatry, 112(6):*613–616, 1966.

31. HEINICKE, C. M., and GOLDMAN, A., "Research on Psychotherapy with Children," *American Journal of Orthopsychiatry, 30(3):*483–494, 1960.

32. Joint Commission on Mental Health of Children, *Crisis in Child Mental Health: Challenge for the 1970's,* Harper & Row, New York, 1969.

33. KAFFMAN, M., "Short-Term Family Therapy," *Family Process, 2(2):*216–234, 1963.

34. KARDINER, A., *The Traumatic Neuroses of War,* Hoeber, New York, 1941.

35. KELLEHER, D., "A Model for Integrating Special Educational and Community Mental Health Services," *The Journal of Special Education, 2:*263–272, 1968.

36. KENNEDY, W. A., "School Phobia: Rapid Treatment of 50 Cases," *Journal of Abnormal Psychology, 70(4):*285–289, 1965.

37. KERNS, E., "Planned Short-Term Treatment, A New Service to Adolescents," *Social Casework, 51(6):*340–346, 1970.

38. KLIMAN, G., "Discussion," *American Journal of Psychiatry, 128(2):*145–146, 1971.

39. LESSING, E. E., and SHILLING, F. H., "Relationship Between Treatment Selection Variables and Treatment Outcome in a Child Guidance Clinic: An Application of Data Processing Methods," *Journal of the American Academy of Child Psychiatry, 5(2):*313–348, 1966.

40. LESTER, E. P., "Brief Psychotherapy in Child Psychiatry," *Canadian Psychiatric Association Journal, 13(4):*301–309, 1968.

41. LEVY, D. M., "Release Therapy," *American Journal of Orthopsychiatry, 9(4):*713–736, 1939.

42. LEWIN, K. K., *Brief Psychotherapy,* Warren H. Green, St. Louis, Mo., 1970.

43. LINDEMANN, E., "Symptomatology and Management of Acute Grief," *American Journal of Psychiatry, 101(2):*141–148, 1944.

44. MACKAY, J., "The Use of Brief Psychotherapy With Children," *Canadian Psychiatric Association Journal, 12(3):* 269–279, 1967.

45. MAHER, B. A., and KATKOVSKY, W., "The Efficacy of Brief Clinical Procedures in Alleviating Children's Problems," *Journal of Individual Psychology, 17:*204–211, 1961.

46. MALAN, D. H., *A Study of Brief Psychotherapy,* Charles C Thomas, Springfield, Ill., 1963.

47. MELTZOFF, J., and KORNREICH, M., *Research in Psychotherapy,* Atherton Press, New York, 1970.

48. MINUCHIN, S., CHAMBERLAIN, P., and GRAUBARD, P., "A Project to Teach Learning Skills to Disturbed, Delinquent Children," *American Journal of Orthopsychiatry, 37(3):*558–567, 1967.

49. NEBL, N., "Essential Elements in Short-Term Treatment," *Social Casework, 52(6):*377–381, 1971.

50. PARAD, H. J., and PARAD, L. G., "A Study of Crisis-Oriented Planned Short-Term Treatment: Part I," *Social Casework, 49(6):*346–355, 1968.

51. PARAD, L. G., and PARAD, H. J., "A Study of Crisis-Oriented Planned Short-Term Treatment: Part II," *Social Casework, 49(7):*418–426, 1968.

52. PATTERSON, G. R., *Families,* Research Press, Champaign, Ill., 1971.

53. ———, and GUILLION, M. E., *Living With Children,* Research Press, Champaign, Ill., 1968.

54. PHILLIPS, E. L., "Parent-Child Psychotherapy: A Follow-Up Study Comparing Two Techniques," *The Journal of Psychology, 49(1):*195–202, 1960.

55. ———, and JOHNSTON, M. S. H., "Theoretical and Clinical Aspects of Short-Term Parent-Child Psychotherapy," *Psychiatry, 17(3):*267–275, 1954.

56. PHILLIPS, E. L., and WEINER, D. N., *Short-Term Psychotherapy and Structured Behavior Change,* McGraw-Hill, New York, 1966.

57. PROSKAUER, S., "Some Technical Issues in Time-Limited Psychotherapy with Children," *Journal of the American Academy of Child Psychiatry, 8(1):*154–169, 1969.

58. *Psychiatric News,* "Biofeedback Said to Place Responsibilities on Patient," July 2, 1975.

59. RANK, B., "Case 3, Jerry Hoskins," in Witmer, H. L. (Ed.), *Psychiatric Interviews With Children,* pp. 136–356, Harvard University Press, Cambridge, 1946.

60. RANK, O., *Will Therapy and Truth and Reality,* Knopf, New York, 1945.

61. ROSENTHAL, A. J., and LEVINE, S. V., "Brief Psychotherapy with Children: Process of Therapy," *American Journal of Psychiatry, 128(2):*141–146, 1971.

62. ———, "Brief Psychotherapy with Children: A Preliminary Report," *American Journal of Psychiatry, 127(5):*646–651, 1970.

63. SALK, L., *What Every Child Would Like His Parents to Know,* Werner Books, New York, 1973.

64. SHAW, R., BLUMENFELD, H., and SENF, R., "A Short-Term Treatment Program in a Child Guidance Clinic," *Social Work, 13(3):*81–90, 1968.

65. SHULMAN, J. L., "One-Visit Psychotherapy with Children," *Progress in Psychotherapy, 5:*86–93, 1960.

66. SMALL, L., *The Briefer Psychotherapies,* Brunner/Mazel, New York, 1971.

67. SMITH, J. M., and SMITH, D. E. P., *Child Management—A Program for Parents and Teachers,* Ann Arbor Publishers, Ann Arbor, Mich., 1966.

68. SOLOMON, J. C., "Trends in Orthopsychiatric Therapy: Play Technique," *American Journal of Orthopsychiatry, 18(3):*402–413, 1948.

69. SPRINGE, M. P., "Work with Adolescents: Brief Psychotherapy with a Limited Aim," *Journal of Child Psychotherapy, 2(1):*31–37 1968.

70. STOLLAK, G. E., GUERNEY, B. G., and ROTHBERG, M. (Eds.), *Psychotherapy Research, Selected Readings,* Rand, McNally, Chicago, Ill., 1966.

71. TARJAN, G., "And What of the Children," *Hospital and Community Psychiatry, 20(4):*223–227, 1969.

72. THOMAS, A., CHESS, S., and BIRCH, H. G., *Tempera-*

ment and Behavior Disorders in Children, New York University Press, New York, 1968.

73. Wagner, M. K., "Parent Therapists: An Operant Conditioning Method," *Mental Hygiene, 52(3)*:452–455, 1968.

74. Waldfogel, S., Tessman, E., and Hahn, P. B., "A Program of Early Intervention in School Phobia," *American Journal of Orthopsychiatry, 29(2)*:324–332, 1959.

75. Werry, J. S., and Wollersheim, J. P., "Behavior Therapy with Children: A Broad Overview," *Journal of the American Academy of Child Psychiatry, 6(2)*:346–370, 1967.

76. Witmer, H. L. (Ed.), *Psychiatric Interviews With Children*, Harvard University Press, Cambridge, 1946.

77. Wolberg, L. R., *Short-Term Psychotherapy*, Grune & Stratton, New York, 1965.

---

5 / Individual Behavior Therapy

James P. McGee and Donald H. Saidel

Definition of Behavior Therapy

Behavior therapy is defined by Ullmann and Krasner[109] as "treatment deducible from the sociopsychological model that aims to alter a person's behavior directly through application of general psychological principles." More specifically, Wolpe[116] relates behavior therapy to psychological learning theory by describing it as ". . . the use of experimentally established principles of learning for the purpose of changing unadaptive habits." As far as can be determined, the first use of the term behavior therapy appeared in the literature in 1953 in a monograph by Lindsley, Skinner, and Solomon,[66] describing research in operant conditioning with regressed adult psychotics. Although there are currently a number of definitions of behavior therapy, including Lazarus's[62] atheoretical "technical eclecticism—use whatever works" approach, most writers in the field share a common view which includes the following points: (1) the operational definition of concepts so they can be tested experimentally; (2) a broad concept of "laboratory" which includes the clinic setting; (3) research as treatment, treatment as research; (4) an explicit strategy of therapy; (5) establishment of causal relationships between antecedents, behavior, and consequence; and (6) establishment of specific goals of treatment via a functional analysis.[59]

History

The origins of behavior therapy, or to use the more generic term, behavior modification, can readily be traced back to the philosophical tradition of empiricism as characterized by the British philosophers Locke, Hume, and Hartley.[19] Here the mind was regarded as a *tabula rasa*, or blank slate, upon which experience impressed knowledge and behavioral tendencies. This contrasts sharply with the "nativism" of Kant, which assumed the presence of innate ideas, drives, and behavioral tendencies. In many ways psychoanalytic theory, which promotes the importance of instinctual drives, was derived from nativistic philosophy.

In addition to regarding man as essentially a product of his environment, the British empiricists also fostered the development of a specific philosophy of science. They encouraged attention to the observable and measurable while simultaneously deemphasizing speculation and inference. This focus on the observable is also consistent with behavior theory and therapy.

In the United States, the behavioral school of psychology was founded by John B. Watson, who is often regarded as the "father of modern behaviorism." In some of Watson's early work in the 1920s, he applied learning principles to alter behavior patterns in children. His work was greatly influenced by the researches of Pavlov[89] on the conditioned reflex and by the pioneer learning theorist, E. L. Thorndike. It was Thorndike's "law of effect"[108] which articulated the influence of reinforcing consequences on behavior and provided the foundation for Skinner's[101] behavioral psychology of operant conditioning. Krasner[59] regards the work of Skinner as one of the most important of fifteen various "streams of influence" which converged in the early 1960s to give birth to the present field of behavior therapy. Additional sources of influence identified by Krasner[59] range from the Dollard and Miller[31] interpretation of psychoanalysis in learning theory terms to the psychiatric works of Adolph Meyer and Harry

Stack Sullivan, both of whom placed considerable weight on observation of behavior and human interaction. Occurring almost concurrently with, but somewhat independent of, the development of behavior therapy in the United States was a parallel movement in Great Britain. This was led primarily by H. J. Eysenck and S. Rachman and their associates. In addition to the work of Skinner, perhaps the two other most important trends affecting the evolution of behavior therapy were: the development of the social learning theory of psychopathology (see volume 2) as a viable alternative to the disease or medical model; and a growing dissatisfaction with psychoanalysis and psychodynamic psychotherapies because of their alleged inefficacy.[36]

Finally, it seems no accident that the time period (late 1950s, early 1960s) during which behavior modification became an influential school of therapy coincides roughly with the epoch of the emergence of clinical psychology as an independent psychotherapeutic profession. With the notable exception of Joseph Wolpe, a psychiatrist, the major early contributors to behavior therapy were academic psychologists. They came straight out of the laboratory and brought to the clinic empirically established principles of behavior change technology.

Theoretical Assumptions of Behavior Therapy

BEHAVIOR AS LEARNED

Fundamental to the theory of behavior therapy is the assumption that the bulk of human behavior is acquired through various processes of learning or conditioning. No distinction is made between the mechanisms by which prosocial or adaptive forms of behavior and deviant or maladaptive behaviors are learned. Accordingly, the same principles of behavioral acquisition and maintenance apply to adaptive behaviors in children (such as cooperative play or socially acceptable levels of aggression) and to undesirable behavior (such as social withdrawal and isolation) or self-destructive behavior (such as head banging).

DEVIANCE AND SOCIAL JUDGMENT

A corollary to this assumption is the notion that behavior generally is not in and of itself patho-logical or deviant but rather is labeled that on the basis of social judgments. For example, a temperature elevation of 104° is inherently or intrinsically pathological; it is symptomatic of illness regardless of the cultural or geographic setting in which it occurs. In contrast, extreme levels of aggressive behavior may be highly valued and, in fact, rewarded if they occur in a combat zone, while they may result in incarceration when displayed on the streets of a city. The relevance of social judgments in the designation of behavior as adaptive or maladaptive applies even to hallucinations. For example, the inpatient on a psychiatric ward who hallucinates may be regarded as quite sick and receive an increase in psychoactive medication. Certain Indian tribes, however, will give praise and elevate the status of a person who manifests the same behavior. Even subjective feeling states, such as depression and grief, are influenced by social values; for example, there is considerable variation from one cultural group to another regarding what it is appropriate to become depressed about, and how intense and prolonged the depression should be.[109]

Once he accepts this corollary assumption about labeling behavior as deviant, the behavioral practitioner becomes all the more concerned with specific behavioral deficits and excesses, rather than with global psychiatric diagnostic categories and their implication of mental illness. Thus, a whole range of maladaptive behaviors in a child—for example, fire setting, enuresis, poor school performance, and social isolation—can be assumed to arise from a basic source, namely, some internal psychic disturbance or a group of fixations and associated ego problems which have been identified by the diagnosic process. In contrast, the behavioral therapist would view those behaviors as separate entities, each acquired separately through processes of learning, and each most appropriately treated through a specific relearning or retraining program.

MODES OF LEARNING

As mentioned earlier, one of the basic assumptions of the behavior therapist is that behavior has been acquired through learning processes. It follows then that learning principles must be utilized to alter behavior. There are a number of processes of learning (in effect, the modalities of behavioral acquisition) that behavior therapists consider to be important. These are: (1) classical or Pavlovian conditioning, (2) operant or Skinnerian conditioning, (3) modeling (or learning through imitation, or vicarious learning), and (4) cognitive acquisition, a category not included by all authors. In this chapter, these various forms of learning or conditioning will be examined, and examples will be given of how they apply to the development of maladaptive behavior.

CLASSICAL CONDITIONING

Classical, Pavlovian, or reflexive conditioning is a form of learning related primarily to reflexive responses mediated by the autonomic nervous system. It was discovered and initially investigated by the famous Russian psychophysiologist, Ivan Pavlov.[89] Its discovery is a prime example of the principle of serendipity, or finding one thing while looking for something else. Pavlov and his associates were engaged in research on the gastrointestinal activities of dogs with a focus on salivatory and gastric secretion responses. Their typical experiment involved providing one of the research animals with a portion of food and then measuring the secretory process. In the course of this work it was frequently observed that animals would display salivatory and gastric secretion responses in the absence of the food stimuli. This phenomenon was initially regarded as an annoyance; it tended to contaminate the data that the investigators hoped to acquire. Later, however, it was deemed a phenomenon worthy of investigation in its own right. What Pavlov observed was that when a stimulus, such as food which evokes a reflexive response, is repeatedly paired with neutral stimuli (conditioned stimulus), such as the animal's cage or laboratory lights, the neutral or conditioned stimulus will eventually evoke the reflexive response when presented in the absence of the unconditioned stimulus (food). The early experiments typically involved using a tone such as a bell or tuning fork as the conditioned stimulus. This was paired repeatedly and contiguously with an unconditioned stimulus such as meat powder. The ensuing response was salivation. After a series of trials of presenting the two stimuli together, the unconditioned stimulus (food) was removed, and the animal then salivated in response to the presentation of the tone stimulus alone. This classical conditioning procedure has been applied successfully to species throughout the phylogenetic scale, ranging from a lowly earthworm to human beings from infancy onward. A broad array of responses such as sweating, heart rate, gastrointestinal secretions, nausea, vomiting, tendon jerks, and limb withdrawal have been conditioned to stimuli not normally known to effect such a response.[76] The literature on classical conditioning is voluminous, and this particular form of learning is one of the thoroughly researched phenomena in the field of behavioral psychology.

CLASSICAL CONDITIONING AND PHOBIAS

In the early 1920s, John B. Watson[110] conducted one of the earliest studies that demonstrated how classical conditioning could cause a child to acquire a clinical symptom, namely, a fear or phobic response. In this particular study, an intense anxiety response to the presence of a white rat was conditioned in an eleven-month-old boy (Albert) who previously had shown no fear of it. In this experiment, the unconditioned stimulus was a loud noise produced by striking a steel bar with a hammer; the white rat was the conditioned stimulus. After several presentations of a white rat in conjunction with the loud noise, the child displayed a severe anxiety response to the animal. In this study of little Albert, Watson and Rayner also documented the principle of generalization. Generalization refers to the fact that once a conditioned response has been established to a certain stimulus, stimuli that are similar to it in quality and intensity will now evoke the conditioned response. For example, a dog conditioned to salivate to a tone of a certain frequency and amplitude will also show the conditioned response to other tones in adjacent frequency and amplitude ranges. In the case of little Albert, not only did he display a phobic response to the white rat, but also to other furry animals and objects such as a woman's fur coat and a Santa Claus mask with a beard. This is often referred to as being analogous to the establishment of neurotic anxiety or a phobic response.

In Watson's experiment, several presentations of noise (the aversive, unconditioned stimulus), paired with the laboratory rat, were required in order for a conditioned response to be established. Other studies,[23, 52] however, have demonstrated that under certain conditions of intense aversive stimulation, only one trial is required in order for a full-blown conditioned emotional response to be established. Additional studies by Pavlov,[89] Liddell,[65] and Wolpe[116] have provided experimental evidence that intense and persistent conditioned emotional responses can be developed after repeated exposure to mild levels of aversive stimulation, a situation that is probably more typical of the natural development of human anxiety. The one-trial learning experiment may illustrate what happens in the development of a "traumatic phobia" (a phobia that occurs subsequent to experiencing a single highly toxic psychological event). In a particularly amusing paper by Wolpe and Rachman,[118] an effort is made to reopen Freud's famous case of little Hans and explain the child's phobia in terms of a one-trial learning, classically conditioned emotional response. These authors correctly point out that Hans had witnessed a serious accident involving a horse-drawn cart immediately prior to the onset of his "horse phobia," a fact apparently regarded by Freud as unimportant.[118] Thus, some have regarded the disputes between psychodynamic and behavior therapists as essentially a contest between Freud's little Hans and Watson's little Albert.

For obvious reasons, the research conducted on the development of emotional responses through classical conditioning has been restricted to laboratory studies. However, with the help of this conditioning paradigm, it is possible to explain a fairly broad range of human anxieties. For example, the child who repeatedly receives large doses of aversive stimulation in the form of physical punishment from a hostile mother is concurrently exposed to a broad array of otherwise neutral stimuli, involving all the cue properties possessed by an adult woman. These could include such things as feminine attire and hair style, physical stature, voice intonation, odor of perfume, cosmetics, and so on. According to the classical conditioning model, by repeatedly pairing these with an unconditioned stimulus, namely, physical punishment, the mother is inadvertently conditioning an emotional response to these various neutral stimuli. The theory would then predict that once conditioning occurs, when the child is presented with the stimulus characteristics of other women, he would experience an emotional reaction. Since classical conditioning apparently occurs at an autonomic-subcortical level, it would not be essential that the child experience negative cognitions regarding women in order to evoke this emotional response. In fact, recent studies on "attribution theory" by Schachter and Singer[100] have indicated that, in some instances, the belief system or cognitive side of emotional response may be the result of, rather than the cause of, emotional arousal. In the example given, the child concludes, "I must not like women because I feel so uncomfortable when I am with them." This may readily become either: "There is something wrong with me" or "There is something wrong with women," or both.

Thorny issues confront the therapist who attempts to explain the acquisition of anxiety responses in terms of classical conditioning alone. One of these involves the rather extreme variability in the intensity and persistence of conditioned emotional responses among different individuals. In fact, when a large group of people are all exposed to the same traumatic event, they do not acquire an emotional response of the same quality and intensity, nor do they all retain the emotional response for the same period of time. Explanations of this phenomenon range from Eysenck's[37] proposition of a biologically determined factor of conditionability which varies from one individual to the next to the emphasis placed by Marks[72] on the fact that there is a common denominator uniting phobic individuals—that is, their persistent avoidance of the phobic object. He emphasizes the fact that phobic individuals scrupulously avoid that which they are afraid of, and thus never have an opportunity to unlearn or decondition themselves to the phobia. Conditioning theory predicts that repeated exposures to the conditioned stimulus in the absence of the unconditioned stimulus will lead to extinction (the conditioned stimulus loses its ability to evoke a response). When the organism has limited access to the conditioned stimulus however, it does appear that extinction is less likely to occur.

OPERANT CONDITIONING

In its simplest form, the main principle of learning and behavioral acquisition by operant, instrumental, or Skinnerian conditioning can be stated as follows: "Behavior is greatly influenced by its consequences."[11] This principle was originally described by Thorndike as the law of effect and, later, elaborated by B. F. Skinner, one of the most famous and controversial living American psychologists. It forms the foundation of the practice of behavior therapy.

FREE OPERANT CONDITIONING

As was the case with classical conditioning, much of the early research on operant conditioning was done with animals. The typical operant experiment involved placing an animal in a controlled environment where his behavior could be directly altered by systematically applying various rewards or punishments. For example, a laboratory rat might be placed in a T-shaped maze with a food reward placed at the end of the left arm of the T. On early learning trials when the animal was placed at the entry of the maze, he would engage in essentially random search behavior; that is, the probability of his taking a left- or right-hand turn in the maze would initially be equal. However, after the animal made his first left-hand turn and discovered the food reward in the arm of the T, those probabilities would change. On subsequent trials, the animal would be more likely to make a left-hand turn, particularly if the left-hand arm of the T-maze always contained food. After a series of trials, the animal's behavior would no longer be random at all. Instead, as soon as he was placed in the maze, he would head directly for the left-hand portion of the T-maze, the area in which he had always found the food reward.

Another common operant conditioning experiment involves the use of an experimental apparatus called the Skinner box (named after its inventor, B. F. Skinner). Typically this is an enclosed cage large enough to accommodate whatever animal is being used in the experiment in such a way that the animal has some freedom to move about. One side of the cage might be plexiglass so that the animal's behavior can be observed, and there is usually a grid plate in the floor through which aversive stimulation in the form of electroshock can be applied. At one end of the Skinner box there might be a small lever or bar. When pressed by the animal, this lever releases a food pellet reward which is dropped into a tray immediately adjacent to the bar. In experiments on "free operant conditioning," a totally untrained animal is placed in this environment without receiving any direction or cues regarding how to operate the food release mechanism. Initially the animal's behavior will be totally random wanderings about the cage. However, at some point and quite accidentally, the animal invariably hits the lever. This in turn activates the food pellet release mechanism. For the animal, his "operation" on the environment, namely, the lever pressing, has produced a particular reinforcing consequence, the appearance of food. Subsequent to this first reinforcing event, the probability of the animal's movement in the cage changes. No longer is it aimless; now he tends to spend more and more time at the end of the cage where the food tray and bar are located. Once he has narrowed down his field of movement in this way, the odds on his accidentally hitting the bar again are increased. With each subsequent bar press trial which produces food

reinforcement, the probability of the animal's future behavior changes again. Each successful experience makes him more and more likely to engage in bar-pressing behavior. This constitutes free operant learning; it is roughly equivalent to learning by trial and error.

DISCRIMINATION LEARNING

Another common form of operant conditioning involves discrimination learning. Here behavior is reinforced only if it occurs in the presence of a signal, or discriminative stimulus.[101] For example, an animal would receive food reinforcement only if he pressed the bar at the same time that a small light went on in the cage. Once learning has occurred, the animal's behavior is under both stimulus and response control: He will engage in bar-pressing behavior only when the light is on because it is only under those conditions that he receives reinforcement. It appears that a great deal of human behavior is under this type of stimulus-reinforcement, or antecedent-consequence control; it is roughly equivalent to one aspect of "learning from experience."

ESCAPE AND AVOIDANCE TRAINING

The forms of operant or Skinnerian learning described thus far generally fall under the heading of "reward training." Two other common forms of instrumental or operant conditioning are "escape training" and "avoidance training." In escape training, the animal must learn to make a specific response in order to terminate a painful stimulus. In the usual escape-training experiment, the animal receives a series of nonlethal but painful shocks through an electrified grate on the floor of a Skinner box. In order for the animal to terminate or escape the aversive painful stimulation, he must perform some particular act, such as pressing a bar, or withdrawing a limb, or moving to a different part of the cage. After a few such trials, the animal learns to make the escape response as soon as it receives a shock.

In avoidance training, the situation is somewhat different. Prior to receiving the aversive stimulation, the animal receives some type of cue or signal, such as a tone or a light, which indicates that aversive stimulation will follow. If the animal responds to the cue rapidly enough, for example by moving to a different part of the cage or pressing the bar of the Skinner box, he will avoid the aversive stimulation. Once established, avoidance responses are extremely resistant to extinction. Indeed, they frequently persist through hundreds of trials in which no shock has been administered after the warning signal.[103]

Many of the studies of avoidance training and avoidance learning have been used as the analogs for human avoidance behavior or social withdrawal. Thus, the socially isolated and withdrawn individual is regarded as a person who encountered unpleasant, aversive consequences during early social experiences. After a series of such aversive experiences, the individual regards the various cue properties of other human beings as signals that aversive stimulation is imminent; consequently, he withdraws himself from social situations, much in the manner of a laboratory animal exposed to a sequence of avoidance training. This is another aspect of learning from experience.

KINDS OF REINFORCERS

According to operant theory, there are essentially four different kinds of consequences or categories of reinforcers that may follow a particular behavior. These are: positive reinforcement, negative reinforcement, punishment, and the absence of reinforcement. Positive reinforcement is the experience of some pleasurable or positive reward contingent on performance of the specific behavior. The effects of positive reinforcement are to increase the likelihood of a behavior recurring. Negative reinforcement is the termination of aversive stimuli contingent on behavior. Negative reinforcement has the same effect on behavior as positive reinforcement; it increases the probability of some specific behavior recurring in the future. For example, if a person sitting near an open window feels an uncomfortable breeze blowing through the window, he may get up and close the window. In the language of conditioning theory, he "operates" on the environment, performs an operant behavior, the consequences of which are the termination of an aversive stimulus, the breeze.

Punishment, the third category of reinforcers, and negative reinforcement are often confused. Negative reinforcement refers to the termination of aversive stimulation, while punishment refers to the application of an aversive stimulus contingent on behavior. For example, a stray dog may have a continuous shower of sticks and pebbles thrown at him until he runs away. This is quite different from slapping a puppy on the nose every time he jumps up on his master's chair. Here, aversive stimulation is applied contingently only upon the appearance of the undesired be-

havior. The effects of punishment are to suppress behavior or to decrease the probability of behavioral recurrence.

A final behavioral consequence is to give no reinforcement and thus to create a schedule of extinction. This is simply a condition where subsequent to the performance of a behavior, nothing happens. The individual receives neither positive reinforcement, negative reinforcement, nor punishment. Thus, in one respect, extinction conditions are like punishment; they have the effect of reducing the probability of a given future behavior.

Research in categories of reinforcers indicates that extinction schedules and schedules of positive reinforcement achieve the highest predictability in terms of their effects on behavior. In contrast, punishment has the least predictable effects. As a result, it is regarded as the least desirable measure for behavior control purposes.

SCHEDULES OF REINFORCEMENT

Another important factor influencing the acquisition of operant responses is the schedule of reinforcment, that is, the manner in which reinforcement is delivered. It may occur immediately after a response, it may be delayed for some period, or it may take place only after a certain number of responses have been emitted. For example, reinforcement may be delivered on the basis of a predetermined number of responses. There could be a one to one ratio in which every single correct response received an immediate reinforcement, or there could be a ten to one ratio where every ten responses received a reinforcement. Or, rather than delivering reinforcement on the basis of the response rate, it could be delivered according to the passage of time. The reinforcement, for example, could be delivered every two or three minutes after a correct response. The various schedules of reinforcement have highly characteristic effects on the rate of responding and the rate of extinction.[101]

A schedule of reinforcement which seems most closely to approximate what occurs in real-life situations is called a variable intermittent reinforcement schedule. This is a schedule in which reinforcement is delivered in a somewhat unpredictable, almost haphazard fashion. It is quite similar to what one encounters while playing a slot machine; the player knows that reinforcement is possible but is unable to predict exactly when it will occur. It is possible to explain a great deal of human social behavior in terms of variable intermittent reinforcement. One of the most striking characteristics of this type of schedule is its extreme resistance to extinction. In other words, once an individual has had a particular behavior reinforced on a variable intermittent schedule, it is extremely difficult to eliminate that behavior from his behavioral repertoire. This is, of course, precisely the case with something like gambling, where only a small portion of the responses are actually reinforced, and that reinforcement occurs on an unpredictable basis. Contrast this with operating a cigarette or candy machine. Here the individual's learning experience is that each behavioral response, depositing money and pulling the lever of the machine, invariably results in reinforcement, a package of cigarettes or candy. On those occasions when the machine does not operate and deliver, it is rather unlikely that the individual will continue to put more money in the machine and try to operate it.

Tantrum behavior in children seems frequently to be maintained on an intermittent-reinforcement schedule. Parents often report that they only rarely give in to the child's tantrum, but according to operant theory, that is precisely the type of reinforcement schedule which would result in tantrums becoming a well-established part of the child's behavioral scheme.

THE NATURE OF REINFORCEMENT

The question of what, in fact, is a reinforcer is typically answered empirically. In other words, a positively reinforcing stimulus is one which increases the probability of the future repetition of a response. This definition has been criticized because of its circularity; however, since it rests on empirically-observable phenomena, it has operational utility. Reinforcers are classified as either primary or secondary. Primary reinforcers are concerned mainly with basic physiological needs and include such things as food, water, sex, and pain. Secondary reinforcers are inherently neutral. However, because of repeated pairing with primary reinforcers, they acquire the capacity to govern behavior in much the same manner. For example, money is a secondary reinforcer or a token reinforcer. There is nothing inherently or intrinsically satisfying or drive-reducing about currency; however, one can use it to acquire more basic reinforcers such as food.

SHAPING

Finally there is the principle of "shaping" or "reinforcement of successive approximation."[101]

This is given considerable weight by behavior theorists. It refers to facilitating the acquisition of complex sequences of operant behavior, such as language in humans, by selectively reinforcing partial responses which approximate the desired criterion. At the same time, it involves carefully ignoring, or not reinforcing, nonapproximation responses.

OPERANT CONDITIONING AND DEVIANCE

Generally speaking, writers who have attempted to explain psychopathology in terms of operant conditioning view psychiatric symptoms as the result of inadequate reinforcement histories. From this standpoint, deviant behavior is seen as a pattern of maladaptive operant responses which were, in turn, the result of inadequate or inappropriate reinforcement. Once these deviant operant responses become well established, they prevent the individual from acquiring other responses of a more adaptive nature. In reality, behavior therapists are generally not very concerned about the origins of deviant behavior; they would rather focus their efforts at altering it. Clinically it is in precisely this area, namely, modifying deviant behavior, that the principles of operant conditioning have received their most extensive applications. With children, this might include such things as training mute, autistic children in verbal behavior by systematically reinforcing successively more appropriate uses of the mouth and verbalizations. The primary reinforcers might be such items as foods and candy.

IMITATION LEARNING

Until recently, the strong emphasis on operant and classical conditioning and learning theory has tended to obscure the fact that a considerable amount of human learning is a result of the imitation of behavior observed in models.[49] Although some of the research on imitation learning has been done with subhuman species, the bulk of observational learning research has been done with humans. In the case of humans, the overriding importance of observational learning is readily apparent in the acquisition of speech and language. It is inconceivable that children could acquire fluent, intelligible speech by the selective reinforcement of successive approximations of spoken language without reference to a model of the language to be learned. Indeed, the whole of formal education would be hard-pressed to accomplish its tasks without recourse to modeling as a technique for encouraging the learning of new behaviors. There are many situations in which the desired behavior is not likely to be performed, either because the eliciting stimulus is absent or because a dominant response repertoire renders the behavior infrequent or improbable. In such instances, modeling the behavior so that it can be observed and imitated is the only efficient means of generating the desired modification. Trial-and-error learning with differential reinforcement, as is the case with operant conditioning, would be very wasteful of both time and effort. It is not at all difficult to find examples of behaviors humans may wish to acquire in which trial-and-error learning would be extremely hazardous (learning to drive a car), inefficient (learning to tie shoes), or absurd (learning a surgical technique).

FACTORS IN IMITATION LEARNING

The effort to place an appropriate emphasis on observational learning in humans has been led by Albert Bandura.[10] Since the early 1960s, he has generated or participated in a large number of studies designed to demonstrate the effects of an observed model on behavior and to explore the relevant variables. Bandura's typical experiments were designed along the following lines: An experimental group observes a model engaging in a particular behavior, while a control group engages in an activity other than the observation of a model. In the final phase, independent observers record the number and kind of model behaviors emitted by subjects in the two groups. A variation of this procedure begins by selecting subjects on the basis of specific response tendencies and then exposes them to a model of the opposite response tendency. Subsequent observation reveals whether observing the model caused the subjects' behavior to be modified in a direction opposite to their initial tendency.

IMITATION OF AGGRESSION

Early studies of the imitation of model behavior were concerned largely with aggressive behavior.[12] In these studies, Bandura and his colleagues provide rather convincing evidence that children exposed to aggressive models were likely to resort to aggression as a problem-solving strategy in future frustrating situations. Their findings stood in contrast to some psychoanalytic theories which had predicted the opposite effect, that is,

that observation of aggression in others would have a cathartic effect and result in a diminished propensity toward aggression on the part of the observer.[12] Since the ability to control and cope with aggression is clearly an important part of making a prosocial adjustment, the relevance of modeling in the development of psychopathological aggression was noted early in the studies of learning by imitation.[14] Other studies relating learning to psychopathology have provided support for the popular conviction that a large amount of asocial behavior stems from the imitation of asocial models in the home or peer group.[14, 96] The contributions of imitative learning and the effects of models, in the case of maladaptive behavior, may not be regarded as qualitatively different from acquisiton of prosocial adaptive behavior through imitation learning. If the child can learn misinformation from a misinformed teacher, he can also learn maladaptive behavior from a maladapted model.

COGNITIVE LEARNING

Both behavior theorists and behavior therapists in the past have placed little, if any, emphasis on the relationship between thinking, or cognition, and behavior. In fact, some operant theorists have gone so far as to state that most, if not all, human behavior can be understood without any reference to private events or what goes on inside the "black box." The most eminent spokesman of this particular view was in fact B. F. Skinner, who, along with John B. Watson, maintained that thinking was little more than subvocal speech which was often secondary to or an epiphenomenon of overt behavior.[101] Recently, however, behavior therapists, as exemplified by Arnold A. Lazarus[62] have begun to reconsider the importance of cognition in human functioning. According to this new trend, thoughts, attitudes, belief systems, and values are acquired in much the same fashion as overt behaviors. For example, a child who repeatedly hears his parents express the belief that "all dogs are dangerous" is likely to adopt that belief himself. In the future, then, this particular belief will guide his behavior in his dealings with certain animals. The important point here is that a maladaptive behavior, for example, phobic avoidance of dogs, has been acquired in the absence of a concrete learning experience with the phobic object. It is not necessary for the child to have a particular traumatic experience with dogs, as would be necessary with classical and operant conditioning. Nor is it essential, as with imitation learning, that the child observe someone else being attacked or being bitten by a dog. Merely the exposure of the child to the belief system, verbalized by an individual of some importance to him, is sufficient. Surely many prejudices take root in this manner.

RATIONAL EMOTIVE THEORY

A number of studies indicate that the affective meaning of certain words can be determined through processes of conditioning.[85] Furthermore, strict adherence to a particular belief system may be the result of the individual encountering aversive consequences whenever he challenged the belief system, or acted contrary to it. Rational emotive psychotherapy which is described by its developer, Dr. Albert Ellis, as the "kissing cousin" of broad-spectrum behavior therapy, is a school which places particular emphasis on affective meaning, the acquisition of belief systems, and the influence of these belief systems on emotions and behavior.[34] According to this approach, as a result of different life experiences, individuals acquire both rational and irrational belief systems. When an individual operates on his rational belief systems, his feelings and behavior will invariably be healthy and adaptive; whereas, when the individual relies on his irrational belief systems, this produces maladaptive, self-defeating behavior and negative emotional states. For example, a child might be taught by his parents that the judgments and opinions of other people about his behavior are of extreme importance and that dire consequences will befall him if he behaves contrary to the wishes of others. A child who is encouraged to accept this belief system and then later operates on it will be overly inhibited and constricted in his behavior. He will have a strong commitment to the impossible task of pleasing everyone and will be particularly intimidated by the prospect of incurring someone else's displeasure.

Another irrational belief system frequently transmitted from parents to child is that "if you want something very, very badly, you therefore *should* get whatever it is you want, and if you don't get it, that's terrible." Some variation of this particular belief system, Ellis claims, accounts for most, if not all, pathological anger. Children, it seems, are particularly susceptible to developing irrational belief systems since from the developmental standpoint their capacity to think in rational, logical terms is limited. Evidence for this particular position is found in the research on cognitive development generated by the writings of Piaget[90] demonstrating the propensity of children to engage in paleological or magical thinking. According to Ellis, in the childhood of disturbed adults, their innates tendency toward magical-irrational-illogical thinking was unwittingly perpetuated by their own parents who failed to provide them with appropriate models of rationality.

COGNITIVE DEVELOPMENT AND BEHAVIOR THERAPY

One of the more obvious changes that occurs in the course of human development is an increase in the importance of cognitive functioning with increasing chronological age. One of the distinct advantages of behavioral therapy strategies with children is that many of these techniques can be implemented quite effectively with young children with limited cognitive development and linguistic competence. In fact, it appears that with children in particular, irrational belief systems such as "all dogs are dangerous" can be effectively bypassed through the use of direct environmental manipulations based on modeling or conditioning principles.

VERBAL MEDIATION

Finally, cognitive learning is of additional relevance to the field of behavior therapy in that it can facilitate other forms of learning or conditioning. Research in this area has been generated by the "verbal mediation hypotheses" of Luria.[69] In part this refers to the developmentally acquired ability to engage in covert self-instruction regarding the contingencies of learning. The studies suggest that self-instruction enhances the acquisition of certain learned responses. For example, in an operant learning situation, if the human subject cognitively learns the rule "If I do this, I will receive a reward (positive reinforcement)," he can rather quickly reach a level of error-free performance. In this instance, there is a covert verbal mediator between the stimulus and the response. It appears that once correct verbal mediators have been acquired, some forms of learning and performance can take a quantum leap. The role of symbolic mediation in learning is of significance when dealing with children who are at a developmental level (typically after age four) where they have acquired the ability to engage in instructional self-talk.

PRINCIPLES OF DEVELOPMENTAL THEORY

One of the fundamental principles of developmental theory is the concept that there are significant differences in psychological function and ability at different chronological age levels. Furthermore, these differences are qualitative, rather than solely quantitative, in nature. That is, the child is not simply a "little adult." For example, it has been hypothesized (and for some researchers, proved) that there is a qualitative difference in the nature of thinking processes or cognition at different times within the span of an individual's growth and development. Thus, not only are there differences among individuals at different age levels, but inference is made as well that there are qualitative differences within each individual's functioning as his development progresses. Clearly, the infant's mode of relating and perceiving the people around him is different from that of the toddler, the nursery school-age child, the child entering elementary school, and so on through the teens and into adulthood.

Another important characteristic observed in the course of development is the expansion of the child's capacities for coping with his internal and external worlds. The ability to tolerate frustration and to deal with any delays of gratification advance with growth. New functions emerge enabling the child to deal with difficult experiences in an age-appropriate fashion. Thus, one cannot expect to observe certain behaviors before the child has developed the functions necessary to carry them out. The child cannot master bladder and sphincter control until he has developed the physiological capability for doing so. The child cannot carry out complex visual-perceptual tasks until the recognition, storage, recall, and integrative functions necessary to these activities are developed.

It is basic to this approach that certain functions should emerge at particular periods in time. When these functions cannot be observed, the conclusion is drawn that growth and development are not proceeding as they should. Such failures may stem from multiple causes, but generally they are regarded as a form of disturbance or interference in development. Quite often, clinicians have defined these deviations as representative of a "disease" and have developed diagnostic labels for them. In the service of presenting the behavioral orientation toward therapeutics, this orientation will not be used in this chapter. Instead, the emphasis will fall on looking at what is functional and adaptive in the behavior of that child. An-

other important consideration is the confusion that often seems to reign regarding the basic data with which the behaviorist and the dynamically oriented clinician begin. It is not that the behavior or functions attended to are so different. Essentially, what happens in fact is that observations are labeled in a different fashion. The assumption seems therefore to have been made that these basic data are different. To be sure, there are different inferences made from the observed behaviors. What must be stressed, however, is that the initial observables, while labeled differently, are one and the same.

Bringing together the behavioral and developmental points of view will entail designating which of the various behavioral techniques will be most appropriate for dealing with difficulties as they emerge at each level of development. This model requires that different behaviors or functions be present at particular times in the course of growth. When these functions and behavior do not appear, or when they persist beyond expected age levels, then one would proceed to facilitate change in the development of these functions through the application of behavioral techniques. Furthermore, the techniques would be selected so as to be consistent with each level. For example, in the early stages of life where developmental theorists see behavior as essentially reflexive in nature, one would not choose a behavioral technique based upon cognitive learning. The assessment of the child would include a determination of the level of development of his behavior; the introduction of behavioral techniques would then be consonant with the inferred level of development.

Description of Evaluative Methods

BEHAVIORAL ASSESSMENT

The acid test of differential diagnosis, in the traditional medical sense, is the utility of the diagnosis as it relates both to treatment and to etiology. There are many who claim that psychiatric diagnosis, in particular, has not met these requirements adequately.

Behavior therapists have long challenged the utility of traditional psychiatric diagnostic nomenclature. They cite a number of studies which indicate relatively poor validity and reliability for many of the diagnostic categories.[16, 122] In this section, alternatives to that traditional approach, namely, target behavioral analyses, will be described. The emphasis will fall on behavior problems that are considered social in nature, such as troubled peer and parental relationships.

TARGET BEHAVIORS

There is a behavioral alternative to the traditional approach of psychiatric assessment and psychodiagnostic testing. It involves directing the focus of attention exclusively to target behaviors. This form of assessment[82] generally refers to a pattern of observation and data collection that concentrates first on behavior, both appropriate and maladaptive, and then on the salient environmental variables which influence the behavior. One of the important requirements of this target behavior assessment is that it provides information that has direct implications for treatment.

GOALS OF BEHAVIORAL ASSESSMENT

The assessment's task is: (1) to identify the target behavior to be increased or decreased in frequency or changed in topography; (2) to identify the environmental factors that elicit, cue, or reinforce the target behaviors; and (3) to identify what environmental factors can be manipulated to alter the behavior.[82] The selection of target behavior with children usually begins by having the parent, teacher, or guardian present his concept of the problem. Thus, in large measure, maladaptive behavior in children is behavior that is considered inappropriate by the key people who come into contact with the child.[82]

TECHNIQUE OF ASSESSMENT

Since behavior is frequently situation specific, it is sometimes necessary to conduct a behavioral assessment in situ in order to determine what the precipitating and reinforcing events of the child's behavior are. This may require entering the home and observing the child interact with his parents or studying the child in his classroom, if that happens to be where his maladaptive behavior occurs with greatest frequency and intensity. In the classroom, for example, the behavior therapist may want to observe the degree to which the child accepts teachers' demands, remains in his seat, works neatly and quietly, interacts appropriately with other children, uses acceptable language,

and so on. The use of this in vivo assessment approach is based in part on an acknowledgment that parents and other significant persons in the life of a child often fail to report the child's behavior accurately, and in part on the fact that the behavior displayed by the child in a clinic setting may not be characteristic of the way he operates in other situations.

The two primary dimensions along which behavior is measured during a behavioral assessment are its intensity and frequency. Here simplified rating scales can be used, for example, to grade the intensity of tantrums from 1 to 10 (1 being bottom low, 10 being extreme high). The ten incremental values on the scale can be anchored qualitatively to statements such as: child sulks, pouts, and nags but does not engage in high-level screaming subsequent to frustration. This represents point 1 on the scale. The other extreme, point 10, would designate such behavior as screaming, flailing about, and self-injurious acts such as head banging or face slapping. The frequency dimension would be tapped through a simple frequency count, namely, how many times during a particular period—for example, fifteen minutes, one-half hour, or an hour—the child displays the undesired behavior.

DETERMINING REINFORCERS

In addition to specifying the target behaviors, the assessment also involves assembling a list of reinforcers. These are items which might influence the child's behavior in the desired direction. There are two main methods of developing such a list of reinforcers. The first involves ascertaining which rewards most children in that age range find attractive, for example, snack-type food, playtime, or, with very young children, being held and cuddled. The second guideline for selecting reinforcers relies on what is known as the Premack Principle,[91] which refers to the fact that anything the child does with regularity is by its very nature reinforcing. Thus, for any two given behaviors, the one that occurs more frequently will serve as a reinforcer for the one that occurs less frequently. For example, if watching television occurs often and appropriate speech seldom occurs, then appropriate speech may be increased in frequency by reinforcing it with access to a television set. Once the roster of target behaviors has been assembled along with the list of reinforcing events, the two can be arranged contingently in a response-reinforcement sequence designed to bring about desired behavioral change.

BEHAVIORAL ASSESSMENT AND PSYCHOLOGICAL TESTING

The behavioral assessment approach has tended to bypass completely the use of psychometric or psychological test devices. This is due largely to the fact that such techniques as projective tests or figure drawing tests are based on the assumption that the truly important determinants of behavior reside within the child's psychic structure. By the same token, the child's overt behavior and the environmental events connected to that behavior are given less weight. Generally speaking, the only testlike devices used in behavioral assessment are behavior check lists. These are comprised of various do's and dont's of inappropriate behaviors that are to be eliminated or of appropriate behaviors currently absent from the child's repertoire which are to be established. Recently, there has been some use of mechanical devices such as closed circuit TV and telemetry for recording behavior (such as in the case of the Lang and Melamed[61] study that will be described later in the chapter). Finally, pocket counting devices, such as those used by market shoppers or for counting golf strokes, are used as a convenient means for determining frequency rates of behavior.

THERAPEUTIC EFFECTS OF ASSESSMENT

It should be noted that the assessment of behavior in terms of frequency and intensity sometimes serves not only as a method of evaluation but also as a treatment procedure. Occasionally, just by having parents systematically record antecedents and consequences of undesired behavior in their child, they rather quickly see what it is they are doing to provoke this behavior. They then make the necessary alterations in their behavior on their own.

SELECTION OF INITIAL TARGET BEHAVIORS

Subsequent to conducting his assessment, the practicing behavior therapist must decide which of the identified problem behaviors should be dealt with first. O'Leary[82] offers guidelines for dealing with this issue. First, he suggests selecting a behavior that is easy for both the child and his parents to change, so that their early efforts will have a high probability of success. Second, he considers the issue of how alteration of one behavior could produce changes in other areas. For example, a shy child with a low verbal output might benefit most from treatment aimed first at increasing verbal fluency. It is unlikely that the problem of being shy could be properly remedied without first improving verbal skills.

Techniques of Behavior Therapy

This section will simply define and describe the major techniques of behavior therapy without emphasizing the extent to which they do or do not share common features. The present state of knowledge does not justify the placement of behavioral techniques into mutually exclusive categories based on whether the technique is derived from principles of classical or operant conditioning or imitation learning,[93, 113] or whether the goal is to establish a new desirable behavior or eliminate an old maladaptive one, or whether the technique involves primarily positive or aversive controlling stimuli.

SYSTEMATIC DESENSITIZATION (SD)

Also known as reciprocal inhibition therapy, systematic desensitization (SD) was originally developed by Wolpe[116] to treat phobic anxiety. SD involves three main components:

1. Inducing a state of deep relaxation or calm which "reciprocally inhibits" or prevents anxious arousal based on the assumption that an organism can be either relaxed or anxious but that it cannot be in both states simultaneously. The most commonly used method for inducing relaxation is the Jacobson technique,[55] which involves instructing the patient to relax by alternately tensing and relaxing various muscle systems while attending to the marked difference in these two contrasting sensations. Less frequently used for producing relaxation are hypnosis, autogenic training, biofeedback, and various drugs such as sodium pentothal. For those young children for whom the ritual of specific relaxation training is not appropriate, a state of relaxation is produced by having them engage in desired activities such as playing or eating sweets.
2. The next step involves developing a graded hierarchy of imagined scenes related to approaching the phobic object, beginning with an item that produces minimal anxiety; the process then moves in small steps to maximal anxiety-producing images. In the case of a school phobia, for example, items would range from "getting up in the morning and getting dressed

in preparation for school" to "you are sitting in class and the teacher asks you a question."

3. Finally, while the patient is in the relaxed state, he is presented by the therapist with a detailed verbal description and encouraged to form a clear mental image of the first imagined phobic scene. Assuming the patient is able to retain his relaxed state while thinking about this first scene, he is moved on to subsequent items in the hierarchy until he is able to imagine the top item vividly while remaining fully relaxed. The most common variation of SD used with young children is in vivo rather than imaginary desensitization; the child is exposed in reality to small, but gradually increasing, doses of the phobic object. As mentioned earlier, with young children, relaxation is frequently achieved by having the child engage in some type of relaxing activity such as eating or playing while in the presence of the phobic object. This in vivo approach is quite similar to the procedure described by Jones[56] more than fifty years ago.

For the treatment of school phobia, Garvey and Hegrenes[44] used an in vivo desensitization approach in the course of which the child was gradually brought closer and closer to a real school and classroom setting. Patterson[87] desensitized a child by simulating situations in a playroom setting which were gradual approximations of the feared school and classroom setting.

Anorexia nervosa has been treated successfully with both systematic desensitization and operant-based techniques. Lang[60] reported using desensitization as the main form of treatment with a young female anorexic outpatient. In this case, loss of appetite and episodic vomiting were anxiety responses to a wide variety of social-interpersonal situations. Through desensitization, the patient was able to overcome her social-interpersonal anxiety. Her appetite then returned to normal. Similarly, in the course of work with an anorexic, twelve-year-old female, Hallsten[46] used desensitization to reduce anxiety associated with the act of eating itself. The apparently successful desensitization was followed by a rapid return to the patient's normal weight. However, the confounding of other treatment variables in this study makes it difficult to draw firm conclusions about the results.

IMPLOSION

With SD, a gradual approach is made toward feared stimuli under conditions of induced relaxation; in contrast to this, implosive therapy[104] involves having the patient experience a direct, prolonged, imaginary confrontation with a highly elaborated version of the phobic object or situation. In actual practice, the therapist adopts a vivid and theatrical manner, designed expressly to maximize anxiety. He describes the patient as reexperiencing a greatly magnified version of the original traumatic event. The justification for this practice is based on the conditioning theory concept of extinction; that is, over a prolonged period of time the organism is presented with the conditioned or neutral stimulus in the absence of the unconditioned stimulus. The patient is thus encouraged to experience a significant degree of anxiety in the presence of a reconstruction of the precipitating traumatic event without encountering any actual aversive consequences.

Implosion is the only behavior therapy technique which is based on both psychodynamic and learning theory concepts. With implosion, the assumption is made that phobic avoidance and anxiety are invariably based on early childhood trauma connected with dynamic-developmental issues such as sex, aggression, separation, orality, and so on. With this notion in mind, the therapist presents the patient with a description of the phobic situation. This includes not only the patient's account of his fears, but also the therapist's assumptions about the patient's primitive, repressed anxieties connected with topics such as mutilation, castration, cannibalism, and so forth. For example, Hogan[50] described the case of a patient with an intense fear of rejection. The implosion scene included a description of the patient as an infant being deprived of food by a hostile and sadistic mother.

Implosive therapy is a relatively recent behavior therapy development. Although early reports on its effectiveness appear promising, more research is needed to determine its true utility. Although the majority of cases involving implosive treatment of phobias reported in the literature involve adult patients, there are some examples of its use with adolescents. It is not a procedure currently applied to phobic disorders in young children.

FLOODING AND RESPONSE PREVENTION

These terms are essentially synonymous. They refer to the practice of exposing an individual to anxiety-provoking stimuli while preventing escape or avoidance. This procedure is similar to implosive therapy in its extinction aspects; however, it does not involve the psychodynamic interpretations common to implosion. In addition, flooding is typically practiced in vivo, with an actual, rather than an imaginary, approach toward the feared stimuli. One particular version of flooding is called prolonged exposure.[13] Under the guidance and gentle encouragement of the therapist, it involves having the phobic individual gradually approach the feared object in vivo. This seems particularly well suited for use with children in that it is apparently as rapid a treatment for phobias as conventional implosion and flooding. Unlike them, however, it does not require the patient's intense experience of anxiety.

EMOTIVE IMAGERY

This technique developed by Lazarus and Abramowitz[63] is a behavioral procedure designed specifically for eliminating phobic responses in children. The procedure involves first determining the nature of the child's hero images and then having the child imagine himself in association with these heros when he confronts the phobic situation. For example, during the treatment sessions with one of the cases described by Lazarus and Abramowitz, a child with a fear of darkness is encouraged to imagine himself going through his house during the night in association with Superman. Another case describes a child with a dog phobia who is encouraged to imagine himself the owner of a sleek racing car. Situations are described to him in which he experiences the pride and exhilaration of owning the car while in the presence of a dog (the phobic stimulus).

ASSERTIVE TRAINING

This is a term used to refer to a broad array of behavioral strategies designed to increase social-interpersonal assertiveness while simultaneously decreasing passivity, deference, and withdrawal. The main practical components of assertive training are role playing and behavioral rehearsal. Theoretically, assertive training includes aspects of classical and operant conditioning as well as imitation learning. Wolpe[116] maintains that assertive behavior, like the relaxation response, reciprocally inhibits anxiety. Furthermore, in therapy, assertive behavior is modeled by the therapist and imitated by the patient, while the patient's success experiences are rewarded according to operant conditioning principles.

Initially, an assessment is conducted to determine the extent of the patient's lack of assertiveness. This ranges from very simple forms of behavior—for example, does the patient maintain eye contact when speaking, is his voice clear and appropriately loud—on up to determining how well the patient handles complicated interactions with a hostile store clerk or job supervisor. Based on the result of the assessment, the patient is taught new assertive behaviors via didactic and role-playing devices.

In one example of assertive training with a shy and socially withdrawn seven-year-old girl, behavioral rehearsal was placed within the context of a game.[45] The patient and therapist engaged in a game of blocks while the child was skillfully maneuvered into gradually more dominant and assertive behavioral roles such as making up the "rules of the game," talking loudly, and so on. Correct or assertive responses on the part of the child were lavishly praised and reinforced by the therapist.

Using a combination of positive reinforcement and modeling, parents and teachers have functioned as "behavioral technicians" in programs designed to increase assertiveness in children. With older children and adolescents, group assertive training employing role playing and behavioral rehearsal has been successfully employed.[2, 10]

MASSED PRACTICE

In a book entitled *Habits, Their Making and Unmaking*, Dunlap[33] first reported on this procedure, also known as overpractice or negative practice; it is designed to eliminate small motor habits, such as tics. Paradoxically, for prolonged periods the patient must practice intentionally the very behavior (such as a tic) that he is trying to eliminate. Massed or negative practice is based on the theoretical concepts of reactive inhibition and conditioned inhibition.[53] It is assumed that by definition, a behavior such as a facial or vocal tic is occurring at maximum habit strength. It follows that by raising the frequency of the tic well over its normal rate, reactive inhibition or fatigue will be produced along with a desire to stop the tic. Once fatigue builds up and the patient does stop the tic, this stopping is reinforced by the rest or cessation of fatigue (conditioned inhibition).

The literature on this technique gives little information as to the optimal amount of overpractice necessary to eliminate a given habit; in fact, this seems to vary considerably among individuals. Because of the generally favorable results reported in the literature on massed practice, as well as its simplicity and ease of application, it is regarded by many behavior therapists as the treatment of first choice for simple motor habits in both children and adults.

MODELING BASED PROCEDURES

Behavior therapy techniques based on principles of modeling or imitation learning generally fall into two categories: those designed to promote the acquisition of new, adaptive, or prosocial behaviors; and those whose purpose is to eliminate fear and anxiety. In the former category, the usual arrangement is for the therapist or an assistant to demonstrate the target behavior, such as greeting another person, asking directions, and so on; and then having the patient imitate the behavior while being coached. When he does achieve a correct imitation, he is positively reinforced by the therapist. The modeling with reinforced guided performance routine is repeated until the patient masters the new behavior successfully. Behavioral rehearsal or practicing the new behavior is also usually included in the modeling treatment. Modeling procedures lend themselves to the use both of live and filmed models. Through this means, a broad range of behaviors, including language, self-care, cooperativeness, adaptive responses to frustration, and so forth, have now been successfully established in emotionally disturbed, retarded, and normal children.[10] In the behavioral treatment of mute psychotic children, for example, the speech therapist begins by modeling simple verbalizations such as vowel sounds in an effort to get the child to imitate. At first, any sound is reinforced, then only those imitations by the child which approximate the modeled verbalization. Nonapproximation responses are ignored or penalized. Using this approach, a simple vocabulary is established for the child. Subsequently, words are chained together by the therapist, and the child receives reinforcement for emitting word chains or sentences. Depending on the rate of speech acquisition, the therapist gradually moves the child toward the development of increasingly complex verbal skills. Initially, those mute, psychotic, or retarded children who are trained with this type of procedure display a rather characteristic robotlike, mechanical speech pattern; however, over time and with additional practice, their speech does take on a more natural and spontaneous quality.

Modeling can be employed in the treatment of anxiety. Typically, this involves having the anxious individual observe a model with whom he can readily identify (a child model in the case of a child patient) engage in approach behavior toward the anxiety-arousing object or situation. In one study, Bandura and his associates[13] demonstrated that after watching filmed models interact fearlessly with dogs, phobic children were able to approach the animals and even sleep with them. Other studies have shown that children's fear of dentists,[1] nonpoisonous snakes,[94] and water[54] can be significantly reduced through modeling.

PROCEDURES BASED ON OPERANT CONDITIONING

Subsumed under this heading are all the various behavior therapy manipulations designed to increase adaptive-prosocial behaviors while eliminating maladaptive or disturbed behaviors through the systematic use of response-contingent reward and punishment. Some of the most dramatic achievements in the clinical application of operant-based procedures have been made with children. Operant behavior therapy has been broadly applied with normal, emotionally disturbed, and retarded children in both inpatient and outpatient settings. The range of problems successfully treated includes the grossly psychotic and self-destructive behavior of autistic and schizophrenic children, hyperkinesis, hyperaggressivity, school failure, delinquency, psychosomatic problems, tantrums, bedwetting, and so on.

The token economy system first employed by Statts and Statts[105] with children, and later refined by Ayllon and his associates[3] in a state hospital setting, is perhaps the most widely known and frequently utilized behavioral system based on principles of operant learning. Under a token economy regimen, patients are systematically reinforced with points or tokens (for example, poker chips) for engaging in socially appropriate behaviors. Such behaviors might include getting up on time, speaking appropriately, bathing, grooming, attending therapeutical recreational activities. The token rewards serve as the "coin of the realm"; as such, they may be exchanged for backup reinforcers which are not otherwise available, such as various commodities and privileges such as snacks, cigarettes, money, naps, or TV time. Maladaptive behavior is either ignored (not reinforced and thus placed on an extinction schedule), penalized with a fine, or given "time out from reinforcement" (this involves isolating the patient for brief periods in a rapid and perfunctory manner immediately after the display of inappropriate behavior.[71] Azrin[6] has recently described two additional operant procedures for responding to misbehavior which he refers to as positive practice and overcorrection. Typically used in combination, positive practice and overcorrection involve the simultaneous practice of the correct response and punishment for the incorrect one. An illustration of this is the child who soils on the floor: He must not only correct his mistake by cleaning up his mess but must then proceed to "overcorrect" by tidying up the entire room. The child who steals a toy from another child corrects the misbehavior by returning what he stole and then "overcorrects" by giving the victim two or three additional toys. In the course of positive practice, after the individual has performed the incorrect behavior such as fighting, he must repeatedly practice the correct opposite response, which in this instance would involve being cooperative and compliant.

Slightly different from the token economy system is an approach referred to as contingency management. There the environment is arranged so that naturally available reinforcers such as food, leisure time, or recreational activities automatically occur after a display of the desired behaviors. In a classroom situation, this would mean that recess periods occur only after a period of "on task" behavior by the students; at home it might mean implementing the rule "After you eat dinner, then you get dessert," or "after you empty the trash, then you watch TV." With pure contingency management, intermediate reinforcers in the form of tokens are not utilized.

Contingency contracting is a special form of contingency management. To carry it out, members of a social system like a family mutually reinforce one another for desired behavior change according to the provisions of a previously arranged contractual agreement. In the case of the family of an unruly teenager, this might involve the parents agreeing to plan and implement family recreational outings in exchange for the child coming in before 11 P.M. or doing one hour of homework per night. In the case of a married couple, the husband might agree to be more affectionate toward his wife in exchange for her being a more tidy housekeeper.

Although the various operant procedures—token economy, contingency management, contracting, time out from reinforcement, and so on—can be employed alone, it is quite common for them to be used in combination with one another in a single behavior therapy program. A disturbed child at home may be on a token economy system run by his parents in which cleaning his room, grooming, doing homework, and other daily care activities are rewarded with points exchangeable for snacks or money. The child's misbehavior, such as tantrums, are handled with a time out from reinforcement procedure, while overcorrection and positive practice are used to treat his encopresis.

Multidimensional therapeutic considerations regarding mental retardation are discussed in detail in chapter 39. Specific behavior modification programs for the retarded generally rely on operant conditioning procedures, particularly in the case of severe retardation. With the less profoundly retarded, modeling-imitation learning procedures can also be used. There is little difference between the way in which behavioral principles are applied with retarded children and with those of normal intelligence. The differences are more in terms of assumptions made about how intellectual impairment affects the acquisition of new behavior. For example, both might work on acquiring the same element of behavior. However, the retarded individual may require more practice trials of that particular behavior to reach desired performance. He may rely on obvious versus subtle discriminative stimuli. And he may need the more complicated behavioral sequences broken up into smaller elements than would be necessary for a child of normal intelligence.

In general, behavioral programs with the retarded have emphasized three major goals: symptom control, social rehabilitation, and academic or vocational rehabilitation. In the area of symptom control are included such issues as toilet training, stereotyped movements, tantrums, to name a few. For these and other forms of "symptomatic" or maladaptive behavior in the retarded, the behavioral techniques of positive reinforcement of incompatible behavior, extinction, punishment, and so forth, previously described with non-retarded children, are applied in similar fashion. For example, Hamilton and associates[47] used time out from reinforcement to eliminate self-injury, property damage, and other disruptive behaviors in institutionalized retardates; while Henriksen and Doughty[48] eliminated undesirable maladaptive behavior in retarded boys using a combination of time-out, punishment, and positive reinforcement. Repp and Deitz[92] reduced aggressive and self-injurious behavior in institutionalized retarded children using various operant techniques, alone and in combination. For example, with a severely retarded twelve-year-old boy who regularly had violent unremitting temper tantrums, they reinforced gradually, increasing periods of compliant behavior with candy, while simultaneously penalizing aggressive behavior with rapidly applied physical restraint. During the pretreatment baseline period, the youngster's rate of aggressive responses was one or more incidents every two minutes, while compliant nonaggressive behavior rarely occurred. During the treatment phase, aggressive behavior dropped off almost completely, while cooperative behavior increased significantly. A "reversal" technique, in which the reinforcement was abruptly withdrawn, produced a rapid return of the aggressive behavior. The reinforcement was then reinstated, with an equally prompt cessation of tantrums. This was used to demonstrate the relationship between treatment variables and outcome.

In a classroom setting, working with an eight-year-old boy with an IQ of 47, the same authors used "gold stars" to reinforce gradually increasing periods of nonaggressive-disruptive "on task behavior." The child's teacher used a kitchen timer to time first five-, then ten-, then fifteen-minute intervals of the child's behavior. For each interval of time when no aggressive incidents occurred, the child was rewarded with stars, which could be exchanged for a gift. If an aggressive response did occur during a timed interval, the teacher said no and the timer was reset. Again, using a "baseline-treatment-return to baseline-return to treatment" experimental design, Repp and Deitz[92] demonstrated a clear relationship between the reinforcement contingencies and the elimination of disruptive behavior.

In working with social skills, one of the first goals which must be achieved with many retarded children is to teach them to "pay attention" and to follow instructions reliably. Many retarded children have severe attentional deficits, which must be remedied before more ambitious behavioral changes can occur. Zimmerman and associates[123] worked with a group of seven mildly to moderately retarded boys (IQ range 25 to 70) with severe attentional deficits. They used social and token rewards to reinforce appropriate attention to instructions and correct responses. In daily half-hour treatment sessions of the entire group, a teacher instructed the children verbally to perform various classroom relevant behaviors. These included items such as "sit down at the table and raise your hand" and "bring me the crayons and paper." Prompt and appropriate compliance with the instructions was immediately reinforced with praise and with tokens which could be exchanged for toys and snacks.

Assuming attentional problems and difficulties in following instructions have been overcome, the next aspect of social rehabilitation with retarded children involves establishing self-care behaviors such as bathing, brushing teeth, selecting clothing, dressing appropriately, feeding, and so on. Using a combination of modeled demonstration, gradual shaping, and selective reinforcement, a remarkable degree of independent self-care behaviors have been established, even in severely retarded children. Minge and Ball,[78] for example, using the aforementioned approach, trained a group of severely retarded girls (IQ 10 to 25) in dressing and undressing skills. Similarly, after three months of fifteen- to thirty-minute daily operant-based training sessions, Bernsberg and associates[18] succeeded in doubling the scores on a test of social maturity (grooming, bathing, dressing, feeding) of a group of retarded boys.

The final aspect of the behavioral treatment of retarded children has to do with educational and vocational rehabilitation. Again, the primary treatment modalities in this area are operant conditioning and procedures based on imitation learning. In the operant-based programmed instruction techniques, the material to be learned is broken into its smallest components and gradually "chained" together. Along with this, immediate feedback of correct and incorrect responses and rewards for correct responses are used extensively. This approach is much used with retardates. It includes the use of "teaching machines," automated devices which provide the child with the material to be learned according to the principles of operant programmed instruction. One interesting example of programmed instruction and the teaching machine concept is the "talking typewriter," a computerized device involving a typewriter keyboard connected to a TV monitor. When the child operator types his name, the machine responds by selecting the computerized lesson plan which had previously been programmed specifically for the child. The machine may even be programmed to greet the child by name, for example: "Hello, John, today we will have a spelling and reading lesson." At that point, a picture of a cat along with the word cat is displayed on the TV screen. The child then receives from the machine audio instructions to spell "cat" while the word is removed from the screen. The child types his response on the keyboard. If it is correct, the word cat appears on the screen, and the machine "praises" the student by saying "Good boy, John, that's correct." At that time, the machine may also dispense a tangible reinforcement in the form of tokens or points. If the child hits the wrong key, nothing appears on the screen; all the keys except C-A-T in sequence are automatically locked out to prevent an erroneous response. The machine says, "No, that's wrong. Look again. C-A-T spells cat. Now try again." This routine continues until the child responds correctly. Then, after the reward, the machine moves on to the next element of the lesson plan. There are obvious advantages of this mechanized approach. The child can work at his own pace, the machine never tires or becomes bored at the retarded child's lack of rapid progress, and erroneous responses on the part of the child are less likely to occur while correct responses are always promptly reinforced.

It should be noted that the use of the programmed instruction and teaching machines is not restricted to retarded children. Currently, it is being employed on the college and university level to teach subjects as complicated as foreign languages and advanced mathematics. Nor is it essential to have access to highly complex and expensive "teaching machines" in order to apply the principles of operant programmed instruction with retarded children.

Vocational training of the retarded also relies heavily on operant and imitative approaches. The main components include modeled demonstration, gradual shaping, and reinforcement. Increasingly, sheltered workshops for the retarded are implementing "token economy" programs for their clients. Punctuality, regular attendance, appropriate work habits, and quality and volume of work are the usual target behaviors in these programs. The tokens used for reinforcement are exchangeable for money, cigarettes, toilet articles, food, and so on.

There is one issue of considerable concern, particularly with retarded children, in the use of operant-based treatment methods. This has to do with transfer of training and generalization. These issues are related to the question of how to ensure that new behaviors acquired under a contingent reinforcement system will be maintained in the natural environment where contingent reinforcement occurs less systematically and predictably. In fact, the data bearing on response maintenance and transfer of training are not encouraging. They indicate that behaviors developed under operant reinforcement systems are frequently not maintained when contingencies are eliminated; only rarely do they transfer automatically to non-treatment settings.[57] This finding suggests that after formal treatment, in order for positive change to be maintained at follow up, the initial treatment program must include provisions to maximize the likelihood of a solid transfer-of-

training effect to occur. In a review of token economy research, Kazdin[57] suggests programming response-maintenance through the use of the following steps:

1. Systematically substituting social reinforcers for tangible reinforcers. This is based on the assumption that in the "natural" noninstitutional environment, much of human behavior is under the influence of intermittent social reinforcement—praise and censure.
2. Gradual fading from the early treatment stage of immediate constant reinforcement for small bits of behavior to a "level" system where consistent appropriate general social behavior is rewarded with unlimited access to a wide range of reinforcers.
3. Training those individuals who form the subject's human environment (such as parents, teachers, siblings, and so on) to use behavioral techniques in their day-to-day relationships with the patient. This will facilitate the retention of treatment acquired behaviors (see chapter 11).
4. Scheduling intermittent reinforcements so as to have the patient eventually responsive to an extremely "lean" reinforcement schedule—the type which laboratory studies identify repeatedly as most resistant to extinction.
5. Varying the stimulus conditions of training (or, in other words, arranging for training to occur under a variety of stimulus conditions) so as to include those which simulate the living-working conditions in which the child will eventually be placed.
6. Self-reinforcement training. Teach the patient to monitor and reinforce his own behaviors.
7. Self-instruction training. Train the child to "talk to himself," that is, give himself verbal prompts, cues, and statements of encouragement to guide his behavior in new settings.
8. Manipulating reinforcement delay, both by delaying the receipt of reinforcement after admission of a behavior and by increasing the time between the receipt of token reinforcement and the exchange of tokens for backup reinforcers.
9. The simultaneous manipulation of several reinforcement parameters (such as magnitude, delay, place, quality, and schedule) in order to increase resistance to extinction.

TECHNIQUES OF AVERSIVE CONTROL

There are two main classes of behavioral procedures which involve the use of aversive or painful stimulation: those based on classical conditioning, and those based on operant conditioning. In the former category, the aversive stimulus occurs at the same time as the performance of the undesirable behavior or the perception of the inappropriate stimuli. This procedure may be viewed as a form of "sensitization." After the conditioning trials, the patient experiences a negative emotional state in the presence of stimuli which previously elicited approach behavior. With alcoholics, for example, one aversive-based procedure involves having the patient see, taste, and smell an alcoholic beverage while receiving a painful electroshock. In the language of classical conditioning, the beverage is the conditioned stimulus, the shock, the unconditioned stimulus, and anxiety or negative emotional arousal, the response. After repeated pairings of the beverage and shock, the shock is removed, and the beverage stimulus alone evokes the negative emotional response and subsequent avoidance of the alcoholic beverage. Similarly, in an effort to reduce the attraction of male homosexuals to men, according to classical conditioning principles, the patients receive painful electroshocks while viewing pictures of nude males.[38]

The other main form of aversive behavioral control involves the use of "response-contingent punishment." Here an undesirable operant behavior, such as self-mutilation by a psychotic child, is immediately followed by a punishing painful shock in an effort to suppress the behavior. This therapeutic use of punishing stimulus is sometimes called aversion therapy. It frequently involves aspects of both classical and operant conditioning. For example, with a self-destructive child, the therapy sequence may be as follows— The child begins to self-injure, the therapist shouts "stop" (a conditioned stimulus), and then shocks the child (unconditioned stimulus). When the child ceases to self-injure, the shock is terminated. In other words, stopping self-mutilation is reinforced in operant terms by the termination of aversive stimuli—a negative reinforcer.

Though aversive control techniques are the least commonly used of all the behavior therapy procedures, they are undoubtedly the most controversial. It does seem, however, that with self-destructive psychotic children, where the behavior may lead to permanent injury or even death, aversive techniques are justified.

BEHAVIORAL METHODS OF SELF-CONTROL

Over twenty years ago, Skinner[101] proposed a behavioral formulation for self-directed human behavior. It is only recently, however, that this topic has been seriously considered by practicing behavioral clinicians. Generally speaking, in behavioral terms, self-control is seen as a process in which the individual manages his own behavior by systematically reinforcing himself for engaging in desired behaviors. In addition, the self-controlling individual is seen as manipulating his environment so that only certain controlling stimuli are present. In the case of an overweight person who is trying to diet, he may remove high-calorie foods (controlling stimuli) from his home and reward himself for skipping a meal by going to a movie. He could also punish himself for going off the diet by destroying a five-dollar bill. The self-control aspects of this program would be within the individual himself, manipulating the controlling and reinforcing stimuli, and thereby influencing his own behavior in a particular direction.

One significant aspect of many behavioral self-control programs is self-monitoring, or having the person keep a record of his own behavior. The advantage of this procedure is that the individual develops a clearer understanding of the conditions under which his behavior occurs, and what environmental antecedent and consequent events influence it. In one behavioral program for outpatient hyperaggressive children,[32] the children used self-ratings of their own classroom behavior to record the time spent in seat, quiet, and on task, as well as episodes of disruptive behavior. Nondisruptive cooperative behavior was reinforced along with those self-ratings which were consistent with the ratings of independent observers. Once a child became reliable at evaluating his own classroom behavior, he was permitted to reinforce himself accordingly. This self-monitoring in combination with self-reinforcement was effective in reducing disruptive behavior significantly while simultaneously improving academic performance.

COVERT CONDITIONING AND COVERT REINFORCEMENT

Some behavioral theoreticians[51] have proposed that covert cognitive events such as thoughts and images can be manipulated according to the principles of operant and classical conditioning in much the same fashion as overt behavior. According to this assumption, imagining something pleasurable such as lying on the beach is an event which can serve as a positive reinforcer. Conversely, thinking about something unpleasant such as getting nauseated can serve as a punisher. By having these "covert reinforcers" follow a real or fantasy behavior, they influence that behavior in the same manner as an overt reinforcer. Cautela[26] has developed a procedure called covert sensitization. This involves having the patient imagine himself engaging in some undesirable behavior (in the case of an alcoholic, this might be an image of drinking alcohol) and then imagining himself getting violently ill. In other sessions, the patient imagines himself turning away from alcohol and being rewarded with lavish praise from his wife and family and a sense of physical well-being. There is some suggestive evidence that similar covert sensitization procedures can be useful in treating obesity, excessive cigarette smoking, and homosexuality.

Covert reinforcement procedures have also been used to change cognitions such as a negative self-image. Thus, a person with a negative self-image might be encouraged to spend a few minutes each day thinking of himself in positive terms, such as, "I am a good person, kind, sincere. . . ." He is then instructed to reinforce these self-statements positively by following them with a pleasurable fantasy. The assumption is that the pleasurable fantasy reinforces the positive self-statements; according to operant theory, this makes them more likely to occur in the future. Covert extinction procedures[25] have also been developed in which an individual imagines an undesired behavior such as exhibitionism or homosexuality; he thinks of it as being ignored or not receiving reinforcement. Cautela[24] undertook the behavioral treatment of a child with a seizure disorder which was unresponsive to medications. He used a combination of relaxation training, covert reinforcement, and covert extinction to bring about a significant reduction in her seizures. During therapy sessions, the child was encouraged to imagine first that she was having a seizure which was not reinforced afterward (by receiving adult attention); she was then to imagine herself relaxing as an alternative to having a seizure and being reinforced (praised and encouraged) for not having a seizure.

While the behavior therapy literature contains numerous examples of the successful application of covert procedures such as those just described, the assertion that private, cognitive events are influenced, that is, reinforced, punished, extinguished, and conditioned in the same fashion as overt behaviors remains unproven.

COGNITIVE BEHAVIOR MODIFICATION—
THERAPEUTIC SELF-INSTRUCTION

Closely related to self-control methods and the covert techniques are a group of behavioral strategies that are called self-instructional. These approaches involve supplying the patient with self-instructional scripts which they can use to guide and control their own behavior.[74] With a hyperactive child, a self-instruction designed to slow the

child down might be: "Remember, slow down, take it easy. You make a lot of mistakes when you move too fast. Your friends and teachers like you better when you take it easy and go slow. You feel a lot better too when you slow down." Initially, the self-instructions are spoken out loud, but later they are done subvocally. Self-instructional scripts are developed by the therapist after conducting an assessment to determine what kind of cognitions precede, accompany, and follow a particular behavior. The therapist then designs replacement scripts to be substituted for the ones that the patient currently uses.

Preliminary reports on the use of self-instruction appear particularly promising, and many behavior therapists feel that cognitive and self-instructional behavioral techniques are the "wave of the future." It seems a bit ironic that a school of therapy which originally rejected the importance of cognitive and other internal psychological events should have come full circle in its maturity and begins now to attach considerable importance to these very same processes. There are, however, some behavior therapists who still seriously question the appropriateness of including techniques which are largely cognitive in nature within the rubric of behavior therapy.

BIOFEEDBACK

As was the case with the cognitive approaches just described, there is a lack of complete agreement among behavior therapists as to whether biofeedback techniques should be included among the behavior therapies. The justification for doing so is based on the fact that the early investigators in this area, for example, Neal Miller and his associates, conceptualized their research on controlling autonomic functions in rats in terms of operant conditioning. Although other theoretical explanations for biofeedback have been offered and some of the research casts doubts on a strict conditioning explanation for these phenomena, there does remain some tendency to regard biofeedback as a special form of operant learning.

In a broad sense, biofeedback refers to the process by which an organism can regulate its own behavior on the basis of information arising from that behavior. The term is usually applied to situations in which an organism acquires control over an autonomic physiological response, such as blood pressure, by being provided with direct on-line information about the status of that function.

The historical antecedents of biofeedback can

be traced back at least as far as the work of Luthe[70] early in the century. The research of Neal Miller[77] in the early 1960s, however, was the major influence on the development of the field. In these studies, Miller demonstrated that operant control of autonomic functioning could be achieved with respect to heart rate, blood pressure, intestinal contractions, peripheral vasomotor responses, the amount of blood in the stomach wall, and the formation of urine in the kidney. In a typical experiment, the heart rate of a laboratory rat was monitored and any slight increase above its normal baseline was rewarded. Or alternatively, an animal would be punished (shocked) for having its heart rate or blood pressure fall below a certain level. Using such contingent rewards and punishments, Miller found that he could train the animals to develop a remarkable degree of control over physiological processes not normally thought to be controllable. It should be noted that to rule out the possibility that the changes in heart rate, blood pressure, and so forth were occurring secondary to the animal regulating a skeletal process such as breathing rate, all the research animals were injected with curare to induce paralysis (and thus make skeletal learning impossible).

On the basis of his findings, Miller speculated that biofeedback phenomena might account for the development of psychosomatic illness. He proposed, for example, that a child who fears going to school because he is unprepared for an examination may, in his anxiety, display a variety of autonomic symptoms such as increased heart rate, gastrointestinal activity, pallor, and faintness. Upon observing these symptoms, the child's parent might decide the child was ill and keep him home from school. The child is relieved of his fear; at the same time, in biofeedback terms, he has been inadvertently rewarded by his parent for having produced those autonomic changes. If this experience of autonomic change followed by reward occurs frequently enough over time, the child may "learn" to generate those symptoms in order to receive the reward of anxiety relief. Consistent with Miller's speculation, most clinical applications of biofeedback technology have been in the area of psychosomatic illness. For example, tension headaches have been successfully treated by training the patient to reduce electromyogram (EMG) activity in the frontalis muscle. An electrode is attached to that area and the activity level in the muscle is communicated to the patient either visually (on an oscilloscope) or by auditory clicks. As muscle tension decreases, the activity

on the oscilloscope or the frequency and intensity of clicks decreases. Under these conditions, patients can learn to reduce tension significantly in the frontalis and thus eliminate the tension headaches.[22] Contrary to the animal studies where feedback was provided in the form of reward and punishment, with human subjects, informational feedback seems adequate for the subject to bring about change.

Migraine headaches have also been treated with biofeedback using peripheral skin temperature as the target of biofeedback control. Since migraine attacks involve significant blood flow increase in the head, this blood flow is accompanied by a decrease in peripheral skin temperature in the extremities. Using biofeedback, migraine patients were trained to increase skin temperature in the hand, while simultaneously decreasing it in the forehead. This altered the blood flow which produced the migraine, and the headaches were eliminated.[99] Another major area of clinical application of biofeedback has been in cardiovascular disorders; persons suffering from essential hypertension were trained to reduce their blood pressure, thus eliminating arrhythmias and reducing tachycardia.

Although the bulk of the work on psychosomatic illness and biofeedback has been done with adults, some studies have involved children. Davis and associates[30] used EMG frontalis muscle feedback to teach relaxation to asthmatic children. Previous studies have indicated that ease of expiratory respiration was directly linked to relaxation level. In another study, aversive stimulation was applied in response to preseizure electroencephalogram (EEG) activity in a biofeedback paradigm. This successfully reduced the rate of seizures in an epileptic five-year-old.[119]

Biofeedback has also been applied to the treatment of speech disorders in children. For example, a troublesome problem in patients with cleft palate is a lingering nasal resonance which may persist even after surgical repair. This was treated by converting vibrations in the nasal cavity indicative of hypernasality into visual feedback in the form of a red light.[95] By altering speech patterns to produce less nasality, the patient could dim and eventually turn off the red light (visual feedback).

Finally, biofeedback procedures have been used in rehabilitation medicine to improve fine motor control and decrease spastic movements in cerebral-palsied children. For example, Sachs and his associates[97] improved the manual dexterity and coordination of an eleven-year-old cerebral-palsied child. They accomplished this by providing him with visual feedback in the form of flashing light patterns contingent on correct finger and hand movements.

As was the case with cognitive and self-instructional techniques, it seems that biofeedback and related procedures will receive increasing clinical experimentation and application. This represents one of the major future trends in behavior therapy.

The listing of behavior therapy techniques previously described, while not all-inclusive, does contain what most writers in the field would regard as the more important and commonly practiced behavioral strategies. There is a large variety of behavior therapy procedures used in the treatment of sexual disorders (both inadequacy and deviance). These were purposely omitted as not applicable to children. Also excluded were a large number of innovative procedures described in single case studies in the behavior therapy literature because of uncertainty regarding the range of their applicability.

Clinical Applications of Behavior Therapy

Attention will now be focused on the application of behavioral techniques to selected illustrative problems characteristic of various developmental levels.

PREVENTIVE BEHAVIORAL INTERVENTION

One of the most recent and innovative applications of behavior therapy principles with children is being conducted by Mednick, Schulsinger, and Vennables.[73] They have identified a population of children who are at risk for the development of schizophrenia on the basis of constitutional and genetic grounds. They placed these children in an operant-based training program with an aim toward fostering in these children constructive peer interaction and play participation. They systematically reinforce social approach behaviors while simultaneously reducing withdrawal tendencies in these children. They train them to respond adaptively to frustrating events and encourage their leadership skills, initially by introducing them into play groups of younger peers, followed by the gradual introduction of same-age peers into the group. The study is longitudinal in nature, so the

outcome of their efforts to train children in social and executive competence will not be known for some time. Chandler[27] has been utilizing a similar approach with delinquent populations or with children vulnerable to develop delinquent tendencies, whose treatment is discussed in detail in chapter 33. Chandler's preventive intervention is focused on developing more socially adaptive behavior in children. The focus of these studies is on identifying people who, while not yet disordered, have a high probability for future disorder as suggested by the presence of certain factors in their lives. The research acknowledges the relationship between premorbid competence and recovery rate in severe forms of psychopathology. The strategy then taken by the investigators is to try to develop premorbid competence in the population at risk, using operant conditioning and imitation learning procedures to develop social and interpersonal skills.[43]

FEEDING DISTURBANCE IN INFANCY

The literature on behavioral intervention during infancy deals primarily with feeding disturbances during the first year. The classic paper in this area is by Lang and Melamed,[61] describing a nine-month-old male infant who displayed persistent vomiting and chronic rumination to an extent that they were life-threatening. The patient had achieved a normal weight of seventeen pounds by age six months when he began vomiting his food. By nine months, he vomited all the food he ingested within ten to fifteen minutes after each meal. A complete physical work up, including gastrointestinal fluoroscopy, EEG, and neuropsychological testing, failed to show any organic basis for the condition. A variety of treatment procedures (including dietary changes, administration of antinauseants, and intensive nursing care) had been tried without success. At the time of the behavior therapy intervention, which was turned to, according to the attending physician's clinical notes, as a last resort, the child was down to a weight of twelve pounds and in critical condition. Initially the child was closely observed for two days and baseline data were collected on vomiting immediately before, during, and after normal feeding periods. This assessment revealed that the child persistently regurgitated most of the food that he had taken in within ten minutes after each feeding, and that he continued to bring up small amounts throughout the rest of the day. In order to get more precise data on the vomiting response, EMG recordings of the muscles involved in vomiting were taken and used in conjunction with direct visual observation. Subsequent to the collection of this baseline data, the following treatment program was instituted. Electrodes were placed on the calf of the patient's leg to allow for the delivery of a painful electroshock contingent on his vomiting. Treatment sessions were conducted directly following feeding; each session lasted less than one hour. The child's response to this treatment procedure was dramatic, and after two sessions the shock was rarely required. The authors reported that initially the infant reacted to the shock by crying and immediate cessation of vomiting. By the sixth treatment session, the infant no longer vomited at all during the procedure and would typically fall asleep during the middle of the treatment hour. Over the ten days of treatment in the hospital, the patient had a 26 percent increase in body weight. Follow up revealed that one month after leaving the hospital his weight was twenty-one pounds, and five months later he weighed more than twenty-six pounds. At the one year follow up, he had apparently continued to thrive in a normal fashion, both physically and psychologically.

LEMON JUICE THERAPY

In a more recent report, a similar form of treatment was employed for a six-month-old infant who engaged in life-threatening rumination. This treatment involved the use of what the authors called "lemon juice therapy."[102] The patient was a six-month-old female who was hospitalized when her weight fell below her initial birth weight. She was then in the second percentile for her age, and her condition was described as critical. For a number of practical reasons, including the reluctance of the pediatric ward staff to use electroshock with such a young child, the investigators decided to use squirts of lemon juice deposited in the child's mouth as the aversive stimulus contingent on vomiting. In a rather short period of time, they achieved the same successful results as Lang and Melamed. Again there was no return of the symptom at a ten-month follow up. It should also be noted that there was no evidence of "symptom substitution" found in either case, and that by contrast positive social behavior seemed to increase to a considerable extent as the vomiting decreased. Lang and Melamed[61] report that their patient "became more responsive to adults, smiled more frequently, and seemed to be more interested in toys and games than he had been previously." In the "lemon juice therapy"

case, after the symptomatic behavior had terminated, the patient "became more attentive to adults about her, smiling appeared, and she began grabbing at objects near her."

Both of these case examples illustrate rather dramatically the use of conditioning principles to eliminate a serious life-threatening psychogenic behavior in a human infant. These treatment procedures, which generally come under the heading of aversion therapy, involved components of both classical and operant conditioning. From the point of view of classical conditioning, there was a contiguous pairing of certain neutral stimuli, namely, the physical movements and muscular changes in the child which were precursors of vomiting, and an unconditioned stimulus, the electroshock in the one case and the lemon juice in the other. Learning theory would predict that this pairing would create a classically conditioned response. However, since it was possible in both cases for the infant to terminate and later to avoid the aversive stimulus by performing a particular operation, suppression of the vomiting-regurgitation response, there were obviously operant components at work as well.

In both cases the patient was at a developmental level where cognitive abilities were limited and verbal skills totally absent. Behavioral treatment, therefore, seems particularly appropriate. In fact, the use of reflexive conditioning procedures is consistent with the emphasis placed by Piaget and other developmental theorists on the reflexive nature of learning typical of the period of early infancy.

Such aversive conditioning techniques have also been applied to older children with the same problem. There are also reports in the literature of the application of similar procedures with retarded adults with psychosomatic rumination.[102]

In later childhood, feeding difficulties typically take the form of episodic hunger strikes or restricting food intake exclusively to certain special foods which are frequently of poor nutritional quality. Behavior therapy techniques for this type of refusal to eat or selective eating typically involve strategies based on operant conditioning. For example, among the reinforcers that may contribute to the child's refusal to eat are high levels of attention by concerned parents. These are consistently eliminated at the same time that appropriate eating behavior is reinforced positively in whatever way has been found to be rewarding to the child. For the "finicky eater," the special or highly desired foods can be used as reinforcers. They are delivered to the child contingent on his eating foods he likes less. The rule here is the very commonsense one of "after you eat your vegetables, then you get your dessert."

ANOREXIA NERVOSA

This syndrome which is characterized by marked weight loss that usually starts around puberty is discussed in volume II. Bachrach and associates[8] achieved dramatic success in the treatment of a severely anorexic woman with a program based on operant conditioning. At the outset, the patient was in critical condition with a body weight of twenty-one kilograms. Social interaction and privileges such as TV watching time were dispensed on a strictly contingent basis, first for eating and later for weight gain. Refusal to eat was penalized by isolation in a bare room devoid of social or material reinforcers. At the conclusion of treatment, the patient's weight had doubled. It continued to be maintained at that level after one year of follow up. Stunkard[107] observed that hospitalized anorexic females had a significantly higher activity level (walking, as measured with a pedometer) than normal-weight women. On the basis of this finding, he used access to physical activity as the predominant reinforcer for appropriate eating. Stunkard reports consistent weight gains averaging four to six pounds per week with a number of cases of severe anorexia treated in this fashion; he claims that these results equal or surpass the best reported in the anorexia nervosa medical literature.

OBESITY

Obesity has also been treated with operant-based behavioral techniques. The typical treatment package derives largely from the work of Ferster[40] and Stuart.[106] It involves removing from the patient's environment those stimulus cues which elicit eating behavior, penalizing overeating, and rewarding reduced food intake and weight loss. Although the behavior therapy literature includes a number of single-case and small group studies of behavioral treatment of obesity with successful outcome, after reviewing the relevant literature, Yates[120] concludes that this is an area in which behavior therapy has failed. In summarizing his conclusions, he states: "The results [of behavior therapy with obesity] are not particularly impressive given the time and effort involved and the studies are plagued frequently by high attrition rates and inadequate follow up."[121]

ENURESIS

Perhaps the most commonly observed developmental difficulty displayed by children, be they normal or disturbed, has to do with the acquisition of bowel and bladder control. Enuresis, which is discussed in detail in volume II, is conceptualized behaviorally by viewing the phenomenon of bowel and bladder control as a highly complicated behavioral skill which includes both reflexive (classically conditioned) and respondent (operantly conditioned) components. Yates,[121] for example, states that the achievement of bladder control "represents a high-level skill of considerable complexity" and "that it is not therefore surprising that some children have difficulty in achieving such control." (Indeed, it may be argued that the really surprising fact is not that some children fail to achieve such control, but that most children do achieve it.) Enuresis, then, is not seen as a symptom of mental illness. It is, rather, a failure at skill acquisition which results from either insufficient or incorrect training procedures applied by the child's parents.

Perhaps the most widely practiced behavior therapy technique known both to layman and professional alike involves the use of the bell and pad device[76] for the treatment of nocturnal enuresis. The pad is a soft and comfortable cloth square, approximately the size of a small electric blanket. It contains a cloth cushion sandwiched between two mesh or wire screen squares constructed of some highly conductive material, such as copper. This pad is placed in the child's bed so that the child sleeps upon it. The pad itself is actually a switch, and when the child wets the bed, the urine closes the circuit between the two wire meshes. With this, a loud bell starts to ring. This wakes the child, and micturition is inhibited until he reaches the bathroom. In classical conditioning language, the bell is the unconditioned stimulus, while the bladder distension and relaxation of the urinary sphincter comprise the conditioned stimulus. The response is sphincter contraction and awakening. When successful, the repeated pairing of these two stimuli produce a situation in which the stimulus of bladder distension alone is sufficient to evoke sphincter contraction. Crosby[28] devised a similar apparatus in which, in addition to the bell sounding upon micturition, an electroshock is delivered to the child's leg. This device has been criticized as being no more efficient than the Mowrer pad and having the disadvantage of sometimes being upsetting to the child.[121] Currently the bell and pad device may be either purchased or rented from a variety of commercial firms.

Although the outcome studies on this particular treatment modality for enuresis tend to leave something to be desired in terms of experimental design and rigorous research procedures, the data available do tend to be rather impressive. In reviewing fifteen follow up studies, Yates[121] found that success rates (measured in terms of percentage of subjects dry or practically dry at the end of a follow-up period) varied from 100 percent to 21 percent. He felt that an extremely conservative estimate of the number of children who benefited from this type of treatment was more than 50 percent and probably closer to 90 percent. Many of the follow-up studies done on children treated with the bell and pad device addressed the issue of symptom substitution. In these reports, there was no clear evidence that symptom substitution did occur; in fact, in many instances the opposite happened. A high proportion showed positive personality changes after becoming dry.[29, 80] With older children, this positive change may be particularly striking. Frequently the older enuretic child feels considerable embarrassment and anxiety about his "problem." In addition, his mother is bothered by the unpleasant task of cleaning up the child's soiled bed linens. This frequently leads to abrasive exchanges between parent and child. Once the child acquires bladder control, however, this attitude can change considerably. The child develops a feeling of mastery and confidence at having acquired a new skill indicating greater maturity. Simultaneously, the parents experience pride at their child's accomplishment, and the mother is freed of an unpleasant task.

With all its assets, this classical conditioning procedure is fairly complicated, and the Mowrer pad device is not always available. As a result, this approach is currently being replaced by more straightforward training procedures based on operant conditioning. Kimmel and Kimmel[58] describe a method which emphasizes selective reinforcement of a child's increasing ability to avoid urinating until he has a full bladder. The child is encouraged to increase his fluid intake to the maximum during the daily training periods and then to indicate to his parents when he feels the need to urinate. At this point the child is encouraged to wait first for a very brief period, a few minutes, and then, during subsequent trials, for increasing durations of time before urinating. Successful waiting periods are reinforced with some type of tangible reinforcement, such as candy or small amounts of money, and lavish praise from the parents. The advantage of this procedure, according to the authors, is that it trains the child to tolerate a full bladder and, if successful, gets the child to the point where he can sleep through the entire night without getting up to urinate. This is in contrast to the classical conditioning techniques which teach the sleeping child to respond to a full bladder by awakening. Because of its use of complex verbal instructions, the Kimmel and Kimmel[58] approach is perhaps better suited for older children.

One of the critical features of this method is the assumption that daytime training will effectively carry over to the night. Exemplifying this contention is the case of a four-and-one-half-year-old boy who had never been completely bladder trained. His bowel training was generally quite good, although he occasionally had "accidents." He was enrolled in a nursery school at the time he entered treatment, and other than his problem with elimination, he showed no significant deviations from normal development. After an initial interview with the child's parents and a meeting with the child, the parents were instructed to keep a daily record of both successful bowel and bladder movements and any "accidents." During this base rate collection period, the parents solicited the assistance of the child's nursery-school teacher. The assessment revealed that during the baseline period the child had an average of 1.5 episodes of enuresis during his waking hours and was nocturnally enuretic every night. In addition, over that fourteen-day time period he had two incidents of diurnal encopresis. Prior to formal therapeutic intervention, in their own efforts to train the child, the parents had tried a number of "home remedies" without success. These included reducing his fluid intake and trying to anticipate his urination by taking him to the bathroom a number of times during the day, sometimes as frequently as once every forty-five minutes. This latter procedure may have, in fact, served to maintain the child's difficulty. It appeared that the child, rather than relying on his own internal cues to void, awaited external cues from his mother or teacher.

The treatment program for this child was initiated over a weekend. The parents explained to the child that over the next two days they were going to attempt to have him learn to go to the toilet without having any accidents. They explained to the child that for every successful trip he would receive a point, and with this point he could get something that he wanted. It had been previously determined that "horseplay" type activities with the child's father were extremely pleasurable to the child and of obvious reinforcing value. The arrangement then was to reinforce the child with points which could be exchanged for "horseplay time." Under this arrangement, during the first day the child successfully voided in the toilet on all occasions and had no accidents whatsoever. The same was true for the second day of the program. Both evenings, however, the child still experienced nocturnal enuresis. During the third day, the child was home with his mother during the day and achieved 100 percent success as his mother continued the program, namely, encouraging the child to drink large quantities of fluids and then giving him points for successfully voiding in the toilet. Those points could be exchanged later in the day for horseplay time when his father returned home from work. On the fourth day, the child was returned to nursery school, and the program was continued there, with the nursery-school teacher giving the child points on the same basis as he received them at home. This first day at nursery school under the program, the child had a slight accident in that he was somewhat late getting to the bathroom. However, he had no further accidents that day after leaving the nursery school. After two weeks of maintenance on this program, the child was completely dry during all waking hours. It should be noted at this point that there was no direct intervention with the problem of nocturnal enuresis or encopresis, but the parents noted that over this two-week period, the child seemed to be showing some improvement in both of those areas. The parents were encouraged to continue the daytime program and, over the next three-week period, to continue collecting data on the frequency of both day and evening accidents. The child maintained his 100 percent success rate during the day and also showed gradual improvement in the evening. By the end of two months, the child was completely dry, both day and evenings, and the encopresis had disappeared. Follow up on this child one and a half year later reveal that he has retained the progress he made and has not displayed any symptom substitution. In this case the simple development of bladder control during the waking period had the added effect of eliminating episodic encopresis and frequent nocturnal enuresis.

A recently reported approach to toilet training utilizes a combination of operant conditioning and imitation learning procedures. Although the approach was originally devised for use with a clinical population composed of both retarded and emotionally disturbed children, Azrin and Foxx[7]

found that it is quite successful when used with normal children. Their procedure is described in the book aptly titled *Toilet Training in Less Than a Day*.

According to this method (which the authors claim is appropriate for use with children as young as eighteen to twenty months of age), use of the toilet is demonstrated to the child employing a doll that wets. In addition, during the training period the child is encouraged to drink large quantities of fluid to increase the probability of urination. After the child has taken in a quantity of liquid and has had a number of demonstrations with the doll, he is placed on the toilet. Successful trials of urinating in the toilet are lavishly reinforced with both tangible and social rewards. The authors conducted a formal study evaluating the effectiveness of this procedure with a study group of almost 200 children, over twenty months of age. All the children who were responsive to instructions and whose parents desired the training were successfully trained. The average child required less than four hours to be trained to toilet himself independently without assistance or reminder. Some children were trained in as little as thirty minutes. The longest time required by any child was two days, fourteen training hours. Girls trained slightly faster (by one-half hour) than boys. Children over the age of twenty-six months tended to train faster (in about two and one-half hours) than children younger than twenty-six months (who averaged about five hours).

ENCOPRESIS

In contrast to the rather voluminous literature on enuresis and its treatment, the problem of encopresis, which is discussed in volume II, has received relatively little attention from either psychodynamic or behavioral theorists. Behavioral treatment of this syndrome, with a few exceptions, involves operant conditioning procedures in which the child is reinforced positively for having bowel elimination at the proper time and in the appropriate place. In contrast to such methods for enuresis as the Mowrer pad, there is no single systematic behavioral approach for the treatment of encopresis. In the literature, it is said that approximately one-half to three-fourths of the children treated with a reinforcement approach show some improvement. Again, there are no reports of symptom substitution associated with successful behavioral treatment of encopresis, despite the fact that many writers acknowledge encopresis to be more frequently associated with other forms of psychopathology than is enuresis. Yates[121] argues that the behavioral-reflexive mechanisms of bowel control are similar, if not identical, in nature to those of bladder control. Consequently, he advises the development of a mechanical device similar to the Mowrer pad which would provide some sort of signal to the encopretic child that a bowel movement is imminent. The device would be self-contained and would probably allow for the placement in the area of the anal sphincter of a monitoring electrode which would pick up pre-elimination sphincter contractions and, in response to these, sound a signal.

TANTRUMS

The occurrence of extreme, persistent tantrum behavior in children in response to frustration is not limited to any one particular developmental level. However, the behavior patterns of both parent and child that ultimately result in firmly established tantrum behavior usually begin between the first and second year. This is the time when children in general begin to assert themselves and make more complicated demands on their parents. When frustrated, the toddler responds naturally with intense crying and rage. If the parents begin at this stage to give in to the tantrums periodically, the tantrum behavior achieves for the child the desired outcome, and the pattern may become well established. As mentioned earlier, the reinforcement schedule which establishes behaviors extremely resistant to elimination is one where the reinforcement is delivered on just such an intermittent, unpredictable basis. Reports from animal literature, for example, document instances where pigeons so trained and then placed on an extinction or no-reinforcement schedule persist in a bar-press response for literally thousands of responses before finally giving up. There are suggestions also that a human behavior maintained on the same type of reinforcement schedule would be extremely resistant to extinction. This is obviously the case with many children who throw temper tantrums. Indeed, a study by Etzel and Gewirtz[35] suggests that crying in infants even as young as six weeks of age was under operant control. They demonstrate in a compelling fashion that the attention such a young infant receives for crying greatly influences the frequency and intensity of the crying behavior. This finding stands in some contrast to the position taken by many developmental theorists that crying in infants is entirely reflexive.

One of the more common etiological factors in the background of tantruming children arises when a child has a severe physical illness at some point in his early development. This warrants a great deal of attention from the adults around him. Frequently, after the child recovers from the illness, he still demands the same intense attention he received while sick. This was the case in one of the reports in the literature on the behavioral therapy treatment of tantrum behavior in a twenty-one-month-old child.[114] This child suffered a severe illness, during which his parents were in almost constant attendance. Subsequent to his recovery, he cried incessantly whenever the parents left the room in which they were attempting to put him in for a nap. The treatment proposed for this child was elegant in its simplicity. It involved having the parents first ensure that the child was in no physical discomfort. They then placed him in his room and left, without returning at all despite the child's crying. On the first trial of this extinction schedule, the child cried for more than forty-five minutes before finally falling asleep. It was, of course, only with considerable reassurance from the therapist that the parents avoided responding to this intense crying; however, on the very second trial there was therapeutic payoff in that the child did not display any crying behavior at all. During subsequent episodes of putting the child to bed, there was a slight recurrence of the crying, but it was gradually eliminated entirely and, in fact, the behavior pattern followed an extinction curve much like that displayed by infrahuman subjects when exposed to the same type of operant paradigm.

Generally speaking, behavior therapy tactics for eliminating tantrum behavior include two components: first, nonreinforcement of the tantrum behavior, and second, positive reinforcement of behavior incompatible with the tantrum. Some cases involve the additional use of punishment. This is true for the aversive conditioning procedures used with autistic children whose tantrums involve mutilation and self-injury. Behavior therapists typically discourage parents from using punishment as a control method at home since it can lead to so many undesirable consequences.

Illustrative of a two-phased treatment package involving elimination of reinforcement for the tantrum and positive reinforcement of a competing response is the four-and-one-half-year-old boy who consistently responded to even mild frustration by collapsing on the floor and screaming and crying for prolonged periods. His parents reported that the child had been doing this rather regularly since age two and one-half. Their own efforts at dealing with the tantrums had been unsuccessful. Baseline data collected by the parents and by observations in the home revealed that roughly 15 percent of the child's tantrum behavior would receive what could be construed as positive reinforcement. This came in the form of attention; the parents unwittingly reinforced the child when, with good intentions, they tried to "talk the child out of his tantrum." The tantrums were particularly trying for the parents when they would occur in public, perhaps in a store, in the presence of other people. Subsequent to collecting the baseline data, the first phase of the treatment program involved time out from reinforcement, a procedure routinely used by behavior therapists to eliminate maladaptive tantrum and crying behavior. If the child displayed maladaptive behavior, he was to be removed from the social situation and isolated for a relatively brief, predetermined period of time in a small utility room in a remote area of his house. (Since the child had no history of self-destructive behavior, it was felt safe to employ this time-out procedure.) The parents were instructed to remove everything from the room that might either be a source of positive reinforcement or hazard for the child and to place a soft mat or carpet on the floor of the room, which was approximately the size of a large closet. The parents were then instructed to explain to the child, who at age four and one-half was quite competent verbally, that all future tantrums would be responded to by his being placed immediately and without fuss in the time-out room. As soon as the child stopped crying for one minute in the time-out room, a small kitchen timer would be set for five minutes and placed where he could see it. If he remained quiet for that next five minutes, he would be allowed out. If he resumed crying, the timer would be stopped and restarted again for five minutes when the crying ceased. The parents were instructed to inform and demonstrate to the child quite clearly when the timer was started.

It goes without saying that in conducting an assessment on tantrums, it should be determined to what extent, if any, they are actually provoked by the parents who, for example, might be frustrating legitimate demands on the part of the child. With this particular child, the first instance the time out from reinforcement procedure was used, he cried for approximately fifteen minutes before quieting down for the required one minute prior to the setting of the timer for five minutes. After three minutes he began crying again; he was reminded by the parents that he must be quiet for five minutes. They reset the timer and after five

minutes of quiet, he was removed from the room. The parents at that point lavishly praised him for quieting down and continued this use of the time-out room every time a tantrum occurred for the next three-week period. In addition, they placed a chart on the bulletin board of their kitchen readily visible to the child and broke up the day into three periods, morning, afternoon, and evening. For each of those periods the child went without having a tantrum, he would be rewarded by having a star placed on the chart; for every three stars the child earned, he would receive a candy bar. In this way, behavior incompatible with tantrums, namely, cooperative quiet activity, was systematically reinforced side by side with the time-out procedure. During the treatment period, in order to avoid tantrums outside the home where the parents had no good way of controlling them, the child was not taken any place where he was likely to have a tantrum. This resulted in the child staying home with a sitter while his mother went shopping. It was hoped that if control could be achieved at home, there might be generalization outside the home, which actually proved to be the case. By the end of three weeks of this program, the child's tantrum behavior was eliminated entirely. The decline in tantrum behavior again followed the learning curve characteristic of operant extinction trials for both human and infrahuman subjects. At one-year follow up, there had been a brief emergence of the tantrum behavior which was again treated successfully with the time-out room. There was no evidence of symptom substitution.

ANXIETY REACTIONS, FEARS, AND PHOBIAS

Severe anxiety phobiclike reactions in children have been seen to occur during the first year of life. This includes the commonly observed "separation anxiety" displayed by a child removed from his parents and given to the care of a stranger, as well as anxieties connected to specific objects, analogous to the true phobic reaction. Bentler[17] describes the behavioral treatment of a water phobia in an eleven-and-one-half-month-old child involving a series of procedures which resembled the systematic desensitization technique devised by Wolpe.[116] Systematic desensitization is based on the principle of "reciprocal inhibition." The therapist creates an autonomic state in the phobic person which competes with or prevents the presence of anxiety and simultaneously presents the patient with gradually increasing doses of the phobic object. This eleven-and-one-half-month-old girl displayed intense fear characterized by crying and general violent emotion when she was placed in a bathtub or tub of water, or washed in the hand basin. She displayed a similar response to faucets, to a wading pool, or to water in any other part of her house. The phobia was precipitated when she slipped and fell in the bathtub and sustained a moderately painful injury.

Treatment involved having her play with desired toys near the bathtub. On each successive day, the toys were gradually moved closer until they were eventually placed in the tub of water, and she had to immerse her hands in order to get access to them. In addition to this gradual desensitization, the child received a substantial amount of support and encouragement from her mother. The treatment lasted approximately a month and resulted in the complete elimination of the phobia. This method utilized the principles of classical or reflexive conditioning. It included the simultaneous pairing of traumatic stimuli, the water and bathtub, with pleasurable stimuli such as desired toys. These evoked a pleasure response which competed with the anxiety.

A four-and-one-half-year-old boy had an intense phobia of balloons and inflated toys following an episode a year earlier when a large helium-filled balloon had burst in his face. Subsequent to that incident the child would display a characteristic phobiclike response, including screaming and fretting and clinging to his parents, when exposed to balloons or inflated plastic toys. After he entered nursery school and displayed the phobic response when other children played with balloons or inflated toys, he was brought into treatment.

The therapy was actually carried out by the child's parents. They were instructed to spend approximately an hour with the child each evening. At this time, they provided the child with a large bowl of one of his favorite foods, ice cream. While the child was eating the ice cream, the parents were instructed to display a small uninflated balloon in the room at such a distance that the child could observe it without becoming frightened. (It had previously been determined that uninflated balloons did not provoke so intense a fear response.) During subsequent evening training sessions the parents were instructed to inflate the balloon gradually to somewhat larger size and to bring it slightly closer to the child. They gauged the child's fear response each time in order to determine how large to make the balloon and how close to bring it to him in each successive session. Over the course of approximately three weeks and two and one-half gallons of chocolate

ice cream, the parents were able to place a fully inflated balloon directly in front of the child while he was eating. Subsequent to his being able to tolerate this, the child began playing with balloons. Not only did his fear of balloons diminish, but it also decreased with other inflated toys. Follow up indicated no return of the phobia after one year, and no evidence of any type of symptom substitution. The treatment procedure used with this patient is almost identical to the classical one described by Mary Cover Jones[56] more than fifty years ago. In essence, she reversed Watson and Rayner's[110] earlier demonstration of conditioning a phobia by treating a three-year-old child with a fear of furry animals and furry objects by means of a direct conditioning procedure, which included the association of the phobic object with food that the child liked.

Recently, modeling procedures have been emphasized in the treatment of anxiety responses in children. Here nonphobic children with whom the phobic child can readily identify are encouraged to approach and actively engage the phobic object. Thus, in the case of a dog phobia, the model might be asked to play with a dog and receive considerable reinforcement for this. The observing child is then encouraged and reinforced to imitate the behavior of the model. A number of studies have indicated that the use of live or filmed models engaging in approach behavior toward what are phobic objects for the observers are a particularly efficient and rapid method of eliminating a phobia. It should be noted that both the outcome of the model's behavior in terms of receipt of positive reinforcement, and the degree of similarity between the observer and the model greatly influence whether or not the observer will acquire the modeled response. Because of the importance of similarity between observer and model, it seems that coping rather than mastery models are more effective. This refers to the fact that a phobic observer has great difficulty identifying with a person approaching the feared object and displaying absolutely no anxiety and, in fact, a great deal of confidence. The more hesitant, slightly anxious though still willing-to-approach model seems to provide greater payoff. It is interesting that children are more likely to imitate approach behavior to threatening objects modeled by other children rather than by adults or parents.

HYPERKINESIS

The importance of early correct identification and treatment of childhood hyperactivity or hyperkinetic syndrome has received considerable attention from the medical, psychological, and teaching professions as described in chapters 23, 37, 38 and volume II. After reviewing three well-controlled treatment outcome studies comparing the relative effectiveness of behavior therapy and stimulant drugs for hyperactive children in a classroom setting, Safer and Allen[98] reached the following conclusions:

1. For control of classroom behavior, stimulants are the simplest, most effective treatment; where the children respond dramatically to stimulants, behavior therapy has little to add.
2. For increasing academic performance, behavior therapy is the most successful approach. Stimulants improve attention and completion of classroom assignments, but they do not improve the rate of learning. It is not known whether stimulants added to behavior therapy would be better for academic performance than behavior therapy alone.
3. For more severely hyperactive children, behavior therapy may fail to decrease hyperactive behavior significantly in the regular school classes; for some hyperactive children, within special institutions and over short periods, behavior therapy can be as effective as stimulant drugs in reducing hyperactive behavior in the classroom.

When behavioral programs are implemented with hyperkinetic children, they tend to focus on the following areas at home and in school: reducing persistent and excessive motor activity, increasing attention span, improving general academic performance, decreasing behavioral problems such as fighting and quarrelsomeness, diminishing temper outbursts, and compensating for low frustration tolerance. Somewhat less common targets of intervention have been impulsivity, peer difficulties, and low self-esteem.[98]

In a classroom, behaviors such as "in seat—on task" are incompatible with hyperactive responses. The behavioral treatment of hyperactive children involves the use of operant-based procedures such as positive reinforcement, shaping, extinction, and so on to establish such patterns. Ayllon and his associates[4, 5] reinforced responses such as academic performance which were incompatible with hyperactive behavior. They were thus able to demonstrate the effectiveness of an approach in which direct rewarding of academic success resulted in both improved "on task" academic behavior and decreased classroom misbehavior. Their emphasis on the reinforcement of academic success was based on a previous study[39] which indicated that reducing hyperactive behavior in

children per se did not necessarily result in improved academic performance. Ideally, in treating hyperactivity, both disruptive behavior and learning problems should be dealt with. However, it is important not to assume that quieting a hyperactive child in class automatically produces increased learning.

Perhaps even more important than controlling the classroom behavior of hyperactive children is training parents to manage these youngsters in the home. In a five-year follow-up study of hyperactive children, Weiss and associates[112] found a significant relationship between successful treatment outcome and positive home factors in combination with appropriate medication. Safer and Allen[98] also stressed the importance of home management. They mention that in order to minimize side effects, stimulant drug regimens (small morning dosages) are usually aimed at suppressing hyperactivity during the time the child was in the classroom. In the late afternoon, on weekends, and during vacations, the hyperactive child is frequently unmedicated. This necessitates the use of nonchemical behavioral control approaches during these periods. The issue then becomes one of training the parents. They must learn to use operant-reinforcement techniques to increase the rate of adaptive responding while simultaneously reducing hyperactivity and misbehavior. Again, the usual approach is contingent reinforcement of appropriate behavior along with simultaneous extinction and punishment of misbehavior.

Patterson[86] has listed over twenty of the most frequently reported home behavioral problems of hyperactive children. These range from destructiveness, lying, and stealing, to sleep disturbance and oversensitivity to criticism. When generating target behaviors for a home-based treatment program, this list can serve as a guide. Once the target behaviors have been identified and their rate of occurrence determined, contingent rewards and punishments can be introduced. This will serve to establish adaptive responses which are incompatible with hyperactive misbehavior. The actual procedures of reinforcement, extinction, punishment, shaping, and so forth used are identical to those previously described for the treatment of other childhood disorders such as mental retardation and childhood psychosis.

One of the most recent developments in the behavioral treatment of hyperactivity involves the use of self-instructional self-control training. Meichenbaum and Goodman,[75] for example, used a self-instructional treatment approach to reduce hyperactivity and increase "on task" behavior in a group of school-age "impulsive" children. The self-instructional training proceeded as follows:

1. The therapist modeled a task while talking aloud to himself.
2. The child imitated the therapist's behavior while the therapist instructed aloud.
3. The child then performed the task talking aloud to himself while the therapist whispered softly.
4. The subject performed the task whispering softly while the therapist made lip movements but no sounds.
5. The child performed the task making lip movements without sound while the therapist self-instructed covertly.
6. The subject performed the task with covert self-instruction.

Using a similar approach, Bornstein and Quevillon[20] dramatically increased "on task" non-hyperactive behavior in a group of overactive preschool boys. The self-instructional scripts contained statements about following teacher's instructions and cooperative-complaint classroom behavior. After only two hours of self-instructional training for the children in this study, at a five-month follow up their improved performance was maintained.

BEHAVIOR THERAPY WITH PSYCHOTIC CHILDREN

The behavioral treatment of autistic and schizophrenic children, which is also discussed in chapter 34, does not differ significantly in theory or practice from the behavioral treatment of less serious disorders. The difference lies in the fact that the extreme severity of this form of psychopathology requires more extensive and elaborate treatment programs aimed at the wide-ranging behavioral deficiencies of the psychotic child. While behavior therapists tend to acknowledge a difference between the two major categories of psychosis in children, autism and schizophrenia, they do not regard a precise diagnosis as essential to the formulation of a treatment program. In both categories, behavioral treatment usually begins with an effort toward eliminating the grossly deviant behaviors such as self-mutilation or bizarre, repetitive mannerisms which characterize many psychotic children. The assumption is that the occurrence of these highly deviant responses precludes the acquisition of more adaptive behavior. Sometimes efforts to get rid of the highly noxious behavior of psychotic children, such as head banging and other forms of self-mutilation, include the use of high-intensity aversive procedures like electroshock, which is one of the more controversial aspects of behavior therapy. In psy-

chotic children, self-injurious behavior is by no means a mild behavioral problem, since it frequently takes such severe forms as gouging eyes, biting one's flesh down to the bone, and head banging causing skull fractures. Often when extinction programs alone, such as ignoring the behavior, are used, the initial response of the child is to increase his rate of self-destructive behavior. It is for that reason that response-contingent high-intensity punishment has been resorted to as a treatment procedure. Bucher and Lovaas[21] treated a seven-year-old schizophrenic boy who had engaged in self-injurious behaviors since the age of two. During a ninety-minute period of observation, the child engaged in over 3,000 self-injurious behaviors! With four sessions and twelve contingent shocks, the self-injurious behavior was almost completely eliminated. Aversion therapy for this type of problem usually involves having the therapist shout "Stop" to the child after self-injurious behavior has begun and then applying a high-intensity electroshock through a grid plate on which the child is standing. Again, it should be noted that this procedure is used only in extreme cases, where the alternative—namely, allowing the child to continue the self-injurious behavior—may result in serious injury or even death.

Following the elimination of grossly deviant behaviors through the use of contingent punishment or extinction procedures, most behavior therapy programs then focus on the development of adaptive social skills. With autistic children, this typically starts with a focus on language acquisition. In some cases, the program becomes even more basic and deals with reinforcing the child's paying attention to an adult therapist and imitating the therapist's gross bodily movements. With schizophrenic children, where the capacity to relate is somewhat greater, treatment can start at a higher level. In general, the programs involve direct tangible and social reinforcement of adaptive behavior such as eye contact, socialization, and verbalization. Later, self-care behavior including personal hygiene and dressing appropriately, and then, at more advanced levels, participating in a remedial education program, become the targets of the program. Finally, behavior therapy programs with autistic and schizophrenic children frequently include training parents in behavior therapy techniques which they can then implement with their children.

Follow-up studies on such treatment programs with psychotic children generally show fairly significant improvement. In most, if not all, instances, children remain to some extent deviant; however, the behavioral programs do seem useful in eliminating most of the highly disturbing and, in some instances, self-destructive behaviors of the psychotic child, while at the same time building in more adaptive living skills. Lovaas and associates[68] conducted one follow-up study on twenty psychotic children who had participated in a behavior therapy program. The degree to which children maintained improvement gained in the behavior therapy program seemed directly related to whether they returned to their own parents at the end of treatment or were institutionalized. At the termination of the formal behavior therapy treatment, all the children were showing approximately the same degree of improvement; however, those who were institutionalized regressed considerably, whereas those who returned to their parents in most cases maintained their improvement. One study[81] compared the effectiveness of behavior modification with psychotic children with more traditional play therapy. It was found that in terms of reaching the treatment goals of elimination of grossly deviant behavior and the establishment of more adaptive age-appropriate behavior, behavior therapy programs were more effective than the play therapy.

Controversial Issues

The advent of the behavioral therapies has brought with it considerable controversy. Criticism has not been limited to those who favor the psychodynamic approach but has also included criticism from within. That is, those who place heavy reliance on behavior modification techniques in their clinical work have not only sought to refine procedures but have also recognized the greater complexity of human learning as compared with animal learning. This is best exemplified by the increasing interest in imitation learning and cognitive learning on the part of many prominent "behaviorists." Furthermore, the criticism from "within" has not been solely directed to refinements of techniques and to a broadening of the theoretical models of learning and, subsequently, behavior modification procedures. Rather, the critiques may be seen as well within the mainstream of ethical, scientific, and clinical examination of the implications of any new understanding regarding the influence the clinician has on the behavior of others.

It was not the purpose of this chapter to examine in great detail the several issues stimulated by the increased application of behavior modification but rather to present a framework for understanding how behavioral therapies are used. However, it would seem useful to briefly touch upon some of the controversial issues.

SYMPTOM SUBSTITUTION

One of the initial criticisms of the behavioral approach came from the dynamically oriented therapies and regarded symptom substitution. An oversimplification of this criticism might be: All the behavorist has changed is the overt symptom, leaving untouched the underlying cause. New symptoms may emerge, and these may, in fact, be more serious than the initial symptoms. Reference has been made at several places in the chapter to studies which tend to refute this criticism. There are, however, other important considerations. To view behavior simply as a symptom seems to be a rather narrow view of human functioning. It leaves out the richness and complexity not only of the individual's behavior but also of the consequences of that behavior upon both the individual and the significant people in his environment. Finally, one may look upon "symptom substitution" from a different perspective. Almost all theories of personality include the concept of "habits" designated by one term or another. For the dynamically oriented, these habits represent behaviors that originated in conflicts but persist following conflict resolution. If nothing else, the behavioral approaches should be able to eliminate these "habits" without resulting in the development of new symptoms.

EXTRINSIC REINFORCEMENT

In general, this controversy relates to the use of external reinforcements when it is felt that the behavior should be its own reward. For example, a parent gives a child a prize for doing his homework, but it is felt the completion of the task should be reward enough. O'Leary, Poulos, and Devine[84] point out that while tangible reinforcers have been shown to be useful in inducing behavioral changes, they are often misused. They do not feel tangible reinforcers should be equated with bribes inasmuch as the primary dictionary definition of bribery includes the concept of "corruption of conduct." They carefully assess the various criticisms of the use of tangible extrinsic reinforcers and conclude that treatment programs making use of such procedures should be implemented only after other methods have been tried.

Levine and Fasnacht[64] take a slightly different tack in approaching the question. After noting the reported effectiveness and widened application of the use of token rewards in producing behavior change, they question the efficacy of the use of extrinsic reinforcers. Using a cognitive learning model, they begin with the position that it is that to which we attribute the causality of our behavior that will determine future behavior. They cite several studies in which behavior was established through the use of extrinsic rewards. However, the maintenance of the behavior was contingent upon the continuation of these rewards. Thus, while the extrinsic rewards do help produce the desired response, the response then extinguishes when the reinforcement is removed. Levine and Fasnacht[64] do not discredit the role of operant analysis in determining those instances where the behavioral excesses or deficiencies are inadvertently reinforced. However, it is their position that since the extrinsic rewards were generally not necessary for the development of the behaviors or for their maintenance, one should first search for "natural" reinforcers as the point of intervention. However, Levine and Fasnacht are in agreement with O'Leary, Poulos, and Devine[84] regarding the potency of extrinsic reinforcers and would recommend their use when there is danger to the person or when other alternatives have failed.

To sum up, extrinsic reinforcers are not bribes. They can serve as powerful influences on behavior. Several studies suggest that maintenance of target behaviors is contingent upon continued application of the extrinsic reinforcements, and, therefore, it is preferable to first use other sources of reinforcement.

TEACHING CONTROL TECHNOLOGY

The controversy here relates to the teaching of control technology to parents and teachers, which is described in detail in chapter 11. (The broader issue of behavior control will be discussed.) Winett and Winkler[115] raise the question of the application of behavior modification in schools, expressing concern regarding the behaviors that have been reinforced. They question whether the techniques have been applied more in the service of the institution than the child. They contend that a questionable status quo is maintained. O'Leary[83] questions the basis for Winnett and Winkler's con-

clusions. He further maintains that behavior modification provides an approach and a set of procedures to alter behavior, but the procedures do not determine the goals.

In considering the implications for parents, it seems most important to recognize that regardless of the extent of their knowledge of behavioral techniques, they already play a significant role in influencing the behavior of their children. One would hope that as they learn behavioral principles, they will be able to do so in a more functional fashion. In fact, one often hears the dynamically oriented clinician express dismay regarding parental behaviors that are viewed as having a detrimental effect on the child.

BEHAVIOR CONTROL

One moves quickly from the issue of control technology to the much broader issue of behavior control. London[67] has written at great length on this subject but does not limit his discourse to behavior modification. He maintains that there has been an emergence of a "behavior technology" which includes the use of drugs, psychotherapy, and advances in knowledge and control of brain functioning, as well as the conditioning procedures. He views efforts to control others not as merely a contemporary issue, but emphasizes that the present and future developments of behavioral control technology can make it easier to maintain power over others if one chooses to do so. He maintains that in considering the issue of freedom versus control, one is speaking in relative terms, for with the concept of a social system the first negation of freedom occurs—that is, there are many controls imposed on the individual by his society. The behavioral control technology then only serves to threaten our "myths" regarding freedom and control.

Although Bandura[9] views the issue from, perhaps, a less broadly defined perspective, he nonetheless presents a somewhat similar viewpoint. While he indicates that there is a considerable body of research that demonstrates behavior is oftentimes influenced by its consequences, he maintains there are other determinants of human behavior besides external consequences. He stresses the capacity of humans to defer immediate rewards and especially emphasizes that without awareness of what is being reinforced, behavior is not much affected by its consequences. External consequences are seen as having their greatest influence on behavior when they parallel those that are self-produced. Unless there are strong coercive forces at work, external influences are not viewed as likely to override opposing self-reinforcing functions. External reinforcers are viewed by Bandura as a means of designating appropriate conduct. Nevertheless, he would maintain that people can exercise some control over their behavior. But perhaps even more significant is his contention that not only does changing contingencies change behavior but also the reverse occurs—by changing behavior one changes contingencies.

It is at this point that Bandura's and London's views tend to merge. To them the crucial, although not the sole, counterbalance to behavior control is awareness. The more information one has regarding contingencies, the greater capacity for self-control. If behavior control is dependent upon sources of stimulation, then awareness is viewed as a major key to self-control, since it enables the individual to effect his own sources of stimulation.

Inherent in all this are one's views regarding the nature of man. In questions of this order, frequently our value system strongly influences our theoretical orientation. Our beliefs regarding the nature of man affect which aspects of human functioning we focus on and what we choose to disregard. As professionals, it would then seem important that we recognize our value systems as we make theoretical and clinical judgments, regardless of whether we begin with a behaviorist or dynamic viewpoint. This should then enable us not only to ensure that those we work with receive the most appropriate forms of therapy, but also that the necessary monitoring of treatment modalities continues.

REFERENCES

1. ADELSON, R., and LIEBERT, R. M., "A Modeling Film to Reduce Fear of Dental Treatment," *International Association of Dental Research Abstracts*, vol. 2, p. 114, 1972.

2. ALLEN, K. E., et al., "Effects of Social Reinforcement on Isolate Behavior of a Nursery School Child," *Child Development*, 35:511–518, 1964.

3. AYLLON, T., and AZRIN, N., *The Token Economy: A Motivational System for Therapy and Rehabilitation*, Appleton-Century-Crofts, New York, 1968.

4. ——, and ROBERTS, N., "Eliminating Discipline Problems by Strengthening Academic Performance," *Journal of Applied Behavior Analysis*, 7:71–76, 1974.

5. ——, LAYMAN, D., and KANDEL, H. J., "A Behavioral-Educational Alternative to Drug Control of Hyperactive Children," *Journal of Applied Behavioral Analysis*, 8:137–146, 1975.

6. AZRIN, N., *Positive Practice and Overcorrection*, Paper presented at Association for Advancement of Behavior Therapy, San Francisco, December, 1975.

7. ——, and FOXX, R., *Toilet Training in Less Than a Day*, Simon & Schuster, New York, 1974.

8. BACHRACH, A. J., et al., "The Control of Eating Behavior in an Anorexic by Operant Conditioning Techniques," in Ullman, L. P., and Krasner, L. (Eds.), *Case Studies in Behavior Modification*, pp. 153–163, Holt, New York, 1965.

9. BANDURA, A., "Behavior Theory and the Models of Man," *American Psychologist*, 29(12):859, 1974.

10. ——, "Psychotherapy Based on Modeling Principles," in Bergin, A. E., and Garfield, S. L. (Eds.), *Handbook of Psychotherapy and Behavior Change*, pp. 653–708, John Wiley, New York, 1971.

11. ——, and WALTERS, R., *Social Learning and Personality Development*, Holt, Rinehart & Winston, New York, 1963.

12. ——, "Aggression," in Stevenson, H. L. (Ed.), *Child Psychology: The Sixty-Second Yearbook of the National Society for the Study of Education*, pp. 364–415, University of Chicago Press, Chicago, 1963.

13. ——, BLANCHARD, E. B., and RITTER, B., "Relative Efficacy of Desensitization and Modeling Approaches for Inducing Behavioral, Affective and Attitudinal Changes," *Journal of Personality and Social Psychology*, 13:173–199, 1969.

14. ——, ROSS, D., and ROSS, S. A., "Imitation of Film Mediated Aggressive Models," *Journal of Abnormal and Social Psychology*, 66:3–11, 1963.

15. ——, "Transmission of Aggression Through Imitation of Aggressive Models," *Journal of Abnormal and Social Psychology*, 63:575–582, 1961.

16. BECK, A. T., et al., "Reliability of Psychiatric Diagnosis: A Study of Consistency of Clinical Judgment and Ratings," *American Journal of Psychiatry*, 19:351–357, 1962.

17. BENTLER, P. M., "An Infant Phobia Treated With Reciprocal Inhibition Therapy," *Journal of Child Psychology and Psychiatry*, 3:185–189, 1962.

18. BERNSBERG, G. J., COLWELL, C. N., and CASSEL, R. H., "Teaching the Profoundly Retarded Self Help Activities by Behavior Shaping Techniques," *American Journal of Mental Deficiency*, 69:674–679, 1965.

19. BORING, E. G., *History of Experimental Psychology*, Appleton-Century-Crofts, New York, 1950.

20. BORNSTEIN, P. H., and QUEVILLON, R. P., "The Effects of a Self-Instructional Package on Overactive Preschool Boys," *Journal of Applied Behavior Analysis*, 9:179–188, 1976.

21. BUCHER, B., and LOVAAS, O., "Use of Aversive Stimulation in Behavior Modification," in Jones, M. R. (Ed.), *Miami Symposium on the Prediction of Behavior, 1967: Aversive Stimulation*, pp. 77–145, University of Miami Press, Coral Gables, Fla., 1968.

22. BUDZYNSKI, T. H., et al., "EMG Biofeedback and Tension Headache: A Controlled Outcome Study," *Psychosomatic Medicine*, 35:484–496, 1973.

23. CAMPBELL, D., SANDERSON, R. E., and LAVERTY, S. G., "Characteristics of a Conditional Response in Human Subjects During Extinction Trials Following a Single Traumatic Conditioning Trial," *Journal of Abnormal Social Psychology*, 68:627–639, 1964.

24. CAUTELA, J. R., *B. F. Skinner and Behavior Change* (Film), Research Press, Champaign, Ill., 1975.

25. ——, "Covert Extinction," *Behavior Therapy*, 2:192–200, 1971.

26. ——, "Covert Sensitization," *Psychological Reports*, 74:459–468, 1967.

27. CHANDLER, M. J., "Egocentrism and Antisocial Behavior: The Assessment and Training of Social Per-

spective Taking Skills," *Developmental Psychology, 9:* 326–332, 1973.

28. CROSBY, N. D., "Essential Enuresis: Successful Treatment Based on Physiological Concepts," *Medical Journal of Australia,* 2:533–543, 1950.

29. DAVIDSON, J. R., and DOUGLASS, E., "Nocturnal Enuresis: A Special Approach to Treatment," *British Medical Journal,* 1:1345–1347, 1950.

30. DAVIS, M. H., et al., "Relaxation Training Facilitated by Biofeedback Apparatus as a Supplemental Treatment in Bronchial Asthma," *Journal of Psychosomatic Research,* 17:121–128, 1973.

31. DOLLARD, J., and MILLER, N. E., *Personality and Psychotherapy,* McGraw-Hill, New York, 1950.

32. DRABMAN, R. S., SPITALNIK, R., and O'LEARY, K. D., "Teaching Self-Control to Disruptive Children," *Journal of Abnormal Psychology,* 82:10–16, 1973.

33. DUNLAP, K., *Habits, Their Making and Unmaking,* Liveright, New York, 1932.

34. ELLIS, A., *Reason and Emotion in Psychotherapy,* Lyle Stuart, New York, 1962.

35. ETZEL, B. C., and GEWIRTZ, J. L., "Experimental Modification of Caretaker Maintained High-Rate Operant Crying," *Journal of Experimental Child Psychology, 5:* 303–317, 1967.

36. EYSENCK, H. J., "The Effects of Psychotherapy: An Evaluation," *Journal of Consulting Psychology, 16:*319–324, 1952.

37. ———, and RACHMAN, S., *The Causes and Cures of Neurosis,* Knapp, San Diego, 1965.

38. FELDMAN, M. P., and MacCULLOCH, M. J., *Homosexual Behavior: Therapy and Assessment,* Pergamon Press, Oxford, England, 1971.

39. FERNITOR, D., et al., "The Non-Effects of Contingent Reinforcement for Attending Behavior in Work Accomplished," *Journal of Applied Behavior Analysis, 5:*2–17, 1975.

40. FERSTER, C. B., et al., "The Control of Eating," *Journal of Mathetics, 1:*87–109, 1962.

41. FLAVELL, J. H., *The Developmental Psychology of Jean Piaget,* D. Van Nostrand, Princeton, N.J., 1963.

42. FREUD, A., *Normality and Pathology in Childhood, Assessments of Development,* International Universities Press, New York, 1965.

43. GARMEZY, N., *Intervention with Children at Risk for Behavior Pathology,* American Psychological Association, Distinguished Scientist Award Speech, New Orleans, 1974.

44. GARVEY, W. P., and HEGRENES, J. R., "Desensitization Techniques in the Treatment of School Phobia," *American Journal of Orthopsychiatry, 36:*147–152, 1966.

45. GOLDFRIED, M. R., and DAVISON, G. C., *Clinical Behavior Therapy,* Holt, Rinehart & Winston, New York, 1976.

46. HALLSTEN, E. A., "Adolescent Anorexia Nervosa Treated by Desensitization," *Behavior Research and Therapy,* 3:87–91, 1965.

47. HAMILTON, J., STEPHENS, L., and ALLEN, P., "Controlling Aggressive and Destructive Behavior in Severely Retarded Institutionalized Residents," *American Journal of Mental Deficiency, 71:*853–856, 1967.

48. HENRIKSEN, K., and DOUGHTY, R., "Decelerating Undesired Mealtime Behavior in a Group of Profoundly Retarded Boys," *American Journal of Mental Deficiency, 72:*40–44, 1967.

49. HOEMAN, H. W., *The Relevance of Imitation Learning Through Modeling for Psychopathology and Behavior Therapy,* Unpublished manuscript, Catholic University of America, Washington, D.C., 1968.

50. HOGAN, R. A., "Implosively Oriented Behavior Modification: Therapy Considerations," *Behavior Research and Therapy,* 7:177–184, 1969.

51. HOMME, L. E., "Perspectives in Psychology: XXIV Control of Coverants, The Operants of the Mind," *Psychological Record, 15:*501–511, 1965.

52. HUDSON, B. B., *One Trial Learning in the Domestic Rat,* Genetic Psychology Monograph, vol. 13, pp. 94–146, 1950.

53. HULL, C. L., *Principles of Behavior,* Appleton, New York, 1943.

54. HUNZIKER, J. C., *The Use of Participant Modeling in the Treatment of Water Phobias,* Unpublished masters thesis, Arizona State University, 1972.

55. JACOBSON, E., *Progressive Relaxation,* University of Chicago Press, Chicago, 1938.

56. JONES, M. C., "The Elimination of Children's Fears," *Journal of Experimental Psychology,* 7:382–390, 1924.

57. KAZDIN, A., "Recent Advances in Token Economy Research," in Hersen, M., et al. (Eds.), *Progress in Behavior Modification,* vol. 1, pp. 252–256, Academic Press, New York, 1975.

58. KIMMEL, H. D., and KIMMEL, E., "An Instrumental Conditioning Method for the Treatment of Enuresis," *Journal of Behavior Therapy and Experimental Psychiatry,* 1:121–123, 1970.

59. KRASNER, L., "Behavior Therapy," *Annual Review of Psychology,* 22:483–531, 1971.

60. LANG, P. J., "Behavior Therapy with a Case of Anorexia Nervosa," in Ullman, O. P., and Krasner, L. (Eds.), *Case Studies in Behavior Modification,* pp. 217–221, Holt, New York, 1965.

61. ———, and MELAMED, B. G., "Avoidance Conditioning Therapy of an Infant with Chronic Ruminative Vomiting," *Journal of Abnormal Psychology, 74(1):*1–8, 1969.

62. LAZARUS, A. A., *Behavior Therapy and Beyond,* McGraw-Hill, New York, 1971.

63. ———, and ABRAMOWITZ, A., "The Use of 'Emotive Imagery' in the Treatment of Children's Phobias," *Journal of Mental Science, 108:*191–195, 1962.

64. LEVINE, F. M., and FASNACHT, G., "Token Rewards May Lead to Token Learning," *American Psychologist, 29(11):*816–821, 1974.

65. LIDDELL, H. S., "Conditioned Reflex Method and Experimental Neurosis," in Hunt, J. (Ed.), *Personality and the Behavior Disorders,* Ronald Press, New York, 1944.

66. LINDSLEY, O. R., SKINNER, B. F., and SOLOMON, H. C., *Studies in Behavior Therapy,* Status Report 1, Metropolitan State Hospital, Waltham, Mass., 1953.

67. LONDON, P., *Behavior Control,* Harper & Row, New York, 1969.

68. LOVAAS, O., et al., "Some Generalization and Follow-up Measures on Autistic Children in Behavior Therapy," *Journal of Applied Behavior Analysis, 6:*131–166, 1973.

69. LURIA, A. R., *Higher Cortical Functions in Man,* Basic Books, New York, 1966.

70. LUTHE, W., *Autogenic Training,* Grune & Stratton, New York, 1969.

71. McGEE, J. P., "Broad Spectrum Behavior Therapy with a Chronic Schizophrenic," *Journal of the National Association of Private Psychiatric Hospitals, 6(2):*5–19, 1974.

72. MARKS, I. M., *Fears and Phobias,* Academic Press, New York, 1969.

73. MEDNICK, S., et al., "Studies of Children at High Risk for Schizophrenia," in Dean, S. R. (Ed.), *Schizophrenia: The First Ten Dean Award Lectures,* pp. 247–293, M.S.S. Information Corporation, New York, 1973.

74. MEICHENBAUM, D. H., *Cognitive Factors in Behavior Modification,* Research report 510,25, Department of Psychology, University of Waterloo, Ontario, Canada, 1971.

75. ———, and GOODMAN, J., "Training Impulsive Children to Talk to Themselves: A Means of Developing Self Control," *Journal of Abnormal Psychology,* 77:115–126, 1971.

76. MEYER, V., and CHESSER, E., *Behavior Therapy in Clinical Psychiatry,* Penguin Books, Middlesex, England, 1970.

77. MILLER, N. E., "Learning of Visceral and Glandular Responses," *Science, 163:*434–445, 1969.

78. MINGE, M. R., and BALL, T. S., "Teaching of Self-Help Skills to Profoundly Retarded Patients," *American Journal of Mental Deficiency, 71:*864–868, 1967.

79. MISCHEL, W., *Personality and Assessment*, John Wiley, New York, 1968.

80. MOWRER, O. H., and MOWRER, W. A., "Enuresis: A Method for its Study and Treatment," *American Journal of Orthopsychiatry, 8:*436–447, 1938.

81. NEY, P. G., PALVISKY, A. E., and MARKELY, J., "Relative Effectiveness of Operant Conditioning and Play Therapy in Childhood Schizophrenia," *Journal of Autism and Childhood Schizophrenia, 1(3):*337–349, 1971.

82. O'LEARY, K. D., "Diagnosis of Children's Behavior Problems," in Quay, H. C., and Werry, J. S. (Eds.), *Behavior Disorders in Children*, pp. 111–161, John Wiley, New York, 1973.

83. ———, "Behavior Modification in the Classroom: A Rejoinder to Winett and Winkler," *Journal of Applied Behavior Analysis, 5(4):*505, 1972.

84. ———, POULOS, R. W., and DEVINE, V. T., "Tangible Reinforcers: Bonuses or Bribes," *Journal of Consulting and Clinical Psychology, 38(1):*1–8, 1972.

85. OSGOOD, C. E., SUCI, G. J., and TANNENBAUM, P. H., *The Measurement of Meaning*, University of Illinois Press, Urbana, Ill., 1957.

86. PATTERSON, G. R., "A Learning Theory Approach to the Treatment of the School Phobic Child," in Ullman, L. P., and Krasner, L. (Eds.), *Case Studies in Behavior Modification*, pp. 279–285, Holt, New York, 1965.

87. ———, "An Empirical Approach to the Classification of Disturbed Children," *Journal of Clinical Psychology, 20:*326–337, 1964.

88. PAUL, G. L., *Insight versus Desensitization in Psychotherapy*, Stanford University Press, Stanford, Calif., 1966.

89. PAVLOV, I. P., *Conditioned Reflexes*, trans. G. B. Anrep, Oxford University Press, London, 1927.

90. PIAGET, J., *The Origins of Intelligence in Children*, International Universities Press, New York, 1952.

91. PREMACK, D., "Towards Empirical Behavior Laws I: Positive Reinforcement," *Psychology Review, 66:*219–233, 1959.

92. REPP, A. C., and DEITZ, S. M., "Reducing Aggressive and Self Injurious Behavior of Institutionalized Retarded Children Through Reinforcement of Other Behaviors," *Journal of Applied Behavior Analysis, 7:*313–325, 1974.

93. RIMM, D., and MASTERS, J., *Behavior Therapy Techniques and Empirical Findings*, Academic Press, New York, 1974.

94. RITTER, B., "The Group Treatment of Children's Snake Phobias, Using Vicarious and Contact Desensitization Procedures," *Behavior Research and Therapy, 6:*1–6, 1968.

95. ROLL, D. L., "Modification of Nasal Resonance in Cleft Palate Children by Informative Feedback," *Journal of Applied Behavioral Analysis, 6:*397–403, 1973.

96. ROSS, S., *The Effects of Deviant and Nondeviant Models on the Behavior of Preschool Children in a Temptation Situation*, Unpublished doctoral dissertation, Stanford University, Stanford, Calif., 1962.

97. SACHS, D. A., MARTIN, J. E., and FITCH, J. L., "The Effect of Visual Feedback on a Digital Exercise in a Functionally Deaf Cerebral Palsied Child," *Journal of Behavior Therapy and Experimental Psychiatry, 3:*217–222, 1972.

98. SAFER, D. J., and ALLEN, R. P., *Hyperactive Children, Diagnosis and Management*, University Park Press, Baltimore, 1976.

99. SARGENT, J. D., WALTERS, E. D., and GREEN, E. E., "Psychosomatic Self Regulation of Migraine Headaches," *Seminars in Psychiatry, 5:*415–428, 1973.

100. SCHACHTER, S., and SINGER, J. E., "Cognitive, Social and Physiological Determinants of Emotional States," *Psychological Review, 69:*379–399, 1962.

101. SKINNER, B. F., *Science and Human Behavior*, Macmillan, New York, 1953.

102. SOJWEJ, A., LIBET, N., and AGRAS, S., "Lemon Juice Theory—The Control of Life-Threatening Behavior in a Six-Month-Old Infant," *Journal of Applied Behavior Analysis, 7(4):*557–566, 1974.

103. SOLOMON, R. L., and WYNNE, L. C., *Traumatic Avoidance Learning: Acquisition in Normal Dogs*, Psychology Monographs, vol. 67, no. 4, page 354, 1954.

104. STAMPFL, T. G., and LEVIS, D. J., "Essentials of Implosive Therapy: A Learning Theory Based Psychodynamic Behavior Therapy," *Journal of Abnormal Psychology, 72:*496–503, 1967.

105. STATTS, A. W., and STATTS, C. K., *Complex Human Behavior*, Holt, Rinehart & Winston, New York, 1963.

106. STUART, R. B., "Behavioral Control of Overeating," *Behavior Research and Therapy, 5:*357–365, 1967.

107. STUNKARD, A. J., "New Therapies for the Eating Disorders," *Archives of General Psychiatry, 26:*391–398, 1972.

108. THORNDIKE, E. L., *Reward and Punishment in Animal Learning*, Comparative Psychology Monograph, vol. 8, no. 39, 1932.

109. ULLMANN, L., and KRASNER, L., *Case Studies in Behavior Modification*, Holt, Rinehart & Winston, New York, 1966.

110. WATSON, J. B., and RAYNER, R., "Conditioned Emotional Reactions," *Journal of Experimental Psychology, 3:*1–14, 1920.

111. WATSON, J. P., GAIND, R., and MARKS, N., "Prolonged Exposure: A Rapid Treatment for Phobias," *British Medical Journal, 1:*13–15, 1971.

112. WEISS, G., et al., *The Effect of Long-Term Treatment of Hyperactive Children with Methylpheridote*, Paper presented at the American College of Neuro-Psycho-Pharmacology, 1975.

113. WENRICH, W. W., *A Primer of Behavior Modification*, Wadsworth Publishing, Belmont, Calif., 1970.

114. WILLIAMS, C. D., "The Elimination of Tantrum Behavior by Extinction Procedures," *Journal of Abnormal and Social Psychology, 59:*269, 1959.

115. WINETT, R. A., and WINKLER, R. A., "Current Behavior Modification in the Classroom: Be Still, Be Quiet, Be Docile," *Journal of Applied Behavior Analysis, 5(4):*499, 1972.

116. WOLPE, J., *The Practice of Behavior Therapy*, p. 7, Pergamon Press, New York, 1969.

117. ———, "Experimental Neuroses as Learned Behavior," *British Journal of Psychology, 43:*243–268, 1952.

118. ———, and RACHMAN, S., "Psychoanalytic 'Evidence': A Critique Based on Freud's Case of Little Hans," *Journal of Nervous and Mental Diseases, 130:*135–148, 1960.

119. WRIGHT, L., "Aversive Conditioning of Self-induced Seizures," *Behavior Therapy, 4:*712–713, 1973.

120. YATES, A. J., *Theory and Practice in Behavior Therapy*, John Wiley, New York, 1975.

121. ———, *Behavior Therapy*, John Wiley, New York, 1970.

122. ZIGLER, E., and PHILLIPS, L., "Psychiatric Diagnosis and Symptomology," *Journal of Abnormal and Social Psychology, 63:*69–75, 1961.

123. ZIMMERMAN, E., ZIMMERMAN, J., and RISSELL, C. D., "Differential Effects of Token Reinforcement on Instruction Following Behavior in Retarded Students Instructed as a Group," *Journal of Applied Behavior Analysis, 2(2):*101–112, 1969.

6 / Hypnosis as a Psychotherapeutic Adjunct

Daniel T. Williams

Hypnosis can accelerate and augment the impact of psychotherapeutic intervention. Despite this, only a small minority of practicing child psychiatrists are trained in the use of this potentially helpful technique. This under utilization can be traced to a long-standing proliferation of theories, controversies, and misconceptions about the nature of hypnosis and its use in psychiatry.

It is true of hypnosis, as of all modalities of psychotherapeutic intervention, that the mechanism of its action is imperfectly understood. Similarly, when used inappropriately, it can generate untoward effects. It is worth noting, however, that in recent years a growing body of clinical and experimental data have been leading to a better understanding of hypnotic phenomena. The result has been an increasing grasp of the capacity of hypnosis to facilitate changes in emotional-cognitive perspective. One salutary, demystifying effect of objective inquiry has surely emerged: It has established that in terms of final outcome, everything done in psychotherapy with hypnosis can also be done without hypnosis. At the same time, cumulative experience suggests that the increased therapeutic leverage afforded by hypnosis can often facilitate both the conversion of insight into action and the more rapid relief of disabling symptoms. In this sense, once its limitations and the range of its clinical usefulness are appreciated, hypnosis can be a valuable addition to the child psychiatrist's therapeutic armamentarium.

It is a common observation that human beings are capable of many levels of awareness, entailing different degrees of conscious attention to various aspects of their environment. The spectrum of different levels of consciousness includes varying degrees of dissociation; these can range from transient daydreams or reveries to fully developed hypnotic trance states. It is evident that a variety of such hypnotic phenomena occur spontaneously. It follows, then, that the psychiatrist can enhance his clinical skills by learning to identify trance capacity in a patient. He is then in a position to activate, control, and channel it for defined therapeutic purposes.

In addition to the quality of dissociation, another basic ingredient in hypnosis is the element of transference. Originally, transference was conceived of as pertaining primarily to the psychoanalytic setting. Today it is best understood as part of the universal subjective coloration of interpersonal relationships that is based on previous experiences. Because of events early in life, each individual has certain ongoing desires and expectations which tend to emerge within his interpersonal relationships. These introduce certain perceptual distortions which have special clinical implications in psychotherapeutic settings.

In this context, Spiegel's definition of hypnosis is most useful.[13] He describes hypnosis as an altered state of intense and sensitive interpersonal relatedness between hypnotist and subject. It is characterized by the subject's nonrational submission and relative abandonment of executive control in a somewhat regressed, dissociated state. In the clinical situation, this state is actively instigated and knowingly enhanced by the hypnotist for therapeutic purposes. At the same time, hypnosis entails a structured form of aroused concentration that can be disciplined and directed toward specific goals. In practice, the therapist provides cues that activate the patient's capacity for a shift in attention to specified areas. This shift in attention is constantly sensitive to and responsive to guidance from the therapist. It thereby permits the patient to concentrate intensively on thoughts or feelings. The clarification of these can then lead to designated therapeutic reorientations.

The preceding definition is helpful in clarifying the illusory similarity between hypnosis and sleep. It is all the more important to emphasize this distinction because of the confusing etymological derivation of the term hypnosis from the Greek word *hypnos*, meaning sleep. In both of these states, peripheral awareness contracts, but for different reasons. In sleep, peripheral awareness contracts as part of a general withdrawal of attention with respect to the environment. In hypnosis, peripheral awareness contracts because this facilitates a heightened level of focal concentration.

Historical Development of Hypnosis

More rudimentary forms of hypnotic phenomena probably date back to prehistoric times. Various kinds of trance experience have played important roles in the earliest recorded religious practices of many cultures. They have continued to play a part in the more sophisticated religious systems which subsequently evolved.

The theoretical constructs developed to explain hypnotic phenomena and to guide their application (in both the earlier religious and later clinical settings) have followed a continuum. Initially, there was a belief in the exclusive role of external forces. This moved to a postulation of physical or physiological processes, and finally arrived at a recognition of the significance of psychological factors.

The first effort to bring hypnotherapy into the realm of science was made by Mesmer during the eighteenth century.[20] In line with the scientific thinking of his day, he formulated a psychopathology based on disturbances of the "universal fluids" in which man and all planets were immersed. He viewed his cures as being mediated through the power of "animal magnetism." It is noteworthy that he numbered several children among his cures.

During the nineteenth century, Braid at first considered "mesmeric phenomena" as strictly neurophysiological occurrences; he explained his therapeutic efforts as attempts to excite or depress the "nervous energy" of the patient. Subsequently, however, he stated that the important point was the subjective or psychological character of these phenomena, and he introduced the term "hypnosis" to denote the technique of eliciting them.

During the 1890s, a bitter and extended struggle developed between the "physicalists" of Paris, led by Charcot, and the "suggestionists" of Nancy under Liebeault and Bernheim. Later, this was shown by Janet to be no more than a sophisticated revival of the historic struggle between Braid and the early mesmerists. Janet himself emphasized the role of "dissociation" in hypnosis, though he lacked the dynamic psychology which Freud was subsequently to develop.

Freud's early applications of hypnotherapy for the release of charged emotions was of central importance in his thinking. They led to his elaboration of the concepts of repression and associated unconscious processes; these in turn gradually gave rise to the techniques and theories of psychoanalysis.[3] As Freud developed this new framework, he became concerned about what amounted to unclarified transference issues and accordingly abandoned the exploration of hypnotherapy. This established a precedent for its similar neglect by his followers. It should be noted, however, that Freud himself came to foresee how public health needs would probably reactivate a role for hypnosis to enable the more widespread therapeutic application of psychoanalytic insights in a more expeditious manner.[4]

There was some intervening physiologically based study of hypnotic phenomena by Pavlov; aside from this, little was done until the 1930s. At that point, however, there was a resurgence of interest in the medical use of hypnosis, influenced largely by Schilder[12] and M. H. Erickson.[8] In 1956, Ambrose[1] published the first book attempting a systematic empirical survey of the range of clinical efficacy of hypnotherapy with children. He hoped that this approach might expedite treatment in child guidance clinics where growing patient volume pointed to the need for more rapid and effective means of intervention.

Contemporary Theoretical and Empirical Considerations

Modern understanding of cognitive and affective processes has been strongly influenced by the experimental elucidation of the role of the reticular formation as a selective stimulus filter in the brain. Also of importance has been the delineation of the variations in the level of electrical brain wave activity over time, reflecting the individual's state of arousal. These developments have laid the groundwork for a growing understanding of the neurophysiological basis of focal attention and altered states of consciousness, including hypnosis.[2, 14] From another source, the work of several experimental psychologists has established objective ways to measure the degree of hypnotizability in a given subject. With appropriate sampling techniques, it was then possible to ascertain the distribution of this trait in the population at large. A crucial fact thus was brought to light: that hypnotizability is a rather stable and distinct psychological capacity characterizing an individual, similar to intellectual capacity or musical ability; it is not something "projected" onto the subject by the hypnotist. This, in turn, has led to clearer distinctions between the features which form the essence of hypnosis, and those artifacts which result from sociocultural influences or the idiosyncratic communications of a given hypnotist.[5] Finally, reactivated interest in hypnosis by some psychoanalysts has led to a reformulated theory of hypnosis in ego-psychological terms; this has highlighted the interdependence between sensorimotor and transference factors,[7, 10, 17] Such a reformulation views hypnosis as a circumscribed, guided regression in the service of the ego; it thus makes more understandable how hypnosis can be structured most effectively for therapeutic purposes, using a psychodynamic frame of reference.

Special Considerations with Children

In a series of 2,000 consecutive cases, Spiegel[14] has found that roughly 70 percent of the adult population is hypnotizable to a clinically significant degree; it has also been clearly established that children are more hypnotizable than adults. Cross-sectional and longitudinal surveys concur in finding increases in hypnotic susceptibility scores between the ages of five and ten, a peak in the preadolescent years, and a gradual decline thereafter, which continues through adulthood.[11] During childhood and adolescence, there are no significant sex differences in hypnotizability.

There are a number of major variables which influence children's hypnotizability; an understanding of these can contribute to more effective therapeutic use of hypnosis with them.[6]

THE PATIENT

The cognitive skills of the child are not fully developed. As a result, he generally focuses more on the immediate present and tends to be entirely absorbed in what he is doing. This focused attention is required in hypnosis. This stands in contrast to the usual adult waking state, which is characterized by more complex intellectual processes. These involve logical and critical thinking and the integration of different ideas across time and space; together, these constitute a potential source of resistance to hypnosis, which requires their temporary suspension. Further, Piaget's description of the young child's natural tendency toward concrete, literal thinking helps explain the child's more ready acceptance of appropriately worded hypnotic suggestions; the child gives mini-

mal consideration to the intrinsic nature of hypnosis and related abstract issues. Thus, children's more limited capacity for reality-testing plus the greater ease with which they intertwine fantasy and reality tend to facilitate their acceptance of the hypnosis ceremony.

Many emotional factors contribute to the greater hypnotizability of children; these include their general openness to new experience, their emotional malleability, their intrinsic orientation to learning new skills, and the greater ease with which they can accept regressive phenomena. In this regard, the hypnotic relationship more closely approximates the ways in which children generally relate to adults, as compared to the ways in which adults usually relate to each other. Children's propensity for trusting responsiveness to suggestion and their readiness to accept help from a respected adult authority are part of their natural developmental tendencies.

THE PARENTS

As with any therapeutic intervention, parental cooperation and support will increase the likelihood of a child's responsiveness. Because of lingering popular misconceptions about hypnosis as shamanistic or dangerous, it behooves the therapist to explain to the parents how hypnosis can be a safe and useful component of the therapeutic strategy. This adds the important force of their consensual validation to enhance its acceptability to the child.

THE THERAPIST

Again, as with any therapeutic modality, appropriate intervention presupposes empathic understanding of the patient and a cogent assessment of the existing problems and available resources. Another important consideration is the need for sensitivity regarding what linguistic and metaphorical style will be most suitable. This must meet the individual child's cognitive level, range of experiences, and emotional needs. This dimension of rapport is of particular significance with adolescents, who would, for example, be offended by language and imagery that would be quite appropriate for a younger child.

THE ENVIRONMENT

The physical setting for hypnosis should optimally engender a sense of comfort, security, and freedom from distracting stimuli. In the social milieu, consensual validation is important, not only from parents but also from the referring physician, nursing staff, and any others who are in a position either to aid or to hinder therapeutic movement.

Indications for Hypnosis

Having designated hypnosis as a facilitating therapeutic adjunct, it is clear that the method, in itself, is not a substitute for comprehensive therapy. The task of a child psychiatrist who uses hypnosis is first to devise a sound overall treatment strategy. This must aim both at modifying pathogenic influences in the child's life situation and augmenting the child's capacity for mastery of ongoing intrapsychic conflict.

Once the outlines of this plan have been established, hypnosis may begin to play its part. It can increase therapeutic leverage by tapping the patient's capacity to participate in the therapeutic experience in a more intense and concentrated way. The patient's intensified transference and attention become focused on the treatment situation; with this, an atmosphere of receptivity develops which enhances his capacity for reorientation and change. Moreover, where appropriate, the patient can be taught self-hypnosis. This allows him to reproduce the improved response in his daily life, and he can thus implement and reinforce the gains made in the clinical setting.

With adults, hypnosis has been demonstrated to promote uncovering of repressed material. This is accomplished through abreaction or by means of complex exploration in "hypnoanalysis." In contrast to this, there appears to be little or no advantage to using hypnosis for such purposes in children.[9] The prevalent, conventional methods of play, drawing, storytelling, and free discussion seem better suited to fostering spontaneous expression in younger patients.

The primary value of hypnosis in child psychiatry is its capacity to generate a new sense of mastery. When a child experiences this, it can enhance the process of attitude alteration and facilitate the more rapid relief of disabling symptoms.[21, 22, 23] In this sense, once a therapy plan has been developed, hypnosis can be used to focus on key dynamic elements in a welter of complex environmental and intrapsychic variables. The patient is frequently embroiled in a symptom-complex to which he has retreated under duress. Hypnosis then presents him with a simple, sound, and palatable route by which he can relinquish this defensive encumbrance with honor. By calling the patient's attention to more resourceful and effective coping methods available to him, the ceremony of hypnosis can constitute an occasion for the patient to realign his emotional-cognitive perspective dramatically. Thus, if the therapeutic strategy has been judiciously formulated under the supportive-protective authority of the hypnotherapist, the patient can incorporate a healthier perspective of adaptation.

There are several diagnostic categories in which hypnosis has been found empirically to be most helpful in child psychiatry. Their range includes psychophysiological disorders, neuroses, behavior disorders, and special symptoms (such as enuresis, encopresis, stuttering, learning problems, fingersucking, nail biting, factitious dermatitis). Children with clear-cut psychosis or substantial organic brain damage generally lack the necessary ego strength and capacity for concentration to utilize hypnosis effectively. However, for selected children with borderline conditions or minimal brain dysfunction, hypnosis may be of value; a determination of the individual child's capacity for trance experience will indicate whether or not hypnosis is applicable. Indeed, reports of some workers suggest that even psychotic patients have periods of lucidity during which they may be capable of the necessary concentration and cooperation. Circumscribed therapeutic changes can sometimes be achieved by using hypnosis with psychotic patients; these gains are unlikely to be sustained, however, unless accompanied by the associated intensive psychotherapeutic support that the overall condition requires.

To the extent that hypnosis is most often introduced as an adjunct within the larger framework of ongoing individual and/or family therapy, the reader is referred to the chapters 3, 4, and 7, which deal with these primary modalities. Their proper management is a prerequisite to the appropriate use of hypnosis. Once this is appreciated, a number of indications can be delineated for the introduction of the hypnosis as a supplementary resource.[9]

1. In the course of phychotherapy, a therapist may judge that his patient can achieve clinical improvement by means of insight. Nonetheless, the conversion of insight into changed behavior does not take place. Clearly, the patient's capacity to implement the new planned task should be realistically assessed. Here the introduction of hypnosis can provide an opportunity to "shift gears" from a more exploratory to a more actively direct approach.
2. There are many instances where symptoms can lose their original emotional significance and

persist on a self-perpetuating basis as a sort of established habit. Hypnosis can catalyze the active escape from a previously semiautomatic repetitive pattern in which the patient had felt trapped, yet which he had previously lacked the confidence or motivation to overcome.

3. At the beginning of a therapeutic relationship, hypnosis can be valuable in advancing urgently needed behavioral changes. This presupposes that the psychiatrist's initial evaluation has furnished sufficient psychodynamic data to justify application of hypnosis. This implies assessment of both the presenting problem as well as the child's and family's capacity for change. Such an approach is particularly valid in crisis intervention, which is discussed in chapter 32, though it need by no means be restricted to such situations. There is a "ripple effect" of relief and increased self-confidence generated by initial symptomatic improvement; this generates a more conductive atmosphere for further psychotherapeutic work.[15]

4. In cases of emergency—bronchial asthma, for example—the persistence of the symptom may be based in part on pervasive anxiety. Here the use of hypnosis serves as a form of "relaxation technique." The therapist allays the patient's anxiety through interpretation of the assumed causative factors and a reassuring demonstration of the corrective resources at hand.

Some therapists have had substantial experience with the use of hypnosis in child psychiatry. They feel that, rather than turning to it as a last resort after other measures have failed or bogged down, there is merit in employing hypnosis as a first resort whenever it appears likely to expedite ongoing psychotherapeutic progress.

Precautions and Contraindications

When used with sound clinical judgment in an appropriately goal-directed manner, hypnosis is a remarkably safe therapeutic aid. Nevertheless, there are some precautions to be observed. Hypnosis is of particular value in treating conversion reactions and psychophysiological disorders. It is, however, worth emphasizing the principle that applies to any psychotherapeutic intervention—that is, the need to consider carefully the possible role of organically based pathology before embarking on psychiatric treatment of such cases.

A therapist may find himself the target of the demands of parents, the referring physician, or of his own ego. It can then be tempting to try to satisfy all these by using hypnosis to remove a symptom coercively. It is clearly inappropriate to try to deprive a patient of a symptom which is serving a defensive function. One must first help him restructure his perspective for alternative adaptive maneuvers, and do this in a way that takes into account his own autonomy. Attempts at blind symptom removal through hypnosis or any other suggestive method will not only fail, but will undermine the patient's confidence in the therapist. These pitfalls are avoided when hypnotic suggestions take into account existing psychodynamics, the patient's self-esteem, and his capacity to achieve designated goals.

It is a popular misconception that hypnosis is necessarily followed by symptom substitution or recurrence. It has been amply demonstrated that such results have derived most often from either self-fulfilling prophecies conveyed inadvertently by the misguided hypnotherapist[16] or through otherwise inappropriate technique, as noted previously. It should also be observed that even when symptoms have been appropriately removed with hypnosis, they may recur. This happens if excessive adverse life stresses are reactivated, or if the psychotherapeutic support needed to consolidate gains is terminated prematurely. This observation is no more characteristic of hypnosis, however, than other therapeutic modalities.

Technique

Many different procedures can be used to identify, encourage, or induce hypnotic trance states. Indeed, the specific induction technique used is almost inconsequential in the production of the trance, as long as it is esthetically acceptable to the patient. Of primary importance, however, is the expectation of both the patient and therapist that the ceremonious transaction between them will engender a change in the patient's subjective experience. The operation signaling this change may involve any one of the myriad of disciplined tasks that involve concentration, with the associated tacit expectation that this will lead to a heightened state of receptivity to the therapist's further comments or suggestions.

The "Eye-Roll Levitation Method" of Spiegel,[18] is particularly useful in clinical settings, and the wording of its instructions for inducing hypnosis can readily be modified according to the age and individual needs of a given child. This method affords a quick. convenient, semiquantitative and reproducible way of measuring hypnotizability, which has advantages both for clinical and research purposes. Further, this method has been demonstrated to have satisfactory statistical correlation with existing standardized scales that are laboratory-based but which are much more cumbersome and time-consuming.[19] Here only the broad outlines of the Eye-Roll Levitation Method will be delineated. The instructions include a series of directions and suggestions; the patient's degree of behavioral responsiveness and compliance constitutes the basis of assessment of hypnotizability. Evidence to date suggests that both the neurophysiological endowment and psychological makeup of the subject determine this measured capacity to experience the hypnotic trance state.[14]

Initially, the patient is asked to look upward as high as he can and, while continuing to look upward, to close his eyelids slowly (eye-roll). Then the patient is asked to take a deep breath, exhale, and imagine a sensation of floating. This sensation is heightened by having the therapist stroke a finger of one of the patient's hands while also suggesting that this will generate physical concomitants of the floating sensation, so that the patient will allow his hand to float upward into the air (arm levitation). Supportive verbal reinforcement and gentle physical assistance by the therapist are employed, if necessary, to aid in the development of this response. Then a series of instructions are given regarding the anticipated "post-induction phase." Namely, the patient is told that even after he is told to open his eyes, were the therapist to put the patient's hand down, it would float back up into the air (posthypnotic motor compliance). Further, the hand would tend to remain there until the therapist touches the patient's elbow (cut-off signal). Observation is then made of the patient's capacity to comply with these suggestions, while also noting the amount of verbal reinforcement necessary to enable the patient to do so. Finally, note is made of the patient's report of posthypnotic subjective sensations, such as an awareness of a difference in his sense of control between his two hands during the post-induction phase.

Spiegel's Hypnotic Induction Profile[18] provides a systematic method of clinically measuring and correlating the patient's pattern of response to signals for eye movements, arm levitation. posthypnotic motor compliance, and posthypnotic subjective experience. By using this standard format for hypnotic induction, these various measurements are combined to convey a composite index of the patient's relative ability to maintain a disciplined level of concentration and cooperation in a relaxed, dissociated state. Degrees of hypnotizability are designated on a scale of zero to four, with

zero indicating nonhypnotizability and four indicating maximal responsivity.

As with any psychotherapeutic technique, textbook description can provide only a basic frame of reference to which practical clinical experience must be added in order to cultivate and refine an effective clinical methodology. A growing number of didactic workshops held periodically at medical centers around the country currently are available to convey this initiating personal exposure.

Aside from ascertaining hypnotizability, administration of Spiegel's Hypnotic Induction Profile has another advantage. It is a helpful way of providing the patient with a "practice exposure" in which to experience hypnosis free from concomitant concern about its therapeutic application.[21] Once this has been accomplished, the demonstration of the patient's hypnotizability generates enhanced confidence that a new resource is available with which to tackle the problem in question. As long as the child is hypnotizable to some degree, there appears to be little correlation between the specific grade of hypnotizability and the subsequent pattern of therapeutic response. Rather, the critical factor is the therapist's ability to integrate existing data and field forces in formulating an effective therapeutic strategy. This appears to be of much greater significance in determining clinical outcomes.

Using this approach, the child can now be guided easily back into the trance state. His attention is focused on postulated causes of the presenting problem. Emphasis is placed on his capacity to reorient his own contribution to it autonomously by directing his thoughts and efforts along new lines. Often a symptom has evolved as the patient's symbolic expression of unresolved intrapsychic conflict. This is interpreted to the child at a level he can understand; concomitantly, he is offered a more felicitous adaptive metaphor with which to confront his life situation. Thus, the stage is set for him to incorporate a more "grown-up" coping mechanism, with the associated intrinsic appeal this has for children. These thoughts can be summarized in a dialetical format of two or three short statements which convey the crux of the new orientation; this is often helpful in dramatizing and reinforcing the ceremony of hypnosis as the occasion for a new mastery experience. Alternatively, particularly for younger children or those with less verbal ability, a visual or experiential image can be utilized to convey the sense of mastery which is central to the desired therapeutic reorientation. Thus, the child can be told. where appropriate, to imagine a scene in which his favorite television or sports hero provides support and encouragement for a new approach to solving a given problem.

It is often helpful to teach the patient self-hypnosis. This further encourages autonomous carryover of key therapeutic messages for implementation in daily life circumstances. For older children and adolescents, this teaching can be made easier by having a set of general instructions for self-hypnosis printed, with room left to insert the therapist's particular message for each patient. (This will be illustrated in a clinical example later.) For younger children, in some cases the parents may be recruited as surrogate hypnotherapists to administer the exercise at home. In these instances, it is best to do initial hypnotic induction of the patient without the distracting presence of the parents. Once the patient has mastered it, the parents can appropriately be brought back into the room to observe the technique so that they, in turn, can administer it to him at home. Alternatively, a tape recording of instructions and suggestions can be used to help bridge the gap from the treatment setting to home.

Further discussion of hypnotic technique with children[6] along with a variety of case summaries illustrating specific applications of this approach in therapy,[21] are available elsewhere. Here, only a brief clinical vignette will be used to highlight how hypnosis can play a pivotal role in therapeutic reorientation.

CASE ILLUSTRATION

Gary was a thirteen-year-old boy who had injured his back in a football game three months previously. He was admitted to the pediatric service of a medical center for neurological evlauation of persistent lower back pain. He had already been seen by orthopedists at two other medical centers with inconclusive findings. At the time of the current admission, he had missed five weeks of school because of the recommendation for bed rest, made in hope of relieving the pain. Physical findings were essentially negative, and the neurologist observed inconsistencies in the pain pattern. Psychiatric evaluation was then requested.

Psychiatric evaluation included one session with Gary, one with his parents, and one family session, during which it was noted that there was a family history of lower back pain suffered by Gary's father and paternal uncle, as well as substantial sibling rivalry between Gary and his fourteen-year-old sister. At the time, she was doing considerably better than he was at school. Further, Gary had shown some previous tendencies toward occasional hypochondriacal complaints.

The psychodynamic formualtion viewed the data as suggesting a probable conversion reaction, based on a variety of contributants. These included Gary's and his parents' anxieties arising from the initial injury,

Gary's concern about physical vulnerability deriving from identification with his father and uncle, the developmental uneasiness normally associated with the approach of puberty, and Gary's preexisting tendency to somatization. Further, the symptom afforded Gary considerable secondary gain in the form of both additional parental attention and solicitude, as well as a regressive escape from responsibilities at school and at home. All these factors combined to foster the persistence of pain on a psychogenic basis, pain that continued even after the physical sequelae of the injury had subsided.

Supportive explanation of the nature of psychosomatic pain was given both to Gary and to his parents. The potential role of hypnosis as a facilitator of "relaxation" was described. Gary was then tested for hypnotizability using the Hypnotic Induction Profile and was found to be a good subject (grade 3). In the same individual session, the following exercise was thereupon offered to Gary:

1. Look up toward the top of your head.
2. Close your eyes and take a deep breath in.
3. Let your breath out, let your eyes relax, and let your body float. As you feel yourself floating, let one hand or the other feel like a big balloon and let it float upward. When it reaches the upright position, this becomes your signal to enter a deeper state of relaxation in which you concentrate on these three important points:
   a. Worried feelings can cause tension.
   b. Tension can cause lower back pain.
   c. By relaxing, I can reduce the tension and eliminate the pain.

After reviewing these important thoughts, you then bring yourself out of this state of relaxed concentration by counting backward this way:

3. Get ready.
2. With your eyes closed, take a deep breath in.
1. Let your breath out and let your eyes open slowly. Then, when your eyes are back in focus, make a fist with the hand that is up and let your hand float downward. That is the end of the exercise, but you continue to have a pleasant feeling of floating.

Having been additionally prepared by the helpful reassurance of the referring neurologist, both Gary and his parents accepted the proposed strategy. Gary was taught how to do the preceding exercise on his own, using self-hypnosis; the instructions for this are essentially the same. Gary was advised that he could enter the trance state on his own by simply following steps 1 through 3. Similarly, he could terminate the trance when ready by following the final steps 3 through 1. He was pleased with his new-found skill and was discharged the next day to return to school with only temporary restriction on contact sports until his condition had fully cleared. A follow-up outpatient visit was scheduled for ten days later.

By two days after discharge, telephone contact with Gary's father yielded a report of "miraculous" improvement with essentially no further complaints of pain. Gary's clinical improvement continued to be maintained when reviewed in two follow-up sessions in which therapeutic gains were consolidated. Gary's parents also reported noticeable improvement in his general social and emotional demeanor. It was agreed at this juncture that no further formal psychotherapy was indicated. The positive impact of psychotherapeutic intervention had opened a channel of communication and help, however, which would clearly be available, should any further need for it arise. Aside from one mild athletic injury which subsided uneventfully, Gary has subsequently been symptom-free over a two-year period, with no further psychiatric treatment.

Preparation of the Patient and Family

Establishment of a trusting rapport is a prerequisite for effective therapeutic application of hypnosis. Under favorable circumstances, this rapport will be established during diagnostic evaluation. If hypnosis then appears indicated, tentative dynamic formulation is presented to the patient, the parents, and the referring physician in appropriate terms. Along with this, the associated suggestion is offered that hypnosis may serve as a helpful therapeutic aid. In lay terminology, hypnosis can often best be explained as a "relaxation exercise," one that can help the child concentrate on a new approach to dealing with his problems. Concomitantly, of course, there may be important areas of educative therapy for the parents. This is designed to help them modify those aspects of their own behavior that may have contributed to the genesis and maintenance of the presenting problem. In the case of Gary, this is exemplified by the manner in which the initial parental conviction of somatic etiology of a psychosomatic symptom gave way to the understanding of its probable psychogenic causes. This change on their part enabled Gary to incorporate a similar explanation much more readily.

Economic Implications

Clearly, anything which effectively accelerates the impact of therapeutic intervention has significant economic and public health implications. It is obvious that a child psychiatrist must have a sophisticated grasp of the subtle and complex factors operative in the diverse intrapsychic, interpersonal, and environmental fields that surround his patient. Yet, it is by no means clear that the patient must attain a full level of insight to achieve effective therapeutic results. Extended analytic working-through can certainly add new dimensions of self-understanding to those with the resources to utilize that approach. However, for

the many for whom a protracted and costly approach is simply not possible, hypnosis affords an opportunity to achieve certain therapeutic results more rapidly. Actively guiding a patient to surmount a developmental obstacle with hypnosis is clearly different from helping him to overcome it gradually by greater reliance on his own efforts. There is merit to having both of these approaches available to the child psychiatrist so that either or both can be applied where indicated.

Integration of Hypnosis with Associated Practices and Modalities

In addition to the already-noted introduction of hypnosis into larger individual and/or family therapy framework, other considerations also warrant mention. Any therapeutic strategy oriented toward symptom relief must both take cognizance of and deal with the secondary gain features of the symptom. With children, the long-range therapeutic benefits of a procedure may be particularly difficult for the patients to appreciate. It is, therefore, essential that any ongoing secondary gain features of a symptom be diminished or eliminated; indeed, this is critical in order for the symptom's removal to be sustained. This can often be achieved by means of parental counseling, environmental manipulation or a concomitant behavior modification program. The therapist's awareness of the operating contingencies of reinforcement and what can be done to influence them are vital to the success of any psychotherapeutic strategy, including the use of hypnosis (see chapters 5 and 11).

Frequency of Administration and Patterns of Follow Up

No pro forma guidelines can reasonably be stated regarding optimal frequency or duration of hypnosis as a therapeutic adjunct. These will vary widely, depending primarily on the unique constellation of features present in each case. For some patients, such as Gary, only a few sessions may be necessary to achieve the desired therapeutic results. For others, there may be valid reason for continued or periodic use of hypnosis within the context of a more conventional and extended therapeutic format; this is determined by the patient's ongoing needs. These same considerations apply to patterns of follow up. It is usually wise to schedule some follow-up sessions in order to reinforce therapeutic gains. This is true even when therapeutic intervention has been quickly and dramatically successful. Experience has shown that it takes some time for a child and family to assimilate all of the ramifications of the new level of adaptation.

Evaluating the Therapeutic Results of Hypnosis

Follow-up studies show that when it has been appropriately applied, the therapeutic results achieved with hypnosis in child psychiatry demonstrate a respectable stability.[9,21] However, its appropriate use entails concomitant combination with other therapeutic modalities. Hence, it is difficult to separate out the particular contribution of hypnosis and to compare its efficacy to that of other modalities in a controlled way. A reasonable interim goal is to render a clinical judgment about the impact of hypnosis when introduced in the course of ongoing psychotherapy. One method of doing this is by using the patient as his own control and evaluating the therapeutic responses before and after hypnosis was added.[9] While much remains to be learned about hypnosis and its therapeutic applications, to date the results of such studies suggest that it can be a valuable psychotherapeutic tool. It therefore merits inclusion in the education and practice of child psychiatrists.

REFERENCES

1. AMBROSE, G., *Hypnotherapy with Children*, Staples Press, London, 1956.
2. CHERTOK, L. (Ed.), *Psychophysiological Mechanisms of Hypnosis*, Springer-Verlag, New York, 1969.
3. FREUD, S., "An Autobiographical Study," in Strachey, J. (Ed.), *The Standard Edition of the Complete Psychological Works of Sigmund Freud* (hereafter: *The Standard Edition*), vol. 20, pp. 3–74, Hogarth Press, London, 1959.
4. ———, "Lines of Advance in Psychoanalytic Therapy," in *The Standard Edition*, vol. 17, pp. 159–168, Hogarth Press, London, 1955.
5. FROMM, E., and SHOR, R. E. (Eds.), *Hypnosis: Research Developments and Perspectives*, Aldine-Atherton, Chicago, 1972.
6. GARDNER, G., "Hypnosis with Children," *International Journal of Clinical and Experimental Hypnosis, 22:* 20–38, 1974.
7. GILL, M., and BRENMAN, M., *Hypnosis and Related States*, International Universities Press, New York, 1959.
8. HALEY, J. (Ed.), *Advanced Techniques of Hypnosis and Therapy: Selected Papers of M. H. Erickson*, Grune & Stratton, New York, 1967.
9. KAFFMAN, M., "Hypnosis as an Adjunct to Psychotherapy in Child Psychiatry," *Archives of General Psychiatry, 18:*725–738, 1968.
10. KUBIE, L., and MARGOLIN, S., "The Process of Hypnotism and the Nature of the Hypnotic State," *American Journal of Psychiatry, 100:*611–622, 1944.
11. MORGAN, A., and HILGARD, E., "Age Differences in Susceptibility to Hypnosis," *International Journal of Clinical and Experimental Hypnosis, 21:*78–85, 1973.
12. SCHILDER, P., *The Nature of Hypnosis*, International Universities Press, New York, 1956.
13. SPIEGEL, H., "Hypnosis: An Adjunct to Psychotherapy," in Freedman, A., Kaplan, H., and Sadock, B. (Eds.), *Comprehensive Textbook of Psychiatry*, vol. 2, pp. 1843–1849, Williams & Wilkins, Baltimore, 1975.
14. ———, "An Eye-Roll Test for Hypnotizability," *American Journal of Clinical Hypnosis, 15:*25–28, 1972.
15. ———, "The 'Ripple Effect' Following Adjunct Hypnosis in Analytic Psychotherapy," *American Journal of Psychiatry, 126:*53–58, 1969.
16. ———, "Is Symptom Removal Dangerous?" *American Journal of Psychiatry, 123:*1279–1283, 1967.
17. ———, "Hypnosis and Transference," *Archives of General Psychiatry, 1:*634–639, 1959.
18. ———, and SPIEGEL, D., *Trance and Treatment*, Basic Books, New York, 1978.
19. SPIEGEL, H., et al., "Psychometric Analysis of the Hypnotic Induction Profile," *International Journal of Clinical and Experimental Hypnosis, 24:*300–315, 1976.
20. TINTEROW, M. M., *Foundations of Hypnosis*, Charles C Thomas, Springfield, Ill., 1970.
21. WILLIAMS, D. T., and SINGH, M., "Hypnosis as a Facilitating Therapeutic Adjunct in Child Psychiatry," *Journal of the American Academy of Child Psychiatry, 15:*326–342, 1976.
22. WILLIAMS, D. T., SPIEGEL, H., and MOSTOFSKY, D. I., "Neurogenic and Hysterical Seizures in Children and Adolescents: Differential Diagnostic and Therapeutic Considerations," *American Journal of Psychiatry, 135:*82–86, 1978.
23. WILLIAMS, D. T., et al., "The Impact of Psychiatric Intervention on Patients with Uncontrolled Seizures," *Journal of Nervous and Mental Disease* (in press).

PART B
Family and Group Therapies

7 / Family Therapy

Mary French Whiteside

Description of the Method

Defining family therapy for the "Family and Group Therapies" section of this volume on child psychiatry is difficult, for family therapy is often considered to be more than a specific method of treatment. Rather, it can be a way of viewing personality structure and psychopathology, an approach which has implications for therapeutic interventions of all sorts. Family treatment methods are based on the assumption that an outbreak of symptoms in any member of the family is related to transactional difficulties within an intricately balanced family organization. The"patient" is the family—not as a collection of related individuals, but as an emotionally meaningful unit with clear psychological boundaries. In fact, many family therapist, when receiving a child referral, will spend as little time as possible discussing the child's difficulties. Right from the start, he will move toward dealing with the strengths and weaknesses of the family system as a whole. Interactions among parents and siblings are not regarded as environmental factors which influence or historically cause a child's problem. Instead, it is precisely these interactions which are considered central to the understanding of the child's distress.

The child's overt behavior and intrapsychic organization simultaneously reflect the influence of the family system and also influence that system. The family, in turn, is not an independent unit; it is a subsystem of larger societal and cultural organizations. The history of the movement toward work with families illustrates the gradual evolution of this point of view.

Review of the Development
of Family Therapy

Twenty-five years ago, there were the stirrings of a conceptual revolution within the scientific community. Linear notions of causality and determinism were being revised in favor of a concept of organized systems, an approach which was being explored by a number of independent investigators. Such ideas as circular feedback mechanisms, multiple causes for a given effect, characteristics of wholes independent of the sum of the parts, and the like were introduced. They enabled discussion of goal, purpose, and evolution toward higher states of order. These ideas, essential in biology and the behavioral sciences, no longer raised the spectors of vitalism and teleology. They could now be analyzed in terms of objective events. To prove the point, cyberneticists constructed mechanical devices which were goal-directed, motivated, learned from their errors, and gave an uncanny impression of being alive and intelligent.

A major impetus for the spread of system concepts came from a series of symposia in the 1940s and 1950s, sponsored by the Josiah Macy, Jr. Foundation. At these conferences, scientists from a number of disciplines studied cybernetics, teleological mechanisms, and circular causal systems. Principles which had developed in seemingly disparate fields soon showed exciting promise of universal application. Another series of conferences chaired by Roy Grinker, Sr., in the 1950s brought system concepts more specifically to the behavioral sciences. The discussions ranged over concepts of homeostasis, principles of reciprocating relationships, and the transactional processes of communication and information.[18, 27]

Within general psychiatric theory, there was a gradual shift. Initially, the disease model located mental illness within the individual and regarded causes as a linear sequence of internal and environmental influences. Presently this changed to a redefinition of psychopathology and of personality theory in transactional terms. Behavior was seen as a process of circular or reciprocal causation that arose within exchanges between people, rather than as a straight line series of causes and events. When applied to families, this movement toward interpersonal systems made particularly good sense. At first, the picture of family function was pieced together from individual data; in time, however, it evolved into an image of family gestalt. Whole families were then observed as they interacted together, and an entirely new set of observations and understandings emerged. This fit well into the ideas of system organization germinating in other fields. As larger societal influences are described and multigenerational dynamics come to be better understood, the picture of the family continues to evolve.[15, 51]

In some areas there had been a growing dissatisfaction with traditional modes of treating and understanding psychopathology. Sometimes bravely and sometimes with a high degree of charismatic flamboyance, a number of independent therapists followed through their new ideas and revolted against what they saw as the professional status quo. The result was the formulation of important new theories of mental illness. As early as 1938, Nathan Ackerman published an article discussing the utility of the family unit in dealing with individual difficulties.[4] Throughout his career, he continued to work with family clinical material and was perhaps family therapy's best-known pioneer. As an outgrowth of the Macy Conferences, Gregory Bateson provided a specific link when he applied ideas from cybernetics to the communication processes. He then joined with Don Jackson, who had independently been developing ideas of homeostatic mechanisms operating in families of schizophrenics. With the individual mode of treatment there had been several nagging problems which these critics could now regard in a new light. For example, treatment failure when a child was treated alone frequently could be understood in terms of the reciprocal nature of his relationships. That is, the child's difficulties were only part of a complex interplay with parental marital problems. The parade of siblings through the doors of the child guidance clinic suggested that individual difficulties might well be more accurately related to family problems. Also, there were hospitalized patients who made significant gains in treatment. Once back home from the hospital, however, they fell into immediate and discouraging regressions. Ideas of need complementarity now began to explain such phenomena.

It was observed that following the improvement of the identified patient in treatment, other family members might appear with symptoms. This encouraged the extension of therapeutic responsibility to all family members. The view grew that any taboo on seeing the family members as part of treatment was inappropriate and therapeutically limiting. Rather than seeing the family as potentially contaminating the intrapsychic focus in therapy, there was a move to deal directly with primary relationships, both as a central mode of problem resolution and as a valuable healing resource. It was recognized that pain in one family member was sometimes tolerated and even encouraged by the rest of the family, and that any improvement might be actively resisted. This led to the realization that individual symptoms served a homeostatic function for the family status quo. It was observed that disruption of family organization might generate even higher levels of anxiety and more intense feelings of crisis than those produced by maintaining a psychologically crippled member within a stable family equilibrium. This suggested, as well, that an intervention which enabled the family as a whole to move to a more adaptive level of functioning might release a correspondingly greater impetus toward health.

Institutional recognition of the use of family

therapy techniques came in the late 1950s. The National Institute of Mental Health and other sources began to fund several large clinical research projects in the exploration particularly of schizophrenic pathology. These included the collaboration of Jackson, Bateson, and colleagues[36] in Palo Alto, Friedman and associates,[25] Bowen,[16] Laing,[43] Lidz,[45] MacGregor,[46] and Wynne.[65] These early works provided solid theoretical and clinical underpinnings for further development of the theory of family functioning and change.

An equally strong impetus came as clinicians began discussing more and more openly their experimental therapies with families. Early books on clinical technique by Ackerman,[3] Bell,[12] and Satir[55] encouraged this process. An interdisciplinary journal, *Family Process*, was established in 1962. During the mid 1960s, family institutes for therapy and training were established in most of the major United States cities. By 1970, clinicians such as Friedman[24] could speak with a sense of stability and confidence that the theory of family systems and therapy was already solidly beyond the early stages of development.

Finally, as emphasized by Ackerman,[1] one cannot underestimate the influence of the social changes of the 1960s on the family movement. This was a period of profound instability and questioning of values. These led to an increased concern with the ways that social and environmental forces influenced individual behavior, as well as to the study of how disturbances in family structure bring about increased individual distress.[27, 37, 68]

Theory

Although the theory of family therapy is certainly beyond its initial stages of development, it is, at the same time, in a state of continual growth. It is not yet conveniently concise, integrated, or agreed upon. Rather, there are a number of ideas drawn from systems theory, communications theory, cybernetics, structuralism, social role theory, psychoanalytic theory of object relations, social psychology, and cultural anthropology. These are ordered and weighted differently, depending upon the family therapist's background and predilections. Some of these assumptions are commonly accepted, others debated. A few have been chosen here to provide an introduction to the area. When

integrated with the growing store of clinical findings, they can help in organizing a rationale for therapeutic interventions into the ongoing family process.

The basic assumption required for an understanding of family therapy is that the family group operates as an open, dynamic system. To elaborate the idea of the family gestalt requires a brief discussion of the ideas of wholeness, interdependence, feedback loops, equilibrium, structure, communication, and first- and second-order change. A second important set of ideas comes from the family theorists with a psychoanalytic background; this deals with the inextricable linking of family generations via conscious and unconscious processes. This chapter will also discuss the ideas of projective identification, pathological need, and complementarity, as well as advance suggested definitions for adaptive and pathological system functioning.

WHOLENESS

The basic premise is that a system is the product of the dynamic interaction among a set of mutually interdependent objects. The family system can then be seen as the set of patterns developed over time from the transactions among the individual members. This evolving organization has new characteristics which cannot be explained just by the nature of the personalities of individual members. It is a unique unit with its own structure and history. In this vein, one needs to describe a family in terms which reflect pertinent characteristics of its existence as a unit. Each family, for example, has its own unique style, cultural requirements, and role interrelationships; in effect, its own manner of dealing with stress and of expressing emotions. Therapists speak, for example, of "slippery" or "tough" families,[b] the "united front" family,[41] the "enmeshed" or "disengaged" family,[48] or, as in one of the delightful descriptions by Mitchell, "the Turtle Family, in which everyone stays in his shell, fearful of sticking his neck out."[5]

INTERDEPENDENCE

System organization develops for a family because its members are functionally interdependent. For example, there is division of labor around vital family functions; members are interdependent as primary drive objects for one another; and they have the biological irreversibility of blood ties. Because of these multiple levels of interdependence, the family system is formed into highly complex interlocking relationships organized out of extremely powerful forces. There is a built-in complementarity of needs, so that a change in the emotional state of one person will necessarily be followed by changes in all remaining family members. The resultant interaction will have effects on all members which are not predictable from the individual input.

In the following summary from a family therapy session, even the timing of a biological need —the urge to urinate—can be seen to be closely related to the process of the family interaction:

CASE ILLUSTRATION

Through the session, as soon as either Mr. or Mrs. V showed anxiety, nine-year-old twin daughters, Carol and Rose, were immediately on their laps, cuddling and kissing. This distracted the conversation and reassured everyone. When conversation became too threatening, such as Mr. V mentioning old problems with alcoholism, Carol rushed out of the room, needing to go to the bathroom. Rose evidently felt the same urge in unison, and Mrs. V followed immediately, ostensibly to show them the way. The twins' agitation, distraction, and attention seeking—labeled by Mrs. V as "hyperactivity"—could thus easily be linked to the family's need to avoid conflictual interactions. As the women left the room, Mr. V got off the hook; Mrs. V did not have to deal with her anger at him; the girls obtained mother's separate attention and, like all good peacemakers, separated their parents at a critical moment, avoiding dangerous arguments and relieving everyone. The V's described the home situation as similar to the interview: All might be in the same room watching TV, but there was continual interruption and moving about.

FEEDBACK

As can be sseen in the preceding example, the dynamic processes of interdependence in system organization are of circular character. Mr. V's open revelations in response to therapist probes and support triggered anxiety in his daughters and his wife. Their sudden departure effectively curtailed the discussion; as a result, anxiety dissipated and the customary level of joking and tangential talk was resumed.

This is the critical characteristic of feedback loops. It removes system operation from a linear conceptualization of cause and effect to a circular conceptualization of multiple influences and reverberating effects. Interpersonal feedback loops refer to the fact that the behavior of each person affects and is affected by the behavior of every other person in the system. Moreover, the system is self-regulating since one's subsequent behavior is affected by the feedback from what one just did. Mr. V's initial statement led to a message by the rest of the family in so many words: "If you say this to the therapist, we can't tolerate it," leading him to drop that line of discussion and introduce more lighthearted jokes. In this manner, the level of anxiety tolerance in the family was clearly delineated.

HOMEOSTASIS

The family system's characteristic of self-regulation corresponds to a definition of limits on the variations in behavior allowed each member—a characteristic which is critical for the stability of the system. A state of balance within these limits is an equilibrium state. Because of feedback, whenever the ongoing status quo is disturbed beyond given limits, correction will be applied, and the system will attempt to return to homeostasis. Clinical concepts of family functioning, such as that of family myths, can be seen as idiosyncratic, unspoken, but clearly understood formulations of rules. These define desired or feared states of family equilibrium which then dominate a whole range of family interactions.[21] For example, a family may believe that a healthy unit is always harmonious, and that any expression of conflict is associated with craziness and signals imminent disintegration. Interactions will, therefore, always be aimed toward the maintenance of overt harmony; avoiding, suppressing, and condemning the expression of differences over even minor issues. In other words, the presence of conflict will signal disequilibrium and touch off mechanisms to restore the balance. A more adaptive rule system would define health in a way which allowed and which had modes for dealing with a broader range of conflict, but which included limits to the intensity and degree of permitted rage.

RULES AND STRUCTURE

The persistent and observable regularities in family relationships which evolve over time are termed the "rules" of the family system. The set of rules and the corresponding organization of family roles defined by them constitute the family structure. Rules refer to the mundane agreements about style, territoriality, or division of labor necessary for the smooth functioning of several persons living together. (For example, the jokes frequently heard about marital disputes over the way in which toothpaste tubes are rolled; the symbolic protection by the husband sleeping on the side of the bed toward the door; sex differences reflected in whether the toilet seat is left up or down—all illustrate unnoticed regularities in living, which come to awareness only in early stages of relationships when new family styles are being evolved.) Rules also refer to the more heavily loaded patterns in family structure referred to as coalitions, splits, alliances, and so on. For example, a common rule of a family brought together in a remarriage is that "we are a happy family, not repeating past problems from divorce." As a consequence, the "ours" child can become the symbol of the new marriage. To fulfill this role, confirming the parents as good, he or she must always be happy. Even normal irritability signals unusual trouble and must be suppressed. Similar family rules, such as "discipline rests only in the natural parent and not in the stepparent," may reflect unresolved issues in the family's history and crystallize splits into the "yours" and "my" side of the family.

At any period of time the family structure is a static concept, that is, one may draw a picture of who is on whose side for which issues, who asks whose permission, and so on. Over time, the structural organization can change gradually as new situations are encountered and members change in developmental needs and skills. Or it may change abruptly if a member is suddenly gained or lost.

COMMUNICATION

The functionally dynamic aspect of family interaction is the communication process. Communication is seen as family behavior. It is the manner in which the system responds. The form which communication processes take is determined by the structure. Conversely, as regularities of communication patterns develop, structure is established. As described particularly clearly by Jackson[37] and Watzlawick and associates,[60] all communications convey both a content ("report") message and a relationship ("command") message. The report gives the data to be transmitted, and the command states the "nature of the relationship between the communicants" or "how this information is to be taken." Over time, the exchange of communication acts essentially as ongoing negotiation about the relationship between persons. The resultant organization forms the structure of the relationships.

In the V family previously mentioned, the twins regularly received simultaneous, conflicting messages about important aspects of their expected relationship with parents. On the one hand, it was important that they have no problem; yet on the other. if mother did not receive concerned calls from the school continually, she became exceedingly anxious. The twins reacted to the confusion by developing an irritating, puppy-dog clinginess. They displayed constant smiling, coupled with an inhibition of all assertive questioning. When this was internalized, it created a generalized learning inhibition. Their message to mother was thus complementary—it reassured her that they (and, therefore, she) were loving and happy; at the same time, they continued her involvement with the school. Mr. V supported this stance by his message "Whatever keeps mother active and focusing her anger at school will keep our delicately balanced marital relationship stable." The content of the exchanged messages amounted to: "everything is fine and loving," while the nonverbal qualifiers established a state of affairs in which Mrs. V fought the outside world for her family, the children were innocent victims, and Mr. V was the quiet supporter and protector.

To be sure, the structure or form of the family system, with its self-perpetuating states of dynamic equilibrium, maintains stability in the face of external pressures; at the same time, it is important to note that it is not a closed system. As in all interpersonal organizations, the family is open to environmental input, which can change the structure of the system. Although it is a steady state (that is, fluctuations are kept within bounds), the equilibrium within the family is a continually changing one. There are pressures. both from forces outside the family and from the developmental changes within the family, which must be accommodated; these tend to force modification of the rules and structure of the system.

FIRST- AND SECOND-ORDER CHANGE

A full understanding of the operation of a family system thus includes two levels of description. It involves both the mechanisms which change behavior in order to maintain equilibrium and the mechanisms which allow structural change. Watzlawick and associates[61] discuss this distinction in terms of the differences between first- and second-order change. First-order change is behavior variation occurring within the rules of the system. That is, a move by one member will be countered by another, and the state of the system as a whole remains invariant. For example, if a family is organized so that the husband and wife have no disagreements, they must maintain a stance which preserves the myth of marital harmony without the threat of disruption by inevitable differences. The behavior difficulties of their child may provide both a way in which they can argue (about the child's problem) without acknowledging marital disagreements, and a way in which they can unite in a common cause. It is possible for this child to improve his functioning greatly and for difficulties to appear in another child without altering the overall organization of the system. Thus, change had indeed occurred, but it is first-order change, and the basic pattern of one child or another child functioning as a bridge and buffer between the parents is continued.

Second-order change is change in the way of behaving. It is a change which alters the system organization itself so that new and different equilibrium states are formed. In the preceding example, a new definition of marital harmony might be arrived at which included the rule that spouses argue out their differences between themselves. This would result in a strengthening of the coalition between the couple and would free the children from their role as buffer. They could then develop more autonomously. Thus, an understanding of system organization can explain why a small amount of therapeutic input at a critical point may sometimes lead to far-reaching changes, whereas, in contrast, there are instances where a tremendous investment of energy can be simply absorbed and negated by the system with no appreciable change.

As Haley[33] suggests, family problems frequently occur when the conflict is not over what behavior should take place, but over *who is going to decide* the rules of behavior. The patterns of rule negotiation, as well as the rules themselves, are a critical aspect of the functions of a family system. In addition, the situation becomes particularly complicated when there exist side by side a rule and another rule which states that there is no rule. For example, a child may complain about being restricted only to be told, "You're crazy. We don't have rules, it is just that you don't love us and want to do those awful things."

In planning therapeutic interventions, it is important to distinguish between situations requiring second-order system change and those in which the capacities of the system, as currently functioning, are sufficient. For example, new parents may be quite upset over the stubborn, bossy, recalcitrant behavior of their toddler. They may fear that they are failures when, in fact, allowing their child's self-assertive protest is a sign of adequate protection and parenting which is strong enough to push against. Attempts to change the system by modifying the parental stance would simply cause a problem, stifling the necessary growth of the toddler. On the other hand, if the child's new autonomy threatens a very weak sense of self on the part of the mother, if his growth alters a symbiotic comfort which has substituted for a secure reciprocal relationship with her own mother and which has made possible a comfortable withdrawal on the part of the father, then the parental anxiety is a signal of the disruption of a rigid, nongratifying system organization. This situation has the potential for severe defensive restrictions to be placed upon the toddler, which would then require substantial painful reworking on the part of the whole family.

In general, system concept of feedback, homeostasis, first- and second-order change, and so on illuminate both the manner in which individual symptomatology makes sense and the way it is balanced within the framework of the family system as a whole. What can be called pathological system organization is stable in its functioning —in spite of the amount of emotional pain and crippling its members endure. Modes of relating described in the clinical literature, such as pseudo-mutuality,[65] mystification,[42] transmission of irrationality,[45] double bind,[7] scapegoating,[3] and the like are mechanisms for maintaining stability while observing and denying the need for change and altered rules or roles. These mechanisms appear at sensitive points in family interaction; these are the points at which a member pushes the limits of permitted behavior. They achieve their destructive effects by bringing about an escalation of the difficulties. They place demands on the participants which can only be resolved by symptom formation and impoverishment of functioning. Thus, equilibrium is maintained at the cost of individual emotional growth. As Boszormenyi-Nagy and Spark[15] observe, these are "exploitative" techniques which inevitably induce guilt in the participants which must be balanced in the course of subsequent transactions. This balancing, particularly in severely distorted systems, perpetuates the progressive crippling and deprivation of both children and parents for generation after generation.

PROJECTIVE IDENTIFICATION AND PATHOLOGICAL NEED COMPLEMENTARITY

Because of the interdependence of system organization and individual personalities, the history of the system (that is, the history of parental families of origin as well as the history of the current family) along with the unique developmental experiences of each member all contribute to the particular opportunities or constraints that come from family membership. Some maintain that a knowledge of the current organization and functioning of a family unit is sufficient to plan therapeutic involvement.[61] However, other therapists, particularly those with a psychoanalytic and/or developmental orientation, place additional emphasis on the manner in which the current system became organized. They assert that there is some way in which the family history, with its unresolved unconscious emotional balances, is kept alive, a way that is potentially crippling and distorting to family members.[14]

It is evident that the formation of family organization is influenced both by the members' reactions to each other as separate individuals and by their unconscious projections onto one another of internalized object images. As a result, at any one point, it can be very difficult to separate out current reality factors from historical residues. The more conflicted the parent's experiences with his family of origin, the greater his disposition to be torn by internal conflict and to be at odds with some aspect of himself. The more intense the conflict, the more likely will his choice of marital partner mesh with his needs to externalize what are seen as undesirable aspects of his own personality. It is also more likely that the children of this marriage will have been cast in the role of wish-fulfilling objects; children accommodate to such pressures so that they become the living embodiment of the projected images. In addition, since the family's version of events is a major part of the child's perceptual reality, the organization of the child's object identifications reflects the introjection of whole family patterns.

Among family theorists,[23] the importance of these "projective identifications" in the understanding of dysfunctional family transactions has been widely acknowledged. However, there continues to be debate as to the possibility of resolution of unsatisfied longings and hurts stemming from past object relationships by means of change in current family interactions. This issue has relevance to the need to reverse the legacy of deprived relationships from parental families of origin, as well as to the need to deal with children who bring to treatment internalized residues of years of family messages. It is obvious that intervention into the current family system can make a substantial difference in the alleviation of family suffering. It can increase feelings of self-worth and open new channels of experience for both parents and children. Renewed autonomy and freedom of emotional expression would then feed back into the system and facilitate the individual growth of

all members. This, then. is accompanied by a change in the internalized structures of self and object relationships. Such changes can come from individual therapy with the parents or child, from family interviews, or through the normal disruptive and growth-producing effects of developmental maturation. In their discussions of parenthood as a developmental stage, Anthony and Benedek[6] describe the opportunities for adults to rework old conflicts as they help their children resolve developmental crises. Boszormenyi-Nagy and Spark[15] emphasize that an important way of balancing the ledger with parents is to be an effective parent with one's own offspring. Rapoport,[54] Pittman,[53] Langsley and Kaplan,[44] and others have discussed the opportunities for crisis intervention to make major changes in families by taking advantage of structural flux. It is just such structural flux caused by developmental regressions which allows growth in relation to developmental crises. MacGregor and associates,[46] Haley,[33] and Watzlawick, and associates[61] emphasize the use of a brief intervention to change system parameters with resultant major change in everyday behavior. On the other hand, Framo,[23] and Boszormenyi-Nagy and Spark[15] focus on the importance of modifying internalized introjects over a long period of time as critical for the achievement of lasting change. They discuss the need for the slow emergence and working through of the unconscious identification which link parents and children. This comes about through the clarification of projections in the immediate family, along with the reworking of the present relationships with extended families. At one level, initial presentations of family structure are immediately available; the underlying unconscious interlocking mechanisms only emerge over time. The authors[14] emphasize the distinction between "intensive family therapy," which works through transference distortions projected onto family members, and "supportive family therapy," which clarifies communication and changes interaction patterns. thus helping the family deal with concrete stress situations.

The possibility of change is discussed not only in terms of level (unconscious—conscious) of relationship but also in terms of degree of disorder. For example, Lidz is pessimistic about the likelihood of change in "schism" and "skew" families if the sole therapeutic intervention consists of family interviews.[45] Bowen[17] also is discouraging about the degree of change possible in families low on his scale of self-differentiation. Both investigators are describing families having one hospitalized schizophrenic member. Such severely troubled families have deficits on many levels. Not only are the children severely disturbed (i.e., borderline or schizophrenic), but the parents too have severe interpersonal difficulties. In addition, there is a dysfunctional family structure and continuing interference from parental families of origin. Clarification of these issues is most likely to come from studies which relate processes of long- and short-term therapies with diagnostic assessments of families in system terms.

FLEXIBILITY

Normal parenting facilitates the introjections and identifications necessary to the child's increasing independence. In the usual course of development, increasing differentiation from the original symbiotic ties leads the system toward its own dissolution, that is, the children leave their families of origin for their own families of procreation. More rigid systems result in inadequate separation of child from parent, immature levels of object relationship, and disturbances of identity. The pathological family functions much like a closed system; it presents enormous resistance, and experiences intense anxiety over glimmers of system change. In any family, transition periods (for example, periods of adjustment after the loss or addition of family members, periods of transition between family developmental stages) produce transitory symptoms as a means of handling the feelings produced by the disruption.[22] However, what is important is the variation among families in their tolerance to disruption, in their capacity to employ alternative transactional patterns in order to accommodate stress, and in their vulnerability to the crystallization of symptom into structure. Watzlawick and associates[61] suggest that the ability to generate second-order changes is one of the characteristics of the healthy family system. The goal of most family therapeutic interventions is to help the family evolve transactional modes which will allow for the structural change necessary to permit individual growth, and which will build in the necessary flexibility to accommodate for the inevitable accompanying stress and disruption.

Technical Considerations

The central characteristic of family therapy is an understanding of and focus on the functional and dysfunctional characteristics of the family system itself. It is, therefore, misleading to attempt to think of a specific repertoire of techniques characterizing "family therapy." (Nevertheless, later in this chapter there will be a discussion, with illustrative clinical vignettes, of various maneuvers a therapist can employ to facilitate family assessment and therapeutic change.) Since family members are interdependent in their emotional functioning, all therapeutic interventions, even those directed toward a single individual, have certain ramifications within the family network. As pointed out by Montalvo and Haley,[50] individual therapy for the child can be a powerful therapeutic intervention in the family system. There is a wide range of therapists who have used different combinations of experience and personal style, and who have invoked highly diverse conceptualizations of the interactional relationships among family systems. Their techniques are sometimes contradictory. pointing up discrepancies in theories about family change. They intervene at different places and at different levels in the family system. Rather than being discouraging, this diversity of family therapeutic approaches can, in part, confirm the utility of a system conceptualization of therapeutic interventions. The organized nature of the family system makes it possible for significant restructuring to occur as a result of input from a number of different points of entry. Any change will throw off the balance of the rest of the system and open new possibilities for alternate transactions. The result of input at different points will differ depending on the organization. Assessment of the system leads to the conceptualization of a range of strategies of intervention. Employment of a given strategy will close out some alternatives and open others.[48]

A therapist may choose to work with one family member,[21, 45] perhaps seeing this person as the one trying the hardest to change the system, or as the one bearing the brunt of the family's problems. Individual work can be done with cognizance of the resultant effect of change on the system. This is, however, a very difficult view to formulate without seeing the patterns of communication which arise when the family group is together. In doing individual work, one may anticipate the need for support from other members, particularly the parents, as the carefully worked-out balances are shifted. There is one reaction to individual change which regularly leads to potential difficulties. Here the shift in the family equilibrium is responded to by sabotaging the individual treatment. For example, parents frequently terminate a child's treatment just as he is beginning to improve. Sometimes the system is too rigid to accommodate adaptively to the change; in such instances, another common occurrence is the development of symptoms in a different family member. For example, in one family, the fourteen-year-old boy began to move from a distractible, hyperirritable stance at school to one of showing his depressed feelings more directly at home. With the situation no longer stirred up by the identified patient, the father deeveloped migraine headaches and the mother felt increasingly helpless. They decided to send the boy to his grandparents' home, out of state, for the rest of the year.

Another important factor can influence the course of individual therapy. This is the awareness that commitment to change in individual treatment may be seen as an act inherently disloyal to the family. Paradoxically, getting well can then become an extra source of guilt. Illustrating this point vividly was the case of a teen-age boy who was running away from home and being disruptive in school. It turned out that the emergency conferences arising from his behavior were the only times when his divorced parents talked with one another. For the boy to give up his symptoms would mean abandoning commitment to the old family system; it would leave his parents without a way of being together. In this case, the boy had first to be freed from the responsibility of maintaining family ties, before he could afford to change his behavior.

Another treatment strategy rests on the assumption that the most effective road to change is through the most powerful family members. Therefore, some therapists move quickly to the parental unit, sometimes by way of family interviews, perhaps never seeing the symptomatic child.[16, 40, 56] Bowen[16] discusses the feasibility of beginning treatment with the member of the family most able to make a positive move toward differentiation. He assumes that a successful step taken by this person will influence other members of the system to make similar moves. Again, interventions are made with a view to the family system as a whole.

An alternative approach views the family as a subsystem within a wider network and employs what may be termed third-order change. These interventions use the forces in the "family network"—the forty to fifty members of the family's social community—to change parameters affecting the family systems as a whole.[59]

Clearly, the techniques of family therapy are not defined by the membership of the therapeutic interviews. In fact, the more sophisticated one's understanding of the workings of the family system, the more one can manipulate the membership to therapeutic ends. Minuchin[48] describes the effectiveness of working with different subsystems (e.g., the spouse system, the subgroup comprised of adolescent siblings, community groups) in order to strengthen the boundaries around the group and to reinforce the important functions carried on by that subgroup for its members.

Some therapists exclude children under age eight from family group sessions. Bell, for instance, feels that in terms of the way in which he conducts sessions,[11] children that young are not mature enough verbally or intellectually to participate on an equal level. Other therapists assert that there is value in the presence of younger siblings; they bring about a positive, relaxed tone in the otherwise argumentative sessions.[9, 48, 63] In fact, the role of the baby in the family is often just that—to bring out the nurturance within the family. This often provides an important balance to the rejection of an adolescent. In addition, the fantasy play of younger children can bring in important material during the session.[30, 66] A given child may not be enmeshed in the triangular relationship with the parents as tightly as is the identified patient. Since he can thus receive more support from them, he may be free to speak in a way which spurs on the therapeutic process unexpectedly. For example, in one initial family interview, the mother was asked by the therapist how she typically expressed her anger within the family. The mother answered blandly, "Oh, I very rarely get angry." The eight-year-old looked at her, surprised, and said, "But what about last night when you were yelling at Dad for so long?"

Perhaps the most important advantage of the approach is the fact that seeing the family unit as a whole will bring to the surface interactions which would not be seen in any other context. The picture is then elaborated as one explores different dimensions of the family. Differences can be identified in patterns of interaction when only a subsystem is seen, or when the grandparental generation is included.

Indications and Contraindications

It should be obvious from the preceding discussion that the usual question of indications and contraindictions for a treatment mode need to be restated. In relation to family therapy, the questions might be: Is an intervention needed in the system? If so, at what point in the system and in what manner? Clinical data necessary to refer to the issue would then have to be given in terms of categories of system diagnosis, as well as individual diagnosis. At this point, there are several carefully worked out schedules of evaluation of important areas of family life that can be helpful to the therapist making an assessment.[19, 26, 48] Most generally, the important areas attended to are:

1. *The meaning of the presenting symptom in the current family homeostasis.* For example, in one case, a young teen-age girl was having intense battles with her stepbrother, was depressed, and doing poorly in school. When seen individually, her difficulties appeared to relate primarily to an adolescent resurgence of unresolved feelings from an early traumatic sexual molestation. Within a family interview, her symptoms played an additional and central role in serving to mask intense splits within a newly remarried family. Her behavior served both to unify the new marital couple and as a convenient scapegoat for their difficulties in the early stage of their marriage.
2. *Assessment of family structure.* For example, what are the characteristic constellations of family conflict and patterns of control and expression of feelings? Are defensive patterns flexible, with many alternatives, or rigid and brittle? Is there a clear distinction between adults and children and between older and younger siblings, or is there a denial of parental authority and a delegation of responsibility to one of the children?
3. *Flexibility of the structure and accessibility of alternative action patterns.* Is there an ability to accommodate to the therapist's presence, can they relax the focus on the identified patient?
4. *The family's developmental stage.* Is the family experiencing heightened tension and confusion because of an expected developmental transition? For example, has the last child become a problem in order to help mother delay her transition? The mother is about to move to a stage in which immediate caretaking is less demanding, and where she and her spouse will be home alone together in a new and threateningly intimate way. Or is the family showing the results of chronically impaired relationships, a continuing stress which has impaired its ability to meet the developmental needs of all members? How does the family structure accommodate to the new abilities of the older children or to the demands of parental careers?
5. *Sources of external stress and support.* How well does the family value system fit with the surrounding community? Is there increased strain on the family because of sudden increased wealth, or from actual or anticipated unemployment?

The family diagnosis continues to change as therapy proceeds. Gradually, as structural changes begin, surface conflicts give way, deeper splits are revealed, and unconscious material about interlocking interactions becomes more available. However, the exploration of areas of family blocking and of effective actions, with their relationship to the presenting complaints, should point the way to specific areas of difficulty. It is here that interventions should focus. Exemplifying this is a family which came to a child psychiatric clinic in the midst of a hopeless stalemate between the thirteen-year-old daughter, Rose, and her parents, Mr. and Mrs. N.

In the preceding two years, Rose had begun to spend time with a delinquent crowd at school and to act much older than her age. She became involved with a married man in his twenties. She was described as the odd one in the midst of a well-controlled, law-abiding, hard-working family. In the first few interviews it became clear that the presenting difficulties related to the long-standing special position this favored last child had occupied between the marital couple. With her budding adolescent feelings, this had now become intolerable to Rose. More than that, however, it was also connected with significant family shifts. There was a handicapped older brother, for whom the family had had to devise many protections and accommodations. At the time of the referral, he was about to marry and leave home. The family had recently moved to a more isolated and upwardly mobile community. In addition, the identified patient was the last child; Mr. and Mrs. N had to anticipate the idea of once more being alone together at home. In the sessions, family members worried about Mrs. N's depression; humorously, but with underlying seriousness, they speculated about which member would have a crisis to help mother continue her nurturing, worrying role.

Several therapeutic strategies were designed to help with different areas of stress. The goal was to aid the family in finding new ways of relating, so that they would regain what was formerly an effective mode of functioning. Least obviously relevant to the presenting problem, but resisted by the family with an insistence which indicated immediate concern, was the issue of the older brother's marriage. When the therapists insisted that the family discuss these upcoming events, it became clear that the uproar over Rose obscured anxiety over the brother's leaving and the potential parental conflict. The brother had played an important role in the family equilibrium, supporting his mother's worrying role. Rose's substituting an older boyfriend was an attempted solution; it served cerain system functions, but ultimately escalated the level of stress. Discussion of mixed feelings about the young man's departure from home decreased the covert pressure on Rose to act up. The wedding could then occur in a period of calm, which was markedly different from the emotional climate of the preceding months.

Clarification of the immediate crisis made it possible to move to more long-standing family patterns which had left Rose in a scapegoat position. Mr. and Mrs. N had an unspoken rule in their marriage that they would not argue. Potential disagreements were resolved by calm discussion with one or the other giving in. Typically, Mrs. N took a submissive role and turned her anger into depression. For a number of reasons this stance had worked less and less effectively over the years, and Rose was drawn into a position between her parents. They took her along on occasions formerly reserved for the two of them alone; disagreements between them surfaced more and more frequently in relation to her discipline. Fearful of too intense arguments, Mr. and Mrs. N delegated much parental authority to the older children. Everyone watched Rose's actions carefully and had strongly held opinions about the best way to discipline her. In this manner, the entire family was drawn together around discussions of Rose's difficulties.

On the basis of this assessment, the therapists used two primary intervention strategies in attempting to help the family members break out of these frustrating patterns. When the parents complained about Rose's defiance and disrespect, they were given the task of working out together, in the session, a rule and the expected consequences for breaking the rule. They were not allowed to slide off the hook by the immediate submission of one parent. When the interruptions by Rose and by the older siblings were blocked, the disagreements between the parents became painfully clear. Over time a relationship between Rose's "incorrigibility" and the parental inability to compromise was demonstrated. Each time Mr. and Mrs. N would work effectively together, Rose surprised the family with her relaxed, confident behavior. When Mr. and Mrs. N were split—even if they had come to a quick superficial agreement— Rose would have a new episode of misbehavior which pushed a confrontation with her parents until the three of them were united in prolonged and unproductive arguments.

In addition to the work with Mr. and Mrs. N, the therapists tried to lessen the isolation of Rose within the family by emphasizing the bonds between her and her sister. This led to less rigid role expectations for each. The "pretty one" was allowed to be sloppy; the "fat one" began losing weight. The "good sister" became less depressed and much more openly assertive. She gradually became an important spokesperson during the meetings, on several occasions carrying out important confrontations with her parents.

In sum, once a picture of the entire family system was drawn, interventions could be designed in relation to a number of different subunits: the spouse subsystem, the triangle between parents and daughter, and the sibling subsystem. These all were seen as pertinent to the relief of the initial painful situation.

Obviously, a complete family assessment presents a complex array of choices, and one can easily get lost in the richness of multiple patterns. One of the difficulties in doing family interviews, in fact, is dealing with the overload of input. The therapist must make sense out of the rapid and confusing exchanges—all given in a language familiar to family members but foreign to the therapist. Haley[32] claims that the experienced family therapist spends less time on diagnosis than the novice, and moves immediately toward the therapeutic interventions. One function of experience, of course, is quick recognition of common patterns and a sense of clarity in what, to a beginner, is overwhelming confusion. Another important distinction, however, is that between diagnosis of individual difficulties in the traditional sense and diagnosis in terms of the family system. In addition, at this point, even with a careful description of a family system, the literature does not offer a great deal of information about the relationships of differing family structures to therapeutic strategies. For example, the therapist who agrees to meet with a mother and her children without seeing the divorced husband may fall prey to the family myth that the father was consistently bad and useless. This leaves little opportunity for allowing the children to develop a new, postdivorce relationship with father, which may be valuable to their continuing identification needs. On the other hand, a contract which includes the presence of both parents in the sessions would deny the reality of the separation and might, indeed, rekindle both old battles and the nostalgic hope of reunification.

In terms of specific indications and contraindications for family interview per se, a common view is that stated by Bloch and LePierre.[13] This suggests that unless specific contraindications can be established, in all cases in which psychotherapy is indicated, family interviews are preferred. Lists of potential contraindications are given by Ackerman,[3] Kramer,[40] and Wynne.[64] These generally center on families with extremely severe disturbances and families without a commitment to working together.

In any case, the family system operates with great power. As a result, the dangers of family interviews loom larger in the mind of the novice than they actually appear in reality. Bell,[10] for example, states that in his extensive experience with families, toward the end of a stormy session he had found a tendency for the family to regroup. They begin to get back in touch with one another in small ways, as they shift once again into their usual interactions. The characteristic problem is less a concern about upsetting a precarious equilibrium than it is how to make a dent in the family structure.

An assessment of the presenting situation may lead to a choice among a number of alternative therapeutic approaches. Nonetheless, it would be misleading to fail to emphasize that a body of therapeutic techniques has been evolving for dealing with the most common family group, the nuclear family. It is on these techniques that the rest of this discussion will center.

Interviews with the Nuclear Family

The important tasks of the initial contacts with the family are: (1) the establishment of a role for the therapist (or cotherapists) in relation to the family that is at once a positive one, yet not a part of the dysfunctional organization; (2) defining the problem and the necessary intervention in terms of family interaction—this is a definition which allows all members to receive some benefit from the family's improvement and in which the family is seen as taking responsibility for finding solutions; and (3) the formulation of specific, attainable goals for the therapeutic work. From the first session onward, some part of all the more specific moves the therapist makes are directed toward the accomplishment of these tasks.

Ground Rules

Some therapists begin the work by the establishment of certain ground rules. They make a statement which introduces the idea of problems in the mutual influences of all family members.[10, 34, 39] The idea is then demonstrated and underlined by the therapist's method of conducting the session. Satir[34] initially makes the rounds of the family getting a statement from each member, no matter how terse, of his view of the family problems. Boszormenyi-Nagy and Spark[15] state that the therapist has to "extract commitment for participation from all members of the family." Families will usually come in with an identified patient, and this member is presented as the cause and expression of all the difficulties experienced in the family. Immediately challenging this assumption, the therapist expects all members to share their opinions, discomforts, and wishes for help. Inquiry may proceed into the parents' situation, listening to their quickly exposed hurt feelings. Focus on other family dyads elaborates the family picture and enables the therapist to avoid getting drawn into battles between parents and child. If at the outset, the family is too rigid to abandon the scapegoating focus, one can work through a discussion of the symptom. Other family members can be drawn out by having them give their reactions to the identified patient's behavior.[24] These techniques weave the members consciously into an awareness of family interactions. Simultaneously, they give each member the message that his opnions and feelings will be listened to, respected, and considered useful. The initial complaints, scapegoating, and hidden guilt about parenting failures are thus gradually elaborated into a conception of a family process in which each person plays a role. This counters the initial feelings that family events are out of the members' control. As Ackerman states, "The first responsibility of the therapist is to arouse the dormant hope of these troubled people. . . . He tries to enhance the quality of interchange among the family members and with himself, to make it more live, more meaningful."[1]

There is an agreement established as to the membership expected in the initial sessions. In spite of this, it seems almost axiomatic that during the first few sessions a family resistance to the contract of working with the family system will surface through the "absent-member maneuver."[57] Either one member will absent himself intermittently with a threat to leave permanently, or it will be discovered that there is an important family member who has been absent from the start, but who is having significant impact on the therapy issues. As Sonne and associates[57] observe, when a member is absent, there may be no indication in the family that they miss him and a blandness in reaction to the therapist's attempts to discuss the absence. At the same time, their continued interest ensures that the member remains alive in the sessions. This family maneuver signals resistance to the development of the family group process. As the defensive patterns of interaction are interrupted, it serves as a way of handling the ensuing anxiety. By keeping certain relationships out of treatment, the family prevents critical changes from occurring; if this is not addressed, the entire therapy may flounder.

Strategies for handling this problem vary. Bell[10] simply states from the outset that if the whole family does not come, he will not see any of them. To emphasize, he gives an example of simply walking out of a session in which two of the children had been left home. Kramer,[41] on the other hand, takes a more analytic stance by confronting the family with the resistance and making interpretations about what seem to be the dynamics of the resistance. He conducts the interview as though the absent member were there. He continues to focus on all dyads, discourages blaming the absent one, and speculates what the absent member's reactions might be to the current action. Another important contribution to these family maneuvers may be the therapist's own reactions. At times, the therapist inevitably becomes over-identified with one or more members of the family, preoccupied with what is happening inside a member, or becomes negative toward some person(s). When this occurs, the members may feel pushed out or not properly attended to, and they will communicate these feelings through their actions. The therapist does well to heed these family messages and to correct the imbalance by returning to a focus on the relations among the members.[10]

A similar maneuver viewed as a family resistance is the request for one member to have a confidential discussion with the therapist dealing with "personal issues" or "material which might damage the relationships in the family." While in individual therapy, a confidential relationship with the therapist typically is thought to be axiomatic for therapeutic work, in family sessions, as private conversation is seen as a defense against the confrontation of interactional issues. It sets up a secret which allies the therapist on one side of the family alignments and carries the message that the other persons are too vulnerable or insensitive to deal with important issues. It reinforces family myths that certain topics are too explosive, as terrible as imagined, and that the family structure is weak and vulnerable.

On the other hand, at the therapist's discretion, separate interviews may be held with subsystems of the family in order to reinforce the boundaries between them and the rest of the family. For example, the therapist may meet with the parents alone at times to discuss subjects such as intimate sexual details which they feel should not be discussed with children present, yet which must be brought into the open before the associated conflicts can be resolved.[2, 41] Haley, however, states another point of view, pointing out that the process of working out a sexual problem is part of the larger problem of defining a relationship in a mutually satisfying way. The subtle transactions which go on between a married couple sexually are similar to other patterns in their lives together. Thus, he feels that the explicit sexual aspects of a marriage do not necessarily need to be dealt with directly. As they work out their relationships in other areas, the sexual area becomes less conflictful.[33]

Defining the Problem in Family Interactional Terms

The most power lever to commitment to a family contract is through the definition of treatment goals which are explicitly laid out in interactional terms. The family's initial goal is to have the therapist change the identified patient, without changing their own comfortable status quo. The therapist must work to broaden the conceptualization of the problem, to shift it from the focus on the individual to a focus on the family's current interactions. Therapeutic styles for doing this can differ widely. On one end of the continuum, there is the combination of an active, directive stance with a commitment to a brief therapeutic contract. In this type of work there is an early emphasis on specific, concretely defined problem areas (perceptively diagnosed by the therapist to be nodal points of system dysfunction). This is sometimes accompanied by dramatic manipulations of the interactions which interrupt the former stalemates and make new alignments and interaction possibilities appear quickly. These interventions may be made with very little conscious understanding on the part of the family members as to the underlying interactional dynamics. However. the interviews are accompanied by a sense of relief. The problem situation is felt to have been meaningfully redefined. The changes in interactional feedback around the new alignments then become self-reinforcing. If the intervention has been successful in hitting a central organizational point, one would expect further impact on the relationships without additional therapeutic interventions. For example, Minuchin presents a case in which the initial problem, firesetting, is dealt with, in part, by the prescription of a task. In the first session, rather than worrying with the mother about the girl's problem with fires, the therapist tells the mother to teach the child how to handle matches without burning herself. This creates a new interaction between mother and daughter based on competence, giving each a positive reason to change.[48, 61]

A contrasting therapeutic stance is one which may be no less active, but which takes more time with the family; time devoted to the mutual exploration of recurrent interactional patterns. It puts less emphasis on solving immediate, concrete problems, and looks more toward altering pervasive dysfunctional family interactional patterns. Initial contracts are made on the basis of pointing out the role other family members play in the sequence of events. Attention is focused on areas of conflict, tension, and pain within the family structure, and in a variety of ways additional emphasis is placed on the power and responsibility of these other family members in facilitating the recovery of the patient. This type of work is illustrated well in the writings of Framo,[23] Friedman and associates,[24, 25] Boszormenyi-Nagy and Spark,[15] Kramer,[40] and Bloch and LaPierre.[13]

In this regard, an interesting sidelight should be noted. It is frequently stated that with family treatment there will be significant alleviation of the presenting symptoms within the first ten to twenty sessions. This results from a shifting in the balance of the family structure so that with the clarification of underlying conflicts, less pressure is placed on the identified patient; he then finds it less necessary to handle anxiety by symptom formation. In addition, because of the family's new awareness of its functions, the centrality of the symptom in the family equilibrium loses its power. With these changes, the family and the therapist may be satisfied. Some see this as successful reorganization of the meta-rules of the system and feel that further treatment only prolongs and encourages difficulties.[61] Kramer[40] reports that two-thirds of his cases terminate at this point. It would not be surprising to see this figure borne out in the work of numerous clinics. Obviously, this point in treatment poses choices for family members. They may be content with symptom reduction and the resulting new possibilities of interaction, or they may agree to seek deeper more radical system change. At this point, Kramer[40] sees the appropriate shift as one from the externalization onto the child to a focus on the underlying conflicts within the marital dyad. Other therapists[15, 23] see this new contract as a commitment to work with the whole family; this leads to a reworking of unconscious projections.

Variations in technique in the two stages of therapy may not be as radically diverse in process as they are represented in the claims of different therapists. However, they do vary all the way from an exclusive focus on specific problem resolution to an encouragement of broader based role modifications. In addition, as discussed earlier, there remain differences of opinion as to how much the therapist needs to be involved in order to influence the introjected residues of individual member's developmental histories to a significant degree.

Frequency of Interviews

Aside from specialized intensive team interventions in crisis work, which is discussed in chapter 32,[44,46] family interviews are commonly conducted once a week for one to two hours. More frequent sessions are sometimes used. However, realistically, when there are a number of family members involved, more numerous sessions are usually difficult to arrange. In addition, because of the ongoing family interaction during the week, a frequency of once a week is experienced as fairly intensive. This stands in contrast to individual therapy.

The Process of Change: Analysis of Problems and Working Through of Solutions

As the family begins treatment, it is usually caught up in defensive maneuvers which obscure basic issues and accelerate the family's feelings of helplessness. Its members are caught in a bind, as self-defeating as it is self-perpetuating. Behavior designed to solve problems does not touch the original sources of anxiety. Their defenses have the destructive effect of blocking growth and spontaneity and of distorting reality. From the start of treatment, there are a host of therapist maneuvers which can be employed to facilitate openness, to cut through ineffective displacements and substitutions, and to lead to the admission of hurts and resentments. The goal of this part of the work is a reduction in diffuse anxiety (although there will be a heightened expression of feeling around specific issues), an increase in empathetic support, and a clarification of basic issues so that adaptive solutions become possible.

Different "schools" of family therapy technique have been contrasted according to a number of criteria, such as degree of overt directiveness versus more covert facilitation of the flow of the interview. degree of emotionality encouraged, and amount of attention to unconscious projections versus emphasis on concrete task orientation. All these are important distinctions, and the reader is referred to references 8, 9, and 29 for further elaboration.

Common objectives are characteristic of family interviews across the several schools; these reflect the original aims of the family therapy movement. Thus, the major aim of interventions is to study the ongoing transactions with primary objects—the other members of the family as opposed to analysis of displaced projections within the transference to the therapist. Within a family interview, there may be a great deal of one to one interaction between a family member and the therapist. However, it is always done with cognizance of the presence of the rest of the family. What transpires affects their perceptions, and they know that they will quickly be drawn into the exchange. Changes in one member's perceptions and behaviors immediately force an accommodation in other members of that family system. The resultant interaction becomes part of the ongoing family history and has the potential for being reinforced by any member of the family. This stands in contrast to individual treatment sessions in which the new transactions tried out with the therapist are less likely to be successful in between sessions—the burden of change rest entirely upon one member of the complementary dyad. With all the members present, the focus falls not only on one member's input into the interaction, but on the complementary dyadic process itself—a second-order change. For example, in a family interview, the therapist was gradually able to elicit the father's expression of intense feelings of isolation. As in individual treatment, this move was intended to free up and clarify previously warded-off emotions, leaving him less likely to withdraw when needed in the family. However, just as the father began talking, his wife turned to the youngest child, fussing with her clothes and answering her well-timed request to go to the bathroom. When asked what her husband had just said, she replied casually she was sorry but she wasn't listening. When the therapist requested that the couple turn their chairs toward one another to talk more directly. the stored-up resentment behind the wife's turning away began to pour forth. After this, she was able to listen to his feelings of loneliness, and the two of them could draw closer together.

In clarifying the chronic patterns of exchange among family members, a good deal of importance is attached to nonverbal communication—the body signals of unspoken, but clearly communicated affective messages. The therapist notices when a slight turning away of the mother can set off a major battle between father and adolescent daughter. The therapist brings this to their attention and asks for explication of its meaning. Pointing to a parental smile as the son's delinquent escapades are discussed can lead to an elaboration of profound mixed messages and intense unspoken feelings. Ackerman's work[2, 3] is filled with examples of the way in which he used these cues to "tickle the family's defenses," to challenge reluctances in sharing feelings and, through his support, to validate genuine expression of emotion on the whole range of topics whose discussion at first was forbidden.

Attention is paid not only to the nonverbal messages per se, but also to the mixed, contradictory, and double-binding structure of the communications. The therapist helps members to express and to understand their conflicting needs and to notice the self-defeating results of these defensive protections.

During a typical sequence, as the interview progresses toward areas of family conflict, the identified patient begins to make his demands in an especially provocative manner. Observations of the sequence has some value (e.g., with the therapist's help, one member will sometimes be able to say "Here we go again"), but it is even more clarifying to underscore the gains that each member received from the interruption. For example, just as the mother is feeling particularly helpless in counteracting her husband's authoritative demands, the child may begin to act in a way demanding her succor. She immediately feels better and the father remains unchallenged.

A variety of therapeutic devices are available to manage the session in such a way that the uncovering of complementary needs are facilitated and observation can occur. Minuchin,[48] for example, describes the use of the therapist as a block, changing seating arrangements of members, sometimes moving an intrusive member out of the room to observe behavior through a one-way screen. Bowen[16] directs all conversation through himself, maintaining a calm, supportive continual questioning attitude. He takes a "researcher" stance, which forces the couple to think about the events that trigger their emotional responses, rather than allowing them to react as usual to customary provocations without awareness of what is setting them off. Satir and associates[56] use role play, interpersonal exercises, and teaching of communication techniques to accomplsih similar ends. Also common are simple rules of procedure (which are quickly broken by the family as interactions begin to heat up), such as not speaking for another person in the room, not interfering with interruptions, insisting that each person be allowed to speak and be heard, and maintaining a focus on here and now interactions.

It is just at points of incipient anxiety that conversation tends to break up into several different subgroups with a confusing increase in noise level, multiple message directed toward the therapist, and increased moving about the room. When the focus is brought back to the precipitant (for example, when the therapist reminds the family that pandemonium broke out just as the mother began to suggest that she might be depressed), feelings can be clarified for all members. This is likely to be accompanied by sudden calming.

The process of changing these family sequences of interactions rests on two main categories of therapist maneuvers: (1) those which are supportive of the system (e.g., discussed in terms of accommodation,[48] development of "trust"[56] in terms of developing a framework in which one can begin to intervene,[39] and (2) maneuvers which upset the system's equilibrium, creating stress. Supportive maneuvers are those which reduce anxiety to tolerable levels. Such interventions are congruent with the family system and tend generally to facilitate the development of trust in the therapist, so that individual family members can risk expressing themselves in a manner different from their customary practice. The therapist operates with a basic respect fo the ultimate adaptive functioning of the family unit and defines a role in which he alternatively engages and disengages from the family process. For instance, in the treatment with the N family previously discussed, the therapists agreed fully with the parents' insistence that their daughter needed strong parental controls. They also were sympathetic with the frustration and helplessness engendered by the parents' fruitless arguments. They did not, however, go along with the implication that the family could never resolve its dilemma. A reminder of the N's ingenuity in dealing with the complex problems of their son's handicap served both to support their competence and to challenge their current despair. Further, support of the parents' need to assert effective authority led to the more upsetting interventions, such as interrupting the displacement of disciplinary functions onto the older children. In general, "joining" interventions allow entry into the family group so that the therapist can experience the pressures, understand the pain, and become a meaningful object to family members. However,

at the same time, the therapist does not assume responsibility for family functions. He retains the freedom to be spontaneous in interventions and not to be provoked or caught up in the system.

Disequilibrating interventions are those which disrupt the usual sequences of interaction. This category of therapeutic interventions allows underlying issues to emerge more clearly and directly, and thus places a greater range of exchanges under the family's control. Hopefully, this will allow for new and more productive sequences to be established. The clarifying interventions described earlier are examples of the disruption of sequences. Another highly effective means for illuminating interactional sequences for the family in a new way is what Jackson and Weakland[39] term "reframing," or inverting the messages of family members. Waltzlawick and associates[61] define reframing as changing the conceptual and/or emotional setting or viewpoint in relation to which a situation is experienced and placing it in another frame which fits the "facts" of the same concrete situation equally well or even better, thereby changing its entire meaning. For example, the therapist may talk about the sensitivity and helpfulness shown by the naughty child as he protects his parents from their arguments by his behavior. Or, he may comment how pleasant it is for the nonsharing wife to save her husband from unnecessary burdens by not telling him about the difficult issues with the children until they are settled.

Minuchin[48] describes similar techniques in terms of confirming one aspect of the personality while simultaneously disconfirming another. Thus, the child's delinquent acts are destructive and upsetting to the family. Yet, at the same time, they may be related to his positive attachment to the parents. Thus, he may wish to spare them the intolerable feelings aroused by his becoming grownup, responsible, and independent of them. The effect of such interpretations is to "detoxify" the effect of original behavior and to suggest new ways of helping in the situation. For example, the therapist can suggest to the adolescent that he can be more helpful to his parents by letting them fight their own battles, no matter how hard they may try to get him to fight for them. This then gives the adolescent a more adaptive way of fighting for autonomy.

The goal of interventions, which are designed to break through dysfunctional communication patterns and to encourage more direct acknowledgment of emotional messages, is in no way simply a cathartic venting of pent-up feelings. Rather, the therapist's moves are always made within a context of respect for the importance of individual privacy and for the boundaries of appropriate autonomy. As defined by Minuchin,[48] clear boundaries are those which are delineated well enough to allow subsystem members to carry out their function without undue interference but that also allow contact between members of the subsystem and others. A clear boundary around the individual enables the person to take the differentiated "I position." This is described by Bowen[16] as a position which defines principle and action in terms of "This is what I think or feel or stand for" and "This is what I will do or not do." The responsible "I" assumes responsibility for one's own happiness, comfort, and well-being. It avoids thinking that tends to blame one's own unhappiness, discomfort, or failure on others. The responsible "I" avoids the posture of an irresponsible or narcissistic "I," which makes demands on others such as "I want or deserve" or "This is my right and privilege." Taking this position cuts through battles for control. By not trying to force the other's position, paradoxically, one assumes control. By clearly stating a position, one draws the other into a complementary response. This results in a reduction of anxiety and more effective functioning as a unit.

Families in distress frequently employ a pattern of boundaries that are either too rigid or too diffuse. In either situation, the members are tied together in such a way that they cannot function independently. When boundaries are diffuse, any differentiating move threatens disintegration. Thus, whole areas of experience must be denied and reality testing and sense of self are profoundly distorted. In families where boundaries are too rigid, adequate functioning of one member may depend on the distress of another. Feelings are rigidly apportioned, and again, major aspects of personality are stunted. Supportive and disequilibrating interventions have the effect of clarifying boundaries and restructuring the family system.

CASE ILLUSTRATION

Illustrative of this is a family with a son who was referred to the clinic showing symptoms of phobias, confusion, and infantile behavior. Early in the family interview, the mother gave rambling explanations about the necessity for continually remaining home with the boy—an explanation filled with vague worries about his actions, couched in terms of what he needed, what her husband agreed with, and so on. All the time this account proceeded, it was punctuated by bizarre noises from her son. The therapist encouraged clearer statements from her about her desires to do something outside the home, and forced the woman and her husband to discuss their social life directly and to talk about their disagreements over their son's ability to care for himself. The therapist listened to tthe son's opinions on the subject and had the parents negotiate a plan for babysitting during the session. The result of these and similar interventions over several interviews was to bring into the open a clear picture of long-standing marital noninvolvement. Paradoxically, by drawing the battle lines where they belonged, the spouses became closer. The husband abandoned a long-term extramarital relationship and suported his wife's new interest in teaching. Because the distance increased between mother and son, the boy no longer needed to be the sole supporter of her needs. He became less fearful and, for the first time, began spending time with boys his age, instead of absorbing himself in the cartoon world of TV.

Termination

The principles that govern the termination of family treatment are similar to those which prevail in individual treatment. Ending contact with the therapist represents separation, an issue which is at the heart of difficulties for many families. In line with their concept of operational mourning, Paul and Grosser[52] discuss the use of termination as an active experience in which old feelings around separations can be reworked. This results in enhanced affective freedom and increased reciprocal empathy. As termination is anticipated and carried through, there is an opportunity to master competently an experience which in the past was avoided and denied. This experience is especially crucial to short-term interventions. Here the termination experience becomes a central therapeutic focus to activate and to work through difficulties with separation.

Effective separation also implies autonomy. It suggests that the family members feel that new ways of handling difficulty have become integrated into the family system in a way which does not rely upon the therapist's presence. The therapist's role in the family should not have become a functional role—as parent, scapegoat, healer, or the like. The continual disengagement required of the therapist to allow him to reflect on the family's progress, and to allow family members to struggle for themselves, is a model for the ultimate disengagement at termination. From the outset, the framework is one in which the family takes responsibility for its own functioning. Families will recognize their growth as they report continued success and as they realistically assess their goals and progress toward them.

The assessment of such achievements generally results from a compromise between family expectations and therapist values. As with all literature about treatment, much of the family therapy literature has statements about ideal or optimal family functioning. Such ideals are rarely approximated, but they do serve as powerful motivating forces. Families have their own values, priorities, and practical compromises. As Zuk[67] puts it, they terminate when the family convinces the therapist that they no longer need to come. A more idealistic statement, given by Boszormenyi-Nagy, is that he looks for "a genuine dialogue among the family members regarding important issues of family life, conducted in a manner which recognizes differences and conflicts as valuable, reconcilable ingredients, rather than obstacles to relating and growth."[15]

Follow Up

As with most therapies, follow-up procedures vary more with clinic policy and therapist predilection or research interests than with theoretical considerations. Usually it is hoped that the therapy experience will have taught the family to recognize signals of problems which require second-order change, and that the family members can engage in a realistic assessment of the limits of family coping devices. If this has been achieved, when they decide that outside help is again needed, the family is expected to recontact the therapist. It is also likely that one positive legacy of the relationship with the therapist will be a continuing interest by the therapist as well as the family in their continued progress.

Economic Implications

Since family treatment requires interviews longer than fifty minutes, initially it may be considered an expensive type of intervention. If cotherapists are used. there is extra time required outside of the interviews to work out cotherapy relationships. In addition, from the family's point of view, all members must sacrifice many other activities and employment in order to come in. And when members of the extended family are brought in for interviews from far away, it is additionally expensive and time-consuming. On the other hand, family treatment can be considered highly economical, in that all members benefit from one intervention. With system changes, one avoids the requirement that different members of the family are seen individually, concurrently, or sequentially for years. There are cases described in which five or six family members were each in individual treatment—a situation which actually may have prolonged and exacerbated the original conflicted situation. In addition, crisis intervention programs such as that described by Langsley and Kaplan[14] have demonstrated that by maintaining the identified patient in the family, the costs of hospitalization and the painful effects of separation are avoided.

Relationship to Other Modalities of Treatment

As has been stated throughout this chapter, no matter what the eventual treatment modality, a family system point of view is valuable in conceptualizing the difficulties experienced by a child. If introduced at the beginning of the contract with the therapist, family interviews can be used most easily in conjunction with other interventions. In this manner, they may serve as a bridge to marital work, individual treatment, filial therapy. and the like. A therapist who has begun with a traditional individual contract may encounter some technical difficulties if a move to family interviews is indicated. There are different ground rules as to confidentiality; the view of the presenting problem may be conceptualized in a radically different manner; and most important, the therapist may not be able to extricate himself from his initial strong alignment with those family forces which demand an identified patient. Sometimes, this is best accomplished by another therapist who is not similarly encumbered.

Treatment Results

The assessment of the process of family interviews, much less the validity of their outcome, is a task which is only beginning to be attacked in a rigorous manner. In a recent review of outcome studies of family treatment, Wells and associates[62] found few which met their requirements for adequate research design. They suggest, however, that promising outcome measurement methodology can be developed for family therapy. In addition, they conclude that at this point, the accumulation of case studies using clinical evaluations of outcome suggests that improvement does take place in a majority of the cases treated by family therapy. With adults, their figures show that family treatment of identified patients shows an overall success rate comparable to that of individual treatment. Where the identified patient is a child or an adolescent, the figures for family treatment show a somewhat higher success rate than those reported for individual treatment with similar populations.

REFERENCES

1. ACKERMAN, N. W., "Family Psychotherapy and Psychoanalysis: The Implications of Difference," *Family Process, 9:*5–18, 1970.

2. ———, *Treating the Troubled Family*, Basic Books, New York, 1966.

3. ———, *The Psychodynamics of Family Life*, Basic Books, New York, 1958.

4. ———, "The Unity of the Family," *Archives of Pediatrics, 35:*51–62, 1938.

5. ———, BEATMAN, F. L., and SHERMAN, S. N. (Eds.), *Expanding Theory and Practice in Family Therapy*, Family Service Association of America, New York, 1967.

6. ANTHONY, E. J., and BENEDEK, T. (Eds.), *Parenthood: Its Psychology and Psychopathology*, Little, Brown & Co., Boston, 1970.

7. BATESON, G., et al., "Toward a Theory of Schizophrenia," *Behavioral Science, 1:*251–264, 1956.

8. BEAL, E. W., "Current Trends in the Training of Family Therapists," *American Journal of Psychiatry, 133:*137–141, 1976.

9. BEELS, C., and FERBER, A., "What Family Therapists Do," in Ferber, A., Mendelsohn, M., and Napier, A. (Eds.), *The Book of Family Therapy*, pp. 168–232, Jason Aronson, New York, 1972.

10. BELL, J. E., *Family Therapy*, Jason Aronson, New York, 1975.

11. ———, "A Theoretical Position for Family Group Therapy," *Family Process, 2:*1–4, 1963.

12. ———, "Family Group Therapy," *Public Health Monograph Number 64*, United States Government Printing Office, Washington, D.C., 1961.

13. BLOCH, D., and LAPIERRE, K., "Techniques of Family Therapy, A Conceptual Frame," in Bloch, D. (Ed.), *Techniques of Family Psychotherapy: A Primer*, pp. 1–19, Grune & Stratton, New York, 1973.

14. BOSZORMENYI-NAGY, I., and FRAMO, J. L., *Intensive Family Therapy*, Harper & Row, New York, 1965.

15. ———, and SPARK, G. M., *Invisible Loyalties: Reciprocity in Intergenerational Family Therapy*, Harper & Row, Hagerstown, Md., 1973.

16. BOWEN, M., "Family Therapy and Family Group Therapy," in Kaplan, H. I., and Sadock, B. J. (Eds.), *Comprehensive Group Psychotherapy*, pp. 384–421, Williams & Wilkins, Baltimore, 1971.

17. ———, "The Use of Family Theory in Clinical Practice," in Haley, J. (Ed.), *Changing Families*, pp. 159–192, Grune & Stratton, New York, 1971.

18. BUCKLEY, W., *Modern Systems Research for the Behavioral Scientist*, Aldine Publishing Co., Chicago, 1968.

19. EPSTEIN, M., RAKOFF, V., and SIGAL, J. J., *The Family Category Schema*, Unpublished manuscript, Department of Psychiatry, Jewish General Hospital, Montreal, Quebec, 1968.

20. FERBER, A., MENDELSOHN, M., and NAPIER, A., *The Book of Family Therapy*, Jason Aronson, New York, 1972.

21. FERREIRA, A. J., "Family Myths," in Cohen, M. (Ed.), *Family Structure, Dynamics, and Theory*, pp. 85–90, Psychiatric Research Report no. 20, American Psychiatric Association, Washington, D.C., 1966.

22. FRAMO, J. L., "Symptoms from a Family Transactional Viewpoint," in Sager, C. J., and Kaplan, H. S. (Eds.), *Progress in Group and Family Therapy*, pp. 271–308, Bruner/Mazel, New York, 1972.

23. ———, "Rationale and Techniques of Intensive Family Therapy," in Boszormenyi-Nagy, I., and Framo, J. L. (Eds.), *Intensive Family Therapy*, pp. 143–212, Harper & Row, New York, 1965.

24. FRIEDMAN, A. J., et al., *Therapy with Families of Sexually Acting Out Girls*, Springer Publishing Co., New York, 1971.

25. FRIEDMAN, A. S., et al., *Psychotherapy for the Whole Family in Home and Clinic*, Springer Publishing Co., New York, 1965.

26. GLICK, I. D., and KESSLER, D. R., *Marital and Family Therapy*, Grune & Stratton, New York, 1974.

27. GRAY, W., DUHL, F. J., and RIZZO, N. D. (Ed.), *General Systems Theory and Psychiatry*, Little, Brown and Co., Boston, 1969.

28. GROTJAHN, M., *Psychoanalysis and the Family Neurosis*, W. W. Norton, New York, 1960.

29. Group for the Advancement of Psychiatry, *The Field of Family Therapy*, Group for the Advancement of Psychiatry, New York, 1970.

30. HAJAL, F., "Post Suicide Grief Work in Family Therapy," *Journal of Marriage and Family Counseling, 3:*35–42, 1977.

31. HALEY, J., "A Review of the Family Therapy Field," in Haley, J., (Ed.), *Changing Families*, pp. 1–12, Grune & Stratton, New York, 1971.

32. ———, "Family Therapy," *International Journal of Psychiatry, 9:*233–242, 1970.

33. ———, *Strategies of Psychotherapy*, Grune & Stratton, New York, 1963.

34. ———, and HOFFMAN, L., *Techniques of Family Therapy*, Basic Books, New York, 1967.

35. HOWELLS, J. G., *Family Psychiatry*, Charles C Thomas, Springfield, Ill., 1963.

36. JACKSON, D. D., *Therapy Communication and Change: Human Communication*, vol. 2, Science and Behavior Books, Palo Alto, Calif., 1969.

37. ———, "The Study of the Family," *Family Process, 4:*1–20, 1965.

38. ———, and SATIR, V. M., "A Review of Psychiatric Developments in Family Diagnosis and Family Therapy," in Ackerman, N. W., Beatman, F. L., and Sherman, S. N. (Eds.), *Exploring the Base for Family Therapy*, pp. 29–51, Family Service Association of America, New York, 1961.

39. ———, and WEAKLAND, J. H., "Conjoint Family Therapy: Some Considerations on Theory, Technique and Results," *Psychiatry, 24:*30–45, 1961.

40. KRAMER, C. H., *Psychoanalytically Oriented Family Therapy: Ten Year Evolution in a Private Child Psychiatry Practice*, The Family Institute of Chicago, Oak Park, Ill., 1968.

41. ———, et al., *Beginning Phase of Family Treat-*

ment: Proceedings of a Workshop on Family Therapy, The Family Institute of Chicago, Oak Park, Ill., 1968.

42. LAING, R. D., "Mystification, Confusion and Conflict," in Boszormenyi-Nagy, I., and Framo, J. L. (Eds.), *Intensive Family Therapy: Theoretical and Practical Aspects*, pp. 343–363, Harper & Row, New York, 1965.

43. ———, and Esterson, A., *Sanity, Madness and the Family: Families of Schizophrenics*, Penguin Books, Baltimore, 1964.

44. LANGSLEY, D. G., and KAPLAN, D. M., *The Treatment of Families in Crisis*, Grune & Stratton, New York, 1968.

45. LIDZ, T., *The Origin and Treatment of Schizophrenic Disorders*, Basic Books, New York, 1973.

46. MACGREGOR, R., et al., *Multiple Impact Therapy with Families*, McGraw-Hill, New York, 1964.

47. MEISSNER, W. W., "Thinking about the Family: Psychiatric Aspects," in Ackerman, N. W. (Ed.), *Family Process*, pp. 131–170, Basic Books, New York, 1970.

48. MINUCHIN, S., *Families and Family Therapy*, Harvard University Press, Cambridge, 1974.

49. ———, et al., *Families of the Slums: An Exploration of Their Structure and Treatment*, Basic Books, New York, 1967.

50. MONTALOV, B., and HALEY, J., "In Defense of Child Therapy," *Family Process*, 12:227–244, 1973.

51. PAPAJOHN, J., and SPIEGEL, J., *Transactions in Families*, Jossey-Bass, San Francisco, 1975.

52. PAUL, N. L., and GROSSER, G. H., "Operational Mourning and Its Role in Conjoint Family Therapy," *Community Mental Health Journal*, 1:339–345, 1965.

53. PITTMAN, F. S., "Managing Acute Psychiatric Emergencies: Defining the Family Crisis," in Bloch, D. A. (Ed.), *Techniques of Family Psychotherapy: A Primer*, pp. 99–107, Grune & Stratton, New York, 1973.

54. RAPOPORT, R., "Normal Crises, Family Structure and Mental Health, *Family Process*, 2:68–80, 1963.

55. SATIR, V., *Conjoint Family Therapy: A Guide*, Science and Behavior Books, Palo Alto, Calif., 1964.

56. ———, STACHOWIAK, J., and TASCHMAN, H. A.,

Helping Families to Change, Jason Aronson, New York, 1975.

57. SONNE, J. C., SPECK, R. V., and JUNGREIS, J. E., "The Absent Member Maneuver as a Resistance in Family Therapy of Schizophrenia," *Family Process*, 1:44–62, 1962.

58. SPECK, R. V., "Some Specific Therapeutic Techniques with Schizophrenic Families," in Friedman, A. S., et al. (Eds.), *Psychotherapy for the Whole Family*, pp. 197–205, Springer Publishing Company, New York, 1965.

59. ———, and ATTNEAVE, C. L., *Family Networks*, Pantheon Books, New York, 1973.

60. WATZLAWICK, P., BEAVIN, J. H., and JACKSON, D. D., *Pragmatics of Human Communication*, W. W. Norton, New York, 1967.

61. ———, WEAKLAND, J. H., and FISCH, R., *Change: Principles of Problem Formation and Problem Resolution*, W. W. Norton, New York, 1974.

62. WELLS, R. A., DILKES, T. C., and TRIVELLI, N. C., "The Results of Family Therapy: A Critical Review of the Literature," *Family Process*, 11:189–207, 1972.

63. WHITAKER, C., "My Philosophy of Psychotherapy," *Journal of Contemporary Psychotherapy*, 6:49–52, 1973.

64. WYNNE, L. C., "Some indications and Contraindications for Exploratory Family Therapy," in Boszormenyi-Nagy, I., and Framo, J. L. (Eds.), *Intensive Family Therapy: Theoretical and Practical Aspects*, pp. 289–322, Harper & Row, New York, 1965.

65. ———, et al., "Pseudomutuality in the Family Relations of Schizophrenics," *Psychiatry*, 21:205–220, 1958.

66. ZILBACH, J. J., "The Family in Family Therapy: Discussion," *Journal of the American Academy of Child Psychiatry*, 13:459–467, 1974.

67. ZUK, G. H., *Family Therapy: A Triadic-Based Approach*, Behavioral Publications, New York, 1971.

68. ———, and RUBENSTEIN, D., "A Review of Concepts in the Study and Treatment of Families of Schizophrenics," in Boszormenyi-Nagy, I., and Framo, J. L. (Eds.), *Intensive Family Therapy*, pp. 1–32, Harper & Row, New York, 1965.

8 / Parent Counseling and Therapy

Edward Sperling

Description of the Method

In this chapter, parent counseling and therapy are conceived of as therapeutic measures undertaken with parents for the primary purpose of helping their children. Parent *counseling* refers to a relationship between a therapist and parent in which educational methods directed primarily toward the conscious ego of the parent are used in order to further some therapeutic goal for the child. Parent *therapy* refers to psychotherapy of the parents focused around issues of the parent-child relationship. Its purpose is to shed light on the conscious and unconscious structure and dynamics of these

relationships so that they can be improved for the benefit of the child. The borderline between parent counseling and parent therapy is not always sharp, and the therapist may shift from one approach to the other, even within a single session. Nonetheless, at times, the centers of gravity of the two approaches are sufficiently wide apart that they need separate consideration. At other times, these two techniques can be discussed under the umbrella term of counseling.

Parent counseling and therapy are usually adjuncts to child psychotherapy. However, some children, particularly young ones, may be treated by working with the parents exclusively.[16,39] In the therapy of older children, the parents may be seen by the child's therapist or by another therapist. In the traditional child guidance team, the child is seen by the psychiatrist while the mother (the more usual parent seen in counseling) is seen by a social worker. However, today this division of labor is more varied and flexible, being shared by psychologists, special educators, nurses, and child development specialists of varying backgrounds.*

Parent counseling can take place with an individual parent, a married couple. in a family interview, or in a parent group. It can have as its aim the amelioration of ongoing suffering in the child (as well as in the family), or it can have a preventive function, such as counseling parents how best to handle the child's feelings about the death of a beloved grandparent.

History

It is well known that the history of modern child psychotherapy begins with a variant of parent counseling—in this case with the father of "Little Hans."[15] In effect, the father blended the roles of father and therapist under the tutelage of Freud. At that time, Freud felt that only because the authority of both father and physician were united in a single person, who possessed a combination of affectionate care and scientific interest, was it possible to apply the psychoanalytic method to a child. While it later became evident that this restriction did not hold, it is ironic that later child psychotherapists felt uncomfortable in dealing directly with the parents of the children whom they were treating. In 1948, Bruch[5] "confessed" that when she first went into the private practice of child psychiatry, she labored under the conviction that dealing with the parent when the child was under treatment was not quite right in that the parents should be handled by someone else.

When child psychoanalysis began to develop in Europe in the 1920s (coinciding approximately with the development of child guidance clinics in the United States), it became apparent that dealing with parents was an indispensable part of treating children. In clinics, the child guidance "team" of pediatrician, child psychiatrist, psychologist, and social worker became the model for child psychiatric care.

* See references 2, 4, 5, 6, 7, 9, 12, 14, 16, 21, 22, 31, 35, 38, 39, and 42.

As the field of child psychotherapy widened its scope to include psychotic children, institutionalized children, and very young children, and as experience in the practice of child psychotherapy accumulated, various patterns of parent involvement were added to the pattern of the traditional "team." In private practice, individual psychotherapists began dealing regularly with parents as part of the child's treatment, sometimes treating mother and child in joint sessions, and sometimes conducting parallel individual treatment of parents and children. The model of the treatment of Little Hans was rediscovered and extended so that some children have been treated exclusively through their parents under the direction of a child therapist. More recently, techniques of family therapy (see chapter 7) have combined elements of parent counseling with the examination of family dynamics.[1] In addition, group counseling of mothers, fathers, and of parental pairs has become part of the broadened range of parent counseling.[10, 30, 44]

Theory or Rationale

WHO IS THE PRIMARY PATIENT?

When a child is brought for psychiatric care, some special questions arise as to how to conceptualize his psychopathology. Is his symptom a reflection of a family disturbance? If it is, does the symptom have "a life of its own" or is it dependent entirely upon a set of intrafamilial dynamics? What are the boundaries between the child as a self-contained individual and his family? It is evident that the type and variety of treatment ap chosen will depend upon how such questio answered.

The age and stage of development of the child, the degree of his psychopathology, the emotional intactness of the family, the role of specific traumata (e.g., death of a parent or severe physical handicap), and the degree of emotional individuation of each member of the family, will all influence conceptions of psychopathology and treatment strategies. The philosophy, training, and goals of the therapist will also have an influence. A family therapist will be prone to conceptualize childhood disturbances as part of family pathology, and may recommend family therapy. A child psychoanalyst may aim at unraveling rigid and maladaptive psychic structure in the child through child analysis. The judgment about how to proceed will depend on the therapist's evaluation of the psychological openness of the family and the motivations of the family members for help. Once they make the decision to seek psychiatric aid, some parents are open to self-examination. Others resent any implication that they play a significant role in the child's difficulties. The therapist must synthesize these elements into a therapeutic approach which will be practical for the particular child and family. In addition, the approach must be flexible, so that the parent counseling, child interviews, and family interviews can be brought into play as clinical needs demand.

In any case, each professional should make his judgment on the basis of a careful diagnostic appraisal of the child within the family and should be aware of the limitations of his own particular training and experience. However, since no hard and fast rules exist, these judgments are not easily made.

FORGING A THERAPEAUTIC ALLIANCE WITH PARENTS

In order to achieve successful child treatment, a therapeutic, or perhaps more accurately, a *caretaking alliance* must be created between therapist and parents.[9] In describing an introductory phase to child psychoanalysis, Anna Freud[14] told of how she lost a patient because of the failure to establish a proper bond with the parents. When this bond is formed, it enables the parents to join the therapist in making a contribution to their child. This serves to raise the self-esteem of the parents and to strengthen their parental abilities. It allows them to transmit to the child a feeling of trust in the therapy. This will help minimize the child's conflict of loyalty between his attachment to the therapist and to the parents. Ultimately, this critical bond enables the parents to sustain the treatment through its difficult episodes.

When child therapy fails, it usually founders on the rock of poor therapist-parent communication.[31]

TECHNICAL LIMITS IMPOSED BY THE IMMATURITY OF CHILDREN

The young child in therapy cannot be expected to provide the therapist with an ongoing account of his daily life. He may spend sessions after session elaborating a special theme in play; through all this, he may never mention that he is failing in school, or that his father is suffering from a severe depression. While certain information can be gleaned from the child's productions, it is gener-

ally the parent who must supply the everyday context for the child's therapy.

In addition, the child's commitment to treatment may be fragile due to his emotional lability, his inability to escape his egocentrism, and his inability to understand long-range goals. In these respects, too, the parents must serve as auxiliary egos.

EDUCATIONAL FUNCTION OF COUNSELING

Counseling may be used to educate the parent regarding:

1. Normal child development—for example, the natural curiosity of children; their interest in genital play; their need and capacity to understand how their bodies function.
2. Children's reaction to stress—for example, how children respond to stress, death of a beloved pet, or friend, or family member.
3. The nature of the child's psychopathology—for example, how to understand the diagnosis of specific learning disability, or childhood autism; how to understand the dynamics of symptomatic acts such as stealing or fire setting.
4. Enriching the parent's pattern of parenting—for example, expanding the repertoire of parental responses[3, 18, 19, 32] and offering alternative frameworks for understanding and dealing with problems of discipline.[13]
5. Instructing and elucidating parental reactions to stress in the child and in the family—for example, parental reactions to loss of a child. An illustration:

A one-year-old boy died on the operating table while undergoing surgery for the removal of a brain tumor. His three-year-old sister was later told that God took her brother to heaven. No other explanation was offered. In addition, in order to protect their daughter from their grief, the parents did not show signs of sadness or depression in front of the girl. The girl reacted by frantically searching the house for her brother. She could not believe he was gone. She developed a general fearfulness, especially about being separated from her parents and at going to sleep. She became generally cranky, clinging, and immature. In desperation, the parents sought help in a child guidance clinic. They were advised to tell their daughter that her brother had had a terrible illness which the doctors could not cure and that her brother died. Also, the parents were urged to share their sad feelings with the child. When the parents explained the death of her brother, the daughter listened with intense interest. Her response was to be vary angry with the doctors for not saving her brother, and with her parents for not even feeling sad that he was gone. It was only then that the parents could overcome their own reluctance and tell the girl how much they had loved her brother, how hard everyone tried to save him, and how unhappy they were that he died. The parents cried, and for the first time, the daughter cried as well. Her fear and other symptoms dramatically abated.[37]

The parents' reluctance to explain death to a young child and their attempts to shield their daughter from what they fear might be overwhelming feelings are not unusual responses to such a painful event. The girl's reaction, in turn, could also be anticipated. Her mistrust of the inadequate explanation of her brother's disappearance, her resulting fear of this threatening unknown, her anger at her parents and the doctors for having allowed this tragedy to occur, all are the expected reactions of a young child in these circumstances. While one can question whether these parents have a pathological need to avoid painful events and to be overprotective, one does not have to resort to account of personal psychopathology as the only possible explanation. Cultural patterns. education, experience in living, and psychological understanding all play a role. Simply informing the parents about how people behave under such circumstances can frequently go a long way toward resolving traumatic reactions. Further delving into the personality structure of the parents or child may not be necessary; indeed, it may even be inappropriate.

Parents who are confronted by a situation in which a child is placed under unusual stress usually need counseling. Such events may include divorce, adoption, placement of a child outside the immediate family, major illnesses in the child or in the immediate family, debilitating accidents affecting the child or family, major psychiatric illness in the child or family, and developmental disturbances in the child. For example, parents need a great deal of information and guidance about how to deal with a schizophrenic child, or with a diabetic child, how to anticipate and cope with children's reactions to a parent who develops multiple sclerosis, and so on—for so many of life's vicissitudes.

6. Preparing a parent for his or her own psychotherapy—Some parents see their own role as merely dropping the child off at the office—the "doorstep case"[5] or the "garage syndrome"[39] (like leaving your car to be fixed). They expect the therapist to do the entire job. Most parents, however, sincerely want to take an actvie role in helping their children. In counseling, such parents may be stimulated by the understanding of the therapist, by the chlid's improvement, or by acquiring insight into themselves. They may request personal psychotherapy. The counselor must explore this carefully and make an appropriate recommendation. (See the section on technique.)

Indications for Parent Counseling

Parent counseling can be used as a method of child therapy, as an adjunct to child therapy, and as an educational aid in difficult. stressful circumstances such as preparing a child for surgery.

As a method of child therapy, parent counseling alone may suffice for the treatment of developmental disturbances in the first three or four years of life.[16, 39] (See the case illustration described later in this chapter and for more details about this approach, consult chapter 9).

As an adjunct to therapy with young children, it is essential that parents be seen for the reasons previously mentioned. In the case of older, more mature or less pathological adolescents, parental counseling may be held to a minimum.[42]

For tiding parents and children over stressful events, such as hospitalization, surgery, or divorce, parent counseling may be helpful.

CASE ILLUSTRATION

Fred, a four-year-old boy, was admitted for abdominal exploration of his undescended testes. By the morning of surgery, the parents had not yet explained anything to Fred about the purpose of his hospitalization and had not mentioned surgery. This lack of preparation resulted more from ignorance than from parental pathology; when offered the possibility, the parents responded very favorably to counseling on the pediatric ward. Surgery was performed and no testes were present. All that could be found were some rudimentary nubbins of testicular tissue. The parents then asked for advice as to how to explain this to Fred, and how to respond to questions of friends and family about the surgery. Their own concerns about Fred's development were also discussed. Telephone follow up a few months later indicated that the family weathered the entire incident well, as evidenced by Fred feeling free to discuss his experiences and questions with his parents, and they in turn feeling more assured in their handling of these issues.

Complications, Disadvantages, or Side Effects

Parent counseling as a part of child therapy is subject to the following difficulties or pitfalls: (1) issues of confidentiality; (2) adverse emotional responses by parent or child to the counseling arrangement; and (3) difficulties of coordination within the therapeutic team.

CONFIDENTIALITY

The bedrock of psychotherapy is the trust of the patient in the integrity of the therapist. An important element in this trust is the therapist's commitment to keep confidential the patient's communication. Adolescents, with their intense concerns about autonomy, integrity, and emerging sexuality, are particularly unwilling to have their inner life exposed to their parents. However, even rebellious adolescent patients understand the need for their therapy to be safeguarded by a trusting relationship between their parents and the therapist.

CASE ILLUSTRATION

A fourteen-year-old boy was referred for consultation after the breakup of previous psychotherapy. His original treatment was undertaken because he was constantly defiant and furious with his parents, culminating in his trying to run away from home by stowing away in an airplane. His first therapist saw him three times per week and had no contact with the parents. The results of psychological testing also were not shared with the parents. The father suspected that his son was psychotic and that this was being withheld from him. He arranged for a physician friend to receive a copy of the test results. In this way, the father learned that his son had some "schizophrenic features," information which he repeated to his son. At this point, the therapy was terminated by the parents and a new consultation requested. The second psychiatrist, who worked primarily with the boy, communicated with the parents enough to allay their anxiety and win their confidence. It was possible then to proceed with long-term therapy. The youngster never questioned the necessity of the parental counseling; indeed he understood that it was necessary to his treatment.

In treating children, the issue of confidentiality arises in a different way. Children expect their parents to know a great deal about them, to choose the therapist, to make all the arrangements, and to "run the show." Confidentiality is not uppermost in their mind, and it becomes important only when there is a family tradition of secrecy or when special sexual, aggressive, or antisocial secrets come to the fore. At those times, the child may have to be reminded that what he says is confidential. However, such issues are not usually encountered until an advanced stage of treatment. In contrast, the adolescent frequently enters treatment with conscious guilt. If he can be assured of confidentiality, he is often quite ready to speak. In general, it is fair to say that although confidentiality must be maintained, concerns about confidentiality are not as prominent in the therapy of children as in the treatment of adolescents. In either case, it is important for the therapist to be sensitive to the youngster's attempts to ask for help in being able to share burdensome secrets with the parents under the guise of a concern about confidentiality.

ADVERSE EMOTIONAL RESPONSES TO COUNSELING ARRANGEMENTS

Adverse responses to counseling usually occur in two circumstances: the mistrustful adolescent and the reticent parent. The adolescent who is angry, rebellious, and has to be coerced into treatment presents a familiar. if not too promising, clinical picture. Under these circumstances, it is frequently helpful to meet with the adolescent before seeing the parents. This allows an opportunity to forge a therapeutic alliance with the youngster which can later withstand the stress of involving the parents. An initial family interview may serve a similar purpose. Here, separate clinicians for the youngster and for the parents may diminish this problem, although such a team arrangement should not completely cut off the youngster's therapist from the parents.

As previously mentioned, there are parents who want little or no participation in their child's treatment. This attitude may arise from a number of different sources, including a painful feeling of being a failure as a parent, a fear of opening up old areas of trauma, or as part of a more general rejection of the child. At times, the therapist must content himself with working exclusively with the child. (For a discussion of why the parent should not be seen by the same therapist who is conducting the child's *psychoanalysis*, see Weiss[43]). This can be successful if the parent's underlying attitude is a wish for the child to get well. Sometimes, after beginning work directed primarily toward the child, the parent overcomes his or her reluctance to being involved, especially after seeing some improvement in the child. At other times, the therapist may judge that treating the child without working with the parent might be yet another step in the alienation of the parent from the child. If this appears to be the case. the therapist may direct his efforts toward working this problem through with the parents, or he may consider advising a more radical separation of child from parent, as described in chapters 15 and 18.

COORDINATION DIFFICULTIES IN THE THERAPEUTIC TEAM

The traditional team approach in which the child and parents are treated by different members of the team provides certain advantages—for example, it is time-saving, in that parent and child can be seen individually at the same time—but this approach also entails difficulties in coordination between the therapists. The two therapists must communicate regularly with each other so that each may benefit from the other's work. They must also maintain a consistent view of the clinical issues involved and the way to approach them. Each therapist must avoid the tendency to overidentify with his own client at the expense of a sympathetic understanding of the other patient. While those pitfalls can be overcome by a team of professionals who have a high regard for each other and who are used to working together, there still remains the difficulty of professional time spent in coordinating their efforts. This is best overcome in clinics, where the professionals work side by side and can communicate about several patients and other matters as a regular part of their work.[23] In private practice, this is more difficult to achieve, and more rarely accomplished.

Contraindications

There are a few instances in which parent counseling is either contraindicated or approached with the utmost caution. These instances usually involve clinic care in the face of strong objection of one or more family members toward counseling. An unusual, although not a rare instance, is that of an adolescent who applies for psychiatric help at a clinic but only under the condition that this be kept secret from his family. Sometimes this wish for secrecy is realistic and rests upon the knowledge that the parents would disrupt the therapy if they knew about it. At other times, this secrecy is part of an exaggerated mistrust which needs working out in treatment. In either case, an immediate contact with the parents against the wish of the adolescent is generally contraindicated. The exception to this rule arises when the adolescent is in danger of seriously destructive behavior, either toward himself or others, in which case the therapist may have to alert both the parents and/or other authorities.

Another contraindication arises when one parent, usually the mother, insists that the other parent not be told about the treatment. This type of situation also arises mainly in clinics and frequently involves fathers who are paranoid or dangerous. Here the therapist must be careful to be alert to the possibility that this view of the father is distorted. but this can only be ascertained as the relationship with the mother and child unfolds.

Another contraindication arises when only one parent has custody of the child and does not wish the therapist to be in touch with the other parent. Here, one must respect the wishes of the parent who has the responsibility for raising the child. Of course, such parental attitudes may change as therapy progresses.

The parent in individual therapy—is this a contraindication for counseling? If a child is about to begin psychotherapy, what should be recommended for a parent, especially the mother. who may herself be in therapy or in psychoanalysis? Should the parent's therapy be relied upon to help the mother cope better with the child? The answer seems to be: in the long run, yes; but in the short run—and in a child's timetable[20] this may be a long time—no. Every psychotherapy, especially if it is nondirective, uncovering therapy, has its own agenda. The treatment of a parent may or may not focus upon the parent-child relationship. The parent's treatment might even interfere with the treatment of the child. An example:

> The mother of a child in treatment was herself in personal analysis. She developed a hostile attitude toward the child's therapist, even while acknowledging that the child was improving in treatment. The two therapists met to discuss this situation, and the mother's analyst explained that the mother had a "split transference," the positive transference directed toward her analyst, the negative toward the child's therapist. Eventually, the child had to be transferred to another therapist.

The counseling of a parent need not interfere with the parent's own treatment. In fact, the counseling can serve as a means of pointing out patterns of difficulties to the parent, who may then find this a fruitful stimulus for his own treatment.

Technique of Counseling and Parent Treatment

TREATMENT OF THE CHILD BY MEANS OF COUNSELING THE PARENT[16, 39]

This is a method which, for a number of reasons, has been used particularly for preschool children[16] and is discussed in more detail in chapter 9. In the preschool years, the youngster's life is centered in his home, and particularly in the relationship with his mother. The young child is particularly susceptible to the mother's moods and to her means of handling him. The mother, in turn, is in close touch with the child, both physically and emotionally, even where there are gross misinterpretations of the child's behavior. Any increase in the mother's understanding and competence in handling the child has profound, long-term consequences. Enhanced competence makes the mother feel closer and happier about herself and her child. The child is then exposed to a twenty-four-hour-per-day "therapy" in the form of enriched openness and understanding from the parent. Another benefit of such treatment is that the lessons learned in caring for one child can be generalized to the care of other children (and adults) in the family.

CASE ILLUSTRATION

A young married, professional couple were concerned about the development of their twenty-one-month-old daughter, Clara, their first and only child. She was described as beautiful and intellectually precocious. Her development had been smooth for the first year of life, but then she gradually became progressively more tense and anxious. At the time of referral, she was described as clinging to the mother and happy only when she was alone with either parent. She was frightened not only of strangers but also of her grandparents, aunts, uncles, and young cousins, all of whom she knew well. The mother was embarrassed to visit her family, because Clara would cling to her for hours at a time, not relaxing until the visit was over. In addition, Clara was afraid of loud noises and afraid to go to sleep. She appeared to be soothed more easily by her father than by her mother. Since the parents were planning to move to another part of the country in three months, there was a definite time limit for the intervention. Sessions with the mother were arranged, with the father joining whenever his schedule would permit. There were eight sessions in all, with the father participating in four.

Within the first two sessions, the following picture emerged. The mother, an intelligent, lively, energetic, strong-willed woman, was dismayed to see her daughter display qualities of fearfulness and clinging, which were entirely the opposite of mother's personality. The mother was afraid that her daughter would always remain a frightened and dependent shrinking violet. She had been dealing with this behavior by admonishing Clara not to be afraid and to stand on her own two feet. When Clara tried to climb on her lap, she would push her away, thus trying to foster independence. The father, who was generally more relaxed and openly warm, had less trouble dealing with Clara, such as when putting her to bed. Mother was aware of this discrepancy and felt pained that her daughter seemed more relaxed with her husband. She attributed this partly to her husband's being too "indulgent" with Clara but admitted that her husband had a more easygoing, relaxed approach.

The turning point in the counseling came when the mother was asked what she thought would happen if she complied with all of Clara's demands. The mother was startled by this question. She then sputtered out that she assumed Clara would become increasingly demanding and lose whatever independence she had. This attitude was questioned. Discussion was directed toward the developing child's own thrust to mature and become independent.

The mother was urged to reduce her efforts to push Clara into independence; instead it was suggested that she allow herself to trust the child's own drive to develop. She was able to accept this advice in an intellectual way, and the next few sessions were devoted to going over mother-child interactions in some detail, as they were lived out in various settings, and in helping the mother prepare the child for their move. Father participated by encouraging his wife to experiment and by avoiding interposing himself too quickly between wife and daughter.

The mother was able to translate the counseling into a more indulgent and less pressured attitude toward Clara. The girl responded quickly, first by being more clinging, and then by becoming more relaxed. Greatly encouraged and stimulated by her daughter's improvement, the mother began to shed her fears about her daughter's ultimate development. Shortly before the move, remarking on the virtual disappearance of Clara's anxious, clinging behavior, the mother remarked, "I never could have believed that a child would change so much in such a short time."

During the counseling, the mother inadvertently dropped hints about her own struggle for independence, but she quickly shied away from even the slightest show of interest in her own history. At the end of this brief counseling, she was perfectly content with the results and showed no curiosity about why she had had the trouble with Clara in the first place. She did, however, state that if she needed help for Clara in the future, she would not hesitate to look for it.

COUNSELING PARENTS AS AN ADJUNCT TO THE CHILD'S TREATMENT*

In arranging for the psychotherapy of a child or a young adolescent, the therapist may wish to see the child one or more times per week, and the mother at weekly interviews. As clinical necessity and schedules permit, fathers may be invited to join the mothers in their sessions. An understanding is reached with mother and child that the purpose of the parental interviews is twofold: to obtain information about the child's life and to help the mother better understand the child. It is often wise to stipulate that what the child has to say will be kept confidential, but what the parents say will, in general, not be kept from the child. The therapist can respect the parents' wishes to maintain

---

* See references 5, 6, 8, 9, 14, 21, 23, 27, 31, 33, 36, 41, and 42.

parental secrets, for example an adopted child who has not been told of his adoption, but the therapist cannot be used as an ally in concealing such information indefinitely if the child indicates that he already suspects the truth. Nor can the therapist steer the child away from such material. as this would be antithetical to the basic thrust of the treatment. (Instead the parents will be asked to reconsider their policy of secrecy.) Parents almost invariably accept these conditions, and children rarely object to their parents' having independent sessions with the therapist. Occasionally, children will fear that the parents will reveal some very embarrassing information which the child has not yet expressed to the therapist, such as that the child has wet the bed or stolen something. But this is grist for the therapeutic mill as the child comes to trust the nonjudgmental attitude of the therapist.

In their sessions, the parent is encouraged to keep the therapist informed about the daily life of the child and to discuss any difficulties which may arise in his management. Issues which frequently arise during counseling include parental guilt over having failed the child, the ambivalent wish to be given magical formulas for soothing problems, and competition with the therapist for the affection of the child. Where the parents have been emotionally deprived, there may be competition with the child for the affection of the therapist.

Once the child's therapy is under way, new emotional hurdles are raised for the parents. The child's behavior begins to change, he may become more symptomatic, and he often begin to view his parents in a different way. Parents, who already feel outwitted or defeated by their children, may find that the child has now become a more sophisticated adversary, and all with the help of his new-found ally, paid for by the parents themselves.[16] It is no wonder, then, that when a child's therapy collapses, it is almost invariably due to a breakdown in the therapeutic alliance between therapist and parent rather than between therapist and child.

Just as there are pitfalls and dangers in child therapy, there are rewards and gratification which accrue when therapy is successful. As the therapy of an adult offers him a "second chance" to alter, make corrections, and repair the deprivations and distortions of his own childhood, so does the therapy of a child offer the parent a second chance at raising the child, correcting old maladaptive approaches, and finding new resources for helping the child grow. At the very least, the parent can feel helpful in supporting the treatment by bringing the child regularly, supplying vital information, and by demonstrating his or her helpfulness as an ally of the therapist.

In his role as counselor, the therapist must judge the mother's capacity for differentiating herself from the child, for objectively appraising the child's thoughts and difficulties, for tolerating an objective appraisal of her mothering function, and for being able to accept the implied criticism of suggestions on the part of the therapist. In addition. in that borderland between counseling and therapy, the therpist must appraise the mother's capacity to observe and absorb constructively the revival of issues which played important and sometimes traumatic roles in her own childhood.

CASE ILLUSTRATION

A mother of a five-year-old boy reacted to his sexually tinged attempts at "cuddling" by a passive withdrawal. This provoked the boy to increase his demands, now in a more aggressive way. In exasperation, the mother would then strike the child. In discussing her initial handling of the boy's request for affection, the mother linked her own sexually repressive upbringing with her withdrawal from her son.

Counseling has now crossed into therapy. The child therapist must be careful to realize the transference (and countertransference) potentials which may be stimulated by the parent becoming a patient, but the mother's capacity to make such connections and to generalize upon them must be respected. Such a parent may then go on to engage in therapy for herself or may be content with the occasional insights gained while examining her relationship to her child.

With these thoughts in mind, the counselor is guided by the following principles.

1. The goals of the parent and therapist for the child are fundamentally the same: to enhance the child's growth so that he can become a happier, more productive person. If these goals are not shared, for example, if the parent's attitudes and actions are overly constricting or sadistic, and if these attitudes are not subject to influence, then consideration has to be given to sending the child away from home or to helping the child cope with his difficult home situation.

2. The child's therapist should share with the parent the general nature of his work with the child. While the parents do not need to know the details of the child's fantasy life, they are entitled to know by what rules the child therapist operates, what sort of influences or values are being brought to bear on the child, how sensitive issues as religion and sexual enlightenment are handled. The parents should also be invited to periodic discussions of the goals of therapy and the child's progress.

3. The therapist or counselor should encourage the

parent to be an active participant in efforts to help the child. Particularly during the treatment of psychotic children, the educational and counseling role of the psychiatrist may be his most important contribution.

CASE ILLUSTRATION

The parents of a psychotic boy vacillated between seeing his behavior as the product of a completely disorganized mind, which was responding randomly to all stimuli, and regarding his behavior as almost entirely the product of willful malice. Careful and repeated attention to his psychotic outbursts convinced the parents that there was usually a discernible emotional precipitant to the upset, and that the disturbed behavior was frequently the result of overwhelming panic. After a while the parents could anticipate and avoid most of these episodes.

In dealing with less flagrant pathology, the focus of counseling shifts toward an examination of the more subtle dynamic interplay between mother and child.

CASE ILLUSTRATION

On eight-year-old boy was referred for difficulty in learning, disruptive behavior in school, and negativistic behavior at home. Previous psychological testing revealed difficulty in fine motor coordination and a diagnosis of mild brain damage. His parents had written off any future academic career for him and were concerned that he might not develop sufficient skills to finish high school and become self-supporting. In therapy, the boy revealed himself to be of above average intelligence but suffering from depression and low self-esteem. The mother was devoted to the boy but constantly criticized him. She could find little to like and nothing to admire in him. His father dealt with this problem mainly by withdrawing and remaining aloof. In addition to constantly finding fault with the youngster, the mother, in the course of her counseling sessions, also revealed her utter inability to help him. Not only was the boy a faliure, but she was constantly failing him. The therapeutic approach was to be accepting of and sympathetic with the difficult position of mother and child while simultaneously pointing out some of the strengths of both, for example, the mother's commitment to the child's treatment and the child's good athletic ability. As the mother saw improvement in her son, her own depression and self-criticism eased. She began to glimpse that she had identified her son with some aspects of her own unhappy childhood experiences.

JOINT TREATMENT OF CHILD AND PARENT

In this approach, mother and child are seen together in joint therapeutic sessions.* This technique is particularly well suited to the treatment of

* See references 2, 4, 12, 27, and 35.

young children and to children with separation problems. With the latter, the therapist frequently has no choice; if he is to treat the child at all, then the mother must be in the same room.[4]

CASE ILLUSTRATION

Greg, a three-year-old boy, was brought to treatment for excessive clinging to the mother and for general fearfulness. The parents were in the process of getting a divorce; the father had already moved out of the home. The mother was a full-time student in a professional school, and during the afternoon, the boy was left in the care of a babysitter. Greg attended a nursery school in the mornings, where he was quiet, overly polite, and somewhat withdrawn. There was a noticeable lack of self-assertion and complete absence of age-appropriate aggressive behavior.

Although he formed a rapid attachment to his warm, understanding, female therapist, he could not tolerate being in the office with her alone, even with mother sitting directly outside the room. The mother was, therefore, invited into the playroom, where she became an observer and passive participant in the treatment. At first, the child played polite tea party games and made numerous drawings. Gradually, he began to test the therapist by becoming more demanding and aggressive. He revealed fears about his father and anger toward him for leaving the house. He also noted mother's acceptance of his criticisms and angry outburts. After several months of weekly therapy, he was able to allow mother to remain in the waiting room throughout the session. He gradually became normally assertive at nursery school and generally more outgoing and lively.

The mother made many observations during the therapy. She became aware of the complexity of the boy's behavior and was able to see the link between his anger and his fear. She observed the therapist at work and learned how to be more sensitive to Greg's anxiety instead of being overwhelmed by it. She became open to Greg's newly voiced complaints against her and was able to respond without being defensive. At the end of the year, it was felt by both therapist and parents that Greg no longer needed treatment. Mother, however, planned to continue seeing the therapist to discuss some of her own reactions to her divorce.[40]

Seeing mother and child together has manifold benefits. It allows for a gradual separation of children and parents who are tightly bound together. It allows the mother to view her child with a new objectivity, first by sitting back and being an observer, second by seeing the child through the eyes of the therapist. It enables the mother to be a participant in the therapy, strengthening her role as caretaker of her child. It allows the mother to see the entire interaction between therapist and child so that projection and jealousy are held to a minimum. It provides the mother with a deeper understanding of the child and of her interaction with the child, and understanding which the mother will carry with her long beyond the therapy itself. From the child's point of view, this technique eliminates the child's dilemma of loyalty, split between therapist and mother, both of whom. in this arrangement, are seen to be working together harmoniously.

PARALLEL TREATMENT OF CHILD AND PARENT

"Parallel treatment" means that child and mother are each in independent psychotherapy. They may be treated either by the same or by different therapists.* While some authorities advise against the same therapist for parent and child, others have found this a useful approach.[12, 38] This technique requires great skill and experience (see discussion of Elkisch's paper by Kestenberg[12]), but it does have the great advantage of one therapist correlating the work between parent and child. With adolescents it is frequently wise to have a different therapist for the adolescent patient and for the parent. (See "Counseling Parents of Adolescents.")

COUNSELING OF FATHERS[10, 21]

In clinical work with children and adolescents, fathers are frequently the neglected member of the family. In our increasingly urbanized society, with fathers away at work during the day, child care becomes primarily a maternal responsibility. In disturbed families, this polarity in child rearing is frequently exaggerated and added to by sharp differences of outlook and continuing conflicts between the parents.[41] A mother may be concerned about her son's fighting in school and poor scholarship, while the father may see this behavior as a normal part of growing up. Some families are dominated by the mother, with the father taking a passive, peripheral role. Some disturbed fathers, who perceive themselves as destructive, will attempt to protect their children by keeping a great distance from them. The mother then fills the vacuum as best she may. It is important for the therapist not to support such pathological arrangements unwittingly by going along with comments from the mother as "my husband is too busy to get involved" or "he is not interested" or "he is against psychiatry." The therapist can show his interest in and respect for the father's position by involving the father from the start, and by pointing out to both parents that the father's help is needed for

evaluation and treatment of the child. For many fathers, the fact that their opinion and involvement is sought and valued is a novel and deeply gratifying experience. Even for those fathers who do not accept the invitation to participate, the door is left open by the therapist's interest and by his refusal to fall in automatically with the family's neurotic patterns, or with the father's problem of low esteem. Fathers who are at first reluctant to engage in counseling, or who even refuse to speak to the psychiatrist at all, quite often change their minds as they witness in their wives and children some constructive influences of the therapy. In particular, they are often encouraged if the wife's reports tell of the therapist's nonjudgmental attitude toward parents. The father may then spontaneously join the mother in counseling sessions or may finally respond to the therapist's repeated invitation. Sometimes, the father can be more easily reached if he is given an appointment for himself alone.

The experience of being a helpful participant in the child's therapy can initiate a positive sequence of events. In being a helper, the father's self-esteem is enhanced. He may then feel less threatened by his own punitive superego and become less defensive and more open to understanding his family. The potential for more harmonious relationships in the family and for a more effective working together are evident.

If the father's work schedule interferes with sharing all the counseling sessions with the mother, periodic sessions should be arranged for the father's convenience.

GROUP COUNSELING OF PARENTS†

Counseling of parents in groups has been used successfully as an adjunct to the therapy of children, both in residential centers and in clinics. In addition to reaching more parents in a given time, group counseling allows the parents to help each other. Parents in a group can accept observations, comments, and interpretations from their peers which might prove devastating if they came from a therapist. In addition, the group allows parents to identify with each other, to share feelings and problems in common, and to arrive at a more objective appraisal of their own functioning as parents. In recounting his experience with a mothers' group in a child guidance clinic, Jones[24] describes how the mothers set up their own meetings independent of any therapist. Mothers were

---

* See references 2, 7, 12, 22, and 38.

† See references 21, 22, 24, 31, and 44.

able to go on to provide supportive group treatment for other children. A fathers' group provides the special insights of parents "in the same boat." Also, it is a particularly good medium for fathers who are accustomed to keeping all their thoughts and feelings to themselves.

Within the group, there is a dilution of transference feelings. Hostile feelings toward the therapist can be supported by other group members, can be expressed vicariously through other group members, or can be displaced to other members of the group. This allows for a gradual and flexible working through of such feelings without the threat of a direct unsupported one to one confrontation with the therapist.

In hospital or residential treatment settings, group counseling, both short-term and long-term, has been helpful in allowing parents to overcome their guilt feelings about having raised children so seriously disturbed that they require inpatient care.[2, 11] A more humane approach to themselves and to the caretaking institution can be fostered by the group experience.

COUNSELING PARENTS OF ADOLESCENTS[2, 17, 42]

Because of the developmentally appropriate drive toward independence from parents, special attention needs to be given to the involvement of parents in the treatment of adolescents. In planning the counseling program for the parents of an adolescent in treatment, the critical elements are the maturity and degree of pathology of the youngster. The relatively healthy and mature older adolescent is able to provide the kind of information about his life which in child therapy is expected from the parent. In addition, such an adolescent is capable of running his own life well enough so that the parents are not excessively threatened and can support the therapy with relative equanimity from a distance. Frequently, an end-of-the-year meeting with the adolescent and his parents for a progress report is all the contact which the parents need. On the other hand, an adolescent who is seriously disturbed, truanting from school, running away from home, or endangering himself or others in any way creates a situation in which responsibility must be shared among the patient, therapist, and parents. What is most essential is that lines of communication are kept open, so that each can carry out his own responsibility in an open and mutually respectful way.

Younger adolescents who are not so verbal or so able to transmit a picture of their lives also need to be treated in conjunction with parent counseling. Counseling should be offered to parents who are motivated to help their adolescent youngsters or who need help themselves in maintaining their own equilibrium in dealing with their youngsters. If the parent is a candidate for personal psychotherapy, then it is usually advisable to refer the parent to another therapist. Provisions can then be made for communication between the parents and youngster's therapist, either directly or through the two therapists.

Preparation of Family and Child

As previously outlined, from the outset, the counseling of parents should be taken for granted as part of child psychotherapy. Children simply assume that their parents will be involved and rarely raise objections. When objections are raised, they can be discussed openly and the child assured of the confidentiality of his personal communications. Even more important, children can understand that a good working relationship between parent and therapist is necessary for safeguarding the treatment. The same considerations hold for young or very disturbed adolescents.

In preparing the parent, it is important to state what the therapist sees as the role of the counseling. Parents frequently feel strongly that any involvement implies that they, the parents, are being told that they need psychiatric treatment. Many parents resent this implication since they are satisfied with their own functioning and are convinced that the pathology lies only within the child. It is important to make clear that the parents are not being asked to enter psychiatric treatment for themselves. Rather, they are expected to aid in the treatment of the child by supplying vitally needed information about the past history and the ongoing life of the youngster and family. In addition, the counselor should enhance the parent's understanding of the child's functioning and pathology in order that the parent may have a broader and more appropriate range of responses to the youngster.

Parents frequently assume that after a few visits, the child therapist will be able to give advice on important decisions, such as whether to send the child to another school or to a summer camp, or that the therapist will have a ready answer for the daily interpersonal problems that arise at home. In some instances, that is, in fact, possible. As a rule, however, the patterning of maladaptive behavior may not be sufficiently visible at first either to the therapist or to the parent. The therapist will then have to point out that only after knowing the child and family over a period of time will he be able to give opinions based on knowledge. By then, he will be in a position to make connections between precipitants of disturbed behavior and the meaning of the behavior. Alternative solutions to the problem can thereupon be suggested or may suggest themselves.

CASE ILLUSTRATION

A fourteen-year-old girl disturbed her mother and stepfather by wanting free access to their bedroom during the evenings. She spent more time with them than in her own room. The mother regarded this behavior as one further example of the youngster's disregard of the mother's needs—the need for privacy. Despite many fights, the youngster persisted. Counseling sessions revealed that this girl, who had been her father's favorite, was in a chronic depression precipitated by her father's death several years before. When father was alive, the same parental bedroom was used as a combination family room and bedroom, so that the girl's behavior can be seen as her attempt to recapture the love she used to experience in that room. The mother saw spontaneously that this explanation tied together a number of observations and made sense out of them. Her attitude thereupon softened, and she found ways of supplying affection which avoided this conflict.

Economic Implications

In planning the therapy of a child, parent counseling must be included as part of the overall expense. Group work with children and parents reduces the financial burden of treatment, while seeing the parent and child simultaneously (either in a team arrangement or by one therapist) reduces the parent's burden of traveling. Because of the high level of parental involvement, child therapy tends to be very expensive, a factor which must be weighted in all mental health programs for children.

Frequency of Sessions

While child psychotherapy can range in frequency from one to five times per week, parents in counseling are seldom seen more often than once a week. After a solid working relationship is established between the therapist and parent and after the main educational goals of the counseling are met, the sessions may taper off to once every two weeks or even less often. As mentioned previously, for the more mature adolescents the frequency of counseling sessions for parents may be as little as once or twice per year. Of course, during acute crises, parents of any age child should be involved in a flexible way.

Patterns of Necessary Follow Up

Although there is a growing literature on follow-up studies in child psychiatry, and it is a critical factor in our understanding of psychopathology,[25, 34] this area remains underdeveloped. Until additional data are amassed, it is important to stress in this connection that successful parent counseling should leave the door open for future and follow up.

REFERENCES

1. ACKERMAN, N. W., *The Psychodynamics of Family Life*, Basic Books, New York, 1958.
2. BERRYMAN-SIMPSON, E., "The Simultaneous Treatment of a Mother and Child: The Mother's Side," *American Journal of Psychotherapy*, 17:266–274, 1963; also in Noland, R., *Counseling Parents of the Emotionally Disturbed Child*, pp. 195–205, Charles C Thomas, Springfield, Ill., 1972.
3. BETTELHEIM, B., *Dialogues with Mothers*, Free Press, New York, 1962.
4. BORNSTEIN, B., "The Analysis of a Phobic Child," in Eissler, R. S., et al. (Eds.), *The Psychoanalytic Study of the Child*, vol. 3/4, pp. 181–226, International Universities Press, New York, 1949.
5. BRUCH, H., "The Role of the Parent in Psychotherapy with Children," *Psychiatry*, 2:169–175, 1948; also in Noland, R., *Counseling Parents of the Emotionally Disturbed Child*, pp. 44–54, Charles C Thomas, Springfield, Ill., 1972.
6. BURLINGHAM, D., "Child Analysis and the Mother," *Psychoanalytic Quarterly*, 4:69, 1935; also in Haworth, M., *Child Psychotherapy*, pp. 69–92, Basic Books, New York, 1964.
7. ———, GOLDBERGER, A., and LUSSIER, A., "Simultaneous Analysis of Mother and Child," in Eissler, R. S., et al. (Eds.), *The Psychoanalytic Study of the Child*, vol. 10, pp. 165–186, International Universities Press, New York, 1955.
8. BUXBAUM, E., *Troubled Children in a Troubled World*, International Universities Press, New York, 1970.
9. CAREK, D. J., *Principles of Child Psychotherapy*, Charles C Thomas, Springfield, Ill., 1972.

10. CHALPIN, G., "The Father's Group," *Journal of the American Academy of Child Psychiatry, 5:*125–133, 1966; also in Noland, R., *Counseling Parents of the Emotionally Disturbed Child,* pp. 333–342, Charles C Thomas, Springfield, Ill., 1972.

11. EDWARD, J., "Extending a Hand to Parents of Disturbed Children," *Children, 14:*238–243, 1967; also in Noland, R., *Counseling Parents of the Emotionally Disturbed Child,* pp. 106–117, Charles C Thomas, Springfield, Ill., 1972.

12. ELKISCH, P., "Simultaneous Treatment of a Child and His Mother," *American Journal of Psychotherapy, 7:* 105–130, 1953; also in Noland, R., *Counseling Parents of the Emotionally Disturbed Child,* pp. 165–194, Charles C Thomas, Springfield, Ill., 1972.

13. FRAIBERG, S., *The Magic Years,* Charles Scribner's Sons, New York, 1959.

14. FREUD, A., *The Psycho-Analytical Treatment of Children,* Imago, London, 1946.

15. FREUD, S., "Analysis of a Phobia in a Five-Year-Old Boy," in Strachey, J. (Ed.), *The Standard Edition of the Complete Psychological Works of Sigmund Freud,* vol. 10, pp. 5–147, Hogarth Press, London, 1955.

16. FURMAN, E., "Treatment of Under-Fives by Way of Parents," in Eissler, R. S., et al. (Eds.), *The Psychoanalytic Study of the Child,* vol. 12, pp. 250–262, International Universities Press, New York, 1957.

17. GELEERD, E., "Some Aspects of Psychoanalytic Technique in Adolescence," in Eissler, R. S., et al. (Eds.), *The Psychoanalytic Study of the Child,* vol. 12, pp. 274–275, International Universiies Press, New York, 1957.

18. GINOTT, H., *Between Parents and Teenager,* Macmillan, Toronto, 1969.

19. ———, *Between Parent and Child,* Macmillan, New York, 1965.

20. GOLDSTEIN, J., FREUD, A., and SOLNIT, A., *Beyond the Best Interests of the Child,* Free Press, New York, 1973.

21. HAWORTH, M., *Child Psychotherapy,* Basic Books, New York, 1964.

22. HELLMAN, I., FRIEDMAN, O., and SHEPHEARD, E., "Simultaneous Analysis of a Mother and Child," in Eissler, R. S., et al. (Eds.), *The Psychoanalytic Study of the Child,* vol. 15, pp. 359–377, International Universities Press, New York, 1960.

23. JACKSON, L., and TODD, K. M., *Child Treatment and the Therapy of Play,* Methuen, London, 1947; also in Haworth, M., *Child Psychotherapy,* pp. 76–80, Basic Books, New York, 1964.

24. JONES, B. H., "Group Therapy for Mother and Children in Parallel," *The American Journal of Psychiatry, 125:*1439–1442, 1969. also in Noland, R., *Counseling Parents of the Emotionally Disturbed Child,* pp. 263–268, Charles C Thomas, Springfield, Ill., 1972.

25. KOHLBERG, L., LACROSSE, J., and RICKS, D., "The Predictability of Adult Mental Health from Child Behavior," in Wolman, B. B. (Ed.), *Manual of Child Psychopathology,* pp. 1217–1286, McGraw-Hill, New York, 1972.

26. LANGFORD, W. S., and OLSON, E., "Clinical Work with Parents of Child Patients," *Quarterly Journal of Child Behavior, 3:*240–249, 1951; also in Noland, R., *Counseling Parents of the Emotionally Disturbed Child,* pp. 94–104, Charles C Thomas, Springfield, Ill., 1972.

27. MAHLER, M. S., *On Human Symbiosis and the Vicissitudes of Individuation,* vol. 1, International Universities Press, New York, 1968.

28. MELLSOP, G. W., "Psychiatric Patients Seen as Children and Adults: Childhood Predictors of Adult Illness," *Journal of Child Psychology and Psychiatry, 13:* 91–101, 1972; also in Chess, S., and Thomas, A., *Annual Progress in Child Psychiatry and Child Development,* pp. 689–702, Brunner/Mazel, New York, 1973.

29. MILLER, D., "Family Interaction in the Therapy of Adolescent Patients," *Psychiatry, 21:*277–284, 1958; also in Noland, R., *Counseling Parents of the Emotionally Disturbed Child,* pp. 29–43, Charles C Thomas, Springfield, Ill., 1972.

30. MOE, M., WAAL, N., and URDAHL, B., "Group Psychotherapy with Parents of Psychotic and of Neurotic Children," *Psychotherapy and Psychosomatics, 8:*134–146, 1960; also in Noland R., *Counseling Parents of the Emotionally Disturbed Child,* pp. 368–380, Charles C Thomas, Springfield, Ill., 1972.

31. NOLAND, R., *Counseling Parents of the Emotionally Disturbed Child,* Charles C Thomas, Springfield, Ill., 1972.

32. OLSHAKER, B., *What Shall We Tell the Kids,* Dell, New York, 1971.

33. PEARSON, G. H., *A Handbook of Child Psychoanalysis,* Basic Books, New York, 1968.

34. RUTTER, M. L., "Relationships Between Child and Adult Psychiatric Disorders," *Acta Psychiatrica Scandinavica, 48:*3–21, 1972; also in Chess, S., and Thomas, A., *Annual Progress in Child Psychiatry and Child Development,* pp. 669–688, Brunner/Mazel, New York, 1973.

35. SCHWARTZ, H., "The Mother in the Consulting Room," in Eissler, R. S., et al. (Eds.), *The Psychoanalytic Study of the Child,* vol. 5, pp. 343–357, International Universities Press, New York, 1950.

36. SMIRNOFF, V., *The Scope of Child Analysis,* International Universities Press, New York, 1971.

37. SPERLING, E., personal communication.

38. SPERLING, M., "Children's Interpretation and Reactions to the Unconscious of their Mothers," *International Journal of Psychoanalysis, 31:*36–41, 1950.

39. SZYRYNSKI, V., "Psychotherapy with Parents of Maladjusted Children," *Canadian Psychiatric Association Journal, 10:*350–357, 1965; also in Noland, R., *Counseling Parents of the Emotionally Disturbed Child,* pp. 72–85, Charles C Thomas, Springfield, Ill., 1972.

40. TOLCHIN, J., personal communication.

41. VOGEL, E. F., "The Marital Relationship of Parents of Emotionally Disturbed Children: Polarization and Isolation," *Psychiatry, 23:*1–12, 1960; also in Noland, R., *Counseling Parents of the Emotionally Disturbed Child,* pp. 5–28, Charles C Thomas, Springfield, Ill., 1972.

42. WEINER, I., *Psychological Disturbance in Adolescence,* John Wiley, New York, 1970.

43. WEISS, W., "Parameters in Child Analysis," *Journal of the American Psychoanalytic Association, 12:*587–599, 1964.

44. WESTMAN, J. C., et al., "Parallel Group Psychotherapy with the Parents of Emotionally Disturbed Children," *International Journal of Group Psychotherapy, 13:* 52–60, 1963; also in Noland, R., *Counseling Parents of the Emotionally Disturbed Child,* pp. 345–355, Charles C Thomas, Springfield, Ill., 1972.

9 / Filial Therapy

Erna Furman

Description

Filial therapy is the treatment of the child by his parent. It is probably the most widely used means of assisting a youngster with troubles. In its broadest sense, it is applied long before, and long after, professional advice is sought; indeed, it is simply one of a parent's many functions. When a young child has a cold, the mother turns doctor and nurse; as he learns how to dress himself, she is his teacher; when he fearfully encounters a steamshovel, she may say: "The man makes it pick up the soil. He makes it do the right thing in a safe way. It is not angry and it does not hurt anyone." Sensitive to his stage of personality development, she explains its realistic uses and helps the child to dissociate it from his animistic concepts and aggressive projections. She, thus, becomes his therapist and furthers his ego's capacity for mastery by offering insight and increased reality testing. The professional teacher and physician may supplement, but they never supplant the parent. It follows, then, that when a child's emotional difficulties require expert help, it is also often indicated that the parents maintain their therapeutic role. They can, however, extend, deepen, and perfect what they do through their contacts with a specialist in child development.

Such work with parents may follow three main approaches:

1. "To advise the mother directly as to educational methods, to suggest specific ways of handling certain situations, e.g., feeding, toileting, and to give her intellectual understanding of the child's emotional needs in his different developmental phases. This approach presupposes that the mother is emotionally capable of absorbing and utilizing such knowledge to the benefit of the child and without causing an untoward upheaval in her own personality. [This approach is utilized in many books on child development for parents and is, in various forms, described by several anuthors.[13, 33, 35]]
2. "To treat the mother [and/or father]—by psychoanalysis, psychotherapy, or various social work techniques—in order to bring about changes in her own personality. This will in turn enable her to alter her attitude toward her young child and effect changes in his behavior without direct educational advice. The approach assumes that the mothers' relationship with her child is primarily shaped by deep-rooted, unconscious factors and that the mother can, and will, change her actual handling of her child only after she has gained insight into her own early conflicts."[18] [pp. 250–251]
3. The third approach consists of treatment of the child via the parent in the specific circumscribed form to which this chapter is devoted. This method, too, aims at helping the parents as educators (furthering all aspects of ego development and lending age-adequate support in dealing with internal and external demands). But there are two further goals: to enable parents to help their child with conflicts with his environment (including conflicts with the parents) and to help them treat certain forms of internalized neurotic conflicts. These tasks make great demands on the parent. They require both the capacity for a considerable degree of insight into oneself and into the nature of the parent's interaction with his child, as well as an ability to understand and interpret the child's unconscious defenses, feelings, and thoughts.

Historically, the first recorded treatment of a young child by his parent was that of Little Hans, described by S. Freud.[11] Analytic interest in this type of work then subsided until the special conditions during and after World War II provided a new impetus. A. Katan[25] described a mother's analysis of her young child. Ruben,[34] Bonnard,[5] and Rangell[30] recorded similar cases. Buxbaum,[7] Friedlander,[12] and Jacobs[21] reported on their work in assisting mothers to treat their young children's developmental difficulties. Undoubtedly, many therapists have since then used variations of this method of work with parents. The only consistent and systematic efforts at developing and studying treatment via the parent as a technique took place in Cleveland, in connection with the Hanna Perkins Therapeutic Nursery School and Kindergarten.[20] Katan's interest and experience with filial therapy led her to organize this center with a staff of child analysts and child therapists, several of whom had been trained in working with parents at A. Freud's Hampstead Child Therapy Course. Since the early 1950s, many of the emotionally disturbed children at the Hanna Perkins School have been treated via their parents. The many theoretical and practical aspects of this work have been continuously evaluated and compared with work with parents of children outside the nursery-school age group, from babyhood to adolescence. The findings were reported in some detail[18, 20] and illustrated by clinical case material.* The present chapter draws substantially on these experiences and publications.

Theory Underlying Filial Therapy

Psychoanalytic thinking has long known and strongly stressed that the parent-child relationship is a unique bond. It plays an important part in the child's life and in the development of his personality. This is especially so with the infant and preschooler; in different forms, however, it holds true throughout later childhood and adolescence. The parents' central role in the child's life continues until object removal[24] is accomplished and the adult personality established. At that point, the parents may appear to lose their importance. Actually, they are destined soon to assume a new and significant role. Their parenting of the now grown-up "child" plays a large part in his development as a parent; this configuration is further enhanced by their attitudes, as grandparents, toward his children.

Parental Development

It is now recognized that adulthood does not represent the end point of maturation; indeed, it contains new developmental stages of which parenthood is perhaps the most important. Coleman, Kris, and Provence,[8] Benedek,[3] Bibring,[4] and Winnicott,[36, 37] described aspects of this process. Our experiences with parents at the Cleveland center led us to formulate independently the concept of parenthood as a developmental phase. We studied it especially as it related to filial therapy.[16].

Parenthood shares certain characteristics in common with other developmental phases. Newly experienced stimuli from within and without weaken habitual defenses, produce a relative flux and flexibility within the personality, and lead to new masteries and means of integration. Conception, pregnancy, birth, nursing, and intimate daily care of the baby form parental development. These experiences reactivate and impart new significance to memories of having been parented and

* See references 1, 2, 17, 20, and 32.

to infantile fantasies of being a parent. In many instances, these early memories and fantasies reach a new level of conscious or preconscious awareness. The baby's individual behavior and characteristics also play their role (his activity in utero, his looks, good or ill health, responsiveness), as do the attitudes of those who participate in the new parental experience: the obstetrician, pediatrician, nurses, relatives, and the psychotherapist. Through their interaction, all these contribute to shaping the parent aspect of the individual's personality makeup. Parental development is most flexible in its early phases; at this point it can integrate new methods and aims of child rearing most readily—that is, during the child's prelatency years. To a certain extent, this process renews itself with each child and brings about individual parenting for children within the same family

The most crucial maturational task of parenthood is to achieve an appropriate parental attachment to, or cathexis of, the child. This consists, in part, of extending one's love for oneself to the baby and, in part, of relating to him as a loved person in his own right. When both object love and self-love extended to the child are sufficiently positive and are maintained in a flexible balance, the parent is able to empathize to a unique degree with all aspects of the child's mental life and to respond effectively to his many bodily and emotional needs. This special parent-child relationship is not achieved suddenly, nor is its initial version likely to persist without change.

During a child's prelatency years, his relationships with mother and father differ. The child enhances maternal development through the bodily unity with the mother (pregancy, nursing), as well as through the continuing intimate interactions of care and play. The father experiences fewer bodily stimuli and interacts to a more limited extent. The mother's parental function focuses on empathic fulfillment of bodily and mental needs; the father's serves at first to shield the mother-child relationship during its initial most vulnerable period. Later, the father provides an additional specific relationship for the child.[6, 16, 36] As a result of these differences in parental development, the mother of the prelatency child is more closely attuned to all aspects of the child's personality. After the resolution of the Oedipus complex, the child's personality acquires a more independent structure, and many aspects of his parental attachments undergo repression. Parental functioning changes correspondingly to meet a new configuration, and the unique closeness of the mother-child relationship diminishes greatly.

The enormous demands of parenting are outweighed by its gratifications. These inhere in the relationship with the child, as well as in the increase in self-esteem derived from functioning as a responsible parent. This sense of responsibility for all aspects of his child's well-being is a hallmark of parenting. It provides the major motivation for the parent's willingness to undertake the child's treatment and to persevere in the difficult task. The parent's intuitive therapeutic skill, and the child's ready response, stem from their conscious and unconscious closeness. This is further enhanced by the parent's intimate knowledge of the child's lifelong experiences. In helping his child, the parent also gains. Both experience the rewards of a richer and better relationship.

Indications

It is evident from the foregoing discussion that the optimal timing for filial therapy obtains when a mother is assisted in treating her prelatency child. The father participates most helpfully when he adjusts his handling of the child so as to support the mother's work. He discusses with her, and, periodically with the therapist, specific areas of his relationship with his child. He can also supplement the mother's role in instances where she may find it difficult.

Selection of Parent

It is essential that the mother who undertakes this work has already entered the developmental phase of motherhood. Sometimes a mother's maternal development has been invaded by interferences at specific levels or in particular areas. Whether the source of these interferences is internal or external, their net effect is to interrupt her growth. This is not necessarily a contraindication as long as her motivation suggests a potential for overcoming her difficulties and progressing in her maternal maturation.

CASE ILLUSTRATION

Mrs. M was very much concerned about her clever three-and-one-half-year-old son, Martin, who had been excluded from two nursery schools for sudden uncontrollable attacks on other children and periods of wild hyperactivity. She was at a loss; she didn't understand him, didn't know how to handle him, and hoped to learn what to do from books or from the therapist. Mrs. M had felt close to Martin until his second year. She had enjoyed his early speech and motility. She was still relating to him as a young toddler by ministering to all his body needs and speaking of his activities as "we did" this or that. During Martin's second year, Mrs. M had been bedridden with a difficult unsuccessful pregnancy. This was followed by several months of depression. During this interval, Martin had been cared for intermittently by various relatives; he had not been helped to understand or master the many events and changes. He developed symptoms, and his ego functioning remained infantile. The mother's maternal development was also arrested at that early level. The work showed that her maturation was impeded by her unfortunate experiences and Martin's pathology, and by her fear of identifying with her own parents' unhelpful models. Filial therapy enabled her to understand and help Martin and to resume her parental development with newly integrated aims and methods.

The therapy is much more likely to succeed if the father has also entered the developmental phase of fatherhood. In some instances, it is possible for father to be the therapist for his young child. This is especially true when he functions as the sole or primary parent. This may come about if the mother is dead, absent, or severely handicapped by bodily or mental disease.

It is not easy to assess parental development. The overall adult personality functioning cannot be used diagnostically. Some very disturbed adults are surprisingly capable as parents. By contrast, some well-adjusted adults show a circumscribed deficiency in parenting. Prior to treatment, and during its initial phases, the best prognostic indicator is the amount of healthy guilt the parent experiences. It is in the nature of the parent's relationship with the child that the parent feels both a narcissistic hurt and guilt when something is bodily or mentally wrong with the child. This holds true even when the parent knows that he or she has in no way caused the condition, but it is usually heightened when the child's difficulties are of emotional origin. Parental self-esteem is diminished, and the parent blames himself for real or imaginary mistakes in handling his child. Many factors determine the intensity of these feelings, the relative proportion of narcissistic hurt and self-blame, and the manner in which the parent deals with them. For example, the parent may need to deny the child's problems or blame others in order to ward off awareness of his pain, or may have such a pathological need for self-punishment that unconscious feelings of deserving a damaged child prevent working toward improvement. When much of the hurt and guilt are within normal limits, however, the parent can recognize them and correct the situation that causes them. Healthy guilt thus contributes to a parent's dedication and responsible commitment. Under optimal circumstances, the parent feels responsible for helping the child overcome his difficulties, regardless of their origin and despite the hardship and sacrifice.

It is only during the later stages of therapy that the second major factor can be assessed. This involves the capacity to identify with the aims and the means of the work. This manifests itself, for example, in the ability to apply acquired insight and methods of handling to new situations and to maintain gains during temporary interruptions of the work, such as vacations. There are a number of circumstances under which parents *cannot* cooperate. This is especially true when their disturbance has prevented them from entering the developmental phase of parenthood or when personality pathology has so seriously invaded their normal functioning that it leaves no room for healthy maturation (for example, when parents suffer from psychoses, borderline states, depressions, some severe obsessional neuroses and character disorders, incapacitating psychosomatic disease, and from consistent inability to assume responsibility for the care of the child).

Selection of Child

For children under five, the following diagnostic categories are potentially suitable for filial therapy:

1. In spite of some manifest behavior disturbances, the personality growth of the child is essentially healthy.
2. The forms of pathology (symptoms, defenses, economic factors) are products of developmental conflicts, which are age- or phase-appropriate.
3. The pathological formations (symptoms, defenses, economic factors) are not phase-appropriate. An under-five child is placed in this group when the neurotic conflicts appear to endanger the proper resolution of the oedipal conflict.[9] These disturbances include manifestations of external and, to some extent, internalized conflicts; they exclude crystallized neuroses, character disturbances, and atypical or "borderline" pathologies.

Filial therapy with school-age children and adolescents cannot, and should not, include treatment of internalized neurotic difficulties. Such treatment involves interpretation of unconscious infantile contents. This, in turn, would "seduce" the child to regress to the corresponding prelatency relationship with the parent. Along with this, it would interfere with an age-appropriate investment in love-objects outside the family. Shifts of this kind would impede development, rather than enhance it. There are, however, a number of other specific goals which filial therapy may attain successfully at these later developmental stages. Among these are:

1. The resolution, or lessening, of the child's difficulties which arise from external conflicts. Thus, filial therapy can bring insight into the parent-child interactions and enable the parents to understand and meet the child's developmental needs.
2. Preparing the child for direct treatment. With older children, their ability to involve themselves in necessary individual treatment depends not only on parental support but on their own insight and motivation. Ignorance and unconsciously employed defenses prevent this. Filial therapy allows the parents to recognize the child's need for help, and enables them to work with the child's defenses to increase his awareness. For example, the child's pattern of externalizing conflict may provide a powerful defensive screen. As a result, the parents or school become involved in such a way as to obscure the child's internalized difficulties.

CASE ILLUSTRATION

Five-year-old Randy engaged his mother and teacher in constant battles by refusing to cooperate in daily routines. All disciplinary measures proved useless. For example, he insisted that an adult dress him, and he had a temper outburst if no one would comply. During filial therapy, the mother told Randy that sometimes children make a big fight with grown-ups when they are scared of a fight inside themselves. She would rather help him with the inside fight than be always at odds with him. As Randy now attempted to dress himself, his obsessional agony became clear to him and to his parents: As soon as he put on a boot he was compelled to take it off, then put it on, then off. He never knew how long the compulsion would continue, or whether it would stop when he was dressed or undressed. The parents could now sympathize with Randy, and he began to wish for treatment.[14]

3. Helping the child master specific stresses which interfere with development.[26] Such stresses may be acute or continuing, and may involve the child primarily or affect a member of his family (for example illness, hospitalization, bodily or mental defects, bereavement, sexual experiences, imprisonment, and the like).

In most instances these goals overlap. They are also limited aims in filial therapy with children under five when either the parent's or child's pathology prevents fuller utilization of the treatment.

The Therapist's Professional Background

This is a very real factor in the choice of this therapeutic method. The method involves an extension of psychoanalytic understanding and technique. The therapist should accordingly be a child analyst, or someone who commands unusual intuitive insight plus intellectual familiarity with analytic concepts and practice. A detailed knowledge of normal and pathological child development, of parental—as opposed to adult—functioning, and of educational techniques are also essential. Moreover, these qualifications have to be integrated in the context of a sensitive empathy for the parent, the child, and the parent-child relationship. It is a demanding task that no one is likely to fulfill perfectly. With full recognition of our limitations, however, it is one toward which we can strive.

Complications, Disadvantages, Side Effects, and Contraindications

In the earlier years of its use, it was feared that, through prolonged treatment via the parent, mothers would become too dependent on the therapist, their relationship to him would become too intense, or that mother and child would find it difficult to relinquish the gratifications of their special closeness and to progress toward a relationship appropriate to the onset of the child's latency. These misgivings were not borne out.

Complications can, however, arise during the course of the work. Some of them are caused by an initial failure to assess the true depth of the child's or parent's pathology. Subsequently, this necessitates limiting the therapeutic goals as previously described. For example, young children sometimes develop a full-blown neurosis at the height of the phallic-oedipal phase or in response to new major stresses.

A mother sometimes shows initial limiting factors which take the form of danger signals. It is only as she faces new aspects of her child's diffi-

culties, recognizes her own weaknesses, and strives to overcome them that the extent of her incapacities emerges. Among these are: a pathological attitude toward the expression of drives in herself and/or in the child (e.g., inability to control aggression, to frustrate libidinal gratifications, or to tolerate the necessary minimum of drive satisfaction in the child at some or all levels); the fact that mother and child share(d) important conflicts or prominent defenses, either in the past or present; disturbances in the cathexis of the child (e.g., excessive narcissistic investment in the child, extension to the child of self-hate rather than self-love, inconsistent cathexis leading to interference in caring for the child or in protecting him, seeing the child as though he were some person from the parents' past); gross educational inconsistency (e.g., alternately punishing or allowing certain behaviors, overgratifying some drives and prematurely frustrating others); pathological guilt (e.g., unconscious guilt that requires that the child "fail," or guilt that gratifies the mother's masochism but prevents her working toward an improvement); inability to integrate the means and aims of educational and therapeutic principles (so that she is unable to apply the principles without the therapist's help, or she slips back to earlier methods once the child's symptoms have subsided).

These factors often coexist and interact. Nonetheless, it is possible for some mothers to achieve sufficient insight and self-control to overcome their noxious effects. Other mothers fail in their efforts. In favorable cases, a mother may have sufficient insight to seek psychiatric help for herself.

CASE ILLUSTRATION

John's mother was working to help her four-year-old correct his wetting and soiling. Presently, she came to understand with him that his trouble was his defense against being a bigger boy. It took her much longer to recognize that she was contributing to this, that she had an underlying need to keep him little and to spare him the frustrations that she had herself often found so hard to bear. She never showed disgust or appropriate annoyance at his messing, she thought up excuses for each "accident," she failed to engage his help in the clean-up, and she carried and cuddled him like a toddler. When she realized the effect of this behavior on the child, she struggled to alter her management. She also told John that she had a problem about this. In a way, she wanted to keep him little, although she also wanted him to grow up. He could help her and himself by not requesting toddler care and by reminding her when she offered it. In spite of many lapses on the part of mother and child, in time their joint efforts succeeded.

Complications can also arise from the therapist's limitations in understanding or technique. The mother's or child's difficulties may touch on the therapist's own blind spots or, in the course of the work, he may unduly mobilize the mother's unconscious conflicts. They then interfere with her handling of the child, as well as with her relationship to the therapist. Such a situation would perhaps be the one instance in which filial therapy could, at least temporarily, interfere with average expectable parenting. Experience suggests that only rather disturbed parents continue their involvement in such a pathological interaction with a therapist. Relatively healthy parents, by contrast, sense the dangers of an inappropriate technique and, on one or another pretext, interrupt the treatment.

Given proper selection and technique, the outcome is usually positive. The progressive development of parent and child continues through subsequent maturational phases without further assistance. Moreover, the parents are able to apply their new understanding and skills to their other children. Younger siblings, particularly, are often the greatest beneficiaries as earlier intervention prevents later pathology.[20]

Technique

The therapist's initial task is to establish a goal-directed working relationship with the parent. This consists of outlining the therapeutic techniques and aims and of mobilizing the parent's healthy guilt as a motivating force. The parent is told that he or she will be the main partner in the joint effort and will decide which of the child's difficulties should be the focus of the therapeutic work. The parent is in charge of observing the child's behavior and verbalizations. In time, the parent will learn to understand from them the underlying causes and connections in the child's mind. The therapist is the parent's assistant and contributes his knowledge of child development and experience with other children. But it is up to the parent to weigh these suggestions carefully and to use them only as and when they are pertinent to the child. Most parents need reassurance that they and their child have a good chance at working successfully. At the same time, allowance should be made for possible limitations which parent and therapist will observe and discuss together as they emerge in the course of therapy. It needs to be stressed also that the focus of the work will be on the child.

It is not part of the contract that the parent will derive benefit for his personal difficulties; his only promised reward is the satisfaction of helping his child. This is usually a relief to those parents who fear exposure of their own mental life. It helps others to set aside potentially interfering personal problems which do not immediately affect their parenting. Above all, it calls upon the active participation of the parental aspect of the adult's personality.

Utilization of Parental Guilt

The establishment of such a working relationship depends to a large extent on the therapist's empathy with the parent's guilt. The therapist acknowledges that this feeling is not a sign of incompetence. On the contrary, it is the hallmark of parental responsibility. All parents make mistakes, and the parent who embarks on this work to help the child has already begun to correct the past in a responsible way. Such discussions are most readily initiated when the parent remarks on his guilt or reproaches himself for specific shortcomings in handling the child. They are harder to approach when the parent's guilt shows indirectly, for example, in terms of a fear of criticism or in defensive interrogation or criticism of the therapist. In such instances, it is safe to assume that the guilt is too painful for direct expression, and it is, therefore, even more important to find a way to approach it. Although these topics arise repeatedly throughout, initial discussion sets the stage for the actual work to get under way.

The Therapeutic Process

The parent presents a weekly account of observations of the child. This material is used to help in recognizing and resolving existing external struggles between the parent and the child. In the case of internalized conflicts, the parent is helped to proceed gradually, first to an understanding of the child's defenses against emerging anxiety and the uncovering of heretofore unconscious struggles, and then to their interpretation. Thus, the process engaged in is similar to that of direct psychotherapy or psychoanalysis. At the same time, the parent is helped to give the child age-appropriate support of ego functions and to provide guidance toward healthy mastery. Young children's immature ego functions make it difficult for them to think in terms of time sequences and causal connections. Their feelings and thoughts often surface "out of the blue." At the same time, their inner struggles, so acute in specific conflictual situations, may become inaccessible moments later. As a result, it is usually not helpful for a parent to work with the child during scheduled therapeutic sessions. The parent needs to be observant at all times, in tune with the child, responsive to his communications, and ready to utilize appropriate moments for educational and therapeutic interventions. The best time for this may be when the child actually experiences difficulty, or later when the intensity of affect has subsided and his self-observation and wish to overcome his problem are more at his disposal. Quite often, however, parents do find a period during the day which is calm and mutually agreeable for discussion—story time, the car ride to and from nursery school, afternoon snack time. Even these times cannot be used regularly for therapeutic purposes, and the parent needs to make sure that "talking about troubles" does not become the only way to have a pleasant time together.

In the nature of things, work never proceeds smoothly; interferences manifest themselves at each turn. These stem from many sources: the parent's difficulties in the relationship with the child, current extraneous concerns which divert the parent's focus away from the child, and aspects of the parent's relationship to the therapist. At no point does the therapist interpret the parent's unconscious defenses or repressed content. In some instances, he may encourage the parent to exercise a measure of conscious control over the interference for the sake of helping the child; in others, he utilizes the parent's mental closeness to the child, that is, in understanding the child's defenses and conflicts the parent will gain some insight himself.

CASE ILLUSTRATION

Erin's mother tended to deal with stresses by arranging elaborate outings, visits, or parties. Instead of facing her feelings and mastering the situation at hand, she ended up overwhelming both herself and others. It was an effective defense and caused important material to escape discussion with the therapist on many occasions. As a result, it interfered with the therapy. In a similar fashion, whenever Erin was anxious, she overwhelmed herself and her mother with frantic busyness and endless requests. After the mother had come to understand Erin's defense and, with the therapist's help, to interpret it, she commented one day, "I guess I do that too and it doesn't help either of use." This insight enabled her to overcome her difficulty to a considerable extent. Subsequently, it could be used by the therapist at appropriate times to remind her what her behavior meant.

The final stage of the work is reached when the child's difficulties are resolved, when the child is freed for maturational progress, when the parent has sufficiently identified with the means and aims of the work to be able to meet the child's age-appropriate needs, and when the parent is prepared as well for the demands of the child's next developmental phase. This identification is not necessarily rooted in a positive relationship to the therapist. Experience shows that some mothers who are very critical and trying in their interviews can integrate the substance of the work successfully, whereas others who are appreciative and readily accept suggestions are never able to make the therapist's approach their own.

Therapist's Contact with the Child

It is assumed that the recommendation for treatment via the parent is based on a diagnostic study that includes interviews with the child. As is well known, such interviews with children under five unfortunately yield only limited and sometimes misleading information, owing to the lability of the young child's inadequately structured personality and immature ego. The presence or absence of the parent may reveal differences in the youngster's functioning, whose significance is difficult to evaluate. Isolated subsequent interviews similarly are not apt to contribute significantly to the overall assessment but also require the parent's help in preparing the child and in working through the experience with him afterwards. For these reasons, the therapist may decide not to see the child himself, as long as he knows what transpired during the initial evaluation interviews. Under special circumstances, however, he may wish to meet with the child; for example, when a mother is particularly anxious for some of her child' ssymptoms to be observed professionally or when the therapist feels that the mother's accounts of her child's behavior obscure the true picture. Moreover, most youngsters want to "visit" the therapist at least once. In any case, the child does need to know of the work in order to understand changes in the parent's approach and handling and in order to participate in the treatment. Many children do this, not only by bringing their material to the parent but by sending pertinent messages to the therapist. They ask the parent to discuss some issues and utilize what the parent tells them about some of the talks with the therapist.

Preparation of the Family and Child

No special preparation for this work is necessary. Parents are usually quite willing to follow a recommendation of "As far as I can understand from our evaluation, your child's difficulties are of such a nature that you yourself will be able to help him resolve many or even all of them." Misunderstandings and misgivings, however, are voiced frequently. "You mean I should have treatment?" "How could I help him? I am not trained." "What if it doesn't work out?" Clarification is necessary about the rationale for filial therapy, its methods, and its aims. Indeed this comprises the initial part of the work, as does the discussion of possible limited goals. When therapy actually gets underway, one of the first topics is usually: How is the parent to prepare the child and elicit his cooperation? In doing so, the parent tests and confirms his own understanding.

Economic Implications

The parents pay only for their interviews with the therapist. This makes it perhaps the least expensive method of individual psychotherapy, especially when one considers its prophylactic effects on later developmental phases for parent and child and the frequent beneficial spread to other children in the family.

Necessary Associated Activities

In treatment of children under five via the parent, it is particularly helpful when the child attends a therapeutic nursery school. Such a setting makes an important contribution in the areas of observation and education.[20, 22]

With young children, diagnosis is an ongoing process, and the nursery school setting is its most valuable tool. It is a site where teachers, therapist, and parents can observe the daily shifts in the child's conflicts and his means of coping with them.[15, 23, 27, 28] The varied nursery school activities and interactions with nonfamily members reveal different aspects of the child's functioning and supplement home observations.

Nursery school data have been found to be especially valuable in the following cases:

1. Children whose pathology involves areas of ego-functioning (in contrast to isolated symptoms).
2. Children whose disturbance is largely rooted in traumatic experiences that occurred during an earlier separation from the mother, such as hospitalization or seduction (with these children, the nursery school often becomes the setting in which derivatives of the original reactions are displayed, whereas the home serves as a protection against a possible repetition of earlier incidents).
3. Children whose difficulties tend to become apparent when they are separated from their mothers, such as fear of loss of control, difficulties in peer relations, castration anxiety, or separation fear.
4. Children who have a tendency to displace conflicts from the home to other settings.
5. Children whose mothers have prominent blind spots and are unable to observe some areas of the child's behavior.[16]

In the area of education, the school provides the child with the optimum support for his developing ego functions. It programs activities which help master inner and outer stresses. It also provides guidance in using freed-up energy for sublimatory interests and achievements. For the mother, the school's educational methods serve first as a chance to see how a different approach works in practice and, later, as a model for identification.

When a therapeutic nursery school is not available, specially selected, dynamically oriented, and educationally sound conventional schools can, to some extent, fulfill this role.[15, 19, 31]

In working with older children, parents and therapist do gain some additional data from school reports. However, the child's personality structure at these later stages is of such character that school observations and methods cannot contribute anything comparable to those of the nursery school.

Frequency and Intensity

Filial therapy usually proceeds best when weekly fifty-minute interviews with parents extend over one to two years. This period may be much shorter in the case of children under five with developmental conflicts of recent onset, or when limited goals are set for latency children or adolescents.

Sometimes, fortnightly or even longer intervals between sessions are indicated. (This might be appropriate in the last stages of therapy when the parent is getting ready to carry on independently.) Such an arrangement is unavoidable when distance or illness make more frequent contacts impossible. However, the parent must be aware that long intervals between sessions may handicap the work and that the task will be difficult.

Patterns of Follow Up

A formal follow-up program is usually not necessary. At the conclusion of filial therapy, the parent is sensitive to his child's strengths and weaknesses and is alerted to the tasks of the next developmental phases. The parent has also identified with the means and aims of the work. Taken together, these factors enable the parent to gauge the need for follow up or additional help, and to utilize appropriately the therapist's assurance that he will be available and interested in good and bad news.

Having shared in the parent's and child's development at a crucial time, the therapist may be treated as a family friend and receive periodic news for many years. In other instances, parents and child put the treatment behind them, along with other childhood experiences, so that contact is renewed only in case of need. Both are appropriate outcomes.

The Relationship of Filial Therapy to Other Modalities of Treatment

As mentioned in the section devoted to indications for filial therapy, it sometimes has to work toward limited goals. This is either specified initially or comes about as a result of unforeseen complications. In these instances, the work is used to pave the way for other forms of treatment which can then be utilized better by parent and child. This is particularly true if the work includes the choice of and planning for the next step.[16, 29]

For example, recognition of the extent and nature of the child's internalized conflicts can lead to preparation for direct psychotherapy for the child; the parent's realization of personal difficulties may lead to seeking help. Sometimes serious family difficulties create insurmountable external conflicts for the child. Under such circumstances, the child cannot progress developmentally or even utilize treatment. The parents may then be helped to plan for the child's treatment at a later stage (when emotionally less dependent) and/or to enroll him in a boarding school or residential treatment center.

Treatment via the parent should not be burdened by having to succeed. The parent needs to know that the therapist will assist in arranging other forms of treatment should the need arise, that the work can be used as a means of preparation, and that this will not jeopardize the child's chances of benefiting from other therapies.

Therapeutic Outcome

The only available research study[20] suggests that positive results are often achieved and maintained. Children treated via the mother at the Hanna Perkins School were reassessed up to eleven years later. Among twenty-four such cases, twenty-one showed diagnostic improvement on leaving nursery school or kindergarten.[10] Seventeen of these maintained or improved their diagnosis by the time of follow up. Three others showed some difficulties as, in addition to adolescence, they were currently coping with serious stresses (disease, parental bereavement). Of special interest was the group of nineteen children who were originally quite disturbed. Sixteen of these manifested only minor developmental conflicts on leaving school and maintained their improvement at follow up. At the start of nursery school, these sixteen children's neurotic conflicts intereferred with their maintaining themselves at the phallic or oedipal level. Seven of them showed regressive trends which, in turn, impaired their ego functioning. With all of them, severe impairment was noted in the areas of drive development, defense organization, object relationships, and economic functioning. These children's improvement shows convincingly that treatment via the mother can be the appropriate treatment for a significant proportion of prelatency children whose disturbances are of greater severity than transitory developmental conflicts.[10]

157

REFERENCES

1. BARNES, M., "Kathy," in Furman, G. (Ed.), *A Child's Parent Dies*, pp. 154–162, Yale University Press, New Haven, 1974.

2. ———, "Reaction to the Death of a Mother," in Eissler, R. S., et al. (Eds.), *The Psychoanalytic Study of the Child*, vol. 19, pp. 334–357, International Universities Press, New York, 1964.

3. BENEDEK, T., "Parenthood as a Developmental Phase: A Contribution to the Libido Theory," *Journal of the American Psychoanalytic Association*, 7:389–417, 1959.

4. BIBRING, G., "Some Considerations of the Psychological Processes in Pregnancy," in Eissler, R. S., et al. (Eds.), *The Psychoanalytic Study of the Child*, vol. 14, pp. 113–121, International Universities Press, New York, 1959.

5. BONNARD, A., "The Mother as Therapist, in a Case of Obsessional Neurosis," in Eissler, R. S., et al. (Eds.), *The Psychoanalytic Study of the Child*, vol. 5, pp. 391–408, International Universities Press, New York, 1950.

6. BURLINGHAM, D., "The Preoedipal Infant-Father Relationship," in Eissler, R. S., et al. (Eds.), *The Psychoanalytic Study of the Child*, vol. 28, pp. 23–48, Yale University Press, New Haven, 1973.

7. BUXBAUM, E., "Psychotherapy and Psychoanalysis in the Treatment of Children," *Nervous Child*, 5:115–126, 1946.

8. COLEMAN, R., KRIS, E., and PROVENCE, S., "The Study of Early Variations in Parental Attitudes," in Eissler, R. S., et al. (Eds.), *The Psychoanalytic Study of the Child*, vol. 8, pp. 20–47, International Universities Press, New York, 1953.

9. DAUNTON, E., "Diagnosis," in Furman, R. A., and Katan, A. (Eds.), *The Therapeutic Nursery School*, pp. 204–214, International Universities Press, New York, 1969.

10. ———, "Description, Evaluation and Follow-up of Cases Treated via the Mother," in Furman, R. A., and Katan, A. (Eds.), *The Therapeutic Nursery School*, pp. 215–230, International Universities Press, New York, 1969.

11. FREUD, S., "Analysis of a Phobia in a Five-year-old Boy," in Strachey. J. (Ed.), *The Standard Edition of the Complete Psychological Works of Sigmund Freud*, vol. 10, pp. 5–149, Hogarth Press, London, 1955.

12. FRIEDLANDER, K., "Psychoanalytic Orientation in Child Guidance Work in Great Britain," in Eissler, R. S., et al. (Eds.), *The Psychoanalytic Study of the Child*, vol. 2, pp. 343–357, International Universities Press, New York, 1947.

13. FRIES, M., "The Child's Ego Development and the Training of Adults in His Environment," in Eissler, R. S., et al. (Eds.), *The Psychoanalytic Study of the Child*, vol. 2, pp. 85–112, International Universities Press, New York, 1946.

14. FURMAN, E., "Some Aspects of a Young Boy's Masturbation Conflict," in Marcus, I. M., and Francis, J. J. (Eds.), *Masturbation*, pp. 185–204, International Universities Press, New York, 1975.

15. ———, "Use of the Nursery School for Evaluation," in Glenn, J. (Ed.), *Child Analysis: Technique, Theory, Applications*, pp. 128–159, Jason Aronson, New York, 1978.

16. ———, "Treatment via the Mother," in Furman, R. A., and Katan, A. (Eds.), *The Therapeutic Nursery School*, pp. 64–123, International Universities Press, New York, 1969.

17. ———, "Observations on a Toddler's Near-fatal Accident," *Bulletin of the Philadelphia Association for Psychoanalysis*, 14:138–148, 1964.

18. ———, "Treatment of Under-fives by Way of Parents," in Eissler, R. S., et al. (Eds.), *The Psychoanalytic Study of the Child*, vol. 12, pp. 250–262, International Universities Press, New York, 1957.

19. FURMAN, R. A., "Experiences in Nursery School Consultation, Young Children," *Young Children, 22(2):* 84–95, 1966; and in Baker, K. (Ed.), *Ideas That Work with Young Children*, pp. 225–236, National Association for the Education of Young Children, Washington, D.C., 1972.

20. ———, and KATAN, A., *The Therapeutic Nursery School*, International Universities Press, New York, 1969.

21. JACOBS, L., "Methods Used in the Education of Mothers: A Contribution to the Handling and Treatment of Developmental Difficulties in Children Under Five Years of Age," in Eissler, R. S., et al. (Eds.), *The Psychoanalytic Study of the Child*, vol. 3/4, pp. 409–422, International Universities Press, New York, 1949.

22. KATAN, A., "Some Thoughts about the Role of Verbalization in Early Childhood," in Eissler, R. S., et al. (Eds.), *The Psychoanalytic Study of the Child*, vol. 16, pp. 184–188, International Universities Press, New York, 1961.

23. ———, "The Nursery School as a Diagnostic Help to the Child Guidance Clinic," in Eissler, R. S., et al. (Eds.), *The Psychoanalytic Study of the Child*, vol. 14, pp. 250–264, International Universities Press, New York, 1959.

24. ———, "The Role of Displacement in Agoraphobia," *International Journal of Psychoanalysis*, 32:41–50, 1951.

25. ———, "Experience with Enuretics," in Eissler, R. S., et al. (Eds.), *The Psychoanalytic Study of the Child*, vol. 2, pp. 241–255, International Universities Press, New York, 1947.

26. NAGERA, H., *Early Childhood Disturbances, the Infantile Neurosis and the Adulthood Disturbances*, International Universities Press, New York, 1966.

27. NEUBAUER, P., and BELLER, E., "Differential Contributions of the Educator and Clinician in Diagnosis," in Krugmann, M. (Ed.), *Orthopsychiatry and the School*, pp. 36–45, American Orthopsychiatric Association, New York, 1958.

28. ———, ALPERT, A., and BANK, B., "The Nursery Group Experience as Part of a Diagnostic Study of a Preschool Child," in Esman, A. (Ed.), *New Frontiers in Child Guidance, J. H. W. van Ophuijsen Memorial Volume*, pp. 124–138, International Universities Press, New York, 1958.

29. OPPENHEIMER, R., "The Role of the Nursery School with the Children Who Received Direct Treatment," in Furman, R. A., and Katan, A. (Eds.), *The Therapeutic Nursery School*, pp. 274–292, International Universities Press, New York, 1969.

30. RANGELL, L., "A Treatment of Nightmares in a Seven-Year-Old Boy," in Eissler, R. S., et al. (Eds.), *The Psychoanalytic Study of the Child*, vol. 5, pp. 358–390, International Universities Press, New York, 1950.

31. REDMOND, S., "Evaluating the Child Study Group: Psychoanalytic Consultation with Preschool Teachers," Doctoral Thesis, Department of Education, Case Western Reserve University, Cleveland, 1975.

32. ROSENBAUM, A. L., "Hank and Sally," in Furman, E. (Ed.), *A Child's Parent Dies*, pp. 129–139, Yale University Press, New Haven, 1974.

33. RUBEN, M., *Parent Guidance in the Nursery School*, International Universities Press, New York, 1960.

34. ———, "A Contribution to the Education of a Parent, in Eissler, R. S., et al. (Eds.), *The Psychoanalytic Study of the Child*, vol. 1, pp. 247–261, International Universities Press, New York, 1946.

35. ———, and THOMAS, R., "Home Training of Instincts and Emotions," *Health Education Journal* (London) 5:1–6, 1947.

36. WINNICOTT, D. W., "From Dependence Towards Independence in the Development of the Individual," in *The Maturational Processes and the Facilitating Environment*, pp. 83–92, International Universities Press, New York, 1965.

37. ———, "The Theory of the Parent-Infant Relationship," in *The Maturational Processes and the Facilitating Environment*, pp. 37–55, International Universities Press, New York, 1965.

10 / Group Therapy

Irvin A. Kraft

History

Pratt's work[65] in 1907 was the beginning of group therapy in this country. It was not until 1934, however, when Slavson[82] originated activity group therapy with latency-age children, that group psychotherapy was seriously addressed to children. Early on, Slavson and his students differentiated group psychotherapy from children participating in group activities such as camping and scouting. Group psychotherapy implied that an objectively stated theory of personality and behavior was present, and that its implications were available for testing. The leader predicated his actions and verbalizations on his theortical position; usually he utilized deliberately designed situations for the therapy. As a corollary, it was assumed that the behavior of the participants in that context were responses to the treatment.

Activity group psychotherapy as well as later forms of group therapy for children were all based on classical psychoanalytic theory as exemplified by Bender's[8] use of group therapy with children on a hospital ward in 1936. Once several basic therapeutic group techniques became known, the other factors asserted themselves: Various age groupings of children required different methods of treatment. This became especially important in working with adolescents. Also, the settings in which patients were treated influenced the choice of techniques; these settings included residential treatment centers, public schools, pediatric specialty clinics, units for delinquents, and hospitals.

The 1950s witnessed several elaborations and variations of group treatment, although all were within the basic framework of psychoanalytic theory. Adolescent group psychotherapy expanded beyond its initial confinement to situations for delinquents and inpatient units. It came to be employed in a wide range of outpatient settings, including private practice. The mid-1960 cultural and social occurrences flooded both clinic facilities and staff faculties with new patients, unusual phenomena, and novel treatment challenges. The adolescent and young adult counterculture, new role and old role expansions in femininity and masculinity, and the many aspects of drug abuse pressed the psychiatric caretakers to reexamine their therapy procedures. Many of these factors remain, and the emerging methods have still to be refined so that they may eventually be utilized productively in routine situations.

Description of the Method

Group psychotherapy is a process in which therapeutic forces are deployed in a setting where several (two or more) patients meet with one or more therapists. The patients are carefully selected deviant children and adolescents brought together for the purpose of helping each other change in the direction of "normal development."[74] The procedures involve intrapsychic, interpersonal, transactional, and group psychodynamic frameworks. These play roles of varying importance, depending on the leader's philosophy and techniques. The therapist's inputs interweave with the interactions of the group members, although this operates differently than is the case in dyadic therapy. Each patient receives multiple inputs, processes them, and utilizes his output in the group as well as in life.

In contrast to the general schemata of group therapy, for which several classifications are available, age and developmental considerations have dominated the group therapies utilized for children. One such grouping bases itself on psychoanalytic approaches: (1) psychodrama, which rests on techniques for the symbolic expression of conflicts; (2) nondirective therapy, in which structure and the active interference of the therapist are kept to a minimum; (3) psychoanalytic therapy; and (4) transactional analysis, another educative type of therapy which gives the child some understanding of his actions and encourages him to apply this knowledge. Therapists differ in their reliance on verbalization and conceptualization as opposed to symbolic expression of conflicts, in the degree to which group interaction is spontaneous or structured, in their views of the role of the therapist, and in their understanding of how group therapy actually works.

Group psychotherapy of children sets as its goal

the education and control of the emotions. This is accomplished in various ways; basically it comes down to conveying an acceptance of the child's feelings and specific types of behavior as simply and effectively as possible. In his role as leader of the group, the therapist provides situations that encourage behavior containing messages which lend themselves to emotional interaction and intellectual translation. For example, a situation in a psychotherapy group may provoke a child to an outburst of rage. The therapist can respond with acceptance and understanding: "Sometimes it is really difficult to control anger." The child feels better and may indeed have gained insight at several levels of personality organization. The experiential insight arises from two sources: from the verbalization of this violent feeling, and from realizing that retribution need not necessarily follow the expression of a true, albeit misplaced, emotion. Additional ways for this insight to come about arise through interactions with other group members. The patients utilize such defense mechanisms as identification, rationlization, denial, catharsis, and identification with the aggressor in an atmosphere of impunity and safety.

The listed approaches do not adequately describe the techniques that have been developed for children over the years. As noted, more perhaps than any other factor, it is the characteristics of the different developmental stages that have influenced the growth of psychotherapy techniques. Since the standard diagnostic nomenclature does not adequately discriminate among the psychiatric disorders of childhood, therapists tended to group children first by age and then by the nature of presenting difficulties. They assumed also that the children could not utilize verbalization to any meaningful extent much before puberty or adolescence; as a result, play and activities dominated their approaches. Aside from psychotic children and several types of sexual deviates, the categories that appeared were: (1) preschool and early-school age; (2) late latency, ages nine to eleven; (3) pubertal, ages twelve and thirteen; (4) early adolescence, ages thirteen and fourteen; and (5) middle adolescence through late adolescence, ages fourteen to seventeen.[41, 84]

Rationale

Systems require means for the exchange of information. The behavioral patterns of children and adolescents strongly reflect the influence of data exchange for living, especially in the to-and-from transmission with the child's parents and other caretaking persons. The child's data processing often seems overwhelmed by rapidly oscillating, changing inputs, so that he lacks adequate dwelling, reflective, and associative time for purposive decision making. Part of the therapist's responsibility in group psychotherapy of children and adolescents consists of sifting with the patients and helping them sort out faddish messages. Gibson[26] pointedly tells us that "we have arrived at the stage where the time required to make decisions (i.e., assemble and examine all necessary information), even simple ones by human beings, is considerably longer than the time required to transmit the information over a communication system." He makes the further point that either valid or misleading information gets transmitted with equal ease and fidelity. In life, and in group psychotherapy, more and more time becomes allotted to securing accurate information, be it cultural, interpersonal, and/or intrapsychic, in order to aid in reality-oriented decision making.

As children learn to operate in varying systems, they constantly call for rearrangements of equilibria. In their group psychotherapy experience, the children encounter settings and techniques by which they glimpse, at varying levels of abstraction, the role of their families, primarily as a message center and processor. The systems of negotiation become the focus rather than the individual psychopathology (the person; the small group, including the family; larger interest groups, such as scouts; and so forth); the group leader and the group itself confront this structured segment of their lives primarily in the here-and-now of the group session.

The leader's operational assumptions and his definitions of how people function determine how he handles these transactions. He may construe a child's behavior in the group as the result of intrapsychic and social field forces. He could then point out to that child and to the group how the family system elsewhere required the patient to be disturbed in order to maintain family balance. It quickly becomes evident in the group that the patient tends to initiate in this arena the schisms, secret alliances, and power plays of his family of origin.[53] Combatting this trend, especially with children and adolescents, is the built-in capacity for identification as part of growth. Bandura[3] describes modeling behavior and its importance in personality formation. A study by Patterson and Anderson[61] postulates that peers serve as effective agents to provide social reinforcers. As a therapy group anneals and grows, group values permeate the behavior of the patient. These serve to counter the nonadaptive family-sponsored behaviors. The latency child also takes in data from his social, educative, and group experiences. Under normal circumstances, this will enhance his industriousness and transfer sufficient libidinal energy to out-of-home activities to lead him out of the family embrace.

Early on, children and parents sense this; they feel buffeted. Diminished time together reduces their ability to monitor and filter the bombardment of overt and covert stimuli. These include both information for rational decision making and subliminal messages designed not to inform but to influence. The family must fulfill the tasks of providing emotional support to its members and of training the children in competency (age- and sex-adequate control of the body and the symbolic environment). These functions falter amid the welter of megamachine living.[56] Increased tension and decreased control lead to faulty communication, especially in the interpersonal areas, and, in time, to familial disorganization. We assume, therefore, the family offers the child initial training in adaptation at one level of a hierarchical organization into which he will gradually fit. Survival, however, may not be equivalent to health.

Yalom[98] lists eleven curative factors which play significant roles in group psychotherapy. Their applicability will be reviewed here, with the recognition again that developmental and reality factors (such as real dependency on parents) may alter them.

1. *Instillation of hope:* In adults, this involves the placebo-effect phenomenon. In children, however, it is difficult to assess; many children do not see themselves as troubled or as not coping adequately. Adolescents are better able to see themselves as needing to and capable of change, and thereby having hope. Once young children do get involved with the group, they tend to begin to have hope in combination with other curative factors.
2. *Universality:* Since children and adolescents seek peer conformity, it is immensely reassuring to find that there are others of like age with similar feelings and experiences.
3. *Imparting of information:* Depending on the patient population involved, the giving of didactic information by the therapist is of varying value. As will be observed, clinical judgment always determines when, how much, and what should be said.
4. *Altruism:* Even with the counterculture surge "to do one's own thing," to do something for others still fosters good feelings in doer and recipient, both in children and adolescents. The patients might not see their interactions as altruistic, yet they do utilize this in the group process.
5. *The corrective recapitulation of the primary family group:* Again, as with most therapy with children and to a lesser extent with adolescents, the patients relive the distortions of their original family experiences in portions of their present. Much, if not most, of these corrective experiences occur in the lower levels of awareness.
6. *Development of socializing techniques:* Social learning plays a large role in a number of different kinds of child and adolescent group psychotherapy. Modeling often occurs on the therapist's behavior as well as that of other group members. Deliberate use is made of this tendency in varying formats, especially in groups for the retarded and for pubertal and early adolescent girls, among others.
7. *Imitative behavior:* This includes role modeling, as before, but in the sense that the patient will observe how one group member deals with a difficulty that he himself also encounters and imitate it: "it worked for him, so why not for me?" With children and adolescents, role playing, brief psychodramatic exercises, and other activities often lead to trials or experiences in behaving a certain way, as demonstrated. What works then tends to become incorporated into a behavioral repertory.
8. *Interpersonal learning:* Since the range of group structures is so much greater for the child population, this factor becomes difficult to evaluate in terms of comparison with adult groups. There is evidence, especially in adolescent groups, of the patient becoming aware of his behavior, appreciating some of its quality, and sensing its effects upon others in the group. Generally, the youths develop more rewarding relationships with peers and often with parents.
9. *Group cohesiveness:* Although not often verbalized, this factor soon appears. Where the parents support attendance at outpatient settings, the children tend not to miss sessions; the resulting continuity provides a good basis for cohesiveness. The "group" becomes quite important to the members, usually with a core who attend regularly and with a few who are more peripheral and less regular.
10. *Catharsis:* Under appropriate conditions, it is helpful for children and youth to express strong emotions, especially those hostile to authority figures. However, it is probably the interpersonal process involved in the group more than the "release" of feelings that enables the patient to utilize the experience for growth.
11. *Existential factors:* So many children see parents and other grownups as unfair and unjust that the fact of their inherent dependency becomes lost amid their distortions. Facing life alone, for example, has limited meaning to eight-year-olds. Probably a sense of being responsible for one's behavior is the most meaningful of Yalom's five items of existential factors. In any case, these factors have less ap-

plicability in groups for younger patients, the retarded, and for the mild behavior disorders.

Ordinarily, one excludes from an outpatient group the grossly psychotic, very active sexual deviates, children who are murderers or extremely assaultive, the extreme sociopaths, and low-functioning retardates. Inevitably many exceptions arise, either from expediency or from a therapist's experimental bent. It is important to keep in mind, however, that ultimately the clinician must decide on the basis of self-knowledge, external circumstances, and clinical hunches whether to include a child who would ordinarily be excluded. Inpatient groups offer other means for treating otherwise excludable children. For example, homogeneous groups of sociopaths or of homosexuals might do very well. In sum, even exclusion criteria for group psychotherapy prove to be flexible according to the circumstances of the setting and the therapist.

In general, group psychotherapy has been able to accommodate itself to a number of theoretic positions and subsequent variations of techniques. Now, newer formulations, such as reality therapy, gestalt therapy, and transactional analysis, are nudging the traditional dominance of Adlerian concepts, classical psychoanalytic principles, and client-centered psychotherapy. Yet, if one examines closely the conceptual frameworks of therapists, certain assumptions are likely to be found in common. These include Freudian constructs of the mind (such as the ego and the defenses), psychic determinism (which coexists more and more uneasily with a philosophical allegiance to the free will of other theoreticians), infantile sexuality, and the unconscious.

Activity, such as artwork, play, dancing, gestures, and interactions, allows the inner fantasies of the child to seek expression and resolution in development, in family transactions, and in other aspects of growth—promoting adaptation.[76] The child exerts his will and engages in "power plays" in his constant search for need gratification within his time-space complex. To the perceptive therapist, the child's behavior reveals and communicates content, whose meaning is inferred within the therapist's theoretical orientation. To deal with the healthy, as well as the sick (distorted), complexities of the child's behavior call for special skills and empathic qualities. From his background and his training, the therapist evolves his individualized treatment style.

Development plays an overriding role in all treatment considerations. All therapy, and especially group psychotherapy, attempts restoration of the child as closely as possible to his own path of individuation and normal development. At most stages of childhood and adolescents, positive peer interactional experiences promote such growth.

Indications for Group Therapy

Judging from the wide range of childhood diagnostic categories for which groups have been utilized, there are few disturbed children who would not benefit at some point from a group therapy experience. However, good clinical judgment needs to be exercised to determine when to use it. For example, from one point of view, group therapy might not be indicated for a severely neurotic youngster of six, at least not until he has undergone intensive individual therapy. However, experience has demonstrated that concomitant participation in a group often augments the individual therapy. In general, if good group therapy is available for a certain age child, then one should seriously consider it as part of that child's treatment regime.

The criteria for group psychotherapy of children lack the clarity they possess for adults. Most types of group therapy for children and adolescents essentially strengthen and aid ego mechanisms. At their meetings, the children tend to avoid dipping into unconscious material. The groups deal with here-and-now productions, which often seem superficial and banal. However, the patient population does involve itself intensively in customary life patterns, as well as in each patient's life, with growth, development, and consolidation of ego functions well in the foreground. Generally, the reasons for referral to group psychotherapy are manifold. There are comparatively few reasons for not referring a child to a group (either as a main or adjunctive procedure). Exclusion criteria dominate the process of selection unless training and theoretical bias skew the therapist's viewpoint against group psychotherapy, so that he simply does not consider it at all in his treatment recommendations.

Complications, Disadvantages, or Side Effects

Again, there are a few issues to be pursued in this connection, for group composition affects them drastically. The major complications encountered have been with outpatients whose parents complained that their offspring had acquired a new vocabulary or new behavioral patterns (such as seeking straight communications). Moreover, the children were telling tales of outlandish activities that supposedly were going on in the group. The patient tests his parents and the group leader in a variety of ways, with the result that the parents sometimes withdraw the child from therapy.

Contraindications

The major factor here is the clinical judgment as to how much stress the patient can tolerate. Some borderline adolescents might find outpatient group treatment too stressful, althiugh they might well be able to handle it as part of a total inpatient regimen. In an office setting, schizophrenic boys in their early teens were able to do well; they did even better when patients were added who were only mildly upset. Thus, the acumen and skill of the therapist remain overriding factors in deciding what are contraindications.

Techniques

In recent years, there has been increased use of group psychotherapy within such settings as hospitals, private offices, and community clinics. Experimentation in this field has expanded as well. This growth has been augmented as the limitations of activity group therapy became ever more pronounced. Interview-activity techniques appeared[21, 42] with variations, such as interactional emphasis, employment of selected encounter group techniques,[44, 66] tranactional analysis methods, psychodrama exercises, modified marathon regimes, gestalt modalities, and behavioral therapy programs. Along with this stimulating experimentation was a state of confusion; this has not yet been replaced by any truly clear, systematic synthesis. Since children's group therapy encompasses a wide spectrum of ages, developmental crises, and potential for receptivity on the part of the children, the basics of techniques that pervade the various types of group psychotherapy for children must be touched upon.

The setting can vary widely, consistent with the practicalities of the therapist's working arrangements. Often, this requires a room with the primary purpose of servicing group functions. The usual office probably would not offer enough floor space and moving area for a group of eight children, at least not eight-foot by ten-foot carpeted and undercushioned area. Most therapists feel more at ease with the group if furniture and other items in the room are durable and not too valuable because of the inevitable nicks and bruises in this work.

Some therapists use chairs and perhaps a low, central table, whereas others prefer a rather bare room. There may be tools, models, games, or other artifacts available to the group. As with the basic rule that the therapist does not permit injuries to self or to others in the group and does not allow destruction of furniture, lights, or windows, he also clearly delineates what will be permitted and what will not be allowed in the use of tools, furniture, food, audiovisual instruments, and the like.

The literature is not sufficiently explicit about those practical details that the beginner learns with difficulty. For example, the optimal size for a group tends to be six to eight children. In defence to usual school circumstances, most groups for school-aged children meet in the mid-to-late afternoon, although some therapists report that Saturday mornings work out well.

The sessions with younger children tend to be weekly, lasting one hour or even less, except in the use of classical activity group psychotherapy, where the time is one and one-half hours or more. In those cities with urban sprawl and poor public transportation, this means that a parent, usually the mother, brings the child and waits for the group to end. Clinics often utilize this opportunity for the mothers' group or some other work with the mother, which is more difficult to arrange for the child clinician in private practice.

The group usually takes five to ten minutes to settle into its work. The children, especially the boys, exchange information, boasts, taunts, and challenges. The therapist has the option of one of several approaches for openings, which children quickly pick up on, comment about, and then comply with. The approach chosen may reflect the interest of the therapist, who, for example, might inquire about dreams since the last session or about emotional events that stirred anyone in the past week. In effect, this encourages the group to be activity-interactional with emphasis on verbalizations. In contrast, others may want the children to do things together (such as games) and deemphasize their more personal and possibly introspective verbal productions.

The last ten to fifteen minutes of the session could entail some free or organized play activity involving all the members. Some therapists find this an extremely useful means of ascertaining other facets of the children. For example, fifteen minutes of kickball on a nearby playground can elucidate productive interactions, revealing body damage concerns, skills, and competitiveness. Having food to share (doughnuts, cookies, sodas, etc.) enables observation of how food is used with each other and individually.

Whether to have more than one therapist is best answered with reference to the overall setting: private office, clinic, or inpatient. Most reports suggest two therapists, preferably of opposite gender. Within broad limits, each therapist can hew to his own therapeutic approach and the children handle the differences nicely.

As will be described in more detail, the major emphasis emanating from the therapist is confidentiality and seeing the child as a person, not a culprit assigned to the therapist for correction and change. When indicated, the therapist protects the weak child from the overly aggressive ones by taking the heat off verbally or by physically intervening. At times he intervenes in other circumstances, as with contagion of excitement, by pointing out the group process underlying the turmoil. At other points, he may be authoritative in forcibly telling someone to sit down or to halt what he is doing until the emotional elements behind it are explored.

The text that follows offers a pragmatic discussion of the major modalities employed for each developmental period.

Preschool and Early School-age Groups

Most of the work during the preschool years utilizes play therapy with or without accompanying supervised observational interaction by mothers. The therapist aims at individual emotional expression with the materials, as in one-to-one treatment, but with the process facilitated by peer interactions. When indicated, interpretations are used in keeping with the theoretic proclivities of the therapist.[27, 82, 83] The mothers may observe and/or meet as a parallel group with another therapist. This tends to emphasize each woman's cognitive grasp of her child's problem and to enhance the mothers' understanding and skills in parenting.

The therapist usually structures the situation by using a specific approach, such as artwork, puppets, or a permissive play ambience. Children project their fantasies onto puppets, and they find a means to express their feelings, an experience of considerable value. The child utilizes the group setting perhaps more as a site for the observation and imitation of others than as an opportunity for direct interactions.

A useful tool for infants to three-year-olds is Nielson's method.[57] This is conducted in a family living project in which the mothers sit in a group with a therapist while watching their children interacting with school personnel and with one another. The focus of these informal, leisurely meetings is on the nature of play and on its role and importance in the child's development. Hopefully, other workers will study this in different settings, such as Sunday School nurseries or day-care centers.

Hansen and associates[33] used modeling theory to show that socially isolated, early elementary students of low socioeconomic background would respond well to peer "models." When compared to control groups, they retained their gains. Behavioral intervention of this sort interrupted their somewhat fixed interactional repertoires.

Play-group therapy emphasizes the propensities of the children to interact with one another and the therapist in a permissive playroom setting. Slavson[82] suggests a female therapist who would induce the children to produce verbal and played-out fantasies; the therapist would also use active restraint when the children translated excessive tension into hyperkinetic patterns. The room offers the traditional artifacts of toys, water, plasticine, toy guns, and a doll's house. Children usually respond by reproducing their home difficulties and acting out aggressive impulses. By catalyzing each other, the children obtain libido-activating stimulation from their play materials.

Group play therapy effects basic changes in the child's intrapsychic equilibrium in his capacity for relationship and in his reality testing through catharsis, insight, and sublimation.[27] The child finds significant opportunities to change in a positive direction as he identifies himself with other group members and with the therapist. Ginott[27] places little emphasis on the group as a unit, since each child assumes the focus of the therapy. Frequent shifts occur in the play relationships, attachments to toys and peers, and the subgroups which come and go.

Haizlip, McRee, and Corder[32] found that only

one of ten randomly selected clinics provided group therapy for the younger child. In those that they studied, as well as in their own program, staff resistance was expressed in terms of theoretic issues and a lack of referrals; underlying these were more basic anxieties deriving from insufficient experience with this age group.

There are reports of programs[49, 64] with children under five in general hospital physiotherapy units. These were retarded children with histories of insufficient environmental stimulation and/or minimal cerebral damage. The groups utilized maternal participation with staff to help the children control behavior, enhance mobility, and increase peer communication.

A basic requirement for selection as a group member is the presence of social hunger, a need to be liked and to be accepted by other children. If the child has never experienced a primary relationship with a mother figure, Ginott[27] excluded him and referred him for individual psychotherapy. He also rejected children who felt murderous toward their sibs, sociopathic youngsters, those with perverse sexual experiences, extremely aggressive patients, and habitual thieves. The symptom picture of those who were selected included: phobic reactions, effeminacy in boys, excessive shyness and withdrawal, separation anxiety, and the milder primary behavior disorders.

Speers and Lansing[86] went beyond these criteria and utilized group therapy along with art therapy and parent group therapy for autistic children. They began with four children under the age of five who showed withdrawal from reality and severe disturbances in self-identity. Among these children language deficits, lack of bowel and bladder control, severe sleeping and eating disturbances, and stereotyped behavior were prominent. The investigators reported that within their group setting these psychotic children were able to change through obtaining the rudiments of self-identity. At the outset, the physical and psychological closeness of the group members panicked some of the children; over time, however, it helped them establish relationships. After the autistic defenses had been repeatedly penetrated, a group ego developed much in the form that E. J. Anthony had originally described for older children in group therapy. This provided part of a therapeutic symbiosis for each patient. Safety in the group fostered emancipation from the sick relationship with the mother.

Another variation of group therapy has been employed for preschool youngsters with special disability problems, such as retardation, brain damage, and cerebral palsy. The usual emphasis was to offer the child opportunity for age- and ability-appropriate activities, especially communication with peers An essential ingredient of such groups was the active involvement of the mothers; the end result was to enhance both their physical care of the child and their communication with him.[64]

Latency-age Groups

In addition to activities and play, verbalization techniques enhance group experience. Thus, activity-interview group therapy differs from the "pure" activity type in that the therapist actively intercedes and interprets to the children the meanings of both their verbal productions and their actions. These groups are able to accept more severely disturbed youngsters. The therapist encourages the telling of dreams, the expression of dynamically laden material, and peer-to-peer interpretations. These groups usually meet after school hours and last about an hour; the terminal ten minutes are devoted to refreshments. As with pubertal and adolescent groups, the children talk around problems, often enclosing them in a pastische of commonplace gossip. At the same time, they are well aware that their difficulties have brought them together and that there exists a group goal of changing them.

The children are usually told that none of their verbalizations will undergo censure, and that the therapists will not permit behavior destructive to persons or to the building. Beginning about 1968, an injunction had to be added that drug usage (marijuana, alcohol, LSD, etc.) would not be allowed in the sessions. The therapists reserve the responsibility and the attendant right to notify the parents if a serious matter arises that significantly affects health. The children in turn will be notified of telephone calls or other contacts their parents make with the therapists. The therapists explain to the children that they are trying to get the parents to understand their children and to perhaps change their interaction; in the service of that goal, many therapists feel free to tell parents of the general concerns of the patient, while not quoting his words per se. Although some children test out these regulations, no one seriously opposes them.

Composition of the Group

Generally speaking, late latency children (ages nine to eleven) handle the activity-interview type of therapy well. If the patient flow permits, one can place girls as well as boys in the group. In child psychiatric work with latency children the sex ratio runs about three boys to one girl. As a result, finding enough girls for these groups becomes a problem. If possible, equal numbers of each sex should be sought. The girls tend to act as a modulating influence and diminish the extremes of behavior. Their selection will depend more on the overall structure of the group than on each patient's characteristics. The optimum number of group members usually is six, although some therapists (especially if they operate with cotherapists) go to eight.

The leader may be of either gender. Sometimes the therapist talks with and sometimes for the children. As the children relate daily experiences, make comments about their parents, and discuss their interactions with other group members, the therapist offers occasional psychodynamic generalizations. The therapist's discipline of origin may be any of the traditional fields, or he may come from the newer paraprofessional training programs in mental health. A cotherapist of the same or opposite sex can be useful in these groups and has been creatively used on a pediatric ward.[45]

It helps to differentiate types, so as not to include more than a limited percentage of withdrawn and taciturn members. Such groups do not function well if they include the incorrigible or psychopathic child, the homicidal child, and the child with overt sexual deviance. The severely threatened, ritualistic, socially peculiar children who cannot establish effective communication with other group members at any useful level also do poorly in these groups; they do better if placed in more homogeneous groups with their own kind. If too many retardates are in the group, they impede interaction and tend to enhance motoric patterns for all the group members. On the other hand, children with physical deformities, protruding teeth, tics, or behavior based on maturational brain dysfunction generally find the group situation helpful. Groups tend to respond with support as the victim's sensitivities and feelings are revealed when one or two members vehemently taunt the child about his disability.

As freedom of expression and activity evokes responses among the members, different roles emerge. There are the instigators, who enable the group to stay alive dynamically; the neutralizers, who, in response to their stronger superegos, keep impulsive acts down and help regulate behavior; the social neuters, who seem impotent to accelerate or impede the flow of group activity; and the isolates, who are so neurotically constricted that they initially find the group too frightening to join in its activities.

In general, within the group, the child reproduces his customary and usual adaptational patterns. For example, all his life he may have utilized helplessness to elicit dependency fostering and psychological feeding responses from adults and peers. In the group, however, he is likely to find peers and the therapist "failing" him. The neutrality of the therapist impedes these characteristic patterns and in time creates enough frustration to initiate different behavior. Similarly, the provocative, extremely aggressive child finds no rejection or punishment for his behavioral distortions; instead he meets with acceptance, and controls. In time, he begins to react differently to the therapist and to follow group members.

Frequently, therapists report that latency-age children can be caught up in irrepressible behavior with strong contagious elements. Impulsive, acting-out children usually cow their more inhibited, conforming group-mates, though sometimes even these more reserved children catch on and join the bedlam. A recent report[89] recounts such an experience. The therapists coped with it by eliminating the play period and its regressive magnetism; instead they took a very active role in an hour-long discussion session and emphasized self-control as a value. Their work illustrates what often occurs, that is, given clearly defined limits and expectations, the children in a therapeutic group will feel more comfortable and adopt more age-appropriate behavior.

A related technique with the primary emphasis on the associative element, rather than on the activities involved, is the club formed by the children themselves.[16, 59] The members name the club, determine its goals, and elect its leadership. The very fact that the club is chosen, not imposed, generates enthusiasm and enables members to participate actively in the therapeutic process itself—as agents rather than "patients." The club forms a therapeutic milieu which allows members to face competitors and to dramatize conflicts which, without the support of an integrated group, might have destroyed them. Parental participation is sometimes encouraged. Therapeutic clubs have been successful with disadvantaged children of minority groups, with psychotic children, and with severely disturbed pubertal boys. The reported results include the strengthening of impulse control, reality testing, and self-esteem, and the improvement of object relations.

Most therapists agree that the function of group psychotherapy at this age is to aid the organization of drives into socially acceptable behavior modes.[75] The child gains in coping patterns as well as finding his place in the group. Thus, beyond certain fundamental rules established by the therapist, children set their own group behavioral standards. These take forms that are open and explicit as well as covert and concealed, a pattern that holds true for all group processes.

In some groups, videotaping of the initial twenty minutes of the group interview has been utilized. Dreams, negative and positive reports about any aspect of the children's lives, and specific comments about what the therapist defines as each child's major problem area might be recorded. Then, if meaningful material emerges, the group reviews the tape and any further material is also noted. The recording equipment presents no deterrent.[52]

Behavior modification approaches to the latency child vary in terms of the nature of the proffered rewards, the extent to which they are provided, and how they are used. Rose[72] developed an extensive program based on earning points that could be translated into material rewards. His patients showed varying kinds of emotional problems. In such a program the therapists must find the details and exigencies of such an approach rewarding for themselves as well; otherwise they would be better advised to utilize the more traditional group procedures. A variation of this is to countercondition test anxiety through Wolpe's systematic desensitization procedures in a classroom setting.[1, 88]

An increased interest in sexual dyconformities in adults has led to efforts to change the life-styles of effeminate boys, aged four to nine. No work appears on similar projects with masculine girls, if in fact they can be identified as such. Green and Fuller[31] describe a first effort in working with seven effeminate boys concomitant with a mothers' group, a fathers' group, individual psychotherapy each for mother, father, and boy, and a home-based token economy system for reinforcing masculine behavior. This total push produced reductions in effeminate patterns and an increase in closeness of the father-son relationships. The team believed the group experiences were essential for the boys and for parents.

Group therapy of boys with absent fathers[90] strives to meet their unresolved dependency and other oral conflicts, their oedipal distress at replacing the father, and the associated general authority conflicts. Obviously, the therapist must be male and able to bear up well and respond flexibly to both the overt and the even more powerful covert demands such a group makes upon him. Sessions with mothers and sons help highlight the core problems; optional ways of handling them can then be offered.

Activity-interview techniques can be modified especially for girls. In late latency with its overlap with early pubescence, girls readily discover common problems and concerns. These center about maturational problems and quests, such as clothing, makeup, boys, closeness with fathers, and physical changes. Change in such girls reflects both inherent and social maturational factors along with group cognitive and experiential learning. One study[80] utilized repeated Rorschach testing to assess progress and found positive changes in the girls' records.

In working with latency-age children, primarily boys, and especially those who are hyperactive, the therapist often ends up letting the members have at it with movement.[17, 22] Sometimes, if allowed to get too involved in activities, the group gets physically out of control. Schacter[76] attempts to harness this by suggesting that games stimulate emotional responses as in real-life situations. When the therapist perceives such an expression of feelings, he can freeze the action and have the participants stop and get in touch with the feelings. Similar work has also made use of videotapes and replay to enhance the recognition of the feelings being discussed.[95]

Group therapy in school settings has been controversial. Some therapists contend that group permissiveness carries over to classroom behavior, creating separation and dissonance. Pasnau and associates,[60] after twelve years of experience, suggest this does not necessarily occur. Teachers can be used as leaders under continuing supervision and friendly psychiatric liaison is encouraged by this. Moreover, small activity groups provide a service to children as a bridge between classroom and clinic. Schiffer[77] describes over twenty years of work with therapeutic play groups in elementary schools. He sees the group following a psychodynamic evolutionary timetable over several years; it develops from a preparatory, to a therapeutic, to a reeducative, and finally, to a termination phase.

In the form of group counseling, group therapy lends itself readily to school settings. DeLara[20] used gender and problem as criteria for the selection of homogeneous groups of six to eight students to meet once a week during school hours. The group might meet over a time span of two to three years. The commonality of the presenting problems underlay the ultimate success of the groups.

Yet, contrary to other school group therapy reports, Minde and Werry[55] found that intensive group treatment of a verbal nature in a low socioeconomic neighborhood school demonstrated no overall treatment effect. Other inner city work shows mixed results. Barcai's work demonstrated that children were capable of acquiring verbalizing skills when taught carefully in a remedial manner.[5]

In clinic and school settings, where large numbers of children need to be processed or screened, various group screening methods have been devised. In the procedure used by Gratton and Pope,[30] three investigators put five or six children into a diagnostic group for an hour a week for three weeks. They also conducted weekly group psychotherapy for twelve weeks with two groups of five children each. This was carried out in keeping with play therapy models with the goal of modifying the child's classroom behavior. Their work, and that of others, indicates that group techniques can be applied to school settings in flexible ways in order to achieve limited goals of social behavior alterations. Rhodes[68] found that conventional verbal treatment along with clear behavioral limits worked well in a short-term (six or eight sessions) program when carried out by very active therapists in an elementary school setting. The therapy directed itself to exploring the child's classroom difficulties and to gathering information for further referrals.

In a day hospital setting, Kraft and Delaney[43] utilized what may be called "discovery" therapy, employing a form of dance-movement therapy. It offers an opportunity for the child to function with others in a literally harmonious fashion so that through rhythmic and expressive movements, positive relationships emerge between individuals and the group as a whole. Feelings of isolation and alienation diminish as the group members spontaneously share their feelings actively and esthetically. The casual and enjoyable associations that come about through their rhythmic movements allow the children sufficient individual freedom to permit their dancing and moving by themselves without feeling that they disrupt group activity. The changing actions of the group bring on one-to-one relationships, as well as group relationships. These result in a sense of acceptance and influence on others that bolsters feelings of independence and self-esteem. This enhanced sense of personal strength and identity often provides the first steps toward participation in other forms of individual or group therapy.

The rhythmic movements make it possible to express emotions in ways that hurt no one; and at the same time they allow for the discharge of tension. This leads to relaxation and the freedom to go on to other things. Rhythmic action allows expressive behavior without great physical strain. It provides control over emotion rather than allowing the emotion itself to take control. Movement communication makes use of the natural kinesthetic responses to musical rhythm and leads to satisfying structured action. In responding to rhythm, the child becomes more aware of his body; it moves at a time and in a way that he wants it to. For children who have difficulties in relating directly to what is outside of the self, this technique allows them a combination of relationship and shared action which occurs in the here and now. The movements transcribe themselves into functions which are at once expressive and reality-oriented.

In group dance therapy the physical movement allows the children a means of "speaking" with each other, a method of tuning into and sharing what other people are "saying" with their actions. Movement communication establishes direct relationships, makes initial contacts, and offers access to sharing the experience of feelings. This provides an opportunity for "working through," of obtaining emotional release with symbolic body action via the rhythmic, expressive, physical movements of the group. Being in a group feels safer and is more conducive to individual risk-taking.

Art therapy is another relatively new technique employed in group therapy. Once again, providing the patient with the opportunity to speak freely and to express himself while occupied with an activity, in this case an art or a craft, has proved to be of great value. Socialization is enhanced through the group, and patients are able to express emotional conflicts symbolically through artistic productions. Such material helps the therapist clarify the diagnosis. Family participation can be encouraged or may occur spontaneously. Art therapy thus helps to reestablish lines of communication within the family. This is particularly likely to occur if the therapeutic group is the family itself rather than a children's group. Originally, art therapy relied heavily on psychoanalytic concepts; at present, many other theoretical constructs serve as the bases for interpretation and diagnosis. It has become an increasingly common technique in psychiatric hospitals, clinics, and special schools. Art therapy is especially valuable with younger children; for them it is a more "natural" mode of expression, and they find it easier to say graphically what they lack the ability to communicate verbally.

Pubertal Groups

Similar group therapy methods can be used with pubertal children, who are often grouped by gender rather than mixed. Their problems resemble those of late latency children, but they are also beginning to feel the impact and pressures of early adolescence. This is especially true of girls. In a way, these groups offer help during a transitional period. Group structure appears to satisfy the social appetites of preadolescents, who tend to compensate for feelings of inferiority and self-doubt by the formation of groups. This form of therapy takes advantage of the "natural" pressure toward socialization during these years. Since children of this age experience difficulties in conceptualizing, pubertal therapy groups tend to use play, drawing, psychodrama, and other nonverbal modes of expression. The therapist's role is active and directive, as opposed to the more passive role clasically assigned him.[19]

Activity group psychotherapy has been the recommended type of group therapy for preadolescent children. The children are usually of the same sex, and there are not more than eight members in the group. They are encouraged to act freely in a setting especially designed and planned for its physical and milieu characteristics. Slavson[82, 83] pictured the group as a substitute family in which the passive neutral therapist becomes the surrogate for the parents. The therapist assumed different roles, mostly in a nonverbal manner, as each child interacted with him and with other group members. More recently, however, therapists have tended to regard the group as a form of peer group, with all its attendant socialization processes, rather than as a reenactment of the family.

Activity therapy involves games, structured forms of play, and projects which must be planned and carried out. For children with neurotic-type difficulties,[85] the work is designed to achieve maximal elicitation of fantasies and expression of feelings about others. In order to reduce the potential for frustration and failure, the equipment supplied the child is minimal. Anxiety, however, is allowed to develop, and the therapist works to help the group members cope with it. In the ego-impaired group, the sessions are highly structured and anxiety is reduced to a minimum, although the structure is progressively loosened as the children's frustration tolerance rises. For these children, all destructive behavior is actively discouraged. In the neurotic-type groups, on the other hand, limit setting is maintained only to protect personal safety and to prevent property damage.

This therapeutic medium can help children with deficient and distorted self-images, inadequate role identifications, habit and conduct problems, and mild psychoneuroses. Neurotic traits that may be present in behavior disorders diminish in this type of group. Characterological disorders—as exemplified by the passive, dependent, infantilized child —tend to alter as these personality traits persistently fail to achieve satisfaction, are worked with, and are gradually replaced by other behaviors.

There are different forms of group therapy for latency and for prepubertal children. These vary between the modes of the activity interview and the pure activity format (which will be described later). The group procedure has been used as a diagnostic tool in child guidance work; small, short-term groups have been brought together to provide data on peer interactions. In effect, the clinic sets up a group milieu to furnish the staff with pertinent observations of the patient's behavior, while concomitantly engaging the child in a therapeutic experience.[18]

In selecting patients, one can strive for homogeneity; for example, brain-damaged youngsters can be placed in one group and neurotic children in another, and both groups are modifications of activity group therapy. The neurotic group emphasizes the verbalization of fantasy and the expression of feelings. The ego-impaired group devotes itself to structured physical activity and to carefully designed group discussions about current events.[24]

Another form of homogeneity is to give group treatment in an outpatient clinic to patients, usually boys, who have been recommended for residential or day treatment. The children gain impulse control, enhanced reality testing, and elevated self-esteem.[48]

Inpatient facilities offer other opportunities for selecting fairly homogeneous populations; yet even here the therapist cannot use only one procedure as the basic treatment process. He must match his armamentarium of techniques flexibly to the behavior patterns of the group members.[38, 95] In most latency groups that are not designed as varieties of activity therapy, the therapist involves himself in determining goals and structures of the therapy and actively pursues topics or activities.

Egan[22] suggests a modification of the routine activity group therapy in the form of activity discussion group therapy. Certain dynamisms occur in the groups: first, identification with the therapist, with group members, and with the group as a "family." Second, reinforcement and other behavioral techniques modify behavioral patterns. Third, direct (verbal), or indirect, or derivative insight develops. As with routine activity group therapy, gymnastic and other equipment is necessary, a factor which discourages practitioners who occupy cramped quarters.

When boys (especially those in residential treatment) reach the preadolescent age range, their aggressive feelings often perplex them and drive them to impulsive actions; group therapy, especially when it is combined with other techniques, can help in many ways. It affords opportunities for positive interpersonal transactions which can serve to diminish their basic mistrust, it provides ways to enhance low self-esteem, and it can affect dependency-independency conflicts for the better. Bardill[6] utilized behavioral contracting as a means of scheduling the exchange of positive reinforcements. Great pains were taken to clarify explicitly the expectations of each party to the contract. Points were awarded for certain specified behaviors during therapy.

In contrast to the residential setting, Barcai and associates[5] worked in a school setting with fourth-and fifth-grade students from a low socioeconomic area. The goal of the undertaking was to increase the students' school achievements. The therapists set up groups, counseling, remediation, and art. They found that performance improved differentially in relationship to the specificity of interventions used and the climate of the classroom. They hypothesized that underachievement could be tied to lack of reward for language-oriented communication in the children's homes. Hence, specific interventions would effect more change than generalized interest and care. Their work agrees with findings reported elsewhere of the generalization effects of psycholinguistic remediation programs.[7]

Underscoring that the specificity of intervention, when insistent and constant, plays a major role in change are experiences with a transactional analysis (TA) approach with a late latency group of boys and with groups of thirteen-year-old girls and with fourteen-year-old girls in a clinic setting.

In this technique, the initial interviews occupy an important place. At this point, the therapists set up contractual guidelines with the parents. They are told how much involvement there will be for them with the leaders and what types of data will be given to them about what their child does and says in the group. A commitment is usually obtained from the parents for at least a three-month group stay before they make any decision about terminating therapy. This has been used in both all-girls' and all-boys' groups. Strong emphasis is placed on the confidentiality that the therapists will enforce for themselves, and the patients for themselves. It is made very clear, however, that there will be an active response to any hints of destructive behavior a patient plans to direct at himself or at others. If there are data whose seriousness requires telling the parents, as when a girl is not certain but feels that she might be pregnant, the patient is urged to tell the parents directly, usually in a family session. The patient can do this with the therapists' help, with tutoring and protection.

At the time of the initial interview it is stated as well that the therapists are available to patient and parents at all times: any hour and any day, and the child is asked: "Why are you here? What is it you want to change about yourself? What is it you'd like to see altered in your family?" The therapy contract is then constructed on the basis of his replies. When resistances emerge ("Talk to my parents; they send me and pay for it."), in this TA framework, it is assumed that the rebellious adapted child ego state prevails; it is stroked, and the contractual negotiations proceed. The children catch on quickly to the ego states paradigm and work astutely with game classification, both on each other and the therapists. This approach is used consistently with them, endeavoring to achieve symptom amelioration and behavioral change.

In sum, when the physical situation permits in latency and puberty, activity groups provide an opportunity for an emotionally corrective experience. This is accomplished by utilizing a highly permissive setting to encourage freedom of expression of pent-up feelings along with regression.[81] Interview-activity and other variants along the spectrum of therapeutic techniques also provide opportunities for effective experiential insight. The therapist's consistency, warmth, flexibility, and empathic qualities, coupled with adequate knowledge of personality theory and of therapeutic techniques, provide the ingredients for good group therapy in these and other age bands.

Parent Groups

As is true with most treatment procedures for children, parental difficulties present obstacles. Sometimes uncooperative parents refuse to bring a child or to participate in their own therapy. In extreme cases, severely disturbed parents use the child as their channel of communication to work out their own needs. The child then finds himself in the intolerable position of receiving positive group experiences at the clinic that create havoc at home.

Parent groups have therefore been a source of valuable aid to the children's group therapy.[23] The parent of a child in therapy often has difficulty in understanding the nature of his child's ailment, in discerning the line of demarcation between normal and pathological behavior, in relating to the clinical establishment, and in coping with feelings of guilt. A parents' group assists in these areas. More than that, it helps members formulate guidelines for action. Participation in discussion groups has been valuable for mothers of disadvantaged children. Mothers acquired changed attitudes and new understanding of their children; this, in turn, improved the behavior of the children. In fact, in the author's experience with one group, the most lasting changes in the younger children occurred when the changes in parental attitudes were greatest. By the same token, the greatest failures occurred where the mothers were least influenced. In the community at large, parent groups were designed to further understanding of preschool development and emotional needs. Health personnel then tried to persuade the mothers to join, but their efforts were largely in vain.

Adolescent Groups

In early and middle adolescence, boys and girls tend to differ in social awareness and responsivity. Therapists assume that the main streams of emotional striving are present in both genders and run throughout these two periods. However, as the youth acquires more social tools within his peer group and with adults, the strivings are expressed and handled somewhat differently. Adolescent deviance proceeds by characteristic stages that seem to occur and be gone through as if of necessity. This process has been studied extensively; unfortunately each observer attaches significance to only one element or another that commands his attention. Goldberg,[28] for example, suggests that in the search for identity some adolescents lack the ability to love adequately, thereby feeling that they have missed out on something. As a result of this, they use other people primarily in the service of their own narcissism rather than as objects loved for their own qualities.

As Josselyn[39] points out, peer identity processes are important keys to the successful transit of latency and adolescence. In the teens especially, the youngster's recognition of ". . . himself as a child of his past and an adult of his future" becomes fundamental to maturity. For the normal youth, the turmoil of adolescence is the process of abandoning his childhood patterns for adult ones.

As described previously, when cultures undergo rapid and massive changes, the trial and error necessary for learning and growth are hindered; there is simply not enough time and opportunity. The current almost total emphasis on twosomes—"going steady"—in contrast to multiple dating adds to the difficulties of learning about one's self through brief and varying heterosexual encounters. Therapeutic efforts which employ mixed gender groups offer opportunities for some degree of honest experimentation with feelings and thoughts.[10, 12, 81, 84]

The adolescent's use of drugs as a pathway to insightful growth usually fails. Theoretically, its goal is oneness with the universe, or to spend hours searching for one's self in an unshackled inner world, or to provide overall meaning to existence.[15, 66] By way of contrast, peer group affiliations offer an opportunity for identification, working on self-esteem, devices to enhance ego strength, personal consistency, and a feeling of environmental mastery. Again, when the adolescent fails to obtain these structural elements in his family, he can retrieve his lost opportunity through group psychotherapy. Working in this helpful psychosocial therapeutic context, he can head on to adulthood with more direction.

Many an adolescent embraces the counterculture mores and strictures summed up in "Do your own thing!" Ironically, as with drug use, he again places himself in situations where there is less opportunity for growth. To the extent that he adheres rigidly to the countergroup, gains in separateness and independence are less likely to occur. When girls' groups were formed,[44] they soon developed a degree of cohesivenesses that came in direct conflict with the call of the countergroups. This was especially true when the countergroups were involved with extensive drug usage. Interestingly, the clamorous craving for excitement that is so characteristic of these patients[73] was satisfied by the use of encounter and other modalities in the group.

Techniques of group therapy with adolescents vary rather widely; usually they correlate with the therapist's background and present outlook. Ackerman,[1] in 1955, readily placed both genders, ranging in age from fifteen to twenty-three, in the same group. Each patient had previously undergone individual psychotherapy, and the group therapy experience supplemented it. Ackerman suggested that the group functioned to "provide a social testing ground for the perceptions of self and relations to others." He emphasized the importance of nonverbal behavioral patterns as material for group discussion.

Subsequent reports tended to agree that group therapy dealt more with conscious and preconscious levels than did the individual intensive, deeply introspective approach. Hulse[37] listed clarification, mutual support, facilitation of catharsis, reality testing, superego relaxation, and group integration as ego-supportive techniques. Adolescent group therapy provides constructive experiences, support for the youth's attempt to behave differently, opportunities to look at problems in everyday life, and a chance to see the adolescent's impact on others.[9]

Composition of the Adolescent Group

Group therapy with adolescent patients can be conducted in an outpatient clinic,[36] private office, hospital[35, 70] or in special settings, such as a detention home, with modifications appropriate to the setting.[92] The setting itself strongly influences the total group process. The group format is that of an open-ended interview-interaction. The preferred number of adolescents for these groups is eight to ten; circumstances often require the screening of perhaps thirty or more youths in order to produce a group of fifteen. Of these, about six will form a core group with constant attendance and effort; another three or four will constitute an intermediate group who attend more than they miss; and the remainder will make up a peripheral group that attend occasionally. Attendance and therapeutic achievement are difficult to predict for the individual patient, since these factors do not seem to be related to age, presenting problem, or diagnosis. Some therapists suggest the separation of patients in early adolescence (ages thirteen and fourteen) from later adolescent patients, since boys of thirteen and fourteen and seventeen-year-old girls live in quite different worlds and would find one another difficult to deal with in these groups. Robinson[71] used role play with retarded adolescent girls in a vocational school setting to teach appropriate job behavior and to enhance their management of interpersonal relationships.

Here again, the diagnostic categories fail to distinguish among patients sufficiently to serve as guideposts to patient selection. Certain behavioral patterns (such as overt homosexuality, a flagrant sociopathic history, drug addiction, and psychosis) contraindicate inclusion in these groups. Group methods for these patients can be used, particularly with alcoholism, homosexuality, and drug addiction, but they require special conditions.[14]

AIMS AND TECHNIQUES

Mixed group psychotherapy offers adolescent boys and girls an opportunity to relearn peer-relating techniques in a protected and supportive situation.[79] Under favorable circumstances, diminution of anxiety over sexual feelings and consolidation of sexual identity can be expected to occur. In time, as he begins to participate in the group interaction, the youth feels the pull of group cohesiveness. He reacts to the group's pace and its changes. The group will shift its content level frequently and rapidly, often within a single session. In the course of this, he experiences relationship, catharsis, insight, reality-testing, and sublimation. The boy presently begins to identify with other group members and with the therapist. In the course of these processes, the mechanisms of identification afford major opportunities for therapeutic gain. The individual adolescent constitutes the focus of treatment, but he and the therapist are continually involved with the group as a sounding board and testing ground.

Inevitably, the adolescents employ numerous diversionary tactics to avoid discussing threatening subjects. A favorite maneuver is to change the focus by a question or a comment about some unrelated topic. Sometimes diversion masks itself behind physical activity, such as throwing a gum wrapper at the wastebasket or showing the others a picture in a textbook. These and other behaviors frequently evoke precise confrontations and/or interpretations from other group members; if not, the therapist calls attention to them.

Several investigators[21, 42, 50, 78] comment that the therapist must be active, ego-supportive, and in control of the group situation at all times.

The therapist interprets cautiously to avoid the patient's misconstruing interpretation as personal criticism. Such interpretations focus on reality rather than on symbolism. They involve simple direct references to basic feelings; statements about the unconscious intent of behavior may be made when the meaning lies close to awareness. In this connection, transactional analysis has the advantage of a simple, easily understood interpretative terminology. It fulfills a basic requirement of group therapy by encouraging the individual or the group to also analyze behavior.

The therapist can be of either sex. Cotherapists and observers do not deter group process and interaction. When the cotherapists are of different sexes, differential responses are made to each. Leadership involves identifying goals for the group, showing the group how to function, keeping it task-oriented, furthering its cohesiveness, serving as a model, and representing a value system. In carrying out these tasks, the leader may offer clarification of reality, analysis of transactions, brief educational input, empathic statements acknowledging his own feelings as well as those of the members, and, at times, delineating the feeling states that occur in the group.

The content of the discussions varies enormously, ranging over school examinations, sibling competition, parental attitudes, difficulties with self-concepts, and sexual concerns. Sexual acting out or impulse eruption rarely occur. For the usual patient, brief group responses to significant experiences that he narrates fulfill his needs, for he can return to the subject later if necessary. The group often prefers short discussions, since the anxiety level is too high to dwell on a significant topic at length.

One valuable type of therapy is the encounter group. Here the emphasis falls on intense activity, and the therapy utilizes psychodrama, role playing, and other more active forms of interaction.* The raw material offers numerous opportunities from which insight can develop. The group becomes the vehicle for heightened emotional interaction between therapist and patient and between patient and patient. Encounter techniques insist that it is not enough merely to be present while a patient goes through some emotional turmoil. In order to increase group interactions the group is expected to experience and share the feelings of each member. A key concept is "free role experimentation." This facilitates the resolution of the adolescent ego identity crisis by allowing the adolescent to experiment with a wide variety of

* See references 44, 54, 58, 59, and 97.

feelings, thoughts, and behaviors, in the group setting. Group cohesion is fostered, however, by common emotional experiences in which all share, by field trips undertaken together, and by other group activities. One of the most useful of these is the camping trip which is popular with adolescents and serves to bind them together.[46]

Recently, minithons have been tried with a mixed group of adolescents. This consists of meeting for four to six hours consecutively, either at the regular place or somewhere else. After about two hours of the usual group session, a thirty- to forty-five-minute break is taken for food and stretch; the group then resumes for several additional hours. Essentially, the longer time allows for more intensive exploration of a number of topics without everyone succumbing to malaise and fatigue, as frequently occurs in adult marathons lasting for long weekends. Themes that occur in the regular group meetings attain greater depth and are explained with more intensity.

Transactional analysis is being used increasingly with adolescent therapy groups. It emphasizes treatment directed toward very specific goals. These are defined in terms of observable changes in behavior as well as attitudinal changes. The concepts of transactional analysis provide a common vocabulary and frame of reference that are readily intelligible and acceptable to adolescents and preadolescents, and which can be the focus of group discussions and analysis. Group members learn to detect "games" in their own behavior and in that of others, to analyze transactions, and to put into practice various techniques which enable them to solve "crossed transactions" and to acquire "stroking."

For example, a very common game is "kick me," which involves the adolescent offering some verbal or behavioral "hook" or ploy to a peer or adult. The other person then responds predictably, with some sort of put-down or criticism of the adolescent, who then righteously feels badly and offended. The leader and/or group members point out how the adolescent has maneuvered himself into this situation to obtain a negative stroke since he feels undeserving of straight or positive strokes, which are egosyntonic, supportive actions, or verbalizations.

Ulterior transactions are those in which the true message is covert and perhaps subtle. Adolescents love to detect these in their peers, parents, and authority figures. In one of the author's own groups such an incident involved an adolescent girl who kept telling the group she did not behave enticingly to boys or to her father, but the group picked up her tone and manner which conveyed the sexual seductiveness she really portrayed. Behavior is changed primarily by increasing the group members' understanding of themselves and of each other. Transactional analysis uses role playing, gestalts, psychodrama, and other group therapy techniques which involve verbalization and analysis, and relies as well on verbal contracting, in which the patient specifies the goals toward which he will work and the length of time he expects it will take to achieve them.

Behavioral contracting is a technique which involves scheduling the exchange of positive reinforcements between two or more persons. Although in many ways similar, transactional analysis differs from behavioral contracting in its "black box" basis. A good contract fulfills five requirements: (1) the privileges each party expects for fulfilling responsibilities, (2) the responsibilities essential to securing each privilege, (3) a system of sanctions for failure to meet responsibilities, (4) a bonus clause, and (5) a feedback system to keep track of reinforcement given and received.[72] It is crucial that the expectations of each party to the transactions be clearly understood.

The theory of modeling has shown that adolescents will respond to new stimulus situations in a manner consistent with that of the models' even if they had never observed the models responding to these particular stimuli. Modeling influences thus produce not only specific mimicry but also generative and innovative behavior. Group therapists working with disadvantaged children succeeded in introducing "star" students into the group and encouraging the members to model some aspects of their behavior on that of the "stars." Peers have also been used as agents who dispense social reinforcers. This has resulted in significant change in the behavior of group members, especially when reinforced by friends rather than by nonpreferred peers.

In brief, the tendency to regard the group as an object acted on by the therapist is now giving way to the view of the group itself as an active therapeutic factor. Transactional analysis, encounter therapy, modeling, and peer reinforcement all seem to be part of this trend.

GROUP THERAPY FOR DELINQUENT ADOLESCENTS

In Western society, many special caretaking facilities have been devised for children and ado-

lescents. In many instances group psychotherapy techniques have been adapted to these different settings. Among others, the delinquent has received a good deal of attention, including group work, field workers who work directly with neighborhood gangs, and group psychotherapy with neighborhood gangs, and group psychotherapy with probationers. Special considerations in the treatment of delinquents are discussed in detail in chapter 33.

The customary procedures for group psychotherapy require modification when employed for delinquent adolescents. These changes are in response to the contingencies arising from the character disorders of the delinquents. These adolescents differ in their dyssocial patterns from those who violate the legal, moral, and social values of the community during an adjustment reaction of adolescence or a transitional neurotic acting-out incident. The adolescent with a delinquent character structure is persistently truant, steals, vandalizes, runs away, or engages in other activities which usually mean removal to an institution.

INSTITUTIONAL GROUP THERAPY

Schulman[78] pointed out that the complexities of group psychotherapy are increased by the characterological antagonisms and chronic uncooperativeness of delinquent patients. These factors combine with those inherent in institutional settings to make it difficult to study the role of group therapy for the antisocial adolescent. Psychotherapists have pressed for the humanization of institutions and, whenever possible, for the use of alternatives such as homes and halfway houses.

Several reports indicate favorable results with groups of delinquent patients.[13] In Gersten's 1951 study, group psychotherapy with male delinquents in an institution resulted in improved intellectual and school functions. Psychological tests indicated some enhancement of emotional maturity.[25] Another report by Thorpe and Smith[93] in 1952 described sequential steps in the youngsters' responses. At first, there were episodes of testing, and later, a series of acceptance operations. In 1954, Peck and Bellsmith[62] used group methods for delinquent adolescents with reading disabilities. Richardson and Meyer[69] used the peer group as a catalyst for change by encouraging a high level of interaction within various autonomous groups. In some instances, they used the therapist roles to harass the patient in his "hot seat" and had the group itself verbally pummel the transgressor until he "gave out" to the group.

Schulman[78] emphasized a three-fold purpose in blending psychotherapy into the totality of care for these patients: (1) intellectual insight and reality testing occur in the group milieu, (2) alloplastic symptoms and superego development can be observed, and (3) the group situation readily tests the developmental stage of new attitudes since the patient continues to perform in a homogeneous group of delinquents.

Delinquents use aggression predominantly to reduce internalized anxiety. The delinquents show a weak ego structure and a defective superego. Schulman suggested that their inherent difficulty with society and its authority symbols serves as the nidus for a therapeutic relationship. Modifications of the traditional therapist-patient relationship can allow the delinquent to develop a shallow emotional attachment. Schulman initially used variations in activity and unexpected refreshments; later he modified this to focus on the authority-dependency relationship built into the institutional situation. From the beginning, the adolescent knows that his release from the institution depends on the therapist, who then assumes a certain omnipotence and, thereby, becomes a person with whom the youngster can identify. As the therapist continues to evoke a sense of early life experience for the adolescent—but without the inconsistencies, exploitations, and dishonesties that were formerly present—he becomes somewhat of an ego ideal for the embryonic superego.

Other therapists challenge this type of therapy precisely because it is based on the authority-dependency relationship. As they see it, the goal for the patient is real autonomy, not merely good adjustment to the institution; they stress that the delinquent's release must depend on him. They strive to present a leader role characterized by permissiveness and support. At times, their stance may be contrary to the overall patterns of the institution. However, they maintain that despite their stated aims, these institutional arrangements do not so much prepare the delinquent for life in society as they incapacitate him. Thus the permissive approach in their view promotes therapeutic readiness.

Schulman and others described the sexual preoccupations of adolescent female delinquents; they assert that the therapist needs to control these preoccupations in order to avoid group deterioration through continuous perseveration. This sort of deterioration occurs in the male group as well, often with the onus falling on some group scapegoat. Directed discussion by the therapist can change the tone of the session and/or block group disintegration.

Among the many variables that need to be examined, one of the most pertinent seems to be the duration of the group therapy process. Generally, the longer the group can function effectively, the better the chances for positive change among its members. Other techniques employing audiovisual methods such as videotapes are beginning to be employed and show considerable promise.

Other Group Therapy Situations

A number of investigators[11,40] have used group therapy in the management of pregnant teenagers. Medical complications ordinarily met with in this group include an increase in weight and toxemia with a higher risk of infant mortality and prematurity. Thus, an effective procedure should result in a decrease of these risks, as well as an improvement in the quality of certain psychological variables such as caring for self and the baby, subsequent pregnancies, and others. A study by Goldman and associates[29] involved eight poverty-level Puerto Rican and black females in twenty short-term, goal-directed group sessions. The young women who completed the sequence turned out to have shorter labor periods than did the dropouts of the therapy group and an untreated matched control group. The group members proved to be more consistent in keeping clinic appointments. No differences appeared in weight gain and hemoglobin level.

Group therapy has been employed in school settings for underachievers and for the underprivileged. In addition to traditional techniques, the therapists have relied on reinforcement and on modeling theory and have supplemented their work with the children by forming parent groups. Such groups have resulted in improved skills, better classroom behavior, more regular attendance, and in a decrease in disruptive behavior and hostile attitudes. Some of the most notable improvements have been achieved in reading skill groups.

As detailed in chapters 14, 15 and 16, inpatient settings provide more complex situations. The group method, in turn, must work differently to achieve the "genuine internalization of positive treatment goals by a majority of members" of the group.[47] One agency turned to a very forceful use of the group.[47] The patients met four times a week and focused strongly on group restrictions. When one member engaged in significantly deviant behavior, for example, a suicidal attempt or physical assault, three requirements had to be met: (1) each member had to explore his own role in the deviance of his confrere, (2) everyone's feelings about the incident and its perpetration had to be expressed openly, and (3) the group then had to help the patient by showing him alternative ways of handling his feelings. Working in a private, intensive-care hospital, Masterson found psychoanalytic group therapy very ". . . effective in reinforcing control of behavior and focusing the patient's consideration of therapy as an instrument to deal with his problems."[51] The therapists confronted behaviors in the group, thereby enhancing input that was dealt with much more intensively and deeply in the concomitant individual therapy.

In view of the opportunity they afford for more controlled conditions, residential treatment units have been used for specific studies in group therapy, such as behavioral contracting.[34, 67] Bardill[6] used such a setting as a site for the exchange of positive reinforcements among preadolescent boys who showed severe concerns in basic trust, low self-esteem, and dependency conflicts. In contrast to this planned, specific behavioral modification approach is the work of Celia in Brazil. There a group club was used as a means for group interaction and the integration of individuals. According to the reports, the children formed their club, used its structure to face competitors, dramatized conflicts, and corrected fantasy by reality outreach.[16] Osario[59] utilized a similar technique with psychotic children in forming a therapeutic community or home. He believed this model involved the children more than a therapeutic schoolroom model. In time, the therapeutic club, which incorporated group therapy as a part of its program, became the axis around which patients and team acted in the therapeutic task of reintegrating the child.

Somewhat akin to formal residential treatment units are social group work homes.[20, 94] The children in these settings have undergone many psychological assaults before placement; supportive group therapy offers them the opportunity for ventilation and catharsis. More often, however, it succeeds in letting these children become aware of the enjoyment of sharing activities and developing skills.

Evidently, there are many indications for the use of group psychotherapy as a treatment modality.[91] Some can be described as situational, for example, where the therapist works in a reformatory setting (in which group psychotherapy has seemed to reach the adolescents better than individual treatment). Another indication is the economic one; theoretically, at least, group therapy offers a way in which more patients can be reached at less expense. Perhaps a more appropriate indication would be the necessity to use a treatment procedure that will best help the child at a given age, a given developmental stage, and with a specific type of problem. In the younger age group, the child's social hunger and his potential need for peer acceptance help determine his suitability for group therapy. Criteria for unsuitability are controversial and have been progressively loosened.

The Role of the Therapist

The traditional passive role of the therapist has come under attack increasingly.[63] Encounter therapy, for instance, incorporates several "active" techniques, such as environmental intervention, to foster a positive transference to the therapist, to motivate group members to attend sessions, and to stimulate positive, meaningful, and concerned encounters between the therapist and his group. Transactional analysis requires an active, intervening role for the group therapist, and the very nature of contractual techniques assures that he will state his expectations and premises in a manner that would ordinarily be proscribed by a classic psychoanalytic posture. Some argue that the therapist should in fact impress his individual tastes and personality upon the techniques he uses. There is increasing agreement that the therapist can and should use positive rewards and reinforcement, and many of the techniques outlined previously are based upon this premise. Thus, the therapist actively directs the group and may even be expected to provide it with a model.[87]

Another aspect of the therapist's task is specificity of intervention. Therapists upholding the value of specific, highly directed intervention maintain that it is not enough for them to project a benevolent, supportive, and permissive presence. One comparison found that specific intervention and direct rewards had a more effective impact on the achievement of children from a low socioeconomic area than did undirected "love and care" Specific intervention on the part of the therapist necessarily involves the projection of his values and expectations upon the group; to the extent that he does this, as Azima cogently points out, it is his responsibility to be aware of his countertransference.[2]

The use of parapsychiatric personnel reflects another change in the role of the therapist. In increasing numbers of programs where the model for responsibility has remained a medical one, the model for the therapy, however, may be nonmedical. The entire issue of responsibility for becoming a therapist, for supervision, of patient care, and for clinical judgment comes into sharp focus when the traditional triad of psychiatry, social work, and psychology yield clinical space to paraprofessionals.

Leadership, preferably with male and female cotherapists, involves developing cohesiveness, identifying goals for the group, showing the group how to function, keeping the group task-oriented, serving as a model, and representing a value system. In carrying out these tasks, the leader may offer clarification of reality, analysis of transactions, brief educational input, empathic statements acknowledging his own feelings and those of members, and at times delineating the feeling states at hand in the group.

Preparation

In most circumstances, preadolescent children can enter outpatient groups without any special preparation. If the therapist is so inclined, he can brief the parents and the child; for the most part, in fact, the experience itself quickly indoctrinates the child. Adolescents often need one or more introductory sessions with a family orientation in order to make sure that both the parents and the adolescent child understand what each is contracting for in the forthcoming experience.

Frequency

Customarily, in office settings, the group meets once a week. Often mechanical problems, including travel to and from the group, confine the members to that pattern. In other settings, such as inpatient units, the group may meet with greater frequency if indicated by therapeutic considerations. There are little data about office or clinic practice with groups that met more often than once a week.

Simultaneous Practices

The major questions here involve parents, other caretakers, and sometimes siblings. Often the therapist and the appropriate school persons need to collaborate, especially when the child has a history of rebellions and acting-out behavior. Ideally, the patient's family should participate in the therapeutic process, even if only episodically (such as once monthly, or every two to three months). In reality, this often proves difficult. An alternative is to utilize parent group meetings at one- to three-month intervals for the parents to compare notes and selves. (This assumes the father and/or mother is not in some type of formal therapy.) Family therapy, which includes the presence of the patient, also aids in the treatment. This is discussed in detail in chapter 7.

Economic Factors

Obviously, in an office setting, a group experience provides care at less cost than does individual therapy. Paraprofessional training programs suggest that these personnel can be utilized to offer even lower unit-cost care than do the professionals. With the ever-increasing number of children needing help and with inflation and other economic factors disrupting the traditional pattern of providing care, more pursuit and use of group psychotherapy is in order for children and their families.

Follow Up Patterns

As indicated previously, the family system often has used the child as the scapegoat or as the emotional radar signal for its hidden interactional discomforts. Presumably, the child's therapy, often coupled with some form of family intervention, has altered the family's patterns enough that follow-up procedures can be instituted. Some therapists make clear to the child that he is free to return to the group for a visit or to attend to other problems that might arise subsequently.

After children leave the group, it is wise to see them individually two or three times at intervals of perhaps three or four months to check on progress and any possible regressions. Interval histories from parents covering the original and associated problems over the same period also prove useful. In sum, the family must be aware that problems can reoccur or surface in other ways, so that the child and the parents remain vigilant, especially for the six to twelve months after the child leaves the group.

Evaluation

The results of group therapy with children are difficult to evaluate. Several reports using control groups show favorable results with nondirective play therapy and with specific intervention group therapy for underachievers, and even for delinquents. Milieu therapy has resulted in striking improvement with ghetto children. It has also been a basic modality with childhood psychoses. Evaluating the results of group psychotherapy with children proves as difficult as assessing the outcome of their individual psychotherapy. At this point, impressionistically, it can be reported that children seem to feel unconditionally accepted by the therapist and the group members. The child gains the impression that "failures" are part of his development as a person. Through group therapy the child has obtained some inklings or more definitive insights into himself and his family's system for handling life's stresses. He has experienced, sometimes with cognitive awareness, group cohesion and his growth responses to it. Feelings of anxiety, inferiority, guilt, and insecurity find relief. Usually, years later, he recalls the group and its happenings more than he recalls the therapist, often not even remembering the therapist's name. This finding emphasizes the overall value and productivity of the experiential nature of group psychotherapy.

REFERENCES

1. ACKERMAN, N. W., "Group Psychotherapy with a Mixed Group of Adolescents," *International Journal of Group Psychotherapy, 5*:249–260, 1955.

2. AZIMA, F. J., "Transference Countertransference Issues in Group Psychotherapy for Adolescents," *International Journal of Psychotherapy, 1(4)*:52–70, 1972.

3. BANDURA, A., "Modeling and Vicarious Processes," in Bandura, A. (Ed.), *Principles of Behavior Modification*, p. 118, Holt, Rinehart, & Winston, New York, 1969.

4. BARABASZ, A. F., "Group Desensitization of Test Anxiety in Elementary School," *Journal of Psychology, 82*:295–301, 1973.

5. BARCAI, A., et al., "A Comparison of Three Group Approaches to Underachieving Children," *American Journal of Orthopsychiatry, 43*:133–141, 1973.

6. BARDILL, D. R., "A Behavior Contracting Based Program of Group Treatment for Early Adolescents in a Residential Setting," *International Journal of Group Psychotherapy, 22*:1–15, 1972.

7. BATTIN, R., and KRAFT, I. A., "Psycholinguistic Evaluation of Children Referred for Private Consultation to a Child Psychiatrist," *Journal of Learning Disabilities, 1*:46–51, 1968.

8. BENDER, L., and WALTMAN, A. S., "Use of Puppet Shows as a Psychotherapeutic Method for Behavior Problems in Children," *American Journal of Orthopsychiatry, 6*:341–348, 1936.

9. BERKOWITZ, I., "On Growing a Group: Some Thoughts on Structure, Process and Setting," in Berkowitz, I. (Ed.), *Adolescents Grow in Groups: Experiences in Adolescent Group Psychotherapy*, p. 6, Brunner/Mazel, New York, 1972.

10. ———, and SUGAR, M., "Indications and Contraindications for Adolescent Group Psychotherapy," in Sugar, M. (Ed.), *The Adolescent in Group and Family Therapy*, p. 3–21, Brunner/Mazel, New York, 1975.

11. BLACK, S., "Group Therapy for Pregnant and Nonpregnant Adolescents," *Child Welfare, 51(8)*:516–517, 1972.

12. BRANDES, N., "Group Psychotherapy for the Adolescent," *Current Psychiatric Therapies, 11*:18–23, 1971.

13. BRANDT, D. E., "A Descriptive Analysis of Selected Aspects of Group Therapy with Severely Delinquent Boys," *Journal of the American Academy of Child Psychiatry, 12*:473–481, 1973.

14. BRATTER, T., "Reality Therapy: A Group Psychotherapeutic Approach with Adolescent Alcoholics," *Annals of the New York Academy of Sciences, 233*:104–114, 1974.

15. ———, "Treating Alienated, Unmotivated, Drug Abusing Adolescents," *American Journal of Psychotherapy, 27*:585–597, 1973.

16. CELIA, S. A., "The Club as an Integrative Factor in a Therapeutic Community for Children," *American Journal of Orthopsychiatry, 40*:130–134, 1970.

17. CERMAK, S. A., STEIN, F., and ABELSON, C., "Hyperactive Children and an Activity Group Therapy Model," *American Journal of Occupational Therapy, 26(6)*: 311–314, 1973.

18. CHURCHILL, R. R., "Social Group Work: A Diagnostic Tool in Child Guidance," *American Journal of Orthopsychiatry, 35*:581–588, 1965.

19. CROWDES, N. E., "Group Therapy for Preadolescent Boys," *American Journal of Nursing, 75*:92–95, 1975.

20. DELARA, L. E., "Listening is a Challenge: Group Counseling in the School," *Mental Hygiene, 53*:600–610, 1969.

21. DUFFY, J. H., and KRAFT, I. A., "Beginning and

Middle Phase Characteristics of Group Psychotherapy of Early Adolescent Boys and Girls," *Journal of Psychoanalysis in Groups, 11:*23–29, 1966.

22. EGAN, M. H., "Dynamisms in Activity Discussion Group Therapy," *International Journal of Group Psychotherapy, 25(2):*199–216, 1975.

23. EPSTEIN, N., "Brief Group Therapy in a Child Guidance Clinic," *Social Work, 15(3):*33–38, 1970.

24. GERSTEIN, A. I., "Variation in Treatment Technique in Group Activity Therapy for Children," *American Journal of Orthopsychiatry, 39:*261–263, 1969.

25. GERSTEN, C., "An Experimental Evaluation of Group Therapy with Juvenile Delinquents," *International Journal of Group Psychotherapy, 1:*311–317, 1951.

26. GIBSON, R. E., "The Ambassador and the System (Electronic and Otherwise)," *Johns Hopkins Magazine, 24:*2–3, 1973.

27. GINOTT, H. G., *Group Psychotherapy with Children,* McGraw-Hill, New York, 1961.

28. GOLDBERG, A., "On the Incapacity to Love: A Psychotherapeutic Approach to the Problem in Adolescence," *Archives of General Psychiatry, 26:*3–7, 1972.

29. GOLDMAN, A. S., MURPHY, R. J., and BABIKIAN, H. M., "Group Therapy in Obstetric Management of Pregnant Teen-Agers," *New York State Journal of Medicine, 73:*407–411, 1973.

30. GRATTON, L., and POPE, L., "Group Diagnosis and Therapy for Young School Children," *Hospital and Community Psychiatry, 23:*40–42, 1972.

31. GREEN, R., and FULLER, M., "Group Therapy with Feminine Boys and Their Parents," *International Journal of Group Psychotherapy, 23:*54–67, 1973.

32. HAIZLIP, T., McREE, C., and CORDER, B. F., "Issues in Developing Psychotherapy Groups for Preschool Children in Outpatient Clinics," *American Journal of Psychiatry, 132(10):*1061–1063, 1975.

33. HANSEN, J. C., NILAND, T. M., and ZANI, L. P., "Model Reinforcement in Group Counseling with Elementary School Children," *Personnel Guidance Journal, 47:*741–744, 1969.

34. HAUSERMAN, N., ZWEBACK, S., and PLOTKIN, A., "Use of Concrete Reinforcement to Facilitate Verbal Initiations in Adolescent Group Therapy," *Journal of Consulting and Clinical Psychology, 38(1):*90–95, 1972.

35. HERRICK, R. H., and BINGER, C. M., "Group Psychotherapy for Early Adolescents—An Adjunct to a Comprehensive Treatment Program," *Journal of the American Academy of Child Psychiatry, 13(1):*110–125, 1974.

36. HODGMAN, C. H., and STEWART, W. H., "The Adolescent Screening Group," *International Journal of Group Psychotherapy, 22(1):*177–185, 1972.

37. HULSE, W., "Psychiatric Aspects of Group Counseling of Adolescents," *Psychiatric Quarterly, 34(Suppl.):*307–373, 1960.

38. JOHNSON, D. L., and GOLD, S. R., "An Empirical Approach to Issue of Selection and Evaluation in Group Therapy," *International Journal of Group Psychotherapy, 21:*456–468, 1971.

39. JOSSELYN, I. M., "Adolescent Group Therapy: Why, When, and a Caution," in Berkowitz, I. H. (Ed.), *Adolescents Grow in Groups: Experiences in Adolescent Group Psychotherapy,* Brunner/Mazel, New York, 1972.

40. KAUFMANN, P. N., and DEUTSCH, A. L., "Group Therapy for Pregnant Unwed Adolescents in the Prenatal Clinic of a General Hospital," *International Journal of Group Psychotherapy, 17:*309–320, 1967.

41. KRAFT, I. A., "An Overview of Group Therapy with Adolescents," *International Journal of Group Psychotherapy, 18:*461–479, 1968.

42. ———, "Some Special Considerations in Adolescent Group Psychotherapy," *International Journal of Group Psychotherapy, 11:*196–203, 1961.

43. ———, and DELANEY, W., "Movement Communication with Children in a Psychoeducation Program at a Day Hospital," *Journal of the American Dance Therapy Association, 1:*6, 1968.

44. ———, and VICK, J. W., "Flexibility and Variability of Group Psychotherapy with Adolescent Girls," in Schwartz, E., and Wolberg, L. (Eds.), *Group Therapy: An Overview,* pp. 72–90, Intercontinental Medical Book Corp., New York, 1973.

45. LAYBOURNE, P. C., SHUPE, S., and SIKKEMA, S. J., personal communication on open-ended brief group therapy on a pediatric ward.

46. LEATHERMAN, E. H., and NEHRING, S., personal communication on a unique camping program for adolescents.

47. LEWIS, J. M., et al., *Development of a Protreatment Group Process Among Hospitalized Adolescents,* Timberlawn Foundation Report no. 40, Dallas, 1970.

48. LILLESKOV, R. K., et al., "A Therapeutic Club for Severely Disturbed Prepubertal Boys," *American Journal of Orthopsychiatry, 39:*262–263, 1969.

49. LOVELL, L. M., "The Yeovil Opportunity Group: A Play Group for Multiple-Handicapped Children," *Physiotherapy, 59(8):*251–253, 1973.

50. MARVITT, R. C., LIND, J., and McLAUGHLIN, D. G., "Use of Videotape to Induce Attitude Change in Delinquent Adolescents," *American Journal of Psychiatry, 131(9):*996–999, 1974.

51. MASTERSON, J. F., *Treatment of the Borderline Adolescent: A Developmental Approach,* John Wiley, New York, 1972.

52. MELNICK, J., and TIMS, A. R., "Application of Videotape Equipment to Group Therapy," *International Journal of Group Psychotherapy, 24(2):*199–206, 1974.

53. MELVILLE, K., "Changing the Family Game," *Sciences, 13:*17–19, 1973.

54. MILLER, A. H., "The Spontaneous Use of Poetry in an Adolescent Girls' Group," *International Journal of Group Psychotherapy, 23:*224–227, 1973.

55. MINDE, K. K., and WERRY, J. S., "Intensive Psychiatric Teacher Counseling in a Low Socioeconomic Area: A Controlled Evaluation," *American Journal of Orthopsychiatry, 39:*595–608, 1969.

56. MUMFORD, L., *Pentagon of Power,* Harcourt Brace Jovanovich, New York, 1970.

57. NIELSON, G. H., "A Project in Parent Education," *Canadian Journal of Public Health, 61:*210–214, 1970.

58. OLSSON, P. A., and MYERS, I., "Non-Verbal Techniques in an Adolescent Group," *International Journal of Group Psychotherapy, 22:*186–191, 1972.

59. OSARIO, L. C., "Milieu Therapy for Child Psychosis," *American Journal of Orthopsychiatry, 40:*121–126, 1970.

60. PASNAU, R. O., WILLIAMS, L., and TALLMAN, F. F., "Small Activity Group in the School," *Community Mental Health Journal, 7(4):*303–310, 1971.

61. PATTERSON, G. R., and ANDERSON, C., "Peers as Social Reinforcers," *Child Development, 35:*951–960, 1964.

62. PECK, H. B., and BELLSMITH, V., *Treatment of the Delinquent Adolescent,* Family Service Association of America, New York, 1954.

63. PHELAN, J. R., "Parent, Teacher, or Analyst: The Adolescent-Group Therapist's Trilemma," *International Journal of Group Psychotherapy, 24(2):*238–244, 1974.

64. POOLE, A., and RUCK, R., "Remedial Play Groups for the Under-Fives in a General Hospital," *Physiotherapy, 58:*132–134, 1972.

65. PRATT, J. H., "The Principles of Class Treatment and Their Applications to Various Chronic Diseases," *Hospital Social Service, 6:*401–403, 1922.

66. RACHMAN, A. W., "Encounter Techniques in Analytic Group Psychotherapy with Adolescents," *International Journal of Group Psychotherapy, 21:*319–329, 1971.

67. RAWLING, E. I., and GAURAN, E. F., "Responders and Non-Responders to an Accelerated, Time-Limited Group," *Perspectives in Psychiatric Care, 11:*65–69, 1973.

68. RHODES, S. L., "Short-Term Groups of Latency-Age

Children in a School Setting," *International Journal of Group Psychotherapy, 23:204–216, 1973.*

69. RICHARDSON, C., and MEYER, R. G., "Techniques in Guided Group Interaction Programs," *Child Welfare, 51(8):519–527, 1972.*

70. RISSO, A. E., OSSARIO, A., and SAXON, L., "The Organization of an Adolescent Unit in a State Hospital: Problems and Attempted Solutions," in Sugar, M. (Ed.), *The Adolescent in Group and Family Therapy,* pp. 69–84, Brunner/Mazel, New York, 1975.

71. ROBINSON, L., "Role Play with Retarded Adolescent Girls: Teaching and Therapy," *Mental Retardation, 8(2):* 36–67, 1970.

72. ROSE, S. D., *Treating Children in Groups,* Jossey-Bass, London, 1972.

73. ROSENTHAL, L., "Some Dynamics of Resistance and Therapeutic Management in Adolescent Group Therapy," *Psychoanalytic Review, 58:353–366, 1971.*

74. SADOCK, B. J., "Group Psychotherapy," in Freedman, A. M., Kaplan, H. I., and Sadock, B. J. (Eds.) *Comprehensive Textbook of Psychiatry,* vol. 2, p. 1850 Williams & Wilkins, Baltimore, 1975.

75. SANDS, R. M., et al., "Breaking the Bands of Tradition: Reassessment of Group Treatment of Latency Children in a Community Mental Health Center," *American Journal of Orthopsychiatry, 43:212–214, 1973.*

76. SCHACTER, R. S., "Kinetic Psychotherapy in the Treatment of Children," *American Journal of Psychotherapy, 28(3):430–435, 1974.*

77. SCHIFFER, M., *The Therapeutic Play Group,* Grune & Stratton, New York, 1969.

78. SCHULMAN, I., "Delinquents," in Slavson, S. R. (Ed.), *The Fields of Group Psychotherapy,* pp. 196–207, International Universities Press, New York, 1956.

79. SHAPIRO, Z., and BERKOWITZ, I., "The Impact of Group Experiences on Adolescent Development," in Sugar, M. (Ed.), *The Adolescent in Group and Family Therapy,* pp. 87–103, Brunner/Mazel, New York, 1975.

80. SHERE, E. S., and TECHMAN, Y., "Evaluation of Group Therapy with Preadolescent Girls: Assessment of Therapeutic Effects Based on Rorschach Records," *International Journal of Group Psychotherapy, 21(1):99–104, 1971.*

81. SINGER, M., "Comments and Caveats Regarding Adolescent Groups in a Combined Approach," *International Journal of Group Psychotherapy, 24(4):429–437, 1974.*

82. SLAVSON, S. R., *Analytic Group Psychotherapy with Children, Adolescents, and Adults,* Columbia University Press, New York, 1950.

83. ———, and SCHIFFER, M., *Group Psychotherapies*

for Children, International Universities Press, New York, 1975.

84. SOBLE, D., and GELLER, J. J., "A Type of Group Psychotherapy for Withdrawn Adolescents," *American Journal of Diseases of Children, 68:86–90, 1964.*

85. SOO, E., "The Impact of Activity Group Therapy Upon a Highly Constricted Child," *International Journal of Group Psychotherapy, 24(2):207–216, 1974.*

86. SPEERS, R. W., and LANSING, C., *Group Therapy in Childhood Psychosis,* University of North Carolina Press, Chapel Hill, 1965.

87. SPRUIELL, V., "Adolescent Narcissism and Group Psychotherapy," in Sugar, M. (Ed.), *The Adolescent in Group and Family Therapy,* pp. 28–40, Brunner/Mazel, New York, 1975.

88. STAMPS, L. W., "The Effects of Intervention Techniques on Children's Fear of Failure Behavior," *The Journal of Genetic Psychology, 123:85–97, 1973.*

89. STRUNK, C., and WITKIN, L., "The Transformation of a Latency Age Girls' Group from Unstructured Play to Problem-Focused Discussion," *International Journal of Group Psychotherapy, 24(4):461–469, 1974.*

90. SUGAR, M., "Group Therapy for Pubescent Boys with Absent Fathers," in Sugar, M. (Ed.), *The Adolescent in Group and Family Therapy,* pp. 49–63, Brunner/Mazel, New York, 1975.

91. ———, "Office Network Therapy with Adolescents," in Sugar, M. (Ed.), *The Adolescent in Group and Family Therapy,* pp. 105–117, Brunner/Mazel, New York, 1975.

92. ———, "The Structure and Setting of Adolescent Therapy Groups," in Sugar, M. (Ed.), *The Adolescent in Group and Family Therapy,* pp. 42–47, Brunner/Mazel, New York, 1975.

93. THORPE, J. F., and SMITH, B., "Operational Sequences in Group Therapy with Young Offenders," *International Journal of Group Psychotherapy, 2:24–33, 1952.*

94. TIETZ, W., and RAMER, M., "Establishing a Small Group Treatment Home in the Mexican Ghetto," *American Journal of Orthopsychiatry, 40:242–247, 1970.*

95. VANSCOY, H., "Activity Group Therapy: A Bridge Between Play and Work," *Child Welfare, 51(8):528–534, 1972.*

96. ———, "An Activity Group Approach to Seriously Disturbed Latency Boys," *Child Welfare, 50(7):413–419, 1971.*

97. VICK, J., and KRAFT, I. A., "Creative Activities," in Brandes, N. S. (Ed.), *Group Therapy for the Adolescent,* pp. 127–138, Jason Aronson, New York, 1973.

98. YALOM, I. D., *The Theory and Practice of Group Psychotherapy,* 2nd ed., Basic Books, New York, 1975.

PART C

Counseling

11 / Behavioral Counseling: The Environment as Client

Ralph J. Wetzel, Philip Balch, and Thomas R. Kratochwill

There is now considerable evidence that a number of children's behavioral problems can be eliminated through the use of behavior modification procedures. Moreover, it appears that these techniques effect a lasting change in the deviant patterns of responding. The application of behavior modification has expanded at a phenomenal rate; it is being used in a wide variety of settings, on highly diverse populations and target behaviors.[46] Behavioral counseling has played a primary role in this proliferation, undoubtedly because of its capacity to effect change through "significant others" (for example, parents, teachers, peers, etc.) in the child's environment. While it is easy to discern how behavioral counseling has made major inroads into treating deviant child behavior, it is not easy to provide a specific definition of the term behavioral counseling. As discussed here, behavioral counseling refers to the dissemination of knowledge and skills, derived from learning theory, to assist those persons who traditionally have child-rearing responsibilities to be more effective managers of child behavior.

Some years ago, the problems of defining behavioral counseling were addressed in an entire issue of the *Counseling Psychologist*.[36] Clearly, definitions will depend on the meanings given to the terms "behavioral" and "counseling." Today, most writers in the field would acknowledge that behavioral counseling falls under the general rubric of behavior modification, but even a clear definition of the latter is not available.[1, 21, 46] Without entering into the ongoing debate over these issues, it seems safe to say that behavioral counseling has extended far beyond the earlier conceptualizations of operant conditioning. Although many of the procedures that will be discussed here are based on operant approaches,[83] operant conditioning and behavior modification are not synonymous.[48] For example, many of the behavior counseling procedures employ vicarious processes,[7, 8, 9] self-control strategies,[89] and cognitive approaches.[62, 65] Moreover, behavioral counseling departs from some of the practices of child treatment commonly associated with traditional dynamic psychotherapy approaches. Although some authors have tried to reconcile the two[63] the basic assumptions and the modes of treatment differ. At the same time, behavior therapists do use certain traditional clinical procedures

181

(for example, interviewing, rapport building, etc.).

Behavioral counseling interventions frequently derive their uniqueness and utility from viewing behavior in a context of stimulus situations or environmental events and from targeting significant people in the natural environment as change agents.[86] This chapter describes some rationales and techniques which make this form of counseling one of the most important skills for the child therapist. It is argued that since the primary datum is the observable and operationally specified behavior of the child in relation to the environment, behavioral counseling best focuses on techniques for organizing and maintaining the environmental forces surrounding the behavior of the child.

Characteristics of Behavioral Counseling

Because of their general relevance to the modification of deviant child behavior, four particular qualities of the behavioral approach are described here. (Expanded discussion of these and other factors are in chapter 5 and in volume II.) First, behavioral counseling places primary emphasis on the environmental, situational, and social determinants of behavior.[47, 91, 96] Ullman and Krasner[91] characterized the behavioral approach as using "systematic environmental contingencies to alter the subject's response to stimuli." The focus on the environment directs the therapist's attention away from an exclusive focus on hypothesized internal traits, motives, and other psychodynamic conceptualizations that could explain this behavior.[9,91] The focus of behavior change is not on problems "within" the child but rather on the environment where inappropriate behaviors are maintained. This model implies that the child therapist must act on the child's environment. It is not enough simply to see the child in one setting, such as a clinic or hospital. If a real change is to be effected, the scope of treatment must include a careful examination of situations where the problem behavior exists,[45,68,69] such as the home or the classroom.

Second, the behavioral counseling approach regards the majority of child behaviors as learned and hence alterable through additional learning procedures. It is assumed that children can be taught appropriate responses to replace behaviors which are not appropriate to a given situation. Frequently, the new responses which are taught are incompatible with old or established ways of responding. In concert with this view of behavioral counseling, the significant others in the child's environment must also be taught new ways of responding.

An increasingly important component in learning or relearning during the therapeutic process involves modeling or *vicarious learning procedures*.[5, 6] Social model learning involves matching (imitation) of the behavior of a social model by the child (the therapist or significant other in the environment can play this role). Those individuals affiliated with the social learning paradigm argue that behavior is learned and organized chiefly through cognitive processes which do not require actual performance at the time of learning.[6] Certain patterned behavior is guided by symbolic representation rather than formed through more direct reinforcement of behavior. Thus, when modeling is used, in many cases it is not necessary to gradually shape and reinforce behavior by approximations. For example, the therapist (or significant others in the environment) can demonstrate the desired behavior for the child.[56]

Hasford[36] indicated that one of the main advantages in the use of modeling in the course of behavioral counseling is its adaptability to both group and one-to-one settings. Further, the behavioral counselor can make use of video and film technology to present appropriate models and teach certain skills during the counseling process. Modeling is also useful in the development of self-control behavior.[89]

A final point regarding the importance of modeling is the need for the clinician to assess and intervene in the child's natural environment. In these contexts, children are exposed to potent sources of imitative learning (for example, the family and school). Only if these areas are included in the therapeutic process can the counselor hope to effect potent changes in client behavior.

A third characteristic of the behavioral approach to counseling is the view that normal and abnormal behavior do not represent qualitatively different processes in personality development. Instead, "acceptable" and "deviant" are social judgments about behaviors which are acquired through basic (and the same) learning processes. Such social judgments are influenced by the normative standards of certain individuals promoting the judgment, the context in which deviant behavior is exhibited, specific attributes of the behavior, as well as the unique characteristics of the child.[9] For example, it has been found[10] that aggressiveness in children was reinforced by some parents and regarded as a masculine and healthy aspect of behavior; at the same time, other individuals in the child's environment regarded such responding as deviant and a symptom of personality disorder.

The fourth and, perhaps, the most unusual aspect of the behavioral counseling approach is its data-base, and the integral role of data in the therapeutic process. A data-oriented methodology must be the basis for the treatment of devient child behavior just as the scientist-practitioner method should guide the therapist in clinical practice.[17] While the more strict operant approach to treatment has been characterized by the single subject research strategy,[38, 47, 51, 82] research procedures have expanded to a number of diverse methodologies.[71, 88]

The data-based approach to behavioral counseling has three important features. First, it provides the child therapist with direct feedback about behaviors in the natural environment. It also takes note of the relationship of these target behaviors to other individuals who may be maintaining the behaviors.[16] Second, the data-gathering activities of significant others in the child's environment provide parents and teachers feedback which demonstrates how their behavior directly influences child behavior. For example, if a teacher is asked to record child behavior, the graphing of these results can have a great impact, both for monitoring the investigation as well as suggesting relationships between what the teacher does and how the child behaves. Finally, since the approach is data-based, actual change in the client's behavior is documented and can be shared with other professionals and individuals responsible for the welfare of the child. For example, results are frequently displayed in graphic form; this provides a potent means of communication not characteristic of many other therapeutic approaches.

Experience has shown that behavioral counseling principles are complex and require careful application. Far too many of the aforementioned technical aspects of the approach are not understood; as a result, when individuals employ "behavioral procedures" indiscriminately, more problems are created than solved. Behavioral counseling procedures have been found to be extremely effective in bringing about change in a variety of settings. The application of these procedures will greatly advance the practice of child psychiatry, but this will occur only when they are used appropriately by individuals with firm knowledge of the principles of learning and with a grasp on the technology of application as communicated in a large and growing research literature.

Basic Techniques of Behavioral Counseling

Some investigations have applied behavior counseling techniques to groups of elementary school children, high school, and college students.[54,80,90] This chapter, however, will focus not so much on the application of techniques to the child directly as is discussed in chapter 5, but rather on the dissemination of knowledge and skill in the realm of behavior management to significant individuals in the child's environment, especially parents and teachers. In this process of dissemination, the child therapist teaches principles and techniques of behavior management, first to enable the adult to deal with the specified referral problems and later, to help the adult cope with a broader array of behavioral issues as they arise in the course of the child's development. In this sense, as noted earlier, the process of behavioral counseling described here involves the dissemination of professional knowledge and skills to those individuals in this culture who traditionally have child-rearing responsibilities.

The process begins with the identification and precise description of the referral behaviors. Once identified, the behaviors in question become the point of reference for all other operations. An analysis of the functional relations between these behaviors and their environments generally seeks answers to the following questions: (1) what does the child currently do or not do which is of concern (that is, what are the behaviors in question; these behaviors must be observable and discrete, hence countable); (2) under what circumstances and conditions do the behaviors occur; (3) what environmental responses to the child's behaviors account for their current excessive frequency or infrequency; (4) what alternative and more appropriate behaviors can be established; and (5) what environmental reorganizations will establish the alternative behaviors?

Very often, a functional analysis of behavior is performed by actual intervention in the behavior-environment interaction.[45] For example, a counselor may assess the function of parental attention in tantrum behavior by having the parents ignore tantrums for a few days. In other words, the assessment procedure may involve an actual intervention. Hence, the procedures of assessment and treatment are not always discrete and sequential, though they are presented here as such for purposes of description. The following material describes some common assessment or information-gathering techniques.

GATHERING INFORMATION

The basic problem for the therapist is to obtain enough reliable information about the behavior to determine what environmental factors are maintaining it and what changes in the environment can be made to bring about improvement. Several different information-gathering procedures are used in behavioral counseling, either singly or in combination.

Behavioral Interviewing. Behavioral therapists can draw on traditional clinical interview procedures and content in the process of behavioral interviewing.[12,40,65] Techniques for establishing rapport and content areas such as developmental and social histories are as important to the behavioral interview as any other. Professionals interested in learning the techniques of behavior analysis need not feel that their current professional skills are superfluous. Nevertheless, a number of sophisticated interview procedures are available[12] which move this information-gathering technique well beyond subjective impressions.

The informants in the interview may be any significant individual in the child's environment or, of course, the child himself. The behavioral interview tends to pursue the present situation in greater detail than most traditional procedures, emphasizing current behavior and its ecology rather than feeling states and other intrapsychic phenomena.

The initial interview converts the presenting complaints into precise and measurable descriptions of behaviors, their frequency, duration, and/or intensity.[45] Since many informants do not think in descriptive, behavioral terms, as a rule, the interviewer must elicit this information. When a parent says, "He's always fighting with his brother," the interviewer must ask, "What does he actually do?" A common technique is to ask the informant to recall the most recent behavioral incident and describe it in detail. This also permits the counselor to judge the informant's style and skill at behavioral observation.

In addition to the behavioral descriptions, the counselor must know the relevant environmental events. These are: (1) the *antecedent events* (the setting, conditions, circumstances; who, where, and when) of the designated behavior; and (2) the *consequent events* (what happened then; the response of the environment to the behavior, the reinforcing events). "When does this usually happen?" "With whom and where?" "What happened then?" and "What did you do?" are typical questions of the therapist who is pursuing relevant environmental events. Because of the critical role which reinforcement plays in the maintenance of behavior, the interviewer pays particular attention to behavioral consequences. Behavioral frequencies are determined by a variety of effects which behaviors produce in the physical and social environment. Behavior-environment interactions can be such that privileges, goods, and various forms of stimulation are actually contingent on maladaptive behavior. For example, research data indicate that mild teacher scoldings can increase the frequency of disruptive behavior in the classroom.[87] By the same token, the social environment may fail to support and reinforce appropriate, adaptive behaviors and/or their approximations.

Of special importance in the analysis of response consequences is the powerful influence of social attention. Parents, teachers, and peers influence the child's repertoire through the interplays between the behavior and the attention of others. Often enough, the adults in the child's environment are not only unaware of the powerful influence of attention, but they are also unaware of the subtle shifts and directions of their own attention. For example, they may not recognize the reinforcing value of eye contact, physical proximity, mild scoldings, and verbal responses. These contingencies can often be teased out by the interviewer (for example, "What did you do then?"; "Did you see it happen?"). The more the interviewer can direct adult informants toward precise descriptions of their own responses to the behavior of the child, the more likely he is to identify possible sources of behavioral maintenance or reinforcement of failure.

There is another important aspect to the initial discussions with significant others in the child's environment; this is the exploration of acceptable alternative behaviors. The therapist and adults must settle on target behaviors which are appropriate to the status of the child and to the situation. Once again the therapist may call on a range of traditional clinical procedures to help adults establish reasonable behavioral goals for the child in their care. It is critical to behavioral techniques that the goals be observable and measurable (countable).

In sum, the hallmarks of behavioral techniques are the step-by-step programming of goal behaviors, the setting of subgoals so as to insure success (reinforcement) by the child, and the development of complex skills from the combination and chaining of simpler competencies.

Direct Observation. Because behavioral approaches have developed largely from the application of research techniques to clinical problems, direct observation of children in their natural environments is another common information-gathering procedure.[15,49,71] The trained observer enters the child's environment to gather the same information pursued in the interview: precise behavioral descriptions together with the antecedent and consequent environmental events. The observer may be the therapist himself or an individual specially trained in observation techniques: Students and other paraprofessionals have often functioned as behavioral observers.[4] The techniques of observations and recording are becoming increasingly complex and sophisticated and are currently receiving considerable attention.[35,53] Instruments have been developed for recording the behaviors of both individuals and groups in the classroom, home, and other natural environments.[19,86]

Generally, an observation instrument permits the recording of specified behaviors over time. Various coding systems have been developed in which the observer marks the occurrence of one or more behaviors along time divisions. Relevant antecedent and consequent events are also frequently recorded. Direct observations may be used instead of extended interviews or to supplement information from the interview.

In behavioral research, experimental variations introduced into the environment have a measurable effect on behavior. This effect is monitored by careful observation and recording of behavioral frequencies. Similarly, the initial observations (baselines) of both the child's behavior and the behavior of others in the environment (usually frequency counts) provide a basis on which to evaluate later intervention procedures. For example, a pattern of observation such as the following might be employed: Baseline observations are made prior to experimental intervention, some experimental intervention is performed, baseline conditions may then be reinstituted, and the ex-

perimental intervention again introduced. Variation in the behavior frequency coincidental with the introduction and withdrawal of the experimental intervention is typically accepted as evidence that the experimental variable is a controlling event.[38,47,82]

Reliable observations from the environment avoid the distortions in information introduced by the untrained informant. Precise descriptions, behavior frequencies, setting events, and behavioral consequences are the major objectives of direct observation. A large and technical literature on the development of behavioral definitions[33,37] observer training,[67,73] the nature and complexity of behavioral coding,[43,60,95] and related issues have developed over the past decade.

Controlled Observation. It is common in behavioral counseling to gather initial information through observation of the child's behavior and of his interaction with significant others under controlled conditions in the clinic or laboratory. Observation facilities and technology such as one-way mirrors, sound systems, and television permit the observer to sample behavior and relevant antecedent and consequent events directly. Standardized tests can also be regarded as procedures for sampling behavior under controlled and specified conditions.

At the University of Oregon Health Sciences Center, Constance Hanf and her colleagues[33,34] have developed a particularly promising technique of controlled observation. The child-parent interaction is observed under two conditions, the "child's game" and the "parent's game." In the child's game, the adult is instructed to permit the child to initiate an activity with whatever materials are provided. The adult's task is to follow the child's lead in the activity. In the adult's game, the adult establishes the activity and guides and instructs the child. An observation and recording procedure permits the observer to count the frequencies of certain relevant categories of adult and child behaviors (for example, commands, instructions, questions, descriptions, praise, criticism, compliance, etc.).

The resulting profiles are used in consultation with the parent, who can practice new interactions under the counselor's direction until the profile of interaction meets specified criteria. Similar procedures can be used in classroom consultation with teachers.

Interview and observation procedures are often combined as an information-gathering technique. Observation of the parent-child interaction directly following an interview permits the therapist to assess the informant's reliability as an observer and to develop some definitive behavioral goals for the parents.

The Client-observer. The behavior therapist may ask parents and teachers to observe and record (count) the frequencies of certain behaviors and other relevent events in the natural environment. The recording procedures are usually simple enough to permit the parent or teacher to cound such diverse behaviors as tantrums,[14] disruption,[92] opposition,[81] and firesetting,[40] to name just a few. It is the clinician's responsibility to instruct the client in the procedures of observation and recording, to specify the task clearly, and to keep it manageable and relevant to the client. Properly designed, a procedure of observation and recording helps parents and teachers develop a clear picture of the child's actual behavior and their own relation to it. They achieve this as they note the setting and reinforcing events with respect to the targeted behaviors. This procedure involves the client at the outset and prepares him for a later role as the therapeutic change agent.

A special case of the client-observer with older children is *self-monitoring* in which the child himself records the occurrence of certain categories of behavior and the relevent environmental events. There are numerous examples of self-monitoring procedures in the literature.[89] Data indicate that, in some instances, merely the observation of behavior and circumstances by adults and/or children is sufficient to bring about therapeutic reorganization of the behavior-environment interaction.[76]

Aims and Methods of Behavioral Counseling

The general aim of behavioral counseling procedures described here is to lead significant individuals in the child's natural environment to rearrange the behavior-environment interactions. In this way, inappropriate (undesirable, "pathological") behaviors are no longer modeled, prompted, or reinforced by the environment, while appropriate behavioral alternatives are identified, developed, and maintained. The characterizing and significant aspect of the procedure is that important individuals in the child's own environment become the agents of therapeutic change; it is they who rearrange the environment under the direction of the counselor. The therapist is both consultant and teacher of the clients and aims to transmit to them specific skills of behavior management. These skills include the ability to:

1. *Observe behavior.* As described in the preceding section, the clients must learn to view the *behaviors* of the child, to become aware of behavioral frequencies over time, and to notice their own and other environmental responses to the behaviors in the forms of attention, ignoring, praise, punishment, allowances, privileges, and the like. They must learn especially to notice appropriate behavior (for example, "to catch the child being good").

2. *Identify reinforcers.* Frequently, parents, teachers, and others in the child's environment are unaware of those events which have reinforcing properties for the child's behaviors. What does he like? Whom does he seek? What activities, privileges, and materials are functional reinforcers? All these are potential maintaining consequences for appropriate behavior.

3. *Manage reinforcement contingencies and shape behavior.* Once the client understands the functional relationships between the child's behaviors and his own reinforcement, nonreinforcement (extinction), and punishment, he is in a position to arrange these events to the benefit of the child's behavioral development. Particularly stressed by most behavioral therapists is the reinforcement (shaping) of approximations: attempts by the child to engage in a behavior, however rough or approximate. Many children fail to develop appropriate behavior because initial attempts either go unreinforced or are punished. Although most behavioral counselors are not opposed to the use of punishment in behavior management (especially the withdrawal of positive reinforcers), most contingency management techniques stress the positive control of appropriate behavior.[61]

4. *Model and demonstrate new behavior.* Learning theory suggests that an appropriate behavior will not automatically appear as a maladaptive response disappears. New responses must be carefully developed. Until relatively recently, imitation has been neglected by most theories of learning; now it has been shown to be a powerful learning phenomenon.[9] Parents, teachers, and other responsible individuals in the child's environment are currently being instructed in how modeling and demonstration are critical to the learning of new behaviors.

5. *Prompt and instruct appropriate behavior.* Many adults need assistance in learning how to make instruction effective and how to support new responses in the form of "cues" or stimulus prompts. Also important is the focus of instruction on what to do rather than what *not* to do.

6. *Fade instructional control gradually and to generalize new behavior.* Once new behaviors are established, the therapist teaches the adult client how to withdraw gradually from the controlling position and to bring the behavior

under the direction of appropriate situations and events. This process is basic to social development and eventual independence on the part of the child.

There are several ways in which maintenance and generalization can be promoted. The counselor can treat the problem behavior in several settings in order to associate new behavior with a number of situations and people. Many people in the child's extended environment can be taught to maintain (reinforce) new responses. Reinforcement can be varied and new reinforcing events paired with old. For example, social reinforcers can be paired with tangibles which are gradually faded. The delay between behavior and reinforcement can be gradually lengthened. Additionally, various self-reinforcement procedures can be developed so that the child can reinforce himself.[58,61]

Stokes and Baer[86] reviewed an embryonic technology which offers a series of what-to-do possibilities to promote generalization. They emphasized first that the therapist should look for a response that enters natural reinforcer communities to reinforce desirable behaviors. Second, the therapist must train many examples of the behavior to be generalized; in particular, diversify them. Third, he must loosen control over the stimuli and responses involved in training; specifically, train difficult examples concurrently, and vary instructions, discriminative stimuli, social reinforcers, and back-up reinforcers. Fourth, the therapist must make unclear the limits of training contingencies; in particular, conceal the point at which those contingencies stop operating, possibly by delayed reinforcement. Fifth, he must use stimuli that are likely to be found in generalization settings and in training settings as well. Peers or tutors can help in this situation. Sixth, the therapist must reinforce accurate self-reports of desirable behavior; also, apply self-recording and self-reinforcement procedures wherever possible. Finally, when generalizations occur, he must reinforce at least some of them at least sometimes, as if "to generalize" were an operant response class.

Models of Counseling

Different training and counseling models have been described, depending on the therapist's initial relationship to the situation. Therapists may begin with a specific referral problem (for example, headbanging, tantrums, noncompliance, etc.) and give the client detailed instructions for observing, recording, and modifying those behaviors. Gradually, they may begin to impart to the client general principles and skills which will enable the adult to handle new behaviors and to take a more active and effective role in the child's behavioral development. Under other conditions (such as a position as general consultant), behavioral counseling may begin with the teaching of general principles and skills which can later be focused on the specific behaviors of different children. The latter approach is more common when the therapist is working with groups of parents and teachers and/or in a preventive capacity.

Since the aim of behavioral counseling described here is the acquisition of new skills by responsible adults in the child's environment, the principles of learning underlie the techniques of counseling as well as the content. Hence, therapists rely on the principles of modeling, instruction, shaping, programming, fading, and generalization in the design of their counseling activities. Numerous books and manuals have been developed for use with parents and teachers* and child care workers and houseparents.[75] These publications vary in the level of complexity and the degree of sophistication needed by the reader. Many of them are programmed texts. Andrasek and Mayhy[2] reviewed thirty-nine behavior modification training manuals and primers, sampling various topical areas, and found that the texts ranged from very difficult (appropriate for college graduates) to fairly easy (appropriate for readers at the seventh-grade level). Counselors have used them as adjuncts in their work with both individuals and groups. Research data indicate that these manuals and texts are more effective when used in conjunction with practical experience.[59] Films, tapes, and workshop formats have also been developed to provide a theoretical foundation to a variety of audiences.

Behavioral counselors frequently demonstrate procedures of behavioral control to parents and teachers. Through a one-way mirror, parents have observed a behavioral worker with their own child;[94] teachers have stood to the side and observed demonstrations of classroom management in their own classrooms;[22] trained workers have gone directly into homes to demonstrate procedures of behavioral management before parents.[77] Clients are often given the opportunity to practice new skills in the presence of the therapist, who prompts and gives immediate corrective

* See references 11, 18, 32, 41, and 73.

feedback. The techniques of proper programming, insured success, and reinforcement maintenance are important aspects of behavioral counseling methods. The evaluation of different techniques of training for parents and teachers has only recently become an active research endeavor.[77]

Consultation with an entire family is also possible in the behavioral model.[70] The establishment of target behaviors and appropriate reinforcement is best accomplished through total family involvement. Chores, responsibilities, and reinforcing consequences can be negotiated in family conference with the clinician occupying the position of arbitrator. Written contracts between the parents and/or the teacher and children are common techniques[23, 41, 86] In these contracts, the behaviors of the child are detailed and the responses of the adults to the behaviors specified. Developing a contract puts the counselor in the role of negotiator with the family and gives the family an opportunity to develop the skills of listening, negotiating, and living up to contracted responsibility. The counselor teaches the family to plan, to put demands in behavioral terms, and to arrange satisfactory token economies and/or other reinforcement contingencies.

An illustration combining the use of teachers and parents, and home and school environments, to modify a child's disruptive classroom behavior was provided by Tharp and Wetzel.[86] They report the case of Teddy, who was referred to the project's behavior consultant for aggressiveness, classroom management problems including getting out of his seat without permission and talking out, as well as underachievement. A token contract system was established whereby Teddy was able to earn tokens (a note from his teacher) for the agreed-upon behavior of not talking without permission. These school-earned tokens were each cashable for fifteen minutes of playing time with Teddy's father, an activity previously identified as reinforcing. After several weeks, this system was working so well that the contract was altered so that earning a note became contingent on the absence of both talking out and getting out of seat without permission. It is also noted that the teacher found this system so successful that it was begun with other children's problem behaviors.

Behavioral therapists have developed considerable skill at working with public school personnel.[12, 22] Visits with the teacher and observation in the classroom give the clinician valuable information about the nature of the child's environment and behavioral problems. Many school professionals have now been trained in behavioral techniques.

The Evaluation of Behavioral Counseling

Behavioral counseling has been evaluated from several different points of view. Ethical and philosophical concerns, such as issues of behavioral control and the focus on "symptomatic" treatment, have been extensively discussed and debated and are well summarized for the interested reader.[36] Two additional dimensions of evaluation are discussed in this chapter, economic implications and the effectiveness of persons in the natural environment as therapeutic change agents.

ECONOMIC IMPLICATIONS

The economic implications of behavioral counseling may be viewed from several perspectives. One is the cost in number of therapy hours of direct treatment services by professionals or paraprofessionals, either to individuals or to groups who have been defined as clients. Somewhat apart from this perspective is the use of behavioral processes to *prevent* the occurrence of problems, or to foster an environment which maximizes the possibilities of "healthy" child development. The reader should bear in mind that any comprehensive economic appraisal of therapeutic interventions is intricately related to the efficacy of the process in achieving and then maintaining its objectives, as well as the efficiency and generalizability of the intervention.

The situational and problem orientation of behavioral interventions has generally facilitated therapy of considerably shorter duration than that traditionally associated with nonbehavioral approaches.[57] It is clear that duration of specific interventions carried out by professional or paraprofessional therapists is related to the type, severity, and chronicity of the behavior being treated; nonetheless, the relative efficiency of behavioral techniques, as well as the usual small attrition rate, has been noted in the literature. In a review of behavior modification and childhood psychoses,[9] emphasis has been placed on the relative speed with which operant procedures produced desired, if not curative, effects. It has also been noted[57] that with this population, paraprofessionals seem equally capable and efficient in the use of these techniques. Others working with less severe, though often chronic, behavior problems have similarly noted successful treatment of relatively short duration. Mira[67] reported that to train parents successfully to modify common problem behaviors of their children has required an average of two hours in individual sessions.

Group treatment provides a built-in economy of money as well as time; moreover, there is evidence that training parents to modify their own behaviors so as to effect changes in their children's problem behaviors can be efficiently accomplished. The impressive parenting programs which have been reported[33, 34, 74, 93] were accomplished over periods of six weeks (fifteen half-hour lab sessions), fifteen weeks, and ten to twelve weeks, respectively. Rinn, Vernon, and Wise[78] conducted successful parent training groups that consisted of five two-hour meetings. They report that the cost of group training plus the cost of individual treatment for the group failures amounted to approximately one-third of the expense of giving all the parents single-family intervention. Further, no differences were found in the effectiveness of groups conducted by doctoral versus master's level therapists. Several recent reviews serve to document the frequency with which parents,[13, 70] as well as diverse groups of paraprofessionals (for example, aides. college students, indigenous and community workers) are being trained as behavioral counselors,[4] with increasing attention being focused on training technology.[28] In each of these reviews, the evidence supports the practical feasibility of behavioral paraprofessionals and suggests that they are effective over a broad range of activities and with various client populations. Training is often relatively brief in nature, and salary differentials, relative to those of professionals, make this an economical use of effective therapeutic skills.

Behavioral counseling approaches have additional important economic implications because of the ease with which they can be adapted to preventive efforts. The view that the same processes underlie the learning of normal as well as deviant behaviors underscores the relevance of behavioral programs and techniques to normal child development. Child management, parenting skills, and the other useful interventions which behavioral technology has now amassed should be routinely available to parents, teachers, child care workers, and others who interact significantly with children. This will help insure that they will have the skills necessary to anticipate and solve the problems which predictably arise as children grow and develop. In the past, arguments have been advanced that efforts directed to the prevention of childhood disorders and to the facilitation of positive child development would, in the long run, yield both economic as well as social gains. The use of behaviorally trained paraprofessionals working within this preventive context would serve to maximize these efforts (see volume 4).

EFFECTIVENESS OF PARENTS AND TEACHERS AS BEHAVIOR MODIFIERS

Much research interest has focused on the training of parents to modify the behaviors of their children.[31] Single-family interventions have been assessed as well as group training of parents, with varying levels of responsibility and autonomy granted the parents in the course of treatment. A series of recent reviews has established the effectiveness of parents as behavior modifiers.[84] They are particularly successful when training focuses on changing their responses toward their children,[70] and when training combines teaching of concepts of behavior modification with opportunities for the parents to apply these concepts.[29] Berkowitz and Graziano[13] have served an important function by presenting the several techniques in order of increasing methodological sophistication and degree of parental responsibility and involvement. Johnson and Katz[42] have reviewed the variety of childhood problem categories for which parents have served an effective therapeutic function (that is, antisocial and immature behavior; speech dysfunction; school phobia; encopresis and enuresis, seizures, and self-injurious behavior).

More recently, work with parents has shifted from patterns of training designed to modify discrete behaviors to methods for giving parents a broad and generalized range of competence in dealing with children's behaviors, and with the parent-child interaction system. This training has been accomplished using various formats which include: (1) didactic instruction with individual parents, (2) group training, (3) laboratory training, and (4) combined home and laboratory training. The study noted earlier[78] provides a particularly comprehensive examination of the effectiveness and efficiency of an operantly oriented parent effectiveness training program with 1,100 parents seen over a three-year period. Findings for this program, collected both at end of treatment and at follow up, indicated that 92 percent of the parents showed much improvement relative to goal attainment, and 88 percent of the parents indicated much or moderate improvement at the follow up. Additionally, 84 percent indicated further services had not been sought, 77 percent rated the instruction as very good, and 97 percent indicated strong or moderate approval of the behavioral training approach. Although no differences were found related to instructor's title, middle-income parents attended more sessions and had greater goal attainment than parents of low income. Contingent reimbursement to parents was found to increase their attendance and rate of project completion.

As with parents, teachers have been used effectively as modifiers of discrete classroom and academic behaviors of children and have also been trained in general principles and techniques. In a review of the application of these techniques to school settings, Dorr[25] concluded that behavior modification has clearly been effective, and that successful interventions have been carried out by teachers with the guidance and support of mental health professionals. After they had received specific behavioral instructions, teachers have successfully modified such problematic classroom behaviors as isolation, crying, uncooperative playing, and poor study habits. Thus, with training in the use of such techniques as contingent social approval and attention, token reinforcement systems, and verbal and physical praise, teachers have been successful in producing desired, appropriate behavior changes.

General training programs have also been developed for teachers and appear promising. When they were given group training via didactic and didactic plus videotape feedback techniques, the teachers displayed evident increases in their behavioral knowledge.[20] After their teachers had received such training, it has also been reported that target children showed desired changes in deviant behaviors.[50] Dorr[25] also discussed the potential advantages of future applications of behavioral technology. He envisaged applications by school counselors to behaviors which occur outside the regular classroom and to the academic learning process itself.

Based on this brief overview, an encouraging picture emerges. It documents the effectiveness of behavioral counseling techniques applied to children. A less well researched area is the durability of these treatment effects and their generalizability to other settings.[85] Based on the available comprehensive follow ups with parents, results in nearly all cases indicate that behavioral improvements were maintained beyond pretreatment levels; moreover, there is no indication of undesirable after effects.[47] The use of realistic reinforcers, mediators from the client's natural environment, and treatment conducted in whole or in part within the natural environment together tend to contribute to the long-range effectiveness and cross-situational generalizability of this approach. Systematic retraining, perhaps in conjunction with routine follow ups, is likely to be important in maintaining the effects of treatment.

The techniques of successful child management are not new. Skilled parents and teachers have always existed. What is new is the formulation of testable principles of behavior management. These give rise to rules which can be learned and applied systematically by the many people in responsible child-rearing positions, people who, for a variety of reasons, may not have acquired the necessary skills. Behavioral counseling is the link between an important and developing body of scientific research and those individuals in our society in the position to apply the research findings.

REFERENCES

1. AGRAS, W. S., "Toward the Certification of Behavior Therapists?" *Journal of Applied Behavior Analysis*, 6:167–173, 1973.
2. ANDRASEK, F., and MURPHY, W. D., "Assessing the Readability of Thirty-nine Behavior Modification Training Manuals and Primers," *Journal of Applied Behavior Analysis*, 10:341–344, 1977.
3. BAER, D. M., WOLF, M. M., and RISLEY, T. R., "Some Current Dimensions of Applied Behavior Analysis," *Journal of Applied Behavior Analysis*, 1:91–97, 1968.
4. BALCH, P., and SOLOMON, R., "The Training of Paraprofessionals as Behavior Modifiers: A Review," *American Journal of Community Psychology*, 4:167–169, 1976.
5. BANDURA, A., *Social Learning Theory*, Prentice-Hall, Englewood Cliffs, N.J., 1977.
6. ———, *Social Learning Theory*, General Learning Press, New York, 1971.
7. ———, "Psychology Based Upon Modeling Principles," in Bergin, A. E., and Garfield, S. L. (Eds.), *Handbook of Psychotherapy and Behavior Change: An Empirical Analysis*, pp. 653–708, John Wiley, New York, 1971.
8. ———, *Psychological Modelings: Conflicting Theories*, Aldine-Atherton, Chicago, 1971.
9. ———, *Principles of Behavior Modification*, Holt, Rinehart & Winston, New York, 1969.
10. ———, and WALTERS, R. H., *Social Learning and Personality Development*, Holt, Rinehart & Winston, New York, 1963.
11. BECKER, W. C., *Parents and Teachers: A Child Management Program*, Research Press, Champaign, Ill., 1969.
12. BERGAN, J. R., *Behavioral Consultation*, Charles E. Merrill, Columbus, Ohio, 1977.
13. BERKOWITZ, B. P., and GRAZIANO, A. M., "Training

Parents as Behavior Therapists: A Review," *Behavior Research and Therapy, 10:*297–317, 1972.

14. BERNAL, M. E., et al., "Behavior Modification and the Brat Syndrome," *Journal of Consulting and Clinical Psychology, 32:*447–455, 1968.

15. BERSOFF, D. N., "Silk Purses into Sow's Ears: The Decline of Psychological Testing and a Suggestion for Its Redemption," *American Psychologist, 28:*892–899, 1973.

16. BIJOU, S. W., PETERSON, R. F., and AULT, M. H., "A Method to Integrate Descriptive and Experimental Field Studies at the Level of Data and Empirical Concepts," *Journal of Applied Behavior Analysis, 1:*175–191, 1968.

17. BROWNING, R. M., and STOVER, D. O., *Behavior Modification in Child Treatment,* Aldine-Atherton, Chicago, 1961.

18. BUCKLEY, N. K., and WALKER, H. M., *Modifying Classroom Behavior,* Research Press, Champaign, Ill., 1970.

19. CANTELLA, J. R., *Behavior Analysis Forms for Clinical Intervention,* Research Press, Champaign, Ill., 1977.

20. CANTRELL, R. P., "Efficacy of Inservice Training of Teachers in Operant Techniques," Ph.D. thesis, George Peabody College for Teachers, Ann Arbor, Michigan (University Microfilms no. 70–7626), 1970.

21. CIMINERO, A. R., CALHOUN, K. S., and ADAMS, H. E. (Eds.), *Handbook of Behavioral Assessment,* John Wiley, New York, 1977.

22. CLARK, H. B., et al., "The Role of Instructions, Modeling, Verbal Feedback, and Contingencies in the Training of Classroom Teaching Skills," in Ramp, E., and Semb, G. (Eds.), *Behavior Analysis, Areas of Research and Application,* pp. 187–222, Prentice-Hall, Englewood Cliffs, N.J., 1975.

23. DeRESI, W. J., and BUTZ, G., *Writing Behavioral Contracts: A Case-stimulation Practice Manual,* Research Press, Champaign, Ill., 1973.

24. DICKSON, C. R., "Role of Assessment in Behavior Therapy," in McReynolds, P. (Ed.), *Advances in Psychological Assessment,* vol. 3, pp. 341–388, Jossey-Bass Publishers, San Francisco, 1975.

25. DORR, D., "Behavior Modification in the Schools," in Gentry, W. D. (Ed.), *Applied Behavior Modification,* C. V. Mosby, St. Louis, 1975.

26. EVANS, I. M., and NELSON, R. O., "Assessment of Child Behavior Problems," in Ciminero, A. R., Calhoun, R. S., and Adams, H. E. (Eds.), *Handbook of Behavioral Assessment,* pp. 603–681, John Wiley, New York, 1977.

27. FRANKS, C. M., and WILSON, G. T., *Annual Review of Behavior Therapy: Theory and Practice,* Brunner/Mazel, New York, 1975.

28. GARDNER, J. M., "Training Non-Professionals in Behavior Modification," in Thompson, T., and Dockens, W. S. (Eds.), *Applications of Behavior Modification,* Academic Press, New York, 1975.

29. GLOGOWER, F., "Training Parents as Effective Behavior Modifiers: A Group Approach," Master's thesis, West Virginia University, 1972.

30. GOLDFRIED, M. R., "Behavioral Assessment," in Weiner, I. B. (Ed.), *Clinical Methods in Psychology,* pp. 281–330, John Wiley, New York, 1976.

31. GRAZIANO, A. M., "Parents as Behavior Therapists," in Hersen, M., Eisler, R. M., and Miller, P. M. (Eds.), *Progress in Behavior Modification,* vol. 4, pp. 251–298, Academic Press, New York, 1977.

32. HALL, R. V., *Managing Behavior, Parts I, III,* H. & Y. Enterprises, Marriam, Kan., 1970.

33. HANF, C., "Modifying Problem Behaviors in Mother-Child Interaction: Standardized Laboratory Situations," Paper presented at the meeting of the Association of Behavior Therapies, Olympia, Wash., 1968.

34. ———, "A Two Stage Program for Modifying Maternal Controlling During Mother-Child (M. C.) Interaction," Paper presented at the meeting of the Western Psychological Association, Vancouver, B.C., 1968.

35. HARTMANN, D. P., "Notes on Methodology: On Choosing an Interobserver Reliability Estimate," *Journal of Applied Behavior Analysis, 10:*103–116, 1977.

36. HASFORD, R. E., "Behavioral Counseling—A Contemporary Overview," *Counseling Psychologist, 1:*1–32, 1969.

37. HAWKINS, R. P., and DOBES, R. W., "Behavioral Definitions in Applied Behavior Analysis: Explicit or Implicit," in Etzel, B. C., LeBlanc, J. M., and Baer, D. M. (Eds.), *New Developments in Behavioral Research: Theory, Methods and Applications,* pp. 167–188, Lawrence Erlbaum Associates, Hillsdale, N.J., 1977.

38. HERSON, M., and BARLOW, D. H., *Single Case Experimental Designs: Strategies for Studying Behavior Change,* Pergamon Press, New York, 1976.

39. HOLLAND, C. O., "Elimination by the Parents of Fire-Setting Behavior in a Seven-Year-Old Boy," *Behavior Research and Therapy, 7:*135–137, 1968.

40. HOLLAND, C. J., "An Interview Guide for Behavioral Counseling with Parents," *Behavior Therapy, 1:* 70–79, 1970.

41. HOMME, L. E., *How to Use Contingency Contracting in the Classroom,* Research Press, Champaign, Ill., 1971.

42. JOHNSON, C. A., and KATZ, R. C., "Using Parents as Change Agents for Their Children: A Review," *Journal of Child Psychology and Psychiatry, 10:*107–121, 1969.

43. JONES, R. R., "Behavioral Observation and Frequency Data: Problems in Scoring, Analysis and Interpretation," in Hamerlynck, L. A., Handy, L. C., and Mash, E. J. (Eds.), *Behavior Change: Methodology, Concepts and Practice,* pp. 119–145, Research Press, Champaign, Ill., 1973.

44. ———, REID, J. B., and PATTERSON, G. R., "Naturalistic Observation in Clinical Assessment," in McReynolds, P. (Ed.), *Advances in Psychological Assessment,* vol. 3, pp. 42–95, Jossey-Bass, San Francisco, 1975.

45. KANFER, F. H., and SASLOW, G., "Behavioral Diagnosis," in Franks, C. M. (Ed.), *Behavior Therapy: Appraisal and Status,* pp. 417–444, McGraw-Hill, New York, 1969.

46. KAZDIN, A. E., "Characteristics and Trends in Applied Behavior Analysis," *Journal of Applied Behavior Analysis, 8:*332, 1975.

47. ———, "Methodological and Assessment Considerations in Evaluating Reinforcement Programs in Applied Settings," *Journal of Applied Behavior Analysis, 6:*517–531, 1973.

48. ———, and CRAIGHEAD, W. E., "Behavior Modification in Special Education," in Mann, M. L., and Sabatino, D. A. (Eds.), *The First Review of Special Education,* vol. 2, pp. 51–102, JSE Press, Philadelphia, 1973.

49. KENT, R. N., and FOSTER, S. L., "Direct Observational Procedures: Methodological Issues in Naturalistic Settings," in Ciminero, A. R., Calhoun, K. S., and Adams, H. E. (Eds.), *Handbook of Behavioral Assessment,* pp. 279–328, John Wiley, New York, 1977.

50. KOZIER, K. P., "Effects on Task-oriented Behavior of Teacher Inservice, Charted and Video-taped Feedback and Individual Consultation," Ph.D. thesis, University of Wisconsin, Ann Arbor, Michigan (University Microfilms no. 71–3469), 1971.

51. KRATOCHWILL, T. R. (Ed.), *Single Subject Research: Strategies for Evaluating Change,* Academic Press, New York, 1978.

52. ———, and BRODY, G. H., "Methodological and Statistical Considerations in 'Behavior Modification' Research," in Kazdin, A. E., *Use of Statistics in N–1 Research,* Paper Presented at the 83rd Annual Convention of the American Psychological Association, Chicago, 1975.

53. ———, and WETZEL, R. J., "Observer Agreement, Credibility and Judgment: Some Considerations in Presenting Observer Agreement Data," *Journal of Applied Behavior Analysis, 10:*133–139, 1977.

54. KRUMBOLTZ, J. D., and THORESEN, C. E. (Eds.), *Behavioral Counseling: Cases and Techniques*, Holt, Rinehart & Winston, New York, 1969.

55. LAZARUS, A. A., "The Elimination of Children's Phobias by Deconditioning," in Eysenck, H. J. (Ed.), *Behavior Thearapy and the Neuroses*, pp. 114–122, Pergamon Press, London, 1960.

56. LEBOW, M. D., *Behavior Modification: A Significant Method in Nursing Practice*, Prentice-Hall, Englewood Cliffs, N.J., 1973.

57. LEFF, R., "Behavior Modification and Childhood Psychoses," in Graziano, A. M. (Ed.), *Behavior Therapy with Children*, pp. 133–153, Aldine-Atherton, Chicago, 1971.

58. LOVITT, T. C., and CURTISS, K. A., "Academic Response Rate as a Function of Teacher and Self-Imposed Contingencies," *Journal of Applied Behavior Analysis*, 2:42–53, 1969.

59. MCKEOWN, D., ADAMS, H. E., and FOREHAND, R., "Generalization to the Classroom of Principles of Behavior Modification Taught to Teachers," *Behavior Research and Therapy*, 13:85–92, 1975.

60. MCLAUGHLIN, T. F., "An Analysis of the Scientific Rigor and Practicality of the Observational and Recording Techniques Used in Behavior Modification Research in Public Schools," *Corrective and Social Psychiatry* and *Journal of Behavior Technology Methods and Therapy*, 21:13–16, 1975.

61. MADSEN, C. H., and MADSEN, C. K., "Teaching/Discipline," in *Behavioral Principles Toward a Positive Approach*, Allyn & Bacon, Boston, 1970.

62. MAHONEY, M. J., "The Sensitive Scientist in Empirical Humanism," *American Psychologist*, 30:864–871, 1975.

63. MARMOR, J., "Dynamic Psychotherapy and Behavior Therapy: Are They Irreconcilable?" in Franks, C. M., and Wilson, G.T. (Eds.), *Annual Review of Behavior Therapy, Theory, and Practice*, pp. 57–71, Brunner/Mazel, New York, 1973.

64. MARTIN, R., *Legal Challenges to Behavior Modification: Trends in Schools, Corrections and Mental Health*, Research Press, Champaign, Ill., 1975.

65. MEICHENBAUM, D., *Cognitive-Behavior Modification: An Integrative Approach*, Plenum Press, New York, 1977.

66. MEYER, V., LIDDELL, A., and LYONS, M., "Behavioral Interviews," in Ciminero, A. R., Calhoun, K. S., and Adams, H. E. (Eds.), *Handbook of Behavioral Assessment*, pp. 117–152, John Wiley, New York, 1977.

67. MIRA, M., "Results of a Behavior Modification Training Program for Parents and Teachers," *Behavior Research and Therapy*, 8:309–311, 1970.

68. MISCHEL, W., "Toward a Cognitive Social Learning Reconceptualization of Personality," *Psychological Review*, 80:252–283, 1973.

69. ———, *Personality and Assessment*, John Wiley, New York, 1968.

70. O'DELL, S., "Training Parents in Behavior Modification," *Psychological Bulletin*, 81:418–433, 1974.

71. O'LEARY, K. D., and KENT, R. N., "Behavior Modification for Social Action: Research Tactics and Problems," in Hamerlynck, L.A., Handy, L.C., and Mash E. J. (Eds.), *Behavior Change, Methodology, Concepts and Practice*, pp. 69–96, Research Press, Champaign, Ill., 1973.

72. ———, and KRANOWITZ, J., "Shaping Data Collection Congruent with Experimental Hypotheses," *Journal of Applied Behavior Analysis*, 8:43–51, 1975.

73. PATTERSON, G. R., and GULLION, M. E., *Living with Children: New Methods for Parents and Teachers*, Research Press, Champaign, Ill., 1968.

74. PATTERSON, G. R., COBB, J. A., and RAY, R. S., "A Social Engineering Technology for Retraining Aggressive Boys," in Adams, H., and Unikel, I. (Eds.), *Issues and Trends in Behavior Modification*, Georgia Symposium in Experimental Clinical Psychology, vol. 2, pp. 139–210, Pergamon Press, Oxford, 1972.

75. PHILLIPS, E. L., et al., *The Teaching Family Handbook*, Research Press, Champaign, Ill., 1974.

76. PIERSEL, W. C., and KRATOCHWILL, T. R., "Self-Observation and Behavior Change: Applications to Academic and Adjustment Problems Through Behavioral Consultation," *Journal of School Psychology*, in press.

77. RAMP, E., and SEMB, G., *Behavior Analysis, Areas of Research and Application*, Prentice-Hall, Englewood Cliffs, N.J., 1975.

78. RINN, R.C., VERNON, J.C., and WISE, M. J., "Training Parents of Behaviorally Disordered Children in Groups: A Three Years' Program Evaluation," *Behavior Therapy*, 6:378–387, 1975.

79. ROMANCZYK, R. G., et al., "Measuring the Reliability of Observational Data: A Reactive Process," *Journal of Applied Behavior Analysis*, 6:175–184, 1973.

80. RYAN, T. A., and KRUMBOLTZ, J.D., "Effect of Planned Reinforcement Counseling on Client Decision-Making Behavior," *Journal of Counseling Psychology*, 11:315–323, 1964.

81. SAJWAJ, T., and HEDGES, D., "A Note on the Effects of Saying Grace on the Behavior of an Oppositional Retarded Boy," *Journal of Applied Behavior Analysis*, 6:711–712, 1973.

82. SIDMAN, M., *Tactics of Scientific Research*, Basic Books, New York, 1960.

83. SKINNER, B. F., *Science and Human Behavior*, Free Press, New York, 1953.

84. SLOOP, E. W., "Parents as Behavior Modifiers," in Gentry, W. D. (Ed.), *Applied Behavior Modification*, pp. 4–36, C. V. Mosby, St. Louis, 1975.

85. STOKES, T. F., and BAER, D. M., "An Implicit Technology of Generalization," *Journal of Applied Behavior Analysis*, 10:349–367, 1977.

86. THARP, R. G., and WETZEL, R. J., *Behavior Modification in the Natural Environment*, Academic Press, New York, 1969.

87. THOMAS, D. R., BECKER, W. C., and ARMSTRONG, M., "Production and Elimination of Disruptive Classroom Behavior by Systematically Varying Teacher's Behavior," *Journal of Applied Behavior Analysis*, 1:35–45, 1968.

88. THORESEN, C. E., *Let's Get Intensive: Single Case Research*, Prentice-Hall, Englewood Cliffs, N.J., forthcoming.

89. ———, and MAHONEY, M. J., *Behavioral Self-control*, Holt, Rinehart & Winston, New York, 1974.

90. TOSI, D. J., et al., "Group Counseling With a Non-Verbalizing Elementary Student: Differential Effects of Premack and Social Reinforcement Techniques," *Journal of Counseling Psychology*, 18:437–440, 1971.

91. ULMANN, L. P., and KRASNER, L. (Eds.), *Case Studies in Behavior Modification*, Holt, Rinehart & Winston, New York, 1965.

92. WAHLER, R. G., "Oppositional Children: A Quest for Parental Reinforcement Control," *Journal of Applied Behavior Analysis*, 2:159–170, 1969.

93. WALDER, L. O., et al., "Teaching Parents to Modify the Behaviors of Their Autistic Children," Paper presented to the 74th Annual Convention of the American Psychological Association, New York, 1966.

94. WETZEL, R. J., and PATTERSON, J. R." Technical Developments in Classroom Behavior Analysis," in Etzel, B. C., LeBlanc, J. W., and Baer, D. M. (Eds.), *New Developments in Behavioral Research: Theory, Methods and Applications*, pp. 363–388, Lawrence Erlbaum Associates, Hinsdale, N.J., 1977.

95. WETZEL, R. J., et al., "Outpatient Treatment of Autistic Behavior," *Behavior Research and Therapy*, 4:169–177, 1966.

96. YATES, A. J., *Behavior Therapy*, John Wiley, New York, 1970.

12 / Dynamic Counseling

Doris Olch and Maurice Freehill

Definition and Description

Counseling denotes the professional work carried out by those who call themselves counselors. It is a generic term used to refer to a good deal of the work carried out by the helping professionals. A general definition of counseling is: a processs involving a relationship between a counselor and a client, or clients, through which those who are counseled become able to make positive changes in behavior and mental health.

There has been much debate and some attempts at analysis aimed at determining whether counseling and psychotherapy are equivalent, or even distinguishable. Many books on counseling address this issue from the start, inasmuch as the particular viewpoint biases the conception of process, techniques, and goals. Some maintain there are no essential differences between counseling and psychotherapy.[1, 50, 61] Tyler[78] sees a difference; she contends that therapy is concerned with personality reconstruction, whereas counseling aims for better utilization of existing personal resources. Brammer and Shostrom[13] posit a continuum with counseling characterized by short-term problem solving with normals in a rational mode, while psychothcraphy centers on the alleviation of pathological conditions in severely disturbed people with the help of a focus on the unconscious.

Blocher[6] differentiates the two on the basis of goals. Counseling goals are felt to be developmental, educative, and preventive, whereas psychotherapy goals are remedial, adjustive, and therapeutic. He indicates that such a bifurcation cannot be maintained in practice. Indeed, the appeal of the "yavis" syndrome (the young, attractive, verbal, intelligent, successful people) to the psychoanalyst and to other highly trained therapists suggests that precisely those cases which are most handicapped will be left to community and publicly supported programs staffed by counselors! Nor can student services in schools refuse to work with highly aggressive, suicidal, or marginally psychotic children.[17] Such realities underline statements that distinctions are quantitative more than qualitative,[7] that there are more commonalities than differences,[65] and that only practical and political considerations dictate recourse to separate terms.[68]

As Szasz's[73] contention that mental illness is a myth has gained acceptance in medical and legal circles, the person seeking or needing help is increasingly defined as having "problems in living," and psychotherapy is viewed not as curing a disease but as a "process of learning new techniques for getting along."[71] That viewpoint, combined with need for service and a desire to reach greater numbers of clients, suprred the development of brief psychotherapies which present themselves as counseling. These trends increase the blurring of an already uncertain demarcation between psychotherapy and counseling.

Obviously, there is considerable overlap between counseling and psychotherapy. At the same time, there are differences in emphasis that can be listed. Counseling is recognized and described as dealing with developmental, more than with remedial, problems; it focuses rather more on specific problems and rather less on pervasive personality disturbance; it views the client not as "sick" but as having learned maladaptive or unsuitable behaviors; it tends to be brief rather than extended in time; it concerns itself more with contemporary than with historical events, thoughts, and feelings; it attends more to conscious ego than to unconscious id phenomena; it regards the client as capable of growth and control and it is active rather than reactive.

Whether the process is labeled psychotherapy or counseling may depend on the setting in which it is exercised and the background and training of the practitioner. It is most certain to be labeled counseling if it occurs in an educational institution, or an employment, vocational, or rehabilitation center. The term is employed increasingly in mental health clinics, churches, community programs, and in private practice; it is least likely to be utilized in a medical setting. Counselors are usually master's degree graduates of a counseling program within the framework of education or psychology; some are psychologists with a doctoral degree; others have diverse college backgrounds with social welfare orientations and are employed in institutions such as prisons. In many such instances, the assignment, not the training, determines the title. In all, there are approximately 75,000 counselors in the United States, with 54,000 of these employed in educational institutions.[65]

A significant portion of all counseling may be termed "dynamic." Broadly conceived, the term "dynamic" implies a degree of inwardness in both the motivation and the organizational pattern of behavior. The view denies David Hume's thesis that behavior is externally caused and externally organized, with experience being the sole source of knowledge. Dynamic thinking assumes that the overt and observable structures of behavior depend on, but do not directly reflect, underlying, deeper, or covert structures—Freud's "unconscious," Maslow's "deeper side," or Chomsky's "transformational rules." The approach of dynamic counselors diverges widely; for some, the human task is to find expression for a blind and biologic impulse; others argue that the human is self-defining with cognitive factors modifying, limiting, and creating the affective or impulsive aspects.[55]

Under the larger definition of dynamic, there are two possible shades of meaning. First, it may connote adherence to the Freudian or analytic tradition in psychology, the psychodynamic principle that mental life is governed by both conscious and unconscious forces, that behavior is a product of an interwoven pattern of these processes, some of which are only dimly perceived by the individual.[14] This position is in contrast to the behaviorist's explanation, couched in terms of learning principles and acknowledging only observable behavior (with both unconscious causes and consciousness dismissed from the realm of viable concepts). The endorsement of psychodynamics implies acceptance of the phenomena of defense, resistance, and transference, although it does not insist that these be emphasized in the counseling process.[7] Behavior is multiply determined, and the counselor may choose to develop his working alliance with conflict-free, ego aspects of personality or with the client's competency and growth drives.[9]

A second element of "dynamic" work is related to systems theory. This takes into account the person's neurological and psychological structure, and the interrelations with family, school, community, society, and culture.[33, 64] The person is the microcosm, the whole system is the macrocosm, and there is complexity and interdependence of parts in each and together. Minor changes in the system or in attitudes, feelings, or behavior may have far-reaching consequences, although the impact may not be direct or immediately manifest. On the other hand, change may arise in part of the system without repercussions registering elsewhere. Consultation with parents or school personnel may prove more profitable than working directly with the child. A more formalized method might be abandoned in order to engage the client in his world.

Theory

Multiple and mixed theories underlie dynamic counseling for children. Freudian formulations are basic; the theory of psychosexual development and the importance of early childhood experiences and family relationships provide the background for understanding children and the development of personality. Freud's discoveries led to a systematic treatment of children, including Anna Freud's work with young children (see chapter 2), August Aichhorn's efforts with delinquents (see chapter 33), Bettelheim's care of severely disturbed youngsters in a special school (see chapter 14), and Slavson's group psychotherapy for children and parents (see chapter 10), which have been prototypes for dealing with children.

The neo-Freudians rejected some of Freud's biological orientation, attached greater importance to socioenvironmental and cultural factors as they bore on the individual, and focused on the pull of the future as well as the push of the past. Alfred Adler's views of man as a social creature have been amplified in writing and teaching by Rudolf Dreikurs[20] and continue as the basis for a major counseling thrust in children's services.[19, 41]

Otto Rank influenced Carl Rogers, the originator of client-centered counseling[61] and a major figure in the development of counseling. Rogers's insistence that the person is rational, social, realistic, forward-moving, and active in his own behalf seriously challenged more negative assumptions about the nature of man, while his specifications for necessary conditions in a therapeutic relationship sharpened interest in the role of the counselor, the process of counseling, and the conduct of research. Play therapy practiced by Axline[2] and relationship therapy by Moustakas[44] followed the so-called nondirective method advanced by Rogers, which is discussed in chapter 13.

Sullivan's attention to interpersonal relationships is probably more closely connected with communication and systems theories,[80] and family therapy.[4,82] The idea that the individual can develop and be understood only in the context of the family and mileu provides a rationale for insistence on dealing with systems in order to relieve personal distress (see chapter 7).

Ego psychologists gave impetus to the trends in education and therapy which addressed themselves to the development of competence and effective transactions with the environment.[9] In particular, Erikson[23] developed an expanded and broadened treatment of psycho-sexual growth, and Robert White,[83] along with Hartman and Rapaport, conceptualized notions of conflict-free ego energy. The "psychoeducational approach," elaborated by Long, Morse, and Newman[38] and linked with Redl and Wineman,[57] rests upon an integration of individual psychodynamics, group forces, and growth principles (see chapters 19 and 20).

The worth and dignity of human life and a belief in the freedom of the individual to set goals and find meaning in relation to the universe— these are existential ideas brought into counseling by philosopher/psychologists such as Allport, Maslow, May, Frankl, and Binswanger. With technology's encroachment into every segment of society and the proliferation of change almost beyond human tolerance,[77] the search for personal identity and values became a prime objective in handling adults as well as youth and children.

There are many varieties of counseling which are labeled dynamic. These comprise a rather loose family of divergent theories, which encompass broad similarities and significant differences.

Indications

The report of the Joint Commission on Mental Health of Children stated that for all its wealth, the United States had witnessed a decline during the twentieth century in the care of its emotionally disturbed children.[58] In the latter 1960s this led to a renewed interest in children. Ultimately it yielded a "promise unfulfilled"[59] when the comprehensive Child Development Bill to insure a widespread preventative and remedial mental health system failed to be enacted. Of the 93 million young people (under twenty-four) in this country, 0.6 percent are considered psychotic, an-

other 2 to 3 percent are labeled severely disturbed, and an additional 8 to 10 percent require professional mental health attention.

Schools are often a primary site for the recognition and care of emotional disturbance in children. A Canadian study[17] noted that 15 percent of its child and adolescent population suffered from serious mental health problems and suggested that counselors in the school system should be used more frequently as a resource. Bower[10] verified that early identification of the adjustment status of a child could be determined fairly accurately through ordinary information available to teachers. He urged the adoption of school programs on the assumption that early detection might initiate help at a time when it could be most beneficial and economical.

According to Bower and Lambert,[11] there are patterns of behavior discernible in children which are sufficient cause for further study. These are: an inability to learn, an inability to build or maintain interpersonal relationships with peers and teachers; inappropriate or immature types of behavior or feelings under normal conditions; a general pervasive mood of unhappiness or depression; and a tendency to develop physical symptoms, such as speech problems, pains or fears, associated with personal or school problems.[12] Another way of stating what might be an indication for counseling is found in the definition of a "psychological problem" by Buhler and associates:[16] "a hindrance that disrupts the continuity of processes within the individual or in group. A problem in school disrupts the work, the desirable cooperation of the group, or the individual's ability to function adequately." "Disturbances" that are significant in contrast to more trivial difficulties are further characterized as repetitious, involving a succession of different types of disturbance, or as a serious single episode.

Freud proposed, and Erikson expanded, a view of development as a sequence of stages with special problems and accomplishments connected with each stage. Research and clinical experience give some evidence that the acceptable curiosity of the scientist rises from oedipal stress[43] or that many human impulses are rooted in the uncertainties of adolescence.[18] These concepts have influenced every variety of counselor other than those who are the most strict disciples of conditioning theories. In practice, it is critical to determine which problems are developmental only, and which are significantly different. Where problems are identified early, immediate brief intervention may eliminate the need for later protracted treatment.[79]

developmental and personal attributes may be enhanced.[31]

Complications, Side Effects, Disadvantages, and Contraindications

The hazards of brief therapy enumerated by Small[67] are applicable to counseling. They include oversimplification of interpretation to produce quick clinical results, development of transference which proves difficult to resolve, and the possibility of overlooking associated somatic problems. On the positive side, however, since neither interpretation nor the exploration of transference are pursued in counseling, such dangers may be minimal.

There is the risk that in order to insure progress with the case, serious disorders may be masked or there may be an understatement of severity. Too-early termination carries disadvantages, in that a client may require additional treatment for more favorable functioning even though diminished anxiety has by then reduced therapeutic motivation. Frank's[25] admonition that any treatment which heals can also hurt, bears remembering; "the fact that psychotherapy harms some people is, paradoxically, evidence of its power."

Contraindications for accepting a client for counseling customarily include the need for hospitalization, desirability of medication for the disturbance, or a combination of emotional difficulties with physical symptoms as a clear-cut psychosomatic ailment. Nevertheless, with medical consent and cooperation, counselors do work even with the preceding conditions.[7]

The method for selection of clients for group counseling varies. Frequently anyone too deviant from the others or with insufficient controls is excluded.[72] Segregation of children by sex and age is followed inconsistently.[47]

Antisocial children and children with chronic severe conditions present serious challenges to even the most highly trained professional and in the most favorable milieu.[74] Difficulties in their management are therefore expected. Nonetheless, the service given to such children in institutional and clinic settings is often in the hands of counselors. With cases of retardation and neurological damage, the ceilings for expected change are necessarily lowered. Elevation of academic scores in nonachievers should not be expected although

Technique

As implied in the definition of counseling, the relationship between client and counselor is the basis for and the essence of the whole process. Transference and countertransference reactions were first studied as uniquely significant dimensions of psychoanalytic therapy. Traditional clinical training has emphasized technical skills and encouraged perception of the therapist as a relatively passive, neutral observer. Counselor training, on the other hand, emphasizes the "therapist's personality and the attitudes he brings to bear on the treatment situation as the key to therapeutic influence and perhaps of greater importance than any technique."[71]

To the extent that the counselor can communicate to the client feelings of acceptance, understanding, and congruence (a genuineness and sencerity in what is being said and done), the client can feel safe, secure, and free to change and grow.[60] Such counselor characteristics as empathy and attentiveness,[65] counselor values,[63] and even "healing qualities that elude precise definition"[25] contribute to the effects that may "come with care from one knowledgeable adult" in dealing with disturbed children.[26]

The relationship is the means through which goals are achieved; the techniques used are for the purpose of establishing and maintaining that relationship. Techniques vary widely. In some instances, they are closely tied to counseling philosophy; more often still they reflect personal style and are geared to the particular problem and individual involved. Parent, group, and individual methods in verbal and multiform action modes are all utilized.

Since counseling is relatively brief, abbreviated identification and clarification of the problem sets the stage for active, focused, and straight-forward intervention. A contract is established so that the child and/or others involved will know the time limits and other arrangements, and goals are mutually developed. The counselor keeps in mind the pragmatic question: What will help most, and most quickly?

Because the child is brought into counseling by parents, school, or other agencies and does not come of his own volition, and because there are limitations to verbalizing, understanding, and controlling the environment, the usual practice is to involve other concerned persons. For example, the Adlerian-Dreikurs model of family counseling takes place in a family education center using a combination of techniques encompassing educational methods and group dynamics.[69] The format includes interviewing the parents before the group of parents assembled in the counseling room, while the children are in the playroom with the playroom director. After the interview is completed, the parents leave, and the children enter to be counseled before the group. Then, the parents return for the playroom director's description of observations of the children's interactions in the playroom. This is followed by the counselor structuring a discussion with the parents aimed at designing a program for working with the child. "This discussion of mutual problems in a democratic spirit of respect leads to an understanding by all parents of the method used to influence and stimulate their children toward harmonious family living."[69] The counselor's task, in essence, is to interpret the dynamics of the family situation to the parents, clarify for the child goals toward which he is striving, and to instruct both about ways to seek a more satisfying living style.[41]

More often, family counseling follows the practices of Satir,[64] as discussed in greater detail in chapter 7. The entire family is seen together, the problem is elicited from parents and child, family interactions are observed firsthand, and the counselor confronts each person with how he or she appears and how family members seem to be affecting each other. Impressions are shared and exchanged; attitudes and perceptions are brought into the open; and different ways of behaving, of viewing behavior, and of dealing with behavior are explored together. Weinberger[81] suggests that in the case of children under seven years, the main focus of the work should be with the parents (see chapter 9). When the child is between seven and eleven, parents and children can be seen separately and, occasionally, together. And when the children are over eleven, all can be seen together. Granger[29] suggests that tasks be devised to be performed by the family focusing attention on the family as a unit and allowing for inclusion of the younger child.

Counseling goals tend toward problem solving rather than toward uncovering internal conflicts. The counselor may, however, develop hypotheses regarding the nature of the conflicts present. These hypotheses sharpen counselor participation and give direction to plans for altering the family

pattern.[3] The Bartens state that parents need to learn how to observe and listen to the child, to see the value of positive reinforcement, and to appreciate each child's role in the family system. The following case illustrates such intervention techniques:

CASE ILLUSTRATION

Johnny, age seven, was referred to a school counselor because he was not learning to read despite evidence that he was unusually bright. He appeared shy and markedly attached to his attractive mother. His parents were from diverse backgrounds; differences in interests and goals made the marriage rancorous and had brought it near dissolution. Nevertheless, the mother shielded the child, hid her anger, and pretended the father's absences were routine. Attempts were made to help the family see how the child was confused by unacknowledged family tensions and become aware of how they might help and support him in carrying out school tasks. Immediate tutoring was undertaken, designed to give Johnny personal reassurance and pleasure in learning to read.

Group parent counseling alone, without the children present, has long been advocated.[66] It is much practiced, although with diverse emphases which extend all the way from teaching skills[28] to open discussion of problems.[5] Parents may view the group leader as a child-rearing expert, but his task is to lead parents to search for their own solutions. In organizing groups of parents, counselors find it efficient to select them according to the age and the presenting problems of the children.[22]

Disorder in children is traditionally ascribed to early parent-child interaction; its treatment, in turn, requires modification of intrapsychic factors in both child and parent. Another view holds that the child's disturbance does not necessarily reflect parental pathology.[76] The latter view supports the belief that the goal is not always basic change in child or parent personality structure but that parental guidance alone may alter the child's world sufficiently to induce behavioral change. Furthermore, say Phillips and Johnston,[53] it is not necessary to be concerned with "this" before tackling "that"; instead, the total relationship is made the focus. Similarly, the theory behind consultation with teachers and school administrators, which is discussed in chapter 21, asserts that the school system itself contributes to the child's malfunction.[38, 45]

In working with the child, as with the adult, a counselor may use techniques which reflect feeling, reassure, restate content, interpret, accept, clarify, encourage, and so forth.[65] It is essential that vocabulary be consonant with the child's mental development. On a nonverbal level, the counselor acts as a model for the child, allows behavior rehearsals, and sanctions alternative methods for dealing with situations. The counselor arranges a corrective and an enhancing environment, permits release of emotional tention, gives support, and tries to provide satisfaction by acceptance.

The child's acquisition of competence signifies the achievement of some degree of control. This, then, will lead to confidence and self-respect. "Labeling," or developing language for mediation, increases the child's cognitive control. Children with problems can be taught to alter their behavior in response to verbal cues and to acquire the habit of talking about things in order to gain better control over events.[32]

Cognitive restructuring thus becomes a goal. The child and those about him are helped to develop new attitudes toward themselves and to develop viewpoints which differ affectively and cognitively from former conceptions and which are functionally more fruitful.[55] Even the well-known behaviorist Lazarus[35] departs from traditional behaviorist language in noting the value of having clients alter their thoughts; thus, along with desensitization, he teaches the client to engage in cognitive restructuring, that is, to consider behavioral alternatives. No longer is emphasis only upon insight, appreciating the connectedness between causal events and consequence; rather the counselor shares with the client the actual process of attitudinal change,[40] of how to alter beliefs so that they are more congruent with reality and productive of emotional well-being.

Physical activity is most important for a child, and the possibilities of action-oriented counseling are manifold. Ohlsen[48] and Long and associates[38] include descriptions of counseling via different media—dance, art, music, and theater. It is, however, free play which is the child's natural means of communicating. Moreover, this is an avenue for understanding the child, as well as for allowing the child to work out feelings and to try out and rehearse behavior. Slightly different techniques of play therapy are described by Ginott, Ross, Moustakas, and Axline in Haworth's collection.[30] Bosdell[8] discusses the play experience for the child, both individually and in groups. Suitable play equipment must match age and level of maturity. The intent is to elicit different forms of expression and to provide opportunity for the child to gain mastery over self and materials (see chapter 25).

Group counseling for children is increasingly utilized by schools and agencies. An excellent presentation of the appeal of group counseling, its values and limitations, operational practices, and related research appears in Shertzer and Stone.[65] Ohlsen[46] summarizes the method thus:

When a counselor is most successful in counseling children in groups he facilitates change in behavior by conveying to prospective clients what they may expect before they join a group, by helping those who volunteer for group counseling to define undecided goals and make essential commitments for behavior change, by selecting those who believe that they can be helped and can convince him of this conviction, by conveying his confidence in their ability as individuals to profit from the experience, and by teaching them to be helpers as well as clients. [p. 328]

In one school, group counseling was undertaken with six eighth-grade boys, each selected by a teacher because he was failing a class or causing disturbance. The group met in a multipurpose room, surrounded by painting materials, unused books, and media equipment. The objective was to provide opportunity for airing problems and, perhaps, establish a relationship with an attentive adult. Follow up after five weekly sessions provided evidence of success. Three boys secured passing grades in target subjects and five of the six were reported to be more social and better-behaved in class. Only one appeared to profit very little. He was, in fact, suspended, but on his return to school, he asked that the special group be started again.

Some of the boys may have established a new relationship with an adult, while others obtained better understanding of important old relationships. The following fragment from a tape may prove illustrative:

Student A: My dad jumps all over me about school work.
Student B: What's he say?
Student A: Well, you know, he says, "Why ya gotta be the dummy in the family?" and "Your sister did good in school." And sometimes he says he was valedictorian for his class, whatever that is.
Counselor: Valedictorian means outstanding student, one who gets the best grades.
Student A: Well, that sure ain't me.
Counselor: Do you think your father wants you to be like he was?
Student C: I'll bet that's it.
Student A: Maybe, but I ain't got the brains.
Student D: My old man doesn't care what I do in school.
Student E: How'ja know?
Student D: He never says nothin' about it.
Student B: Well, don't he talk to ya?
Student D: Sure, but not about school.
Student B: Well, what about?

Student D: Sports and things and he tells me to do stuff.

Student B: What?

Student D: Tells me to clean my room or take out the garbage or get milk from the store.

Student B: Does he say you do that OK?

Student D: Sometimes but sometimes he says, "Don't do it like you do your schoolwork," or if I bring back change from an errand he says "Any eighth-grader should be able to count that much."

Counselor: Then he does say something about schoolwork.

Student E: Yeah, I suppose.

Counselor: Do you know how your father liked school or got along?

Student D: Not much, but Grandma says he was the dummy of the class and sometimes when both of my folks are lookin' at my report card Mom says "like father, like son."

Student B: Maybe he doesn't like rememberin' and he doesn't talk much about school.

Student D: I never thought about that before.

For adolescents, group counseling is often preferable to individual work. With this age group's preference for peers and its distrust of and rebellion against adult figures, the group provides a natural setting for its work. The group allows for a social practice arena, decreases feelings of being isolated or different, and fosters new ways of dealing with relationships and situations.[72] The response is often most favorable when the group sessions are offered in some form of outreach programs, outside the existing formal channels. Use of audio and video recording with feedback to the participants stimulates interest and heightens learning.

Ghetto children[34] do especially well in group counseling, because this setting resembles their experiences on the neighborhood block. The ghetto child is acculturated to gut-level responses and accustomed to trusting peers rather than adults to assist in solving problems. Role playing and behavior modification techniques have been used in such groups (see chapter 27).

Diagnosis and the use of psychological tests in counseling have been in and out of favor and have aroused considerable controversy between supporters and detractors. The client-centered school in particular was most opposed to these practices. It argued that they were antithetical to client self-actualization and therapeutic practice of unconditional acceptance of the client and, further, that tests interfered with an effective relationship. In recent years, however, this position has been tempered.[70]

Bordin[7] indicated four ways in which testing had value for psychological counseling: "to provide information for the counselor; to develop

more realistic expectations of what is to be the purpose of counseling; to give the client information; to stimulate self-exploration." While advantages and disadvantages continue to be debated,[65] the trend is to avoid traditional psychiatric classifications. Instead, there is a trend to use individual assessment as a vehicle for exploration rather than as an immutable prescriptive decision.[26] As a description of functional ego processes, psychodiagnostic testing facilitates accommodating the therapeutic modality to the case,[56] deepens understanding of the client and the problem, and permits a sharper focus on an individual's strengths and weaknesses.

One of the authors initiated a project for teaching graduate students, which involved the individual administration of a battery of intelligence, projective, and interest tests to a number of adolescent girls attending a school for unwed mothers. Test data became the basis for a popular and useful program of educational and vocational counseling for these girls, as well as a source of understanding for the professional staff. The test process itself proved valuable in that these high school girls, usually poorly motivated in academics, met and received attention from students only slightly older than themselves but models of achieving and purposive life.

Conditions Required

The necessary conditions for successful dynamic counseling include client cooperation, commitment to change, and client understanding of such arrangements as punctuality, confidentiality, and probable process. There is very rarely a written contract, but there is a verbal understanding about the conditions for referral to other professionals, termination, or renegotiation of the arrangements. Because parents have expectations that influence the counseling relationship and process, they are often party to this understanding.

Counseling is provided within a system. Its objectives must have some congruence and support from agents and institutions, particularly from family and schools but also from courts, churches, and others. Counselors then find themselves working either cooperatively or parallel with behavior modification in schools, pharmacologic management of some children by pediatricians, or environmental programs various agencies are providing for delinquents. The practical necessity for working together is supported by the view that in many cases "a balance of etiological forces seems to be on the situational side."[4]

Any therapeutic effort may be hampered by a resistance that arises within the broader societal context. In some instances, there is a rejection of mental health goals and methods, such as that voiced in the now-defunct *American Mercury* or on the "Stamp Out Mental Health" signboards. The argument is that the goal of mental health intervention is adjustment, or mediocrity, and that the methods employed are both improperly authoritarian and an invasion of privacy. Socially alienated groups object on other grounds. Their argument is that therapists are agents of the establishment, categorizing others in pejorative ways, unable to overcome social distance in treatment, and confusing improvement with compliance. While all counseling is beset with these problems, they are most acute in work with children and persons in institutional settings since these are not clients by choice.

Frequency

Individual sessions are held for one-half to one hour; group sessions run from one to three hours; both are usually conducted on a weekly or semi-weekly basis. A time span of approximately six to ten weeks may be average, but a number of cases are disposed of in one or two interviews; at the other extreme, counseling may extend for a year, or even longer. Duration is flexible, based upon practice, and readily altered.

Economic Implications

Counseling services are frequently offered by public agencies and are either no-fee, as in schools, or on a low-fee sliding scale, as in mental health clinics. Since many counseling positions can be filled by individuals with master's-level training, costs remain modest compared with traditional medical-psychological services. In the private sector where counseling is carried out chiefly by doctoral level personnel, costs for services tend to be competitive with the lower economic range of medical counterparts.

Follow Up

Follow up is not often required except for research purposes. Good counseling teaches personal responsibility along with a recognition of danger signals, and alertness to cues of diminished functioning in daily living. It encourages return for additional counseling when this occurs. Self-monitoring is thus basic to preventive mental health.

Outcome

The ultimate questions facing any mode which purports to help people is: Does it do any good? What is it good for? And the accompanying question: Is it better to do it a special way? The pitfalls which await the would-be unraveler of these fundamental queries are legion.

Shortly following Eysenck's[24] blistering attack upon the efficacy of psychotherapy with adults, Levitt[37] published comparable findings with respect to children. He added the cautionary note, however, that until research methodology improved, conclusions should not be drawn. At the same time, a study of delinquency prevention[54] yielded results that were entirely negative. In 1961, Tyler[78] said

various kinds of follow-up researches . . . have produced almost no evidence that measurable personality changes occur as an outcome of counseling. What does happen is that limited problems are solved, workable decisions are made, the client moves forward with more assurance than before. [p. 14]

Smith[68] located a study by Caplan in 1957 which reported improved grades and self-concept following group counseling with socially maladjusted boys at the junior high level, and another study by Roman which noted improved reading skills and psychosocial adjustment of emotionally disturbed adolescents. However, Broedel, Ohlsen, and Proff[15] using group counseling, discerned no improvement in grades, although self-acceptance and behavior showed positive change. Negative results were reported by Ohlsen and Gazda[49] after group counseling with underachieving fifth-graders. Steffre[70] in the *Encyclopedia of Educational Research* observed that "it remains to be shown that counseling has value in improving academic achievement," and Ohlsen[47] noted "improved achievement test scores are more easily obtained than improved grades."

That which fails by a frontal attack, however, may be influential by a less direct maneuver. Ohlsen[47] reports a project by Sonstegard in 1961 in which teachers and parents and the fifth-grade students were counseled, and reading achievement scores were improved. Perkins and Wicas[52] reported significant increase in grade-point average and self-acceptance by bright, underachieving ninth-grade boys when counselors worked with the mothers, with or without the students. Taylor and Hoedt[75] cite three additional sources corroborating this finding. A recent, well-designed research project[39] reported an upward trend in grades with parent involvement, but not with child therapy.

In all, the data overwhelmingly attest to the relation between school effectiveness and the child's interpersonal environment; the data point up also the importance of counseling with the one who bears the grievance. Such an intervention should be matched with parental characteristics. Lower socioeconomic level families respond favorably to more structured counseling approaches that include suggestion and advice, while upper socioeconomic level families, with greater educational assets, do better with sessions which make use of their verbal problem-solving capacities.[39, 41]

Inasmuch as brief psychotherapy and dynamic counseling share many similarities, the recently developing body of research which relates to the former may be applicable to the latter. Rosenthal and Levine[62] studied children coming to a psychiatric outpatient clinic, where the mean length of treatment in the experimental group was 8.1 weeks, as compared with a length of 39.9 weeks for the control subjects. The therapists for the experimental subjects used a direct approach "utilizing areas of psychological strengths within the family in a coping and adaptational framework." There was 76 percent improvement in briefly treated cases compared with the 79 percent by means of the longer, more conventional treatment. On the basis of 3,000 children seen in a clinic, Weinberger[81] estimates that brief therapy which focuses on current behavior is sufficient for 50 percent of those treated, that 30 percent require more extensive therapy, and that other types of service are relevant for 20 percent of the cases. In a mental health center for children and adolescents, a brief therapy program, based upon a "competence model" conducted over a four-year period, was "highly efficient and effective" on the basis of multimeasure evaluations.[36] It produced a low withdrawal rate, reduced waiting lists, and satisfactory termination of 42 to 47 percent of cases. While the proceding data are not conclusive, the implications are that "long" is not necessarily better, and that "brief" may certainly be sufficient.

The values of group counseling in general have been increasingly explored, and a number of reviews attest to its capabilities for behavior change.[27,51] After examining a number of studies of group counseling with children published in the late 1960s and early 1970s, Ohlsen[46] claimed positive results in development of interpersonal skills, self-acceptance, and classroom behavior.

Isolation of those qualities which belong distinctively to dynamic counseling of children is almost impossible to find in the literature and in the observation of practice. This has a pervasive influence on most counseling and is affected in turn by the experience of others. Successes and failures are not predicted simply by the age of the client or the nature of the problem, an observation which lends support to the wisdom of an eclectic dynamic view. The dynamic orientation profits by strengthening coping tendencies, mobilizing cognitive review, and realigning environmental systems in ways that foster the natural growth tendencies of children.

REFERENCES

1. ALBERT, G., "If Counseling Is Psychotherapy—What Then?" in Smith, C. E., and Mink, O. G. (Eds.), *Foundations of Guidance and Counseling*, pp. 447–454, Lippincott, Philadelphia, 1969.

2. AXLINE, V. M., *Play Therapy*, Houghton Mifflin, Boston, 1947.

3. BARTEN, H. H., and BARTEN, S. S., "New Perspectives in Child Mental Health," in Barten, H. H., and Barten, S. S. (Eds.), *Children and Their Parents in Brief Therapy*, pp. 1–21, Behavioral Publications, New York, 1973.

4. BEISER, M., "Etiology of Mental Disorders: Socio-Cultural Aspects," in Wolman, B. B. (Ed.), *Manual of Child Psychopathology*, pp. 150–188, McGraw-Hill, New York, 1972.

5. BETTELHEIM, B., *Dialogues with Mothers*, Avon, New York, 1971.

6. BLOCHER, D. H., *Developmental Counseling*, Ronald Press, New York, 1966.

7. BORDIN, E. S., Psychological Counseling, 2nd ed., Appleton-Century-Crofts, New York, 1968.

8. BOSDELL, B. J., "Counseling Children with Play Media," in Ohlsen, M. M., (Ed.), *Counseling Children in Groups: A Forum*, pp. 27–45, Holt, Rinehart & Winston, New York, 1973.

in Waetjen, W. B., and Leeper, R. (Eds.), *Learning and Mental Health in the School*, pp. 23–46, Association for Supervision and Curriculum Development, National Education Association, Washington, D. C., 1966.

10. ———, *Early Identification of Emotionally Handicapped Children in School*, Charles C Thomas, Springfield, Ill., 1960.

11. ———, and LAMBERT, N. M., "In-School Screening of Children with Emotional Handicaps," in Long, N. J., Morse, W. C., and Newman, R. G. (Eds.), *Conflict in the Classroom*, Wadsworth Publishing Co., Belmont, Calif., 1965.

12. ———, *Pupil Behavior Rating Scale*, Publisher's Test Service, CTB/McGraw-Hill, Monterey, Calif., 1978.

13. BRAMMER, L. M., and SHOSTROM, E. L., *Therapeutic Psychology*, Prentice-Hall, Englewood Cliffs, N.J., 1960.

14. BRENNER, C., *An Elementary Textbook of Psychoanalysis*, rev. ed., International Universities Press, New York, 1973.

15. BROEDEL, J., OHLSEN, M., and PROFF, F., "The Effects of Group Counseling on Gifted Adolescent Underachievers, *Journal of Counseling Psychology, 7:*163–170, 1960.

16. BUHLER, C., SMITTER, F., and RICHARDSON, S., "What Is a Problem?" in Long, N. J., Morse, W. C., and Newman, R. G. (Eds.), *Conflict in the Classroom*, Wadsworth Publishing, Belmont, Calif., 1965.

17. COUCHMAN, R., "Counseling the Emotionally Troubled, a Neglected Group," *Personnel and Guidance Journal, 52:*457–463, 1974.

18. DEUTSCH, H., *Confrontations with Myself: An Epilogue*, W. W. Norton, New York, 1973.

19. DINKMEYER, D., *Guidance and Counseling in the Elementary School*, Holt, Rinehart & Winston, New York, 1968.

20. DREIKURS, R., *Psychology in the Classroom: A Manual for Teachers*, Harper & Row, New York, 1968.

21. ENTWISTLE, N. J., and CUNNINGHAM, S., "Neuroticism and School Attainment—a Linear Relationship?" *British Journal of Educational Psychology, 38:*123–131, 1968.

22. EPSTEIN, N., "Brief Group Therapy in a Child Guidance Clinic," in Barten, H. H., and Barten, S. S. (Eds.), *Children and Their Parents in Brief Therapy*, pp. 203–213, Behavioral Publications, New York, 1973.

23. ERIKSON, E. H., *Childhood and Society*, W. W. Norton, New York, 1963.

24. EYSENCK, H. J., "The Effects of Psychotherapy on Evaluation," *Journal of Consulting Psychology, 16:*319–324, 1952.

25. FRANK, J. D., *Persuasion and Healing*, rev. ed., Johns Hopkins University Press, Baltimore, 1973.

26. FREEHILL, M. F., *Disturbed and Troubled Children*, Spectrum Publications, Flushing, N.Y., 1973.

27. GAZDA, G. N., and LARSEN, M. J., "A Comprehensive Appraisal of Group and Multiple Counseling," *Journal of Research and Development in Education, 1:*57–132, 1968.

28. GORDON, T., *Parent Effectiveness Training*, P. H. Wyden, New York, 1970.

29. GRANGER, J. A., "Including the Younger Child in Conjoint Family Evaluation and Therapy," *Psychiatric Forum, 4:*21–26, 1974.

30. HAWORTH, J. R., *Child Psychotherapy*, Basic Books, New York, 1964.

31. HEWETT, F. M., and BLAKE, P. R., "Teaching the Emotionally Disturbed," in Travers, R. M. W. (Ed.), *Second Handbook of Research on Teaching*, pp. 657–688, Rand McNally, Chicago, 1973.

32. HOBBS, N., "The Re-education of Emotionally Disturbed Children," in Bower, E. M., and Hollister, W. G. (Eds.), *Behavioral Science Frontiers in Education*, pp. 339–354, John Wiley, New York, 1967.

33. JACKSON, D. D. (Ed.), *Therapy, Communication and Change*, vol. 2, Science and Behavior Books, Palo Alto, Calif., 1968.

34. JEFFRIES, D., "Counseling Ghetto Children in Groups," in Ohlsen, M. M. (Ed.), *Counseling Children in Groups: A Forum*, pp. 228–241, Holt, Rinehart & Winston, New York, 1973.

35. LAZARUS, A. A., "Desensitization and Cognitive Restructuring," *Psychotherapy: Theory, Research and Practice, 11:*98–102, 1974.

36. LEVENTHAL, T., and WEINBERGER, G., "Evaluation of a Large-Scale Brief Therapy Program for Children," *American Journal of Orthopsychiatry, 45:*119–133, 1975.

37. LEVITT, E. E., "The Results of Psychotherapy with Children: An Evaluation," *Journal of Consulting Psychology, 21:*189–196, 1957.

38. LONG, N. J., MORSE, W. C., and NEWMAN, R. G. (Eds.), *Conflict in the Classroom: The Education of Emotionally Disturbed Children*, Wadsworth Publishing, Belmont, Calif., 1965.

39. LOVE, L. R., KASWAN, J. W., and BUGENTAL, D. B. *Troubled Children: Their Families, Schools and Treatments*, John Wiley, New York, 1974.

40. LOVELESS, E. J., and BRODY, H. M., "The Cognitive Base of Psychotherapy," *Psychotherapy: Theory, Research and Practice, 11:*133–137, 1974.

41. LOWE, R. N., *Dreikursian Principles of Child Guidance*, College of Education, University of Oregon, Eugene, Ore., 1974.

42. LYNN, R. "Two Personality Characteristics Related to Academic Achievement," *British Journal of Educational Psychology, 29:*213–216, 1959.

43. MCCLELLAND, D. C., "On the Psychodynamics of Creative Physical Scientists," in Gruber, H. E., Terrell, G., and Wertheimer, M. (Eds.), *Contemporary Approaches to Creative Thinking*, Atherton Press, New York, 1963.

44. MOUSTAKAS, C. E., *Psychotherapy with Children: The Living Relationship*, Harper & Row, New York, 1959.

45. NEWMAN, R. G., *Psychological Consultation in the Schools*, Basic Books, New York, 1967.

46. OHLSEN, M. M., "Comparisons and Conclusions," in Ohlsen, M. M. (Ed.), *Counseling Children in Groups: A Forum*, pp. 307–329, Holt, Rinehart & Winston, New York, 1923.

47. ———, "Counseling Children," in Ohlsen, M. M. (Ed.), *Counseling Children in Groups: A Forum*, pp. 3–23, Holt, Rinehart & Winston, New York, 1973.

48. ———, *Counseling Children in Groups: A Forum*, Holt, Rinehart, & Winston, New York, 1973.

49. ———, and GAZDA, G. M., "Counseling Underachieving Bright Pupils," *Education, 86:*78–81, 1965.

50. PATTERSON, C. H., *Theories of Counseling and Psychotherapy*, Harper & Row, New York, 1966.

51. PATTISON, E. M., "Evaluation Studies of Group Psychotherapy," *International Journal of Group Psychotherapy, 15:*382–393, 1965.

52. PERKINS, J. A., and WICAS, E. A., "Group Counseling Bright Underachievers and Their Mothers," *Journal of Counseling Psychology, 18:*273–278, 1971.

53. PHILLIPS, E. L., and JOHNSTON, M. S. H., "Theoretical and Clinical Aspects of Short-Term Parent-Child Psychotherapy," in Barten, H. H., and Barten, S. S. (Eds.), pp. 22–39, *Children and Their Parents in Brief Therapy*, Behavioral Publications, New York, 1973.

54. POWERS, D., and WITMER, H., *An Experiment in the Prevention of Delinquency*, Columbia University Press, New York, 1951.

55. RAIMY, V., *Misunderstanding of the Self: Cognitive Psychotherapy and the Misconception Hypothesis*, Jossy-Bass, San Francisco, 1975.

56. RAPAPORT, D., GILL, M. M., and SCHAFER, R., *Diagnostic Psychological Testing*, rev. ed., Holt, R. R. (Ed.), International Universities Press, New York, 1968.

57. REDL, F., and WINEMAN, D., *Controls from Within: Techniques for the Treatment of the Aggressive Child*, Free Press, Glencoe, Ill., 1952.

58. REPORT OF THE JOINT COMMISSION ON MENTAL HEALTH OF CHILDREN, *Crisis in Child Mental Health, Challenge for the 1970's*, Harper & Row, 1970.

59. RICHMOND, J. B., "The State of the Child: Is the Glass Half-Empty or Half-Full?" *American Journal of Orthopsychiatry, 44*:484–490, 1974.

60. ROGERS, C. R., *On Becoming a Person*, Houghton Mifflin, Boston, 1961.

61. ———, *Client-Centered Therapy*, Houghton Mifflin Boston, 1951.

62. ROSENTHAL, A. J., and LEVINE, S. V., "Brief Psychotherapy with Children: A Preliminary Report," *American Journal of Psychiatry, 127*:106–111, 1970.

63. SAMLER, J., "Change in Values: A Goal in Counseling," *Journal of Counseling Psychology, 7*:32–39, 1960.

64. SATIR, V., *Conjoint Family Therapy*, rev. ed., Science and Behavior Books, Palo Alto, Calif., 1967.

65. SHERTZER, B., and STONE, S. C., *Fundamentals of Counseling*, 2nd ed., Houghton Mifflin, Boston, 1974.

66. SLAVSON, S. R., *Child-Centered Group Guidance of Parents*, International Universities Press, New York, 1958.

67. SMALL, L., *The Briefer Psychotherapies*, Brunner/Mazel, New York, 1971.

68. SMITH, D. C. "Counseling and Psychotherapy in the School Setting," in Magary, J. F. (Ed.), *School Psychological Services*, pp. 142–170, Prentice-Hall, Englewood Cliffs, N.J., 1967.

69. SONSTEGARD, M. A., and DREIKURS, R., "The Adlerian Approach to Group Counseling of Children," in Ohlson, M. M. (Ed.), *Counseling Children in Groups: A Forum*, pp. 51–77, Holt, Rinehart & Winston, New York, 1973.

70. STEFFLRE, B., "Counseling Theory," in *Encyclopedia of Educational Research*, 4th ed., pp. 252–267, Macmillan, New York, 1969.

71. STRUPP, H. H., *Psychotherapy and the Modification of Abnormal Behavior*, McGraw-Hill, New York, 1971.

72. SUGAR, M. (Ed.), *The Adolescent in Group and Family Therapy*, Brunner/Mazel, New York, 1975.

73. SZASZ, T. S., *The Myth of Mental Illness, Foundations of a Theory of Personal Conduct*, Hoeber-Harper, New York, 1961.

74. SZUREK, S. A., and BERLIN, I. N. (Eds.), *The Anti-Social Child, His Family and His Community*, vol. 4, Science and Behavior Books, Child Psychiatry Services, Palo Alto, Calif., 1969.

75. TAYLOR, W. M., and HOEDT, K. C., "Classroom-Related Behavior Problems: Counsel Parents, Teachers, or Children," *Journal of Counseling Psychology, 21*:3–8, 1974.

76. THOMAS, A., CHESS, S., and BIRCH, H. G., *Temperament and Behavior Disorders in Children*, New York University Press, New York, 1968.

77. TOFFLER, A., *Future Shock*, Random House, New York, 1970.

77. TYLER, L. E., *The Work of the Counselor*, Appleton-Century-Crofts, New York, 1961.

79. WALDFOGEL, S., TESSMAN, E., and HAHN, P. B., "A Program for Early Intervention in School Phobia," in Barten, H. H., and Barten, S. S. (Eds.), *Children and Their Parents in Brief Therapy*, pp. 163–175, Behavorial Publications, New York, 1973.

80. WATZLAWICK, P., BEAVIN, J., and JACKSON, D., *Pragmatics of Human Communication*, W. W. Norton, New York, 1967.

81. WEINBERGER, G., "Brief Therapy with Children and Their Parents," in Barten, H. H. (Ed), *Brief Therapies*, pp. 196–211, Behavioral Publications, New York, 1971.

82. WHITAKER, C. A., "The Symptomatic Adolescent —An AWOL Family Member," in Sugar, M. (Ed.), *The Adolescent in Group and Family Therapy*, pp. 205–215, Brunner/Mazel, New York, 1975.

83. WHITE, R. W., *Ego and Reality in Psychoanalytic Theory*, Psychological Issues (Monograph no. 11), International Universities Press, New York, 1963.

13 / Rogerian Counseling

Cecil H. Patterson

Carl A. Rogers developed an approach to counseling, or psychotherapy, which he called client-centered. Today, it is perhaps more commonly known as Rogerian. It grew out of his experience as a psychologist during the 1930s with the Child Study Department of the Rochester (New York) Society for the Prevention of Cruelty to Children. His training at Columbia University (Ph.D., 1931) was psychoanalytic; during the years in Rochester, however, he was more influenced by Rankian theory than by Freud.

The first description of his approach appeared in 1942 in *Counseling and Psychotherapy: Newer Concepts in Practice*.[11] This style of work became widely known as nondirective. In 1951,[10] he published a revised statement in which he adopted the term "client-centered" as his preferred designation. His 1961 book[7] supplements the basic 1951 statement. In addition to his theoretical writing and his teaching, treating, and counsulting, Rogers has engaged in a tremendous amount of research on the nature and outcomes of counseling or psychotherapy.[12,13]

The Nature of Client-centered Counseling or Psychotherapy

CONDITIONS FOR THERAPEUTIC PROGRESS

In 1957, Rogers[9] published a paper in which he listed the necessary and sufficient conditions of therapeutic personality change. Three of the conditions involve the counselor or the therapist:

unconditional positive regard, empathic understanding, and congruence. Currently these are designated as respect (or nonpossessive warmth), empathic understanding, and therapeutic genuineness. They are known as the core conditions and merit specific description.

Respect or Nonpossessive Warmth. This is similar to Rogers' unconditional positive regard: "To the extend that the therapist finds himself experiencing a warm acceptance of each aspect of the client's experience as being part of that client, he is experiencing unconditional positive regard."[8] Warmth includes acceptance, interest, concern, prizing, respect, liking. It is not necessarily acceptance of behavior or making no judgments about it; it refers to the client as a person. Truax and Carkhuff, in defining their "Tentative Scale for the Measurement of Nonpossessive Warmth," say that: "it involves a nonpossessive caring for [the client] as a separate person, and thus, a willingness to share equally his joys and aspirations or his depressions and failures. It involves valuing the patient as a person, separate from any evaluation of his behavior or his thoughts."[14]

Empathy or Empathic Understanding. A second major characteristic of the atmosphere or conditions for client progress is understanding on the part of the counselor, and the communication of this understanding to the client. It is important to recognize just what this means. The kind of understanding which appears to be most effective in counseling is not knowledge of or about the client. It does not consist of the results of a battery of tests, nor of the data in the client's record, nor of extensive case studies, no matter how voluminous or complete. What is critical is the understanding that emerges from empathy. An empathic understanding is a "feeling with" another, the entering into his frame of reference—the internal rather than the external frame of reference—so that one sees the world and the other person, insofar as possible, through the eyes of the other. No one responds to the word as it exists, or is assumed to exist, "in reality"; one can only respond to the world one perceives. The counselor then attempts to put himself in the client's place. He realizes that in order to fully understand another's feelings, attitudes, and behavior, he must see things as the other sees them.

Therapeutic Genuineness. The third major condition of a good counseling relationship is genuineness. The counselor must be real, honest, freely and deeply himself. He is not playing a role. There is no such thing as a professional role, which a counselor assumes when he enters the

counseling office or when the client enters his office. He places no facade between himself and the client. In addition, there is no conflict between what he thinks and feels and what he says. This does not mean that the counselor must blurt out all his positive or negative feelings; this would not help the client. But the counselor does not present a false friendship or pretend a liking for the client.

Genuineness is often misinterpreted to mean an "anything-goes" policy. "Genuineness must not be confused, as is so often done, with free license for the therapist to do what he will in therapy, especially to express hostility."[2] There is a difference, as Carkhuff and Berenson point out, between a construct of genuineness and the construct of facilitative or therapeutic genuineness; untempered genuineness can surely be destructive. It is unlikely, for example, that a highly paranoid or an authoritarian person will be therapeutic no matter how genuine he is.

In addition to these three conditions identified by Rogers, there are other qualities which facilitate a counseling relationship. Carkhuff and Berenson mention therapist spontaneity, confidence, openness, flexibility, and commitment, and the intensity of the therapeutic contact.[2]

Concreteness. There is one quality which is probably not closely related to the three core conditions but which, nevertheless, merits designation as a fourth condition. This is concreteness, or specificity. Concreteness means that the therapist and the client deal with specifics, with desirable feelings, with remembered experiences, and with overt behavior. It is the oppisite of generality and abstraction, or vagueness and ambiguity. Carkhuff and Berenson suggest that concreteness serves at least three important functions: It keeps the therapist's response close to the client's feelings and experiences; it fosters accuracy of understanding by the therapist, allowing for early client corrections of misunderstanding; and it encourages the client to focus on specific problem areas.[2]

Concreteness and specificity would appear to be the opposite of much that is included under interpretation. Many interpretations are generalizations, abstractions, higher levels of labeling, or the application of higher level categories to specific experience. Such activity is often not useful. Many interpretations are threeatening in character and tend to cut off self-exploration by the client; in particular, abstract or overly general interpretations appear to do this. To take an extreme example, after a client has explored his relationship with his parents, the therapist might suggest that he "has" an Oedipus complex. The client might agree, he might well feel that he has insight. But there would probably be little if any change in his behavior. He is likely to feel that there is no point in discussing the matter or in engaging in further self-exploration along that line.

These core conditions, as they are now known, are general and, no doubt, complex. It is possible they might be broken down into more specific conditions, much as any general factor may be broken up into groups of specific factors. It is also possible that there are other core conditions present in successful therapy which remain to be discovered. Hopefully, these will become apparent as the present categories are better isolated, defined, and measured.

When these conditions prevail, a central element of the ensuing counseling relationship is the absence of threat. Although it may appear to be a negative way of looking at counseling and mental health, the concept of threat is extremely important. Threat to the self and to the self-concept seems to be the basis for many personality disturbances and for much poor mental health. One basic need of every individual is the preservation and enhancement of the self; all other needs or drives may be subsumed under this. Frustration of, or threat to, the satisfaction of this basic need results in a lowered evaluation of the self; a loss of self-esteem is the core of much personality disturbance.

The influence of threat upon behavior has been demonstrated in many areas. In the face of threat, perception is narrowed, so that the individual literally does not see many aspects of the situation. Often the individual will withdraw, even to the point of freezing, becoming literally paralyzed with fear under extreme threat. On the other hand, where the threat is less, the individual may become defensive or aggressive. It may be that what has been designated as instinctive or natural aggressiveness is in fact always a reaction to a threat. This reaction is universal because threat, in some form or other, is also universal. That is, while threat, or frustration, may lead to reactions other than aggressiveness, aggressiveness is always a result of threat or frustration.

The variety of the possible responses to threat is very large. The behavioral patterns described range all the way from excessive compliance and self-destruction to self-deception. In one way or another, these serve to avoid loss of self-esteem or to restore it.

In everyday life, we are aware of these phenomena. In the face of pressure or threat, the individual is unable to perform effectively or efficiently.

He may be unable to learn easily; he may persist in ineffective attempts at problem solving rather than in fruitful exploration. We know that we can create resistance when we attempt to change people by pressure or threat; examples are when, in the face of correction, the child becomes even more insistent on doing what he wants to do, or in the face of parental objection, the girl becomes still more determined to marry the obviously unsuitable boy.

Changes in attitudes and behavior, in self-actualization, and in the development of independence and responsibility—in short, in mental health and adequacy of personality development—occur only under conditions of absence of serious threat to the self and the self-concept. The goals of counseling include the preservation or restoration of good mental health and of self-esteem, along with the fostering of self-actualization. It then follows that the counseling situation must be characterized by an absence of threat. Respect for the client, interest in and acceptance of him as a person, absence of evaluative attitudes, and empathic understanding that sees the client's point of view —all these contribute to an atmosphere devoid of threat.

In addition to these elements that characterize the counselor, there are certain conditions which must be met, or provided, by the client.

Client Incongruence. Incongruence, as used by Rogers, indicates that the client is in a state of emotional need. Essentially it means that he feels vulnerable or amiss; he is disturbed, distressed, upset, angry, troubled, stressed, in conflict, unhappy, discouraged, depressed, dissatisfied. In short, the client hurts psychologically, is aware of the hurt, and wants to do something about it.

Client Perception of Therapist Conditions. If empathic understanding, respect, and therapeutic genuineness are to be effective, they must be perceived and recognized by the client, at least to some degree. The offering or providing of the conditions by the therapist is not sufficient; they must get through to the client. The client must be receptive, able to recognize and be affected by the therapist's efforts to reach him.

Client Self-Exploration. The basic activity required of the client is that he engage in a process of self-exploration or intrapersonal exploration. In every approach to psychotherapy, the client talks about himself. The talk may be about his memories, or dreams, or it may be about his beliefs, attitudes, feelings, experiences, thoughts, and actions. However it is pursued, the client explores some aspect of the self. Considerable research has shown the existence of a relationship between such client self-exploration and success or favorable outcomes.[14] There is also a considerable body of research indicating that the level of client self-exploration is related to, and influenced by, the level of facilitative conditions provided by the therapist.

The process of self-exploration is a complex one, involving several aspects, or, perhaps, stages.

1. *Self-disclosure.* Before the client can explore himself, he must disclose or reveal himself. In the beginning of counseling, this most often consists of the disclosure of negative aspects of himself —his problems, failures, inadequacies, and so forth. These constitute the basis of his dissatisfaction and unhappiness; they are the reasons he has sought counseling. It is recognized that most children and adolescents are referred to counselors rather than seeking counseling on their own. Others, mainly parents and teachers, provide the counselor with information about the client's problems and difficulties. But if counseling is to be productive, the child or adolescent must himself recognize and accept his problems. Since the problems are negative, revealing a low or negative self-concept, they are often difficult for him to express. Self-disclosure at this level represents self-exposure.

Among students of counseling, the question of the desirability of accepting, or listening with acceptance, to such material often arises. Given free reign, the client may engage in extensive disclosures of negative feelings and emotions, self-negation, and self-criticism; he may express feelings of worthlessness, discouragement, depression —even suicide. Isn't this likely to reinforce these feelings and make the client worse? Shouldn't the counselor reassure the client that things aren't as bad as he thinks they are, that he isn't as bad as he thinks he is?

The therapist must remember that the client has sought treatment just because he has problems, negative feelings, and a negative self-concept. His low opinion of himself is not (usually) merely unrealistic, a misperception—it has some basis in reality. He is failing to be his best self, to be a self-actualizing person. To deny this, to challenge his feelings that this is the case (even if it is not so), or even to disagree with the extent to which he holds these opinions to be true will not help. Indeed, it is likely to prevent the client from going further and thus, in time, from coming to recognize the positive aspects of himself and his situation. The process of working through his distress cannot be short-circuited. If the client is to reach the positive elements, he must be allowed to express the negative. And the counselor must be willing and able to go with him into the depths and face the worst with him. It is only when he has plumbed the depths and seen himself at his worst that the client can rise again and, knowing the worst, build a new and positive self. The counselor must be ready to embark on this process despite his own discomfort, anxiety, or fears.

The following excerpt, in which a twelve-year-old boy discusses his difficulties with some of his teachers, illustrates the process.

Client: . . . even if I told my side of the story it wouldn't do much good.
Therapist: Mmhm. You feel that no one would listen if you argued. . . .
Client: Yeah. It wouldn't do. . . .
Therapist: What's the use?
Client: About that.
Therapist: You really feel bad about the predicament you're in.
Client: Well, it's not the most fun in the world to have your teacher for your worst enemy. And it's not very healthy either.
Therapist: Have to, sort of, live with it.
Client: It's always a lot easier if you can get along with your teachers. . . .
Therapist: And you don't know quite how to. . . .
Client: Uh huh. Seems like everything I do is wrong.
Therapist: Just no use in doing anything. There's nothing you can do about it.
Client: Well, I wouldn't say that. I still try.

2. *Exploration of the Self.* Once a client has begun to disclose himself, to put himself on view to himself and the therapist, he is able to look at himself more as a whole and to engage in the process of exploring what and who he is. He can *be himself* in a way in which he cannot in ordinary interpersonal relationships; he can be open, real, and honest, with himself as well as with the therapist. He begins to be able to face himself as he is.

The process of self-exploration does not proceed simultaneously and at equivalent levels in all areas of the client's life, with all of his problems or all aspects of his difficulties. Some progress may occur in one area and then be blocked or slow down. The client shifts to another area only to reach again a level beyond which he is not yet ready or able to go. This process may repeat itself in still other areas. Eventually, the client returns to the first area and to each of the other areas, to progress further. Exploration in each sector makes it possible to explore the other dimensions of the self more deeply. It is not useful, or possible, to insist that the client stick to one area, or to one problem, until it is thoroughly explored, before moving on to another. The total process is not logical, it is psychological; it is in the nature of personality that all the difficulties are interrelated in complex ways and cannot be explored completely as separate problems.

The client begins where he is able to begin, and usually where he is most conscious of a problem. He moves to other relevant areas and problems when he is ready and able to do so within the context of the relationship. To attempt to push the client, to direct him toward areas considered important by the therapist, is to introduce threat and to risk retarding, rather than facilitating, the client's self-exploration. Parents who send their children for counseling or teachers who refer students to counselors often have great difficulty understanding or accepting this aspect of the work.

3. *Self-awareness.* The process of self-exploration leads in many directions. Among other things it catalyzes self-discovery, self-understanding, and self-awareness. This is more than is commonly meant by intellectual insight. (Insight in that sense usually means some form of cognitive awareness, a theoretical grasp of a problem in terms of its origins or etiology.) Self-understanding is not limited to intrapersonal processes but includes an understanding of the impact the client has on other people or the nature of his functioning in interpersonal relationships. To some extent, he begins to see himself as others see him.

Self-exploration reveals inconsistencies and contradictions. Attitudes and feelings that have been experienced, but denied to awareness, are discovered. Experiences inconsistent with the self-concept, or self-image, previously denied or distorted, become symbolized in awareness. The client becomes more open to his experiences.

With increasing self-awareness, the client's self-concept becomes clearer. And with increasing clarity, his vague dissatisfactions with himself become more specific. He begins to see in particular how he is failing to actualize himself, and in just what ways he fails to measure up to his self-ideal. He begins to reorganize his self-concept, to assimilate all his experiences of himself; his self-concept becomes more congruent with his experiences, and thus more realistic. In turn, his perception of his ideal self becomes more realistic and more attainable, and his self has the possibility of becoming more congruent with his ideal self. To the extent that he can achieve positive changes in the self and the self-concept, the client becomes more accepting of himself. He is likely to feel more confident and better able to order his life. As he perceives more realistically and accurately his changed self is likely to elicit more positive reactions from others. He then experiences a greater measure of social acceptance. Given such developments, he will presently become a fully functioning *person*, a more self-actualizing person.[8] His feelings of adequacy and of self-esteem increase.

Not all that the client discovers about himself is negative or bad. In the process of developing self-understanding and self-awareness, both positive and negative attitudes toward himself arise. Experiences, which at first do not seem to belong to and cannot be integrated into the self, become accepted as part of the self.

As the process continues, negative attitudes toward the self decrease and positive attitudes increase. "The client not only accepts himself—a phase which may carry the connotation of a grudging and reluctant acceptance of the inevitable—he actually comes to *like* himself." The self which emerges—the deep, basic nature of the client, is not repugnant. The core of the self "is not bad, not terribly wrong, but something positive. Underneath the layer of controlled surface behavior, underneath the bitterness, underneath the hurt, is a self that is positive, that is without hate."[7]

In a very significant way, then, therapy does not necessarily require change of the basic self. Therapy assumes the essence of a positive core of the self; it seeks discovery, and it strives to free the self so that the client can be this real, basic self. The conditions of therapy provide a nonthreatening environment in which the client does not have to respond negatively, aggressively, or defensively, but is free to strive to become the self that he really is, or is capable of being. Therapy, then, is a situation in which the client can be his best self, the potential self which has been covered up, or not allowed to develop. The self-concept and the self-ideal must both undergo changes; indeed, the discrepancy between them may be reduced by change in the self-ideal, as much, if not more, than, change in the self-concept. Or, perhaps more accurately, changes in the self-concept may occur without changes in the basic self.

It is important that the process of self-exploration not be confused with the client's talk *about* himself. This is often a problem with beginning counselors. By continued questioning, they persuade the client to make statements about himself and mistake this for client self-exploration. But in such talk, the client is viewing himself as an object (as is the counselor) and is not actually expressing or disclosing himself. His talk is externally oriented, abstract, generalized—an intellectual or rational discourse about himself as an object.

Implementing the Conditions

LISTENING

If the therapist is to reach any understanding of the client, he must allow the client to persent himself. Only the client can tell the therapist how he feels, what he thinks, how he sees himself and the world; and only by listening to the client can the therapist enter his world and see things as he does. The first rule of therapy is to listen to the client.

It should be obvious that one cannot listen if one is talking. Yet beginning counselors seem to find it extremely difficult not to talk. Perhaps they have been trained to initiate conversation in social situations. Many of them have had experience in teaching or preaching, where they have assumed the initiative and have taken responsibility for directing or guiding conversations. Now they are unable to relinquish the initiative to another. Or perhaps they have read somewhere about the necessity for the counselor to begin by establishing rapport in some way, such as by attempting to find some common experience, acquaintance, activity, and so forth. At any rate, the problem is so common that beginning students in the counseling practicum are initiated with a simple, concrete rule: Keep your mouth shut. This is an objective, easily observed criterion for the instructor and the counseling student to evaluate in a tape recording. Someone has suggested that with beginning counselors adhesive tape might be more useful than recording tape.

For a counselor to listen it is of course necessary that the client talk. It is true that many children do not initiate a conversation with the counselor. They may not trust the counselor, they may be there only at the suggestion or command of someone else, they may feel they have no problem, or they may have learned, literally, that a child doesn't speak until spoken to or given permission to speak. Perhaps because of these factors, it is widely believed that children, particularly below the secondary school level, are not sufficiently verbal nor sufficiently capable of verbalizing their problems to be suitable for counseling or psychotherapy of a verbal nature, or for "talking therapy."

Those who are familiar with children, however, would certainly question this. Most children, when they feel comfortable with an adult and do not feel threatened by the situation, can be highly verbal. Their lack of verbalization is often related to a situation, such as the school setting, where they are not expected to talk spontaneously, but rather to remain quiet.

In such cases, while it is a good rule for the counselor to remain quiet long enough to allow the child to initiate the conversation, the counselor may need to make the first move. It may be sufficient simply to give the child permission to talk. Beyond that, the approach mentioned later in the discussion of structuring and responding may be used. For the child who cannot (or perhaps will not) verbalize, play therapy, also to be discussed later, is appropriate.

The difficulty created by counselor initiative and activity in the early part of counseling lies in this: It tends to impose the counselor's frame of reference on the client, who is often all too eager to comply. Rather than speak from his own frame of reference, the client then presents himself as he thinks the counselor wants him to. There is a school of thought that feels that to understand the client, the counselor needs certain kinds of information about him, which he should obtain in the initial interview. But such an approach does two things: (1) it sets the structure of counseling as one in which the counselor leads and the client follows; and (2) it may lead to knowledge *about* or understanding *about* the client, but not to the necessary empathic understanding of the client's frame of reference. Such an approach protects the counselor from any need to tolerate ambiguity and from the fear of an unstructured encounter, rather than helping the client or the progress of therapy.

It is difficult to listen to and allow another person the freedom to present himself without forcing him into one's own frame of reference. There must be genuine interest in the other person and what he has to say. In most social conversation, the listener doesn't focus his attention on what the other is saying; he is thinking about what he is going to say when his turn comes. Listening then amounts to the necessary waiting for one's turn to speak. Too many counselors engage in this kind of listening. Real listening is difficult. The auditor must not be preoccupied by his own thoughts or thoughts about himself. Real listening is active, not passive. The listener's complete attention must be given to the speaker. While he is listening to the client—indeed, during the entire therapy process—the therapist must be totally committed to the client. Moreover, listening is a potent reinforcer. It reinforces verbal productiveness by the client, and without such verbal productiveness, therapy could not progress.

Real listening is hard work. Some years ago, a cartoon presented two psychiatrists in an elevator. One was impeccably neat and fresh; the other looked bedraggled, with tie askew and suit rumpled. The one asked the other: "How can you listen to people's problems all day and still look so fresh?" To which the other replied: "Who listens?"

In the course of his listening, the therapist must not only suspend thinking about his own experiences and problems but must also suspend all evaluation and judgment of the client. This turning away from his own concerns, however, does not mean that the therapist represses all the feelings which arise in response to what the client is saying. These feelings and associations are useful in understanding the meanings of what the client is saying.

STRUCTURING

Many clients, particularly children, have misconceptions about the nature of psychotherapy and its practice. They do not know how to act or what do to. The counselor or psychotherapist is a professional person; people often have certain conceptions of their relationships with professionals. The professionals are experts and authorities; one listens to them and is passive or subordinate in the relationship. Students often identify counselors with teachers. Thus they often remain silent, expecting the counselor to interrogate them. Older children often equate the psychotherapist with the physician. Thus, they may begin by stating their complaints or problems. But they then wait for the therapist to question them. They expect the therapist to give them advice or to offer them solutions to their problems.

Structuring is the orientation of the client to his role and responsibility in the relationship, and to the role and responsibility of the therapist. Overt or verbal structuring may not be necessary. If, on entering the relationship, the client takes the responsibility for presenting his problems and concerns, it is not necessary for the therapist to engage in formal structuring. He informs the client of his own role by his behavior, by modeling rather than by verbal discussion. Formal verbal structuring is necessary only where: (1) the client has no idea about what he is expected to do, or what the therapist's role is; and (2) the client has

a misconception of what he is expected to do or what the therapist's role is.

In the early period of client centered therapy, structuring was often routinely practiced by many counselors, and many instructors taught their students to structure as a matter of course. In most cases, it was probably necessary to structure since the approach was new and different from that used by many other counselors. In many cases at present, the educated public knows what to expect. Popular magazines have carried articles on how to behave when seeing a psychotherapist. They have indicated that the client is expected to do the talking, that the therapist listens and probably will not even ask many questions. Nonetheless, many segments of the public and many clients (including perhaps most children of school age) do not know what psychotherapy is really like.

Thus, the therapist should be prepared to structure when necessary. One of the problems regarding the practice of client-centered therapy has occurred here. There are those who have claimed that the client-centered approach is not appropriate for counseling in the public schools because students are dependent and not able to take responsibility for themselves in the counseling process. This opinion has arisen in part, at least, from a misconception on the part of many would-be client-centered counselors about the client-centered approach. In this misconception, to be client-centered is to be passive. Thus, when a student comes to see the counselor, he is silent. Waiting for permission to speak, or not knowing what he should do, he remains silent. The counselor does not structure. As a result, no relationship is established, and the student leaves, does not return, and is not helped. And the blame is placed on "client-centered counseling." The counselor may conclude that client-centered counseling is not appropriate for students, abandons all its principles, and becomes directive in his approach. But all that may be necessary is to give the student permission to speak and to define counseling as different from the classroom situation. Simply saying "Can you tell me why you are here?" may be sufficient to enable the student to enter a relationship.

Where structuring is required, it should be provided only to the extent necessary. It is undesirable, and unnecessary, for the counselor to go into a long lecture on the nature of his approach —probably saying that he is not going to do much of the talking or to dominate the relationship, at the same time as he is doing exactly that! Structuring should be brief, given only to the extent necessary at the moment, and provided again, or more explicitly later as needed. As the relationship gets started, the behavior of the therapist provides the necessary structure.

Where structuring is routinely engaged in, even where not necessary, it may confuse the client. A high school student, highly verbal, began the interview by presenting his concerns about himself and his future. After fifteen or twenty minutes there was a slight pause, and the counselor structured the process: "Well, you see, it's your time, just use it as you want to; feel free, relax. . . ."

The client, no doubt feeling that this is what he has been doing, appears to be puzzled, wondering what he might be doing that is wrong. After a pause, he says: "Well, I don't know what to say, exactly . . . what. . . . Well . . . do you think it would help if I tell you a lot about my background . . . things like that?"

It is some time before the student returns to his real concerns.

RESPONDING

In the beginning of therapy, and, indeed throughout, the function of the therapist is to respond to the client. Interviews in which the client responds to the therapist are not therapy interviews, they are interrogations. (It is very easy to determine from a tape recording who is responding to whom.) A simple rule for beginning counselors, which avoids a pattern where the client responds to the counselor, is: Never ask a question —except when you don't understand what the client is saying. Again, this provides a very simple, objective criterion.

If the client is responding to the counselor, it is clearly the counselor's interview. He is leading and guiding the exchange, usually along his own preconceived lines of what is important, relevant, or interesting to him. He is superimposing his own structure and frame of reference on the client; it is not likely he will be able to enter the client's inner world and develop an empathic understanding of him.

A question which always arises in discussions of therapist listening and responding is what to do with a silent or inarticulate client. Can one listen to or respond to silence? To some extent one can. A sensitive therapist can sometimes feel what a client is thinking, or he may hazard a guess. He can then respond to this, perhaps in a tentative way. The client may display or communicate discomfort, uncertainty, hesitation, confusion, and so forth. The counselor may respond with "You don't know where to start," or "You find it hard

to decide what to say first," or "You find it hard to talk," or "You don't know what you are supposed to do." If the client is completely inarticulate, or says that he cannot talk or express himself, the counselor is in a dilemma. It appears he wants the client to take responsibility for his therapy and wants to avoid a relationship in which the client is responding to him. The client may be dependent in the beginning, but the counselor wants him to move toward independence and does not want to reinforce dependent behavior.

There is a possible way out of his dilemma. If it is necessary for the counselor to initiate the interaction, he can do so in a way which will insure that at least 50 percent of the time he will be responding to the client. He can achieve this simply by responding to every response he elicits from the client, before going on, if necessary, with another initiating action. Fifty percent reinforcement is perhaps not particularly effective; with most clients, however, it will be greater than this, and the client is thus taught that the counselor responds to him. If the counselor assumes the initiative and continues to hold it, he is reinforcing the client as responder. This will make it difficult, if not impossible, to develop a therapy relationship.

Another basic function of the therapist's responses (as least in the early phases of therapy) is to communicate to the client an understanding of what the client is saying, or trying to say. There are a number of ways in which the counselor can respond to the client to convey both his understanding, as well as his interest in, and concern about, what the client is saying.

Acceptance Responses. These responses tell the client that the therapist is there, listening, with him, following him. They are simple indications of understanding: "Uh huh," "Yes," "I see," "I understand," "I follow you." Silence may also convey acceptance.

Reflection. Reflection responses go somewhat beyond simple acceptance responses. Reflection of content, or restating what the client is saying in different words, lets the client know that the therapist is hearing what he is saying, that he understands the content, if not what is behind the content. Reflections of feelings go beyond or behind the content. They are responses to the more obvious feelings which the client has about the content. They let the client know that the counselor is aware of what he is feeling. Simple acceptance and reflection of content responses need not represent empathic understanding. The therapist can offer such responses as a technique. They are easily faked. But reflection of feeling is more difficult to fake and requires some real, or empathic, understanding. Beginning students often find it difficult to respond to feelings rather than simply to content. Sometimes it is helpful to a student to begin a response, to himself if not aloud, with the words "You feel . . ." to help him focus on just what the client is feeling.

Clarification. The client's verbalizations, especially when he is disturbed and feeling deeply, are not always easy to understand. They may be confused, jumbled, hesitant, incomplete, disordered, fragmentary. In clarification responses, the counselor attempts to put together what the client is saying or trying to say, to put into words ideas that are vague or feelings that are implicit if not explicit in what the client is saying. What is confused to the client may not be clear to the therapist, so that clarification responses are not easy to formulate, and the therapist often is not sure of their accuracy. The responses, therefore, are often tentative or phrased in the form of a question.

Specificity or Concreteness. The counselor, by his responses, attempts to make concrete and specific what may be general and abstract in the client's verbalizations. Concrete and specific responses help the client be more specific, help him to move from vagueness to clarity, and to focus upon reality, upon the practical. This will help him move from feeling to action as therapy progresses.

By avoiding abstractions and generalizations, specificity helps the client analyze his problem in detail. Generalizations and abstractions give him the feeling that his problems are resolved because he can now give them names, or broad labels. Labeling has often been advocated to help the client understand by providing discrimination and avoiding overgeneralization. This may be true if the labeling is specific and discriminating in nature. But much labeling is generalization, often overgeneralization. It consists of assigning a specific item to a higher order category or concept. The effect of such labeling or generalization is to discourage the client from further discussion or exploration of the problem. Much so-called insight is simply labeling. It becomes the end of the process rather than making possible further exploration of specific behaviors.

Consider this example of a student who comes for counseling because of vague dissatisfactions about his relations with his parents.

Client: I don't know just what the problem is. I don't get along with my parents. It's not that I don't like them, or that they don't like me. But we seem to disagree on so many things. Maybe they're small and unimportant, but . . . I don't know, we never

have been close . . . there has never been a time, as far as I can remember, that they gave me any spontaneous affection. . . . I just don't know what's wrong.
Therapist: It seems that your present situation is of long standing and goes back to a long series of difficulties in your developmental process in a cold home.

This kind of abstract response, attributing the situation to a "cold home," is unlikely to help the client to focus upon specific aspects of his problem. Compare this with a more concrete response which the therapist might have made:

Therapist: Although you say you don't know what's wrong, and although you say your parents like you, they never seem to have shown any specific evidence of love or affection.

Another student comes in to see the counselor, all steamed up about his teachers:

Client: They're so bossy—you have to do everything just the way they say—even if it doesn't make sense. There's nothing you can do about it. You can't reason with them—if you try, you're labeled a troublemaker and your grades suffer. It's just—just so unfair.
Therapist: Your trouble seems to be that you can't accept authority.

Silence. Silence on the part of the therapist has varying effects, depending upon how it is perceived by the client. To a verbal client, silence on the part of the therapist may be welcomed—as long as he knows the counselor is listening. But silence can be ambiguous. Silence on the part of the psychoanalyst is probably one of the bases for transference, encouraging the client to project onto the therapist. Therapists are sometimes warned about the dangers of catharsis in the beginning of therapy. While experience does not bear out the predicted dire results, there are clients who do not return after a first interview. It is possible that, since their disclosure of themselves brought little or no response from the therapist, they fail to return because they are uncertain whether the therapist really was listening, was interested, or understood them. They fear that because they have voiced undesirable thoughts or revealed unadmirable behavior, the therapist did not understand or accept them. Therefore, it is desirable that the therapist break in occasionally to let the client know he is heard, understood, and accepted.

When the client pauses, he usually (though not always) expects and desires a response from the therapist. Not to receive a response may be perceived as rejection. Or at least it may be interpreted by the client as not talking about what he should be talking about. Silence on the part of the counselor is a means of discouraging irrelevant talk. When used in other situations it can extinguish *all* talk. Responsiveness by the therapist will facilitate deeper exploration by the client, avoiding a one-way recital.

Thus, the therapist silence has different effects. The therapist must be aware of these possible effects and allow silence to continue or break it, depending upon his sense of what the client perceives the silence to mean. Therapy may be taking place even during long silences. But long silences in the first interview should usually be avoided.

INTERPRETATION

Clarification responses deal with what is explicit or implicit in the client's behavior, verbal and/or nonverbal. Interpretations go beyond this, involving a contribution by the therapist. In interpretation, the therapist is adding to what the client is saying, going beyond his verbalizations, adding something of his own.

The line between clarification and interpretation is a fine one. They would appear to be on a continuum. There will often be disagreement as to whether a therapist's response is a clarification or an interpretation. Whether it is classified as one or the other will depend, in part, on the sensitivity of the observer. What is clarification to a highly sensitive observer (or therapist) may appear to be interpretation to one who is less sensitive to what is implicit in what the client is saying. Rogers writes: "When the client's world is clear to the counselor and he can move about in it freely, then he can communicate his understanding of what is vaguely known to the client and he can also voice meanings in the client's experience of which the client is scarcely aware."[6] The counselor who thoroughly enters into the client's frame of reference, who perceives in the same way the client does, can often speak *for* the client when the client is not able to speak adequately for himself. But it is important to emphasize that the counselor is operating within the client's frame of reference. It would perhaps be as well to use this as a criterion on which to base the distinction between reflection and empathic responses on the one hand, and interpretive responses on the other. Interpretation views the client from the outside. It attempts to fit him into a system, a theory or some other cognitive structure which the counselor applies to him. It derives from the counselor's frame of reference, or from an external frame of reference. In addition, since interpretation involves generalization or

higher order labeling, it ignores or departs from the uniqueness of the client and is thus less meaningful and helpful to him.

QUESTIONING

Little has been said so far about questioning as a technique (except in regard to the silent client), although textbooks on counseling and psychotherapy often discuss this topic extensively. The reason is simple—questioning by the therapist has little place in counseling or psychotherapy. Interviews in which the client does little else but respond to questions by the therapist are not therapy interviews. Neither Sergeant Friday nor Perry Mason are proper models for counseling interviews. Questioning and probing are counterindicated for at least two reasons—they may be threatening to the client, and they set up the interview as an externally oriented process. The therapist then fails to assume the internal frame of reference of the client. In addition, questioning or probing often leads to an intellectually or cognitively oriented process. The result is that the client does not take the initiative and is discouraged or prevented from engaging in the process of exploration.

Client-Centered Play Therapy

Verbalization is the normal means of communication among adults and older children. However, some children find it difficult to talk. This may be more a matter of not having been taught or allowed to express their feelings—or having been taught not to express feelings, particularly to adults—than of inability to do so. Younger children normally express themselves through both play and talk and, at the preschool level, may be able to express themselves more easily through play than through verbalization. All children, however, may accompany their play with covert or overt verbalization.

Thus, play therapy may be the method of choice with many young children, either singly or in groups. But it should not be used routinely with all children; particularly older children who, though they may be reluctant to talk or have difficulty in talking about themselves and their feelings, are able to do so with an accepting, understanding therapist. It may be argued that progress in therapy is more likely to occur when the client engages in verbal exploration, which leads to self-understanding, which can be stored in verbal memory and recalled, repeated, and reviewed outside the therapy situation. Verbalization certainly aids one in dealing with ideas, attitudes, feelings, and so forth.

On the other hand, overt verbalization is apparently not necessary for therapeutic change. Every play therapist is familiar with the child who comes in, spends his hour playing without much talking, leaves, and returns to do the same thing session after session. Nothing seems to be happening—his play may not even appear to be related to his problems. Or he may not even play. Yet, parents and teachers report changes in his behavior!

Axline says:

That is why it does not seem necessary for the child to be aware that he has a problem before he can benefit by the therapy session. Many a child has utilized the therapy experience and has emerged from the experience with visible signs of more mature attitudes and behavior and still has not been aware that it was any more than a free play period.[1] [p. 23]

Dorfman[3] reports a session with a nine-year-old boy who had spent the hour painting in silence. Near the end, the following interchange occurred:

Dick: How much time do I have left?
Therapist: Seven minutes, Dick.
Dick: I might as well go rock for a while. (He goes and sits in the rocking chair. He closes his eyes and quietly rocks.) How much time do I have left now?
Therapist: Five more minutes, Dick.
Dick: (Sighs very deeply): Ah, five more minutes *all to myself.*
Therapist (very softly): Five more minutes *all your own,* Dick?
Dick: Yes! (Said with much feeling. He rocks silently for the rest of the hour. His eyes are shut, in apparent enjoyment of peace.)
Therapist: It feels good just to sit and rock?
Dick: (Nods.)
Therapist: That's all the time we have for today, Dick.
Dick: O.K. (He gets up immediately and goes to the door with the therapist. They say good-bye, and he goes out. A minute later he knocks at the door.) I thought I'd get you some clean water.
Therapist: You want to help me, Dick?
Dick: Yes, I do. (He gets the water. The therapist thanks him and he leaves, skipping down the hall. This is the first time that he has ever made any effort to clean up after his painting.)[3] [p. 246]

It is apparent here that the therapist accepts the child, permits him to use the time as he wishes, and attempts to understand him and communicate this understanding. That is, the conditions for verbal client-centered therapy considered earlier are also the conditions for client-centered play therapy. In play therapy, the child is free to express his feelings, emotions, confusions, ideas, in play and/or verbally. The therapist responds with interest and understanding. His responses reflect or clarify the feelings and thoughts of the child as they are expressed in his play. Where there is no verbalization by the child, it may be difficult to discern the meaning of his activities. Thus, responses may often be a statement of what the child is doing, indication that it is acceptable, and permission to continue; or they may take the form of questions, indicating uncertainty and a desire to understand. Interpretations are avoided for the same reasons as they are in verbal therapy.

The presence of an accepting, understanding, friendly therapist in the playroom gives [the child] a sense of security. The limitations, few as they are, add to this feeling of security and reality. The participation of the therapist during the therapy contact also reinforces the child's feeling of security. The therapist is sensitive to what the child is feeling and expressing through his play and verbalization. She reflects these expressed, emotionalized attitudes back to him in such a way as to help him understand himself a little better.[1] [pp. 17–18]

The play therapist, then, offers the child in play therapy the same conditions which are offered clients in the usual counseling or therapy interview process. These conditions lead to self-exploration on the part of the child.

In the security of this room where the *child* is the most important person, where he is in command of the situation and of himself, where no one tells him what to do, no one criticizes what he does, no one nags, or suggests, or goads him on, or pries into his private world, he suddenly feels that here he can unfold his wings; he can look squarely at himself, for he is accepted completely; he can test out his ideas, he can express himself fully; for this is his world. . . .[1] [p. 16]

He can become a more self-actualizing person.

Theoretical Orientation

Client-centered therapy is based upon a particular view of the nature of man and the goal of life, or of man as an individual. It is possible here only to summarize the theoretical basis in a series of statements which may be viewed as postulates or assumptions.[4, 5, 8, 10]

1. Each individual lives in his own private world.
2. Behavior is determined by the perceptions of

the individual; the individual's perceptual field is, for him, "reality."

3. The individual behaves as an organized whole in relation to his phenomenal field.

4. Man has a single basic motivation—the preservation and enhancement of the self—or the striving for self-actualization.

5. Behavior is not simply reactive, but actively directed toward the maintenance and enhancement of the self.

6. Since behavior is a function of the individual's phenomenal field, the best way to understand that individual is from within his internal frame of reference; that is by putting oneself, as best as one can, in the place of the other.

7. An individual's values may derive from his direct experiences, or may be introjected from others (and perceived as related to one's own experience).

8. Experiences are organized and given meaning in relation to the self or self-concept. Experiences which are inconsistent with the self-concept are threatening and are distorted or denied, or ignored.

9. Psychological "maladjustment" or disturbance exists when there is a discrepancy between the individual's self-concept (including his self-ideal) and his experiences; that is, the individual becomes aware of a discrepancy between what he is and what he wants to be or is capable of being. In other words, he is not achieving his potential; he is not a self-actualizing person.

10. In the absence of threat to the self, the individual is able to perceive and deal with experiences inconsistent with the self-concept and with the associated discrepancies.

11. The psychological conditions which minimize threat are the core conditions of counseling or psychotherapy: empathic understanding, respect, warmth, and therapeutic genuineness. The absence of these conditions leads to psychological disturbances (failure to be self-actualizing). The presence of these conditions in psychotherapy frees the client, enabling him to become a more self-actualizing person—a person who is able to take responsibility for himself, to explore and understand himself, to make adequate choices and decisions, and to engage in other behaviors and actions which express his emerging self. Among the results of client-centered therapy is the client's movement toward becoming more empathic, more respecting of others, and more genuine.

Indications and Contraindications

The development and the early application of client-centered therapy took place in a university setting; the clients were mainly college students. Rogers was very cautious in his claims. As a result, many who are unfamiliar with the development of client-centered therapy during the past thirty-five years still consider it to be a limited approach, applicable only to young individuals of somewhat above average intelligence.

However, client-centered therapy has been used and has been effective with a wide variety of clients and with a wide variety of problems of varying degrees of severity, including hospitalized mental patients. Its efficacy has been demonstrated, both by experience and by a great deal of research.

It is not going too far to suggest that client-centered therapy is applicable to all psychological problems or functional emotional disturbances. If one accepts the notion of emotional disturbance as a unitary disorder, differing in its manifestations and symptoms, but having the same origin or etiology (psychological "mistreatment" or the lack of the conditions for positive personality development), then client-centered therapy is the specific treatment. It provides the missing conditions. Thus, the major contraindication for its use is disturbances of an organic (neurological or physiological) origin.

The method minimizes action, control, or intervention by the therapist. As does medicine, it depends on the natural healing qualities inherent in the organism. It is thus consistent with the medical principle of conservative management and minimizes the dangers, or undesirable side effects, of active intervention.

Some Practical Implications

CLIENT AND FAMILY INVOLVEMENT

As is true for all psychotherapy, client-centered therapy requires a voluntary or cooperative client. Unlike medical treatment, psychological treatment cannot be imposed upon a person against his will. To some extent at least, behavior can be changed without the person's desire to change, or even his awareness that he is being controlled. Client-centered therapy, however, recognizes the right of the individual to refuse to be changed; it is offered only where the individual himself wants to change. In the case of children, the cooperation—and patience—of the family is desirable. Parents should be involved to some degree; although, if the child is seen in an institution (including a school) and the parents refuse to become involved, results can be achieved if the child is allowed to participate in therapy. Where parents are willing to be involved, work with the parents can take several different forms: (1) if the child's problems do not revolve around parental treatment, for example, with a school or classroom problem, parents may be seen occasionally for feedback or reports of progress; (2) parents may be seen in consultation at the beginning of therapy and irregularly thereafter, to discuss progress or changes and external factors which may be involved; (3) where the problem involves poor parent-child relations or mistreatment of the child because parents lack information, parents may be brought into teaching or tutoring sessions or they may be referred to classes in parent education or child psychology; and (4) where the problem involves emotional disturbances in the parents, counseling or psychotherapy may be provided for them, either by the same therapist who sees the child or by another therapist who shares the orientation of the child therapist.

FREQUENCY OR INTENSITY OF TREATMENT

Weekly sessions are most common in client-centered therapy. If the client and therapist deem it desirable, sessions may be held twice a week or even daily. Daily sessions are, however, seldom resorted to, because, in part at least, unlike psychoanalysis, the method does not emphasize the recovery and discussion of childhood memories but is more concerned with the here-and-now life of the client.

RELATIONSHIP TO OTHER METHODS

In common with all other methods of psychotherapy, client-centered counseling or psychotherapy is a form of psychological treatment. It is possible that to the extent that they are successful or effective, all psychological methods of treatment include some common elements. Certainly they all involve a psychological relationship with the client. To some extent at least, this relationship partakes of elements of the placebo. If it were nothing more than that, however, it is unlikely that it would be effective in terms of general or long-term results. There is no denying that the placebo quality, deriving from the authority, prestige, and status of the therapist, and from the use of suggestion, persuasion, reassurance, advice, and direction, does obtain immediate results, particularly in client satisfaction. Some methods of psychotherapy consist of little more than this. Client-centered therapy, however, minimizes the placebo element and is still effective. Thus it appears that there are other factors in the relationship which are therapeutic. These other factors, it can be maintained, are present in other methods of psychotherapy, such as psychoanalysis and its derivatives, which do not depend heavily upon the placebo.

The core conditions previously described are believed to be necessary and sufficient for therapeutic change. Research has demonstrated their efficacy in treating a wide variety of clients with a wide variety of problems. Moreover, these conditions have been identified in the actual practice of counselors and therapists professing different theories of psychotherapy. Finally, an analysis of the major existing theories indicates that the conditions are always present, implicitly if not explicitly.

The client-centered method differs from other methods in that: (1) the conditions are explicit and are described and defined, and scales have been developed to measure the degree of their presence or absence; and (2) it is assumed that the conditions are not only necessary but sufficient for positive or therapeutic personality change.

REFERENCES

1. AXLINE, V. M., *Play Therapy*, Houghton Mifflin, Boston, 1947.
2. CARKHUFF, R. R., and BERENSON, B. D., *Beyond Counseling and Therapy*, Holt, Rinehart & Winston, New York, 1967.
3. DORFMAN, E., "Play Therapy," in Rogers, C. R. (Ed.), *Client-centered Therapy*, pp. 235–271, Houghton Mifflin, Boston, 1951.
4. PATTERSON, C. H., *Relationship Counseling and Psychotherapy*, Harper & Row, New York, 1974.
5. ———, *Theories of Counseling and Psychotherapy*, 2nd ed., Harper & Row, New York, 1973.
6. ROGERS, C. R., "The Interpersonal Relationship: The Core of Guidance," *Harvard Educational Review*, 32:416–429, 1962.
7. ———, *On Becomming a Person*, Houghton Mifflin, Boston, 1961.
8. ———, "A Theory of Therapy, Personality, and Interpersonal Relationships," in Koch, S. (Ed.), *Psychol*ogy: *A Study of Science: Study I. Conceptual and Systematic*, vol. 3 *Formulations of the Person and the Social Control*, pp. 184–256, McGraw-Hill, New York, 1959.
9. ———, "The Necessary and Sufficient Conditions of Therapeutic Personality Change," *Journal of Consulting Psychology*, 21:95–103, 1957.
10. ———, *Client-centered Therapy*, Houghton Mifflin, Boston, 1951.
11. ———, *Counseling and Psychotherapy: Newer Concepts in Practice*, Houghton Mifflin, Boston, 1942.
12. ———, and DYMAND, R. F. (Eds.), *Psychotherapy and Personality Change*, University of Chicago Press, Chicago, 1954.
13. ROGERS, C. R., et al., *The Therapeutic Relationship and Its Impact*, University of Wisconsin Press, Madison, 1967.
14. TRUAX, C. B., and CARKHUFF, R. R., *Toward Effective Psychotherapy*, Aldine, Chicago, 1967.

PART D
Environmental Therapies

14 / Milieu Therapy: The Orthogenic School Model

Bruno Bettelheim and Jacquelyn Sanders

Roots of Milieu Therapy

The need for a special environment to house severely disturbed mental patients has been recognized since the middle ages, as exemplified by Bedlam and the German "Fools' Towers" (*Narrentuerme*). Historically this "need" to place deranged people in a special environment was motivated by the community's desire to lock them securely out of its way. When Pinel, Rush, and others made valiant efforts to improve the lot of such patients, they were motivated mainly by humanitarian, rather than specific, considerations. It took a long time, well into the twentieth century, before the best institutions began to assign precedence to the patient's need for therapy over the community's wish to have him safely removed from its midst.

The first psychoanalytic sanatorium was organized in Berlin after World War I, with the belief that not only should the community be made safe against the impact of mentally disturbed people and the patient protected against his self-destructive tendencies, but also with the new realization that the patient must be protected against further traumatization originating, for example, in the attitudes of his family or in events occurring in the institution. Once this safety and decent environment, free of punitive attitudes, was provided for the patient, the institution felt it had met its obligations when it provided some individual psychotherapy for the patient in carefully set-aside times and places. Other institutions, including some in the United States, adopted similar regimes.

At the beginning of the 1930s, Harry Stack Sullivan recognized that the attitudes of ward personnel had an important influence on the behavior of patients. He therefore trained nurses and attendants to be responsive to the patients' needs. Following his lead, others, for example the Menningers in Topeka, began to work out detailed programs of activity for each patient. The ward personnel were expected to organize the lives of the patients not only in accordance with the institution's routines, but also with regard to the patients' anxieties and other psychodynamic factors. Despite the new understanding that had been achieved, this recognition of what various activities ("occupational therapy," for example) could contribute to the well-being of the patient and of the importance of sympathetic handling of his anxieties by a trained, understanding nurse was still kept in the background. When it came to "definitive treatment" and cure, the institution relied on individual therapy, carried on in accordance with classic psychoanalytic procedures.

Essentially, the institution's task was to keep the patient in "cold storage" (a term first used by Redl), from which he was removed only to meet his psychiatrist in the office.[19] The term "cold storage" is an apt one, because the prevalent notion was that the best an institution could do for the patient was to see to that in between his therapeutic sessions (which were at worst once in a long time, and at best nearly daily) the patient did not deteriorate, the same reasoning by which food is kept in "cold storage."

The spiritual roots of milieu therapy go even further back into history and are as old as man's concern with how to deal with severe psychological difficulties in living. Long before man achieved any systematic understanding of the workings of his personality, its delicate interrelation with his body, and the impact of his physical and human environment on his existence, he had discovered practical palliatives for some of the ills that beset him. The medieval man, oppressed by feelings of sinfulness (in psychoanalytic terms by a conflict between id desires and superego strictures), sought and found relief through pilgrimages to religious relics or shrines. From antiquity, generations found "taking the bath" an effective cure for what ailed them, from depression to a whole catalog of real or psychosomatic physical problems. Though modern scientific knowledge has repudiated the curative properties of both holy relics and sulphur springs, let along thermal baths, many were helped by them.

It is possible that what accounted for the success of these cures is that they offered their participants a radical, if temporary, change in their conditions of life. Both the pilgrim and the visitor to a hot spring left behind them all the pressures, responsibilities, and irritations of their daily routine to join in an engrossing new enterprise with like-minded but new and stimulating acquaintances. The pilgrim's sense of religious mission during the journey helped to bolster his superego, while some quite different experiences he was likely to have in the course of the pilgrimage satisfied otherwise frustrated id desires, with the cumulative result being relief of inner tensions. The spa-goer had ample opportunity and encouragement to pay attention to his body, the demands of which he neg-

lected in the course of his workaday life. An inner belief shared by the multitude in the value of pilgrimages and bathing supported their efficacy. Relics and baths do not in fact work wonders on the body; however, the inner experiences they evoke can greatly help the psyche and, in this sense, benefit the body. Such experiences provided relief and restored neglected physiological and psychological functions by satisfying basic needs, but they did not lead to a change in what had originally produced the pathology. Hence the "cure" had to be repeated over and over.

Psychoanalytically speaking, it could be said as far as the patient's personality was concerned, the balnearic cure at its best provided primitive bodily satisfactions acceptable to ego and superego. In this fashion, it invested the ego with additional psychic energy. Outside the setting of the balnearic cure, such satisfactions were tabooed or created too much guilt for the person to derive benefit from such indulgence of the body.

The physician who advised patients to visit a spa (or, in different social and economic circumstances, to take a trip around the world) did so because he understood that the patient required a radical change in his human and physical environment in order to be restored to bodily and mental health. Even Freud, despite his complete commitment to psychoanalysis, occasionally advised a radical change in environment—with separation from all familial, occupational, and hence psychological, demands—either as a substitute for or an aid to psychoanalytic treatment.

In the course of developing psychoanalysis, Freud's experiences led him to create a very special physical and human setting: the analytic situation. Seclusion in the treatment room during the analytic hour, the absence of any stimuli other than those coming from the patient's introspection and the analyst's reflections on it, the absence of any physical exertion reinforced by the supine position, the assurance that nothing from the outside will interrupt the concentration on psychic processes—all these suggest the degree to which Freud felt psychoanalysis needed a unique environment if it was to succeed. Toward this same end, Freud took all possible steps to ensure the patient's security, including the very important protection that whatever the patient said, or did in the analytic situation would have no deleterious consequences in reality but would remain a secret between him and his therapist.

The psychoanalytic setting is also characterized by the absence of any demands for age-correct or socially appropriate behavior. In their place it creates its own protocols: the supine position, the silence that is essentially broken only by the patient, the encouragement to engage in primary process thinking and to follow one's fantasy rather than to suppress it, the rule that the patient is to say everything that comes to his mind, no matter how absurd, obscene, or illogical it may seem. All these induce regression to earlier forms of experience and make it safe to do so. In short, the setting encourages reexperiencing in fantasy material that was traumatic when experienced in reality—and not only the content of the memories but, in particular, the associated strong emotions. Because of the protective nature of the setting, that which was once so emotionally destructive in reality may now be safely worked through. Often enough, without such protection it would still be overwhelming. In short, the therapeutic milieu is a vital factor in psychoanalytic treatment.

The pilgrimage could temporarily relieve a feeling of sinfulness originating in the conflict between id and superego. A permanent cure, however, would have required a restructuring of the personality (for example, by a turn to asceticism or a change in patterns of inhibition) with a new and more viable balance struck between these two institutions of the mind. To achieve this today, we can rely on outpatient psychotherapy or psychoanalysis. For neurosis and hysteria, for example, and for certain of the character disorders, such ambulatory treatment is the preferred method of therapy. But it is not nearly so effective for the more disorganizing and deep-seated psychiatric disturbances. Those who suffer from them need hospitalization. The transition from extra- to intramural status in itself, then, becomes a first level in intervention. Sometimes, even very severe disturbances undergo rapid spontaneous remission at this point. This may well occur because the radically different, though often harsh, environment of the mental hospital may by chance meet deep inner needs. When these needs are satisfied, the person is permitted to go on with the tasks of living. Milieu therapy is designed to take such matters out of the realm of chance and submit them to careful scrutiny and planning.

The Total Treatment Design
for Children

The total treatment design of "milieu therapy" originated in the field of children's treatment. It was facilitated by at least two separate factors.

First, a child is much more vulnerable to the impact of his parents—from whom he may have to be protected, as exemplified by the "battered" child—than is the average adult to the influence of his closest relatives. Second, for some centuries, society has been convinced that the young, for their own good, must be removed for considerable periods of time into a very special institution, supposedly designed to meet their needs: schools. Overtly, schools are designed only to teach what children need to learn; covertly, schools also serve to free adult society for a time of the burden of its children so that they do not interfere unduly with its operations. Since all children attend some institution especially planned for them, the idea that special children, such as the severely disturbed, need institutions especially designed for their needs is easier to accept.

For many years, it was a canon of education that children suffering from severe physical defects should be placed in institutions which provided classroom teaching and other guidance geared to the nature of their deviation. For example, it was accepted that blind children required from the institution not only methods of teaching different from normal children, but special arrangement of all other life activities. This was true long before the need for the special institutions for mentally disturbed children was recognized.

After World War I, in an all too short-lived experiment, August Aichhorn[1] treated a group of wayward youngsters in an institutional setting. While this in itself was not new, Aichhorn's experiment was critical in the history of the development of milieu therapy for children. Here, for the first time, was a deliberate effort to apply psychoanalytic understanding to the "life" structure of the child. For example, Aichhorn used the strength of his own transference relationship to guide the lives of some of his patients. In the institution, he, the doctor, became involved in the life of the group, supporting and guiding the "child care" staff to make use of the living situation to rehabilitate the youngsters. For instance, a group of boys was permitted to act out and destroy things in accordance with the notion that this would have a cathartic effect. Then, rather than being punished, they were given new quarters. Thus, psychoanalytic theory was applied not only in the traditional analytic sessions, but to a whole life situation. Years later, Slavson, Redl, and others applied Aichhorn's principles to group or camp settings, and out of their efforts grew the procedure now known as group therapy (see chapter 10). Redl pioneered summer camp settings for delinquent youngsters in which the camp activities and the group life were designed to have a therapeutic impact independent from, or in addition to, individual and group treatment.

Among psychoanalytically trained therapists, it became accepted that as much attention must be paid to all details of the setting in group psychotherapy as was necessary in individual therapy. But within institutions, except for Aichhorn's work, the prevalent conviction persisted that the setting need only be humane and protective, while the true therapeutic impact would come from individual or group therapy sessions, or from a combination of both.

In the United States during the 1940s, a number of psychoanalytically trained people began to apply psychoanalytic principles to the treatment of very disturbed children within a residence. Stanislaus Szurek[25] at Langley Porter Clinic in San Francisco, Fritz Redl[20] in Detroit, those working at Southard School in Topeka,[17] and the staffs at settings associated with the Jewish Board of Guardiens in New York[2] are among the most noteworthy. Under the stimulus of the new thinking, residential institutions for disturbed children proliferated widely at that time. All these efforts contained some element of concern for the effects of the environment on the rehabilitation of the children. It was during this same period that Maxwell Jones[16] began working on the development of a therapeutic community for adults in England.

In 1944, the University of Chicago entrusted Bruno Bettelheim with the task of reorganizing its Orthogenic School in line with the most advanced ideas on the treatment of severely disturbed children. He was able to secure Emmy Sylvester's help in that work. Bettelheim and Sylvester undertook to formulate a more comprehensive approach: What would the setting and life within an institution for children suffering from severe functional disorders be like, if every detail was in line with psychoanalytic thinking on child development and child psychotherapy? It immediately became apparent that how a child was fed, bathed, toileted, treated on getting up and being put to bed were just as important as what occurred during his daily psychotherapy. In fact, it soon turned out that such events, when handled with understanding and skill, were even more important than what could be achieved for the child in his individual treatment hour. Since all children with major emotional illnesses suffer from severe ego disturbance, they need to have help in mastering all those life experiences that lead to ego growth.

This was the situation which led not only to much of the thinking that went into the creation of milieu therapy, but also prompted the selection of its name. When Bettelheim and Sylvester felt ready to report on their common work, they were hard-pressed to find a suitable name for it. The term "milieu therapy" finally occurred to one of them, and a consultation of the *Oxford Dictionary* indicated its appropriateness. "Milieu" was defined as "a medium, environment, surrounding." This was exactly what Bettelheim and Sylvester had in mind, for what they had tried to create was a medium—an enveloping matrix within which one lives; an agency; an environment. Within the framework of psychoanalytic thinking, they strove to create an environment, both physical and human that would in itself function as an agency for therapy. "A Therapeutic Milieu" was the title for their first publication describing the work of the Orthogenic School,[10] shortly followed by another, "Milieu Therapy—Indications and Illustrations."[9]

In these first publications, Bettelheim and Sylvester stressed that theirs was not a new technique. Their article "Milieu Therapy" begins:

> Milieu Therapy is not new as a psychotherapeutic technique. It is no more than the application of psychoanalytic concepts to the specific task of creating a setting for emotionally disturbed children who are in need of residential treatment . . . Nor is the idea of creating a psychoanalytic milieu for emotionally disturbed children a new one. Anna Freud considered it, though not without skepticism, when she spoke of the need for a milieu which would be suited to child analysis, and Aichhorn reported favorably on his experience in an institutional setting which had therapeutic value in itself.[9] [p. 54]

Treating the Whole Patient

Even in the best of today's private children's institutions (which often are far superior to the public ones), directed and staffed by psychoanalysts, an abyss separates therapeutic opportunities afforded the child during his individual or group psychoanalytic sessions from what he encounters at other times. The personality of the psychotic child is by definition badly fragmented and lacking in cohesion. Occupational and recreational therapy and other features of a daily or weekly program, while breaking the monotony of institutional living, often tend to fragment the child's life further, by parceling it out. Only a unified institution can present an image by which the child can integrate the disparate aspects of his own life and personality. Fragmentation not only seriously interferes with the goals of the institution but runs counter to them. This has been convincingly demonstrated by the experiences of those who voluntarily subjected themselves to living with psychiatric patients for a short time.[11,12,21]

The attitudes toward the patient's symptomatology is an instance of this fragmentation. The analyst will view the symptom as a significant manifestation of, as well as an effort to solve, a conflict, while the rest of the staff is likely to view it as an evil. The mental patient's symptoms, as distressing as they may be to him, as upsetting and even dangerous as they may be to his surroundings, are nevertheless his highest achievement. They need to be recognized and respected as such not only by his psychiatrist but by the entire institution. But more often than not, in the reality of today's institutions, the techniques of conditioned-reflex psychology (under the name of behavior modification) show utter disrespect for the symptoms and, with it, for the child. Be it via physical restraint, cold packs, shock therapy, drugs, or schedules of reinforcements, attempts to eliminate symptoms convince the child only that his environment wishes to shape him as it thinks best, and not as he through a strenuous and tortuous process of self-discovery may wish to become. Even if restraints or drugs are not used or employed only with the best of therapeutic intentions, for the child his placement in an institution itself can be a massively dehumanizing experience.[13]

Rather than to try to give a generalized picture of milieu therapy to which no reality conforms, since each therapeutic milieu is unique in some respects, we deemed it more useful to the reader to base our discussion on the Orthogenic School in Chicago, which exists in reality and has proven its viability for over thirty uninterrupted years. Invariably, the path by which the creators of institutions arrive at their conviction about the unique therapeutic merits of their methods of treatment will exercise some influence on the nature of the therapeutic milieus they create and operate. Therefore, a few remarks on how Bettelheim came to develop his notions about the need for a total therapeutic milieu for the treatment of psychotic children may be of some interest. It also demonstrates that, initially, errors can hardly be avoided but that much may be learned from them to improve the future.

Bettelheim's involvement with total treatment milieus began in the early 1930s as an experiment in treating an autistic American child brought to Vienna by her parents. She had been sent to Freud by Piaget, and by him to Anna Freud. Anna Freud immediately realized that psychoanalysis by itself offered no chance of recovery for this girl. She thought, however, that psychoanalysis might bring results if combined with placement in a home where the child could receive round-the-clock care, arranged entirely in accord with her psychological needs, as understood on the basis of psychoanalytic insights. So an arrangement was made whereby the girl was treated psychoanalytically by one of Anna Freud's colleagues, while the Bettelheim couple—not at all realizing what they were letting themselves in for —agreed to have the girl live in their home. They reorganized their home life to meet the child's physical, emotional, and psychological needs as far as humanly possible. The arrangement endured for over seven years, until Hitler's invasion of Austria ended it prematurely.

After thinking about these years, two things became evident. First, a total therapeutic milieu was the only way to help such desperately sick children. Second, this is no task for a private family. Even if they have no children of their own and are deeply committed to the enterprise, the demands of such an effort are overwhelming. The emotional burden is too heavy, and the interference with the lives of those who serve the patient, too far-reaching. The girl had made remarkable progress over the years, but complete recovery had not been achieved. In retrospect, it became obvious that what the girl would have needed most was a setting especially designed to meet *all* her treatment requirements. Such children need not only daily psychoanalytically oriented therapy sessions, combined with a home environment arranged as much as possible to provide whatever is required for their rehabilitation, but also a very special school setting.

It also became obvious that ideally, the task required an organization. In that way, those caring for the psychotic child would be able to share the burden with others, and, despite long hours and arduous demands, the caretakers could still continue to have a life of their own. Such caretakers would have to be in complete philosophical accord about what was best for the children under their care. They would need the ability to put this into practice in the widest variety of situations, while doing so within the terms of their own personalities. All this could be possible only if consistency and deep commitment to a clearly understood common treatment philosophy were to transcend all individual differences. That is, there would probably be many different ways of dealing with the child, since different people would be doing so, but they would all have to share a basic, underlying agreement.

These considerations evolved out of the realization that despite the best efforts of all concerned in Vienna, some serious discrepancies persisted which the experiment had failed to overcome. These involved unrecognized or unacknowledged tensions between the various aspects of the girl's therapeutic experiences. Her analyst, her foster parents, and later her school teachers—all shared a common orientation and a common overwhelming commitment to the patient's well-being. But that was not enough. There was still not a sufficiently thorough integration of all efforts to prevent fragmentation in the girl's life experiences. Cooperation and consensus are prerequisites, but they are not all that is required. There is a need for complete integration of all aspects of the total life within the therapeutic community—from analysis to caretakers to service personnel. (In Vienna, the Bettelheims had discovered that uncomprehending, uninvolved cooks and maids could threaten the integrity of the milieu they were struggling to create. They had quickly realized the importance of making sure that every person who encountered the patient understood her needs and could accept with understanding what was at times unpleasant and seriously upsetting behavior.)

The impasse in treating the girl in Vienna had to do with a preconceived hierarchy according to which the psychoanalyst knew best what was good for the child, and how things ought to be done. While the foster parents and teacher had tried to respect this, in retrospect, it appeared doubtful that deep down they had accepted it, or accepted it without resentment. They *had* accepted the psychoanalyst's superior understanding of the child's unconscious, but the same had not been true for suggestions about what they should do for the child in home and classroom. After all, it was a private home; the foster parents were present and observed how the girl acted and seemed to feel in the bathtub and on the toilet, while the analyst remained a relative stranger to such experiences. The foster parents-therapists lived with the child not fifty minutes but many hours a day. Similarly, the teachers also resented being told how to understand the child. They never doubted that the psychoanalyst had special knowledge derived from experiences in treating the girl; but so had they, gained from their different experiences. In order to provoke as little resentment as possible, the psychoanalyst was reluctant to make as many or as forceful suggestions as she might have, with detrimental consequences for all therapeutic endeavors.

The Organization Needed for Milieu Therapy

For these and many other good reasons, the decision was made that in the reorganized Orthogenic School there would be no hierarchies—everybody would be equally important, and common psychological understanding of the children's needs would form the basis of the institution's integration. Each staff member would possess his own special skills and knowledge, but this must never confer any special prerogatives. If the institution were to become a total therapeutic milieu, the greater importance any one staff member assumed would interfere with the unity of the environment. It was agreed that there was one most important single factor in treating the psychotic child. It was this: that despite the complexities, vagaries, and crises of his life, the child should be surrounded at all times by the reality of a unified setting. This view has been supported by the findings of Caudill,[11] Goffman,[13] and others who brought this concept to wider attention, and Henry[15] who, for a few years, joined in the work of the Orthogenic School and published his findings.

The theory of staff equality was correct. However, it became clear in practice that this ideal equality was an artificial way to achieve what was sought. First, there were obvious differences in each person's individual capacities to understand a particular child's needs and what might best be done about them. Second, as soon as a child came to the institution, some staff members became more involved with him than others, and often the child singled out some of them as most important to him. Each child, when given the opportunity, created his own hierarchy, and the staff was compelled to respect this. The child's own hierarchy had little to do with any special training a staff member possessed but was determined by what kind of a person the staff member was and how deeply he, at this moment in his life, was able to commit himself to a particular child as a person and to meeting the child's therapeutic needs, whatever they might be.

It became apparent that utter equality in importance for the patient, common philosophy in regard to his treatment, or common understanding of psychology and pathology—although they are all important ingredients—could not singly, or in their combination, create that integrated and total treatment design which was the common goal. Nevertheless, as they worked together to make that goal become reality, the staff realized that they were achieving the integration for which they all were striving. What made this possible was not so much a working together for the patients' benefit, though this remained the ultimate aim. What counted more in practice was that problems were dealt with together, hopes were shared along with anxieties, successes as well as defeats. In short, they shared what the work with and for the children meant to each of the staff as individuals and meant to them as a group committed to the idea of a therapeutic milieu as the main instrument of treatment. This sharing bound them together in their common endeavor much more intimately than anything else. All that they poured of themselves personally into their task made life much more meaningful to each of them who shared in it.

As this became clear, the various efforts that were made to achieve an integrated institution assumed a different order of importance. For example, conferences where the psychoanalyst added to the staff's understanding of the child on the basis of his insights became less important than working together to explain why one staff member had not been able to achieve such insight on his own. What they now sought to comprehend fully was why one person had handled a situation this way, and another had done so differently; and what this told about a staff member's inner attitudes toward himself, the child, the philosophy of the setting, and the challenge of the work. Just as effective and exciting as understanding a particular child was coming to understand how and why the way a particular staff member handled a child and his problems flowed from his personality and past experiences, and how their aftereffects could be mastered to the staff member's own benefit, to the child's benefit, and, above all, to the benefit of the treatment design of the institution.

As they devoted themselves to the task of scrutinizing all aspects of the institution with the same careful attention that had been given to trying to understand the children, increasingly beneficial effects began to emerge for the children, for the treatment team, and for the total institution. They realized that they had started out with a too-static, not sufficiently alive concept of what really makes for a total therapeutic milieu.

What was finally discovered (and all their subsequent effort has been basically a continuous process of refining and implementing this discovery) is that the integration of the total treatment institution is never complete. It is in fact a vital process of *becoming* integrated, an ideal always to be striven for, never to be fully achieved. To be alive is to be continuously becoming; an institution is moribund if it believes that its integration can be accomplished once and for all, remaining happily the same forever after. It was discovered that the ongoing process of analysis must be applied to all aspects of the situation—from human interaction on all levels down to the smallest detail of the physical setting. And this discovery provided the true paradigm for the work: that it is of crucial importance for children working toward the integration of their own personality to live in a setting continuously striving for its own better integration. This spirit, pervading the institution and all of the life that unfolds within it, transcends the myriad specifics through which one may endeavor to realize it.

With such insights, and as a direct consequence of them, a different organization of the therapeutic milieu developed. The original ideal of total equality had proven unworkable. The ideal of equality was then replaced by one of becoming, of facilitating. As much as possible, the organization strove to guarantee a continuous process of achieving higher integration to individual staff members, to the institution, and, ultimately, to the patients it served. Basically, the idea of equality gave way to that of social solidarity around a common goal. After it had been achieved and was found working well for the patients, a well-known social anthropologist, Jules Henry, was invited to come in and evaluate the process. He had wide experience in the children's field and in the study of mental hospitals, and he was given complete freedom in making his evaluation.

For several years, Henry studied the therapeutic milieu that had been created and subsequently published his findings.[14,15] In order to present what he considered the most salient factors of the therapeutic milieu, he devised two categories: "simple undifferentiated" subordination (SU), and "multiple differentiated" subordination (MD). He, then, contrasted the structure of the Orthogenic School milieu (SU) to that of the typical mental hospital or psychiatric ward (MD). He summarized his findings about the two systems in the following abridged table.[15]

The social solidarity of all staff members neither requires nor implies that there are no divergencies of opinion, or that there will be no arguments

TABLE 14–1

In the SU System	*In the MD System*
The Physical Plant	
Living is packaged around the dormitory.	Living is split up and distributed over the hospital floors.
Task Performance	
Almost complete responsibility for task execution is in the hands of the workers.	Task responsibility is distributed among several departments and persons.
Most of the workers' time is given over to caring for the patients; no sharp distinction is made between on-the-job time and off-the-job time.	Personnel work on a standard eight-hour day; a sharp distinction is made between on-the-job time and off-the-job time.
One person is with the patient through all phases of the illness.	Different persons pace the patient through different phases of the illness.
The worker has complete autonomy in the execution of the task.	The worker does not have autonomy in the execution of the task.
Worker Personality	
The large energy output drawn from inner needs is accepted and utilized.	Inner needs are masked under routine and frozen professional competence.
. . .	
The worker is deeply involved with the patient.	Involvement of the worker with the patient is an obstacle to the functioning of the system.
. . .	
The Director	
The director is limited by his staff because of its autonomy.	The staff is subordinate.
He permits autonomy to the staff.	He governs by "policy decision."
His responsibility, since it is for the total task, is heavy and oppressive.	His responsibility is only for his department task.
He is close to all operations.	He tends to be distant even from his own departmental operations because of the delegation of tasks to executive officers.
. . .	
There is a deep mutual involvement of director and workers.	There is little involvement of the department head in workers.
The Patients	
There is a diminution of separation between the patient system and the worker system.	The two systems are strictly separated.
The patient is internalized by the worker.	Internalization of the patient by the worker does not occur.
Status of the worker is dependent on his involvement with the patient.	Status of the worker is dependent on his relative detachment from the patient.

NOTE: This table is reprinted, in abridged form, with permission of the publisher from "Types of Institutional Structure," by Jules Henry, *Psychiatry, 20:*59, 1957.

about them. On the contrary, since the solidarity is based on commitment to what the institution stands for, it stipulates defense against those who seem, rightly or wrongly, to act out of line with its ethos. If the battles concern how to achieve a more therapeutic operation of the institution, they do not threaten solidarity but strengthen it. The open venting of disagreement holds the staff together; avoiding it would erode the staff's trust in the institution.

Such social solidarity requires the most ample communication among the staff. Since Sullivan first brought it to wider attention, much has been written about the need for communication among the staff of mental institutions. It has recently been demonstrated that the existence of the necessary level of communication among the staff members of a psychiatric hospital may be decisive for the life or death of some patients. In addition to that, however, it may be critical for the very life and death of the hospital itself.[24] A decade earlier, the same was implied in the findings of Stanton and Schwartz.[23] Not even daily staff meetings, as is the practice at the Orthogenic School, are sufficient to assure the free flow of communication. A certain formality is inescapable in a definitely scheduled staff meeting. It is the many informal get-togethers—prompted by personal friendship, the wish and need for mutual reassurance, and the desire to learn more about the patients and how to handle them—which assure that social solidarity and meaningful communication exist. Communication is the consequence of this interactive process; it would not work if it were sought for itself. That is why many institutions fail to achieve good communication, even though they realize its importance and try to facilitate it.

Housing the Spirit

It is evident that emphasis on the specifics of one setting would be parochial, whereas the goal here is to define therapeutic principles whose universal applicability make them useful in many different kinds of settings. The details of application and implementation have to be in line with the particular conditions that prevail. The organic growth of the philosophy underlying the work at the Orthogenic School was dwelt on at some length in order to illustrate these principles. Whatever the specifics, that which goes on in a therapeutic milieu must be "all of one piece" and therapeutic in every respect. Just for these reasons, it is difficult to give an adequate account of how milieu therapy actually operates, since the details will necessarily vary. One cannot describe an organic process without simplifying and distorting it.

The essential requirement of growth and integration must be stressed, even in regard to the physical plant: Things must never be frozen at any one level but always be flexible to provide what each patient needs most. Since the inner integration of the individual is the goal, some aspects of the institution must represent id gratification, others superego control, and still others ego achievement. And these aspects must at all times regulate and influence each other, as any true personal integration requires. How this is done can most adequately be illustrated by detailing the treatment of individuals[56,7,8] and by a description of the setting in which it is done.[4]

It is characteristic of milieu therapy that in regard to its physical setting, specific details are of little importance and must depend on the means available. It is the spirit underlying the physical structures and their furnishings that is significant. In that sense, however, the way the elements of physical structure are designed and put together are the great importance. In the same way that psychoanalysis demands a very special physical environment, so does milieu therapy. Psychoanalytic knowledge of oral experiences, for example, convinced the Orthogenic School staff that if they wanted to get across to their children (preferably nonverbally so as not to make a fuss about it) how important they thought it was that children should enjoy eating and the human interactions it encompasses, they had to make the institution's dining room as beautiful as possible. So they made sure that only elegant china, glasswear, and silverware were employed there, but of an elegance that appeals to children and not the sort preferred by sophisticated adults. Before new china or glasses or whatever were acquired, several desirable patterns were presented to the children for their final selection. The result was that everybody used more elegant table settings than are usually found in most homes, except when entertaining. However, the meals at the institution are not formal but extremely relaxed. The intention was to convey in symbolic fashion that in the institution, each of the children's meals is considered as important as is a formal meal to the host, hostess, and guests when they share in such entertaining.

The children are not expected to, nor do they eat with, any regard to what are considered polite table manners. Nonetheless, breakage is practically nonexistent. Without saying so, the children appreciate the milieu's intentions. Very rarely is any deliberate damage done. And when a child does break a few dishes to make a point, the willing acceptance of such expense and the staff's understanding of the situation that provoked the action provide a yield far beyond price in terms of continued progress.

Similarly, bathrooms and toilet facilities (places so closely associated with the anal period of development) must also convey the milieu's respect for the body and its functions. And, not so incidentally, being with a child while he is on the toilet or giving him a bath and accepting whatever he does is much easier if the surroundings are attractive. Use the beautiful tiling and fixtures and avoidance of an all-too "hygienic" white, for example, make it clear to the child that the milieu is committed to the notion that elimination should be enjoyable, that it is an important human activity, and nothing to be ashamed of. No therapeutic milieu can recreate the splendor of the Roman baths. But one can try as far as possible with limited funds to approximate it. None of this is lost on the children.

But dining room, bedrooms, and bathrooms, as important as they are, are only parts of a building. Unless the building in its entirety is a creation in the right spirit, its isolated features will have little effect in conveying the message to the child. A building's outer appearance, inner structure, and furnishings reflect the style of life that goes on inside it. An essential part of the desired style is the constant growth of the physical plant. Children not only need to give up old crippling defenses, have essential needs met, and conflicts resolved, but they need to grow continually, both from the primitive levels that have been thwarted by disturbance and from the more or less "normal" levels common to all children. Thus, physical growth of the institution must go on both in terms of remodeling and new construction. Both are done slowly with thought and consultation with the child, so that the new growth is appropriate and related to the existing structure.

One account of the treatment of a psychotic girl is significantly called *Symbolic Realization*.[22] It is true, for psychotics of all ages, that every experience they meet becomes a symbol of intention and attitude much more important to them than the rational purpose and meaning it may have generally. For example, while to most people one color is more pleasing or cheerful or depressing than another, to the psychotic one color (or form) means good will, another evil; one means that he may take hope, another that he will be destroyed; one

object may mean safety, another persecution or despair—and this quite irrespective of the ordinary person's view and use of the object in everyday life. For everyone, there are, of course, certain symbols that convey much deeper meanings than are easily put into rational words—the crucifix, the cap and gown, the passing hearse. But to the psychotic, everything becomes a symbol of intention and attitude. He reacts intensively to symbols and their private meanings. If the therapist wants to reach him, he too must resort to the symbol, long before he can communicate through rational expression.

Evan a normal child will gauge an adult's intention by how the adult treats the child's teddy bear or doll. He will also gauge intentions by how his room is arranged, and most of all, by whether he can keep his room the way he wants it or must keep it the way others want. Mere words, however encouraging, will make little difference. The more disturbed a person, the less he believes what is said to him and the more crucially interested he is in what actually transpires. Because of his past experiences with double-bind messages, a disturbed child knows better than to trust what he is told. He is a little bit more ready to believe the meaning conveyed by what is done and how he is approached. But most of all he believes what he can touch, feel, smell, and see for himself.

Recognizing these facts, the therapeutic milieu most take very seriously the problem of how to convey meaning not only through rational arrangements but also through the attitudes reflected by the physical setting. This is the carrier of symbolic meaning. How the institution is built and furnished, down to the last detail of lighting and furniture, must all be designed to convince the patient that this is a place where he can afford to let down his defenses, because everything is here to satisfy all his needs. Further, he must become convinced that these satisfactions will not endanger him, and that he will not be destroyed, even if he relaxes his controls over his anger and anxiety. But he will believe this only if even inanimate objects tell him that everything is here for him, that he is terribly important to the staff, and that life can be good even for him. Only then can he dare to begin to trust the institution's intentions and begin to get well.

Physical settings, like words, can also deceive. That is why the new child "cases the joint"—to see if the milieu really is what it seems to be, and if it really is trustworthy and safe. Psychotic children know that locked doors signify only the staff's fear of them, and locked cupboards, the staff's distrust of them, whatever else may be claimed. Whatever rational explanations may be given, children know that those who place them in drab structures care little that drabness may further depress them. Even the argument that locked doors and barred windows are there primarily to protect the child from harming himself is unacceptable. The danger of harming himself exists only if the child is left alone or placed in a physical and human setting lacking in concern for his needs.

The suicidal person, more than others, needs liberation from impersonal restraints like bars. These only prove to him what he already believes, that life is not worth living. The suicidal child needs to live under conditions that convince him that life is worthwhile, even for him, and that he matters a great deal to those who take care of him. He does not need maximum security or isolation "to think things over." To isolate a child only means to him that the adult does not even try to have empathy with his distress. The more upset or violent he is, the more a child needs maximum human care to counteract his feelings of isolation. He does not need barred rooms that are virtually empty and barren, but the most attractive surroundings possible in order to counteract his overwhelming sense of depression and desperation.

All this gives only a small glimpse of how a generally ignored detail of institutional life—the physical setting—must be given the closest scrutiny if it is to enhance and support therapeutic work and not detract from it. It is just one element of all those which taken together constitute the total treatment milieu.

Some Preconditions for Milieu Therapy

Unless there is need for it, one should not remove a child from his home into an institution, especially for a considerable period of time. Milieu therapy is not short-term treatment. Given the seriousness of a disturbance which indicates treatment in a very special environment, the treatment must often extend over several years to be successful. There are many reasons for this, over and above the severity of the disturbance.

First, it takes time for the child to accept this new therapeutic milieu as "real." He has experienced trips away from home, perhaps he has also lived in a different environment for a time. As long as the child expects to return shortly to the environment which was so destructive to him (given the paramount importance parents hold for all children), the child cannot believe that his parents could or would accept him if he developed a very different personality, even if they tell him they want him to do so. The child has developed his pathological defenses in response to his perception of his parents. He will not give those perceptions up if he thinks he will soon need them again when he returns to living with his parents.

It can easily take a year before a severely disturbed child begins to believe that from now on, he will be living in a situation where the old defenses are no longer necessary for his survival. But only after this conviction has taken hold does the child begin to restructure his personality, although he may, from the first, have taken advantage of the relief a total therapeutic milieu offers him. Therefore, for milieu therapy to be fully effective, the milieu must be so constructed that the child becomes convinced that his parents no longer exercise their old domination over his life, and that the milieu even abrogates the parents' right to arrange the details of his life. However, the legal giving up of parental rights is disadvantageous because it results in a reduction in parental self-respect. Parental cooperation is essential for what must be a common enterprise, in which the parent's role is defined by the therapeutic process.

Removing the child from the old pathogenic environment will have lasting effects in promoting a better integration of personality only if the new environment provides all the ingredients compatible with it. If the patient continues to be exposed to double-bind messages,[3] for example, one set coming from the milieu and contradictory messages originating with his parents, then the split in the patient's personality will not be healed. Nothing is more effective in convincing a child that the therapeutic mileu indeed protects him so that his old defenses are not only unnecessary but counterproductive than his discovery that it is the milieu, and not the parents, which controls communications between parents and child, including arrangements for visits.

For the milieu to thus control such communication, fullest parental cooperation is necessary. It is, therefore, the prime precondition for milieu therapy. However great a child's need for milieu therapy because of the severity of his disturbance, it is useless to place him in such a milieu unless the parents are fully cooperative.

It must be made clear from the very beginning

of placement that milieu therapy is purposeless unless the parents fully cooperate. Given such a condition, only very seldom do parents decline to place the child. In nearly all cases, the parents understand, not infrequently on the basis of their own experience with psychotherapy, the need for relinquishing their parental prerogatives, even for years. At the Orthogenic School, during years of treatment, most parents cooperated. From time to time, they found it difficult to do so and needed help to continue their cooperation. Even those parents who at the beginning were psychologically unsophisticated responded to their child's dire need. As the need grew less dramatic, the parents would then deal with the child's improvement.

Once the child has been in the milieu for a certain length of time, the human and physical environment begin to convince him that the old pathogenic forces can no longer exercise influence on him. This conviction, when well handled, disintegrates the child's old pessimistic views that there is no hope for things being different, which becomes replaced by a first tentative hope that a "new beginning," a new form of life may be within his grasp. Even quite psychotic children can gain this hope, as is rather dramatically demonstrated by the spontaneously expressed desire of some children to be called by a different name once they came to believe that the old environment would no longer directly affect them. The Orthogenic School staff learned from this experience to ask each child as soon as he had begun to believe that his parents or other significant figures of his past environment would no longer influence his life, whether he wanted to be known by a different first name than before. While only some children chose a different name, all were pleased to be offered the choice.

The fact that some children choose to change their names is reassuring to those who do not. It seems to say that freedom from old restraints and the right to change one's personality is guaranteed by the therapeutic milieu.

Much more important to all patients is the guarantee that their parents will not know the details of their life in the milieu and will, therefore, be unable to exercise control over it. This is made clear from the start, since on their initial visits, only they and not their parents are shown the Orthogenic School. Also, if information is sought, it is sought mainly from the children, although naturally, later on, additional information is also sought from the parents. Further, only the children, and not their parents, meet those staff members who work most closely with them. Most important of all, the final decision on whether or not to join the therapeutic milieu is the individual child's and the institution's, but nobody else's. Obviously, this is a decision which can be implemented only by the parents, both because of their legal rights and also because, in most cases (the only exception are children who are wards of public or private agencies), the parents have to be responsible for the payment of fees.

In order to secure such far-reaching cooperation from the parents, they must receive all possible support. Some parents have had experience with psychotherapy in various forms and, from their own experience, readily understand that their treatment would never have succeeded if some of their closest relatives, marital partners, siblings, parents, had been regularly informed of what went on in the therapy or had been permitted to interfere with it. On the basis of such personal experience, it is easier for them to understand that the relative speed and completeness of their child's recovery depends on their refraining from interfering with his life in the therapeutic milieu. They also must be satisfied with being informed only of those aspects of the child's life and progress which can be conveyed to them without betraying the confidentiality and privacy which the child needs for his recovery.

Those parents who have not had such personal experiences sometimes require more explanation. It is very important that they be informed regularly about those things that can be revealed to them. Monthly reports that convey the flavor of the life of the child are greatly appreciated. The parents do not have contact with the child's counselor or teacher, but they are free at any time to consult the director.

There are those parents (but they are a small minority) who are pleased to be rid of the child and to know he is in good hands, so that they need not feel guilty about it. Relief of guilt about having caused the child's disturbance and about placing him in an institution is one of the most important services the total therapeutic milieu can, and as far as possible must, render to all parents in return for their cooperation.

In this respect, the experience at the Orthogenic School has been that the most difficult period is the first year of the child's placement; sometimes the difficult period extends well into the second year. By then, in the vast majority of the cases, the child's improvement is so obvious, even to the most skeptical parent, that parental cooperation is assured by their desire not to jeopardize what has been accomplished or to impede further progress.

Indications for Milieu Therapy

Milieu therapy is indicated for those children suffering from undeveloped or very weak egos. These include autistic, psychotic, borderline, schizophrenic, and severely neurotic children. There are certain groups of children, often referred because of the difficulty of differential diagnosis or because they suffer from more than one disability, for whom psychoanalytically oriented milieu therapy is not indicated.

The Orthogenic School has had only limited success with children who had been considered severely retarded for several years, and had lived in institutions for feeble-minded children, where they were taught and treated as feeble-minded. They were accepted by the Orthogenic School only when there was serious doubt about the correctness of the original diagnosis. A few such children were worked with when it became quite apparent that the diagnosis was indeed incorrect.

This limited success may well be due to a shortcoming of this particular form of milieu therapy. But so long as others do not report different results, it seems reasonable to believe that there is a certain timetable in intellectual development. When serious intellectual stimulus deprivation has continued for too long during an age when the child is particularly susceptible to his pernicious effects, the damage may become to some degree irreversible. Certainty in this respect will be gained only if many more prolonged experiments with milieu therapy for such children are undertaken. With more care in diagnosis, it is to be hoped that in the future, not many children will be misdiagnosed and mistakenly treated as retarded.

A more difficult problem is that of brain damage. The Orthogenic School has been very successful with children who had been diagnosed as brain damaged when there were no hard neurological signs, or when the diagnosis was based on behavioral indices only. Here again, the likelihood is that the original diagnosis was incorrect. When there are no hard neurological signs, it may well be that a prolonged therapeutic test is the best way to arrive at a definite decision. If the child responds well to milieu therapy, then it is indicated, because more often than not it then leads to complete recovery.

On the other hand, children who had been subjected to a series of shock treatments showed some improvement at Orthogenic School but failed to make a complete recovery. The younger the child had been when subjected to shock treatment, the less the institution was able to help him. It, therefore, discontinued accepting children who had been exposed to shock treatment, although they may, too, improve considerably when exposed to milieu therapy. Given the small number of children who can be taken care of by institutions which presently practice milieu therapy, it seems reasonable to reserve the available places for children who in all likelihood can be completely rehabilitated.

Over the years, the Orthogenic staff worked with a number of children who had been on tranquilizing drugs for years before they were admitted. These children have always been taken off drugs immediately, and the medication replaced with devoted human care, respect for their symptoms, and the offer of ample, age-correct, and therapeutically indicated regressive instinctual gratifications. The result was always the same: even the most difficult child became much more manageable under such a regime than he had been under the influence of drugs.

In general, the Orthogenic School found that tranquilizing drugs hinder rather than help the therapeutic task. After some experimentation, it was found that patient and institution were both better off when the principle was established never to use tranquilizing drugs. By not using such drugs to solve impasses in living, the staff is forced to do full justice to the patient's needs—to his anxieties and deepest hopes and desires—and in this way, the nonuse of drugs speeds final recovery.

There is another group of disturbed children who benefit greatly from milieu therapy, and whom it can readily and completely cure. These are children whose placement is determined not on the basis of the severity of the underlying pathology, but on whether or not they can be kept within society or within their families. The decision to institutionalize them is most often made on the basis of the nuisance value of their symptomatology rather than on the severity of the disturbance. These children are so upsetting to their parents or siblings that they cannot be kept within the home; they are so disruptive to the school or the community that they should be placed in a special setting.

The total therapeutic milieu is ideally suited for the treatment of psychotic children, anorexic children, drug addicts, severe delinquents, and others who suffer from such serious personality arrest or misdevelopment that they cannot be kept and treated within their customary, or even in an improved "normal," environment. In general, milieu therapy is the treatment of choice for youngsters with severe ego-disturbance. In discussing the theory of residential treatment, Noshpitz says "generally speaking, youngsters in residence confront us primarily with the problem of massive ego weakness. . . ."[18] This logically requires a massive ego cure which can be provided by a total environment specifically designed for ego strengthening experiences.

Economic Implications

Milieu therapy is a relatively inexpensive treatment. Tuition at the Orthogenic School, which includes room, board, laundry, schooling, swimming instruction, recreation, accompaniment to dentist, doctor, clothes shopping, celebration of major and minor holidays and birthdays and other expenses is only about as much per year as the cost of full psychoanalysis, or approximately two times the salary that a working parent must pay a housekeeper to look after a normal child.

Of course, the cost of milieu therapy in a hospital setting is much higher. However, since hospital-type medical procedures are not necessary, a hospital setting is neither required nor advisable. Moreover, it is possible to staff the institution with bright, young, dedicated people who are willing to work for relatively little pay in exchange for an intensive and rewarding learning experience. Those who are able to understand and practice milieu therapy tend to stay at the Orthogenic School from four to nine years. Teachers tend to stay longer and thus provide important institutional continuity. The counselors, the teachers, two social workers, two consultant psychiatrists, and the director comprise the basic professional staff for fifty children. The operating budget is therefore not heavily weighted with high-salaried people who spend relatively few hours with the patient. Thus, tuition is within the range of many families without medical insurance coverage.

Often, when treatment for these children is covered by medical insurance, the program is at the mercy of the policies of the insurance company. Residential institutions that meet hospitalization requirements are usually three to four times as expensive as the nonhospital treatment. While the expenses for this treatment are covered by certain insurance programs, the duration of the funding is almost invariably for a limited amount of time: after so many weeks or months, the expense of continuing the patient's treatment falls fully on the family.

State funding is variable. Many states provide for the education of all children and will contribute a portion of the costs to approved schools. Some states consider it the child's right to be educated and will therefore pay for all other costs such as room and board since they are necessary for the child's attendance at a special school. At present, the cost of the Orthogenic School is less than the cost to the state of maintaining a child in its own facilities.

However, there is also a danger in state funding. The state must have some way of keeping track of what it is paying for and thus may require evaluation measures. If these evaluations are at odds with the treatment philosophy, a toublesome situation may arise. For example, the tendency to require behavioral objectives is distressingly paradoxical when the goal of treatment is strengthening the individual's ability to determine his own destiny.

Results of Milieu Therapy

The therapeutic results of milieu therapy depend upon the nature of the disturbance treated. For example, neglected children who may need institutional placement for their rehabilitation will respond much more readily and positively to a benign environment than will a hardened delinquent, a severely neurotic or psychotic child, a drug addict, or an anorexic child. When the placement is the first effort at treatment of a psychotic child, for example, the outcome has to be evaluated differently than in the case of another psychotic child who has continued to deteriorate despite repeated and intensive therapeutic attempts. Thus, the treatment results of the Orthogenic School have to be evaluated in the light of the fact that practically only "hopeless" cases were accepted. These were children in whose cases serious efforts at treatment, sometimes repeated efforts, had failed. In the light of such an admission policy, the Orthogenic School's effectiveness as a therapeutic system seems quite remarkable, since 85 percent of the children treated for a prolonged period recovered sufficiently to make a life on their own. A vast majority of these "successes" finish college and have since held responsible positions in society. The group includes university professors, businessmen, teachers, social workers, and so forth.

Since the data are based on only one relatively small institution, the numbers are not large, although they cover a couple of hundred cases. Detailed data must be much more guarded in respect to the outlook for those who suffered from infantile autism.[5] Treatment results were markedly better for all other groups.

Patterns of Follow Up

The relationship of the school with the student after graduation is determined solely by the student. The task of milieu treatment is to strengthen the ego so that the individual can be master of himself, no matter what his environment. When a student is graduated, in effect he is told that the staff believes he is now strong enough for this mastery. If the staff were then to "look over his shoulder," it would belie this implicit statement. Furthermore, the students should not be made to feel any pressure to continue the attachment. The staff is always delighted to hear from them, but only as they wish to communicate.

Some students want to stay nearby and continue to come back for a time to talk with a trusted staff member. Some maintain no communication at all. However, most manage to let the staff know what they are doing, albeit rather erratically. Various members of the staff have learned of former students, either from direct communication or from communication from another student (some form lasting friendships), so that just about all former patients can be accounted for.

Conclusion

Milieu therapy is still very much a becoming, not a being. It is an idea which has to be new in every institution practicing it every single day, every single moment, in order to be realized. But even at this early stage in its development, milieu therapy has shown its value in returning to society those children so disturbed as to have been declared hopeless. Such children are entitled to a better chance. Milieu therapy gives it to them.

REFERENCES

1. AICHHORN, A., *Wayward Youth*, Viking, New York, 1939.
2. ALT, H., *Residential Treatment of the Disturbed Child*, International Universities Press, New York, 1960.
3. BATESON, G., et al., "Toward a Theory of Schizophrenia," *Behavioral Science*, 1:251–264, 1956.
4. BETTELHEIM, B., *A Home for the Heart*, Alfred A. Knopf, New York, 1974.
5. ———, *The Empty Fortress*, The Free Press, New York, 1967.
6. ———, *Truants from Life*, The Free Press, Glencoe, Ill., 1955.
7. ———, *Love is Not Enough—The Treatment of Emotionally Disturbed Children*, The Free Press, Glencoe, Ill., 1950.
8. ———, "A Psychiatric School," *The Quarterly Journal of Child Behavior*, 5:86–95, 1949.
9. ———, and SYLVESTER, E., "Milieu Therapy—Indications and Illustrations," *Psychoanalytic Review*, 36:54–67, 1949.
10. ———, "A Therapeutic Milieu," *American Journal of Orthopsychiatry*, 18:191–206, 1948.
11. CAUDILL, W., *The Psychiatric Hospital as a Small Society*, Harvard University Press, Boston, 1958.
12. DEANE, W. N., "The Reactions of a Non-Patient to a Stay in a Mental Hospital Ward," *Psychiatry*, 24:61–68, 1961.
13. GOFFMAN, E., *Asylums*, Doubleday, Garden City, N.Y., 1961.
14. HENRY, J., "The Culture of Interpersonal Relations in a Therapeutic Institution for Emotionally Disturbed Chil-

dren," *American Journal of Orthopsychiatry*, 27:725–734, 1957.
15. ———, "Types of Institutional Structure," *Psychiatry*, 20:47–60, 1957.
16. JONES, M., *The Therapeutic Community*, Basic Books, New York, 1953.
17. Menninger Clinic Children's Division, *Disturbed Children*, Jossey Bassey, San Francisco, 1969.
18. NOSHPITZ, J. D., "Notes on the Theory of Residential Treatment," *Journal of the American Academy of Child Psychiatry*, 1:284–296, 1962.
19. REDL, F., and WINEMAN, D., *Controls from Within: Techniques for the Treatment of the Aggressive Child*, The Free Press, Glencoe, Ill., 1952.
20. ———, *Children Who Hate*, The Free Press, Glencoe, Ill., 1951.
21. ROCKWELL, D. A., "Some Observations on 'Living In,'" *Psychiatry*, 34:214–223, 1971.
22. SECHEHAYE, M. A., *Symbolic Realization*, International Universities Press, New York, 1951.
23. STANTON, A. H., and SCHWARTZ, M. S., *The Mental Hospital: A Study of Institutional Participation in Psychiatric Illness and Treatment*; Basic Books, New York, 1954.
24. STOTLAND, E., and KOBLER, A. L., *Life and Death of a Mental Hospital*, University of Washington Press, Seattle, 1965.
25. SZUREK, S. A., BERLIN, I. N., and BOATMAN, M. J. (Eds.), *Inpatient Care for the Psychotic Child*, vol. 5, The Langley Porter Child Psychiatry Series, Science and Behavior Books, Palo Alto, Calif., 1971.

15 / Residential Treatment

Lawrence A. Stone

To comprehend the many faces of residential treatment, it is necessary to understand the complex nature of youthful health and ill health. It is also important to have a working grasp of the character of the adults, the societies, and the environments which influence young people.

History of Residential Treatment

History tells of genesis and has meaningful implications for the future. In this context, the entire section of the handbook devoted to the history of child psychiatry might be viewed as an account of residential treatment. In a similar way, every other section of this work speaks in detail to the several aspects of the totality of this mode of intervention. Certain facets of the historical background, however, require emphasis in order to provide a clear understanding of the emergence of residential treatment.

ADULT-ORIENTED ROOTS

Most of man's endeavors to relieve suffering arose from recognition of the need to protect the existing adult society. To achieve this it was necessary to remove, punish, and, at times, even sacrifice those who troubled that society. "Humane" and "corrective" efforts have always sought initially to benefit the adults; as a result, either directly or indirectly, the needs of young people have been often relegated to a secondary—at best—level of effort. The tale of residential treatment can be linked to this history of human strivings to cope, adapt, improve, or even destroy. Most of these trends, albeit initially adult focused, have nevertheless set patterns which continue to persist in the treatment of children. Indeed, these patterns are intimately involved in operational considerations of residential treatment.

In order to manage the complexities of human nature and to stabilize and sustain social organizations, productive retrospection and realistic foresight are necessary. Only with these is it possible to meet increasing societal and environmental demands. For man to manage and direct his perpetual revolutionary and evolutionary processes effectively, understanding the past and anticipating the future are of critical importance. It seems safe to say, however, that these abilities are to be found only among adults. This may make the previously mentioned historical developments seem less harsh. It also provides an important perspective for reviewing the history of residential treatment. This should lead, then, toward preparation for future challenges and refinements.

PRESCIENTIFIC SOURCES

Prior to the development of scientific knowledge, the accepted wisdom was based on the mythologies of human nature and of the environment. It included demonology and a mystic orientation. Within this framework, disturbing behavior was defined, reacted to, and presented as the saga of the "possessed." This may still be seen today in many basic adult attitudes toward children's natural instincts and impulses, and frequently toward their developmentally immature thinking and behavior. Later, the efforts to understand behavior became more organized and gave rise to ideological and religious beliefs. In time, a series of mores and traditions gradually emerged. These in turn became powerful factors in the continuing endeavors to deal with troubled individuals and their impact on society. They took form during a long-lasting era of belief in good and evil spirits and resulted in a series of "purging phenomena." With time, the social order became more demanding, and these attitudes and practices became "institutionalized" for the benefit of society—the age of removal, confinement, punishment, penance, and penitence.

YOUTH-ORIENTED EFFORTS

The emphasis of social order shifted from the adult's concerns about survival toward materialism and personal possessions. Youth-related problems began to be distinguished and viewed in terms of their meaning as a burden for adult society; presently "deranged" youth and youthful "offenders" were identified. This led to the isolating of youth in institutions and settings which embodied the principles of punitive control and management that were the prevailing orientation of that period. As feudalism gave way to the rise of cities, attention focused on the juvenile delinquent as a major cause of disruption, and more "specialized" institutions appeared for the "seclusion" and "correction" of delinquents.

At the same time another problem for society became recognized: the homeless, abandoned, parentless youth. At this point, charitable individuals, religious groups, and other humanitarian organizations began to come to the aid of both society at large and the rapidly growing number of burdensome, "lost and neglected" children; with this came the advent of orphanages and a variety of other institutions. Such institutions developed not only in response to the distress to society caused by the homeless; they were also the response to such realities as poverty (those who required poor houses), the presence of the socially disadvantaged (who were placed in group homes), and the fact of societal drifters (who, when caught, could be remanded to work farms). This was progress of a sort, but unfortunately the models of institutional management which prevailed in those times were, to say the least, traumatizing.

HUMANIZATION—INSTITUTIONALIZATION

Other factors developed during the eighteenth century that were later to have special meaning for the future development of residential treatment. In founding the Pennsylvania Hospital, Benjamin Franklin introduced a concept which may properly be called preventive medicine, and he included a ward for the mentally ill. Although it did not grow consistently, more humanitarianism was beginning to develop. Thus, a true picture of those times would encompass the extremes of human degradation and hardship to the most advanced attempts then known to individualize and humanize care. The advances in care were almost equal in proportion to the regressions. It was during the latter part of the eighteenth century and the beginning of the nineteenth that the most significant struggles developed between progressive *humanization* efforts and restrictive *institutionalized* forces. The never-ending effort to balance these two was eventually to become one of the essential functions of an effective residential teratment facility.

From this point on, many of the important implications of humanization and institutionalization can be observed more specifically in terms of significant events and changes. A conception of the humane and orderly management of individuals and groups began to pervade the penal, custodial, and medical endeavors of the time. Generally such innovations were prompted by the activities of magnanimous individuals and charitable associations. Presently, under this pressure, public programs began to be established. In a sense, mental hygiene was becoming recognized as some sort of entity.

Education was not yet a dominant factor in the hierarchy of societal concerns. Nevertheless, it was the source of the most potent statements ever made about the effect of the setting on children's functioning. Jean Jacques Rousseau's noted book *Emile* dealt with education and was a powerful influence on it. Thereafter, individualized human care was linked with a recognition of the importance of the environment.

Toward the end of the eighteenth century, a new work house, Maison de la Force, was opened in Ghent by Jean Jacques Phillippe Vilain. It introduced disciplined and orderly ways of treating its inmates. Among its principles were: (1) grouping prisoners—felons and vagrants were housed separately, as were women and children; (2) adequate medical care; (3) provision for individual cells; and (4) productive work as an essential element in the service of personal reform.

Under John Howard's influence, the Philanthropic Society of London opened cottages for deprived children in need of reform, and an attempt was made to create a familylike structure by combining "cottage parents" and farm work. Later, the Society for Relief of Poor Widows and Small Children was founded in the United States by Isabelle Graham, Elizabeth Seton, and others. It provided valuable recognition of the important mother-child relationship.

In France, Phillipe Pinel and his "unshackling" of the insane had a profound influence on humane care; his approach gave considerable thrust to the concept of a proper milieu. This included attitudes of respect for the dignity of the inmates—a concept which was the forerunner of milieu therapy, human rights, and in many respects, modern psychiatry.

Shortly after 1800, Dr. Jean Marc Gaspard Itard of France described an experience with a feral child. Though not completely successful, it nonetheless demonstrated that massive damage could be remedied by planned treatment. Madame Guerin, who handled the child for Itard, might be considered the first child-care worker to provide treatment under the direction of a physician.

More and more public facilities were opening. Fiscal, legal, administrative, and political complexities were becoming part of the spectrum of human care services. By and large, education was still in the hands of private or religious agencies. Institutions provided only apprenticeship or coercion.

Under the influence of increasing social need, there was ever more pressure for learned skills necessary for productivity. Free-school societies began to appear and brought pressure for public participation in education. This led to conflicts between church and state. From these conflicts came yet another dimension to the development of residential treatment facilities: an awareness of the essentials of education and the public domain's concerns for productivity, as well as a recognition of the importance of the individual's beliefs, faiths, and practices.

SCIENTIFIC SPECIFICITY AND INDIVIDUALIZATION

During the early and mid-1800s there were many attempts to apply rudimentary humane and moral treatment in private and public human care (penal, welfare, educational, medical) institutions. It was a period of active trial-and-error efforts to create milieu programming. Out of these efforts came even greater demands for improved specific methods. Differences in individual pathological conditions began to be noted and problem areas began to be distinguished. The Hartford Institute for the Deaf opened in Boston, and separate groupings of the insane, feebleminded, and criminals began to occur in other places. Gradually, the awareness arose that children, even bad ones, were different and that they needed special kinds of settings and programs. In 1823, the Society for Prevention of Pauperism (later to become the Society for Reformation of Juvenile Delinquents) focused almost exclusively on juvenile delinquency. It later developed landmark advances in milieu care with a total plan for reeducation.

Two major facilities for specific disabilities helped further to identify the needs of special children. Samuel G. Howe, director of the Perkins School for the Blind in Boston, taught a blind deaf-mute to communicate. A few years later, Dr. Guggenbuhl at Abendberg Asylum in Switzerland brought help to many cretins by genuine loving care, good air, diet, and supervised exercise. Each of these developments was a significant addition to the knowledge of specific problems and the fundamental needs of children and adolescents; each became another essential component of today's residential treatment.

These many advances led to other steps forward: experiments with the probation and supervision of young offenders; use of the family as a base for planning and management of the child; various intensive educational efforts for idiots or for the feebleminded; and attempts at classification of mental disorders with consequent groupings and individualized approaches.

From the mid-nineteenth century on changes came more rapidly; these developments affected the institutional care of children both directly and indirectly. The advances fall into several major areas. There was an increase in political, legislative, and judicial government interest, as well as an increase in the inherent powers, regulations, and organizational effects this implies. Scientific and clinical advances were beginning to produce methods which seemed to be at once more systematic and reproducible. Individual professionals became interested in the field and began to publish studies. Eventually this led to the formation of national associations of special interest groups, as well as to the development of more sophisticated institutions.

Thus, a more refined mental hygiene gave way to a mental health orientation. As this took place, medicine began to address itself to mental diseases and later to children. In time, neurology, pediatrics, and child psychiatry emerged as medical specialties. The shift from the problems of the child's behavior in society to the behavioral problems of children was hastened by the advancing knowledge of developmental psychology. Genetics made important contributions to the problems of mental retardation and mental illness, and new methods were developed in the areas of care and treatment.

Clinical psychology developed and contributed detailed behavioral studies, management methods, and specific testing techniques. The nature of important variables of emotional, behavioral, learning, and organic disorders was studied, and their understanding was continually refined. The value of systematized case studies which included the family and environmental influences was recognized; this significantly helped to promote the growth of psychiatric social work.

Medicine and other mental health disciplines accumulated ever more knowledge relating biological and psychological interactions to many afflictions. New hospitals were opened; initially they were primarily for organic problems, but in time isolated mental hospitals also came into being. In 1931, the first psychiatric hospital for children in the United States, the Emma Pendleton Bradley Hospital in Providence, Rhode Island, was founded. With clinical discoveries of organic causes and cures of some known mental disorders —those due to syphilis and encephalitis, for example—there arose a never-ending conflict between the organic and psychodynamic factions. Freud and many others meticulously laid formidable basis for the importance of psychodynamics in the spectrum of human mental disorders; with the passage of time, the psychobiological, psychodynamic, and psychosocial aspects of human behavior all gained greater relevance. These began to be pursued vigorously in highly specialized medical facilities, including residential treatment.

An integral part of this era of developing specialized skills was the coming of the psychiatric nurse, who uniquely bridged many disciplinary gaps. Child-care workers and psychiatric nurses developed their specific skills and methodologies to care for and help disturbed children. Today they are both vital clinical participants in the effective functioning of residential treatment facilities. Additional important personnel categories with highly valuable skills have recently emerged. These include mental health workers and other mental health paraprofessionals.

All of these individual, societal, governmental, scientific, and organizational developments were taking place at once; as they grew they were continually influencing the nature and types of delivery of child mental health care. Penology relating to children made initial progress under the impetus of forceful humanitarians, whose objectives were therapeutic rather than punitive, and they shifted the juvenile justice system toward a new clinical and preventive orientation. Child welfare efforts led to significant refinements in the care of children and youths who would otherwise have been lost. Individualized placements became the rule along with greater continuity of care in adoptive procedures, guardianships, foster parent placements, children's shelters, and boardinghomes. The educational shifts produced special education, reeducation, psychoeducation, and therapeutic residential education facilities.

The mental hygiene movement begot special clinics which reached out to large segments of the population and influenced many child-related institutions and organizations. Interest in these clinics grew, and support was extended by many groups, foundations, and governmental agencies. As a result, child mental health outpatient services came

into being. There was ever more community concern along with a growing knowledge of child development and family processes; together these led to the emergence of the day-care concept. Alternatives to hospital treatment, continuity of care, and community relationships became vital concepts in an important network of services within which residential treatment would find its place.

The importance of play, fun, and games in child development and family unity was recognized by Joseph Lee, "The Father of the American Playground Movement." The approach to this essential aspect of families' and young peoples' needs became formally institutionalized in 1906 when Lee organized the National Playground Association, which later became the National Recreational Association.

Child labor was finally abolished by legislation after many years of struggle. Untenable abusive practices had long been thrust to the forefront of public awareness. During this time the importance of productive activities plus the advances in psychological, educational, and child development knowledge produced a "reformed" vision of children and of work. This vision combined with the many previous experiments to help children through work-oriented endeavors; eventually it resulted in planned therapeutic activity and vocational programs with treatment and rehabilitation as their goal.

PERIOD OF RAPID CHANGES

From this early historical overview and schematized perspective, an image of the primordial residential treatment facility begins to take form. To follow the detailed chronology of developments into the twentieth century would provide a fully formed picture of present-day residential treatment. However, too many details make up the picture to allow for an individual appreciation of each. The richness of each and the blending of all, though, must be valued by those studying the whole tapestry of residential treatment. Here one can select only a few examples from the recent historical panorama.

GOVERNMENT

In the mid-1800s Dorothea Dix published harrowing accounts of the observations she had made studying the mental health care systems. These served to ignite the consciences of legislators and government officials. Since that day, the flame of legislative concern has flickered, died down, and blazed up with remarkable inconsistency. Nonetheless, local, state, and federal laws have slowly but surely become an inseparable component of the mental health care systems. Yet the search still goes on for the right mixture of humanitarian concern, scientific knowledge, and governmental mandate to eradicate even a few of the ravages of mental disorders among younger people.

There are laws today which regulate, control, and give directions for newer developments. Although publicly pressured political, legislative, and judicial actions have often created many dark clouds, they have also contributed to progress. The recent developments of community mental health centers, child rights, third-party payments. and provider accountability suggest that further advances are likely. These are already foreshadowed by peer review, continuing education, and the proliferation of standards for the evaluation of mental health delivery systems. Such developments and others will undoubtedly find a place in the mosaic of residential treatment. These are explored in greater detail in volume IV.

ORGANIZATIONS

Many creative organizations whose effects on residential treatment have been powerful were established on behalf of young people. The many associations of mental health clinicians working with children and adolescents also played instrumental roles in residential treatment. In the course of their scientific, philosophical, and scholarly endeavors the different disciplines have also given basic support to the multiple types and models of residential treatment.

RESIDENTIAL FACILITIES AND THE INDIVIDUALS CONNECTED WITH THEM

Finally, the host of innovative and forward-reaching children's and adolescents' residential treatment facilities themselves need mention. It is to their painstaking organizational and therapeutic trials and errors and to the labors of their creators, supporters, staff, and patients that the discipline today owes its foundation. Their individual institutional contributions must be analyzed in order to continue the search for the best modalities for residential treatment. Descriptions of their programs can provide pathways to guide the progress of residential treatment. The contributions of the many individual torchbearers in this field form an exciting and extensive list. A meticulous study of their work is part of the task of all concerned students and practicing clinicians These are exemplified by the writings of Aichorn,[1] Alt,[3, 4] Bettelheim[11, 12, 13, 14] (see also chapter 14), Mayer,[62] Redl,[74, 75, 76] and Szurek.[85, 86]

HISTORICAL SUMMARY

There is now a long history of efforts to distinguish the natural differences and needs of children from those of the adults, and to systematize approaches to the management of these needs. Such efforts have been advanced primarily by the combination of a solid knowledge base and the prevailing cultural attitudes at any given period of time. These have included concepts of sacrifice; exclusion; separation and isolation; punishment; correction; penance and penitance; economic values; labor or work; social welfare; family practices; education; organic, genetic, or neurological determinants; psychological, psychobiological, and psychosocial interrelationships; individual and group processes; and the dynamics of child and adolescent development. In summary, then, the search for improved humanitarian caring practices continues to evolve from mystiques, ideologies, and traditions; philosophy; the art of caring; and science.

Today, residential treatment has grown into a variety of institutional arrangements. Paralleling the historical parameters of this growth has been the development of the caretakers themselves. Inevitably, the practices of care emerged from the existing base of understanding and knowledge. Thus, those persons who later formed the care staff continued to develop their expertise. They learned from trial and error; from experience and practice; from supervision by and counsultation with others; and from formal training. Today the results of this diverse genesis are clearly evident.

Residential Treatment Today

With the passage of time, numerous conflicts arose among the many aforementioned human, scientific, and organizational developments. Out of these, however, have emerged some of the important axioms for the discipline, namely: the importance of clarification of goals, roles, patterns of authority and lines of communication; the essential need for unity of purpose; the emphasis on individualization of care and treatment; the recognition of psychological, psychobiological, and psychosocial interactions as critical treatment elements; the importance of an adequate theory of child dynamics and development and family and group processes; the specialized attention to every detail of the child's and family's condition and to whatever affects them; a comprehension of, coordination, and collaboration with all other significant forces, organizations, and persons both within the facility and outside; a commitment to continuity of care; and an acceptance of the true meaning and importance of an integrated team approach.

Residential treatment for children and adolescents is a specialized form of highly organized and planned therapeutic intervention which is utilized to treat some of the most serious mental, emotional, and behavioral disabilities. Its practitioners employ widely differing organizational structures and many varieties of staffing patterns, treatment practices, and modalities. Nevertheless, it is not simply a random, alternative method, nor only a last resort. It is a definitive therapeutic modality designed to deliver specified results for a defined group of problems. Although the nature of the programs, problems, and results vary widely within different centers, certain fundamental features are common to all.

To examine the differences and the essential common elements, it is best to consider first the particular characteristics of the children and adolescents requiring this form of treatment, then to proceed to a study of the facilities themselves. Chapter 1 noted that nosological categorizations as such do not provide absolute indicators for specific therapeutic modalities. In fact, they sometimes function as justifications for misuse, which must be guarded against at all times. Scientific specificity which links the evaluative, diagnostic, and treatment processes definitively must be pursued. This will require additional systematic clinical research, longitudinal studies, and determinations of outcome and follow up. These are fundamental considerations and must be shared by all residential treatment facilities.

Indications for Residential Treatment:

Its Advantages and Disadvantages

Residential treatment is the therapy of choice for children and adolescents with a wide variety of severe disturbances. The growth of the young person into a capably functioning adult rests primarily upon maturational and developmental processes and the environmental influences of his early life. It is always difficult to know when to remove a child from the mainstream of his life and to place him in a special setting. A decisive factor is the need to protect his development. The importance of timely and adequate relief and correction of early major disturbances, as well as the prevention of resulting potential future disabilities, must be given great weight.

The complex maze of health services required for some children is often overwhelmingly complicated, too much so for their families to integrate into their patterns of life. This often results in serious deficits in the child's ego growth and leads to lags in his normal developmental progression. Consider the following case.

Jamie was a ten-year-old fourth-grade student who had physical limitations from birth, which later caused him to have serious emotional and behavioral problems. He had been diagnosed early in his school life as hyperactive with accompanying specific learning disturbances. Additionally, he had been found to have poor vision and hearing; these had gone unnoticed until routine school examinations. He had been treated with methylphenidate (Ritalin), which helped his hyperactivity, and he had attended special education classes, which helped his academic progress. Glasses and a hearing aid were prescribed for his visual and auditory deficits. Unfortunately, in Jamie's case, because of his large and disorganized family and the fragmentation and lack of continuous coordination between all of the necessary family, medical, educational, and social support systems, there was very inconsistent follow-through of the correction of these problems. Jamie missed medication; felt "freakish" in the special education program; and broke, lost, or seldom wore his glasses or hearing aid. His socialization skills became as disruptive as his poor learning habits. He withdrew more and more and began looking and acting "strange." He developed intense preoccupations with daydreaming and compensatory regressive visual and auditory hallucinations. Prior to his admission to residential treatment, he was variously labeled by family, mental health professionals, the school, and friends as bizarre, impulsive, autistic, minimally brain damaged, retarded, hyperactive, and probably psychotic with a schizoaffective disorder. Following a complete evaluation and assessment at the residential treatment center, it was determined that treatment there (including special education at the center school) was necessary in order to coordinate all of the therapeutic programs necessary for his recovery. A treatment plan was set up emphasizing education of the parents through casework and appropriate special educational support. Jamie consistently received his medications and was required to wear his corrective glasses and hearing aid. Child-care work was geared to help him regain a realistic orientation to the world and to his own sensory systems. He had individual and group counseling to clarify the nature of his bizarre thoughts and to aid him in his self-acceptance. It was hoped this would allow him to achieve further socialization skills. He changed rapidly, never showing any clear indications of psychosis. His whole concept of himself and his world began to alter as he learned that he could realistically see, hear, and interact with himself and others in newly discovered, meaningful ways. The therapeutic qualities of the family, school, medication, mental health, and environment had been harnessed to correct and reverse the seriously debilitating processes of Jamie's life.

The impact of the family as well as on significant societal systems is a vital part of the consideration for residential treatment. In addition, there are the disadvantages and complications of the treatment itself. These include: the problems of disruption of family and community relationships; financial hardships; parental denial or guilt; confused and distorted preceptions by other siblings; removal of the young person from the the continuum of his educational system; predictable noxious stigmata and labeling; and the potential for intense and unresolved transference and dependency attachments to the institution. This last factor may lead to difficulties in getting the patient back into the mainstream of community life. All these must be appraised carefully and thoughtfully.

There has been an increasing tendency for society to "tolerate" serious emotional and behavioral disturbances in children and adolescents especially since the advent of the "youth culture" and the rapid changes ins social structures and order.

Bill, age nineteen, represents one of the unfortunate consequences of these phenomena and one that residential centers are encountering more and more. Following a very "successful childhood" through high school, Bill quite unexpectedly became "everything his parents never dreamed of." While maintaining a facade of normality and an "I-know-what-I-am-doing" response, he progressively involved himself in drugs, alcohol, antiestablishment movements, asocially oriented groups, and cultisms. Simultaneously, he isolated himself from his previous friends, disdained further education, and derided gainful employment. During all this, he was moving around the country as a "free spirit." He alternately alienated his family and friends, but then addressed himself squarely to their guilt and sense of responsibility for his support when he "felt the need." After innumerable internal confrontations with this tormenting dilemma, the family turned to all known sources of help—friends, schools, church, juvenile authorities, and mental health professionals. They received empathy but direct help usually came in the form of "that is the way the young people are today." From some of these encounters, however, the parents learned that Bill had transient episodes of "free-floating psychosis" along with other serious characterlogical and situational maladjustments. However, he also always had

his own set of cultist authorities to offer counterclaims that he was just "doing his own thing." The family felt confused, frightened, angry, guilt-ridden, and relatively immobilized by the resulting ambivalence and indecision. Eventually, after consultation with a child psychiatrist friend, the family was able to sustain sufficient determination to cope with their ambivalence meaningfully and "force the issue" with their son: either residential treatment for a thorough evaluation or no further support of any kind, including no money or home "rest stops." Bill resented his family's ultimatum but believed they were determined. He also felt that the psychiatrist had somehow gotten through his unreal world into his troubled turmoil and that his parents were finally "buying" this expert's understanding. He offered token resistance but gave in to their combined "force." Fortunately, with close collaboration of the consulting psychiatrist and the family with the residential treatment center, the admitting staff was immediately prepared to move in and follow up by dealing directly and realistically with Bill's two worlds. Gradually, this painstaking preparation paid off. After the initial evaluation it was determined that Bill had a severe schizoid personality with passive-aggressive and depressive features, and a drug-related organic brain syndrome with transient psychotic episodes. The residential treatment staff set up an intensive program of milieu therapy, special education, job training, individual therapy, and activity and group therapy. They worked directly with the referring psychiatrist, who continued close contact with the family. This contact became even more crucial as the parents went through various traumatic stages of doubt, abandonment, guilt, sorrow, and anger. Sustaining Bill in treatment depended upon sustaining the parents' hope and their commitment to the program. From their past experiences they had heard a great deal about the "horrors of confinement," the "brainwashing" of residential treatment, the denial of civil rights, and "restrictions of free choice." Fortunately, they found these not to be true. For their son, his illness and his previous particular choices of environments were handicapping him. Bill progressed slowly but well, relearning social skills while working with the staff to clear up his drug-induced disorganized thoughts and impulse controls.

At this point of entry into residential treatment, there are the problems of new restrictions and new authorities with different expectations and responsibilities. These often create a type of "culture shock." When such factors are overlooked or inappropriately perceived, pathologic regressive reactions can readily occur early in residential treatment. These same circumstances as well as new group pressures may lead to troublesome contagion phenomena, for example, the adolescent's stating, "I'm crazy like they are" or seriously imitating others' "acting out" behaviors. On the other hand, these same "culture shock" effects can be applied as a rational justification for residential treatment.

Residential treatment programs are often called

upon to treat young people whose backgrounds, life experiences, family, and environment have become totally disrupted. The child's continued existence may entail no more than a maintenance and reenforcement of his alienation, identification with regressive behavior, and development of a- or antisocial characterological coping styles. Yet, there may be no one definitive diagnosis as such that fits these very troubled children. Consider the following case.

John, a nine-year-old, came into residential treatment from such a disorganized background. He was admitted with well-developed manipulative behavior, a limited capacity for trust, a belligerence toward all authority, and a hostility toward adaptive or developmentally appropriate activities. He exhibited the often-seen paranoid style: "I know what to expect from everyone and everything—nothing but a kick in the teeth or worse, and I am ready for anything." He had a thorough individual psychiatric evaluation, including psychological and medical assessments, and his past school failures, delinquency records, and family and social upheavals were reviewed. It was concluded that a "totally different environment" seemed necessary, even though this meant going far away from his "familiar territory." A local mental health team was to help the family, while John was sent to encounter a very different "external real world": a working ranch-type residential treatment center. He brought with him his own "mental world," which very quickly failed radically to fit his "new environment." The immediately ensuing "culture shock" was disorganizing for him, and he experienced a strong sense of vulnerability. This was a strange new place that was operated by people with trust, care, respect, and expectations of success. There was genuine appreciation for task-oriented work, achievement-oriented study, developmentally appropriate fun and games, age-appropriate controls, and a clearly delineated "healthy and normal expectable environment." His initial shock, confusion, and vulnerability were met quickly by thoughtful understanding staff acting in unity to move into his life quite differently from his built-in expectations. They immediately appeared consistently solid and cohesive in their therapeutic plans even while each staff member carried out distinctively different parts of the program. They set up individual and group activities totally new to John's previous experiences. These new experiences—such as caring for and riding horses, shearing sheep for pay, planting flowers and landscaping to beautify his cabin, washing dishes and cleaning tables with respect, organized team athletics, riflery and archery, and motorcycle riding—were unaffected by his dwindling and fragile old patterns of regressive manipulation. At the same time, he unexpectedly experienced an appeal to his age-appropriate ego needs for mastery, self-confidence, autonomy, and fun. After a brief initial period of resentment and testing, a depression appeared. Then came a steady reconstruction of his previously arrested ego growth and developmental progress. His consistent interaction with the staff and the totally new

environment (with its opportunities for unanticipated mastery coming from special previously unexperienced activities and achievements) enabled John to grow, change, and eventually find a new and productive place for himself outside the residential treatment program.

The decision to utilize residential treatment is a major therapeutic step. It should always be based upon a careful, complete clinical evaluation. Among the objects of study should be the individual child or adolescent, the family and significant others, and the effects and influences of their environment. This study must be coupled with a clear comprehension of the potentials, capabilities, and limitations of the specific residential treatment program and of other alternative therapeutic modalities. Together these guide the decision for or against residential treatment. This decision *should always* rest with the *responsible evaluating clinical professional staff* of the residential treatment facility. In varying degrees, they share this decision with the child or adolescent, the family, and other specifically involved individuals and organized units of society. In the course of deciding on treatment modality, the attempt is made to predict the impact each will have on the young person's future mental health, growth, and social adjustments.

All attempts to specify a set of conditions or certain designated syndromes as definitive indications for residential treatment have failed. Those children and adolescents who most require such treatment are those with serious intrapsychic pathological disturbances; severe developmental difficulties; and major relationship problems with their environment. Generally it is a critical combination of these factors that suggests residential treatment. Such a combination has either clearly precluded or has produced failures of other less intensive methods of treatment.

Maggie, a seventeen-year-old college freshman, was admitted for residential treatment following an acute severe psychotic episode. Until that event, she had been a "straight" "All-American type," highly achievement-oriented. While on a trip alone in Europe, she experienced her first heterosexual relationship. Upon returning home to her depressed, disorganized, narcissistic, widowed mother, Maggie became progressively disoriented. Shortly thereafter, she entered her first year at a private, Eastern girls' college. During that year, she could no longer cope with the multitude of internal conflicts and the resumption of her "Snow White" image. After admission to residential treatment, the initial evaluation revealed a paranoid psychosis with a reversal of roles in her nonnurturing, mother-daughter relationship. She also expressed intense social and academic ambivalence resulting from primary conflicts in her adolescent dependency and independency demands. Her previous high achievements and successes no longer compensated for her long-standing unfulfilled oral and nurturance needs. Nor did they begin to resolve her painful oedipal conflicts left after her father's early death or the intensity of her ambivalent adolescent strivings. Initially, she responded well. Her treatment included antipsychotic medications and a close relationship with nonthreatening yet authoritative, maternally caring, understanding psychiatric nurse. Maggie was involved in group and activity therapy with a progressive emphasis on task achievement, not performance. There was limited casework-supervised contact with her mother. She also began to develop a therapeutic alliance with a concerned, dynamically aware but reality-oriented male psychotherapist. She was beginning to confide in and explore her conflicts with her therapist and was developing a predominantly paternal transference when he had to leave the program unexpectedly. All of the involved staff attempted to pick up and continue the treatment plan. However, the significance of the special relationship with her individual therapist and his unexpected departure was difficult to deal with directly at that time. Maggie progressively withdrew and regressed into a full catatonic state. Upon the return of her therapist she went through a full cycle of hebephrenic activity for months before she slowly began increasing her adaptive functioning. The therapist used the previously gained analytic insight and understanding, especially of her object loss, to work closely around these issues with Maggie and the staff. She finally reestablished a positive relationship with the staff and worked diligently with her psychotherapist toward further insight and awareness. As she again utilized the entire treatment program and milieu, she gained a new reality-orientation both toward herself, her parent figures, and her environment. She was later discharged, but continued in psychotherapy and used the residential program and personnel as back-up. She subsequently required two brief reentries into the residential program. These were precipitated by conflicting social and environmental pressures, a crisis involving another family member, and a period of major anxiety while working through some intense issues in psychotherapy. After her last discharge, she continued in long-term analytically oriented psychotherapy. Today she is happily married, a good mother, a college graduate, and holds a very responsible job.

This case history briefly highlights the multidimensional problems that a residential treatment program encounters. There are the considerations of the dynamics of the patient's disorder, the family problems, environmental influences, and the intricacies of the changes in the therapeutic personnel and program for each individual patient. In this particular case, if the staff had placed more emphasis on working with Maggie's reaction to the unexpected temporary loss of her therapist, would the subsequent intense regression have been avoided? Or was that regression inevitable? Were the continuous availability and persistence of the program and the return of her therapist essential?

Did the shared analytic understanding working in harmony with the other staff facilitate recovery? Was the follow-up support a factor in the girl's eventual stability? And, finally, did the analytic therapist's insistence that she work through the object loss and basic object mistrust in the residential program and in long-term psychotherapy prevent her from becoming a "back ward" chronic schizophrenic, as she had been thought by some staff and outside consultants? Clinical work suggests such questions; some form of controlled research may eventually begin to answer them.

The target population of children and adolescents for whom residential treatment should be considered can now be presented by a general schematic outline.

1. Severe individual *intrapsychic* disorders (mental, emotional, and behavioral)
   a. Disturbances of object relations, capacity for attachment, and basic trust
   b. Imbalances in response to age-appropriate need gratifications and realistic limitations
   c. Failures in the development of maturationally adequate reality testing
   d. Unrealistic self-concepts and self-image
   e. Disruptions in the integration of active, passive, aggressive, and libidinal impulse-control patterns
   f. Inappropriate affective responses
   g. Disorganization and confusion of symbolic and formal thought processes
   h. Difficulties in the sequential development, organization, and utilization of informal and formal learning capacities
   i. Neurological and other organic or psychophysiological impairments and complications with primary manifestations in the behavioral or emotional area
2. Serious *developmental* disturbances
   a. Failure to achieve progressive psychomotor development and mastery of psychobiological functioning, or pronounced fixations or regressions, for example, motor, speech, cognitive, social, psychosexual
   b. Developmental deviations likely to produce severe future impairments
   c. Acute situational crisis related to a developmental stage with inadequate, inappropriate, or ineffective support for remediation
   d. Failure of necessary self-sustaining initiative, motivation, and adaptive capabilities
   e. Behavioral patterns with destructive psychological, physical, or social consequences, for example, chemical addiction, lack of self-protective responses, excessive risk-taking and social isolation or conflict
   f. Impaired or inappropriate anticipatory responses
3. Significant disturbances in *environmental* relationships
   a. Severe disruptions of relationships within the family or with significant others

b. Pathological relationships which cause the internalization of inappropriate models
c. Persistent maladjustment of peer and other social relationships
d. Environmental disturbances in family, peers, or other influencing systems which interfere with learning and social development
e. Maladaptive or unrealistic development of social behavior
f. Overwhelming or seriously traumatizing environmental conditions or events

As elaborated in the chapter on nosology in volume II, children and adolescents can be evaluated from many perspectives. For residential treatment, the emphasis falls on children's management in the face of serious conditions. In general, nosological terminology does not draw the necessary distinctions. Most often the paramount indication is a *critical combination* of serious disturbances in the young person's psychodynamic, psychobiological, psychosocial, development, and environmental stability. Other contributing factors are the nature of strengths in the young person, the family, his group affiliations, and environmental resources; the influence of time in terms of the onset and duration of prior pathological conditions; the anticipated length and intensity of the necessary treatment; the requirements for continuity of care, in particular in relationship to the young person's future development; the severity of societal conflicts; the results of previous remediation efforts; financial considerations; and the availability of other potentially effective less intensive therapeutic resources.

The residential treatment is not merely an alternative to family placement or simply a means of providing a singular form of therapy or rehabilitation. It becomes the treatment of choice when a disturbed young person is in need of the care of a total *residential* environment and the appropriate *treatment* modalities are available within the residential treatment programs.

Organization

Residential treatment facilities differ from one another in respect to their organization and therapeutic programs. There is considerable variation in the time structure of residential treatment: short-term diagnostic evaluation, acute crisis intervention, and short- to long-term intensive care and treatment. Different disorders and varying circumstances necessitate numerous adaptations in the concomitant utilization of family and significant others and of community, and social resources (community, schools, recreational and vocational programs, specialized medical facilities, judicial and legal authorities, and welfare agencies).

Crisis intervention recently has been added to the traditional resources of residential treatment. Most often it deals with intervention in cases of acute drug-induced psychosis, dangerous impulsive behavior, serious antisocial activities, or life-threatening conflicts.

Louise, a thirteen-year-old adolescent, found an approach to her problems through quite a different use of the crisis intervention unit of residential treatment. She had been transferred there from an acute emergency pediatric ward. She had been walking with some friends and smoking pot when she was hit by an automobile. Her initial examination revealed cuts, abrasions, contusions, a probable concussion, and questionable internal organ damage. The parents were understandably frightened. The pediatric staff and nurses were cautious and hospitalized her for further observation, examination, and medical tests. She was on strict flat bedrest, intravenous fluids, and no visitors except her parents. She was told what was going on and all precautionary procedures were explained to her, but she was not told of the extent nor the potential seriousness of her injuries (which were still undetermined). These she could only guess from the implications of the medical restrictions, the concerned faces of the physicians and nurses, and the poorly veiled terror evident on her parents' faces. Though everyone concerned felt she was going to be fine with no residual injuries, this fact was not communicated to her pending results of all the tests. Louise had previously been an average, healthy, well-adjusted preadolescent, and the pot smoking on that evening was only a one-time peer group experiment. However, to everyone's surprise, during her parents' first hospital visit, she became a "raving maniac." Quite out of character for her, she cursed them and everyone who approached her. She became totally uncooperative, to the point of sitting up in bed, pulling out IV's, refusing examinations, vomiting after any oral intake, and demanding to see her friends and no one else. This behavior considerably complicated the medical picture and management, with suggestions of an intracranial lesion, serious intra-abdominal pathology, or an acute psychotic organic brain syndrome. There was also speculation that perhaps she had been on some "hard stuff" before the accident. Because of the major management problem she presented and medical reluctance to give her sufficient sedatives, a child psychiatric consultation was requested. It was decided after team consultation to transfer her to the crisis intervention unit of a residential treatment center where she would continue to be followed by the pediatric team. It was noted by the child psychiatric nurse that the patient became lucid and cooperative when she talked confidentially about her friends. Other factors were noted, such as Louise's fear of imminent death and her feelings of guilt relative to a family scandal if her pot smoking were to become known. As these insights were assimilated, emphasis was placed on understanding Louise from a child developmental point of view. The focus was directed toward the intensity of the preadolescents' need for peer attachments, their ambivalent dependency-independency and love-hate conflicts with parents and other authoritative persons, and their tendency to dramatize submissiveness and passivity into catastrophic helplessness and hopelessness. The family caseworkers dealt immediately with the parents' apprehensions and anguish at being "thrown out" by their beloved daughter. The residential treatment staff in conjunction with the pediatric staff then convincingly reassured Louise of her recovery, even though the tests were not in. They permitted only her friends to visit her, and extended her movement to the maximal range consistent with the best pediatric judgment. She became cooperative, and with the help of the casework team, her parents were able to accept this program as they came to understand the dynamics employed in this very special case. Soon Louise was told that medically all things checked out absolutely fine. She was also reassured that her parents would probably be realistically understanding about her indiscretion with the pot, if she could trust herself and them enough to talk it over with them. She soon asked to see her parents along with her child-care worker, in order to work out this guilt and reestablish the meaningful family relationship that had existed prior to the accident. Louise was discharged after a week with follow-up plans through pediatrics and child psychiatry, which required only a few return visits.

In addition to the primary consideration of treating the child or adolescent, other aspects of residential treatment centers play major roles in the way they operate and thus in their organization and programs. Among these important influences are such variables as:

1. Number of children and adolescents served
2. Age range of patients
3. Sex of patients
4. Philosophy of therapeutic orientation
5. Aegis under which the institution functions—courts, schools, child welfare, hospitals
6. Local, state, and federal laws, regulations, and requirements
7. Availability of special resources and personnel
8. Physical location and plant, including size, space, structures, and environment
9. Nature of financial support

These influences are inseparable from the development, operation, and effective utilization of the resources of residential treatment, and they provide determinants which establish both the potentials and the limitations of any such facility. In certain instances, these factors are responsible for the provision of residential treatment where it would not otherwise exist. At times, however, some of these influences are out of phase with current knowledge and run counter to the most successful therapeutic operation of the facility.

Under the impact of new clinical knowledge and evaluation of experiences, changes are occuring steadily in milieu management and specific treatment methods. In addition, many changes have resulted from the influences exerted by funding sources, governmental and judicial procedures, and changing attitudes of society. Indeed, these influences have given rise to issues that are both complex and serious. Among the clinically important determinations that have been affected are such elements as selection for admission, length of stay, legal implications of guardianship rights, and type of treatment to be provided. Further changes and innovations will doubtedly flow from other currently emphasized areas. These include rights of the child; child, family, and consumer participation; and shifts in the balance between governmental and professional regulatory functions. More than that, processes designed to achieve quality assurance, determinations and issues of clinical accountability and responsibilities, and matters of documentation and records are especially likely to affect clinical practices. The responsible residential treatment facility, and all persons concerned with this particular area of care for children, must keep abreast of these multidimensional issues. Indeed, the facility must attempt to influence the issues from the standpoint of the best available knowledge and experience. Only then can continuing efforts to achieve the primary goal of this field—the establishment and maintenance of new residential treatment facilities which provide the most efficient and therapeutically effective results for children in need and which do so at the least cost—be assured.

Administrative complexities affect the personal feelings of the staff of residential treatment centers and therefore play a vital role in the demanding and tedious work with severely disturbed children and adolescents. A continuous dedication to the therapeutic process is essential. The foundations of success of residential treatment rest heavily on the training, experience, personal characteristics, and endurance of each staff member. These characteristics can become problematic for a variety of reasons. Negative countertransference reactions, conflicts between personal and institutional philosophies, lack of responsible institutional support, individual pathological attitudes, and problems between different cultural or value judgments have the potential to emerge during the course of treating troubled youth in an intensive-care setting. The following case history illustrates problems that might arise.

Dr. G, a thirty-two-year-old child psychiatrist, took over as ward chief for residential treatment in a large psychiatric hospital. He had an outstanding record in a high-quality community mental health center. He was energetic, innovative, and dedicated. In the new job, his good clinical skills, fine organizational abilities, and leadership charisma helped him recruit an outstanding multidisciplinary staff, even at low wages. The program grew, and effective treatment became a consistent standard. He utilized a full range of mental health professionals as consultants. They operated on a limited budget, but this was initially not a major obstacle. Two years later, however, the scene had changed drastically. The innovative treatment modalities were no more than regimented series of behavior restrictions and punishments: few consultants showed up; the living conditions had deteriorated and were hazardous; isolation in a bare "cell" with the floor for toileting were the hallmarks of "behavior modification" and "a quiet room"; and patients and staff seemed to have reached a symbiotic state of mutual hate and apathy. "Treatment" had deteriorated to merely existing from day to day. At this point in time, because of new regulations, the residential treatment program had an initial evaluation survey by an outside team. At the onset of the survey, Dr. G and the staff were defensive and angry, then ashamed and guilty. They later became ambivalently excited that someone was actually coming to evaluate the program. Dr. G described the disillusionment that had slowly but progressively come into their work. Because of the stagnant system in the parent hospital, he felt helpless in his losing "battles" for improved support for children and adolescent services. He became hostile and jealous, and even developed an attitude of "class discrimination" toward the unit's school program, which had an extra educational subsidy. No such extra subsidy was available for improvements in the residential living conditions, activity equipment, and other basic needs. He described "a society class syndrome" in which he even "rationalized" to himself "well, the kids don't need any better, since this is the way it is where they come from." He had also begun to hire staff who had "minority hostilities." Dr. G "justified" this as "equal and fair employment" practices representing a "constituency balance." Finally, he confided that "the youth culture invasion" had gotten to him. "What the hell—let them [the young patients] do their own thing" was his attitude. "Why fight all these crazy professional battles for good treatment, when everyone out there is running around looking for their own quickie cure or magic, and all the responsible tried and true techniques are suspect and considered rip-offs anyway." Dr. G and the entire residential treatment program had become vulnerable and had professionally regressed to cynicism and defeatism: "We'll join 'em if we can't lick 'em." However, the new, educationally oriented emphasis on peer review, quality assurance, and standards compliance brought a new hope and enthusiasm as they evaluated the future. Time will tell whether these efforts to apply standards will serve to liberate residential treatment, and all the Dr. G's and their staffs, or whether they will only add to the repetition of the stifling processes this experience represents.

Administrative responsibilities—staffing, fiscal plant operations, and maintenance—and clinical treatment decision making are inseparably linked. Their interaction has an immense impact on the programmatic effectiveness of residential treatment for children and adolescents. These administrative and therapeutic functions should be a responsibility of the the staff directly involved in the management and treatment processes. Therefore, all necessary arrangements must be made to establish and maintain the staff's essential autonomy and authority.

Fundamental Concerns and Responsibilities

Despite the numerous influences at work and the wide variations among the programs, certain fundamental considerations apply to all residential treatment facilities. To comprehend these multiple considerations, it is necessary to combine a historical perspective of the past, an objective analysis of current influences, and a thoughtful consideration of future developments.

The Evaluation

When examined holistically, these fundamental concerns and responsibilities are directed toward the primary care and remediation provided the individual child or adolescent. They also shed light on what goes into the efficient functioning of an organized residential treatment facility. From the very outset, the impact of entry into residential treatment is considerable. It affects the young person, the family, and the significant others in their social system. When the facility operates thoughtfully and with understanding, it plans and anticipates their responses from the moment of first contact through the time of their last follow up. As a result, much therapeutic advantage is gained and many distressing consequences can be prevented or relieved. Regardless of the distance between the child's home and the facility, an appreciation of the background of the young person and family along with an understanding of their experiences, frustrations, fears, and expectations continue to form the basis for meaningful responses by the residential treatment staff. As a rule, the

TABLE 15–1

Residential Treatment for Children and Adolescents:
Fundamental Concerns and Responsibilities

Care and Remediation	Processes: Outside and Within the Facilities
Healthy growth and development Disorders and pathological processes Effects of disorder on future growth and development	Individual Groups—family, significant others, peers, staff Environment Social

Individual	Clinical and Administrative
Physical Psychological Developmental Age Sex Family Education Social Environment Recreation Vocation	Assessment—Evaluation and Examination Formulation—Diagnosis Treatment Follow up Prevention Continuity of Care Documentation Confidentiality Patients' Rights Research Training Quality Assurance Organization Administration Physical Plant Political Legislative Legal Financial

(↑ CLINICAL ↔ ADMINISTRATIVE ↓)

residential treatment facility operates as a link in the chain of services for children and adolescents, among, for example, private clinicians, out-patient, day-treatment programs, and schools. It is, therefore, most important for the setting to maintain an integrative awareness of and the necessary collaborative contacts with these outside resources.

A great deal of information is accumulated by the evaluating team of residential treatment personnel, information which can often be pivotal in helping the young person, family, or social agency to determine the most appropriate alternatives for care and treatment. Decision making should be accomplished with as much clarity and with as little disruption and confusion as possible. Safeguards for the rights of the young person and family, and due respect for their dignity, are basic.

The initial assessment for residential treatment includes the necessary specific clinical evaluations of all the processes and individual considerations in table 15-1.

While the initial individual assessment methods will vary within different residential treatment programs, the thoroughness should not. A uniform evaluation of the staff processes in relation to their clinical and administrative implications should be universal. A number of elements are essential to effective decision making, to planning and carrying out the evaluative and therapeutic programs. These rely on the skillful integration of two functions: an understanding of the child's total needs and an awareness of the residential treatment facility's special organizational capabilities and limitations.

Detailed descriptions of the methods available for evaluating the individual child and family are set forth in volume I. For residential treatment, these are utilized in combination with the fundamental concerns and responsibilities outlined in table 15-1. A comprehensive care and treatment plan are developed from these. From the onset, this plan forms the basis for every aspect of the staff's planning and functioning. It is a living plan, working within a time frame, and with established objectives and goals. The plan includes clarification of roles and important lines of communication; sets out specific as well as general guidelines for staff responses; indicates special programmatic needs and requirements; and describes appropriate limitations, controls, privileges, and opportunities. The treatment plan process continually undergoes evaluation and modification, when needed. It involves consideration not only of the individual child or adolescent, but of the other young people in the program, the personnel, the various services and, in brief, the total internal environment, as well as of the resources utilized outside the program.

The Milieu

In chapter 14, one vital part of residential treatment is presented in the form of a descriptive analysis of an approach milieu therapy. Though few residential treatment facilities are set up in the fashion described in that chapter, the principles of ongoing concern for the detailed planning elaborated there do apply quite generally. This is true regardless of the facility's primary organizational orientation and structure.

At the time of the patient's entry, and throughout his course of stay in residential treatment, a number of issues must be considered. The child or adolescent should be placed in the living arrangement—single, double, or multiple—that will best meet his needs. Factors that bear upon specific placement include the child's interactions with other patients, the possible effects of his presence on the other patients and groups, and the degree and types of forces generated by the nature and size of the group. Of importance here are such influences as: the nature and severity of the patients' problems; their ages—chronological, psychological, and developmental; sex; capacities and deficits in interpersonal relationships-object constancy; specialized requirements—medical, educational, rehabilitative, recreational, vocational, and so on; security—controls, limitations, and boundaries.

These aspects of residential treatment are planned to achieve a number of goals: to promote appropriate individual interaction of the patients, staff, and the environment; to provide close observation as a basis for continuing planning; to support the patients in mastering individual and social conflict; and to establish a sense of security that would enable the patients to manage their dependent, independent, and interdependent needs successfully. Within the treatment setting the disturbed young person is to achieve age-appropriate management of tension; a sense of competence,

individuality, and self-esteem; and sufficient cognitive, interpersonal, behavioral, and motor skills for future living at home or within the community.

When treatment progresses well, the young person gradually develops a capacity to define himself and to gain a sense of security. This work is influenced by his internal and external experiences with *consistency* and *stability*, along with the nature of the *changes* and *complexities* in his living environment. Of special importance in residential treatment are such factors as:

1. Human
   a. Individual and group interactions
   b. Specialized or generalized responsibilities and functions
   c. Frequency and intensity of contact
   d. Closeness and intimacy, or distance and superficiality
   e. Conflict and resolution
   f. Direct and indirect communications
2. Structural
   a. Closed or open
   b. Single or multipurpose
   c. Nature of usage or nonusage
   d. Implicit expectations from humans or from objects
3. Environment
   a. Human, material, and geographic
   b. Limited or multiple stimuli
   c. Clarity or ambiguity
   d. Simple or complex
   e. Demanding or permissive
   f. Offering protection, control, or freedom
   g. Functional or aesthetic

The Environment

The influence of special factors is constantly present. It involves patients, staff, structures, activities, and the total environment. The continuous planning and skillful understanding and application of the processes themselves establish the therapeutic potential of the residential treatment milieu.

Among the important milieu elements of the residential treatment facility are the significant characteristics of the architecture, furnishings, equipment, decorations, and indoor and outdoor spaces. The young person tends to develop immediate and often long-lasting impressions and transferences to the human and natural structures, processes, and usages that surround him. All areas should be structurally definable so that their functions can be clearly understood by the patients. Special arrangements should be sensibly planned with an eye always to the children and adolescents to be served. The initial perceptions of these youngsters are influenced by their parental and peer attitudes. Their outlook is also colored by the values from their community and culture, and by their previous experiences. These form the basis for their initial biases. However, the nature of the personnel attitudes, things, structures, places, and activities they encounter in the residential treatment facility impart special meanings and expectations which influence the total experience.

Historical perspectives and the institutional influences previously mentioned must be dealt with thoughtfully. Ghosts from the past can all too readily be carried over into the facility's environment; the staff and patients will hear them as important messages. They will seem to mean that the expectations are dehumanizing, punitive, impersonal, disrespectful, or monetarily oriented. Whatever the nature of the institution's history and its current organizational needs, these should not divert it from its goal: Its plant and personnel must communicate clearly and comprehensibly the overt and covert expectations of respect, thoughtful concern, understanding, trust, and the many other positive attitudes necessary for the young person's health and happiness.

For this form of treatment, safety factors are intrinsic considerations of special importance, due to the average expectable dangers inherent in such a group-living environment. These dangers include the proclivity for destructive behavior that stems from the young patients' background exeriences. Such maladaptive responses are likely to arise in the face of any disturbing events in the young patients' lives. In particular, they may appear as interpersonal conflicts either with other patients or with staff. Necessary safety features and programmatic precautions should therefore be an integral part of the design, use, and maintenance of the plant. They should also affect the utilization of therapeutic programs and techniques of care and treatment. These children often need special clinical modalities or equipment, along with specific structural characteristics for the responsible management and treatment of their disturbed conditions. These special requirements, however, should not overwhelm those elements of the environment designed for meaningful child and adolescent care.

In some residential treatment facilities special safety features—for example, locked areas, shatterproof glass, and security screens—are indicated. Where necessary, these should be incorporated in an unobtrusive blend with the healthy orientation of the entire milieu, in consonance with the therapeutic orientation and expectations of the staff.

They thus add emphasis to a sense of prevailing concern for the individual patient's protection and to the expectations for progressive improvement. The goal is to strive toward more adequate individual self-controls and responsible social and environmental interactions. It is clear that the physical environment as well as interpersonal and programmatic circumstances may foster, modify, or nullify therapeutic efforts and may enhance or impede healthy development.

Therapeutic Modalities

It is evident that many things flow from the initial and comprehensive evaluation and formulation of the individual youth's strengths and disabilities. Among these are: the decision for placement; the studied integration of programs and staff for the provision of daily living needs; the planned creation of a protective and therapeutic milieu; the decisions for specific modalities of treatment; the necessary activities for continuity of care both throughout the stay and in preparation for and after discharge; and the important follow-up functions. All of these vary depending upon the patients served and the institutional characteristics of the residential treatment facility. The most variable aspect of residential treatment, however, is the nature of the special treatment modalities provided in different settings.

Historically, there have been a multitude of practices based on mystique, tradition, art, and diverse philosophic and scientific perspectives. These have yielded a large range of treatment methods. Their variety, however, is not due merely to historical developments. They are also subject to new advances, current trends, changes within the mental health disciplines, organizational attitudes, funding sources, and outside pressures, for example, consumer, governmental, and judicial. In many instances they are affected by the availability or by the lack of the necessary trained and competent clinical staff. Changes in the availability, the diversity, and the modes of delivery of specific treatment methods are occurring more rapidly than alterations in any other aspect of residential treatment. In recent years, treatment has been influenced most by advances in the grasp of child and adolescent psychodynamics, and psychobiological and psychosocial interrelationships. There have been many steps forward in the understanding of child and adolescent development and the dynamics of family, group, and social processes. Variations of emphasis exist concerning such specialized therapeutic techniques as individual psychoanalysis and other psychotherapies, group-oriented treatment, family therapy, behavior modification techniques, special education, activity and work-oriented programs, and psychopharmacologic usage. Today residential treatment programs tend to utilize specific treatment approaches in conjunction with outside community resources. These are integrated into the total network of the therapeutic milieu.

There are times when organizational arrangements for service delivery can be both good and bad, and the difference seems almost indistinguishable. All good residential treatment programs must therefore engage in a continuous process of reevaluation of their goals, and their methods of achieving these goals. Consider the following case.

Sally and Jane were both patients in a well-run residential treatment program which was doing a highly successful job with difficult young patients. Nine-year-old Sally was being treated for a passive-aggressive personality, with a hysterical neurosis and multiple phobias and hypochondriacal symptoms. Jane, on the other hand, was a thirteen-year-old antisocial delinquent with "runaways," truancy, involvement in drugs, and a defiance of all authority. Each child was in need of a therapeutic environment with appropriate limits and controls, as well as a treatment plan that was aimed at both their internal conflicts and their distortions in their perceptions of their environment. The residential treatment center had skillfully established the staff and the treatment program as a respected authority for Sally. With the help of a responsive family casework relationship, her troubled parents were able to turn over the necessary authority and responsibility to the residential treatment staff. All attempts to create such an arrangement with Jane and her family had failed; no way could be found to overcome her pervasive defiance and negativism and her family's lack of understanding and cooperation. Jane had become a ward of the court under the direct supervision of the local juvenile court judge. While Sally's acting out and troubled behavior was always worked with directly by the residential treatment staff, Jane's destructive antisocial behavior occasionally brought the juvenile officers into the residential treatment, where they acted directly as agents of the judge. They dealt with her primarily legalistically; thus for "time out" she was taken for a day or so to the Juvenile Detention Center, from where she had originally been admitted. This seemed to be an ideal collaboration between the psychiatric mental health team and the juvenile justice authorities. Unfortunately, it created a serious problem—an impression of a double standard with conflicting authorities and confusing consequences. Sally began to "get into the act" each time the officers came to take Jane away for her "time outs." Sally, too, seemed to seek out this "ultimate omnipotent authority" that Jane had found. In addition, the procedure of juvenile officers entering the milieu to investigate "one of theirs" created a good deal of fear. There was a sense of invasion of privacy, implied loss of confidentiality, and other concerns, both real and subjective. The judge rightly felt his legal responsibility for those under his jurisdiction. Yet the unclarified double jeopardy involved in this mode of decision making created an atmosphere which prompted the young people to act out their most severe ambivalence. Their object-splitting symptomatology and their double bind with authority figures increased. With the help of an outside child psychiatrist consultant working with the staff, the judge, the families, and representatives from the community, the problem was clarified. A more realistic plan for responsibility and authority was worked out between the residential center and the juvenile judge, an innovative arrangement for that particular location. The judge agreed to maintain the final authority over those under his mandate but to turn over to the residential treatment staff the responsibility for the fundamental treatment and child care decision making, including issues involving delinquent behavior. Arrangements were then made for monthly (or more frequent) briefing meetings between residential staff, the judge, and the families involved. This was not merely an administrative arrangement unrelated to the actualities of treatment. As it became clear to Jane that the staff had the responsibility and the direct authority from the judge to deal with her therapeutically, she began to cease her pathological "acting out," searching for the "one great authoritarian," and started working things through with this newly identified "judge"—the staff. In turn, Sally lost the gratifications from her "contagious" acting out and reinvested herself in her own treatment program and in her own staff team.

A detailed description of specific treatment modalities used in residential treatment are available in other chapters of this handbook. These include:

1. Psychoanalysis
2. Psychotherapy
3. Play therapy
4. Family therapy
5. Group therapy
6. Reality therapy
7. Child care techniques
8. Impact therapy
9. Life-space interviewing
10. Socialization engineering
11. Behavioral therapy
    a. Behavior modification
    b. Reconditioning
    c. Token economy
12. Special education
    a. Reeducation techniques
    b. Psychoeducation
13. Speech, language, and hearing therapy
14. Activity therapy
    a. Art therapy and music therapy
    b. Dance therapy
    c. Recreational therapy
    d. Psychodrama
15. Occupational therapy
16. Vocational therapy
17. Rehabilitation

18. Counseling
    a. Pastoral counseling
    b. Personal counseling
19. Specialized physical medical treatments
20. Medications

Substantial as it is, this list is incomplete. When the variables for specific types of emergency care, crisis intervention, short- to long-term treatment, and specific differences between younger children and adolescents are added, the complexity of this range of therapeutic interventions becomes clear. When such treatment modalities are utilized, they should be provided by competent staff who make sufficient observations, document all significant responses, and have appropriate back-up resources to ensure optimal benefits and necessary follow up. Specific treatment modalities—for example, individual psychotherapy—may require unique arrangements for personal relationships, specialized activities, or confidentiality. The interests of patients and staff are best served by continuous evaluation, clarification, and open communication regarding the effects of such methods. In this area in particular, the integrity, integration, and continuity of the entire residential treatment program is of signal importance.

INDIVIDUAL PSYCHOTHERAPY

Individual child or adolescent psychotherapy often plays a major role in helping both to understand and work through the most serious intrapsychic disorganizations. While the dynamic processes may not vary, the unique circumstances of the total care within a therapeutic milieu place special demands on the person undertaking or continuing individual psychotherapy within such a facility. Among other factors are the ubiquitous intense interactions with other staff, the omnipresent activities and programs, the overall integration of the facility's threapeutic orientation, and the special relationships with family and outside community. Here the child psychiatrist may bring a particularly important dimension to this specialized form of clinical treatment. He has a background in medicine, transference phenomena, and child and adolescent psychodynamics, along with experience in play therapy, individual child and adolescent psychotherapy, family and group dynamics. He may provide these valuable skills directly through supervision or consultation, or by participating in the training of other staff.

Total isolation of psychotherapy from other parts of the program has generally created more problems than it has solved. Thoughtfully and skillfully managed individual provisions should be worked out for confidentiality, while avoiding or clarifying destructive attitudes of absolute secrecy. The psychotherapist usually benefits from participation in the overall treatment planning. In many circumstances he is a part of the ongoing decision-making team; sometimes he is the primary decision maker. Within each individual psychotherapy arrangement there are different and often changing transference consequences and other psychodynamic implications; the individual therapist should be aware and skilled in these special considerations.

GROUP PROCESSES

Group dynamics play an important part in residential treatment, both within the overall therapeutic milieu and in formally organized therapy groups. The techniques of group therapy are often beneficially utilized both in informal programs within the living units and in activity-centered groups. Of particular importance in any group work are the vicissitudes of the different disorders and their impact on the young people who are continuously living and interacting together. Likewise, the significance of various holidays and memorial dates vary widely from child to child because of differing backgrounds and experiences. At the same time, each event may have a profound effect on the individual, the other young patients, or the entire patient group. Thus, the staff must deal with a wide range and diversity of circumstances within the facility as well as with family and community events that affect the young patients. This is a continuing challenge to the group leaders' comprehension and management abilities. They must, therefore, be skilled in handling the individual, cultural, and social ramifications that are special to the residential treatment facility's patient population.

Some of the other group process considerations especially common to residential treatment are:

1. Management of rivalries among groups or individuals
2. Dealing with problematic special relationships formed among patients and between patients and staff
3. Influencing particular behavioral problems, for example, withdrawal, hostility, self-destructiveness, scapegoating
4. Implementing constructive techniques for conflict and grievance resolution
5. Emphasizing unity of purpose without sacrificing respect for the individual autonomy
6. Developing healthy attitudes for self-determination by instituting various arrangements for self-government

7. Advancing individual initiative and socialization skills through task-oriented activities and project planning

An understanding of individual psychodynamics and child development is vital to residential therapeutic endeavors. Sometimes, however, the focus gets concentrated totally on the individual, and essential dynamics of group processes become overlooked or poorly utilized. It is important to keep both individual and group psychodynamics and developmental understanding in proper perspective. In the following case history, no resolution of the problem could occur until the prevalent group processes were recognized.

An open setting utilizing reality therapy, a work orientation, behavior modification, close personal staff interactions, and group dynamics had recently been through a horrifying period of glue, paint, and gasoline sniffing. Fortunately, no serious ill effects occurred. Through their interaction and treatment review conference, the multidisciplinary staff arrived at a concensus that these incidents were being instigated as tests of omnipotence and counterphobic "bullying techniques." There was competition for the "ringleader" position in the groups by means of threats, scare tactics, and various forms of intimidation. All this was evident within the context of both individual and group processes, but predominantly the latter. Once they grasped this, the staff could readily collaborate. They tried to eliminate the sources and availability of toxic substances. They consistently confronted the perpetrators with the foolishness and dangers of the acts. They invoked clear restrictions and loss of privilege as punishment without becoming hostile to or rejecting the children. They were united in their determination that this dangerous behavior and all of the individual and group bullying and intimidation tactics were expected to stop. These would be dealt with directly, both by one-to-one and group pressures. The sniffing gradually stopped. The staff's use of individual and group dynamics had paid off. Therapeutic group functioning and respected staff limits were established. Shortly thereafter, a patient had to be transferred to a closed residential treatment setting because of other uncontrollable dangerous behavior. This sixteen-year-old boy was a "proclaimed homosexual" and was constantly "on the make" with any of the staff or the other young male patients. His forced termination had not been the result of his sexual activities or "sniffing" but rather some life-threatening hysterical behavior that the residential treatment program had been unsuccessful in managing. The next "outbreak" of group problems was an "epidemic" of "queering off." The entire staff immediately became anxious, tense, and felt a real sense of lack of direction. They experienced personal turmoil in trying to find a response that would cope with this new form of maladaptive behavior. This ignited some of their own personal identity conflicts, as well as their repressed prejudices against "homosexuals." This served to arouse their guilt; perhaps they had "run off" the one boy because of his homosexual activities. Initially,

the entire staff sought desperately and painfully to analyze this new "homosexual" behavior from the point of view of their own intrapsychic and psychosexual dynamics as well as those of each individual patient involved. This was both unrewarding and nonproductive, and the "queering off" increased. With the help of their outside child psychiatrist consultant, the individual analytic and psychosexual point of view was shifted to include consideration of the group dynamics. After interviewing many of the young boys, it became clear that the boys did not see their behavior as homosexual. In fact, it had all the dynamics of the previous "epidemic" of sniffing. This was a meaningful breakthrough for the staff, as it enabled them to deal more comfortably with their own guilt about "all of their boys being homosexuals." With this new perspective, the staff and the boys began referring to these acts by a more direct and demeaning name, "butt fucking." Little if any oral-genital involvement was taking place. With this new emphasis, the deinstitutionalization of the status of the term "queering off" began to take place. The staff regrouped to handle "butt fucking" primarily as a group phenomenon involving the same testing, bullying, and control issues encountered with the sniffing episode. As the staff revised the treatment strategies to deal with this more directly, both as individual and as group processes, their effectiveness increased and the "butt fucking" decreased. Unexpectedly, the boys seemed relieved and became more interested in exploring with the staff such areas as appropriate, "healthy" sexual activity and peer-group interactions.

FAMILY INVOLVEMENT

Family involvement has achieved a considerable role in the overall approach to and the long-range effects of residential treatment. It is an integral part of many residential treatment facilities. In some it may be highly structured as family therapy, while in others it is utilized more as an adjunctive or resource modality. Regardless of its nature or its degree of integration into the treatment program, family therapy serves multiple and important purposes. One prime purpose is to help correct contributing family psychopathological processes. Other goals include the clarification of misperceptions, fears, and tensions regarding both the young patient's condition and the nature of residential treatment; the continuing acquisition of significant information; the maintenance of important family relationships; building the necessary alliances for continuity of care and aftercare; working out difficult social, financial, legal, or community-related problems; resolving conflicts created by developmental crises, generation gaps, or changing cultural patterns (especially with adolescent patients); and aiding the family in the effective and appropriate utilization of other necessary community resources.

Family therapy and therapeutic work with the families and significant others of those in residential treatment involve multiple skills and a wide variety of techniques. Some of these are specific to the modality of family therapy itself, which is discussed in chapter 7; others arise from adaptations to the particular programs, staff, child or adolescent, and family's needs. Parent counseling and therapy is also discussed in chapter 8.

EDUCATIONAL PROGRAMS

The education of any young person is vital to his ego growth. It affects the organization of cognitive functioning, socialization processes, acquisition of self-sustaining abilities, and mastery of productive skills. For the seriously disturbed youth, the intramural school very early became one of the mainstays of residential treatment. Today in some facilities the entire therapeutic approach is organized principally around the educational program. Here, special educators and educational techniques are the primary therapeutic forces; around them are woven the skills of other necessary specialized mental health staff. Other residential treatment facilities include the educational component and staff in more separate and formally designated areas and programmatic dimensions, for example, adjunctive therapies; still others have their educational elements woven into the total milieu with close interaction with other therapeutic programs. Finally, facilities turn to various arrangements with outside educational personnel or institutions: In such instances, the public school system may provide the academic programs both within and outside the facility.

Although arrangements for the provision of both formal and informal education may vary, the emphasis on meeting the individual child's needs for learned knowledge and skills should never vary. Special remedial, tutorial, psychoeducational, self-pacing, formally structured, and daily living-learning experiences are but a few of the educational tools utilized. Whatever their nature, and however they are carried out, the curriculum and teaching techniques should be geared to the young patient's social and emotional needs as well as to his intellectual and vocational development. All of the varieties of teaching in residential treatment are directed toward developing the young patient's ego strengths. These include his capacities for communication, for self-help and management, for social skills, for the acquisition of and adaptive utilization of knowledge, and for the achievement of other mental and physical skills necessary for a rewarding quality of independent living.

While the educational arrangements for any seriously disturbed child must be flexible, all young patients need to achieve the maximum amount of formal education of which they are capable. The realties of the world outside residential treatment require this. A continuing preparation for reentry into the mainstream of academic and vocational life is extremely important. It should not, however, overshadow the vital importance of acquiring the knowledge, judgment and skills so necessary for a healthy, well-adjusted, self-sustaining life.

In some seriously disturbed children and adolecents, their learning abilities have not been impaired by their disorder. In others, as part of their condition, intellectual abilities may have accelerated to the point that they are out of phase with the rest of their development. Such youngsters may require advanced academic challenges, but special sensitivity is required to integrate their exceptional abilities into a meaningful and rewarding pattern. For the majority of youth requiring residential treatment, however, their emotional, mental, or behavioral disturbances (with or without certain specific central nervous system disabilities) make it difficult or them to learn. Special educational experiences must be provided to remedy previous deficits in their education (where they may have fallen behind due to their disorder) or often enough, to allow them to begin any kind of successful academic learning.

The strengths, deficiencies, and *fundamental* needs of the *individual* child or adolescent must be assessed in relation to the *processes* (see table 15-1). This assessment forms the basis for coordinating the full range of educational approaches with all of the other required therapeutic efforts. Meaningful learning and effective internalization of skills seldom, if ever, take place in an interpersonal vacuum. It is, therefore, vital that appropriate and integrated educational reinforcements come from the milieu, from specific treatment modalities, and from other staff caring activities. The necessary administrative arrangements to achieve these goals include policies, procedures, periodic reviews, clear lines of communications, and multidisciplinary team meetings. The specifics will vary, but it is of central importance that this integration always be present.

The needs of each patient and of groupings of patients change significantly over time. These changes often occur very unevenly, during different stages of treatment and at different developmental periods. Accordingly, special educational attention and staff functioning are required to adapt in quite a variety of forms at different times. At certain times, the emphasis is on individual or special tasks, while at others the focus is more on the group or general achievements. Overall educational resources must be utilized flexibly both within and outside the residential treatment setting; and provision should be made for well-thought-out changes in approaches, materials, utilization of staff skills, and teacher-student ratios. Throughout treatment, the essential element is to maintain and foster progress, and to keep alive a reasonable expectation for continued progress in the future. (Detailed discussion of psychoeducation is available in chapters 19 and 20.)

BEHAVIORAL THERAPIES

The history of residential treatment is probably nowhere better illustrated than in a consideration of the methods of behavioral control. Purgings, penance, spiritualistic rites, cultist rituals, isolation, hard labor, forced imitation, and coerced responses are but a few of the methods which gave rise to many acclaimed behavioral "therapeutic" programs for seriously disturbed young people. Today there are diverse and, at times, problematic dissentions within the total mental health field and within many individual residential treatment facilities concerning this critical area of therapy and habilitation. Controversy has swirled about the nature, orientation, definitions, goals, organizational arrangements, roles, functions, and results of behavioral methods. From these diversities, however, have come many major technical and clinical advances; bit by bit these are entering into the total care and treatment armamentarium. Under closer scrutiny, utilizing today's knowledge, many behavioral techniques seemed to be no more than advancements of "meaningless" rituals and traditional practices. This discovery has led to continuous reevaluation in order to make the application of new knowledge generate better and more "meaningful" behavioral methodologies.

With the accumulation of clinical experience and advances in the scientific basis of behavior therapy, there have been many organizational improvements as well as progress in therapeutic care. In many residential treatment facilites, the primary organization, including administrative and clinical functioning, is essentially oriented around the principles of behavioral therapy. In other settings, behavioral therapies are applied in more focal programatic ways, for example, in ad hoc applications of behavior modification and operant conditioning to deal with individual symptoms. These may employ token economies and behavioral scales with both self- and group-rating systems in order to determine rewards, privileges, or deprivations. The skillful use of these methodologies has achieved significant success in restoring a sense of self-confidence to seriously disturbed young persons, in strengthening their behavioral controls, and in improving their reality orientation. When competently utilized, these behavioral methods can work in harmony with other treatment programs for the mutual benefit of each.

Most of the fundamental considerations outlined previously for educational programs and milieu therapy apply as well to behavioral therapies, which are discussed in chapters 3 and 11. The *complete assessment* of the young patients' *total needs* remains the hallmark of clinical decision making in residential treatment. The clinical determination of those needs should provide the primary basis for the utilization of behavioral therapy programs.

As in most other areas of residential treatment, further research and well-organized follow-up studies are much needed here. Because of the relative newness of behavioral therapies and the rapid advances in their systematic theoretical application, special attention should be given to determining their most effective therapeutic implementation. The previously mentioned primitive practices provided a harsh laboratory; they produced many methods which were dehumanizing and often cruel. The tendency to revert to such approaches is always present, and constant attention is needed to prevent this. At the same time, the more sustaining, individualized, mastery- and growth-promoting ingredients must be fostered and further developed. This is most likely to happen when ongoing work is designed to increase the understanding and motivation of the entire staff. No attempted procedure should remain outside the crucial, perpetual integrative review and evaluation processes, and each should be melded as smoothly as possible into the schema of the other ongoing administrative and therapeutic practices. In this manner, all of the youngsters' "meaningless" behavior has the greatest potential to become productively "meaningful."

ACTIVITY AND VOCATIONAL PROGRAMS

Activity and vocational therapy programs might well be thought to have acquired their significant place in residential treatment via a special rhetorical process: the conversion of the word "purposeless" to "purposeful" when applied to young people's activities. A wide variety of activity and vocational therapies are currently contributing to the total treatment impact of residential care.

Many facilities, due to their historical bases, are now almost totally oriented toward activity and recreational programs. In a large number of instances, the primary therapeutic emphasis and programmatic orientation resemble counterparts in society at large: They are designed around farming, ranching, business training, vocational schools, recreational camps, and others.

The diversity of therapeutic techniques speaks primarily to the multitude of integrating forces that are now known to be at work within the seriously mentally, emotionally, or behaviorally disturbed young person. Any or all of the forces can be utilized in the quest for well-being. Recently society seems to have shifted from a primary emphasis on material productivity to a more child-centered personal growth orientation. This has opened the way for new and rewarding insights into the essential ego processes and developmental needs of all growing and maturing young people. From these insights many outstandingly successful designs have developed for new activities and vocationally oriented therapeutic processes. For the seriously disturbed young person, new stabilizing, integrating, and satisfying efforts are now developing. These include measures which allow for the mastery of purposeful activities, opportunities for team participation, supervised competition, and the development of a capacity for consistent pursuit of pleasurable and gratifying interests.

Based on these foundations, today residential treatment includes a wide assortment of special programs and specially skilled staff integrated into the therapeutic program in many different fashions. These programs include activity therapy, vocational and occupational therapy, recreation therapy, and even more specific forms such as art, drama, dance, and music therapy. When utilized effectively and in harmony with other therapeutic programs and activities, these can often "reach" certain seriously disturbed young patients and provide initial important breakthroughs. At the same time, these programs provide other children with opportunties for the development and maintenance of valuable self-satisfactions and potential skills and keep interest alive for many future "purposeful" endeavors.

An appreciation of the patients' activity efforts and the inherent gratifications from body control and coordinated performances frequently gives rise to important increases in attention span and impulse mangement. Not only do such effects result in better internal stability, but the all-important body awareness, ego boundaries, and respect for others may be positively affected.

The acquisition of productive skills or technical knowledge helps children orient themselves toward the future. They can begin to view themselves as self-supporting and valuable members of the work environment within the community. This is especially true for the adolescent. Work and other productive activities are frequently combined with resources within the facility as well as outside it. For many young patients in residential treatment, earning real money is often a valuable incentive. Some recent legislation has limited or prevented this practice completely. The value of earning wages as part of the total therapeutic resources in such treatment should not be lost, and responsible efforts should be made to preserve this. However, any program involving work and monetary exchange should be judiciously monitored; it must be based clearly on the *clinical assessment* of the child or adolescent's needs, and there must be clear indications that such work and payment would meet these needs. Abusive practices in this area have, at times, resulted in flagrant violations of young persons' rights; among its other undesirable effects, these violations would totally destroy the treatment benefit.

Many of the activity and vocational programs once considered innovative have now become accepted therapeutic modalities. Further work to determine their most effective utilization within residential treatment will continue to enchance their beneficial effects.

PHYSICAL HEALTH CARE

The residential setting assumes full responsibility for the young person's health, including his physical health and any special physical needs. This responsibility begins at admission and continues throughout the entire course of residence; it includes appropriate arrangements for any necessary medical aftercare.

The details of the intricate interrelationships between a young person's physical health and his emotional, mental, characterlogical, and behavioral characteristics are subjects specifically highlighted in other sections of this handbook. The varieties of arrangements for qualified staff and availability of specific medical resources to residential treatment are touched upon elsewhere in this chapter. The *Accreditation Manual for Psychiatric Facilities Serving Children and Adoles-*

cents[48] elaborates specific guidelines for such medical care practices in residential treatment.

There are often special medical regimens or corrective procedures necessary to help young patients with such problems as central nervous system disease, birth defects, allergies, functional limitations acquired from previous illnesses or injuries, chronic disease, or special sensory limitations in, for example, speech, vision, and hearing. These or other such physical problems should be managed through integrated teamwork involving all of the required medical specialists and the residential treatment staff. Timely availability and collaboration is essential. To achieve these goals, it is necessary to avoid some common pitfalls, such as: staff denial or feelings of pity and helplessness; staff ignorance or indifference to appropriate backup resources; staff "fears of personal failures" if they "call for help"; medical-nonmedical battles; and psychiatric-medical disunity. Clear responsibilities and procedural practices must be established, along with regular reviews for carrying out all ongoing physical medical care and emergency procedures. These and related issues are discussed in greater detail in chapters 35, 36, 37, 38, 39, 40, 41, and 42.

At times, minutes are critical. A cook or a maintenance worker with the right training could make the difference. Thus, not only do physical diseases or abnormalities need to be detected, corrected, or properly managed, but unexpected accidents must be dealt with as quickly and as effectively as possible. All staff should have first aid knowledge. Such training as Red Cross emergency first aid and Emergency Medical Services training, as well as others, are now available in most locales to all personnel.

Staffing

It is clear that in such diverse facilities the staffing must differ considerably from one setting to another. There are so many areas of variation: in the nature of disturbances of the children and adolescents served, in the varieties of therapeutic goals and potentials, and in the diversity of organizational structures. Staffing is essentially determined by the needs of the patient population. This mandates the special care, the kinds of treatment, and the specific environment required; ultimately,

it determines the operational requirements for the continuing efficiency and the effectiveness of the organization.

Thus, in different settings, the patterns of staffing and staff composition may follow quite different lines. These vary from departmental organization by disciplines or special functions on the one hand, to service unit organizations based on patient groupings on the other. There are many alternatives in between. Experience has demonstrated one significant principle: Whatever the staffing composition and patterns of organization, there should be a sufficient number of competent staff members available to carry out the necessary therapeutic functions of the program effectively, and there should be respect and understanding for staff differences in expertise and responsibilities. Understaffing should never be a criterion for the use of any treatment or management modality, nor should it justify overlooking the special need of any patient. Nor should any specific treatment be undertaken without the necessary competent staff available.

Problems arising within the staff most often center around issues of misunderstanding and mistrust, and are usually the product of organizational confusion, poor lines of communication, and hidden personal prejudices about responsibilities and territorial boundaries. In general, organizations do not operate without naturally occuring conflicts. Thus, effective residential treatment facilities will not function well without built-in processes for continuing staff evaluation and for conflict determination and resolution. These are expected of the young people and demanded of the staff.

A number of factors influence the specific variety, numbers, and makeup of the residential treatment staff. Chief among these are the nature of the disturbances of the patient population served and the professionally determined therapeutic philosophies and clinical methodologies required.

Since the organization of the total milieu is of such importance, within each residential treatment facility the specific functions of each staff member are usually unique. These functions seldom follow any of the formal role definitions of the professional disciplines. However, residential treatment should include staff members with the expertise and knowledge base of each of the mental health disciplines to care for the wide range of the young patients' needs.

When the needs of the *individual* and the *processes* of treatment are related to the *care and re-*

mediation goals (see table 15-1), what emerges is some sense of the totality of required specialized clinical expertise. The skills of child and adolescent psychiatrists; pediatricians; pediatric neurologists; other medical specialists; child psychiatric nurses; psychologists; social workers; educators; speech, language, and hearing specialists; child-care workers; and other professional, paraprofessional, and mental health workers are most often involved. Additionally, valuable contributions have recently come from other child-oriented specialists, such as anthropologists, sociologists, lawyers, pharmacologists, and a variety of psychobiological researchers. Because of this complex mosaic of talent, it is most important that the individual contributions be well coordinated; directly and indirectly their collective work affects the lives of the patients in treatment.

The seriously disturbed child or adolescent needs continual clarification of the functions and relationships of those around him. This is of critical importance; it serves to repair his often fearful, confused, and fragmented comprehension of the persons that are a part of his environment. Thus it is vital to help the young patient understand and accept specialized individual functions and the inherent resources and limitations of staff relationships. Properly done, this facilitates the internalization of his self-caring and self-sustaining abilities. Therefore, regardless of the nature of the program, the individual perspectives and the countertransference reactions of every person involved must be actively reviewed. Continual analysis and realistic clarifications of these will serve to reduce the tension-producing misconceptions that are so common to young people and staff members in such settings.

Patient rights, privileges, restrictions, and limitations are not implicit in staffing. Nonetheless, they are major factors in individual staff member's functioning and responsibilities. Important clinical decisions regarding these areas of the young patient's life must be determined on the basis of a clinical assessment and be consistent with the established care and treatment plan. Such issues as visitation, mail and phone privileges (or limitations), holidays, weekend and vacation arrangements, all should be joint clinical-administrative staff determination. They require clear communication between the young patient and the responsible adults, and should be reviewed and modified according to a current evaluation of the therapeutic needs and progress.

In correcting many of the more serious disorders, continuity of relationships and consistency of expectations are especially valuable. Continuity and consistency rebuild the capacity for human empathy from mistrust, paranoia, antisocial behavior, passive-agressive and oppositional behavior, and aid as well in fostering adequate reality testing. It is useful to assign one staff member as a young patient's primary clinical coordinator or resource worker. However, children in a therapeutic milieu tend to establish their own "most valued" personal relationships and their own staff hierarchy. Often, these are relationships with cooks, maintenance personnel, secretaries, and so on. This factor merely emphasizes the importance of an all-out effort for total staff interaction and the fostering of respectful attitudes throughout the staff, with continuous inservice training of all personnel.

In the day-to-day operation of residential treatment there can arise subtle but potentially serious complications. These stem from the multitudinous complexities of the treatments involved. At times, individual staff roles or "territories" gain an unrecognized power. These may threaten the integrity of the most thoughtfully integrated individual treatment planning. Consider the following case.

Michael, age ten, inadvertently found himself in such a dilemma. He had come into the residential treatment program after a painstakingly well-documented case history and a thorough psychiatric evaluation and assessment. He was a severely handicapped young boy with extreme obsessive-compulsive thought patterns and behavioral rituals; these had created a total impasse in his development. Despite the efforts of his family and the schools, all attempts to handle these by outpatient therapy, including medications, and individual, family, and group work, had failed. Every detail of his fundamental needs had been appropriately assessed, and his strengths, weaknesses, and therapeutic needs determined. A highly individualized treatment plan was worked out, utilizing the expertise of all of the multidisciplinary staff and including family involvement and educational resources. Michael initially responded well and progress seemed rapid. This, however, changed drastically after the initial "honeymoon period," and Michael reverted back to his incorrigible and manipulative avoidance of all self-fulfilling activities. He conned each individual staff member by placation and the development of a superficial, special, "private" relationship with each of them. He became each staff's most important patient, and the one that supposedly no other staff member could satisfactorily understand. In treatment review conferences the various personnel realized that they each felt Michael was progressing. But, when it was all put together, serious doubt emerged as to the reliability of any of this. The "special" child-care worker, the "understanding" teacher, the "sympathetic" group therapist, and the "confidential" psychotherapist began to realize that Michael was playing up to their magnanimity and their prestigious role images, and was thus avoiding confrontations with much of the work expected of him. His avoidances and procrastinations had gone unchallenged under the guise that the "other" staff did not understand him or expected too much. He had "outobsessed" them all, and, as a result, had involved the staff in playing the game "whose role is the most important?" Homework was unattended so Michael could participate with the group; team activities were avoided because he did not have enough time to study; individual and group therapy sessions were missed because he needed to do his housekeeping, and so on. Michael had found one of the weaknesses in the human institutional process. Before the staff came to deal with it, he had exploited it for his maladaptive purposes. In interaction conferences, the staff opened themselves up concerning this "territoriality" and the "role dominance" pitfall; they spoke of their individual "rescue fantasies" common to all residential treatment. They then reorganized themselves and re-established the essential, respected peer collaborations. More meaningfully for Michael, they began following through more explicitly the details of his treatment plan, which, after all, they themselves had worked out in the beginning. The total staff's continuing intra- and interpersonal reviews and revisions of his treatment plan were essential in order to interrupt Michael's demanding neurotic conflicts and character disorders. Eventually, this enabled him to integrate people, functions, purposes, and goals realistically without perpetually trying to split them.

In addition to reviewing the benefits of primary staff responsibility, continuity of relationships, and special alliances, children and adolescents in residential treatment must be prepared repeatedly to deal with special circumstances and specialized functions involving limited contacts with staff. Anticipatory preparation and clarification of these can often convert panic into cooperation. Careful attention should be given to the special needs of all the patients, and skilled staff should be available to handle these needs with as little confusion and disruption as possible. Provisions should be built into the program to respond to medical emergencies or critical events involving the child's family or peers outside the residential facility immediately, thoughtfully, and in as reassuring a manner as possible. These interventions should not take place in isolation, apart from the rest of the clinical staff, although considerations of confidentiality and privacy may sometimes justify such special handling.

The personnel of the residential treatment facility have additional responsibilities. These emanate from principles of humane care, sound child-rearing practices, considerations about the rights of the child, and newer medical knowledge pertaining to specific treatments. Periodic reviews and revisions of what is actually happening within their designated divisions of responsibility should be carried out by the total staff in order to provide safeguards for these principles. This is essential so that cruel, dehumanizing, painful, or severely isolating or restrictive procedures never become rationalized substitutes for the wise and judicious use of experienced interventions, effective programs, or competent medical judgment. Techniques involving planned anticipatory management, individual and group influences, staff relationships, appropriate time outs, and reward systems have proven to be of significant benefit. Psychopharmacological agents also have an important role in helping manage the behavior of certain young patients, as discussed in chapter 23. These should be administered according to specific medical indications and prescriptions, and never primarily for the convenience of the staff or program. Inordinate use of demoralizing punishments, insensitive prolonged seclusion, and unjustified use of medications are legacies of historical practices and fads which are sometimes carried forward into residential treatment. Fortunately in the face of a more conscientious child-oriented approach, the upgrading of child-caring knowledge, and the use of more effective combinations of clinical staff expertise, these methods of dealing with patients are rapidly disappearing from the scene.

Residential treatment facilities utilizing trainees or volunteers or conducting research incur special responsibilities. The particular effects on each patient and patient group of the unique aspects of these undertakings must be reviewed. Disruptions in patient care and treatment programs must be avoided, and patient stability and rights must be safeguarded. The patients' welfare, both in respect to their current condition and to their future, must remain the primary consideration in all treatment programs. The utilization of specially skilled outside persons can often enhance the child's appreciation of such unusual abilities and talents; it may also serve to counteract institutionalizing forces by providing continuing bridges to the outside. Descriptions of many such detailed staffing considerations have been set forth in the *Accreditation Manual for Psychiatric Facilities Serving Children and Adolescents*[48] developed and utilized by the Joint Commission on Accreditation of Hospitals. The standards described there provide guidelines for alternative staffing patterns, recommendations for methods of organization, and review mechanisms. Many of the processes and procedures aimed at enabling the residential treatment facility to carry out these principles most effectively are emphasized.

THE CHILD PSYCHIATRIST

The field of residential treatment is particularly appropriate for the child psychiatrist. Here a professional can see some of the most beneficial results to emerge from his total medical and clinical expertise. The foundations of residential treatment are built upon the total needs of the seriously disturbed young person; the work itself takes expression in the design and development of care and treatment plans to correct the existing damage. Reviewing the fundamental concerns listed in table 15-1, it is evident that they reflect the studies of a well-trained child psychiatrist. Clearly the degree, depth, and range of experience in each of the vital areas detailed there will vary from one professional to another. Nonetheless, each psychiatrist's background, training, and clinical experience uniquely provides him with a certain basis upon which to build for optimal effectiveness in residential treatment.

Child psychiatrists cannot be all things to any given residential facility. Their functions must be incorporated into the treatment process along with those of the other required staff. Due in part to the multifaceted historical development of residential treatment, neither the role nor the most effective utilization of the child psychiatrist in these programs is exactly alike, and each changes considerably depending upon the environmental conditions.

Certainly no child or adolescent should be treated in an intensive manner under residential care without having a complete clinical assessment. This must include the individual and process considerations listed in table 15-1 and involve periodic reviews.

The child psychiatrist should be a primary member of the team that carries out this assessment and plans for the implementation of the required care and treatment. Child psychiatry has grown rapidly as a scientific clinical profession. In the past more attention was paid to the central areas pertaining to physical and psychodynamic examinations, diagnosis, and specific treatment of the individual child. Today, however, the total spectrum of child development, family and group dynamics, education and activities, systems and organizational consultation, environmental influences, and psychopharmacology have all been interwoven. The effort now is to synthesize the totality of psychological, psychobiological, and psychosocial interrelationships and their total effects on mental illness in children and adolescents. Also, biological growth, hereditary, and genetic influences are rapidly becoming a more central part of the child psychiatrist's study.

Advances have been rapid in the development of newer and more effective medications for the emotionally, mentally, or behaviorally disturbed child or adolescent as well as in the more efficacious usage of older ones. This newer knowledge has brought a great deal of help to many suffering patients, help that has resulted in an increase in the overall effectiveness of many aspects of residential treatment. These advances have carried with them an ever more vital role for the child psychiatrist. His knowledge of new psychopharmacological treatments now combines with the special psychobiological, dynamic, and developmental training and experiences he has had with young people. The mix forms a powerful therapeutic instrument, one whose efficacy is sure to continue to advance.

Psychopharmacological treatments must be injected by the psychiatrist into the residential milieu with painstaking skill, in close cooperation with other staff members. Just as in any medical practice, the well-known "placebo" effect and newly discovered side effects must be considered. In residential treatment, however, these effects often become more significant, in that they join with many other salient considerations, including staff and patient prejudices (for example, consideration of a drug as "the golden pill" that cures all, leading to overusage and eventual frustration, or flagrant misconceptions that medications have only harmful effects on the mind and behavior, which leads to underusage and resentment). Various negative transference reactions tend to occur based on ambivalent and conflicting feelings that the "medicine man" knows all or thinks he does, or inappropriate and disruptive dependencies are attached to the omnipotent man with the "black bag" or the "couch." Finally, there are ingrained institutional therapeutic philosophical differences which play no small role in the way treatment works. The psychobiological and psychopharmacological knowledge of the child psychiatrist must be worked into a harmonious blend with the differing orientations, attitudes, and responsibilities of other staff members. Clearly these considerations place the child psychiatrist in an important position. However, by no means do they define his total role, authority, or responsibilities. These must be determined individually by each residential treatment facility.

Today many such facilities claim to be "psychiatric" yet have only token psychiatric input. Other residential centers have tried to obtain psychiatric participation only to find that the contributing child psychiatrist would participate only minimally. Often enough, he has little comprehension of the total therapeutic program, or of his own role, authority, or responsibilities. Worst of all, sometimes he hardly knows the children or adolescents or whom he supposedly had accepted medical responsibility. None of these circumstances should exist. Residential treatment facilities and child psychiatrists must work together to avoid these occurrences; outside agencies that perhaps do not know the fundamental principles according to which residential treatment best functions cannot monitor the psychiatrist's participation.

Sometimes child psychiatrists are overall directors of residential units and bring their wide range of administrative and clinical knowledge to the entire facility. In other cases, the child psychiatrist has more specialized clinical functions. A serious problem in residential treatment, one that creates major programmatic disruptions and often impedes therapeutic effectiveness, is the lack of clear operational definitions for the work of those child psychiatrists who serve as clinical consultants. Their responsibility for patient care is often totally ambiguous. While this type of confusion should never exist, it has in fact proliferated, as more regulations regarding clinical accountability, quality assurance, and criteria for funding have been promulgated. Every residential treatment facility, along with the child psychiatrists, should make definitive and accurate determinations about who is accountable for what. In policies, procedures, and especially practices, a clear delineation of medical responsibility and authority is needed as well as a definition of the administrative or other programmatic participation of the child psychiatrist. These, along with all the other necessary staff functions, should blend with and complement the most effective care and treatment programs.

CHILD-CARE FUNCTIONS

Child care has emerged in residential treatment as the final chapter in a history of ancillary parenting, which includes foster parents, cottage parents, and group living. In child care there has been a progressive development from institutionalization to humanization, and an emphasis on individual and group care. As knowledge of early child development increased, an understanding of the crucial role of mastery of early motor skills,

simple self-help methods, and body functions grew rapidly.

Child-care workers initially took care of the important daily living requirements, such as handling appropriate clothing and dressing skills, toileting, and sleeping routines. From these came additional valuable child-care functions and responsibilities, most often carried out under the supervision of professional clinicians—for example, adequate general health monitoring and care, specific personal hygiene skills and habits, and nutritious child-oriented meals and snacks.

Dynamic perspectives began to emphasize the importance of psychosexual progress for young children, and the vicissitudes of their dependency-independency-mutual interdependency struggles. These ushered in a recognition of the vital role of child-care workers; for many children, the workers' close understanding and consistently effective personal response formed the basis of their first continuing, trusting relationship. This laid the cornerstone for object constancy, adequate reality testing, age-appropriate adaptive behavior, and progressive maturation. The child-care worker thus became instrumental in providing the seriously disturbed young person a central object to interact with and to react to and against as developmentally necessary.

Child care is rapidly becoming an organized clinical discipline. It is "professionalizing" around the broadening base of a constellation of functions involving critical care and habilitation. As such, it parallels the emergence of other "paraprofessional" mental health workers. In residential treatment, the child-care worker often occupies a position in relation to the young patient of nurturance, nursing, primary caretaker, teacher and guidance counselor, social engineer and conflict resolver, therapist and nontherapist, older sib, adult companion and rival, and, in varying degrees, the authority, judge, interpretor of society and the "establishment." These workers serve as primary caretaker and go-between, they do and have others do, and they manipulate and are manipulated. Evidently, the child-care worker has a variety of functions; additionally, his judgments, values, and perceptions all could produce a positive or negative therapeutic impact on the seriously disturbed young patient.

Within different settings, child-care workers are utilized in widely diverse fashions. Equally diverse is their background and training within the field. In some settings, these workers come solely from the clinical mental health professional disciplines. In others, they come from different backgrounds and varieties of experience, such as foster parents, teachers, or caring nonprofessional adults. When a residential treatment setting is formally organized around a particular or mental health orientation, the child-caring staff tend to be represented by more formally designated disciplines; thus in the child psychiatric hospital these activities fall to the child psychiatric nurses and their aides; in the therapeutic residential school, to teachers, counselors, and teachers' aides.

Some deem it unfair to include child psychiatric nursing in the same discussion as child care. This is an unfortunate and short-sighted view, since not only does child psychiatric nursing belong within the realm of child care, it also offers many specialized medical, theoretical, and clinical management dimensions that are of singular importance in residential treatment. A collaborative blending of the specialized medical and child psychiatric nursing skills with the essential elements of child-care attitudes and methods holds forth enormous promise. In fact, the residential treatment field sorely needs many more child-trained nurses. Psychiatric nurses, and particularly child psychiatric nurses who have developed their clinical skills within the framework indicated in table 15-1, are of critical importance. Their valuable contributions should be more widely available to residential treatment facilities and to disturbed children.

As things stand, the majority of residential treatment facilities provide child-care functions out of an amalgam of professional and paraprofessional disciplines. Today the work of child care is becoming more and more demanding; it is in fact, central to the effectiveness of residential treatment. From this treatment have developed many outstanding theories and practices.

Among the child-care workers primary functions within residential treatment are the making of skilled observations around the clock and the consistent accurate analysis and interpretation of these data. Without these, residential treatment loses much of its special advantage as an assessment and therapeutic resource. All recorded observations of the young patient, whether administrative in nature or clinical, are the *sine qua non* of the therapeutic planning processes. Such information should include: verbal and kinetic behavior, both spontaneous and reactive, and cognitive processes, including thought content and judgments. The important staff inferences drawn from these observations must also be noted. These might detail: developmental levels and the age-appropriateness of the responses; resistances and their origins—symbolic, cultural, value-derived; conscious and unconscious fantasies; and transferences—to individuals, groups, objects, environment, and the total institution.

Emphasis must also be placed on the skills required for effective communication and organizational responsiveness. These include the capacity to work with a wide range of staff disciplines, to cope with administrative requirements, and to make use of resource persons and organizations outside the facility, including both families and significant others. Obviously, those staff members who function in a child-care capacity cannot be totally confined to a single clinical prescription or administrative directive. They must have the knowledge, autonomy, and flexibility to translate goal-oriented treatment plans into operational methods. Knowing who, when, what, where, and how not to do are equally essential. Last, knowing the significance of appropriate and timely communications of all of these considerations to other residential treatment staff often makes the difference between a positive and a negative outcome.

Administrative Functions

An analysis of the history and the implications of the fundamental concerns outlined in table 15-1, along with the other specific criteria set forth in this chapter, can elucidate many of the important pieces of the puzzle of residential treatment. However, skillful and effective administrative work is necessary to bring them together as an efficient working entity. This in turn must be related in the most efficacious manner possible to the population to be directly served, the families and significant others, the gallery of outside resources, and the vast and ever-changing influences of the community at large.

Such an administrative structure is usually developed around either of two models. One involves a specifically qualified and trained professional administrative staff, and the other a staff with more diverse administrative and clinical backgrounds which functions according to specialized guidelines. A great deal has been written about these two sides of the same coin. Organizational considerations exert major influences on the total picture of residential treatment, and it is clear that the administrative staff and its functions must be coordinated and integrated with the work of the clinical staff members and their functions. It is essential to delegate special duties according to a well-organized plan. Lacking this, a number of complications is possible. Considerable coordination and teamwork is always required. In work with adolescents, this is particularly demanding since their return to a responsible place in society is often fraught with many variables that are outside the control of the residential treatment staff.

Administration deals with interrelated issues which involve complex inside and outside processes. Administrative personnel often serve as the bridges between the community and the residential treatment as a whole. Thus they become the intermediary between internal affairs involving many clinical and maintenance activities and numerous ongoing outside community changes and influences.

Many laws, regulations, standards, funding guidelines, and other outside mandates must be interpreted and compiled with. In order to achieve the necessary complience, additional and often laborious synchronized administrative and clinical work becomes important. There will be times when meeting certain conditions will be deemed inappropriate or even contrary to well-established operational or clinical practices. On such occasions, major efforts must be directed to influence the sources of such inappropriate regulating and controlling forces.

Administration also involves acting as go-between for the staff and the agency's governing body; this too may be quite complex. At times the actual existence of the residential treatment facility rests upon this interaction; at other times, major clinical decisions and responsibilities are at stake. Administrative and clinical authority and responsibilities must be carefully integrated. The residential treatment facility needs a real measure of autonomy. It needs a sufficient measure of organizational authority and independence from its parent body, the many funding sources, community agencies, governmental and judicial controls, mental health discipline politics, and other so-called "jurisdictions" with which it deals. Only then is the administrative-clinical staff most effective in making the necessary decisions for the benefit of its seriously disturbed young patients.

Termination and Follow Up

Aftercare

Advance administrative and clinical planning for follow up is part of the provision of aftercare. Certain considerations are sometimes overlooked.

The young person needs the sense of continuity of care. Also, the "culture shock" of residential treatment termination needs to be minimized. At discharge, the young patient often regresses because he is leaving a protected environment, one where new skills were learned and old problems resolved. The patient has changed, and his individual needs are new. Likewise the "old environment" has changed, and there are different resources to be utilized. The farther the young person was moved from his old environment during residential treatment and the greater the growth and changes, the more different the outside may seem to him, and he to the "outsiders"—family, peers, schools. Changes too have occurred in the young person's relationships to dependency and authority, and in many of his need-gratifying activities. Predischarge planning and strategy sessions with the young person, the family, and significant others, along with preliminary visits and increased community involvements, are helpful. Also, specially trained aftercare and follow-up personnel attached to the center are invaluable. Families often need as much help in establishing new and healthier relations as do the young patient. Sometimes the gaps that previously existed or the new ones to be dealt with are simply too much to be resolved. Other community resources can be used in these cases. The availability of halfway houses, foster placement, boarding schools, or other self-sustaining individual living arrangements are vital. Unfortunately, these latter are all too often scarce and their arrangement demands considerable effort. Liaison with community resources —including the great chain of educational, vocational, and judicial systems, outpatient clinics and day-treatment programs, and privately practicing clinicians—helps keep residential treatment optimally aligned with other mental health agencies. This linkage usually works two ways: as a source of ancillary clinical information in evaluating referral to residential treatment and as a vital resource for appropriate disposition planning, aftercare, and follow up. In addition, good community and public relations often play a much needed part in obtaining program necessities, including funding, advocacy, outreach, and increasing public acceptance and awareness·of availability.

Economic Considerations

Since residential treatment varies in so many of its significant aspects, not even a general statement can be made about specific cost factors. The treatment is constantly subject to changes produced by new discoveries, altered conditions within the facilities, and uncontrollable outside influences. Nevertheless, it can be asserted that residential treatment is among the most costly of all child psychiatric treatment methods.

Residential treatment is often condemned—unfairly—for its high cost. The cost must be evaluated in relation to the life-long damage to a young person's and a family's mental health that would be evident were this treatment modality deemed clinically necessary but not provided. Continuing efforts are required to improve all areas of cost efficiency and therapeutic efficaciousness, and, where possible, to develop less intensive treatment methods that do not compromise outcome. The total field of residential treatment provides a fertile ground for research; in particular, outcome studies are of critical importance. However, all such studies also carry a price. While many improvements have occurred in the important fiscal-to-clinical relationship, significant distortions have also been created.

At this time, most of the efforts to develop financial accountability have pursued greater specificity of cost-to-outcome relationships. Unfortunately, these are often modeled upon inappropriate definitions borrowed from therapeutic endeavors not truly equivalent to residential treatment. Realistic cost formulas for the determination of financial responsibility, reimbursement, or cost-sharing arrangements need to be developed and continuously reviewed. All such approaches must take into account the necessary specific treatments,—for example, psychotherapy—as well as all other required therapeutic processes,—for example, milieu therapy, special and remedial education, therapeutic recreation, and the full range of activity programs.

Outcome

While there has been a good deal of follow up of individual children and adolescents who had been in residential treatment, a search of the literature for systematic scientific outcome studies of sufficiently large groups is disappointing. With only a few exceptions, findings in this most important area have not yet been sufficiently documented to allow for reliable comparison and adequate evaluative studies. Most often, the benefits of this modality are recorded only in the obscure clinical rec-

ord, indelibly in the hearts and minds of the providers of the service, and in the uncertain awareness of the child, family, and significant others who have benefited.

Neither the successes nor the failures of residential treatment can be definitively tallied. They are subject to numerous variables, such as clinical criteria of objectives and goals, definitions of outcome, extraneous events during and after treatment, availability and changes of necessary outside supporting resources, and, finally, society's precariously changing attitudes, values, and demands.

When dealing with young people, the problems inherent in any systematic follow-up study are magnified. Those persons doing follow-up studies must take responsibility for accumulating, analyzing, and publishing data which will be of continuing benefit both to other young people with serious problems, and to those working to help them. In addition to requesting information from the young person and family, it is often necessary to request information from other sources and institutions. Both those asking for the information and those providing it must ponder the issues of confidentiality and patient's rights.

In recent years, there has been more awareness and acceptance of the need to analyze and document outcome findings. This has served both the advancement of knowledge and the demand for accountability. Increasingly sophisticated data collection systems and methods will add an important dimension to the ever-increasing knowledge of results. These technological advances will become increasingly important. Concomitantly, the individual rights of those involved will need to be considered and adequate safeguards developed.

Distribution of Services

Residential treatment facilities exist throughout the United States. However, it would be pointless to detail their specific locations or to offer numbers, for there are simply too many differences in the populations they serve, their program orientations, the characteristic emphasis in their milieus and environments, and the varieties of therapeutic services they provide. When residential facilities are counted and located, one ends up with a morass of descriptions, titles, and localities. No single nomenclature covers either what they are called or what they call themselves and much less what they do best. General descriptive information is available about the many programs which fall under the overall rubric of residential treatment. When placement of any seriously disturbed young person is being considered, such data should be consulted. There is, however, no substitute for securing first-hand information about the specific program.

Proximity to the individual child or adolescent's family and community is often a critical factor; it provides essential outside support and continuity of care. In certain cases, however, a degree of geographic separation of the young patient from his original environment may be of significant benefit. This is especially true for adolescents, particularly those with histories of long-standing delinquency. In these cases, a complete environmental change with attendant dramatic alterations in expectable and acceptable patterns of thinking, values, and behavior (and sometimes even the "last resort" before the "end of the line" phenomena) can bring about significant therapeutic changes. These considerations should always be a well-though-out part of the total clinical plan. Sending a child away should never be used as a "discard" practice, nor derived from a veiled punitive, threatening "or else" orientation; such maneuvers are likely to compound previous pathological experiences and ultimately end in further failures.

The real problem for the field of residential treatment consists of the intricate and difficult task of locating the right facility for the seriously disturbed young person. Appropriate psychiatric treatment facilities may include psychiatric hospitals therapeutic schools, reality and work-oriented milieus, wilderness groups, "hospital without walls," and many others. At the same time there are enormous variations in the patterns of needs presented by seriously disturbed young people. As a result, the matching of these for the most efficacious and least costly therapeutic outcome remains a most demanding challenge. This is not, however, too different from the agonizing and costly efforts to bring together the patient with a seriously damaged heart and other life-threatening complications and the right specialist team in the right cardiac facility.

In the past all too many seriously disturbed young people went without available corrective help or were mistreated or misplaced. Today a "great step" forward must be achieved in grasping the implications of residential treatment. This must be accomplished by child psychiatrists and by all others involved with the mental health of young people. Thus, further clarification is needed concerning the therapeutic characteristics and programs, along with the many practical details that pertain to each residential treatment program. An equally forthright detailing of the nature of the disturbances of the young persons best served is also necessary. And, finally, a much broader integration and dissemination of this information is basic to future progress.

ACKNOWLEDGMENT

The author appreciates the collaborative work of Margaret A. Murphy of Chicago, Illinois, which was invaluable in the development of this chapter.

REFERENCES

1. AICHORN, A., *Wayward Youth*, Viking Press, New York, 1925.
2. ALLERHAND, M. E., et al., *Adaptation and Adaptability: The Bellefaire Follow-up Study*, Child Welfare League of America, New York, 1966.
3. ALT, H., "The Concept of Success in Residential Treatment—An Administrator's View," *Child Welfare*, 43:423–426, 430, 1964.
4. ———, *Residential Treatment for the Disturbed Child: Basic Principles in Planning and Design of Programs and Facilities*, International Universities Press, New York, 1961.
5. American Psychiatric Association, *Standards for Psychiatric Facilities Serving Children and Adolescents*, American Psychiatric Association, Washington, D.C., 1971.
6. ANTHONY, E. J., and KOUPERNIK, C. (Eds.), *The Child in His Family*, Wiley-Interscience, New York, 1970.
7. BEHRENS, M. L., and GOLDFARB, W., "A Study of Patterns of Interaction of Families of Schizophrenic Children in Residential Treatment," *American Journal of Orthopsychiatry*, 28:300–312, 1958.
8. BENDER, L., *Child Psychiatric Techniques*, Charles C Thomas, Springfield, Ill., 1952.
9. BERLIN, I. N. (Ed.), *Bibliography of Child Psychiatry*, The American Academy of Child Psychiatry, Human Sciences Press, New York, 1976.
10. ———, and CHRIST, A. E., "The Unique Role of the Child Psychiatry Trainee on an Inpatient or Day Care Unit," *Journal of the American Academy of Child Psychiatry*, 8:247–258, 1969.
11. BETTELHEIM, B., *A Home for the Heart*, Knopf, New York, 1974.
12. ———, "The Director's View," *American Journal of Orthopsychiatry*, 28:256–265, 1958.
13. ———, *Love Is Not Enough*, Free Press, Glencoe, Ill., 1950.

14. ——, and SYLVESTER, E., "Milieu Therapy: Indications and Illustrations," *Psychoanalytic Review, 36:* 54–68, 1949.

15. BOATMAN, M. J., PAYNTER, J., and PARSONS, C., "Nursing in Hospital Psychiatric Therapy for Psychotic Children," *American Journal of Orthopsychiatry, 32:*808–817, 1962.

16. BRADLEY, C., "Indications for Residential Treatment of Children with Severe Neuropsychiatric Problems," *American Journal of Orthopsychiatry, 19:*427–431, 1949.

17. Center for Urban Studies, University of Chicago, *Population of Children's Residential Institutions in the United States,* Project on Physical Facilities for Group Care of Children, Project no. 3, 1968.

18. Child Welfare League of America, *From Chaos to Order: A Collective View of the Residential Treatment of Children,* Child Welfare League of America, New York, 1972.

19. ——, *Standards for Services for Child Welfare Institutions,* Child Welfare League of America, New York, 1964.

20. ——, *Annotated Bibliography, Residential Treatment of Emotionally Disturbed Children,* Child Welfare League of America, New York, 1952.

21. CHRIST, A. E., and WAGNER, N. N., "Residential Treatment. Iatrogenic Factors in Residential Treatment: The Psychiatric Team's Contribution to Continued Psychopathology," *Americal Journal of Orthopsychiatry, 35:*451–461, 1965.

22. COHEN, R. L., CHARNY, I. W., and LEMBKE, P., "Parental Expectations as a Force in Treatment: The Identification of Unconscious Parental Productions onto the Children's Psychiatric Hospital," *Archives of General Psychiatry, 4:*471–478, 1961.

23. D'AMATO, G., *Residential Treatment for Child Mental Health,* Charles C Thomas, Springfield, Ill., 1969.

24. DAVIDS, A., "Personality and Attitudes of Child Care Workers, Psychotherapists, and Parents of Children in Residential Treatment," *Child Psychiatry and Human Development, 1:*41, 1970.

25. ——, and SALVATORE, P. D., "Residential Treatment of Disturbed Children and Adequacy of their Subsequent Adjustment: A Follow-up Study," *American Journal of Orthopsychiatry, 46:*62–73, 1976.

26. *Directory of Facilities for Mentally Ill Children in the United States,* The National Association for Mental Health, New York, 1967.

27. EASSON, W. M., *The Severely Disturbed Adolescent,* International Universities Press, New York, 1969.

28. EISSLER, K. R. (Ed.), *Searchlights on Delinquency,* International Universities Press, New York, 1949.

29. EKSTEIN, R., *Children of Time and Space,* Appleton-Century-Crofts, New York, 1966.

30. ——, WALLERSTEIN, J., and MANDELBAUM, A., "Countertransference in the Residential Treatment of Children," in Eissler, R. S., et al. (Eds.), *The Psychoanalytic Study of the Child,* vol. 14, pp. 186–218, International Universities Press, New York, 1959.

31. ELKIN, R., and CORMICK, D., *Analyzing Costs in a Residential Group Care Facility for Children,* Child Welfare League of America, New York, 1969.

32. FRAIBERG, S., "Some Aspects of Residential Casework with Children," *Social Casework, 37:*159–167, 1956.

33. FREUD, A., and BURLINGHAM, D. T., *Infants Without Families,* International Universities Press, New York, 1973.

34. ——, and DANN, S., "An Experiment in Group Upbringing," in Eissler, R. S., et al. (Eds.), *The Psychoanalytic Study of the Child,* vol. 6, pp. 127–168, International Universities Press, New York, 1951.

35. GAIR, D. S., and SALOMON, A. D., "Diagnostic Aspects of Psychiatric Hospitalization of Children," *American Journal of Orthopsychiatry, 32:*445–461, 1962.

36. GLASSER, W., *Reality Therapy,* Harper & Row, New York, 1965.

37. GOLDFARB, W., *Growth and Change of Schizophrenic Children: A Confidential Study,* Winston, Washington, D.C., 1974.

38. ——, and GOLDFARB, N., "Evaluation of Behavioral Changes in Schizophrenic Children in Residential Treatment," *American Journal of Psychotherapy, 19:*185–204, 1965.

39. GOLDSMITH, J. M., *The Communication of Clinical Information in a Residential Treatment Setting,* Casework Papers, Family Service Association of America, New York, 1955.

40. ——, SCHULMAN, R., and GROSSBARD, H., "Integrating Clinical Processes with Planned Living Experiences," *American Journal of Orthopsychiatry, 24:*280–290, 1954.

41. GOOD, L. R., SIEGEL, S. M., and BAY, A. P., *Therapy by Design. Implications for Architecture for Human Behavior,* Charles C Thomas, Springfield, Ill., 1965.

42. HAGAMEN, M. B., "Family-Support Systems, Their Effect on Long-Term Psychiatric Hospitalizations in Children," *Journal of the American Academy of Child Psychiatry, 16:*53–66, 1977.

43. HARRISON, S. I., and BURKS, H. L., "Some Aspects of Grouping in a Children's Psychiatric Hospital," *American Journal of Orthopsychiatry, 34:*148–152, 1964.

44. ——, McDERMOTT, J. F., JR., and CHETHIK, M., "Residential Treatment of Children: The Psychotherapist Administrator," *Journal of the American Academy of Child Psychiatry, 8:*385–409, 1969.

45. HIRSCHBERG, J. C., and MANDELBAUM, A., "Problems of Administration and Supervision in an Inpatient Treatment Center for Children," *Bulletin of the Menninger Clinic, 21:*208–219, 1957.

46. HYLTON, L. F., *The Residential Treatment Center—Children, Programs, and Costs,* Child Welfare League of America, New York, 1964.

47. INGLIS, D., *Authority and Reality in Residential Treatment,* Child Welfare League of America, New York, 1954.

48. Joint Commission on Accreditation of Hospitals, *Accreditation Manual for Psychiatric Facilities Serving Children and Adolescents,* Joint Commission on Accreditation of Hospitals, Chicago, 1974.

49. JONES, M., *Beyond the Therapeutic Community: Social Learning and Social Psychiatry,* Yale University Press, New Haven, 1968.

50. ——, *The Therapeutic Community,* Basic Books, New York, 1953.

51. KONOPKA, G., "Implications of A Changing Residential Treatment Program," *American Journal of Orthopsychiatry, 31:*17–39, 1961.

52. ——, "Institutional Treatment of Emotionally Disturbed Children," *Crime and Delinquency, 8(1),* 1962.

53. KRUG, O., "Application of Principles of Child Psychotherapy in Residential Treatment," *American Journal of Psychiatry, 108:*695–700, 1952.

54. LANDER, J., and SCHULMAN, R., "The Impact of the Therapeutic Milieu on the Disturbed Personality," *Social Casework, 41:*227–234, 1960.

55. LEVY, E. Z., "Long-term Follow-up of Former Inpatients in the Children's Hospital of Menninger Clinic," *American Journal of Psychiatry, 125:*47–53, 1969.

56. LINN, L. S., "Measuring the Effectiveness of Mental Hospitals," *Hospital and Community Psychiatry, 21:*381, 1970.

57. McDERMOTT, J. F., JR., FRAIBERG, S., and HARRISON, S. I., "Residential Treatment of Children: The Utilization of Transference Behavior," *Journal of the American Academy of Child Psychiatry, 7:*169–192, 1968.

58. McTAGGERT, A. N., "The Psychiatric Care of Children in a Teaching Hospital," *Canadian Psychiatric Association Journal, 10:*332, 1965.

59. MAIER, H. W. (Ed.), *Group Work as Part of*

Residential Treatment, National Association of Social Workers, New York, 1965.

60. Marsden, G., McDermott, J. F., Jr., and Minor, D., "Selection of Children for Residential Treatment: A Study of Evaluation Procedures and Decision-making," *Journal of the American Academy of Child Psychiatry*, 16:427–438, 1977.

61. Masterson, J. F., *Treatment of the Borderline Adolescent*, Wiley-Interscience, New York, 1972.

62. Mayer, M. F., and Matsushima, J., "Training for Child Care Work: Report on a National Conference," *Child Welfare 59(9)*, 1969.

63. Mitchell, H. E., and Mudd, E. H., "Anxieties Associated with the Conduct of Research in a Clinical Setting," *American Journal of Orthopsychiatry*, 27:310, 1957.

64. Moller, C. B., *Architectural Environment and Our Mental Health*, Horizon Press, New York, 1968.

65. Noshpitz, J. D., "Training the Psychiatrist in Residential Treatment," *Journal of the American Academy of Child Psychiatry*, 6:25–37, 1967.

66. ———, "Notes on the Theory of Residential Treatment," *Journal of the American Academy of Child Psychiatry*, 1:284–296, 1962.

67. Perkins, G. L., "The Consultant's View," *American Journal of Orthopsychiatry*, 28:266–275, 1958.

68. Petrick, A. C., and Godbout, R. A., "Graduate Collegiate Education in Nursing in Child Psychiatry," *American Journal of Orthopsychiatry*, 32:794, 1962.

69. Polsky, H., *Cottage Six: The Social System of Delinquent Boys in Residential Treatment*, Russell Sage Foundation, New York, 1962.

70. *Profiles on Children*, White House Conference on Children, United States Printing Office, Washington, D.C., 1970.

71. Provence, S., and Lipton, R., *Infants in Institutions*, International Universities Press, New York, 1962.

72. Rabinovitch, R. D., "Observations on the Differential Study of Severely Disturbed Children," *American Journal of Orthopsychiatry*, 22:230–236, 1952.

73. Rabinow, B., "An Agenda for Educators Working with the Emotionally Disturbed in Residential Settings," *American Journal of Orthopsychiatry*, 31(3), 1961.

74. Redl, F., "The Concept of a 'Therapeutic Milieu,' " *American Journal of Orthopsychiatry*, 29:721–736, 1959.

75. ———, "A Strategy and Technique of the Life-Space Interview," *American Journal of Orthopsychiatry*, 29:1–18, 1959.

76. ———, and Wineman, D., *The Aggressive Child*, Free Press, Glencoe, Ill., 1963.

77. Reid, J. H., and Hagan, H. R., *Residential Treatment Centers for Emotionally Disturbed Children: A Descriptive Study*, Child Welfare League of America, New York, 1952.

78. Riley, M. J., "The Child Care Worker's View," *American Journal of Orthopsychiatry*, 28:283–288, 1958.

79. Rinsley, D. B., "Psychiatric Hospital Treatment: With Specific Reference to Children," *Archives of General Psychiatry*, vol. 9, 1963.

80. Robinson, J. F. (Ed.), *Psychiatric Inpatient Treatment of Children*, American Psychiatric Association, Washington, D.C., 1957.

81. Rossman, P. G., and Knesper, D. J., "The Early Phase of Hospital Treatment for Disruptive Adolescents," *Journal of the American Academy of Child Psychiatry*, 15:693–708, 1976.

82. Rousseau, J. J., *Emile; or Education*, Dutton, New York, 1974.

83. Shore, M. F. (Ed.), *Red Is the Color of Hurting: Planning for Children in the Hospital*, National Institute of Mental Health, Bethesda, Md., 1965.

84. Stanton, A. H., and Schwartz, M. S., *The Mental Hospital*, Basic Books, New York, 1954.

85. Szurek, S. A., "Dynamics of Staff Interaction in Hospital Psychiatric Treatment," *American Journal of Orthopsychiatry*, 17:2815–2857, 1947.

86. ———, Berlin, I. N., and Boatman, M. J. (Eds.), *Inpatient Care for the Psychotic Child*, Science and Behavior Books, Palo Alto, Calif., 1971.

87. Toussieng, P. W., "The Role of Education in a Residential Treatment Center for Children," *Mental Hygiene, 45*:543–551, 1961.

88. Treffert, D. A., McAndrew, J. B., and Dreifurst, P., "An Inpatient Treatment Program and Outcome for 57 Autistic and Schizophrenic Children," *Journal of Autism and Childhood Schizophrenia, 3*:138–153, 1973.

89. Trieschman, A. E., Whittaker, J. K., and Brendtro, L. K., *The Other 23 Hours*, Aldine Publishing Company, Chicago, 1969.

90. Wallin, P., and Koch, M., "The Use of Goal Attainment Scaling as a Method of Evaluating Clinical Outcome in an Inpatient Child Psychiatry Service," *Journal of the American Academy of Child Psychiatry*, 16:439–445, 1977.

91. Winnicott, D. W., "Children's Hostels in War and Peace," *British Journal of Medical Psychology*, 21:175–180, 1948.

92. ———, and Britton, C., *Residential Management as Treatment for Difficult Children*, vol. 1, Human Relations, London, 1947.

93. Wollin, M., "Some Theory and Practice in Child Care: A Cross-Cultural View," *Child Welfare, 52(8)*, 1963.

94. Wright, B., "The Psychologist's View," *American Journal of Orthopsychiatry*, 28:276–282, 1958.

95. Young, D. R. (Ed.), *The Directory for Exceptional Children*, 7th Ed., Porter Sargent, Boston, 1972.

16 / Hospital Treatment of the Adolescent

David Zinn

Psychiatric hospitals have always admitted adolescent patients, but the development of programs for the special needs of youth has been a relatively recent phenomenon. Early reports described special programs for adolescents at Bellevue,[14] at Michael Reese Hospital,[26] in Britain,[10, 112] at the University of Michigan,[41] and at the C. F. Menninger Hospital.[72] Subsequently, there has been a dramatic increase both in the number of adolescents referred for hospitalization and in the population actually resident there. This increase has been coincident with a decrease in total admissions and shorter lengths of stay for adults. As a result, adolescents are occupying a larger proportion of hospital beds than was true just a few years ago.[101] This increased use of hospitalization has been attributed to one or more of several factors; it is not clear to what extent each plays a role. Among these factors are: increased professional appreciation of adolescent psychopathology; difficulties in working with adolescents as outpatients; an increase in symptomatic behavior within the adolescent population (this, in turn, may well reflect increasing social stress, earlier puberty, and a possible increase in the number of vulnerable young people entering adolescence); or merely increased bed availability.

Despite this trend, however, treatment of adolescents in hospital facilities is currently the focus of controversy. Insurance companies increasingly question hospital stays longer than a few days; they find support for their position in some segments of professional opinion. The revision of mental health laws is extending to the adolescent the right to object to voluntary placement by his parent; the consequent involvement of the courts, in the treatment process can be demoralizing to parents and physicians alike. Hospital administrators are concerned about the often turbulent behavior of the hospitalized adolescent, the wear and tear on physical facilities, and the expense of the necessary special programming. Taken in aggregate, these factors make it difficult to treat the adolescent in the hospital and to administer and maintain such treatment programs. This should not obscure the fact that these measures, painfully evolved over the past two decades, have an important place in psychiatric intervention with certain types of disturbed adolescents. It does underscore, however, that hospitalization, like any medical intervention, should be a thoughtful, carefully considered process.

The term "hospital" is used here to refer to programs in a variety of facilities which include general, state, and private psychiatric hospitals. This can be confusing, especially when contrasted with "residential treatment," which is addressed in chapters 14 and 15. Indeed, those involved in environmental programs for adolescents have discovered that regardless of *locus* (that is, a Joint Commission on Accreditation of Hospitals–accredited "hospital" or some other type of facility) adolescents do best in programs which: promote productive activity and interpersonal involvement, are allied with the strengths of the individual young people, and provide as age-appropriate an experience as possible. One could argue that hospitalization and residential treatment of adolescents are fundamentally more alike than they are different, and that such differences as do exist have more to do with institutional traditions, resources, and ambiance than with program substance. Nevertheless, the hospital facility, with its wide range of adolescents with severe difficulties and its theoretical eclecticism, is a distinct entity within the spectrum of mental health work with adolescents.

Hospitalization and Adolescent Psychopathology

ADOLESCENCE AND ADOLESCENT PSYCHOPATHOLOGY

The term "adolescence" commonly refers to both a chronological age period (usually the teenage years plus or minus a year on either end) and to behavioral immaturity. Phrases such as "the awkward years" and "gangling teenager" suggest an image of adolescence as a time of transition, of disjointedness between body and spirit, of a painful struggle to become adult. This view is a misleading one, however. Adults tend to view adolescents stereotypically; and these stereotypes influence adolescent behavior, hence confirming the popular conception.[4] Research with normal adolescent populations indicates that the view of adolescence as a time of personal turmoil, behavioral instability, and internal reorganization has been overemphasized, and that adolescent experience and behavior has more organization and stability than the stereotype would suggest.[82] It is difficult to conceptualize this organization, however; unlike much of preadolescent development, adolescence is not so clearly defined in psychobiological terms. It is true that early and middle adolescence are associated with the onset of puberty and subsequent physical maturation.[37] Indeed, a biologically induced "adolescence" is characteristic of human development generally.[30] In Western industrialized society, however, the experience of "adolescence" has expanded to involve much more than an adaptation to puberty and subsequent physical maturation; it has come to encompass the broad process of achieving social maturity. This process, in turn, introduces issues of social attitude and organization. In particular it has brought the opportunities provided by society for growth and mastery into direct consideration in individual development. The psychoanalytic view of adolescence,[7, 29] has emphasized the internal psychological shift from infantile self and object representations to their mature forms accompanied by the development of the capacity to achieve true interpersonal intimacy. Erikson, in particular, uses the term "ego identity" to refer to the individual's organization of a sense of self out of the turbulence of adolescent development.[24] Research on a normal adolescent population, however, suggests that the reality is somewhat different: the autonomy struggles of the contemporary adolescent focus more on superficial than on substantive issues, and the late adolescent moving into young adulthood is fundamentally a more compliant creature than the conventional image would have it. This tends to belie the notion of a true "psychosocial moratorium."[1, 16] For the "normal" (or perhaps, modal) adolescent, then, the substance of adolescent development is embedded in the transactions between the individual young person and social organization and attitude. Social process and individual development are directly and inextricably intertwined. While psychological development in adolescence tends to be thought of in terms of interpersonal maturity, it needs to be emphasized that the adolescent years are characterized equally by maturation in cognitive functioning and the capacity to conceptualize and organize experience.[23, 77] This, in turn influences one's sense of morality and one's view of the world.[50] Adolescent development, in fact, involves maturation in virtually all areas of personality functioning.[37]

One can think of the developmental thrust in adolescence as reflecting two interlocking processes: the internal, physiological "push" of puberty and physical development, and the "pull" of social expectation. Historically, neither of these two processes are stable. The median age of onset of puberty has been consistently declining, a fact insufficiently appreciated in the organization of schools. The present onset age now corresponds to the point at which most young people move from the less demanding and relatively more structured elementary school to the larger and more anonymous junior high. This usually interrupts their passage from latency. It creates extraordinary stress and a particular hazard for the early adolescent.[37] More than that, social expectations and the support patterns for middle and late adolescent development have changed dramatically over the past thirty years. Activities which formerly began at this period, such as scouting and social clubs, are now initiated at an earlier age. By the middle teens, the adolescent is expected to have moved beyond most "youthful" community activities. Simultaneously, there has taken place an erosion of community standards for adolescent behavior; in urban areas particularly, personal conduct is governed largely by individual and family. Police or neighbors become concerned only with flagrant delinquency. For the middle-class late adolescent, social support consists essentially of the colleges, though they, too, have become less structured. There is an ever-increasing pace of change and mobility within the society. Perhaps in response to this, young people are expected to "grow up" more quickly and to function more autonomously at earlier ages. The "freedom" and lack of structure of middle and late adolescence is a two-edged sword: on the one hand, there would appear to be less infantilization and fewer artificial constraints than was previously the case; on the other, there is less aid to growth. In Spartan fashion, the net effect would appear to be a toughening of the well endowed and a further weakening of the vulnerable.[70]

Throughout adolescence, there is an expectation of movement toward more autonomous functioning. This is associated with both progressive and regressive feelings.[4] Ultimately, the adolescent's overall outlook will be determined by the extent to which he feels comfortable with mastery of the developmental challenge. An adolescent with a good sense of self and reasonable social expectations and support will approach the future optimistically. By way of contrast, the adolescent with a poor sense of self who faces confused or unreasonable social expectations and a lack of social support will find it difficult to avoid giving in to the regressive pull. The contemporary adolescent probably has more opportunity and a wider range of means with which to engage in regressive functioning than has heretofore been the case. The minimum means for sustenance are relatively easily obtained, as are drugs and alcohol; a job, on the other hand, can be more difficult to find. As a group, unemployment is higher among adolescents than it is in the population at large; among particularly vulnerable inner-city youth it approaches 50 percent.[87]

The phenomenology of personal difficulty during adolescence is not unique to this age period, though perhaps it is more predictable. Failure to perform well and to achieve personal goals leads to poor self-esteem; this, in turn, engenders feelings of helplessness and vulnerability. These create further problems which perpetuate the cycle. Occasionally, the adolescent experiences the sense of failure as something that occurs within the self and describes it accordingly; more often, however, he is likely to use externalization as a way of preserving self-esteem. Thus, the problem is not in him, but in something or someone else. This defensive attitude is abetted by the developmental thrust away from dependence on adults and the wish to "go it alone" in order to maintain at least the illusion of independence. In addition, the adolescent may have a perceptual set which causes him to see the world as exploitative and noncaring; this then justifies social withdrawal. A sense of alienation, of expecting things to go poorly, protects a vulnerable self from the challenge of a fair test.

The "alienated adolescent" is, however, one version of interpersonal style, a cultural stereotype. Such a formulation does not address the issue of what is reactive to social reality and what reflects a true internal problem likely to result in continuing difficulty. Longitudinal studies of adolescents would tend to support the view that transient anxiety and depression, unassociated with complete withdrawal from significant adults or with major behavior problems, are within the range of normal adolescent development and unlikely to indicate long-term disability. A thought disorder, alienation

from all adults, or significant behavior problems, on the other hand, is associated with continuing difficulty.[65, 75, 82] This research is of considerable significance in modifying earlier stereotypes about the inevitability of "adolescent turmoil." It needs to be noted, however, that all these studies involved relatively small samples; in two cases, relatively homogeneous populations; and, in the sample that was most systematically studied and longest followed, a group selected for their normative adaptation within a stable social milieu. The interrelationship of social structure and adolescent behavior, and the significance within this framework for long-term development of various kinds of adaptation, has not been studied systematically.[17] Continuing difficulties tend to be associated with family disorganization[65] and a history of separations in early childhood.[40] Overall, however, research is somewhat unclear as to long-term prognosis for those cases which constitute the bulk of psychiatric work with adolescents: a young person who is not psychotic, but who is doing poorly in school, not getting along with parents, who is involved with peers, perhaps using some drugs, and who "doesn't want to see a shrink." There is no question but that such young people are not making productive use of their teenage years and feel badly because of it. The optimal site for intervention, however, whether the community and schools, the family, or the individual young person, cannot be stated with certainty.

For most troubled adolescents, the decision to intervene, as well as the extent and type of intervention, must be judged according to a careful evaluation of the stress-vulnerability equation. Such an evaluation must be embedded in an empathic appreciation of both the adolescent's personality and the family and social milieu. Given the enormous variability of adolescent development, the social disorganization experienced by many adolescents, and the imprecision of current concepts of "vulnerability," this task is inherently ambiguous. Ambiguity, however, should provide only minimal difficulty so long as one is guided by a primary concern for the individual young person. It is not the symptom per se which is at issue, but the personal failing, the subsequent impediment to personal growth, and the *inability of the young person to correct the difficulty himself.* The difficulty must be defined from the young person's perspective, and the alliance must be developed around his own particular aspirations and goals. Intervention on behalf of the family or community agency in the interest of "control" may collude with the youth's infantile view of the self and a view of the world as persecutory; presuming a set of values for the adolescent will leave the adolescent with, at best, a feeling of irrelevance, and, at worst, a sense of empty isolation.

Intervention is directed toward helping the young person with the problem underlying his particular difficulty. It may range from exploratory psychotherapy or psychoanalysis aimed at resolving a neurotic fixation, to more direct address to the school, family, and community. The aim is to promote developmental growth by helping the young person with the performance of personal tasks. This presumes an understanding of the full range of possible interferences with functioning difficulties which are essentially environmental; character improverishment resulting from developmental interferences rooted in family or community problems; neurotic symptoms secondary to well-structured internal conflict; learning disorders caused by problems with attention and comprehension; body image problems secondary to socially asynchronous physical development or medical illness; and so forth.

THE ROLE OF THE HOSPITAL

Within the broad spectrum of psychiatric interventions with adolescents, the hospital can offer protection and shelter, containment, and the opportunity to create a therapeutic life space for the young person. Disturbed adolescents adrift in the community are vulnerable to exploitation and physical harm, and the role of shelter and protection in the treatment of symptomatic adolescents should not be minimized. Given the disadvantages of hospitalization, however, this role is hardly sufficient to justify anything other than the briefest stay. Protection and shelter can be offered in a more developmentally appropriate manner and at less expense than in a hospital, for example by temporary foster care or a group home. Containment raises problems as to the practical difficulty of engaging the young person who is alienated from adults, may be on the run, and may be deeply involved in delinquency, drugs, or promiscuous sexuality. None of the interventions of outpatient practice, individual or family therapy, or medication can interrupt the gratifications of an entrenched regressive pattern of behavior. Further, containment can be useful for the psychotic adolescent whose symptoms are too disruptive for his family, and for the suicidal adolescent who cannot be sufficiently stabilized as an outpatient. Containment provides the opportunity to assess

the usefulness of the therapeutic relationship, of medication, and of family and community interventions in dealing with an otherwise alienated adolescent in trouble. Simple containment, however, quickly becomes aversive; and however beneficial such an admission may be initially, the disadvantage of the young person's increasing preoccupation with his "confinement" will quickly make itself evident. It will significantly impair whatever initial alliance may have been developed and may, in fact, give credence to a persecutory view of the world. To deal with this problem, the hospital may add various "activities" intended to make containment appear something else; but the adolescent will easily see through such an approach. A not insignificant portion of the historical difficulties with adolescents in the hospital can be attributed to the fact that activities programs which work well with adults, for example, craft classes and the like, are often viewed by the adolescent as too reminiscent of childhood pursuits. This tends to provoke intense defensive maneuvers against their regressive pull.

CASE ILLUSTRATION

Barbara was an intelligent and articulate sixteen-year-old who was admitted to an adolescent inpatient unit for evaluation of a variety of behavior problems. On the third day of her admission, Barbara was shown through the occupational therapy area, and the occupational therapist explained the various projects which could be undertaken. Barbara became rude to the worker and insisted that she wanted no part of "basket weaving and making ashtrays" despite the fact that these were not among the projects suggested. For the next few days, Barbara refused to return to the occupational therapy area or to talk further with the therapist. She told her physician that she was "into glass blowing" and would like to bring her outfit onto the ward, including butane tanks prohibited by hospital fire regulations. The physician suggested that she talk to the occupational therapist about this, and an opportunity was arranged for Barbara to spend some time in the chemistry department's glass shop and to report on these activities to the occupational therapist. Barbara followed this suggestion enthusiastically; the initially defensive maneuver was dealt with, and the youngster's interests channeled in an adaptive manner. During her subsequent treatment, she told her psychotherapist much later that the occupational therapy projects reminded her of "summer camp and junior high school."

Finally, hospitalization offers the opportunity to create a therapeutic life space for the young person, an environment which is responsible to his particular developmental problems and needs. Hospitalization is not merely the sum total of a collection of specific interventions; instead, the entire therapeutic program can be integrated in a manner which will develop an alliance both with the treating physician and with the overall *process* of hospitalization. This is particularly useful in the modification of developmentally maladaptive but environmentally syntonic behavior patterns. Hospital programs will vary in the degree to which they emphasize these various roles of hospitalization, and different types of emphasis will be appropriate for various patients. Thus, the combination of hospital-based protection and containment may be most useful for the acutely psychotic patient pending symptomatic response to medication and a supportive environment, whereas containment plus the therapeutic life space are most appropriate for the treatment of character disorders.

In considering the role of the hospital, it should be noted that some referring agencies confuse "placement" with "treatment." The search for "placement" usually involves a primary emphasis on finding an appropriate *environment* for a young person who, for one reason or another, cannot continue to live with his family. Only secondarily does it imply considerations of *individual change*. All too often, social agencies are left with the responsibility for a young person but lack suitable resources to meet his need. They may then attempt to "place" their ward in a hospital, particularly if he is in any way problematic. The hospital may indeed help to determine the best environment for the youth's ultimate disposition, or it may be able to help out in a crisis. Hospital treatment, however, should focus on active interventions which would correct an individual's difficulties, not on the simple provision of environmental support.

TYPES OF PROGRAMS

The themes of protection, containment, and an active milieu environment are present in all hospital facilities; nonetheless, programs can differ in a variety of important ways. They may emphasize a particular *conceptual approach* for treating adolescent psychopathology (individual psychodynamic, family, behavioral, and so forth); they may be thought of according to *predominant length of stay* (acute, intermediate, long-term); they may be thought of according to *locus of treatment* (general hospital, private psychiatric hospital, state hospital); a program may organize its milieu around a particular *age group* within the adolescent period (early or late adolescence); the program may be *"open"* or *"closed"* or both. The program may *mix* the adolescents with adult patients or it may physically *separate* the adolescent from the general patient population. The diversity of programs reflects the complexity of adolescent psychopathology and attests to the fact that no one treatment approach will be appropriate for every patient.

The typical adolescent entering a hospital program is likely to display a considerable degree of alienation and a high level of symptomatic behavior. This leads to the general assumption that in the initial stages of treatment, adolescents need to be maintained in "closed" settings. In theory, a "closed" setting is one where the young person's movement and activities are strictly controlled within the confines of the treatment program; in practice, "closed" has come to mean a locked ward and an architecturally restricted environment. This latter connotation gives credence to the frequent confusion between "closed" and "secure." "Closed" should refer to the degree of supervision and intensity of involvement with staff and patients. "Secure," on the other hand, is a term derived from the penal system. It assumes that for social reasons, the facility has an overriding concern in preventing the patients from running away. Parents may confuse "secure" and "closed" and should have this difference explained to them at the time of the young person's admission. In a treatment program, every effort should be made to control impulsivity and delinquent behavior; the efforts to control, however, should not be at the expense of overall treatment goals. It has come to be recognized that "control" of the adolescent centers largely on human relationships and has relatively little to do with locks or security. An adolescent who does not at some level recognize the appropriateness of his admission or who does not feel involved with the staff of the hospital will usually manage to run away from even the most restricted ward. Locked doors may prevent a momentary, impulsive AWOL (an important consideration with some patients), but they will not contain an adolescent determined to leave. Conversely, open settings do not necessarily mean that the young people are continually running away. A more meaningful dimension than open-closed is the degree of community or nonhospital activities in the program. Some settings routinely use "off-ward" facilities such as the public schools or YMCA as parts of the program, and such an approach may be desirable for patients not in need of continual direct supervision.

The historical debate over whether or not to mix adolescents with adult patients should be resolved in terms of which patients do best in which environment. Isolated, highly vulnerable young people, for example patients with an acute exacerbation of chronic schizophrenia, often do best in a mixed setting. The more varied environment offers them a measure of group anonymity while at the same time protects them from the intensity of an adolescent peer group. On the other hand, contact with older, regressed schizophrenics may frighten them about their future prospects. The frequent statement that mixed programs are desirable because of the greater variety of adults with whom the adolescents can relate should be balanced by one's sense of the appropriateness of psychiatric patients as identification models. The involvement of the adolescent in regressive group behavior and the formation of delinquent adolescent groups is more easily prevented in mixed settings; less behavioral disturbance is reported under these conditions.[6] More than that, mixed wards can usually accept a wider range of patients and do not have to be as preoccupied with the issues of group composition that are such important considerations in the all-adolescent milieu, which will be further discussed later in this chapter. On the other hand, amid the diffuse and somewhat anonymous atmosphere of mixed wards, character-disordered young people are often able to continue patterns of regressive acting out simply because the nursing staff is unable to provide the special monitoring and involvement their behavior requires.

CASE ILLUSTRATION

Jane was a seventeen-year-old admitted to a general hospital psychiatric unit following a suicide attempt. She had a history of several years of alienation from parents, of school difficulties, of disturbed peer relationships, and of drug abuse. She remained on this unit for two months, at which time it became apparent to her physician that "nothing was happening"; and she was transferred to an adolescent unit. She became acutely disorganized and intensely upset at the time of the transfer, and this persisted for the first few weeks of her stay on the new ward. Finally she was able to bring herself to admit that throughout her two months on the general unit she had continued to obtain drugs surreptitiously from one of the staff and was simultaneously involved in a sexual relationship with an older patient. The nursing notes from Jane's general hospital stay were reviewed, and there was no indication of her disturbed behavior. The situation was discussed with Jane's original physician and with the conscientious and well-meaning people who comprised the nursing staff. It became apparent that they were neither attuned to nor organized in a way that would have allowed them to supervise Jane and be cognizant of this behavior. Her apparent compliance had been interpreted as a positive response to the milieu program, and her fear

of losing the gratification of her regressive behavior had prevented her from confiding in her psychiatrist.

Mixed adult-adolescent wards are probably preferable for short-term admissions, since frequent turnover in an all-adolescent milieu can be disruptive to group process. The creation of a milieu exclusively for adolescents and the opportunity to develop special programming and staff skills offer definite advantages in the intermediate and long-term treatment of character disorders. There is a strong evidence, however, that adolescents do best in an environment in which at least some of the setting is specifically tailored to their needs.[34] In those cases where adolescents are housed with patients of other ages it is important to develop specifically youth-focused activities programs., for example, an adolescent "day program" or "peer group."

As adolescence is prolonged into the early twenties, its several phases (early, middle, and late) are becoming increasingly distinct.[37] A given program may therefore choose to focus its therapeutic milieu around a particular age group. Although there is an advantage to maintaining some continuity in patient mix through the entire adolescent age range, as a practical matter, middle and late adolescents require a more flexible structure than is appropriate for the younger group. If all ages are to be grouped together, some means of allowing for this must be found.

One way of conceptualizing various types of hospital treatment programs is to consider the interrelationship between adolescent problems and the environments designed to deal with these problems. One can postulate a spectrum; at one end would be the essentially reactive disturbances in young people who have demonstrated adequate capabilities in psychosocial adaptation but who have become severely symptomatic around a particular stress. Ideally, such patients would not require admission to a hospital, as is discussed in chapter 32; but if no more appropriate resource was available, they might be admitted to a facility close to home for a very brief period. Their treatment would emphasize family and social milieu issues and specific coping skills.

Next to be considered is that group of patients who have demonstrated long-term deficiencies in adaptation and whose symptoms appear to be caused by the current interaction with family and social milieu.

CASE ILLUSTRATION

Tanya was a sixteen-year-old seen in a hospital emergency room at the request of parents and police.

She was brought following a fight with her parents in which she had allegedly grabbed a knife and threatened her mother. The difficulty with her parents was precipitated by Tanya's staying away from home for two days. On examination in the emergency room, Tanya presented the typical picture of a highly symptomatic adolescent: on the one hand, she was manifestly troubled, appearing both sad and frightened; on the other, she was resistant to telling her side of the story or talking with the evaluating physician. The parents said that Tanya had always been "a compliant child." Following a precocious puberty at age nine, however, she had become "withdrawn and distant." At thirteen, when Tanya was in seventh grade, medical problems arose with two other members of the family; this resulted in Tanya's effective abandonment within the family group. Later she would tell a clinician that throughout this year she felt "sad and empty." Her school work subsequently deteriorated, and she became involved with drugs. During the next two years she continued to use drugs, and her academic performance was at best marginal. During this period, the parents were too preoccupied with their own difficulties to notice what was happening. Several months prior to Tanya's appearance in the emergency room, the parents came to realize that things "were not right" with her, and they sought psychiatric consultation. On the first occasion, Tanya went for one session but would not return. She refused to see a second psychiatrist at all. Tanya told the emergency room evaluator that she was "sick of shrinks . . . they promise a lot but don't do anything." The evaluator felt that, given Tanya's previous experience and current alienation, any further attempt at outpatient treatment would be useless. He therefore arranged admission to an adolescent inpatient program. Interventions included: individual psychotherapy with a focus on Tanya's disturbed self-concept, parent work focusing on the parents' guilt over withdrawing from Tanya and on more productive ways of relating to her, occasional family sessions to clarify family communication, and a remedial school program. Tanya and her family made rapid gains over several months, and she was discharged to the continuing care of the inpatient psychotherapist. At one year follow up she was continuing in psychotherapy and doing well.

Patients such as Tanya are best served by a hospital stay of intermediate duration, that is, several months to a year or so. The emphasis falls both on helping the young person cope with individual difficulties and attempting to alleviate problems with the family and social milieu.

The third group of patients to be considered manifest chronic difficulties in adaptation; for them family and social milieu issues seem secondary to longstanding, well internalized problems. There are the patients who are most likely to be in long-term psychiatric care and hence for whom the risk of institutional syndromes is highest; ideally they should be treated in as normal an environment as possible, as, for example, partial hospitalization programs or sheltered workshops. Where there are intractable difficulties in maintaining them in the community, however, or where the clinician believes that the internal difficulties can be resolved by intensive treatment in a more controlled environment, long-term inpatient hospital or residential treatment may be indicated. There are conflicting opinions in the literature over the relative merits of closed hospital settings and open residential environments in long-term treatment.[88, 113] The discrepancy between these two points of view appears to have less to do with theoretical treatment issues than with the fact that the term "severely disturbed adolescent" encompasses at least several disorders: discrete developmental fixations and concomitant specific ego defects; multiply traumatized young people with a broad spectrum of ego defects; physiologically defective young people with organic difficulties in impulse control; and essentially unsocialized young people who have grown up in a milieu centered around antisocial behavior and dehumanization. More research is needed to delineate specific interventions for these various problems; it is unwise to generalize about long-term treatment as a unitary treatment modality.

The Process of Hospitalization

ADMISSION

Hospitalization of the adolescent is a significant interruption in normal development. However well intended, it should never be attempted without careful consideration of both the presumed advantages and the possible ill effects. For some difficulties, hospitalization is clearly an important part of the treatment. It is, however, potentially stigmatizing; it may damage a young person's self-esteem, coping capacity, and subsequent identity formation; and it is expensive in terms of both money and professional effort. The decision to hospitalize an adolescent should be based on a clear judgment that he has a *significant problem* which he *cannot correct himself* and which is *not amenable to a less intensive and less developmentally disruptive intervention*. There should be a *reasonable expectation that the admission will help the young person cope more adequately*.

If possible, the appropriateness of admission should be evaluated prior to hospitalization. Occasionally, truly life-threatening situations justify short-term admissions for the purposes of "control." Such an admission, however, should be the exception rather than the rule. As noted in chapter 32, crisis intervention should be attempted on an outpatient basis for a few days. If nothing else, this will provide both the individual and the family an opportunity to demonstrate their capacity to deal with the situation on their own and will permit an evaluation independent of the invariably distorting influence of hospitalization. Once removed from his home, the very fact of admission can alter the young person's concerns in a way that makes it difficult to assess actual adaptive problems in the community.

In the case of character disorders, the phrase "significant problem" presumes a value judgment. But it is one that is relatively easily and accurately made, particularly when the problem cuts across several areas of functioning. The young person refuses to go to school *and* has no friends, preferring instead to spend time alone in his room. The young person runs away from home *and* indulges in potentially self-destructive behavior with a deviant peer group. One gets the sense of a driven quality to the behavior; the young person has lost the capacity to make choices in what he does. By considering manifest behavior in the areas of home, peers, and school, one gets a sense of the breadth of the difficulty. From this, it is relatively easy to estimate what is an entrenched developmental difficulty as opposed to what might be situational.

A family diagnostic interview can be an important component of the admissions process. One needs to get a direct sense of the extent to which the young person's difficulties are syntonic with the family style or even specifically stimulated by family members. Often, a family meeting reveals intrasystemic emotions and processes which remain obscure in individual discussions. Observing how the adolescent and the family cope with the stress of the evaluation process can provide some insight into broader coping skills, but it is important to assess not only psychological but external reality as well. A family may be under real financial pressure which overwhelms its capacity to care for its individual members. This, in turn, gives credence to a feeling of abandonment and rejection. Though systematic evidence on the point is lacking, it seems that the complaints of pubertal girls about seductive, if not outright incestuous, behavior on the part of family members and older men is far more often based on some reality than it is a total product of the imagination. Before one can confront a psychological defensive maneuver,

one must have an alliance with the individual; this requires a certain sensitivity to and understanding of all aspects of his psychological world, including those perceptions which are founded in reality. In the early process of working with an adolescent, a common error is to move too quickly to a confrontation of the distortions without having first demonstrated to the young person that one clearly understands what is distortion and what is not. Confrontation is the essence of early treatment with the adolescent, but, like all effective interventions, it entails a possible deleterious side effect, the capacity to undermine a developmentally and/or pathologically tenuous sense of self. This must be balanced against its therapeutic advantage.

Aside from individual psychological and family process issues, during the evaluation it is important to assess the young person's level of physical development and the effect that this may have on his presenting difficulties, medical status, cognitive maturity, and intelligence.

The chronological timing of puberty should be evaluated both in terms of the particular developmental status of the individual as well as the level of pubertal development of his peer group. Dysynchronous onset of puberty influences personality formation; early puberty is particularly stressful for girls, and the reverse is true for boys.[45] In clinical practice, though, there are enough exceptions to this to suggest that each case must be considered individually. The processes of puberty may exacerbate a number of previously subclinical neurological and endocrine problems, and a careful medical history and examination should be carried out with every patient. Conversely, the stress of puberty coupled with an illness may produce symptoms in a vulnerable ego organization. One must be wary of attributing all psychological difficulties in the medically ill adolescent to "reactions to illness." The diabetic adolescents' difficulties in following a treatment regimen, for instance, may reflect reactive denial to the stress of their illness. It may also obscure personality difficulties which predate their diabetes. Given the fact that intelligence is a consistently good predictor of response to treatment, it is surprising that relatively little has been done to further refine techniques of cognitive and intellectual assessment. Tests such as the Wichsler Intelligence Scale for Children provide a good estimate of a particular kind of adaptive functioning, that is, the capacity to work with verbal material in the typical school setting. At the same time, they do not necessarily indicate an overall level of cognitive development.

A careful developmental history is part of the evaluation of every child and adolescent. There is, however, much to suggest that parental reporting of the adolescent's development is even less reliable as objective evidence than has been demonstrated to be the case with children.[67, 93, 114] Cases have been found where the family distorts such relatively objective information as the time of occurrence of major events like deaths, births, and the like.

CASE ILLUSTRATION

Mark was a seventeen-year-old seen in consultation at a state hospital where he was diagnosed as suffering chronic brain syndrome, reportedly secondary to injuries sustained in an automobile accident when he was five. The clinical findings were not consistent with this diagnosis, however, and previous medical records were requested and reviewed. Mark had been hospitalized for three years in a residential facility during latency, and several consultations had been carried out by neurologists and neurosurgeons. They found no evidence of organic difficulty nor, in the extensive history taken at that time, was there any mention of an automobile accident. Nevertheless, the family had recalled a minor accident during Mark's adolescence. Though he was not even seen by a physician at the time, they attributed his lack of improvement to his "injuries." The family distortion allowed them to deal with the pain created by his chronic schizophrenia.

The developmental history is most useful as a hypothetical construct through which one understands the "family mythology" and from which one gleans clues that suggest further psychological exploration. The more disturbed the individual and the family, both in terms of severity and duration of symptoms, the more likely that the family will significantly distort reality, and this despite the absence of any clear-cut deficiency in reality testing on the part of any of its members. School records can provide an important source of objective information about adaptation during latency. These can serve also as a predictor of treatment outcome, but these data should be reviewed from the perspective of the individual's active involvement with teachers and peers, and not in terms of simple behavioral compliance, a possible negative predictor. The association of hyperactivity in childhood with problems in adolescence is well documented,[100] although its implications for treatment are unclear.

One must have experienced both the advantages and disadvantages of hospitalization as well as the process of working with the highly symptomatic adolescent in order to assess the relative merits of hospital care as compared to other inter-

ventions. There is an unfortunate tendency for mental health clinicians to ally themselves with particular treatment modalities and treatment settings and to see all psychopathology and intervention from this perspective. Family therapists, psychoanalytic psychotherapists, and hospital psychiatrists often view problems from the vantage point of their parochial treatment interests; the net effect is to lose sight of the relative merits of a given approach for a particular problem. This is particularly serious in dealing with disturbed adolescents for whom the verbal interchange and office encounter can provide only a portion of the transaction between patient and clinician. The adolescent, especially when under stress, should be understood as much through his behavior as his words. At a difficult moment, his anxiety about dependency can interfere with his capacity to conceptualize and articulate personal difficulties in any meaningful way. A therapist dealing with such a patient must have the capacity to see through the obfuscation and the avoidance the youngster stirs up in order to study the young person's capacity to control himself. Only through developing such a sense can the clinician gauge the young person's potential for maladaptive behavior. And only then can he estimate which therapeutic interventions will be effective in dealing with the patient's problems. Evaluating this in the outpatient setting is often a herculean task even for the most seasoned clinician.

CASE ILLUSTRATION

Tom was an attractive, highly intelligent and verbal fourteen-year-old from a prominent family. He had volunteered for outpatient treatment because of increasing school difficulties. Tom's parents were reluctant to involve themselves either with the therapist or a clinic social worker, and Tom shared their reluctance. He insisted that his problems were between himself and his therapist, and there was no need to involve anyone else. Indeed, Tom appeared to enter treatment enthusiastically and seemed able to discuss his impulse-control difficulties with his therapist. The therapist was confident that their frequent meetings were effective in helping Tom control his expression of intense affect aroused within the family, and to resist temptations to revert to drug abuse and school truancy. At 3:00 A.M. one weekend morning, however, the therapist was awakened by a call from the police who told him they had a young man in their custody who "won't give us his name but says you are his doctor." Tom had stolen a car, robbed a liquor store, and was apprehended only after a high-speed chase. In retrospect, it was apparent that Tom's impulse control was not aided at all by his outpatient treatment, and that his facility with words had obscured his ego capacity to deal with tension. Tom was admitted to an adolescent inpatient unit and subsequently did well.

Denial of difficulties by parents and school personnel often colludes with an adolescent's need to maintain an illusion of competence and mastery.

CASE ILLUSTRATION

Mary was a seventeen-year-old who was admitted to a psychiatric hospital on an emergency basis. She had made a serious suicide attempt following difficulties with a boyfriend. Routine educational screening revealed marked academic deficiencies, though none of this was noted in the school report. School attendance had been regular. Mary had been seeing an outpatient psychotherapist for the past nine months; he reported that he and Mary had discussed her frequent marijuana use but that it did not appear to be a problem. In fact, her treatment appeared to be helping her adapt both at home and at school. Direct discussion of the matter with Mary's teachers and with her parents cast a different light on the matter. Mary's school operated under "a flexible module system," which meant, in effect, that a young person could come and go from classes at will. There was an unsupervised area in the school building which was used for marijuana smoking; and Mary had been observed to spend considerable time there. Her enthusiasm in such classroom discussions as she did take part in, despite the lack of any objective measures of achievement, convinced the teachers that "nothing was really wrong." Mary's involvement in therapy and the lack of concern from the school helped the parents ignore the fact that Mary's room was often full of "funny-smelling smoke." A detailed retrospective review of Mary's situation revealed that she had been massively regressed for months.

Failure to meet a social or family expectation, however, can lead to reactive symptoms which may mimic more severe pathology.

CASE ILLUSTRATION

Holly was the fifteen-year-old daughter of a university professor. She was brought to the emergency room by her parents following her return from a runaway. Without apparent cause, Holly had left home, traveled by herself to a neighboring city, and checked into a hotel for five days. During this time, she had apparently done nothing but sleep and eat a few room-service meals. Personnel at the hotel became concerned and called her parents, who brought her home and then to the hospital emergency room. On examination at that time, she was reported to be "detached and distant." The examiner felt that Holly "didn't relate well," and she was admitted to the hospital with a preliminary diagnosis of possible incipient psychosis. During the next few days in the hospital she continued to appear detached, uninvolved with people, and somewhat chronically depressed. There was, however, no evidence of a psychotic process. During a family diagnostic interview, her father, almost as an aside, mentioned that "Holly isn't living up to her potential." At this point she began to cry and mumble that "nothing I ever do is right." Exploration of this interchange revealed that the parents, both successful academics, had high expectations of Holly's school performance; Holly, in turn, had little interest in academic accomplishment. A concurrent educational evaluation revealed that Holly was of only average intelligence; projective psychological testing disclosed enormous performance anxiety associated with her failure to meet her parents' expectations. Holly was discharged and the family began intensive family treatment focusing on their expectations. At follow up two years later, Holly and her parents were content with each other, and Holly had experienced no further difficulties. Her school work had improved, and she was indeed planning to go to college "because I want to." In retrospect, a better initial immediate decision in the emergency room would have been the scheduling of a next-day outpatient family evaluation, where Holly's feelings of helplessness could have been explored and the family confronted more directly about their relationship.

Gauging motivation for change and the willingness of the adolescent to involve himself in treatment can be a problem. Even in the midst of the most overtly traumatic difficulties and manifestly self-destructive behavior, the adolescent will often say that he "doesn't need help." Acknowledging a desire for psychiatric hospitalization runs counter to the normal developmental push of adolescence; one cannot expect the adolescent to agree to hospitalization in the same spirit as an older, overwhelmed person who looks on the hospitalization as a welcome relief from excessive pressure. Implicitly, hospitalization conveys a statement of an inability to cope. In order to protect their fragile self-esteem, most adolescents quite normally need to see admission as externally imposed. Phrases such as "if you say so," "well, since I have no choice," "I really don't like this, but . . ." are common and should not necessarily be construed as unwillingness to enter treatment. On the contrary, more often than not they indicate a developmentally appropriate, if maladaptive, defense of the self, and the adolescent, again more often than not, will comply behaviorally while vigorously protesting verbally.

The characteristic ambivalence of the adolescent toward hospitalization reflects several things. On the one hand, at some level, he sees the need for hospitalization. On the other, however, he does not like to acknowledge its implications for his capacity to manage himself. All patients with emotional difficulties feel ambivalent about giving up their symptoms, and all adolesacents have mixed feelings about growing up. Faced with hospitalization, the adolescent may act out these tensions.

The initial ambivalence toward hospitalization may be more centrally rooted in developmental difficulties. For example, these may be fixations around relationships to infantile omnipotent objects. In the course of hospitalization, these may shade into a more enduring psychological theme.[88, 92] Finally, it is important to note that cognitive immaturity may make it difficult or impossible for the adolescent to see what he is doing in any objective fashion or to think of his personality as evolving in historical time; his perception of the implications of his difficulties, then, may be entirely different from that of an external observer's. The capacity to look at oneself, particularly one's thoughts and feelings, and to think of one's self as having continuity over time in any abstract sense presumes the achievement of what Piaget calls formal operational thinking. Even by late adolescence, the mastery of this developmental stage is far from a universal accomplishment.[18, 23, 77] Adolescents with emotional difficulties which reflect their limited growth generally are more likely to be cognitively immature.

A negative attitude toward hospitalization does not necessarily reflect ambivalence, however; it may reflect an uncomplicated wish not to be hospitalized. The most difficult task in arriving at a decision to hospitalize is probably the differentiation between ambivalence and a resolute negativism. Ambivalence implies a tie to an object, in this case symbolized by the hospital; and one expects to feel this tie, however diffusely, during an evaluation interview. On experiences the intermixing of pleas for help with manifest rejection of one's efforts to be helpful. The ambivalent adolescent reveals his difficulties at the very time he is denying any need to change. This is not the case with the truly negative adolescent, who presents a more consistent picture of denial of symptoms, active efforts to "look presentable," and denial of the need for help. Often such negativism arises from an incapacity to enter into human relationships, usually consequent on severe developmental trauma.[98]

It is the practical experience of most programs that for psychological treatment to occur the patient must have both the capacity to enter into relationships and the wish to do so, no matter how obscurely expressed. Often, these cannot be effectively assessed prior to admission; and a trial of treatment may be indicated. In such cases, the therapist must be prepared to recognize any inability to respond which will lead to a treatment failure. Often enough, the wish to help a young person is so strong that it completely obscures the young person's total rejection of the helper's efforts.

Most clinicians consider the potentially or actually homicidal adolescent unsuitable for conventional hospital treatment. This view rests on both the refractory nature of the patient's difficulties and their potential impact on the hospital milieu. The problem is to determine who is potentially homicidal and who is not. Though some authors maintain that the potential for violence against persons can be predicted,[73] the consensus of psychiatric opinion tends toward an opposite opinion.[96] The issue is further complicated by the task of differentiating between nonspecific psychotic rage on the one hand and the wanton violence of certain nonpsychotic persons on the other. As a practical matter, such differentiation must be based on the history of previous behavior and on a continuing diagnostic evaluation, with special attention directed toward the possibility of insidious paranoid trends and covert delusion formation. Psychodynamically oriented clinicians often overlook subclinical psychotic functioning until flagrant decompensation occurs; conversely, biologically oriented clinicians often medicate young people excessively and futilely in cases where the potential for violence arises not out of a psychotic syndrome but out of profound character pathology. What can be done for the latter? In theory, behaviorally oriented programs should provide external controls while at the same time allowing the young person to remain emotionally detached. Whether such a program would lead to enduring change is an unanswered question.

In the preceding context, however, it is important to note that delinquency, that is, the commission of antisocial or illegal acts, is characteristic not only of virtually all types of adolescent psychopathology but of presumably normal adolescents as well.[38, 103] Delinquent behavior does not in and of itself imply either "antisocial character disorder" or the lack of capacity to enter into human relationships. "Sociopathy" is much more likely to be a part of the lives of severely disturbed adolescents than of severely disturbed adults. Conversely, truly "antisocial characters" often appear initially to be "model patients," usually because it is more comfortable to be a "psychiatric patient" than "a juvenile delinquent." Adolescents adjudicated "delinquent" are a clinically heterogenous group, and some types of delinquents are quite treatable,[56, 62] as is discussed in detail in chapter 33.

In evaluating suitability for hospital treatment, one should be wary of overemphasizing a history of drug use.[33] Some degree of drug abuse will be found in the vast majority of severely disturbed adolescents, and this practice can obscure the presenting picture. It is not uncommon, for instance, to see late adolescent patients with schizophrenia increase hallucinogenic drug use at times of stress. In such cases, the drug abuse functions essentially as a defensive process analogous to what Cain[9] has called "playing crazy."

Some *special situations* deserve mention. Long-term treatment of schizophrenic young people should be reserved for those few institutions specializing in such treatment. Such youngsters share a propensity to develop institutional syndromes and in any case, a special expertise is required for the long-term intensive treatment of schizophrenia. The usual acute-onset schizophrenic adolescent is best served by a brief hospitalization focusing on symptomatic treatment of the psychosis. This usually involves medication, consistent and nonintrusive environmental structure, careful exploration of family issues contributing to the decompensation, and intensive follow up. The aftercare should include both psychological and environmental interventions, and, when necessary, a program for partial hospitalization. Brain-damaged young people have the same risk for institutional syndromes as do schizophrenic adolescents. Once an adolescent with poor impulse control is diagnosed as suffering from organic impairment and the recommendation is made for environmental structure, placement in a residential facility is preferable to continued hospital treatment.

Serious suicide attempts and self-destructive behavior of nonlethal intent have different implications for treatment; every effort should be made to distinguish between them early in the evaluation period. While occasionally associated with schizophrenia or major affective disorder, serious suicide risk is usually present in an adolescent with brittle character defenses and a profound sense of helplessness; these traits often reflect a rigid, covertly rejecting family background.[99, 109] Treatment usually involves separation from the family and intensive individual work. Suicide threat or self-mutilation, on the other hand, may represent the acting out of ambivalence toward an important object. Here the context involves a looser, less consistently rejecting family milieu. Once hospitalized, these patients tend to act out their ambivalence tenaciously.[36, 81, 83] Family-focused treatment in combination with continued outpatient work is therefore more likely to be successful at the time of crisis.[76]

The successful treatment of a young adolescent

female transsexual in a hospital setting has been reported.[15] This suggests that the commonly held belief that core identity disorders are untreatable beyond latency may be in error, and that a combination of separation from parents, intensive individual psychotherapy, and a therapeutic environment may be helpful in such cases.

Treatment

THE INDIVIDUALIZED TREATMENT PLAN

The overall *goal of treatment* for the hospitalized adolescent is no different than the goal of adolescent intervention generally: to promote growth and the mastery of appropriate developmental tasks. Quite aside from the immediate circumstances surrounding the admission, the severely disturbed adolescent usually manifests developmental failure in many areas. More often than not, he is several grades behind his chronological level at school; relationships with peers may be characterized by pathological dependency and neurotic distortion rather than movement toward true interpersonal intimacy; relationships with adults may be strained or absent; he may lack frustration tolerance; and he may be impulse ridden and unable to perform productive work. Psychological conflict and problems with self-esteem may be obscured by compulsive drug use, sexual promiscuity, or delinquent behavior. Character problems may mask disorders of thought, perception, or emotion. Medical problems are more common among disturbed adolescents than in the normal population.

The goal of hospitalization is to interrupt symptomatic behavior, to design a therapeutic program to deal with the underlying causes of developmental failure, to support healthy functioning, to provide as developmentally appropriate a living experience as possible, and to maintain the patient's ties to family and community. The basis of the working alliance is an empathic appreciation of the adolescent's developmental difficulties as well as of his strengths and aspirations. This is true whether the therapist's goals are symptomatic and short-term or focused on broader issues of personality. Empathy allows the therapist to keep in touch with the internal shifts which are the essence of adolescent experience; this kind of emotional resonance can lead to the tempering of therapeutic rigidity that is both theoretically and practically appropriate. Indications for therapeutic interventions are rarely clear-cut, and, more often than not, the adolescent himself is a better guide to the appropriate intervention than the textbook.

The hospitalized adolescent will invariably require a variety of interventions, and it is the task of the therapist to prescribe them in the context of an overall *treatment plan*. This, in turn, is based on a clear understanding of the problems prompting admission and on a diagnostic formulation. The plan should specify measures to evaluate the success of the interventions. Child psychiatry has yet to develop an adequate general language for developmental treatment; while psychoanalytic metapsychology is useful as a framework for individual psychotherapy and for understanding the patient's relationships with milieu members, it does not suffice for a variety of other interventions. Academic deficiencies, for instance, may reflect a combination of motivational problems best described psychodynamically, delayed cognitive maturation conceptualized in a Piagetian framework, or neuropsychological deficits which rest on physiological concepts. None of this may be helpful for a teacher attempting to work with the young person, an essentially social psychological task.

There is increasing interest in the conceptual integration of treatment and adolescent psychopathology. Out of an interest in the relevance of the psychoanalytic theory of object relations for adolescent psychopathology, Masterson[64] and Rinsley[88] have described a theory of treatment process. Their work has focused on the interrelationship of symptomatic behavior in a milieu, defective self-esteem, and developmental difficulties with formation of the self. They emphasize confronting the symptomatic behavior in the milieu and working through the self-esteem problems in individual psychotherapy. Zinner and R. Shapiro[118, 119] and E. Shapiro and colleagues[104] have described an approach integrating individual and family work, focusing on the interrelationship between the young person's failure to develop autonomy and a family style which both undermines self-formation and provides a pathologic identity. Though not specifically directed toward work with adolescents, Kernberg[47, 48] has presented an even broader integration of the interpersonal presentation of self, the development of object relations, group process, and hospital administration. The use of behavioral techniques has been described by Lehrer and colleagues[53] and Rossman and Knesper.[95]

The specific *process of therapeutic change in hospitalization* can be described in terms of a number of parameters. Identity consolidation may be aided through identification with the therapist, particularly with the therapist's personal autonomy and reflective style of thinking. The adolescent may have the opportunity to learn and practice both specific ego skills and new styles of interpersonal functioning. His self-esteem is improved by finding that he can function well and productively in a more neutral and less charged atmosphere than was present in his community milieu. Increased self-esteem improves his capacity to tolerate frustration.

The *role of the hospital physician* is to integrate his psychiatric understanding of the patient's difficulty into the patient's life space. He seeks to do this in a way that gives the patient a sense that "being in the hospital" is more than just an opportunity for a variety of specific interventions; that it is in itself helpful. Information about the patient comes as much from the accounts of the patient's behavior in the milieu as it does from the patient's direct report. Adolescent experience is bound up in action, and the disturbed adolescent will invariably reveal much of himself outside the office. Similarly, response to the patient occurs through both specific and general interventions in the milieu. For instance, academic deficiencies may be revealed during the initial evaluation process, and the therapist might work with a school teacher to explore their psychodynamic significance. More specifically, a patient might be involved in individual or family therapy in which, from time to time, particularly upsetting issues may arise. At such moments, he may need to give very close attention to day-to-day structure. Often, "hospital therapist" is seen as synonymous with "psychotherapist." While hospitalized adolescents at times may benefit from the exploration of psychological conflict, more often than not the nature of the therapeutic task is not to remove pathologic defenses but to function as an auxiliary ego.[78, 79] The therapist assesses the patient's strengths and weaknesses and makes appropriate environmental prescriptions for structuring the adolescent's experience according to his needs and the goals of treatment.

An important part of the environmental prescription is to guide the milieu staff. They must be aware not only of the patient's characteristic defensive maneuvers and transference distortions but of the weaknesses and strengths in other areas of his personality functioning. They should know something of the tolerance of the young person for interpersonal contact. The acutely psychotic adolescent, for instance, needs to be allowed a certain amount of distance and the opportunity to initiate contact in his own terms. The adolescent with a character disorder, on the other hand, will need to be much more actively involved in the milieu and should be discouraged from withdrawing. The therapist should develop a sense of the appropriate balance of support and pressure for change, and should maintain an overall view of the patient's growth in the hospital environment.

THE MILIEU

For all but the briefest admission, the living environment of the hospitalized adolescent will be the focus of most of his attention; accordingly the success of hospitalization will depend on developing an alliance between patient and milieu. While this is true for adolescents with all types of disturbance, it is particularly necessary to the intermediate and long-term treatment of character disorders.

The severely disturbed adolescent admitted to a hospital is accustomed to dealing with defective self-esteem in regressive fashion. Typically, the young person will alternate between extremes of idle passivity and impassioned protestation that he can take care of himself. He may be accustomed to gratifying his passive impulses by indulging in drugs or certain forms of sexual behavior. In the hospital, he may be inclined to obtain substitute gratification through continually watching TV, listening to music, or participating in regressive group behavior. The *milieu task* is to confront this regressive behavior and the associated use of externalization and projection, and at the same time to support and encourage constructive activity and appropriate developmental functioning. It must be emphasized that support and confrontation are interlocking processes; both are necessary to develop an effective working alliance between patient and milieu. Excessive confrontation at the expense of appropriate support will quickly alienate the young person and lead to a paranoid stance. Excessive support, on the other hand, only rewards his regressive tendencies. The psychological tone of the effective milieu staff member appears to be a blend of a "no funny business" attitude with an affectionate wish for the adolescent to succeed. Confrontation tinged with sadism or affection tinged with indulgence only perpetuates regressive functioning. Most adolescents sufficiently symptomatic to warrant hospitalization suffer from highly troubled interpersonal relationships, both contemporaneously and historically; they carry within themselves many images of frustrating relationships with people. Support by therapists and mil-

ieu staff in the mastery of developmentally appropriate tasks can provide alternative images. These will sustain the adolescent after hospitalization.

Interruption of regressive behavior usually reveals deficient self-esteem; this may be related both to past experience and to current reality. Not only does the adolescent feel badly about himself because of experiences in the past, but he re-creates situations in the present which perpetuate a negative view of self. Deficient self-esteem, in turn, leads the adolescent to avoid situations in which mastery is appropriate and expected. The task of the milieu is to reverse the cycle and to support positive self-esteem both by interrupting regressive behavior and by providing and supporting attempts at mastery. Most troubled adolescents are very much bound up in the immediacy of their experience. They tend to act and react depending on environmental circumstances, and hence do not have the capacity to elect options. Developing a stronger sense of self provides the nidus for a reflective capacity which allows them to consider alternatives and to make decisions.

It should be emphasized, however, that conscious awareness and acknowledgment of deficient self-esteem is not an end in itself. It only serves as an intermediary stage that enables the patient to recognize the compulsive and driven quality of his self-defeating behavior and to make connections between feeling states and action. A certain amount of denial of personal inadequacy, however, is concomitant with passing through adolescence; the therapist should recognize that "blundering through" is a necessary part of healthy growth. Further, the often raw instinctual behavior of adolescents is not in and of itself pathological. The end toward which this activity is turned determines the issue. Too often, people think of quieting the adolescent down rather than directing energy in developmentally appropriate channels. The goal is to promote sublimation rather than to strengthen reaction formation.

What are specific developmentally appropriate *milieu activities*? In large measure, this must be decided through careful consideration of the goals and aspirations of the particular adolescents with whom one is working. Forestry projects, for instance, may be developmentally appropriate but may not match the interests of inner-city youth. Content should be defined according to the aspirations of the individual adolescent; process, according to its assessed role in promoting ego development. The program should offer depth of experience and should not focus narrowly on a particular environment or specific activity. Therapeutic camping, for instance, may be helpful not only for instilling a sense of self-reliance but in releasing tension built up within the intense environment of a hospital ward.

Historically, there have been two views on the character of a school that is part of a hospital setting. One is that this academic experience should strive to parallel the normal school environment and curriculum, with similar expectations for appropriate classroom behavior; difficulties in the classroom may require exclusion and should become issues within the psychotherapy. The other view is that the classroom experience should be modified to meet the needs of the disturbed adolescent; the young person should remain with the teacher no matter how mutually uncomfortable their encounter becomes. While both views have forceful proponents, the latter approach appears to have advantages, particularly for closed hospital settings. If an adolescent can function in a conventional classroom, then every attempt should be made to place him in a public school setting. This may be difficult if the adolescent is exposed to regressive opportunities which undermine his potential adequacy, for example, drugs in the public school; but within a closed setting, "a normal classroom" will not seem like "normal school" to the adolescent no matter how conventional the curriculum or the teacher. Further, many disturbed adolescents, and particularly those in need of intensive hospitalization, cannot effectively use such a conventional experience. For them, the classroom has been a source of frustration which chronically undermined their self-esteem;[32] by this time they have become alienated from the educational process. "Unlocking" their difficulties with learning depends first on creating an environment where they feel comfortable and interested. Only then can they be engaged in the academic task. Performance anxieties can be "worked through" around specific classroom tasks.

CASE ILLUSTRATION

Mrs. Stone, a teacher in an adolescent inpatient unit, was faced with several withdrawn young people who were inhibited in the classroom environment. She developed a class in "animal care." The young people served as volunteers in a local humane society, feeding and caring for the animals. By encouraging their affection for the animals, she was able to stimulate their interest in conventional academic topics. On another occasion, faced with a group of young girls with poor body image, she instituted a course in grooming and hygiene. She had a good relationship with the girls and was able to serve as a model in promoting self-care.

The requirement of "constructive activity" should include attention to developmental appropriateness and should reflect normal adolescent experience. Adolescents need intergenerational relationships, for instance, and work with the elderly can be particularly valuable in providing a perspective on the life cycle. Regular visits to a retirement home can be arranged where the adolescents are expected to become involved in activities with the residents. This type of experience can give the young person the opportunity to be helpful to someone else, just as milieu personnel are being helpful to him. Work in day-care or nursery settings can have a similar function; in particular, it may be a useful way of dealing with the fantasies about pregnancy and babies characteristic of many emotionally disturbed early and middle adolescent girls.

While emphasizing the importance of constructive activity, it is nevertheless equally important that the adolescent have some breathing room. A milieu can be too intrusive and, by its very intensity, block just those goals it is attempting to attain. The adolescent should be allowed the opportunity to regress appropriately. While milieu work offers an invaluable opportunity to correct interpersonal distortion, exaggerated expectations, and paranoid fantasies, genetic interpretation of psychic content generally should be avoided. Milieu work should focus on the present, and a more reflective view of personal difficulties in historical perspective should be reserved for individual psychotherapy.

Sexual anxieties are inevitable, and it is an error to presume that separate treatment environments for males and females will reduce them. On the contrary, single-sex treatment programs often induce homosexual anxieties which are far more difficult to deal with than heterosexual concerns. At the same time, when the sexes are housed together there must be appropriate monitoring of behavior. Programs vary in the degree to which some heterosexual activity such as holding hands is allowed, but extensive "coupling" in a milieu spells trouble. While it is true that heterosexual experience is part of normal adolescent development, it needs to be emphasized that the adolescent in a psychiatric unit is rarely capable of developmentally appropriate sexual functioning; behavior which may appear normal is usually regressively motivated.[21]

As a rule, *milieu structure* centers on a system of expectations, responsibilities, and privileges; however, there is often an unfortunate tendency to equate structure with some formal system or set of rules governing behavior. While formalized "policy" provides a concrete basis for discussion, the essence of therapeutic structure is an empathic appreciation of the personal strengths and weaknesses of the individual adolescents for whom it is intended. The adolescent needs to feel that he is dependent upon persons and not governed by regulations. Adolescents vary from day to day in their capacity to manage themselves, and what is appropriately firm and reassuring treatment one day appears punitive and arbitrary the next. The capacity to be flexible in response to behavior is essential. Often a formal system is developed in the hope that it will quiet arguments with the adolescent. This misses the crucial fact that the struggle over privileges is the essence of relationship, and that referring the young person to a policy book is regarded as a copout.

Some of the negative impressions about inpatient work with adolescents have stemmed from the tendency of these patients to engage in major *group disturbances.* Episodic self-destructive behavior,[81] absconding,[35, 55] destruction of property[28] and rioting[63] have been described. Indeed, it would appear that group disturbances are far more common than the rather slim literature about them would suggest. Group disturbance is a particularly telling example of the cumulative impact of a variety of systems in determining adolescent behavior. Riots, for instance, usually involve an adolescent group with a predisposition toward aggressive outbursts; this, in turn, reflects the presence of individuals whose psychodynamics in part revolve around issues of oppression and control of rage. There is often a charismatic leader somewhere in the picture, usually a profoundly disturbed individual whose ties to people are limited; and all these are contained within an administrative structure which has lost touch both with the needs of the individual adolescents and the overall shift in the patient group toward delinquency. Often there are associated staff problems such as conflict, turnover, and so forth. A group disturbance usually means that the young people are looking to each other for structure rather than to staff; membership in the delinquent group has more meaning than involvement in the tasks of the milieu. The riot, thus, reflects a sense of group helplessness and lack of support by staff. For adolescent patients, this process is the analog of the increase in psychotic symptoms seen among adult patients during periods of staff conflict.[12, 106] It should occasion a thorough analysis of program operations.

The major disadvantage of the all-adolescent milieu is the necessity for *patient selection,* illustrated by the process of group disturbance. Regressive group functioning is a continual possibility, and effective milieu work depends on maintaining not only individual involvement with the milieu, but a group alliance as well. The admission of a patient to an all-adolescent milieu must be evaluated in terms of his potential effect on overall group cohesion.

SPECIFIC INTERVENTIONS

There are serious difficulties in forming a true psychotherapeutic alliance with many hospitalized adolescents. This in addition to the recognition that their symptoms do not always reflect well-structured internal conflict have led to modifications of *individual psychotherapy* to meet their special needs. Early papers by Noshpitz[80] and Hendrickson, Holmes, and Waggoner[42] on engaging the hospitalized delinquent in psychotherapy describe techniques for involving the young person in treatment. Subsequent developments have centered on the use of the therapeutic relationship to improve ego functioning by promoting the patient's identification with the therapist's strength and mastery. Such identification allows the patient to recognize the therapist's perceptions and judgment as acceptable alternatives to his own. In the course of discussing perceptions of reality, the patient acquires an increasing capacity to reflect about himself and to put words between impulse and behavior. One might conceive of the course of psychotherapy as beginning with an initial period of developing attachment and identification. This progresses through an intermediate phase of working toward mastering appropriate developmental experience and reaching a final period in which the patient recognizes the inevitable separation from the therapist and his anxiety at his own emerging autonomy. This process is accompanied by a concomitant psychological internalization of the therapist. It may be especially useful in dealing with problems of a defective sense of self resulting from interference with separation-individuation in early childhood.[64, 88] The unique aspect of individual psychotherapy within the framework of hospital treatment is the opportunity to put contemporary problems in historical perspective. The hospitalization provides a reflective situation and allows the patient to develop a sense of himself as a person evolving in historical time. The psychotherapist working with adolescent patients must be more active than is the case with adults.[69] This is particularly true in the case of severely disturbed, hospitalized adolescents; for them ambiguity can often cause an intensification of a paranoid process. A confrontative, confining milieu combined with a lack of focus in individual psychotherapy can lead to an entrenched negative transference; once developed, this can rarely be worked through without some major modification of treatment approach. Often, another therapist will have to be provided.

How active should the psychotherapist be in the milieu? The answer to this question rests on the patient's needs rather than on theory.[78, 79] Some patients will be so alienated from adults or so anxious in an office-based encounter that attachment to the therapist and the milieu program can come about only by an entirely different approach. Someone, most often the therapist, must take an active role in the overall direction of their treatment and, in effect, communicate with them through action. Only then are they able to relate. Further, assigning psychotherapy and milieu administrative functions to two different persons can collude with internal object splitting. The result may be an unworkable arrangement unless there is very close communication between the two therapists. There are other patients, particularly those with sexual perversions rooted in well-structured neurotic conflict who respond to a more traditional, conflict-oriented psychotherapeutic approach. In this case ward management and psychotherapeutic treatment should be separated.[39] The psychotherapist must have a sense of the individual treatment in the context of the patient's total life. If the adolescent lives in an unempathic and aversive environment, it will be difficult for him to assume anything approximating a reflective stance.

Group work is an important aspect of the treatment of the hospitalized adolescent in two very different ways. The adolescent's propensity to involve himself in groups is well known, and "community meetings" can be an important site for developing a task orientation in the patient group in connection with the functioning of the milieu. Group sessions specifically directed at interpersonal problems within the group should be defined for staff and patients as a distinctly different activity. When such a group meeting is convened, continued concentration on some real milieu problems can create a sense of helplessness for the individual patients. This is likely to be acted out elsewhere. Conversely, discussing individual personalities in a meeting designed to make decisions about a camping trip, for instance, can be regressive and again can provoke a sense of helplessness.

The importance of *family involvement* has been emphasized, and it needs to be seen in three contexts: The family must provide support for the hospitalization, both materially and emotionally; adolescent psychopathology has an important family dimension and diagnostic work with a disturbed adolescent requires an evaluation of this aspect of his life; and finally, from the treatment point of view, pathological family functioning must be improved if the adolescent is to return to his parental home. There is growing appreciation of the fact that historically hospitals have not been sufficiently sensitive to family issues. Most families experience a real sense of loss at the hospitalization of the adolescent and are subject to considerable guilt.[110] This is often exacerbated by the attitudes of the hospital personnel, who tend to identify with the patient and to make the family a scapegoat for the patient's difficulties. It should be recognized that a family's functioning may be relatively healthy and adaptive in areas not involving the patient or the hospital and that only rarely is it possible to treat an early or middle adolescent from an intact family unless the parents favor the hospitalization.

The alliance with the family begins with respect for the fundamentally healthy decision to seek treatment for the adolescent; it continues by the therapist providing support for their involvement. Just as one can become excessively confronting and alienate the adolescent, so can one alienate the family by moving into an interpretive stance too quickly. Family guilt is invariably a complex phenomenon. One should never stimulate it, but one should also avoid excessive reassurance that "you aren't the problem." The parents of adolescent patients often experience extreme and unwarranted guilt alternating with bland denial. In all too many cases, the motivation for family change must be found in what initially appears as irrational self-accusation.

It is difficult to work with an adolescent whose parental situation is unclear. A young person who does not have some definite tie to a family and social milieu invariably will begin to think of the hospital as "home" and the hospital personnel as "parents." For such young people, these feelings are, of course, of more than symbolic significance; indeed, they come to assume preeminence in psychological adaptation. Not only does such an adjustment make change difficult, but it encourages a developmentally inappropriate adaptation as well. The adolescent in the hospital should always "be from somewhere . . . and headed some place."

Family pathology underlying adolescent difficulties has become an increasingly productive area of investigation. Wynne and Singer[117] have established the relationship between family communication patterns and thought disorder. Lidz[58] has described the connection between parental relationship and schizophrenia in adolescence, while Stierlin[107] has correlated adolescent behavior and styles of family integration. Zinner and Shapiro[118] and Shapiro and colleagues[104] describe pathologic family process and the adolescent's failure at self-differentiation. It is clear that family process has a significant influence on adolescent behavior and plays a particularly important role in adolescent psychopathology.

It is important, however, to distinguish between assessing the family dimension of an adolescent's difficulties and a decision to treat these difficulties through direct intervention in the family. Separation from the family and intensive individual work may be as effective as attempting to modify the family milieu. In fact, experience suggests that the more tenacious the symptom, the more rigid the family structure; as a corollary of this, the less likely is the family to be workable as a group. In such cases, family meetings may well be useful to confront externalization and denial directly, and to leave the actual process of working through personal difficulties to individual sessions. Timing of interventions is an issue. Masterson,[64] for instance, prefers to separate parents and adolescent in the early phase of hospitalization, while Shapiro and colleagues[104] contend that family therapy early in hospitalization expedites formation of the individual alliance.

Age is also an important consideration. Direct family intervention is more appropriate and probably more effective with the younger adolescent. He is still very much a part of the nuclear family relationship, unlike the older adolescent who is trying to establish a measure of independence. Overall, the decision as to the form of family intervention means selecting among family therapy —conjoint treatment of parents with individual treatment of the patient, or parents and patient all seen individually. The specific method should be judged according to practicability and developmental appropriateness, and not merely because family pathology is present.[116]

Parent groups can be an important adjunct to family work. The sharing of experiences with adolescents can encourage a more expressive mode of thinking about parenting and family process, and groups can provide support during difficult periods of treatment.

In view of the extent to which they are given *medications*, it is surprising how little systematic research has been done on clinical psychopharmacology in adolescence. This aspect of clinical practice tends to follow that of adult psychiatry but with some important variations. As one would expect from someone who is growing and adjusting to a new body image, adolescents are acutely aware of side effects, particularly of the major tranquilizers; the possibility of their occurrence should, therefore, be explained with special care. The target symptoms of medication, for example, "peculiar thoughts . . . panic . . . sadness . . . trouble controlling yourself," should be pointed out and the advantages of the medication in dealing with these symptoms should be explained. More than that, the help that medication offers in dealing with these symptoms in contrast to the disadvantages of the side effects should be thoroughly discussed.

The phenothiazines are known to reduce agitated behavior in character-disordered adolescents. There is a question as to whether this is the result of some specific therapeutic action of the drug or merely reflects chemical restraint brought about through the drug's sedative and extrapyramidal effects. Antipsychotic agents are clearly indicated in manifest psychosis and contraindicated where psychosis can be absolutely ruled out. Antipsychotic agents may be indicated on an empirical basis for those patients who are behaviorally agitated and who demonstrate thought disorder and significant reality distortion under stress or on psychological testing. It is likely that transient "micropsychotic" episodes are much more common with adolescents than with adults, though this remains to be conclusively demonstrated. Sedatives and minor tranquilizers should be used with extreme caution with adolescents. Their value is questionable, they have a regressive effect, and there is a possibility that the therapist's behavior will collude with a youth's delinquent attitude toward drugs.

Lithium and the tricyclics are clearly indicated in major affective disorder.[44] The use of imipramine in the treatment of pathological separation anxiety in adolescents is being investigated,[31] though this drug's potential for cardiotoxicity requires that it be used with caution. Imipramine is also reported to be helpful in dealing with the depression following withdrawal from amphetamines.[69]

DISCHARGE AND AFTERCARE

The decision to discharge is based on the goals of the hospitalization. In the case of short-term admissions for symptomatic treatment, the issue is relatively clear-cut. For the longer term treatment of character disorders, however, the situation is more complex. In this latter instance, one generally looks for the patient's increased capacity to make choices, to look at himself, and to become more reflective. One watches for behavior which is less driven and more adaptive. "Adaptation" is a criterion full of pitfalls, however, since adaptation to an artificial environment, the hospital, is not in itself a desirable outcome. A rigid treatment program, in fact, can exacerbate the difficulties of the patients.[33] Any estimate of adaptation made in the hospital is at best an inferential process based as much on examination of the hospital milieu as on evaluation of the adolescent. Weekend passes and home visits provide an opportunity to judge the extent to which self-control can be maintained in the environment—which is really what matters. Following discharge, continued care in the community is almost always indicated. It consistently emerges from follow-up studies as a positive predictor of good treatment outcome.

As with most psychological interventions, there is a tendency toward regression at discharge and in the period that follows. When symptoms return during or following discharge, one should be wary of jumping quickly to the presumption that treatment has failed. A very brief short-term readmission may be indicated, but emphasis should be placed on adaptation to the community and on outpatient support. There is a growing feeling that for most adolescent problems, very long periods of hospitalization, that is, several years, are counterproductive.[33] It has been observed after a period of successful inpatient work that some young people act out so as to force their administrative discharge. In retrospect, the therapeutic staff often realizes that the youngster was capable of a better non-hospital adaptation than was recognized at the time. It cannot be emphasized enough that hospitalization must be seen as an aid to growth, not as the growth process itself, and that the overall process of achieving personal maturity extends beyond hospitalization and other psychiatric interventions.

LEGAL ISSUES

There is a trend in mental health legislation to permit the adolescent to object to hospitalization initiated by his parents. The specific procedures vary from state to state; in the face of the adolescent's objection to hospital admission or to continued stay, the usual process is to allow for involuntary confinement for a few days pending a formal review by the court. A decision is then made as to whether treatment is justified or not, and the parents' request for treatment is either supported or denied. Criteria for continued hospitalization vary from state to state, but there is an unfortunate tendency to apply adult standards. Thus, "dangerousness to self or others" interpreted literally is more likely to be the standard than "need for treatment," either in terms of psychiatric syndrome or developmental difficulty. The legal position on this matter is reviewed by Lessem.[54] While it stems from abuses in the hospitalization of juveniles,[8] several problems are created. It may place parents and adolescent in a legitimized adversary relationship over the issue of what is in the young person's best interest, and it undermines the view that child rearing is primarily the responsibility of the family. In many states, mental health hearings are a matter of public record, and the legal process may contribute to the stigma of hospitalization. Preparation for a hearing and the actual process of testifying can consume a vast amount of professional time; and the criterion of "dangerousness" is not relevant to the psychiatrist's primary area of expertise, "treatment."[108]

At the time of this writing, the U.S. Supreme Court has refused to consider further the case of *Bartley* vs. *Kremens*, a class action suit brought on behalf of minors in state hospitals in Pennsylvania. The case was declared moot on the basis of subsequent modification of state statute. The plaintiff in the suit had requested and won in the lower courts the right of court review of all admissions of minors, whether or not the child or adolescent formally objected. The issue came down to the applicability of due process standards to the hospitalization of juveniles. The American Psychiatric Association, the American Academy of Child Psychiatry, the American Society for Adolescent Psychiatry, and the American Association of Psychiatric Clinics for Children entered a joint brief in the case[105] arguing that

Balancing the children's rights and the other considerations . . . this court should except from due process hearing requirements those cases in which (1) a parent in an intact family wishes to admit a (2) pre-adolescent child to (3) an accredited institution (4) for a short-term period. . . . The professional literature establishes that when children reach a developmental age of approximately 13 they *begin to be* significantly more capable of rational and analytical evaluation of their own best interests, as well as articulate expressions of their views. Amici believe that Pennsylvania has appropriately determined that adolescent children should be entitled to an opportunity to present their views whenever they disagree with the parents' decision to seek residential care for them. Adolescents will be far less threatened by the hearing procedures and will be much more capable than pre-adolescents of using these procedures effectively. . . . [pp. 25, 27–28, italics added]

The plaintiffs in *Bartley* vs. *Kremens* represent a significant point of view regarding the issue of treatment programs for juveniles, and it is to be expected that further actions of this sort will be undertaken. There is a tendency to react to these developments with undue pessimism. It does indeed emphasize the responsibilities of the psychiatrists and of those hospital programs that treat severely disturbed adolescents. Psychiatrists must be able to describe their treatment goals clearly, and they must pay careful attention to their alliance with the young person. The appropriate stance for psychiatry would appear to be a concerted effort to educate the public and the legal profession. They must be better informed about the nature of adolescent communication, the capacities of adolescents to make judgments about their own best interests, and the significance of development difficulties for functioning in later life.[115]

The difficulties with the process notwithstanding, legal issues can be brought into the treatment process. Often, the psychiatrist's involvement can be a powerful statement to the patient that the doctor is committed to his long-term welfare.

CASE ILLUSTRATION

Philip was a fifteen-year-old, hospitalized for school refusal and increasing anxiety about any activity other than staying at home and watching television. Shortly after admission, in reaction to pressure to participate in an active ward program, he filed an objection to his hospitalization. A court hearing was scheduled seven days thereafter. His therapist met with Philip and his family and advised them together that in his view, Philip "needed treatment" for his difficulties and that he, the therapist, would assist the parents in court if that was their wish. The family was encouraged to retain a lawyer to present their point of view, and they did so. Two hours before the court hearing, Philip withdrew his objection saying that he wouldn't be able to go to court because he wanted to participate in a school activity. The firm stand in response to Philip's objection in effect mobilized Philip to involve himself in his treatment program.

An objection to continued hospitalization can also be an appropriate reaction on the part of the patient to problems in the working alliance; hence, notice of an objection should always prompt a review of the patient's overall treatment status. Testimony in court should focus not only on the specific issues with the individual young person, but on more general issues as well. These might include: the nature of adolescent ambivalence, the capacity of the adolescent to make judgments in his long-term best interest, and the extent to which developmental difficulties in adolescence may be the precursors of more pronounced difficulties later on.

Program Administration

Theoretically, the administration of an adolescent inpatient program is essentially no different from the administration of any other organizational activity; the administrator defines overall goals, develops various tasks through which the goals are to be accomplished, assigns the tasks to members of the organization in a way that provides coherent and workable job descriptions, and monitors performance of the group. In an adolescent inpatient program, however, the difficulties in accomplishing this can be enormous. Historically, the problems appear to have been of two kinds. First, the approach to the adolescent tended to be either adult-oriented or child-oriented, neither of which provided these youngsters with an age-appropriate environment. As experience has developed in treating adolescents in hospital settings and their special needs have been recognized, this difficulty appears to have become less significant. The second problem, however, arises from the fact that under the best of circumstances, adolescents are not an easy group with whom to work.

Much of what goes into administration involves supervision of the staff in their work with the patients. Those directly involved with the severely disturbed adolescent are continually dealing with someone who says one thing but tends to convey the direct opposite by his behavior. The adolescent says he wants autonomy, yet will not accept responsibility without protest. For example, he will complain about the food but involve himself only with great reluctance in a committee to work with the dietician to develop new menus. Presently, staff members are tempted to take care of any problem themselves instead of encouraging the adolescent to deal with it. The severely disturbed adolescent is a master at making other people feel they are inadequate in caring for him and, in effect, at getting them to take over for him. In the face of this attitude, maintaining a task orientation with ward staff can be an enormously time-consuming process. Staff members need to be reminded constantly that their job is not simply "to care for" the adolescent but to help him care for himself.

The manifest helplessness of the patients combined with the difficulties they create for the staff can be extremely debilitating. These difficulties can lead to various kinds of regressive processes, perhaps most commonly the wish for magical solutions. The administrator must help to keep such feelings in perspective. At the same time, administrative realities must be clearly separated from psychological distortion. Given the complexity of the modern hospital environment and its status hierarchies, it is inevitable that there will be miscommunication and confused responsibilities which have nothing to do with the patient population. The administrator must evaluate both the reality of staff difficulties and look for psychological determinants in the staff-patient interactions. For instance, a common event is staff "splitting," that is, tensions arise between staff groups or individual staff members. These may result as readily from competitive feelings among staff members, poor delineation of tasks, and so forth, as from disturbances by the patients themselves. It is important to consider intramilieu conflict not only in terms of patient pathology but in terms of administrative organizational issues as well. The association of impersonal patient care and administratively complex hospital organizations has been described[43, 85] and is particularly an issue with adolescents. Every effort should be made to promote staff members' autonomy in their work with young people. Insofar as possible, decisions should be made by those responsible for their implementation.

Administrative techniques are a matter of individual preference, but some issues are worth noting. It is important for the milieu leadership to have good individual working relationships with line staff. This can be achieved better by individual supervisory sessions than by group supervision. In order to understand a transaction with an adolescent, some capacity to reflect on one's personal reaction to working with him is essential. Regressive group pressures can often inhibit personal disclosures in group sessions; for their part, staff members may feel more comfortable talking with a supervisor individually. Group sessions, however, are useful in clarifying tasks and establishing a consensus on milieu policies. The age of staff members can be an important consideration. A young staff can be energetic and provide the adolescents with an important identification model. However, they are often so close to their own adolescent conflicts that out of a need to support their own sense of mastery, they may deny the adolescent conflicts of the patients. An energetic, middle-aged staff is an invaluable resource; however, individuals of this age working as staff in mental hospitals often have a passive impersonal quality which is frightening to adolescents.

It is probably impossible to pacify a group of severely disturbed adolescents completely; but even if it were, it would be psychologically undesirable. The therapeutic task is to channel the energy in productive ways, not to make the adolescent submissive or to encourage reaction formation as a defense. Staff and hospital administration must understand that the patients' behavioral difficulties are very much a part of the treatment process. A certain amount of AWOL's, disturbed group behavior, and physical wear and tear on the building are inevitable. In the adolescent unit, furniture will take more punishment than on other wards. Again, recognition of this can be utilized in the treatment process; for instance, one can create an expectation that damaged furniture will be repaired in the occupational therapy shop. AWOL's should be handled by stressing the psychological meaning of the behavior as part of the treatment process,[55] and group disturbances should be examined in terms of overall milieu functioning.

Program Evaluation

Inpatient settings tend to become isolated from the broader world of adolescents in the community. The ward can come to represent a particular professional perspective, which may or may not be relevant to the actual world of adolescence. Professionals working in such units can become unduly optimistic about their professional efforts—or the reverse. It is imperative that every program develop systematic methods of evaluating treatment, a topic comprehensively reviewed by Durkin and Durkin.[19] They describe several evaluation strategies: *goal attainment*, either outcome or long-term follow up; *process*, evaluating the internal functioning of the treatment milieu in light of its goals; and *systems*, looking at the treatment process in the context of its relationship to family and community systems of influence. The first is in the mainstream of traditional medical research, while the latter two involve involve organizational and adaptational concepts that are more a part of social science research. Goal attainment studies of environmental treatment present major problems: choice of outcome criteria; difficulties delineating the relative contribution to outcome of the various components of the program; and delay in providing to the program relevant feedback about treatment effectiveness. Further, outcome or long-term evaluation studies present a problem in terms of controls; the long-term history of young people with difficulties is not well known[51, 98] (although there are sound reasons for supposing that spontaneous remission of difficulty is more the exception than the rule[65, 86, 94]).

Treatment outcome reflects treatment variables as much as aspects of patient and family, and the evaluation of treatment environments is an increasingly important area of interest. The ideological stance of a program may not reflect the program's actual operation, and systematic techniques have been developed for measuring variables such as ward atmosphere, staff cohesion, and overall program homogeneity.[52, 74] These techniques provide an important independent monitor of program functioning. As experience with them broadens, these techniques should become an ever more practical component of program administration. It should be emphasized that evaluation of both treatment outcome and program operation can be integrated with program activities. If this is accomplished properly, it will promote throughout the staff realistic attitudes about the task of hospitalization. Individual staff members might be encouraged, for instance, to follow the subsequent course of patients discharged to the community, thereby gaining a broader perspective on their efforts. Every program should provide a frequent opportunity for the staff to examine program organization and communication in a critical way. Just as the adolescent needs to be involved actively in the milieu structure, so does the line staff need to be included in shaping program goals and operations.

Another consideration in program evaluation is recent PSRO legislation, which has been prompted by increasing government concern with the cost of hospitalization. This requires that institutions perform utilization studies and review clinical practice. Recent publications by the American Academy of Child Psychiatry,[2] the American Psychiatric Association,[84] and Knesper and Miller[49] are helpful in dealing witrh this important task.

Inpatient programs serving adolescents can be accredited by the Joint Commission on Accreditation of Hospitals according to the standards for either a general psychiatric facility or for special facilities serving children and adolescents. Descrip-

tions of both are reviewed in accreditation manuals available from the Joint Commission, and the choice of which standard to employ is usually dictated by the nature of the institution with which the program is affiliated. These issues are discussed in greater detail in volume IV.

Research

Given the extent of hospitalization of adolescents, it is somewhat surprising that research in this field is so limited. Gossett and colleagues[34] reviewed published reports of the results of inpatient treatment and isolated six variables that correlate with good outcome. Three concerned the patient: severity of psychopathology, process versus reactive evolution of symptomatology, and intelligence. Two had to do with the hospital: presence of a specialized adolescent program and completion of recommended inpatient treatment. The final positive variable was continuation in outpatient treatment following hospital discharge. They also conducted their own research into treatment outcome of a group of adolescents treated by long-term hospitalization; the findings supported the distinctions drawn in their literature review.[33] Further, they found that the severity of the initial psychopathology and the fact of process versus reactive onset presented a consistent pattern of interaction: neurotic young people have a good prognosis, regardless of the nature of onset, while those with psychotic disorders have just the reverse. Young people with character disorders accompanied by reactive symptoms do well, while "process behavior disorder" patients have a mixed outcome. The youth's overall status of ego functioning would appear to be a more powerful predictor than his specific adaptive course. Further, they found that completion of the recommended plan of intervention is a predictor of good outcome that is quite independent of the level of pathology or the pattern of symptom development. Interestingly, they also comment that "it has been our experience that it is far easier to help youngsters learn to channel high levels of energy into more productive pursuits than it is to motivate profoundly passive, apathetic, or lethargic adolescent patients." The problem with the study, as the authors acknowledge, is the lack of controls; this work, nevertheless, provides an important perspective on the results of hospital treatment.

A group at the Illinois State Psychiatric Institute is currently completing a five-year study of juvenile delinquents treated intensively in a hospital program; this work is significant in that it uses the hospital setting to describe the functioning of these young people more precisely. A preliminary report[62] tells of how factor analytic techniques were used to subdivide the overall patient group into four distinct subgroups. This further validated the finding of clinical heterogeneity within delinquent populations and provided an objective basis for the prescription and evaluation of treatment. From the perspective of nosology in general psychiatry, Hudgens[44] has reviewed the clinical presentation of 110 adolescent psychiatric inpatients, comparing these data to medical hospital controls. This work is notable in revealing the strengths and weaknesses of such an approach. Over 50 percent of the psychiatric inpatients could not be classified effectively according to these criteria, although anticipated longitudinal follow up may clarify their status. Some members of Anthony's[3] sample of children vulnerable to schizophrenia are now in adolescence, and the study of their clinical difficulties and coping styles in longitudinal perspective should provide important insights into the use of hospitalization, as well as other interventions, with young people similarly at risk.

The direction of research in the hospital treatment of adolescents appears to be striving for ever greater precision in describing the relationship between the treatment process and the young person's developmental course, conceptualized in terms not only of clinical difficulties but of overall life adaptation.

Conclusion

The evolution of hospital-based psychiatric treatment programs for adolescents reflects the pioneering efforts of many people—all of whom shared a common interest in promoting therapeutic change and growth in young people. The opportunity to gain asylum for the adolescent or his confinement for society's protection is a negligible part of this tradition. In the midst of increasing financial pressure on program operation, legal concern with the rights of juveniles, and social concern with adolescent misbehavior, it is imperative that this overall goal be at the forefront of consciousness.

REFERENCES

1. ADELSON, J. B., "The Mystique of Adolescence," *Psychiatry, 27*:1–5, 1964.
2. American Academy of Child Psychiatry, in Silver, L. B. (Ed.), *Professional Standards Review Organization: A Handbook for Child Psychiatrists,* American Academy of Child Psychiatry, Washington, D.C., 1976.
3. ANTHONY, E. J., "A Risk-Vulnerability Intervention Model for Children of Psychotic Parents," in Anthony, E. J., and Koupernik, C. (Eds.), *The Child in His Family: Children at Psychiatric Risk,* vol. 3, John Wiley, New York, 1974.
4. ——, "The Reactions of Adults to Adolescents and Their Behavior," in Caplan, G., and Lebovici, S. (Eds.), *Adolescence: Psychosocial Perspectives,* pp. 54–78, Basic Books, New York, 1969.
5. BAUMRIND, D., "Early Socialization and Adolescent Competence," in Dragastin, S. E., and Elder, G. H., Jr. (Eds.), *Adolescence in the Life Cycle,* pp. 117–143, John Wiley, New York, 1975.
6. BESKIND, H., "Psychiatric Inpatient Treatment of Adolescents: A Review of Clinical Experience," *Comprehensive Psychiatry, 3*:354–369, 1962.
7. BLOS, P., SR., "The Second Individuation Process of Adolescence," in Eissler, R. S., et al. (Eds.), *The Psychoanalytic Study of the Child,* vol. 22, pp. 162–186, International Universities Press, New York, 1967.
8. BURT, R. A., "The Therapeutic Use and Abuse of State Power over Adolescents," in Schoolar, J. C. (Ed.), *Current Issues in Adolescent Psychiatry,* pp. 243–251, Brunner/Mazel, New York, 1973.
9. CAIN, A. C., "On the Meaning of 'Playing Crazy' in Borderline Children," *Psychiatry, 27*:278–289, 1964.

10. CAMERON, K., "Symposium on Inpatient Treatment of Psychotic Adolescents," *British Journal of Medical Psychology, 23*:107–119, 1950.
11. CAPLAN, G., "Elements of a Comprehensive Community Mental Health Program for Adolescents," in Caplan, G. and Lebovici, S. (Eds.), *Adolescence: Psychosocial Perspectives,* Basic Books, New York, 1969.
12. CAUDILL, W., "Social Processes in a Collective Disturbance," in Greenblatt, M. Levinson, D. I., and Williams, R. H. (Eds.), *The Patient and the Mental Hospital,* pp. 438–472, Free Press, Glencoe, Ill., 1957.
13. CUMMING, J., and CUMMING, E., *Ego and Milieu: Theory and Practice of Environmental Therapy,* Atherton Press, New York, 1967.
14. CURRAN, F. J., "Organization of a Ward for Adolescents in Bellevue Psychiatric Hospital," *American Journal of Psychiatry, 95*:1365–1371, 1939.
15. DAVENPORT, C., and HARRISON, S. I., "Gender Identity Change in a Female Adolescent Transexual," *Archives of Sexual Behavior, 6*:327–340, 1977.
16. DOUVAN, E., and ADELSON, J., *The Adolescent Experience,* John Wiley, New York, 1966.
17. DRAGASTIN, S. E., "Research Themes and Priorities," in Dragastin, S. E., and Elder, G. H., Jr. (Eds.), *Adolescence in the Life Cycle,* pp. 291–302, John Wiley, New York, 1975.
18. DULIT, E., "Adolescent Thinking *à la* Piaget: The Formal Stage," *Journal of Youth and Adolescence, 1*:281–301, 1972.
19. DURKIN, R. P., and DURKIN, A. B., "Evaluating Residential Treatment Programs for Disturbed Children," in Guttentag, M., and Strikning, E. L. (Eds.), *Handbook*

of Evaluation Research, vol. 2, pp. 275–339, Sage Publications, Beverly Hills, 1975.

20. EASSON, W. M., *The Severely Disturbed Adolescent*, International Universities Press, New York, 1969.

21. ———, "Adolescent Inpatients in Love: A Therapeutic Contradiction," *Archives of General Psychiatry*, *16*:758–763, 1967.

22. EDELSON, M., *Sociotherapy and Psychotherapy*, University of Chicago Press, Chicago, 1970.

23. ELKIND, D., "Recent Research on Cognitive Development in Adolescence," in Dragastin, S. E., and Elder, G. H., Jr. (Eds.), *Adolescence in the Life Cycle*, pp. 49–62, John Wiley, New York, 1975.

24. ERIKSON, E. H., "The Problem of Ego Identity," *Journal of the American Psychoanalytic Association*, *4*: 56–121, 1956.

25. ESMAN, A. H., "Consolidation of the Ego Ideal in Contemporary Adolescence," *Psychosocial Process*, *2*:47–54, 1971.

26. FALSTEIN, E. I., FEINSTEIN, S., and COHEN, W. P., "An Integrated Adolescent Care Program in a General Psychiatric Hospital," *American Journal of Orthopsychiatry*, *30*:276–289, 1960.

27. ———, et al., "Group Dynamics: Inpatient Adolescents Engage in an Outbreak of Vandalism," *Archives of General Psychiatry*, *9*:32–45, 1963.

28. FINE, P., and OFFER, D., "Periodic Outbursts of Antisocial Behavior: Outbursts Among Adolescents in a General Psychiatric Hospital," *Archives of General Psychiatry*, *13*:240–254, 1965.

29. FREUD, A., "Adolescence," in Eissler, R. S., et al. (Eds.), *The Psychoanalytic Study of the Child*, vol. 13, pp. 255–258, International Universities Press, New York, 1958.

30. GADPAILLE, W. J., "A Consideration of Two Concepts of Normality as it Applies to Adolescent Sexuality," *Journal of the American Academy of Child Psychiatry*, *15*:679–692, 1976.

31. GITTELMAN-KLEIN, R., "Pharmacotherapy and Management of Pathological Separation Anxiety," in Gittelman-Klein, R. (Ed.), *Recent Advances in Child Psychopharmacology*, pp. 255–272, Human Sciences Press, New York, 1975.

32. GOLD, M., and MANN, D., "Delinquency as Defense," *American Journal of Orthopsychiatry*, *42*:463–479, 1972.

33. GOSSETT, J. T., et al., "The Adolescent Treatment Assessment Project: Lessons Learned in Process," *Timberlawn Foundation Report* no. 89, April 1976.

34. ———, et al., "Follow-up of Adolescents Treated in a Psychiatric Hospital: I. A Review of Studies," *American Journal of Orthopsychiatry*, *43*:602–610, 1973.

35. GREENBERG, H. R., BLANK, R., and ARGRETT, S., "The Anatomy of Elopement from an Acute Adolescent Service: Escape from Engagement," *Psychiatric Quarterly*, *42*:28–47, 1968.

36. GRUNEBAUM, H. V., and KLERMAN, G. L., "Wrist Slashing," *American Journal of Psychiatry*, *124*:527–534, 1967.

37. HAMBURG, B. A., "Early Adolescence: A Specific and Stressful Stage of the Life Cycle," in Coelho, G. V., Hamburg, D. A., and Adams, J. E. (Eds.), *Coping and Adaptation*, pp. 47–68, Basic Books, New York, 1974.

38. HANEY, B., and GOLD, M., "The Juvenile Delinquent Nobody Knows," *Psychology Today*, pp. 49–55, September 1973.

39. HARRISON, S. I., McDERMOTT, J. F., JR., and CHETHIK, M., "Residential Treatment of Children: The Psychotherapist-Administrator," *Journal of the American Academy of Child Psychiatry*, *8*:385–410, 1969.

40. HASLAM, M. T., *Psychiatric Illness in Adolescence: Its Psychopathology and Prognosis*, Butterworths, Boston, 1975.

41. HENDRICKSON, W. J., and HOLMES, D., "Control of

Behavior as a Crucial Factor in an All Adolescent Ward," *American Journal of Psychiatry*, *115*:969–975, 1959.

42. ———, and WAGGONER, R. W., "Psychotherapy of the Hospitalized Adolescent," *American Journal of Psychiatry*, *115*:965–970, 1959.

43. HENRY, J., "Types of Institutional Structure," in Greenblatt, M., Levinson, D. J., and Williams, R. H. (Eds.), *The Patient and the Mental Hospital*, pp. 73–90, Free Press, Glencoe, Ill., 1957.

44. HUDGENS, R. W., *Psychiatric Disorders in Adolescents*, Williams & Wilkins, Baltimore, 1974.

45. JONES, M. C., "Psychological Correlates of Somatic Development," *Child Development*, *36*:899–911, 1965.

46. KAUFMAN, I., et al., "Delineation of Two Diagnostic Groups Among Juvenile Delinquents: The Schizophrenic and the Impulse-Ridden Character Disorder," *Journal of the American Academy of Child Psychiatry*, *2*:292–318, 1963.

47. KERNBERG, O. F., "Modern Hospital Milieu Treatment of Schizophrenia," in Arieti, S., and Chrzanowski, G. (Eds.), *New Dimensions in Psychiatry: A World View*, pp. 201–220, John Wiley, New York, 1975.

48. ———, "Psychoanalytic Object-Relations Theory, Group Processes, and Administration: Toward an Integrative Theory of Hospital Treatment," *Annual of Psychoanalysis*, *1*:363–388, 1973.

49. KNESPER, D., and MILLER, D., "Treatment Plans for Mental Health Care," *American Journal of Psychiatry*, *133*:45–50, 1976.

50. KOHLBERG, L., and GILLIGAN, C., "The Adolescent as a Philosopher: A Discovery of the Self in a Postconventional World," *Daedalus*, *100*:1051–1086, 1971.

51. ———, LaCROSSE, J., and RICKS, D., "The Predictability of Adult Mental Health from Childhood Behavior," in Wolman, B. B. (Ed.), *Manual of Child Psychopathology*, pp. 1217–1284, McGraw-Hill, New York, 1972.

52. LAWTON, M. P., and COHEN, J., "Organizational Studies of Mental Hospitals," in Guttentag, M., and Struening, E. L. (Eds.), *Handbook of Evaluation Research*, pp. 201–238, Sage Publications, Beverly Hills, 1975.

53. LEHRER, P., SCHIFF, L., and ANTON, K., "Operant Conditioning in a Comprehensive Treatment Program for Adolescents," *Archives of General Psychiatry*, *25*:515–521, 1971.

54. LESSEM, L., "On the Voluntary Admission of Minors," *Journal of Law Reform*, *8*:189–216, 1974.

55. LEVY, E. Z., "Some Thoughts About Patients Who Run Away from Residential Treatment and the Staff They Leave Behind," *Psychiatric Quarterly*, *46*:1–21, 1972.

56. LEWIS, D. O., and BALLA, D. A., *Delinquency and Psychopathology*, Grune & Stratton, New York, 1976.

57. LEWIS, J. M., et al., *No Single Thread: Psychological Health in Family Systems*, Brunner/Mazel, New York, 1976.

58. LIDZ, T., *The Origin and Treatment of Schizophrenic Disorders*, Basic Books, New York, 1973.

59. MAIN, T. F., "The Ailment," *British Journal of Medical Psychology*, *30*:129–125, 1957.

60. MALUCCIO, A. N., and MARLOW, W. D., "Residential Treatment of Emotionally Disturbed Children: A Review of the Literature," *The Social Service Review*, *46*:230–250, 1972.

61. MAROHN, R. C., *Hospital Treatment of the Juvenile Delinquent*, in press.

62. ———, et al., "Psychodynamic Types of Institutionalized Juvenile Delinquents—A Reformulation," mimeographed, September 1976.

63. MAROHN, R. C., et al., "A Hospital Riot: Its Determinants and Implications for Treatment," *American Journal of Psychiatry*, *130*:631–636, 1973.

64. MASTERSON, J. F., *Treatment of the Borderline Adolescent: A Developmental Approach*, Wiley-Interscience, New York, 1972.

65. ———, *The Psychiatric Dilemma of Adolescence*, Little Brown, Boston, 1967.

66. ———, and RINSLEY, D. B., "The Borderline Syndrome: The Role of the Mother in the Genesis and Psychic Structure of the Borderline Personality," *International Journal of Psycho-Analysis, 56:*163–177, 1975.

67. MEDNICK, S. A., and SHAFFER, J., "Mother's Retrospective Reports in Child Rearing Research," *American Journal of Orthopsychiatry, 33:*457–461, 1964.

68. MEEKS, J. E., "Psychiatric Treatment of the Adolescent," in Freedman, A. M., Kaplan, H. I., and Sadock, B. J. (Eds.), *Comprehensive Textbook of Psychiatry—II*, pp. 2262–2270, Williams & Wilkins, Baltimore, 1975.

69. ———, *The Fragile Alliance: An Orientation to the Outpatient Psychotherapy of the Adolescent*, Williams & Wilkins, Baltimore, 1971.

70. MILLER, D., "Adolescent Crisis: Challenge for Patient, Parent, Internist," *Annals of Internal Medicine, 79:*435–440, 1973.

71. ———, "The Etiology of an Outbreak of Delinquency in a Group of Hospitalized Adolescents," in Greenblatt, M., Levinson, D. J., and Williams, R. H. (Eds.), *The Patient in the Mental Hospital*, Free Press, Glencoe, Ill., 1957.

72. ———, "The Treatment of Adolescents in an Adult Hospital," *Bulletin of the Menninger Clinic, 21:* 189–199, 1957.

73. ———, and LOONEY, J. G., "Determinants of Homicide in Adolescents," *Annals of the American Society for Adolescent Psychiatry, 4:*231–254, 1975.

74. MOOS, R. H., *Evaluating Treatment Environments: A Social Ecological Approach*, John Wiley, New York, 1974.

75. MORIARTY, A. E., and TOUSSIENG, P. W., *Adolescent Coping*, Grune & Stratton, New York, 1976.

76. MORRISON, G. C., and COLLIER, J. G., "Family Treatment Approaches to Suicidal Children and Adolescents," *Journal of the American Academy of Child Psychiatry, 8:*140–153, 1969.

77. NEIMARK, E. D., "Intellectual Development During Adolescence," *Review of Child Development Research, 4:*541–594, 1975.

78. NOSHPITZ, J. D., "The Psychotherapist in Residential Treatment," in Mayer, M. F., and Blum, A. (Eds.), *Healing Through Living*, pp. 158–175, Charles C Thomas, Springfield, Ill., 1971.

79. ———, "Notes on the Theory of Residential Treatment," *Journal of the American Academy of Child Psychiatry, 1:*284–296, 1962.

80. ———, "Opening Phase in the Psychotherapy of Adolescents with Character Disorders," *Bulletin of the Menninger Clinic, 21:*153–164, 1957.

81. OFFER, D., and BARGELOW, P., "Adolescent and Young Adult Self-Mutilation Incidents in a General Hospital," *Archives of General Psychiatry, 3:*194–204, 1960.

82. OFFER, D., and OFFER, J. B., *From Teenage to Young Manhood: A Psychological Study*, Basic Books, New York, 1975.

83. PAO, P., "The Syndromes of Delicate Self-Cutting," *British Journal of Medical Psychology, 42:*195–206, 1969.

84. Peer Review Committee, *Manual of Psychiatric Peer Review*, American Psychiatric Association, Washington, D.C., 1976.

85. PERROW, C., "Hospitals: Technology, Structure, and Goals," in March, J. G. (Ed.), *Handbook of Organizations*, Rand McNally, Chicago, 1965.

86. PICHEL, J. I., "A Long-Term Follow-Up Study of 60 Adolescent Psychiatric Outpatients," *American Journal of Psychiatry, 131:*140–144, 1974.

87. RASKIN, A. H., " 'The System' Keeps the Young Waiting," *The New York Times*, December 5, 1976.

88. RINSLEY, D. B., "Theory and Practice of Intensive Residential Treatment of Adolescents," *Annals of the American Society for Adolescent Psychiatry, 1:*479–509, 1971.

89. ———, "Intensive Residential Treatment of the Adolescent," *Psychiatric Quarterly, 41:*134–143, 1967.

90. ———, "Intensive Psychiatric Hospital Treatment of Adolescents: An Object-Relations View," *Psychiatric Quarterly, 39:*405–429, 1965.

91. ———, and HALL, D. D., "Psychiatric Hospital Treatment of Adolescents: Parental Resistances as Expressed in Casework Metaphor," *Archives of General Psychiatry, 7:*286–294, 1962.

92. RINSLEY, D. B., and INGE, G. P., "Psychiatric Hospital Treatment of Adolescents: Verbal and Nonverbal Resistance to Treatment," *Bulletin of the Menninger Clinic, 25:*249–263, 1961.

93. ROBBINS, L. C., "The Accuracy of Parental Recall of Aspects of Child Development and of Child Rearing Practices," *Journal of Abnormal Social Psychology, 66:* 261–270, 1963.

94. ROBINS, L. N., *Deviant Children Grown Up*, Williams & Wilkins, Baltimore, 1966.

95. ROSSMAN, P. G., and KNESPER, D. L., "The Early Phase of Hospital Treatment for Disruptive Adolescents," *Journal of the American Academy of Child Psychiatry, 15:*693–708, 1976.

96. ROTH, L. H., and MEISEL, A., "Dangerousness, Confidentiality, and the Duty to Warn," *American Journal of Psychiatry, 134:*508–511, 1977.

97. RUTTER, M., *The Qualities of Mothering: Maternal Deprivation Reassessed*, Jason Aronson, New York, 1974.

98. ———, "Relationships Between Child and Adult Psychiatric Disorders," *Acta Psychiatrica Scandinavica, 48:*3–21, 1972.

99. SABBATH, J. C., "The Suicidal Adolescent—The Expendable Child," *Journal of the American Academy of Child Psychiatry, 8:*272–289, 1969.

100. SATTERFIELD, J. H., and CANTWELL, D. P., "Psychopharmacology in the Prevention of Antisocial and Delinquent Behavior," in Gittelman-Klein, R. (Ed.), *Recent Advances in Child Psychopharmacology*, pp. 228–238, Human Sciences Press, New York, 1975.

101. SCHONFELD, W. A., "Comprehensive Community Programs for the Investigation and Treatment of Adolescents," in Howells, J. G. (Ed.), *Modern Perspectives in Adolescent Psychiatry*, pp. 483–511, Brunner/Mazel, New York, 1971.

102. SCHWARTZ, M. S., "What is a Therapeutic Milieu?" in Greenblatt, M., Levinson, D. J., and Williams, R. H. (Eds.), *The Patient and the Mental Hospital*, pp. 130–144, Free Press, Glencoe, Ill., 1957.

103. SCHWARTZ, G., and PUNTIL, J. E., *Summary and Policy Implications of the Youth and Society in Illinois Reports*, Institute for Juvenile Research, Chicago, 1977.

104. SHAPIRO, E. R., et al., "The Borderline Ego and the Working Alliance: Indications for Family and Individual Treatment in Adolescence," *International Journal of Psychoanalysis, 58:*77–87, 1977.

105. SNYDER, A. R., *Brief of American Psychiatric Association, American Society for Adolescent Psychiatry, American Academy of Child Psychiatry, and American Association of Psychiatric Services for Children, As Amici Curiae*, Press of Byron S. Adams Printing, Washington, D.C., 1976.

106. STANTON, A. H., and SCHWARTZ, N. S., *The Mental Hospital*, Basic Books, New York, 1954.

107. STIERLIN, H., *Separating Parents and Adolescents*, Quadrangle, New York, 1974.

108. STONE, A. A., "Overview: The Right to Treatment—Comments on the Law and Its Impact," *American Journal of Psychiatry, 132:*1125–1134, 1975.

109. STONE, M. H., "The Parental Factor in Adolescent Suicide," *International Journal of Child Psychotherapy, 2:*163–201, 1973.

110. VEIGA, M., "The Missing Child: Family Reactions to Hospitalization of Children with Mental Disorders," *American Journal of Orthopsychiatry, 34:*145–148, 1964.

111. WARREN, W., "Treatment of Youths with Behavior Disorders in a Psychiatric Hospital," *British Journal of Delinquency, 3:*234–249, 1953.

112. ———, "Inpatient Treatment of Adolescents and Psychological Illnesses," *Lancet, 1:*147–153, 1952.

113. WEINTROB, A., "Long-term Treatment of the Severely Disturbed Adolescent: Residential Treatment versus Hospitalization," *Journal of the American Academy of Child Psychiatry, 14:*436–450, 1975.

114. WENAR, C., "The Reliability of Mothers' Histories," *Child Development, 32:*491–500, 1961.

115. WESTMAN, J. C., "The Legal Rights of Adolescents from a Developmental Perspective," in Schooler, J. C.

(Ed.), *Current Issues in Adolescent Psychiatry,* pp. 252–262, Brunner/Mazel, New York, 1973.

116. WILLIAMS, F. S., "Family Therapy: Its Role in Adolescent Psychiatry," *Annals of the American Society for Adolescent Psychiatry, 2:*324–339, 1973.

117. WYNNE, L. C., "Communication Disorders and the Quest for Relatedness in Families of Schizophrenics," *American Journal of Psychoanalysis, 30:*100–114, 1970.

118. ZINNER, J., and SHAPIRO, E. R., "Splitting in Families of Borderline Adolescents," in Mack, J. E. (Ed.), *Borderline States in Psychiatry,* pp. 103–122, Grune & Stratton, New York, 1975.

119. ———, and SHAPIRO, R., "Projective Identification as a Mode of Perception and Behavior in Families of Adolescents," *International Journal of Psychoanalysis, 53:* 523–529, 1972.

17 / Psychiatric Day Treatment

Jack C. Westman

Historical Perspective

Healing the seriously emotionally disturbed child poses a fundamental dilemma. The healthy development of children depends upon normal living conditions and is stunted by institutionalization. However, the intensive treatment of troubled children necessitates major interventions in their lives. In the past, when outpatient therapy was not sufficient, nothing could be done while children remained in their homes since the only intensive treatment available required hospitalization.

In 1943, with the opening of a therapeutic nursery school in the J. J. Putnam Children's Center in Roxbury, Massachusetts, it became apparent that the psychiatric team could build therapeutic experiences into the daily life of disturbed young children without removing them from their families.[27] In 1950, the Dayton Children's Psychiatric Hospital opened a day treatment service.[28] Three years later, the League School for Emotionally Disturbed Children was established by Fenichel as an outgrowth of the Children's Psychiatric Unit of Kings County Hospital in Brooklyn, New York.[12] Previously the concept of the "day hospital" for the psychiatric treatment of adults[6, 8] had been introduced in 1947 by Cameron in Montreal.

By 1963 ten day treatment programs for children were reported by the National Institute of Mental Health's Biostatistics Division. The concept of day treatment caught hold, and the following decade saw a ninefold increase in such programs for all ages. Yet, in 1972 only 60 of 344 residential treatment centers for children reported day units, and only 2.8 percent of all treatment episodes for both adults and children took place in day treatment programs.[25]

Despite its great intellectual, economic, and clinical appeal, the day-treatment concept did not proliferate as rapidly as had been anticipated. The reasons for this are not clear; undoubtedly they relate to many factors. Several considerations may be mentioned, however. One is that additional time was needed to properly evaluate and stimulate adoption of the new program. Another is that the general climate was one of giving the highest priority to the establishment of community mental health centers.[17] Children's psychiatric facilities could only grow slowly as attention to them was deferred to this primary concern. The appearance of specialized educational services in public schools also eclipsed the need for children's psychiatric services within the health-care system. A further development was the emphasis upon family therapy which tended to obscure the specific needs of individual children for intensive treatment. The continuing potential for day-treatment growth, however, is indicated by the heavy use of existing programs, the inclusion of day treatment in model children's psychiatric centers, and the persistent pressure to reduce psychiatric treatment costs for children.

Rationale

Although conceptually a simple and obvious means of treating the troubled child, day treatment came into existence as a reaction to the disadvantages of institutional treatment. The long experience of institutions and community child guidance clinics led each modality to expand toward day treatment. The institution initially expanded day treatment in order to extend bridging services to discharged patients and the clinic followed suit in an effort to care for children too handicapped to profit from outpatient treatment alone.[9, 29]

The regressive potential of hospital care has been recognized as antitherapeutic. "Institutionalization" is a result of continued dependency of children upon the protected environment of a residential setting. In some instances, this has served to condition the child to an artificial existence. The "closed ranks" phenomenon is another force that operates to discourage reentry of the child into his home community.[7]

More recently, day-treatment programs have been conceptualized and planned in more positive terms. They have been employed as the primary initial treatment modality, as a transitional phase after residential care, and as an extension of the diagnostic process. However used, day treatment challenges the patient, family, and staff to maintain community ties. Because the parents have daily responsibility for the child, day treatment provides leverage for change in the family.

As mandatory state education laws increase the number of special education programs, their capabilities and limitations have become evident. For those children who need more than an education program is able to provide, psychiatric day treatment offers a comprehensive interdisciplinary resource.

Disadvantages

Although a part of the child's community, a day-treatment program is not a part of the mainstream of children's lives. As with residential treatment and special education classes, the child's presence in a day program may encourage dependence upon a protected environment and hence promote regression. Social isolation of the child can also develop if care is not taken to preserve the child's role in a neighborhood peer group.

Another disadvantage may arise as a result of a child's removal from association with healthier children and immersion into a group of handicapped peers. The possibility of regression through exposure to more disturbed peers is a significant factor to be balanced against the possible therapeutic benefits.

Because of their availability in the community and separation from local schools, day programs can be used as enclaves for children regarded as school misfits or uneducable. Subsequent reentry into schools can later be impeded by the community's tendency to exclude deviant children. An adequate liaison service and integration with the network of community services are necessary to minimize both of these tendencies.

A significant risk in the day treatment of a child is the possibility that removal of the child from the visible mainstream may mask a disintegrating or neglectful home. There is likely to be a temporary reduction of community concern about the family because the child is in treatment. A child may, therefore, be allowed to remain in an environment that resists change and fosters subtle deterioration. Conversely, a disturbed child living at home during day treatment may pose an overwhelming burden for the parents and adversely affect the development of siblings.

The continued presence of the children in pathogenic families may serve to reinforce familial scapegoating. The net effect may well outweigh whatever gains are made by day treatment. This is particularly true for antisocial children. In such instances, the acting out serves unconscious parental motives of enormous intensity, so much so that progress cannot be made while the child lives at home.

Most of the disadvantages of day treatment relate to the severity of family pathology and to the fact that day treatment is apart from the educational mainstream.

Program Description

Day-treatment programs offer intensive psychiatric treatment resources to children who remain with their families. An effective program of this sort provides total, comprehensive treatment for all aspects of a child's problem, encompassing the individual child, family, peer group, educational experience, and community living. To meet a child's total treatment needs, no element of an interdisciplinary program can be omitted. It is for this reason that day-treatment programs tend to be within the health-care system and are difficult to carry out in an adequate fashion within the educational system.

The aims of day treatment are those of any psychiatric program for children: to relieve anxiety and to promote the development of adaptive skills, interpersonal relationships, self-knowledge, self-control, and self-esteem. In brief, the aim is to overcome those factors that prevent the forward sweep of individual development. In order to achieve these objectives, the program employs diagnostic resources, a structured therapeutic milieu, specialized educational services, individual psychotherapy, group therapy, family therapy, activity therapy, language therapy, psychopharmacological treatment, community liaison resources, and meaningful parent participation.

Indications and Contraindications

Because day treatment can be a primary, transitional, or adjunctive treatment modality, the indications for its use vary widely. Generally, day treatment is for children who are unable to function in community school programs and who require comprehensive, interdisciplinary management. It is indicated, particularly, for children with academic or behavioral disabilities that result from faulty ego development or from disabling levels of anxiety. These should be children who may remain in the home as long as they are simultaneously receiving the benefit of intensive treatment.

Reports are becoming available describing the characteristics of day-treatment populations. These patients resemble inpatient populations and may be diagnosed as suffering from psychoses, developmental disorders, organic syndromes, character disorders, severe neuroses, and moderate neurotic conditions.[2, 5, 13, 18] The admission criteria frequently include a relatively favorable prognosis; ultimately the children are assumed to be capable of functioning in a community school, either at a regular or at a special educational level. Brief day treatment has been used to facilitate a child's ability to remain in regular classes. Day treatment ordinarily is not a terminal track in itself. For very seriously disturbed children, day treatment may be useful in preparing a child for self-care in an institution.

The critical factor in deciding between day treatment and residential care is whether or not remaining at home and in the community will facilitate the child's treatment. Of greatest importance is the family's capacity to care for their child, support the day program, and benefit from what it offers them. When the pathological influences of the family outweigh the therapeutic benefits provided by the child's presence in the home, day treatment should not be elected even though the family prefers it and/or it costs less. When separation from the family is to the child's advantage, residential treatment is the treatment of choice. The presence of both residential and day-treatment resources within the same facility permits the flexible use of each modality.[11]

The distance to be traveled may be a critical factor in discouraging day treatment. Extended distances, involving over one hour of travel time, may pose undesirable burdens on the troubled child. The decision about treatment has to weigh the factors of fatigue and stress caused by travel to and from the program. Extended travel time may further deprive the child of neighborhood peer associations.

Program Content

The formats of day-treatment programs vary with their aims. Some are oriented toward educational and others toward psychotherapeutic techniques. All psychiatric day programs, however, are distinguished from educational programs by the availability of a full range of mental health, health, and educational disciplines.

ADMINISTRATIVE ORGANIZATION

Two basic lines of organization are required to ensure both the integrity of the program and the individualization of each child's therapeutic care. The first line fixes responsibility for the overall operation in a director and heads of the various functional components. A democratic atmosphere is necessary for the appropriate recognition of each staff member's competence and contribution; nonetheless, the demands of program accountability require fixed points of responsibility.[19] Unfortunately, many psychiatric programs have suffered from the ambiguity of lines of authority. There are pressures from many directions—staff, families, patients, administrative boards, and peer-review mechanisms. These necessitate both the maximum participation of all disciplines in decision making and the designation of individuals with budgetary, personnel, and program responsibility. Successful programs reflect a coherent treatment philosophy implemented by a broadly trained and experienced director with ultimate responsibility for personnel and budgetary matters.

A second administrative line is utilized to coordinate the components of the program so that they meet the unique treatment needs of each child and family. This integration of disciplines can best be achieved through a therapeutic team comprised of the individual staff members working directly with each child. Of the essence, however, is their coordination by a case manager who assumes responsibility for planning, documenting, and monitoring the child's program and its relationship with extramural elements.

The program's administrative organization and the therapeutic teams interdigitate by frequent staff meetings plus regular intake, progress, and discharge conferences. The frequency of these meetings should ensure continuous review and revision of each child's program objectives and management plan. The ongoing study of the staff's efforts with each child minimizes the inevitable tendency to develop favorites or scapegoats.

PROGRAM SCHEDULE

The effective use of each child's time maximizes the therapeutic impact of day treatment. Activities are planned with the rhythms and the capabilities of children in mind. The interplay of structured and free time, of recreational and work activities, and of individual and group interaction are critical elements in the therapeutic structure. At the same time, the morale of staff members must be protected; disturbed children tax the energies and motivation of even the most dedicated workers.

Figure 17-1 is a prototype schedule developed by combining several model day-treatment programs.

PHYSICAL PLANT

Day-treatment programs may take place in a variety of settings; in every case, however, the basic facilities should take into account the needs of growing children. The location should minimize the distraction of traffic noise and the restrictions of competing adult activities. This benefits the program and reduces the danger of offended neighbors. Accessibility to parking and to drop off points helps minimize inconveniences of transportation. The division of space into quiet and noisy areas provides environmental cues for work or play. In addition to classroom and activity rooms, both indoor and outside play areas are needed. Access to a swimming pool is not a luxury for children. They profit from sensory contact with water as a stimulus to skill development and as a site for physical contact with others and the learning of self-confidence.

PROGRAM ELEMENTS

The proximity of the day service to the child's home brings the staff into close association with the realities of the child's life. Conversely, because there is no hospital ward to absorb disruptive behavior, the ups and downs of the child's treatment have visible repercussions in the community. Both of these factors necessitate sensitive responsiveness of the staff to the child's family and community. Occurrrences in the child's home become staff concerns, and events within the day service can be utilized in helping the family. The staff will identify issues and crises for use in family therapy.

The flexibility demanded by the numerous points of contact between all disciplines and the child's family and community results in blurring of professional roles. For those familiar with hospital or residential care, it is important to note that children in day treatment are continuously within the physical space of the service. This requires the staff to relate more closely to each other than is the case in a residential setting, where the child moves back and forth between an activity area and a ward or living unit, as discussed in chapter 15. Furthermore, in day treatment, activities are compressed in a back-to-back sequence, placing a high premium on efficient and coordinated schedule and curriculum planning.

The strength of each individual component is essential to the effectiveness of the interdisciplinary team. The complexity of child psychiatric treatment makes it impossible for any one discipline alone to provide for a child's total care. In addition to the child's need for attention throughout a full day, the number of technical skills required are beyond the competence of a single discipline.

The range of disciplines for work with children

FIGURE 17–1

Composite Schedule of Several Model Day-treatment Programs

	Monday	Tuesday	Wednesday	Thursday	Friday
8:00					
	Staff meeting	Staff meeting	Staff meeting	Staff meeting	Staff meeting
9:00					
	School	Arts and crafts	School	Arts and crafts	School
10:00					
	Tutoring	School	Tutoring	School	Tutoring
10:45					
	Morning snack	Morning snack	Morning snack	Morning snack	Morning snack
11:00					
	Arts and crafts	Tutoring	Arts and crafts	Tutoring	Arts and crafts
12:30					
	Mealtime	Mealtime	Mealtime	Mealtime	Mealtime
1:00					
	Recreational therapy	Group psychotherapy	Recreational therapy	Group psychotherapy	Recreational therapy
2:00					
	School	School	School	School	School
3:00					
	Individual psychotherapy	Recreational therapy	Individual psychotherapy	Recreational therapy	Individual psychotherapy
4:00					
	Staff intake conference	Staff case review	Family therapy	Parent liaison	Staff development seminar

deserves special comment. Day programs have grown either from hospital or community services; the specific disciplines involved in a given program are likely to reflect the staffing patterns of the parent programs as much as they do the actual skills and training needed to serve the children. For this reason, nurses and child-care workers may play a prominent role in a program with a hospital base and not be represented at all in a program developed from a community clinic. A basic staffing pattern includes a sufficient variety of professionals to provide for the following necessary functions.

Therapeutic Milieu. Every aspect of the child's day should be used for therapeutic purposes. Some of the most important opportunities for therapeutic intervention occur at unscheduled and informal moments. Among the common problems for children in day treatment are an intolerance to change and disorganization. Consequently, the ways children handle arrival, departure, and the moving from one activity to another may both expose personality problems and offer opportunities to deal sensitively with them therapeutically. The service must assign specific responsibility for supportive handling of transitions, routine liaison with parents, mealtimes, and crisis intervention; unless all of this is built in, a major program element is lost.

The effective management of the children's crises is a vital requirement of both the scheduled and unscheduled aspects of the therapeutic milieu. It is facilitated by resources such as classroom telephones and "time out" spaces. Specific routine techniques for dealing with problem behavior include: (1) labeling affects and behavior to help children see themselves as others see them; (2) life-space interviews;[26] (3) arranging "time outs" from activities for "cooling off" with a staff member; (4) giving children feedback on the effect of their behavior on others; (5) helping children distinguish fantasies from actions; (6) helping children learn to accept failure and tolerate frustration; (7) providing firm, supportive management when self-control is lost; (8) desensitizing children to activities with unpleasant feelings and associations; (9) guiding peer pressure constructively when a child's behavior is offensive to the group; and (10) selectively prescribing medications.

The staff responsible for the supportive milieu should be skilled in life-space interviewing, behavioral therapy, first aid, the administration of medications, parent liaison, and supportive psychotherapy. With these skills, the staff members can deal with the informal events and back up the formally scheduled parts of the day. These functions may be performed by nurses, child-care workers, and other trained in these skills.

Psychotherapy. The definitive treatment of the emotionally disturbed child is based upon an understanding of each child, his defensive operations, coping behaviors, and his view of self and the world. Without understanding why a child is not adapting successfully, no rational treatment plan can be designed. There is no substitute for the intimate knowledge gained both from ongoing behavioral observations and sensitive interactions with each child. A staff member who is familiar with psychodynamics and is skilled in interviewing techniques can infuse the child's program with an understanding of motivations and defenses. This will have application in all aspects of the child's treatment.

Depending upon each child's needs, the program may provide individual psychotherapy, group therapy, child-oriented family therapy, or some appropriate combination of modalities. These are discussed in chapters 2, 3, 7, and 10. The child's psychotherapist should be prepared to handle case managerial responsibilities.[3] Without professionals trained in these responsibilities, a program cannot be sufficiently informed and flexible to meet each child's needs.

Specialized Educational Services. Most children who need day treatment show deficits in academic skills. They may have learned socially disruptive skills all too thoroughly, but their ability to function competently in school is likely to be impaired.

In our society, school is an essential part of every child's life. The school thus forms the backbone of day treatment. It provides for the child's formal education, and it is the site for key interpersonal experiences with both adults and peers. The classroom curriculum, atmosphere, grouping, scheduling, and routines, and how they are handled by the teacher, all have implications for socializing experiences that can induce change and growth.[12]

The basic educational objectives can be met through individual planning and work with each child. However, a small-group environment is also necessary because it provides children with the opportunity to work effectively with peers.

The educational philosophy should stress the acquisition of socially useful information. At the same time, it should seek to provide coping skills, competencies which capitalize upon family activities and events of immediate and concrete significance to each child. In addition to small-group teaching, the special education staff should be skilled in behavioral therapy, individual remedial tutoring, life-space interviewing, group leadership, and team functioning. Behavioral therapy and counseling is discussed in detail in chapters 5 and 11, and the other psychoeducational approaches are discussed in chapters 19 and 20.

Family Therapy. In keeping with one of its basic missions, family therapy occupies a prominent place in day treatment. The child's presence in the home and the family's support of day treatment provide a natural matrix for therapeutic work with the child's entire family. In the course of such work, particular emphasis falls on the child's role both as victim of and source of pathogenic processes in the family. Experience suggests that at least half of the parents may be expected to be functioning at psychotic or character disorder levels. Although practical considerations may limit the degree to which such family treatment can be carried out, the responsibility to the child of the day program includes an exhaustive exploration of these possibilities.

Professionals trained in the techniques of family therapy can be called upon to address the family itself as the focus of treatment. They seek to produce change in family relationships and style of interaction. When indicated, the day program should also either provide for or refer family members (other than the child) for individual treatment. Parent counseling and therapy is discussed in chapter 8 and family therapy is discussed in chapter 7.

Parent Liaison. Quite apart from family therapy, the parents, relatives and other community figures are given significant roles in the ongoing life of the day service. They participate in the activities, treatment, and administration. Liaison with parents is vital to the child's progress in school and recreational activities. Parents aid in social and recreational activities, and assist in fund raising. A direct role for parents in the program's administration is offered by such mechanisms as a community-parent advisory committee.

For some parents, an intermediate goal of family therapy is to bring them to participate in such parent-oriented activities. For others, parent activities may be an introduction to family treatment. In either case, parent involvement strengthens the day program and enhances the parents' ability to relate to their child and to deal with their psychiatric problems with dignity.

One of the aims of parent liaison is to make parents members of the treatment team. Training programs for parents can teach them how to aid their children in developing self-care, communication, socialization, and academic skills.[10] In this way, parents can continue the therapeutic management in the home.

It is necessary to distinguish clearly between the parents' role in liaison activities and in family therapy. This establishes an important model for the child—one in which both the parents' strengths and ability to help and deficits and need for help are openly acknowledged. All staff members can contribute to this function.

Recreational Therapy. An often underestimated source of satisfaction and growth for children is in the achievement of recreational and athletic skills. Some children require physical therapy and many need training in gross motor skills. All children, however, profit from a sense of heightened coordination and a feeling of mastery of their bodies. A range of activities can be offered from eye-hand coordination training through swimming and dance to tennis. An all-weather program should have access to an indoor gym, swimming pool, and outdoor areas. Since performance in recreational games can be a source of either peer rejection or acceptance, each child should be encouraged to develop his capacities to the maximum. Achieving physical fitness is a neglected and, often enough, a problem-laden area in the lives of troubled children. Its meaning goes far beyond the mere development of recreational skills.

Recreational activities help children learn how to play and to translate fantasies into actions. An important opportunity for learning how to relate to peers is gained through games and team membership. Sharing, taking turns, and satisfactions in group efforts can be acquired in this way as well.

It is in this area in particular that coordination with community facilities can both benefit the day program and provide greater visibility for and acceptance of the children in the community. The recreational therapist should be skilled in games, athletic instruction, gross motor coordination training, group leadership, life-space interviewing, and team functioning.

Craft, Art, and Music Therapies. The relevance of this group of skill-mastery activities depends to some extent upon the ages of the children. Creativity is an important part of every child's life. To help a child to discover and use natural talents is an engaging and exciting experience. The wide variety of modern craft, music, and art materials offers stimulating opportunities (many of which were unknown during the earlier days of diversionary craft programs).

In addition to their direct benefits, these activities offer opportunities for cooperation in sharing equipment and materials. An appreciation of others' work and a collaborative relationship with the adult therapist provide concrete ways of developing interpersonal relationships. The therapist should be skilled in teaching crafts, arts, and music, as well as in training children in fine motor coordination, and in group leadership, life-space interviewing, and team functioning.

Language Therapy. Larger day-treatment services may justify the inclusion of a language therapist. Each service, however, should have access to a specialist in communicative disorders. This discipline can provide both direct treatment for the children and consultation to the staff on how best to approach a child's communication problem.

Community Liaison. This function is an area of vital responsibility. Since it is so often taken for granted, it is frequently neglected. It includes the range of extramural resources such as public relations materials, community speaking and education resources, referral channels, relations with funding sources, the provision of orientation information, participation in community councils, and representation within the day service's parent organization.

Liaison with the child's school is crucial to day treatment. Although the ability of the program to prescribe educational management, either during a diagnostic admission or at the time of school entry, is limited, practical coordination with the curriculum and schedule of the school can be carried out with the child's teachers.[20]

Unless responsibilities for this liaison function are specifically assigned to staff members, the whole area is likely to be slighted, and, in the long run, the program will suffer.

Psychopharmacology. Provisions should be made for the prescription, monitoring, and administration of psychoactive and anti-convulsive medications. These are likely to be used with approximately one-third of the patients (see chapter 23). The inclusion of children with psychophysiologic and somatic illnesses also necessitates the presence of a staff member with designated medical responsibility (see chapter 36).

Health Consultation System. The day-treatment service must establish lines of referral to the existing spectrum of health services. It is essential that full cooperation exist in this area. The sporadic and unsystematic use of consultation may lead to an inadequate understanding of the child's psychiatric program by the consultant or to incomplete communication of useful information by the consultant to the day service.

Staff Development. At first glance, an adequate staff in-service training program may appear to be unrelated to program functions. In fact, it is essential to the practical operation of the interdisciplinary team. Idealism or exhortation cannot replace the mutual respect and interdependence fostered by factual knowledge of each other's fields and an understanding of the different points of view of the several disciplines. The result of staff education is usually a simultaneous expansion of each discipline's horizons. It clarifies areas where true overlap exists and sharpens the definition of disciplinary function in areas where expertise is clearly evident.

SUMMER PROGRAM

A valuable option for day services is a summer program. This can operate either as a self-contained experience or as a modification of the regular program to accommodate to children's summer schedules. If the day program continues throughout the year, when summer comes the content of the program can be adapted to include camping and other warm-weather adventures.[21]

In a discrete summer program, specific objectives can be set, such as evaluative-prescriptive studies to aid school programs, attitude-changing experiences for parents, and bolstering the regular school program through intensive skill development.[11]

THE COURSE OF TREATMENT

An optimal sequence for a course of day treatment might begin with the initiation of outpatient psychotherapy with the child and family at the earliest opportunity. This may precede admission to the day-treatment service. The child then moves to the day program when he is unable to function in a community school.

At times the integrity of a child's treatment may be threatened, necessitating special efforts to re-solve conflicts and misunderstandings. The point of transition to community school attendance deserves special comment as well. Because day treatment is not a complete treatment modality in itself, a child may be ready for school reentry before all of the problems are resolved. In fact, as with psychotherapy itself, maximum improvement will not be achieved until the child assumes responsibilities within the educational mainstream. Anxiety in all quarters about a child's readiness for school entry and his potential for success may obscure recognition of signs that he is in fact ready to leave. It may, thus, lead to overprotectiveness, both before, during, and after school entry. For this reason, when entry or reentry into a community school is possible, a transitional period of part-time day service may be meshed with the school schedule.

When he becomes capable of full-time community school attendance, the child's treatment and that of his parents continues on an out-patient basis. This clearly establishes for the child, family, and community that the child is in day treatment only as long as his needs require, and that his treatment is basically outpatient and community-centered.

Preparation of Family and Child

The most important step in preparing a child and family for treatment is a thorough assessment of the child's needs. At least two central purposes are served by the evaluation of a child under consideration for day treatment. The first is to assess the child's general need for treatment which might be met in a variety of ways. The second purpose is to determine specifically whether or not day treatment is the treatment of choice. The initial point of contact with the day service or its parent organization is the first opportunity for obtaining whatever services the child needs. With this in mind, the evaluation of the child is not simply to determine whether or not he may be admitted to the program, but to augment the family's and the community's understanding of the services that the child needs.

The diagnostic process should be based upon information about the child's past, present, and anticipated performance. The parents, school files, and health records provide background information on the child's developmental progress. In complicated situations, the cooperation of social agencies is helpful in obtaining an accurate picture of the child's developmental course. Evidence for developmental arrests and previous regressions can be useful prognostic information. It is helpful to gain an appreciation of the constitutional, cognitive, motor, language, and temperamental factors in the child's developmental history, with particular emphasis on their interdigitation with parenting. When the child's developmental course is placed within the context of the history of the family and the medical history, the child's critical life experiences can be viewed in better perspective. Regardless of the treatment disposition, such a comprehensive developmental history is invaluable to the child's health record.

An understanding of the child's family can be obtained through exploring the family history and the life stories of the parents. Particular emphasis should be placed upon each parent's developmental course, and, when appropriate, a complete genetic history should be elicited, Interviews with the entire family, the parents together, and each parent alone can yield valuable information about family background and interactions.

An appreciation of the child's present assets and liabilities can be gained from direct observation of the child at home, in school, in test settings, and within the day program itself. Information is needed about the child's capacity to function independently, to work in a group, to respond to men and women, to tolerate frustration and control impulses, to test and deal with reality, to concentrate on tasks, to relate to peers, and to pursue special interests and talents.[5]

Although extensive information may be available about the child's behavior and skill levels in school, it is usually worthwhile to draw upon the program's staff for an independent psychoeducational assessment of the child. In the day setting, the child's actual cognitive and academic skill levels may be testable under favorable conditions, and the program staff can use instruments and seek data that relate directly to their treatment objectives.

Psychiatric interviews are used to assess the child's relationship capabilities, handling of drives, strength of internal controls, current dynamic issues, symptom formation, affect and view of self and life. Psychological testing can assess ego strengths and weaknesses, intellectual functioning, dominant fantasy themes, favored defense mechanisms, behavioral reinforcers, and provide information on which to base prognosis. Further knowledge of the child's fine and gross motor performance adds to the information on his current status.

The resulting diagnostic assessment is most usefully cast in the form of a problem-oriented description from which specific treatment objectives can be based. This description sets forth the extent of the child's present handicaps, presents the family picture, permits a determination of the child's need for day treatment, and also provides a baseline from which treatment achievements can be measured, and, ultimately, readiness to leave the program determined. A nosological diagnosis can be made for administrative purposes; however, the most useful formulations relate to psychosocial and competence issues. The diagnosis is a working formulation which changes over time as a result of clarification or change in the clinical picture. A detailed discussion of nosological issues in child psychiatry is available in volume II. Section 3 in volume I is devoted to processes of assessment.

Throughout the diagnostic process, the child and family become acquainted with the service and take a fresh look at the child's problems. If the child is accepted for the program, a more explicit orientation is needed, both to clarify the aims of the service and to deal with such practical matters as financing, schedule, transportation, and treatment techniques. Frank discussions should be conducted with the parents and child to provide dependable information. In addition, brochures and audiovisual aids can be helpful. The child in particular needs help in understanding the reasons for admission to day treatment as well as an explanation of his problems in a way he can grasp. The projected course of treatment should also be outlined so that the child and family understand the role that day treatment is to play in the child's life. The informed consent of the parents is required not only for the treatment techniques themselves, but also to authorize communication with related agencies and the school.

A useful way of spelling out and measuring the attainment of treatment objectives is to start the work by collaboratively devising therapeutic contracts with parents and, when possible, with the child. This step forces confrontation with child and family pathology in a rational and open manner. It can be assumed that the subsequent course of treatment will be dominated by irrational forces. Nonetheless, the existence of an agreed-upon contract provides a foundation in reality that can save the treatment process at moments of crisis. The contract can also minimize the inevitable disappointment that arises from unrealistic expectations for change. The staff benefits from a documented list of treatment objectives. The list provides a management prescription that is shared by all members of the therapeutic team and that sets the tone for the treatment of that child.

Depending upon the program's case load, size, and philosophy, the use of trial admissions can be helpful. The advantage of trial admission is that it provides a direct in vivo test of the program's suitability for that specific child. It must be smoothly coordinated with an alternative disposition, however, lest a negative outcome constitute one more failure for the child without counterbalancing benefits.

Economic Implications

Beyond its therapeutic advantages, the most important advantage of day treatment is economic. With the costs of inpatient child psychiatric care mounting astronomically, the economic benefits of providing equivalent care by day treatment are obvious. The expenses of day treatment are one-third to one-half the cost of hospitalization. Moreover, states with mandatory education legislation may be able to provide school district funding for the special education component of day treatment.

An often overlooked, but significant, factor which should be taken into account in the total cost of day treatment is the daily transportation of the children.

Supportive and Adjunctive Elements

As with other treatment modalities, day treatment is not an end in itself. The integration of day treatment with past, ongoing, and future services for the child necessitates close collaboration with the range of child-caring systems. A practical means of ensuring continuity and integration of services is by developing a tentative plan at the time of admission for the child's eventual disposition. Referring agencies and the community school system should remain involved throughout the course of treatment. From time to time, they should be asked to initiate or to continue their services to the child.

While in day treatment, some children may profit from other community services. For example, children in one-parent homes may be able to use Big Brother or Big Sister services. A change in

home circumstances might also lead to the use of foster or group home placement in lieu of residential care, particularly with adolescents. In other situations, protective or homemaking social services may be valuable adjuncts.

Treatment Duration and Intensity

The intensity of day treatment varies with the age group served. A therapeutic nursery school may operate on a half- or full-day basis five days a week throughout the year, depending upon the family's ability to provide for child care.[14] Most programs for all ages follow public school schedules. They provide daily service five days a week for approximately six or seven hours including the lunch period. The structure of treatment throughout the year can be thought of in terms of the school calendar. A summer program may be used for special supplementary work or as a separate treatment unit in itself.

Especially during the transition from day treatment to the next program, partial use of specially selected components of the day-treatment service is appropriate according to the needs of each child.

Follow Up

Children can easily be lost sight of in communities with fragmented services. The day-treatment program should therefore assume an advocacy role for each child. The parents may require particular support during the period of school reentry. As the logical point for the coordination of subsequent services and follow up, the day service can aid in the later school management of the child and help bridge the yearly transitions which are frequently accompanied by changes in personnel and shifts in program emphasis. Progression in age also poses new developmental issues for the child's treatment. Another agency or service may assume the coordination or advocacy function. That shift of responsibility, however, should be clearly planned with and understood by the family so that they know to whom to turn as the need arises.

Family therapy or counseling will generally continue after the child's discharge from day treatment. If this cannot be handled by the day-treatment staff, transfer of responsibility can be arranged along with the advocacy function. Prior to discharge, plans for community recreational and peer-related activities can be made and subsequently followed up to ensure their fulfillment.

Some children who are initially unable to profit from individual psychotherapy may later mature sufficiently to use such interpretive work. Follow up can ensure identification of such readiness and the provision of help in obtaining service.

Role of Day Treatment
in the Network of Services

As an element of psychiatric services for children, day treatment is at the same time a part of the broader spectrum of educational, welfare, and health services for children.[24] Its prominence currently is a part of the network serving the elementary school-age child. But the early identification of vulnerability and intervention now possible with younger children has emphasized the need for therapeutic nursery programs to serve children from three to six years of age.[15, 16] These programs will continue to expand and, at least theoretically, should be the principle future use of day treatment. Most of the children now served at the elementary school level could have been identified and more profitably treated at an earlier age.

Day treatment for adolescents is provided in some large urban areas, primarily as a transition from residential care. Programs for adolescents place particular stress on enhancing peer interactions, developing recreational skills, and vocational training.[23]

Evaluation and Outcome Studies

Although limited in number and scope, outcome studies of day-treatment programs have validated their effectiveness. At the same time, community demand for day services has secured their place in the network of mental health services.

The day-treatment service of the University of Colorado Department of Psychiatry followed fifty former patients between 1962 and 1970. The duration of treatment was one year for 15 percent and two years for 85 percent. At the time of follow up, ranging from one to six years, 82 percent of the children were functioning in public school

programs, 4 percent had graduated from high school, 4 percent were in special education classes, 2 percent were in residential treatment, and 8 percent had dropped out of school or had unknown outcomes.[4]

Dealing with a population of severely handicapped children unable to function in their schools or communities at the time of admission, the League School in Brooklyn reports a general "salvage rate" of 80 percent who ultimately are able to function outside of institutions.[13]

The most definitive study of day treatment was carried out at the Ittleson Center for Child Research in Riverdale, New York, in a five-year comparison of day and residential treatment.[18] In this study, thirteen day-treatment children were matched according to psychiatric and neurological diagnoses with thirteen children in residential treatment. The study found that organic schizophrenic children who attained low ratings on the Wechsler Intelligence Scale for Children and who possessed formally intact families improved equally in both day and residential treatment. In contrast, nonorganic schizophrenic children in residence improved more than those in day treatment. The study concluded that the nonorganic schizophrenic child, exposed to more pathogenic family forces, might respond best to separation from the family through residential treatment, whereas the organic schizophrenic child with less family pathogenicity may respond as well to day treatment as to residential treatment.[18]

LaVietes[22] reported on seven years of experience with day treatment and found 76 percent of the children improved significantly and 24 percent did not. She concluded, as did Goldfarb,[18] that schizophrenic children with massive parental pathology responded better to inpatient care than to day treatment.

Further evaluative studies are needed, both to make clear which population is best suited for day treatment and to assess treatment effectiveness. Another emerging control group, in addition to residentially treated children, is the growing population of emotionally disturbed children in special education classes in community schools.

Summary

Psychiatric day treatment for children utilizes the intensive resources of a hospital and yet allows children to remain with their families. It is indicated for children who are unable to function in community school programs and who require comprehensive, interdisciplinary management. It can serve as the primary, a transitional, or an adjunctive treatment modality.

The components of day treatment are psychotherapy; specialized educational services; family therapy; parent liaison; milieu therapy; recreational therapy; craft, art, and music therapies; community liaison; psychopharmacology; and consultation resources within a therapeutic milieu.

For children whose families are able to participate in the program, day treatment offers a significant resource within a community network of mental health services.

REFERENCES

1. BENEDEK, E. P., and SALGUERO, R., "A Summer Day Treatment Service Program," *Journal of Child Psychiatry, 12:*724–737, 1973.

2. BENTOVIM, A., and LANDSDOWN, R., "Day Hospitals and Centres for Disturbed Children in the London Area," *British Medical Journal, 1:*536–538, 1973.

3. BERLIN, I. N., and CHRIST, A., "The Unique Role of the Child Psychiatry Trainee on an Inpatient or Day Care Unit," *Journal of Child Psychiatry, 8:*247–258, 1969.

4. BLOM, G. E., FARLEY, G. K., and EKANGER, C. A., "A Psychoeducational Treatment Program: Its Characteristics and Results," unpublished manuscript, 1975.

5. BLOM, G. E., et al., "A Psychoeducational Approach to Day Care Treatment," *Journal of Child Psychiatry, 11:* 492–510, 1972.

6. CAMERON, D. E., *The Day Hospital,* American Psychiatric Association Monograph, Washington, D.C., 1958.

7. CONNELL, P. H., "The Day Hospital Approach in Child Psychiatry," *Journal of Mental Science, 107:*969–977, 1961.

8. CRAFT, M., "Psychiatric Day Hospitals," *Journal of the American Psychiatric Association, 116:*251–254, 1959.

9. DINGMAN, P. R., "Day Hospitals for Children," in Epps, R. L., and Hanes, L. D. (Eds.), *Day Care of Psychiatric Patients,* Charles C Thomas, Springfield, Ill., 1964.

10. DORNBERG, N., ROSEN, B., and WALKER, T., *A Home Training Program for Young Mentally Ill Children,* League School for Seriously Disturbed Children, Brooklyn, N.Y., 1968.

11. EVANGELAKIS, M. G., *A Manual for Residential and Day Treatment of Children,* Charles C Thomas, Springfield, Ill., 1974.

12. FENICHEL, C., "Special Education as the Basic Therapeutic Tool in Treatment of Severely Disturbed Children," *Journal of Autism and Childhood Schizophrenia, 4:*177–186, 1974.

13. ———, "Psychoeducational Approaches for Seriously Disturbed Children in the Classroom," in Knoblock, P. (Ed.), *Intervention Approaches in Educating Emotionally Disturbed Children,* Syracuse University Press, Syracuse, N.Y., 1966.

14. FROMMER, E. A., "A Day Hospital for Disturbed Children Under 5," *Lancet, 1:*377–379, 1967.

15. FURMAN, R. A., and KATAN, A. (Eds.), *The Therapeutic Nursery School,* International Universities Press, New York, 1969.

16. GLASSCOTE, R., and FISHMAN, M. E., *Mental Health Programs for Preschool Children,* American Psychiatric Association, Washington, D.C., 1974.

17. ———, and SONIS, M., *Children and Mental Health Centers,* American Psychiatric Association, Washington, D.C., 1972.

18. GOLDFARB, W., GOLDFARB, N., and POLLACK, R. C., "Treatment of Childhood Schizophrenia," *Archives of General Psychiatry, 14:*119–128, 1966.

19. GOODMAN, M., "Day Treatment: Innovation Reconsidered," *Canadian Psychiatric Association Journal, 19:*93–97, 1974.

20. HIGLEY, L. W., and BLUMENSTEIN, B., "The Day Diagnostic Center," in Hetznecker, W., and Forman, M. A. (Eds.), *On Behalf of Children,* Grune & Stratton, New York, 1974.

21. HOBBS, T. R., and SHELTON, G. C., "Therapeutic Camping for Emotionally Disturbed Adolescents," *Hospital and Community Psychiatry, 23:*298–301, 1972.

22. LAVIETES, R., et al., "Day Treatment Center and School: 7 Years Experience," *American Journal of Orthopsychiatry, 35:*160–169, 1965.

23. LECKER, S., HENDRICKS, L., and TURANSKI, J., "New Dimensions in Adolescent Psychotherapy," *Pediatric Clinics of North America, 20:*883–900, 1973.

24. LOCKETT, H. J., "The Day Treatment Center," *Journal of the National Medical Association, 64:*527–532, 1972.

25. National Institute for Mental Health, "Residential Treatment Centers for Emotionally Disturbed Children, and Psychiatric Services in General Hospitals," *Mental Health Statistics,* Series A, nos. 6 and 11, National Clearinghouse for Mental Health Information, Washington, D.C., 1972.

26. REDL, F., "The Life Space Interview," *American Journal of Orthopsychiatry, 29:*1–18, 1959.

27. REXFORD, E. N., "The Role of the Nursery School in a Child Guidance Clinic," *American Journal of Orthopsychiatry, 19:*517–524, 1949.

28. SIMPSON, C. B., Personal communication, 1975.

29. VAUGHAN, W. T., and DAVIS, F. E., "Day Hospital Programming in a Psychiatric Hospital for Children," *American Journal of Orthopsychiatry, 33:*542–544, 1963.

18 / Environmental Interventions

Rena Schulman

"How shall we order the child and what shall we do unto him?" According to the Bible, Samson's parents put this question to an angel of the Lord and received the surprising reply, "Never cut his hair." In *The Little Darlings*, a popular history of United States child-rearing practices, Mary Cable[6] cites this biblical quotation as the earliest recorded example of child guidance offered to parents. The question, however, demonstrates something fundamental underlying environmental intervention. It is a technique that consists largely of working with the multiple factors that order a child's existence. Historically, when this approach was originally employed, a child's normal development was thought to recapitulate the evolution of the human race. Thus, the child was assumed to begin as a savage and, eventually, to achieve civilized status. Consequently, principles of character building and methods for achieving this were invoked. Environmental manipulation was part of the child-rearing approach of the early twentieth century, and handmaiden to improving child welfare.

In no branch of medicine does the success of treatment depend so muich upon the patient's general environment as it does in psychiatry. For the still developing young patient, the environment remains a particularly important source of change. Initially, all psychiatric endeavors directed toward children employed environmental changes as their primary means of intervention. As Kanner[17] has pointed out:

The early students of children's problems centered their investigations around the gross and obvious disorders and tried to remedy them largely by providing adequate community facilities which were then pitifully lacking . . . the main emphasis lay on environmental cushioning of the decidedly delinquent, the noticeably retarded, the woefully neglected and mistreated.

Changing environments is no longer one of the basic approaches of child psychiatry. However, environmental modification remains an integral part of therapeutic planning for the child and his family. When caretakers ponder which school a child is to attend, which after-school recreational activities the child is to pursue, or what will be an appropriate camp, this is simply no longer referred to as "environmental manipulation."

To define this activity as a distinct dimension of therapeutic intervention is difficult. Today such intervention may be subsumed under a variety of therapeutic modalities, such as placement in residential treatment institutions or foster homes, the planning of milieu treatment experiences, or the provision of substitute or ancillary relationships as part of outpatient treatment. A formal definition of environmental intervention is those activities that add or change experiences; or any efforts that alter a child's environment physically and/or psychologically. Such changes may be for the purpose of removing impediments to the child's development and/or for the creation of a more positive growth-enhancing life situation. This may involve changing, substituting for, or improving upon the emotional climate in which a child is being reared. The purpose of all these changes is to permit positive developmental progress to take place. Frequently, any environmental intervention is but one aspect, often an incidental one, of the main or primary therapeutic approach.

Historical Considerations

The first systematic social efforts to assist children were essentially environmental in nature. They were the work of child welfare and juvenile protective services. Early in the nineteenth century, children's institutions were established to provide vagrant, homeless, and runaway children with humane and benign environments. Formerly, such youngsters were allowed to roam the streets, to become delinquent and/or criminal, or to end up in adult almshouses which were all too often combined with the local insane asylums and orphan homes. Removal of the child bodily to another environment become the major modality of help for the troubled child. This continued into the earlier years of the present century.

For instance, when Jewish Board of Guardian's Hawthorne Cedar Knolls School was established in 1906, and presently issued its first annual report,[3] it was stated that the children would be exposed to fresh air, sunshine, and clean living, accompanied by military drill and religious practices, and would be protected from the sources of their difficulties in the ghettos and the slums. The school would also expose them to positive social experiences, which would change them. As the director of the institution wrote again in 1909:[19]

It has been the aim of the School to surround the boys with influences tending to happiness, contentment and the formation of right ideals. They are provided with an attractive and comfortable home. They are given suitable clothing and food. Pleasant work and wholesome play fill their days. They find helpful friends in the teachers and cottage parents . . . [who] give the child adequate breathing space, decent living conditions, and opportunities for healthy and legitimate enjoyment and most of the problems of juvenile delinquency are solved.

Indeed, removal to institutions and other benign children's homes, often *did* reshape the child's life. For many, this was their first experience with caring adults whom a child could grow to trust. At the same time, they were freed from the noxious stimuli of slum companions. In the era preceding residential treatment as we know it today (see chapters 14 and 15), many markedly disturbed children emerged from such institutions and foster homes obviously improved by the experience. The assumption was that change took place as a result of the removal from a pathological, depriving and/or neglectful environment. Undoubtedly, the positive results were due to the presence of caretaking and nurturing adults and the opportunity for new identifications; the environmental change, however, gave enormous support to these factors.

Other such efforts to deal with disturbed and delinquent youth included the establishment of the juvenile court system and the subsequent addition of juvenile probation. It was up to the court-appointed guardian, the probation officer, to look after the child, to steer him toward wholesome recreational facilities as well as to protect him from parental mismanagement.[13] Though foster homes were developed in the mid-nineteenth century, it was not until about 1915 that they began to be used for disturbed children. During this period, "child guidance classes" were begun as forerunners of what is now known as special education. These classes sought to make sure that school placements were appropriate to the children's needs. The emphasis was on promoting achievement of success. The "visiting teacher" movement was started at this time and became the forerunner of today's school social worker. The visiting teacher's tasks were manifold: to study a child's problem, to observe and to visit the home as well

as the classroom, to advise both parents and teacher, to insure correct class and school placement, and to try to change the negative circumstances of a particular child's home environment.

Before and after World War I, as part of the mental hygiene movement, psychiatrists increasingly emphasized the social sources of mental illness and the role of "environmental factors" in the causes, prevention, treatment, and ultimate cure of mental disease. Later, after the war, the child guidance movement had its first flowering with the establishment of so-called demonstration clinics. In these clinics, an increasingly systematic approach was applied to the study and treatment of the problem child and his family.

Psychiatric Social Work

Social workers had long-standing experience with poorhouses and prisons, and had come to know the mentally ill who in the past had been confined there. Eventually, psychiatrists called on social workers to provide the necessary "treatment" expertise. As Deutsch[8] has noted, this "stimulated the rise of psychiatric social work as a profession." Meanwhile, social workers were placing increasing stress on personality factors in the problems of dependency, delinquency, and family breakdown with which they dealt. In 1922, Mary E. Richmond[29] defined social case work as consisting of those processes which developed personality through adjustments consciously affected, individual by individual, between men and their social environment. The close collaboration between psychiatry and social work during this period was epitomized by the pioneer cooperative efforts of Dr. Elmer E. Southard and the social worker, Mary C. Jarrett, at the Boston Psychopathic Hospital.

From the beginning, the social worker was assigned the task of environmental modification. In defining case work, Mary Richmond drew the distinction between "direct" and "indirect" treatment. Indirect treatment was described as those changes brought about in the clients' human and physical environment.[29] Such techniques are still important to the social work treatment method. These techniques are designed to influence various factors in the social and psychological environment of the patient in a positive way.

In describing the organization of one of the first child guidance clinics in the country, Reymert[28] delineated the duties of the psychiatric social worker. He noted that:

The social service activities include an active part in selection of cases appropriate for study and treatment . . . The caseworker represents the point of contact between the clinic and the home. Throughout the clinical treatment, she undertakes to enlist and maintain the full cooperation of the parents or other adults concerned with the child both by interpreting to them the efforts of the clinic and by trying to enlist their cooperation in the actual procedures recommended . . . Some work is done with the parents themselves in these interviews in attempting to modify somewhat undesirable attitudes or undue anxieties they might have in regard to the child.

In the 1924 book, *Three Problem Children*,[33] the case of Mildred was presented. She was referred to the clinic at the age of twelve, shortly after having been transferred from a parochial to a public school. There she had fared so badly that she was demoted to the first grade, where she towered above her schoolmates. The experience made her even more shy, inhibited, enuretic, and she became the family's scapegoat. The team psychiatrist developed a treatment plan: The social worker was to get Mildred into another class, to find a tutor for her, and to see that the child went to see him. She was taken to the Girl Scouts, where she was taught how to knit. This was one means of gaining a special skill and thereby raising the child's self-esteem. After an outing with the social worker that included a visit to a museum, the child even gained enhanced status within her family. The major and hidden medical problem within Mildred's family was the father's syphillis, an illness he denied. A major task of the social worker was to induce the infected mother to visit a clinic and to accompany her there. She also planned for the medical care of Mildred and her siblings. The social worker, then known as the "visiting teacher," was asked to "meddle" in family's affairs on behalf of the child.

"The visitor tried to get into the friendliest relations with the child and to carry out personally many items in the program,"[33] as part of the reconstruction of the environment to make it more favorable. The visitor overlooked nothing. Getting down to basics, she advised the mother to let Mildred sleep in a bed of her own, so that her continuing enuresis would not disturb the sister with whom she slept, and who had been teasing and raging at Mildred for her bedwetting. Such environmental minipulation in situ worked wonders. Ultimately, the child was encouraged to utilize the social and recreational resources that the social worker helped make available to her. Under this positive nurturing approach, little Mildred literally blossomed.

The treatment plan for Mildred, as outlined by the psychiatrist, focused on stimulating the growth of her personality. As noted in the case record:

A policy of attempting to broaden Mildred's field of interests was outlined by the psychiatrist with 2 points in mind: first, that new interests would waken her mentally and take her out of herself, help to overcome her absorption in her own inner life; and second, that they would remove her, for certain definite periods, from the depressing influence of the home.[33]

Of the three problem children described in the book,[33] the most drastic of the many possible environmental manipulations was avoided in that not one had to be removed completely from home. The three case vignettes illustrate the function of concrete supportive efforts, advice, and direct help and encouragement provided by the visiting teacher-social worker.

Under the impetus of the Commonwealth Fund grants, the establishment of child guidance clinics proliferated and had a tremendous influence upon child treatment. At the same time, however, an even greater influence in child psychiatry was exerted by the psychoanalytic contributions of Sigmund Freud which were slowly drawing increasing attention from psychiatrists. Such psychoanalytic studies of the child were to have the most profound influence on the practice of child psychiatry and the theories and practices of social work.

Child Guidance Clinic Psychiatry

Despite the important influences of dynamic psychiatry, the work of the early child guidance clinics remained largely environmental in nature, particularly as it related to the younger child. The approach involved two stages, first psychiatric study, and then prescription. The child psychiatrist sought changes in the home, school, or recreation that would bring about the alleviation of problems. Most often, the prescription called for changes in external circumstances, usually in the school, or even more often, in the attitudes and behaviors of the parents, particularly the mother. The early child guidance clinic developed the concept of the interdisciplinary team approach. The social worker manipulated a great many situations involving the child. She gathered information for the psychiatrist and served as a conduit for his recommendations.

Changes in this approach were inevitable. It was soon realized that parents were unable to take an objective, intellectual attitude toward their children's problems, nor could parents alter their behavior in accordance with a psychiatrist's prescription. It was recognized also that despite the theory of dynamic psychiatry, the children's difficulties were *not* the result of some specific undiscovered trauma but arose rather from the pathological emotional relationships between parents and children. Intellectual advice-giving approaches were therefore found to be inadequate; they failed to create the required attitudinal changes. As a consequence, a therapeutic responsibility replaced the advisory function. Treatment of parents was begun by the social workers and was directed towards resolving their emotional conflicts. It was hoped that because of treatment-induced changes, parents would be able to do what was required of them on behalf of their child and, indirectly, for themselves. The simultaneous treatment of parent and child continues to be the practice in many child guidance and child psychiatry clinics. Today, however, treatment of parents is no longer directed solely toward environmental modification. But the goals continue to have such elements as: to bring about changes in the child's environment, in attitudes toward the child or in the handling of specific behavioral or developmental problems (see chapters 7, 8, 9, 11, 12, and 13).

The practice of child psychiatry in this country has been subjected to two sets of influences. One is the unique native brand of child guidance that encompasses simultaneous parent-child treatment or parental guidance, and the other the European-derived psychoanalytic approach that emphasizes not only the dynamics of development, but also the direct treatment of the young child (see chapters 2 and 3). The introduction of play therapy techniques made direct work possible with ever younger children. This accentuated the trend toward individual therapy and resulted in even greater concentration on direct treatment of the young child.

With the increasing influence of child psychoanalysis, there tended to be considerable variation in the degree of emphasis placed on environmental interventions or on the utilization of experiences outside the therapy room. It was believed by many that change in children could take place through direct psychotherapy alone and did not require the ancillary assistance of environmental changes. As a result of the popularization of psychoanalytic concepts, the knowledge and attitudes of parents and teachers became more sophisticated; presently they require less in the way of educational and guidance efforts. Those problems that remained were less subject to change through parental education or advice-giving; sometimes they also proved recalcitrant to treatment efforts.

There continued to be controversy about the necessity of parental involvement in a child's therapy. Yet, for the most part, it is generally agreed that psychiatric treatment of a child cannot take place unrelated to the social and psychological realities of his life. If and when changes take place in the child, these require a great deal of environmental support. Modifications in parental attitudes or resolution of parent-child conflicts are basic. They are required in order for changes in the child to be received and supported by his environment. The degree of parent-child interaction in pathological development, as well as in the healing process, is enormous. This indicates that a good deal of environmental change will continue to be required in the course of child treatment regardless of modality.

As the twentieth century has progressed, the modalities of treatment for parents and children have evolved and changed. There has been increasing recognition that the family system contains the seeds of emotional pathology; indeed, it is often considered to be the principal determinant of the behavior of individual family members. Accordingly, family therapy developed as a prime method for intervention in a pathological family system. The use of family therapy techniques, which are discussed in chapter 7, may remove the need for a certain amount of environmental modification. The parent-child conflict is dealt with in situ; the focus of treatment is on attitudinal and behavioral changes, as these are modified in the interaction between family members. On the other hand, the systems approach has also developed the concept of "network" therapy. This brings the field right back to the environment; here the focus is directed toward mobilizing the networks within the community and the extended family systems in order to serve the interest of the child and family. With this approach, direct manipulation of the environment is basic.

The community mental health center movement has also thrust psychiatric attention back onto the environment. According to the movement's philosophy, mental health efforts were no longer to concentrate on the individual and his pathology. Instead, they were to be directed toward societal ills. Social advocacy and social action were to deal with specific environmental issues, whether to serve the interests of an individual or of an entire group. In any case, environmental interventions were designed to bring about social and institutional change. Dealing with social issues was expected to deal with the causes of individual stress and thus benefit larger numbers of children.

At the same time, early intervention and preventive programs were stressed. These often provided concrete services embedded in a psychiatric and psychoanalytic framework as discussed in volume IV. Programs of early mother-child interaction, infant care services, and special day care programs emphasize the modification of child-rearing practices. They thus provide concrete services as well as environmental alteration. Thus, the attention of child psychiatry has once again been concentrated on environmental change. The approach has come full circle.

Theoretical Considerations

The possibility of bringing about change in the child through environmental experiences and milieu relationships derives from basic developmental concepts. The child's personality and behavior are the result of the interacting forces of his intrinsic makeup and his external circumstances. These include his immediate family and the larger environment of society around him. During his earlier years, the child's personality structure continues to be fluid. This permits the impact of environmental experiences and relationships to be constructive throughout childhood and even into adolescence. Ego development may be enhanced or impeded by the type of life experiences encountered by the child. Later life events may also play a significant role in determining personality development. In his *Outline of Psychoanalysis*, Freud states:

> . . . the ego is principally determined by the individual's own experience, that is to say by accidental and current events. . . . An individual's superego in the course of his development takes over contributions from later successors and substitutes of his parents, such as teachers, admired figures in public life, or high social ideals.[12]

The process of ego growth is thus enhanced by positive life experiences. Conversely, traumatic experiences or deprivation will retard ego development. The growth of mastery and skill are necessary for the development of ego strength; experiences of failure may undermine the ego's potential. Throughout childhood, constructive experiences may be planned to support ego development. Whether such positive experiences can actually undo pathology depends on the extent and nature of the disturbance. In particular, it reflects the extent to which internalization has taken place. There are those children whose pathology requires the most intensive and professional therapeutic work. Even in such instances, the nature of the child's interaction with his environment continues to play an important role in resolving pathology and in the healthy development of his personality.

Corrective emotional experiences provide opportunities for corrective identifications that are of primary therapeutic value. As Augusta Alpert has stated:

> The best therapeutic hope, in our present state of knowledge, is that by strengthening the ego, the balance between ego and instinct may be modified in favor of mental health. The earlier this occurs, the less interference with maturation and the fewer secondary pathological developments. These considerations favor the introduction of a corrective identification earlier rather than later . . .[1]

Alpert was then discussing an educational therapeutic approach. It was designed to be used with prelatency children who showed disturbance in developmental progression and balance. Over time, however, corrective identification has been utilized as a therapeutic tool in a wide variety of therapeutic endeavors and with a wide range of child, adolescent, and adult patients. It has been regarded as especially indicated when a pathological mother-child relationship has blocked the child from mastering its primary identification with the mother. Such corrective identification provides need-satisfying relationships with a protective object; this in turn helps spur maturation and development. Corrective relationships may be provided by high specialized professionals or may result from pivotal encounters with a significant figure. The impact of such confrontations may be a turning point in the child's life. Such encounters with older students, a teacher, a club leader, or other friendly adult may be the result of planful intervention or an accident of fate. The introduction of such a person with whom the child may develop a relationship provides a possibility for corrective identifications and ego modeling.

Experiences of success, achievement, or mastery enhance self-esteem and support ego development. The resultant appreciation or approval of parents, or of other significant figures, further supports this. In the course of normal childhood, such experiences are part of every child's life. Where such interactions are missing or fragmented, special opportunities may be provided for the child to make up for what is lacking or to support beginning efforts at mastery.

The extent to which external manipulation is utilized to help the individual child may depend as much on the treatment plans theoretical orientation as on the nature of the problem and the availability of resources. It has been suggested that the more intensive and psychoanalytically oriented the approach, the less involved will the therapist be with the environment of the child, lest these "contaminate" the purity of the intrapsychically oriented therapy. The less intensive the individual treatment, the more essential the utilization of environmental change or ancillary treatment devices. Earlier, it had been assumed that intensive treatment could in itself restore the child to mental health or normal developmental progress. In the early days of child analysis, all that was required of the parents was permission for the child's therapy. This did not mean total disregard of the parents. As Anna Freud stated, the patient's family cannot be:

wholly excluded from the analysis. Insight into the seriousness of the neurosis, the decision to begin and to continue treatment, persistence in the face of resistance or of passing aggravations of the illness are beyond the child and have to be supplied by the parent. In child analysis, the parent's good sense plays the part which the healthy part of the patient's conscious personality plays during adult analysis to safeguard and maintain the continuance of treatment.[11]

Burlingham's[5] sensitive discussion more than four decades ago emphasized the need for maintaining the interest and sympathy of the parents throughout a child's treatment. It is still valuable advice for clinicians today.

It was evident, however, that more was demanded of the family than merely to treat the child and to have the parents' support the treatment. A great deal of parental patience was required while waiting for behavioral change to appear. There was the expectation that the child's environment would become child-focused, that the family's activities would be geared to the needs of the child-patient. There are instances in which it was suggested that the father not make an eagerly sought important career move, since this would interfere with the continuation of the child's treatment. In another instance, a child was not allowed the bimonthly overnight visits to father as authorized by the legal separation agreement. They were deemed too stimulating for the little girl, who had to share her father's one-room studio apartment.

Since the mother had been requested not to have male friends stay over when the child was there, this assumed that mother would be ready to give up her own social relationships. These are indeed examples of manipulation of the environment in the interest of the child's individual psychotherapy.

Environmental interventions may also be a function of the level of disturbance of the child. The sicker the child and the more pathological his environment, the greater the need for environmental changes. This may even lead to the removal of a child from the home. With the less disturbed or the merely neurotic child, environmental interventions are less important and less likely to be utilized.

In these cases, ancillary devices such as the introduction of new relationships or some modification of experiences are not ordinarily used. Nonetheless, therapists are concerned about securing the appropriate camp or the right school or class and do make specific recommendations to the parents as to what management is optimal. All this still falls under the rubric of environmental manipulation.

The treatment setting largely determines the extent of environmental intervention. Thus, in the child guidance clinic, the usual approach is to extend simultaneous treatment to parent and child. Typically, work with the parent is geared to environmental and attitudinal modifications. This has not been so common in individualistic private child psychiatric practice. The private practitioner tends to avail himself less of the range of environmental interventions that are available to the community clinic. The individual practitioner is often inclined to feel he has neither the resources nor the time nor the support of third party payers to make many school or home visits. The simple economics of therapy too often preclude this or other nondirect activities. The same economics may determine the type of patient to be treated by the private practitioner; if so those requiring extensive environmental interventions or supportive services are best referred for treatment to a community clinic.

Techniques of Environmental Interventions

There is no single technique of environmental intervention. There are instead a host of interventions. New experiences, activities, or services may be introduced for the enrichment or support of ego development. In those situations where the child's own environment is deficient, substitute relationships may be provided that can be the basis for new identifications. Or there are instances where a family's pathology prevents them from mobilizing their own or the community's resources on their child's behalf. Modification in the school situation, or possibly a different educational program, may be required. In any case, some sort of concrete service must be invoked to modify or supplement the child's reality, or his present situation.

There are social realities which may be destructive to the child's development or sense of self. Short of removal from the family environment, these may demand a number of changes in the social circumstances of the child's life. What are needed here are concrete services, such as assistance with housing, vocational guidance, skill training, job finding, camp or day care placements which will actually remove a child from the city streets, tutoring, homemaking services, assistance in securing new housing, school and class changes, and the mobilization of community resources for recreational and other supportive help. These services often rely on a student aide or paraprofessional person for a Big Brother type of relationship. This is a major help with socialization. Such forms of assistance for seriously disturbed and disorganized multiproblem families, in which it is often impossible to focus on an index patient and in which there is insufficient motivation, trust, or a capacity for regular office interviews, are usually categorized as "social services." As such, they are often distinguished from, and sometimes dismissed from, child psychiatric activities; however, it is wise to embed them in a clinical child treatment program and integrate them with whatever modality of treatment is employed, be it individual, group, or family psychotherapy; pharmacotherapy; or some combination thereof.

These concrete services symbolize also the genuine interest an agency feels for its client/patient. Moreover, these services are not merely evidences of caring; they are important and necessary environmental supports. Changes in neighborhood are achieved by moving into a new apartment away from the "junkie" and rat-infested street. Assistance in organizing the household is extended to a disorganized, alcoholic mother, who simultaneously receives some nurturant attention from the homemaker. All these are essential interventions which make possible other treatment of the child and family. Such services, and others as well, are among the services provided by many community mental health centers.

CASE ILLUSTRATION

The S family, of mixed ethnic background, was referred to a special preventive services project within a child psychiatric agency. Diane, the oldest girl, had been turned down by a succession of residential treatment institutions, and the younger boy, Harry, had been placed on the waiting list for an institution for the retarded. After her intake interviews for placement, Mrs. S broke all subsequent appointments. Home visiting by a therapist was begun. During the first visit, Mrs. S was not home but was at the local fast-food restaurant where she hung out. The two children were home and vied in their "craziness" for the worker's attention. The three-room apartment was bare except for a broken-down couch and two beds without bedclothes. Closets were empty and the refrigerator was bare. Diane had not been in school for almost a year. Harry was about to be thrown out of school again. He had been sent to a children's shelter, had run away after two days, and had then been sent home. There was a primitive, unsocialized, pseudo psychotic, pseudo retarded quality to the family interaction. Indeed, the three members of this family, presented as a *folie à trois*, huddled together in a symbiotic, phobic way. Mrs. S had been deserted by her husband, twenty years her senior, because he could no longer bear her peculiar behavior, and she had become estranged from her entire family as well.

Treatment of this family continued on an outreach basis. Because of their phobic nature, the family could not leave their neighborhood or even the house, except for the local restaurant, where in fact many interviews with Mrs. S were held.

After six months, the worker recorded distinct changes in the family. Diane had been registered in a class for the emotionally handicapped and had been attending regularly for the first time in years. She had begun to communicate with the worker and had developed excellent insights into her own and her mother's behavior. Harry was no longer on the waiting list for the institution, since it turned out that he now had an IQ of 101! Furniture had been secured, including a separate bed for Diane. The family had been registered at a local community center for recreational activities. As yet they had not been able to use it since the settlement house was a little outside of their immediate neighborhood. But the worker was hopeful that eventually they would go there. Harry no longer came to school scratched and bruised from injuries that the school suspected had been inflicted by the mother. Mrs. S had been helped to get a Medicaid number and to begin to get some medical care for herself. This included new teeth to replace several broken front teeth that had given her an aged and derelict appearance. She had also been brought into contact with members of her family. Most important, it was felt that the children might be ready for individual therapy and that Mrs. S might permit them to come into the preventive services project office.[27]

This case is strikingly reminiscent of the 1924

case of Mildred and suggests that environmental intervention as a technique is not as obsolete as it is often presumed to be. Today such environmental manipulation is rare but obviously can have a great impact on a disorganized, ill family. It can still restore them to some measure of equilibrium and prepare them for more formal child psychiatric help.

Foster Care

Institutional or foster home placement provides therapeutic benefits for many children. In a reasonably benign environment, children who have experienced object loss or have been exposed to severe environmental pressures have been able to reconstitute their lives. Children whose difficulties were reactive to environmental circumstances and whose problems were not yet internalized are frequently able to respond favorably to placement in a benevolent environment. They do best with warm, devoted, and intuitively sensitive foster mothers or houseparents. For some, a renewal of family living is helpful. Once again they become part of an intact and stable family. For others, the less personal atmosphere of the institution is best. They do well with its emphasis on peer group interaction and impersonal routines. Continued development can take place when ego growth permits better object relationships and the ability to function in school and in the group is developed. In case of death or of serious parental illness, the object loss can be handled constructively. It is necessary for responsive and sensitive foster mothers to accept the child's continuing tie to the absent parent. The child's ties, even with a neglectful or emotionally disturbed parent, remain close and positive. As a rule, placement in a small institution does not threaten those ties. It provides nurturance and care instead of neglect and can be most helpful by permitting the child to retain his unambivalent relationship with his fantasied "good parent."

FOSTER PLACEMENT

Max, an extremely well-endowed child of ten, was brought to the child guidance clinic because of his increasing difficulties in school and his exposure to destructive and dangerous experiences in his community.

Max's parents were separated. His mother, who had custody, was on drugs, mentally ill, and in and out of mental hospitals. His father worked and earned a marginal income; when mother was away, he took over care, but was unable to provide for the child's basic needs. It was evident that for the mother even in her periods of remission, Max's care provided too much stress. Still, she was unwilling to give him up. In view of the extreme neglect, the clinic felt Max could not be treated on an outpatient basis. The clinic recommended placement in a normal child-care institution. However, placement could not be accomplished because of parental and child resistance. Considerable work by the clinic and child placement agency was required, as was understanding of the subtle manipulation of the parents by the child, before Max was finally placed in a suburban group home where he has done extremely well.

For many years, a successful mode of treatment for most youngsters consisted of removal of delinquent urban youth from the crowded deteriorated slums and from delinquent companions to the fresh air, discipline, and routines of a child-care institution in the country. Here, he would receive appropriate educational and vocational training. However, with cultural and socioeconomic changes, the population of these institutions changed as did the effectiveness of their program for delinquent youth. Their development must be viewed in a historical perspective.

The first explicit use of foster homes for what may be designated as disturbed children seems to have taken place in the second decade of this century.[17] Thus, foster care, whether in institutions or in foster family boarding homes, appears to be one of the earliest and still continuing forms of environmental interventions. As has been true of the development of outpatient child psychiatric services, the treatment of emotionally disturbed children in institutions evolved frequently out of changing programs serving delinquent youth.

In eighteenth-century America, such "homeless" children were cared for in almshouses. Early in the nineteenth century, institutions for children were founded, often by religious groups. The first institution for delinquent youth in the country, the New York House of Refuge, was established by the Society for the Reformation of Delinquents, an offshoot of an earlier Quaker organization. It later developed into the New York State Training School for Boys which has continued to this day.

Child-care institution and foster family care programs were designed to serve "dependent and neglected children." These were youngsters made homeless by parental death or destitution or whose parents, for various reasons, could not care for them any longer. In line with advances made in child welfare and child psychiatry, these programs were largely transformed, and foster family boarding care became the major method for caring for these children. Ultimately some of the early institutions were transformed into today's residential treatment programs.

Late in the nineteenth century, Charles Loring Brace, a minister and philanthropist, became interested in the homeless and destitute slum children of eastern big cities. He was convinced that the children would fare better with foster families on farms in the Midwest than in the institutions then available. As a consequence, tens of thousands of youths were so placed. However, controversy raged over the merits of such placements versus institutional care; there were charges of exploitation and indenture. Eventually, in the early 1900s, many of the denominational organizations added foster family boarding care, called "placing out," as adjuncts to their institutional programs. Further controversy has continued over the respective merits and specific indications for foster family versus institutional care. There have been several pendulumlike swings of opinion favoring one or the other. Presently, there is general agreement as to the disadvantages of large institutions for any group of children and a preference for small institutions and/or community based group homes for those children for whom foster family care is not indicated or possible.

In recent years, there has been much discussion of the hazards of foster care. The major concern has been for the potential impermanence of the arrangement and for the fact that children's lives may be subjected to a multitude of changes. Transfers may result from a wide variety of causes. Among these are personal difficulties of the foster parents, the inability of foster parents to tolerate aggressive or rebellious behavior, or simply the decision of foster care agencies to transfer children from home to home for unstated reasons. It is charged that these transfers have sometimes been motivated by a desire to prevent development of too close ties between child and foster family. By now, most professionals have agreed on the desirability of "permanence" for children. This is particularly true for those destined to be raised through most of their childhood by other than their own parents. There has also been general agreement on the undesirability of placing preschool children under institutional care.

During the 1930s and 1940s, many child-care agencies, residential institutions, and foster care agencies began to make a singular observation. They noted that the children who were being referred to them comprised a population that was considerably more disturbed emotionally than that which they had seen in the past. Institutions for de-

linquents found that the "hard-core delinquents" did not respond to separation from their "unhealthy" life situations, nor did they accept the new benevolent environment. Presently, psychiatric consultants and psychiatric social workers were brought in to assist in the study and treatment of children with "special problems." Thus began the transformation of many institutions into progressive residential treatment programs.

Concurrently, a number of agencies experimented with the development of specialized foster boarding homes to serve children with emotional and behavior problems. They hoped to help even the more seriously disturbed and psychotic children, as well as those who could not be served in the available residential treatment facilities.

The child welfare literature of the mid 1950s and early 1960s contain the reports of a number of such projects. Wildy[35] described the children for whom such specialized foster homes were used as consisting of three groups:

1. Young children, generally preschool age, who have suffered severe maternal deprivation and, often, early physical abuse and neglect. Such children may also be autistic or otherwise severely disturbed.
2. Children who show emotional pathology or behavioral problems as a result of parental pathology. These children may also have physical handicaps or illnesses. In these children, the degree of disturbance does not seem severe enough to warrant removal from the community to residential treatment institutions. But they are difficult to serve in the usual foster family.
3. Children who may be ready for discharge from a residential treatment institution, but who continue to require some specialized "transitional experience" in order to consolidate their progress before returning to family and community living. Special foster families were found and developed by intensive casework support and supervision. Dramatic progress was shown by all of the children in the program.

A project described by Waskowitz[34] was designed for children who could not be served in regular foster family homes or in normal child-caring institutions. Though in need of residential treatment, such facilities were not available for these youngsters. They represented all ages up to sixteen and varied behavioral problems that could not be tolerated in the usual foster home. Their family backgrounds were replete with neglect, abuse, inconsistency, and severe emotional psychopathology. Recruitment of suitable foster families involved great effort and additional payments. Sustaining such homes required intensive casework support for the foster parents.

Kaplan and Turitz[18] described a project designed to serve children aged three to eight, of potentially average intelligence, who required psychiatric treatment. Diagnosed as childhood schizophrenics or severe character neuroses, these children were provided a subsidized foster home with a high tolerance for difficult behavior, intensive casework services, and psychotherapy. Adjunctive therapeutic facilities were utilized as well, including remedial tutoring, special schools, camps, and so forth. In addition to psychiatric treatment of the individual children, intensive services were provided to the natural parents, the foster parents, and the children. The psychiatrist participated in all aspects of the project including selection of the special foster parents. Evaluation of the project at the end of four years revealed extraordinary gains by many of the children; only one of them required subsequent residential treatment.

Such individualized programs require the recruitment of special foster homes. This may be accomplished by unusual efforts, payment of higher rates than usual, and the provision of additional supports to the foster parents, such as maids, housekeeping, and babysitting services. Sometimes, foster parents are regular agency employees, or they occupy an agency-owned house. Invariably, intensive casework, psychiatric consultation, and treatment services are provided. Generally, the child's psychiatric treatment is provided by the foster care agency staff, or arrangements are made with clinics or hospitals. An important aspect of these programs is the consultation provided to the foster parents by both psychiatrists and social workers. It is this support, training, and supervision that helps make the foster home a therapeutic setting.

Even without such special projects, at times it may be possible to secure a specialized foster home for an individual child who presents extraordinary problems. In some sections of the country, the unusual requirements of children with special needs are recognized by varied scales of payment from public funding sources for foster home care. Such scales are based on the extent of the child's special needs.

The 1970s have witnessed a renewed interest in the concept of special-treatment family care homes for disturbed children. The large numbers of such children with special needs, the excessive cost of residential treatment, and the lack of available resources in many parts of the country combine to pose a major management problem. It is evident that a flexible, creative, and experimental approach must continue in order to develop special treatment resources.

Specialized foster family care should be considered for groups of children who require complex forms of help but for whom existing residential treatment services are not appropriate. These may be severely disturbed children, or less disturbed youngsters with multiple handicaps. It also includes older adolescents for whom a larger group setting would be countertherapeutic; indeed, many of them are the failures of residential programs. They may also be unsuitable for, or unacceptable to, psychiatric hospitals. These take only the most disturbed and are also committed to short-term care and deinstitutionalization. The hospitalized children tend to be violent and assaultive in group settings, or they require more intensive one-to-one care than is available in treatment centers. Homes designed for such children must be supported by appropriate therapeutic resources and, in many instances, by special educational facilities. In addition, the foster parents need intensive help and a variety of supportive services.

The most crucial issue in offering this form of care is the recruitment and selection of such foster parents. Past efforts in this area have included seeking candidates with professional backgrounds, or relying on natural self-selection and challenge, combined with incentive payments. The latter approach has within it the liabilities of the foster care system generally, that is, reliance on the "natural" and intuitive foster parent. Although this might work out for average situations, special treatment homes require greater certainty regarding the foster parent's attitudes, consistency, and symptom tolerance. Such foster parents are as much a part of the treatment team as is the child-care staff of residential treatment centers. They require training and supervision, and an understanding of the nature of the disturbances of the children with whom they are living. Self-awareness and an ability to deal with their own feelings are also essential. The foster family carries greater responsibility for the day-to-day dealings with such children than the staff of a residential institution. The foster parents must therefore be fully prepared for the children, able to anticipate difficulties, and ready to handle them on the spot. Recourse to the agency's supervisory or administrative personnel should be available on an emergency basis when required. With the very best of selection, training, and support systems, one must be prepared to remove children from such homes when, and hopefully before, they reach a breaking point. This serves both to avert total decompensation of the child and the loss of the home's availability for another child. When used in conjunction with a backup institution, such homes can increase the range of treatment services offered. A number of communities are presently reporting such services both for delinquents and disturbed youth. There is wide variation in the nature of these programs. Further evaluation will be required to determine their efficacy.

The Boarding School as a Therapeutic Resource

Just as the *normal* child-caring institution can provide a therapeutic resource for troubled children, so can the private boarding school. In the absence of special funding, the costly boarding school is limited largely to affluent families. For some youngsters, it provides an acceptable solution to their need for a consistent, caring environment. For others, it may be the most palatable solution to serious parent-child conflicts.

Boarding schools may be divided into three groups. There is the personalized, small boarding school that provides a substitute family setting for neglected and/or deprived children who require such an environment. Such resources may be known only by word of mouth. At times, they may be known to school advisory services of large communities.

CASE ILLUSTRATION

Ralph was subjected to an extremely litigious custody battle between his seriously disturbed parents. Finally, the lawyers for both had agreed to abide by the recommendation of a child psychiatrist as to the fate of the child. It was determined that neither parent provided custody conducive to the wholesome development of this child. Because these parents would never accept a foster home recommendation, the psychiatrist suggested a small, family-type boarding school. Such a school was found where approximately twenty-five children lived. The owners of the school, who were personally involved in the care of all the children, were apprised of Ralph's needs and the fact that he might not be able to spend holidays or vacations with his disturbed parents. Arrangements were made for him to visit with the school owner's family during such periods, until his parents were again ready to have him for short visits.

Another type of boarding school caters to children with special learning difficulties or personality problems. While not providing a formal residential treatment setting, they may be run by a person especially attuned to the needs of difficult or troubled youngsters. Such schools provide a setting and staff that are able to provide the required type of relationships, leadership, and guidance. Some schools are near psychiatric facilities where therapy may be available. However, for most youngsters, separation from their own family plus the environment alone, with its accepting, tolerant, and understanding adults, may prove to be sufficient. Such schools usually have a particularly creative headmaster or director, whose charismatic qualities and special interests may bridge the gap to the rebellious youngsters who frequently resist authority. The programs provided for such youngsters may be flexibly designed to challenge their abilities and support individuality, rather than enforcing conformity.

CASE ILLUSTRATION

Ellen was a child for whom such a boarding school provided a respite from a smothering mother, whose domineering, controlling, and demanding qualities were contributing to Ellen's self-defeating behavior. Ellen's life was made up of association with undesirable companions, school failure at a special public high school for talented youngsters, and runaways from home. Ellen did not require a residential treatment setting, and her therapist felt that she would function well in a different environment. The boarding school challenged her intellectually and, supported by close staff-student relationships, supplied her need for caring adults. Ellen continued to be a somewhat "offbeat" youngster, whose functioning depended in good measure on the adults with whom she worked. But she was able to finish high school and, having done well, went on to college.

The third group of boarding schools provide no special services. They accept children in accordance with the student's intellectual functioning, social status, and financial circumstances. These are the usual boarding schools that provide a good education, a degree of discipline, and some separation from families. For some children, attendance at such schools is part of their family or social class tradition; it may also be necessitated by parental circumstances, such as absence from the country. However, for some children, at the point of adolescent rebellion, planning for boarding school plays a part in dealing with serious parent-child conflict.

CASE ILLUSTRATION

Fourteen-year-old Christine's parents were divorced and her mother had recently remarried. Christine's functioning at a fashionable private day school for girls had been excellent but had begun to deteriorate about six months previously. Her behavior at home was unacceptable to her new stepfather and disruptive as well to the marriage. At age fourteen she was leading a double life, including active sexual involvements and beginning drug experimentation. Midnight assignations were kept, in spite of her mother's attempts to enforce a 10 P.M. curfew. Christine still aspired to excellent school performance and desired to go to college. The school felt betrayed and confused by the changes in the girl and recommended boarding school. Though intrigued and responsive in therapy, Christine was extraordinarily suspicious and resistant to treatment; she viewed her participation as another demand of her mother's and refused to comply. She and her family were at loggerheads, and her behavior was disrupting the new marriage. At this point, Christine and her mother simultaneously decided on a boarding school. The girl selected a school recommended by her headmistress and the therapist whom the family had consulted.

For such children, separation from frustrating, controlling parental authority, a loosening of unreasonable restrictions, and the presence of impersonal authority may provide an atmosphere conducive to intellectual and personal development, even if underlying problems remain. In cases where no serious ego breakdown and disruption of cognitive functions has occurred, this can be a reasonable solution. It is also a useful therapeutic tool in treating youngsters since they derive great support from their peer group membership.

The Volunteer Big Brother

The use of volunteers in mental health, social welfare, and child-guidance settings has a long and honorable history. In many programs that now relegate the volunteer to an auxiliary role, the presence of the volunteer often antedates the introduction of professional services. Moreover, in many instances, the volunteer Big Brother or Big Sister plays a primary role in providing basic, urgently needed emotional relationships. The volunteer is a growth-producing factor and provides a therapeutic influence in the child's everyday life. A volunteer may be assigned to a child to help build a relationship of trust and to enhance the youngster's sense of worth. Use of a Big Brother or Big Sister introduces substitute relationships to make up for those that are missing or inadequate in a child's immediate family. The existence of this relationship in itself can convince a child that he is worthy, which many professionals may not be able to do in quite the same way. The assignment of the volunteer to a child in psychiatric treatment may lend support to new-found capacities for socialization or may assist the child in the negotiation of social realities. The volunteer provides a "friend" who shares in the child's real life and who often sets no time limit on the relationship. Ultimately, this provides a corrective emotional experience.

The most common form of this relationship is probably the volunteer Big Brother for the fatherless boy. The Big Brother may be ancillary to psychiatric treatment or, as in many Big Brother organizations throughout the country, this may be the only form of treatment intervention. For the fatherless boy, even in an extended family, the absence of any close adult man means an absence of a needed relationship, a major block to any opportunity for male identification. This lack may pose a serious threat to the boy's development, dependent on the nature of the loss, and the extent to which the mother and/or the extended family have dealt with the loss and with the child's needs.[25] In many such instances, psychotherapy will be necessary. In others, where more reality relationships and supports seem required, the Big Brother may be employed in a manner that is ancillary to therapy. Or, there are situations where the introduction of the volunteer alone may be sufficient, either because the pathology is not that crystallized, or when the assessment suggests that this relationship alone may be of help to both the boy and his family. In some cases, a family has been too resistant to acknowledge the need for psychiatric help. Mental health service may then have to be initiated through response to the specific request of a mother for a Big Brother "to help her child in his masculine identification."

The Big Brother usually undertakes to provide regular contact with the child, whether weekly or bimonthly. In order to avoid the "promise and the hurt" of an abortive relationship, he is generally asked to commit himself to such a relationship for a specific period of time. The success of such programs usually depends on the nature of the selection and training process, and the extent to which professional supervision and guidance are available to the volunteer.

A FATHERLESS BOY

Ten-year-old David's mother felt that the boy had become too attached to her and she had, therefore, requested a Big Brother. David experienced a good deal of anxiety when away from his mother. When he was with her, however, he was angry and resentful. David's father had deserted the family when his son was six months old, leaving the child to be reared by the mother and the grandmother (with whom they lived). There were no available male relatives.

David had few friends and felt picked on by other children. A Big Brother was introduced to support the boy in his emerging strivings for separation from his mother and to help him achieve greater independence. It was also hoped that this arrangement would provide a greater opportunity for masculine identification.

David's mother was angry and disappointed that he did not develop a number of interests which she favored. Though David seemed anxious and immature, it was also evident that he felt distinct urgings for independence. He had been able to go on overnight camping trips and seemed eager and ready for a relationship with a Big Brother. This was thereupon provided.

On his first few trips with his Big Brother, David seemed anxious about being away from his mother; he even asked to be taken home early. However, this behavior quickly disappeared. He became less anxious and his enjoyment of their activities soon became obvious. He also became less anxious and demanding at home, and more independent of his mother. With this, the mother's own anxiety about her son diminished. In this instance, the introduction of the Big Brother served to strengthen the positive side of the ambivalence on the part of both mother and son about their imminent separation.

The Big Brother provides the influence of a responsible older male figure who offers concrete help, friendly guidance, acceptance, interest, and a masculine image with which to identify. His major influence is supportive. The Big Brother may also be helpful in reducing stress experienced by the mother. As a single parent, she often feels pressured; she may be frightened by the closeness of the mother-son relationship, and sometimes she is quite consciously anxious about her feminizing influence on her son.[31]

Therapeutic Use of Camp

The possibilities of camp as a therapeutic experience for youngsters has been much discussed and has, indeed, proven to be of considerable value. Whether at a special therapeutic camp or merely in a well selected and well planned private setting, the summer experience can prove highly constructive for many youngsters. In terms of the family, it provides a socially acceptable, well structured separation experience. Peer group support is provided, as well as nurturance and protection emanating from the interested, intelligent, and energetic young people who serve as counselors. The emphasis on activities may initiate or strengthen special interests and encourage the development of skills. In turn, skill mastery advances the process of ego development. For some

children, even the competitive structure of camps may provide stimulation towards accomplishment. Other children will do better in a camp which plays down competition in the group and deals with children on the basis of individual accomplishment.

CASE ILLUSTRATION

Donald was an eleven-year-old in psychotherapy for some years. After an unpleasant day camp experience at age seven, he had refused to attend camp again, just as he avoided other new experiences. Donald could not bear to be separated from his family with whom he was involved in a deeply ambivalent and, frequently, mutually hostile relationship. For such a child, when he is finally able to separate from home and go to camp, there is a sense of relief from the manifold pressures of home and school. For Donald's parents, who were at the end of their rope with him, it permitted a breather which diminished the intense stress they were under. The constant irritation and counterirritation of life together, which had escalated to extreme intensity before the summer, was now abated, at least for a few months. The parents' visits to the camp were pleasant and they were surprised and pleased at the way Donald welcomed them. Donald, on the other hand, was pleased that his parents had come to see him, though he did not deign to acknowledge this directly.

Thus, during the summer, an acute parent-child conflict went through a cooling off period. Reunion in September proved to be a happy occasion; both the child and the family welcomed life together. For Donald, who had always felt vastly inferior to a successful and adored older brother, excelling in horseback riding gave him his first taste of success. This was the first achievement he was able to accept. It was also something he had chosen and achieved on his own without his intellectual and artistically creative family exerting any pressure on him. Riding became a special interest that permitted him to compete with his older brother's excellence in judo. On their visits, Donald's parents were extremely pleased with his enthusiasm for riding and Donald benefited from their pleasure in his achievement. A better equilibrium had, at least temporarily, been established in this family.

During the subsequent year, the previous conflicts may again escalate within the family but they will be dealt with in psychotherapy. The summer experience will, however, serve as a reminder to the family of the pleasurable possibilities of life together when family problems are resolved. For Donald, the success at camp provided increased confidence for his return to school. He was now better able to cope with school pressure and with his anxieties about achievement. During the previous year, he had responded to pressures with frustration, tantrums, and destruction of his own work. Now he was better able to withstand frustration and also began to experience some success in school. His greater degree of confidence also allowed him new relationships with his peers. He was less prone to impulsive and aggressive outbursts towards them and began to develop some relationships. While his boasting about his riding achievements might alienate some children, his newer relationships seemed to be lasting through the school year.

This kind of positive spiral of development illustrates how external experiences, exemplified by successful camp placement, can interact with intrapsychic phenomena to accomplish gains for a child in therapy. For some children, camp may provide in miniature the positive effect of a residential treatment experience without the specific intervention of therapy. The camp experience relates itself to the child's ego and his strengths, not to his pathology. It is ego-supportive and ego-developing. However, to benefit from this type of environmental change, the child has to be ready to encounter new things and also have the capacity to experience success. Some children may be able to accomplish this at any good camp. Others will make headway only through the use of a special therapeutic camp, where the experiences are tailored to the individual needs and capacities of the child. As a result, skill mastery and small successes can be afforded to even the most seriously disturbed child, with obvious therapeutic impact.

Therapeutic Use of Court Authority

In therapeutic work with delinquents, external authority can be used to provide the necessary leverage for the treatment of an unmotivated adolescent, as well as the control that will limit his acting out behavior. For those delinquents who are considered unsuitable for therapy, the court structure and probation experience becomes the treatment modality of choice.

ILLUSTRATION OF USE OF AUTHORITY

Nir[26] cites the case of Barry M., a thirteen-year-old boy, brought into court as a sexual offender. Both the boy and his parents denied problems or the need for psychiatric help. Assessment of the boy showed him to be isolated, affectively impoverished, with paranoid ideation and fears of being attacked or knifed. He was diagnosed as suffering from a schizophrenic reaction, paranoid type. In view of his own and the parents' refusal to cooperate with psychiatric treatment, indefinite probation was recommended. It was assumed that such external controls would strengthen Barry's ego defenses and enable him to contain the erupting sexualized aggressive impulses. During the time he remained on probation, with periodic reporting to his probation officer, he remained asymptomatic and even did well in school. In view of his good behavior, the probation department pressured the agency to recommend the boy's termination from probation. Four weeks after such termination, Barry was arrested again for another sexual offense. Nir comments: "Barry's case illustrates the possibility of translating a basic therapeutic technique into the area of social interaction with authority and the law."[26]

For a variety of psychodynamic reasons, the concept of providing support for ego defenses by the use of court authority and the impersonal structure of the court has a good deal of merit. It is useful and effective in certain individual cases. For other children who, at first, are not motivated for treatment or cannot "publically" acknowledge their interest, the beginning phase of therapy may be accelerated if the child is placed on probation. The proviso is set that the child attend psychotherapy sessions as one of the conditions of his probation.

This is another example of environmental manipulation in the interests of support to the ego and as a means of containing acting out behavior. For similar reasons, one may recommend that a child be placed in a detention shelter for a few days. This may be done to present reality to the child very rudely; indeed it may become a test of his sense of reality, as well as a means of interrupting a surge of delinquent behavior which he himself cannot consciously control. A brief period of hospitalization may accomplish the same purpose; that is, awakening the child's reality sense or shifting the balance of forces within the personality. The interruption in the acting out behavior by means of the confinement may, by itself, be sufficient to establish a new balance. This may succeed in making the youngster more accessible to the more usual modalities of treatment.

The preceding material has presented a few examples of environmental intervention. These may be multiplied many times to include a far wider range of activities and experiences. In some instances, these environmental activities may avoid the need for direct psychiatric intervention. In others, they are obviously ancillary to treatment. One must learn to distinguish between two kinds of situations, those that respond to such direct interventions without continued treatment, and those in which such activities are clearly secondary or optional. Case assessment must include evaluation not only of the immediate social-psychological environment but also of the broader environmental circumstances. Only thus can one assess the necessity for or the value of specific environmental interventions.

REFERENCES

1. ALPERT, A., "A Special Therapeutic Technique for Certain Developmental Disorders in Prelatency Children," *American Journal of Orthopsychiatry, 37(2):*256–270, 1957.

2. AMBINDER, W., et al., "Role Phenomena and Foster Care for Disturbed Children," *American Journal of Orthopsychiatry, 32(1):*32–41, 1962.

3. Annual Report, Jewish Protectory and Aid Society, New York, 1908.

4. BAUER, J. E., and HEINKE, W., "Treatment Family Care Homes for Disturbed Foster Children," *Child Welfare, 55(7):*478–491, 1976.

5. BURLINGHAM, D. T., "Child Analysis and the Mother," *Psychoanalytic Quarterly, 4(1):*69–92, 1935.

6. CABLE, M., *The Little Darlings,* Charles Scribner & Sons, New York, 1975.

7. DEFRIES, Z., JENKINS, S., and WILLIAMS, E. C., "Treatment of Disturbed Children in Foster Care," *American Journal of Orthopsychiatry, 34(4):*615–624, 1964.

8. DEUTSCH, A., "The History of Mental Hygiene," in Hall, J. K. (Ed.), *One Hundred Years of Psychiatry,* pp. 325–365, Columbia University Press, New York, 1944.

9. FINE, R. V., "Moving Emotionally Disturbed Children from Institutions to Foster Family," *Children, 13(6):* 221–226, 1966.

10. FRAIBERG, S., "A Therapeutic Approach to Reactive Ego Disturbances in Children in Placement," *American Journal of Orthopsychiatry, 32(1):*18–31, 1962.

11. FREUD, A., "Indications for Child Analysis," in Eissler, R. S., et al. (Eds.), *The Psychoanalytic Study of the Child,* vol. 1 pp. 127–149, International Universities Press, New York, 1945.

12. FREUD, S., *An Outline of Psychoanalysis,* W. W. Norton, New York, 1949.

13. GLASSCOTE, R., FISHMAN, M., and SONIS, M., *Children and Mental Health Centers,* Joint Information Service, Washington, D.C., 1972.

14. GRAY, B., "A Foster Family Program for Disturbed Children," *Child Welfare, 36(9):*10–15, 1957.

15. HIKEL, V., "Fostering the Troubled Child," *Child Welfare, 48(7):*427–431, 1969.

16. HOPKIRK, H. W., *Institutions Serving Children,* Russell Sage Foundation, New York, 1944.

17. KANNER, L., *Child Psychiatry,* 4th ed., Charles C Thomas, Springfield, Ill., 1972.

18. KAPLAN, L., and TURITZ, L., "Treatment of Severely Traumatized Young Children in a Foster Home Setting," *American Journal of Orthopsychiatry, 27(2):* 271–285, 1957.

19. KLEIN, J., *Superintendent's Report, Annual Report,* Jewish Protectory and Aid Society, New York, 1909.

20. LAWDER, E., ANDREWS, R., and PARSONS, J., *Five Models of Foster Family Group Homes,* Child Welfare League of America, New York, 1974.

21. MCMANUS, J. E., "The Proctor Program for Detention of Delinquent Girls," *Child Welfare, 55(5):*345–352, 1976.

22. MALUCCIO, A. N., "Selecting Foster Parents for Disturbed Children," *Children, 13(2):*69–74, 1966.

23. MILLER, C., "The Agency-Owned Foster Home," *Child Welfare, 33(9):*9–17, 1954.

24. MORA, G., "Foster Families for Emotionally Disturbed Children," *Child Welfare, 41(3):*104–106, 1962.

25. NEUBAUER, P. B., "The One-Parent Child and His Oedipal Development," in Eissler, R. S., et al. (Eds.), *The Psychoanalytic Study of the Child,* vol. 15, pp. 286–309, 1960.

26. NIR, Y., "The Use of Court Authority in Psychiatric Treatment of Delinquent Adolescents," paper presented at the Annual Meeting, American Association of Psychiatric Clinics for Children, Philadelphia, 1970.

27. RAAB, M., Personal communication.

28. REYMERT, M. I., "The Organization and Administration of a Child Guidance Clinic," in Harms, E. (Ed.), *Handbook of Child Guidance,* pp. 225–248, Child Care Publications, New York, 1947.

29. RICHMOND, M. E., *What is Social Casework? An Introductory Description,* Russell Sage Foundation, New York, 1922.

30. SMITH, E., RICKETTS, B., and SMITH, S., "The Recommendation for Child Placement by a Psychiatric Clinic," *American Journal of Orthopsychiatry, 32(1):*42–49, 1962.

31. STARK, R., "The Fatherless Boys Project: Some Therapeutic Implications," paper presented at the National Conference for Jewish Communal Services, Boston, 1976.

32. TAYLOR, D., and STARR, P., "Foster Parenting: An Integrative Review of the Literature," *Child Welfare, 46:* 371–385, 1967.

33. *Three Problem Children,* Narratives from the Case Records of a Child Guidance Clinic Publication, The Joint Committee on Methods of Preventing Delinquency, New York, 1924.

34. WASKOWITZ, V., "Foster-Family Care for Disturbed Children," *Children, 1(4):*125–130, 1954.

35. WILDY, L., "The Professional Foster Home," in Child Welfare League of America, *Foster Family Care for Emotionally Disturbed Children,* pp. 1–8, Child Welfare League of America, New York, 1962.

36. WOLINS, M., and PILIAVIN, P., *Institution or Foster Family,* Child Welfare League of America, New York, 1964.

19 / Psychoeducation in the Clinical Setting

Gaston E. Blom

Definition and Description

The term "psychoeducation" has appeared for some time in special education, but only recently has it entered the psychiatric and psychological literature. Generally speaking, it connotes the integration of psychological and educational approaches in the evaluation, remediation, and programming for handicapped children. It is often applied to settings where the work is carried out by a single professional discipline; but it is based on principles and on understanding that various professional specialties have developed in the course of working with the handicapped child.

Within the larger realm of special education, psychoeducation for the most part stresses emotional sensitivity and awareness, along with those approaches described in chapter 20. Nonetheless, the emphasis in remediation efforts continues to fall primarily on educational techniques and strategies. Mental health professionals tend to ignore education and training methods or to take them for granted. This results in a relative separation of two major professional groups. The net effect is to reduce the opportunity for more effective remediation of various handicapping conditions. In management of most handicapped children, integrated interdisciplinary effort is required. This can rarely be accomplished by the work of a single professional from any one specific discipline. In order to understand this more unified kind of psychoeducational approach, this chapter will examine the concept, both in theory and practice, in terms of a number of related issues.

There are two major professions that guide efforts to help handicapped children: (1) the training and teaching professions, and (2) the treatment professions. These two groups are defined broadly to include educators, speech (language) therapists, and other didactic specialists on the one hand, and the various health professionals, both mental and physical, on the other. Each of these groups has its own set of theories, principles, values, and practices, which differs from and, indeed, stands in contrast with that of the other. It is, therefore, all too easy to understand why conflict so commonly arises between them, and why it is a challenging task to integrate their efforts.

In Table 19-1 contrasts between the operations of teaching and treatment have been organized according to goal, focus, value orientations, behavioral views, and behavioral approaches. For heuristic purposes, the contrasts have been somewhat polarized and exaggerated. Teaching and treatment share the common purpose of helping children, but they seek to do so by different methods. Teaching places its emphasis on skill and competence development with a focus on the influence of external environments and reality. Treatment strives first to diagnose and then it focuses on changing inner psychological events and feelings to remediate pathology. The expectation here is that as blocks to development and normative functioning are removed, inner personality resources and environmental opportunities will in turn give rise to competence.

Thus, different value orientations determine how behaviors are viewed and approached. Teaching holds the following to be important: content, performance, cognition, present and future time emphasis, immediacy of events and short-term goals, empiricism and pragmatism in operations, conformance in behavior, and simple unitary cause for behavior. Treatment holds contrasting orientations: process, inner psychological change, emotion, past to present time perspective, present events in relation to long-term goals, theoretical propositions to understand behavior, individuality, and multiple complex causes often stated in a special language.

It follows that teaching views behavior in terms of what is manifest and observable, its frequency and consequences, conscious communication, and its evaluation according to normal and morality standards (good-bad, acceptable-unacceptable, desirable-undesirable, age appropriate-inappropriate, and high-low ability). Treatment, on the other hand, views behavior in relation to what it means, the salience or significance of behavioral events, antecedent causes, less conscious communication —feeling, conflict, and relationships to other people, and nonevaluative and nonjudgmental attitudes. As a result, the concept of normality is blurred, and behavioral variabilities are viewed as normal or pathological along with some vague, not agreed upon continuum.

From different goals, focus, value orientations, and behavioral views, approaches to behavior differ as well. Teaching makes use of talking, modeling, advising, reacting to behavior, presenting consequences, emphasizing control, decreasing tension, structuring events, and attending to the group. On the whole, the professional tends to take the initiative. Treatment employs listening, understanding, interpreting, reacting with emotional neutrality, uncovering and expressing, increasing tension, exploring events, and attending to the individual. The subject is usually encouraged by the professional to initiate his own pattern of behavioral activity.

There have been differences noted in the assumptions of school personnel and mental health clinicians[18] regarding how change in behavior of children is brought about. LaVietes and Chess[25] have contrasted these professional groups in relation to the difficulties encountered in school consultation. When one recognizes that the operations are induced through training, maintained by professional experience, and influenced by personality style, then the task of combining these two professional streams of thought presents some formidable difficulties. Yet to appreciate and respect these

TABLE 19–1

Contrasts Between Teaching and Treatment

		Teaching	Treatment
1.	Goal	Competence and skill	Remediation of pathology
2.	Focus	External environments Reality	Inner psychological events Feelings
3.	Value orientations	Content Performance Cognition Present-future time Short-term goals Empiricism and pragmatism Conformance Simple unitary cause	Process Inner change Emotions Past-present time Long-term goals Theory Individuality Multiple complex causes
4.	Behavioral views	Manifest observation Behavioral frequency Consequences Conscious communication Norms Moral evaluation	Latent meanings Behavioral salience Antecedents Feelings, conflict, relationships Blurring of normality Nonjudgmental
5.	Behavioral approaches	Talking Modeling Advising Reacting-consequences Controls and suppresses Decrease tension Structuring events Initiation by professional Group	Listening Understanding Interpreting Emotional neutrality Uncovers and expresses Increase tension Exploring events Initiation by subject Individual

differences can facilitate bridging. This in turn can lead to an integration that increases the potential power of intervention strategies in psychoeducation. Furthermore, the integration will in many instances result in a positive change in the way things are done.

Instead of having an "either-or" point of view, it is possible to take an "as-well-as" or "both-and" stance. The remediation of pathology and skill development may coexist, and treatment and training will then facilitate one another. Positive motivation does modify or overcome handicaps and skill achievement will influence pathological states. While assisting parents with their emotions, they can be helped at the same time to develop more competence in child caring. One can focus simultaneously on environments and on the inner lives of children; the emphasis can be allowed to fall on wherever the need is greater or where potential results are more likely to be positive. More flexible strategies are possible if there is freedom of movement within and between the two professional streams of thought. Value orientations can be combined so that one's method includes content and process, short- and long-term goals, empiricism and theory (understandably communicated in simple language), past-present-future time perspectives (without becoming obsessive about the past), and individuality within sensible conformance. It is possible to be aware of both the cognitive and emotional domains of the personality, of reality performance as well as inner psychological change. A simple unitary cause should be accepted when it is operationally useful; by the same token, multiple causality has value only as it clarifies rather than complicates.

The "as-well-as" stance also applies to behavioral views. As detailed in chapters 5 and 11, it is important to be clear about what is observable and how often it occurs before inferring meanings from and salience to behavior. Both antecedent causes and behavioral consequences should be considered. Consequences have a powerful influence in maintaining behavior. It is also best to proceed from conscious face value communication to unexpressed feeling, partially perceived conflict, hidden relationships, and other meanings. Yet, to deny that behavior has meaning beyond its immediate concrete content is to miss the richness in human communication. Positive behavioral expectations can be defined in terms of desirability and normality. It is important to establish such expectations in a way that is realistic and achievable for individuals and groups. This has a more favorable influence than the confusion of "supposed" nonjudgmental attitudes with the consequent blurring of normality. "Supposed" indicates that there will always be attitudes anchored in a helper's value systems. Evaluation does not have to be offered with a heavy hand and without tolerance. But to refute, to deny, or to keep evaluation totally implicit are neither helpful nor realistic.

In considering approaches to behavior, there should be balance and flexibility between talking and listening, modeling and understanding, advising and interpreting, controlling and expressing, decreasing and increasing tensions, and structuring and exploring. Mutuality about who initiates interaction presents a more usual form of communication. It is possible to work with children individually and in groups. Again it is not realistic to assume that a helper can remain emotionally neutral to behavioral events and that he/she will not have reactions. This does not condone presenting reactions and consequences in a haphazard manner.

The following clinical case example illustrates one variety of conflict that arises in a clinical psychoeducational setting between therapist and teacher.

FEELINGS AND CONFLICT VERSUS SKILL TRAINING

Tracy, age eight and one-half, was one of identical twin boys. He displayed fearfulness, inhibition, and multiple phobias, maintained close ties to his brother and mother, and elaborated an aggressive inner fantasy life. In body-motor training class, he was reluctant to become involved in various exercises. On one particular day, a distinguished psychomotor specialist visited the program, noted that Tracy had difficulty in eye convergence with rope climbing, and discussed some possible training activities together with desensitization. This provided the teacher with a ready, authoritative program. He later met with the therapist in a team meeting and presented this suggestion in a convincing firm way. The therapist reacted both to the idea and to the associated affect. He stated that such activities might heighten Tracy's anxieties since he would view action as dangerous in accordance with his violent inner fantasy world. The therapist asserted that Tracy was not ready and needed more time to develop trust in his environment and to explore feelings and meanings. The teacher

held to his views, and in short order an impasse resulted. Both therapist and teacher embraced the goals, focus, values, views, and approaches of their professional orientations ever more firmly. It required third-party mediation and time before these two professionals could see their efforts as complementing each other.

In the preceding example, the child under discussion had presented symptoms of anxiety and immaturity. His difficulties in learning and socialization were primarily psychologically determined, although there was evidence of maturational lags. If it was deemed necessary and useful, he could be considered emotionally handicapped and an appropriate psychiatric diagnosis could be made.

The term "handicapped child" has been here employed in order to indicate a more general view of disabilities. Psychoeducation is viewed as the generic mode of therapy for children with a variety of handicaps—in particular, those children with problems in the physical, sensory, emotional, mental, and educational realms. The specifics of method may vary with different handicaps, but the overall philosophy remains the same. Furthermore, this approach can be utilized within different clinical and educational settings—schools, clinics, day programs, residential facilities, and other specialized environments.

Theory and Rationale

Unfortunately, there is no unified comprehensive theory of personality functioning and development. The complexities involved in human mentation and behavior make such a formulation difficult to achieve, if not impossible. Yet, one can only agree with Baldwin[2] who states that the aim of developmental studies turns ever "towards an integrated and unified theory." Psychoeducation represents an eclectic attempt to bring together a number of different points of view. It seeks to integrate the strengths and ingredients of different theoretical and empirical models of behavior that have pragmatic usefulness.

Other chapters in this volume review the many existing approaches to understanding and dealing with behavior. Elsewhere, Rhodes and Tracy[28] have depicted various treatment-education models applied to emotional disturbances. This chapter will briefly discuss some of them from a clinically oriented, psychoeducational perspective, emphasizing: etiologic, psychodynamic, behavioral, adaptive, and ecologic perspectives.

An *etiologic* view stresses the causation of pathological behavior. Diagnostic procedures are used to determine one or more causes, whether biologic, psychologic, familial, or educational. As specific cause(s) can be sorted out, they may be corrected, modified, or altered through treatment procedures. One limitation to this view is that diagnosis all too frequently does not lead to specific interventions, that is, it does not indicate what needs to be done and how. Another limitation arises from the assumption that normal behavior will resume after a pathogenic cause has been remedied. Etiology does not make a distinction between what initiates and what perpetuates maladaptive behavior(s). The latter may be just as significant as the former. Furthermore, what initiated the behavior(s) originally, may no longer be operative; once established, the pattern may maintain itself.

The *psychodynamic* model is based on the concept that inner conflict, emotional states, disturbed relationships to others, and unconscious meanings are causally related to manifest maladaptive behavior. Conflict(s), emotions, relationships, and unconscious elements are approached psychotherapeutically with the expectation that as psychodynamics are modified, manifest symptoms will diminish and appropriate, adaptive behavior will develop. In some instances this may indeed occur, especially if environmental factors and past experiences are favorable to change. However, behavior frequently becomes syntonic and autonomous, that is, little underlying conflict exists, and the symptom has a somewhat independent status of its own which resists change. In the course of time, long-standing symptoms may acquire all kinds of secondary elaborations, and the environment's response may support their continuation. The psychodynamic view does not give adequate recognition to this phenomenon of symptom autonomy. As a theory, it is also deficient in conceptualizations about cognition and learning and in failing to recognize the large number of children who lack inner controls and are otherwise deficient on a structural basis.

The *behavioral* model is based on learning theory. It asserts that maladaptive behavior is learned and perpetuated by various environmental contingencies and reinforcements. Through careful programming of reinforcements and methodologic strategies, maladaptive behaviors can be modified and alternative patterns generated. The tasks may be academic, social, motor, and emotional. The program can be used for both management and instructional purposes.

This model has been extensively applied to a wide variety of problems in clinical and educational settings. However, its claims seem overstated and its exclusive use can be questioned.[3] It does not deal with inner feelings, psychological states, nor the meanings of behavior. In particular, the psychology of success-failure in tasks is ignored, and the assumption that natural contingencies will maintain an acquired behavior is not always warranted.

The *adaptive* model stresses that skills and competencies need development in their own right. Opportunities for their generation are provided in therapeutic, educational, family, and other settings. In part, they can be taught, and as they are generated, they will favorably influence the child's conflicts, emotions, and relationships. Skills are not limited to the academic realm; they involve emotional, social, body and other realms as well. Behavioral change can occur from the outside-in as well as from the inside-out, and approaches from both directions add power to the effectiveness of treatment.

An *ecological* model offers a strategy for dealing with pathological and maladaptive behaviors in a variety of ways. Hobbs[23] describes and conceptualizes the child within an interacting system. The system consists of family, school, and community elements. Each of these elements in the ecological system can be considered a site for intervention, particularly when it can be demonstrated that this element influences the child's behavior. Furthermore, each element in the system can be viewed as a subsystem with its own subelements. The ecological system then can be studied in terms of its elements, subsystems, and subelements. Places are selected for intervention according to: (1) their significance, (2) their accessibility, (3) the possibility for effecting change, and (4) the availability of professional assistance. At any given time, intervention strategies operate that are based on evaluative data. Both the data and the form of intervention may change over time as additional information and experience become available. The character and nature of the problems will also change. As is the case with more traditional educational and therapeutic strategies, in the ecological system too, it is possible to focus on a limited number of elements. Yet if one recognizes that behavior is strongly determined by environmental contexts, then a limited focus may not yield results that are sufficiently effective or efficient in terms of time and cost. The ecological system can make use of the problem oriented approach and regular utilization review in a way that is both easy and natural. Problem priorities, timing, the selection of intervention strategies, and continued problem solving become ongoing processes.

From these theoretical and empirical models of behavior, a number of practices have been selected that have served the test of pragmatic usefulness. These are outlined in Table 19-2. Several have been discussed more fully in other publications.* Most of them have a central adherence to Erikson's[15] psychosocial developmental theory and White's[34] concepts of competence. Both of these theories provide bridges between the individual and his/her environment, between normality and pathology, and among the body, motor, cognitive, language, and emotional domains of the individual.

Three case histories provide illustrations of practices used during the course of a clinical psychoeducational program.

HOME ENVIRONMENT MODIFICATION

Kent, age ten, presented a manifest picture of thought disorganization, difficulty in attending to tasks, and a preference for fantasy activities. Although he was a highly intelligent boy, his academic performance was below grade level, and he remained isolated from other children. It was observed that as the week progressed from Monday through Friday, with structure, labeling, reality encouragement, and other measures, his disorganization progressively decreased and his capacity for attention increased. However, on Mondays, Kent was usually back in the same disorganized state again. Discussions with his parents did not reveal any unusual events that occurred over the weekends. Nor were their relationships with Kent so obviously unusual as to account for this phenomenon. When sufficient trust had been established with his parents, a staff social worker made a home visit on a Saturday morning. He discovered that Kent was watching television programs and dramatizing their content in action, adding his own elaborations. Kent's parents, particularly his mother, did not consider this unusual; to some extent they viewed it as evidence of creative fantasy and an indication of talent. When it was explained that this contributed to his problems, it was possible to enlist their cooperation in stopping this activity. At the same time the psychological basis for her acceptance of this behavior was explored with Kent's mother. She presently revealed that when she was ten years old, a heart murmur had been detected, she had been diagnosed as suffering from rheumatic heart disease, and her physical activities had been restricted. As a consequence, she turned to her fantasy life, daydreaming extensively, wrote, and developed an ambition to become a famous author. A number of years later, the heart murmur was determined to be benign and normal activity was resumed. However, the pleasure and daydreams of her

* See references 5, 6, 7, 8, 9, 10, 11, 12, 14, and 31.

fantasy world persisted and were accentuated through her son, Kent.

TABLE 19–2

Psychoeducational Practices

A. Information Collection
1. Broad sampling of behaviors in different contexts by screening instruments
2. Observations in naturalistic settings
3. Information from other agencies and sources

B. Information Processing
4. Descriptive behavioral data base
5. Developmental viewpoint including various areas of functioning
6. Etiologic and biologic awareness
7. Problem oriented system—identifications, priorities, goals, strategies, and progress over time

C. Program Principles
8. Interdisciplinary team and staff collaboration
9. Ongoing problem solving
10. Programming in real life contexts and environments
11. Time limited goals and plans/steps for normalization
12. Periodic utilization review—clinical and test assessments
13. Trial-and-error procedures

D. Program Emphasis
14. Flexible and combined therapeutic and educational strategies
15. Structure, predictability, and clarity
16. Interaction of management and instruction
17. Management of stimulation
18. Success/failure dimension
19. Attention to individual and groups
20. Child/parent accountability and reinforcement

DEALING WITH FEAR OF SUCCESS

Kelly, age nine, came from a family in which his father's relatives were accomplished professionals and his dominating mother had married in part to achieve the status which she felt was lacking in her own background. Kelly, therefore, was expected to meet special ideals. Moreover, he had two older sisters who were academically and socially successful. He developed a pattern of passive-aggressive behaviors and took little responsibility for learning. In reinforcement learning exercises where tasks were designed for his presumed ability levels, Kelly was very uneven in his performance. Nor did changing tasks, procedures, and rewards have any substantial effect. At times it was difficult to determine whether he "couldn't" perform or "wouldn't." The issue of success-failure was dealt with by both the teacher and the therapists of the child and parents. It was difficult to modify the parental pressures and expectations. Eventually, Kelly revealed his great fear: that if he succeeded in small tasks, then the demands to learn more would be unceasing and limitless. If he read a page successfully, then he would have to read the book, then many books, then he would have to go to college, and, finally, to become a lawyer. To him, all this seemed devoid of pleasure and meaning. When the staff were able to convince Kelly that they were not the agents of his parents, that they would respect his own goals and not overwhelm him with work, he began to achieve. At this point, however, he lacked the academic skills appropriate to his grade level and needed help to develop them. Periodically, he would fail, and it was often helpful if the teacher labeled this behavior as a fear of success.

STRESSING SOCIAL SKILLS

Another child, Wanda, age seven, had failed first grade in public school. She was depressed and had not received consistent attention, care, and stimulation from her young parents. When she first entered the psychoeducational program, she did not behave in socially appropriate ways. She ate with her fingers, was not personally clean, and did not know how to adjust to the classroom. As a result, she was rejected by the other children. The team decided the first priority was to work on her social skills and manners—to teach her to eat with utensils, wash her face and hands on arrival in the morning, greet people when she came in, ask permission to do things, and carry out other tasks related to classroom behavior. At first Wanda responded only to extrinsic rewards for task achievements. Gradually she began to respond to social rewards, and in time the effective reinforcers became self-satisfaction and peer acceptance. It took a much longer time to facilitate change in the parents' behavior.

Historical Background and Development

Over the past fifteen years a number of diverse sources have challenged traditional mental health, social, and educational programs for handicapped children and families. The critique has been directed variously to their goals, philosophies, policies, efficacy, costs, and limited services. The Joint Commission studies and reports[29, 30] highlighted many of these issues. In the 1960s, the Great Society programs were planned, legislated, funded, and implemented (in some instances with limited mental health professional input). They were addressed to large numbers of the handicapped and disadvantaged who had previously been ignored or who had not been helped.[27] The prevention and remediation efforts of these Great Society programs emphasized educational and training methods designed to develop skills and competence. In 1965, the National Institute of Mental Health sponsored a conference on "Social Competence and Clinical Practice" which addressed the existing national conflict between clinical and educational approaches and considered ways in which this might be resolved.[17] Unfortunately, this heated professional dialogue has waned. Currently, for the most part, the clinical and competence groups continue to be isolated from each other and to operate independently.

The mental health and education fields have of course expanded and developed in a variety of ways. The tracks on which they run are usually parallel but seldom integrated. It is not possible to provide an adequate concise critique of these ongoing historical trends. Special education programs within both private and public areas have understandably broadened the categories of handicapped children they serve. The categories now include not only physical, mental, and sensory handicaps, but a proliferation of specifically identified handicaps—language disabled, dyslexic, perceptually handicapped, autistic, aphasic, brain damaged, learning disabled, and others. The area of developmental disabilities is being defined to include both traditional and newly established entities. The diverse professional sponsorship of these programs includes pediatrics, education, and interdisciplinary groups. Normalization, child advocacy, and mainstream philosophies have emerged only to encounter responses that range through questioning, resistance, reasoned perspective, and unbridled enthusiasm from public and professional groups.

As a result of studies by the Joint Commission and by other sources, community mental health programs have developed on a national scale. They emphasize integrated and expanded treatment services, community based activities, citizen participation, and prevention programs. Special population and problem groups have been addressed, alternative patterns to hospitalization have been provided, traditional treatment modalities continue to be available, and the use of new professional and paraprofessional staff has become characteristic of their operation. Nonetheless, in spite of all their changes in philosophy, these programs have not always fulfilled their objectives. Indeed, in many instances they are merely old programs with new faces and increased funding.

Hospital and community treatment groups have oriented themselves toward the funded dollar and the establishment of a professional power base. Hospitalization has in turn become something vastly different from a judiciously indicated, useful, time-limited procedure, occupying one point on a spectrum of services. The issues of efficacy, efficiency, quality care, restricted services, and evaluation are lively issues, but withal still not sufficiently addressed. The rapid expansion of community mental health programs with large amounts of funding has led to an inflation of ambitions without the technologies or the adequately trained staffs necessary to realize such grandiose goals. The lack of capable evaluation procedures has contributed to the problems. One can only laud the directions and philosophy of community based programs. Better methodology however is sorely needed.

Within both mental health and education a trend can be identified which fortunately has received some professional response. Human services need greater public accountability and monitoring of their professional activities in relation, both to their funding sources and to the people they serve. This has led to open records legislation and policies. to improved and specified standards of care, to public and private accreditation groups, to continued education requirements of professionals, to periodic licensing, to utilization and peer review processes, to more representative citizen participation in decision making and on advisory and administrative boards, and to improved and standardized record keeping and evaluation of progress. Pressure groups, legal suits, audits, and public visibility are among the less comfortable events taking place in our society. But human service professionals should be responsive to reasonable and reasoned criticisms, expectations, and human rights. At times, these developments become politicized and are exploited in the service of nonhealth related or irrational motives. Anti professional attitudes and movements have both rational and irrational components. The positive and rational elements within intelligent humanistic young adults who provide dedicated help to disabled and troubled children and adults should be recognized.

There are of course new professionals, paraprofessionals, and related professionals who should be integrated within mental health and educational programs. Language therapists, occupational therapists, child development specialists, nurse practitioners, and other professionals are increasing in number and have special contributions to offer within interdisciplinary programs. The roles, functions, and operations of paraprofessionals with special experiences are yet to be clarified.

On another level, a proliferation of different and, often, novel treatment methods cannot be ignored. Some of these, though not all, are patently absurd, exploitive, irresponsible, and harmful. Many procedures affect behavior profoundly, but for reasons that are different from their "official" rationale. Factors such as suggestibility, increased attention, positive relationships, and chance happenings may do more to bring about changes in patients than anything new in the proposed method. As a result, it is most difficult to evaluate such approaches.

In 1961, at the University of Colorado, a child psychiatrist and psychoanalyst, and a number of colleagues from other disciplines (pediatrics, education, social work, and clinical psychology) came together in response to the dissatisfactions which had arisen in their professional experiences and because of their desire to develop coordinated and flexible approaches to treating and teaching handicapped children and families. This small group was impressed by the limitations imposed on professional work by biases of setting, tradition, limited staff composition, lip service to multidisciplinary approaches, fragmented professional efforts, and restricted environmental contexts. Over the next fourteen years, a psychoeducational program gradually evolved and became larger in scope and size to include a medical center-based, day-care program for children with school-related problems and extramural activities in community schools.[15] In part, the program has tried to keep pace with historical trends, to integrate conflicting views, to incorporate other and new professionals, and to be responsive to criticisms of the several professional fields.

Resolving Problems in
Services to Children

THE CLINIC AND EDUCATIONAL SETTING

The structure, organization, traditions, attitudes, and social dynamics of a setting strongly influence the kinds and quality of services that it renders to handicapped children and their families. In studying settings, one sometimes wonders if they are designed to function for those who are the intended recipients of services or for the staff who are the providers of care. A number of interactive characteristics of settings will be briefly examined in relation to the nature of the services they provide: (1) sponsorship, (2) administrative direction, (3) staff composition and functions, (4) traditions and operating procedures, (5) populations served, and (6) special attitudes.

The sponsorship of a setting may come from any source, for example, medicine, education, welfare, psychology, university, community, research, or combined. Whatever it is, it will influence all the other characteristics that are present in that agency. The sponsorship will determine the setting's location and thus its accessibility to certain recipients of care. The director of the program is in the nature of things selected by the sponsor and is usually expected to be a generalist and stimulator and to develop constructive staff relationships and dialogue. At the same time, his professional discipline, training, experience, and special interests will influence setting operations profoundly.

A further consideration is the composition of the staff—its diversity according to sex, ethnicity, and profession. The question arises: How many of what types of professional staff are carrying out what kinds of tasks? What activities are being performed and what ignored? How much staff participation is there in decision making and what degree of responsibility occurs?

It is difficult to change the traditions or standard operating procedures of any setting. These may have arisen from a specific professional field, from a given theoretical orientation, or from the history of the setting itself. What were once bright innovations may have quickly become traditionalized. A preference for long, complex diagnostic studies may be maintained even though this approach has limited usefulness to referring agencies. In some settings, the child therapist may be the center of the universe, and often enough his power to make decisions may far exceed his knowledge and capacity. In others, a rule about confidentiality, as unrealistic as it is rigid, will hamper staff communication.

There are many additional factors that will also influence the nature and operations of the setting. These include the kinds of problems referred, the character of the children and families, and the decisions that determine who is selected and who rejected. Cumulatively, these will also lead to an image within the professional and lay community which in turn will reinforce the selected population. Based on such a specific patient group, the setting and its individuals may generalize their experiences into a viewpoint about all handicapped children. To some extent, community pressures, consumer advocacy, and citizen representation on boards may modify these tendencies but only to a limited degree.

There are certain attitudes which will also influence settings. Fad and fashion play their role here as elsewhere in human affairs. At a given time, certain problems are popular—perceptual handicap, minimal brain dysfunction, dyslexia, and others. Such "entities" may receive special funding and public support.

Sarason[33] has studied the culture and dynamics of schools. He described the inevitable loss of innovativeness unless the possibility and process of change are built into setting operations and leadership. Many other studies of mental health hospitals[19] and of treatment practices[16, 24, 30, 32] have documented the fact that many nonclinical factors within settings influence delivery of care. While few question this conclusion, it is striking that settings rarely make provision to evaluate and modify these influences in an ongoing way.

In a particular city, it is possible for a given child with a reading disability to be referred to any one of the following services: (1) a neurology clinic where dyslexia will be diagnosed and Orton-Gillingham tutoring advised, (2) a child psychiatric clinic where a neurotic learning problem will be identified and psychotherapy recommended, (3) a psychology clinic where a structured reading skills program with behavioral reinforcement will be instituted, (4) an educational remedial service where a learning disability will be diagnosed and a special class or school will be recommended, and (5) a developmental center where an extensive diagnostic study will be carried out and a series of prescriptions given to the school which the child attends. Nor do these five possibilities exhaust the list.

CLINICAL EFFECT OF CONFLICTING SERVICES

The case of Donald, age ten, illustrates the problem of settings. Donald and his parents came to a psychoeducational day center after having been evaluated by a number of professionals and centers. The following diagnoses had been communicated to the parents: mental retardation, brain damage, schizophrenia, family psychopathology, and psychoneurosis. Various treatment approaches had been instituted: psychotherapy, a private school for retarded children, and family therapy. The impact of such confusion on Donald's self-image could be observed in his behavior. His teacher reported behavior patterns that could successfully be described as retarded, brain damaged, and "crazy." While Donald and his parents had difficulties enough, all too often his behavior was determined by what he thought, and had been told, was wrong with him.

LIP SERVICE

While considerable lip service is given to multidisciplinary evaluation and remediation of handicaps, in practice, service delivery is often fragmented into activities that are geographically and conceptually separated. Such a multidisciplinary evaluation involves a great deal of time and expense. The step that is so often omitted is the critical integration of the multiple findings along with their translation into meaningful statements of problems and remediation strategies. Without this, it is impossible to use such an evaluation.

Biases operate in what is done and what is ignored in delivering services to children. The "whole child" concept is often a shibboleth. The child is defined as both a psychological and biological developing organism influenced by constitution and his/her environment. This sort of formulation is commonly stated but its implications are ignored. Major areas of development may be overlooked, as well as the importance of constitutional-environment fit. Children live in many social contexts—family, school, neighborhood, peers, and social institutions. Despite the multidisciplinary approach, little conceptual and practical effort is made to influence these different contexts.

CONCEPTS OF HANDICAP AND DIAGNOSIS

A large variety of categorical systems exist. These are based on different concepts of handicap which in turn arise from professional biases. These concepts include: disease, disability, deficiency, defect, learned behavior, abnormality, and others. The concept(s) will influence diagnostic or categorical systems evolving from them. In separate studies, Hobbs has reported the findings of an extensive project on the issues in the classificiation of exceptional children[21] and critique of existing systems, that suggests the need to include competencies children need rather than capabilities they lack.[22] Morse has expressed concern about the tendency to use numerous categories in identifying limited characteristics of children in special school programs, "like Howard Johnson's ice cream flavors."[26] In a similar fashion, Hewitt[20] refers to how school systems "cafeteriorize" handicapped children.

Children who are described as having school-related problems can be categorized in multiple ways: emotionally disturbed, educationally handicapped, dyslexic, learning disabled, developmentally disabled, culturally disadvantaged, and others. Such children have difficulties in various areas of development (body, emotional, social, language, cognitive) from a variety of interactive causes. The most useful conceptual diagnostic approach has been a descriptive behavioral one. On the basis of reports and direct observations, manifest behaviors are noted in various areas of developmental functioning and in many situational contexts. These may include the classroom, particular learning situations, therapy, physical activities, lunch, music, home, neighborhood, physical examinations, psychological testing, achievement testing, before and after school behavior, structured and unstructured situations, and many others. These observations provide a wealth of real-life data about the child and his family life. The crucial issue is the synthesis of these data and the establishing of problem priorities on which interventional strategies can be developed. No single system of diagnostic categorization is useful. Biological awareness and evaluations are important. Psychiatric diagnosis and psychodynamic formulation(s) may be helpful in sorting out patterns of behavior. However, their usefulness is measured by the degree to which they contribute to therapeutic and educational programming. Strategies of remediation should be developed based on observation and information in an ongoing process. The central question in diagnosis is: How much of what kinds of information is necessary for specific decision making about treatment and education at a given point?

Difficulties in the Psychoeducational Approach

It is far easier to identify and to pose central questions about the problems in current educational and treatment services for handicapped children than it is to offer ready solutions. There are fewer obstacles to applying the principles of psychoeducation within a single setting than there are to integrating operations in a number of settings simultaneously. It takes time, energy, and patience to work with professionals in a problem-solving way in several settings over an extended period. There are limits to what a single professional psychoeducator can do by himself. More can be done when sharing the work with others, but his interest and willingness may not be shared by others.

Within a given setting, it takes time for a psychoeducational program to evolve.[14] With the best of intentions, past professional experience and training are not always helpful in developing interdisciplinary operations. One has to tolerate the ambiguity that comes from trying different approaches and evaluating these interventions. Programs work best when they are flexible. What works well for one child may not work for another.

Leadership of a psychoeducational program calls for characteristics and qualities that are not readily available. Such a director needs to be a generalist without being a general. One might draw an analogy to an orchestra leader (director) who can value all elements of the orchestra (professional staff), blend them together when necessary, and identify limited elements (specific professional staff and activities) when they are sufficient. The dangers are to oversimplify or to overcomplicate. The former leads to weak, less effective forms of intervention, and the latter, to noisy, confusing ones. A staff should value what each individual can do but have an identification with what the entire group can do.

In the eclecticism that characterizes psychoeducation, how diverse can the number of professionals and theoretical orientations be? It is of course not just a matter of numbers; it is rather the ability and interest that different professionals bring to the task of bridging with one another. Given the difficulties, the process can be both exciting and stimulating. The realistic and tolerable position for a professional to take is that of seeking solutions to problems over time rather than through immediate action. Decisions about further evaluation, observations missed by others, and suggestions for strategy may come from different staff members.

A companion difficulty is how to process a great deal of information about a given child from a wide variety of areas and sources. Sometimes, the information is discordant and needs clarification. At other times, one feels overwhelmed by too many problems and too much information. It is easy to understand why many professionals limit the number of behavioral elements to be observed and treated, and why the reduction of these many factors to some oversimplified theme or explanation is so appealing. There is good reason to question both the restriction of information and the overreductionism that characterize the operations of many clinicians in the teaching and treating professions. Initial screening of a broad sweep of information and the continued collection of data will often allow for more effective intervention strategies. The use of a problem-oriented approach can provide a way to list problems, select those that appear to have salience, develop appropriate intervention strategies, and assess progress. As indicated previously, an ecological approach provides a great deal of information about a child. But one can select sites for intervention on the basis of accessibility, responsiveness to change, and many other criteria.

Professional Staff and Program

MULTIPROFESSIONAL STAFF

There should be some diversity in a full-time professional staff by professional discipline, theoretical orientation, and special areas of knowledge. Part-time and consultation staff can provide additional information, evaluation, and intervention inputs both to the overall program and to the work with individual children. This is important in order to expand the operation base of the core staff and to develop a positive eclectic viewpoint. Trainees and students from various professional groups will strengthen diversity and interdisciplinary experience. One should question the appropriateness and effectiveness of a traditional child guidance staff which will restrict program opportunities.

In general, a staff member has some role functions that are exclusive and some that overlap with those of other staff. This provides interfaces which facilitate the communication of many viewpoints about a child. Sharing duties and responsibilities will thus tend to expand staff contributions. A therapist may have something to offer to the didactic program, and a teacher to therapy. Special perceptual-cognitive-motor assessments should lead not only to specific remedial training, but also to formulating how these findings can be incorporated in the program of the child's every day activities. Otherwise, specific limited interventions may become splintered off from the main body of care and have limited generalization effects. Nor should one lose sight of the power of motivation to overcome and modify skill deficits and difficulties.

In any setting, an individual staff member should be assigned primary responsibility for a single child or for a small number of children. In some settings, it may be possible to have an interdisciplinary team assigned to every child or group.

In either case, the individual or the team should be open to other staff contribution, to periodic case utilization conferences, and to independent, objective assessments of children.

PROGRAM BASE

A psychoeducational program for handicapped children should be organized around the every day life of the child. As many life contexts as possible should be considered. School and home are central, but each has many different activities, constellations, and times. In many developmental and personality areas, both problems and strengths will emerge within real life settings. These provide prime opportunities for intervention and facilitation. Day-by-day observation and experiences supply continuing input on the basis of which program ingredients are developed.

An initial decision needs to be made regarding educational placement: regular class, special class, day program, or residential facility. This may change or involve transitional steps. The guiding principle should be realistic normalization.[35] A good deal of current controversy exists regarding educational placement. The advocates at one extreme recommend mainstreaming under almost all circumstances, whereas those at the other speak for special categorical settings. There is no question that special placement of children, which may be ideal intervention (chapter 15), may also result in a child remaining in a setting for inordinate periods of time, too well adapted to the special setting, and isolated from normal and real life experiences. It is understandable that parents, professionals, and planners have criticized this practice. The child advocacy concept has evolved as a response to these and other abuses; unfortunately, its operations have often not been well organized or implemented. A spectrum of placements should exist for dealing effectively with different degrees of handicap and capacities for adaptation. Assessments should be made frequently enough to avoid long or unnecessary placement, and regular monitoring should be performed by the program staff as well as by outside peer review.

The question of setting placement also applies to treatment. Here again, the adaptive capacities and degree of handicap of the child must be realistically assessed in relationship to parents, family, school, neighborhood, and other ecological elements. It is not only the child who needs evaluation but also those who interact with him.

What receives little attention in treatment is a rationale for treatment choice. Blom[4] has conceptualized the various interacting elements which may change over time. These are presented in Figure 19-1. A rationale should begin with what the

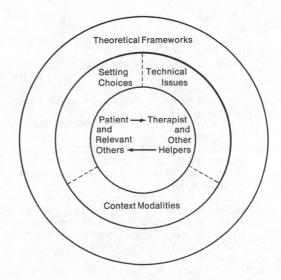

FIGURE 19–1
Elements to Consider in Treatment Choice

patient and his relevant others think, want, and can do. These opinions are related to what professionals consider as treatment options for particular problems. Setting choices would include: office, clinic, school, home, substitute home, general hospital, day or night programs, and residential facility. Then there are context modalities of individual, group, family, and combinations. A large number of technical issues of treatment include: time duration, frequency, support, relationship, interpretation, modeling, advice, focus, unspecified goals, role playing and rehearsal, training procedures, medication, consultations with other helpers, fees, single therapist or treatment team, and many others. There are many theoretical frameworks for treatment which are largely influenced by professional training, experience, and bias. These include: psychoanalytic, individual psychology, client centered, interpersonal, existential, family, rational-emotive, behavior modification, Gestalt, transactional, common sense, and others. Psychoeducation is eclectic in viewpoint, making use of the concepts, principles, and practices from a number of theoretical frameworks including the cognitive, biological, and ecological aspects.

PROGRAM CONTENT

It is less difficult to formulate and implement program content for a given day care or residential setting for handicapped children than for other types of settings. However, the elements listed should be considered in all treatment and educational settings:

1. The basic academic skills of language and mathematics
2. Related skills—body motor, perceptual, cognitive, language, socialization
3. Other subject areas according to age-grade curriculum such as science, social studies, music, and others
4. Reinforcement learning of practiced and/or rote skills
5. Activities and interests for individual pleasure and accomplishment
6. Body, sex, and health education
7. Biological and health issues—evaluation, medication, treatments, nutrition, and management by self and others
8. Behavior management including crises
9. Home-initiated activities by self and with others including television monitoring, other entertainment, sleep, meals, work, conversation, outings, peer relations, value teaching, and others
10. Formal and informal therapeutic activity for the child and his/her parents or guardians
11. Periodic accountability to child and parents by the setting staff through conference, report cards, and setting visits.

It is possible to consider this wide scope of program content through a number of procedures previously noted: (1) application of the ecological viewpoint, (2) problem-oriented approach, (3) periodic case and program utilization review by the staff and (4) periodic case and program peer review by outside staff.

CASE ILLUSTRATIONS

A few clinical examples illustrate the content and operations of the psychoeducational approach. They are vignettes at particular points in time that exemplify problem-solving around salient issues.

EXPERIENCE IN CARING FOR OTHERS

Nelson, age ten, was an overly dependent, narcissistic boy who demanded that his parents, therapist, and staff do things for him. He resisted taking responsibility for his own learning and was content to read at a first-grade level while conversing in an age-appropriate fashion. Nelson persisted in wearing the kind of T-shirts normally worn by three- or four-year olds. His clothing provoked his schoolmates to call him a baby. This sequence of arousing criticism from his peers and then complaining about it to adults was a repetitive pattern. The staff tried to label this behavior pattern, but to no avail; nor did parental negotiations with him about his clothing fare any better. Albeit narcissistically oriented, he liked his therapist and enjoyed being with her. It was, therefore, decided to ask and encourage Nelson to do favors for the therapist and for others. He helped her shop for groceries and assisted the dietician and teachers in age-appropriate tasks. This was carried out initially around a token economy and later shifted to social reinforcement. However, it was difficult to maintain caring behaviors through self-satisfaction, even though they were instituted at home as well as school. A small gain was made which was not particularly accelerated through the psychotherapeutic exploration of dynamic issues from the past and present with Nelson and his parents, separately and together in family meetings. Despite his lack of pleasure in more adequate functioning, in time he did take more responsibility for his learning and gained a measure of reading skill. The criticism-complaining pattern diminished to some extent as well.

PROGRAMMING FOR ATTENTION SPAN

Terrance, age seven, was a borderline autistic boy who had some language skills but showed a good deal of disorganized thinking and acting. Periodically he would crawl on the floor and make animal noises. He and his parents had been treated in an outpatient setting for one and one-half years before admission to a day program. He had become more manageable at home, but various attempts to have Terrance attend public school special education classes had failed. Thioridazine medication was also being used. During diagnostic classroom observation it was noted that Terrance had a strikingly short attention span, timed at forty-five seconds. It was therefore decided to limit school attendance to two hours a day according to staff tolerance, and for the same teacher to program Terrance for his attention span in forty-five-second segments. While a good deal of aberrant behavior existed, whenever learning did take place it was within his attention span. It was possible to structure teaching in a forty-five-second, pause, forty-five-second, pause, etc. sequence. Many other psychoeducational operations were going on at the same time, but attention span was used as a major organizer of behavior. Successful performance and some added social reward were sufficient motivators for this program. Gradually, Terrance's attention span increased and his bizarre behavior decreased. Little by little, he began to attend school for longer periods of time. At the end of one and one-half years, Terrance, at eight years of age, was able to enter a public school developmental class with primary mental ability age ranges of 6.1 to 8.4 and with behaviors that were containable and tolerable for six hours a day.

BEHAVIORAL CHANGE THROUGH NARCISSISTIC APPEAL

Nort, age nine, was a hyperactive, aggressive, provocative boy of at least bright normal intelligence.

When he was motivated, he could perform academically in an adequate fashion. He had two older brothers who were also reported by their schools to have behaved similarly although not to the same degree. The family's children had a reputation in the community for trouble making; inevitably school expectations were that another member of this "clan" would behave the same way. A home visit discovered a noisy, physically aggressive, and hectic household; the parents were defensive about their children and about the complaints leveled against them. It was clear that when Nort came to school in the morning, he was already stirred up by the excitement that began at home as soon as the family awakened. Neurological assessment did not demonstrate any abnormalities, and a clinical trial of methylphenidate was carried out without much benefit. A number of other measures had some success: using a shield board to reduce the amount of visual stimulation input, and having him read and do math problems wearing earphones that played soothing background music. Later on, in play therapy, he identified his behavior, impulses, and problems through a doll character he called Gardo Pack. At this same time, his troublesome behaviors diminished to some extent, presumably from channeling and limiting them in psychotherapy sessions three times a week. After one year, Nort's therapist left the program for another city, and in the second year of psychoeducational treatment, Nort had a new psychotherapist. His progress began to level off, as did his parents' progress. The family decided to move to another city where there was a good job opportunity and a chance, as they saw it, to start afresh. The staff decided to support the parents' hopes even though there was uncertainty about the realism of some of their expectations. Even though improved, Nort at this time was not particularly responsive to relationships, either with the adult staff or his peers. His team teacher commented that she had never experienced any giving comments from him. It was decided to try to get him to change his behavior through a narcissistic appeal—to get him to control his anger, settle down to work, use his intelligence, and get along with others. Both therapist and other staff commented repeatedly on his brightness and how he would benefit by performing according to his capabilities. Nort did respond to these efforts, and the staff accepted this as sufficient feedback although many wished for a more mutually satisfying relationship.

Transitions and Follow-up Services

NORMALIZATION PLANS

When a handicapped child is placed in a specialized setting or program, plans for his progress toward normalization along the spectrum of services and experiences need to be made realistically. These plans should also include a time estimate, and both should be communicated to staff, child, parents, and referral source. The estimate and plans may be revised as experience accumulates, although this should not be done lightly. The program strives to provide the child with normal life contacts to the degree that he is able to handle them with assistance. Discharge or movement are based on this normalization principle. It is relatively easy for a child, parents, and staff to become settled into a program for long periods of time. One can make transition trials or move flexibly back and forth along the continuum of services. Maintaining contact with the referral source can modify the tendency to "dump" problem children or to have the attitude, "out of sight—out of mind." This can be accomplished through periodic reports and discussion. Such communication will facilitate the child's eventual return.

TRANSITIONS

As a child progresses in a program, transition experiences must be carefully planned, implemented, and evaluated. Their nature, duration, and frequency are planned in desensitizing steps. Specific factors to be considered are a child's strengths and areas of weakness. When the receiving agency is given the rationale for transition, some knowledge about the child, recommendations for managment and instruction, consultation, and the option to return the child if necessary, the experiences are usually successful. These are times when the child and parents may need special support and assistance. It may not be possible for a child to be moved immediately into the class, school, or program he will eventually enter. That has both advantages and disadvantages. The transitional experience may be home focused or include some other element in the ecological system.

REENTRY

Transitions pave the way for entry into another program or back to the referral source. The psychological elements in the entry-reentry phase must be understood. Regressions may occur which should be viewed as a response to anxiety about the new situation as well as to loss of the familiar settings. Children develop gratifying, stable staff relationships which they are reluctant to sever. The staff usually have similar feelings. Since "cure" has not occurred, they are concerned about how the child will function in the future and how this will reflect on their own competence. The parents' feelings are also significant factors in the dynamic equation of change. It is obvious that these feelings need to be expressed, appropriately shared, and worked through in an understanding way.

With the child, specific interpretations may be helpful such as "Jim, you are behaving somewhat like when you first came—I think that means you want to stay here and not leave." Comments such as, "I am going to miss you too, but we can remember each other," can be helpful. The receiving agency will also have concerns about a child from a special program. Discussions between the referring and receiving staff on each other's turf will focus realistically on the current functioning of a child and diminish the intensity of the emotional issues. A short written report on the child may be prepared which sets forth his strengths and weaknesses, testing results, grade and age level performances, interventions which have helped and hindered, and notes difficult areas. This will facilitate discussion and planning. The availability of a referring staff member for consultation and practical follow-up services provides emotional and material help. At the same time, the use of the recipient agency's own resources and those of the family and community need to be encouraged.

FOLLOW-UP SERVICES

The forms of frequency of follow-up activities vary from case to case. They should, therefore, be determined in as thoughtful a way as possible. Consultation is often sufficient and may be particularly helpful on occasions of stress or change in the childs' and family's life, such as a move, a new school, or parent illness. Direct short-term services may be indicated. Yet it is important not to overreact to these stress events.

Follow-up services should focus on the site of greatest identified need. This may be specific tutoring, ongoing psychotherapy, parental guidance and training, medication monitoring, training activities, or consultation with other helpers. Some case examples will illustrate the what, why, and how of some follow-up decisions.

NO NEED FOR FOLLOW UP

Vernon, age eight, had an intractable school phobia for two years which had been resistant to outpatient psychotherapy and school management measures. Upon entering a psychoeducational day program, the management of phobic and anxiety symptoms was accomplished relatively easily in a period of a few months. Albeit an intelligent boy from a psychologically unsophisticated family, Vernon had lagged behind in academic skills and needed time to catch up. However, a phobic cognitive style was identified in his learning. It became necessary to desensitize him to new learning situations and unfamiliar academic content, and to allow some cognitive regression before requiring him to master new material. As he gained in confidence, skills, and exploratory modes, the carefully designed instruction was gradually withdrawn. It became clear that Vernon could return to a regular public school at a grade level appropriate for his age. Although he was somewhat anxious, he did not regress during the transitional steps. Indeed, at home he was influential in facilitating more content and affect expression in his family. It was decided that neither he nor his family required follow-up services. An outcome study done two years later revealed that he had continued to progress well.

THE MEDICATION AND SUPPORT FOLLOW UP

Dick, age ten, demonstrated primarily inhibited behaviors with periodic aggressive outbursts almost seizurelike in character. His father expected a great deal of manly, assertive behavior from him at an early age. Dick was somewhat clumsy, and the strong paternal pressure for motor skills added to his difficulties. A borderline electroencephalogram, some soft neurological signs, and the presence of visual perceptual problems suggested minimal brain dysfunction without epilepsy. A trial of methylphenidate resulted in more evenly modulated behavior. Specific body motor training focused on graded skills in a number of areas. He made slow but definite academic gains and at the end of two years, was considered ready for discharge to a regular public school class, one grade level behind his age level. Follow-up services consisted of periodic assessment of his methylphenidate medication by a pediatrician, and some attention to general family issues. One year later, medication was withdrawn for the summer and resumed for the school year. Three years later, an outcome study revealed that he was adjusting well with average academic performance.

FLEXIBLE MAINTAINED FOLLOW UP

Teresa, age ten, and her brother, Victor, age eight, had a variety of anxiety and psychosomatic symptoms. Teresa was obese and highly allergic to a number of substances. She had episodes of urticaria and angioneurotic edema. Victor was phobic and had asthma. Both the parents had had cancer, and hypochondrical concerns dominated family life. They had undergone successful surgical treatment but were concerned about recurrences, early death, and worried over who would care for the two children. Father, in part, denied his worries by assuming a posture of forcefulness, attacking and criticizing the world. He was a successful businessman who could be unscrupulous in his work. Mother was dramatic, gave unusual attention to her dress and body, and was anxious, demanding, and complaining. She was angry at Teresa about her obesity. The parents pestered doctors, teachers, and other helpers about themselves and their children. They were distrustful and had an angry attitude toward an unfair fate. They resented and envied those who were healthy and lucky. Both parents were secretive about their cancers, reasons for hospitalization, surgical operations, and health checkups. Illness received a great deal of anxious attention and led to many school absences. Inevitably, it was used by the children to manipulate their parents into gratifying various wishes and to maintain some element of control over them. It took considerable staff tolerance, patience, and flexibility to respond to this family constructively. For a time, the staff director had to keep adrenaline in his office and Teresa and Victor were the only children to bring allergen-free sack lunches. A host of events, learning situations, and objects had symbolic death meanings for the two children. Victor could not tell time; Teresa was fearful about being late; both had multiple phobias, among them fear of dark, injury, illness, doctors, dentists, food, religious holidays, and so forth. The parents were afraid to leave the children even for an evening, but resented being tied down by them. When something went wrong at school, the parents phoned the teacher, therapists, and director to criticize and complain. At times, they all wanted to change therapists, especially Teresa. The staff did not react with anger, defensiveness, or rejection as so many other helpers had before. Whenever possible, small accommodations were made. When some progress was made in the therapeutic examination and discussion of the issues of death threat, anger, disappointment, mistrust, fate, envy, and jealousy, there would be periodic crises that functioned as a defensive smoke screen. The staff had to ride these out and again pursue the task of redeveloping trust and fostering communication. What was later related by the parents as significant to them was the fact that the staff persisted and did not reject them. During the second year it was decided to have family therapy sessions. Gradually, secretiveness decreased and it was possible to talk about illness and death threat with diminished anxiety. The manner in which the children manipulated their parents' anxieties to get their own way was pointed out. The family began to have discussions at home, modeled somewhat after their treatment sessions. This contrasted to their previous dramatic crises around the dinner table and on going to bed. The parents were able to take a week's vacation in spite of mother's fear of air travel and their worries about the children's welfare. The children's school attendance became regular; they ate normal food and began to devote some of their energies to school. When transitions began, fears were activated again and the parents viewed discharge as rejection, desertion, and death. It was decided that the staff social worker would maintain contact with the family, at first on a regular basis, then with slowly diminishing frequency, and finally only on parent initiation. The family still receives occasional phone calls and personal visits after five years. Several times they made calls to inform the staff about progress, as if in part to say, "you see, we are still alive."

Ongoing Evaluation

A striking aspect of both teaching and treatment efforts is the lack of adequate ongoing evaluation of programs for individual children. This is even more characteristic of treatment activities. What evaluation does exist is often fraught with unsystematic data collection; and unclear and general statements about the nature of problems, interventions, goals, and outcomes. Considerable defensiveness is evoked in professionals when programs are asked merely to demonstrate effectiveness, costs, numbers served, and efficiency. Such requests are viewed as criticisms, attacks, and impositions on humanistic endeavors. While this may sometimes be true, a rational basis for evaluation exists.

Many defenses are reflected against record keeping and evaluation. It takes too much time. We are not trained to do that. More staff would be required. Record keeping wastes time since the essential things are remembered. No one can assess what we are doing unless they are trained by us and part of our group. There are too many variables involved in the process and outcome, many of which are not measurable; objective instruments and statements do not consider feelings elements that are highly important in human behavior. Latent and interpreted behaviors have greater significance than descriptive ones. Professional training, certification, and experience vouch for competence. The treatment situation is private, confidential, and nonevaluative; therefore, assessment of progress and outcome is ethically wrong, an invasion of privacy, and a disturbance to the treatment process. Reassurance comes from the assumption that what is being done is effective; if one enjoys teaching or treatment, then it must be beneficial; if a recipient reports progress or feeling better, that is sufficient.

The recently instituted developments of a minimum data base, standardized record keeping, problem-oriented approaches, utilization review, and peer review have encountered resistances, especially within the mental health field. Comparable activities in education have also been reacted to in a negative fashion. Professionals do not like to provide or collect the supportive evidence for problem statements and resist organizing their work according to a generally agreed upon format. It is interesting that utilization and peer review are confused by professionals. Utilization is an evaluation of progress and remediation activities by the professional or by his group. Peer review is evaluation by someone else, or by an outside group, using acceptable standards and criteria for diagnosis and treatment.

While professionals are quick to express concerns about the abuses of evaluation, they fail to be equally concerned about the inadequacies of current practices within educational and treatment programs. Unnecessary polarities develop between clinical and scientific attitudes, the subjective and objective, openness and secrecy, impressions and test measures, manifest and latent behavior, isolation and accountability, and between the abuses that come with change and the inadequacies of the status quo.

There is no question that evaluation must be an essential element of any therapeutic or educational program. It can be simple or complex depending on the number of staff and program goals. When such as evaluation is introduced into a program that has well established operations, resistances and irrational expectations are likely to occur. Fortunately, sufficient social pressure exists today to make evaluation necessary. It is an ongoing process that is performed at periodic intervals, during treatment, at discharge, and at follow up. It is facilitated by an initial minimum data base, a problem-oriented scheme, and the use of standardized behavioral measurements. These procedures are adaptable for program fit, feasibility, and efficiency.

In practice, a sufficient, though limited, amount of information is obtained and constitutes the minimum data base. Then a problem-oriented scheme provides a systematic format for listing problems in a number of areas of developmental functioning, for identifying their subjective and objective criteria, for establishing priorities, for specifying intervention strategies including the collection of further information, for making changes over time, for recording progress, and for dating various entries. The scheme, complex or simple, can be mastered with some practice. Periodic, objective test measurements will fit into the overall program. It is not necessary, and often a waste of time, to include psychological test batteries. Tests and objective measures should be selected according to initial indications and later employed to measure progress.

Many aspects of what has been described previously have been used by some professionals for many years, though not as systematically and broadly as advocated here. Behavior modification and prescriptive teaching are examples, though both may be characterized as too restrictive in their focus of behavior.

A problem-oriented scheme is used by a group at the University of Colorado Medical Center.[36] It is one of many schemes which are currently being developed. The initial minimum data base consists of information obtained from intake and limited diagnostic study: (1) family, medical, and social history; (2) developmental questionnaire; (3) pediatric examination; (4) home and school behavior checklists; (5) interview reports; (6) information from other sources; and (7) intelligence, achievement, cognitive, and personality test according to indications.

A case team generates a written problem list from these data organized into a number of domains—academic, affective, interpersonal, language, sensory-motor, cognitive, medical, child rearing, and family issues. The team decides which problems are most pressing and gives them first priority. Existing subjective and objective information regarding each problem are recorded. A short analysis of the problem examines its significance, possible causation, relationship to other problems, specific need for change, and ways to effect change. A treatment plan is developed by enumerating courses of action and intervention which may include further data collection.

At ongoing team meetings the status of these problems is reviewed, adding new information and further analysis, and reviewing the intervention strategies. New problems can be generated and former problems given attention. Modifications in information are provided, as well as analyses. Problem resolution is noted. All entries are entered on uniform record sheets, dated, and signed by a team recorder.

Psychoeducational Results

The number of systematic studies of the outcome of treatment and educational program is limited. Those few which do exist have many inadequacies. Some results of a psychoeducational day program for fifty children have been reported.[13] The study has several limitations—a special sample of children, no comparison group, unsatisfactory objective behavior rating scales, retrospective rating of information, not analyzing achievement test data, and others. However, it has led to an improvement in design and methods which will be used in future outcome studies.

Of the fifty children studied, follow-up information was obtained on forty-eight, a response rate of 96 percent. The mean (average) time between discharge and follow up was 34.1 months. Ten population characteristic variables were rated and three others described. Three treatment variables (duration, parent participation, age begun) were rated and teaching variables were described in general terms.

About one-third of the children received psychoactive medication at some time. Behavioral ratings in academic, peer relations, adult relations, and self-esteem areas were scored at intake, discharge, and follow up. Parent reports of school placement, academic performance, and the psychoeducational program were also obtained. These data constituted thirty-three rated variables and more than twenty descriptive variables.

The population may be described in the following terms: three times as many boys than girls, mostly white Protestant, mean age of 8.65 years at the start of treatment, 50 percent having personality disorders (GAP classification), and 56 percent with central processing disorders. The children tended not to be first born and had two or more siblings. There were usually two parents in the home although some were step-parents. Their mean education was eight years and combined mean family income $8,700.

At follow up, 90 percent of forty-eight children either had graduated from high school or were in regular public school classes. Of the remaining 10 percent, two were in special education classes, one in a residential treatment center, and two had dropped out of school in adolescence without becoming delinquent. Seventy percent of the group performed at an average or better academic level. All the mean behavioral rating scores showed statistically significant changes between intake and discharge, and stability of change beatween discharge and follow up (on the average close to three years later). The greatest change scores were noted in the academic and self-esteem areas.

Some of the results of further follow-up data analyses and impressions included:

1. More favorable outcomes were associated with being white, having two parents at home, parents with more education, earlier age at the start of treatment, and lower ordinal position.
2. The amount of parent participation in treatment showed no discriminative differences between children, although more family crises were associated with poorer adult relations scores.
3. Borderline children adapted better and were able to control fantasy and bizarre thinking and action.
4. The children as a group tended to be indistinguishable from their peer mates as reported by the schools; originally, they were "sore thumbs" who now fitted in but were not outstanding achievers.

5. Forty-seven of forty-eight families reported being satisfied with the program.
6. Siblings of the patient complained a good deal about the attention he/she received during the program.
7. All the children recalled their teachers by name but had difficulty recalling the names of their psychotherapists.

On the whole, these results seemed quite promising, but one can still wonder how they will hold up over time, how they might compare to untreated and differently treated groups, and whether another group of children similarly treated would have similar outcomes. There also seemed to be evidence that while the children adapted better, those with tested higher abilities were not outstanding performers. Perhaps creativity was sacrificed for adjustment. Beyond ensuring child attendance and limited cooperation, the amount of parent participation in treatment did not seem to matter, a somewhat provocative finding. However, most of the parents reported satisfaction with the program. Perhaps, for children at this age, an intensive day experience of six hours, five days a week, has considerable impact with or without strong parent involvement. A number of the children benefited when they could be helped to come to terms with their parents as they were. This was often associated with the staff accepting parent limitations and not expecting too much or putting such strong pressures on them.

Implications of Psychoeducation

As indicated previously, psychoeducation is regarded as applicable to a wide spectrum of settings, both clinical and educational. The integration of treatment personnel, teaching staffs, and program elements requires time. This implies careful sorting out of the most effective utilization of available resources. The decision to have an individual treatment session should be balanced against the importance of a school conference or a home visit. Perhaps the advantage of a more intensive investment in psychoeducation for a short time should be weighed against prolonged, restricted, and limited remediation by a professional operating alone. The latter may still have a place within the various dimensions of treatment, but such an approach may sacrifice effectiveness for the great majority of handicapped children. The few follow-up studies on the results of traditional child psychotherapy[1] support such an opinion.

There is another implication of psychoeducation: Clinics and programs need to have greater diversity in staff and include wider professional representation of teaching, training, and treatment approaches. The traditional child guidance model of stereotyped and restricted operations should be seriously questioned. The knowledge and experience base of a staff must be broadened so that more flexible remediation approaches can be developed. Conceptual and practical approaches exist for intervening in the environments of children; these should be appropriately used.

A further implication is the need for a unified eclectic approach to handicapped children. It is no longer sufficient to know only about the emotional life of children and neglect the cognitive, body, language, motor, environmental, and other factors. There are limits to what a generalist can know, but at least he/she can know enough to bridge effectively to others who are knowledgeable about other domains.

These implications point to important educational needs for those professionals who would teach and treat. This education should consist of interdisciplinary training and experience. It should include exposure to different conceptual models in therapy and education, including their strengths and weaknesses. There should be a thorough knowledge of child development. A helping professional should have knowledge and experience with different individuals, groups, families, and societies, including considerable contact with normal children and families.

Is this too much to expect? The author believes not. Many training programs are haphazard, inefficient, redundant, limiting, and undemanding. They tend to be poorly conceptualized, planned, and organized. Prevailing psychodynamically oriented training can be particularly sloppy, unscientific, and lacking in information. Pre-service education may be an easier place to begin before practices become rigidly established with experience. Yet, inservice and continuing education are also necessary not only for the preservice graduate but also for those who are more established. To focus momentarily on the child psychiatrist, a long, broadening, ongoing education should be a satisfying and stimulating endeavor. Ultimately, one has the right to expect that the child psychiatrist should have something special to offer handicapped children and their families.

Summary

Psychoeducation is an eclectic approach to handicapped children that integrates two major streams of professional thought, experience, and practice. It uses both treatment and teaching methods to develop skills and competence and to remediate pathological behaviors. The concepts, principles, and practices of many theoretical models of behavior are selected according to their pragmatic usefulness. A developmental viewpoint is applied to many areas of child behavior. The ongoing processes of problem identification and problem solving are employed over time guided by the principle of normalization.

In this chapter, a number of issues related to psychoeducation have been examined: problems with interprofessional collaboration, the rationale of psychoeducation, historical and developmental background, current problems in services to children, difficulties in the psychoeducational approach, professional staff and program ingredients, transitions and follow-up services, ongoing evaluation, and study of outcomes. Case vignettes have been utilized to illustrate the approach, its problems, and its operations. The implications of psychoeducation for clinical and educational settings are discussed in terms of staff diversity, time utilization, flexible intervention strategies, interdisciplinary knowledge and experience, and the nature of training for human service professionals. Psychoeducation in the educational setting will be discussed in greater detail in chapter 20.

REFERENCES

1. ANTHONY, E. J., "The Behavior Disorders of Childhood," in Mussen, P. H. (Ed.), *Carmichael's Manual of Child Psychology*, pp. 667–764, John Wiley, New York, 1970.
2. BALDWIN, A. L., *Theories of Child Development*, John Wiley, New York, 1967.
3. BLOM, G. E., "A Psychoanalytic Viewpoint of Behavior Modification in Clinical and Educational Settings," *Journal of the American Academy of Child Psychiatry*, 11(3):675–693, 1972.
4. ———, "A Conceptual Model of Therapy," unpublished paper, 1972.
5. ———, "The Psychoeducational Approach to Learning Disabilities," *Seminars in Psychiatry*, 1(3):318–329, 1969.
6. ———, "The Psychoeducational Approach to Emotionally Disturbed Children," *Medical Records and Annals*, 61(11):348–351, 1968.
7. ———, "Psychoeducational Aspects of Classroom Management," *Exceptional Children*, 32:377–383, 1966.

8. ———, and Parsons, P. C., "The Education of the Emotionally Disturbed Child of Elementary School Age," in Jenkins, R., and Harms, E. (Eds.), *Understanding Disturbed Children*, pp. 240–270, Special Child Publications, Seattle, 1976.

9. Blom, G. E., Farley, G. K., and Guthals, C., "The Concept of Body Image and the Remediation of Body Image Disorders," *Journal of Learning Disabilities, 3(9):* 440–447, 1970.

10. Blom, G. E., Rudnick, M., and Searles, J., "Some Principles and Practices in the Psychoeducational Treatment of Emotionally Disturbed Children," *Psychology in the Schools, 3(1):*30–38, 1966.

11. Blom, G. E., Rudnick, M., and Weiman, E., "A Psychoeducational Treatment Program: Implications for the Development of Potentialities in Children," in Otto, H. (Ed.), *Explorations in Human Potentialities*, pp. 454–468, Grune & Stratton, New York, 1966.

12. Blom, G. E., Waite, R. R., and Zimet, S., "The Motivational and Attitude Content of First Grade Reading Textbooks," in Levin, H., and Williams, J. (Eds.), *Basic Studies in Reading*, pp. 188–221, Basic Books, New York, 1971.

13. Blom, G. E., et al., "A Psychoeducational Treatment Program: Its Characteristics and Results," in Blom, G. E., and Farley, G. K. (Eds.), *A Report on the Activities of the Day Care Center of the University of Colorado Medical Center to the Commonwealth Foundation*, p. 65, University of Colorado Medical Center Press, Denver, 1973.

14. Blom, G. E., et al., "A Psychoeducational Approach to Day Care Treatment," *Journal of the American Academy of Child Psychiatry, 11(3):*492–510, 1972.

15. Erikson, E. H., "Identity and the Life Cycle," *Psychological Issues, 1(1):*171, 1959.

16. Gardner, J. W., *Self Renewal: The Individual and the Innovative Society*, Perennial Library, Harper & Row, New York, 1971.

17. Gladwin, T., *Social Competence and Clinical Practice*, National Institute of Mental Health Report, U.S. Government Printing Office, Washington, D.C., 1966.

18. Glidewell, J. C., "The Education Institution and the Health Institution," in Bower, E. M., and Hollister, W. G. (Eds.), *Behavioral Science Frontiers in Education*, pp. 273–285, John Wiley, New York, 1967.

19. Greenblat, M., Levinson, D., and Williams, R. M. (Eds.), *The Patient and the Mental Hospital*, Free Press, Glencoe, Ill., 1957.

20. Hewitt, F., Personal communication, 1970.

21. Hobbs, N., *Issues in the Classification of Children*, Jossey-Bass, San Francisco, 1974.

22. ———, *The Futures of Children*, Jossey-Bass, San Francisco, 1974.

23. ———, "The Re-Education of Emotionally Disturbed Children," in Bower, E. M., and Hollister, W. G. (Eds.), *Behavioral Science Frontiers in Education*, pp. 339–354, John Wiley, New York, 1967.

24. Hollingshead, A. B., and Redlich, F. C., *Social Class and Mental Illness: A Community Study*, John Wiley, New York, 1958.

25. LaVietes, R. L., and Chess, S., "A Training Program in School Psychiatry," *Journal of the American Academy of Child Psychiatry, 8(1):*84–96, 1969.

26. Morse, W., Personal communication, 1971.

27. Rae-Grant, Q., Gladwin, T., and Bower, E. H., "Mental Health, Social Competence and the War on Poverty," *American Journal of Orthopsychiatry, 36:*652–661, 1966.

28. Rhodes, W. C., and Tracy, M. L., *A Study of Child Variance: Conceptual Project in Emotional Disturbance*, University of Michigan Press, Ann Arbor, 1972.

29. Report of the Joint Commission on Mental Illness and Health, *Crisis in Child Mental Health: Challenge for the 1970's*, Basic Book, New York, 1969.

30. Report of the Joint Commission on Mental Illness and Health (Final), *Action for Mental Health*, Basic Books, New York, 1961.

31. Sadler, J., and Blom, G. E., "Standby: A Clinical Research Study of Child Deviant Behavior in a Psychoeducational Setting," *Journal of Special Education, 4(1):* 89–103, 1970.

32. Sanford, N., *Self and Society*, Atherton, New York, 1966.

33. Sarason, S. B., *The Culture of the School and the Problem of Change*, Allyn and Bacon, Boston, 1971.

34. White, R. W., "Ego and Reality in Psychoanalytic Theory," *Psychological Issues, 3(3):*210, 1963.

35. Wolfensberger, W., *The Principle of Normalization in Human Services*, National Institute on Mental Retardation, Toronto, 1972.

36. Zimet, S. G., et al., Personal communication, 1974.

---

20 / Psychoeducation in the School Setting

William C. Morse and Mark M. Ravlin

The purpose of this chapter is to provide an overview of recent developments in school mental health. This is a realm with which mental health professionals of all sorts are becoming increasingly involved in a variety of ways. It is critical that those who enter the schools as part of this movement do so with maximum understanding of the development of these agencies and how they function.

The foremost trend in school mental health has been away from tertiary intervention by highly specialized mental health personnel. Instead, the emphasis has fallen on primary and secondary prevention, accompanied by the use of new approaches implemented by a wide variety of personnel. Broadly speaking, this new emphasis has been called *affective education* or, as preferred here, *psychoeducation*.

Several forces have combined to produce this new direction in school mental health. We live in a complex, heterogeneous society of diverse cultural heritage. As a result, at all stages of development and socialization children are confronted with a confusing array of beliefs, values, and life styles. America's "child centeredness" has been subject to scrutiny by such authors as Bronfenbrenner,[5] who have expressed concern about the high-risk status of children in our polymorphous culture. One primary reason for the new emphasis on school mental health is recognition of the need for close collaboration between families and schools in assuring the child's healthy development and socialization. A second reason is the popularization of psychology and the associated increased interest in the understanding of oneself and others. Yet another important contributing factor is the increased attention to prevention (see volume IV) brought about by the community mental health movement. More than that is the ever growing interest in new methods for developing prosocial behaviors. Finally, the very proliferation of psychoeducational programs and materials has in itself increased interest in the field.

Schools and the Affective Domain

It has long been recognized that schools exert a powerful influence on the psychological development of children. Schools share with families a primary responsibility for socialization. They can facilitate a child's capacity for mutually satisfying human relationships, for facing and coping with reality, for experiencing independence and self-determination, and for developing positive personal identity. Or they can induce the sense of failure, defeat, disillusion, despair, and dependence that are the stuff of cynicism and alienation from the society-at-large. Despite their obvious influence on the affective aspects of children's lives, historically, their systematic attention has been confined to the cognitive and motor aspects of development. Minuchin and associates[40] have concluded, however, that "schools cannot choose to limit the scope of their impact by fiat," and that they clearly influence the interests, attitudes, emotions, and values of their students. The psychoeducational movement is by no means new: Indeed, the McGuffy readers were moral tracts. Schools must now face the charge, framed by Jersild[27]

some time ago that they have dealt with affective concerns "so haphazardly, and with so little perspective and often negative consequences."

Schools and education have always occupied a central position in American culture: How well they have adapted to the currents of social and cultural change continues to be the subject of vigorous debate. Should schools emphasize and reinforce the cultural status quo? Or should they act as agents of social change? Responses to such fundamental inquiries are grounded in philosophical positions seldom articulated explicitly. We have failed, Silberman[67] has noted, to come to grips with the values which underlie this dilemma.

American schools have come to be popularly viewed as a panacea for all sorts of social and cultural ailments. As a result, high expectations have developed, and responsibility has been thrust on schools that is far beyond their capacity to fulfill. Such expectations render them vulnerable to criticism for failure to attain goals they were never designed to achieve. It is thus important to maintain a balanced perspective regarding goals and prospects as we examine the current movement.

Description of Psychoeducation

Psychoeducation is the study and application in schools of principles derived from the behavioral sciences. It involves classroom use of knowledge drawn from the study of human development and dynamics, group process, mental health, motivation, and learning. The overarching objective is for children and youth to understand themselves and others better, and to be able to apply this understanding to everyday life situations much as they use the computational skills learned in mathematics in their everyday encounters with numbers.

Rationale

A number of guiding principles comprise the theoretical foundation of psychoeducation:[16, 34, 47] (1) Human behavior is a complex and inseparable weave of cognitive and affective processes; (2) A wide range of instructional methods are necessary to coordinate emotional and cognitive learning in the classroom; (3) Schools should be milieus which invite the expression of affect for the purpose of enriching the curriculum and enhancing its relevance; (4) Inadequate consideration of these processes, and/or neglect of students' needs for self-understanding and empathy results in subversion both of the intellectual aims of education and of positive mental health; (5) Numerous findings of the behavioral sciences are relevant to students and teachers and can be made available to them in schools. Miller[39] has suggested that the most important responsibility borne by mental health professionals is to make their knowledge readily accessible to all. Psychoeducation is one mode by which such access can be maximized.

The role of psychoeducation in schools is threefold. First, psychoeducation is proactive: It is concerned with building strengths and with promoting and enhancing positive personality development in all children. Hollister[25] has coined the term "strens" to denote experiences which build such strength of personality, contribute to positive development, and enhance the self.

Psychoeducation's second role revolves around prevention of mental and/or emotional disturbance and the provision of support to students who are experiencing stressful life events. The National Institute of Mental Health[49] has reported an alarming incidence of emotional disorders among school-age children. The Joint Commission on Mental Health of Children[28] has suggested, furthermore, that fully 80 percent of the children with emotional and mental difficulties could have received adequate support from parents, public health and school nurses, and guidance counselors —all of whom are present in the everyday life space of children in our society. Psychoeducation is a mode of intervention which school personnel can apply to reduce the incidence of emotional disorder.

Legislation that is mandating education for *all* children is creating a third role for psychoeducation in the schools. An ever increasing number of states are enacting statutes which, supported by pursuant litigation, require public education for all children, regardless of retardation, emotional disturbance, or the presence of other handicap(s). Among the cardinal principles articulated in the new legislation is that children have the right to be placed in the program or setting of least exclusion from the regular classroom. This right is being realized through "mainstreaming"—the integration into regular classes of children who had theretofore been excluded and placed in specialized, separate programs. The welfare of the special children, however, depends on how both the teacher and the peer culture respond to them. Psychoeducation, then, can play a significant role in facilitating the proper implementation of such mainstreaming.

Support for the Concept of Psychoeducation

Support for psychoeducation is widespread. Federal and state governments, teachers, parents, and children have all expressed interest in the concept. A the federal level, the Joint Commission on Mental Health of Children[28] has strongly endorsed it:

There is a close association between the child's mental health and his education. Schools have a tremendous potential for enhancing the mental health of all children who attend them, preventing the development of serious emotional disorders. [p. 383]

It seems entirely appropriate to introduce into the curriculum of elementary and secondary schools new theories and knowledge from the social and behavioral sciences which are, indeed, closely related to the concept of mental health and society. [p. 401]

Integrated learning which is lasting and usable to the child must be addressed to his emotional and social needs as well as to his intellectual and rational ones. [p. 393]

At the state level, the goals and principles promulgated by state education departments reflect increasing interest in issues of deep concern to psychoeducation. For example seven of Michigan's twenty-two Common Goals pertain directly to the affective domain. They are: morality, citizenship, and social responsibility, physical and mental well-being, self-worth, social skills and understanding, preparation for family life, and preparation for a changing society. Since local districts must be able to demonstrate compliance with these goals, the goals, in turn, shape the programs which the local schools will offer.

Teachers and parents are also aware of the importance of the affective domain in education. Teachers spend a great deal of classroom time on such affect-laden issues as control and the quality of interpersonal interactions. A recent survey by the National Education Association[48] indicated that teachers rank affective issues high on any list of areas in which they need support. Values and attitudes of the school-age generation, student disruptiveness, and the psychological climate of the school are among the problems mentioned.

Parents, too, reveal considerable interest in the affective dimension of the school's goals. They want children and youth taught facts and skills, but they also want schools to give more attention to respect for law and authority and to teaching students how to get along with others.[19]

Finally, a survey of 5,000 children, *Teach Us What We Want to Know,* by the Connecticut

State Department of Education[8] has revealed that such affect-related concerns as understanding of oneself, others, and interpersonal relations are of particular concern to children from kindergarten through high school.,

Unresolved Issues in Psychoeducation

A number of problematic issues continue to plague psychoeducation and lend substance to the resistance expressed by critics of the movement. They include : (1) the unclear role of the schools vis à vis the affective domain, (2) the confusion created by the multiplicity of approaches and materials in the field, (3) unclear terminology and the resultant difficulty of evaluative research, and (4) uncertainty regarding the nature of adequate training to conduct psychoeducational programs.

Rhodes[59] has observed that according to national consensus. Americans are wary of governmental organization and regulation of the personal and social aspects of learning and socialization. Thus, educational efforts intended to complement and support families, and the efforts of other institutions that share the responsibilities of child rearing, are often perceived as invading family privacy. In the area of affective development, there is a lack of consensus as to the rights and responsibilities of the schools. The fact that children come to school with functionally inseparable melanges of affective, cognitive, and motor domains is ignored by those who continue to labor under the illusion the schools deal only with "disembodied intellect."[62]

The nation's cultural heterogeneity leaves schools and psychoeducators hard-pressed to define affective development in terms that are universally acceptable, to say nothing of fostering it. Production of materials has accelerated, and the proliferation of programs has created confusion about what is appropriate and useful. Moreover, little effort has been made to examine philosophical underpinnings or to integrate common philosophies and methods.

Further, there are a number of peripheral and/or unrelated approaches that are often included under the rubric of psychoeducation. The inclusion of such questionable and explosive approaches as advocating the abandonment of traditional, academic subject matter in favor of encounter groups and "touchy-feely" activities has heightened fears of invasion of personal and family privacy. The boundaries between psychoeducation and psychotherapy must be clearly drawn.

Admittedly, the many nebulous or ambiguous terms that comprise the prolific jargon of the field[33] make it difficult to define its parameters. Kirsner[31] has striven to define "awareness" in behaviorally specific terms, but the going is rough. Vague terminology renders research and evaluation exceedingly difficult. Work by Jersild,[27] Ojemann,[53] Roen,[61] and Weinstein[71] reads convincingly but is at best only provocative.

Finally, there is the issue of competence in the training of psychoeducators. While Aspy[1] has conducted research regarding one form of training, his efforts stand alone in the field. Personnel involved in psychoeducation range from teachers, school psychologists, social workers, and guidance counselors working in the schools to a variety of mental health professionals from outside. Any of these personnel may or may not have participated in training experiences which in some sense qualify them as psychoeducators. The fact is that too many of the training programs and workshops spawned by new approaches are inadequately conceived, superficial, and only marginally governed by ethical standards.

The challenge facing those interested in psychoeducation is twofold; to meet the needs of children, teachers, and parents as outlined previously; and to channel the enthusiasm and demonstrated potential of the field into resolution of these concerns. Psychoeducational efforts should not remain haphazard and intuitive: It is necessary to make decisions concerning the kind of human development we wish to foster.

Approaches to Psychoeducation

At the programmatic level, psychoeducation defies systematic, integrated description. The present alternative is a compilation of the major approaches and curricula in the field under two discrete headings: (1) those approaches which are most obviously teacher-focused; and (2) those most obviously child-focused. These categories are for purposes of organizational convenience only, for in practice there can be no such discrete separation: Most programs include both components. Neither teacher-focused nor child-focused approaches are ends in themselves. Training in congruent communication, for example, should permeate the classroom and affect the entire milieu. Child-focused approaches such as classroom meet ings obviously involve teachers, at least in their role as group leaders.

These approaches vary in a number of ways. Some, for example, are *intrinsic* and part of the natural school context, while others are *extrinsic* and represent specialized operations or curricula. Most approaches are concerned with process as opposed to product, and most conceive of the teacher as facilitator rather than pedagogue. Psychoeducation is intrinsic to the extent that the principles and practices are broadly implemented throughout the curriculum. George Brown[7] has referred to this as "confluent education," denoting the perpetual intermingling of cognitive and affective. Psychoeducation is extrinsic to the extent that its principles and practices supplement preexisting curricula, occupying a prescribed period of the day.

A second way in which psychoeducational approaches may vary is that of *formality*. Toward the informal extreme of the continuum are psychoeducational approaches to everyday, unplanned real-life activities such as the breakup and resolution of a fight, a quarrel over supposedly shared equipment, or the fear of a given child by peers. Richard Jones[29] has discussed such informal opportunities at length and found them to be richly present during the average school day. Activities of a more specific, preconceived, planned kind, such as curricula or projects involving explicity psychoeducational components, occupy the formal end of the continuum.

For convenience, the substantive descriptions of programs which follow are presented in two sections: teacher-focused and child-focused. The sections are comprised of more or less complete descriptions of prominent psychoeducational programs. The references provide a source for the total program descriptions. There are literally dozens of programs, some local and some national in scope. The nineteen presented here are among those better known and are representative of the types of programs presently functioning for which materials are available.

Teacher-Focused Approaches

CONGRUENT COMMUNICATION: GINOTT

Congruent communication is founded on awareness of and respect for human affect. Haim Ginott[21] has defined congruent communication as harmonious and authentic verbal interchange in which words fit feelings. It is his premise that the quality of the communication process between teachers and children is pivotal to teaching and learning. Teaching is replete with overloaded classes, endless demands, and sudden crises that would even tax the likes of Job. Yet, too few teachers have been adequately forewarned during training to expect children to frustrate them, cause them to lose patience, and make them angry. Ways of accepting and dealing with anger and other such affect states are seldom explored. The unspoken message which this implies is that good teachers do not get angry at children.

Two tenets lie at the core of the theory of congruent communication. The first is that adults must address the situation in which children find themselves, rather than judge their characters and personalities. For example, a child who forgets to return a book to the library may be addressed in one of at least two ways: "Your book is overdue. It needs to be returned." or "You forgot to return your book. Why did you forget it? You're so irresponsible." The first makes a factual statement about the situation; the second, a critical judgment of the child.

The second tenet, which follows from acceptance of human feelings, is that feelings must be "owned." There are, for example, at least two ways that a teacher might react to a child who continually talks out of turn. One would be to say, "I am annoyed by that"; the other, to say, "You are pestering me." The first "owns" the feeling of annoyance; the second does not, but rather places blame on the child.

A number of the techniques and attitudes advocated by Ginott grow out of the observation that children are highly dependent on teachers; this creates a situation which can readily breed hostility. The deliberate provision of opportunities for autonomy and self-determination can mitigate this counterproductive relationship: One such opportunity lies in avoiding direct commands. "The social studies assignment is on page sixty" is a request, whereas "Take out your social studies book and turn to page sixty" is a command. Another opportunity lies in the way in which praise is delivered. Praise consists of one's remarks to a child and what the child in turn thinks to him- or herself regarding the remarks. Praise which speaks to specific acts, such as "That sentence is tightly constructed," leaves it to the child to judge him- or herself. This is significantly different from praise which evaluates the child, such as "You are a good writer," in which the judgment is imposed by the adult authority figure.

THE LIFE SPACE INTERVIEW (LSI): REDL

Pioneered by Fritz Redl,[57, 58] the Life Space Interview (LSI) is a psychoeducational approach designed to facilitate therapeutic working through, and learning from, critical events which transpire in the classroom milieu. To variations on the LSI theme have been distinguished:[57] emotional first aid and clinical exploitation of life events. The purpose of the former is essentially ego-support for a child or children in stress. The latter is directed at more far-reaching exploration of the situation, with the aim of transferring educational or clinical insight to the child or children.

The LSI process may be broken down into seven component steps.[44] First, an incident calling for adult intervention must occur. Emotional first aid will suffice in most cases, but when an incident worthy of broader and deeper exploration occurs, clinical exploitation is in order.

A CASE IN POINT: THE INCIDENT

N is a twelve-year-old boy, six years in this country from Europe. His teacher was unable to cope with his behavior in the classroom. At her request a helping or crisis teacher (I) is working with him in the classroom. His behavior is characterized by daily name calling, swearing, fighting, and lying. His only defense was hitting. Because his older siblings had always protected him, he did not think he could ever get in trouble regardless of his behavior. He is of average intelligence and has reasonable academic achievement.

The interview of one and one-half hours followed a crisis which came when he entered the class swearing which upset his peers and started a shoving-fighting episode. The main target, D, is the son of a family with whom N's family is feuding.

Second, the student's perception of the event is sought by the interviewer. The point is not objective "truth" but the child's perception, however distorted. All sides must be heard when more than one child is involved.

THE STUDENT'S PERCEPTION

N: "My brother will come and change me from this school. If both people get into a fight at the other school, they send both people to the office, but here they send me all the time."
I: "When some people swear, they can just go sit down and do their work."
N: "I do my work and then D comes over and hits me and I have the right to hit him back."
I: "Well, it's not just D, is it?"
N: "Well, there's J and all of D's friends. I know they all like D and I don't care—that's why I'm moving out of this school."

He feels he is always getting caught and must fight back. His aim is to escape.

Third, the interviewer (whether teacher or other adult) assesses the depth and breadth of the issue. Is the incident isolated or is it related to a larger pattern of events? Is it, in other words, symbolic of the child's life experience? Through nonjudgmental reconstruction, the interviewer should attempt to ascertain the course of events and attendant feelings that comprise the incident-at-hand before moving on.

SCANNING FOR DEPTH AND SPREAD

I: "When you're in school, is it cool to fight?"
N: "If I feel like it—yeah."
I: "What happens?"
N: "You usually get in trouble."
I: "Okay, what might happen now that your father knows about it?"
N: "He'll just talk to me and try to convince me, but I'll just talk to him and tell him I ain't going to stay in this school. I ain't walking in that classroom—nobody's going to tell me to go and I'm taking karate and I'm going to kick that kid's ass. He ain't gonna have no teeth—and I don't care what they're going to do—it ain't going to stop me."
I: "You know what happens to people when they get in bad fights?"
N: "What? Go to juvenile?"
I: "Yes."
N: "So."
I: "You want to go there?"
N: "No."
I: "That would be the worst thing that could happen, wouldn't it? You'd be away from your family, policemen would be watching you all the time, you'd have to go to court."
N: "I don't care—I've been to court once, my parents have been to court twice now."
I: "Does it make them happy?"
N: "I don't know. Anyway, it's all of D's family's fault. D's mother thinks I'm lying all the time."
I: (Tells story about the boy who called wolf.)
N: "I don't care—no one's going to stop me from getting in fights because I'm so mad right now I'm going to kick his ass. He ain't gonna have no luck this time . . ."
I: "You think that the reason you're in trouble is because of D?"
N: "Yeah. He's the one who started it."
I: "When did this trouble start?"
N: "Monday or Tuesday. Everybody in the class said I went to the bookshelf and then D comes charging and I had the right to hit him."
I: "After you came back from your weekend Did you have a good time?"
N: "Yeah."
I: "How come you came back swearing like that Saying those sentences?"
N: (pause) "I didn't come back swearing. D go me mad and if I get mad—I ain't gonna do nothin but fight—nobody can stop me, if I get mad I'm gonna knock 'em out. I don't care what happens."

I: "N, how come you were swearing? I heard you were using those words in sentences."

N: "Who told you—that Ms. R?"

I: "Well, you wrote it down on paper and I read it."

N: "Yeah, I wrote it and I said it and I had the right to and nobody is going to stop me."

I: "But how come you said it?"

N: "Cuz he got me mad."

I: "Who's he?"

N: "D—he comes over and slaps me all the time. I have the right to get mad at him and kick his ass."

His perceptions become clear, as well as his projection of blame. Ventilation, catharsis, and empathy have been central to the LSI process thus far. At this point, there is a turn in strategy to a more conceptual, problem-solving orientation. The essence of the fourth step is embodied in the question, "Well, what should be done about this?" This step offers simultaneous opportunities to assess how the student's value system relates to the area of concern and to begin establishing alternative resolutions of the issues involved.

MOVEMENT TO RESOLUTION

I: "You think the reason you are in trouble is because of D?"

N: "Yeah."

I: "Do you really believe that?"

N: "Yeah, he's the one who started it, that's why my sister went down to the office and said that we wanted an appointment, and if this doesn't get settled, I'm not coming back to school."

I: "So in other words, you think the whole problem is with D?"

N: "Yeah, why don't they just try us in another class?"

I: "Because they think you should be able to get along, not to talk to him, ignore him, so you don't get into fights with him. If you didn't talk with him and he didn't talk to you, do you think that would help?"

N: "No."

I: "You don't?"

N: "That wouldn't help at all."

I: "Why not?"

N: "His mother tells him to fight."

I: "Okay, maybe we should get D in here. Would that help?"

N: "Yeah, go get him."

I: "But what are you going to talk about with D? You can't fight him, right? I don't want to see any fights—I won't get him if you are going to fight. What can we do so that you two can get along in the same classroom?"

N: "We never will get along. I know that."

I: "Wait a minute—you have to get along."

N: (No response)

I: "You have to get along—that's the rule. Now how are you going to do it? If D didn't fight you and you didn't fight him, then would everything be cool?"

N: "Probably."

I: "Okay, but what will happen if you get mad at D, and you get in a fight?"

N: "Nothin'—I won't get in a fight."

I: "Okay—I'm going to get him."

There followed a joint session which included D's perceptions of the situation. It is best to include the relevant others in the discussions. The goal here was interaction without fighting and facing the reality that he did have to get along. This represents the fifth component step of LSI in which the interviewer brings reality factors present in the milieu to bear on these alternatives, remaining cognizant of the psychological context in which the student can be expected to hear them. Step six revolves around the juxtaposition of the student's thoughts about resolution with the reality factors in the milieu: How does the student think he might be assisted and what steps should comprise such a plan?

COMMITMENT TO A PLAN

After the interview with N and D; N was reluctant to make any kind of commitment, although D did make a commitment to N.

I: "N has to do something to get along with other people."

N: "What about if he doesn't?"

I: "Well, then he's going to get in trouble."

N: "I ain't going to get in trouble."

I: "When I say trouble, I don't mean getting spanked or any of that stuff. When I say trouble, I mean trouble like a problem—like it'll be hard to get along with a person and that is not a very nice thing, is it?"

N: "No, but if it's going to come up, I'll just do it."

I: "But that's the whole point—you just said it—if it's going to come up. But the point is not to let it happen. The only way with D is to ignore him, like he said he's going to ignore you."

N: "I don't think he's really going to."

I: "Well, do you always keep your promises? Have you ever made one?"

N: "No, and I never will."

I: "How come?"

N: "Because I'll forget one time."

I: "That's right, it's very difficult to remember."

N: "That's why I never promise." (Lunch bell rings)

I: "How many fights do you usually get into in a day?"

N: "One or two."

I: "I want you to try this afternoon not to get into any fights."

N: "If I come back this afternoon."

N needed some alternatives for getting along with D, ignoring D, and a contract. The supportive measures taken were the tools for a plausible resolution.

Finally, a follow-through plan must be developed as to what should take place if the resolution proves inadequate.

A daily behavioral chart was made. Every day after school, N's teacher evaluated him. He got nearly twenty points every day that week—a complete behavior change over. The chart was brought home on Friday for his father to sign. Seldom does one achieve a turnabout in a single interview, as in this instance. While this was at the ego level, skilled interviewers will clarify affective feelings as well. Though the past can be examined when relevant, more time is spent on the future linked to goals, hopes, and strategies. With children, attention to the concrete reality, both of the inner life and external conditions, is crucial.

These steps are in no sense doctrinaire. The LSI is a highly flexible way of communicating with children and youth and, as such, is adaptable to diverse situations. Considerable training is necessary to master Life Space Interviewing, for it involves many of the same subtleties found in psychotherapeutic processes.

LOGICAL CONSEQUENCES: DREIKURS

Rudolf Dreikurs[14] has defined logical consequences as existing in "situations where the consequence is, in effect, arranged by the parent or other adult." These are explicitly differentiated from natural consequences, which flow from actions without arrangement. Four criteria distinguish logical consequences from punishment. First, logical consequences should express the reality of the social order, with minimal interpretive bias by their administrator. Punishment, on the other hand, represents arbitrary personal authority. Second, logical consequences are intrinsically related to the behavior from which they spring, whereas punishment bears only arbitrary, extrinsic relation to the inducing behavior. Third, logical consequences, unlike punishment, are not intended to be morally judgmental. Finally, logical consequences are only concerned with what will transpire henceforward, whereas punishment is concerned with the past.

By way of example, situations in which children for one reason or another demand frequent repetition of directions and explanations are common fare in schools. One example of punishment for the behavior transpiring during direction and explanation might consist of sending the children to the principal's office. A logical consequence would consist of explaining the unfairness to others of in-terrupting the class to repeat directions, informing the children involved that directions would not be repeated again, and placing responsibility for understanding and completing assignments in their hands.

The four criteria serve to articulate the conceptual distinction between logical consequences and punishment; but, at the practical level, it is children who must draw the phenomenological distinction between the two. This issue is of particular importance when conditions of emotional arousal or disturbance prevail, for under such conditions, consequences will seldom be experienced as the results of the children's actions. It is equally important that the teacher understand the purpose and function of the behavior to which a consequence is to be assigned. Only by such understanding can we assure the perceived logic of the consequence. One child's need for repetition of directions may be based on insufficient skills to master the task, while another's may be based on inattention due to conversation with a neighbor. The request for repetition is functionally different for these two children, so for them, logical consequences must be differentially defined. Finally, it is important to be aware that the choice inherent in any consequence is intended to be logical. The previous example presents the children with the choice as to how and when to master directions and complete the work assigned. Teachers must be certain that they can live with all of the choices implied in a logical consequence. Thus, logical consequences must be framed in terms that: (1) are perceived to be logical by the child(ren) and (2) define alternatives which are acceptable to the teacher.

THE PSYCHOLOGICAL CURRICULUM: WEINSTEIN AND FANTINI

Developed at the University of Massachusetts, the core of the Psychological Curriculum is a resource bank of experiential teaching procedures containing source materials for projects and units. The teaching procedures are designed to focus on the concerns of a particular group of students. The subject matter is derived directly from student concerns as they may be reflected in behavior, cognition, and/or affect. The Psychological Curriculum must thus be individually designed on a group-by-group basis.

Weinstein and Fantini[71] have developed a model assessment process with which teachers can evaluate the relevance of existing curriculum, content, and techniques; on the basis of this they can then develop a psychological curriculum for their classes. The process includes: (1) identification of the learning group in maximum detail, (2) identification of shared concerns, (3) diagnosis of underlying factors, (4) definition of desired outcomes, (5) recognition of organizing themes, (6) planning of content vehicles for relating concerns and themes to outcomes, (7) delineation of skills necessary for mastery, and (8) examination of teaching procedures most appropriate for developing the learner's skills so that mastery and intended outcomes become feasible. The Psychological Curriculum is intended to assist children in development in three key areas of human concern: sense of identity, sense of potency, and sense of connectedness.

TEACHER EFFECTIVENESS TRAINING (TET): GORDON

Teacher Effectiveness, as articulated by Thomas Gordon,[22] is founded on differential assessment of student-owned, teacher-owned, and conflict-of-needs problems in the classroom. Teacher effectiveness is comprised of explanations of this nomenclature, differential strategies for approaching each kind of problem, and the techniques for implementing each strategy. *Teacher Effectiveness Training* (TET) is both the title of the book by Gordon in which Teacher Effectiveness is explicated, and of the courses conducted throughout the country by his organization, Effectiveness Training Associates, which is responsible also for Parent Effectiveness Training (PET).[23]

Student-owned Problems. Gordon has found teachers to be better trained to recognize classroom problems than to know how to respond effectively. TET is intended to fill this training void. According to Gordon, when dealing with student-owned problems, teachers regularly throw up one or more of a dozen "roadblocks to communication." These include commanding, threatening, advising, moralizing, interpreting, and interrogating. He advocates that such responses be replaced with: (1) passive listening, (2) acknowledgment responses, (3) door openers, and, perhaps most importantly, (4) active listening.

Active listening consists of reflective verbal responses which provide feedbacks to the student as to what the teacher has understood to be the problem. For example, an active listening response to "Are we going to have a test this week?" would be "You're worried that we're going to have a test soon." Seven attitudes, or "sets" are discussed

from which one must work in order to be an effective active listener. Finally, active listening has been noted to have six specific effects: (1) it can defuse strong feelings, (2) it can help students accept their emotions and work with them, (3) it can facilitate problem solving, (4) it places ultimate problem solving responsibility on students, (5) it can increase student willingness to listen to teachers, and (6) it can promote less dependent student-teacher relationships.

Teacher-owned Problems. Teacher-owned problems are indicated by teachers' feelings of annoyance, frustration, resentment, anger, distraction, irritation, and so forth. Student behaviors such as leaving supplies all over a room or talking while directions are being given often stimulate teacher-owned problems. The crux of effective response to teacher-owned problems lies in the acknowledgment of ownerships in the form of "I"-messages such as "I can't work when I have to first clean up a lot of left-around materials," and "I get tired of having to repeat directions because people are talking."

"I"-messages must contain three components: (1) nonjudgmental description of the behavior which creates the problem, (2) statement of the concrete effect of the behavior on the teacher, and (3) statement of the feelings generated in the teacher by the concrete effect.

When a teacher confronts a student directly, it often creates a problem for the student. It is vital that the teacher be alert to cues that this is happening, in order to shift strategy to one more appropriate to student-owned problems.

Problems Arising From Conflict-of-needs. Confrontation may, on the other hand, reveal a situation in which conflict-of-needs is the basic issue, that is one in which the problem is mutually owned by teacher and student. Gordon notes that two approaches to such situations prevail in schools. Rather than further labor the terms "authoritarian" and "permissive," he labels the two approaches Method I and Method II. Both are win/lose strategies: the teacher wins and the student loses under Method I, and vice versa under Method II. Gordon delineates certain things that are known to be true about each approach and notes that in relation to their effectiveness, their ultimate cost is high.

Method III is offered as an alternative in dealing with problems of conflict-of-needs: it is a no-lose approach both parties join in mutual problem-solving negotiation. Method III is a process which uses confrontation, active listening, and other TET tools in a six-step problem-solving model grounded in the work of John Dewey. The steps are:

1. Defining the problem.
2. Generating possible solutions.
3. Evaluating the alternative solutions.
4. Deciding on the best solutions(s).
5. Determining how to implement the solutions(s).
6. Assessing the effectiveness of these solution(s).

The benefits of Method III include minimization of dependence and a resentment, increased motivation for problem solution, mutual participation, and encouragement of student responsibility in the workings of the classroom.

TRAINING TEACHERS IN INTERPERSONAL SKILLS: ASPY

David Aspy[1] has conducted extensive research in psychoeducation, particularly on the impact of teacher attitude on learning, problem-solving ability, and classroom morale. He has analyzed classroom interactions along the Rogerian dimensions of empathy, congruence, and positive regard. These three conditions have been found to correlate positively and significantly with cognitive growth, while low levels of these conditions may actually retard learning and encourage absenteeism.

A second phase of Aspy's work involved a shift in focus from diagnosis to intervention. Could teachers increase their levels of these interpersonal skills? He and his colleagues developed a fifteen-hour "didactic-experiential" training program modeled after that of Carkhuff,[10] in which: (1) a trainer explains the scales for measuring empathy, congruence, and positive regard, (2) the teachers-in-training apply these scales to audiotapes of classroom sessions, and (3) the teachers respond to standard stimulus statements and score their responses using three scales. Significant gains in the three facilitative conditions were reflected in pre- and postcodings of audio recordings made of these teachers' classrooms.

Aspy's research approach is noteworthy in a field suffering a lack of objective data. His work includes a fully articulated model for training treachers to be more empathic towards, congruent with, and respectful of children.

TRANSACTIONAL ANALYSIS: BERNE

Transactional Analysis (TA) is based on the delineation and articulation of three "ego states" which are said to exist in all human beings. The *parent*-ego state includes systems of feelings and patterns of behavior which resemble those of parental figures; the *adult*-ego state, those which are "autonomously directed toward objective appraisal of reality"; and the *child* state, those archaic but active relics which are grounded in early childhood. These ego states are normal phenomena, much as the id, ego, and superego of traditional psychoanalytic classificatory schemata.[3]

Harris[24] has delineated a developmental sequence of four basic life positions which are also integral to TA: (1) "I'm not OK—You're OK," (2) "I'm not OK—You're not OK," (3) "I'm OK—You're not OK," and (4) "I'm OK—You're OK." These life positions are composed of multiple transactions with the world, and each implies a different *weltanschauung*.

Transactions are "units of social interchange," and analysis of a transaction (TA) consists of assessment of which ego state(s) is (are) involved in a particular interaction. Transactions may be complementary or crossed. Complementary ones are those in which one person's response to another's stimulus remark is appropriate and expected. For example, adult interacting with adult, and parent interacting with child are complementary transactions. On the other hand, an interaction in which adult addressed adult, but child responded as if to parent, represents a crossed transaction.

The primary strength of TA as it is applied in schools lies in its view of parent, adult, and child states as normal phenomena to be found in all human beings—adults and children alike. The result can be a construction of human existence which incorporates a wide range of behavior without resorting to perjorative concepts such as deviance or pathology. *TA for Kids*[18] describes ways in which TA can be used in schools.

Student-Focused Approaches

CLASSROOM MEETINGS: GLASSER

According to William Glasser,[21] children and adolescents must learn to care and to be responsible for themselves and for one another. Schools must in turn provide experiences conducive to such learning or accept responsibility for the failure begotten of loneliness. Personal responsibility lies at the core of the social responsibility, which children need to learn. Central to Glasser's work is the facilitation of children's capacity and willingness to make value judgments about their own behavior. Simply to tell children what is **right** and wrong, administering consequences accordingly is to absolve them of personal responsibility. The result can be thoughtless conformity or even belief in forces such as luck and chance, in the face of which one is helpless. In Glasser's words, "Responsibility is learned only by evaluating the situation and choosing a path that a person thinks will be more helpful to himself and to others."[21]

Glasser has observed how tragic it is that in schools so little use is made of indigenous group situations. The notion of youngsters learning to help one another cope with and/or solve the everyday problems of life is seldom associated with school; whereas such groups might serve as laboratories for fostering social responsibility. Noting the severe limitations of "fact and memory" education in this regard, Glasser advocates the classroom meeting as a tool for developing personal and social responsibility. The philosophy and technique of the classroom meeting are fully described in Glasser's *Schools Without Failure*,[21] and are illustrated in film and tape cassette series.[37]

There are three kinds of classroom meetings. The first takes the form of teacher-led, nonjudgmental, problem-solving discussions about topics important to members of the class. Such discussion is not aimed at finding fault but rather at solving problems. The second kind of meeting involves open-ended discussion of any issue which proves thought-provoking to the class, whether it be a news item or a recent event in class or school. The object of such meetings is to stimulate children to think and to relate what they know and feel to the subject at hand, not simply to arrive at factual conclusions. The relationship between subjects of discussion and the larger curriculum may at times be explicit or remain implicit, depending on the situation. The third kind of meeting is an educational-diagnostic one which pertains directly to the content and/or the process of the subject matter that the class is studying. The leader's judgments have no place in such meetings. Rather, they are settings in which the opinions and feelings of the children are encouraged and considered. Teachers may be invested in their classes so intensely that it is difficult for them to lead educational-diagnostic meetings; leadership of such meetings may then be assumed by a consultant or other outsider.

The classroom meeting is a mode through which children and adolescents can experience autonomy and self-determination; and consequently, learn personal and social responsibility. For example three third-grade boys demonstrated such understanding one day. After the class had experienced several problem-solving class meetings on issues of communication, teasing, and fighting; the third-graders asked to reserve the conference corner. They were having a problem and wanted to have a "triangle meeting." The teacher acceded and stopped by the corner several minutes later in time to hear the boys exchanging perceptions of the problem, then brainstorming possible solutions and choosing the best alternatives for implementation.

Practice with the problem-solving format and teacher support for the classroom meeting are crucial to such learning. The nonjudgmental and open-ended nature of the meeting is also crucial. Right and wrong, success and failure have no place in classroom meetings.

COMPREHENSIVE CURRICULA FOR
HUMAN DEVELOPMENT AND
INTERPERSONAL INTERACTION

The following curricula are designed to foster better understanding of social-emotional behavior, interpersonal interaction, and the individual's relation to larger social contexts. All employ listening, inquiry, discussion, and experiential approaches to learning.

1. *Developing Understanding of Self and Others (DUSO) (K–3) and Toward Affective Development (TAD) (3–6)*
2. *Dimensions of Personality (K–12)*
3. *Focus on Self-Development (K–6)*
4. *Lifeline (7–12)*

DUSO[14] employs a range of activities, such as role play, puppet play, group discussion, reading, art, and music to develop the understanding of eight central themes: understanding and accepting self, feelings, others, independence, goals and purposeful behavior, mastery, resourcefulness, and choices and consequences.

TAD[15] is an activity-based curriculum which is aimed at: (1) expanding children's openness to experience; (2) helping children learn to recognize, label, and accept feelings and to understand the relationship between them and interpersonal events; (3) helping children develop social collaboration skills; (4) assisting children in developing their unique characteristics, aspirations, and interests; and (5) facilitating the development of thought processes in order to maximize personally satisfying and socially constructive behavior.

The *Dimensions of Personality*[30] program develops such themes as making friends, cooperation, and dealing with shyness and fear at the kindergarten level. Cooperative group interaction is utilized to allow children to experience competence in the small group setting and to support self-discovery and acceptance in the elementary curricula of levels one through six. The secondary materials address the issue of personal identity in larger social contexts and confront matters of day-to-day decisions and their relationship to values.

The Focus on Self-Development program* consists of three stages: Stage I, for Kindergarten through grade 1, focuses on awareness of self, others, and the environment through development of several subthemes. Stage II, for grades two through four, includes such subthemes as self-concept and communication. Stage III is designed for grades four through six and is organized around the theme of involvement.

Designed for secondary-level use (ages twelve to eighteen), Lifeline is comprised of three units based on actual real-life situations.[37] The program rests on two essential factors: (1) the importance of motivating students to become involved in and committed to taking others' needs, interests, and feelings into account in the course of everyday interactions; and (2) the importance of work with children and youth which encourages putting values into actual practice. Lifeline's themes are clustered around sensitivity, referring to ways of encouraging sensitivity to self and others; and consequences, referring to means of facilitating awareness of moral and social consequences of any universe of alternative behaviors.

Lifeline is not concerned with inculcating any particular values beyond that of conscious attention to others' needs. Rather, it focuses on the process of confronting and acting on value-laden issues. The program is based on the premise that in a majority of situations, adults working with adolescent youth in the school setting should "come off the fence" and let their value positions be known. While Lifeline recognizes the risks inherent in adults coming forward in this manner, it should be noted that the traditional wariness regarding how much, how, when, and what is said does not produce real neutrality.

DELIBERATE PSYCHOLOGICAL EDUCATION:
MOSHER AND SPRINTHALL

Deliberate psychological education is a secondary-level curriculum focusing on individual and human development. It was designed by the Psy-

* This program was developed by J. Anderson and M. Henner. See their *Focus on Self-Development* (Chicago: Science Research Associates, 1972).

chological Education Group at Harvard. The work is grounded in a critique of most guidance and psychological services offered by schools and in an appraisal of the unintentional, but potent, psychological experiences of children in school. With regard to the former, the group has concluded that "no genuinely significant psychological provision exists" for the majority of students in secondary schools.[46] Concerning the latter, the group has suggested that schools are indeed affecting students' attitudes, self-concepts, and values; but that this is done through a "hidden curriculum" which is implicit in formal academic instruction.

Deliberate psychological education is a half-year course, most of which can be taught in school, though certain aspects must take place in the community. The central theme of the program is "personal history"; it is approached from two perspectives. The first is a cognitive one, in the form of a "core course." This is built around resources such as the writings of prominent authors in human development, contemporary novels, films, and comprehensive case studies. The second is an experiential one. It takes the form of an internship chosen from an array of possibilities, including theater improvisation, psychology of interpersonal behavior, teaching, counseling, and film making. This dual format is intended to offer students maximum opportunity to understand more fully and to apply psychological resources to everyday life.

The group has undertaken curriculum development focused on other issues of intense concern to adolescents, such as drugs, sex, and authority relationships.

EDUCATION FOR PARENTHOOD:
OFFICE OF CHILD DEVELOPMENT

The Office of Child Development (OCD) of the Office of Education has, since 1973, supported numerous programs for teaching parenting to youth in grades seven through twelve. The thrust of Education for Parenthood has also included development and field testing of Exploring Childhood (Educational Development Center, Cambridge, Massachusetts), a one-year curriculum on child development intended for secondary students. Parenting, as conceived by the OCD, includes the full range of activities, concerns, knowledge, and skills needed for fulfilling parental roles. The thrust behind Education for Parenthood is that our laissez faire approach to parenthood is grossly inadequate. The Education for Parenthood approach is grounded in the findings of the 1970 White House Conference on Children. Bronfenbrenner's[5] work also supports such efforts. It is specifically not the OCD's intention to undercut or replace the family as primary parent-training institution, but rather to offer families and communities integrated support in meeting this challenge.

Among the strategies being implemented under the aegis of Education for Parenthood are the use of child development laboratories and other such settings in which training experiences for secondary school youth can be developed; use of films, filmstrips, and so forth for case presentation and discussion; discussion of material and concerns grounded in practical experience; and use of observation and assessment instruments such as rating scales to assist in conceptualizing and analyzing the behavior and dynamics of young children. The OCD has also engaged in clearinghouse activities, surveying and describing materials available in the area of parenthood education.

THE HUMAN DEVELOPMENT PROGRAM: PALOMARES

A developmentally sequenced program spanning preschool through sixth grade, the Human Development Program revolves around the Magic Circle. The first level (for preschool and kindergarten) is designed for groups of eight to twelve children, while Level I (first grade) includes gradual progression to groups of thirty or so children who may occupy two concentric circles. The program is designed to present children with a series of challenges, geared to their state of readiness, which emphasize affective development. The subject matter for the Magic Circle is the children's own experience, which is "gently structured by the teacher so that the children can learn about it and from it."[4]

The program is organized around three central themes: awareness, mastery, and social interaction; which Bessell and Palomares[4] have described as the three "focal settings" through which the human being can be viewed. Operationally, the program is described in Lesson Guides, one for each level. Each of these includes 180 daily activities in the form of lesson plans, as well as supporting theoretical discussion pertaining to child development, group dynamics, and the like. The activities begin with low-threat exercises and build on increasing children's group experience. One fourth-grade class that had been holding Magic Circles—some by the book, some not—for several months was doing a series of exercises to find out more about each other. Children could ask other children any question they wished; to which the response "that's private" was permissible if a question touched on matters which the questioned child did not wish to discuss publicly. One boy in the class was asked why his voice was "so funny." After an audible gasp from an adult visitor to the class, the child explained calmly that he had had an operation on his vocal chords. Further questions regarding the reasons for the surgery were answered in considerable detail after a nonverbal gesture of support from the teacher. The class proved quite able to deal with the highly sensitive subject, and the interview and discussion went on without interruption. Two weeks later, the teacher observed that teasing around this subject—a frequent occurrence before this circle meeting—had ceased.

The program also includes an assessment tool, the developmental profile, which is used for ongoing evaluation of the program's impact in the classroom. The Human Development Program is designed specifically for use in schools. Its developmental sequencing is an asset offered by too few programs. Bessell and Palomares[4] warn, however, that even the highly motivated teacher should not expect instant success. Acquisition of full competence with the Human Development materials may take a full year.

MORAL EDUCATION: KOHLBERG

Lawrence Kohlberg is well known for his research in the area of moral reasoning. According to his theory of moral development, human beings pass through six universal stages: the preconventional (stages one and two), during which one is minimally influenced by societal norms; the conventional (stages three and four), during which societal expectations are paramount; and postconventional (stages five and six), during which one's actions are governed by personal conscience.[32] Dividing the stages of moral development between three and four reveals that the first three are more dependent on external cues, rewards, and sanctions. In contrast, the latter three revolve around personally "owned" beliefs and values.[36] Mattox[36] has defined the sequence of themes which characterize the six stages of moral development as avoidance of punishment (stage one), self-benefit (stage two), acceptance by others (stage three), maintenance of the social order (stage four), contract fulfillment (stage five), and ethical principles (stage six).

Moral education is the facilitation of progress

through the six stages. The process centers around the presentation of "dilemmas" by the teacher, who functions as facilitator and stimulator. Essentially, dilemmas are scenarios which turn on a situation involving some moral decision. Dilemmas may be the basis for group discussion, simulation, or role-play (numerous examples have been provided by Mattox[36]). Student involvement is central to all of these procedures. It is important also that no single answer be presented as correct: the process should be divergent and nonjudgmental.

Children experience moral dilemmas and make moral decisions every day. The process of moral education entails planned exposure of children to the wide range of their peers' moral reasoning. Its aim is to facilitate understanding of the interactions between people and their environment, as well as the relationship between values and behavior. The skills in acquiring, organizing, and evaluating data required for resolution of moral dilemmas have obvious application to traditional subject matter such as mathematics, language arts, and social studies.

THE SELF-CONTROL CURRICULUM:
FAGEN, LONG, AND STEVENS

Fagen, Long, and Stevens[16] have defined self-control as "one's capacity to direct and regulate personal action flexibly and realistically in a given situation." Self-control is viewed not from the perspective of inhibition of behavior but as freedom of choice among a finite universe of alternatives present in any situation. Self-control, thus defined, is comprised of eight developmentally-sequenced processes: storage (or retention of information), sequencing and ordering, selection, anticipating consequences, appreciating feelings, managing frustration, inhibition and delay, and relaxation. The self-control curriculum is intended to facilitate the development of competence in these areas in order to enhance children's abilities to confront, to arrive at, and to act upon difficult decisions. The curriculum is explicitly not a complete or definitive program. Rather, it seeks to articulate specific areas of concern and to develop learning activities pertinent to each.

Teaching children self-control addresses all eight areas of competence. For each, it provides a theoretical outline, a statement of rationale, a description of the component curriculum units and their goals, and suggested learning activities. Each of the curriculum units is aimed at a specific skill within one of the areas of competence. Selection, for example, is broken down into: (1) focusing and concentration, (2) mastering figure-ground discrimination, (3) mastering distractions and interference, and (4) processing complex patterns. Appreciation of feelings is broken down into: (1) identification of feelings, (2) development of positive feelings, (3) management of feelings, and (4) reinterpretation of feelings.

The description of the curriculum includes discussion of matters such as alternatives for its use and instructional schedule, techniques of particular salience to its implementation, the need for evaluation, and the importance of facilitating generalization of competence to real-life situations.

SELF-ESTEEM EDUCATION PROGRAM:
COOPERSMITH

Stanley Coopersmith[12] is the central figure in psychoeducation who focuses on self-esteem. His program is based on the assumption that individuals' concepts of themselves as learners and their expectations for success and increased competence are vital components of learning and development. Two theoretical issues follow from these assumptions. The first concerns the way children come to see themselves as effective learners; and the other, the way they come to regard themselves as successful. Coopersmith has articulated several interrelated variables which contribute to these developmental processes: internal versus external locus of control, a sense of powerlessness versus competence, positive and negative valences attributed to oneself, expectations held by parents and teachers, and the use of information and cues to confirm or alter one's self-conception.

These variables in turn define the intended goals of Coopersmith's approach; that is, increased individuality, development of intellectual curiosity and skills, facilitation of self-expression and self-control, opportunity for increased personal responsibility and endurance of the consequences of one's actions. Coopersmith asserts there are three general conditions which facilitate movement toward these goals in the classroom: (1) acceptance of children as they are; (2) clearly structured, focused, and relatively demanding standards, expectations, and limits; and (3) latitude for individuality, autonomy, and expression within such limits.

Techniques include contract-based individual instruction, learning centers, and cross-age tutoring. All can be instituted in most classrooms and form the operational backbone of the self-esteem education program.

SOCIAL ADJUSTMENT—A COGNITIVE APPROACH: SPIVACK AND SHURE

Concentrating on early childhood, Spivack and Shure's[69] approach to psychoeducation is based on the premise that those who develop a cognitive problem-solving style grounded in real-life problems and the ability to generate alternative approaches to interpersonal problems will be better able to cope effectively with everyday realities. Spivack and Shure contend further that such effective coping will be manifest in overt behavioral adjustment. Thus, "children must possess certain skills . . . and must be taught how to use these skills in solving real interpersonal difficulties."[69]

The social adjustment program is comprised of two components, prerequisite and problem-solving skills, and focuses on people and interpersonal relations rather than objects and impersonal situations. The program is designed to teach prerequisite language and thinking skills, the habit of seeking and evaluating solutions on the basis of their potential consequences, and problem-solving skills in relation to adaptive behavioral adjustment. Basically its aims are:

1. To teach prerequisite language and thinking skills before teaching problem-solving strategies.
2. To teach new concepts in the context of familiar content.
3. To base program content on people and interpersonal relations rather than objects and impersonal situations.
4. To teach generally applicable concepts rather than correct grammar.
5. To teach the habit of seeking solutions and evaluating them on the basis of their potential consequences rather than the absolute merits of a particular solution to a problem.
6. To encourage the child to create his own ideas and offer them in the context of the problem.
7. To teach problem-solving skills not as ends in themselves but in relation to the adaptiveness of overt behavioral adjustment.[69] [p. 29]

Spivack and Shure's 1974 book, *Social Adjustment of Young Children*,[69] presents verbatim a program script developed over three years and research results suggesting that children in the program demonstrate more substantial gains in social adjustment than those in control groups.

TEACHING PROGRAM FOR EDUCATION IN HUMAN BEHAVIOR AND POTENTIAL: OJEMANN

The late Ralph Ojemann was a pioneer in the field of psychoeducation. He contended that mental disorder might be prevented and emotional strength and stability encouraged through facilitation of adaptive thinking strategies.[53] The causal orientation which forms the core of his work considers both historical and futurist perspectives: dynamic causal thinking involves both sensitivity to how behavior has developed in the past and to its probable future consequences.

The thinking strategies with which children approach given situations develop as functions of the concepts and attitudes which they have learned as pertinent to such situations. Classrooms and schools may, for example, be experienced as milieus in which process and control appear arbitrary or capricious or in which behavior is placed in past and future contexts for greater understanding, and consequences appear dynamically logical. Ojemann's concern with the predominance of the arbitrary and of "surface orientations" to behavior led him to analyze the content of selections from fifteen elementary school social studies readers. He found that less than 1 percent included causal approaches to human behavior.[54]

Such diagnostic work led further to a two-pronged intervention strategy involving teacher training and alteration of the content and process of school curricula. Both were aimed at teaching causal orientations to human behavior. The teacher training component is comprised of three aspects: (1) development of appreciation for past cultural influences on one's own and others' behavior, (2) extension of knowledge of child behavior and development, and (3) exploration of ways to cope with children's feelings in classroom settings.

The curriculum design component includes presentation and discussion of vignettes reflecting surface and causal orientations, and role playing of such episodes. One vignette, for example, portrays a boy who fights with his peers daily. The teacher, who is about to deal with this aggressive behavior in a "surface" way, stops to reflect that the fights do not "just happen." A search for causes reveals that the boy is the subject of frequent teasing for having to go straight home from school to babysit his little sister. This "causal" approach leads to different intervention than the "surface" one would have.[53]

Also included in Ojemann's scheme are room council sessions, discussions similar to Glasser's classroom meetings, which were mentioned earlier in this chapter. Finally, curriculum units such as "Where Behavior Comes From" have been designed and can be presented in social studies or English classes.[53]

Pre- and postmeasurement of experimental and control fourth-, fifth-, and sixth-grade classes, using Ojemann's Problem Situations Test, revealed that his strategy produced measurable differences —not withstanding methodological difficulties. Ojemann's concepts and programmatic strategy have been made operational in the form of curriculum materials available from the Educational Research Council of America in Cleveland, Ohio.

VALUES EDUCATION: RATHS

Values education[55] grows out of the fact that this century has placed such emphasis on emotions and intelligence in human development that values and their relation to behavior have been largely neglected. Though it is noted that no consensual definition of the term value exists, this approach is clearly grounded in the work of Dewey, Allport, and Rogers. The focus is not so much on values as entities, as on the process of valuing.

Valuing is defined as the process of choosing freely among alternatives, the consequences of which have been considered; a position which is prized or cherished, willingly affirmed, and acted upon repeatedly. Values education involves seven processes for facilitating valuing, each of which flows from one of the seven aspects outlined. They are: (1) encouraging children to make choices with maximum freedom, (2) helping them to discover and examine the universe of alternatives present in a choice situation, (3) helping them weigh the alternatives in light of their consequences, (4) encouraging children to consider what they prize and cherish, (5) offering opportunities for children to affirm their choices, (6) encouraging them to act, behave, and live in accordance with their choices, and (7) helping them examine repeated behaviors and patterns in their lives. Values education turns on the "clarifying response." There are a number of criteria by which a clarifying response can be assessed; avoidance of moralizing, criticizing, and evaluating.

In its broadest sense, values education is a general approach to teaching within which an extensive variety of activities has been developed.[68] It should be repeated that values education has nothing to do with teaching any particular values, for its concern is with the process of valuing.

The Bases of Sound Program Development

Certainly interest is on the upswing in the prevention of mental disorder and in the promotion of emotional strength through planned educational experiences which emphasize the affective domain. Numerous authors,[9, 50, 64] havet advocated mental health consultation in schools as one means to these ends, and experience suggests that psychoeducational insights and practices can be shared effectively with school personnel through this mode of intervention. Educators and mental health professionals are indeed being called upon for consultation and collaboration in the conception, planning, and implementation of psychoeducational programs (see chapter 21).

It would be difficult—particularly in light of the unresolved issues previously outlined—to overstate the importance of painstaking care in the design of psychoeducational programs. The diverse issues relevant to sound program development can be ordered in three categories, according to their focus on children, teachers, and systems, respectively. Issues within these three areas are presented to alert mental health consultants to certain basic problems of program design.

CHILD-CENTERED CONSIDERATIONS: DEVELOPMENT AND READINESS

The psychology of child development involves a sequence of patterns which must be considered in designing psychoeducational programs. Piaget, Kohlberg, and others have provided guideposts for cognitive and moral development. For example, attempts may be made to foster the attitudes and skills involved in empathy. These will be doomed to failure if the children involved are not yet able to view the world from perspectives other than their own. Another example of the importance of developmental readiness is provided by the work of Schelkun[65] He found significant differences between the abilities of fourth- and fifth-graders to master labels for feeling states such as "scared" and "proud."

One element that is central to many approaches to psychoeducation is open-ended discussion. Children do not as a rule achieve the stage of cognitive development in which abstract thinking is the norm until they are between twelve and fourteen years of age.[26] Thus, the concrete content of discussion-stimulating anecdotes intended to facilitate abstract learning must be carefully assessed.

Among the approaches described earlier in this chapter, the Human Development Program, the self-control curriculum, and the work of Spivack and Shure are all exemplary in discussion of the issue of developmental readiness. Developmental readiness must be assessed with reference to specific individual children as well as to norms which apply to whole classrooms or grade levels. For example, a child may be struggling with the presence of a mentally impaired sibling in his home. The special concerns he presents may be addressed by planning activities which focus on the acceptance of individual differences. Special planning and implementation is obviously called for in situations which involve children who are somehow more volatile or vulnerable than the norm. Psychoeducational programs must be situationally specific according to the needs and strengths of both particular classrooms and individual children.

Other child-centered considerations pertain to intent and purpose. A number of the approaches composing psychoeducation's armamentarium of technique do define goals and objectives more or less clearly and specifically. It is important that these be scrutinized from at least two perspectives. First, how do they apply to specific classes or groups for which the psychoeducational program has been designed: Are they applicable verbatim, or is class-by-class or even session-by-session individualization in order? Second, how do they relate to the overall reasons for and intentions of the program as a whole?

Few of the approaches are explicit regarding the underlying values. It is crucial that these be articulated in their own right and that they be analyzed in the light of the social context of the community. Psychoeducation can ill afford to ignore the admonition contained in Silberman's[67] commentary on the failure of schools to come to grips with educational goals and values.

A final child-centered issue addresses the large number and wide variety of settings which comprise children's life space. There must be some assurance that the skills and attitudes fostered through psychoeducation will be adaptable to such diverse environments as structured and unstructured elementary and secondary classrooms, supervised and unsupervised peer groups, athletic field, household, and sites of eventual occupation.

TEACHER-CENTERED CONSIDERATIONS: COMPETENCE AND ATTITUDES

For most psychoeducation programs, the teacher is obviously pivotal as the primary agent of planning and implementation. Research suggests that programs which train teachers in affective and interpersonal skills produce greater mental health benefits than do programs which focus on children alone. Teachers' attitudes and skills thus seem to sift out at critical variables which deserve considerable attention.

Obviously not all educators and mental health professionals are competent in the area of psychoeducation. Unfortunately, teachers' exposure to the behavioral sciences upon which psychoeducation is grounded is often less than adequate. Schools hold teachers accountable for academic subjects such as arithmetic and language arts. Teacher-training programs in turn stress mastery in these areas, reducing the behavioral sciences to elective status.

The prevalence of faddish, dazzling techniques in psychoeducation increases the problems of the inexperienced. A weekend workshop on values clarification or communications skills can certainly serve as a beginning for work in the affective domain. Buyt, viewed from the broader perspective of psychoeducation in toto, it is at best a limited experience. Nonetheless, experience has shown that limited training combined with competent professional support can enable many teachers to implement a number of approaches effectively.

The eventual goal of all psychoeducational activities is the development of daily integrated psychoeducational skills and attitudes by classroom teachers. Classroom meetings and Magic Circles, which were described earlier, are among the approaches which focus most obviously on the development of children but are designed to influence teachers and the overall process of education as well. Such activities provide time-limited, low-threat settings in which teachers can develop necessary skills. By observing and modeling on a collaborating mental health consultant, they acquire competence in the nonjudgmental facilitation of classroom process. Hopefully, these competencies will generalize to the classroom milieu.

It would be naive, however, to consider teacher involvement in psychoeducation or the role of mental health professionals in schools only from the standpoint of competence. Attitudes and values—those of mental health professionals as well as those of school personnel—play crucial roles in these involvements. The nature of teacher training and of the schools' cursory excursions into the affective domain, on the one hand, and of the minimal experience of many mental health professionals in education, on the other, speak clearly to such issues.

Teachers may or may not conceive of their roles as including psychoeducation. Some may welcome the growing concern with the affective domain; others may see such concern as appropriate for mental health professionals but *not* for teachers. Mental health personnel may or may not conceive of these school programs as suitable for their involvement.

SYSTEMIC CONSIDERATIONS: CONSTITUENCIES AND SOCIAL CONTEXT

Perhaps the most complex and subtle issues which influence psychoeducational programs are found at the system level. To understand these concerns requires an assessment of the available human and material resources. Funds for the purchase of new materials, as well as for provision of inservice training and consultation, are always limited. Scrounging, doing-it-yourself, and brokering are often in order. Human resources are most important: It may be inadvisable to start a program with just one teacher in a school. There is a risk that the teacher involved may be viewed as particularly needy or inept or might be accused of grandiose self-conception by peers. This danger must be judiciously weighed, for such repercussions can have immeasurable ripple effects in schools.

The Classroom Milieu. The most far-reaching system considerations pertain to the cultures in which a program is to be embedded. The classroom is perhaps the most evident subcultural entity and involves at least three constituencies: teacher, children, and parents. Considerations pertaining to the first two, discussed previously, are diverse and must be carefully weighed. In addition, the parents and the universe of their possible concerns about psychoeducation must also be anticipated, and the issues addressed at every step of program development.

The Culture of the School. A second, broader perspective involves the culture of the entire school. The school's constituencies include parents, other chidren than those of the classroom in question, other teachers, pupil personnel staff, the principal, and such groups as the parent-teacher organization and the local education association. Each of these may have very different perspectives on the issue of psychoeducation, for they may each be influenced by different concerns, values, and norms. Relations with pupil personnel such as school psychologists and social workers are critical; their ascribed and assumed roles (those which are defined in job descriptions and those defined by themselves) are similar to and may be isomorphic with those of the outside mental health consultants. These in-house mental health workers may view external mental health personnel as intruders.

The School System. Of course any particular school is but one component of the larger cultural entity that is the school system. It is important to be aware of the concerns that influence the central administration of the schools, the teachers' association, and the school board. Each may bring highly variant perspectives to bear on the issue of psychoeducation.

The Community Context. The values of the surrounding community influence all of the constituents. Communities often have strong convictions about such issues as family privacy, roles of teachers and "psychology types," and the prerogatives of schools in the context of the community. It would be difficult to overemphasize Rhodes's[59] observation regarding the American's sensitivity to any hint of overt control of learning and socialization.

Communities have been known to exhibit sensitivity to some of the specific issues which arise in the course of psychoeducational programming. "Sensitivity training" in the schools, for example, has generated extensive and vigorous debate. Specific approaches to psychoeducation, such as moral education and values clarification, may be particularly high-risk in this regard. It might well be considered outrageous for schools to usurp such family-held territory.

The strength of community reaction is illustrated by a bill recently enrolled in the Michigan House of delegates, which reads in part that:

> Psychological or psychiatric methods shall not be practiced in the public schools. This prohibition includes role-playing, sensitivity training, or any other method of dealing with or probing the psyche of the student. "Sensitivity training" when used in this act means group meetings, large or small, to discuss publicly a student's intimate and personal matters, opinions, values, or beliefs; or to act out emotions and feelings toward one another in the group.[38] [pp. 2–3]

While Bill 4951 may never pass, it is all but impossible to measure the extent to which the forces behind it impact on the state's department of education and/or local school boards. Knowledge of the political history of issues to which a community is sensitive should be integral to the consideration of psychoeducation.

In summary, it is clear that mental health consultants must be aware of difficulties attendant on psychoeducation in the schools. It is possible to ignore some of the more problematic issues. The long-run risk involved must, however, be carefully weighed against the short-run convenience. If psychoeducation is to become a trustworthy component of school life and the educational process, these problems must be given the fullest consideration.

FUTURE

The future of psychoeducation is difficult to predict. Educational movements ostensibly concerned with improvement often lose out to vested interests.

Several authors have offered perspectives on the future: Sarason[63] has discussed the culture of schools, while Berlin[2] has written of change in schools; Brown[6] has reached beyond confluent education to examine educational trends; and both Ringness[60] and Schmuck[66] have presented syntheses of new directions in school mental health. There is a continual expansion of resources in psychoeducation. Those who wish to examine the movement further will find ample suggestions in the bibliographies of Morse and Munger.[41, 42]

REFERENCES

1. ASPY, D., *Toward a Technology for Humanizing Education*, Research Press, Chicago, 1972.
2. BERLIN, I. (Ed.), *Advocacy for Child Mental Health*, Brunner/Mazel, New York, 1975.
3. BERNE, E., *Games People Play*, Grove Press, New York, 1964.
4. BESSELL, H., and PALOMARES, U., *Methods in Human Development*, Human Development Training Institute, LaMesa, Calif., 1972.
5. BRONFENBRENNER, U., "Who Cares for America's Children," unpublished paper, Cornell University, 1975.
6. BROWN, G., "Training of Teachers for Affective Roles," in Ryan, E. (Ed.), *Teacher Education, The 74th Yearbook of the National Society for the Study of Education*, Part 2, pp. 173–203, University of Chicago Press, Chicago, 1975.
7. ———, *Human Teaching for Human Learning*, Viking, New York, 1971.
8. BYLER, R., LEWIS, G., and TOTMAN, R., *Teach Us What We Want to Know*, Mental Health Materials Center, New York, 1969.
9. CAPLAN, G., *The Theory and Practice of Mental Health Consultation*, Basic Books, New York, 1970.
10. CARKHUFF, R., "Training in Counseling and Psychotherapy: Requiem or Reveille," *Journal of Counseling Psychology*, 13:360–367, 1966.
11. CHASE, L., *The Other Side of the Report Card: A How-to-do-it Program for Affective Education*, Goodyear, Pacific Palisades, Calif., 1975.
12. COOPERSMITH, S., *Developing Motivation in Young Children*, Albion, San Francisco, 1975.
13. DINKMEYER, D., *Developing Understanding of Self and Others*, American Guidance Service, Circle Pines, Minn., 1970.
14. DREIKURS, R., and GREY, L., *A New Approach to Discipline: Logical Consequences*, Hawthorn, New York, 1968.
15. DUPONT, H., et al., *Toward Affective Development*, American Guidance Service, Circle Pines, Minn., 1974.
16. FAGEN, S., LONG, N., and STEVENS, D., *Teaching Children Self-Control: Preventing Emotional and Learning Problems in the Elementary School*, Merrill, Columbus, Ohio, 1975.
17. *Focus on Self Development*, Science Research Associates, Chicago, 1971.
18. FREED, A. M., *TA for Kids*, Jalmar Press, Sacramento, Calif., 1971.
19. GALLUP, G., *Fourth Annual Gallup Poll*, Phi Delta Kappa, Bloomington, Ind., 1972.
20. GINOTT, H., *Teacher and Child*, Macmillan, New York, 1972.
21. GLASSER, W., *Schools Without Failure*, Harper & Row, New York, 1969.
22. GORDON, T., *Teacher Effectiveness Training*, Wyden, New York, 1974.
23. ———, *Parent Effectiveness Training*, Wyden, New York, 1970.

24. HARRIS, T., *I'm OK—You're OK*, Harper & Row, New York, 1969.
25. HOLLISTER, W., "The Concept of 'Strens' in Preventive Interventions and Ego Strength Building in Schools," in Lambert, N. (Ed.), *The Protection and Promotion of Mental Health in Schools*, pp. 30–35, Public Health Service Mental Health Monograph no. 5, U.S. Government Printing Office, Washington, D.C., 1965.
26. INHELDER, G., and PIAGET, J., *The Growth of Logical Thinking from Childhood to Adolescence*, Basic Books, New York, 1958.
27. JERSILD, A., *In Search of Self*, Teacher's College Press, New York, 1952.
28. Joint Commission on Mental Health of Children, *Crisis in Child Mental Health: Challenge for the 1970's*, Harper & Row, New York, 1969.
29. JONES, R., *Fantasy and Feeling in Education*, Harper & Row, New York, 1968.
30. KIMBACHER, W., *Dimensions of Personality*, Pflaum/Standard, Cincinnati, Ohio, 1969.
31. KIRSNER, D. A., "Instrumentation of Bloom and Krathwohl's Taxonomies for the Writing of Educational Objectives," *Psychology in the Schools*, 6:227–231, 1969.
32. KOHLBERG, L., "Development of Moral Character and Moral Ideology," in Hoffman, M. (Ed.), *Review of Child Development Research*, vol. 1, pp. 383–432, Russell Sage, New York, 1964.
33. KRATHWOHL, D., et. al., *Taxonomy of Educational Objectives: The Classification of Educational Goals, Handbook II: Affective Domain*, McKay, New York, 1964.
34. LONG, N., MORSE, W., and NEWMAN, R. (Eds.), *Conflict in the Classroom*, Wadsworth, Belmont, Calif., 1971.
35. McPHAIL, P., et al., *Learning to Care: Rationale and Method of the Lifeline Curriculum*, Argus, Niles, Ill., 1975.
36. MATTOX, B. A., *Getting It Together: Dilemmas for the Classroom*, Pennant Press, San Diego, Calif., 1975.
37. Media Five, *Media Five 1976 Film Catalog*, Media Five, Hollywood, Calif., 1976.
38. Michigan House of Delegates, *House Bill 4951*, Lansing, Mich., 1975.
39. MILLER, G., "Psychology as a Means of Promoting Human Welfare," *American Psychologist*, 24:1063–1075, 1969.
40. MINUCHIN, P., et al., *The Psychological Impact of the School Experience*, Basic Books, New York, 1970.
41. MORSE, W., and MUNGER, R., *Affective Development in Schools: Resource Programs and Persons*, Behavioral Science Education Project, Ann Arbor, Mich., 1975.
42. ———, *Helping Children and Youth with Feelings*, Affective-Behavioral Science Education Resources for the Developing Self/Schools, Washtenaw County Community Mental Health Center, Ann Arbor, Mich., 1975.
43. MORSE, W. C., "The Schools and the Mental Health of Children and Adolescents," in Berlin, I. (Ed.),

Advocacy for Child Mental Health, pp. 158–198, Brunner/ Mazel, New York, 1975.

44. ———, "Training Teachers in Life Space Interviewing," *American Journal of Orthopsychiatry, 33:*727–730, 1963.

45. ———, and SMALL, E. R., "Group Life Space Interviewing in a Therapeutic Camp," *American Journal of Orthopsychiatry, 29(1):*27–44, 1959.

46. MOSHER, R., and SPRINTHALL, N., "Psychological Education in Secondary Schools: A Program to Promote Individual and Human Development," *American Psychologist, 25:*911–924, 1970.

47. MUNGER, R., and RAVLIN, M., *Furthering the Development of Children in Schools: The Role of Community Mental Health Centers in the Synthesis of Cognitive and Affective Development,* Behavioral Science Education Project, Ann Arbor, Mich., 1975.

48. National Education Association, *A Comparison of Teacher and Educational Leader Assessments of Teacher Needs,* National Education Association, Washington, D.C., 1973.

49. National Institute of Mental Health, *Mental Health and Learning,* Rockville, Md., 1972.

50. NEWMAN, R. G., *Psychological Consultation in the Schools: A Catalyst for Learning,* Basic Books, New York, 1967.

51. ———, "The School-Centered Life Space Interview as Illustrated by Extreme Threat of School Issues," *American Journal of Orthopsychiatry, 33(4):*730–733, 1963.

52. Office of Child Development, *Children Today,* vol. 2, no. 2, U.S. Government Printing Office, Washington, D.C., 1973.

53. OJEMANN, R., "Investigation into the Effects of Teaching Understanding and Appreciation of Behavior Dynamics," in Caplan, G. (Ed.), *Prevention of Mental Disorders in Children,* pp. 378–397, Basic Books, New York, 1961.

54. ———, "Sources of Infection Revealed in Preventive Psychiatry Research," *American Journal of Public Health, 50:*329–335, 1960.

55. RATHS, L., et al., *Values and Teaching: Working with Values in the Classroom,* Merrill, Columbus, Ohio, 1966.

56. READ, D., and SIMON, S. (Eds.), *Humanistic Education Sourcebook,* Prentice-Hall, Englewood Cliffs, N.J., 1975.

57. REDL, F., *When We Deal with Children,* Free Press, New York, 1966.

58. ———, *Strategy and Techniques of the Life Space Interview, The School-Centered Life Space Interview,* Washington School of Psychiatry, Washington, D.C., 1963.

59. RHODES, W., "Psycho-Social Learning," in Bower, E., and Hollister, W. (Eds.), *Behavioral Science Frontiers in Education,* John Wiley, New York, 1967.

60. RINGNESS, T. A., *The Affective Domain in Education,* Little, Brown, Boston, 1975.

61. ROEN, S., "Primary Prevention in the Classroom Through a Teaching Program in the Behavioral Sciences," in Cowan, E., et al. (Eds.), *Emergent Approaches to Mental Health Problems,* pp. 252–270, Appleton-Century-Crofts, New York, 1967.

62. SANFORD, N., "The Development of Cognitive-Affective Processes through Education," in Bower, E., and Hollister, W. (Eds.), *Behavioral Science Frontiers in Education,* John Wiley, New York, 1967.

63. SARASON, S., *The Culture of the School and the Problem of Change,* Allyn and Bacon, Boston, 1971.

64. ———, et al., *Psychology in Community Settings,* John Wiley, New York, 1966.

65. SCHELKUN, R., *Measurement of Children's Ability to Attach Cognitive Labels to Situational-Affective Cues,* Washtenaw County Community Mental Health Center, Ann Arbor, Mich., forthcoming.

66. SCHMUCK, R. A., and SCHMUCK, P. A., *A Humanistic Psychology of Education,* National Press Books, Palo Alto, Calif., 1974.

67. SILBERMAN, C., *Crisis in the Classroom,* Random House, New York, 1970.

68. SIMON, S., et al., *Values Clarification: A Handbook of Practical Strategies for Teachers and Students,* Hart Publishing, New York, 1972.

69. SPIVACK, G., and SHURE, M., *Social Adjustment of Young Children: A Cognitive Approach to Solving Real-Life Problems,* Jossey-Bass, San Francisco, 1974.

70. THOMPSON, J., *Beyond Words: Nonverbal Communication in the Classroom,* Citation, New York, 1973.

71. WEINSTEIN, G., and FANTINI, M., *Toward Humanistic Education: A Curriculum of Affect,* Praeger, New York, 1970.

72. WINEMAN, D., "The Life Space Interview," *Social Work, 4:*3–17, 1959.

PART E

Consultation as Therapy

21 / Mental Health Consultation to Child-Serving Agencies as Therapeutic Intervention

Irving N. Berlin

Mental health consultation is taught and practiced as an indirect method of helping a child client. Typically it addresses problems about which a consultee or line worker has some concern. The approach has been described by Coleman[27, 28] Caplan,* Berlin† Rapoport,[66] Bindman and others.[18] It attempts to identify and to help the worker with his own internalized problems. This rests on the assumption that it is precisely these internal difficulties which interfere with his ability to be helpful to the disturbing and disturbed child who is his student or client.

This is different from psychotherapy. The focus is on the consultee's work problems, not his personal psychopathology. In fact, however, when it is effective, it is therapeutic both for the worker consultee and the child client.

History

Mental health consultation has become a defined and systematic method of helping consultees confronted with client problems. This way of working

* See references 22, 23, 24, 25, and 26.
† See references 6, 7, 8, 9, 10, and 11.

was first described by Julius Coleman.[28] In his work with a public welfare agency, he encountered case workers struggling with troubled and troublesome clients. He recognized that he could best help the process by attending to the consultees' anxieties. Presently, he began to focus on understanding how the consultees' difficulties were reflected in their feelings; in this way he legitimized these feelings as issues for discussion. He emphasized the need to bring into the open how the clients made the worker feel. This was considered the factor which prevented the professional from doing his best work with the clients. In contrast, the traditional method of giving advice to the consultee about how to deal with the client turned out to be far less helpful. Thus, the consultant's most useful input occurred when he could find a way to reduce the consultee's anger about the overwhelming dependency and resulting demandingness of the welfare clients. This, then, resulted in the consultee providing service with much greater effectiveness.

Later, Gerald Caplan,[23, 24, 25, 26] at the Laboratory for Community Psychiatry at Harvard began to study the consultation process systematically. The result was the first clear delineation of the different types of mental health consultation.

At the same time, there gradually evolved a description of the methodology of each type of consultation and the steps that occurred in the development of each variety of consultative process.[36, 65, 73, 78]

At about the same time that Caplan was publishing his first systematic findings, Berlin,[*] Susselman,[76] Maddux,[56, 57] Parker,[62, 63, 64] and somewhat later Bindman,[18] Rapoport[66] and others began to publish reports of their similar experiences in a wide variety of settings. Some of the theoretical differences seemed to result from the different settings in which the practice occurred. A striking and unexpected finding was the general concurrence of all these workers that consultation was not to be regarded as psychotherapy but as an indirect method, once removed from the client who needs help. Thus, in the mid to late 1950s there were developed a number of centers throughout the nation to promote teaching, practice, and research in mental health consultation.[†]

Of special interest was the effort to work out the distinctions between consultation with groups and with individuals.[‡] As the work became more sophisticated, efforts were made to develop methods of program consultation, administrative consultation, and systems consultation. Here the break with the past was complete; the client populations were no longer individual children. Instead, the new targets were the administrators' concerns with faculty as individuals and groups, problems within an administrative hierarchy, and with problems which affected how the total system functioned.[§]

Agency Specificity

For our present purposes, we will confine ourselves to an examination of consultation aimed at helping individual children or classes of children served by an agency.

The growing literature on mental health consultation with child-serving agencies began to demonstrate that each class of agencies had its own kind of problems, both with the children and with the workers. The character of these problems was determined by the specific function of the agency.[||]

In the school, the problems had to do with failure to learn and behavior problems in the classroom. These behaviors interfered with the learning of others. They were of a special nature because they challenged the authority of the teacher and the teacher's capacity to discipline children. Most important, however, they made it difficult for the teacher to maintain a "learning atmosphere" in the classroom and to gain personal satisfaction from helping children learn and become effective students. Recently, in inner city schools, disruptive behaviors have been taken for granted and little done to alter the class atmosphere. In effect, this state of affairs destroyed the teacher's reason for existing—to promote learning by at least some children.[¶]

Most juvenile detention and probation workers were confronted by the youngster's antisocial, hostile, aggressive, or sexual acting-out behavior. While such behavior was generally at odds with the morality of society, it impacted with special force on the particular code of the lower middle-class workers in that setting. Most of these workers were raised in a neighborhood where antisocial, hostile behavior and sexual acting out occurred frequently. However, as children, they had not been permitted by their parents to take part in such behaviors during their growing up. They could only look on and envy. As a result, the detention or probation workers' reactions to such behavior by their clients was frequently angry or retaliatory. This interfered with their playing a possible therapeutic role or providing role models for their clients or their clients' parents.[**]

In the welfare department, various divisions seemed to have idiosyncratic problems. Thus, one group of workers dealt with general welfare and aid to dependent children. Here they felt overtaxed by the dependency and continued demands of the clients, which resulted from inadequate budgets and from special needs for medical aid, housing, or other help. The workers were angry at the clients. The clients characterized each worker as a harsh, denying mother figure. The result was an atmosphere of mutual hostility.[††]

Another group of workers dealt with dependent children. These were youngsters taken from their families or referred by the courts for foster home placement. The staff viewed each child as a bur-

---

* See references 6, 7, 8, 9, 10, 11, 12, 13, and 14.
† See references 7, 16, 23, 24, 40, 41, 43, 47, 50, 60, 66, 69, and 72.
‡ See references 2, 17, 19, 35, 48, 51, and 55.
§ See references 5, 6, 22, 24, 31, 33, 35, 42, 49, 51, 52, and 74.

|| See references 17, 36, 65, 73, and 78.
¶ See references 1, 3, 5, 10, 12, 14, 21, 26, 50, 55, 60, 61, 62, and 71.
** See references 11, 13, 31, 34, 35, 38, and 76.
†† See references 17, 28, 30, 35, 39, 45, 48, 57, 64, and 66.

den. Each foster home was seen as a potential haven and repository, and each foster mother, as a sacrificing martyr. The desire to care for foster children was perceived as a result of the foster mother's affection for children, especially in view of the paltry pay received. Inevitably, crisis followed crisis. The failure to work on a continuing basis with each foster parent to help with the child's personality problems led to a recurrent need to find a new foster home for the child. Each failure caused the worker to view the child as more malevolent and hopeless. Presently, the workers began to regard themselves as foster home shufflers; they felt inadequate, hopeless, and angry, both at the children and at the foster parents who promised so much and delivered so little. Thus, they rarely tried to understand or learn how to study each child's needs or to assess and understand the needs and capacities of the foster parents. They did not perceive themselves as the child's advocate in a child-serving division; nonetheless, they felt guilty and angry. As a result, they often failed to make the home visits necessary to get to know the child and the setting.[27, 58]

A different state of affairs prevailed in the child protective services which dealt with child abuse and neglect. There, the workers identified with the hurt child and behaved as opponents of the parents. Their hostility toward the parents and their efforts to have the child made a ward of the court often made it difficult for them to work with those parents who perhaps could have learned to be more effective in managing their children. The workers often identified with the neglected, hurt child within themselves. They repeatedly placed their charges with foster parents who were overly solicitous and permissive. They soon found that these children learned to provoke anger and abuse from most adults, including these very foster parents. This group of workers was misled by an amorphous, hopeful wish that love would cure all. They were angered that they had to work to understand the problems and to provide consistent help both to foster parents and natural parents.[58, 59]

Public health nurses in both urban and rural settings possess a great many skills which make them potentially important mental health workers. Their medical background and agency identification, however, make it difficult for them to work easily with families who will not follow advice or directions. They are especially disturbed by individuals who defy the authority of the physician at the clinic or their own authority as nurses during home or clinic visits. This anger at defiance of direction is especially evident when parents do not follow instructions designed to help or alleviate the disorders of children.[*]

Other child-serving agencies such as foster homes, day-care centers, and treatment centers have special problems. Often these are the result of frustrations that occur when they try to deal with a particular child who is difficult to handle, treat, or teach.[†]

Methodologies of Consultation

Most authorities view mental health consultation as a technique in which a consultant helps a colleague from another profession with a work problem. The interaction which evolves is essentially collaborative or horizontal rather than the kind of therapist-patient, teacher-student model which places the consultant in a one-up postion. Most recent literature strongly emphasizes the value of a collaborative, sharing roll which helps the consultee become a partner with the consultant in the effort to help the client.[‡]

Phases in Consultation

Each author who has described a particular method of consultation has generally divided the process into various phases. The first phase establishes a contract with the agency and defines how, where, and when the consultant will work, and how much it will cost. The second phase is introductory, a time for getting acquainted and reducing anxiety. The consultant may accede to a variety of requests from the consultees to prove his willingness to be helpful. The first efforts to delineate client problems are utilized to demonstrate that the consultant will not try to analyze or treat the consultee. Instead, consultant and consultee will interact as colleagues, and the consultant will place his special expertise in understanding human behavior, its development, and its disturbances at the service of the consultee.[§]

The third phase is the beginning of problem solving. It delineates the client's problems and ex-

* See references 12, 13, 20, 32, and 56.
† See references 20, 32, 64, 65, 66, and 70.
‡ See references 6, 7, 9, 17, 18, 22, 25, 33, 54, and 58.
§ See references 6, 17, 18, 22, 24, 36, and 46.

plores the client's past life experiences to help elucidate present behavior. There is also an effort to collaborate with the consultee to obtain specifics of the client's current behavior. When and where does the disturbing behavior occur?

Possibilities of intervention are explored to find a plan that the consultee feels might work and is willing to try. The plan should make sense in terms of the behavioral data accumulated. The interventions are then mutually appraised and amended in terms of their effectiveness. This process involves a mutual analysis of the interventions; it continues until the consultee has evolved a program which succeeds in altering the troublesome behavior of the client.

Once a consultee has learned to work effectively with a particular client or child, there is substantial agreement that he will be able to deal with other clients who present similar problems.

The last phase of consultation is the disengagement. The consultant and consultee agree that the problem has been dealt with and that the consultee is indeed now effective with the client presented. Often enough, the consultee, as collaborator, accepts an equal share in the success of the effort and does not express any special appreciation. The consultant should learn to obtain his gratification from the enhanced functioning of the consultee rather than from explicit acknowledgment of how helpful the consultation has been. The lack of feedback about one's effectiveness is especially difficult for young consultants who have experienced the gratification of direct rewards in the course of effective direct clinical work.*

Group Consultation

The work in group consultation is of essentially similar character to the work with individual consultees. Altrocchi, Spielberger, and Eisdorfer;[2] Berken and Eisdorfer;[4] Eisdorfer and Batton;[29] Rowitch;[71] and Berkowitz[5] are among those who have graphically described the process. In most groups, the problem client, which one member elects to discuss, usually represents a class of clients of major concern to the group.

A perennial worry in this manner of working is that one of the consultees may attack the presentor and uncover personal problems. This invariably disrupts the process. Most consultants are

* See references 1, 6, 7, 12, 15, 16, 18, 22, 25, 44, 49, 63, 68, 69, 70, and 75.

able to deal with these issues in the group and protect the person presenting. On the positive side, the process of helping one group member with his client's troubles has carry-over for the other consultees in their work with similar clients. A few consultants view their work as essentially educational.

The Dynamics of the Process

THE CONTRACT

The contract negotiating phase is described in a variety of ways. The dynamics depend on the consultant and his status, the organization he represents, and the recognized needs of the agency for consultative help. Most child psychiatrists make individual arrangements with an agency based on their relationship with various people in the administration. Thus, the contract is usually negotiated with someone in the upper structure of the hierarchy. This may be an assistant superintendent, an assistant director in welfare, or assistant chief probation officer who agrees that some agency staff members have problems that require the consultant's skills.

There is an important dynamic in this phase of negotiation that the consultant often fails to recognize. The central administrator hires the consultant to rid himself of problems in a subsystem. If the consultant accepts the assignment without first requesting an opportunity to explore the feasibility of consultation in the subunit, he gravely compromises his effectiveness. A school may have problems, but to agree to work there without gaining the confidence of the principal, whose domain it is, means trouble. The consultant must obtain the principal's collaboration and acceptance that the consultant's skills might be helpful to him and to the teachers who deal with difficult students. Unless he can do this, he will never gain entrance into the school. The same principle applies in other settings as well. After the central hierarchy agrees to pay for the time spent in consultation, a working agreement must be negotiated with the operational heads of every unit of the organization. [6, 22, 42, 49]

There is one common phenomenon in the contract-setting phase which regularly troubles young consultants. No matter what arrangement is made with the unit administrator, the first few appearances of the consultant at the agreed-upon time will be greeted with astonishment or bewilderment. In the press of daily activities, the unit head, or his designee, has forgotten about the consultation and has not scheduled anything. There is no better way to deflate the ego of a high-status child psychiatrist than to indicate they really haven't had time to work out how to use him. He will just have to wander around for the time being, and they will certainly schedule counselors or teachers for his next visit. The inexperienced consultant, unaware that the principal must assert his authority in the school, will continue to be surprised that for some weeks the schedule is not clarified.

The experienced consultant may ask the principal's permission to visit some classrooms that the principal recommends and thereby try to get a feel for the school and its problems. He therefore makes clear his need to depend upon the principal and his staff to clarify the educational goals, methods, and problems which are not in his own realm of expertise. He also acknowledges the educator's sphere of competence and his own role as learner. The consultant should make clear his desire to learn from the principal and staff about the educational process, the hierarchical lines of communications, and the expectations of various individuals in the hierarchy. He should also indicate his willingness to spend whatever time the administrator feels is necessary to understand the school and how it functions. Often the principal will introduce the consultant to teachers in the coffee room. As part of the introduction, he may state that in order for the consultant to learn about the school, he will be visiting the classrooms to learn about the kinds of problems with which teachers are faced. Thus, in time, the operational contract is adhered to, but only as the principal begins to feel comfortable with the consultant and accept him as an equal who understands and acknowledges the administrator's importance in the school.

THE INTRODUCTORY PHASE

This phase may take many weeks. The consultant attempts to reduce the apprehensions which psychiatrists arouse in members of other professions that their behavior and statements will be analyzed and that they will be found lacking both as human beings and as professionals. The omnipotence generally attributed to mental health professionals will be tested. Characteristically, the staff will present horrendous cases not amenable to educational or to usual mental health interventions and tell of children so disturbed that they

cannot be kept in school. All this serves as an occasion for seeing what kinds of outlandish recommendations the expert will make. The staff wants to learn that the consultant can admit ignorance and defeat and can say "I don't know" without feeling threatened.

In this period of testing, the consultant will often be asked to perform various tasks that are not part of the job description he has outlined. The consultant may be asked to see various children to confirm the diagnosis of other specialists or teachers; he may be asked to give lectures on mental health principles or on child development or to provide a mental health point of view on an inservice training program which is primarily educationally oriented.

The initial readiness of the consultant to make himself useful is important. He can use this testing period as an opportunity to delineate the areas of his expertise and to communicate his understanding of affective, psychophysiological, and social development, and their behavioral manifestations. As he reveals himself to be a compassionate and understanding human being, willing to learn from his colleagues and not tempted to "analyze" those who present information to him, he begins to develop the initial trust required for consultation to proceed.

After a period of testing, the experienced consultant will again sit down with the administrator. He will attempt to redefine the way in which he can be most helpful now that he has some understanding of the workings of the school.[6, 16, 18, 22]

INITIATING CONSULTATION

The next phase, or the beginning of the consultation, contains a honeymoon period which the consultant must understand. As the consultant works with teachers on the problems with disturbing children, the teachers may at first experience relief at having a high-status person listen to them so carefully and even provide a few sensible suggestions. At this point, the consultant has not really begun the actual helping process. His reduction of teacher anxiety, however, may produce feelings of euphoria in his consultees who agree that the consultant is really very helpful. After a period, however, they discover that they have not actually learned any new ways of coping with their difficult students. They don't voice their disenchantment to the consultant directly, but he learns from others (the principal or counselors) that the teachers are less eager and have not found the consultant as helpful as they thought he was going to be. To the beginning consultant, such dis- enchantment may come as a surprise and cause feelings of hurt and inadequacy.

At such a point, the more experienced consult- ant addresses the issue with his consultees. Now that they know each other better and now that the consultant understands the nature of the problems the consultee has with the student, they need to redefine their work together. It becomes necessary for them to look more carefully at the information available from early records, health records, and parent interviews to try to understand why the stu- dent behaves as he does, and how and when such behavior began, because there must be antecedents to the present behavior. Thus, gradually, the mu- tual problem-solving attitudes are developed.

TRANSFERENCE AND COUNTERTRANSFERENCE PROBLEMS

Throughout the consultation process, phenom- ena occur which can best be understood in terms of transference and countertransference.[8] The consultees appear to react to the consultant as if he were an authority figure from their past. Thus, irrational anger may appear because the consult- ant does "not give enough." Or it is asserted that he is "too demanding" in the collaborative work, when, in fact, no demands have been made and, on the surface, the collaboration seems to be going well. Also, states of considerable dependency often represent transference phenomena brought about by the consultant's position and his tendency to be nurturant and helpful. When such overdependence is not acceded to and the collaboration is insisted on, temporary rages occur. Unless they are under- stood within this framework and dealt with firmly and kindly, they can become overwhelming and undermine the collaboration.

On the other hand, the school setting reminds the consultant of his own past and his erstwhile youthful awe of teachers, principals, and authority figures. Such residual feelings, if they are uncon- scious, may make it difficult to be explicit about his expectations. He may find himself trying to please and placate his consultees rather than collaborating with them. For example, a particu- larly arbitrary and irrational principal evoked in this writer not only memories of an awesome prin- cipal of his own childhood, but also elements of parental behavior. All this needed to be under- stood so that the meaning of the principal's behav- ior in the present situation could be placed in perspective. Otherwise, the angry, irrational ele- ments of behavior in an authority figure would

have evoked responses which would have inter- fered with integrative problem solving in consulta- tion. The task-oriented approach of how do we aid the consultee with the problems of the client helps put both transference and countertransference be- havior into perspective.

RESISTANCE TO COLLABORATION

Resistance by the consultee to doing the neces- sary work is a frequent occurrence. It is often dif- ficult to help a teacher search out and bring to- gether relevant data from previous records. The consultee often feels and expresses a sense of anger, for not only has the consultant not solved the problems, but he has further burdened the teachers by requiring extra work. When this expe- rience is encountered repeatedly, it begins to be understood dynamically. The fact that extra de- mands are being made should be balanced by the realization that the requests for additional data offer the consultee the possibility of understanding more about the student's problems. The sense of "I have to do it all myself; you could help me and solve this problem if you would" often reflects of old interaction patterns. It speaks as well for continuing resistance to the kinds of self-growth and self-reliance which would reduce the need to be dependent on others. One teacher had patiently worked through this phase and expressed gratifica- tion at understanding the problem better with the consultant's help by saying "I had a feeling that if I learned how to do this, I would have to give up being helpless. Almost like I'd have to stop having any child-like feelings and could never ask anyone for help."[6, 7]

THE DATA-GATHERING COLLABORATIVE PHASE

Once the consultant and consultee have worked through the resistance to mutual data gathering, a true collaboration develops. The con- sultee-teacher needs to gather data about the stu- dent, his early development, and behavior in school and at home which the consultant and con- sultee agree may provide clues to the student-cli- ent's present problem. When the consultant is a physician, he can offer to obtain and evaluate medical data from the pediatrician and school nurse. In this way, all the data can be shared, and from its accumulation, a picture may evolve.

This data-gathering collaboration has an impor- tant consequence. Together, consultant and con- sultee begin to understand the factors leading to the onset of the student's problems. They learn where and how these difficulties seem to become most manifest and how the home setting and various previous school experiences have exacerbated or reduced these problems. Thus, the teacher begins to feel less personally to blame for the student's difficulties. He can place the origin of the problems in a developmental context in which other individuals have had an important part.

Usually such a delineation leads to the next phase of data collecting. The consultee becomes aware that the circumstances surrounding the student's current disturbed behavior need to be studied. On the basis of his experience, the consultant can usually help structure such observations. For example, he might suggest keeping a log, which shows when and where the disturbing behavior and nonlearning occur, in order to grasp the meaning of patterns of behaviors. Such patterns would then be of aid in planning where, when, and how to intervene. Thus, the daily behavior log can become clearer, and the different variables can be explored. In spontaneous ways, the consultee will often begin to include his own interactions with the student as one of the significant variables that merits study. Occasionally, in the course of exploring the times, places, and social context in which behavior problems were most disturbing, the consultant may inquire, "Where were you in the classroom when this happened? Could the student's behavior reflect a need to get you involved with him in some way because he really can't get your attention and approval simply by doing his job of learning?" Usually when the teacher begins to tell of his impact on the student as a negative or positive force in the student's behavior, he does so without at first talking about the feelings the student evokes in him. As the observations continue, however, or at the beginning of the intervention phase, the teacher as consultee feels safe enough to begin to reveal the kind and the degree of intensity of feeling evoked by this student.[6, 7]

THE INTERVENTION OR
HYPOTHESIS-TESTING PHASE

As the data from the past and present are gathered and discussed, various hypotheses are generated about why this student behaves as he does. The consultant may then suggest that they begin to consider some tentative hypotheses about what might change the behavior.

The consultant again reminds the consultee that basically they have been using the scientific model. First there was a data-gathering process; from this, a hypothesis was developed about possible causes; and now one must consider possible solutions which must be tested in action. With this framework in mind, the teacher-consultee can more readily work together with the consultant to generate ideas about the kinds of interventions that may be helpful to the student. Inherent in this phase of consultation is the clarification of method. Based on the data gathered and the hypotheses formulated about the reasons for the behavior, there is now a need to speculate about alternate possibilities for intervention. The effectiveness of these interventions will determine any need to modify the strategies employed. This, in turn, will alter the hypotheses about both why the behavior occurs and how it can be managed.

It is in this process of trying various interventions that the teacher-consultee becomes aware of his own importance to the student. As each intervention effort is examined and assessed in terms of whether it is working, what it is doing, and whether or not a totally different approach is required, the teacher begins to think creatively about what is in fact required to bring about changes in the student's behavior. Since each intervention is designed as a trial effort to be assessed, the teacher-consultee does not feel blamed for any failures. He shares these with his collaborator as they continue to try to understand the behavior, its history, and the implications of what has not worked for further intervention.

As the effective degree of teacher involvement with the problem student becomes clear, the teacher may angrily remonstrate that while the time spent may help this student, the rest of the class is suffering. Often, then, teachers can evaluate with the consultant how much actual teacher time a disturbing student has required.

As the interventions become more effective and the student begins to settle down to learn, perhaps the most important benefit of consultation begins to emerge. The teacher gradually becomes aware of how important a successful learning experience with a facilitating teacher can be to the mental health of a student.

In most instances, the hypotheses which generate the interventions reflect the need for an accurate assessment of where the student is in every aspect of his learning. Usually, such careful assessment has never been done. Typically, what is found is the need for help in major academic areas at a primary grade level. Then, a stepwise program must be devised for helping the student to be effective and successful in each area. The intervention begins to work because the concerned teacher provides consistent, positive encouragement and practical, assimilable increments of help. Instead of derogation and shame, with which the student has become too familiar, this new approach produces a sense of competence and being cared about.

In this process, the consultant has behaved as a model. He has provided consistent encouragement for small incremental efforts on the part of the consultee. He has been able to live through his moments of discouragement with the teacher without giving up. The consultant's persistence has led to continued efforts by the consultee until the consultee's own persistence pays off.

One of the inadvertent gains from this process occurs when teachers recognize after such an experience that they can only help a few of the most disturbing students and that many more require help. At this point, the teacher-consultee may arrange for assistance by teacher aides, parent helpers, student tutors, for whom he, in turn, provides a modified training program and consultation to assist them to help some of his students.[6, 7]

THE DISENGAGEMENT PHASE

When a teacher-consultee has successfully helped a disturbing student and can begin to generalize the method so as to help other students, there are clear signs that consultation is no longer required. Many teachers will suggest other colleagues who require the consultant's help. Others will simply indicate that they need no further help, sometimes with only a perfunctory statement of appreciation for the consultant's aid. Certainly one of the signs of effectiveness in consultation is the lack of further need for the consultant. When the usual process of testing various interventions with the student and modifying them to find the most helpful approach has occurred, the consultant can feel satisfied with his work. The consultant may properly indicate his general availability to the consultee should other problems occur. This statement can be coupled with a statement of the pleasure the consultant has experienced in working with the teacher and observing the evolution of his successful work with a difficult student. With the expressed satisfaction by the consultant, the teacher can accept the possibility of future use of the consultant and, from time to time, he may, in fact, let the consultant know of his effectiveness as well as about some different problems which now confront him. Then, perhaps another short consultative effort may be undertaken.*

* See references 6, 7, 15, 22, and 47.

Evaluation of Effectiveness in Consultation

In the past, the effectiveness of the mental health consultation process was determined by the consultee's subjective sense of how well he or she was now able to cope with certain problem children. The consultant also added his subjective evaluation. When the work had gone well, administrators, too, could often verify the increased capacity of the consultee. Questionnaires have been used with consultees and administrators to indicate the presence or absence of satisfaction with the consultation process.

Since most consultation occurs around severe behavior problems, two general methods of evaluation have evolved. The first is a detailed behavior inventory of the student prior to and after consultation. This inventory is based on some formulated problem lists with assigned degrees of severity. This has been filled out by the teacher, counselor, and administrator in contact with the student.

Students of concern to teachers tend to have other behavioral indicators of disturbance which can be described more objectively. First is absenteeism, days in school, or a record of skipping difficult classes. One concrete way of demonstrating the student's increased capacity for learning and improved adaptation to the school environment is more regular attendance.

It is also clear that most of these students are sufficiently disturbing to class and teacher to be excluded frequently from the classroom. Thus, a count of the actual visits to the vice-principal's office, the number of exclusions from the classroom, or the occasions of being sent to the counselor for help provide another objective measure of the effectiveness of the consultation process. An evaluation of academic achievement before and after consultation has also proved to be an important assessment tool.

In general, with the consultative approach described, most evaluations are positive. Where actual behavior and academic data are gathered, there is clear evidence of quantitative and qualitative improvement.

In a few instances of group consultation, the data were gathered on a number of students with severe behavior problems in several teachers' classrooms. It turned out that the frequency of visits to the office or to the counselor showed a marked decrease.†

† See references 3, 6, 36, 50, and 60.

One of the problems in examining outcomes is that of continued assessment when the student moves on to another class. There are, as yet, too few follow-up data to give a sense of long-term results. There are some impressionistic data, questionnaires, and so forth regarding how students with behavior and learning problems do in subsequent years. These suggest that if the student has begun to obtain satisfaction from learning and there is good communication between teachers, the improvement is sustained.

Contraindications for Using Consultation

In some settings, the turmoil in the school, the disorganization in the classrooms, and the feelings of confusion among the teachers reflect inadequate administrative capacity to deal with problems. Under such conditions, consultations with individual teachers may prove fruitless because the teachers are unable to operate differently. However, such consultation may be a lead into discussions with the administrators, resulting in eventual consultation with teachers. Preliminary consultation with teachers in groups or individuals may be the only effective way to approach the administrators.

When the consultant is new to the system, the need for urgent answers to acute crises may make it difficult to insist on appropriate data gathering in order to understand the genesis and nature of the crisis. In such situations, the inexperienced consultant may become a "fall guy" for the administrator because all he has to offer is a process through which crises can be understood, perhaps dealt with, and avoided. He cannot provide instant answers.

In each of the preceding situations, the consultation may be used by the administration as a palliative measure designed to show that every effort is being made to provide help, but that even the high powered consultants can't find the answers.

When psychiatrists are cast in the role of consultants, sometimes their narcissism and omnipotence make it difficult for them to realize that they are being used as "cat's paws" and will not be permitted to help with actual problem solving. When a consultant does recognize the dimensions and nature of problems in which he has little or no expertise, he is most effective when he declines to consult and indicates that other experts in systems approaches or management methods would be better for this task.

Economic Implications of Consultation

When it works well, the method has important implications for the total economics of help for children. A consultee affects many children. Once the consultee is helped to be effective with those children who are most disturbing, he can deal ably with that kind of child thereafter. The method is not only therapeutic for the child in terms of a different relationship with his teacher, but, on an ego level, the enhancement of the client-child's actual competence is critical to improved self-concept and therefore to his mental health.[6, 8, 22]

Group consultation may increase the numbers of consultees reached. However, the process requires considerable skill with group process as well as competence in the methodology of consultation.

The frequency of mental health consultation optimally is once a week. Consultation every two weeks is possible but not optimal. Less frequent involvement does not seem to work because of the dilution of intensity and the difficulty in working through acute problems at such an infrequent rate. If optimal frequency is not possible, the contract should be renegotiated. If no change can be effected, except in rare instances, such consultation should not be attempted (or continued).

Relationship of Consultation to Psychotherapy or Behavior Modification

For the client or student with very severe problems in interpersonal behavior and learning or for the psychotic child, consultation along may not be effective, because the student and family require help beyond the skills of the teacher. The alteration of relationship and efforts to promote learning may not be helpful if internalized conflicts in the child make it difficult for him or her to relate. or to attend and learn.

In such instances, recommendations for psychiatric evaluation (with an eye toward individual and family therapy) may need to be made. Usually the consultant is also aware of community facilities. In conference with teacher, counselor, school social worker, or psychologist, the consultant may assist in interpreting the data about the child's behavior. In a discussion of referral sources used by the school, the consultant may add his knowledge of facilities especially appropriate for a particular child's problems.

Behavior Modification as a Treatment Modality in the School

Many teachers have been taught to utilize behavior modification methods in the classroom. Some have been taught to use these with behavior problems, learning problems, and so forth. However, they usually learn to use the methods in a small laboratory setting where the contingencies are carefully evaluated and an individualized program can be designed to modify specific behaviors. Since the learning and practice are with individual children in a highly individualized setting, carryover into a large classroom poses problems that limit effectiveness. While the reinforcements may be the teacher's encouragement, the piecemeal versus the total approach to the child's needs may defeat the program in a classroom setting.

In mental health consultation, when one learns to deal with one class of behavior problem, one can usually deal with all similar behavior problems. In behavior modification, each problem child requires a separate search for contingencies and reinforcers. The most successful behavior modification programs occur in very small classes.

Summary and Conclusions

Mental health consultation is a specific therapeutic tool. It engages the consultee as a collaborator in solving the problems created by the client, thus helping the consultee to learn to deal with specific behavior problems of the client. Consultation indirectly deals with the individual consultee's internal conflicts about such behavior. It is not psychotherapy. The consultee is always a collaborator and never a patient. Group consultation dealing with a client's behavior problem of common concern to most consultees extends the therapeutic impact of the consultant. It also demands the consultant's increased awareness of the group process.

The phases of the process need to be learned both didactically and in supervised experiences.

As a therapeutic modality, mental health consultation can be very effective and lead to greater competence of nonmental health professionals in working with clients' serious mental health problems which present themselves as behavior problems.

Evaluation of effectiveness is only now being attempted. However, early efforts indicate its effectiveness as a tool that should be in the armamentarium of most child psychiatrists.

REFERENCES

1. ALTMAN, M., "A Child Psychiatrist Steps into the Classroom: Report of a Training Experience," *Journal of the American Academy of Child Psychiatry*, 11:231–242, 1972.

2. ALTROCCHI, J., SPIELBERGER, C. D., and EISDORFER, C., "Mental Health Consultation with Groups," *Community Mental Health Journal*, 1:127–134, 1965.

3. BALSER, B. H., "Further Report on Experimental Evaluation of Mental Hygiene Techniques in School and Community," *American Journal of Psychiatry*, 113:733–739, 1957.

4. BERKEN, G., and EISDORFER, C., "Closed Ranks in Microcosm: Pitfalls of a Training Experience in Community Consultation," *Community Mental Health Journal*, 6:101–109, 1970.

5. BERKOWITZ, I. H., "Mental Health Consultation to School Personnel: Attitudes of School Administrators and Consultant Priorities," *Journal of School Health*, 15:348–352, 1970.

6. BERLIN, I. N., "An Effort to Update Mental Health Consultation Methods," in Plog, S. C. (Ed.), *Mental Health Consultation to the Schools: Directions for the Future*, pp. 23–44, Behavior Science Corporation, Los Angeles, 1973. (BASICO No. 645–02; Proceedings of a Conference at San Diego, March 15–16, 1973. NIMH Contract.)

7. ———, "Mental Health Consultation for School Social Workers: A Conceptual Model," *Community Mental Health Journal*, 5(4):280–288, 1969.

8. ———, "Transference and Countertransference in Community Psychiatry," *Archives of General Psychiatry*, 15:165–172, 1966.

9. ———, "Consultation and Special Education," in Philips, I. (Ed.), *Prevention and Treatment of Mental Retardation*, pp. 270–293, Basic Books, New York, 1966.

10. ———, "Mental Health Consultation in Schools: Who Does It and Why?" *Community Mental Health Journal*, 1:19–22, 1965.

11. ———, "Mental Health Consultation with a Juvenile Probation Department," *Crime and Delinquency*, 10:67–73, 1964.

12. ———, "Mental Health Consultation in Schools as

a Means of Communicating Mental Health Principles," *Journal of the American Academy of Child Psychiatry,* 1:671–679, 1962.

13. ———, "Psychiatric Consultation on the Antidelinquency Project," *California Journal of Secondary Education,* 35:198–202, 1960.

14. ———, "Some Learning Experiences as Psychiatric Consultant in the Schools," *Mental Hygiene,* 40:215–236, 1956.

15. BERNARD, V. W., "Roles and Functions of Child Psychiatrists in Social and Community Psychiatry: Implications for Training," *Journal of the American Academy of Child Psychiatry,* 3:165–176, 1964.

16. ———, "Education for Community Psychiatry in a University Medical Center," in Bellak, L. (Ed.), *Handbook of Community Psychiatry and Community Mental Health,* pp. 82–123, Grune & Stratton, New York, 1964.

17. ———, "Psychiatric Consultation in the Social Agency," *Child Welfare,* 33:3–8, 1954.

18. BINDMAN, A. J., "Mental Health Consultation Theory and Practice," *Journal of Consulting Psychology,* 23:473–482, 1959.

19. BLUMBERG, A., "A Selected Annotated Bibliography on the Consultation Relationship with Groups," *Journal of Social Issues,* 15:68–74, 1958.

20. ———, "A Nurse Consultant's Responsibility and Problems," *American Journal of Nursing,* 56:606–608, 1956.

21. BONKOWSKI, R. J., "Mental Health Consultation and Operation Head Start," *American Psychology,* 23: 769–773, 1963.

22. CAPLAN, G., *The Theory and Practice of Mental Health Consultation,* Basic Books, New York, 1970.

23. ———, "Problems of Training in Mental Health Consultation," in Goldston, S. (Ed.), *Concepts of Community Psychiatry: A Framework for Training,* pp. 91–108, NIMH, Bethesda, Md., 1965.

24. ———, "Types of Mental Health Consultation," *American Journal of Orthopsychiatry,* 33:480–481, 1963.

25. ———, *Concepts of Mental Health and Consultation,* U.S. Children's Bureau, Washington, D.C., 1959.

26. ———, "Mental Health Consultation in Schools," in Caplan, G. (Ed.), *The Elements of a Community Mental Health Program,* pp. 72–85, Milbank Memorial Fund, New York, 1956.

27. COLEMAN, J. V., "Mental Health Consultation to Agencies Protecting Family Life," in Caplan, G. (Ed.), *The Elements of a Community Mental Health Program,* pp. 69–76, Milbank Memorial Fund, New York, 1956.

28. ———, "Psychiatric Consultation in Casework Agencies," *American Journal of Orthopsychiatry,* 17:533–539, 1947.

29. EISDORFER, C., and BATTON, L., "The Mental Health Consultant as Seen by His Consultees," *Community Mental Health Journal,* 8:171–177, 1972.

30. EISENBERG, L., "An Evaluation of Psychiatric Consultation Service for a Puplic Agency," *American Journal of Public Health,* 48:742–749, 1958.

31. ELKINS, A. M., and PAPANEK, G. O., "Consultation with the Police: An Example of Community Psychiatry Practice," *American Journal of Psychiatry,* 123:531–535, 1966.

32. FARLEY, B. C., "Individual Mental Health Consultation with Public Health Nurses," in Rapoport, L. (Ed.), *Consultation in Social Work Practice,* pp. 99–116, National Association of Social Workers, New York, 1973.

33. FERGUSON, C. K., "Concerning the Nature of Human Systems and the Consultant's Role," *Journal of Applied Behavioral Sciences,* 4:179–194, 1968.

34. GIANOSCOL, A. J., "Psychiatry and the Juvenile Court: Patterns of Collaboration and the Use of Compulsory Psychotherapy," in Szurek, S. A., and Berlin, I. N. (Eds.), *The Antisocial Child: His Family and His Community,* vol. 4. (The Langley Porter Child Psychiatry

Series), pp. 149–159, Science and Behavior Books, Palo Alto, Calif., 1969.

35. GIBB, J. R., and LIPPITT, R., "Consulting with Groups and Organizations," *Journal of Social Issues, 15:* 1–74, 1959.

36. GILDEA, M. C., GLIDEWELL, J. C., and KONTAR, M. D., "The St. Louis School Mental Health Project: History and Evaluation," in Cowen, E. L., Gardner, E. A., and Zax, M. (Eds.), *Emergent Approaches to Mental Health Problems,* pp. 290–306, Appleton-Century-Crofts, New York, 1967.

37. GLIDEWELL, J. C., "The Entry Problem in Consultation," *Journal of Social Issues,* 15(2):51–59, 1959.

38. GOLDIN, G. D., "The Psychiatrist as Court Consultant: A Challenge to Community Psychiatry," *Community Mental Health Journal,* 3:396–398, 1967.

39. GORMAN, J. F., "Some Characteristics of Consultation," in Rapoport, L. (Ed.), *Consultation in the Practice of Social Work,* pp. 21–32, National Association of Social Workers, New York, 1963.

40. GRIFFITH, C., and LIBO, L., *Mental Health Consultants: Agents of Community Change,* Jossey-Bass, San Francisco, 1968.

41. HAYLETT, C. H., and RAPOPORT, L., "Mental Health Consultation," in Bellak, L. (Ed.), *Handbook of Community Psychiatry and Community Mental Health,* pp. 319–339, Grune & Stratton, New York, 1964.

42. HOLLISTER, W. G., "Some Administrative Aspects of Consultation," *American Journal of Orthopsychiatry,* 32:224–225, 1962.

43. HUME, P. B., "General Principles of Community Psychiatry," in Arieti, S. (Ed.), *American Handbook of Psychiatry,* vol. 3, pp. 515–541, Basic Books, New York, 1966.

44. ———, "Principles and Practice of Community Psychiatry," in Bellak, L. (Ed.), *Handbook of Community Psychiatry and Community Mental Health,* pp. 65–81, Grune & Stratton, New York, 1964.

45. ———, "Community Psychiatry, Social Psychiatry and Community Mental Health Work: Some Interprofessional Relationships in Psychiatry and Social Work," *American Journal of Psychiatry,* 121:340–343, 1964.

46. JARVIS, P. E., and NELSON, S. E., "Familiarization: A Vital Step in Mental Health Consultation," *Community Mental Health Journal,* 3:343–348, 1967.

47. KAZANJIAN, V., STEIN, S., and WINBERG, W. L., *An Introduction to Mental Health Consultation,* Public Health Monograph, vol. 69, U.S. Public Health Service, Washington, D.C., 1963.

48. KEVIN, D., "Use of Group Method in Consultation," in Rapoport, L. (Ed.), *Consultation in Social Work Practice,* pp. 69–84, National Association of Social Workers, New York, 1963.

49. KIDNEIGH, J., "The Philosophy of Administrative Process and the Role of the Consultant," *Public Health Nursing,* 43:474–478, 1951.

50. KLEIN, D. C., *Consultation Process as a Method of Improving Teaching,* Boston University Human Relations Research Report, no. 69, 1964.

51. KYSAR, J. E., "The Community Psychiatrist and Large Organizations," *Mental Hygiene,* 52:210–217, 1968.

52. LEININGER, M., "Some Anthropological Issues Related to Community Mental Health Programs in the United States," *Community Mental Health Journal,* 7(1): 24–28, 1971.

53. LIBO, L., "Multiple Functions for Psychologists in Community Consultation," *American Journal of Psychology,* 27:530–531, 1966.

54. LIPPITT, G. L., "Operational Climate and Individual Growth: The Consultative Process at Work," *Personnel Administration,* 23(5):12–19, 1960.

55. MACKEY, R. A., and HASSLER, F., "Group Consultation with School Personnel," *Mental Hygiene, 50:* 416–420, 1966.

56. MADDUX, J. F., "Consultation in Public Health," *American Journal of Public Health, 45:*1424–1430, 1955.

57. ———, "Psychiatric Consultation in a Public Welfare Agency," *American Journal of Orthopsychiatry, 20:* 754–764, 1950.

58. MANNINO, F. V., "Developing Consultation Relationships with Community Agents," *Mental Hygiene, 48:* 356–362, 1964.

59. MERCER, M. E., "Mental Health Consultation to Child Protecting Agencies," in Caplan, G. (Ed.), *The Elements of a Community Mental Health Program*, pp. 47–56, Milbank Memorial Fund, New York, 1956.

60. NEWMAN, R. G., *Psychological Consultation in the Schools: A Catalyst for Learning*, Basic Books, New York, 1967.

61. ———, REDL, F., and KITCHENER, H. L., *Technical Assistance in a Public School System*, Washington School of Psychiatry, Washington, D.C., 1962.

62. PARKER, B., "Some Observations on Psychiatric Consultation with Nursery School Teachers," *Mental Hygiene, 46:*559–566, 1962.

63. ———, "The Value of Supervision in Training Psychiatrists for Mental Health Consultation," *Mental Hygiene, 45:*94–100, 1961.

64. ———, *Psychiatric Consultation to Nonpsychiatric Professional Workers*, Public Health Monograph, no. 53, U.S. Public Health Service, Washington, D.C., 1958.

65. PERKINS, G. L., "Psychiatric Consultation in Residential Treatment: The Consultant's View," *American Journal of Orthopsychiatry, 28:*256–290, 1958.

66. RAPOPORT, L. (Ed.), *Consultation in Social Work Practice*, National Association of Social Workers, New York, 1963.

67. RIEMAN, D. W., "Group Mental Health Consultation with Public Health Nurses," in Rapoport, L. (Ed.), *Consultation in Social Work Practice*, pp. 85–98, National Association of Social Workers, New York, 1963.

68. ROBBINS, P. R., and SPENCER, E. C., "A Study of the Consultation Process," *Psychiatry, 31:*362–368, 1968.

69. ROGAWSKI, A. S., "Teaching Consultation Techniques in a Community Agency," in Werner, W., Mendel, W., and Solomon, P. (Eds.), *The Psychiatric Consultation*, pp. 65–85, Grune & Stratton, New York, 1968.

70. ROSENFIELD, J. M., and CAPLAN, G., "Techniques of Staff Consultation in an Immigrant Children's Organization in Israel," *American Journal of Orthopsychiatry, 24:* 42–62, 1954.

71. ROWITCH, J., "Group Consultation with School Personnel," *Hospital and Community Psychiatry, 19(8):* 45–50, 1968.

72. SARASON, S., et al., *Psychology in Community Settings*, John Wiley, New York, 1966.

73. SCHOWALTER, J., and SOLNIT, A., "Child Psychiatry Consultation in a General Hospital Emergency Room," *Journal of the American Academy of Child Psychiatry, 5:*534–551, 1966.

74. SHELDON, A., "On Consulting to New, Changing, or Innovative Organizations," *Community Mental Health Journal, 7(1):*62–71, 1971.

75. STRINGER, L. A., "Consultation: Some Expectations, Principles, and Skills," *Social Work, 6:*85–90, 1961.

76. SUSSELMAN, S., "Interrelationship of the Correctional Worker, the Offender, and the Legal Structure," in Szurek, S. A., and Berlin, I. N. (Eds.), *The Antisocial Child: His Family and His Community*, vol. 4 (The Langley Porter Series), pp. 134–148, Science and Behavior Books, Palo Alto, Calif., 1969.

77. VALENSTEIN, A. F., "Some Principles of Psychiatric Consultation," *Social Casework, 36:*253–256, 1955.

78. WODINSKY, A., "Psychiatric Consultation with Nurses on a Leukemia Service," *Mental Hygiene, 48:* 282–287, 1964.

22 / Hospital Consultation as Therapy

John E. Schowalter

Description

Hospital consultation is a form of therapeutic intervention. It usually takes place on a pediatric service, although some smaller general hospitals still group together patients of all ages. The very term consultation suggests that the child psychiatrist is not the patient's primary physician but that his evaluation, opinion, or treatment have been requested by the doctor.

Hospital consultation is usually directed toward individual patients and their families. It can also be used to provide resource knowledge to the pediatric staff and to develop hospital policy. Direct consultation with the child is most commonly requested to help patients cope with the fears and ravages associated with their physical illness or with its treatment. At times, however, children are admitted to a pediatric service for psychiatric illness, and, in these cases, the consultant may become the primary physician in much the same way that he would on an inpatient child psychiatry service.

Is his roles as a resource person for staff and as a developer of hospital policy, the consulting child psychiatrist strives to provide an emotionally therapeutic atmosphere in the hospital. This work falls more within the purview of primary prevention.

In describing the technique of hospital consultation, it is important to make clear at the outset that consultation and collaboration are not the same thing. It is just this difference that may be critically important in separating a successful intervention from an unsuccessful one.[19] A consultant has a job to do and he comes in and does it. In hospital consultation, there may be little contact between the child psychiatrist and those who requested his consultation. Communication is often chiefly through notes in the patient's chart. Collaboration, on the other hand, requires the mutual efforts of consultant and consultee working together in an ongoing process. Optimally, consultations should all be collaborations, but there is no such thing as "instant" collaboration. Collaboration is based on familiarity, mutual respect, empathy, and an adequate supportive structure. These factors require time and association. Usually a number of consultations are necessary before genuine collaboration between consultant and consultee develops.

Historical Review

Prior to the nineteen fifties infectious disease was such a constant peril to children in hospitals that the psychologic needs of pediatric patients were seldom considered. The goal was to get the child out alive before he or she contracted another, perhaps a worse, infection. In 1923, Fisk[3] advocated the psychologic utility of parental visits, but the fear of infections brought by visiting parents was overriding and lasted into the antibiotic era. For example, in 1954 in New York City, less than 25 percent of the pediatric beds were in hospitals where daily visiting was permitted.[7]

Of course, fear of infection was not the only argument against the presence of parents. Parents often asked unwelcomed questions and got in the way of hospital routine. Young children tended to cry disruptively following every parental visit, whereas after a few days of continuous separation from their parents, the children usually only whimpered softly. It has been shown that nurses and doctors tend to agree on who are the popular and unpopular patients, and the crying is an important factor in their reactions. The popular patients are those who work with the system and who make the staff feel effective in carrying out their hospital duties. The unpopular group are the criers and demanders who cause staff members to feel helpless and ineffective.[24]

EARLY CONSULTATION

Psychiatrists have long been viewed with suspicion or as superfluous by other physicians. Like parents, their presence on pediatric wards was generally regarded as more of a problem than a help. In 1931 Brenneman, a distinguished pediatrician of the day, wrote an article entitled "The Menace of Psychiatry."[2] In the course of protesting Watsonian behaviorism, he decried the use of "science" to undermine a more natural approach to pediatrics. He believed that too much emphasis was being placed on emotional upset and that so much talk about abnormal psychology would only cause more of it to occur.

In the middle decades of this century, a number of pediatricians came under the influence of Freudian psychology. This theory stresses that childhood events are crucial to the person's lifelong adjustment. Well-known pediatricians and child psychiatrists such as Frederick Allen, Edith Jackson, Leo Kanner, William Langford, David Levy, Grover Powers, Milton Senn, Hale Shirley, Benjamin Spock, and Henry Work lent their prestige to the exploration of children's reactions to illness and hospitalization. The importance of the mother-child dyad and the concept of signal anxiety in Freudian theory aided the movement to miniature adults who just get bigger, but that at different ages within childhood, there are specific goals and needs at each developmental level.

RECENT HISTORY

Spitz[23] reported on the differences in outcome between one group of infants cared for by their mothers and another group cared for by the rotating staff of an institution. This report had an immense effect on the pediatric community in this country. That psychologic care, apart from nutrition and proper hygiene, can make a life or death difference for babies was an impressive concept. That it was a psychoanalyst who demonstrated that this was true was difficult to ignore. Spitz's research findings had special impact because they were expressed physiologically rather than in ward roming-in and careful preparation of children for hospitalization. The epigenetic point of view helped clinicians realize that children are not terms of "complexes" or "psychic structures."

In 1950, a child analyst and a clinical psychologist reported on a rooming-in project for newborns and their mothers.[6] The practice of parents rooming-in with their hospitalized children has since grown to include pediatric patients of all ages.

One of the most important and seminal papers written in this field is Anna Freud's "The Role of Bodily Illness in the Mental Life of Children," published in 1952. Without jargon, the author discussed the developmental tasks compounded by illness and hospitalization. Utilizing the psychoanalytic framework, she depicted the defenses the child uses to cope with various specific stresses. She gave special emphasis to the problem of regression and its impact on development.

During the 1950s, child psychiatrists began to appear on hospital wards and to replace the psychologically oriented pediatricians as the chief purveyors of psychologic counsel to hospitalized children. Blom, Mason, Prugh, Solnit, and many others advocated the importance of parental involvement with their hospitalized children. They began to describe the pediatric patients' reactions

to specific problems such as surgery, mutilation, and approaching death. It was during the 1950s that child psychiatric involvement in hospital consultation reached its peak. This was the decade of the specificity theories in psychosomatic medicine, and optimism ran high that much that was physiologically abnormal could be modified or cured with the correct psychiatric treatment. Child psychiatrists, however, were not in the forefront of the specificity movement. They were neither as optimistic during the era nor as discouraged following its demise as were their colleagues in internal medicine.

In 1967, however, a paper by McDermott and Finch[10] was representative of a more recent point of view. Working with children who had ulcerative colitis, they found that psychotherapy led to emotional improvement in almost all the treated cases, but it neither improved the patients' bowel disease significantly nor reduced the eventual need for surgery.

In the early 1970s, a new concept began to exert an increasing influence on the care of children in hospitals. With the coming together of hospital social workers, child-care workers, and the pediatric nurse practitioner, a third group of care-givers has emerged. Unlike most pediatricians, the members of these disciplines are usually trained to be equally concerned with the psychologic and the physical well-being of the patient. Unlike most child psychiatrists, they are involved directly and daily with the totality of the patients' life in the hospital. Emma Plank was an early source of inspiration to this group in much the same way that Anna Freud kindled the interest of the child psychiatrists.

Theory and Rationale

PHYSICAL ILLNESS CAN CAUSE PSYCHOLOGIC PROBLEMS AND PSYCHOLOGIC PROBLEMS CAN CAUSE PHYSICAL ILLNESS

Physical and psychologic problems often go together. Although it is not always easy to separate out etiology, it is generally accepted that children hospitalized for physical illness are psychologically at risk and in need of attention.

Pless and Roghmann[15] reviewed the findings of the English National Survey of Health and Development, the Isle of Wight Survey, and the Rochester, New York, Child Health Survey. All three had studied the adjustment of chronically ill children and adolescents. Each of the surveys found more psychiatric illness and academic problems in the physically ill children than in the controls. The review concludes that the psychologic maladjustment of the young, chronically ill patient is probably due to his perception of himself as a person of diminished value and worth. In a study of a large number of adolescents, Rosenberg found that ". . . without exception each step down the self-esteem scale finds a larger proportion of respondents with many psychosomatic symptoms."[18]

Two other studies yield further evidence that hospitalized children frequently have psychosocial problems. In one study,[12] sick children of latency age hospitalized with nonpsychosomatic illnesses were compared to control children who were not ill. Examined were the psychologic and social factors occurring in the six months preceding the illness. It was found the ill children suffered more threatening, more frequent, and more recent changes in their environment than the controls, and that the families of the sick children were less well organized. The second study reported the results of a child psychiatrist's evaluation of all the patients on a pediatric ward.[25] While pediatricians requested psychiatric consultation in 11.3 percent of the cases, the child psychiatrist believed 63.7 percent actually warranted consultation. Since the rate of child psychopathology in the general population is usually given as from 6 to 12 percent, the authors concluded that a pediatric hospital must be considered a target area for mental health concern.

PSYCHOLOGIC FACTORS IN PHYSICAL ILLNESS

Although specificity theories are presently held in low esteem among many psychosomaticists, there is little question that psychologic factors may contribute to the formation or the severity of physical disability. With regard to nonpsychosomatic illnesses, it has been reported that children who became sick were more likely to have sustained recent real or threatened losses than children who remained well.[12] Children hospitalized with failure to thrive, weight disturbances, accidents, or sleep difficulties are especially likely to have had preexisting psychosocial problems. In addition, it can be shown that patients with asthma, diabetes, peptic ulcer, ulcerative colitis, and many other disorders have more somatic difficulties when they are emotionally upset.

PSYCHOLOGIC REACTIONS TO PHYSICAL DISORDER

In many ways one's body is oneself, psychologically as well as physically. Shame, anxiety, and fear are all common concomitants of illness and disability. Shame is especially prominent when newly formed developmental tasks are lost or, during adolescence, when strength, beauty, and independence are such important issues for self-esteem. Children are often plagued with separation, mutilation, and death fears which are accentuated whenever they are hospitalized. Younger patients are especially vulnerable, but older youths are affected as well. Langford[7] has described a number of variables which help determine how a child reacts to his disorder. These include his age; the status of his personality development at the time of the illness and hospitalization; his past ways of dealing with new and difficult situations; the nature of the physical symptoms; their severity and duration; the type of treatment required; the general meaning of illness to the child and the family; the child's relationships with physicians, nurses, and other hospital personnel; the hospital personnel's attitudes, feelings, and policies concerning children; and the preparation for hospitalization the child receives. It is obvious how complex such situations are. Prugh[16] has noted that it is often very hard to separate the child's reactions to his illness from his responses to hospitalization.

CRISIS INTERVENTION

As just noted, hospitalized children have a higher likelihood for psychopathology than average. They are additionally at risk because of their separation from their families and because of their fears of treatment and the outcome of their disorder. Two theories form the bases for much of direct hospital consultation and intervention: these are crisis intervention and signal anxiety.

Hospitalization of a child is always a family crisis. At such a moment, family members are often willing to look at and allow change in the family structure and the way they interact. When things are running relatively smoothly, their defense mechanisms, albeit maladaptive, are not perceived as requiring readjustment. They will not even allow discussion of change. Under the spur of the anxiety elicited by the hospitalization, however, families are often willing to face issues and make changes if it is explained they are necessary to help make the patient well and to have him return home. For example, there are two conditions in which change is very difficult without both hospitalization and alteration of family patterns. These conditions are failure to thrive in infants and anorexia nervosa in adolescents.

SIGNAL ANXIETY AND PREPARATION

Anxiety has a useful function; it serves as a signal. It warns of the need to avoid or prepare for a dangerous situation. When a patient is provided with an appropriate warning, he has the chance to prepare for and to respond to traumatic events in a more expedient manner. Probably the most important task a consulting child psychiatrist performs in a hospital is to aid the patient and the family to learn what is in store for them so they have an opportunity to prepare themselves. His task is to facilitate communication.

Preparation of parents and children for hospitalization and the attendant experiences is a prime example of the salutary use of signal anxiety. Clinicians know well that if children know something is going to happen to them, they can mobilize defense and other coping mechanisms to help them face it. The difficulty in preparation is not whether to do it, but how and when, how much information should be given the child and how long in advance. If the information or the time given are insufficient, the ego will be unable to prepare appropriate defenses. If the preparation is overly detailed or the child is informed too far in advance, either the knowledge is repressed or fantasies have time to develop and perhaps become overwhelming. In a classic study published in 1953, Prugh, and associates[17] compare one group of pediatric patients who received careful preparation for hospitalization and daily parental visiting, to another group of patients who, as was then customary, received no preparation and only a two-hour weekly visit. The children who received preparation and support had fewer adverse reactions to hospitalization, both at the time and at a three-month follow up. Three other variables were noted. Adjustment tended to be better in older rather than younger patients, in those children having better relationships with their mothers, and in children who were generally in better mental health before hospitalization.

Child psychiatrists can also use the principle of signal anxiety to help relieve children's physical pain and discomfort. If patients know what is going to happen and can express their fears to someone who can discuss them sensitively, they can prepare themselves psychologically for tests, surgery, sequelae, and so forth. Pain remains a rather poorly understood phenomenon, but it is clear that if proper preparation for a procedure can lessen anxiety, pain will also be decreased. Probably the most widely accepted current theory of pain perception is that of Melzack and Wall.[11] Their "spinal gate control" theory suggests that impulses from the afflicted peripheral area pass through the substantia gelatinosa "gate" in the dorsal horns of the spinal cord on their way to the brainstem. This "gate," however, can be modulated by fibers from the whole cortex, particularly the frontal area. These efferent fibers impinge on the brainstem reticular formation which in turn acts as a central biasing mechanism for the "gate." In this way, attention, anxiety, and past experience can play major roles in how much suffering a child feels.

Consultations are often requested for patients with severe or exaggerated pain. Since anxiety is a major potentiator of pain, the provision of insight, knowledge, or just the comforting of a caring person is frequently sufficient to lessen the patient's discomfort materially. With younger children, the most effective help is often given indirectly, through the parents. When the parents are comfortable with the hospitalization, the child is comforted. With older children and adolescents, discomfort is most often allayed by acquainting the patient as fully as possible with his condition, with what will happen to him, and how he can become actively involved in his own care.

Indications for Consultation

The indication for child psychiatry consultation to a hospital is that it is there and it houses children. The children are taken from their homes and families at the very time when their bodies are not functioning well. Psychologically, their plight makes them vulnerable to begin with and, as has already been noted, they tend to bring with them a degree of psychopathology much greater than that of the general population.

The child psychiatrist however, does not determine when and where he is needed; he must wait to be sought out by a pediatrician who has a problem. Optimally, the child psychiatrist should be sufficiently immersed in the life of the ward to be himself cognizant of needs for consultation.

DIRECT INPATIENT CONSULTATION

In most pediatric inpatient services, consultation requests for direct patient and parent contact fall into five categories.

1. The largest category includes those patients whose physical disorders and hospitalization burden them with unusual psychologic stress. These most frequently requested consultations seek to help the patient to cope with an overwhelming situation. The work here is often anticipatory; it seeks to prepare the patient to face traumatic events. It typically involves patients facing disfiguring or especially hazardous surgery, those in frames or total body casts, and those with chronic, debilitating, or fatal illnesses.
2. A second group of patients have illnesses triggered or intensified by emotional upset. Their illnesses include the "psychosomatic" disorders. With this group, the consultant strives to assess the quality of the patient's emotional makeup and the degree to which it determines his discomfort.
3. A third group of patients referred for consultation consists of those who were admitted with a diagnosis of organic disease but whose symptoms are found to be secondary to depressive or anxiety neuroses, conversion reactions, or malingering. Here the child psychiatrist's greatest contribution may be his differential diagnosis.
4. A fourth category represents children with primary psychiatric disorders. Some pediatric departments are comfortable with, and able to care for, children with psychotic, suicidal, or severely neurotic behavior. In these cases, the consulting child psychiatrist may become the primary physician for the patient.
5. A final category, usually rather small, involves patients whose home situations are so disorganized or unsatisfactory that the consultation request is for help in determining how long the child should remain hospitalized and how best to think about the discharge environment. In some cases, the diagnosis and optimum treatment plan become clear only when the child is removed from his environment and observed around the clock. Patients for whom this may be especially important include those with failure to thrive, cases of suspected child abuse, diabetes, asthma, and anorexia nervosa.

OUTPATIENT CONSULTATION

Many patients come to pediatric outpatient departments with school learning problems, developmental disorders, enuresis, feeding problems, sleep difficulties, and a variety of other disorders caused or aggravated by psychosocial circumstances. For an efficient approach to diagnosing and treating these children, a team of experts is necessary. This should include a pediatrician, plus colleagues from one or more of the fields of child psychiatry, social work, nursing, and psychology. The diverse skills of the team members and the empathy each participant shares with the others makes this an ideal unit to decide issues of referral and service delivery. However, it also carries with it the inherent hazards of team interaction.

EMERGENCY ROOM CONSULTATION

Another important site for child psychiatry consultation is the emergency room.[21] Here, adolescent suicide attempts, drug problems, and psychoses usually dominate the emergencies. As with other consultations and, perhaps here in particular, an ability to work with pediatricians in such a way that neither consultant nor consultee feels let down, or put upon, is crucial. Every response to an emergency call, especially during the night or during a busy time of day, is inherently a fragile situation for everyone. In this regard, it is helpful if the pediatrician has done a reasonable evaluation of the situation before calling the consultant, and the child psychiatrist is gracious in his availability (see chapter 32).

STAFF CONSULTATION

Another reason for consultation is to help with staff problems. Staff consultations are usually requested only after the consultant has proved himself in direct patient care. The request may include teaching inservice training classes or helping with devising and facilitating policy (for example, on preparing children for hospitalization or for procedures or surgery). Since he is both a physician and a person especially interested in the child's reaction to care, the child psychiatrist can often act as mediator when pediatricians, nurses, social workers, child-care staff, or others disagree.

Complications and Disadvantages

One disadvantage of hospital consultation is that the child psychiatrist is often working in an environment in which he is an alien. Aside from the exceptional pediatric ward with a long tradition of collaboration, the consultees may show little respect for psychiatry; they ask for consultations when they are driven to it, for example, after every etiology except the psychologic has been ruled out. When the latter occurs, it is often impossible to convince patient and parents that a belated psychiatric diagnosis following thousands of dollars of medical tests is not a diagnosis of convenience.

A real but subtle factor is the difference in temperament between pediatricians and child psychiatrists. Some complications common in hospital consultation are the result of this difference. Pediatricians often demand answers in hours or, at most, days, while child psychiatrists may be accustomed to evaluations that take weeks or months. Successful collaboration demands that the pediatrician temper his impatience and the child psychiatrist his comtemplation. It is also important that the child psychiatrist report his findings directly and succinctly to the consultee. Cryptic notes in the chart, jargon, impractical musings, and impossible recommendations are not long endured.

Another disadvantage of hospital consultation is that hospitals are usually run for the staff and not the patients. Although hospitals often provide well for the physical needs of patients, their policies just as often oppose psychologic needs. For the child psychiatrist this means that not only must he deal with patient and family resistances, but, often enough, with staff resistances as well. Recommendations for greater involvement of patients in decisions about their own care and for greater participation in it; for more parental performance in areas that have traditionally been nursing tasks; for greater honesty to patients who have serious or fatal conditions; and for psychologic, as well as physiologic, considerations to be weighed prior to procedures and surgery—any of these may be experienced by staff as provocative and may tend to give rise to resistance.

Contraindications

Two types of patients should not be seen for hospital consultation.

The first is the child who could be evaluated as effectively, or more effectively, outside of the hospital, and who is being kept in the hospital longer just for the consultation. Especially for younger children, separation from the home is a potentially pathogenic event; it is paradoxical to evaluate a child's emotional health while jeopardizing it.

The second is the child for whom the consultation is requested to answer general developmental or emotional questions, but who is at the time upset by his illness or hospitalization. Since the evaluation usually reflects the present turmoil at the expense of general issues, it will not serve its purpose in these cases and must usually be repeated later. Under such circumstances, parsimony, plus the wish not to cause unnecessary expense and bother, dictates that the consultation be delayed until the period of acute stress has passed.

Technique Involved

INDIRECT CONSULTATIONS

Indirect consultation seeks to improve the emotional climate for patients in the hospital. It involves the provision of resource knowledge to the ward staff and help in the development of ward or clinic policy. Ultimately such interventions facilitate direct consultations.

To be a resource person for issues of child development, group dynamics, crisis intervention, and policy formation, the child psychiatrist should be trusted and considered an "insider," one of the staff. Hospitals are stratified communities and the credibility given an insider is much greater than that given to anyone on the outside. Intermittent presence on an ad hoc basis is seldom satisfactory; ultimately the child psychiatrist find that his availability and the use made of him are directly proportional. If the consultant's ideas are good, they will be applauded, but if he is considered an outsider, they will probably not be accepted in practice. One reason why so many sound psychologic principles show up in print but not in pediatric practice is that the researchers were in fact just that, researchers. They did not continue to give service and to oversee the program following collection of the research findings. When collaboration stops, so do principles. This is striking in the area of preparation of pediatric patients for hospitalization and procedures. Numerous studies emphasize the need for sensible preparation, but few places actually provide it. It is important to add that collaboration with pediatricians is essential for hierarchical acceptance; but collaboration with nurses, social workers, and child-care workers often proves to have more impact on the patient's daily care.

Regular, weekly staff meetings are useful in promoting psychological mindedness. They provide a forum at which to discuss the implications of patients' conditions and to review patient-staff and intrastaff relationships. A proven procedure is for the house-staff to present a problem to the consultant. In the first of such meetings, only "pure" psychiatric cases tend to be discussed. If the meetings prove successful, cases of patients with psychosomatic illnesses or with psychosocial difficulties begin to be presented, or the cases of youngsters who are having difficulties adjusting to their physical disorders or treatment are examined. Only much much later are issues in staff interaction or ward personnel problems likely to be raised.

Although it is often difficult, pediatric house officers should be persuaded to attend these meetings. The easiest way to achieve this is for a child psychiatrist to colead the meeting. The other leader should be a respected pediatrician whose presence legitimizes the activity and provides a valuable role model. In addition, if the child psychiatrist makes medical ward rounds regularly, he is in turn more likely to be assured of attendance at his meetings. With or without a coleader, the consultant is often looked to as the source of answers. However, a good staff meeting will evolve into one where participation by all the permanent ward staff increases. The formation and revision of general policy can then be discussed with the anticipation that some action will be taken.

While the general staff meeting may include pediatricians, nurses, child-care workers, social workers, chaplains, teachers, dietician, aides, ward secretary, and other personnel, nonetheless a separate weekly meeting, chiefly for the nurses, is often indicated. As with the general staff meeting, this should be held regularly and not on an ad hoc basis. Nurses are often the most permanent professional staff on a hospital floor. Inevitably their support is crucial not only for good physical care but for perpetuating a philosophy advocating the importance of psychologic issues. Topics raised at a nurses' meeting tend to deal more with direct patient care and personnel problems than with theoretic or academic discussions. Immobilized patients, children in great pain, the fatally ill child, and the uncooperative patient are commonly discussed. So are raises, promotions, firings, jealousies, and authority conflicts. Since the supervision of volunteers is often best done by nurses, problems with volunteers may also come up.

Within an outpatient department, staff meetings can focus on the large percentage of children whose chief complaints are psycho-social, and on the frustration most staffs experience in helping these patients. The technique here is not only to give treatment advice but to help the staff feel relatively comfortable facing problems they were often not well trained to deal with. Among the practical subjects which can be discussed are methods of alerting staff to appropriate community resources and the bases for making sound referrals.

DIRECT CONSULTATION

In direct consultation to an individual patient, the child psychiatrist must first know what is being asked of him and why. This is often the most important, and it may be the most difficult step in the whole procedure. Sometimes the question is inappropriate; at other times no question at all is actually formulated. When consultations are unsuccessful, it is all too often because the consultant answers, or tries to answer, questions he has formulated himself rather than those that come from the consultee. Even when the consultant is correct in focusing chiefly on something other than what was asked, he must be aware of what he does and be able to explain it.

It is also important that before beginning a consultation the consultant makes sure that the patient and parents are prepared for it. And it is important to know what went into their preparation, of what it consisted. Pediatricians are often reluctant to tell people that they have asked a psychiatrist for help. They may use a euphemism for the consultant's specialty or not mention it at all. While some parents and children would rather think of the consultant as "a doctor who is interested in children's feelings" or "a talking doctor," it is simpler, more honest, and avoids later confusion and embarrassment to have the child psychiatrist known to be a child psychiatrist from the beginning. Feelings, be they distorted or valid, are usually best faced from the start. Subterfuge and sugar coating often convey accurately the biases of the referring doctor, he projects these onto child and parents, he assumes they feel as he does, he talks to them in such terms, and presently it all becomes a self-fulfilling prophecy. On the other hand, sometimes the consultee uses referral to the child psychiatrist as a threat or a punishment for patients or parents who are not responding the way they are supposed to. When this occurs, it must be recognized and discussed with the consultee.

Although most consultation requests are written, it is wise in any case to talk with the consultee before beginning. This allows the consultant to ask questions as well as to pick up nuances of anxiety, frustration, anger, and other affects. These, in turn, will alert him to expectations or concerns that are often omitted from the written page. The consultant should know what the preparation for his visit was and should inform the consultee what he believes he can do in the situation.

While most consultants read the chart more or less thoroughly prior to the first interview, nurses' notes are usually underused. Good nursing notes provide observations that are often available nowhere else.

In practice, the form of the actual evaluation is usually not much different from what the psychiatrist does habitually. However, there are some differences. With the hospitalized child, it is usual to take a more thorough medical history and to conduct a special scrutiny for signs and symptoms indicating organicity or conversion reactions. At the same time, disability and debilitation sometimes interfere with the patient's ability to communicate through speech and play.

Often enough, a very real difficulty is to find a place private enough to conduct an interview. The availability of such a facility should be part of the agreement to offer consultation services. Whether or not the child psychiatrist consults in a white coat or street clothes is a matter of local option and probably of minor importance as long as the consultant is comfortable and the decision does not cause animosity among coworkers. Although some young patients are automatically afraid of white, it is the uniform of the hospital. When asked why they do not wear a white coat as other physicians do, child psychiatrists usually first answer that it would make the child uneasy. Their second answer is that they would be uneasy.

The first interview may be with the patient, with the parents, or with both. With young children, the parents are often seen first, both to obtain historical information and because the therapeutic work may be carried out chiefly through the parents (see chapters 8 and 9). With adolescents, the work often begins with an interview with the patient, although family therapy may be utilized in this age range. Recent work with anorexia nervosa has emphasized the latter approach.[9] It is obvious that the determining factor may well be the individual consultant's preferred style of interviewing. He will usually do what he is most comfortable doing.

Once the evaluation has been completed, the conclusions and recommendations must be communicated. Although approaches differ, it seems important to speak to the consultee in addition to writing a note in the chart. The latter proves a problem for some child psychiatrists who err in being either too inclusive or too exclusive. Hospital charts are available to many persons, and intimate details should be avoided in the write-up; however, the note should not be so short and cryptic that nothing is conveyed but tantalizing hints. A brief history, a complete mental status examination, specific findings, conclusions, and rec-

ommendations will usually suffice. Some consultants privately keep a record of data too personal for the hospital chart. The consultant should also share his impressions with nurses and other staff who can use it to the patient's advantage.

Usually the consultant will discuss his findings directly with the patient and family. Whether he does this alone, jointly with the pediatrician, or whether the pediatrician is the primary interpreter of the findings will depend on the circumstances of the particular situation. A major guideline here is which approach will allow this patient and family to best take advantage of the recommendations. Some families can accept things from a trusted pediatrician that they could not from an unknown child psychiatrist. On the other hand, some pediatricians resist involvement in matters psychologic and routinely turn over complete psychiatric care to the consultant.

Preparation of Patient and Parent

Preparation is important if a consultation is to "work." The relationship between consultant and consultee and between consultee and family both bear materially on the outcome. In preparing the patient and parents for the consultant's visit, the who, why, what, and when are fundamental. However, the tone conveyed will probably prove to be still more important. When the referring physician has faith in the consultant and the family has faith in their doctor, preparation is usually optimal. When there are doubts or ill feelings between the parties, preparation is of dubious value.

One of the possibilities to emerge from consultation may be preparation for further psychiatric involvement. As a rule this preparation is for further evaluation and treatment for the child and/or family when the patient leaves the hospital. The pediatrician's support is usually crucial for the acceptance of such a recommendation.

Economic Implications

The fact that consultations are carried out in the hospital allows for the possibility of third-party payment. For many families, this is often not available on an outpatient basis. Advantages and disadvantages result.

An obvious advantage is that consultation is available to all hospitalized patients, regardless of social class. This means that certain patients who could either not afford or would not find their way into an outpatient system can receive psychiatric consultation.

A common disadvantage is that children who do not need pediatric hospitalization or removal from the family are admitted solely so that insurance can pay for the consultation. Aside from the ethical issues involved, the disadvantage of the trauma the patient sustains through separation from the family almost always outweighs the value of the consultation.

Support Activities

In modern hospitals, there are both an increasing abundance of and an increasing sophistication in support services. Many nurses are obtaining advanced training in the psychologic aspects of patient care, and the burgeoning of the profession of child-care worker has been phenomenal. Social workers and chaplains are becoming more and more frequent on pediatric wards. Specially trained psychologists offer a great service in determining organic brain damage and, especially in the out patient clinic, in helping to sort out the various types of learning disabilities.

For a given patient, there may be specific areas of conflict and anxiety assigned to these professionals for individual work. However, they also help in the more general realm of facilitating many patients' understanding and control of their situation. Activities and information are most useful in combating the passivity and regression so common to "being in the hospital." During the past decade there have been widespread attempts to have the hospitalized child actively enact and reenact what has already occurred and what is yet to happen to him. Doll play and role modeling are among the modalities most commonly employed. Books by Plank[14] and by Petrillo and Sanger[13] offer detailed advice on how child-care workers and others can use play therapy, stories, classes, drawing, and so forth to aid patients' adjustment. Becker,[1] however, has voiced a warning that enthusiasm sometimes leads workers to "prepare" every child in the same way; there are some individual children for whom such role play may be contraindicated.

Frequency of Consultation Visits

This is extremely variable, but evaluations can often be accomplished in two to four interviews. It is sometimes very difficult and time-consuming to reach all the members of the family who should be seen, and an important factor is that the consultant is often on an hourly schedule, while ward work is not. Another variable is the amount of support available. In some hospitals, social workers, child-care workers, nurses. teachers, and others are available to carry out many missions which, in other settings, the child psychiatrist must perform himself. A third and often crucial variable is the success in involving the parents. Parental attitudes toward hospitalization and their child's condition may have the greatest influences on his adjustment. When the consultant is able to gain cooperation from mother and father both, the consultation is much more likely to be successful.

Follow Up

It usually helps if the consultant continues to show interest as long as a child remains hospitalized. Continuity of care is a concept too seldom honored in most hospitals. The frequency of contact depends on the seriousness of the psychopathology; it may range from daily psychotherapy to occasional "social" visits.

Follow up after discharge depends very much on local conditions. Some visiting nurse organizations are adept at helping mothers improve their parenting. A number of pediatric outpatient departments have pediatricians, social workers, nurses, psychologists, and others who, with or without continued psychiatric consultation, can follow children with psychosomatic and somatopsychic difficulties. A few pediatric outpatient departments have a pediatric psychiatry specialty clinic in which continued psychotherapy is available. Most often, however, children suffering from primarily psychiatric disorders must be referred to child guidance clinics. In larger communities there are always child psychiatrists and pediatricians in private practice who have become known for their expertise in treating children with combined psychiatric and somatic disorders. Unfortunately, once the child is discharged, third-party payment usually ceases and, as documented by Harrison and his colleagues,[5] this fact often blocks the child of poorer parents from obtaining the intensive psychotherapy he needs.

Relationships to Other Modalities of Treatment

In considering outpatient consultation, a common question to be answered is whether the child is better served by the family pediatrician or by a child psychiatrist. The average general pediatrician's longitudinal knowledge of the families he treats and the trust which they have in him provide him with the background required to care for a majority of the adjustment problems of childhood. To do so, however, he has to be willing to take the time, to charge for it appropriately, and to maintain a continuing relationship with a child psychiatrist with whom he can collaborate whenever necessary.[22]

With some inpatient consultations, a common question is whether the child should be transferred to an inpatient psychiatric facility. Patients who are dangerous to themselves or others, who greatly disrupt the physically ill patients around them, or who require a total therapeutic environment often fall into this category. However, in many communities, the rule that calls for selecting the least detrimental alternative dictates that the pediatric ward offers care superior to that in the psychiatric institutions which are available. This is especially true for younger children. When this is the case, it is the responsibility of the child psychiatric community to offer the pediatric staff the degree of support necessary for them to tolerate all but the most difficult patients.

Outcome

By now, the salutary results of taking into regard the psychologic life of the sick and hospitalized child has been compellingly demonstrated in many studies. A sampling of this diversity ranges from the study of Prugh and associates on total patient support,[17] to preparation for specific surgery,[26] to consultations for infants,[8] to consultations with adolescents,[19] to work with groups,[20] to work focusing on family therapy and behavior modification.[9]

The tragedy in hospital consultation is that so much more is known than is used. Psychiatry has much to offer the hospitalized child, but these benefits can be delivered to the patients only when pediatric staff and child psychiatrists collaborate.

REFERENCES

1. BECKER, R. D., "Therapeutic Approaches to Psychopathological Reactions to Hospitalization," *International Journal of Child Psychotherapy*, 1(2):65–97, 1972.
2. BRENNEMAN, J., "The Menace of Psychiatry," *American Journal of Diseases of Children*, 42(2):376–402, 1931.
3. FISK, A., "Psychology," *American Journal of Nursing*, 23(12):1011–1014, 1923.
4. FREUD, A., "The Role of Bodily Illness in the Mental Life of Children," in Eissler, R. S., et al. (Eds.), *The Psychoanalytic Study of the Child*, vol. 7, pp. 69–81, International Universities Press, New York, 1952.
5. HARRISON, S. I., et al., "Social Class and Mental Illness in Children: Choice of Treatment," *Archives of General Psychiatry*, 13(5):411–417, 1965.
6. JACKSON, E. B., and KLATSKIN, E. H., "Rooming-In Research Project: Development of Methodology of Parent-Child Relationship Study in a Clinical Setting," in Eissler, R. S., et al. (Eds.), *The Psychoanalytic Study of the Child*, vol. 5, pp. 236–274, International Universities Press, New York, 1950.
7. LANGFORD, W. S., "The Child in the Pediatric Hospital: Adaptation to Illness and Hospitalization," *American Journal of Orthopsychiatry*, 31(4):667–684, 1961.
8. LEONARD, M. F., RHYMES, J. P., and SOLNIT, A. J., "Failure to Thrive in Infants," *American Journal of Diseases of Children*, 3(6):600–612, 1966.
9. LIEBMAN, R., MINUCHIN, S., and BAKER, L., "An Integrated Treatment Program for Anorexia Nervosa," *American Journal of Psychiatry*, 131(4):432–436, 1974.
10. McDERMOTT, J. F., and FINCH, S. M., "Ulcerative Colitis in Children: Reassessment of a Dilemma," *Journal of the American Academy of Child Psychiatry*, 6(3):512–525, 1967.
11. MELZACK, R., and WALL, P. D., "Pain Mechanisms: A New Theory," *Science*, CL(Nov. 19):971–979, 1965.
12. MUTTER, A. Z., and SCHLIEFER, M. J., "The Role of Psychological and Social Factors in the Onset of Somatic Illness in Children," *Psychosomatic Medicine*, 28(4):333–343, 1966.
13. PETRILLO, M., and SANGER, S., *Emotional Care of Hospitalized Children: An Environmental Approach*, Lippincott, Philadelphia, 1972.
14. PLANK, E. M., *Working with Children in Hospitals*, 2nd ed., The Press of Case Western Reserve University, Cleveland, 1971.
15. PLESS, I. B., and ROGHMANN, R. J., "Chronic Illness and Its Consequences: Observations Based on Three Epidemiologic Surveys," *Journal of Pediatrics*, 79(3):351–359, 1971.
16. PRUGH, D. G., "Investigations Dealing with the Reactions of Children and Families to Hospitalization and Illness: Problems and Potentialities," in Caplan, G. (Ed.), *Emotional Problems of Early Childhood*, pp. 307–321, Basic Books, New York, 1955.
17. ———, et al., "A Study of the Emotional Reactions of Children and Families to Hospitalization and Illness," *American Journal of Orthopsychiatry*, 23(1):70–106, 1953.
18. ROSENBERG, M., *Society and the Adolescent Self-Image*, Princeton University Press, Princeton, 1965.
19. SCHOWALTER, J. E., "The Utilization of Child Psychiatry on a Pediatric Adolescent Ward," *Journal of the American Academy of Child Psychiatry*, 10(4):684–699, 1971.

20. ——, and LORD, R. D., "Utilization of Patient Meetings on an Adolescent Ward," *Psychiatry in Medicine, 1(3):*197–206, 1970.

21. ——, and SOLNIT, A. J., "Child Psychiatry Consultation in a General Hospital Emergency Room," *Journal of the American Academy of Child Psychiatry, 5(3):*534–551, 1966.

22. SOLNIT, A. J., "Eight Pediatricians and a Child Psychiatrist," in Bibring, G. (Ed.), *The Teaching of Dynamic Psychiatry*, pp. 158–174, International Universities Press, New York, 1968.

23. SPITZ, R. A., "Hospitalism. An Inquiry into the Genesis of Psychiatric Conditions in Early Childhood," in Eissler, R. S., et al. (Eds.), *The Psychoanalytic Study of the Child*, vol. 1, pp. 53–74, International Universities Press, New York, 1945.

24. SPITZER, S. P., and SOBOL, R., "Preferences for Patients and Patient Behavior," *Nursing Research, 11(4):* 233–235, 1962.

25. STOCKING, M., et al., "Psychopathology in the Pediatric Hospital: Implications for the Pediatrician," *American Journal of Public Health, 62(4):*551–556, 1972.

26. VAUGHN, G. F., "Children in Hospital," *Lancet, 272(June 1):*1117–1120, 1957.

PART F
Biological Therapies

23 / Psychopharmacology

Magda Campbell

> If we first knew where we are and wither
> we are tending, we could then better judge
> what to do and how to do it.
>
> ABRAHAM LINCOLN

Psychotropic agents are chemical substances which modify the functioning of the central nervous system. Biological interventions in the course of mental health work for children and adolescents are today largely confined to the use of such substances.

History of Psychopharmacology

Drugs which alter behavior have been in use for more than four thousand years. The Old Testament reports on the effects of alcohol, which were already known in ancient Egypt. Marijuana and opium were known long before the discovery of more "modern" drugs. However, pharmacology can be dated back only to the early nineteenth century, and the first utilization of behavioral pharmacology by man can be traced to the end of the same century, to Freud's (1884–1887) experiments on the action of cocaine and to Kraepelin's (1882) systematic investigations of the subjective effects of tea, alcohol, bromides, formaldehyde, and ether on mental processes.

The early use of drugs was intended mainly to sedate agitated hospitalized patients. But all such agents involved risks. Even the barbiturates, one of the first major psychoactive drugs synthesized, had untoward effects on perception and mental processes and often resulted in addiction. With the advent of chlorpromazine,[90] the therapeutic use of drugs in treating psychiatric disorders of adults underwent a revolution. Many other neuroleptics have since developed along with the anxiolytics and lithium.

In children, the more systematic use of psychoactive agents began in the 1930s with the administration of amphetamines to a variety of children with behavior disorders.[21, 28, 29] Since these early trials, the superiority of stimulants over placebo in the treatment of hyperactive (MBD) children has been confirmed. Hypnotics and anticonvulsants had been widely used, particularly in the management of disorders accompanied by excitement and agitation. The discovery of chlorpromazine created hope that with its antipsychotic effect, it would arrest or decrease the psychotic process. The sick child who was initially in a state of withdrawal and/or apathy would then become less resistant to educational and other therapies. It was anticipated, too, that this substance would decrease anxiety, hyperactivity, or aggressiveness, and permit the child to develop more adaptive and socially acceptable patterns of behavior which would facilitate learning. Unfortunately, those hopes were not fulfilled. Indeed, in recent years, the use of drugs for the treatment of children with behavioral disorders (particularly for those suffering mental retardation*) has come under attack. Although many of the accusations are emotional, extreme, and not constructive, they may produce a useful response: the researchers and clinicians may (1) reassess or redefine the role of drugs in child psychiatry (in various diagnostic categories); (2) conduct long-term follow-up studies; (3) employ a more individualized dose schedule; and (4) better inform themselves about both, behavioral and other possible untoward effects of the few drugs that may be indicated, and which they may wish to use.

Rationale That Underlies Psychopharmacology

It is likely that the earliest rationale for the use of psychoactive drugs in the treatment of abnormal behavior are Thudicum's[296] concept of schizophrenia as a behavioral manifestation of body poisons acting upon the brain, and Pavlov's[219] assumption that chemical receptors of the nervous system must underlly normal functions (receptor theory). In any case, it is evident that the biochemical alterations caused by drugs at the cellular level affect organ functions and result in both physiologic and behavioral changes. Localization of the site of systemic drug actions (by the use of surgical procedures, electrical stimulation, or chemical blocking agents) has shed light on, and even brought some insight into, behavioral pharmacology.[264] The psychoactive agents have

also yielded some insights into the biochemical bases of mental illness, such as the role of biogenic amines.[157, 173, 307] Biochemical and pharmacologic approaches to schizophrenia in adults were discussed by Kety.[173] The hypothesis that adult schizophrenia, or at least some types of schizophrenia, is due to a functional over-activity of dopaminergic neurons was reviewed by Meltzer and Stahl;[203] the neuroleptics currently in use in the treatment of these patients are believed to act by blocking dopamine. There have also been a number of attempts to alter biochemical parameters. To this end, in treating psychotic children, pharmacologic approaches have been employed in relation with behavioral phenomena.[30, 31, 46, 241]

It is believed today that the hyperkinetic child with MBD syndrome suffers from an attentional deficit (DSM III); there is supportive evidence that a subgroup of these children have low central nervous system arousal and inhibitory levels. The beneficial effects of stimulants on behavioral symptoms and on cognition are viewed as correcting these abnormal thresholds of arousal and inhibition.[254]

In the present state of knowledge, no specific drug is available for the reliable treatment of any of the diagnostic categories of early life, although in the cases of many MBD children the stimulants are effective. Even in treating adults, except for the specific efficacy of lithium in the treatment of the manic phase of manic-depressive illness, currently used drugs are most effective in reducing "target symptoms"[132] such as insomnia, hyperactivity, impulsivity, irritability, disorganized behavior, psychotic thought disorder, and certain types of aggressivity. Thus, aiming drug treatment at target functions of disturbed behavior would perhaps be a more effective approach,[164, 166] and there is some evidence that supports this view.[74, 254, 256] Until clinical distinctions are correlated with or improved by biochemical, neuroendocrine, and physiological criteria, psychopharmacological treatment of children will remain on an empirical basis.

Methodology of Drug Studies

In behavioral disorders of childhood and adolescence, the unsatisfactory state of diagnostic classification makes it particularly difficult to obtain an accurate assessment of therapeutic drug effects. Such factors as the natural history of the illness,

---

* Independent surveys disclose that almost 50 percent of the institutionalized mentally retarded are receiving psychotropic drugs; dosages are high and duration of medication excessively long. The children receive from two to eight drugs at the same time; there is little evidence of drug monitoring and few drug holidays. Moreover, the use of sedative levels of phenothiazines probably suppresses cognitive-learning functions of critical importance[189, 191] (Lipman, personal communication).

its severity and duration; the child's chronological age, maturation, development, IQ; and parental influences are all variables which can influence the outcome of treatment.[43, 54, 116, 121] If research trials are prolonged, then changes due to drug administration can be confounded with maturation. Milieu treatment and other environmental manipulations can also act to obscure or confound drug effects, or can interact with drugs.[43, 61, 288] Actually, particularly where the psychiatric disturbances are less severe and the psychoactive agents less potent, these environmental variables are frequently more powerful influences than are the drugs.

In assessing the therapeutic efficacy of a given drug, the first step is usually a *single-dose study*. This may be the initial administration of the drug to a child (after sufficient knowledge about safety and efficacy has been accumulated in work with adults). At this point, after enough washout, a few patients are studied in depth. Behavioral evaluations, blood pressure, pulse rate, eating and sleep patterns, and other measurements are carried out before the administration of each dose, and then at regular intervals.

After the safety and efficacy of the single dose have been established to the investigator's satisfaction, the next stage of investigation is frequently an *open study*. On the basis of the single-dose study, the dosage is increased until a therapeutic response, or untoward effects, are observed. If the adverse effects, including behavioral toxicity, are significant, further increases may be precluded. These careful observations provide information on the spectrum of drug activity, effective therapeutic dosage range, dosage producing untoward effects, therapeutic margin, and the duration of drug effect (both therapeutic and toxic). The observations serve as the basis for experimental hypotheses which may then be tested.

If the drug shows therapeutic effectiveness, a more formal *clinical trial* is usually conducted. Patients are randomly assigned to investigational drug or placebo groups; or, to standard drug, investigational drug, and placebo groups. The purpose of this procedure is to reduce bias. Even with *randomization,* the groups may not be alike; only very large samples give balanced groups. It is desirable to stratify the sample for age, sex, IQ, or chronicity[190] and randomize theralter. Even though patients are assigned randomly to treatment groups, on baseline there may be differences among the groups which need adjustment.[209] As an alternative to randomization, *matching* is often employed. It is not desirable, however,

because it is not certain whether matched variables are the important ones. Some investigators prefer a *crossover* design in which each subject serves as his own control in every treatment condition. This method is particularly appropriate in chronic diseases in which, upon discontinuation of the drug treatment, the patients will tend to revert to their baseline condition. In crossover, in the course of statistical analysis of the results, the order of drug administration must be considered. However, in a lengthy study of this type, maturation itself or concurrent psychosocial treatment may be responsible for clinical change.

Chassan[60] recommended a *single subject design,* or the intensive evaluation of each subject. Since individual patients often show different responses, objections have been raised to the application of group statistics within such a design; therefore, others proposed combining the intensive evaluation of each subject with an extensive evaluation across patients.[297]

Controlled studies are usually carried out under *double-blind conditions*. Medication is given and both patients and physician are unaware of what it is; drug(s) and placebo are matched in color, shape, size, and even taste so that they appear identical. Such a procedure also reduces bias.

The assessment of baseline behavior is accomplished in the course of research by the use of psychiatric rating scales; in clinical work, on the other hand, it is achieved by the identification of target symptoms by systematic clinical observations and judgments. Among the prerequisites for the evaluation of drug efficacy are: the assessment of baseline behavior, the development of a behavioral profile, the collection of demographic data, and the formulation of a precise diagnosis. Unfortunately, all too many reports of drug studies, particularly those conducted with psychotic and retarded children, are merely anecdotal.[36, 37, 41, 116] A representative sample of the population under study is essential for the evaluation of drug efficacy.[104]

Responders to a specific drug may be defined by a thorough clinical and laboratory workup using behavioral, biological, biochemical, and neurophysiological parameters. Such an approach would lead to a more rational pharmacotherapy. The determination of etiology is important for treatment but not always possible, but the assessment of pathophysiology is more feasible and equally important.

Prior to the administration of the agent to be investigated, a period of *placebo washout* of adequate length is necessary in order to insure the total elimination of previous medication. With this procedure, placebo responders can be screened out before the administration of an "active" drug,[168] and a stable baseline can be achieved.[41] In crossover studies, such a placebo interval is also required between two drug conditions.

Standardized, sensitive, and appropriate (for the population to be studied) instruments for measuring behavioral changes are necessary in drug effect research. These permit communication with other investigators. Fish[116] has emphasized that the normal variability of a child's behavior creates a great problem in measuring change. Whether a specific behavior is normal or abnormal will depend upon, among other factors, the child's chronological age and the amount of the particular behavior exhibited.

Global evaluations of change are useful but not entirely satisfactory. Standardized rating scales for various psychiatric disorders in adults are available; they are widely used both in individual and in large collaborative National Institute of Mental Health studies. In the 1950s and 1960s, several investigators developed their own rating scales for children, designed to measure "key symptoms" and their severity.[72, 116] The fact that most investigators used their own rating scales impeded comparability.

The rating scales developed by Conners—the Conners Teacher Questionnaire,[79] the Conners Parent Questionnaire[78] and the ten-item Conners Parent-Teacher Questionnaire[226]—are the most widely used for the so-called hyperactive, MBD children. The psychopharmacology branch of NIMH developed a battery of rating scales for pediatric psychopharmacology.[226] These scales were designed for a spectrum of behavioral disorders. The battery contains the Children's Psychiatric Rating Scale (CPRS), Children's Diagnostic Scale (CDS), Children's Diagnostic Classification (CDC), Clinical Global Impressions (CGI), Children's Personal Data Inventory (CPDI), Children's Symptom History (CSH), the Children's ECDEU Battery for Psychologist, and the Children's Behavior Inventory.[34] Objective measures have been developed for retarded[284] and autistic populations.[63] In depressive disorders, scales are currently being tested.[57, 227, 263] The wide range of available rating scales is discussed in more detail in volume 1 of the handbook.

Clinical change should be documented by objective psychological and behavioral ratings which are quantifiable and precise. Performance measures suitable for drug studies have been discussed and critically reviewed by Sprague.[283]

RATING CONDITIONS

Because there are drugs such as amphetamines which have short-term effects and because children's behavior and performance are affected by fatigue even more than they are in the case of adults, it is wise to assess behavioral and other drug-dependent variables at fixed points soon after drug ingestion.[205] In the case of all school-age children and adolescents, the evaluation of behavior during office visits has to be supplemented by information from various observers about the patient's functioning at home and at school. For this purpose, the Conners scales for parents and teachers and the abridged Conners Parent-Teacher Questionnaire are recommended, particularly for the hyperactive MBD child. If the excitable, hyperactive child is sedated by a drug, the parent may be pleased; but in the school or laboratory situation where the sedation may interfere with learning, concentration, and attentiveness, the same change may be perceived as undesirable.

In drug research work with young psychotic children, discrepancies have been found between the ratings of the "blind" research psychiatrist and other staff. The "blind" rater observed and interviewed the child in a standard situation[46, 124] for fifteen minutes prior to drug treatment, at termination of treatment circa two to three months later, and one week after discontinuation of the drug. The patient's variable and unpredictable behavior with occasionally fluctuating symptoms in the standard, fixed-stimulus environment was often an unreliable reflection of his total behavior and frequently differed in the rating situation from that in the more routine circumstances of daily life (classroom, "free play," meals, or weekends with parents at home). As a result, the reports of the staff, who, like the parents, saw the child daily and under various circumstances, often showed a significant discrepancy from those of the "blind" rater. For purposes of rating, it therefore seems desirable that, in addition to the two independent psychiatrists, parents, nurse, and teacher should be rating independently for a more extended period of time under more normal conditions for the child.[43, 54] Moreover, the use of the newly available pediatric battery of rating scales, developed by the psychopharmacology branch of the NIMH[226] should facilitate communication between investigators and clinicians.

When feasible, the last two to four minutes of each "formal" psychiatric rating interview should be videotaped to provide a permanent record.[170] The accumulated tapes on each child can then be assessed in one session by two to three "blind" independent raters who are not otherwise included in the study.[43] This provides an objective method of evaluating drug effects independent of any particular frame of reference or bias.

Issues concerning rating conditions have been discussed by Gleser[146] and Campbell and associates.[41]

DETERMINATION OF APPROPRIATE DOSE RANGE

In many drug studies with children, the dosage employed is either ineffectively low or too high. In our experience, particularly with psychotic children, the great individual differences in metabolism and tolerance indicated the advantage of individually regulated doses. Adequate, effective dosage can be explored by using a flexible dose schedule. Research, chiefly with MBD and retarded children, has offered evidence that dosages should be standardized on the basis of milligrams of drug per kilogram of body weight.[285, 286, 287, 311] The conclusion was that "the titration method used social behavior as the main criterion for determining dosage for stimulant medication. . . . The doses considered optimal . . . are, in fact, deleterious to cognitive performance."[285] Another way to determine therapeutically effective dosage for children is by body surface area.[270, 293]

In studies with children, there is a great deal of disagreement on diagnosis. Further, the samples are not only heterogeneous but also small. As a result, the methods of establishing statistical significance are of great importance.[27] Tabular and/or graphic presentation of data is most informative and cannot be substituted for by statistics.[26]

Methodology in psychopharmacology has been amply discussed and reviewed in cases of adults[17, 181, 295, 300] and in cases of children.* Fisher[126] has reviewed the nonspecific factors influencing behavioral response to drugs, and Sarwer-Foner[252] has presented an overview of the psychodynamics of pharmacotherapy.

Indications for Use of
Drug Treatment

Experience has shown that drug treatment can be a valuable addition to, or the essential modality within, the total treatment of the moderately to severely disturbed child and adolescent. Diagnostic classifications for psychiatric disorders of childhood and adolescence have been unsatisfactory; perhaps the most widely used system is the Ninth Revision of the International Classification of Diseases (ICD-9); and in the United States, the one developed by the committee on Child Psychiatry of the Group for the Advancement of Psychiatry (GAP).† Currently, the *Diagnostic and Statistical Manual of Mental Disorders*. Third Edition (DSM III)[93] developed by a Task Force of the American Psychiatric Association is gaining prominence. The section on childhood and adolescence is considered to be a great improvement over DSM II (1968) for both clinical and research work. An extensive discussion of the diagnostic issues in relation to children's psychopharmacological indications is available in Gittelman-Klein, Spitzer, and Cantwell.[144] The DSM III disorders in which drug treatment has been beneficial, plus some comments are as follows.

1. Mental retardation—A trial of drug treatment is indicated in the biological and intermediate group when retarded functioning is associated with psychosis or with symptoms such as hyperactivity, distractibility, impulsivity, explosive behavior, aggressiveness, or self-mutilation. Learning as such is not enhanced by drugs in this category.[131]

2. Pervasive developmental disorders (infantile autism and atypical psychosis).

3. Schizophrenia—In the psychoses of early childhood and in schizophrenia, a trial of drug treatment is usually indicated, as part of the total treatment. In psychotic children of school age, it is worthwhile to give diphenhydramine first because of its safety. If the child fails to respond, an appropriate neuroleptic should be prescribed. The prepubertal child is frequently oversedated even by low doses of the "sedative" type of neuroleptics, such as chlorpromazine. This interferes with functioning and learning. Since psychosis may be associated with learning disorders and/or mental retardation, and particularly so in the case of the preschool child, this may indeed preclude drug treatment. While diminution of reactivity is a desirable effect in adults with acute schizophrenia, the same kind of change is not therapeutic in the slow, anergic, and apathetic child. The response of adolescents to neuroleptics is similar to that of adults. Experience has shown that the less sedative type of neuroleptics, such as trifluoperazine, thiothixene, and haloperidol, can be therapeutically effective at doses which do not result in excessive sedation.

4. Specific developmental disorders—Imipramine

---

* See references 36, 41, 68, 73, 106, 116, 190, 205, 282, 288, and 309.

† Group for the Advancement of Psychiatry (GAP), *Psychopathological Disorders in Childhood: Theoretical Considerations and a Prepared Classification*, vol. 6, Report No. 62, 1966.

is used frequently in treating enuresis, and its effectiveness has been demonstrated in several double-blind and placebo-controlled studies. But, because enuresis is a nonspecific symptom found in a variety of disorders, despite the effectiveness of imipramine in the management of this symptom, it is recommended that the problems underlying enuresis should be explored and dealt with as indicated by Dische[97] and Forsythe and Redmond.[127]

5. Attention deficit disorders—The efficacy of the stimulants over placebo has been demonstrated in attention deficit disorders with hyperactivity (minimal brain dysfunction with hyperactivity) suffered by children six to twelve years of age. However, in cases of preschool children, the clinical response to these drugs is more variable and unpredictable.[69]

6. Conduct disorders—Undersocialized conduct disorders, aggressive type, frequently fails to respond to treatment with stimulants and a neuroleptic may be indicated. This conclusion is based on clinical experience and not on research.

7. Stereotyped movement disorders—There is good clinical evidence that haloperidol is effective in chronic tic disorder and Tourette's disorder.[320]

8. Affective disorders—While the imipraminelike drugs are effective in adults with major depressive illness, particularly those with psychomotor retardation, comparable results have not been demonstrated in treating children. Depressive states of children are poorly defined conditions; the existence of manic-depressive illness under ten to twelve years of age is questionable. Well-controlled studies with defined homogeneous populations are lacking, both for children and adolescents. Efforts have only recently been made to identify, both systematically and reliably, children who fulfill the adult diagnostic criteria for depression.[227, 263] At the present time, in clinical work, drug treatment (imipramine) is indicated only when environmental manipulations, individual psychotherapy and/or work with parents have failed.

Due to his lack of development and general immaturity, the behavioral repertoire of the young, particularly the preschool child, is small, undifferentiated, and nonspecific. Such a child may respond with the same symptoms (excessive irritability, hyperkinesis, temper tantrums, aggressiveness, or withdrawal) to a variety of causes. At different chronological or mental ages, the same underlying pathology may be manifested in very different forms of behavior. At a young age, a given behavior might be considered a mild response to environmental factors, whereas in adolescence, the same behavior may be an early sign of psychosis (for example, school phobia). Thus, institution of drug treatment or choice of drug will depend on more than diagnosis or symptom. Age, intellectual functioning, and severity and duration of illness are additional variables which must be taken into account.[116]

Where psychosocial factors are prominent if not causative, mild disorders should not be treated with drugs. An exception occurs when the purpose of drug administration is to break a vicious cycle. Delinquency and reactive aggressiveness do not improve much or fail altogether to respond to pharmacotherapy. Eisenberg[103, 104] emphasized that for the child whose symptoms stem from correctable social, familial, biological, or intrapersonal disturbances, it is poor clinical practice to administer drugs without attempting to alter the factors causing the symptoms.

Technique*

Fish[117] stressed that before prescribing drug treatment, the relation of the child and his symptoms to his family needs to be determined. Since many children's symptoms change faster than those of adults, Fish found that the child's response to outpatient or institutional psychiatric treatment could be evaluated in two to four weeks before instituting drug treatment. In emergency situations, such a baseline period of observation and evaluation is not available.

A careful history of prior drug allergy or sensitivity as well as a history of prior drug intake (including the last day of drug ingestion) and dosage should be obtained. This is particularly important in crisis or emergency room situations. Drugs do interact and the potentiation of one agent may take place if another is given.

There are many psychoactive agents, particularly neuroleptics, in use today. The practicing physician should be familiar with two or three of each class of drugs. He must be well acquainted with the therapeutic effects, side effects, and toxic reactions. A large body of information is available in these areas. There are immediate, delayed, and long-term reactions; there are responses specific to the particular drug or class of drugs such as extrapyramidal, gastrointestinal, and so forth; and there are nonspecific reactions, observed with almost any drug or at certain dose level, such as hypersensitivity reactions, loss of weight or appetite, and such behavioral manifestations as irritability, sleepiness, hyperactivity, or hypoactivity.

With the exception of very young retarded chil-

---

* See reference 40 for further discussion of these issues

dren, patients should be told about the medication they are given and what it is expected to do for them. Taking the drug may create fear of loss of control, fear of being poisoned or weakened, or, to the contrary, cause a feeling of being stronger or better. In many patients there is a strong placebo effect which has been demonstrated in placebo controlled studies. The child should be told why he is given drug treatment (for example, to help him in controlling hyperactivity or explosiveness) and what are the limitations of drug treatment (for example, the drug will not perform a miracle, he has to work with his therapist on his problems). Many children are able to verbalize the subjective sensations they experience after drug ingestion (for example, feeling calmer and more relaxed).

Since the child, even the adolescent, depends on an adult, the parent(s) of both in- and outpatients should be informed of the nature of the medication, its expected therapeutic effects, side effects, possible toxicity, and dose regulation. They should be told not only about the usefulness of the drug for their child's condition but also about the limitations and the importance of other treatment modalities which might be of more significance in bringing about change. Parental attitudes toward drug therapy may also vary from using this as means of sadistic control to the hope that the drugs will solve interactional problems or cure uncurable conditions. These issues are discussed elsewhere.[314]

Neuroleptics or potentially harmful drugs should not be prescribed on an outpatient basis if the parents are uncooperative and/or unreliable. The possibility of adolescents making impulsive suicidal gestures with medically prescribed psychoactive agents should be kept in mind. A major problem in the drug therapy of children arises from the psychiatrist's dependence on a reliable, cooperative parent and/or teacher. The availability of the physician, even by telephone, can help eliminate unnecessary anxieties in parents and patient and may also prevent serious complications.

When feasible, a single dose should be used, rather than divided dosage. This is particularly true for the schoolchild, who might be embarrassed by having to take the medication in school, or who might have no one to give the medicine when a school nurse is not available.

DOSAGE

Children usually need or tolerate relatively higher doses of psychoactive drugs than do adults or adolescents. As far as optimal dose is concerned, many investigators have found great individual differences in children and the dosage is frequently unrelated not only to the individual child's weight and age, but even to the severity of symptoms or illness.[116, 258] Thus, weight and age are not always reliable guidelines, and it has been suggested that dosage be determined by body surface.[270, 293] Sprague and coworkers have demonstrated that methylphenidate can be prescribed effectively on the basis of body weight.[285, 311]

It is poor medical practice to maintain the severely disturbed child on excessively high dosage of medication, particularly neuroleptics, which clearly interfere with his functioning and may result in long-term complications, which will be discussed subsequently.

Another frequent error is to place the patient on an ineffectively low maintenance dosage. Underdosage involves exposing the patient to most of the risks without any chance for benefit. Compliance with the most recent *Physicians Desk Reference (PDR)* concerning dosage and age limits is strongly recommended.

DOSAGE REGULATION

In clinical practice with all drugs, particularly with neuroleptics and antidepressants, stepwise progression is recommended. The patient is first placed on a low, usually therapeutically ineffective dose. Increments should be gradual, at regular intervals (twice a week, for example, Tuesday and Thursday, with stimulants, and once a week with neuroleptics or imipraminelike drugs) until therapeutic or untoward effects are noted.

UNTOWARD EFFECTS

Behavioral toxicity has to be watched for. Particularly in young children, it often precedes other side effects (neurological, decrease of appetite, or insomnia). Since, as noted previously, individual differences in what constitutes an optimal dose may be considerable, full dose exploration for each patient is essential. Only then is the optimal dose determined and the patient maintained on it. Negative effects can be the result of overdosage. Some of the undesirable effects will be exaggerated forms of desired effects; for example, in the case of stimulants it may be irritability, excitement, or hyperactivity; whereas with sedatives or neuroleptics the effects may be hypoactivity or sleepiness. Overdosage may be manifested by worsening of preexisting symptoms; this must be differentiated from doses that are ineffective because they are too low.

Untoward effects due to too much drug can be eliminated by decreasing the dosage. At times, especially with neuroleptics and imipraminelike drugs, the medication may have to be discontinued for a day or two. Only then can the dose be lowered. Occasionally, undesirable effects may be transient, or the patient may adapt to the same dose, as evidenced by the spontaneous disappearance of untoward effects. One should be alert to another phenomenon: With time, as the optimal dose continues, untoward effects may begin to occur due to drug accumulation, or because the patient requires less of the agent due to clinical improvement. Again, this must be differentiated from adaptation to the therapeutic effects of the drug, a phenomenon that takes the form of a reappearance of baseline symptoms after a period of improvement.

Children are not as verbal as adults and the physician cannot rely on their statements or complaints. Hence, particularly in the case of a child, the determination of optimal dose must be based on daily observation. Such observation is easy with inpatients. Yet, even then, office observations should be supplemented by reports from parents and teachers. This is all the more necessary with outpatients.

For the adult, it is essential that he be able to function at work; for the child, play or learning and school are important. Where the sedative effect of a drug interferes with the child's or adolescent's functioning, the dosage is excessive and has to be lowered. Or, it may be necessary to switch to another type of drug (for example, from a "sedative" type of neuroleptic to a "stimulating" type). The appearance of sedation at those dose levels which diminish disturbing symptoms presents a major difficulty in the psychopharmacology of children.

Drug-specific untoward effects will be discussed later. Only behavioral toxicity and some general observations will be mentioned here. In young children, in particular, behavioral side effects may differ from those in adults (for review in adults, see references 94 and 266). A child may experience a great deal of discomfort due to an excess of drug. The younger the child, the more apt he is to express this feeling on an affectomotor rather than on a verbal level. As an immature, relatively undifferentiated organism, he reacts to most insults in a nonspecific way; his response may include irritability, hyper- or hypoactivity, or loss of appetite.

Side effects, such as extrapyramidal signs, dystonic reactions, and tardive dyskinesia-like syndromes, are seen less frequently in adolescents than in mature adults, and less frequently in preschool children than in older ones. Careful clinical and laboratory monitoring has shown that impaired liver function, drug-induced jaundice, and bone marrow damage occur less often in childhood.

LONG-TERM PHARMACOTHERAPY

Long-term pharmacotherapy may influence growth, as well as the endocrine, reproductive, and central nervous systems. Information concerning these late effects is limited. The neurotransmitters which control the secretion of the hypothalamic neurohormones are affected by many psychoactive agents. Hence, drugs should be given with caution to prepubertal children. Chlorpromazine is known to decrease growth hormone secretion in adults.[268] In a placebo-controlled trial, acute oral administration of methylphenidate to young adults resulted in marked increase of serum growth hormone, while cortisol concentrations remained unchanged.[32] Chronic dextroamphetamine administration to hyperkinetic children did not affect growth hormone levels in blood, whereas it decreased prolactin significantly.[152, 228] The effect of stimulants on height and weight will be discussed later in this chapter. The foregoing must be viewed against the background that abnormalities of growth and in the onset of puberty have been reported in mentally retarded, brain-damaged, and psychotic children who had not received psychoactive agents.[45, 100, 277] The immediate and long-term hazards of untreated psychiatric conditions have to be weighed against the adverse effects of the drugs. It is often crucial that the patient calm down, concentrate, learn, and be maintained in a classroom.

EFFECTS OF DRUGS ON LEARNING AND IQ

These effects are still controversial. There is some evidence that chronic administration of neuroleptics may decrease cognition in psychotic and retarded children and in children of normal intelligence.[131, 199, 312] Werry and Aman's[310] study of haloperidol indicates that these adverse effects on performance tasks are dose related. Recent studies indicate that stimulants improve attention span and performance in nonretarded MBD children* and in normal controls.[234] It has been

* See references 74, 76, 234, 286, and 289.

suggested that the same drug may have different effects, depending on the individual's IQ.

On the basis of clinical experience, addiction to psychoactive drugs prescribed for behavioral disorders does not appear to pose a problem in the prepubertal child.[129] In this respect, adolescents do not differ from adults, although both instances require further research.

If a patient fails to respond to a drug after a trial period (about four to eight weeks with neuroleptics or imipraminelike drugs and less with the psychomotor stimulants), another drug from the same class, or another agent with similar action should be tried. The MBD patient refractory to dextroamphetamine can be tried on methylphenidate, magnesium pemoline, or even a phenothiazine. Under investigative circumstances, imipramine should be considered. When indicated, it is important to institute drug treatment in the early stage of illness, and not only when all other, often inappropriate, treatments have failed.

FAILURE TO RESPOND

Failure to respond to a drug may be due to several factors: underdosage, overdosage, noncompliance (not taking the drug), the manner in which a drug is being absorbed and metabolized, genetic determinants, and polypharmacy (that is, prescription of several drugs to the same patient, or multiple drug administration). (For review, see references 15 and 160). Overdosage and polypharmacy are frequent in clinical and private practice. It was observed that:

when 5 mg of dextroamphetamine was briefly used to counteract the sedation from chlorpromazine, the sedation was reduced, but this enabled one to use what proved to be excessively high doses of chlorpromazine. Disorganized behavior and mild transient organic syndrome resulted, which disappeared promptly when amphetamine was discontinued and the dose of chlorpromazine was reduced.[51] [p. 327]

The average general practitioner, psychiatrist, and child psychiatrist's limitations in knowledge of psychopharmacology is frequently the cause of "treatment-resistance" by patients; ultimately it deprives the patient of a relatively economical and effective treatment modality. Even worse, perhaps, it creates a false notion that drugs are ineffective.

On the other hand, one must keep in mind that there are individuals whose symptoms or illness are refractory to drug treatment. and that there are conditions, such as personality disorders, in which drugs are of questionable or of no value.

In cases of children and adolescents, the routine use of antiparkinson drugs is unnecessary. As noted previously, extrapyramidal signs are less frequent in the young than in the older age groups. There is evidence that the antiparkinsonian agents may decrease the plasma levels of neuroleptics and their clinical efficacy and cause worsening of psychotic symptoms.[15, 58, 242] If the patient contracts an acute, febrile illness, or one of the common childhood infectious diseases, drug treatment should be discontinued. After the patient has fully recovered, the medication should be reinstituted, starting with gradual increments. The manner of drug discontinuation will depend on the type of drug and dose level. Thus, with amphetamine and methylphenidate, termination may be abrupt. On the other hand, with neuroleptics and imipraminelike drugs, particularly when high doses were used, a more gradual cessation is indicated.

DURATION

Duration of drug treatment is an important issue. While the patient should be given an adequate time on maintenance medication, drugs should not be continued when no longer needed. In acute psychoses, four to six weeks of medication may be sufficient. In chronic psychoses, MBD, and mental retardation or brain damage with a certain behavioral profile, the patient may require maintenance for months or even years. After each three to four months of drug administration, the drug should be decreased gradually and discontinued for a week to reassess the patient's status. If symptoms recur, drug treatment should be reinstituted. Shorter drug-free periods, "drug holidays," are recommended over weekends, or, in the case of MBD children, when feasible during school vacations. There is evidence that drug-induced positive and newly acquired adaptive behaviors and developmental gains can be retained without the drug.[46, 47, 279] It is believed that intermittent discontinuation of drug treatment reduces the risk and incidence of adverse drug reactions.

Neuroleptics

REVIEW OF REPRESENTATIVE LITERATURE

The practice of psychiatry in adults has changed dramatically since the advent of the neuroleptics (antipsychotics or major tranquilizers). Their value in the treatment of schizophrenia. particularly in its acute form, has been inestimable.

TABLE 23-1

Representative Neuroleptics (antipsychotics, major tranquilizers)

Subclass	Characteristics	Generic Name	Trade Name	Range in mg	Daily dosage* Number in Divided doses
I. PHENOTHIAZINES					
A. Aliphatics	Sedative-hypnotic, psychomotor-inhibiting actions; indicated in agitated, hyperactive patients. More likely to produce hematopoetic and hepatic damage and photosensitivity reactions than the piperazines.	Chlorpromazine	Thorazine	9 to 200 (oral) IM max 40 up to 5 years of age	2–4
		Triflupromazine	Vesprin	IM max 75 5 to 12 years of age 1 to 150	2–4
B. Piperidines	More likely to produce lenticular and corneal opacities and retinitis pigmentosa, less likely to produce extrapyramidal effects.	Thioridazine	Mellaril	10–200	2–4
C. Piperazines	Activating, stimulating properties; indicated in with-drawn, apathetic, anergic patients. More likely to produce extrapyramidal side effects.	Fluphenazine	Permitil	0.25–16	1–2
		Trifluoperazine†	Stelazine	1–20	1–2
II. THIOXANTHENES	Less likely to produce hematopoetic and hepatic damage and photosensitivity reactions than phenothiazines	Thiothixene‡	Navane	1–40	1–2
		Chlorprothixene†	Taractan	10–200	1–2
III. BUTYROPHENONES	Decreasing agitation without the hypnotic effect of aliphatic phenothiazines. High percentage of extrapyramidal side effects.	Trifluporidol§			
		Haloperidol	Haldol	0.5–16	1–2
IV. DIHYDROINDOLONES	Activating, stimulating properties; like the piperazine phenothiazines causes fewer side effects, except extrapyramidal reactions, than aliphatic and piperidine phenothiazines.	Molindone‡	Moban	1–200	1–3

* Patients two to twelve years of age. Dosage for adolescents comparable to adult dosage. See current PDR for available dosage forms.
† FDA approval for patients over six years of age only.
‡ FDA approval for patients over twelve years of age only.
§ Withdrawn from investigational use in U.S.A.

There is evidence that these agents not only decrease symptoms but, to some extent, change the course of the illness.[315] Though clinical experience has shown that these medications benefit many children, particularly severely disturbed adolescents, their impact has not been as great nor as clearly established in child psychiatry as in adult psychiatry. This may be due to the fact that: (1) the child is not a fully developed organism; (2) in a child every psychiatric disorder clearly interferes with the course of normal development and thus, the task of treatment is not only to decrease symptoms, but also to enhance development; (3) the prognosis for severe disorders is poorer in the younger age group than for the adult; and (4) large or collaborative studies with sophisticated methodology, using homogeneous, well-defined populations of children are practically nonexistent. (For review, see references 75, 130, 189, 288, and 309.)

Fish[118] found chlorpromazine to benefit schizophrenic and organic children, as well as those with behavior disorders. In her uncontrolled open trial, one important finding was that children with symptoms of hypoactivity and apathy tended to become sedated on this drug. Subsequently, in a controlled study, forty-five hospitalized children, six to twelve years of age, were treated with chlorpromazine, diphenhydramine, or placebo.[119, 120, 177] The diagnoses ranged from mild neuroses and behavior disorders to schizophrenia. Patients were matched for age and symptom severity. Eighty percent of the severely disturbed and intellectually more impaired children showed some improvement on chlorpromazine, 50 percent on diphenhydramine, and none on placebo. Forty-three percent of the children with less severe psychopathology improved on placebo, 60 percent on chlorpromazine, and none responded to diphenhydramine. The differences in efficacy were statistically significant.

By the same criteria, chlorpromazine was found to be superior to placebo in reducing hyperactivity in nonretarded school-age children.[312] In this placebo-controlled, double-blind study, the drug reduced hyperactivity more than it affected distractibility, excitability, and aggressiveness. A history of organicity or the presence of an abnormal EEG did not appear to influence the behavioral response.

Along with chlorpromazine, thioridazine is the most widely used drug in retarded hyperactive, and/or brain-damaged children.[189] In a double-blind study, twenty-one hyperkinetic patients, seven to twelve years of age, with IQs of 55 to 85,

were randomly assigned to either thioridazine. amphetamine, or placebo.[2] Thioridazine was demonstrated to be superior to placebo and amphetamine. Among the positive changes rated were a decrease of aggressiveness along with increases of concentration span, comprehension, sociability, and interest in plus capacity for work. When Fish found that the prepubertal schizophrenic child was often excessively sedated by chlorpromazine at doses which decreased important symptoms,[118] she began to investigate trifluoperazine, a less sedative and potent phenothiazine, for these children. Although not systematically investigated, clinical observation indicated that sedation interfered with the child's learning and functioning.[49, 115, 118] In a double-blind controlled study of preschool psychotics following an open trial, trifluoperazine produced statistically significant changes only in the most impaired children who had no speech.[121] Improvements included increases of language production, alertness, social responsiveness, and motor initiation. The more severely impaired children required higher doses; those with less impairment tolerated lower doses and were responsive to milieu therapy as well. Wolpert, Hagamen, and Merlis[319] compared trifluoperazine (in daily doses of 13 to 20 milligrams) to thiothixene in a homogeneous sample of schizophrenic children, eight to fifteen years of age; the findings are inconclusive, as will be discussed under thiothixene.

Fluphenazine was explored in schizophrenics and autistics in double-blind fashion. Thirty outpatients, nineteen autistics), six to twelve years of age, were assigned to fluphenazine or haloperidol groups.[110] Ninety-three percent showed improvement on fluphenazine, and 87 percent on haloperidol, but the difference in efficacy was not statistically significant. Improvements with fluphenazine were in the areas of self-awareness, constructive play, and decrease of compulsive acts and self-mutilation. Similar results, with no difference in drug efficacy were obtained in a sample of sixty severely impaired, hospitalized five to twelve years olds, fifty-two of whom were schizophrenics.[111]

Trifluperidol, though withdrawn from investigational use in the United States, is still being used abroad. It is a potent antipsychotic agent with stimulating properties and is more effective than either chlorpromazine or trifluoperazine in the treatment of young psychotic children with symptoms of apathy and anergy.[50, 186] However, in trials there was a high incidence of extrapyramidal symptoms and the therapeutic index was narrow.

Haloperidol is similar to trifluperidol, but it appears to be a safer agent with a wider margin of therapeutic index. Acute dystonic reaction can be avoided by starting with a low dose (0.5 milligrams per day) and continuing with gradual, slow increments at regular intervals. With psychotic children, it proved effective both in improving coordination, self-care, affect, and exploratory behavior[110] and in reducing autism and provocative behavior.[111] Others found haloperidol to be particularly effective for decreasing hyperactivity, assaultiveness, and self-mutilation in children with or without mental retardation.*

In a study involving forty young autistic children, haloperidol was compared to behavior therapy, and the interaction of both was critically assessed in a double-blind, placebo controlled fashion.[43] Haloperidol was significantly superior to placebo in decreasing stereotypies and withdrawal. The combination of haloperidol and behavior therapy was effective in facilitating the acquisition of imitative speech. Optimal doses ranged from 0.5 to 4.0 mg/day (mean, 1.65 mg/day); excessive sedation was the most common untoward effect, clearly a function of dosage.

There are reports indicating that behavioral improvement with haloperidol administration is associated with a slowing down in skilled motor tasks and cognition.[88, 310] In a crossover study of twenty-four hyperactive or unsocialized-aggressive children, both low (0.025 mg/kg) and high (0.05 mg/kg) doses of haloperidol were effective in reducing behavioral symptoms.[310] However, while the lower dose facilitated performance, there was a suggestion that the higher dose impaired cognitive functions.

In a trial involving autistic children, there was no effect on performance by any treatment, though haloperidol was clinically effective.[43] The dose-related differential effects of drug on behavioral symptoms and cognition are important findings and require further inquiry.

Anecdotal reports and open studies are available on the efficacy of this drug in the treatment of Gilles de la Tourette's syndrome.[56, 59, 195, 267] A well-controlled and intensive study involving four inpatients, twelve to fourteen years of age, using both objective and subjective assessment measures, has demonstrated that haloperidol is statistically significantly superior to both diazepam and placebo in reducing tics.[67] The results with diazepam were not statistically different from those with placebo, and the patient who improved

on this drug had a relapse after being discharged from the hospital. In a recent paper,[33] a 7- to 103-month follow-up study of seventy-eight patients, ages six to sixty-seven years (thirty-four were below eighteen years of age at the time of the initial evaluation), was presented. Fifty-three were treated by haloperidol alone (or haloperidol with methylphenidate or anticholinergics) and six with haloperidol plus another medication. Improvement increased with increase of length of treatment; patients treated for more than four years averaged a 93.4 percent improvement. The authors concluded that haloperidol appears to be the most effective medication available for the treatment of this syndrome but that its use is limited by the side effects which these patients do not seem to tolerate very well.

Wolpert, Hagamen, and Merlis[319] explored thiothixene in schizophrenics eight to fifteen years of age, in a double-blind study. The sixteen patients were randomly assigned to thiothixene or to trifluoperazine. On the basis of global impressions of the raters, four of the sixteen patients improved on thiothixene and three on trifluoperazine, in the areas of autism, socialization, stereotypies, and appetite. These findings are inconclusive, and the pretreatment washout was too short. Thiothixene was explored in ten preschool-age hospitalized psychotics, after a four-week washout.[53] Decreases in withdrawal, excitability, stereotypies, and psychotic speech were noted; the changes in the scores for single symptoms were not statistically significant, although the change in mean pathological scores for the group was significant. The drug had both stimulating properties and a wide therapeutic margin. In a single-blind study of eighteen schizophrenic outpatients, five to thirteen years of age, significant improvements were noted in motor activity, stereotypies, coordination, sleep, affect, exploratory behavior, concentration and eating habits.[302] The change in mean scores on the symptom rating scale was statistically significant. Simeon, and associates[273] obtained similar therapeutic changes in psychotic boys, five to fifteen years of age; statistically signficant improvements occurred both in global ratings and individual symptoms. The positive behavioral effects were accompanied by changes in the electroencephalogram and in visual evoked potentials. Reports on the use of chlorprothixene are anecdotal and therefore no conclusions can be reached.[212]

Recently, molindone, a dihydroindolone, has been marketed for the treatment of adult schizophrenics. It is a neuroleptic with some antidepressant characteristics. (For review, see reference

* See references 35, 88, 148, 185, 265, and 299.

16). On the basis of the only available report on its use in children, it appears to be of potential value in the treatment of those psychotic children who are usually overly sedated by chlorpromazine.[51] In this pilot study of ten preschool patients, molindone showed antipsychotic effects and "useful stimulant effects." In the hypoactive children, improvement was noted in motility and in the patients with apathy, in affect.

Loxapine succinate, a dibenzoxazepine, was found to be as effective as haloperidol and significantly superior to placebo in (average) doses of 87.5 mg/day.[224] This was a double-blind study involving seventy-five adolescents with acute schizophrenia or chronic with acute exacerbation, where the subjects were assigned to one of the three treatment conditions.

Pimozide was explored in an open and single-blind fashion, in doses of 1 to 2 mg/day, in a small sample of severely disturbed, including eight schizophrenic children.[217]

INDICATIONS

Neuroleptics are indicated as an adjunct in the total treatment of psychotic disorders. They are particularly useful for: the acute types, chronic brain syndrome with psychomotor excitement, mental retardation with psychomotor excitement, and for adolescent character disorders with a marked emotional component (EUCD). Table 23-1 lists the recommended dosage range. Chlorpromazine has been in use for the longest period of time and is the drug of choice. Thioridazine is preferred in cases with an associated seizure disorder.[130] Because its sedative properties are less, trifluoperazine is preferred to chlorpromazine in psychoses where withdrawal, apathy and anergy are prominent features. Should the patient fail to respond to trifluoperazine, the newer drugs with "stimulating" qualities—thiothixene, haloperidol, or molindone—may be tried. In psychiatric emergencies, chlorpromazine can be given intramuscularly.

For the child with MBD, thioridazine or chlorpromazine should be prescribed only if he fails to respond to the stimulants (dextroamphetamine, methylphenidate or pemoline). Haloperidol is recommended as the drug of choice in the treatment of Gilles de la Tourette's syndrome.

RECOMMENDED LABORATORY STUDIES

A pretreatment alkaline phosphatase, serum glutamic-pyruvic transaminase (SGPT), serum glutamic-oxaloacetic transaminase (SGOT), complete blood count (CBC), and urinalysis are recommended. These tests should be repeated weekly during the first two months of treatment, once a month until the sixth month, and additionally when indicated.

SIDE EFFECTS

The most serious reactions are allergic (idiosyncratic). Icterus is rare in children, usually occurring in the early weeks of treatment. When agranulocytosis occurs, it is in the first two months and is unrelated to dosage. It may be manifested initially by elevated temperature, sore throat, and enlarged lymph glands.

The extrapyramidal symptoms (EPS) comprise the parkinsonian complex (tremor, cogwheel rigidity, excessive salivation), dystonic reactions, (abnormal movements of face, neck, tongue, jaw, and torticollis, oculogyric crises, opisthotonos, and difficulty in speech and swallowing), and akathisia. Reduction of dosage is recommended for the parkinson-like symptoms. Administration of antiparkinsonian agents may reduce plasma chlorpromazine levels by 6 percent to 100 percent.[242] Acute dystonic reaction is relieved with diphenhydramine, orally or intramuscularly (25–50 mg).

A few reports are available on the occurrence of a neurologic syndrome in children which resembles the tardive dyskinesia seen in adults.[259] In a retrospective investigation, McAndrew, Case, and Treffert[199] found that after withdrawal of phenothiazines, 10 of 125 hospitalized children (7 schizophrenics and 3 with behavior disorder, ages eight to fifteen years) developed involuntary movements of their upper extremities with akathisia. Six of these ten showed facial tics. The symptoms were first noted three to ten days after drug discontinuation and ceased within three to twelve months. The children who developed this syndrome had been on phenothiazines for a longer time and on higher doses than those who were asymptomatic after drug withdrawal; the differences were statistically significant. The 10 afflicted children were compared to 84 children who remained asymptomatic over a one-month period after an abrupt withdrawal from phenothiazines (chlorpromazine, chlorprothixene, triflupromazine, thioridazine, fluphenazine or perphenazine, received singly or sequentially). All phenothiazine dosages were calculated in terms of chlorpromazine equivalents, in accordance with the standard dose conversion table utilized by Hollister.[161] The median gram intake in the asymptomatic group was 8.7 g; in the symptomatic group, it was 403 g. The median daily termination dose was 99 mg in the asymptomatic group and 400 mg in the symptomatic group. Median duration of drug intake was significantly different: four months in the asymptomatic group, versus thirty-two months in those with tardive dyskinesia.

In another study,[223] fourteen of thirty-five outpatient schizophrenics, six to twelve years of age, showed neurological withdrawal-emergent symptoms after termination of neuroleptics. Five drugs were involved and the mean dosages were as follows: fluphenazine 25 mg; haloperidol, 9 mg; trifluoperazine, 19 mg; thiothixene, 17 mg; and for thioridazine, the mean daily dose was 399 mg. Duration of drug therapy was six to fifteen months. Both abrupt total withdrawal and gradual graded withdrawal with weekly reduction of dose by 25 percent yielded identical results. The involuntary movements associated with ataxia appeared within the first to the fifteenth day after drug withdrawal. In half of the children these symptoms disappeared spontaneously (mean duration of symptoms fifteen days), while in the rest, the symptoms disappeared within two weeks after starting with another neuroleptic. Only one child had oral dyskinesia. The involuntary movements were of a choreiform nature, mainly in the extremities, trunk, and head. Occasionally, myoclonic, hemiballisticlike, athetoid, and head-rocking movements were seen. The most frequently implicated drug was fluphenazine (daily dose range 1–50 mg), and the least implicated with thioridazine (daily dose 50–800 mg). The relationship of this probably reversible syndrome to persistent tardive dyskinesia in adults has not been established.[109]

Convulsive seizures have been reported in patients with no such history prior to treatment with neuroleptics. With chlorpromazine there is an increase in seizures in individuals who had a history of convulsive disorders.[294] Reports indicate that thioridazine does not increase seizures in epileptics.[130] For details, a recent review by Remick and Fine[236] is suggested. Skin and ocular reactions are very rare in children.

For review of side effects, see references 96, 266, and the latest edition of the *PDR*.

Antidepressants

REVIEW OF THE REPRESENTATIVE LITERATURE

The tricyclics are effective treatment for adults with depression, particularly for those with psychomotor retardation. Depression as a symptom is seen in children, but the clinical manifestations may vary, depending on the stage of development. Somatic complaints, insomnia, hyperactivity, antisocial behavior, and phobias have been reported to express depressive states. The existence of manic-depressive illness under ten years of age is contro-

TABLE 23–2

*Antidepressants**

| | Generic Name | Trade Name | Daily Dosage | |
			Range in mg	Number of Divided Doses
A. Tricyclics	Imipramine	Tofranil	6 to 225† (1 to 5 mg/Kg)	2–3
		Presamine		
	Amitriptyline	Elavil	10 to 75	1–3
	Nortriptyline	Aventyl	10 to 75	1–3
B. Monoamine oxidase (MAO) inhibitors	Phenelzine	Nardil		
	Nialamide	Niamid		
	Tranylcypromine	Parnate		

* Except for the use of imipramine for enuresis in patients over six years of age, imipraminelike drugs are not recommended for patients under twelve. MAO inhibitors should not be given to children.
† Recommended dosage for enuresis: 25–50 mg one hour before bedtime for patients six to twelve years of age; 75 mg for patients over twelve years of age.

versial and, in general, depressive states in children are poorly defined entities.*

It is difficult to evaluate the effects of imipraminelike drugs in "depressed" children on the basis of the older literature. In addition to diagnostic problems, controlled studies are lacking and most reports are anecdotal.[133, 134, 135, 290] In an uncontrolled, open trial, nineteen prepubertal depressed children were treated with amitriptyline or imipramine and fifteen were not; three to seven months later, the treated group showed significant improvement.[303] Diagnosis was made on the basis of a ten-item depressive symptomatology index. The patients' families showed a heavy load of affective illness. The efficacy of amitriptyline was explored in a placebo-controlled double-blind study involving a heterogeneous sample of fourteen "depressed" inpatients, ages ten to seventeen.[197] Each child served as his own control in a crossover design. With the exception of sleeping difficulties, ratings on a nine-point depressive symptomatology checklist showed significant decrease in symptoms. Three children improved in four to five of the nine behavioral categories; two were schizophrenic adolescents.

Recently, Puig-Antich[227] has shown some evidence that depressed prepubertal children can meet the Research Diagnostic Criteria (RDC)[281] for major depressive disorder of adults. In a pilot study[227] of thirteen children with depressive disorder, eight boys and five girls, ages six and one-third to twelve years, eight were treated with imipramine in doses of 2 to 4.5 mg/kg/day. After a period of four weeks on optimal dosage, six responded to the drug, and two failed to do so. With careful clinical and laboratory monitoring which included EKG, side effects were minimal. This open trial is being followed by a double-blind placebo-controlled study involving a larger sample of patients.

Nortriptyline was reported to be effective in decreasing hyperactivity, aggressiveness, and destructiveness in retarded autistic children, whose symptoms were refractory to other medications including neuroleptics.[180] Imipramine showed a mixture of stimulating, tranquilizing, and disorganizing effects in a small sample of preschool psychotic children.[52]

Results of controlled, double-blind studies indicate that the tricyclic antidepressants are effective in the treatment of enuresis in children five to sixteen years of age.[1, 225] The single h.s. (before sleep) dosage of imipramine is usually

* See references 5, 9, 89, 149, and 210.

low (25–50 mg), and side effects are thus minimal or absent. There is a paucity of studies comparing the efficacy of drug treatment to other treatment modalities in enuretic children of normal intelligence. Insufficient evidence is available on the effectiveness of tricyclics in the enuretic retarded; the literature has been critically reviewed by Sprague and Werry.[288]

The effects of imipramine were also explored in hyperkinetic children. Rapoport[231] treated a diagnostically heterogeneous group of outpatients, five to twenty-one years of age, with this drug. In most cases, the EEGs showed initial abnormalities; behavioral difficulties ranged from temper tantrums to daydreaming and poor academic work. The greatest improvements were noted in learning skills, attention, and alertness. In another clinical trial involving fifty-two hyperkinetic children, ages three to fourteen, 67 percent showed marked improvement.[162] In a double-blind study in a diagnostically heterogeneous population of thirty-two hyperkinetic and aggressive clinic patients, most with MBD, imipramine was compared to dextroamphetamine and placebo.[318] The children were 63 to 163 months of age, and their IQs ranged from 40 to 113; all were assigned to the three conditions in one of two counterbalanced orders (IPD or DPI). Sixty-nine percent of the children responded to imipramine and only 44 percent to dextroamphetamine; significant decreases in both aggressiveness and hyperactivity were obtained on both active drugs, whereas decrease of inattentiveness occurred only on imipramine. No significant drug effects were noted on various performance tasks.

Imipramine was therapeutic in a homogeneous sample of nineteen hyperactive outpatients, six to twelve years of age.[301] Assessments were made on a variety of rating scales and psychometric measures. Statistical analysis of ratings showed a significant improvement from baseline to termination in hyperactivity, defiance, inattentiveness, and sociability, as well as on Stroop Color-Word Test. However, there was a deterioration of recall, which subsequently improved on placebo. Seventy-eight percent of the group suffered weight loss (average 0.9 kg over eight weeks); an average 1.3 kg of weight increase was noted in four weeks post-treatment on placebo. Four children had enuresis on baseline; this was suppressed during imipramine and, interestingly, returned with placebo treatment.

In a well-designed double-blind study of a carefully defined population comprising seventy-six hyperactive children, imipramine was compared to methylphenidate and placebo.[235] The patients, aged six to twelve years, were middle-class schoolboys, with IQs of 80 and above. Both drugs were rated superior to placebo by several raters using a variety of rating scales and performance tasks; however, all measures favored methylphenidate. Imipramine showed only a weak effect on cognitive tests.

Imipramine was also effective in the treatment of nonpsychotic children, aged six to fourteen years, with school phobia. Most of these youngsters were depressed. The drug was given in conjunction with other treatments.[142, 143] In this well-designed and controlled study, 81 percent of the sixteen children treated with imipramine attended school after six weeks, whereas only 47 percent of the nineteen children who were on placebo did so. Based on the ratings of global improvement by the psychiatrists, mothers, and children, this difference was statistically significant, as was the global therapeutic efficacy. On psychiatric symptom rating scales, depression, phobic behavior, separation from mother, physical discomfort, and fear of going to school (five of six items) improved significantly on imipramine. The authors suggest that the therapeutic effects of imipramine in this group of children were due to the reduction of separation anxiety.

Frommer[133, 134, 135] and Stack[290] used the monoamine oxidase inhibitors, phenelzine and isocarboxazid, in the treatment of depressed children in open clinical trials. As the reports are rather sketchy, it remains questionable as to whether these drugs should be given to children.

INDICATIONS

Imipramine has been recommended for the treatment of enuresis in children over six years of age. Although adequate studies are lacking, it seems that imipramine can be used in adolescents with moderate to severe depressive states. Childhood depressions are poorly defined and, in these conditions, imipramine is restricted to investigational use. In hyperkinetic, nonpsychotic children, the drugs of choice are the psychomotor stimulants; the role of imipramine here, as well as in school phobia, remains to be elucidated. In some settings, this drug may be useful in selected cases.[229]

RECOMMENDED LABORATORY STUDIES

SGOT, SGPT, alkaline phosphatase, CBC, urinalysis, and electrocardiogram (EKG) are recommended.

SIDE EFFECTS

The most frequent side effects with imipramine are: anorexia, drowsiness, insomnia, dry mouth, constipation, and irritability. Increase in blood pressure (diastolic pressure), weight loss[235] orthostatic hypotension,[143] and electrocardiographic abnormalities[316] have been reported in children. The question of epileptogenic effects of imipramine remains controversial as noted in the review by Petti and Campbell.[220] The death of a six-year-old with school phobia has been reported on 14.7 mg/kg/day.[251] The pharmacokinetics of this drug may be different in children than in adults[317] and, therefore, high single doses at bedtime are not recommended. The FDA's new guidelines will approve investigational protocols only if the "total daily dose does not exceed 90 mg for a 40 pound child, 110 mg for a 50 pound child, 135 mg for a 60 pound child, 160 mg for a 70 pound child, and 180 mg for an 80 pound child . . . with recommended regular EKG monitoring when doses approach these limits."[156] The side effects of antidepressants in children are reviewed in references 96, 251 and the latest edition of the *PDR*.

The use of antidepressants in prepubertal psychiatric population has been critically evaluated by Rapoport and Mikkelsen.[232]

Psychomotor Stimulants

REVIEW OF THE REPRESENTATIVE LITERATURE

Of all psychoactive agents used in child psychiatry, the best documented are the effects of psychomotor stimulants. An open clinical trial[28] studied the effects of amphetamine in thirty hospitalized children of normal intelligence, ages five to fourteen years. Their behavioral disorders were severe, ranging from learning disabilities with secondarily disturbed behavior, to withdrawal or aggressiveness. Dramatic improvement was shown in the performance of fourteen children, and fifteen responded to the drug by becoming emotionally subdued; some were noisy and aggressive on baseline. The remaining children showed a variety of emotional responses, from euphoria to crying readily. Side effects were increases of blood pressure, insomnia, loss of appetite, and nausea.

Bender and Cottington[21] reported on the use of amphetamine in forty children, ages five to thirteen years, with a variety of diagnoses and IQs

TABLE 23–3

Psychomotor Stimulants

Generic Name	Trade Name	Daily Dosage	
		Range in mg	Number of Divided Doses
Amphetamine	Benzedrine		
Dextroamphetamine	Dexedrine*	10 to 25	1–2
Methylphenidate	Ritalin†	30 to 60 (0.3 mg/Kg)	1–2
Magnesium pemoline	Cylert	25 to 125 (1.9 to 2.7 mg/kg)	1

* Not recommended for patients under three years of age.
† Not recommended for patients under six years of age.

ranging from retarded to dull normal and to superior. In this open trial, the fourteen children with psychoneurosis and sixteen with neurotic behavior disorders responded favorably to the drug; the children with learning disabilities showed improvement in school work. The most dramatic change was seen in patients with symptoms of aggressiveness and hyperkinesis. The few children with developmental brain anomalies and schizophrenia failed to respond. In the four cases with psychopathic personalities, aggressiveness ceased, and hyperkinesis either ceased or the child became disorganized. All four showed emotional instability, irritability, depression, and tension. It was stressed that amphetamine's use

may be an aid in the differential diagnosis of some obscure problems . . . the successful use of this drug in the behavior problems of children depends on a clear understanding of the causes of the child's problems, the proper choice of children to receive the drug, and the use of the drug only as an adjunct to adequate personal psychotherapy, tutoring and social adjustments.[21] [p. 120]

Eisenberg and associates,[107] in a double-blind, well-controlled study found that dextroamphetamine was statistically significantly superior to placebo or no drug treatment for delinquent boys in a training school. Cottage parents and classroom teachers made the ratings on a symptom check list. Three weeks after the discontinuation of treatment, the differences between experimental groups were no longer present. In a controlled, crossover study,[82] comprising fifty-two school children (average age, 11.6 years, standard deviation = 1.08 years) with learning and school behavior problems, dextroamphetamine was statistically significantly superior to placebo based on

teacher's symptom check list and global ratings as well as a battery of performance tests. Improvements were shown on the factor reflecting assertiveness and drive; the factor reflecting intellectual ability showed no change on drug. In another placebo controlled study of forty-five outpatients (mean age circa ten years), with behavior and/or learning problems, dextroamphetamine showed statistically significant improvement when compared to placebo on achievement tests, the Porteus Mazes, visual perception tests, auditory synthesis, and rote learning.[86] Parent symptom ratings showed significant improvement in hyperkinetic symptoms on drug, while little difference was demonstrated on neurotic symptoms between drug and placebo. There was no drug effect on Wechsler Intelligence Test for Children test scores, oral reading, Bender Gestalt, human figure drawings, auditory discrimination, and memory, and tests of inhibitory control over impulsive movements. Denhoff, Davids, and Hawkins,[92] Steinberg, Troshinsky, and Steinberg,[291] and Finnerty, Soltys and Cole[113] also found that dextroamphetamine was superior to placebo in reducing hyperactivity.

In a double-blind controlled study of sixty-two hyperkinetic schoolchildren, randomly assigned to dextroamphetamine, thioridazine, or placebo, dextroamphetamine was significantly superior to both conditions, though the overall symptomatology decreased in all three groups.[250]

Levoamphetamine was recently withdrawn from use. In some children, it is effective in controlling aggressiveness and hyperactivity.[12, 13, 14]

Both dextroamphetamine and levoamphetamine are ineffective or cause worsening of psychosis in schizophrenic children. Although in some cases the child responded with decrease of hyperactivity, he also became less verbal.[46, 48]

After reports of uncontrolled trials with methylphenidate,[176, 198] Conners and Eisenberg[80] published the results of a placebo-controlled study in eighty-one deprived or emotionally disturbed nonpsychotic children, ages seven to fifteen, with IQs ranging from 65 to 135. The children were drawn from residential care institutions. On the basis of IQ distribution, the children were divided into three groups, and half of each group was randomly assigned to drug or placebo. Methylphenidate was statistically superior to placebo in reducing symptoms, but there were wide individual differences in responsiveness. The authors suggested that for future studies the patients should be more carefully selected and should comprise a more homogeneous group. Methylphenidate had only a mild positive effect on the way the patients scored on the Porteus Mazes; the greatest change being noted in low-IQ children. The decrease of symptoms was thus not related to learning, and there was little or no change in a variety of learning tests.[83] Knights and Hinton[175] reported a double-blind study comparing the effects of methylphenidate and placebo on the motor skills and behavior of forty children with learning problems. Teachers and parents rated the drug group as less distractible and more attentive. The psychological test data showed that the drug treatment was associated with improved attention span, resulting in better motor coordination and performance skills.

In a double-blind, crossover study, Sprague, Barnes, and Werry[289] assigned twelve hyperactive boys (mean age, 94.2 months; mean IQ, 98.6) from a special education class to methylphenidate, thioridazine, or placebo. Each child participated in each of six experimental conditions: three drug conditions at each of two dosage levels (low and high). Both clinical (classroom behavior) and laboratory measures favored methylphenidate. Methylphenidate improved learning performance, whereas thioridazine decreased it. Methylphenidate was investigated in an uncontrolled study in hyperkinetic outpatients of low socioeconomic background.[159] The patients were five to twelve years of age (mean age, 8.3 months), with a mean IQ of 86.8; only five children had IQs of 100 or above. Of the sixty-two children, thirty-one completed the twelve-week schedule. Raters noted statistically significant improvements in various areas of behavior, including hyperactivity, inattentiveness, learning problems, perceptual and perceptual-motor functioning. Methylphenidate was compared to imipramine and placebo[235] in seventy-six middle-class outpatients, six to twelve years of age. The behavioral ratings indicated that both drugs were superior to placebo; on cognitive tests, in particular, methylphenidate was superior to both.

Although Rapoport and associates reported that EEG abnormalities or the presence of soft neurological signs did not predict drug response, others found significant correlations between the degree of brain dysfunction (obtained from EEG abnormalities, skin conduction levels, and neurological findings) and response to methylphenidate treatment.[257] In this double-blind study, thirty-one hyperkinetic children were assigned to methylphenidate or placebo groups. Methylphenidate was superior to placebo. The best responders had greater resting EEG mean amplitudes, greater resting EEG range of amplitudes, more slow-wave activity, more movement artifacts, larger evoked cortical responses, and lower skin conduction levels. This was interpreted as indicating the presence of a low arousal level in the central nervous system.

In an outpatient clinical trial, methylphenidate was found to be therapeutically effective in adolescents with MBD who were twelve to eighteen years old. This was evidenced by improvement in scholastic work on Raven matrices test performance and on the electroencephalogram.[202] The youngsters' IQs ranged from low average to superior. They exhibited hyperkinesis, distractibility, learning problems, soft neurological signs, and abnormal EEGs on baseline. No tendency toward addiction was noted, but the authors recommend caution. Methylphenidate was found to be less effective with very young, hyperactive children. This finding came out of a double-blind placebo-controlled, crossover study comprising twenty-six youngsters whose mean age was four years and whose IQs ranged from 86 to 124.[260] Hyperactivity was reported to be reduced in the home, but psychological tests and school behavior failed to show improvement. Actually, behavioral toxicity (irritability, withdrawal and clinging, and decrease of appetite and insomnia) interfered with the children's functioning. After the termination of the study, the mothers of all but three of the sample decided not to continue methylphenidate. In a similar population of preschoolers, Conners[69] found methylphenidate to be superior to placebo, though he too, came to the conclusion that with this drug the results with preschoolers are more variable and less predictable than with older children.

There is evidence that magnesium pemoline[222]

is a promising therapeutic agent in hyperactive MBD children. A great advantage over other stimulants is that it is given in a single morning dose. This drug has been explored by Conners and associates[84] in eighty-one outpatients, ages 70 to 144 months, with IQs above 80. In this double-blind study, the children were randomly assigned to magnesium pemolone, dextroamphetamine, or placebo groups for a treatment period of eight weeks. Global clinical ratings, symptom ratings, and various psychological tests showed that statistically, both drugs were significantly superior to placebo. Dextroamphetamine acted more quickly, but by the end of the treatment period, the differences in effect were insignificant. Ultimately, circa 96 percent of the patients on dextroamphetamine and 77 percent of those on pemoline were rated improved, in contrast to only 30 percent of those on placebo. However, there were fewer complaints of anorexia with pemoline. Cardiovascular or ophthalmologic changes were absent with both drugs. The authors concluded that magnesium pemoline is a good alternative for the treatment of the child with MBD.

In a collaborative study involving a well-defined population of a total of 413 school children, 238 patients were assigned in random fashion to pemoline or placebo for nine weeks.[216] Maximum effectiveness was at six weeks. All raters on the various measures found pemoline to be significantly superior to placebo, both clinically and statistically. Marked decreases in restlessness, temper tantrums, and other symptoms were accompanied by improvement in cognitive and perceptual functions. Side effects were mild, with insomnia and anorexia noted most frequently. Pemoline was investigated for safety in 407 of the 413 children. Blood pressure and pulse remained stable in both drug and placebo groups. When data analysis was performed on all 413 patients, some of whom failed to meet certain inclusion criteria, the level of improvement of the pemoline group was almost identical to that of the 238 children who had met all of the protocol criteria. In a total of 288 children, the efficacy of pemoline remained stable on administration up to eighteen months.

In the past twenty years or so, more than a dozen open trials and controlled studies have been reported on the use of deanol, a precursor of acetylcholine, for children with behavior disorders or mental retardation. (For review, see reference 73.) Its behavioral effects and its possible influence on performance, along with its apparently mild side effects, warrant a definitive study in hyperkinetic children of normal intelligence.

Casual reports regarding the possible efficacy of caffeine in hyperkinetic children[261] are currently being followed with controlled clinical studies. In a double-blind, crossover study, eight inpatients were randomly assigned to caffeine, methylphenidate, or placebo groups.[137] The subjects were children of normal IQ, ages six to ten years, who were hyperactive as a result of MBD. They were drug-free for two weeks prior to medication. Each child served as his own control and was on medication for ten days; there was a two and one-half day washout period between each course. The assessment measures were the Conners Teacher Rating Scale and perceptual and perceptual-motor tasks. Caffeine in daily doses of 160 mg was inferior to 20 mg of methylphenidate and not significantly better than placebo. Huestis, Arnold, and Smeltzer[163] compared caffeine, d-amphetamine, and methylphenidate in a placebo-controlled, double-blind crossover design. The eighteen hyperactive children were randomly assigned to one of the treatment conditions. Caffeine, in daily doses up to 300 mg/day, was not significantly superior to placebo. A subsequent trial in a sample of twenty-nine children showed similar results: both methylphenidate and dextroamphetamine were significantly superior to placebo and to caffeine.[10] Conners[70] obtained similar results in a double-blind, crossover trial of caffeine and placebo in eight hyperkinetic children. He suggested further research to explore higher doses.

Although beneficial effects from dextroamphetamine with thioridazine were reported in hyperactive schoolchildren with chronic, servere disorders,[274] there is insufficient evidence to conclude that combined drug therapy is more effective than one drug.

There are recent studies which indicate that psychomotor stimulants improve attention span and performance in hyperkinetic MBD children of normal intelligence.* Nonetheless, the effects of drugs on intelligence and learning continue to be controversial.

Several theories have been offered regarding the mode of therapeutic action of stimulants in children.† Some psychophysiological data[81, 254] support the theory that in a subgroup of hyperkinetic MBD children, stimulants raise low central nervous system arousal and inhibitory control, resulting in behavioral improvement.[74, 254]

The medical use of stimulants in preadolescents is not associated with later drug abuse.[19, 129, 179]

Additional reviews on the use of stimulant

* See references 64, 74, 76, 77, 175, 286, 289, and 310.
† See references 64, 76, 114, 182, 280, and 307.

drugs in children are by Cantwell and Carlson,[55] Conners, [71, 75] and Gittelman-Klein.[139, 140]

INDICATIONS

The psychomotor stimulants have been accepted as the drugs of choice for the treatment of hyperactive children with MBD. These drugs may be of help in delinquent children who are inpatients.[107] Fish[114] points out that there are many causes of hyperactivity in children, and these drugs are useful only in some of them. She believes that these agents may be equally effective in some nonhyperactive children. Careful diagnosis prior to medication is essential: stimulants usually cause a worsening in the disorganization of psychotics.[46, 48, 114, 167]

RECOMMENDED LABORATORY STUDIES

In daily practice, baseline SGOT, SGPT, alkaline phosphatase, CBC, and urinalysis are recommended, with checkups twice a year.

SIDE EFFECTS

Anorexia, weight loss, and insomnia are the most frequent untoward effects; behavioral toxicity is seen. Hypoactivity, drowsiness, sleepiness, increase in blood pressure and pulse rates were also reported. (For review, see reference 66.) Hallucinosis has been described with both amphetamine[211, 318] and methylphenidate.[196] A nine-year-old hyperactive child of normal intelligence developed Gilles de la Tourette's syndrome after eight week's administration of 20 mg/day of methylphenidate; it was suggested that the drug evoked the syndrome in a child who was vulnerable.[147]

Safer and Allen[249] reported that administration of dextroamphetamine or methylphenidate over a period of two to three years decreased the growth and weight of hyperactive school children. This is a retrospective study with many flaws. In an anterospective long-term follow up of hyperactive children who received methylphenidate (from 0.3 mg/kg/day to 1.86 mg/kg/day, mean, 0.59 mg/kg/day) for a period of two years, body weight and height did not statistically differ from controls.[201] Gross[154] concluded that there was no stunting of growth from long-term use of methylphenidate, dextroamphetamine, or imipramine/desipramine in one hundred children. Another restropective study indicated that methylphenidate given in childhood did not seriously interfere with growth in height, nor did it contribute to later drug abuse.[19] On the other hand, a one-year follow up of hyperactive boys treated with methylphenidate showed a significant decrease in growth rate for weight, but not for height.[229]

Seventy-two boys treated with methylphenidate (mean dosage 0.52–0.59 mg/kg/day) showed a deficit in height and weight in the first year of treatment, but not in the second year on drug maintenance.[255] Actually, the forty-eight boys receiving medication for two years were taller than expected. Deficits in growth in height were not related to summer drug holidays.

In a prospective study involving seven school-age children with MBD, chronic dextroamphetamine administration resulted in significant growth retardations and prolactin suppression.[152, 228] After three to six months of continuous administration of pemoline, early weight loss returned to the normal curve of weight gain. Unlike the findings with other stimulants, blood pressure and pulse rates remained stable.[216]

Sprague and Werry[287] demonstrated that 0.3 mg/kg/day of methylphenidate was as therapeutically effective as higher doses. Side effects increased with dosage increase until at 1.0 mg/kg/day over 50 percent of the children had some untoward effects (mainly weight loss and worsening of behavior). The same group found that of forty-two hyperactive children on methylphenidate for two years, 26 percent functioned well without drug after a one-month placebo period, while 40 percent still benefited from medication.[279] Since remissions can develop, and on the basis of these findings, periodic drug-free periods were recommended. (For review of clinical management and side effects, see references 55 and 171.)

Sedatives

Chloral hydrate, a sedative and hypnotic, remains important for emergency situations and in the treatment of insomnia. It is given in doses of 25 to 50 mg/kg/day, divided into two to three doses; maximum 2 gm per dose.

Diphenhydramine, an antihistaminic, was explored in an open trial with inpatients, [102, 272] outpatients,[118] and in a controlled, double-blind study of hospitalized, school-age children.[119, 120, 177] The therapeutically effective doses ranged from 3 to 26 mg/kg/day (200–800 mg/day).

According to Fish,[117] thus drug, albeit safe and easy to regulate, has not been sufficiently explored.

Dosages are usually neither individualized nor sufficiently high. It is recommended for behavioral and organic disorders associated with hyperactivity. A trial with this agent is worthwhile prior to placing a schizophrenic child on a neuroleptic. Diphenhydramine is also valuable for the relief of acute dystonic reactions caused by neuroleptics (25–50 mg, P O or I M). (For review, see reference 233.)

Hypnotics and Anticonvulsants

Barbiturates and diphenylhydantoin should be used only as antiepileptics. Anticonvulsants were tried in a group of twenty-six inpatients, ages six to thirteen years, who had various severe behavior problems along with EEG abnormalities.[218] No positive clinical changes ensued. In this open trial, the patients were studied intensively and the methodology was sound. The usefulness of diphenylhydantoin in the treatment of behavioral disorders was not demonstrated in controlled, double-blind studies. Statistically, in terms of decreasing disruptive behavior, including impulsivity and hyperactivity, placebo was significantly superior to this drug. This was determined with institutionalized delinquent boys who were randomly assigned to the treatment conditions.[184] The children, thirteen to sixteen years of age, were of normal intelligence. In a study of forty-three aggressive and disturbed delinquent institutionalized boys, ages nine to fourteen years, behavioral ratings and other measures were subjected to statistical analysis.[85] It turned out that neither diphenylhydantoin nor methylphenidate was therapeutic. Looker and Conners[194] compared diphenylhydantoin treatment to placebo in seventeen nonretarded children, ages five and one-half to fourteen and one-half, with severe temper tantrums and MBD. There was no significant group change on drug.

For review of antiepileptics, a recent chapter by Stores[292] is recommended.

Anxiolytics

In daily practice, these agents are frequently prescribed to individuals with anxiety and neurotic symptoms. However, their value has not been critically assessed in children or adolescents who suffer from the same symptoms.[141]

Chlordiazepoxide was explored in a double-blind, crossover study in a heterogeneous group of sixteen nonpsychotic children, ages seven to fourteen years. It was less effective than dextroamphetamine in diminishing manifestations of hyperkinetic syndrome, although both were superior to placebo.[323] Also, in a double-blind, crossover design, both dextroamphetamine and placebo were more effective than diazepam in reducing symptoms, including hyperactivity and distractibility.[322] In twenty-one outpatients of normal intelligence, ages six to twelve years, most untoward effects were seen with diazepam.

In an open trial involving a diagnostically heterogeneous sample of 130 outpatients, ages two to seventeen years, chlordiazepoxide was effective in children with school phobia.[178] The fact that the ages were not specified is an important weakness in this study. In school phobia, both the response to treatment and the prognosis are different in young children and in adolescents. Those children with brain damage or epilepsy and abnormal EEG responded poorly to the drug. Thirteen children, some with abnormal EEG patterns, developed a "paradoxical reaction," which included loss of control. Chlordiazepoxide may worsen the preexisting psychosis or even create a florid psychosis in patients with borderline schizophrenic features (Campbell and Fish, in preparation); it is not therapeutic and may even be contraindicated in certain diagnostic categories or profiles.[183, 187, 221, 278] For instance, data from studies with adult patients and normals suggest that chlordiazepoxide and some other antianxiety agents should not be given to individuals with poor impulse control or aggressiveness;[95, 136, 165] others have not confirmed these findings.[237] (For review, see references 141 and 233.)

Lithium

Lithium has a well-established role in the treatment of the manic phase of manic-depressive illness and in the prevention of recurrent depressive episodes in adults. Its role has not been established in psychiatric disturbances of childhood. Moreover, affective disorders in children continue to present a diagnostic problem.

Lithium has been given to children with "depressive" and "manic" conditions, reportedly with good results.* However, the populations were not well defined, nor were controls employed.

In clinical trials with hyperactive children, lith-

---

* See references 6, 7, 101, 133, and 134.

ium was ineffective in reducing this symptom.[153, 313]

Rifkin, and associates[238] carried out a study on hospitalized adolescents with emotionally unstable character disorder (EUCD), characterized by chronic maladaptive behavior patterns and non-reactive (usually) depressive and hypomanic mood swings. The twenty-one patients were randomly assigned to lithium or placebo in a double-blind crossover design. Lithium was found to be therapeutically effective and statistically significantly superior to placebo at blood levels of 0.6 to 1.5 mE q/1. On the basis of the patients' drug response, the authors concluded that EUCD is related to affective illness. They also felt that lithium is as valuable as chlorpromazine in the treatment of this condition, particularly because it lacks the sedative effect that is objectionable to adolescents.

Over a period of up to thirty-three months, lithium was administered to twelve boys and girls, ages four to fourteen years, with chronic behavior disorders, "suggesting manic-depressive illness."[91] Daily dosage ranged from 450 to 1,200 mg (blood levels ranged from 0.5 to 1.2 mEq/1). The most marked response to lithium was an improvement in mood in this sample of children, who had exhibited explosive anger and hostility on baseline. Only four of the twelve patients underwent a double-blind crossover trial. It was observed that in "a few children" the effectiveness of the drug diminished over time. Side effects were minimal with clinical and laboratory monitoring. Schou[262] also suggested that lithium maintenance may have a "stabilizing and normalizing action" in children and adolescents with "undulating and periodic disturbances of mood and behavior."

Lithium administration may be effective in decreasing hyperactivity, aggressiveness, and stereotypies in some retarded autistic children.[49, 150] Data suggest that in retarded and psychotic children, whose aggressiveness is associated with explosiveness and excitability, lithium has an antiaggressive effect.[49, 98] The assessment of the efficacy of lithium in children and adolescents depends on further exploration. It may prove of value in certain behavioral profiles of treatment-resistant severe disturbances.[38] (For review, references 42, 138, and 233 are recommended.)

L-dopa

Because of the biochemical and some behavioral effects of L-dopa, this drug was administered to psychotic children.[46, 241] In the first study, after six months of treatment, no behavioral change was evident, although the serotonin blood levels decreased. In the second study, improvements were obtained in several symptoms. For hypoactive children these included a decrease of negativism and increases in play, energy, and motor initiation. Campbell and associates[46] suggested that, because of its stimulating properties, L-dopa merits further exploration in a larger sample of young psychotic children.

Hallucinogens

Both acute and maintenance clinical trials with such agents were carried out in schizophrenic and autistic children. The drugs employed were d-lysergic acid diethylamide (LSD-25) and a methylated derivative of LSD, L-methyl-D-lysergic acid butalamide bimaleate. The results are inconclusive. In some patients, these drugs led to an improvement in behavior with a decrease in withdrawal. In other children, stimulation resulted in an increase in anxiety and disorganization.* (For reviews, see references 207 and 233.)

Megavitamins

Hoffer[158] had reported findings on the superiority of niacinamide and ascorbic acid over placebo in some schizophrenic children. These were not confirmed. In a double-blind study that extended over a period of six months,[151] fifty-seven schizophrenic children, four to twelve years of age, were separated into three groups, each receiving niacinamide, niacinamide plus a tranquilizer, or placebo. Statistical analysis showed no significant difference in the average scores of the three groups. Roukema and Emery[246] arrived at similar conclusions after conducting an open trial for twelve months. In a preliminary report, Rimland[239] described the results of a study of 190 outpatient psychotic children receiving megadoses of vitamins over a period of twenty-four weeks. The subgroup of thirty-seven children with classical infantile autism showed the greatest improvement. The author considered the result only encouraging. A subsequent double-blind placebo controlled study had methodological flaws.[240]

* See references 23, 24, 25, 123, 128, 245, 275, and 276.

An American Psychiatric Association task force concluded that magavitamin therapy was of no value in the treatment of adult schizophrenia.[192] The American Academy of Pediatrics Committee on Nutrition concluded that "megavitamin therapy as a treatment for learning disabilities and psychoses in children, including autism, is not justified on the basis of documented clinical results."[18] A placebo-controlled trial of MBD children concurred with these recommendations.[11]

Triiodothyronine

Triiodothyronine, or T_3, has been tested in a small number of very severely disturbed, young euthyroid children, some of whom were autistic and others nonpsychotic.[39, 47, 48] In these studies, T_3 had both stimulating and antipsychotic effects and was viewed as an agent that is potentially useful in the treatment of autistic children. Further investigations were carried out in a homogeneous group of autistics under controlled conditions, using multiple raters and multiple rating scales.[54] T_3 was significantly superior to placebo only in decreasing loud voice and stereotypies on the psychiatrist's rating scale (Children's Psychiatric Rating Scale) and on parents' ratings (Parent Teacher Questionnaire). The only other significant behavioral finding was that all patients improved over time; thus a lengthy (average eighteen weeks) crossover design is unsuitable even for very chronic psychiatric patients.

Relationships of Psychopharmacology to Other Modalities of Treatment

In medicine, it is essential to know how one treatment compares with another, which is more effective in a specific condition, and whether the efficacy of the best single treatment is enhanced by combining it with another therapeutic modality. How do the immediate and long-term results differ?

In psychiatry, there is some scientific evidence that bears on the efficacy of drug therapy as compared to some other treatment modalities and their relationships in adult patients. (For review, see reference 174).* In the field of child psychiatry

* See also Group for the Advancement of Psychiatry (GAP), *Pharmacotherapy and Psychotherapy; Paradoxes, Problems and Progress*, vol. 9, Report No. 93, 1975.

such well-controlled studies with large samples of homogeneous populations are lacking. In the literature, the reported drug studies casually mention that patients received milieu, individual, or other therapies in addition to the psychoactive agent. However, neither of these studies were designed to compare medications to other treatment modalities.

There are few reports comparing pharmacotherapy with behavior therapy in children, the two most quantifiable of all the available treatments in psychiatry. Young and Turner[321] tested the hypothesis that stimulants would facilitate the conditioning therapy of enuresis in a test group comprised of 299 subjects, aged four to fifteen years. One hundred and five children received conditioning alone, with the Eastleigh buzzer unit; 84 consecutive admissions received conditioning and dextroamphetamine, and the following 110 consecutive admissions received conditioning and methamphetamine. Both drugs facilitated conditioning. Methamphetamine was marginally superior to dextroamphetamine. Dextroamphetamine was associated with a highly significant increase in the frequency of relapse. A follow up of 222 children indicated that combined conditioning and drug treatment yielded a higher frequency of relapse (75.6 percent with dextroamphetamine, and 43.3 percent with methamphetamine) than conditioning alone (31.7 percent).[298] An attempt to replicate these findings failed to show that methamphetamine enhanced the conditioning in either normal or retarded children.[172]

Christensen and Sprague[62] worked with twelve socially maladjusted and conduct problem children (mean age, 114 months; mean IQ, 94.25), who had been referred for hyperactivity. They investigated the effects of methylphenidate and behavior therapy. The children came from special education classes in the public school system. They were divided into a drug and a placebo group, and all received contingent reinforcement. Methylphenidate significantly reduced the number of seat movements (measured by a special apparatus attached to a chair), as did the behavior modification sessions. However, there was an interaction between the drug and the contingent reinforcement sessions: in some ways the combination was superior to behavior modification alone.

In a study with sixteen hyperkinetic institutionalized retardates with IQs of 31 to 68 (mean 51), aged nine to fifteen years, Christensen[61] explored the effects of conjoint drug-behavior therapy. Using a placebo-controlled, double-blind crossover design, with each subject serving as his own control for the first two weeks, the investigators gave each child either placebo or methylphenidate. The alternate medication was given for the last two weeks during each stage of behavior therapy conditioning. Drug trials were nested within the four behavior modification stages so that medication was given only while behavior modification was in effect. On various measures used to assess treatment effects, methylphenidate was significantly inferior to conditioning in reducing hyperactivity and other disruptive classroom behavior. Individual analyses showed that only four children responded to drug, while ten did to behavior therapy. The author suggests that environmental control rather than drug-control should be established over problem behaviors of certain children, either at school or by working with the parents.

However, in a study of ninety-six hyperkinetic school children with significant perceptual-cognitive impairment, those who received dextroamphetamine improved over those who received placebo —both behaviorally and on the Frostig Developmental Test of Visual Perception.[87] Tutoring alone did not make a significant difference. Most children in the experimental groups still required remedial help after the termination of the study. This study had some flaws, including the fact that there was little control over drug administration.

In a double-blind study involving thirty-two hyperkinetic children of normal intelligence, randomly assigned to different treatment groups, the combination of methylphenidate and behavior therapy was the best treatment, followed by methylphenidate alone, and behavior therapy with placebo was the least effective.[145]

For an overview of drugs and psychosocial therapies, reference 3 is recommended.

It would seem that during the formative years, drug therapy alone never suffices. Many colleagues are not opposed to the appropriate usage of psychoactive agents in children and have experience in treating children with drugs. In general, they see medication as an adjunct or important treatment modality in the global treatment of the child.[106, 117, 213, 305] Recently, a comprehensive program for the treatment of hyperkinetic children was discussed,[99] outlined,[112] and the results published.[4] Comprehensive inpatient programs, appropriate for young psychotic children, have also been developed.* The choice of other treatments (environmental manipulation, remedial education, individual psychotherapy, group therapy, family therapy, or counseling) will depend on the etiology, diagnosis, and associated handi-

caps of the individual patient. Even after the cessation of certain symptoms (hyperkinesis, agitation, hallucinations) many patients who no longer need pharmacotherapy may still need follow up and continuation of other treatment(s). Drugs themselves do not create learning and normal cognitive or adaptive behavior, nor do they necessarily alter parental attitudes. However, experience has shown that a therapeutically effective drug can make a child more amenable to environmental variables or to such interventions as remedial work, special education, individual psychotherapy, or parental counseling. Hopefully, these same variables, given in conjunction with the psychoactive agent, will have a more lasting effect on the child.

When calmed by a drug, the hyperactive, distractible child may be able to focus his attention on a task and may, therefore, acquire some reading and writing skills. The child who is excessively aggressive, assaultive, or self-mutilating may require the reduction or abolition of this symptom before he can develop more positive and adaptive social interactions. These, in turn, will help improve his learning. Without drug treatment, such children fail to respond, or respond only minimally, to educational, remedial, milieu, and/or psychotherapy. It has been suggested that pharmacotherapy should be only part of the total treatment of the child and adolescent, which should always include work with parents: This, however, has not been documented with research, as can be seen from the paucity of the literature. Not only are definitive studies about the comparative efficacy of different treatments lacking, but also little is known about their various interactions. In fact, hardly any pilot or controlled studies with adequate sample sizes are available in child psychiatry. Nor will such research alone be sufficient. Only long-term follow up will provide a definitive answer as to what is or what are the most effective and economic approaches to the individual patient.

What Is Known About Outcome or Therapeutic Results

In adults with schizophrenia (particularly, its acute form), depression, and mania, the efficacy of the new psychoactive agents is clearly superior to psychosocial therapies. Pharmacotherapy not only decreases symptoms, but it also modifies the course of the psychiatric disorder. (For review, see references 174 and 315.) Any equivalent

---

* Samit, Nash, and Campbell, in preparation.

effectiveness of drug treatment has not been demonstrated in children and adolescents. It has been barely investigated in a systematic fashion.

Longitudinal studies of deviant infants,[125] psychotic children,[*] hyperkinetic children with MBD.[†] children with unsocialized aggressive behavior,[193, 208, 214, 215] and children diagnosed as sociopathic personality[244] indicate that children do not outgrow these disorders. As adolescents or adults, they are still deviant, retarded, and/or psychotic. Thus, even after the cessation of the hyperkinesis, the child with MBD still has learning and personality problems.

On the other hand, supportive evidence from various follow-up studies indicates that whether or not treated, neurotic symptoms and neuroses in children and adolescents show a high rate of improvement and a very good long-term prognosis. Moreover, such disturbances in early life are not predictive of neuroses in adulthood (for review, see reference 243). Such is the natural history of childhood behavioral disorders.

At present, these disorders are frequently treated with psychoactive drugs; as a rule, however, they should not be treated with drug maintenance. There are no anterospective studies on long-term outcome in which pharmacotherapy is compared with other treatment modalities and with no treatment. Such research is, nonetheless, crucial for the critical evaluation of the therapeutic efficacy of drugs in childhood and adolescence.

The few available studies concern the immediate response or short-term follow up of enuresis, hyperkinetic syndrome, and psychosis.

In a controlled, twelve-month trial, involving 60 enuretics, four and one-half to fifteen years of age, pad-and-bell conditioning was superior to imipramine. Amphetamine was of no value.[200] A long-term follow-up study of 1,129 enuretics indicates a high spontaneous cure rate of this symptom: 3 percent, however, did remain bed wetters after twenty years.[127] In controlled trials, the same authors had disappointing results with psychoactive drugs, including imipramine.

Eisenberg and associates[108] assigned fifty-six neurotic and hyperkinetic children randomly to three groups: psychotherapy without medication, psychotherapy with placebo, and psychotherapy with perphenazine. The therapists were blind as to which patient was on placebo and which on perphenazine. Sixty to 70 percent of neurotic children showed a prompt and enduring response to brief psychotherapy, while only 15 to 40 percent of hy-

perkinetic children attained the same improvement. Addition of placebo did not contribute to the response. There was a suggestion that the hyperkinetic patients benefited more from the active drug than from placebo. In a pilot crossover study involving a diagnostically heterogeneous sample[44] of children with a very wide age range, there was no statistically significant difference between the effects of haloperidol, chlorpromazine, and placebo: instead, an important factor for successful outcome turned out to be improvement in parent-child interaction.[188]

In a study of hyperactive children, three groups were compared: twenty-four were treated with methylphenidate, twenty-two with chlorpromazine, and twenty received no medication[305] (for review see reference 304). Initially, there were notable differences between the groups on ratings of hyperactivity and family diagnosis. However, a five-year follow up of the various measures used showed no significant differences. Over the five years, hyperactivity decreased in all the groups. There was no difference in the degree of improvement among the three groups. Family diagnosis remained unchanged. It was concluded that: "No doubt the stimulants are effective drugs for many hyperactive children, but as the sole method of management their value is limited."[305] Although the hyperactive child on stimulants generally becomes easier to deal with, his ultimate outcome may be affected only slightly, or not at all. A pertinent finding in this study is that only among those taking methylphenidate did initial ratings on family diagnosis predict final outcome by almost every measure of outcome. Only this group showed a significant correlation between family diagnosis and school achievement ($P<0.05$), delinquency ($P<0.05$) and emotional adjustment ($P<0.01$). This strongly suggests that there is an interaction between a useful drug and a healthy family, and that this influences prognosis. Similarly, one can postulate that to change the outcome, a useful drug will interect with other treatment variables such as behavior and modification, family counseling, optimal classroom situations, and skilled, supportive teachers. It is wishful thinking to expect that a useful drug alone will change the outcome of a fairly serious condition with multiple etiologic factors and numerous and various manifestations, such as severe chronic hyperactivity. Satterfield and Cantwell[253] suggest that for many hyperkinetic children, treatment with stimulant drugs not only has a positive short-term effect, but also may serve as a preventive measure for later antisocial behavior.

* See references 8, 22, 44, 105, 169, 247, and 248.
† See references 65, 204, 206, 230, 304, and 306.

A short-term, double-blind procedure was designed to determine whether drug therapy and/or parental counseling are effective in preventing hospitalization and improving the functioning of psychotic children.[271] The forty-eight children, ages four to twelve years, were randomly assigned to one of four treatment groups: trifluoperazine and parental counseling; placebo and parental counseling; trifluoperazine and no counseling; placebo and no counseling. During the treatment period of twenty-six weeks, on four occasions, the progress of each child was evaluated on various measurements. Any one treatment method or combination of methods was found to be of equal effectiveness. On the basis of her clinical experience, Bender[20] maintains that drugs, as well as other treatments, promote the maturation of the psychotic child. In a number of follow-up studies, others failed to find correlation between formal treatment and outcome.[44, 105, 155]

Klein and Davis[174] have offered a superb critique of drug treatment studies in adults and suggested new goals in psychopharmacology. The same applies to children's pharmacotherapy, with the qualification that, for a developing organism, psychosocial interventions may be more effective and, therefore, more important than it is for the adult.

Concluding Remarks

1. Drug therapy has no place in the treatment of mild disturbances of childhood and adolescence, or in conditions which are socially correctable.
2. Drug therapy is a valuable adjunct or an essential treatment modality in many moderately to severely disturbed children and adolescents, but it should never be the sole treatment.
3. In addition to drug and other therapies in the formative years of the patient's life, work with parents is essential.
4. The possible hazards of drug treatment should be weighed against the hazards of the untreated illness.
5. For child psychiatry, psychopharmacology will remain on an empirical basis until its diagnostic entities are defined, not only by behavioral, but also by biological criteria.
6. The effectiveness of drug therapy as compared to other treatments has not yet been critically evaluated.

ACKNOWLEDGMENTS

This work was supported in part by Public Health Service grant No. MHO4665 from the National Institute of Mental Health.

REFERENCES

1. ALDERTON, M. B., "Imipramine in the Treatment of Nocturnal Enuresis of Childhood," *Canadian Psychiatric Association Journal*, 10(2):141, 1965.
2. ALEXANDRIS, H., and LUNDELL, F., "Effect of Thioridazine, Amphetamine and Placebo on the Hyperkinetic Syndrome and Cognitive Area in Mentally Deficient Children," *Canadian Medical Association Journal*, 98(1):92, 1968.
3. AMAN, M. G., "Drugs, Learning and the Psychotherapies," in Werry, J. S. (Ed.), *Pediatric Psychopharmacology. The Use of Behavior Modifying Drugs in Children*, p. 79, Brunner/Mazel, New York, 1978.
4. AMBROSINO, S. V., and DE FONTE, T. M., "A Psychoeducational Study of the Hyperkinetic Syndrome," *Psychosomatics, 14(4):207*, 1973.
5. ANNELL, A. L. (Ed.), *Depressive States in Childhood and Adolescence*, Almquist & Wiksell, Stockholm, 1972.
6. ———, "Manic-Depressive Illness in Children and Effect of Treatment with Lithium Carbonate," *Acta Paedopsychiatrica, 36:*292, 1969.
7. ———, "Lithium in the Treatment of Children and Adolescents," *Acta Psychiatrica Scandinavica* (Supplement), *207:*19, 1969.
8. ———, "The Prognosis of Psychotic Syndromes in Children. A Follow-up Study of 115 Cases," *Acta Psychiatrica Scandinavica, 39:*235, 1963.
9. ANTHONY, J., and SCOTT, P., "Manic-Depressive Psychosis in Childhood," *Journal of Child Psychology and Psychiatry, 1(1):*53, 1960.
10. ARNOLD, L. E., et al., "Methylphenidate vs. Dextroamphetamine vs. Caffeine in Minimal Brain Dys-function," *Archives of General Psychiatry, 35(4):*463, 1978.
11. ———, et al., "Megavitamins for Minimal Brain Dysfunction," *Journal of the American Medical Association, 240(24):*2642, 1978.
12. ———, et al., "Levoamphetamine vs. Dextroamphetamine in Minimal Brain Dysfunction," *Archives of General Psychiatry, 33(3):*292, 1976.
13. ———, et al., "Levoamphetamine and Dextroamphetamine: Differential Effect on Aggression and Hyperkinesis in Children and Dogs," *American Journal of Psychiatry, 130(2):*165, 1973.
14. ———, et al., "Levoamphetamine and Dextroamphetamine: Comparative Efficacy in the Hyperkinetic Syndrome," *Archives of General Psychiatry, 27(6):*816, 1972.
15. AYD, F. J., "Treatment Resistant Patients: A Moral, Legal and Therapeutic Challenge," in Ayd, F. J. (Ed.), *Rational Psychopharmacotherapy and the Right to Treatment*, p. 37, Ayd Medical Communications, Baltimore, 1975.
16. ———, "Moban: The First of a New Class of Neuroleptics," in Ayd, F. J. (Ed.), *Rational Psychopharmacotherapy and the Right to Treatment*, p. 91, Ayd Medical Communications, Baltimore, 1975.
17. BAN, T., *Psychopharmacology*, Williams & Wilkins, Baltimore, 1969.
18. BARNESS, L. A., et al., "Megavitamin Therapy for Childhood Psychoses and Learning Disabilities," *Pediatrics, 58(6):*910, 1976.
19. BECK, L., et al., "Childhood Chemotherapy and Later Drug Abuse and Growth Curve: A Follow-Up

Study of 30 Adolescents," *American Journal of Psychiatry*, *132(4)*:436, 1975.

20. BENDER, L., "Theory and Treatment of Childhood Schizophrenia," *Acta Paedopsychiatrica*, *34*:298, 1967.

21. ———, and COTTINGTON, F., "The Use of Amphetamine Sulfate (Benzedrine) in Child Psychiatry," *American Journal of Psychiatry*, *99(1)*:116, 1942.

22. BENDER, L. and FARETRA, G., "The Relationship Between Childhood Schizophrenia and Adult Schizophrenia," in Kaplan, A. R. (Ed.), *Genetic Factors in "Schizophrenia,"* p. 28, Charles C Thomas, Springfield, Ill., 1972.

23. BENDER, L., and COBRINIK, L., "LSD and UML Treatment of Hospitalized Disturbed Children," in Wortis, J. (Ed.), *Recent Advances in Biological Psychiatry*, vol. 5, p. 84, Plenum Press, New York, 1963.

24. BENDER, L., GOLDSCHMIDT, L., and SANKAR, D. V. S., "Treatment of Autistic Schizophrenic Children with LSD-25 and UML-491, in Wortis, J. (Ed.), *Recent Advances in Biological Psychiatry*, vol. 4, p. 170, Plenum Press, New York, 1962.

25. BENDER, L. et al., "The Treatment of Childhood Schizophrenia with LSD and UML," in Rinkel, M. (Ed.), *Biological Treatment of Mental Illness*, p. 463, Page & Co., New York, 1966.

26. BIGELOW, N., and SAINZ, A., "Pitfalls in Psychiatric Research," *American Journal of Psychiatry*, *118(10)*:889, 1962.

27. BRADFORD HILL, A., *Principles of Medical Statistics*, Oxford University Press, New York, 1971.

28. BRADLEY, C., "The Behavior of Children Receiving Benzedrine," *American Journal of Psychiatry*, *94(5)*:577, 1937.

29. ———, and BOWEN, M., "Amphetamine (Benzedrine) Therapy of Children's Behavior Disorders," *American Journal of Orthopsychiatry*, *11(1)*:92, 1941.

30. BRAMBILLA, F., and PENATI, G., "Hormones and Behavior in Schizophrenia," in Ford, D. H. (Ed.), *Influence of Hormones on the Nervous System*, pp. 482–492, Karger, Basel, 1971.

31. BRAMBILLA, F. et al., "Psychoendocrine Investigation in Schizophrenia," *Diseases of the Nervous System*, *35*:362, 1974.

32. BROWN, W. A., and WILLIAMS, B. W., "Methylphenidate Increases Serum Growth Hormone Concentrations," *Journal of Clinical Endocrinology and Metabolism*, *43(4)*:937–939, 1976.

33. BRUUN, R. D., et al., "A Follow-Up of 78 Patients with Gilles de la Tourette's Syndrome," *American Journal of Psychiatry*, *133(8)*:944–947, 1976.

34. BURDOCK, E. I., and HARDESTY, A. S., "A Children's Behavior Diagnostic Inventory," *Annals of the New York Academy of Sciences*, *105*:890, 1964.

35. BURK, H. W., and MENOLASCINO, F. J., "Haloperidol in Emotionally Disturbed Mentally Retarded Individuals," *American Journal of Psychiatry*, *124(1)*:1589–1591, 1968.

36. CAMPBELL, M., "The Use of Drug Treatment in Infantile Autism and Childhood Schizophrenia: A Review," in Lipton, M. A., DiMascio, A., and Killam, K. (Eds.), *Psychopharmacology—A Generation of Progress*, Raven Press, New York, 1978.

37. ———, "Pharmacotherapy in Early Infantile Autism," *Biological Psychiatry*, *10(4)*:399, 1975.

38. ———, "A Psychotic Boy with Self-Mutilating Behavior and the Antiaggressive Effect of Lithium," Paper presented at the Twentieth Annual Meeting of the American Academy of Child Psychiatry, Washington, D.C., October 18–21, 1973.

39. ———, and FISH, B., "Triiodothyronine in Schizophrenic Children," in Prange, A. J., Jr. (Ed.), *Thyroid Axis and Behavior*, p. 87, Raven Press, New York, 1974.

40. CAMBPELL, M., and SHAPIRO, T., "Therapy of Psychiatric Disorders of Childhood," in Shader, R. I. (Ed.), *Manual of Psychiatric Therapeutics*, p. 137, Little, Brown, Boston, 1975.

41. CAMPBELL, M., GELLER, B., AND COHEN, I. L., "Current Status of Drug Research and Treatment with Autistic Children," *Journal of Pediatric Psychology*, *2(4)*:153, 1977.

42. CAMPBELL, M., SCHULMAN, D., and RAPOPORT, J. L., "The Current Status of Lithium Therapy in Child and Adolescent Psychiatry," *Journal of the American Academy of Child Psychiatry*, *17(4)*:717.

43. CAMPBELL, M., et al., "A Comparison of Haloperidol and Behavior Therapy and Their Interaction in Autistic Children," *Journal of the American Academy of Child Psychiatry*, *17(4)*:640, 1978.

44. CAMPBELL, M., et al., "Childhood Psychosis in Perspective," *Journal of the American Academy of Child Psychiatry*, *17(1)*:14, 1978.

45. CAMPBELL, M., et al., "Some Physical Parameters of Young Autistic Children," unpublished manuscript, 1978.

46. CAMPBELL, M., et al., "Levodopa and Levoamphetamine: A Crossover Study in Young Schizophrenic Children, *Current Therapeutic Research*, *19(1)*:70, 1976.

47. CAMPBELL, M., et al., "Liothyronine Treatment in Psychotic and Non-Psychotic Children Under 6 Years," *Archives of General Psychiatry*, *29(5)*:602, 1973.

48. CAMPBELL, M., et al., "Response to Triiodothyronine and Dextroamphetamine: A Study of Preschool Schizophrenic Children," *Journal of Autism and Childhood Schizophrenia*, *2(4)*:343, 1972.

49. CAMPBELL, M., et al., "Lithium-Chlorpromazine: A Control Crossover Study in Hyperactive Severely Disturbed Young Children," *Journal of Autism and Childhood Schizophrenia*, *2(3)*:234, 1972.

50. CAMPBELL, M., et al., "Acute Responses of Schizophrenic Children to a Sedative and 'Stimulating' Neuroleptic: A Pharmacologic Yardstick,' *Current Therapeutic Research*, *14(12)*:759, 1972.

51. CAMPBELL, M., et al., "Study of Molindone in Disturbed Preschool Children," *Current Therapeutic Research*, *8(1)*:28, 1971.

52. CAMPBELL, M., et al., "Imipramine in Preschool Autistic and Schizophrenic Children," *Journal of Autism and Childhood Schizophrenia*, *1(3)*:267, 1971.

53. CAMPBELL, M., et al., "Thiothixene in Young Disturbed Children, A Pilot Study," *Archives of General Psychiatry*, *23(1)*:70, 1970.

54. CAMPBELL, M., et al., "A Controlled Crossover Study of Triiodothyronine in Young Psychotic Children," *Journal of Autism and Childhood Schizophrenia*, *8(4)*:371, 1978.

55. CANTWELL, D. P., and CARLSON, G. A., "Stimulants," in Werry, J. S. (Ed.), *Pediatric Psychopharmacology, The Use of Behavior Modifying Drugs in Children*, p. 171, Brunner/Mazel, New York, 1978.

56. CHALLAS, G. and BRAUER, W., "Tourette's Disease: Relief of Symptoms with R1625," *American Journal of Psychiatry*, *120(3)*:283, 1963.

57. CHAMBERS, W., PUIG-ANTICH, J., and TABRIZI, M., "The Ongoing Development of the Kiddie SADS," Paper presented at the Twenty-fifth Annual Meeting of the American Academy of Child Psychiatry, San Diego, Calif., October 24–29, 1978.

58. CHAN, T. L., SAKALIS, G., and GERSHORN, S., "Some Aspects of Chlorpromazine Metabolism in Humans," *Clinical Pharmacology and Therapeutics*, *4*:133, 1973.

59. CHAPEL, J. L., BROWN, N., and JENKINS, R. L., "Tourette's Disease: Symptomatic Relief with Haloperidol," *American Journal of Psychiatry*, *121(6)*:608, 1964.

60. CHASSAN, J. B., "Statistical Inference and the Single Case in Clinical Design," *Psychiatry, Journal for the Study of Interpersonal Processes*, *23*:173, 1960.

61. CHRISTENSEN, D. E., "Combined Effects of Methylphenidate (Ritalin) and a Classroom Behavior Modification Program in Reducing the Hyperkinetic Behaviors of Institutionalized Mental Retardates," Ph.D. thesis, University of Illinois at Urbana-Champaign, 1973.

62. ———, and SPRAGUE, R. L., "Reduction of Hyperactive Behavior by Conditioning Procedures Alone and Combined with Methylphenidate (Ritalin)," *Behavior Re-*

*search and Therapy, 11(3):*331, 1973.

63. COHEN, I. L., ANDERSON, L. T., and CAMPBELL, M., "Measurement of Drug Effects in Autistic Children," *Psychopharmacology Bulletin, 14(4):*68, 1978.

64. COHEN, N. J., DOUGLAS, V. I., and MORGENSTERN, G., "The Effect of Methylphenidate on Attentive Behavior and Autonomic Activity in Hyperactive Children," *Psychopharmacologia, 22(3):*282, 1971.

65. COHEN, N. J., WEISS, G., and MINDE, K., "Cognitive Styles in Adolescents Previously Diagnosed as Hyperactive," *Journal of Child Psychology and Psychiatry, 13(3):*203, 1972.

66. COLE, J. O., "Hyperkinetic Children: The Use of Stimulant Drugs Evaluated," *American Journal of Orthopsychiatry, 45(1):*28, 1975.

67. CONNELL, P. H., et al., "Drug Treatment of Adolescent Tiquers. A Double-Blind Trial of Diazepam and Haloperidol," *British Journal of Psychiatry, 113(497):*375, 1967.

68. CONNERS, C. K., "Methodological Considerations in Drug Research with Children," in Wiener, J. M. (Ed.), *Psychopharmacology in Childhood and Adolescence*, p. 58, Basic Books, New York, 1977.

69. ———, "Controlled Trial of Methylphenidate in Preschool Children with Minimal Brain Dysfunction," in Gittelman-Klein, R. (Guest Ed.), *Recent Advances in Child Psychopharmacology, International Journal of Mental Health, 4(1–2):*61, 1975.

70. ———, "A Placebo-Crossover Study of Caffeine Treatment of Hyperkinetic Children," in Gittelman-Klein, R. (Guest Ed.), *Recent Advances in Child Psychopharmacology, International Journal of Mental Health, 4(1–2):*132, 1975.

71. ——— (Ed.), "Clinical Use of Stimulant Drugs," Amsterdam, *Excerpta Medica*, 1974.

72. ———, "Rating Scales for Use in Drug Studies with Children," *Psychopharmacology Bulletin*, Special Issue: Pharmacotherapy of Children, p. 24, 1973.

73. ———, "Deanol and Behavior Disorders in Children: A Critical Review of the Literature and Recommended Future Studies for Determining Efficacy," *Psychopharmacology Bulletin*, Special Issue: Pharmacotherapy of Children, p. 188, 1973.

74. ———, "II. Psychological Effects of Stimulant Drugs in Children with Minimal Brain Dysfunction," *Pediatrics, 49(5):*702, 1972.

75. ———, "Pharmacotherapy of Psychopathology in Children," in Quay, H. C., and Werry, J. S. (Eds.). *Psychopathological Disorders of Childhood*, p. 316, John Wiley, New York, 1972.

76. ———, "The Effect of Stimulant Drugs on Human Figure Drawings in Children with Minimal Brain Dysfunction," *Psychopharmacologia, 19(4):*329, 1971.

77. ———, "Recent Drug Studies with Hyperkinetic Children," *Journal of Learning Disabilities, 4(9):*476, 1971.

78. ———, "Symptom Patterns in Hyperkinetic, Neurotic, and Normal Children," *Child Development, 41(3):*667, 1970.

79. ———, "A Teacher Rating Scale for Use in Drug Studies with Children," *American Journal of Psychiatry, 126(6):*884, 1969.

80. ———, and EISENBERG, L., "The Effects of Methylphenidate on Symptomatology and Learning in Disturbed Children," *American Journal of Psychiatry, 120(5):*458, 1963.

81. CONNERS, C. K., and ROTHSCHILD, G. H., "The Effect of Dextroamphetamine on Habituation of Peripheral Vascular Response in Children," *Journal of Abnormal Psychology, 1(1):*16, 1973.

82. CONNERS, C. K., EISENBERG, L., and BARCAI, A. "Effect of Dextroamphetamine on Children," *Archives of General Psychiatry, 17(4):*478, 1967.

83. CONNERS, C. K., EISENBERG, L., and SHARPE, L., "Effects of Methylphenidate (Ritalin) on Paired-Associate Learning and Porteus Maze Performance in Emotionally Disturbed Children," *Journal of Consulting Psychology, 28(1):*14, 1964.

84. CONNERS, C. K., et al., "Magnesium Pemoline and Dextroamphetamine: A Controlled Study in Children with Minimal Brain Dysfunction," *Psychopharmacologia, 26(4):*321, 1972.

85. CONNERS, C. K., et al., "Treatment of Young Delinquent Boys with Diphenylhydantoin Sodium and Methylphenidate, A Controlled Comparison," *Archives of General Psychiatry, 24(6):*156, 1971.

86. CONNERS, C. K., et al., "Dextroamphetamine Sulfate in Children with Learning Disorders," *Archives of General Psychiatry, 21(2):*182, 1969.

87. CONRAD, W. G., et al., "Effects of Amphetamine Therapy and Prescriptive Tutoring on the Behavior and Achievement of Lower Class Hyperactive Children," *Journal of Learning Disabilities, 4(9):*509, 1971.

88. CUNNINGHAM, M. A., PILLAI, V., and ROGERS, W. J. B., "Haloperidol in the Treatment of Children with Severe Behavior Disorders," *British Journal of Psychiatry, 114(512):*845, 1968.

89. CYTRYN, L., et al., "Biochemical Correlates of Affective Disorders in Children," *Archives of General Psychiatry, 31(5):*659, 1974.

90. DELAY, J., and DENIKER, P., "38 cas de Psychoses Traitées par la Cure Prolongée et Continue de 4560 RP-CR-50 ième," *Congres des Alién et Neurologique de Langue Française*, p. 503, Luxembourg, July 21–27, 1952.

91. DeLONG, G. R., "Lithium Carbonate Treatment of Select Behavior Disorders in Children Suggesting Manic-Depressive Illness," *Journal of Pediatrics, 93(4):*689, 1978.

92. DENIHOFF, E., DAVIDS, A., and HAWKINS, R., "Effects of Dextroamphetamine on Hyperkinetic Children," *Journal of Learning Disorders, 4(9):*491, 1971.

93. *Diagnostic and Statistical Manual of Mental Disorders*, 3rd ed. (DSM III), American Psychiatric Association, Washington, D.C., 1978.

94. DiMASCIO, A., "Behavioral Toxicity," in DiMascio, A. and Shader, R. I. (Eds.), *Clinical Handbook of Psychopharmacology*, p. 185, Science House, New York, 1970.

95. ———, SHADER, R. I., and HARMATZ, J., "Psychotropic Drugs and Induced Hostility," *Psychosomatics, 10(1):*46, 1969.

96. DiMASCIO, A., SOLTYS, J. J., and SHADER, R. I., 'Psychotropic Drub Side Effects in Children," in Shader R. I. and DiMascio, A. (Eds.), *Psychotropic Drug Side Effects*, pp. 235–260, Williams & Wilkins, Baltimore, 1970.

97. DISCHE, S., "Management of Enuresis," *British Medical Journal, 2(2):*33, 1971.

98. DOSTAL, T., "Antiaggressive Effects of Lithium Salts in Mentally Retarded Adolescents," Anneil, A. L. (Ed.), *Depressive States in Childhood and Adolescents*, p. 491, Almquist & Wiksell, Stockholm, 1972.

99. DOUGLAS, V. I., "Are Drugs Enough—To Treat or Train the Hyperactive Child," in Gittelman-Klein, R. (Guest Ed.), *Recent Advances in Child Psychopharmacology, International Journal of Mental Health, 4(1–2):*199, 1975.

100. DUTTON, G., "The Growth Pattern of Psychotic Boys," *British Journal of Psychiatry, 110:*101, 1964.

101. DYSON, W. L., and BARCAI, A. "Treatment of Children of Lithium-Responding Parents," *Current Therapeutic Research, 12(5):*286, 1970.

102. EFFRON, A. S., and FREEDMAN, A. M., "The Treatment of Behavior Disorders in Children with Benadryl," *Journal of Pediatrics, 42(1):*261, 1953.

103. EISENBERG, L., "Psychopharmacology in Childhood: A Critique," in Miller, E. (Ed.), *Foundations in Child Psychiatry*, p. 625, Pergamon Press, Oxford, 1968.

104. ———, "Role of Drug in Treating Disturbed Children," *Children, 2(5):*167, 1964.

105. ———, "The Autistic Child in Adolescence," *American Journal of Psychiatry, 112(8):*607, 1956.

106. ———, and CONNERS, C. K., "Psychopharmacology in Childhood," in Talbot, N. B., Kagan, J., and Eisenberg, L. (Eds.), *Behavioral Science in Pediatric Medicine*, p. 397, W. B. Saunders, Philadelphia, 1971.

107. EISENBERG, L., et al., "A Psychopharmacologic Experiment in a Training School for Delinquent Boys," *American Journal of Orthopsychiatry, 33(3)*:431, 1963.

108. EISENBERG, L., et al., "The Effectiveness of Psychotherapy Alone and in Conjunction with Perphenazine or Placebo in the Treatment of Neurotic and Hyperkinetic Children," *American Journal of Psychiatry, 117(12)*:1088, 1961.

109. ENGELHARDT, D. M., and POLIZOS, P., "Adverse Effects of Pharmacotherapy in Childhood Psychosis," in Lipton, M. A., DiMascio, A., and Killam, K. (Eds.), *Psychopharmacology—A Generation of Progress*, Raven Press, New York, 1978.

110. ENGELHARDT, D. M., et al., "A Double-Blind Comparison of Fluphenazine and Haloperidol," *Journal of Autism and Childhood Schizophrenia, 3(2)*:128, 1973.

111. FARETRA, G., DOOHER, L., and DOWLING, J., "Comparison of Haloperidol and Fluphenazine in Disturbed Children," *American Journal of Psychiatry, 126(11)*:1670, 1970.

112. FEIGHNER, A. C., and FEIGHNER, J. P., "Multimodality Treatment of the Hyperkinetic Child," *American Journal of Psychiatry, 131(4)*:459, 1974.

113. FINNERTY, R. J., SOLTYS, J. J., and COLE, J. O., "The Use of D-amphetamine with Hyperkinetic Children," *Psychopharmacologia, 21*:302, 1971.

114. FISH, B., "The 'One Child, One Drug' Myth of Stimulants in Hyperkinesis, Importance of Diagnostic Categories in Evaluating Treatment," *Archives of General Psychiatry, 25(3)*:193, 1971.

115. ———, "Psychopharmacologic Response of Chronic Schizophrenic Adults as Predictors of Responses in Young Schizophrenic Children," *Psychopharmacology Bulletin, 6(4)*:12, 1970.

116. ———, "Methodology in Child Psychopharmacology," in Efron, D. H., et al. (Eds.), *Psychopharmacology, Review of Progress, 1956-1967*, p. 989, Public Health Service Publication no. 1836, U.S. Government Printing Office, Washington, D.C., 1968.

117. ———, Organic Therapies," in Freedman, A. M., and Kaplan, H. I. (Eds.), *Comprehensive Textbook of Psychiatry*, p. 1468, Williams & Wilkins, Baltimore, 1967.

118. ———, Drug Therapy in Child Psychiatry: Pharmacological Aspects," *Comprehensive Psychiatry, 1(4)*:212, 1960.

119. ———, and SHAPIRO, T., A Typology of Children's Psychiatric Disorders, I: Its Application to a Controlled Evaluation of Treatment," *Journal of the American Academy of Child Psychiatry, 4(1)*:32, 1965.

120. ———, A Descriptive Typology of Children's Psychiatric Disorders. II: A Behavioral Classification, p. 75, Psychiatric Research Report 18, American Psychiatric Association, 1964.

121. ———, and CAMPBELL, M., "Long-Term Prognosis and the Response of Schizophrenic Children to Drug Therapy: A Controlled Study of Trifluoperazine," *American Journal of Psychiatry, 123(1)*:32, 1966.

122. FISH, B., et al., "Comparison of Trifluperidol, Trifluoperazine and Chlorpromazine in Preschool Schizophrenic Children: The Value of Less Sedative Antipsychotic Agents," *Current Therapeutic Research, 11(10)*:589, 1969.

123. FISH, B., et al., "Schizophrenic Children Treated with Methysergide (Sansert)," *Diseases of the Nervous System, 30(8)*:534, 1969.

124. FISH, B., et al., "A Classification of Schizophrenic Children Under Five Years," *American Journal of Psychiatry, 124(10)*:1415, 1968.

125. FISH, B., et al., "The Prediction of Schizophrenia in Infancy: II. A Ten-Year Follow-Up of Predictions Made at One Month of Age," in Hoch, P., and Zubin, J.

(Eds.), *Psychopathology of Schizophrenia*, p. 335, Grune & Stratton, New York, 1966.

126. FISHER, S., "Nonspecific Factors as Determinants of Behavioral Response to Drugs," in DiMascio, A., and Shader, R. I. (Eds.), *Clinical Handbook of Psychopharmacology*, p. 16, Science House, New York, 1970.

127. FORSYTHE, W.I., and REDMOND, A., "Enuresis and Spontaneous Cure Rate," *Archives of Disease in Childhood, 49(4)*:259, 1974.

128. FREEDMAN, A. M., EBIN, E. V., and WILSON, E. A., "Autistic Schizophrenic Children. An Experiment in the Use of D-Lysergic Acid Diethylamide (LSD-25)," *Archives of General Psychiatry, 6(3)*:203, 1962.

129. FREEDMAN, D. X., *Report of the Conference on the Use of Stimulant Drugs in the Treatment of Behaviorally Disturbed Young School Children*, Office of Child Development and the Office of the Assistant Secretary for Health and Scientific Affairs, U. S. Department of Health, Education, and Welfare, Washington, D. C., 1971.

130. FREEMAN, R. D., "Psychopharmacology and the Retarded Child," in Menolascino, F. (Ed.), *Psychiatric Approaches to Mental Retardation*, pp. 294–368, Basic Books, New York, 1970.

131. ———, "Drug Effects on Learning in Children. A Selective Review of the Past Thirty Years," *Journal of Special Education, 1*:17, 1966.

132. FREYHAN, F. A., "Clinical and Investigative Aspects," in Kline, N. S. (Ed.), *Psychopharmacology Frontiers*, p. 7, Little, Brown and Company, Boston, 1959.

133. FROMMER, E. A., "Indications for Antidepressant Treatment with Special Reference to Depressed Preschool Children," in Annell, A. L., (Ed.), *Depressive States in Childhood and Adolescence*, p. 449, Almquist & Wiksell, Stockholm, 1972.

134. ———, "Depressive Illness in Childhood," in Coppen, A., and Walk, A. (Eds.), *Recent Development in Affective Disorders, A Symposium*, Special Publication no. 2, *British Journal of Psychiatry*, p. 117, 1968.

135. ———, "Treatment in Childhood Depression with Antidepressant Drugs," *British Medical Journal, 1*:729, 1967.

136. GARDOS, G., et al., "Differential Actions of Chlordiazepoxide and Oxazepam on Hostility," *Archives of General Psychiatry, 18*:757, 1968.

137. GARFINKEL, B. D., WEBSTER, C. D., and SLOMAN, L., "Methylphenidate and Caffeine in the Treatment of Children with Minimal Brain Dysfunction," *American Journal of Psychiatry, 132(7)*:723, 1975.

138. GERSHON, S., and SHOPSIN, B. (Eds.), *Lithium: Its Role in Psychiatric Research and Treatment*, Plenum Publishing, New York, 1973.

139. GITTELMAN-KLEIN, R., "Review of Clinical Psychopharmacological Treatment of Hyperkinesis," in Klein, D. F., and Gittelman-Klein, R. (Eds.), *Progress in Psychiatric Drug Treatment*, p. 661, Brunner/Mazel, New York, 1975.

140. ——— (Guest Ed.), "Recent Advances in Child Psychopharmacology," *International Journal of Mental Health, 4(1–2)*, 1975.

141. ———, "Psychopharmacological Treatment of Anxiety Disorders, Mood Disorders, and Tourette's Disorder in Children," in Lipton, M. A., DiMascio, A., and Killam, K. F. (Eds.), *Psychopharmacology: A Generation of Progress*, p. 1471, Raven Press, New York, 1978.

142. ———, and KLEIN, D. F., "School Phobia: Diagnostic Considerations in the Light of Imipramine Effects," *Journal of Nervous and Mental Disease, 156*:199, 1973.

143. ———, "Controlled Imipramine Treatment of School Phobia," *Archives of General Psychiatry, 25(3)*:204, 1971.

144. GITTELMAN-KLEIN, R., SPITZER, R. L., and CANTWELL, D. P., "Diagnostic Classifications and Psychopharmacological Indications," in Werry, J. S. (Ed.), *Pediatric Psychopharmacology. The Use of Behavior Modifying Drugs in Children*, p. 136, Brunner/Mazel, New York, 1978.

145. GITTELMAN-KLEIN, R., et al., "Relative Efficacy of Methylphenidate and Behavior Modification in Hyperkinetic Children: An Interim Report," *Journal of Abnormal Child Psychology, 4(4):*361–379, 1976.

146. GLESER, G. C., "Psychometric Contributions to the Assessment of Patients," in Efron, D. H., et al. (Eds.), *Psychopharmacology, A Review of Progress, 1956–1967,* p 1029, U. S. Government Printing Office, Public Health Service Publication no. 1836, Washington, D. C., 1968.

147. GOLDEN, G. S., "Case Report—Gilles de la Tourette's Syndrome Following Methylphenidate Administration," *Developmental Medicine and Child Neurology, 16(1):*76, 1974.

148. GRABOWSKI, S. W., "Safety and Effectiveness of Haloperidol for Mentally Retarded Behaviorally Disordered and Hyperkinetic Patients," *Current Therapeutic Research, 15(11):*856, 1973.

149. GRAHAM, P., "Depression in Pre-Pubertal Children," *Developmental Medicine and Child Neurology, 16(3):*340, 1974.

150. GRAM, L. F., and RAFAELSEN, O. J., "Lithium Treatment of Psychotic Children," in Annell, A. L. (Ed.), *Depressive States in Childhood and Adolescence,* p. 488, Almquist & Wiksell, Stockholm, 1972.

151. GREENBAUM, G. H., "An Evaluation of Niacinamide in the Treatment of Childhood Schizophrenia," *American Journal of Psychiatry, 127(1):*129,1970.

152. GREENHILL, L. L., et al., "Hormone and Growth Responses in Hyperkinetic Children on Stimulant Medication," *Psychopharmacology Bulletin, 13(2):*33, 1977.

153. GREENHILL, L. L., et al., "Lithium Carbonate in the Treatment of Hyperactive Children," *Archives of General Psychiatry, 28(5):*636, 1973.

154. GROSS, M. D., "Growth of Hyperkinetic Children Taking Methylphenidate, Dextroamphetamine or Imipramine/Desirpramine," *Pediatrics, 58:*423, 1976.

155. HAVELKOVA, M. "Follow-Up Study of 71 Children Diagnosed as Psychotic in Preschool Age," *American Journal of Orthopsychiatry, 38(5):*846, 1968.

156. HAYES, T. A., LOGAN PANITCH, M., and BARKER, E., "Imipramine Dosage in Children: A Comment on 'Imipramine and Electrocardiographic Abnormalities in Hyperactive Children,'" *American Journal of Psychiatry, 132(5):*546, 1975.

157. HIMWICH, H. E., KETY, S. S., and SMYTHIES, J. R., *Amines and Schizophrenia,* Pergamon Press, New York, 1967.

158. HOFFER, A., "Childhood Schizophrenia: A Case Treated with Nicotinic Acid and Nicotinamide," *Schizophrenia, 2:*43, 1970.

159. HOFFMAN, S. P., et al., "Response to Methylphenidate in Low Socioeconomic Hyperactive Children," *Archives of General Psychiatry, 30(3):*354, 1974.

160. HOLLISTER, L. E., "Polypharmacy in Psychiatry: Is it Necessary, Good or Bad," in Ayd, F. J. (Ed.), *Rational Psychopharmacotherapy and the Right to Treatment,* p. 19, Ayd Medical Communications, Baltimore, 1975.

161. ———, "Choice of Antipsychotic Drugs," *American Journal of Psychiatry, 127(2):*186, 1970.

162. HUESSY, H. R., and WRIGHT, A. L., "The Use of Imipramine in Children's Behavior Disorders," *Acta Paedopsychiatry, 37(7–8):*194, 1970.

163. HUESTIS, R. D., ARNOLD, L. E., and SMELTZER, D. J., "Caffeine Versus Methylphenidate and d-Amphetamine in Minimal Brain Dysfunction: A Double-Blind Comparison," *American Journal of Psychiatry, 132(8):*868, 1975.

164. IRWIN, S., "How to Prescribe Psychoactive Drugs," *Bulletin of the Menninger Clinic, 38(1):*1, 1974.

165. ———, "The Uses and Relative Hazard Potential of Psychoactive Drugs," *Bulletin of the Menninger Clinic, 38(1):*14, 1974.

166. ———, "A Rational Framework for the Development, Evaluation, and Use of Psychoactive Drugs," *American Journal of Psychiatry,* (Supplement) *124(8):*1, 1968.

167. JANOWSKY, D. S., et al., "Provocation of Schizophrenic Symptoms by Intravenous Administration of Methylphenidate," *Archives of General Psychiatry, 28(2):*185, 1973.

168. JONES, M. D., and AINSLIE, J. D., "Value of Placebo Wash-Out," *Diseases of the Nervous System, 27(6):*393, 1966.

169. KANNER, L., "Follow-Up Study of Eleven Autistic Children Originally Reported in 1943," *Journal of Autism and Childhood Schizophrenia, 1(2):*119, 1971.

170. KATZ, M. M., and ITIL, T. M., "Video Methodology for Research in Psychopathology and Psychopharmacology," *Archives of General Psychiatry, 31:*204, 1974.

171. KATZ, S., et al., "Clinical Pharmacological Management of Hyperkinetic Children," in Gittelman-Klein, R. (Guest Ed.), *Recent Advances in Child Psychopharmacology, International Journal of Mental Health, 4(1–2):*157, 1975.

172. KENNEDY, W. A., and SLOOP, E. W., "Methedrine as an Adjunct to Conditioning Treatment of Nocturnal Enuresis in Normal and Institutionalized Retarded Subjects," *Psychological Reports, 22(3):*997, 1968.

173. KETY, S. S., "Toward Hypotheses for a Biochemical Component in the Vulnerability to Schizophrenia," *Seminars in Psychiatry, 4(3):*233, 1972.

174. KLEIN, D. F., and DAVIS, J. M., *Diagnosis and Drug Treatment of Psychiatric Disorders,* Williams & Wilkins, Baltimore, 1969.

175. KNIGHTS, R. M., and HINTON, G., "The Effects of Methylphenidate (Ritalin) on the Motor Skills and Behavior of Children with Learning Problems," *Journal of Nervous and Mental Disease, 148(6):*643, 1969.

176. KNOBEL, M., WOLMAN, M. B., and MASON, E., "Hyperkinesis and Organicity in Children," *Archives of General Psychiatry, 1(9):*94, 1959.

177. KOREIN, J., et al., "EEG and Behavioral Effects on Drug Therapy in Children. Chlorpromazine and Diphenhydramine," *Archives of General Psychiatry, 24(6):*552, 1971.

178. KRAFT, I. A., et al., "A Clinical Study of Chlordiazepoxide Used in Psychiatric Disorders of Children," *International Journal of Neuropsychiatry, 1(5):*433, 1965.

179. KUGEL, R. B., et al., "Medication for Hyperkinetic Children," *Pediatrics, 55(4):*560, 1975.

180. KURTIS, L. B., "Clinical Study of the Response to Nortriptyline on Autistic Children, *International Journal of Neuropsychiatry, 2(4):*298, 1966.

181. LASAGNA, L., "The Controlled Clinical Trial: Theory and Practice," *Journal of Chronic Diseases, 1(4):*353, 1955.

182. LAUFER, M., DENHOFF, E., and SOLOMONS, G., "Hyperkinetic Impulse Disorder in Children's Behavior Problems, *Psychosomatic Medicine, 19(1):*38, 1957.

183. LAVECK, G. D., and BUCKLEY, P., "The Use of Psychopharmacologic Agents in Retarded Children with Behavior Disorders," *Journal of Chronic Diseases, 13(2):*174, 1961.

184. LEFKOWITZ, M. M., "Effects of Diphenylhydantoin on Disruptive Behavior," *Archives of General Psychiatry, 20(6):*643, 1969.

185. LEVANN, L. J., "Haloperidol in the Treatment of Behavioral Disorders in Children and Adolescents," *Canadian Psychiatric Association Journal, 14(2):*217, 1969.

186. ———, "A New Butyrophenone: Trifluperidol. A Psychiatric Evaluation in a Pediatric Setting," *Canadian Psychiatric Association Journal, 13(3):*271, 1968.

187. ———, "Chlordiazepoxide, a Tranquilizer with Anticonvulsant Properties," *Canadian Medical Association Journal, 86(3):*123, 1962.

188. LEWIS, P. J. E., and JAMES, N. McI., "Haloperidol and Chlorpromazine: A Double-Blind Cross-Over Trial and Clinical Study in Children and Adolescents," *Australian and New Zealand Journal of Psychiatry, 7(1):*59, 1973.

189. LIPMAN, R. S., "The Use of Psychopharmacological Agents in Residential Facilities for the Re-

tarded," in Menolascino, F. (Ed.), *Psychiatric Approaches to Mental Retardation*, p. 387, Basic Books, New York, 1970.

190. ———, "Methodology of Drug Studies in Children," Paper presented at the American Orthopsychiatric Meeting, Chicago Ill., March 21, 1968.

191. ———, et al., "Psychotropic Drugs and Mentally Retarded Children," Paper presented at the Fifteenth Annual Meeting of the American College of Neuropsychopharmacology, New Orleans, Louisiana, December 14–17, 1976.

192. LIPTON, M. A., et al., *Megavitamin and Orthomolecular Therapy in Psychiatry*, American Psychiatric Association, Washington, D. C., 1973.

193. LO, W. H., "A Note on a Follow-Up Study of Childhood Neurosis and Behavior Disorder," *Journal of Child Psychology and Psychiatry*, 14(2):147, 1973.

194. LOOKER, A., and CONNERS, C. K., "Diphenylhydantoin in Children with Severe Temper Tantrums," *Archives of General Psychiatry*, 23(1):80, 1970.

195. LUCUS, A. R., "Gilles de la Tourette's Disease in Children: Treatment with Haloperidol," *American Journal of Psychiatry*, 124(2):243, 1967.

196. LUCAS, A. R., and WEISS, M., "Methylphenidate Hallucinosis," *Journal of the American Medical Association*, 217(8):1079, 1971.

197. LUCAS, A. R., LOCKETT, H. J., and GRIMM, F., "Amitriptyline in Childhood Depressions," *Diseases of the Nervous System*, 26(2):105, 1965.

198. LYTTON, G. J., and KNOBEL, M., "Diagnosis and Treatment of Behavior Disorders in Children," *Diseases of the Nervous System*, 20(3):334, 1959.

199. MCANDREW, J. B., CASE, Q., and TREFFERT, D., "Effects of Prolonged Phenothiazine Intake on Psychotic and Other Hospitalized Children," *Journal of Autism and Childhood Schizophrenia*, 2(1):75, 1972.

200. MCCONAGHY, N., "A Controlled Trial of Imipramine, Amphetamine, Pad-and-Bell Conditioning and Random Awakening in the Treatment of Nocturnal Enuresis," *Medical Journal of Australia*, 2(5):237, 1969.

201. MCNUTT, B. A., et al., "The Effects of Long-term Stimulant Medication on the Growth and Body Composition of Hyperactive Children. II: Report on 2 years," Paper presented at the Annual Early Clinical Drug Evaluation Unit Meeting, Psychopharmacology Research Branch National Institute of Mental Health, Key Biscayne, Fla., May 20–22, 1976.

202. MACKAY, M. C., BECK, L., and TAYLOR, R., "Methylphenidate for Adolescents with Minimal Brain Dysfunction," *New York State Journal of Medicine*, 73(4):550, 1973.

203. MELTZER, H. Y., and STAHL, S. M., "The Dopamine Hypothesis of Schizophrenia: A Review," *Schizophrenia Bulletin*, 2(1):19, 1976.

204. MENKES, M. M., ROWE, J. S., and MENKES, J. H., "A 25 Year Follow-Up Study on the Hyperkinetic Child with Minimal Brain Dysfunction," *Pediatrics*, 39(3):393, 1967.

205. MINDE, K. K., and WEISS, G. C., "The Assessment of Drug Effects in Children as Compared to Adults, *Journal of the American Academy of Child Psychiatry*, 9:124, 1970.

206. ———, and MENDELSON, N., "A Five Year Follow-Up Study of 91 Hyperactive School Children," *Journal of the American Academy of Child Psychiatry*, 11(3):595, 1972.

207. MOGAR, R. E., and ALDRICH, R. W., "The Use of Psychedelic Agents with Autistic Schizophrenic Children,' *Behavioral Neuropsychiatry*, 1:44, 1969.

208. MORRIS, H. H., JR., ESCOLL, P. J., and WEXLER, R., "Aggressive Behavior Disorders of Childhood: A Follow-Up Study," *American Journal of Psychiatry*, 112(12):991, 1956.

209. NASH, H., "The Design and Conduct of Experiments on the Psychological Effects of Drugs," in Uhr, L., and Miller, J. G. (Eds.), *Drugs and Behavior*, p. 128, John Wiley, New York, 1960.

210. *Nervous Child*, 1952.

211. NEY, P. G., "Psychosis in a Child, Associated with Amphetamine Administration," *Canadian Medical Association Journal*, 97(17):1026, 1967.

212. OETTINGER, L., "Chlorprothixene in the Management of Problem Children," *Diseases of the Nervous System*, 23(10):1, 1962.

213. O'MALLEY, J. E., and EISENBERG, L., "The Hyperkinetic Syndrome," *Seminars in Psychiatry*, 5(1):95, 1973.

214. O'NEAL, P., and ROBINS, L. N., "The Relation of Childhood Behavior Problems to Adult Psychiatric Status: A 30 Year Follow-Up Study of 150 Subjects," *American Journal of Psychiatry*, 114(11):961, 1958.

215. ———, "Childhood Patterns Predictive of Adult Schizophrenia: A 30 Year Follow-Up Study," *American Journal of Psychiatry*, 115(5):385, 1958.

216. PAGE, J. G., et al., "A Multi-Clinic Trial of Pemoline in Childhood Hyperkinesis," in Conners, C. K. (Ed.), *Clinical Use of Stimulant Drugs in Children*, p. 98, The Hague, *Excerpta Medica*, 1974.

217. PANGALIA-RATULANGI, E. A., "Pilot Evaluation of Orap^R (Pimozide, R6238)," *Child Psychiatry, Psychiatria, Neurologia, Neurochirurgia*, 76:17–27, 1973.

218. PASAMANICK, B., "Anticonvulsant Drug Therapy of Behavior Problem Children with Abnormal Electroencephalograms," *Archives of Neurology and Psychiatry*, 65(6):752, 1951.

219. PAVLOV, I. P., "Uber die Unvollkommenheit der gegenwartigen physiologischen Analyse der Arzneimittelwirkung, in Holmstedt, B., and Liljestrand, G., (Eds.), *Readings in Pharmacology*, Macmillan, New York, 1905.

220. PETTI, T. A., and CAMPBELL, M., "Imipramine and Seizures," *American Journal of Psychiatry*, 132(5):538, 1975.

221. PILKINGTON, T. L., "Comparative Effects of Librium and Taractan on Behavior Disorders of Mentally Retarded Children," *Diseases of the Nervous System*, 22(10):573, 1961.

222. PLOTNIKOFF, N., "Pemoline: Review of Performance," *Texas Reports on Biology and Medicine*, 29(4):467, 1971.

223. POLIZOS, P., et al., "Neurological Consequences of Psychotropic Drug Withdrawal in Schizophrenic Children," *Journal of Autism and Childhood Schizophrenia*, 3(3):247, 1973.

224. POOL, D., et al., "A Controlled Evaluation of Loxitane in Seventy-Five Adolescent Schizophrenic Patients," *Current Therapeutic Research*, 19:99, 1976.

225. POUSSAINT, A. F., and DITMAN, K. S., "A Controlled Study of Imipramine (Tofranil) in the Treatment of Childhood Enuresis," *Journal of Pediatrics*, 67(2):283, 1965.

226. *Psychopharmacology Bulletin*, "Pharmacotherapy of Children," Special Issue, pp. 196, 222, 1973.

227. PUIG-ANTICH, J., et al., "Prepubertal Major Depressive Disorder," *Journal of the American Academy of Child Psychiatry*, 17(4):695, 1978.

228. PUIG-ANTICH, J., et al., "Growth Hormone, Prolactin and Cortisol Responses and Growth Patterns in Hyperkinetic Children Treated with Dextroamphetamine: Preliminary Findings," *Journal of the American Academy of Child Psychiatry*, 17(3):457, 1978.

229. QUINN, P. O., and RAPOPORT, J. L., "One Year Follow-Up of Hyperactive Boys Treated with Imipramine or Methylphenidate," *American Journal of Psychiatry*, 132(3):241, 1975.

230. QUITKIN, F., and KLEIN, D. F., "Two Behavioral Syndromes in Young Adults Related to Possible Minimal Brain Dysfunction," *Journal of Psychiatric Research*, 7(2):131, 1969.

231. RAPOPORT, J. L., "Childhood Behavior and Learning Problems Treated with Imipramine," *International Journal of Neuropsychiatry*, 1(6):635, 1965.

232. ———, and MIKKELSEN, E. J., "Antidepressants," in Werry, J. S., (Ed.), *Pediatric Psychopharmacology. The Use of Behavior Modifying Drugs in Children*, p. 208, Brunner/Mazel, New York, 1978.

233. ———, and WERRY, J. S., "Antimanic, Antianxiety, Hallucinogenic and Miscellaneous Drugs," in Werry, J. S. (Ed.), *Pediatric Psychopharmacology. The Use of Behavior Modifying Drugs in Children*, p. 234, Brunner/Mazel, New York, 1978.

234. RAPOPORT, J. L., et al., "Dextroamphetamine: Cognitive and Behavioral Effects in Normal Prepubertal Boys," *Science, 199(3):*560, 1978.

235. RAPOPORT, J. L., et al., "Imipramine and Methylphenidate Treatments of Hyperactive Boys," *Archives of General Psychiatry, 30(6):*789, 1974.

236. REMICK, R. A., and FINE, S. H., "Antipsychotic Drugs and Seizures," *Journal of Clinical Psychiatry, 40(2):*78, 1979.

237. RICKELS, K., and DOWNING, R. W., "Chlordiazepoxide and Hostility in Anxious Outpatients," *American Journal of Psychiatry, 131(4):*442, 1974.

238. RIFKIN, A., et al., "Lithium Carbonate in Emotionally Unstable Character Disorder," *Archives of General Psychiatry, 27(4):*519, 1972.

239. RIMLAND, B., "High-Dosage Levels of Certain Vitamins in the Treatment of Children with Severe Mental Disorders," in Hawkins, D., and Pauling, L. (Eds.), *Orthomolecular Psychiatry*, p. 513, W. H. Freeman, San Francisco, 1973.

240. ———, CALLAWAY, E., and DREYFUS, P., "The Effect of High Dose of Vitamin B6 on Autistic Children: A Double-Blind Crossover Study," *American Journal of Psychiatry, 135(4):*472, 1978.

241. RITVO, E. R., et al., "Effects of L-dopa in Autism," *Journal of Autism and Childhood Schizophrenia, 1(2):*190, 1971.

242. RIVERA-CALIMLIM, L., et al., "Clinical Response and Plasma Levels: Effect of Dose, Dosage, Schedules, and Drug Interactions on Plasma Chlorpromazine Levels," *American Journal of Psychiatry, 133:*646, 1976.

243. ROBINS, L. N., "Follow-up Studies Investigating Childhood Disorders," in Hare, E. H., and Wing, J. K. (Eds.), *Psychiatric Epidemiology*, p. 29, Oxford University Press, London, 1970.

244. ———, *Deviant Children Grown Up*, Williams & Wilkins, Baltimore, 1966.

245. ROLO, A., et al., "Preliminary Method Study of LSD with Children," *International Journal of Neuropsychiatry, 1(6):*552, 1965.

246. ROUKEMA, R. W., and EMERY, L., "Megavitamin Therapy with Severely Disturbed Children," *American Journal of Psychiatry, 127(2):*167, 1970.

247. RUTTER, M., "Relationships Between Child and Adult Psychiatric Disorders," *Acta Psychiatrica Scandinavica, 48:*3, 1972.

248. ———, "Autistic Children: Infancy to Adulthood," *Seminars in Psychiatry, 2(4):*435, 1970.

249. SAFER, D. J., and ALLEN, R. P., "Factors Influencing the Suppressant Effects of Two Stimulant Drugs on the Growth of Hyperactive Children," *Pediatrics, 51:*660, 1973.

250. SALETU, B., et al., "Comparative Symptomatological and Evoked Potential Studies with d-Amphetamine, Thioridazine, and Placebo in Hyperkinetic Children," *Biological Psychiatry, 10(3):*253, 1975.

251. SARAF, K. R., et al., "Imipramine Side Effects in Children," *Psychopharmacologia, 37(3):*265, 1974.

252. SARWER-FONER, G. J., "Psychodynamics of Psychotropic Medication," in DiMascio, A., and Shader, R. I. (Eds.), *Clinical Handbook of Psychopharmacology*, p. 161, Science House, New York, 1970.

253. SATTERFIELD, J. H., and CANTWELL, D. P., "Psychopharmacology in the Prevention of Antisocial and Delinquent Behavior," in Gittelman-Klein, R. (Guest Ed.), *Recent Advances in Child Psychopharmacology, International Journal of Mental Health, 4(1–2):*227, 1975.

254. ———, and SATTERFIELD, B. T., "Pathophysiology of the Hyperactive Child Syndrome," *Archives of General Psychiatry, 31(6):*839, 1974.

255. SATTERFIELD, J. H., et al., "Growth of Hyperactive Children Treated with Methylphenidate," *Archives of General Psychiatry, 36(2):*212, 1979.

256. SATTERFIELD, J. H., et al., "Response to Stimulant Drug Treatment in Hyperactive Children: Prediction from EEG and Neurological Findings," *Journal of Autism and Childhood Schizophrenia, 3(1):*36, 1973.

257. SATTERFIELD, J. H., et al., "Physiological Studies of the Hyperkinetic Child," *American Journal of Psychiatry, 128(11):*1418, 1972.

258. SCHAIN, R. J., and REYNARD, C. L., "Observations of Effects of a Central Stimulant Drug (Methylphenidate) in Children with Hyperactive Behavior," *Pediatrics, 55(5):*709, 1975.

259. SCHIELE, B. C., et al., "Tardive Dyskinesia," *American Journal of Orthopsychiatry, 43(4):*506, 1973.

260. SCHLEIFER, M., et al., "Hyperactivity in Preschoolers and the Effect of Methylphenidate," *American Journal of Orthopsychiatry, 45(1):*38, 1975.

261. SCHNACKENBERG, R. C., "Caffeine as a Substitute for Schedule II Stimulants in Hyperkinetic Children," *American Journal of Psychiatry, 130(7):*796, 1973.

262. SCHOU, M., "Lithium in Psychiatric Therapy and Prophylaxis, A Review with Special Regard to Its Use in Children," in Annell, A. L. (Ed.), *Depressive States in Childhood and Adolescence*, p. 479, Almquist & Wiksell, Stockholm, 1972.

263. SCHULTERBRANDT, J. G., and RASKIN, A. (Eds.), *Depression in Childhood: Diagnosis, Treatment, and Conceptual Models*, Raven Press, New York, 1977.

264. SEEMAN, P., and LEE, T., "Antipsychotic Drugs: Direct Correlation Between Clinical Potency and Presynaptic Action on Dopamine Neurons," *Science, 188(6):*1217, 1975.

265. SERRANO, A. C., and FORBIS, O. L., "Haloperidol for Psychiatric Disorders in Children," *Diseases of the Nervous System, 34(5):*226, 1973.

266. SHADER, R. I., and DiMASCIO, A. (Eds.), *Psychotropic Drug Side Effects*, Williams & Wilkins, Baltimore, 1970.

267. SHAPIRO, A. K., SHAPIRO, E., and WAYNE, H., "Treatment of Tourette's Syndrome," *Archives of General Psychiatry, 28(1):*92, 1973.

268. SHERMAN, L., et al., "Effect of Chlorpromazine on Serum Growth-Hormone in Man," *New England Journal of Medicine, 284(1):*72, 1971.

269. SHERWIN, A. C., FLACH, F. F., and STOKES, P. E., "Treatment of Psychoses in Early Children with Triiodothyronine," *American Journal of Psychiatry, 115(2):*166, 1958.

270. SHIRKEY, H. C., "Drug Dosage for Infants and Children," *Journal of the American Medical Association, 193(6):*443, 1965.

271. SILBERSTEIN, R. M., et al., "Avoiding Institutionalization of Psychotic Children," *Archives of General Psychiatry, 19(1):*17, 1968.

272. SILVER, A. A., "Management of Children with Schizophrenia," *American Journal of Psychotherapy, 9(2):*196, 1955.

273. SIMEON, J., et al., "Thiothixene in Childhood Psychoses," Paper presented at the Third International Symposium on Phenothiazines, Rockville, Md., June 25–28, 1973.

274. SIMEON, J., et al., "Clinical and Neurophysiological Investigations of Combined Thioridazine-d-Amphetamine Maintenance Therapy and Withdrawal in Childhood Behavior Disorders (Drug Maintenance in Childhood Behavior Disorders)," Paper presented at the American Psychiatric Association Meeting, Honolulu, May 7–11, 1973.

275. SIMMONS, J. Q., III, BENOR, D., and DANIEL, D.,

"The Variable Effects of LSD-25 on the Behavior of a Heterogeneous Group of Childhood Schizophrenics," *Behavioral Neuropsychiatry*, 3(1–2):10–16, 24, 1972.

276. SIMMONS, J. Q., III, et al., "Modification of Autistic Behavior with LSD-25," *American Journal of Psychiatry*, 122(11):1201, 1966.

277. SIMON, G. B., and GILLIES, S. M., "Some Physical Characteristics of a Group of Psychotic Children," *British Journal of Psychiatry*, 110:104, 1964.

278. SKYNNER, A. C. R., "Effects of Chloridazepoxide," *Lancet*, 1(7186):1110, 1961.

279. SLEATOR, E. K., VON NEUMANN, A., and SPRAGUE, R. L., "Hyperactive Children: A Continuous Long-Term Placebo-Controlled Follow-Up," *Journal of the American Medical Association*, 229(3):316, 1974.

280. SMALL, A., HIBI, S., and FEINBERG, I., "Effects of Dextroamphetamine Sulfate on EEG Sleep Patterns of Hyperactive Children," *Archives of General Psychiatry*, 25(4):369, 1971.

281. SPITZER, R. L., ENDICOTT, J., and ROBINS, E., "Research Diagnostic Criteria (RDC) for a Selected Group of Functional Disorders," unpublished manuscript, 1975.

282. SPRAGUE, R. L., "Principles of Clinical Trials and Social, Ethical and Legal Issues of Drug Use in Children," in Werry, J. S. (Ed.), *Pediatric Psychopharmacology. The Use of Behavior Modifying Drugs in Children*, p. 109, Brunner/Mazel, New York, 1978.

283. ———, "Recommended Performance Measures for Psychotropic Drug Investigations," *Psychopharmacology Bulletin*, Special Issue, "Pharmacotherapy of Children," p. 85, 1973.

284. ———, and BAXLEY, G. B., "Drugs Used for the Management of Behavior in Mental Retardation," in Wortis, J. (Ed.), *Mental Retardation*, vol. 10, p. 97, Grune & Stratton, New York, 1978.

285. SPRAGUE, R. L., and SLEATOR, E. K., "What Is the Proper Dose of Stimulant Drugs in Children?" in Gittelman-Klein, R. (Guest Ed.), *Recent Advances in Child Psychopharmacology, International Journal of Mental Health*, 4(1–2):75, 1975.

286. ———, " Effects of Psychopharmacologic Agents on Learning Disorders," *Pediatric Clinics of North America*, 20(3):719, 1973.

287. SPRAGUE, R. L., and WERRY, J. S., "Pediatric Psychopharmacology," *Psychopharmacology Bulletin*, Special Issue, "Pharmacotherapy of Children," p. 21, 1973.

288. ———, "Methodology of Psychopharmacological Studies with the Retarded," in Ellis, N. R. (Ed.), *International Review of Research in Mental Retardation*, p. 148, Academic Press, New York, 1971.

289. SPRAGUE, R. L., BARNES, K. R., and WERRY, J. S., "Methylphenidate and Thioridazine: Learning, Reaction Time, Activity and Classroom Behavior in Disturbed Children," *American Journal of Orthopsychiatry*, 40(4):615, 1970.

290. STACK, J. J., "Chemotherapy in Childhood Depression," in Annell, A. L., *Depressive States in Childhood and Adolescence*, p. 460, Almquist & Wiksell, Stockholm, 1972.

291. STEINBERG, G. S., TROSHINSKY, C., and STEINBERG, H. C., "Dextroamphetamine-Responsive Behavior Disorder in School Children," *American Journal of Psychiatry*, 128(2):174, 1971.

292. STORES, G., "Antiepileptics (Anticonvulsants)," in Werry, J. S. (Ed.), *Pediatric Psychopharmacology. The Use of Behavior Modifying Drugs in Children*, p. 274, Brunner/Mazel, New York, 1978.

293. TALBOT, N..B., and RICHIE, R. H., "Advantage of Surface Area of Body as Basis for Calculating Pediatric Dosages," *Pediatrics*, 24:495, 1959.

294. TARJAN, G., LOWERY, V. E., and WRIGHT, S. W., "Use of Chlorpromazine in Two Hundred Seventy-Eight Mentally Deficient Patients," *Journal of Diseases of Children*, 94(6):294, 1957.

295. THOMPSON, T., and SCHUSTER, C. R., *Behavior Pharmacology*, Prentice-Hall, Englewood Cliffs, N.J., 1968.

296. THUDICUM, W. L., *A Treatise on the Chemical Constitution of the Brain*, Bailliere, Tindall & Cox, London, 1884.

297. TURNER, D. A., et al., "Intensive Design in Evaluating Anxiolytic Agents," Paper presented at a Symposium on Clinical Pharmacological Methods, New Orleans, May 24–25, 1973.

298. TURNER, R. K., and YOUNG, G. C., "CNS Stimulant Drugs and Conditioning Treatment of Nocturnal Enuresis: A Long-Term Follow-Up Study," *Behavioral Research and Therapy*, 4(3):225, 1966.

299. UCER, E., and KREGER, K. C., "A Double-Blind Study Comparing Haloperidol with Thioridazine in Emotionally Disturbed, Mentally Retarded Children," *Current Therapeutic Research*, 11(5):278, 1969.

300. UHR, L., and MILLER, J. G., *Drugs and Behavior*, John Wiley, New York, 1960.

301. WAIZER, J., et al., "Outpatient Treatment of Hyperactive School Children with Imipramine," *American Journal of Psychiatry*, 131(5):587, 1974.

302. WAIZER, J., et al., "A Single-Blind Evaluation of Thiothixene with Outpatient Schizophrenic Children," *Journal of Autism and Childhood Schizophrenia*, 2(4):378, 1972.

303. WEINBERG, W. A., et al., "Depression in Children Referred to an Educational Diagnostic Center: Diagnosis and Treatment—Preliminary Report," *Journal of Pediatrics*, 83(6):1065, 1973.

304. WEISS, G., "The Natural History of Hyperactivity in Childhood and Treatment with Stimulant Medication at Different Ages: A Summary of Research Findings," in Gittelman-Klein, R. (Guest Ed.), *Recent Advances in Child Psychopharmacology, International Journal of Mental Health*, 4(1–2):213, 1975.

305. ———, et al., "Effect of Long-Term Treatment of Hyperactive Children with Methylphenidate," *Canadian Medical Association Journal*, 112(2):159, 1975.

306. WEISS, G., et al., "Studies on the Hyperactive Child, VIII. Five-Year Follow Up," *Archives of General Psychiatry*, 24(5):409, 1971.

307. WENDER, P. H., *Minimal Brain Dysfunction in Children*, Wiley Interscience, New York, 1971.

308. WERRY, J. S., "Measures in Pediatric Psychopharmacology," in Werry, J. S. (Ed.), *Pediatric Psychopharmacology. The Use of Behavior Modifying Drugs in Children*, p. 29, Brunner/Mazel, New York, 1978.

309. ———, "Childhood Psychosis," in Quay, H. C., and Werry J. S. (Eds.), *Psychopathological Disorders of Childhood*, p. 173, John Wiley, New York, 1972.

310. ———, and AMAN, M. G., " Methylphenidate and Haloperidol in Children, Effects on Attention, Memory, and Activity," *Archives of General Psychiatry*, 32(6):790, 1975.

311. WERRY, J. S., and SPRAGUE, R. L., "Methylphenidate in Children: Effect of Dosage," *Australian and New Zealand Journal of Psychiatry*, 8(1):9, 1974.

312. WERRY, J. S., et al., "Studies on the Hyperactive Child, III. The Effect of Chlorpromazine Upon Behavior and Learning Ability," *Journal of the American Academy of Child Psychiatry*, 5(2):292, 1966.

313. WHITEHEAD, P. L., and CLARK, L. D., "Effect of Lithium Carbonate, Placebo and Thioridazine on Hyperactive Children," *American Journal of Psychiatry*, 127(6):824, 1970.

314. WIENER, J. M., "Developmental Perspective on Psychopharmacology," Paper presented at the Washington Counsel of Child Psychiatry's Institute on Psychopharmacology of Children and Adolescents, Washington, D. C., June 11, 1977.

315. World Health Organization, *Scientific Group on Psychopharmacology: Research in Psychopharmacology*, World Health Organization Technical Report series no. 371, World Health Organization, Geneva, 1967.

316. WINSBERG, B. G., et al., "Imipramine and Electro-

cardiographic Abnormalities in Hyperactive Children," *American Journal of Psychiatry, 132(5):*542, 1975.

317. WINSBERG, B. G., et al., "Imipramine Protein Binding and Pharmacokinetics in Children," in Forrest, I. S., Carr, C. J., and Usdin, E. (Eds.), *The Phenothiazines and Structurally Related Drugs,* p. 425, Raven Press, New York, 1974.

318. WINSBERG, B. G., et al., "Effects of Imipramine and Dextroamphetamine on Behavior of Neuropsychiatrically Impaired Children," *American Journal of Psychiatry, 128(11):*1425, 1972.

319. WOLPERT, A., HAGAMEN, M. B., and MERLIS, S., "A Comparative Study of Thiothixene and Trifluoperazine in Childhood Schizophrenia,' *Current Therapeutic Research, 9(9):*482, 1967.

320. WOODROW, K. M., "Gilles de la Tourette's Disease: A Review," *American Journal of Psychiatry, 131(9):*1000, 1974.

321. YOUNG, C. G., and TURNER, R. K., "CNS Stimulant Drugs and Conditioning Treatment of Nocturnal Enuresis," *Behavioral Research and Therapy, 3(2):*93, 1965.

322. ZRULL, J. P., et al., "Comparison of Diazepam, D-Amphetamine and Placebo in the Treatment of the Hyperkinetic Syndrome in Children," *American Journal of Psychiatry, 121(4):*388, 1964.

323. ZRULL, J. P., et al., "A Comparison of Chlordiazepoxide, D-Amphetamine, and Placebo in the Treatment of the Hyperkinetic Syndrome in Children," *American Journal of Psychiatry, 120(6):*590, 1963.

24 / **Other Physical Interventions**

Alexander R. Lucas

Despite its shortcomings psychopharmacologic treatment is the most widely practiced and the most valuable of the biologic therapies for childhood emotional and mental disorders. As chapter 23 attests, a great variety of drugs is available; there are many indications for their use when they are part of a rational total treatment plan; and there is now considerable documentation regarding their effects, side effects, and contraindications. Since the early 1960s, psychoactive drugs have been increasingly used in child psychiatric practice. They have largely supplanted other forms of physical intervention.

Aside from those which have possible research value, the biologic therapies in child psychiatry are largely of historical interest. Some of the treatments subsumed here border on what is considered legitimate treatment practice; other methods are totally unacceptable.

There are certain metabolic diseases (such as phenylketonuria) which result in mental deficiency and other forms of central nervous system dysfunction in childhood. These were once in the province of child psychiatric practice. As specific dietary therapies were discovered, treatment could be administered by the pediatrician to prevent central nervous system involvement and behavioral complications. It is likely that effective biologic treatment will eventually be found for other disorders of unknown etiology: many types of brain dysfunction, early infantile autism, and childhood schizophrenia. Until that time, supportive, nonspecific, and nonbiological treatment methods for the child and his family will continue to prevail.

For those disorders of childhood still without a specific cure, there is a perpetual search for new modes of intervention. Until the causes are elucidated and rational therapies developed, we can expect the repeated sequence of enthusiastic claims for remedies which will later fall into disrepute and be forgotten. The history of medicine is replete with such occurrences. Kenner[18] referred to an era of indiscriminate prescription of tonics, sedatives, vitamins, appetizers, and other crutches as substitutes for a realistic understanding and treatment of the emotional disturbance. Answers will be found only through research and clinical experimentation. When there is insufficient evidence that a treatment procedure will be of value, there is danger of holding out false hope for a child and his family. In the case of a hopeless condition there can be some justification to "try anything that may be of help." But this should be offered with the family's full knowledge that the procedure is experimental. The hazards of the procedure, including the financial costs, the emotional costs to the parents, and the effect on siblings should be weighed against its possible benefits. Above all, the basic tenet of medicine must be heeded: do not harm.

The other physical interventions to be discussed here will include: convulsive therapies, psychosurgery, nutritional therapies, physical training, and biofeedback. These will be considered from the standpoint of the rationale underlying the technique, the indications for which the technique has been advocated, the disadvantages or contraindications, and the therapeutic results.

Convulsive Therapies

Electroconvulsive therapy (ECT) and, to a lesser extent, Pentylenetetrazol (Metrazol) shock treatment have been used by child psychiatrists to treat young schizophrenic children. Lauretta Bender[6] was an early advocate of these forms of treatment. She advanced the theory that childhood schizophrenia involved encephalopathic interferences in maturational patterning and that these therapeutic methods would enhance integration of the lagging developmental processes and thus help the psychotic children achieve a higher level of functioning. Cottington, working with Bender,[7] administered pentylenetetrazol shock treatment in the 1930s; in the 1940s, Bender and her coworkers employed electroconvulsive treatment.[5, 13] A series of twenty daily convulsive shocks was administered to children under the age of twelve.

Pentylenetetrazol shock is no longer used because of its markedly unpleasant effects, and electroconvulsive therapy is used rarely in preadolescent children. Today, drugs are more effective and easier to administer. In adolescence, the indications for electroconvulsive treatment include severe endogenous depressions, particularly when there is great suicidal risk. It is also resorted to when symptoms of depressive rumination, psychomotor retardation, and anorexia have been resistant to treatment with antidepressive medication. Acutely psychotic adolescents who have failed to respond to adequate trials of antipsychotic medication may, after two months, be considered for a course of electroconvulsive therapy. Child psychiatrists rarely administer ECT, and its actual administration should be left to a physician familiar with the technique. The decision to use this form of treatment should be made jointly by the child psychiatrist who refers the patient and by the psychiatrist who administers it.

Electroconvulsive therapy should be considered only when drug treatment clearly has been ineffective. Kalinowsky and Hippius[17] stated that youth is not a contraindication. They pointed out that no ill effects have been reported in children. The treatment has been used in children as young as three: Use in an epileptic child of that age was reported by Hamphill and Walter[15] and use in a three-year-old schizophrenic child was reported by Bender.[4]

Bender[5] has reported on the follow up of one hundred schizophrenic children treated by convulsive therapies. Positive behavioral changes were observed; these involved the lessening of disturbance, excitability, withdrawal, and anxiety. The kind of remission observed in adults occurred in the cases of only a few children. All of these were near twelve years of age and probably already in puberty. Bender noted that the basic schizophrenic process, including the motility disturbance, vegetative lability, disturbances in thought and language, and perceptual motor patterning was not modified. Secondary symptoms, however, were improved. Thus, her results were comparable to those now achieved with antipsychotic drugs. Intellectual functioning was not impeded by the treatment, and the electroencephalogram continued to indicate maturation.

Psychosurgery

Psychosurgery must be distinguished from neurosurgery. Psychosurgery comprises those surgical procedures which aim at altering behavior by destroying areas of the brain which influence emotion. Neurosurgery deals with the surgical treatment of demonstrably abnormal changes in central nervous system tissue caused by neoplasms, trauma, infections, vascular, and developmental lesions. Older[21] has enumerated the psychosurgical techniques currently in use. In addition to the more traditional methods of prefrontal lobotomy, there is a group of techniques which seek to ablate areas of the brain related to emotion (amygdala, thalamus, and cingulate gyrus). The rationale underlying all of these procedures is to reduce or eliminate severe aggressiveness, destructiveness, and sexual activity. Freeman and Watts[12] reported on eleven psychotic children, four years and older, who underwent prefrontal lobotomies. Reports from the United States,[2] India,[3] and Japan[20, 27] indicate that other forms of psychosurgery have been used, not only in hospitalized, mentall ill adults and prisoners, but also used for children who were aggressive, who had seizures, and who manifested various behavior disorders.

Specific neurosurgical techniques for the purpose of ablating brain foci generating intractable seizure discharges may have a sound rationale, but psychosurgical procedures for children with behavior problems are not indicated. Older[21] questioned the ethics of such surgery because they involved the destruction of irreplaceable brain tissue of a developing child. He suggested that long-term protective hospitalization is preferable to such irreversible procedures. Older recommended categorically that psychosurgery never be permitted on anyone under twenty-one years of age.

Holland and his coworkers[16] reported on the outcome of lobotomy in twelve children and adolescents. Most of these patients were schizophrenic, few had postencephalitic disorders. Selection for the procedure had been based on the very poor prognosis for these children; they appeared to be destined for permanent institutionalization. The presenting symptoms were severe hostility and destructiveness. Follow up after three or more years indicated that only one of twelve remained hostile, and none was destructive. Seven had returned to work or to school. The authors used these data to justify the operation for the amelioration of severe behavioral difficulties; they acknowledged, however, that maturation may have been a factor in the improvement. Freeman and Watts,[11] vigorous proponents of prefrontal lobotomy as a psychiatric treatment for adults, were disappointed by the response of psychotic children they treated.

Nutritional Therapies

Under this category of treatment are included a wide variety of modification in diet, nutrient supplements, amino acids, vitamins, and minerals, which have been advocated in the treatment of the entire spectrum of psychiatric disturbances in children. When a specific metabolic or dietary deficiency is discovered, appropriate treatment is indicated. Various workers have proposed the presence of metabolic deficiencies in certain forms of mental deficiency, psychosis, and hyperkinesis, and have implicated as causative agents hypoglycemia, food allergies, noxious food additives, and deficiencies of trace elements in the diet. As a rule, these theories lacked a sound scientific footing, and treatment claims have not been replicable. Research in all these areas should certainly be encouraged. However, when overenthusiastic claims are made and when the remedies are applied indiscriminately to all disturbed, hyperactive, or psychotic children, violence is done to scientific thinking and a grave injustice meted out to the children and their families.

The most widely publicized of the nutritional therapies is *orthomolecular psychiatric therapy*. Commonly known as *megavitamin treatment*, this term originated with Osmond and Hoffer's[22] use of massive doses of niacin in the treatment of schizophrenia. Pauling[24] coined the term orthomolecular therapy and defined it as the treatment of mental disease by the provision of the optimum molecular environment for the mind, especially the optimum concentrations of substances normally present in the human body. An example he gave is the treatment of phenylketonuric children by use of a diet containing a smaller than normal amount of the amino acid phenylalanine. Thus, some proven methods of treatment fall within Pauling's definition of orthomolecular therapy. Advocates of this treatment are enthusiastic about its application to children with early infantile autism and childhood schizophrenia. Hawkins[14] advocated megavitamin treatment (high doses of niacinamide, ascorbic acid, pyridoxine, and vitamin E) after correction of hypoglycemia in schizophrenic children. A large-scale study, still in progress, of megavitamin treatment for heterogeneous groups of psychotic children, has been undertaken by Rimland.[25] Further careful research on metabolic disturbances in psychotic children is much needed, as are more data on treatment results in comparable groups of children. Evaluating the current state of knowledge, the American Psychiatric Association Task Force on Vitamin Therapy in Psychiatry[1] discounted the claims of orthomolecular psychiatry proponents as neither proven nor replicated.

The continuing controversy surrounding this approach to treatment testifies to the many unresolved questions which remain.[23, 30] The optimum position for the child psychiatric practitioner would be an open mind to new ideas, coupled with an expectation of rigid scientific scrutiny of treatment results.

Physical Training

A method known as "patterning" or the Doman-Delacato Method[8] for training brain-damaged children received much publicity in the 1960s. The originators of this method founded the Institute for the Achievement of Human Potential in Philadelphia. Their methods enjoyed widespread popularity for children with neurologic handicaps, mental deficiency and particularly for those with reading disabilities. The hypothesis underlying the method was based on the premise that man's neurologic organization and development ontogenically recapitulates phylogenetic development, and that failure to follow certain sequences in maturation results in poor neurologic organization or brain damage. "Patterning" was proposed to stimulate critical brain centers to a higher level of functioning. This involved passive manipulation of body parts, active exercises, and the fostering of uniform hemispheric dominance. An elaborate system of prevention and treatment evolved from the hypothesis. It emphasized creeping, crawling, sleep patterns, coordination exercises, and use of the trampoline. A rigorous schedule was prescribed for the child's training, a program which required remarkable adherence by the parents or others to the supervision of this demanding regimen. Reports in popular magazines told of entire communities rallying to the cause.

The prime targets for the application of "patterning" were children with reading disabilities, but profoundly retarded children also received this training. There were even claims that the development of normal children would be enhanced by such a program which would improve their intellectual and academic potential. The medical profession and many educators reacted with skepticism and reproach because of excessive claims and lack of documentation for the results of the procedures. The controversy was delineated by Freeman.[10] In a companion paper by Robbins,[26] a controlled study found the method ineffective in improving reading skills. A joint statement[9] approved by ten American and Canadian associations, including the American Academy of Neurology, the American Academy of Pediatrics, and the National Association for Retarded Children, condemned the Doman-Delacato method because of its questionable theory, the excessive undocumented claims of its adherents, and the extreme guilt-provoking demands placed on parents in carrying out an unproven technique.

In an altogether different realm, eye exercises had also achieved some vogue for poor readers. These were supposed to correct ocular muscle imbalances and to improve tracking. Keeney,[19] an ophthalmologist, pointed out that neither ocular exercises nor gross motor programs have any direct effect on the symbol interpretive function of the brain. Physical training can improve a child's motor skills and can give a poorly coordinated child more confidence in controlling his body. But there is no evidence that central nervous system impairment can be corrected by such methods. Children who read poorly need remedial educational techniques designed to remedy their deficient skills.

Biofeedback

A recent surge of interest has focused on biofeedback as a treatment technique for psychosomatic conditions.[28, 29] The technique, derived from psychophysiologic research, requires the patient to monitor certain of his or her own physiologic parameters, including pulse, respirations, blood pressure, skin temperature, muscle tension, and the electroencephalogram. The rationale is that the subject, by monitoring a visual or auditory record of the measurements of his physiologic state, can learn to control the physiologic processes. Chiefly in adults, biofeedback has already been used with apparent success for treating headache, muscle tension, labile hypertension, cardiac arhythmias, anxiety states, and other conditions. It holds promise for future applications with children and adolescents in psychophysiologic conditions such as vomiting, particularly when used in conjunction with relaxation techniques. Equipment for lay use is readily available. It is important that proper safeguards be established for its use under adequate professional supervision.

REFERENCES

1. American Psychiatric Association, *Task Force Report 7: Megavitamin and Orthomolecular Therapy in Psychiatry*, American Psychiatric Association, Washington, D. C., 1973.

2. ANDY, O., "Thalamotomy in Hyperactivity and Aggressive Behavior," *Confinia Neurologica*, 32:322–325, 1970.

3. BALASUBRAMANIAM, V., KANAKA, T., and RAMAMURTHI, B., "Surgical Treatment for Hyperkinetic and Behavior Disorders," *International Surgery*, 54:18–23, 1970.

4. BENDER, L., "The Development of a Schizophrenic Child Treated with Electric Convulsions at Three Years of Age," in Caplan, G. (Ed.), *Emotional Problems of Early Childhood*, pp. 407–430, Basic Books, New York, 1955.

5. ———, "One Hundred Cases of Childhood Schizophrenia Treated with Electric Shock," *Transactions of the American Neurological Association*, 72:165–169, 1947.

6. ———, "Childhood Schizophrenia," *American Journal of Orthopsychiatry*, 17:40–56, 1947.

7. COTTINGTON, F., "The Treatment of Childhood Schizophrenia by Metrazol Shock Modified by B-Erythroidin," *American Journal of Psychiatry*, 98:397–400, 1941.

8. DELACATO, C. H., *The Treatment and Prevention of Reading Problems*, Charles C Thomas, Springfield, Ill., 1959.

9. "The Doman-Delacato Treatment of Neurologically

Handicapped Children," *Developmental Medicine and Child Neurology, 10:*243–246, 1968.

10. FREEMAN, R. D., "Controversy over "Patterning" as a Treatment for Brain Damage in Children," *Journal of the American Medical Association, 202:*83–86, 1967.

11. FREEMAN, W. J., and WATTS, J. W., *Psychosurgery in the Treatment of Mental Disorders and Intractable Pain,* 2nd ed. Charles C Thomas, Springfield, Ill., 1951.

12. ———, "Schizophrenia in Childhood; Its Modification by Prefrontal Lobotomy," *Digest of Neurology and Psychiatry, Institute of Living, 15:*202–219, 1947.

13. GUREVITZ, S., and HELME, W. H., "Effects of Electroconvulsive Therapy on Personality and Intellectual Functioning of the Schizophrenic Child, *Journal of Nervous and Mental Diseases, 120:*213–226, 1954.

14. HAWKINS, D., "Orthomolecular Psychiatry: Treatment of Schizophrenia," in Hawkins, D., and Pauling, L. (Eds.), *Orthomolecular Psychiatry,* pp. 631–673, W. H. Freeman and Company, San Francisco, 1973.

15. HEMPHILL, R. E., and WALTER, W. G., "The Treatment of Mental Disorders by Electrically Induced Convulsions," *Journal of Mental Science, 87:*256–275, 1941.

16. HOLLAND, H. C., NEWMAN, E. G., and HOHMAN, L. B., "Effects of Lobotomy in Childhood," *Diseases of the Nervous System, 19:*201–207, 1958.

17. KALINOWSKY, L. B., and HIPPIUS, H., *Pharmacological, Convulsive and Other Somatic Treatment in Psychiatry,* Grune, & Stratton, New York, 1969.

18. KANNER, L., Child Psychiatry, 3rd ed., Charles C Thomas, Springfield Ill., 1957.

19. KENNEY, A. H., "Medical Diagnostics and Counseling in Dyslexia," *Medical Clinics of North America, 53:*1123–1129, 1969.

20. NARABAYASHI, H., et al., "Stereotactic Amygdalotomy for Behavior Disorders," *Archives of Neurology, 9:*1–17, 1963.

21. OLDER, J., "Psychosurgery: Ethical Issues and a Proposal for Control," *American Journal of Orthopsychiatry, 44:*661–674, 1974.

22. OSMOND, H., and HOFFER, A., "Massive Niacin Treatment in Schizophrenia: Review of a Nine-year Study," *Lancet, 1:*316–319, 1962.

23. PAULING, L., "On the Orthomolecular Environment of the Mind: Orthomolecular Theory," *American Journal of Psychiatry, 131:*1251–1257, 1974.

24. ———, "Orthomolecular Psychiatry," *Science, 160:*265–271, 1968.

25. RIMLAND, B., "High-Dosage Levels of Certain Vitamins in The Treatment of Children with Severe Mental Disorders," in Hawkins, D., and Pauling, L. (Eds.), *Orthomolecular Psychiatry,* pp. 513–539, W. H. Freeman, San Francisco, 1973.

26. ROBBINS, M. P., "Test of the Doman-Delacato Rationale with Retarded Readers," *Journal of the American Medical Association, 202:*87–91, 1967.

27. SANO, K., "Postero-medical Hypothalamotomy," *Neurologia Medico-Chirurgica, 4:*112–42, 1962.

28. SCHWARTZ, G. E., "Biofeedback, Self-Regulation, and the Patterning of Physiological Processes," *American Scientist, 63:*314–24, 1975.

29. SEGAL, J., "Biofeedback as a Medical Treatment," *Journal of the American Medical Association, 232:*179–180, 1975.

30. WYATT, R. J., KLEIN, D., and LIPTON, M. A., "Comment," *American Journal of Psychiatry, 131:*1258–1267, 1974.

PART G
Special Therapeutic Considerations

25 / Helping Children Cooperate in Therapy

Richard A. Gardner

In this chapter, which will describe some ways of overcoming children's resistance to cooperating in therapy, the term "resistance" will be used to refer to the multiplicity of ways in which the child patient avoids involving himself in meaningful psychotherapeutic endeavors. Although the term originated within the context of psychoanalytic work (where the child avoids psychoanalytic inquiry because of the anxieties associated with the brining of unconscious material into conscious awareness), it willl be employed here for the broader range of psychological and behavioral manifestations associated with the child's not cooperating in therapy. The fact that children are more likely than adults to resist psychotherapy was well appreciated by Freud. In the first paragraph of the first article on the psychoanalytic treatment of a child (the now-classic case of "Little Hans," published in 1909), Freud describes his reasons for having the father, rather than he himself, conduct the analysis.[26]

No one else, in my opinion, could possibly have prevailed on the child to make any such avowals; the special knowledge by means of which he was able to interpret the remarks made by his five-year-old son was indispensable, and without it, the technical difficulties in the way of conducting a psychoanalysis upon so young a child would have been insuperable. [p. 149]

Since the publication of Little Hans's treatment, child therapists have continually attempted to devise ways to reduce, circumvent, work through, and otherwise handle the resistances with which children inevitably confront their therapists. In fact, it is reasonable to view the development of the multiple techniques used in child therapy as, more than anything else, attempts to deal with such resistances.

In 1926, Freud[27] described five kinds of resistance seen in psychoanalytic work. He formulated three ego resistances: (1) repression resistance (the need to maintain ego defenses designed to repress id impulses), (2) transference resistance (the need to repeat with the therapist pathological modes of relating that had once been formed in childhood with significant figures), and (3) secondary gain resistance (the need to maintain a symptom because of "fringe benefits" the individual derives from it). Quite another kind of resistance arises in the id which operates in accordance with the repetition compulsion and thereby maintains the need to release instinctual impulses regardless of how pathological the means of expression may be. And finally, the fifth type of resistance originates in the superego and relates to the sense of guilt and the need for punishment to assuage that guilt—both of which contribute to the patient's need to maintain his pathology. As is readily apparent from this formulation, resistances and defenses are closely related—so much so that their treatment usually occurs simultaneously. Accordingly, if the therapist directs his attention to the treatment of the various resistances that his patient exhibits in the therapy, he will often find himself dealing with the very problems that underlie the presenting symptoms. The therapist does well, then, to view resistances, even the grossly disruptive behavior of disturbed children, not merely as patterns he must somehow circumvent but as manifestations worthy of therapeutic focus. Anna Freud[24] emphasized that it was the *effects* associated with the eruption of instinctual impulses into conscious awareness that contributed most significantly to resistances. (Her descriptions of the kinds of resistances that are characteristic of children will be included in the various types of resistance to be discussed later in this chapter.)

Common Forms of Resistance Seen in Childhood

The overwhelming majority of patients referred to the child therapist do not come like Little Hans— suffering with an ego-alien symptom, motivated to remove it, and willing and able to involve themselves in a psychoanalytic inquiry in the service of alleviating their problems. Most are referred against their will, have little motivation to change themselves, and do not appreciate how their therapeutic experience fits into their life pattern. Commonly, the only thing the child wants is that the therapist be instrumental in getting his parents, teachers, and others who are dissatisfied with his behavior "off his back." Even if the child has some insight into his problems and some motivation to change things, he will often still prefer to play with his friends or watch television, rather than to come to the therapist's office. The child is basically hedonistic and avoids the unpleasant affects whose toleration is so vital for meaningful insight. So strong is this tendency that the child tends quickly to forget disturbing symptoms (such as nightmares) that could serve to motivate him for treatment.[85] Basically the child prefers to live in the present. He will not or cannot take a long-range view of things and is not prone to give up present pleasures (or suffer present discomforts) for future gains and rewards. Rather than intros-

pect, the child tends to act. Rather than view himself as being a contributor to his difficulties, he prefers to externalize and view his problems as caused by forces in his environment.[24, 45]

Accordingly, many children absolutely refuse to come for treatment, or when they do come they refuse to enter the therapist's office. At times, even the child who is forced to come by his parents may ultimately form a successful therapeutic relationship; at other times such coercion may only "sour" him further on the therapeutic process. Many find that allowing the parent(s) to join the child in the initial interview significantly lessens initial anxieties about treatment.[30] The child's primitive thought processes may cause him to entertain and believe the most bizarre fantasies about the therapist. He may believe that the therapist will change him completely, read his mind, operate on his brain, or effect other magical (and often terrible) transformations.[79] The correction of such distortions—and the child's subsequently having the living experience that his fears were unwarranted—can reduce resistances from this quarter. Once in the consultation room the child may run out; or, if he stays, he may refuse to talk; or, if he talks, he may verbalize only trivia. His typical answer is ilkely to be "I don't know." He may prefer to spend his time playing with toys but not verbalizing. He may even begin to search through drawers and destroy property. Some children have been known to cause physical harm to the therapist. Although such behavior provides information about the child, and although such resistances warrant our respect as foci of therapeutic attention, they do not lend themselves readily to intervention.

The child may fear that he is "retarded" or "crazy" and his visit to the therapist may be taken as a confirmation of these apprehensions. Such notions may be reinforced by friends and classmates who, when they learn that the child visits a therapist, may taunt him with epithets like "retard" or "mental." Many children may be afraid to express such concerns to the therapist lest their worst fears be validated. Accordingly, the therapist does well to discuss this issue and to attempt to allay such anxieties with most, if not all, children who begin therapy. The occasional child who is indeed psychotic or retarded has to be helped to appreciate that although the pejorative terms might loosely be applicable, the malevolent intent of the taunters is a sickness in itself.

The chronically angry child may direct the hostility he feels toward his parents onto the therapist in ways that are designed to obstruct the treatment. The anger may be expressed passively by keeping silent or by providing only perfunctory nonrevealing responses to the therapist's inquiries and overtures. Such children may derive morbid gratification from the awareness that they are causing their parents to waste their time and money. The therapist who silently sits, session after session, in the hope that ultimately the patient will speak and relate to him may be an unwitting accomplice to the child's hostile designs and is thereby entrenching rather than relieving the child's pathology. Most therapists ultimately find such silent sessions irritating. Some may deny this both to themselves and to the child—but he knows otherwise. In such situations, the child gains the additional pathological gratification of knowing that he is "getting to" the therapist as well—clearly an undesirable situation. One way to avoid such an antitherapeutic involvement with the child is to see him only in joint interviews with his parents (with siblings present as indicated). In such discussions, decisions are usually made about how to handle various matters that involve the child, and he has to talk if he is to avoid decisions being made that will cause him discomfort.

Some children will try to obstruct therapy not so much to express hostility as to provoke the therapist into retaliatory punishment. To the extent that this succeeds, the child feels less guilt over their anger. The therapist who gets drawn into such involvement, who allows himself to be provoked, and who gets hostile with the child only perpetuates this pathological pattern. Sometimes the expression of anger toward the therapist may serve to provide the child with a sense of power to compensate for feelings of inadequacy. By depreciating the therapist and trying to control him, the child gains a sense of what Alfred Adler called "hidden superiority."[1]

Many, if not most, child patients do not have insight into their problems and are not genuinely motivated to change themselves. The therapist does well, therefore, to avoid trying to get the child to say what his problems are and why he wants treatment. When such declarations are obtained, the child may be mouthing only what he knows the therapist and his parents want to hear. Such avowals are not only worthless but they introduce contaminants into treatment. Urging the child to profess them encourages duplicity in him, and if the child believes that the therapist is gullible enough to be so taken in, his respect for the therapist cannot but be reduced. This is not to suggest that the therapist avoid all attempts to help the child recognize that he has problems. It is merely to assert that he need not feel it necessary to elicit such statements from the child because they are not vital to therapeutic change.

Other forms of compliance can also serve the forces of resistance. The child who agrees with all the therapist says may be doing so without conviction, seeking through professions of agreement to avoid anxiety-provoking interchanges and to ingratiate himself with the therapist. The therapist should be suspicious of the child who is too "good" a patient. More often than not, pathological processes are contributing to the ostensibly happy and smooth course of the treatment. In its extreme form, such compliance brings about transference cures in which there has been no working-through of the fundamental problems, but the child gives up his symptoms so that he can leave treatment. The risk in such situations is that the symptoms are likely to return quickly.

A child who criticizes his parents (the usual case) may consider himself disloyal if he reveals his dissatisfactions to the therapist.[85] The child may have been imbued with the notion that it is wrong to reveal personal family matters to others, and this may inhibit him in treatment.[66] In such cases, the therapist does well to enlist the parents' aid in encouraging the child to reveal himself and to reassure him that there will be no repercussions from the parents for such revelations to the therapist (the usual case).

The child who has been neglected, scapegoated, or otherwise abused is likely to anticipate similar malevolent treatment by the therapist, and this will inhibit him from expressing himself.[10, 69] In such cases, the main goal of treatment may be for the child to find that there are people who treat him benevolently. Words alone will rarely suffice to accomplish this. The child must have the living experience, over a period of time, that such people exist. The child may enter treatment with the assumption (derived from experiences at home and school) that any problem behavior is "bad." Accordingly, he may consider every interpretation a criticism, a proof of his badness.[79] In an extreme case, he may view therapy as the ultimate punishment for all the bad things he has done. In such situations, the child may become quite anxious. He is then not likely to be able to cooperate with, nor to appreciate, what is going on in the treatment.[101] In almost all instances, when the child comes to appreciate that material that has appeared innocuous to him becomes meaningful to the therapist, he may become guarded about revealing himself.[79] The more insecure the child, the greater the likelihood that he will be reluctant to admit to any deficiencies. In fact, one of the reasons why the child (like the adult) does not wish to give up his symptoms is that they may be his main protection against facing his inadequacies.[82] The child may feel that he is the only one in the world who has such problems and insecurities. Such a child has to be helped to become comfortable with the notion that no one is perfect, that all people have some problems, that everyone distorts reality at times, and so forth[79] The child with profound feelings of inadequacy may develop fantasies of omnipotence accompanied by a total denial of difficulties and the delusion that there will be no repercussions whatsoever from the perpetuation of his problems.[58] When such denial exists in the adolescent, group therapy, which will be discussed subsequently, may be useful in helping the youngster see himself more realistically.

Refusal to cooperate in treatment may be a reflection of the child's wish to deny dependency. Oppositional behavior in the service of providing the child with a sense of independence starts as early as the tenth to twelfth month of life. In this period the child typically expresses feelings of independence by refusing to be fed and insisting on holding his spoon himself, or by refusing to accept what is given to him—even something he may value.[70] Some examples of the kind of dependence-denying obstructionism the two-year-old characteristically exhibits are resisting the doctor's examination and refusing to be bowel trained. From the developmental standpoint, such attempts at independence are the first steps toward the child's ultimate necessary separation from his parents.[69] Such resistance to compliance with adult requests can play a role in adapting to therapy. The child may refuse to come as a way of expressing his independence, or he may hesitate for fear that the therapist will change him into just the kind of child he feels his parents want, that is, one who is "good" and compliant, with no sense of individuality.[85] This form of resistance is especially likely to be operative in adolescence. To need help may be equated by the adolescent with residual infantile dependency—the existence of which he is trying his best to deny.[58] Some adolescents may have to be "forced" to come. Often enough, in such cases, the youngster really wants treatment but cannot allow himself to admit it either to himself or to others. By letting himself be coerced into therapy he need not admit to himself or to others that he really wants it; rather, he is convinced that he has only succumbed to overwhelming forces and he cannot but be admired for the courageous resistance he put up before grudg-

ingly submitting. Often in the midst of their professions of absolute refusal to attend, such youngsters will communicate their underlying wish to be forced to go. In such circumstances, it would be doing the child a disservice not to comply with this basic wish.[30]

The adolescent, who bears the additional burden of dealing with confusion over his identity, may fear that through treatment he will lose whatever sense of identity he has or that his confusion will increase. Certain forms of adolescent pathology represent attempts to gain a sense of identity, even if such identity is antisocial, for example, "The toughest guy in the school," "The loosest girl in the neighborhood," or "The kid with a police record since he was thirteen." Such a youngster will look upon therapy as a threat to deprive him of the only personality quality that distinguishes him from others and that calls attention to him as a special human being.[58] A group of related problems are the character resistances (originally described by Wilhelm Reich[91]). Body stiffness, fixed smiles, contemptuous airs, arrogance, and so forth originate in childhood and may contribute to resistance to treatment.[24]

Techniques for Dealing with Children's Resistances to Treatment

Kanner[64] credits Hertha von Hug-Hellmuth with having published in 1913[60] the first article describing the introduction of play into child psychoanalysis. Her 1921 article[59] appears to be the first in the English language on the use of play techniques in child psychoanalytic treatment. Hug-Hellmuth ascribed meaning to just about every act and verbalization of the child, and tended to interpret the child's behavior along strictly classical Freudian lines. Although one might disagree with her specific interpretations, her observation that the child's play fantasies and activities can be a valuable source of information about his psychodynamics was a formidable contribution to the field.

CHILD PSYCHOANALYSIS

Although Freud,[25] as early as 1908, commented briefly on one psychological aspect of play ("The opposite of play is not serious occupation but—reality."), it was Hug-Hellmuth's work that stimulated an interest in play as a tool in child therapy—an interest that persists to the present. In the 1920s Melanie Klein and Ann Freud began using play in child psychoanalysis. Klein[67] considered the fantasies that the child wove around his play to be the equivalent of the adult patient's free associations and the resistances revealed in such verbalizations susceptible to analysis. She directly confronted children as young as one to two years of age with what she regarded as the psychodynamic meaning of their play and believed the child capable of understanding her interpretations and utilizing the insights so gained therapeutically. Klein's critics are generally dubious about the ability of such young children to comprehend the formulations she presented them and consider many of her interpretations to express the content of her own mind rather than the child's.[63] Anna Freud[22, 23] has generally been more cautious than Klein in applying adult psychoanalytic technique to children. She recognized play as a valuable source of information about the child's psychodynamics (although she did not consider play verbalization to be the exact equivalent of adult free association) and as a useful tool in helping the child overcome resistance to treatment. She utilized play in the early phase of therapy to facilitate the child's forming a close and trusting relationship with the analyst; in later phases, she attempted to involve the child in analyzing his play verbalizations (including resistance fantasies). However, her approach to such analysis has always been more cautious than Klein's. In general, she approached the child through his defenses and tried to get him to derive his insights on his own rather than presenting him with the Kleinian kinds of direct interpretations.

Melanie Klein and Anna Freud's studies stimulated an intensive interest in the psychology of children's play that persists to the present. In 1933 Waelder[105] described the value of play as a medium for the child's wish fulfillment, parental emulation, gratification of regressive needs, and dealing with traumatic events (through desensitization and identification with the traumatizer, for example, the dentist). In 1940 Kanner[63] summarized some of the contributions made up through the 1930s. In 1950 Erikson[21] and in 1952 Bender[8] pointed out the importance of the structural configurations and spatial arrangements of the child's play. Subsequent contributions in this area include those of Hartley, Frank, and Goldenson,[51] Herron and Sutton-Smith,[57] Gardner[34] and Millar.[81]

Extensive work has also been done on the meaning of children's fantasies—the understanding of which is so vital to proper utilization of play therapeutic techniques. Pitcher and Prelinger[86] and Ames[3] collected extensive data on the fantasies of "normal" schoolchildren and formulated the frequency with which various themes appeared, for example, violence, food, morality, and so forth. Such data are invaluable because the child therapist is often confronted with the problem of differentiating normal from abnormal fantasies. All fantasies have underlying *psychodynamics*, even those of the child who is relatively free from symptoms. Whether such fantasies also reflect *psychopathology*, however, may be difficult to determine. Like the dream (whether of the child or adult), an analysis that does not take into consideration a multiplicity of additional factors not intrinsically a part of the dream is not likely to be very useful. Studies dealing with the interpretations of children's fantasies and stories and the use of such material in child therapy include those of Gondor,[47] Davidson and Fay,[18] Anthony,[5] and Gardner.[41]

Recognizing the value of the child's self-created fantasies as a valuable source of information about the child's psychodynamics has resulted in therapists' giving the highest priority to the child's expressing such material in the session. Therapists have found, however, that some patients resist revealing themselves in this way, often from an awareness (at some level) that even the symbolic representations may reveal material they do not wish divulged. Many of the techniques to be described subsequently were designed to overcome such resistance. To varying degrees, they have also attempted to solve the problem of how to make therapeutic use of the rich information that the child so often provides us. Exploration of fantasies, based on the assumption that understanding them is a primary therapeutic goal, is questioned by many as lacking the therapeutic power its adherents claim.[63]

One final and most important comment about children's fantasies. The therapist must appreciate that eliciting them too quickly, especially in the very guarded, fragile, and borderline child, may frighten him and thereby induce a resistance to self-revelation that would not have occurred if the therapist had proceeded more cautiously. The therapist does well, therefore, to hold off encouraging such children to reveal themselves until a trusting relationship has been established. The child will then be able to proceed with the genuine security of knowing there will be no untoward repercussions to exposing himself to the therapist.

DOLLS

Figurines representing various family members have traditionally been among the mainstays of the child therapist's playroom. Many consider such dolls to be among the most valuable items in the child therapist's armamentarium—facilitating as they do the production of fantasies that concern the individuals most involved in the child's difficulties. However, there is an intrinsic contaminating aspect to them, a contaminant that exists in all ready-made objects used as foci for the projection of the child's fantasies. Because they have a specific form, they are likely to suggest particular fantasies, thereby altering the purer fantasy that might have been elicited from a less recognizable object or from one that the child himself had created.[110] A preferable "doll" would be one that is more nondescript—a lump of clay on the top of a pencil, for example. To carry this principle further, the ideal "doll" would be no doll at all—because then there would be no contamination of the natural fantasies. The worst kind of doll for therapeutic use is an elaborate, and often expensive, one which presents multiple stimuli that not only restrict fantasies but may be focused upon by the child in the service of resistance. In spite of their potential for fantasy contamination, such dolls are still useful for the child who is too inhibited to verbalize without them. In addition, it is likely that the pressure of impulses to express themselves in fantasies related to the child's unconscious complexes is far greater than the power of the external facilitating stimulus to alter significantly the elicited fantasies.

The therapist does well not only to listen to the stories that the child creates around the dolls, but to observe the child's movements as well. The child's various nonverbal activities and the ways in which he physically structures the doll play can provide additional information of considerable value.[110] Such structuring, however, may be used in the service of resistance. Most therapists have had the experience of a child spending significant time placing the various family members in even rows and then repeatedly becoming dissatisfied with each new arrangement. Or the child may endlessly rearrange the furniture in the dollhouse, never seeming able to get to the story. Accordingly, it seems wiser not to have furniture displayed on the therapist's toy shelves. One may, however, keep certain items in a closet such as a bed and a toilet which, in special circumstances, can be introduced into the play. Similarly, because dolls such as soldiers, cowboys, and Indians tend not particularly revealing (and may thereby serve the forces of resistance), these objects are also to elicit stereotyped, age-appropriate play that is best kept in a closet and only brought out when appropriate.

As therapists acquired experience with psychoanalytic play therapy, it became apparent that only a small percentage of children were motivated to gain insight into their problems as a way of alleviating them. Generally, only the more intellectual and obsessive children were receptive to this approach. Often, they came from homes in which the parents themselves had received psychoanalytic therapy. Such parents were able to transmit to the child a conviction about the value of the psychoanalytic process that enhanced the child's motivation. Obviously, the majority of children lacked such parental involvement. Beginning in the 1930s, a variety of techniques were devised to draw this larger group into meaningful therapy. Some methods attempt to help the child gain insight; others do not consider the development of insight to be crucial to the therapeutic process. All, however, were designed in part to reduce, circumvent, or cope in some way with the child's resistances and failure to cooperate. The remainder of this chapter is devoted to a description of some of these methods. In order to continue the historical perspective utilized thus far, the various approaches will be presented roughly in the chronological order in which they were introduced.

THE PLAY INTERVIEW

One of the earliest modifications of psychoanalytic doll-play therapy was described by Jacob H. Conn, who referred to his approach as the "Play Interview."* Conn considered the fantasies that the child wove around his doll play to be highly valuable sources of information about his basic problems. He defined these, however, as direct reality problems. He believed that the child's gaining insight into these here-and-now issues was more important than inquiries into the "classical" psychoanalytic conflicts or into the past. His therapeutic approach focused on the child's gaining a more objective view of himself, appreciating his own role in bringing about his difficulties, and acquiring more adaptive ways of handling life's conflicts. He frequently urged the child to suppress his everyday anxieties and to desensitize himself to them while entering the anxiety-provoking situation. He took an active role in the play, asked many questions, and often set up specific situations that would channel the child's attention

* See references 13, 14, 15, 16, and 17.

into specific areas that Conn considered to be important. Conn did not have a high opinion of the value of catharsis in the treatment of most psychological disorders, whether such release was obtained from doll play or in other ways. He worked actively with parents in the attempt to change environmental contributions to the child's difficulties.

ACTIVE PLAY THERAPY

During the same period Joseph Solomon, a student of Conn, described a somewhat similar therapeutic approach which he referred to as "Active Play Therapy."[96, 97, 98, 99] He considered his more structured and active therapeutic approach to be indicated when the child exhibited resistance to verbalizing in association with free play. He believed that doll-play catharsis could be salutary, especially for hostile release. He viewed his approach as a modality through which the therapist could reduce guilt, provide therapeutic suggestions, and encourage desensitization through repetition. Although he, too emphasized the importance of focusing on present problems, he considered attention to the past to have a definite, albeit less important, role to play in therapy. As he saw it, the child did not necessarily need to gain insight in order to achieve therapeutic change. He observed that what the therapist transmitted through the doll play had therapeutic value even when it was directed only to the dolls and not ostensibly to the child himself. In fact, keeping the discussion in the third person was, in his view, one of the most efficacious ways to diminish the child's resistance to self-revelation. For the more receptive child, he advised helping him relate the doll fantasies to himself; however, he warned against encouraging such inquiry too rapidly as it might cause the child to become so anxious that he would resist completely any further work through doll-play fantasy.

RELEASE THERAPY

David M. Levy held that catharsis in certain situations could be therapeutic and referred to his techniques for promoting emotional expression in these situations as "Release Therapy."[71, 72] Levy described three types of release therapy. In the first, simple release, a child is allowed free expression of inhibited impulses (usually regressive or hostile): spilling, throwing, aggressive outbursts, and so forth. This form of treatment is indicated for children whose parents will not or cannot allow such release. In the second type, the child is encouraged to express inhibited feelings which are derived from standard situations such as sibling rivalry and curiosity about nudity. For such children the doll material and the therapist's remarks are so structured that comments in these given areas are likely to be evoked from the child. The third type is designed for the child who is reacting pathologically to a specific trauma and whose untoward behavior relates to his having suppressed or repressed his recollection of the event. In the treatment of such conditions, the dolls are set up to resemble the situation in which the trauma occurred; the therapist's comments are then designed to elicit responses related to the event. Generally, the technique worked best for children who were relatively healthy prior to the traumatic event and for whom the symptoms were of short duration. One danger of Levy's method is that the child may be led prematurely to deal with issues with which he is not ready to cope. Great anxiety will then be produced, and the child may become even more resistant to therapeutic work. However, for the situation for which the third type of release therapy is in fact indicated (admittedly a small segment of the children who are brought for therapy), the technique may prove useful.

RELATIONSHIP THERAPY

Frederick Allen considered certain transactions in the therapist-patient relationship to be the crucial elements in successful treatment. He referred to his approach as "Relationship Therapy."[2] Allen considered the experiences of the present, especially those that occurred in the therapeutic situation, to be the most important focus for therapeutic attention. Accordingly, he did not concern himself with helping the child gain insight into past events. He assumed that the child would repeat his past pathological behavior in the session, and worked with the present repetition. This, he felt, was the most efficacious way of alleviating the child's symptoms because then "living and understanding became one."[2] Allen believed the child's problems to stem primarily from environmental repressive forces, the reduction of which he considered to be salutary. Providing the child "freedom" was a paramount element in Allen's approach: " . . . the therapeutic value of talking lies less in the content and more in the freedom to talk."[2] In his view, the child had the innate capacity to discover healthy values and capabilities; the therapist's task was to provide the kind of accepting environment that would allow for their expression. However, Allen still understood that the therapist had to place reasonable controls on the child. The child was aware that these limitations would protect him from the untoward consequences of totally abandoning himself to free expression. Given such controls, he would then be more comfortable in expressing himself. Allen suggested that the therapist concentrate more on what the child is attempting to accomplish with his verbalizations in the therapeutic relationship than on the verbal content per se. For example, the child may be talking about his difficulties not so much in the attempt to resolve them himself but in the hope that the therapist will magically cure his problems for him. Allen appeared to be less concerned than many other therapists with the problem of dealing with resistances. What were often considered to be obstructions to treatment were viewed by Allen as healthy expression and self-assertion. For Allen, these were manifestations of the child's trying to overthrow the restrictive environmental influences that were the primary source of his pathology.

NONDIRECTIVE OR CLIENT-CENTERED THERAPY

Carl Rogers shared many of Allen's views and referred to his approach as "Nondirective or Client-centered Therapy."[92, 93] To Rogers, the term "patient" implied inferior status, whereas "client" connoted responsibility. Rogers considers there to be a "self-actualizing" drive present in all human beings from birth. Its repression by social forces produces various forms of discontent—one type of which is psychopathology. The purpose of treatment is to foster full expression of such self-actualizing impulses. This is most efficaciously accomplished when the therapist exhibits certain important attitudes in his relationship with the client. He must have "unconditional positive regard" for his client, that is, he should be free of judgments, both positive and negative. Only in such a permissive atmosphere will the child be willing to drop his resistances to self-expression. Rogers considers individuals (even children) to have both the innate capacity and the strength to devise (even when unguided) the proper steps toward mature behavior. He therefore suggests that the therapist assume an extremely passive and nondirective role in his work. His technique is to reflect back to the patient the latter's verbalizations and feelings in such a way that self-awareness is accomplished. The therapist encourages the child to take responsibility for his own actions and assumes that he has the capacity to do so. Like Allen, Rogers has a different view of what other therapists describe

as resistances. He sees these as related to the therapist's attempts to channel the child's activities and productions into specific directions. If the traditional resistances are viewed as healthy expressions of the child's basic inner needs, then they no longer appear to be obstructions to the therapeutic process. Presumably, in such a totally accepting atmosphere the child's resistances to revealing himself will be reduced; his revelations will provide the therapist with essential information. His reflections can then serve to clarify the child's awareness of his real, heretofore repressed impulses—and he becomes free to grow in directions natural to him. Taft,[102] like Rogers, was influenced by the work of Otto Rank, but she emphasized more than Rogers the separational elements in therapy (as derivatives of Rankian "birth trauma"). Axline[6, 7] is probably the best known therapist to have applied Rogerian techniques to the treatment of children.

Critics of Roger's work consider it difficult to differentiate the therapist's clarifying reflective communications that Rogers describes from parrotlike echoing of the patient's verbalizations. The technique looks simpler than it is and appears deceptively easy to implement—thereby leading many inadequately prepared therapists into practicing it. In addition, his critics hold that the mere release of emotions is rarely therapeutic in itself.[15] Psychopathological processes and resistances, they argue, are far too complex to respond to such a simple and narrow therapeutic approach.[4, 44] Many are dubious of the inner wisdom that Rogers assumes exists in all of us (even children) and that the "self" that becomes "actualized" in Rogerian treatment is very much affected by social influences, including the therapist's (his passivity notwithstanding). Finally, many would consider providing a child with the degree of freedom proposed by Rogers to be potentially dangerous. A more extensive discussion of Rogerian counseling can be found in chapter 13.

DRAWINGS

Once the immense value of doll play for bypassing and dealing with children's resistances to treatment became evident, therapists in the 1940s began experimenting with other toys to ascertain whether they too could be useful for this purpose. Presently, the use of drawings emerged; this continues to be among the most popular modalities used. It is now generally accepted that a child's self-created drawing is a valuable source of information about him. In the drawing of the human figure, for example, the child (more or less unconsciously) projects onto the picture important information about himself. Practically every part of the figure reveals something significant. Machover[75, 76, 77] was an astute interpreter of such drawings and has provided a wealth of information on how to interpret them. Most psychologists are quite critical of her methodology, but her findings are powerfully suggestive. Not only is the drawing per se a rich source of information about the child's psychological processes, but his behavior while drawing and his verbalizations about what he has drawn can provide the therapist with additional valuable material.

Bender[8] has described in detail the ways in which such productions can be useful in treatment. She found the fantasies that the child wove around his drawings to be useful material for psychoanalytic inquiry. She studied the expression of feelings (especially sexual and aggressive) and the motor release that accompanied the child's verbalizations, and she considered both to be therapeutic. In addition, she found that drawings were useful sources of information for evaluating the child's progress in therapy.

Pencil drawings provide the kind of detail useful for the kind of information Machover derives from a picture. Crayons and paints tell something of the child's use of colors but have the drawback of providing less detail. Many a child resists drawing. He may say that he cannot draw or cannot draw well. In such cases, the therapist does well to impress upon the child that this is not an art contest. Or he may resist revealing himself by drawing a design. When the child starts to do so, the therapist can encourage him to draw something "interesting," "something we can talk about," or tell him that "designs don't count." A common maneuver is to tell a story about the drawing that is mundane and basically nonrevealing. For example, the child may itemize the events of the day: how he got up in the morning, what he had for breakfast, the various subjects he studied in school, and so forth. In such cases, the therapist may mildly challenge the child to tell a more "interesting" or "exciting" story. It is probably true that the fantasies woven around drawings are more restricted than those created without so specific a focus[41] or than those arising around plastic materials such as clay.[110] By its very nature, a picture depicts a concrete scene—no matter how rich and varied its contents. It thereby tends to confine the child's fantasies. One may overcome

this drawback by asking the child to use the picture as a "starting point" for his story and advising him that he can talk about things that might not necessarily be shown in the picture. The child may resist by drawing stick figures when he is intellectually quite capable of providing a richer form. In this event, one can try to spur the child into providing more meaningful drawings: "I know you can do better than that," "You've left out many parts and things," and so forth. Drawing cartoon strips[97] can sometimes increase the child's interest. When a child claims that the figures have nothing to say to one another, or that he cannot think of any conversation that they might have, or he creates a story that is particularly nonrevealing, the therapist can draw cartoon-style balloons over the heads of each of the figures and write in what the child describes each person as saying. (This approach is particularly useful for minimally brain damaged children with auditory perceptual problems who require a visually oriented therapeutic experience.[35] More recently, Elkisch,[20] Rambert, [90] Kellogg and O'Dell,[65] and Hartley[51] have described the meanings of children's drawings and their use in child therapy.

The therapist is well advised to use a variety of approaches to the child's drawings. The freest and most uncontaminated pictures and fantasies come from suggesting that the child draw anything he wants to. Requesting that he draw a picture of a person is more likely to result in a drawing of his projected self. Asking, then, for an opposite-sexed figure can provide additional information. Some therapists have found that suggesting the child draw a family (his, someone else's, or just any family) can also be useful. From such pictures the therapist can learn how the child sees himself in the context of his family.[53]

Burns and Kaufman[12] have developed a technique that they call "Kinetic Family Drawings." They ask the child to draw a picture of the various members of his family with each person doing something. In this way, they claim they obtain more information than arises from a less directive approach. In the experience of others, such family pictures do provide some useful information; however, the stories that the child relates tend often to be stereotyped, mundane, and not particularly revealing—in effect, they serve the purposes of resistance. Suggesting that the child draw other specific items has also been tried. Buck[11] and Hammer[49] describe how valuable information may be derived from drawings of a house and tree, as well as a person. The house-tree-person drawings, however, have become an accepted projective test and are not commonly used for therapeutic purposes.

Winnicott[106, 107] has devised a projective drawing technique that he calls the "Squiggles Game." The therapist scribbles something formless with pencil on a blank sheet of paper. The child is asked to add lines in order to convert the "squiggle" into some recognizable form. The child then makes a squiggle and the therapist transforms it into something distinguishable. Back and forth the game goes. Each drawing serves as a point of departure for a therapeutic interchange. Generally, Winnicott tries to guide the conversation in a direction in which the child can be helped to gain insight (usually along classical psychoanalytic lines) into what the squiggles and the associated verbalizations reveal. The game was designed primarily for situations when only a short-term therapeutic process was possible; however, it can prove useful as a tool in long-term therapy as well. It is certainly a technique with which the child therapist should be familiar. However, it is likely that many of the dramatic cures which Winnicott attributed to the Squiggles Game (often accomplished in one or two interviews) were less related to the interpretations Winnicott employed than they were to the effect of certain aspects of Winnicott's personality and of the situation in which the consultations occurred. Finally, it seems that at this point in our professional development we know much more about how to interpret the meaning of the child's drawings than we know about how to utilize such rich material therapeutically.

CLAY, FINGER PAINTS, WATER, AND BLOCKS

Child therapists have turned to an assortment of other materials with which children have traditionally enjoyed playing. Clay has been one of the more common substances to be used in this way. Its malleability allows for greater alteration of the child's stories and fantasies than do drawings. Drawings have two dimensions, clay has three. Clay can be moved; one can do things with it; this expands the child's fantasy possibilities.[109] It takes less technical skill to work with clay than to draw; it can therefore be used with children younger than those who draw. Clay almost invites the child to pound it, and it therefore serves as a useful vehicle for hostility release and tension reduction.[51, 53] Its resemblance to feces allows the child regressive gratification; with it the child

can get messy and can smear in a manner that is approved of rather than forbidden. It provides the child with motor gratifications and gives him, in addition, a sense of mastery over the things he constructs with it. These creations are foci for fantasies and thus a valuable source of information about the child.[8]

Sometimes a therapist will too quickly make sexual interpretations about the objects that the child creates.[109] A child rolling a piece of clay will inevitably form something resembling a snake. If one invariably assumes that the child has formed a penis, then just about all children will receive the same interpretation—not a very reasonable situation. A ball, too, is commonly made; but if the therapist automatically assumes that this represents a testes or a breast, he may be missing more important communications or ascribing meaning to an activity that has little, if any, sexual significance.

Finger paints are another common play material that has been incorporated into the therapist's armamentarium.[51, 53, 84] Like clay, finger paints can provide regressive gratifications because of the smearing and mess-making outlets that they allow. For the inhibited child, their use encourages freedom of expression. The pictures so produced are generally less structured than crayon drawings and can be altered significantly before drying. Accordingly, they allow for a richer elaboration of fantasies. Moreover, in the course of the finger painting, the child generally becomes more relaxed and the process provides sensory (tactile, kinesthetic, and visual) gratifications that in themselves have therapeutic value. As is true with drawings, the form and content as well as the colors chosen can provide the therapist with useful information. Finally, this activity can give the child the sense of mastery and ego-enhancement that comes from creating something of aesthetic value; since less skill is necessary, the younger child is more likely to achieve this with finger paints than with drawings.

Water play has not enjoyed the same popularity as a therapeutic modality as have crayon drawings, finger paintings, and clay. Perhaps this is related to the greater tolerance for "mess" that water play requires of the therapist. Proponents of its use[50, 51] consider it to be the most flexible of all the play media used in treatment; it produces minimal constriction or contamination of the child's fantasies. Just as clay tends to parallel fecal play, water is likely to simulate urinary play. It can provide tactile pleasure and playing with it can reduce the child's tensions. By spitting, splashing, throwing, and spilling water becomes a useful medium for the release of pent-up aggressive impulses. Finally, playing with water can help open up the inhibited child and give him greater freedom to express himself.

Children's blocks are generally found in the child therapist's playroom. Proponents of their use[51] describe them as providing valuable outlets for repressed hostility: The child can throw them, drop them as "bombs," and so forth. They can be used to build structures that serve as starting points for the expression of revealing fantasies. Such constructions can provide the child with a sense of achievement, power, and motor gratification. Or the child can satisfy regressive, return-to-the-womb fantasies with blocks by building cozy retreats into which he withdraws. Erikson[21] has pointed out the importance of the configurations of the blocks as a useful source of information about the child's psychological processes.

When utilizing clay, finger paints, water, and blocks (and to a lesser degree, other play materials), the therapist does well to differentiate *psychotherapy* from that which is *psychotherapeutic*. Psychotherapy is a process that requires the talents and skills of a person trained in the treatment of psychological disturbances. However, a child can have many experiences that are psychotherapeutic—without the participation of a psychotherapist. Most healthy pleasurable activities are ego-enhancing and thereby contribute to the alleviation of psychological disturbance. The gratifications that flow from creative activity are in general psychologically beneficial. Physical activities can reduce tension and serve to release pent-up aggression. Sexual encounters can reduce tension, give pleasure, and facilitate benevolent human interchanges—all of which can be psychologically salutary. Since individuals can gain psychotherapeutic benefit alone or from interactions with others who are not trained therapists, it behooves the therapist to provide his patients with something beyond what can be obtained elsewhere. Clay, finger paints, water, and blocks along with other traditional toys used in therapy create the possibility that play therapy with them may be more *play* than *therapy*. Mention has been made of their value in providing the child with a greater sense of freedom and in reducing his inhibitions. Obviously such an experience is not valuable for all child patients; there are many children who need just the opposite. Their main problems relate to the fact that they are too *un*inhibited. Providing them with a therapeutic approach that encourages release and free expression may be antitherapeutic and merely frighten them or entrench their pathology. The aforementioned modalities have been described as providing the child with opportunities for regressive satisfactions: with return-to-the-womb gratifications and opportunities for symbolic play with urine and feces. Some hold that such regressive gratifications can be therapeutic, especially for the child who has been deprived of them; however, there is danger in providing too much such satisfaction and thereby entrenching regressive symptomology. Finally, the value of these modalities in releasing aggression should be counterbalanced by recalling the earlier mention of those who consider catharsis to be a naive approach to hostility problems, analogous to pulling the cork out of the spout of a boiling tea kettle without directing one's attention to the flames that are causing the water to boil in the first place.

SPECIAL TOY EQUIPMENT USED IN CHILD PSYCHOTHERAPY

A variety of other traditional childhood toys have been utilized in the therapist's playroom. Some of those described more recently (generally during the 1950s and 1960s) have not enjoyed the popularity of the original methods for engaging the child and reducing resistances.

While palying checkers a child will generally exhibit many aspects of his personality and his modes of relating to others without appreciating that he is revealing himself. The game is particularly useful in providing the therapist with information about the child's reactions to winning and losing, his competitive needs, passivity versus aggressivity level, propensity to cheat, and ability to plan ahead and foresee danger.[4] Loomis[74] has described the specific use of the game in dealing with resistances in child therapy and analysis. Essentially, he uses the pathological manifestations the child reveals while playing the game as points of departure for psychoanalytic exploration. Gardner[43] considers checkers more valuable as a diagnostic than a therapeutic instrument. Insofar as it has therapeutic use, the experiential elements are likely to be more valuable than its potential for providing material for psychoanalytic inquiry; although on occasion it is useful for this purpose as well. Some therapists rely heavily on checkers to help with uncooperative and inhibited children. They hope that some period spent on this relatively low-key activity will groom the child for a deeper, more introspective type of treatment in the future. The danger of such an approach is that many months, and even years, can be spent trying to reach this goal, and it may never be achieved. During this period, other more predictably successful resistance-reducing approaches mentioned in this chapter might have been utilized with a better outcome.

Puppets and marionettes, like dolls, were early recognized as useful means ith which to stimulate fantasies. Experience suggests that the child is more likely to exhibit aggressive play with puppets than he is with dolls; when holding a puppet in each hand he is likely to start striking one puppet against the other, have them grab at each other, wrestle, etc. Because the toy lends itself so well to such activity, the therapist is hard put to know whether significant pent-up hostility is being expressed, or whether the puppet is merely serving as a vehicle for the expression of normal playful activity. As a play medium, marionettes are expressive but of dubious value. So much time may have to be spent untangling their strings that little time may be left for therapeutic play. Accordingly, they are not recommended for office practice. Bender[8] and Woltmann[108, 111] have described a therapeutic technique in which hospitalized children are presented puppet shows designed to elicit comments and reactions of psychological significance. The material so gained is used as a basis for analytically oriented discussions. One of the drawbacks of this approach is that it presents highly specific material to the child and thereby lessens the likelihood of obtaining the more useful, spontaneous fantasies.

Marcus[78] has found the child's donning a costume to be a useful device in helping some children overcome their resistances to revealing their fantasies. Wearing a costume appears to encourage the child to "act" and hence reveal himself. Marcus has found a box of hats to be similarly useful. He found that passive children tend to become more active and less defensive when wearing the costume. The material so elicited is used for psychoanalytic inquiry. Although the child has the opportunity to choose from a variety of costumes and an assortment of hats, one drawback to this technique is that it provides intrinsic contaminants to the child's productions. However, a contaminated fantasy is generally more valuable than no fantasy at all (because the child often introduces idiosyncratic material), and for some children, a costume or hat may enable them to provide material that would not otherwise have been revealed.

Recognizing the child's natural enjoyment of music and dance, these modalities have been used to reduce children's resistances to therapy.

Bender[8] considers dance to be an excellent way to lower the child's inhibitions. And she considers it therapeutic in other ways: It provides pleasure (which in itself is often therapeutic); it can be esteem-enhancing (when the child gains competence in it); it reduces tension; and it serves to sublimate sexual desires. Hartley[51] emphasizes the therapeutic value of dance in lessening tensions, providing primitive pleasure (especially kinesthetic), inducing spontaneity, and as a release for hostility. Self-created songs can, of course, reveal the child's basic fantasies, and these can be used for psychoanalytic inquiry or therapeutic discussion. Heimlich,[54, 55, 56] in a technique that she refers to as "Paraverbal Therapy," attempts to unite the therapeutic elements in music (listening, singing, and playing instruments), mime, dance, and finger painting. Among her techniques, she sings with the child a song that is likely to touch upon issues relevant to his pathology. Her purpose is not only to provide strong and dramatic cathartic release but to use the issues to which the child strongly reacts as points of departure for therapeutic discussions.

Children's books can also be useful in therapy.[46] All psychotherapy involves some education of the child by the therapist, and even in the most passive therapeutic approaches, there occurs a certain amount of learning from the therapist about how to adapt and to cope. There is deep wisdom in the aphorism "knowledge is power." The more knowledgeable one is about the world, the greater one's ability to cope with its inevitable problems, the greater one's capacity to adapt to it, and the less the likelihood one will have to resort to pathological modes of adjusting to life. Knowledge about the world may contribute not only to preventing the formation of psychological disturbances but to the reduction of them as well. Children often enjoy reading books and being read to from them. Books therefore provide a multisensory (visual and auditory) vehicle for communication that might not be possible through simple discussion. Pictures and colors attract the child and enable the message to be delivered "in a pretty package."

Books can help prepare a child for a specific traumatic experience, such as hospitalization.[89] Books designed to help the child deal with a specific problem situation, such as divorce[42] adoption,[94] and minimal brain dysfunction,[38] can provide therapeutic benefit in a palatable format. There are a plethora of books providing sex information for children.[62, 80, 87, 88] It is important that these be properly geared to the child's intellectual and maturational levels. Since ancient times, the allegorical mode has been appreciated as an effective way of communicating messages to which there might be conscious resistance. A story in which the events occur to another person lessens the anxiety the reader or listener would have with a personal confrontation. If the therapist knows of a published story that is relevant to his patient, he does well to recommend it. A literature is now developing which provides such messages in stories designed to deal with common therapeutic issues.[33, 40]

THE MUTUAL STORYTELLING TECHNIQUE

Like many of the aforementioned approaches, the "Mutual Storytelling Technique"[28, 30, 37, 41] is another example of the therapeutic utilization of a traditional childhood activity that children enjoy. Like bibliotherapy, it is based on the observations that children like not only telling stories, but hearing them as well, and that the allegorical mode of communication increases the child's receptivity to unpleasant and anxiety-provoking therapeutic communications. One drawback of bibliotherapeutic approaches is that the stories created for such purposes are likely to be applicable only to a small fraction of the listeners and readers. Providing children generally with such stories is like putting penicillin in the drinking water: Most people will be unaffected, a small percentage of the population will be helped, and a small fraction will develop untoward reactions. With the mutual storytelling technique, this drawback is reduced; the therapist relates a story that is designed specifically to meet the psychological needs of the child at the particular time. In addition, the method is one possible solution to the problem of how the therapist can use the child's self-created stories therapeutically.

When utilizing the technique, the therapist elicits a self-created story from the child, ascertains its psychodynamic meaning, and surmises the pathological element(s) in it. He then creates a story of his own, using the same characters in a similar setting, but introduces what he considers to be healthier adaptations and resolutions than those utilized in the child's story. One might view the method as an attempt to bypass conscious resistance to unacceptable interpretations and insights by communicating directly with the unconscious. That such communications can affect behavior is well established by the ancient appeal of myths and legends. Although subsequent psychoanalytic work may be attempted with the child who is re-

ceptive to such inquiry, such insight might not be crucial to therapeutic change (although it is certainly helpful). It has been observed that the allegorical messages are "heard," reappear in the child's subsequent stories (in both disguised and undisguised form), and contribute to therapeutic change.

As always, the child can readily exhibit resistances when engaged in the storytelling game. He may be unable to think of a story. He may tell one that is short, stereotyped, and essentially non-revealing. Or he may tell a long story, which recounts in detail the mundane events of the protagonist's day ("First, the dog got up in the morning. Then he had his breakfast. He had orange juice and cereal and . . ."), but which yields little basic information. Or the child may ramble on aimlessly, with every new tangent becoming a focus for more comments. Although there may be a common thread in such ramblings that the therapist's story can utilize as a theme, there are often so many themes introduced that the therapist will be hard put to know which one(s) to choose in order to build a useful response. Or the child may try to "pass off" a story about a real event, or one that he has read or heard, instead of truly creating one of his own. To be sure, such "lifted" stories tell something about the child, because they have been selected from among the innumerable stories to which he has been exposed. Nonetheless, they are less revealing than the truly self-created ones. The psychotherapeutic games to be described in the following section were designed. in part, to bypass, deal with, and lessen the likelihood of the appearance of such resistance.

DRAMA

Most children love plays and will welcome the opportunity to act in them. Children spontaneously play act their fantasies, the traditional game of "house" being one of the more common examples. In such games, the child entrenches adult identifications, reflects relationships and experiences, gratifies wishes, releases unacceptable impulses, and attempts to work through various problems and experiences.[34, 51] Play acting a theme of psychological significance provides the child with a far richer experience than merely talking about it and possibly emoting over it. With dramatization, various other sensory elements are brought into the experience: kinesthetic, tactile, an enhancement of the visual, and occasionally the olfactory and gustatory as well. Encouraging children to play act their fantasies enables the therapist to gain a deeper appreciation of their social interactional processes; it may help the child as well to see more clearly how he relates himself to others. Through play acting, the child can desensitize himself to an anxiety-provoking situation, one that he either experienced or anticipated.

The "Projection Action Test" of Moreno can be modified for diagnostic and therapeutic use with children.[48] In this method, the child is encouraged to involve himself in a series of structured dramatic situations the elicit projective material. For example, the child may be asked to imagine himself on a stage with an imaginary person. After a series of questions about who the person is, he is instructed to play act what he is doing with that person. The material so derived then becomes a focus for therapeutic discussion. The stories elicited when utilizing the mutual storytelling technique can also be dramatized. Such an approach enhances the child's receptivity to storytelling and provides him with an even more effective means of therapeutic communication.[30, 32, 41] Dramatization is especially useful in the treatment of children with MBD because of their need for a multisensory therapeutic approach.[35]

PSYCHOTHERAPEUTIC BOARD GAMES

These games make therapeutic use of children's traditional enjoyment of board games, especially when there is a competitive element involved.

(However, in all of them, the therapist does well to discourage the necessary competitive element and encourage involvement in the other aspects of the game.) In *Board of Objects Game* (a modification of a game designed by Dr. Richard A. Gardner and Dr. Nathan I. Kritzberg[28, 30]) figurines, of the kind readily purchased in most toy stores, are placed on a checker board (or a larger board of one hundred squares). The figurines include family members, animals, members of various occupations, and so forth (see figure 25-1). A pair of dice (with one face of each die colored red) and a treasure chest of token reward chips are also used. Each player in turn throws the dice. If a red side lands face up, the player can select any object from the board. If he can say anything at all about the object, he gets one reward chip, and/or if he can tell a story about the object, he gets two reward chips. The winner is the player who has accumulated the most chips when the allotted time is over. The game is generally attractive to children between four and eight years of age and will often result in their revealing their fantasies after other methods have not proved successful. The potential contamination of fantasies when they are formed in response to recognizable objects is reduced by the wide array of objects from which the child can choose. In addition, there is much to suggest that the pressure of unconscious material to be expressed is far greater than the power of a facilitating stimulus to distort the projected mate-

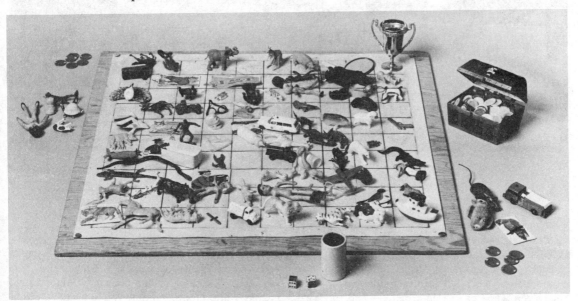

FIGURE 25–1

The Board of Objects Game

rial. The therapist may use the child's verbalizations in a variety of ways: psychoanalytic, mutual storytelling, discussion about the figurine, discussion about the child. and so forth. Derivative games, such as *The Bag of Toys Game, The Bag of Things Game*, and *The Bag of Words Game*[28, 30] can be similarly useful in engaging resistant children.

Resistant, uncooperative children who have reached the second-grade reading level may often be engaged with the *Scrabble for Juniors* game.[95] In a modification of the game devised by Krtizberg and Gardner,[28, 30] each player in turn places two of his seven letter tiles over corresponding letters on the board. When a player completes a word, he receives a token reward chip. If he can say anything at all about the word, he gets another chip, and/or if he can tell a story about the word, he gets two chips. The verbalizations so elicited can be used for a variety of therapeutic interchanges.

*Feeling, and Doing Game** may be useful. Each player in turn throws the dice and moves his playing piece along a path of colored squares (see figure 25-2). Depending upon which color the playing piece lands, the player takes a talking card, feeling card, or a doing card. If the player can respond to the question or directions on the card, he gets a reward chip. As their names imply, the talking cards elicit material of a cognitive nature; the feeling cards attempt to evoke emotional responses; and the doing cards encourage physical expression. None of the cards attempts to obtain responses that would be as anxiety-provoking as free fantasy expression or the relating of self-created stories. The cards range from the low anxiety-provoking ("What is your address?" "What present would you like to get for your next birthday?" "Make believe you're blowing out the candles on your birthday cake." "Make a funny sound with your mouth. If you spit you don't get a chip.") that just about any child can answer and

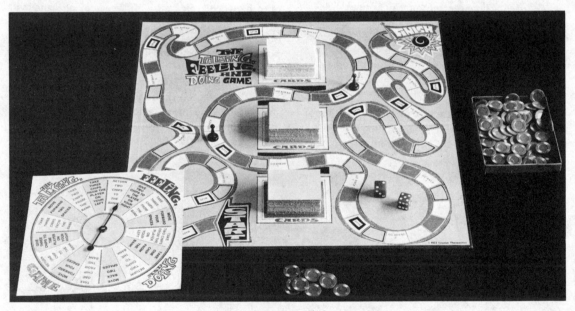

FIGURE 25–2

The Talking, Feeling, and Doing Game

Although the aforementioned games did prove successful in drawing out certain uncooperative resistant children, there were many who still would not or could not involve themselves in therapy. Even with token reinforcement and the pleasures of board game play, they did not reveal their fantasies. For such children (as well as others who are freer to reveal themselves) *The Talking,*

thereby get involved in the game, to the moderately higher anxiety-provoking ("Someone passes you a note, What does it say?" "Make up a message for a Chinese fortune cookie." "Suppose two people were talking about you and they didn't know you were listening. What do you think you

* See references 28, 29, 30, 31, and 103.

would hear them saying?" "What's the worst thing a child can say to his mother?" "A child has something on his mind that he's afraid to tell his father. What is it that he's scared to talk about?" "Everybody in the class was laughing at a girl. What had happened?" "All the girls in the class were invited to a birthday party except one. How did she feel? Why wasn't she invited?"). The playing piece may also land on "Go Forward" and "Go Backward" squares which direct the player to move his piece a specific number of squares, as well as on squares directing the player to spin the spinner (which can result in his gaining or losing chips or squares on the playing path). These elements of the game do not generally bring about revelation of specific psychodynamic material; rather, they enhance the child's involvement in the game and thereby reduce his resistances to the therapeutic activity. The game requires considerable judiciousness on the therapist's part regarding how he answers *his* cards. He must ever keep in mind that he should provide the response that will be in the child's best interests. The complex implications of the therapist's role in this game have been discussed elsewhere,[30] and some of its implications for the therapist-patient relationship will be discussed in the paragraphs that follow.

THE THERAPIST-PATIENT RELATIONSHIP

By far, the most important determinant of whether the therapist will be able to deal effectively with the patient's resistances is the relationship that he establishes with the patient. Although the previously described techniques may contribute to the development of a good therapist-patient relationship, they play only a limited role in this regard; a host of other factors must be operative if this goal is to be achieved. Certain aspects of the child therapist's personality appear to enhance the likelihood that he will be able to form a good relationship with the child. The child therapist should be able to place himself in the child position, to see the world from his vantage point.[5] If he has a good memory of his own childhood experiences, he is more likely to appreciate his patient's situation. Within reason, he should be able to listen with receptivity and interest to the child's verbalizations and be able to converse with the child about the issues that interest him without condescension or baby talk. He must be honest and provide the child with a genuine change from the common duplicities to which children are so often exposed. He must be comfortable enough to admit his deficiencies when the therapeutic situation

warrants such divulgence.[5, 30] The child is surrounded enough by "perfect" people—people who seem always to be doing "right," while he seems always to be doing "wrong." Having a therapist who is healthy enough to admit his shortcomings at appropriate times will engender the child's respect for the therapist and can help lessen the child's unfavorable comparison of himself with adults. *The Talking, Feeling, and Doing Game*[103] provides the therapist with opportunities for just such revelations—without contrivance or artificiality. The therapist must be able to express his feelings as they arise in therapy (again, only when the situation warrants such expression). Therapists encourage patients to express their feelings freely, but often they consider emotional responses of their own to be inappropriate. Many feel that such therapists serve as poor models for their patients, and thereby lessen the likelihood that their patients will freely and appropriately express themselves. Of course, such interactions have to be correlated with the child's needs, the nature of the treatment, as well as variables of the clinician. For instance, children often ask the therapist questions about his personal life. The therapist should be free to provide such disclosures judiciously (again, within reason) because they can serve to bring the child closer to him, to improve their working relationship, and thereby reduce resistances. If the therapist exhibits these and other qualities described in greater detail elsewhere,[30] he is likely to gain the respect and affection of the child. Engendering such feelings is the most efficacious way of preventing the development of resistances, as well as dealing with them. Furthermore, such reactions of the child to the therapist are crucial elements in bringing about a successful therapeutic outcome to many types of treatment.

Children are far more hedonistic than adults and would much prefer pleasurable recreational activities (games, television, and so forth) to therapy sessions. It behooves the therapist to attempt to provide the child with comparable enjoyment if he is to draw him away from "the competition" successfully. The techniques utilized to achieve this goal are the "seductive" elements in child psychotherapy.[30, 36] Many of the play forms described in this chapter serve to provide such seduction. Humor[16] can also serve this purpose.

Many therapists use food in an attempt to entice the child in the belief that providing food can serve to compensate the child symbolically for emotional deprivations he suffers elsewhere.[52] The therapist does well to appreciate that food is a *symbol* of love, and not the real thing. Therapists who may not be providing the child with genuine affection may try to compensate with food and may thereby reproduce a common pathological pattern.[30] Giving the child gifts is another one of the seductive techniques that may serve to foster a therapeutic alliance.[68] Therapeutically, this seems more useful for the deprived child than for the one who has adequate material possessions. One danger of giving gifts parallels that with food: The therapist may be repeating a common parental pathological pattern of substituting material things to compensate for the inability to provide meaningful affection. Another danger of providing gifts is that they may squelch the child's expression of angry feelings that he may harbor toward the therapist.[68] Moskowitz[83] has described the value of magic tricks not only to make therapy more interesting for the child but also as a therapeutic modality in its own right. A danger with all the seductive techniques is that play therapy will become more *play* than *therapy*.

WORKING WITH PARENTS

Most parents feel guilty because their child needs treatment and view it as proof of their having somehow failed in his upbringing.[73] One way that parents commonly assuage such guilt is to find excuses to withdraw the child from treatment or, either overtly or covertly, to sanction his resistances to going. The therapist does well to try to help parents appreciate that at every point in the child's development they did what they considered to be in his best interests (the usual case), and that through misguidance, and/or unfortunate circumstances, and/or the unavoidable effects of their own difficulties their child developed psychological problems. In addition, the therapist does well to inform them that at the present state of our knowledge, we do not understand all the factors that contribute to a child's having difficulty; even if they had themselves been free from psychological problems, if there had been no detrimental circumstances, if they had assiduously followed the best available advice, their child might still have developed problems.[66] When innate temperamental factors[104] may be basic to or contributing significantly to the child's problems, apprising the parents of this can alleviate guilt. Where therapy "takes," the parents may well become jealous of the child's intimate relationship with the therapist and act out such feelings by undermining his work with the child—thereby strengthening the child's resistances. Or they may feel threatened by the anxiety-provoking revelations about themselves that emerge in their child's treatment, which may in turn contribute to their working against the therapeutic process. Some of the common expressions of parental resistance are: lateness to the sessions, canceling sessions for weak or frivolous reasona, forgetting to follow through with the therapist's recommendations, complaining to the child about therapy (its cost, time consumption, and so forth), and withholding payment (one of the most predictable ways of ultimately bringing about a cessation of therapy).

One of the most effective ways of reducing such parental guilt and the resistances that stem from it is to have the parents participate actively in the child's therapy. When parents feel that they are somehow at fault in bringing about the child's illness, actively contributing to the therapeutic process can most directly contribute to the assuagement of their guilt. The younger the child, the less important are considerations of confidentiality[30] and the greater the ease with which one can involve parents. By working closely with the parents, the therapist is more likely to develop a good relationship with them. The child will sense the parents' positive feelings about the therapist and may then be more likely to develop such feelings himself. When the parents have a good relationship with the therapist, they will be more comfortable in expressing resentments and disagreements; the failure to resolve sucn differences and complaints is one of the common sources of parental resistance to the child's treatment. The therapist who feels he must protect the child against indignities suffered at the parents' hands is likely to alienate the parents. The preferable position should be one of impartiality: The therapist should be free to confront equally the child and/or the parents with what he considers to be pathological in their behavior. In this way, he cannot justifiably be accused of "taking sides" and will gain the respect of all parties concerned as being fair.

In addition to the more general ways in which parents may support the child's resistance, they may genuinely not want the child to be relieved of his presenting symptoms despite their protestations to the contrary. Basically, the overprotective mother may want her school-phobic child at home and will undermine the therapist's efforts to get the child to school. The parents of delinquent youngsters often gain vicarious gratifications from their children's antisocial acting out.[61, 100] Many parents have their child referred for treatment by the school because of poor academic performance; in some instances, not only do the parents come with great reluctance, they do not in fact wish that the child do well in his studies. For example, they may fear that the child will surpass them educationally and socioeconomically; in any case, for this or for a variety of other reasons,[34] consciously or unconsciously, the parents undermine his educational pursuits. In brief, parents can play a vital role in augmenting or reducing a child's resistances to treatment.*

Concluding Comments

In closing, it is worth reiterating that the purpose of the various approaches described in this chapter is not merely to reduce and/or circumvent resistances. Resistances are manifestations of the same defenses that contribute to the child's symptomatology. As are symptoms, they are best viewed as objects for the therapist's understanding and treatment.

* See references 9, 15, 16, 26, and 39.

Although it has not been discussed in detail, consideration should always be given to the possibility of the therapist's resistances in child therapy,[85] for example, those related to his inability to tolerate the frustrations entailed in doing psychotherapeutic work with children: his discomfort with regression, his inability to deal effectively with the child's unpredictability, and his exasperation with parental obstructions to the child's treatment. Similar consideration should be accorded the therapist's resistances to new techniques, to methods that question traditional theories and approaches. Ekstein[19] has pointed out that what the therapist calls resistance in the child may be the result of the therapist's own resistance to expanding his view of what child therapy should entail and his too-strict adherence to a particular therapeutic approach. If nothing else, the variety of methods described in this chapter and in this section emphasize the fact that it behooves the child therapist to be familiar with a wide range of techniques if he is to deal successfully with children's resistances.

REFERENCES

1. ADLER, A., *The Neurotic Constitution,* Moffat, Yard & Co., New York, 1917.
2. ALLEN, F. H., *Psychotherapy with Children,* W. W. Norton, New York, 1942.
3. AMES, L. B., *Children's Stories,* Genetic Psychology Monographs, *73(2)*:337–396, 1966.
4. ANTHONY, E. J., "Child Therapy Techniques," in Caplan, G. (Ed.), *American Handbook of Psychiatry,* 2nd ed., vol. 2, pp. 147–163, New York, Basic Books, 1974.
5. ———, "Communicating Therapeutically with the Child," *Journal of the American Academy of Child Psychiatry, 3(1)*:106–125, 1964.
6. AXLINE, V. M., *Dibs in Search of Self,* Houghton Mifflin, Boston, 1964.
7. ———, *Play Therapy,* Houghton Mifflin, Boston, 1947.
8. BENDER, L., *Child Psychiatric Techniques,* Charles C Thomas, Springfield, Ill., 1952.
9. BERMAN, S., "Techniques of Treatment of a Form of Juvenile Delinquency, The Antisocial Character Disorder," *Journal of the American Academy of Child Psychiatry, 3(1)*:29–30, 1964.
10. BRYT, A., "Non-Freudian Methods of Psychoanalysis with Children and Adolescents," in Wolman, B.B. (Ed.), *Manual of Child Psychopathology,* pp. 865–899, McGraw-Hill, 1972.
11. BUCK, J. N., "The H-T-P Technique: A Qualitative and Quantitative Scoring Manual," *Journal of Clinical Psychology, 4(5)*:317–396, 1948.
12. BURNS, R. C., and KAUFMAN, S. H., *Kinetic Family Drawings,* Brunner/Mazel, New York, 1970.
13. CONN, J. H., "Play Interview Therapy of Castration Fears," *American Journal of Orthopsychiatry, 25(4)*:747–754, 1954.
14. ———, "The Play-Interview as an Investigative and Therapeutic Procedure," *The Nervous Child, 7(3)*:257–286, 1948.
15. ———, "The Treatment of Fearful Children,"

American Journal of Orthopsychiatry, 11(4):744–751, 1941.
16. ———, "The Timid, Dependent Child," *Journal of Pediatrics, 19(1)*:1–2, 1941.
17. ———, "The Child Reveals Himself Through Play," *Mental Hygiene, 23(1)*:1–21, 1939.
18. DAVIDSON, A., and FAY, J., "Fantasy in Middle Childhood," in Haworth, M. R. (Ed.), *Child Psychotherapy,* pp. 401–406, Basic Books, New York, 1964.
19. EKSTEIN, R., "Review of R. Gardner, *Psychotherapeutic Approaches to the Resistant Child,* Jason Aronson, New York," in *Psychotherapy and Social Science Review, 9(6)*:4–8, 1975.
20. ELKISCH, P., "Free Art Expression," in Rabin, A. I., and Haworth, M. R. (Eds.), *Projective Techniques in Children,* pp. 273–288, Grune & Stratton, New York, 1960.
21. ERIKSON, E. H., *Childhood and Society,* W. W. Norton, New York, 1950.
22. FREUD, A., *Normality and Pathology in Childhood,* International Universities Press, New York, 1965.
23. ———, *The Psychoanalytical Treatment of Children,* Imago Publishing Co., London, 1946.
24. ———, *The Ego and the Mechanisms of Defense,* International Universities Press, New York (1966), 1937.
25. FREUD, S., "The Relation of the Poet to Day-Dreaming," in *Collected Papers,* vol. 4, pp. 173–183, Basic Books, New York, 1959.
26. ———, "Analysis of a Phobia in a Five-Year-Old Boy," in *Collected Papers,* vol. 3, pp. 149–289, Basic Books, New York, 1959.
27. ———, "Inhibitions, Symptoms and Anxiety," in Strachey, J. (Ed.), *The Standard Edition of the Complete Psychological Works of Sigmund Freud,* vol. 20, pp. 87–175, Hogarth Press, London, 1959.
28. GARDNER, R. A., "Techniques for Involving the Child with MBD in Meaningful Psychotherapy," *Journal of Learning Disabilities, 8(5)*:16–26, 1975.
29. ———, *Psychotherapeutic Approaches to the Resist-*

ant Child (audio-tapes), Psychotherapy Tape Library, Jason Aronson, New York, 1975.

30. ———, *Psychotherapeutic Approaches to the Resistant Child,* Jason Aronson, New York, 1975.

31. ———, *Methods for Involving the Resistive Child in Meaningful Psychotherapy* (audio-tapes), Behavioral Sciences Tape Library, Sigma Information, Leonia, N.J., 1974.

32. ———, "Dramatized Storytelling in Child Psychotherapy," *Acta Paedopsychiatrica, 41(3):*110–116, 1974.

33. ———, *Dr. Gardner's Fairy Tales for Today's Children,* Prentice-Hall, Englewood Cliffs, N.J., 1974.

34. ———, *Understanding Children,* Jason Aronson, New York, 1973.

35. ———, "Psychotherapy of the Psychogenic Problems Secondary to Minimal Brain Dysfunction," *International Journal of Child Psychotherapy, 2(2):*224–256, 1973.

36. ———, "On the Role of Seduction in Child Psychotherapy," *International Journal of Child Psychotherapy, 2(2):*135–137, 1973.

37. ———, *The Mutual Storytelling Technique* (audio-tapes), Psychotherapy Tape Library, Jason Aronson, New York, 1973.

38. ———, *MBD: The Family Book about Minimal Brain Dysfunction,* Jason Aronson, New York, 1973.

39. ———, "Little Hans—The Most Famous Boy in the Child Psychotherapy Literature," *International Journal of Child Psychotherapy, 1(4):*27–32, 1972.

40. ———, *Dr. Gardner's Stories about the Real World,* Prentice-Hall, Englewood Cliffs, N.J., 1972.

41. ———, *Therapeutic Communication with Children: The Mutual Storytelling Technique,* Jason Aronson, New York, 1971.

42. ———, *The Boys and Girls Book about Divorce,* Jason Aronson, New York, 1970.

43. ———, "The Game of Checkers as a Diagnostic and Therapeutic Tool in Child Psychotherapy," *Acta Paedopsychiatrica, 36(3):*142–152, 1969.

44. ———, "Review of H. G. Ginott, *Between Parent and Child,* Macmillan, New York," in *Psychology Today, 1(12):*15–17, 1968.

45. GOLDBLATT, M., "Psychoanalysis of the School-child," in Wolman, B. B. (Ed.), *Handbook of Child Psychoanalysis,* pp. 253–297, Van Nostrand Reinhold, New York, 1973.

46. GOLDINGS, C. R., and GOLDINGS, H. J., "Books in the Playroom: A Dimension of Child Psychiatric Technique," *Journal of the American Academy of Child Psychiatry, 2(1):*52–65, 1972.

47. GONDOR, L. H., "Use of Fantasy Communications in Child Psychotherapy," *American Journal of Psychotherapy, 11(2):*323–35, 1964.

48. HAAS, R. B., and MORENO, J. L., "Psychodrama as a Projective Technique," in Anderson, H. H., and Anderson, G. L. (Eds.), *An Introduction to Projective Techniques,* pp. 662–675, Prentice-Hall, Englewood Cliffs, N.J., 1951.

49. HAMMER, E. F., "The House-Tree-Person (H-T-P) Drawings as a Projective Technique with Children," in Rabin, A. I., and Haworth, M. R. (Eds.), *Projective Techniques in Children,* pp. 258–272, Grune & Stratton, New York, 1960.

50. HARTLEY, R. E., FRANK, L. K., and GOLDENSON, R. M., "The Benefits of Water Play," in Haworth, M. R. (Ed.), *Child Psychotherapy,* pp. 364–368, Basic Books, New York, 1964.

51. ———, *Understanding Children's Play,* Columbia University Press, New York, 1952.

52. HAWORTH, M. R., and KELLER, M. J., "The Use of Food in Therapy," in Haworth, M. R. (Ed.), *Child Psychotherapy* pp. 330–338, Basic Books, New York, 1964.

53. HAWORTH, M. R., and RAIN, A. I., *Projective Techniques in Children,* Grune & Stratton, New York, 1960.

54. HEIMLICH, E. P., "Using a Patient as 'Assistant Therapist' in Paraverbal Therapy," *International Journal of Child Psychotherapy, 2(1):*13–52, 1973.

55. ———, "Paraverbal Techniques in the Therapy of Childhood Communication Disorders," *International Journal of Child Psychotherapy, 1(1):*65–83, 1972.

56. ———, "The Use of Music as a Mode of Communication in the Treatment of Disturbed Children," *Journal of the American Academy of Child Psychiatry, 4(1):*86–122, 1965.

57. HERRON, R. E., and SUTTON-SMITH, B., *Child's Play,* John Wiley, New York, 1971.

58. HOLMES, D. J., *The Adolescent in Psychotherapy,* Little, Brown, Boston, 1964.

59. HUG-HELLMUTH, H. VON, "On the Technique of Child Analysis," *International Journal of Psychoanalysis, 2(3/4):*287–305, 1921.

60. ———, *Aus dem Seelenleben des Kindes,* Deuticke, Leipzig, 1913.

61. JOHNSON, A. M., "Juvenile Delinquency," in Arieti, S. (Ed.), *American Handbook of Psychiatry,* 1, pp. 844–847, Basic Books, New York, 1959.

62. JOHNSON, E. W., *Love and Sex in Plain Language,* Lippincott, Philadelphia, 1967.

63. KANNER, L., "Play Investigation and Play Treatment of Children's Behavior Disorders," *Journal of Pediatrics, 17(4):*533–546, 1940.

64. KANNER, L., *Child Psychiatry,* Charles C Thomas, Springfield, Ill., 1957.

65. KELLOGG, R., and O'DELL, S., *The Psychology of Children's Art,* CRM-Random House, New York, 1967.

66. KESSLER, J. W., *Psychopathology of Childhood,* Prentice-Hall, Englewood Cliffs, N.J. 1966.

67. KLEIN, M., *The Psychoanalysis of Children,* Hogarth Press, London, 1932.

68. LEVIN, S., and WERMER, H., "The Significance of Giving Gifts to Children in Therapy," *Journal of the American Academy of Child Psychiatry, 5(4):*630–652, 1966.

69. LEVY, D. M., "Oppositional Syndromes and Oppositional Behavior," in Harrison, S. I., and McDermott, J. F. (Eds.), *Childhood Psychopathology,* International Universities Press, New York, 1972.

70. ———, *The Early Development of Independent and Oppositional Behavior, Midcentury Psychiatry,* Charles C Thomas, Springfield, Ill., 1953.

71. ———, "Psychotherapy and Childhood," *The American Journal of Orthopsychiatry, 10(4):*905–910, 1940.

72. ———, "Release Therapy," *The American Journal of Orthopsychiatry, 9(4):*713–736, 1939.

73. LIPPMAN, H. S., *Treatment of the Child in Emotional Conflict,* McGraw-Hill, New York, 1962.

74. LOOMIS, E. A., "The Use of Checkers in Handling Certain Resistances in Child Therapy and Child Analysis," *Journal of the American Psychoanalytic Association, 5(1):*130–135, 1957.

75. MACHOVER, K., *Personality Projection in the Drawing of the Human Figure,* Charles C Thomas, Springfield, Ill., 1949.

76. ———, "Sex Differences in the Developmental Pattern of Children as seen in Human Figure Drawings," in Rabin, A. I., and Haworth, M. R. (Eds.), *Projective Techniques in Children,* pp. 238–257, Grune & Stratton, New York, 1960.

77. ———, "Drawing of the Human Figure: A Method of Personality Investigation," in Anderson, H. H., and Anderson, G. L. (Eds). *An Introduction to Projective Techniques,* pp. 341–370, Prentice-Hall, Englewood Cliffs, N.J., 1951.

78. MARCUS, I. M., "Costume Play Therapy," *Journal of the American Academy of Child Psychiatry, 5(3):*441–451, 1966.

79. MARKOWITZ, J., "The Nature of the Child's Initial Resistances to Psychotherapy," *Social Work, 4(3):*40–52, 1959.

80. MAYLE, P., *"Where Did I Come From?"* Lyle Stuart, Secaucus, N.J., 1973.

81. MILLAR, S., *The Psychology of Play,* Jason Aronson, New York, 1974.

82. MONROE, R. L., *Schools of Psychoanalytic Thought,* Dryden Press, New York, 1955.

83. MOKOWITZ, J. A., "The Sorcerer's Apprentice, or the Use of Magic in Child Psychotherapy" *International Journal of Child Psychotherapy, 2(2):*138–162, 1973.

84. NAPOLI, P. J., "Finger Painting," in Anderson H. H., and Anderson, G. L. (Eds.), *An Introduction to Projective Techniques,* pp. 386–415, Prentice-Hall, Englewood Cliffs, N. J., 1951.

85. PEARSON, G. H. J., *A Handbook of Child Psychoanalysis,* Basic Books. New York, 1968.

86. PITCHER, E. G., and Prelinger, E., *Children Tell Stories: An Analysis of Fantasy,* International Universities Press, New York, 1963.

87. POMEROY, W. B., *Girls and Sex,* Delacorte Press, New York, 1969.

88. ———, *Boys and Sex,* Delacorte Press, New York, 1968.

89. PYNE, M., *The Hospital,* Houghton Mifflin, Boston, 1962.

90. RAMBERT, M. L., "The Use of Drawings as a Method of Child Psychoanalysis," in Haworth, M. R. (Ed.), *Child Psychotherapy,* pp. 340–349, Basic Books, New York, 1964.

91. REICH, W., *Character-Analysis,* Noonday Press, New York, 1949.

92. ROGERS, C. R., "Client-Centered Psychotherapy," in Freedman, A. M., and Kaplan, H. I. (Eds.), *Comprehensive Textbook of Psychiatry,* pp. 1225–1228, Williams & Wilkins, Baltimore, 1967.

93. ———, *Client-Centered Therapy,* Houghton Mifflin, Boston, 1951.

94. RONDELL, F., and MICHAELS, R., *The Family That Grew,* Crown Publishers, New York, 1951.

95. SCRABBLE FOR JUNIORS, Selchow & Righter, Bay Shore, N.Y.

96. SOLOMON, J. C., "Play Technique and the Integrative Process," *American Journal of Orthopsychiatry, 25(3):*591–600, 1955.

97. ———, "Therapeutic Use of Play," in Anderson, H. H., and Anderson, G. L. (Eds.), *An Introduction to Projective Techniques,* pp. 639–661, Prentice-Hall, Englewood Cliffs, N. J., 1951.

98. ———, "Active Play Therapy: Further Experiences," *American Journal of Orthopsychiatry, 10(4):*763–781, 1940.

99. ———, "Active Play Therapy," *American Journal of Orthopsychiatry, 8(3):*479–498, 1938.

100. STUBBLEFIELD, R. L., "Sociopathic Personality Disorders, I: Antisocial and Dyssocial Reactions," in Freedman, A. M., and Kaplan, H. I. (Eds.), *Comprehensive Textbook of Psychiatry,* pp. 1420–1424, Williams & Wilkins, Baltimore, 1967.

101. SULLIVAN, H. S., *The Psychiatric Interview,* W. W. Norton, New York, 1954.

102. TAFT, J., *The Dynamics of Therapy in a Controlled Relationship,* Dover Publications, New York, 1962.

103. THE TALKING, FEELING, and DOING GAME, Creative Therapeutics, Cresskill, N. J.

104. THOMAS, A., et al., *Behavioral Individuality in Early Childhood,* New York University Press, New York, 1963.

105. WAELDER, R.. "The Psychoanalytic Theory of Play," *Psychoanalytic Quarterly, 2(2):*208–224, 1933.

106. WINNICOTT, D. W., *Therapeutic Consultations in Child Psychiatry,* Basic Books, New York, 1971.

107. ———, "The Value of the Therapeutic Consultation," in Miller, E. (Ed.), *Foundations of Child Psychiatry,* pp. 593–608, Pergamon Press, London, 1968.

108. WOLTMANN, A. G., "Puppetry as a Tool in Child Psychotherapy," *International Journal of Child Psychotherapy, 1(1):*84–96, 1972.

109. ———, "Mud and Clay, Their Functions as Developmental Aids and as Media of Projection," in Haworth, M. R. (Ed.) *Child Psychotherapy,* pp. 349–363, Basic Books, New York, 1964.

110. ———, "Diagnostic and Therapeutic Considerations of Nonverbal Projective Activities with Children," in Haworth, M.R. (Ed.), *Child Psychotherapy,* pp. 322–330, Basic Books, New York, 1964.

111. ———, "The Use of Puppetry as a Projective Method in Therapy," in Anderson, H. H., and Anderson, G. I. (Eds.), *An Introduction to Projective Techniques,* pp. 606–638, Prentice-Hall, Englewood Cliffs, N. J., 1951.

26 / Transcultural Considerations

Jane Waldron and John F. McDermott, Jr.

Introduction

This chapter will attempt to define and examine culture as it relates to the child psychiatrist's practice. In order to do this, the reader will be taken through several stages. As the reader views a "parade" of cultures and subcultures, he may recognize the faces of many of his patients and their families who are from differing subcultures. The principal aim of this chapter is to make the reader sensitive to and comfortable with cultural factors. More than that, he will feel the need to respect, indeed to utilize the values and beliefs inherent in each case he treats rather than, wittingly or unwittingly, to ignore or oppose them. If the chapter is successful, he should find himself broadening his point of view and increasing the flexibility of his therapeutic armamentarium. Ultimately, he should become aware that he is growing in understanding and skill—from a multicultural, to a cross-cultural, and finally to a transcultural therapeutic position. That is, he should arrive at a point in his work where a variety of approaches are blended to produce the most effective and relevant treatment for his young patients and their families.

Following a general consideration of culture, the material will examine the child rearing practices of several great cultures around the world and then contrast some aspects of child rearing in several contemporary American subcultures. The meaning of children and child-rearing practices and its implication for the diagnosis and treatment of psychopathology in the child and adolescent will receive major emphasis. Next will follow a section on psychopathology, emphasizing the various ways in which cultures may view the cause of emotional and mental illness in children; this will shift to the area of treatment proper which will consider American subculture, and how their values and characteristics match with the particular treatment modalities. While not identifying specific ethnic groups because of the risk of stereotyping them, hypothetical illustrative groups will be presented as subcultures A, B, C, and D. (In reality, these are usually mixed and blended.) The often marginal intercultural family will also be dealt with as a special situation. Next, a discussion of the transcultural therapist will identify characteristics which relate to the formation of such an identity among psychotherapists who work with children and their families, and finally, the authors will present their conclusions.

Definitions of Culture and Children

Kiev[9] defines culture as that which determines the specific ways in which individuals perceive and conceive of their environment. This factor strongly influences the forms of conflict, behavior, and psychopathology that occur in members of that culture. Culture, then, involves transmitted values. beliefs, attitudes, and habits, which are major determinants of the experiences of individuals from infancy onward and which shape the interpretations that the individuals put on their experiences. The link between culture and psychopathology thus becomes clear. The transcultural treatment of children and adolescents requires that the child psychiatrist approach and understand

each child or adolescent as a member of a particular culture or subculture. His approach recognizes that each such entity must have its own special developmental pathways, pitfalls, life crises, symptomatic expressions of stress, and that each one will require different treatment techniques.

The implications of this kind of cultural approach to treatment are many. Studies indicate that time, space, and social systems constitute the primary means of organizing not only human life but large segments of the vertebrate world as well. It is clear, also, that these means of organization are different in different cultures, and that they operate beyond awareness. In order to evaluate the individual's behavior outside of the limited context of the therapist's *own* personal ethnic system and social class background, it is necessary to identify and define these systems for each patient. Without this definition, the psychiatrist cannot be depended upon to understand the behavior of others in any but a distorted fashion. Under such circumstances, he cannot be depended upon to enter into effective treatment relationships.

The definition, understanding, and shaping of childhood and adolescence vary widely among cultures across the world, as well as among subcultures in American society. This is also true historically. In medieval European society, the idea of childhood did not exist; as long as they were dependent, children were considered petlike animals or incomplete adults. It was not until the seventeenth century that adults began to show genuine attachment to children and not until the eighteenth century was the child considered as a person occupying an important place within the family.[1] The length of time a child is coddled, the degree of security and protection to which each child is entitled, the age at which serious learning and work begin, the very existence of adolescence as a transition period from childhood to adulthood, all are heavily influenced by culture and the stage of development of that culture.

The way in which a culture defines its young has a critical determining effect on its conception of behavior and psychopathology, as well as its view of treatment. The child must be seen as a psychological entity before child psychiatry can develop. The term "emotional disturbance" was not applied to children until recent years, indicating that the perception of children as developing individuals subject to debilitating stress and trauma is a relatively new phenomenon. As a result, few studies focus on the role of ethnic and racial factors in child psychiatric disorders and treatment. Indeed, this area in child psychiatry is just beginning to be explored and researched.

Child-rearing Practices

The treatment of children and adolescents in any setting must begin with a clear understanding of the developmental aspects of the young patient. Child-rearing practices play such an important role in personality formation that they must be understood. Only within the framework of such understanding will the transcultural therapist be able to appreciate, diagnose, and treat young patients from other cultures or subcultures. Thus, in this section, the child-rearing practices of several cultures—Chinese, African, and Balinese—will be explored in order to illustrate some of the differences in orientation among groups. Studies which contrast American practices with those of the Japanese will be reviewed, and attention then turned to several American subcultures.

Universal Elements

It seems clear that some expectations about child development, such as walking and learning to talk, are universal and largely biologically determined. Even here, however, the expected age at which a skill is developed may vary from one group to another. Other expectations, such as learning particular forms of interpersonal relations, are presumed to be specific to different groups. Anthropological studies indicate that even at such early ages as three to four months, one can observe differences in the behavior of a child in one culture from one in another.[4] A cross-cultural study was conducted on children in six cultures. The results indicate that certain distinctions in socioeconomic and domestic structures—the living arrangements, daily routine, and the roles assigned to children in each culture—correspond and presumably account for differences in the children's social behavior.[21] It is possible that innate temperamental tendencies play a role in determining the differences among peoples in various cultures. However, there is strong evidence as well that child-rearing practices provide early experiences which are significant factors in the shaping of the ego, that is, the part of the self which relates to the outside world and its various functions. These practices reflect culturally determined systems of values.

The Chinese

In traditional Chinese culture,[19] children are valued as if they were special treasures. In infancy, they are breast fed without question. A Chinese baby is usually carried on his mother's back and sleeps in his parents' bed. An ongoing close attachment to the mother is accepted and encouraged. Such gratification in early infancy lays a foundation for the expectation of continued gratification from the other family members. Much attention is paid to the baby's body, and it is very frequently examined closely. Infants are thought to be extremely delicate and in need of protection. Even when no sign of sickness is present, they are bundled up and herbs are administered frequently. Toilet training is approached permissively and the Chinese mother assumes responsibility for her baby's toileting. However, around six years, when the children reach school age, parental attitudes change abruptly. Both parents and school impose stricter discipline, and older children are expected to help with housework and with the care of the younger children. Although there is almost no privacy in the Chinese home, it is stressed that children must keep information about the family's functioning private from the community outside the family. The minimizing of overt sexual stimulation is one means of social control. Boys and girls are separated in childhood, and chastity prior to marriage is important. In adolescence, Chinese youth traditionally do not revolt against authority and social independence is not encouraged.

The African

Among the Southern Bantu, during the first eighteen months of life, the African infant lives in a state of virtual symbiosis with its mother. This amounts to a state of blissful security with all the baby's needs completely and promptly met. Mother carries the child on her back and feeds him at the slightest whimper. A sharp discontinuity between infancy and early childhood experiences takes place at weaning when the child begins to associate more with his older siblings and grandparents. Extended families provide multiple identification figures and may be responsible for the great flexibility in social and interpersonal relations that characterizes the personality structure of the African. Lambo[11] has suggested that the traditional pattern of child rearing in most parts of Africa aims at building specific ego functions and reducing the vulnerability of the ego to certain types of psychological trauma. There appears to be a central cultural objective here, an effort to insure that the child's primary experience with the common affect-laden interpersonal issues, such as trust, dependence, autonomy, separation, strangeness, and cooperative play will be mastery experiences rather than disorganizing failures. In the cities and urban areas, the picture is often different. Extended families break down and many of the protective buffers are lost.

The Balinese

In Bali, one researcher[8] has described the child-rearing pattern as giving strong encouragement to passivity. The Balinese are described as treating their children like puppets or toys.[2] The child is initially carried in a sling with the right hand bound to his side. He is forced to accommodate himself passively to this situation. Speech is taught by imitation of phrases which others repeat over and over. Gesture is taught by having the teacher move the child's body part until the child moves it himself in the desired manner. This attitude toward training pervades the endless small variations of everyday speech and gesture. Spontaneity or expression of individuality is discouraged, and the child is required to display imposed passivity, limp plasticity, and identification with the model, in word, gesture, and thought. According to Bateson and Mead,[2] a peculiarity of the mother-child relationship which continues throughout the child-rearing process is teasing. This involves stimulating the child to show an emotional response such as affection, desire, jealousy, or anger, and then turning away from him and ignoring him in the midst of his response. This creates frustrating experiences for the child and tends to result in tantrums, sulking, and finally in withdrawal of much responsiveness.

Contrastive Studies

Caudill[4] conducted a cross-cultural, longitudinal study of the behavior of infants and their mothers in Japan and in the United States. He studied their interactions at three to four months, two and one-half years, and six years. His work provides what is perhaps the best evidence that differing child-rearing practices may produce differences in personality that are due to cultural expectations. American mothers seem to encourage their babies to be active and vocally responsive, while the Japanese mother acts in ways which she believes will soothe and quiet her baby. In the two cultures, the responses of the infants seem strikingly in line with the general expectations for behavior. In America, the individual should be physically and verbally assertive; and in Japan, he should be physically and verbally restrained. In Japan, there is less reliance on the refinement of vocal communication between mother and child while, at the same time, more emphasis is given to the importance and communicative value of physical contact. The American mother views her baby as a potentially separate and autonomous being who should learn to do and think for himself. The Japanese mother views her baby much more as an extension of herself, and the psychological boundaries between them tend to be blurred. Compared to Japanese, Americans are more likely to manipulate both their social and physical environments in a functional manner.

Another study[18] involved having Anglo-American, Mexican-American, and Chinese-American mothers teach their children standard tasks. The study demonstrated that the best single predictor of maternal teaching or child response was ethnicity. As teachers, the middle-class Anglo mothers employed an active teaching style. They spent time in giving carefully set up, rich instructions and gave the child a lot of feedback about his performance. Chinese mothers were distinctive in their selective use of specific instructions and in providing a high proportion of enthusiastic positive feedback. Mexican mothers made more use of nonverbal instructions. Chinese mothers considered teaching to be an important component of their maternal role and regular instruction of preschool-age children took place in the home. In contrast to this, the Mexican mothers felt that they were not teachers and that it was the school's job to teach. In contrast to Anglo children, strong cultural demands are made on both Mexican and Chinese-American children, for obedience and respect of elders. It is interesting to note that

Chinese-American children often do extremely well in academic tasks at which Mexican-American children perform relatively poorly. Another study[13] suggests that Mexican mothers react more to what their children feel or might feel, as opposed to their American counterparts. The American mothers reacted more to their children's achievements by rewarding and praising them.

After exploring child-rearing patterns across the world, it becomes clear that most cultures differ from the Western or American emphasis on autonomy, individuality, and independence. Most of the world is still operating a rural agricultural economy from an extended family base. As countries become developed, urbanized, and industrialized, traditional cultural values and processes have been upset, and cultural crises have oftren erupted. The child psychiatrist can begin to function in cultural contexts different from his own only if he appreciates the impact of differences among cultures as well as their changing nature.

A Special Consideration—
Adolescence

A major function of any culture is the transmission of group identity. Because the major developmental task for the adolescent is identity formation, his cultural becomes of special importance. In general, in the course of investigating cultural differences in child-rearing patterns, less attention has been given to adolescence than to childhood.[14] In Western culture, adolescence has been traditionally viewed as a turbulent, rebellious time during which problems can be expected. This is not true across cultures. Mead,[15] for example, reported on fifty Samoan girls who appeared to weather adolescence with no disturbance in personality and role functioning. These findings are especially interesting in view of the recent large-scale studies of normal American adolescent populations[16] which suggest similar patterns, and they call into question previously held assumptions.

Linton[12] found that across cultures adolescence is not usually differentiated as a separate stage. The more commonly recognized stages were the infant, boy, girl, adult male, adult female, old male, and old female. He suggests that there may be an association between symptom prevalence in adolescence and cultural recognition

or nonrecognition of this age group as a stage in the life cycle. It may be that adolescents have an easier time in societies where the stage is recognized and where specific cultural rituals and prescriptions support and aid the child in shifting to adulthood.

Cultural Aspects of Psychopathology

The anthropologist George Devereux[6] has formulated perhaps the clearest theoretical statement on the subject of ethnic neuroses and psychoses. The essential element of his approach is the idea of an ethnic unconscious.

The "ethnic unconscious" is that portion of the total unconscious segment of the individual's psyche which most members of his given cultural community have in common.

Each society or culture permits certain impulses, fantasies and the like to become and to remain conscious, while requiring others to be repressed. Hence, the members of a given culture are likely to have repressed the same things and thereby to have certain unconscious conflicts in common. [pp. 25–26]

Thus, a given wish or conflict, connected, for example, with aggression or sexuality may be deeply repressed in one culture, only minimally repressed in another, and allowed relatively free expression in yet another. Devereux notes that, in various cultures, the same defense mechanisms is present in normal and abnormal personalities. The differences arise in terms of the relative degree of importance which each culture "assigns" to the various defense mechanisms. Although Devereux's theory remains invalidated by substantial research, it does provide a unified view of a diverse array of data on normal and abnormal patterns; at the same time, it takes into account both psychiatric and anthropological data.

Most research and theoretical formulations are still concerned with the effects of culture on the expression of adult mental illness. Yet, it is through children and adolescents that culture develops. It is through them and through their relationship to their families and their society that cultural influences are most active and formative. If one views growing up as a process of enculturation, then deviations or variations from the norm must necessarily be understood against the backdrop of the culture.

Each culture has its own conceptions of illness

437

and its own ideas about etiology. When taken out of context, local explanations for common phenomena often appear bizarre. Nevertheless, in order to evaluate behavior, culturally specific folklore must be understood. Thus, it is clear that the diagnostic significance of any behavior cannot be adequately interpreted until one has taken into account such matters as cultural attitudes toward illness, the channels by which patients reach the therapists, and the ways in which national philosophies and value systems affect an individual's behavior.

For example, a child psychiatrist from culture A which values independence, autonomy, and achievement may be evaluating a youngster from culture B in which dependence and interdependence are prized and in which standing out or above other group members is considered deviant. Under these circumstances, the evaluator may view what are in fact the child's normal characteristics as reflecting some form of psychopathology, such as passivity. Furthermore, the child psychiatrist from culture A may overlook subtle deviations of youngsters from the pattern of normal development in culture B. By the same token a child psychiatrist from culture B will have difficulties in evaluating the dependence-independence values from children in culture A. The same tendency to over- or undervalue according to one's own cultural norms tends to produce other kinds of diagnostic errors as well. Thus, a similar situation could arise in another pair of cultures, one with a high degree of tolerance for motor activity in preschool and school-age children, the other with a low degree of tolerance for such activity. All these views about etiological factors and the requisite therapeutic efforts are necessarily influenced by the culture. However, despite cultural differences, it appears likely that most healers would agree about certain youngsters and families who are in need of help. Symptoms of anxiety, depression, withdrawal, learning problems, the acting out of aggressive hostility, and, to some extent, severe hyperactivity would be recognized almost everywhere as evidence of disorder. This would hold true as well for gross breaks of contact with reality, and disruption, or lack of development, of interpersonal relationships. Their importance and the society's tolerance for their presence would, however, vary considerably. Finally, it appears likely that in most societies, healers are concerned first with the control of violence, both to the community and to the self, next with the reduction of fear and anxiety, and last with the reintegration of the withdrawn or dysfunctional child into the community.[10]

With the initial conceptualization of the young patient's problems, cultural influences become apparent. Ideas about etiology may involve belief that the problem is due to a devil, breaking of taboos, imbalance of vital powers, deprivation or stress in childhood. Historically, man has looked outside himself for the cause of his problems, first to the supernatural world, and later to his natural surroundings and the imbalance in his relationship with them. Only in recent times has he looked to himself, to somatic and then social and psychic origins of disturbance. Prescriptions for treatment follow closely upon this historical process of explanation (this will be discussed in more detail in the next section). First exorcism, then regulation of the patient's life, the supplementation of vital powers, later relearning of behavior, and the expression and understanding of repressed wishes and conflict, all these constitute solutions related to the cultural beliefs of causation. It is clear that cultural factors condition such basic decisions as which psychiatric symptoms are more acceptable and which less, which are actually diagnosed as psychopathology and which are mere eccentricity, and which treatment modalities will be preferred, and, for that matter, effective.

Transcultural Treatment of Children

According to Frank,[7] the high value placed on democracy and science in the United States is reflected in the theory and practice of Western modern psychotherapy. The democratic ideal is made up of such values as the right to seek personal betterment, freedom from inhibition, and a certain degree of independence of thought and action. At the same time, the scientific ideal reinforces the democratic ideal by rejecting dogmatism and upholding objectivity and intellectual comprehension. This, as Frank has suggested, may not be entirely advantageous for psychotherapy. Such an orientation overvalues cognition and unduly stresses interpretation. It avoids therapeutically valuable, emotion arousing techniques such as group rituals, dramatic activities, and the direct influence of the healer; these techniques have wide-spread usage in other cultures. The child's and family's expectations of treatment and their conception of the nature of the problem must be respected if their cooperation is to be gained. Transcultural treatment of children and adolescents must, therefore, take into account the existing culturally approved treatment methods.

Nevertheless, in all therapeutic work with children there are common elements which can be seen as stages or phases, some much longer and more complicated than others. They can be conceived as (1) presentation of the problem, (2) analysis of the problem, (3) explanation of the problem, (4) prescription for change, (5) carrying out the prescription for change, (6) termination and (7) follow up. These stages can be seen in treatment approaches which are based on exorcism, drug therapy, behavior modification, family therapy, short-term or brief intervention, and child psychoanalysis. The extent to which a child patient and family are familiar with and oriented to a treatment procedure will largely determine its effectiveness. Imagine a shaman who is invited to practice his healing ceremonies in an American city or suburb for a child who has never had the opportunity to learn or accept shamanism and the notion of possession; or a child analyst who is asked to practice Western play therapy and analysis in a primitive village in which people have never been oriented to this treatment. Psychopharmacology is also more acceptable in some cultures than in others; for example, in some cultures, medicines are used to treat many illnesses believed to be caused by a loss of strength, and the drug is seen as returning strength to the patient. If family therapy, for instance, involves respect for a particular cultural emphasis or maintaining generational authoritative hierarchies, it can function within a cultural framework with that orientation. For example, in either a mother-centered or father-centered culture, the head of the family can be utilized as the co- or auxiliary therapist. By this alliance, the designated healer can more easily transfer an acceptance and incorporation of therapeutic prescription into the family functioning. By the same token, if behavior therapy is to be effective in a variety of cultures, it must have an underpinning of sound generic clinical judgment. Reinforcing agents are quite different from one culture to another, and patterns of behaviors which identify these agents may be elicited in direct observational pretreatment periods. These will determine the treatment program itself. Thus, there is a preexisting factor in the individual within his cultural setting that influences the appropriateness and chance of success of a particular therapeutic mo-

dality. With sensitive observation and selectivity these can be determined.[20]

Subcultures in the United States

The treatment of racial and ethnic groups in the United States, especially those who have recently immigrated, requires much knowledge and skill in identifying the cultural components of behavior. Part of history taking should include a "cultural history" in which beliefs, behaviors, customs, and symbolism, as well as traditional roles and functions within a family and subculture, are identified. Once a problem is understood within a cultural context, this context can be used to effect change. The following illustrations will refer to subcultures A, B, C, and D rather than to specific ethnic groups. To attempt to do the latter would risk stereotyping American subcultures, such as black, Spanish speaking, Indian, oriental, mountain or hill people, and so forth. Rather, it is preferable to give examples of simulated subcultures. Although these are admittedly defined narrowly, they can be matched with the treatment approaches which may be most appropriate for them. Obviously, there is no such thing as a "pure" subculture in this sense, and in any real situation, many mixtures and combinations will exist. Finally, an attempt will be made to superimpose family structure and socioeconomic grids upon the subcultures described. The intersection of both of these configurations with each subculture is extremely important to consider and would change the nature of appropriate treatment.

SUBCULTURE A

This Subculture A is marked by a belief in the existence of supernatural experiences, either religious in the conventional sense or nonreligious. Historically, such subcultures are often found in farming, fishing, and hunting societies which developed without the aid of modern technology. These are societies which had to find solutions to the overwhelming stresses that arise from natural forces. An understandable belief in the supernatural emerged as the only means of making some kind of order out of chaos and giving people at least some sense of power in the face of overwhelming helplessness. Once integrated into American society, people from these cultures held on to old, familiar ways of interpreting stresses and treating crises. There is often an important figure within such a community (a priest, witch doctor, or holy man) who is believed to have the power to communicate with spirits for religious ceremonies and to receive instructions for dealing with patient's problems. The causes of problems are usually perceived and interpreted as having to do with object intrusion, loss of the soul, spirit intrusion, sorcery, violation of taboos, or having "sinned."

When referred for medical care, youngsters in subculture A may often appear with hysterical or conversion problems. They and their families are highly suggestible and rely heavily on charms, amulets, and superstition to cope with stress. It is most unwise for the therapist to oppose or deprecate their ideas about solutions for problems. Indeed, it may be that understanding the richly symbolic life style will provide solutions in psychotherapy in which a "concrete enemy" (the devil or a spell, and guilt about transgressions) is the issue to be coped with. Short-term directive psychotherapy may be indicated which is consistent with the beliefs and intended to soften their rigid punitive aspects by suggesting experiences which can undo, reverse, or reduce the problem. Drug therapy may be enhanced by beliefs in the power of medicine. Use of the respected "healer" as a cotherapist may often enhance the transcultural psychiatrist's effectiveness. Family therapy may be the best way in which distortions via projected identification, (scapegoating of the child) can be cleared up or changed. Work with dreams in these families is often possible because dreams are given extreme importance, particularly where they are assigned premonitory, warning, or admonishing characteristics.

SUBCULTURE B

In subculture B, the system of reference shifts from the supernatural to the natural, and the problem may be explained as a result of an imbalance or disharmony with the natural principles that rule the universe. The subculture is also concerned with the relationships of forces within the body and with certain somatic predispositions which are ascribed to the individual. Here again the child may be the victim of a projected identification; a particular physical or emotional characteristic which originated from birth or earlier now makes him the bearer of the problem in the family. These subcultures have historical roots in societies which traditionally made use of fortune tellers, astrologists, physiognomists, or herbalists.

Here the treatment of life's problems is focused on working out harmonious ways of adjusting to the natural environment or to natural predispositions existing within the individual. Once again, it is important for the therapist not to oppose, but to supplement and offer additional explanations by brief, directed psychotherapy; both individual and family therapy can be used to explore strategies for coping with imbalances. It is important to try to help the patient to find ways to live compatibly with and adjust to the environment more harmoniously. This is best accomplished through suggestion and advice as to alternate ways of managing life's problems. Treatment can let the patient and family know about themselves and the significant predispositions so that the child can live with what he is and make use of the assets he has. In a way, the child psychiatrist functions as a consultant for coping with the environment; he adds information about personality and the interrelationships between the body, the mind, and nature. Again, since causes and solutions of problems are viewed concretely, therapy is most effective when it is time limited and goal oriented. Drug therapy, the use of vitamins, herbs and health foods, as well as placebos, constitute treatment methods in keeping with the emphasis on nature and bodily concerns; such methods are often readily accepted by subculture B.

SUBCULTURE C

In subculture C, indigenous treatment systems have been based on problems related to a disequilibrium, insufficiency, or decompensation of the individual's psychosociological system. Emotional problems and mental illness are viewed as phychological reactions to external social maladjustment. The modes of therapy generally employed in the folklore in this culture involve recuperation, rest, and compensation. The connection between environmental stress and maladaptive behavior is well understood, and learning theory and behavioral retraining become a natural treatment modalilty for most complaints. Here, social ills are believed to stimulate mental illness, and social psychiatry, with its emphasis on prevention through the elimination of such conditions comes to the fore. Energy channeled toward social action and change are most readily accepted by this group.

SUBCULTURE D

For subculture D, the major factor in emotional distress is internal conflict. The theories of personality most prevalent in this subculture are those developed by Freud and followers which focus on intrapsychic conflict as the major determinant of mental illness. Here psychoanalytically oriented psychotherapy and psychoanalysis become appropriate treatment modalities. It is important to note that these therapies are effective only among peoples whose conceptions of stress and illness involve fairly abstract notions about those internal psychic dynamics which affect behavior. Imagine a therapist exploring parental attitudes toward sex with a family who believes in the devil as the prime factor in the disturbed functioning of their child. Such a family would be confused, bewildered, and shocked by such an approach, and consequently reluctant to remain in treatment.

Family Structure

Running through each cultural subtype are the important issues of family structure, the orientation of each family group, and the hierarchy of specific family roles involving dominance or submission. These may be nuclear or extended families with single or multiple parents. Each subculture has its own value system which defines both roles and tastes, and which stipulates the sources of authority and nurturance for its members. Both matriarchal and patriarchal systems may produce stresses and tensions which are then expressed through the child in the form of symptomatic behavior. The extended family with its multiple generations will emphasize interdependence and authoritative hierarchies; this has considerable influence on the child's mental status. Therapeutically, family therapy can be accomplished with a minimum of stress to the system. The assignment of various functions to family members is likely to be understood and respected, as well as shaped in therapy. Often, approaching the family leader (such as an elderly and esteemed grandfather) can effect changes in stress on a young patient that traditional psychotherapy could not achieve. In strongly authoritarian, extended family structure, environmental approaches become quite appropriate with or without the individual treatment of the child or adolescent. Such methods are particularly effective because of the degree of dependency which exists among most members. For example,[22] a father may block treatment attempts with a child if he sees it as a threat to his authority and prestige. Using such a father as an "overseer," or manager, of the therapy may be useful in order to ensure that the therapy is culturally syntonic. It is important that the father not "lose face" with his child and avoid treatment involvement in consequence; to avoid such an outcome, the transcultural therapist invests him with the cloak of authority saying "You are quite right about your methods, but some children are different from the normal range and your child requires a different kind of approach. We feel it is you who should organize and supervise this approach at home. We would like to see you frequently because you will treat him for six days and we shall see him only one day a week." Thus, the father has been protected and brought in. A method which would imply criticism of him (or her in the case of matriarchal families) would upset the dynamics of the home and might well constitute a greater danger than the primary symptom.

When key individuals in a family have been identified, the therapist can make use of indigenous family "meetings," which occur naturally in many cultures with extended families. He may then simply facilitate the usual course of family discussion (for example, identification of a problem, apology, restitution, punishment, and so forth), or he may elect to shape and influence the resolution more actively in a different fashion. In any of the family structures described, the existing organization and roles can be utilized effectively, with the therapist demonstrating a wide variety of degrees of activity at various points in the process.

Social Class Factors

As previously mentioned, the subcultures described previously are oversimplified for purposes of clarity, and the attempt is made to show how treatment modalities can be matched with primary subcultural characteristics, or identifying factors. It is well recognized, however, that within given American subcultures, there exist further differentiations on the basis of social class or socioeconomic levels. In designing treatment approaches, these must also be considered as key variables. For example, among blacks the following "life styles" have been described[5] which can be related to social class differences: (1) street or urban ghetto life style, (2) the down home or rural extended family life style, (3) the upward bound or "middle-class" life style. Therefore, in working with families from a particular subculture, the economic, environmental, geographical, and philosophical differences among specific socioeconomic groups must be given considerable weight. It is a serious error to superimpose upon a cultural profile only certain commonalities in beliefs, values, and behaviors and to fail to take significant differences into account. Thus, with the "street" group, reality based, here and now, short-term goal oriented therapy might be most appropriate; with the "down home" group, a variety of family therapy approaches which respect the strong religious influences in these families and their orientation towards the supernatural may be effective; while with the "upward bound" group, a more extensive uncovering therapy may be chosen, because it allows for a special relationship between therapist and child which is respected by the parents.

The Intercultural Family

Given a well-adjusted intermarriage where the couple appears to have worked through cultural differences, the arrival of a first child is likely to bring about a resurgence of old conflicts over identity and culture. Earlier identifications must be reworked. For example, a mother-to-be may have openly discussed the issue of a racially mixed child with her husband and thinks herself to be free of racial concerns. Now, however, she may suddenly become extremely worried about the child's looks, the color of his skin, or his facial features. A Caucasian woman may ask herself whether she wants to give birth to a child who is not like her but has facial features of the husband's racial group. The father may fear that his authority will not be respected by a child who does not look like him. If the extended family had subtly or openly objected to the marriage, a different-looking child may increase feelings of rejection by the parent and stimulate further alienation. This, in turn, could result in further resentment of the partner or the child.

In an intercultural marriage, every developmental stage of the child has the potential of producing stress between the parents or between the parent and child. Issues of dependency, autonomy, power, skill mastery, sex identification, values, educational expectations, and peer relations can more easily create conflicts when the culturally different parents adhere to variant prescriptions of how to achieve desired behaviors. A Caucasian father may well feel neglected by his non-Caucasian wife when, after childbirth, she turns her attention exclusively to the baby. This corresponds to her culturally determined perception of her maternal role but not to his. Arguments may arise about mother "pampering" and "spoiling" the children by gratifying their dependency needs rather than fostering independent strivings. A non-Caucasian parent may feel sabbotaged in his or her attempt to raise obedient, achieving children when the Caucasian parent "behind his or her back" allows the youngsters more freedom and does not become upset about occasional fights or complaints from teachers. Which stage in the development becomes problematic will depend on the interplay of many factors, including the cultural mix, the intensity of either parent's adherence to tradition, the parent's personality structure, and the family's integration into the broader social environment.

The racially mixed child often suffers from a loss of cultural identity. This may take the form of excessive self-consciousness, ambivalence in attitude and sentiment, feelings of inferiority or compensatory "superiority," hyper-sensitivity with a tendency to rationalize aggressiveness, or a readiness to be critical in a manner which is more imitative and conformist than creative. Such a child is sometimes referred to as the "marginal person"—that is, one who does not fully belong to any one subculture, or who is on the edge of one or more subcultures. He has been variously spoken of as the apple (Indian or Red on the outside, Caucasian or white on the inside), the Oreo (brown or black-Caucasian) or the banana (Oriental-Caucasian). These youngsters may experience a serious conflict about themselves during adolescence, which is a particularly critical period for identity crystallization. Such problems are best dealt with in individual therapy. There the problems of identity diffusion can be explored, and the work directed toward the integration of the most valued aspects of each cultural part of the youth or to strengthening his identification with the self-perceived "dominant" cultural part.

The Transcultural Therapist

In all modes of treatment, the personality of the therapist is a key factor in the relationship. In the ongoing exchange between the child patient and the therapist, it is this relationship which is the vehicle for change. Kiev[10] believes that the basic features common to all psychological treatment may be more important than the features which differentiate them. When they practice, healers always bring a tremendous amount of personal influence to bear and arouse a multitude of emotions in the patient, as well as in the group. If one were to compare successful with unsuccessful healers practicing various kinds of healing techniques, one would probably find that due weight would have to be given to differences in theoretical orientations and technical approaches. Granted these, however, and quite regardless of culture, it is the healer's personality that is the crucial factor in determining whether he is more or less successful. Thus, a successful shaman, fortune-teller, or modern therapist may have similar skills in relating to other people and in knowing how to maintain socioculturally relevant therapist-client relationships. Within the framework of his technique, each would then be able to function with maximum effectiveness.

In working with children, key personality traits of the healer are most likely related to an ability to empathize with and to "regress" to the child's level in thinking and feeling. The ability to communicate at the child's level is crucial. In many cultures, particularly those in which curse or spirit possession is considered the cause of emotional illness, an ability to sense interfamily and intergenerational conflict is just as crucial as in Western psychotherapy. Only if that conception of the problem is acceptable to the patient will the treatment (for example, a prescription of rituals to undo the curse) be effective. In these cultures, charisma and authoritative qualities may be of greater importance for therapists than in others, although for all such practitioners, the ability to instill confidence and hope are universally desirable qualities.

In looking at the variables involved in the therapist's personality, it is impossible to escape the notion of countertransference. This involves conscious and unconscious attitudes and notions about the patient. These are necessarily biased by the cultural set of the therapist as he evaluates the patient's personality and functioning. The effect of the therapist's own awareness of his culture and of its influence on his perception of psychopathology is, therefore, crucial for effective treatment. As Pierce[17] suggests, at a minimum, and without being pejorative, the doctor should review whether or not a patient requires "middle-class and traditional therapy." For cultures in which less traditional emphases are in order, he specifically recommends: (1) a deliberate loosening of the structure and process of psychotherapy; (2) an emphasis on end products as opposed to process and dynamisms; (3) a deliberate focus on strengths rather than on weaknesses; (4) an emphasis on connotation prior to considerations of cognition; (5) an emphasis on feelings/satisfactions prior to considerations on behavior/achievement; (6) a relatively greater regard for external forces; (7) a relatively great regard for interpersonal and community interactions; and (8) a relatively smaller regard for sexual adjustment.

Conclusions

From birth onward, the infant's biological functions are molded to culturally prescribed limits and patterned after accepted models proffered by his society. Approaches to the treatment of illness are culturally influenced. No cross-cultural treatment of children or adolescents should be attempted without awareness of and respect for the risks, problems, and areas of difficulty involved. A simple transfer of the techniques developed in one culture to application in another cannot be effective.

There are many parts of the world where democracy, rugged individualism, and the equality of all are not part of the psychological set; in such environments, permissiveness and the encouragement to express feelings would be out of place. Drugs, short-term directive approaches, methods oriented toward religion, and supportive techniques are more in tune with the child and family's ideas about healing; as a result, they are more apt to be accepted and respected.

Bolman[3] has advocated the use of "bridging" people; this implies simultaneous cross-cultural psychotherapy. He concludes that in the absence of a single person competent to bridge two cultures, the most feasible approach must involve at least two professionals, one from each culture; for example, a native healer and a Western mental health professional. It would appear, however, that cultural variations in child-rearing patterns, which in turn predispose youngsters to certain developmental and psychopathological problems are becoming increasingly well understood. This complicates the question of which therapeutic intervention will be most acceptable and effective within which contexts. It seems safe to say that cultural bias is gradually eroding, and more and more bicultural therapists are being trained who can bridge one or more cultural gaps in their daily work. To a New York or a Los Angeles child therapist, it may be as important to understand the "hidden" problems which relate to spirit belief and curses, or the imbalance between yang (male) and ying (female), as to understand more traditional methods of formulating problems with children and their families. Treatment incorporating both culturally relevant methods and Western methods of child psychiatry will be most effective.

REFERENCES

1. ARIES, P., *Centuries of Childhood,* Alfred A. Knopf, New York, 1962.
2. BATESON, G., and MEAD, M., *Balinese Character,* vol. 2, Special Publication of the New York Academy of Sciences, New York, 1942.
3. BOLMAN, W. M., "Cross-Cultural Psychotherapy," *American Journal of Psychiatry, 124(9):*1237–1244, 1968.
4. CAUDILL, W., and SCHOOLER, C., "Child Behavior and Child Rearing in Japan and the United States: An Interim Report," *Journal of Nervous and Mental Disease, 157(5):*323–338, 1973.
5. COLE, J. B., "Culture: Negro, Black, and Nigger," *The Black Scholar,* June, 1970.
6. DEVEREUX, G., "Normal and Abnormal: The Key Problem of Psychiatric Anthropology," in *Some Uses of Anthropology: Theoretical and Applied,* pp. 23–48, Anthropological Society of Washington, Washington, D. C., 1956.
7. FRANK, J. D., *Persuasion and Healing, A Comparative Study of Psychotherapy,* Johns Hopkins Press, Baltimore, 1961.
8. HOWARD, J. S., "Schizophrenia and the Balinese," *Conditional Reflex, 7(4):*232–241, 1972.
9. KIEV, A., *Transcultural Psychiatry,* The Free Press, New York, 1972.
10. ———, (Ed.), *Magic, Faith, and Healing,* The Free Press, New York, 1964.
11. LAMBO, T. A., "The Vulnerable African Child," in Anthony, E. J., and Koupernick, C. (Eds.), *The Child in His Family: Children at Psychiatric Risk,* pp. 259–277, John Wiley, New York, 1974.
12. LINTON, R., "Age and Sex Categories," *American Sociological Review, 7(5):*589–603, 1942.
13. MADSEN, M., and KAGAN, S., "Mother-Directed Achievement of Children in Two Cultures," *Journal of Cross-Cultural Psychology, 4:*221–228, 1973.
14. MASTERSON, J. F., TUCKER, K., and BERK, G., "Some Criteria of Psychiatric Disorder in Adolescents," in Murphy, J., and Leighton, A. (Eds.), *Approaches to Cross Cultural Psychiatry,* pp. 187–218, Cornell University Press, New York, 1965.
15. MEAD, M., *Coming of Age in Samoa,* Morrow, New York, 1935.
16. OFFER, D., *The Psychological World of the Teenager,* Basic Books, New York, 1969.
17. PIERCE, C., "Teaching Cross Racial Therapy," unpublished manuscript, 1975.
18. STEWARD, M., and STEWARD, D., "The Observation of Anglo-, Mexican-, and Chinese-American Mothers Teaching Their Young Sons," *Child Development, 44:*329–337, 1973.
19. TSENG, W., and HSU, J., "Chinese Culture, Personality Formation, and Mental Illness," *International Journal of Social Psychiatry, 16(1):*5–14, 1970.
20. TSENG, W., and MCDERMOTT, J., "Psychotherapy: Historical Roots, Universal Elements and Cultural Variations," *American Journal of Psychiatry, 132(4):*378–384, 1975.
21. WHITING, B. B., and WHITING, J. W. M., *Children of Six Cultures,* Harvard University Press, Cambridge, 1975.
22. WIJESINGHE, C. P., "Youth in Ceylon," in Masserman, J. H. (Ed.), *Youth: A Transcultural Psychiatric Approach,* pp. 31–44, Grune & Stratton, New York, 1969.

27 / Socioeconomic and Racial Considerations

William A. Ellis, James P. Comer, and Susannah Rubenstein

Introduction

People of different social classes and races are linked by more commonalities than they are separated by differences. The many universal human needs, tasks, and psychic structures determine this. Yet in the course of psychiatric treatment, differences between the social, economic, racial, and cultural backgrounds of patients and therapists too often complicate the process or inhibit its outcome. This is more frequently the case between middle-class therapists and lower-class patients: It is particularly likely to hold true when the patients are members of a lower-class minority group and the therapists are middle-class whites.

Several factors contribute to the problem. First,

the very principles of psychiatric therapy were developed largely through the study and treatment of middle- and upper-class people. Their behavior became the standard against which all other behavior was compared, measured, and evaluated. Second, not only in the past, but today as well, most therapists are from middle- and upper-class backgrounds. Finally, the training of most therapists continues to be almost entirely in middle-class institutions and settings.

These circumstances are complicated by the overall societal attitudes which attend them. In our society, mental illness and mental anguish are too often viewed as an indication of failure or weakness. Indeed, poverty itself is often thought of as a sign of failure. Racial minority status is perceived by patient and therapist alike as a disadvantage—at some level even a weakness and/or a failure. Middle-"classness," on the other hand, has the implication of goodness, health, strength, and wisdom.

Thus the lower-class patient and middle-class therapist relationship is fraught with dangers of mutual misperception, misunderstanding, doubt, fears, and antagonisms. The therapist is often asked to demonstrate that he or she does not hold the common societal attitudes. The therapist asks the patient to demonstrate that he or she can rise above his or her class. It is not a situation that generates trust, yet trust appears to be a crucial element in successful therapeutic outcome.

In the past decade, a number of efforts have been made to improve the effectiveness of middle-class therapists working with lower-class people. A literature has developed which concerns itself with the culture of poverty, as well as with interracial therapy. Unfortunately, the work done on the psychological effects of poverty does not adequately clarify the effects of socioeconomic conditions on psychological functioning. It overgeneralizes and fails to depict in an adequate fashion the successful psychological and social adaptive functions of lower-class people. On the other hand, the literature on intrerracial therapy is both underdeveloped and underutilized.

Training programs have made some effort to familiarize middle-class therapists with the backgrounds of lower-class patients. Community mental health centers were designed to bring training and treatment into physical proximity with the entire population, including in full measure the lower middle-class and poor people. A variety of new health professionals and treatment modalities have been developed to address the problem—mental health aids, community liaison personnel,

and advocates, environmental problem-oriented therapies, and so forth.

These efforts have had varying degrees of success. Yet, treatment failure remains far more frequent among the poor than among middle- and upper-class patients. Some would argue that this is due to the fact that social conditions create and maintain the excessive stresses which disable the poor; that for this population, *only* massive corrective social changes can improve the level of social and psychological functioning. In fact, they would argue that many psychological problems affecting middle- and upper-income persons are related to adverse social policies and practices.

Without denying the need for more humane and people-oriented social policy, we reject the implications that lower-class patients cannot benefit from therapy or that middle-class therapists cannot be effective in working with lower-income patients. Greater therapeutic effectiveness is possible for both; but it will require more than new approaches and personnel. It demands a commitment on the part of the therapist to learn to appreciate difference. It speaks for a rethinking of our view of the differences in behavior between and within different social class groups. It will necessitate training and research efforts designed to illuminate these differences and the way they may be managed in the treatment situation.

In this chapter, an attempt will be made to identify the kinds of differences that exist among social classes and racial groups and that may intrude upon, threaten, or enhance psychotherapeutic interactions. So armed, the therapist will be in a position to deal more openly and realistically with these issues.

Psychotherapy

INDICATIONS

The indications for psychotherapy are basically the same for all groups. These include intrapsychic conflicts, environmental stress, and developmental crises. Symptoms, too, are the same or similar for all groups. But social, racial, and class differences between therapists and patient *may* make it necessary for the therapist to manage treatment situation differently.

COMPLICATIONS/DISADVANTAGES

As indicated, cultural, class, and racial differences pose complications and disadvantages for patient and therapist alike. A white, middle-class therapist found himself perplexed by the Christmas gift plan of a low-income, black mother. She was planning to buy her hyperactive six-year-old child many elaborate, expensive, and intricate presents. The therapist knew that she was poor and needed many material things; furthermore, he was certain that in short order the toys would be destroyed by this child. To the therapist, the mother's intention represented poor judgment.

He was not aware of the tremendous importance many low-income people place on Christmas gifts. Often it is the only time of the year that children of such families receive any gifts at all. For some of these families, it is the only time of any self-indulgence. The gifts are meant to compensate partially for an otherwise bleak material life and the constant necessity of "doing without." Since the therapist was not aware of the function of gift giving at this period, he was not well prepared to respond to this situation.

Ignorance of cultural factors such as language differences and less repressed, mixed sexual identifications may lead to misperceptions which complicate treatment. The repeated references by a sixteen-year-old patient to "big momma" gave his therapist the impression that this patient had a mother fixation; the liberal use of "you know" had the therapist believing that the patient had empowered him with clairvoyance; and the patient's greeting in the form of "what's happening, my man," caused the therapist to squirm in discomfort. A better understanding of the patient's use of language and of idioms associated with the patient's culture would have facilitated the therapeutic process.

Another complication is racial stereotyping.[6] Fixed notions held by many therapists cause them to eliminate poor and black patients from even a trial of therapy. If they do take poor people into therapy, they have lowered treatment expectations for them. Some therapists assume that *all* poor people have difficulty delaying impulses, that they share an impulsive, erratic life style. Or they take it for granted that all lower-socioeconomic patients view treatment in physical rather than in psychological terms.

After responding to an emergency situation which required medication, a young resident scheduled a low-income mother and her thirteen-year-old child to return to discuss the child's poor school performance. Because of his stereotypic view, he did not expect them to do so. He was quite surprised when they did return and even more amazed when he was able to develop a satis-

factory treatment situation. Certainly there are poor people who respond in accordance with the stereotype. But, too often patients pick up the therapist's expectation even when it is not explicit and live out the implicit, self-fulfilling prophesy. Many treatment opportunities are lost in this manner.[4, 9, 14]

But this does not exhaust the roster of therapist's problems. Some feel that treating lower-status patients lowers one's own status as a therapist. In our present hierarchical arrangement for psychiatric training, it is the young, inexperienced therapist who usually treats the low-income patients. The more experienced therapist rarely sees these patients in individual therapy. The young therapists get the message: These patients are less important. They do not appear among the private patients of the young therapists' mentors and will not be among their own future patients. Thus, treating poor people too often becomes a burdensome "rite of passage" to full professional status.[33]

In addition, without the kind of training which enables one to relate easily to low-income patients or to people from different cultures, working with such persons is apt to be difficult and stressful. Academic, social, and financial rewards will be minimal. Thus, the busy student therapist has many reasons for viewing such patients with less than enthusiasm.

Therapists sometimes have an unwarranted sense of superiority in relationship to low-income patients. This may easily come about when professional status is associated with intelligence, superior effort, good personal organization, and mental health and when poverty is associated with the opposite. A therapist who is not familiar with the historical experience of the group of people he is dealing with, or who does not thoroughly understand the impact of the group's values on individual behavior, can be less empathic than he needs to be.

The opposite situation is also a problem. A therapist may be overconcerned about sociological issues as they affect his patient. He may be so concerned with the factors of poor housing, inadequate diet, and insufficient clothing that the "real issues" of therapy are masked. This, of course, is not to say that these environmental and social issues are not important. But a therapist who is outraged over the patient's life condition may miss psychological problems which, if attended to, might enable the patient to cope better with these very same outrageous conditions.[1]

A youngster in a day treatment center was habitually late for school. When confronted with this, he pointed out that he lived in a subbasement. Further, his family did not have a clock or a telephone and could not be awakened by friends. Rather than lament with the patient over these adverse circumstances, or simply accept the situation of repeated tardiness, the therapist asked the youngster to think about a way that he could manage to make it to school on time. The child asked a friend to knock on his door in the morning, and was not late again.

Through such efforts as these, the therapist helped the child develop ego strength. The child was able to feel successful rather than helpless and dependent. Too often, therapists accept such circumstances with "paternalistic" attitudes while at the same time being irritated by what many of them would term the patient's "lower-class style."

The adaptive and defensive efforts of minority group patients can also complicate therapy. Regardless of race or class, patients often conceal true concerns and feelings from their therapist. This appears to be a more deliberate response among minority group people. There is evidence in folklore, biographies, oral history complications, and the observations of social scientists that in working with or relating to whites, a number of blacks adopt a deliberate strategy of evasion. This is an effort to cope with a social system and with individuals who are either predictably hostile, or whose attitudes toward blacks are assumed to be unpredictable.[23]

A study by Willie and McCord[34] indicated that before they performed well in predominantly white colleges, black students needed some indication that their professors were trustworthy more often than did their white counterparts. The minority patient often assumes that the white therapist will be critical and disapproving because of racial or cultural differences before the therapist has an opportunity to demonstrate otherwise. Conversely, the assumption that the doctor is the helper is less automatic among blacks than whites. Certainly this is the case for those white patients who have experienced unjust early disapproval but not to the extent that it exists among blacks.

Therapists are powerful people and symbols of power in the majority culture. Holding back from the therapist can serve the function of controlling or attacking the powerful; possibly, even probably, it can provide a means of rejecting majority culture. For example, John, a fourteen-year-old black youngster, had been in therapy for several months. He had been quite responsive, and the therapist thought they had a good relationship. However,

for several sessions the patient became hostile, reticent, and angry. On talking with the patient's parents, the therapist learned the reason for John's rage. He had been falsely accused by white administrators and police officials of vandalizing a school. He assumed that the therapist, being white, would not believe him and would agree with his accusers.

It is often said that low-income patients are more often passive and dependent in therapy, that they are, therefore, not able to take the necessary initiative to achieve useful insight and to make confrontation possible.[3, 23] To the extent that this is true, more often than not it is also true that the therapist is dealing with passive-aggressive behavior that can be modified. There is a greater degree of deference to authority among many poor people, and such patients will seem to "accept" interpretations and directives of therapists only to ignore them altogether more often than do other patients. But this is not always passive-aggressive behavior.[6] Often enough it is due to a lack of familiarity with the psychotherapeutic process. Psychotherapy is part of middle-class culture, and there is a clear albeit nonverbal sense about how one is supposed to use the treatment situation. The patient who does not know what he or she is supposed to do, is aware only that he is "out of his element." A low-income patient, referred for feelings he does not understand to a form of treatment he is not at ease with, and concerned about how he or she comes across to a middle-class doctor, is not likely to ask "dumb" questions. He will simply "endure," and continue his usual behavior.

Many poor people *do* enter the health care system with above average dependency strivings. Some approach a therapist or mental health center with the *real* expectation that the clinic or therapist will provide for *all* of their needs. They expect that the therapist and/or clinic will provide transportation, food, clothing, and shelter. In some instances, helping the patient arrange to have such needs met are justified and even therapeutic. But all too often, such requests are designed to exploit the guilt of the therapist, symbol of the powerful white world, in order to maintain a life style of continuing dependency.

Where adults are caught up in such a life style, this may complicate work with the children. Lower-class parents often insist that they want their children to be successful in school and in life. Yet the dependency style they transmit on a day-to-day basis can preclude success or make its achievement much more difficult. For example, Mrs. X telephoned her nine-year-old son's therapist because her welfare check was late. She became quite angry and distraught when the therapist could not provide her with emergency provisions until the check arrived. One of her son's problems was the fact that "something" always prevented him from completing his school assignments. When his excuses were not accepted, he generally felt abandoned and unfairly treated. Mrs. X was asked to consider ways that she might find emergency help on her own. As she did so, she began to develop skills which hopefully she would in time transmit to her youngster.

With the advent of prepaid insurance and other third-party payment programs, increasing numbers of low-income patients are receiving treatment from private psychiatrists. When the payment is thus provided, all too often both the patient and therapist are less concerned about the number of visits than they should be. In addition, the goals of therapy are not made as clear as they need to be. This can be a serious matter when the treatment issues include excessive dependency strivings and organizational problems. Among low-income patients, this is often the case. Thus, inadequate concern about the number of visits and the objectives of therapy may be a disservice to such patients.[24]

Another troublesome characteristic that affects the interaction between minority patients and majority therapists is the inclination of some of these patient to wear a mask.[23] Blacks may put on the mask of "dumb nigger," "street nigger," or "articulate erudite nigger," depending upon what the therapist appears to want or to need. In these cases, the patient perceives that the therapist is amused by or comfortable with a particular black style. Playing the "street nigger" role, a sixteen-year-old student went out of his way to speak "ghettoeze" and to appear slick and "street sophisticated." The therapist was unaware of the pressure the youngster experienced in maintaining this contrived style. He was comfortable with it himself and, therefore, raised no questions about it. He was surprised and confused when he read in the newspaper that his patient was a National Merit Scholar. This sort of role playing has led to such great identity confusion that it caused able black students to fail in school.

Finally, there is the unfortunate propensity of some therapists to assign diagnostic labels and make treatment outcome predictions in response to the patient's social class rather than on the basis of thorough evaluation.[14] So few senior psychiatrists and researchers have been significantly involved with low-income patients that it is reasonable to suspect that there is a lot that we do not know about the meaning of the behavior of such persons. For example, minority patients are overrepresented among those who have paranoid disorders of one kind or another.[7, 22] While there are environmental circumstances which may account for this, one can well wonder if this label is not assigned too readily and without sufficient evaluation. We have often heard therapists claim that the patient's problems were largely social and, therefore, not amenable to therapy. The same can be said of many middle-income patients who are called neurotic. Diagnostic labels and treatment outcome predictions based on the patient's class are too often employed to rationalize inadequate interest and inappropriate disposition of low-income persons seeking therapy.

Many therapists complain that lower-class patients only commit themselves to therapy for the attainment of symptomatic relief. (This will be discussed under the section on brief focused therapy.) But, one must also consider the possibility that the failure to address the issues outlined may in fact influence low-income patients to limit their interest to symptomatic relief.

Fortunately, with very young children, differences in class, race, and culture present fewer problems and are rarely as disruptive, or potentially disruptive, to the therapeutic process as they are with older persons. Yet, recognizing and responding to racial issues can enhance trust and facilitate therapy even with the young child.[3] Statements of awareness and concern by young children may be quite indirect and, therefore, easily missed.

By three years of age, most children are aware of racial differences, and they often raise questions about these differences in one way or another. But, below the age of seven or eight, they generally like or dislike, or are comfortable or uncomfortable, with adults on the basis of personal experiences more than on the basis of societal attitudes, practices, and pressures—except where racial concerns are extreme, pervasive, and carefully taught.

One seven-year-old, white boy, being treated by a black therapist, seated toy figures, an adult and a child, in a toy car, declared that they were gray people and sent them racing down a steep hill. First the car would crash. The youngster would reset the scene and then the car would make the turn. In his play he was saying, "We are two different kinds of people, but it won't get in the way —will it?" After a discussion of how they and their feelings, were different, the therapy proceeded smoothly. Not surprisingly, the parents had voiced similar concerns in the presence of the child without discussing it with the youngster. Sometimes the concern is even more obvious.

A black seven-year-old drew an imaginary line and called one side the black community and the other side the white community and asked his therapist which side he (the therapist) belonged to. The therapist pointed out that he was white but worked with some people who were black and some who were white. He raised the question of whether the youngster might be concerned about whether he (the youngster) was welcome in the clinic and liked by the therapist. This relieved the youngster's anxiety about the issue of racial difference, and again the treatment proceeded smoothly.

ESTABLISHING TRUST

Much has been written about interracial treatment. A smaller, but by no means insignificant, amount of work has been performed in the area of interclass treatment. In general, as is true in all treatment situations, the issue of trust appears to be paramount. The difference is that trust may be more difficult to establish between persons of different races, classes, sexes, and styles than in a situation in which the race, class, and style of the therapist is similar to that of the patient.[19]

Obviously, no therapist has had experience with every class, race, or style of person he is expected to treat. For that matter, of course, he has not shared the personal experiences of any patient. A therapist who is nonjudgmental, fair, interested, naturally empathic, and not influenced by social attitudes toward different groups has the best chance of establishing a trusting relationship with any patient. When society has transmitted a variety of negative attitudes about different groups during the early psychological, social, and intellectual developmental phases of the therapist, this status *is* difficult to achieve and maintain.[20, 30]

Where important differences exist, the degree of difficulty in establishing trust is influenced by a number of factors. One important vector is the degree of awareness and concern about such issues in the society at a given time. Another is the personal experience of a given patient.[15] Yet, even when concerns are pervasive, it is not safe to generalize. A middle-class black youth who grew up in a middle-class or interracial neighborhood and currently attends an interracial school may have little concern about the race and class of the ther-

apist. But, if a major source of the psychic discomfort of this patient stems from problems with racial identity, there may be a great deal of concern about the race of the therapist.

One black adolescent was the first black student in a white southern college. Aa such, he was the subject of a great deal of racial abuse. Simply and understandably, he would not see a white therapist. On the other hand, where persons with a less traumatic experience demand to see a black therapist—particularly in view of the known scarcity of black therapists—this may represent resistance to therapy and should be responded to as such. Thus, each situation must be evaluated on the basis of the facts and circumstances associated with it rather than in terms of a stereotypic set.

Establishing trust is generally easier when the therapist has some familiarity with the people, places, experiences, things, ways, and language of the patient. Patients have less concern about revealing their thoughts and the events in their lives when they sense that the therapist knows about and respects their personal experiences—some of which may be peculiar to their race or class. Black patients will frequently halt in the middle of a vignette about life in a black church, or in the poverty-stricken rural South, and point out to their black therapist that they would be unable to reveal this experience to a white therapist. Sometimes it is because they feel that the therapist would not understand its significance. Sometimes it is because they are ashamed of the experience and feel that the white therapist would find it negative or "low class." Sometimes it is simply a seductive effort to avoid more painful issues with the black therapist—more resistance. Black and white therapists alike must be prepared to prevent such responses from interfering with the course of therapy.[28]

In the past decade, many training programs made an effort to provide trainees with better knowledge about the operation of the social system and its impact on members of minority groups and persons of differing classes.[16, 25] A small number made an effort to help trainees learn to manage their feelings towards persons from different groups.[29] Unfortunately, in recent years, a number of these institutions have dropped such efforts. Yet, the failure to understand the experiences of different groups may lead to excessive antagonism, or sympathy. This, in turn, can make it difficult for a therapist to empathize, establish trust, or respond effectively with patients who are different. Thus, it is important for training program directors to restore and improve these much needed programs. In the meantime, therapists should make an effort to read the most objective literature dealing with the experiences of a variety of groups.

Different Therapeutic Modalities

The basic approaches to therapy are the same for all people. Other sections of this volume have discussed various modalities of therapy in detail. This chapter will discuss certain special considerations in selected types of therapeutic work with persons from different socioeconomic and racial backgrounds.

Group Therapy

ADVANTAGES, COMPLICATIONS, DISADVANTAGES

Group therapy, which is discussed in more detail in chapter 10, is most often used with groups of children or adolescents who have similar problems such as school phobia, drug abuse, or learning difficulties. It is particularly suited for those low-income children and adolescents who have difficulties because of absent parents, poor peer relations, or ego defects. It has proved to be an effective tool for helping children overcome a lack of adequate verbalization skills, a problem seen more often among low-income group children. It is a particularly useful approach in working with such children who are acting up in school.[10, 11] Regardless of their class or racial grouping, group treatment tends to be less useful for youngsters who are extremely hyperactive, are overtly psychotic, or have severe character disorders.[13] In working with lower-income people, problems of transportation and continuity of treatment are predictable complications. This is true regardless of the form of the treatment. It can be particularly troublesome in the group situation because of the necessity for individual patients to "jell" as a group. Frequent absences by different group members greatly diminishes the effectiveness of this approach. Sometimes parents must depend on neighbors, social workers, or hired drivers for transportation and thus have no control over missed appointments. Third parties are often unaware of the importance of regular attendance, particularly if the children appear "normal" to them.

Parents who do not understand the therapeutic process may be threatened by their exclusion from the treatment situation. Conversely, should group treatment prove successful, they may insist that other family members be treated in the same group.

More verbal and aggressive youngsters may provide a mask or cover for their more inhibited and less verbal peers. They may intimidate youngsters who are less verbal and not as aggressive. Middle-income youngsters are more often verbal in a way that is acceptable in the group treatment situation; whereas lower-income youngsters tend to be physically aggressive in an intimidating fashion that tends to cause their exclusion from the treatment process.

TECHNIQUE

In working with low-income children, their family, and third-party persons (involved because of transportation), therapists should make a specific effort to explain to them the therapeutic process thoroughly. Even when working with middle-income patients from groups who regularly utilize psychotherapy, it is assumed far too often that everyone knows what to expect. This is frequently not the case even for middle-income, majority people. It is far less likely to be the case with middle-income minority groups who have had little association with therapists in the past. To low-income persons who have never been able to afford psychotherapy previously, the process is often quite alien.

Parents and others indirectly involved often have important questions which, left unanswered, may undermine the therapy. Who is really taking care of the child? Why does he respond better to the therapist than to me? How could she have a problem when she performs well at one time but not at another? Is this not simply a matter of will? If you leave him alone, won't he grow out of it? Unanswered, these questions can lead to acting out around the transportation issue, lateness, missed hours, withdrawing the child from therapy. Keeping all involved and up to date with the progress of therapy can reduce some of the jealousy and help with the feeling of loss of control and the sense of confusion which is so often felt by many people indirectly involved in the treatment of children.

A therapist must be mindful of class and style differences in the group. Intolerance, jealousies, and antagonisms due to social attitudes must be made explicit. They must be dealt with in the same way that family transferences to group situations are managed. For example, a child may respond to a therapist in a way similar to the way he responds to an authoritarian parent. But he may also respond in a way that he feels that a low-income or minority-group person is expected to respond to an authority figure. There is a great deal of affect involved in such attitudes, and, technically, the socially conditioned aspect of the response cannot safely be ignored.[27]

Brief Focused Therapy

ADVANTAGES, COMPLICATIONS, DISADVANTAGES

This therapeutic approach, which is discussed in more detail in chapter 4, is particularly helpful in working with lower-income patients. It is well suited for persons who seek direct specific relief for specific problems. As a therapeutic form, it utilizes drugs, is time limited, is less expensive and more directive, and is a specially useful approach for people who view psychotherapy in organic rather than psychological terms. However, where short-term ministrations do not bring relief and there are repeated occurrences of a problem (such as running away, drug usage, or school avoidance), then some other more intensive approach is indicated.

Because brief focused therapy is directive and of short duration, it is all the more possible for a therapist whose background differs from that of his patient to misperceive the central problem. For example, a therapist thought that the major cause of a ten-year-old girl's poor school attendance and lack of motivation to do her homework was the absence of her parents' interest. True enough, this was one aspect of the problem. But the child's primary concern was her lack of adequate clothing and the teasing of other children.

Successful brief focused therapy, rather than a less directed open-ended long-term therapy, may require a problem-solving style found more often among middle-class, long-range goal-oriented patients. Lower-class patients who appear not to grasp the importance of the problem-solving style may be exasperating. The resultant negative countertransference can dilute the effectiveness of the therapeutic interaction.

These patients often regard themselves as inherently dependent, and they tend to see the possibility for change and improvement as the responsibility of the therapists alone.

More than that, low-income patients often feel personally powerless. This perception is reinforced by many aspects of their day-to-day functioning with schools, welfare systems, and other service personnel. Such patients often blame the therapists or become angry when the treatment does not work.

TECHNIQUE

Brief focused therapy is a directive approach, which requires that the therapist establish himself quickly as a respected, fair, knowledgeable, and relatively powerful authority figure. At the same time, where excessive dependency exists, it requires that the therapist avoid reinforcing the problem. This can often be accomplished by helping patients deal with concrete problems. For example, chronic tardiness might create a problem with a teacher, an after-school employer, a coach, and so forth. It can be helpful to think these problems through with the patient in a concrete way, probing his or her own understanding of the issues, the possible solutions, how to select the best course and act on it.

To some extent, this is done with all patients. With low-income patients who have not acquired a problem-solving style, this must often be done with a deliberateness which approaches the didactic. It permits the patient to remain active, follow directions, and experience success which will, in turn, motivate more problem-solving behavior.

This approach can be utilized without changing the basic style of the patient. For example, patients who feel that much of what goes on around them is controlled by others may not initially want to, or may not be able to, handle the fact that they can control some of what happens to them. When this is the case, it may be important to help them learn how to solve problems and to deal with just the aspects of their life which are causing psychological pain.

Therapists must comprehend the type of family structure within which the patient functions. It may be far from the free-standing nuclear family style which "goes it alone."[21] Families who receive support from relatives, neighbors, friends, church, and other social institutions may experience pain if they become disconnected. The resultant disturbance in family functioning can affect the children. Sometimes it is better for the therapist to help the family reconnect with supportive institutions rather than encourage it to strive to stand alone. Indigenous mental health workers can be particularly helpful in this regard.

Family Therapy

ADVANTAGES, COMPLICATIONS, DISADVANTAGES

By and large, middle-income persons function within a nuclear family. This is less frequently so among the poor, who are more interdependent. Such an extended family relationship can sometimes be a very desirable situation. It is also a very good reason to consider family therapy in working with low-income youngsters. As mentioned, it is all too easy to arrive at an incorrect assessment of who and what really constitutes the family. Children born out of wedlock prior to a mother's marriage, an informally adopted cousin, other very close relatives, and even friends may constitute the functional family. Both in formation and in function, such a family operates in a way that is a far cry from its traditional middle-class nuclear counterpart. As a result, identity confusion, diffusion of authority figures, and special rivalries, as well as the everyday problems common to all families, may involve persons not ordinarily identified with the middle-class father-mother-child concept.

TECHNIQUE

This type of psychotherapy, which is discussed in detail in chapter 7, can be rewarding. It may be the first and only chance that the whole family has to get together to talk (with direction) about the issues which have given rise to family conflict and malfunction. Again, the therapist may need to be an educator in a more explicit way than he would with middle-class families. More often, lower-income families may not have thought about the range of alternative solutions available. For example, physical punishment is not only a difference of value system between the middle-class therapists and the lower-class patient; the lower-class families have been unaware of any alternative and have accordingly never considered any management style.

Indeed, lower-class patients often view themselves as negligent, or as poor parents, if they do not "beat" their children. Without being critical, therapists can suggest other ways of thinking about the role of discipline—other ways to help children to become responsible persons. They can help adults understand how violence toward children becomes a model for the child's violence toward others, a means for frustration discharge, and a problem-solving method. Again, the therapist need not ask the patients to change their life styles completely; he can seek instead to help them modify practices which cause psychological pain.

Emergency Therapy

ADVANTAGES, COMPLICATIONS, DISADVANTAGES

In the nature of things, emergency intervention, which is discussed in detail in chapter 32, is designed to help patients deal with immediate problems. However, it also provides the opportunity to suggest more effective forms of treatment.[18] One low-income youngster was brought to the emergency room for making suicidal gestures and arson threats. His parents had never heard of psychotherapy before. The youngster proved to be highly intelligent and very perceptive, and eventually he was involved in psychoanalytically oriented psychotherapy. This child's major concern was whether he was wanted and valued at home. There were six children in the family but he, born out of wedlock, had a surname different from the other five. To make ends meet for their many children, his mother held two jobs and his father held three. Frequently this youngster's grandmother cared for him, but she also ran a home-based day care program for five children under the age of five. The suicidal gesture and arson threat were the only means by which this youngster could bring his anxieties and questions to the attention of his family. Had he not been brought to an emergency room he might never have received therapy.

Unfortunately, emergency rooms are generally manned by the most inexperienced clinicians. Too often, they do not understand that poor people live in a state of persistent crises. Beset by multiple difficulties, they sometimes ignore for long periods of time problems that would appear to others to be overwhelming; at other times, they appear to be overwhelmed by problems that would appear trivial to many. For example, people burned out of homes by tenement fires have appeared to be remarkably stoic. Yet when one of these same persons broke up with a boyfriend she "went to pieces." Therapists who simply apply their own value and priority systems in these cases may fail to meet the patient's needs.

When therapists are confronted with alleged emergencies that they do not view as such, they are understandably inclined to be frustrated and angry. Too often they respond with rudeness and hostility. It is not uncommon for mental health professionals to address emergency room patients by their first name, employ derogatory references, and make negative generalizations about all poor people Such an introduction to mental health practitioners will make it difficult to involve these patients in therapy, then or later.

TECHNIQUE

The massive socioeconomic problems of minority groups and poor people in our society can be dealt with only temporarily and superficially in any therapeutic setting. It requires the modification of social institutions to prevent the high level of psychological pain suffered by the many who exist at extreme poverty levels. The most that can be accomplished in the emergency room, or in any other therapeutic setting, is to develop the capacity to respond more sensitively to all people.

It was noted that therapists need a better understanding of the social problems of poor people and minority groups and of the psychological consequences of such status; and it was observed as well that this could be achieved in part through improved training. Periodic inservice training programs can also be useful. Indigenous workers in the emergency room can be helpful when they do not set themselves apart from their own background by overidentifying with the middle-class professional group. When this does happen, they often develop antagonism toward people like themselves. In service programs can be helpful in this regard as well.

Again, reconnecting persons to supportive people and social institutions can be helpful. One very effective emergency room program developed a network of persons in the church and service community on whom they could call for advice and help in "rerooting" their patients. Ministers, deacons, beauticians, and so forth were involved.

Day Treatment and Milieu Therapy

ADVANTAGES, COMPLICATIONS, DISADVANTAGES

Many poor people who would otherwise be banished to large custodial hospitals or sent to juvenile justice institutions are able to function satisfactorily when they participate in day treatment and milieu therapy programs, which are discussed in chapters 14, 15, and 17. However, the involvement of people from different backgrounds in such programs may cause problems. Because of our national commitment to racial and class equal-

ity, we too often deny or ignore the intergroup tensions which occur when representatives of highly diverse sectors of the population come together in structured (for example, treatment) settings. Institutional awareness of the problem potential, preventive planning, and appropriate practices can minimize the problems.

Most mental health institutions have a middle-class orientation. To be sure, persons from all classes work in these institutions. But the values and mores of the middle-class administrative and professional groups set the standards and institutional policy. Thus, regardless of their disturbed psychological functioning, patients from middle-class backgrounds who have similar values and mores often have an "edge" in meeting the expectations of the institution. For example, it is the articulate, reflective, grammatically correct patient who is likely to become the star of the group sessions. It is precisely such relationship issues that need attention. Unless there are ways for patients with different styles to feel valued, to feel adequate and to gain a sense of belonging in the setting, they may well react negatively. Then, in reaction to the implied institutional value system, these lower-income patients with their more physically aggressive styles may well "take over." Under such circumstances, fighting, bringing in drugs and weapons, intimidation of others, and so forth become severe problems.

Given the ordinary tensions prevalent in society, it can be expected that the relationship issues and the potentials for conflict present in all treatment programs will often have racial and class dimensions. All of the problems of understanding and trust that were observed in the interactions between low-income patients and middle-income therapists apply as well to encounters among patients of different backgrounds. Again, this is often less of an issue with very young patients. But it can be a very serious problem among adolescents.

There are other sources of tension and difficulty. Middle-class children are often involved in these programs solely for psychological reasons, whereas lower-class children join them largely because of sociopsychological dysfunctioning. In the case of older children, day treatment programs for many—particularly low-income children—are the last step before incarceration under the juvenile justice system. Because there are fewer family and community resources for the low-income youngster, there is no alternative to incarceration.[30]

Some professionals measure their own adequacy on the basis of the outcome of their therapeutic efforts. They are, therefore, inclined to work more with middle-income youngsters who appear to offer greater likelihood for treatment success. Others view the psychological problems of middle-income youngsters as trivial and unworthy of significant effort when compared with the problems of low-income youngsters. They prefer to concentrate their efforts on the latter. Such staff attitudes and resultant behavior are quickly noted by the patients and affect their responses.

TECHNIQUE

Again, the techniques of therapy are basically the same for all people. It has been pointed out that youngsters from families and communities that have been chaotic and abusive for two or three generations appear to have particularly brittle ego structure. Such patients are physically aggressive and particularly difficult to manage. Even with these youngsters, however, the basic issue continues to be trust. With such children, an even greater sensitivity to the differences discussed previously is crucially important.

In milieu and day treatment programs, youngsters are generally required to relate in a fair, cooperative, and even trusting manner. But the neighborhoods and families of some low-income children function in the opposite way. In order to avoid creating conflict, it is important not to label the neighborhood style as bad, undesirable, or sick. Instead, youngsters should be taught to develop adaptive skills that are appropriate for different situations.[26]

Care must be taken not to overidentify with or romanticize the communities of poor people. Mental health professionals have done this and, in so doing, encouraged acting out, antisocial, and other psychologically harmful, behavior. Low-income youngsters have more than their share of frustration and failure with the ensuing predictable burden of psychological problems. Much of this is due to the fact that no one ever helped them develop appropriate relationship styles to fit different circumstances. Day care and milieu therapy offers such an opportunity.

Rehabilitation Therapy

ADVANTAGES, COMPLICATIONS, DISADVANTAGES

Among middle- and upper-class families, a physically or mentally handicapped youngster causes the family great social and psychological stress. This is even truer when the child has already demonstrated good academic and social potential and an accident or illness has brought about the handicap. Among poor people, however, the expectations for high-level social success are less frequent in the first place. As a result, there is usually less rejection and ostracism of handicapped children.[31]

It is often quite possible to get low-income families to assist the performance or in the recovery of handicapped children. In addition, even though low-income parents from relatively stable circumstances do not have the same expectations for social success for their handicapped youngsters as do middle-income families, they often have higher day-to-day expectations. This situation permitted the highly successful blind singer, Stevie Wonder, to romp and play with his neighborhood playmates when he was a youngster and probably contributed to his success as a musician.

On the other hand, the notion of "God's will" can be a problem. Persons who see handicaps and their consequences as the work of God are too often resigned to accept the condition as it is, resent outside intrusion, and make little effort to find the kind of help that will maximize the child's development. Indeed, a family with this concept may feel that accepting help implies a lack of faith.

Occasionally important relatives advocate "cures" which they insist that parents try even though they are not effective. If that person has an important role or function, such as caring for a youngster so that the parents can work, he or she may prevent the parents from seeking the treatment the youngster needs.

TECHNIQUE

Here it is important to understand that in working with families of poor people a simple listing of the available services will not be sufficient. The critical need here is to consider the factors that may prevent them from seeking these services. The health worker should give thorough explanations and assist families in organizing the special treatments, training, and transportation required. Rather than denigrate the ineffective "cures" favored by relatives, it is better to involve them in the clinic's treatment process. One resistant grandmother was shown the physiotherapy equipment to be employed in treating her grandson and was included in the treatment process. She became an ally of the clinic program while continuing all the while to use her "goose grease." (Additional considerations in the psychiatric treatment of handicapped youngsters are discussed in chapter 40.)

Psychoeducational Therapy

ADVANTAGES, COMPLICATIONS, DISADVANTAGES

Psychoeducational therapy has many advantages for all children (see chapters 19 and 20). It is particularly helpful in working with poor and minority-group children. Education is an adaptive activity highly valued by parents. Many of the same parents who permit psychoeducational therapy would not permit their children to receive treatment in a therapist's office. This therapy facilitates early diagnosis and intervention. Without such diagnosis and intervention, many would eventually be labeled as "bad" or "dumb" children, increasing the probability that they would later develop psychological or learning problems. When the psychoeducational approach includes applying the principles of the behavioral sciences and psychiatry to every aspect of the school program, including staff and parent behavior, even children without specific behavioral problems can benefit.

One of the potential dangers of psychoeducational therapy is that children may be given diagnostic labels of one kind or another. Such labels can follow them and limit expectations. As a rule, diagnostic labels are given at an early formative stage of personality development, or during times of situational stress. Nonetheless, they are too often accepted as permanent and final. The chance of diagnostic error, and certainly of subsequent change, are great.

TECHNIQUE

Schools serving low-income and minority-group children are often under stress. In this situation, one is more likely to find doubt, distrust, and frustration among staff members and between staff and community. Staff members with large classrooms and many problems may envy the therapist who has the luxury of working with one or a few children. More than this, a therapist who works with the children in a one-to-one relationship is likely to overidentify with them. He may then express antagonisms toward staff and parents which will limit his ability to be helpful to all involved. Thus, the first order of the day is for the therapist to establish a bond of trust between oneself (or the mental health team) and the educators and parents.

Trust can best be established by helping teachers and parents work together to accomplish *their* goals. Assisting parents and teachers to accomplish real goals such as planning and scheduling extracurricular activities in a way that is child oriented has been found to be as helpful as individual treatment, case work, group sensitivity sessions, and so forth. Child-rearing workshops, role playing, and other approaches which facilitate insight into group dynamics can be helpful. This is particularly important because there is often great distrust between school staff and low-income and minority groups.

Workshops including parents and teachers permit therapists to pass on to both groups skills based on child development principles. Therapists are in a position to help parents and teachers develop techniques for maintaining discipline without physical punishment or other punitive methods. A useful approach is to help school staffs develop greater awareness of how some of their practices and arrangements contribute to behavioral problems. For example, transfers from one school to another, a frequent occurrence in low-income communities, can be quite disruptive. In one school, a transfer process was examined by the staff. Many changes were made to smooth the entrance of transfer students into the classroom. As a consequence, the major disruptions ordinarily associated with transfers were virtually eliminated.

In many low-income communities, children have not developed the level of social skills expected by the school. Such lags often lead to student-teacher conflict. It is possible to work with parents and teachers to help them understand that this is a developmental lag that stems from the social area rather than deliberate acts of "badness." Teaching the necessary skills in a systematic way can sometimes eliminate what appeared to be serious behavioral problems. A therapist who is mindful of the numerous ways in which the student's low-income background may make things difficult in school can find numerous means of helping children and staff alike.

Psychoanalytically Oriented and Psychoanalytic Therapy

ADVANTAGES, COMPLICATIONS, DISADVANTAGES

The protracted time and cost of psychoanalysis, and even psychoanalytically oriented psychotherapy, are very real problems in working with low-income people and minorities. The need for day-to-day answers to the continuing crises in everyday living makes these approaches difficult. But this is true of all people who have such a life style, and not simply poor people or minorities. There are suitable candidates among poor people and minorities both for psychoanalytically oriented psychotherapy and for psychoanalysis.[8, 17]

Unfortunately, therapists' attitudes have been negatively influenced by leaders in the field. Sigmund Freud[12] wrote that analysands must meet certain prerequisites . . . "those patients who do not possess a reasonable education and reliable character should be refused." For a variety of reasons too many analysts and therapists group all minority and low-income persons in the category of those who do not meet the prerequisites.

Because so few members of these groups have been in analysis, we have too little information about whether there are or are not significant differences between the functioning of minority and majority persons and persons of different income groups. In addition, there are very few black psychoanalysts in the entire country. Thus, the field is deprived of the insight of persons who know the minority's experience from the "inside." It is not surprising then that the field continues to propagate concepts about minorities that are seriously in error.

TECHNIQUE

On the basis of our present knowledge, there is no indication that in working with minorities or low-income people the techniques should be different from those used with any other group. As is true with anyone, it may be important to engage low-income or minority-group persons through some other form of therapy first. This may, however, be more important with these specific populations. Once there is an appreciation of the process and the potential, many persons thought to be unsuitable for psychoanalytically oriented psychotherapy and psychoanalysis are able to benefit by these approaches. This is not to say that these approaches are the highest or best form of therapy. The point is that the full spectrum of therapeutic approaches should be considered and can be utilized with all patients.

REFERENCES

1. ASTRACHAN, B. M., "Values and Treatment," *American Journal of Orthopsychiatry, 43(3):*494–495, 1973.

2. BAUM, O. EUGENE, et al., "Psychotherapy, Dropouts and Lower Socio-Economic Patients," *American Journal of Orthopsychiatry, 36:*629–635, 1966.

3. CHETHIK, M., et al., "A Quest for Identity: Treatment of Disturbed Negro Children in a Predominantly White Treatment Center," *American Journal of Orthopsychiatry, 37:*71–77, 1967.

4. COHEN, A. I., "Treating the Black Patient: Transference Questions," *American Journal of Psychotherapy, 28(1):*137–143, 1974.

5. COMER, J. P., "The Need is Now," *Mental Health, 57(1):*3–6, 1973.

6. ———, *Beyond Black and White*, Quadrangle/The New York Times Book Co., New York, 1972.

7. DOBRENWEND, B., "Social Status and Psychological Disorder: An Issue of Substance and An Issue of Method," *American Sociological Review, 31:*14–34, 1966.

8. EHRENWALD, J., "Psychotherapy—Which Brand to Prescribe?," *Israel Annals of Psychiatry and Related Disciplines, 12(1):*29–36, 1974.

9. ELLIS, W., "A Case Study of Institutional Racism," *Journal of the National Medical Association, 67(2):*158–161, 1975.

10. ———, "Group Work with Latency Aged Boys Within a School Setting," unpublished manuscript.

11. ———, and NELSON, S., "Wheeling and Dealing: Group Work with Lower-Class Latency Age Boys," unpublished manuscript.

12. FREUD, S., "On Psychotherapy," in Strachey, J. (Ed.), *The Standard Edition of the Complete Psychological Works of Sigmund Freud*, vol. 7, pp. 257–268, Hogarth Press, London, 1953.

13. GINOTT, H., *Group Psychotherapy with Children*, McGraw-Hill, New York, 1961.

14. GRAFF, H., et al., "Prejudice of Upper Class Therapists Against Lower-Class Patients," *Psychiatric Quarterly, 45:*475–487, 1971.

15. JONES, E., "Social Class and Psychotherapy: A Critical Review of Research," *Psychiatry, 37:*307–320, 1974.

16. KAPLAN, S. R., and ROMAN, M., *The Organization and Delivery of Mental Health Services in the Ghetto: The Lincoln Hospital Experience*, Williams & Wilkins, Baltimore, 1972.

17. KENNEDY, J., "Problems Posed in the Analysis of Black Patients," *Psychiatry, 15:*313–327, 1952.

18. LaVIETES, R. L., "Crisis Intervention for Ghetto Children: Contraindications and Alternate Considerations," *American Journal of Orthopsychiatry, 44(5):*340–344, 1974.

19. LORION, R. P., "Patient and Therapist Variables in the Treatment of Low-Income Patients," *Psychological Bulletin, 81(6):*344–354, 1974.

20. McDERMOTT, J. F., et al., "The Effect of Social Status on the Evaluation of Emotionally Deprived Children —Observations of Blue-Collar Families," *American Journal of Orthopsychiatry, 34:*253–254, 1964.

21. MAYO, J. A., "The Significance of Sociocultural Variables in the Psychiatric Treatment of Black Outpatients," *Comprehensive Psychiatry, 15(6):*471–482, 1974.

22. MYERS, J. K., et al., "Social Class and Psychiatric Disorders: A Ten Year Follow-Up," *Journal of Health and Human Behavior, 6:*74–79, 1965.

23. OVERALL, B., and ARONSON, H., "Expectations of Psychotherapy in Patients of Lower Socio-Economic Class," *American Journal of Orthopsychiatry, 33:*421–430, 1963.

24. PETTIT, I. B., et al., "Relationship Between Values, Social Class, and Duration of Psychotherapy," *Journal of Consulting Clinical Psychology, 42(4):*482–490, 1974.

25. REISSMAN, F., *New Approaches to Mental Health Treatment for Labor and Low Income Groups,* National Institute for Labor Education, New York, 1964.

26. ROSENBERG, L. A., and TRADER, H. P., "Treatment of the Deprived Child in a Community Mental Health Clinic," *American Journal of Orthopsychiatry, 37:*87–92, 1967.

27. SAGER, C. J., et al., "Black Patient-White Therapist," *American Journal of Orthopsychiatry, 42(3):*415–423, 1972.

28. SHAPIRO, E. T., and PINSHER, H., "Shared Ethnic Scotoma," *American Journal of Psychiatry, 130(12):*1338–1342, 1973.

29. SIEGEL, J. M., "A Brief Review of the Effects of Race in Clinical Service Interactions," *American Journal of Orthopsychiatry, 44(4):*555–562, 1974.

30. STORROW, H. A., "Psychiatric Treatment in the Lower-Class Neurotic Patient," *Archives of General Psychiatry, 6:*469–473, 1972.

31. SUCHMAN, E. A., "Sociomedical Variations Among Ethnic Groups," *American Journal of Sociology, 70:*319–331, 1964.

32. VONTRESS, C. E., "Barriers in Cross-Cultural Counseling," *Counseling and Values, 18(3):*160–165, 1974.

33. WARREN, R. C., et al., "Differential Attitudes of Black and White Patients Toward Treatment in a Child Guidance Clinic," *American Journal of Orthopsychiatry, 43:*385–393, 1973.

34. WILLIE, C. V., and MC CORD, A. A., *Black Students at White Colleges,* Praeger, New York, 1972.

---

28 / Psychiatric Intervention with Infants

Justin D. Call, David E. Reiser, and I. Lee Gislason

> The infant is born out of seeds which possess contrary qualities.
> BARTHOLOMAEUS ANGELICUS, 1230 A.D.

Introduction

In cases of psychopathological development during infancy the rationale now exists for well-formulated intervention. This is recognized by many clinicians, researchers, social agencies, and government agencies. Between conception and age two and one-half* is designated as the period of infancy. Many serious yet treatable problems which occur during this period, are still not clearly enough recognized. They are thus not treated until a later age when more serious disturbances have developed.

Treatment approaches will be emphasized which are based upon an empirical data base, and are applicable to the specifics of each case. The reader may wish to refresh his orientation about normal psychological development from conception through age two and one-half. The sections of this Handbook dealing with normal development

---

* Age two and one-half is chosen as the end of infancy because of the child's capacity to speak in phrases and sentences. Hence, after that time, he can negotiate with others on his own.

covering this area may be useful. It is assumed that the reader has knowledge of treatment principles and approaches utilized with older children and families.

Clinical Assessment

The clinical assessment of infants should always include a carefully obtained medical and developmental history of the child. This should come from the best informed adults in the child's present and past environment. The assessment should include a play interview with the child, evaluation of the child's physical status, psychological testing, social history of the family, home visit, and a nursery school or hospital visit when appropriate. Review of history, physical findings, cultural background, assessment of risk factors, and the utilization of infant tests (such as those designed by Gesell, Brazelton, Bayley, Chess, Ainsworth, Caldwell, Murphy, Frankenburg and Dodds—The Denver Developmental Screening Test, and Knoblock and Pasamanick) have been discussed in some detail in volume I of this handbook.

The term *clinical* assessment is utilized in order to emphasize those things which the child psychiatrist, as a well-trained clinician, should do himself.

In evaluating the maladaptations of infancy, he should review available data from all sources and synthesize this information in the best possible way. The clinician's judgment is based upon a theoretical and clinical understanding of serious symptoms and developmental deviations; in weighting the importance of data coming from all other forms of assessment, it is an indispensable factor. As in other fields of medicine, it is the clinical assessment that should provide an overall synthesis of data.

During infancy, the significance of any sign or symptom of psychological maladaptation must be assessed within a developmental framework. Changes in symptoms and symptom patterns over time must be understood in reference to ongoing maturational change and environmental events. Developmental change occurs throughout life; however, it occurs more rapidly and hence has more influence during infancy. Maturation and experience are interacting vectors whose result is expressed as developmental changes. Such developmental changes provide the context within which the meaning of a symptom or symptom complex can be made comprehensible.

In the clinical assessment of infants a useful starting point can be adopted from clinical pediatrics: evaluation of the child's general physical status. There are many interacting factors that affect the infant's overall behavior and appearance; the capacity to distinguish physical health from illness is based upon their understanding and synthesis. Such factors include the appearance of the skin, color, state of hydration, respirations, responsiveness to external stimulation, general nutritional state, and what is now described as the infant's psychophysiological state. The observations and concerns of an ordinary, devoted, good-enough mother to her infant and her capacity to characterize her infant's state of health or illness are probably based upon her perception of change. She compares the infant's current responsiveness to her to his behavior in the recent past, and to her memory of prior illness. The mother's evaluation is usually expressed in gernal terms, such as, "He's not well," or "She's not interested in playing." Only by dint of careful listening to and questioning of the mother can she be helped to provide the basis for her appraisal. The devoted pet owner or veterinarian seems to utilize the same method of evaluation.

The capacity to differentiate between a healthy infant and a sick one is perhaps the most important distinction that can be made by the clinician. It is based upon observations of a sensitive, informed, involved participant-observer who can integrate both objective and subjective information globally. Such integration may take place preconsciously. Interactional aspects of behavior generated by both the infant and the participant-observer are given weight in the observation. Erikson[23] has observed that infants raise their parents as much as they are raised by them.

The psychologically oriented clinician must be able to compare both his objective and subjective impressions with available standards of expectable behavior and development in a similar setting. In formulating such knowledge, the psychologically oriented clinician makes use of his past experiences. While viewing the clinical problem at hand, he synthesizes them and draws correlations and analogies from them. Symptoms of disturbance in infancy, like words, must be interpreted in terms of context. The most relevant context is a developmental one, emphasizing changing patterns of function over time and according to circumstance.

EXAMPLES

A normal child of sixteen months points to a shiny letter opener on the coffee table, then reaches for it while saying no. The developmentally oriented observer knows that the child's word no in this context means yes as much as it does no. A sixteen-month-old boy has been withholding bowel movements for three to four days. He has been having crampy abdominal pains. His mother consults the pediatrician, who tries unsuccessfully to resolve this problem by reassurance. The child psychiatrist must determine the meaning and context of the symptoms.[11] In doing so, he will ask about such maturational factors as level of growth, fine motor functioning, stage in the development of separation-individuation, that is, individuation phase, practicing phase, or rapprochement subphase.[40] The investigator will determine if fixations in oral and anal development have occurred and will evaluate the circumstances under which these symptoms have occurred previously, that is, under conditions of separation, anxiety, illness and/or threat. What methods of treatment have been used? How has the infant responded? The clinician will obtain a history of bowel training, general modes of "holding on" and "letting go," bodily illness, regressive experiences in the past, history of libidinal attachments, favorite play activities, and previous psychic trauma. Also, if the child has been bowel trained successfully, how was this achieved?

COMMENTS

A "good-enough mother"[65] builds upon her overall feelings of empathy and understanding of the child. She is thus able to evaluate the meaning of and thereby formulate an appropriate response (or nonresponse) to a symptom. The mother's empathy is based upon her identification with the child. Yet this identification is modified by a healthy, observing ego which differentiates her own experience from that of the child. The mother's empathy is a synthesis of her own previous experience as a child and as a sibling, and her experience with her present child—a synthesis of her knowledge of how she felt and of how the child feels undergoing such experience. Thus, in interpreting the child's response to present circumstances, the child's past is taken into account. Some behaviors such as withholding of bowel movements, rumination, bizarre play, food refusal, and vomiting are beyond some mothers' empathic understanding. When this point is reached, that is, when mother's confusion over, repugnance to, or resentment of an infant's particular behaviors rises to a sufficient peak, complaints about the child or his behavior will arise.

As a sole source of diagnostic sensitivity, the child psychiatrist's knowledge of prior development and of currently operating factors in the environment is not sufficient. He must supplement such knowledge and information with his own understanding and empathy. When working with infants, the child psychiatrist must allow himself to become involved, to become identified with the child and with the parent. Such identification must be combined with a capacity to stand aside and objectively study the entire scene, including his own involvement. The clinician is thus like the mother in being able to identify with the infant.[61] Unlike the mother, however, he is, by virtue of his training and experience, able to stand aside from such an identification. With the aid of a professionally disciplined, observing ego, he is then capable of empathic understanding of both the infant and the mother.

Complaints, Signs, and Symptoms

The clinician encounters parental complaints, signs, and symptoms. These, plus combinations and constellations of functioning determine health and disease. With the help of their knowledge of normal development, knowledge of physical illness, and their grasp on bodily health within a framework of psychological understanding, child psychiatrists can intuit the infant's psychic experience. Since infants and young children below the age of two and one-half do not usually express their concerns about themselves in the language of consensual subjective experience, such as, "It hurts here," or "I don't feel good," their feeling states, behaviors, and problems with parents are usually expressed first by parents as complaints or questions about the infant—a statement that something is changed, or wrong. The younger the child, the more necessary it is to distinguish between the complaint of the parent and the symptom of the child. In some areas objective measures of the child's functioning can be obtained by psychological testing.[2, 27, 29] But this gives only a gross approximation of how this child compares to a group of children in testable areas of functioning. The well-standardized test provides some objective determination of the child's functioning in the realm of the complaint expressed by the parent. Clinical work with infants requires the clinician to interpret and translate the parent's complaint about the child within the context of parenting behavior. This is especially necessary if a complaint is not fully substantiated by objective criteria. For example, it is not uncommon for parents of children eighteen to twenty-four months of age, to examine critically and in detail the way in which their youngsters walk. At this age the child is often walking away from the parent. Parents ask many questions about their child's gait. These questions can be understood as displacements of their concern regarding the child's endeavors toward separation, that is, his autonomy from the parents as he seeks liberation from their symbiotic union. This is but one manifestation of the group of *pseudo-orthopedic phenomena*, the psychosocial manifestations of autonomy and mobility in the child, behaviors that are disquieting to parents and projected onto the body of the child as complaints. Such complaints lead the clinician to a consideration of problems inherent in the parent-child relationship rather than to problems in either the child or the parent alone. Parental anxiety, grief, anger, disappointment, guilt, conflict, and confusion often dominate the flow of information between the parent and the clinician about the child. In the mind of the parent, the child is an extension of the self. From this perspective, parenting is a further elaboration of the parental self achieved through projections, displacements, and identifications with the child.* In this way, the child functions as an important force in maintaining the equilibrium within a marriage and in the family. Thus, one can often trace the parent's complaint about the infant to its subjective basis within the parent.

A symptom is different from the parent's complaint. It is a behavioral manifestation of an underlying disturbance in mental functioning within the child himself.[11] Since the infant can seldom express the causes of his own internal hurts or feeling states in psychological terms, the parents and the clinicians working with the infant must consider subtle manifestations in the child's functioning. They must study the cognitive as well as the affective areas as indicators of underlying disturbance. Many common parental concerns and *expectable manifestations* are usually *not* problems of disturbance within the child. Examples which occur at various ages can be listed as follows.

Birth to One Month. Prefers eating every 2 hours; prickly heat rash; not satisfied with feeding; wants to be held "all the time"; grunts with red face during bowel movements; sucks fingers or thumb.

Age Two to Three Months. Cries irritably; colic; "constipation"; does not sleep through night; sucks fingers or thumb.

Age Four to Six Months. Constipation; demands attention; prefers to be propped up; "spoiled"; teethes—bites; sucks fingers or thumb.

Age Seven to Nine Months. Drops things; feeds messily; exhibits disrupted sleep associated with teething, move to new home, or illness; "temper."

Age Ten to Fifteen Months. "Gets into things all the time"; constipation; diminishing appetite; feeds self or insists on being fed; screams; has mild tantrums; exhibits attachment to transitional object (blanket, teddy bear, etc.).

Age Sixteen Months to Two Years. "Gets into things," climbs; is stubborn; exhibits demanding, controlling behavior with the parent (bossiness); clings to parent and cries at the time of separation; has temper outbursts; is "nasty"; Upset easily; "stutters"; "acts like a baby sometimes"; exhibits sibling rivalry; "wants his or her own way."

Age Twenty-five Months to Three Years. Plays messily; "stutters"; won't put thing away; is aggressive and possessive in play; soils or wets

occasionally; is stubborn; won't try new foods; shows babylike behavior with illness or change; wants own way and fusses; has occasional temper tantrums; exhibits short-lived fears without objective basis.

Signs of Psychological Health During Infancy

The preceding material has sought to stress and illustrate the developmental context as a basis for deriving the meaning of clinical data. There is another way of determining the significance of symptoms and deviant developmental trends and of distinguishing between parental concerns and indications of disturbance within the child. That is the process of evaluating and weighting that which is problematic in relation to that which indicates average, expectable normal development.

Certain psychological achievements have an organizing influence on the child's psychological life. These occur at certain times during development and should be given greater weight in making clinical assessments. Such capabilities, listed chronologically from the newborn period to age three, are as follows.

Visual reciprocity with the mother should be established by one month of age. This involves the infant's capacity to fix the gaze of both his eyes on the mother's eyes, and to maintain visual anchorage to the mother's eyes and face as she moves her eyes and changes her expression.[6, 49] It has been said metaphorically that the eye is the second breast.[57] In the visual sphere, reciprocity appears to be organized by underlying, fluctuating states of attentiveness in the infant; even at birth the mother is in synchrony with these. This has been studies in detail by Sander,[52] Brazelton,[6] Robson,[49] and Anders.[1] Physiological reciprocity in the nursing situation is described later in this chapter.

Anticipatory approach behavior in relation to feeding has been observed in the first few days of life.[14] In healthy infants, it is well established by one month of age. This behavior occurs prior to any stimulation of the rooting reflex, and consists of the infant's opening his mouth and moving his head and hands toward the breast or bottle when he is placed in the feeding position. Studies of

---

* See S. Freud, "On Narcissism: An Introduction," in Strachey, J. (Ed.), *The Standard Edition of the Complete Psychological Works of Sigmund Freud,* vol. 14, Hogarth Press, London, 1953.

this behavior showed that each infant organizes his anticipatory approach movements in relationship to the mother's feeding style, and makes an individual adaptation to her specifically. Such behavior emerges as a modification of the complex rooting reflex of early infancy; it indicates the beginning of the infant's specific adaptation to his specific mother, that is, early ego functioning.

The social smile was designated by Spitz[58] as the first personality organizer; it occurs at two and one-half to three months of age. It consists of the infant's fully developed smiling response on presentation of a face or a stimulus resembling it. The social smile must be differentiated from the smiling that is organized endogenously at birth. Shortly after birth, the infant begins to smile in response to nonspecific exogenous stimuli. This is then followed by the social smile. These stages in the evolution of the smiling response have been studied in detail by Emde and Harmon.[20] By three and one-half months of age, the infant usually smiles preferentially at familiar caretakers. By four months, he begins to react negatively to a strange face, and responds more and more positively to a reciprocally engaging familiar face, usually the mother. Smiling and not smiling thereby become ways of eliciting a smile, of attempting to regulate the response of others, that is, of attempting to regulate the libidinal object, as suggested by Winnicott.[61] Winnicott has stated[60] that, for the infant, the mother's face is the first mirror capable of reflecting back that part of the infant's experience which he can subjectively experience. It seems reasonable to suggest that the infant's sense of self emerges from what is (or is not) reflected back to him from the mother's face. If an infant can "turn off" a threatening stimulus, he can thus render the stimulus less threatening. This makes it safer to "turn on" the stimulus and explore it; after all, one has on-off controls. By eight months the infant is capable of suppressing his own smile, even to the familiar maternal figure. At that time, the infant also begins elaborating a series of more subtle facial expressions. Some of this subtlety in facial expression seen in the second half-year of life has been described by Fraiberg.[26]

Playful activities between mother and infant begin at birth. They are often seen after feeding. *Games* are more organized than play and have a predictable beginning, middle, and end.[15] The games of early infancy usually end with a social smile. The earliest games occur at one to two months. They involve head movements (butting games also called "bossing," like goats bumping frontal bones), oral and facial imitation, and extending and elaborating on a theme of reciprocity and mimesis between the infant and mother during periods of relatively conflict-free engagement. Examples of such games described in early literature, include Freud's* description of the child who played the game of the disappearing and reappearing spool, and Winnicott's use of the bowl and spatula[66] in the "set situation." Various infant games and their implications for development have been studied and reported by Call and Marschak,[15] by Fraiberg,[26] and by Kleeman.[34] The capacity of the infant to initiate such games within social context challenged and motivated the authors to devise additional games within social context. These serve as a means of mastering average, expectable life experiences, both as a catalyst for and as a sign of healthy psychological growth. When such games become repetitive and stereotyped, they may indicate psychopathology.[23]

Eight months' anxiety was designated by Spitz[55] as a second organizer of the personality. This is manifest by distressed affectomotor behavior when the infant is confronted with a stranger or separated from the primary mothering figure. Subsequent studies by Benjamin[3] and others[17] have shown that stranger distress occurs earlier, that is, at five months to ten months of age, while separation distress is a later phenomenon which may have its origin around eight months, but which peaks usually around fifteen months and may persist for many months thereafter. In most clinical situations it is difficult to distinguish stranger from separation anxiety. Thus, Spitz's original designation of "eight months' anxiety" appears appropriate as a marker for normal development in clinical settings, and indicates the capacity of the healthy infant to differentiate among mother, stranger, and self.

Affirmation and negation gestures occur in the normal infant's development long before a consistently semantic meaning is organized around the words yes and no. In most infants, negation is clearly organized around the semantic "no" gesture by fifteen months. Spitz[56] has suggested that the infant's use of the "no" gesture is based upon his identification with the frustrator.

* See the following articles in J. Strachey (Ed.), *The Standard Edition of the Complete Psychological Works of Sigmund Freud*: "On Narcissism: An Introduction," vol. 14, 1953; "Instincts and Their Vicissitudes," vol. 14, 1953; "Beyond the Pleasure Principle," vol. 18, 1955.

Deferred imitation[47] marks the beginning of representational and symbolic thought. As an example Piaget cites his daughter L, who at sixteen months pointed to her own nose when Piaget pointed to his, after which she pointed to the nose of her doll, who was not capable of reciprocating with her. A few days later, L imitated her younger brother, J, in a bath when he was not present. She also wiped her own mouth as she had seen her mother wipe J's mouth. At seventeen months, L rocked her doll in her arms as she had earlier seen her sister do. Delayed imitation, as illustrated by these examples, clearly signifies the capacity for representational thought. L's imitation of her sister rocking the baby also indicates L's identification with her sister.

In American culture, the child's active initiation and appropriate use of the "bye-bye" gesture[34] occurs as the parent leaves the child. This marks a very significant achievement not only for the child but also for the parent in mastering the distress of separation. This level of mastery is usually achieved by eighteen months of age; incidentally, this corresponds to the rapprochement subphase of separation-individuation described by Mahler.[39]

Most textbooks suggest that the achievement of *toilet training* by the age of two should be looked upon as a mark of healthy development.[37, 43] The authors have chosen not to dignify this achievement as *the* most significant development at age two. This is not because it is unimportant, but because there is so much variation and unpredictability regarding toilet training in American culture, which probably reflects the degree of stress, conflict, and uncertainty around toileting. For clinical assessment, it is more importrant to know *how* toileting mastery was achieved rather than *when* it was achieved.

An indicator of more fundamental importance in assessment is the *capacity for two- and three-word speech*. This usually occurs at two to two and one-half years of age.[18] The infant of this age may not actually use two to three words effectively in a grammatically correct sentence of his own creation. However, he may show his capacity to comprehend such usage in receptive speech—that is, by responding to a complex grammatical construction of this kind presented to him by others.[42] Or he may combine one or two words with a gesture which accomplishes the same purpose.[9, 31, 32]

The landmarks of normal patterns of communication and language development in infants and young children are currently under renewed study.[8]

Direct Psychiatric Treatment of Infants

The concept of psychiatric treatment of infants is both intriguing and alarming to many parents and professionals. "He'll grow out of it," "Perhaps we should change his formula (or put him in a nursery school") are all examples of the reluctance of many pediatricians and infant careworkers to consider seriously or specifically those aspects of behavior which betoken deviant development in a given infant. Both attitudes, "wait and see" and let's see what will happen if we do this," bypass the important processes of identifying the nature of the disturbance in its developmental and social context, understanding its meanings, and formulating and instituting appropriate intervention. The underlying assumption here is that the behavior and development of infants can be understood, *can be determined*. This presupposes that the mind of the infant has a specific shape at a given point in time and that there is a relatively average expectable set of mental functions characteristic of that period of development. The concept of psychic determinism has already imposed firm clinical rigor in organizing the field's knowledge about older children; but such rigor has been slow to reach infancy. Normal indices of physical growth—such as continuing weight gain, increase in height, walking at the usual time, attaining gross motor function, such as skillful visual tracking behavior (first month), sitting (six months), and pincer gasp (nine months) —are frequently taken as indications that the child's general development is proceeding well enough. This position is often maintained despite whatever other symptoms, unusual behavior, or deviant development might be present. It is all too frequently assumed that no specific understanding (that is, no determination as to cause), no diagnosis, and no rationally conceived intervention is required when such landmark achievements are acquired. Thus serious psychological problems are often not recognized by anyone in the child's environment. Obviously, when problems are not recognized, no thought can be given to the resolution. In some ways society's present reluctance to have its sleep disturbed by notions that infants are more complex than mere cherubs recalls society's attitude to Sigmund Freud's publication of "Three Contributions to Theory of Sex" in 1905.

Typical signs of psychologic or psychophysiologic disturbances which often go unattended during infancy include the following.

Birth to One Month. Failure to gain weight (less than 1 ounce/day); excessive spitting up (more than two mouthfuls at a time); poor eye contact (the healthy, normal infant fixates and actively engages in visual reciprocity when alert); failure to hold head up; failure to show anticipatory behavior at feeding, failure to hold on with hands; ticlike movements of face and head.

Age Two to Three Months. Failure to thrive; indifference to social stimuli (e.g., human face, voice and play overtures); persistent hyperactivity and sleep disturbance; vomiting and diarrhea without physical illness; hyperresponsiveness or hyporesponsiveness to visual, auditory, movement, or other stimuli; turning away from person offering care, especially at feeding; excessive crying (i.e., three or more episodes of more than one hour each in twenty-four hours); inability to maintain sleep or wakeful attention (instability of state of consciousness).

Age Four to Six Months. Persistent sleep problem; hyperactivity and hyperresponsiveness wheezing without infection; lack of interest in social stimuli (preference and fascination with own body, such as fingers, hands); disinclination to assume sitting position spontaneously when awake; Excessive compulsive rocking of self in the presence of easily accessible familiar person (other than at night or when sick); failure or delay in recovery from illness or accident; excessive crying; inability to maintain sleep or attention.

Age Seven to Nine Months. Persistent sleep problems; eating problems (e.g., refusing to use hands or hold glass, refusing all but very familiar bland, soft food; unpatterned sleep and eating (lack of predictability); failure to imitate simple sounds, gestures, or facial expressions; lack of playfulness with familiar persons; lack of clear, affective expressions (i.e., anger, fear, joy, curiosity in appropriate context); bizarre play; poor socialization; absence of distress or caution when first meeting a stranger; excessive self-stimulation and self-destructive behavior; rumination (i.e., swallowing of regurgitated food); withholding of bowel movements; apathy; anaclitic depression; failure to recover from illness or accident; excessive crying, tongue thrust, and other oral habits.

Age Ten to Fifteen Months. No words or word sounds with distinctive meaning identifiable by mothering person; sleep problems—protracted or abbreviated; withdrawn behavior; excessive rocking; stereotypic posturing behavior; bizarre play (grossly unusual play patterns or highly unusual choice of play objects, lack of interest in or fear of new play objects); no distress on separation from mother in presence of stranger; night wandering; excessive distractibility (i.e., easily distracted); withholding of bowel movements; pica (eating nonfood substances, such as dirt, plaster, clay, paint, etc.); failure to make full psychosocial recovery from illness or accident; tongue thrust and other oral habits.

Age Sixteen Months to Two Years. No speech (i.e., no words associated with familiar objects or activities); excessive body rocking; inappropriate play; withholding and other bowel problems; sleep disturbance; retarded development or protracted regression in development in response to stresses such as illness, move, new baby, new persons in household; pica; failure to recover from illness or accident; tongue thrust and other oral habits.

Age Twenty-five Months to Three Years. Disturbed sleep due to persistent frightening dreams; persistent soiling and withholding of bowel movements; persistent eating problems; nonspeaking; inappropriate play; excessive fears of dark, ghosts, burglars, strangers; shyness; excessive body rocking, finger sucking, and tics; serious behavior problems (destructiveness, fighting, attacking, injuring animals, running away); pica; failure to recover from illness or accident.

The Therapeutic Attitude

The therapeutic attitude of the clinician is perhaps the most important feature of all remedies. This is especially true in approaching the treatment of disturbed infants and their families. In addition to an ultimate optimism derived from the adaptive point of view, the therapeutic attitude is characterized by a readiness to listen to parents and to others who have been involved in the life of the infant, a willingness to share questions with parents, a readiness for collaboration with the infant or child, his parents, and others, and above all, a readiness to understand, to remain open, and to be compelled by the data to formulate clinical hypotheses, to modify them, to give them up, and to replace them with other hypotheses as the inferences from data emerge. This therapeutic attitude comprises part of what is known as the "holding function" of the therapist. The capacity to hold within his mind all of the relevant information from the outside together with his own subjective feelings, impressions, and tentative clinical hypotheses is an essential aspect of the therapeutic attitude.

PRIMUM NON NOCERE

As in other medical situations, the clinician must respect the classical diction *primum non nocere* (first do no harm). He must fully appreciate the impact of his own role, including his appearance and his personality as an observer and as a participant, and must be ready to acknowledge that he has been experienced by the patient in the particular way—as the patient expresses it. The therapeutic attitude is one of honesty and candor as well as tact. Clinicians must develop great skill in brief, direct, as well as metaphorical communication designed to raise questions, stimulate thought, and reduce anxiety and guilt reactions, especially in parents. Examples of such communication are: "It must be difficult when your baby's help signals are not clear," "Some mothers I have known have gotten quite angry with their babies when they did that," and "I can tell from what you said that you felt quite embarrassed and guilty and blamed yourself for what happened." The therapeutic attitude allows the patient to make the discovery of what is needed, what belongs, and what does not belong in the therapeutic relationship.

The therapeutic relationship has its own special developmental history. The therapist feels his way along, creating with the patient what is needed. He is involved in the problems of infancy and seeks to apply his skills as the best of mothers does when she strives to integrate a system of communication with the infant. This does not mean that the therapist must win the infant over to his side or be liked and admired by either the parents or the infant. It does mean moving along bit by bit until an understanding, a feeling of balance between elements of trust and mistrust is reached. The end result will mean that the therapist is on cue, can reciprocate with the patient, maintains optimum distance, sometimes leads, sometimes follows in the affective exchanges, knows when to support and when to challenge, and finally learns the subtleties of the infant's and mother's physiological, affective, gestural, and word language.

Most of what has been mentioned thus far can be taught by example and by experience. First, however, the student's barriers to understanding must be adequately identified and resolved.

Breast Feeding as an Intervention in Infancy

There has been a renewed interest on the part of parent groups, educators, hospitals, pediatricians, nutritionists, immunologists, and public health officers the world over in encouraging mothers to breast feed their infants. This renewed interest has stemmed from the well-documented facts that mother's milk produces greater nutritional value, less complications with allergy and gastrointestinal disturbance, and greater protection against infection, particularly gastrointestinal infection and enterocolitis, than does formula. Breast-fed infants show a lower infant mortality rate, especially in high-risk situations (such as prematurity). The major literature on these and related issues has been summarized by Jelliffe.* Moreover, breast feeding is a significant aid to involution of the postpartum uterus. Breast feeding often provides for a closer relationship between mothers and infants, strengthens the development of the family, and provides a more intimate context for the development of future personal relationships.

La Leche League International was founded in 1956 by a group of seven women in Franklin Park, Illinois, who discovered their common interest in breast feeding. The league has since become an international movement now actrive in forty-two countries. The main focus of La Leche League International is on small discussion groups. There were, as of August 1, 1977,[35] 3,528 such groups and 11,865 La Leche–trained group leaders. The league has taken great interest in helping women successfully nurse their infants and has initiated group discussions for parents on infant care, established medical liaison help for physicians and hospitals, and begun to disseminate scientific information on the subject of breast feeding. The league has also developed relactation programs for adoptive parents and for mothers who for various reasons did not establish breast feeding or whose breast feeding was disrupted. Maternity nurses, physicians, public health officials, pediatricians, and general practitioners in the United States and other countries have sought the league's help in order to promote successful breast feeding.

Retrospective studies by Orlansky,[44] Davis,[16] and Sears[53] compared breast and bottle or cup

* See D. B. Jelliffe and E. F. D. Jelliffe, "The Uniqueness of Human Milk: An Overview," *American Journal of Clinical Nutrition,* 24:1013–1014, 1971.

feeding with regard to the development of undesirable personality characteristics[44] as shown on the Minnesota Multiphasic Personality Inventory,[16] by symptom check lists,[16] or by the incidence of oral habits (as listed by questionnaires given to mothers when the children were older). These studies, which suffered from many of the methodological pitfalls of retrospective research were not successful in demonstrating a lower incidence of such phenomena in breast-fed infants as compared to those cup- or bottle-fed. The attempt to test the efficacy of breast feeding from the psychological viewpoint utilizing such gross and remote, retrospectively organized outcome criteria now seems to beg the question. At the time these studies were done, longitudinal studies and prospective studies of infant development had not yet appeared, and much of what is now known of infant development was obscure. Hence, outcome criteria during infancy were not available. The studies were also conceptually weak because the hypotheses being tested were derived from erroneous conceptions of psychoanalytic theory.

Current clinical impressions and recent studies on mother-infant attachment and reciprocity would suggest that the benefitrs of breast feeding are clearly manifest during the period of infancy itself. For example, it has been shown that infants whose relationship with the mother has been disturbed in the first few days of life from any cause are at greater risk for neglect and abuse than infants whose relationship with the mother has not been disturbed. Breast feeding insures a close physiological and hence psychological bonding of infant to mother, and stands as a bulwark against disruption of the relationship during this vulnerable time. Also, for new mother successful breast feeding produces a sense of psychological intactness and functional capacity not unlike that derived from successful completion of pregnancy and delivery. Feelings of self-esteem, psychological competence, and readiness for a nurturant and devoted maternal role are in all probability based upon the underlying feeling of physiological intactness and healthy functioning. What emerges is the sense of an intact functioning bodily self. Thus, maternal self-esteem, competence, and the capacity to provide devoted care for the infant are all enhanced. It has been shown that most of the minor difficulties that tend to disrupt successful breast feeding can, in fact, be resolved by successful education, by psychosocial support from women and groups of mothers who have successfully nursed their infants, and by instruction and proper technique. However, many hospital services continue to engage in such discouraging and disrupting practices as supplemental bottle feeding,* lack of appreciation of rooting reflex in the infant as a means of nipple attachment, rigid schedules, administration of medication which blocks lactation, and disruption of breast feeding in the face of sore nipples and breasts. All of these situations can be remedied and should be remedied if successful nursing is to be promoted.

CASE ILLUSTRATION

Mrs. G, an eighteen-year-old welfare recipient, has been separated from her parents for many years. She had lived in several foster homes, none of which was satisfactory. She had not completed high school when she became pregnant by her current boyfriend. She was about to drop out of school and make arrangements for either abortion or adoption of her infant when she visited an aunt who took an interest in Mrs. G and her predicament. At the aunt's advice, Mrs. G continued in school and enrolled in prenatal classes and was actively encouraged to consider breast feeding. She was given La Leche League International reading materials, including "The Womanly Art of Breast Feeding," and she continued in high school where courses on infant care and parenting were provided. Mrs. G was interested in the *nutritional* aspects of prenatal care. Because of the known advantages of human breast milk, this correlated with her desire to nurse her infant. She read extensively on the nutritional advantages of human milk. She attended prenatal classes regularly, and developed a strong positive feeling for the instructor and for the medical care she was receiving. Her boyfriend renewed his interest in her. They were married at the sixth month of pregnancy. He too participated in the prenatal classes which included instructions in breast feeding and encouragement of mothers to breast feed. Her health and mood remained excellent throughout pregnancy. As delivery approached, Mrs. G was looking forward to the experience of nursing. Labor went smoothly and resulted in the birth of a healthy, full-term male infant with whom she made immediate and enthusiastic visual and bodily contact, including skin-to-skin nursing in the delivery room. Two days later, she was nursing and was progressing smoothly. She made use of the infant's spontaneous rooting behavior in effecting nipple attachment, and held her infant above the crook of the arm, close to her body, during nursing. She was already good at burping, and changing diapers. Although at two days Mrs. G was producing little milk, she was aware that the colostrum the infant was getting was rich in immunogobulins and provided protection against infection.

* Compared to the breast nipple, the bottle nipple is supernormal as an intraoral stimulus for sucking. Hence the bottle nipple is often preferred by the infant and the breast nipple rejected at the very time when sucking stimulation is very much needed to stimulate milk production and the milk-ejection reflex.

Mrs. G's age, unmarried status, lack of education, background of inadequate relations with parents, unsatisfactory foster-home care, and intention of aborting the pregnancy placed both the infant and the mother-child relationship in the high-risk category. Her pregnancy prompted her to visit the aunt, who encouraged Mrs. G to take care of herself and prepare to breast feed her infant. The idea of breast feeding had not occurred to Mrs. G previously, and may have induced within her a narcissistic identification with the infant; that is, she identified with the infant inside herself and became interested in physical needs and nutrition for its sake. She also projected herself into the nursing position; that is, she was (in unconscious fantasy) nursing herself as she imagined nursing her infant. It is doubtful if any of this would have been successful without the continued support of the aunt, who played out the nursing role with Mrs. G. The power and intimacy of the nursing relationship shown in three generations—aunt, mother, and infant—is all too novel in this epoch but quite commonplace before 1920. Contributing factors to the outcome included good prenatal care, preparation for childbirth, and a successfully negotiated marriage. Nursing served as an experience around which Mrs. G's mothering behavior could be organized. Her devoted concern and empathy for the infant could be developed on a narcissistic level. Perhaps this is a basic dynamic of devoted care which exists as a potential in all parents, and which could be utilized more often toward therapeutic goals. However, it is important to note that in less favorable circumstances, this is the kind of situation which could lead to neglect or abuse of the infant. One year followup showed continued nursing, a healthy mother-child relationship, and an infant developing well without a history of physical illness. Mrs. G's relationship with the aunt is still intact, although less intense than during the pregnancy. So far, the marriage seems to be going smoothly. Thus, this infant has traversed the most dangerous period of his life in the care of a mother who, by all demographic criteria available, would have been considered at-risk for deprivation, abuse, and desertion of her infant. The family is, incidentally no longer on welfare.

RELACTATION AS AN INTERVENTION

Mrs. D was a quiet but steady and attentive young woman, well educated and married to a professional older man. She had entered psychotherapy during pregnancy. When her infant, Cheryl, was four months of age, the problems and worries Mrs. D had described concerning the baby during therapy sessions led her therapist to make a referral. This was a planned pregnancy and delivery was uneventful. Jaundice, noticed on the second day of life, resulted in an additional day of hospitalization for tests, which did not reveal a specific cause for the illness. Breast feeding with supplemental bottle feeding seemed to go well at first, but in the second month of life the mother's milk supply began to drop off, and breast feeding was discontinued at the beginning of the third month.

On referral, Cheryl had gained only four ounces in the past month. Circumstances had not been optimal at home. The family had planned to move from an apartment to a newly constructed house at the time of Cheryl's birth. However, construction had been delayed so an interim move to a condominium was necessary during the early weeks of Cheryl's life. Mrs. D's mother, who had been twice hospitalized for depression during Mrs. D's infancy, discouraged her daughter from breast feeding with comments such as "You won't have enough." Mrs. D was not actively encouraged by anyone to nurse her child.

When seen at four months, Cheryl was a small, thin, quiet, somewhat limp little girl. Her maximum social response was a rather wan smile. Her head turned very slowly in the direction of the bell when it was sounded near her ear. The mother was encouraged to try playing with her. The child psychiatrist had been unsuccessful in getting Cheryl to respond enthusiastically to any stimulus. The response to the mother was no better. However, Mrs. D was able to offer her breast, and a delayed let-down* response was observed. Mrs. D held the baby quite loosely. She was able to establish eye contact with Cheryl.

Mrs. D also realized, in retrospect, that when breast feeding was begun, she was not able to feel comfortable nursing Cheryl because of construction workers in the home at the time.

Because of Cheryl's lack of vigor and slow development, together with her inadequate weight gain even on shift to formula feeding, relactation was recommended along with referral to the leader of the local relactation program developed by La Leche League International.† The rationale for recommending relactation was the conviction that both Cheryl and her mother might be able to effect a more intimate and satisfying personal relationship through exclusive breast feeding than had been achieved thus far. This was especially likely if someone in authority

---

* Milk let-down, or the milk ejection reflex, refers to the sudden flow of milk from the nipple. It is first induced by sucking on the nipple and occurs later in response to the infant's hungry cry, holding the infant, or psychic stimuli.

† The authors are indebted to the consultation and assistance provided here by Mrs. Anne McLaren, Medical Liaison Coordinator for Orange County of La Leche International and Volunteer Assistant to the Division of Child and Adolescent Psychiatry, University of California, Irvine, and to Mrs. Barbara Casey, of Long Beach, who has organized La Leche League's Relactation Program in Southern California. See also E. Hormann, "Relactation: A Guide to Breast Feeding the Adopted Baby," La Leche League International reprint, Franklin Park, Ill., 1971.

recommended it, and if psychosocial and educational support for relactation were offered by women who had been successful both in nursing their infants and in establishing firm bonds with them. It was felt that Mrs. D should have adequate models for development of successful nursing, attachment, and social interaction with her infant. The recommendation for relactation was discussed in detail with the parents and their pediatrician. Also, after detailed inquiries, it was recommended to the D's that they restructure their daily routine so as to allow more free time. It was further suggested that Mrs. D take Cheryl to bed with her while nursing. Mrs. D later said, "I was at first reluctant to take Cheryl to bed with me because of all the problems I had heard could result, like smothering the baby in sleep or promoting something which would be difficult to manage later. I needed my husband's approval to try it. The first time I took her to bed with me, she nursed and then we both fell asleep in bed for two hours." A good milk supply with lively let-down reflex was established by Mrs. D within two days. Ten days later, Cheryl was looking more lively and vigorous and had gained ten ounces. The D's were quite happy with the relactation program and with La Leche League discussion groups. Mrs. D continued her psychotherapy and sometimes brought Cheryl with her to the sessions.

At fifteen months, Cheryl was referred again by Mrs. D's therapist because Mrs. D had, for several weeks, seemed preoccupied with details of a business matter and had made little mention of Cheryl. At that time Cheryl appeared very much as she had on the first visit, underresponsive and affectively subdued. She had just begun to walk and did not have a single word in her vocabulary. It was again evident that Mrs. D was quite capable of playing with Cheryl but tended not to do so unless she had psychological support, modeling, and empathically organized direction. She was encouraged to reestablish communication with La Leche League and to find a mother-toddler's observation discussion group so she could discuss and better understand Cheryl's and her own development. Cheryl was about a month and a half behind in her developmental milestones, was still very small (seventeen pounds; twenty-nine inches), and was again without vigor.

Mrs. D was finally able to ask her mother indirectly about her mother's psychiatric hospitalization, and discovered that this had occurred when Mrs. D was three years old, not during the first two years as she had previously supposed. Mrs. D and her therapist had discovered that the estrangement she felt in assuming a nurturant and socializing role with Cheryl was related to her mother's depressive illness.

When Cheryl was seen again at eighteen and one-half months, she weighed twenty pounds, and was thirty inches in length, used six words consistently, could stack three cubes, could play pat-a-cake, was affectively lively, and could hold a pencil and make light random scribbles.

Weaning and Restitution. When solid foods were introduced into the diet at six months, breast feeding was reduced to four feedings per day. At one year, Mrs. D began the process of weaning by eliminating feedings preceding naps. Following the visit at fifteen months, Mrs. D followed through on the suggestions previously mentioned.

Cheryl had been weaned from her night feeding at sixteen and one-half months. Regarding this, Mrs. D commented, "The first night she cried a lot and I held her close and rocked her. She finally cuddled close and went to sleep. The second night she didn't cry as much and I felt she was going to accept it. Each night was easier. She went to sleep easily five or six nights later. I felt closer to her and cried. Every once in a while she makes a play for my breast by feeling my clothes with her fingers. She has eaten well and slept well since she was weaned. We went through it together and somehow I felt much closer to her. At the toddler's group, the teacher tried to get me to leave her without saying or waving good-bye. I told the teacher I couldn't do that to Cheryl. Weaning the way I did it really made a change in the way I felt with her. I felt much closer and it was easier to play with her and respond to her."

In this situation, the mother's psychological state at the time of Cheryl's early infancy could be related to factors in her own early child care, her nonsupport and disappointment stemming from the first years of life when her own mother had been depressed; direct discouragement of infant care and breast feeding by her mother; and a disrupted home setting. Mrs. D seemed unable to establish a firm physical or mental attachment to her infant on her own. She required continuous support for her mothering role. Cheryl's dramatic weight gain and better developmental performance following her first consultation at four and one-half months was due to the reinstitution of breast feeding in the context of psychosocial support from her husband and from mothers in La Leche League. Relactation, including breast feeding Cheryl in bed with her, had played a significant role in helping Mrs. D establish a physical and psychological bond and in enlivening the mother-child relationship. Simultaneous sleep in the mother and infant following the first breast feeding in bed signified the establishment of psychophysiological synchrony in the relationship.

In this case as in the case of Mrs. G, the mother's identification with her infant was facilitated through nursing. It became an avenue through which she could provide an abundance of care and allow the flow of loving feeling to take place between herself and her infant. One might ask whether for Mrs. D nursing provided a bulwark against repressed hostile feeling originally experienced in relation to her own mother, feelings which might be displaced to her infant. Early (four and one-half months) weaning may have exposed Mrs. D to the possibility of acting out such feelings with her infant. Physical distancing and psychological withdrawal may have served to prevent the possibility of acting out these unconscious, hostile feelings. The paradoxical situation in which Mrs. D ended up feeling closer and more comfortable with Cheryl when weaning was completed (at sixteen and one-half months) suggests a resolution of Mrs. D's object loss (the breast-mother) through mourning. Further in-depth case studies and research of the weaning process are very much needed.

Winnicott—Pioneer of Infant Psychiatry

Donald W. Winnicott began writing as a psychoanalytically oriented pediatrician, reporting his experiences with young infants, children, and their families in 1931. For the next forty years, as his psychoanalytic understanding of developmental processes deepened and broadened, he produced a richly textured mosaic of books and articles concerned with theory, treatment, consultation, and prevention at all ages. All of Winnicott's contributions were influenced by his long and deep experience with infants and their families. Like Spitz, Mahler, Erickson, Greenacre, Freud, and many other psychoanalysts, he extended his interest in infancy to the influence and meaning of infantile life as it continues on in the inner psychic life of older children and adults. The converse is also true. Winnicott's work with older children and adults has enriched our understanding of psychic life during infancy. His clinical work, imagery, and conceptualization have helped construct bridges from practice to theory, from genetic propositions to direct observation, and from psychopathological development to normality.

Winnicott's methods of intervention with disturbed infants can be summarized into three main categories: the ordinary, the devoted, and the good-enough holding mother concerned and preoccupied with her infant.* These categories can be used as a model for psychoanalysts, child psychiatrists, pediatricians, and others in orienting themselves to the psychological reality of infants.

Winnicott's conceptualization of transitional phenomena and transitional object attachments is

* Each of these carefully chosen, disarmingly simple adjectives—ordinary, devoted, good-enough, holding, concerned, preoccupied—have within Winnicott's writing acquired a carryover meaning from infancy to later life and from maternal attitudes and functions to therapeutic attitudes and functions.

a fundamental developmental issue in infancy with life-long relevance for psychic life.

Winnicott delineated the "set situaiton" in infancy as a means by which the infant psychiatrist may gain direct access to the mind of the preverbal child and communicate therapeutically with such a child.

Winnicott coined "set situation" as a generic term for any simple, natural, inexpensive, easily administered, interplay—with definition and structure—between infant, mother, and examiner that could elicit responses from an infant that demonstrated the infant's individual way of dealing with particular phase-specific developmental issues.

In his *Collected Papers*[73] a "set situation" which Winnicott described he considered to be a valuable means of eliciting "theme and variations." It involved having a given infant between five and thirteen months confront a person other than the mother who invites him to explore a somewhat novel and engaging item—a cereal bowl and tongue blade. The infant must negotiate the stranger's invitation while in full view and presence of mother. In Winnicott's judgment, for the infant the "outside world" was epitomized in the bowl-tongue blade apparatus and the stranger offering it. The child's response represented his qualitative orientation to that world.

Most infants *younger* than five months are not sufficiently coordinated to sit upright in mother's lap and use their hands to reach for the apparatus that their eye and mind seek. The upper age limit of thirteen months was designated because Winnicott found that beyond that age an infant typically is so fascinated by the world that the mere bowl and tongue blade can hold the baby's attention only briefly.

Winnicott explicitly challenged his readers (as clinicians) to devise additional such "set situations" that could enable "infant watchers" to visualize objectively the human infant's individual idiosyncratic ways of coping with an overlapping series of developmental gauntlets that confront all infants during the first two and one-half years of life.

Winnicott provides two clinical illustrations of how this set situation can be utilized in the service of therapy and of how inferences may be drawn to illustrate the nature of the child's intrapsychic life—his inner reality. The first case was that of an infant whom Winnicott had seen through a gastrointestinal disturbance in the first half year of life. The baby failed to recover, remaining irritable and unsatisfied, and eventually, "fits" developed. This little girl, then about nine months old, was unable to play, was irritable and negative in her responses to people. The "fits," which occurred several times a day, began at eleven months of age. Winnicott states that he took the child on his lap much in the way that he described in the set situation, except that he himself held the child. He saw her every few days for twenty minutes or so, giving her his full attention. While on his lap, she bit his knuckle on two separate days. She eventually began playing with the spatula, biting it and throwing it away, to be retrieved by Winnicott. Following this, she made a recovery, was cheerful, playful, and no longer ill. Fits ceased and a year later she was still well. Winnicott states, "the fluidity of the infant's personality and the fact that feelings and unconscious processes are so close in the early stages of babyhood make it possible for changes to be brought about in the course of a few interviews."

The second case in which Winnicott utilized the set situation in the service of direct therapy with the infant was that of Margaret, a seven-month-old infant, who had been breathing wheezily at night for some time. "Margaret seemed more comfortable with the father than with the mother, who herself had developed asthma when she became pregnant with Margaret and whose own mother was subject to asthma (which began when she became pregnant with Margaret's mother). Breast feeding was proceeding satisfactorily. Onset of asthma in Margaret had been preceded by a three-day period of screaming and trembling in her sleep. She had had a slight cough during that time. In the set situation, Margaret was initially interested in the spatula but unable to make up her mind to take it. Gradually she did take it, while showing a flow of saliva as seen during the second stage, as noted above. In the second consultation with Winnicott, Margaret again hesitated before reaching for the spatula and was excited when it was returned to her. She then threw it down again, brought it to her mouth, and dropped both spatula and bowl to the floor. She obviously wanted to bring the spatula in connection with the bowl, but then separated the two. Eventually, she banged the spatula on the bowl and made a lot of noise. On the two occasions when Margaret was hesitant in reaching for the spatula and bringing ti to her mouth, she was also anxious and began wheezing a little. At the moment she became confident in her handling of the spatula, wheezing ceased. Following the third consultation, she had no more asthma, and twenty-one months later Margaret was without asthma. Winnicott regards Margaret's hesitation in reaching for the spatula as

an indication of anxiety and as "a superego manifestation." He acknowledges the influence of the mother's anxious attitude, but suggests that Margaret's hesitation in reaching for the spatula signified that she expected to produce an angry or perhaps revengeful response in the mother to her (Margaret's) greedy feelings; thus Winnicott reasons that Margaret must have had in mind the notion of an angry mother. In support of this, Winnicott quotes Freud's statement from *Instincts and Their Vicissitudes*: "the external danger must have been managed to become internalized if it is to be significant for the ego." "The idea that infants have fantasies," says Winnicott,[66]

is not acceptable to everyone, but probably all of us who have analyzed children at two years have found it necessary to postulate that even an infant of seven months, like the baby with asthma whose case I have already quoted, has fantasies. These are not yet attached to word presentations, but they are full of content and rich in emotion, and it can be said that they provide the foundation on which all later fantasy life is built. [pp. 60–61]

Winnicott suggests that breathing out (expiration) might have been felt by the baby to be dangerous —linked to a dangerous idea—for instance, an idea of reaching in to take (the breath as an extension of the mouth or hand). To the infant so closely in touch with his mother's body and the contents of the breast which he actually takes, the idea of reaching into the mother's breast is by no means remote, and fear of reaching into the inside of the mother's body could easily be associated in the baby's mind with not breathing. Thus, for Winnicott, a breath or breathing could be the expression of a strong feeling of taking which could be dangerous. Breathing itself could be dangerous once connected with the infant's fantasies. Margaret feared the mother's anger because of what she had projected into the mother. As a result, her own greed had become all the more voracious. Prior to the onset of asthma, the gastrointestinal illness had resulted in feelings of deprivation. All this became part of mother rage.

COMMENT

In both clinical illustrations provided by Winnicott, failure to convalesce from bodily illness played a significant role in symptom formation. Winnicott's capacity to hold and to convey a holding attitude, to endure the infant's oral rage, and to reassure the infant by not retaliating in response to the infant's raging emotions (greedy feelings) were key features to the treatment approach.

A graphic synopsis of infant responses to the set situation is provided in the accompanying illustration, which is based upon Reiser's experience with more than three hundred infants in a six-year period (1971–1977). Some of these infants were presented the same "set situation" at monthly or bimonthly intervals as they passed through their fifth through thirteenth month, revealing both idiosyncratic and constant aspects of their perception, integration, and response to the developmental issues implicit in the set situation.

Figure 28-1 depicts the examiner presenting a cereal bowl and tongue blade, which was substituted for Winnicott's "silver spatula," to infant sitting on the mother's lap. Examiner is seated at right angles, and endeavors to restrain his voice, expression, and posture so that they would not cue and influence. Mother is asked to be similarly restrained during the set situation.

FIGURE 28–2

FIGURE 28–1

FIGURE 28–3

In figure 28-2, the infant visually engages the bowl and tongue blade, usually restraining the initial impulse to reach for it immediately. Infant examines the examiner, apparently inviting his encouragement and mandate to pick up the items.

In figure 28-3, the infant looks away from the bowl-and-donor stimulus, turning head upward to engage mother's face.

The infant may endeavor to "seduce" and/or elicit "soundings" from the bowl's donor (the examiner) with social smile and other beguiling gestures. In this context, examiner must exercise self-discipline and respond somewhere between the extremes delineated by the late Beata Rank of "neither being so intrusive as to be seductive; nor so inert and unresponsive as to be boorish."

In figure 28-4, the infant reveals mounting in-

470

terest by increased salivation and mouthing movements. The crucial quartet of the infant's "eye, mouth, hand, and ego," as designated by the late Willie Hoffer,* may not initially respond in harmonious concerted and integrated fashion. Permutations and combinations among these may reflect uncertainty and conflict. For example, in this figure, *mouth* drools "yes, do it, hold it, mouth and explore it," while *eyes* gaze away from the stimulus.

FIGURE 28–4

In figure 28-5 the infant responds for a period of up to many minutes by avoiding looking at either bowl or examiner.

FIGURE 28–5

In figure 28-6, the infant places fingers in mouth, gazing at examiner with uncertainty.

In figure 28-7 the infant looks away from the bowl, points away, and with other hand touches, strikes, or otherwise "activates" bowl and tongue

* See W. Hoffer, "Mouth, Hand, and Ego Integration," in Eissler, R. S., et al. (Eds.), *The Psychoanalytic Study of the Child*, vol. 3/4, pp. 49–55, International Universities Press, New York, 1949.

blade, then responds as if they were novel materials that suddenly just arrived by means *other* than the stranger-examiner. Winnicott[66] delineated the first phase of this set situation as encompassing the period from examiner's presenting the bowl until the infant picks it up.

FIGURE 28–6

FIGURE 28–7

The second phase includes the wide range of manipulations, gamelike, wandlike, and toollike use of the tongue blade, as well as the myriad ingenious ways the infant invents to bring bowl and blade together (as well as to separate them).

Figures 28-8 and 28-9 depict the characteristic bilateral mirroring style of repeating manipulations by right hand with the left, and vice versa.

As shown in figure 28-10, games that stimulate

feeding self, then mother, and sometimes including feeding of the examiner are common.

Figure 28-11—"Gamelets" or "playlets" appear; these are characterized by pointing *away* with the blade, while holding the bowl near, and vice versa.

In figure 28-12, having extensively explored and played with bowl and blade, the infant briefly disengages all contact, then usually repeats the entire episode of acquisition and exploration: doing/undoing; hello/goodbye.

As figure 28-13 depicts, some infants appear to rehearse holding the bowl and blade over the empty space, with floor below, repeating the sequence of placing them as if to drop, then "saving or rescuing" with a flourish, often accompanied by flashes of pleasure. Inevitably, either bowl or

FIGURE 28–8

FIGURE 28–9

FIGURE 28–11

FIGURE 28–10

FIGURE 28–12

FIGURE 28–13

blade will be dropped, followed by concentration on the remaining item. There may be some constriction of prior bravado, as if sobered and thoughtful following loss of the dropped item. Whether by accident or intention, ultimately both blade and bowl are dropped, concluding the second phase. There may be another brief period of looking away, as if ignoring the loss, followed by phase three, when the infant shows his awareness of the loss, with vocalizations, affective signals that suggest distress, and leading to the scene depicted in figure 28-14, where there is a physical attempt to go after the dropped items, according to the infant's age and degree of neuromuscular coordination. In the five-to-thirteen-month period, many infants lunge after the lost objects, as if oblivious of gravity.

Some infants, as the one depicted in figure 28-15, endeavor to "make the best of what remains,"

FIGURE 28–14

initiating tabletop pounding games and playing with the table cover. When efforts to retrieve bowl and blade fail, or are curtailed, most infants begin to cry, reach back to touch the certainty of mother's breasts, and/or look up to engage mother's face, and may turn around and crawl on her lap, with gestures inviting her embrace.

FIGURE 28–15

Other case studies in infant psychiatry are presented briefly by Winnicott as follows: One-year-old Maisie displayed compulsive rocking and many birth fantasies. Her symptoms were resolved by the utilization of transference interpretations around her anxiety, which stemmed from the mother's pregnancy and Maisie's fear of harming the mother. Queenie, age three, daughter of a charwoman, was referred because of stealing, and was seen two to three times a week for six months. Winnicott interpreted the child's fantasies around penis envy and violent attacks upon the mother's body in relation to primal-scene experience.

Call[11] has reported previously on the treatment of an eighteen-month-old child who was referred because of biting. The boy had experienced several losses and discontinuities of care. Biting was understood and interpreted as the child's way of becoming a "big baby boss" who could hold onto things by biting. At home the child played out his wish to be a big baby boss, told his mother of his wish, and gave up his symptom of biting.

Reiser has made videotape segments of an adopted Indian child at seven, eight and one-half, ten, and twelve months of age, showing her changing response to the Winnicott set situation over that period. On each of these segments each time she dropped the bowl she is shown almost "taking a dive" for the floor out of her adoptive mother's arms. Also apparent in the adoptive mother's response to the child is her own unmourned, unmetabolized grief. The adoptive mother had suffered a severe narcissistic wound, stemming from her longed-for child, her infertility, and her awareness of "the child she herself would not have." This interfered with her relating to the adopted child. Thus, in the videotape the mother's earlier narcissistic wound, her inability to hold the child adequately, and the child's uncertainty about being held are shown. It was discovered that the Indian child had been unsupported in her own home before foster placement. It could not be establiehed whether, in fact, she was literally physically dropped; situationally, however, she was unsupported. It also came to light that in her Indian foster home, she suffered burns on one leg from a defective heating pad. This knowledge repulsed and distressed the adoptive mother and was an affront to her feminine narcissism. She stated, "It will embarrass her when she goes to the beach or when she is married." Thus, the adopted child is burdened with the adoptive mother's displacement of her own conflicts and distress about childlessness, about having a baby to show feminine fullness and completeness. Being female and childless was, in this woman, tantamount to being crippled and castrated.

Finally, the parents were confronted with these issues, particularly the grief of not having a child to show. Afterward, at thirteen months, the child embellished her predictable kamikaze dive to the floor and turned unexpected nonsupport into a game more under her own management and control, according to the repetition compulsion. After wriggling to the floor, she sat with her back adjacent to the drape that extended over the edge of the table. She would pretend to fall backward into the drape as if it were a wall, then catch herself before toppling over backward, and then return to the full sitting position, smiling with those who had observed her pretend fall modified to a "no-fall."

JOSHUA—CASE ILLUSTRATION

Joshua, a fifteen-month-old well child, was seen prior to a scheduled hernia repair. His mother, aware that Josh might be more afraid if he did not comprehend what was happening at the hospital, asked Reiser to devise some play cameos that might help the boy rehearse the "stage actions" and expectable thoughts and feelings as he might encounter them.

Utilizing small play figures, Josh, mother, and therapist sat on the floor as the therapist took initiative to play out going to the hospital, separating from his mother, being held by strangers in white, then rejoining his mother and returning home. The therapist presented phrases appropriate to the play sequences. The condensed "script," improvised on the spot, included the mother doll saying, "Bye, bye, Josh. The nurse will take you to the doctor now." Josh (via therapist) cries, "Mommy, mommy! Don't let me go! I want to stay with you! I can't see you if I go with the nurse! I'm scared! I feel like crying and crying! I'm mad at you, mommy!"

Mother's lines included, "I'm not going away, Josh. I'll be right here when the nurse and the doctor bring you back after he makes your tummy better. I know you are scared. I know you are mad at mommy, 'cause you want me to keep holding you, and I won't go away and I won't leave you 'cause you're mad at me," and so on.

After the initial demonstration, mother took over the play production improvising the themes in her words. Josh watched the dramas intently. Mother was instructed to help Josh hold the figures in subsequent repetitions of the drama, with mother supplying the vocal "sound track" for herself and Josh.

At meetings of the American Academy of Child Psychiatry in 1975, Nelson[42] demonstrated what many mothers, "baby watchers," and psychiatrists studying infancy have long postulated: that the human infant's capacity to *comprehend* verbal communication is present long before the infant is capable of originating words, phrases, and sentences. Josh's vocabulary was limited at the time of the operation, but in play he replicated rudiments of the therapist's original Josh-goes-to-the-hospital drama. It was considered an indicator that he had come comprehension of the actual hospitalization to follow.

He was told, "You'll feel like crying when the nurse picks you up." Subsequent versions of the play were repeated; both mother and Josh contributed elaborations. Josh's recovery from the hernia repair was uneventful. Follow up for sixteen months afterward revealed no symptomatic evidence of residual anxiety discernible in his sleep, eating patterns, mood states, or social relations.

An incidental product of the play sequence outlined above was Joshua's identifying one of the play objects, a toy helicopter, with the doctor. In anticipation of well-baby visits, Joshua would refer to the helicopter as "doctor." Although Joshua had played with the helicopter during several prior well-baby conference visits, his intensified clutching of it during the presurgical preparation session prompted the doctor to give it to him "for keeps." Fifteen months later it was still his constant companion, transitional object, used inventively and adaptively.

RUTH—CASE ILLUSTRATION

Ruth, twelve months old, developed an eye-blinking and squinting tic after hospitalization for umbilical hernia which was elective and cosmetic. No psychological preparation for hospitalization was considered for Ruth by either her parents or her pediatrician. The tic was noted in the course of well-child conference four days after surgery.

It was decided to utilize the play situation in order to abreact the traumatic aspects of the hospital experience. The play drama was enacted on the floor after Ruth had become comfortable with the doctor. Utilizing a mother doll, a baby doll, a nurse doll, and a small automobile and blocks for home and hospital, the central issues in the drama of separation from mother, hospital care, and reunion were articulated in the presence of the mother. The therapist gave a monologue as if it were Ruth's thoughts and feelings. It was spoken slowly, sensitive to Ruth's attention and affectomotor responses. The "script" was somewhat as follows. "Here we go to the hospital in the car, bye-bye home, bye-bye mama, here's the nurse, I'm scared." The baby doll is then covered with a tissue. A bandage is applied to the abdomen under the tissue. Ruth is invited to pull the tissue away and discover the bandage. The baby cries, "Where are you mama, where are you? I can't see you." Then the baby doll says to the mama doll, "I couldn't find you, I couldn't see you." Ruth's response to this is to pick up the mama and baby dolls, hold them closely together, kissing each other, and then to separate them with "bye-bye," and then to reunite them again. This same sequence was dramatized at home several times with the mother's participation, and on Ruth's initiative. The tic cleared after only one visit. Follow up through eighteen months of age showed no further symptoms or other difficulties.

This approach, based as it was on a postulated traumatic experience of recent origin, could be designated "Band-aid therapy," a simple, abbreviated "stitch in time." It is important to emphasize that Ruth's demanding, angry feelings required recognition and acceptance by the mother. It is impressive how simple and therapeutic it is for the therapist to express, *in the mother's and infant's presence*, a burdensome secret,—for example, that the child sometimes feels very angry at mother— and then that the mother *knows* of the child's fury and that they will continue their relationship. The play sequence dramatized this element for both Ruth and her mother so that the unresolved negative side of the ambivalence and self-condemnation (which so often underlies grieflike symptomatology) in such situations could be undone. The importance of this basic issue is reflected in the Psalms where Supplicant says, "turn thy face from my sins and renew a right spirit within me," (or, God, please don't look at my anger).

CORAL—CASE ILLUSTRATION

Nineteen-month-old Coral had persistent screaming and night terrors for five days after the death of her mother at home from cancer. She had witnessed her mother's suffering for nine months.

During initial introductions to therapists, as father held Coral in his arms, Coral scanned their faces and the toys in the room. She protested with a distressed cry when father tried to place her on the floor.

The therapists established an atmosphere intended to be safe for Coral by not moving in intrusively or violating her tempo and integrity, and by affirming her father's accessibility, as he sat with them on the

floor. She could return to his arms when she wished, or when play themes threatened her. These measures respected the principle that an infant will countenance someone or something new after he first discovers how to "turn them off," to prevent being overwhelmed. It then becomes safe to dare to "turn them on," under the infant's regulation.

In a style different from the aforementioned active play interventions (with well-baby clinic children to whom these workers had become familiar figures for months prior to their respective crises), with Coral, the therapists' therapeutic usefulness was mainly in tuning in, observing carefully, and recognizing her concerns as they emerged.

Separation was a constant theme which Coral spontaneously played out by: (1) dropping the dolls to the floor and out of sight, then retrieving them; (2) fitting together nesting cups, then taking them apart, then together, then apart, and so on, for a long series; (3) using the cups to hide, or cover over, dolls, then removing a cup, permitting the dolls to reappear. These sequences were accompanied by Coral gradually separating herself from her father's lap. Coral then (4) covered a doll with a blanket up to its chin. Then she covered it completely, including head, then abandoned the covered doll as she went to other interests. Coral appeared to devote herself in her own play, giving no evidence of listening to her father describe the mother's illness for the therapists. When he mentioned an incident the previous day of taking Coral to see mother's grave, Coral cried out with a wail, arched her back, and struck his mouth with the back of her hand. He stopped talking, hugged her, and said tenderly that he knew she was sad about mother dying. Then she resumed her play.

The usefulness of therapy may have been in responding to this child's natural inclination and capacity to play out what was occupying her mind. Perhaps by nineteen months, an infant has enough play skills to be able to utilize play to express his own concerns. The observant therapist can enhance the infant play by translating the infant's silent, subtle, internal messages into words, making comprehensible to the infant and to others in the his life that which has not been expressed, acknowledged, or comprehended.

MARCIA—CASE ILLUSTRATION

Marcia, age seventeen months, was referred from Protective Services. At ten and one-half months of age, she had been scalded with hot water by her mother and companions who had been high on psychedelic drugs. Marcia had a fear of all household water. In terror, she avoided bathrooms in both her foster and adoptive homes. The scalding incident was reconstructed (according to the therapist's intuitions and the fragmentary information available) in a fashion analogous to therapeutically working through a traumatic neurosis, utilizing dolls and blocks. As with Josh and his mother, Marcia and her adoptive mother viewed the therapist's "modeling" performance of the trauma drama, with verbalizations that the ten and one-half-month-old child did not say but conceivably felt. The dramatic "scenario" included the combinations of fear about mother's unavailabiilty, pain at being scalded, fear and fury at original mother for letting it happen and not making her tormentors stop. The script included community caretakers removing Marcia and taking her to a foster home where she wouldn't be hurt, scared, or made angry. Symptoms of water fears and night terrors ceased, and sustained improvement followed in the constancy of her adoptive home.

Several young children attending the Granite Mental Health Center in Salt Lake City were helped by anticipatory preventive intervention, utilizing play with the child participating and the therapist modeling via speech and play for both child and parent. Play with such young children cannot be adequately described in words, but apparently it can lead to symptom resolution.

One must ask how and why the Winnicott techniques work therapeutically. The question is how such dramatic play resolves symptoms, increases ego strength, and allows normal development to proceed.

Winnicott[66] postulates:

What there is of therapeutics in this work lies, I think, in the fact that the *full course of an experience is allowed*. From this one can draw some conclusions about one of the things that go to make a good environment for the infant. In the intuitive management of an infant, a mother naturally allows the full course of the various experiences, keeping this up until the infant is old enough to understand her point of view. She hates to break into such experiences as feeding or sleeping or defecating. In my observations I artificially give the baby the right to complete an experience which is of particular value to him as an object lesson.

In psycho-analysis proper there is something similar to this. [p. 67]

FOUR FEELING FACES

The following case is presented to demonstrate a technique for eleicting affect-laden information from a very young child.

Alice, age two years eleven months, was brought to the clinic by her extremely anxious young father. She had been living with him for the past six months, following his removal of Alice from her mother. Since birth, Alice had been moved among primary and extended family members at three- to four-month intervals. She saw her mother regularly during these moves, but had developed a very close attachment to an adult female cousin for three months prior to father's removal. The father felt Alice was "too dependent" upon this cousin. After she came to live with her father, Alice cried for her cousin for two months and then stopped asking about her. Symptoms which prompted the father to bring Alice to the clinic included loss of appetite, prolonged crying spells, and day and nighttime terrors of being killed by one of her mother's boyfriends.

Alice was a physically healthy but very subdued child. Despite precocious verbal skills, she was unable to talk about any recent fears, experiences, or her multiple caretakers. In her father's presence, she responded to his requests to show where she had been hurt by her mother's friend. Alice clearly expressed extreme fear. She cried violently and her whole body trembled at the mention of the names of her mother's friends, but she recovered quickly by attempting to put puzzles together.

In an effort to help establish a climate where feelings could be addressed, Alice was asked to sit beside the therapist, who drew "four feeling faces," developed by Reiser, shown in figure 28–16. These 2-dimensional, diagrammatic illustrations can be easily mastered by any therapist. The technique is designed to help a child indicate feelings, and talk about when such feelings are aroused in himself and his family members and how the feelings are expressed and responded to (e.g., "What makes mommy feel angry?" "When you feel like this"—pointing to crying face—"what makes you feel happy again?")

Alice could identify the first three faces as "happy," "crying," and "frowny." The fourth, the therapist labeled as "scared." With this simple vocabulary of affects, Alice could explore her experience: candy made her happy; saying good-bye made her cry; being spanked made her frowny, and nighttime made her scared. She would answer no questions about other people in her life, so to elicit information, the therapist drew three houses below the "four feeling faces" in order to help her focus on the people with whom she had spent most of her life. When the therapist pointed to the first house, asking "Who lives here?" Alice did not answer. The therapist declared, "Daddy lives here." The therapist then drew in a stick figure without facial features. The therapist next asked, "Who lives with daddy?" Alice answered, "I do." So, the therapist drew in a smaller stick figure. They proceeded to the next house. Again, Alice declined to name the inhabitants. The therapist asked if this could be "Mommy's house?" She nodded yes, adding, "And Johnny lives there too." When the third house was pointed to, Alice volunteered that it was the house of her favorite cousin and husband. Each house now contained stick figures.

The therapist returned to the "four feeling faces" above, asking Alice to label them again. "Now," Alice was told, "let's make faces for everyone." "What kind of face shall me make for daddy?" Alice pointed to the happy face. For herself, she pointed to the scared face. As she pointed, the therapist drew in the requested face. She asked for a frowny face for Johnny. She watched carefully as an angry face was drawn. Suddenly she began trembling, then crying, then abruptly said, "No, he's really happy." Of especial significance was her refusal to designate expressions for either her mother or her favorite cousin.

By this time, Alice was leaning comfortably against the therapist as they sat on the floor. Her

FIGURE 28–16

subdued affect had lifted as she engaged in the drawing and conversation. They were then able to talk of the loss of significant people, the many unexplained moves, the fact that no one knew how Alice was feeling, and that Alice's real terror came from experiencing angry feelings in the absence of anyone who could understand or protect her.

The recommendation from this first interview was to restore to Alice direct access to her favorite cousin. Though treatment continued for many months, the presenting symptoms disappeared within two weeks of being moved back to her cousin's home.

Further pursuit of these questions leads to the burgeoning literature on play, some of which is summarized in two recent books, *Play*, a collection of articles from the literature edited by Jerome Bruner, Allison Jolly, and Kathy Sylva,[7] and the volume entitled *Play and Development*, with contributions by Jean Piaget, Peter Wolff, Rene Spitz, Konrad Lorenz, Lois Barclay Murphy, and Erik Erikson, edited by Maria Peers.[46] Both Erikson[22] and Winnicott[60] emphasize the relationship of play to drama and the capacity of play to capture inner experience by making it visually manifest and hence to actualize it. Winnicott emphasizes that inner experience can be represented in playing "when reflected and only when reflected back" and "enables the person to postulate the existence of the self." He states[60]:

this gives us our indication for a therapeutic procedure, to afford opportunity for formless experience and for creative impulses, motor and sensory, which are the stuff of playing. . . . On the basis of playing is built the whole of man's experiential existence. No longer are we either introvert or extrovert. We experience life in the area of transitional phenomena, in the exciting interweave of such activity and objective observation, and in the area that is intermediate between the inner reality of the individual and the shared reality of the world that is external to individuals. [p. 64]

The presently available diagnostic labels for the psychological and psychophysiological disturbances of infancy are inadequate.

Perhaps all these young subjects are suffering in various ways and to various degrees from a fragmentation in the sense of self. If so, reconstruction and/or construction of a sense of self should be the goal of therapy with infants. To do so requires the construction of play space, both internally and externally, and a reflecting back by attitudes, by participation, by the holding attitude. These, the therapeutic tools of the infant psychiatrist, can lead as well as to more specific diagnosis.

Early Intervention with Infants Showing Autistic Behavior

It is now possible to delineate specific behaviors at several developmental levels throughout infancy which mark the onset of "autism." This achievement is the result of accumulated direct clinical experience with young infants showing autistic behavior, of retrospective reconstruction of early development derived from film studies (Massie, 1975), and of some prospective studies of such infants. Several infant studies have now been reported, including those of Massie,[41] Call,[13] Galenson,[28] and Brazelton.[5] In 1957, Call[13] encountered two instructive cases. One case concerned a three-month-old who was showing several signs of withdrawal, lack of reciprocity, and failure to evolve the normal smiling response. The pathology in this case was found to reside largely in the mother-infant interaction. There was a failure of reciprocity, a failure of eye contact, and depressive withdrawal in the mother, which were found to be a defense against underlying feelings of anger and hostility. The therapist verbalized manifest behavior in the infant, and helped the mother express her concerns about herself and the infant. The therapist spoke to the mother through the infant, modeled behavior for holding and infant care, supplied affective stimulation and group support for the mother, and employed a multidimensional psychoeducational approach. This turned out to be successful. Within a few weeks the infant began developing normally. This child is now twenty-two years of age, and is attending college, enjoying a full developed social life, and carrying on part-time work in the family business. In the second case, the child, Glenn, was first seen at two and one-half years of age. He showed fully blossomed developmental deviation due to autism. No speech was present. Gutteral /r/ and /g/ sounds were used in a mechanical way without affect. Behavior patterns were rigidly structured, repetitious, and characterized by stereotypies such as opening and closing doors, turning light switches off and on, and mechanical manipulations of a similar kind. Human contacts were avoided. Eye contact was vacuous. No daily routine of naps, meals, sleep, or play time was established. Treatment techniques were directed toward both Glenn and his family. Particular attention was paid to the mother, whose obsessional-schizoid character traits and schizoid withdrawal covered over a lifetime of intensely hostile feelings which were displaced and concentrated on to the child. Specific treatment techniques utilized with Glenn included dramatization of a play sequence which reenacted one of the major traumatic episodes in his life. In the play, his mother is going to the hospital to give birth to Glenn's younger sister. This occurrence had preceded his regression in language and social behavior and the onset of asthma at eight-

een months. Following this play session, Glenn's light switching, opening and closing rituals, and asthma ceased.

On the basis of some twenty home movies of deviant infants subsequently diagnosed as autistic, Henry Massie[41] developed a scale of attachment indicators which can be applied during the first twenty-one months of life in the course of well-baby care. These indicators may help differentiate between normal and autistic children.

Irving N. Berlin[4] has reported on successful intervention with an autistic child at age two. Galenson[28] has developed an intervention program for infants showing early autistic behavior, and Ruttenberg[51] has developed a multidimensional instrument, the BRIAC interdisciplinary approach, that he has applied to a group of children predisposed by virtue of pregnancy and birth history to autism and to other developmental deviations.

Many years of work with blind infants and their families have prepared the way for Selma Fraiberg[25] and her child development group at the University of Michigan to conceive and establish a unique child development project which unites clinical services for the mental health treatment of children from birth to age three.[24] Training for such work has emphasized detailed studies of normal and deviant development in infancy, utilizing the case-study method, observation of nondeviant infants, and carefully supervised clinical work with disturbed infants and their families. Fraiberg and her group have studied over 150 children in this age group. She emphasizes thorough diagnostic assessment reflected in the light of normal developmental processes, home visits, and emphatic organization of all clinical and developmental data. A sensitive attentiveness to the needs and psychology of the mother, including her past history, is required. In several case illustrations, Fraiberg demonstrates the utility of such techniques as speaking to the mother through the infant, addressing the infant's needs as if they were the mother's needs, providing direct social and psychological support for the mother, utilizing the strengths of the father, and recognizing and responding to stressful situations in a timely way in the home situation.

Sally Provence[48] has long been identified as a basic researcher in issues of early infant development. During the past few years, she has established an alternative group living situation for infants who might otherwise have been exposed to intermittent foster care and institutional placement. Emde[21] demonstrated the prolonged nature of the grief reactions and narcissistic injuries suffered by parents of Down's Syndrome children. He has shown that once such injuries have been dealt with, adequate parenting behavior and family functioning can be established.

Nonempathic Mothering:
A View from the Kneecap

The interface of the mother-infant relationship is intricate and emanates from the mother's past experience and the infant's unique characteristics. In confronting the nature-nurture controversy at this level, one should not be preoccupied with proving that one or the other of these influences is most vital in molding human development. Investigation of exogenous and endogenous factors in development are not a matter of "either/or," but rather one of attempting to assign proper roles to each influence. This case illustrates how a behavior problem in a twenty-month-old infant evolved and is related to the effect of prematurity on the course of development of mother and infant.

It is well known that there is a close relationship between prematurity and the subsequent appearance of behavior disorders. For example, Drillien[19] Pasamanick and Knobloch,[45] and Rubin, Rosenblatt, and Balow[50] have reported that premature infants have a high incidence of subsequent behavior disorders. In these and other studies, the correlation made between these two occurrences is essentially statistical. What has not been shown is whether or not they are causally related, and if so, in what manner. A single case study with a psychodynamic focus is presented here to explore some mechanisms of a behavior disorder in a toddler who was born prematurely.

CASEY—CASE ILLUSTRATION

Casey was a twenty-month-old infant who did not receive what Winnicott termed good-enough mothering. Two outstanding features were noted in Casey's mother: a striving for independence and the experience of repeated emotional traumata before and after this child's premature birth. The severity of perinatal problems shaped the nature of their relationship.

The nuclear family included the natural parents; a brother two and one-half, thirteen months older than Casey; a six-year-old half-sister; and an eleven-year-old half-brother, the latter two children from the mother's previous marriage.

Casey was transferred to the Children's Psychiatric Ward from the pediatric ward of the Orange County Medical Center (now the UCI Medical Center) after they had exhausted their resources. The original admission was for uncontrollable behavior. This had been present for six weeks and was exacerbated by an upper respiratory infection. The mother had expressed to the pediatrician a fear that she might hurt the child. There were times when he was uncontrollable; on such occasions he banged his head, threw himself at furniture, and hit himself with toys. Several superficial abrasions were present on his forehead, presumably from this behavior. Skull X-rays were negative. In the month prior to admission he woke up four times each night. Casey's parents felt that he was "snapping out," and that he was "unable to find peace within himself to rest." Other stresses were: mother's thrombophlebitis, the family's marginal financial status, and the presence of two competitive children, Casey and the brother thirteen months his elder.

The nature of the pregnancy played a significant role in the mother's psychological adaptation to her infant. She became aware of an unplanned pregnancy at four and one-half months' gestation. Recounting her husband's feelings upon learning of the pregnancy, she stated, "I had a feeling he didn't, he couldn't communicate his feelings to me, and we went our separate ways." She was aware of the pregnancy for a total of only two months; the last month was spent in a hospital with vaginal bleeding, secondary to placenta previa. She was told that "More than likely the baby would not live." When he was born two and one-half months prematurely, weighing 1,630 grams (3.6 pounds), she recalled being told, "It is touch and go." His APGAR was 4 at 5 minutes. In the hospital there were numerous medical complications, including respiratory distress, hyperbilirubinemia (with a bilirubin level of 23 mgs percent by the third day), hypocalcemia, and an episode of respiratory arrest. Casey remained in the hospital thirty-four days and had six admissions in the subsequent three months. His parents visited daily, but interaction was limited by his medical condition. Casey was five months old before clothes or furniture were purchased for him.

On the child psychiatry ward, he was a personable twenty-month-old infant, interested in and responsive to his environment. He made an immediate attachment to a nurse and contentment was evident when he was on her lap or near her. In view of the history, this was not anticipated. A Denver Developmental Screening Test,[27] adjusted for prematurity of two and one-half months, placed him at an age-appropriate level. However, he was at the thirty-fifth percentile for height and the third for weight. He was nearing an age when language could be implemented as a tool to cope with his environment more effectively. Nearing but not attaining this developmental milestone contributed to his frustrations, as he could not verbally communicate needs. In consequence, empathy on the part of a caretaking person was important. An analogous situation had occurred when he was sixteen months old. At that time he was almost walking, but wasn't; now he was almost speaking, but couldn't. His mother reported hat he had been tense and irritable while on the verge of walking. These symptoms were similar to those precipitating this admission. In the orthopedic clinic, he could stand, but one foot was everted. Orthopedic boots were obtained and he walked within two days. The behavior disturbance abated. It therefore seemed that, for Casey, nearing attainment of a developmental task, such as walking or talking, was a symptom-producing situation.

There was a history of respiratory difficulties which included asthma; in the father's opinion, this was related to emotional problems. In one situation, his father was convinced Casey had "given himself an asthmatic attack."

A description of the mother's personality and childhood sheds light on her interaction with Casey. An independent style of functioning was evident in many areas of her life. (Independence refers to self-reliance and denial of feelings.) With the death of her parents at thirteen years of age, she felt a need for independence. (Currently she lives far from her brothers and sisters.) Her first marriage was to a man in the navy who was at sea much of the time. Their separation caused further isolation. In a family session with her second husband present, she spoke of the children from her first marriage specifically as "my children," and made their separateness all too clear. In this session, the self-control demonstrated by these children was suggestive of the mother's personality. Her need for autonomy and reaction against dependence led her to refuse a recommended hospital admission for acute thrombophlebitis. This style of functioning was demonstrated with Casey, when she expected him to perform at a level of individuation beyond his capacity.

A description of part of a representative family session, which was typical of observations at other times, will help delineate the problem. In this session, Casey preferred to be with his father, who interacted on his level and accurately anticipated his needs. Irritability was present when he was near his mother. In one situation, he kicked her several times, then bit her fingers, leaving teeth marks, while uttering a sound of ravaging delight. She responded with a kiss and a smile. He reciprocated with rage. The biting and kicking were evidently painful and were not playful in any way. His mother verbalized that he was indeed angry with her. When Casey resumed kicking, his eleven-year-old brother sat between them, apparently understanding the difficulty and attempting to alleviate it. In spite of the fact that Casey related well to this brother, the mother sent him away immediately. Casey stopped kicking long enough to throw some paper onto the floor, and then resumed. Approximately two minutes after the biting, the mother retreated to the opposite side of the room. Casey slid off the sofa and went to his father's lap, where he sat calmly.

Casey's mother did not anticipate his needs. She would not hold him as frequently as he needed. When anxious, he would come to her, settle on her knee, and within seconds she would put him down. A number of reasons for this action were given which varied in each situation. His father, eleven-year-old brother, and various staff members held him until he wanted to leave and explore, and allowed him to return at will.

In the same session in a separation sequence, when the father left there was much anxiety; when he returned, Casey whimpered with joy. When his mother left, there was minimal protest and only the slightest acknowledgment when she returned. This acknowledgment was manifested by his facial expression, which changed from that of active interest in the involvement he had with his father to an attentive but neutral gaze.

DIAGNOSTIC FORMULATION

It was hypothesized that factors secondary to early disruption of the mother-infant relationship were principal determinants of the behavior disorder. Although they could not be entirely discounted, organic factors appeared to be of lesser importance. Such organic factors might include hyperbilirubinemia, with the possibility of bilirubin encephalopathy and respiratory arrest, and the risk of associated brain damage. Other organic disturbances might have arisen because of prematurity or from interactional deprivation associated with hospitalization. On the other hand, evidence against organicity was a favorable rating on the Denver Developmental Screening Test and an absence of neurological signs. Further evidence against organicity was the absence of symptoms when the mother was gone. Casey could relate positively to family members other than mother and to hospital staff members. This suggested that at one time a warm mothering experience had existed. As his mother was the only mothering figure, this experience must have been with her, and had now deteriorated.

What was it that this mother was struggling with and how was this related to the disruption of the mother-infant bond? She had a wish not to conceive, and, when pregnant, a wish to miscarry. When confronted with the prospect of a viable pregnancy, she wanted a normal infant. She then would be able to meet her own needs vicariously by taking care of the infant, attempting to recreate the gaps and master the traumata of her own past.[13] Reality militated against this, she did conceive, did not miscarry, and delivered an imperfect child. The child did not evoke, as Freud termed it, " . . . a revival and reproduction of her own, long since abandoned narcissism as a normal infant would," but rather reminded the mother of her imperfections and was in conflict with her self-expectation to be strong and independent. Grief was experienced, and as Solnit[54] reports, "In the mother's mourning reaction to the loss of the healthy child, her wishes for, and expectations of, the desired child, are crushed by the birth of the defective one." Separation of mother and infant at birth gave time for reflection, which accentuated guilt and allowed for anticipation of problems associated with having four children, the youngest two just thirteen months apart. Weeks of separation also delayed working through an integration of thoughts and feelings. To this was added the realization that only professionals could care for her infant. She felt inadequate.

On the child's release from the hospital, the mother was burdened with caring for him, an imperfect child who might die at any time. Initially she was afraid to become attached; subsequently, in response to his fragility, she became overprotective. This overprotectiveness was also, possibly, a reaction formation to guilt feelings stemming from her wish that the doctor's grave prediction had been actualized.

Overprotection in early infancy preceded the attitude the mother displayed on Casey's admission, her inability to respond empathically. She would slide him off her lap, saying, "Do you want to go and play?" when he was not ready to leave. Behavior necessitating psychiatric intervention and the family's awareness of Casey's preference for the father over her were insulting to her.

Her pattern of reinforcing Casey's negative behavior (for example, kissing him after he bit her) reflected her unconscious feeling that his scorn was deserved. Hostile impulses emerged, followed by the realization that she could harm him. This lack of self-control compromised the mother's ability to set limits, and resulted in feelings of helplessness and rage in the infant, which may have been expressed via his asthma. In early infancy he did not exhibit the negativistic behavior typical of a twenty-month-old infant; therefore, an ability to set limits was not necessary. The mother was comfortable with an infant—this could explain the former warmth in their relationship, warmth that Casey now transferred to accepting adults. The more she was punished by his erratic behavior, the greater the expiation of the guilt associated with her hostile impulses. A sadomasochistic struggle resulted, culminating in the identified behavior disturbance.

It was not until Casey was five months old that his mother was confident he would live. Evidence of her emotional detachment was demonstrated by her reluctance to buy clothes or furniture for him. Klaus and Kennell,[33] Mason and Kaplan,[40] and Leiderman and associates[36] have written about the consequences of early separation for mother and child. Leiderman's research[45] reports:

Separation of a mother from her infant for as short a time as three weeks in the immediate post-partum period can lead to lowered feelings of maternal competency and decreased amounts of attachment behavior sometimes continuing as long as one month following reuniting of the pair. [p. 170]

As a direct response to the difficulties this mother and child experienced, the opportunity for what Winnicott referred to as good-enough mothering was compromised. Winnicott[61] commented that

in my terminology, the good-enough mother is able to meet the needs of her infant at the beginning and to meet these needs so well that the infant, as emergence from the matrix of the infant-mother relationship takes place, is able to have a brief experience of omnipotence. [p. 57]

The mother can do this because she temporarily gives herself over to the one task, that of the care of this one infant. By fitting in with the infant's impulse the mother allows the baby the illusion that what is there is created by the baby; as a result, there is not only the physical experience of instinctual satisfaction, but also emotional union and the beginning of a belief in reality as something about which one can have illusions.

When the mother's adaptation is not good-enough at the start, the infant remains isolated. This is not to imply that this mother was inferior. Extreme needs of this particular infant and the exceptional emotional hardships this mother encountered must be emphasized. When the mothering experience is not good-enough, the clinical picture in the infant, as described by Winnicott,[61] is one of general irritability and of feeding and other functional disturbances. These may disappear clinically, only to reappear in a serious form at a later stage.

OUTCOME

Casey's father became unemployed just prior to the child's discharge from the hospital. It was predicted that Casey would do well at home with his emphathic father and that when the father returned to work, symptoms would recur unless significant change had occurred in the mother. Recommendations on discharge were: for the mother to have individual psychotherapy to help explore the origins of the difficulty she was experiencing with Casey and to develop a treatment plan to change this pattern; for a public health nurse to visit their home; and for Casey to continue attending the Premature Infant Follow-Up Clinic. As Casey was asymptomatic, his mother agreed to come for only one follow-up visit. His father started work six weeks later. The symptoms returned. One month after outpatient visits resumed, symptoms ceased. Therapy was focused on helping the mother develop insight—for example, understanding her hostile impulses and associated guilt. Suggestions were given on how to control her aggression by setting limits (such as, time out rather than spanking for temper tantrums). To facilitate expression of emotion, she was advised to allow Casey to throw pillows to release anger, and to encourage cuddling on her lap in order to experience warmth and closeness. Supportive comments, combined with the therapist's interest in and interactions with Casey, improved her self-esteem. Therapy continued and Casey's behavioral disturbance and the asthmatic disorder have not returned. Videotapes shown to the mother of their interactions before and after establishment of a warm mother-child relationship reinforced treatment gains.

In reviewing the case, one variable that was quite predictable in different situations was this infant's positive response to empathic relationships. His mother had provided this for her first three children with whom there had been no separations in the neonatal period. In Casey's early infancy, she was able to provide good-enough mothering for him as well, when his behavior did not elicit latent hostile impulses. It is therefore plausible that separation at birth had a major effect on this woman's later ability to set limits in response to negativistic behavior and was a precipitant of the nonempathic mothering.

Conclusion

It is widely recognized that mental health care for infants is closely bound up but not exclusively related to the very fabric of life style, tradition, and system of belief. Man emerged as an ape, descended from the trees, engaged in hunting, food gathering, tool making, and play. Stone-age man was a nomad. Only during the past 10,000 years, with the development of an agricultural capacity facilitated by the growth of grains, vegetables (flowers), and the domestication of animals, did man cease his nomadic existence and establish a sense of home which, in turn, strengthened family and kinship ties. This development in man's anthropological and social evolution has posted new problems for the family with an ailing, recalcitrant, difficult-to-understand infant or young child who does not respond positively to caretakers. Concern for the mental health of the infant is only very recent, perhaps the most recent phase in the evolution of man's conscience and consciousness. Each new discovery in the psychological and mental development of the infant has required a long period of "working through" within the matrix of an entire social structure, a reordering of priorities, a redistribution of assets, a new awareness of what a difference a little difference makes, and how something is done rather than what is done. Intervention techniques for mental health in infancy have developed slowly, face much resistance, are forgotten, and must be rediscovered and redefined with each new generation in the language and life style of that generation. Treatment of the mentally disturbed, underdeveloped, or handicapped infant truly imposes for the healer, physician, public health worker, pediatrician, and psychiatrist the recapitulation of man's entire history, as well as the application of his best science and art.

REFERENCES

1. Anders, T., "State and rhythmic processes," *Journal of the American Academy of Child Psychiatry*, in press.
2. Bayley, N., *Bayley Scales of Infant Development*, Psychological Corporation, New York, 1969.
3. Benjamin, J., "Further Comments on Some Developmental Aspects of Anxiety, in Gaskill, H. S. (Ed.), *Counterpoint: Libidinal Object and Subject*, pp. 121–153, International Universities Press, New York, 1963.
4. Berlin, I. N., "A Clinical Note on the Reversibility of Autistic Behavior in a 20-month-old Child," in Szurek, S. A., and Berlin, I. N. (Eds.), *Clinical Studies in Childhood Psychoses*, pp. 529–550, Brunner/Mazel, New York, 1973.
5. Brazelton, T. B., Autism, Personal Communication, 1976.
6. ———, "Early mother-infant reciprocity. *Parent-Infant Interaction*, Ciba Foundation Lymposium 33 (new series), ASP, Amsterdam, 1975.
7. Bruner, J., Jolly, J., and Sylvia, K. (Eds.), *Play: Its Role in Development and Evolution*, Brunner/Mazel, New York, 1976.

8. Call, J. D., "Some Pre-Linguistic Aspects of Language Development," Paper presented at Infant Psychiatry Institute on Recent Advances in Patterns of Infant Development: Relevance for Later Life, February 24–26, 1978.
9. ———, "Some Developmental Aspects of the Pointing Gesture and the Sound 'ush' in a 14-month-old Infant," unpublished manuscript.
10. ———, "The Adaptive Process in Early Infancy: A Research Odyssey, in Anthony E. J. (Ed.), *Explorations in Child Psychiatry*, pp. 167–182, Plenum Press, New York, 1975.
11. ———, "Psychoanalytically Based Therapy for Children and Their Parents," in Dyrud, J., and Freedman, D. X. (Eds.), *American Handbook of Psychiatry*, vol. 5, 2nd ed., pp. 206–234, Basic Books, New York, 1975.
12. ———, "Prevention of Autism in a Young infant in a Well-child Conference," in Morrison, G. C. (Ed.), *Emergencies in Child Psychiatry: Emotional Crises of Children, Youth & Their Families*, pp. 129–143, Charles C Thomas, Springfield, Ill., 1975.
13. ———, "Interlocking Affective Freeze Between an

Autistic Child and His 'As-If' Mother," in Morrison, G. C. (Ed.), *Emergencies in Child Psychiatry: Emotional Crises of Children, Youth & Their Families*, pp. 248–273, Charles C Thomas, Springfield, Ill., 1975.

14. ———, "Newborn Approach Behavior and Early Ego Development," *International Journal of Psychoanalysis*, 45:286–294, 1964.

15. ———, and MARSCHAK, M., "Styles and Games in Infancy," *Journal of the American Academy of Child Psychiatry*, 5:193–210, 1966.

16. DAVIS, R. E., and RUIZ, R. A., "Infant Feeding Method and Adolescent Personality," *American Journal of Psychiatry*, 122:673–678, 1965.

17. DECARIE, T. G., *The Infant's Reaction to Strangers*, International Universities Press, New York, 1974.

18. DE HIRSCH, K., "Language Deficits in Children with Developmental Lags, in Eissler, R. S., et al. (Eds.), *The Psychoanalytical Study of the Child*, vol. 30, pp. 95–126, Yale University Press, New Haven, 1975.

19. DRILLIEN, C. M., "Fresh Approaches to Prospective Studies of Low Birth Weight Infants," *Res. Pub. Assoc. Res. Nerv. Ment. Dis.*, 51:193–209, Williams & Wilkins, Baltimore, 1973.

20. EMDE, R. N., and HARMON, R. J., "Endogenous and Exogenous Smiling Systems in Early Infancy," *Journal of the American Academy of Child Psychiatry*, 11:117–200, 1972.

21. EMDE, R. N., GAENSBAUER, T. G., and HARMON, R. J., *Emotional Expressions in Infancy: A Biobehavioral Study*, Psychological Issues monograph 37, vol. 10, International Universities Press, New York, 1976.

22. ERIKSON, E., *Toys and Reasons*, Norton, New York, 1975.

23. ———, *Childhood and Society*, Norton, New York, 1963.

24. FRAIBERG, S., "Psychiatry and Infant Mental Health," Paper presented at the 23rd Annual Meeting of the American Academy of Child Psychiatry, Toronto, 1976.

25. ———, *Insights from the Blind: Developmental Studies of Blind Children*, Basic Books, New York, 1975.

26. ———, "Blind Infants and Their Mothers: An Examination of the Sign System," in Lewis, M., and Rosenblum, L. A. (Eds.), *The Effect of the Infant on its Caregiver*, Wiley-Interscience, New York, 1974.

27. FRANKENBURG, W. W., and SMITH, J. B., "The Denver Developmental Screening Test," *Journal of Pediatrics*, 71(2):181–191, 1967.

28. GALENSON, E., "Clinical Studies of Young Autistic Children," Personal communication, 1977.

29. GESELL, A., and AMATRUDA, C. S., *Developmental Diagnosis*, 2nd ed., Hoeber-Harper, New York, 1947.

30. GREENACRE, P., *Trauma, Growth and Personality*, International Universities Press, New York, 1952.

31. GREENFIELD, P. M., and SMITH, J. H., *The Structure of Communication in Early Language Development*, Academic Press, New York, 1976.

32. HIRZ, R. H., and CALL, J. D., "The Pointing Gesture: Its Evolution and Meaning for the Development of Language in Infancy," *Psychiatric Spectator*, Sandoz Pharmaceuticals, East Hanover, N. J., 1976.

33. KLAUS, M., and KENNELL, J., *Maternal-Infant Bonding*, C. V. Mosby, St. Louis, 1976.

34. KLEEMAN, J. A., "The Peek-A-Boo Game, Part I: Its origins, Meanings and Related Phenomena in the First Year, in Eissler, R. S., et al. (Eds.), *The Psychoanalytic Study of the Child*, vol. 22, pp. 239–273, International Universities Press, New York, 1967.

35. LA LECHE LEAGUE INTERNATIONAL, *La Leche League NEWS*, 19(5):81–100, 1977.

36. LEIDERMAN, P. H., et al., "Mother-Infant Interaction: Effects of Early Deprivation, Prior Experience and Sex of the Infant," *Res. Pub. Assoc. Res. Nerv. Ment. Dis.*, vol. 51, Williams & Wilkins, Baltimore, 1973.

37. LEWIS, M., *Clinical Aspects of Child Development: An Introductory Synthesis of Psychological Concepts and Clinical Problems*, Lea & Febiger, Philadelphia, 1971.

38. LOZOFF, B., et al., "The Mother-Newborn Relationship: Limits of Adaptability, *Journal of Pediatrics*, 91(1):1–12, 1977.

39. MAHLER, M., *The Psychological Birth of the Human Infant*, Basic Books, New York, 1976.

40. MASON, E. A., and KAPLAN, D. M., "Maternal Reactions to Premature Birth Viewed as an Acute Emotional Disorder," *American Journal of Orthopsychiatry*, 30:539–552, 1960.

41. MASSIE, H., "The Early Natural History of Childhood Psychosis: Ten Cases Studied by Analysis of Family Home Movies of the Infancy of Children," *Journal of the American Academy of Child Psychiatry*, 14:4, 1975.

42. NELSON, K., "First Steps in Language Acquisition," *Journal of the American Academy of Child Psychiatry*, 16:563–583, 1977.

43. NELSON, W., VAUGHAN, V., and McKAY, P., *Textbook of Pediatrics*, 9th ed., Saunders, Philadelphia, 1969.

44. ORLANSKY, H., "Infant Care and Personality," *Psychological Bulletin*, 46:1, 1949.

45. PASAMANICK, B., and KNOBLOCH, H., "Environmental Factors Affecting Human Development Before and After Birth," *Pediatrics*, August, pp. 210–218, 1960.

46. PEERS, M. (Ed.), *Play and Development: A Symposium*, Norton, New York, 1972.

47. PIAGET, J., *Play, Dreams and Imitation in Childhood*, Norton, New York, 1951.

48. PROVENCE, S., "Remarks on Receiving the C. Anderson Aldrich Award," *Pediatrics*, 59:388–389, 1977.

49. ROBSON, K., "The Role of Eye-to-Eye Contact in Maternal Infant Attachment," in Chess, S., and Thomas, A. (Eds.), *Annual Progress in Child Psychiatry and Child Development*, Brunner/Mazel, New York, 1968.

50. RUBIN, R. A., ROSENBLATT, C., and BALOW, B., "Psychological and Educational Sequelae of Prematurity," *Pediatrics*, 52 3:352–363, 1973.

51. RUTTENBERG, B., "Severe Ego Disturbances and Psychoses," Proposal Presented to the Committee on Psychiatric Dimensions of Infancy of the American Academy of Child Psychiatry, Houston, Texas, 1977.

52. SANDER, L., "Some Aspects of Temporal Organization in the Mother-Infant Interaction," in Rexford, E., Sander, L., and Shapiro, T., (Eds.), *Infant Psychiatry: A New Synthesis*, Yale University Press, New Haven, 1976.

53. SEARS, R. R., and WISE, G. W., "Relation of Cup Feeding in Infancy to Thumb Sucking and the Oral Drive," *American Journal of Orthopsychiatry*, 20:123–139, 1950.

54. SOLNIT, A. S. and STARK, M. H., "Mourning and the Birth of a Defective Child," in Eissler, R. S., et al. (Eds.), *The Psychoanalytic Study of the Child*, vol. 16, pp. 523–537, International Universities Press, New York, 1961.

55. SPITZ, R., *The First Year of Life*, International Universities Press, New York, 1965.

56. ———, *No and Yes: On the Genesis of Human Communication*, International Universities Press, New York, 1957.

57. ———, "The Primal Cavity: A Contribution to the Genesis of Perception and Its Role for Psychoanalytic Theory," in Eissler, R. S., et al. (Eds.), *The Psychoanalytic Study of the Child*, vol. 10, pp. 222–240, International Universities Press, New York, 1955.

58. ———, "The Smiling Response, *Genetic Psychology Monographs*, 34:57–125, 1946.

59. WINNICOTT, D. W., *Piggle*, International Universities Press, New York, 1977.

60. ———, *Playing and Reality*, Basic Books, New York, 1976.

61. ———, *The Maturational Processes and the Facilitating Environment*, International Universities Press, New York, 1965.

62 ———, *Collected Papers*, Basic Books, New York, 1958.

63. ———, *The Child and the Outside World*, Basic Books, New York, 1957.

64. ———, *The Child and the Family*, ed. by J. Hardenberg, Tavistock, London, 1957.

65. ———, "Transitional Objects and Transitional Phe-

nomena," *International Journal of Psycho-Analysis*, pp. 1–9, 1953.

66. ———, The Observation of Infants in a Set Situation, *Collected Papers*, pp. 52–69, Basic Books, New York, 1958.

67. ———, *Clinical Notes on Disorders of Childhood*, Tavistock, London, 1931.

29 / Preschool Children

Norbert B. Enzer

The late nineteenth and early twentieth century brought recognition of the importance of early life development and awareness of the unique vulnerabilities of the young child. Among others, the developmental studies of William James and the retrospective reconstructions of Freud were profoundly influential. These investigations began to awaken the scientific community to the diverse factors which can influence the developmental processes. More than that, they highlighted the remarkably long-term effects of these forces and events. The publication of Freud's paper "Analysis of a Phobia in a Five-Year-Old Boy"[9] in 1909 would seem to be the first clear report of the direct treatment of a preschool aged child. This case arose apparently from Freud's urging his friends and students to collect direct observational data on the lives of young children. In essence, this study was not so much an attempt to examine the therapeutic process and the special considerations relevant to the therapeutic approaches with a young child. Instead, it was an attempt to elucidate and further deepen the understanding of infantile sexuality, which prior to then had been derived primarily from the analysis of adult patients. Although the therapeutic effort was conducted in an unusual manner, this received much less attention. By the 1920s, there was a growing awareness that the treatment of children was indeed somewhat different from that of adults. More recently still, attention has been specifically focused on the unique therapeutic needs of the preschool child. This chapter will attempt to examine certain of the specific considerations that apply to the treatment of the child between approximately two and six years of age.

Assessment of the Child

No therapeutic effort can be undertaken without a thorough evaluation of the child, the home, and perhaps the day-care center or preschool program in which the child functions. Such an assessment must include not only problematic areas but strengths and assets as well. It is essential to review all aspects of development against the background of appropriate group norms; in addition, each aspect must be assessed in relation to the individual child's potential, constitutional factors, and temperament. Furthermore, the relationship among the several developmental areas must also be evaluated. Special sensitivities or skills, as well as deviations and deficits, in a given area can in a significant way influence other dimensions of a child's adjustment directly or indirectly. The child with an orthopedic handicap may experience direct interference with locomotion; at the same time, his disability may exert a less direct, but not less important, effect on his self-concept or on his relationship with his parents. Or, an extremely bright and verbal young child may be exposed to disturbing information. This may involve violence, or adoption, or seduction. At his level of development, this will be exceedingly difficult to master emotionally and leaves him vulnerable to excessive and, perhaps, very unusual anxieties.

An assessment of the expectations, attitudes, tolerances, and feelings of parents and other key adults in the child's life is also critical to his evaluation. The importance of the parents should not be underestimated. Throughout these years, the preschool child struggles with a host of issues which relate directly to the pattern of his relationship with his parents. Early in this period, the child is moving toward greater individualization, object constancy, and a sense of autonomy. He does not arrive there, however, without considerable ambivalence. There are frequent attempts to control parents with clinging and aggressiveness combined with negativism and defiance. As a result, the parents are often perplexed and bewildered. Their expectations and affective responses may encourage or impede further individuation. They may intensify the child's fear that the love and concern of parents is fragile and may be withdrawn at any time. If this occurs, his self-worth can be jeopardized. Parents are viewed as omnipotent, which renders them a powerful source of security and certainty on the one hand, but very threatening, on the other. In general, the child's belief that the parent(s) will not allow harm to come to him is a strong protective device that serves him well. Thus, in threatening situations, the mere presence of a parent can prevent the development of acute anxiety in the child. However, the roles and capabilities assigned in his fantasy differ from time to time. Fraiberg[6] points out that a mother may be viewed as a "good fairy" at one time and a "witch" at another. These fantasies are usually related to need gratification.

As the child gradually abandons the expectation of immediate gratification as a major source of his attachment to parents, he begins to have a greater willingness to forego immediate satisfaction. Some level of self-control begins, but whether this control is based on pride or on doubt and shame is largely dependent upon the nature of the full spectrum of interactions with parents. Erickson[3] points out that parental firmness and tolerance are critical, not only in this regard, but also in respect to the child's willingness to be tolerant of others.

Later in development, the oedipal romance provides another framework within which the relationship with parents is played out. Fantasies are rife about sexual differences, about reproduction, and about what goes on between the parents themselves. These provide the precursors for the later development of the desires and yearnings toward the parents themselves, now perceived as differentiated sexual objects. The resultant fantasies and the attendant anxieties place the child in considerable jeopardy. Again, the actions of the parents, their feelings, and their responses become critical. Both play and fantasy are used by the young child as a means of overcoming fears and mastering threatening situations. At the same time, fantasy itself can produce fears. Often, the young child can deal more easily with those fears which arise from fantasy than with those that arise from real threats such as parental absences or anger.

Gould[15] suggests that nursery school children are rather consistent in their fantasies, both in regard to the type of self-representation and the major focus of identification. She asserts that the use of the direct "I" in fantasy as opposed to the more distant-from-self "I'm a witch" represents progress in individuation and in drive-defense. She considers this sequential progression to be a distinct and significant indicator of the times the child is caught up with feelings and content derivative of the aggressive drive. Preschool children differ in the amount of "fluctuating certainty" which is defined as a temporary inability to differentiate a real from an imaginary danger. Continued uncertainty beyond the age of about four years should be viewed as a sign of anxiety-interference, whereas the ability to differentiate further is a sign of developmental progress.

The content of the child's expressed fantasy reflects his experiences with the real world, and the psychological processes which result from and deal with these experiences. Some children have great difficulty in expressing fantasies. In the child who has learned to talk, such difficulties should be viewed as evidence of a problem in affective or cognitive development.

Katan[19] has noted that verbalization itself increases the possibility of distinguishing fantasy and wish on the one hand and reality on the other; it leads to an ever-increasing ego control over affects and drives. The capacity to give verbal expression to internal feelings follows the ability to describe the outer world. Verbalization leads to an integrating process, which in turn results in reality testing and thereby facilitates the establishment of secondary process functioning. Often, the children referred to child psychiatrists have considerable difficulty in verbalization. It is therefore essential that they be approached with great flexibility, and that information be sought from other sources and from behavioral observations rather than solely from spoken words.

In due time, the process of separation and individuation is complete. The child develops a sense of autonomy based more on pride than on shame, and founded firmly on the awareness that he now possesses some level of self-control. With these accomplishments and the resolution of the oedipal romance, the influence of the parents is somewhat diminished. For the preschool child, however, all these are vivid issues. It is for this reason that interactions with parents are critical to the assessment of the child in this period of life. The need for thorough understanding of the parents goes beyond these matters. The parents' feelings, expectations, and values regarding all aspects of a child's life must be explored. Specific deviations, deficits, or handicaps may elicit concern or rejection; certainly they will create some kind of affective responses, often of disappointment, guilt, and anger. And these, in turn, will influence the nature of the interaction with the child. However, sometimes more subtle features may create similar, though often less obvious, responses in parents. These include characteristics which would not universally be viewed as significant limitations. Occasionally. even behaviors which might generally be viewed as assets may produce a negative response by parents. The bright, inquisitive, verbal three-year-old may be seen by some parents as overly intrusive and annoying; in others, such behavior creates a fear for the child's safety.

While the response of parents to matters which currently concern them is of great importance, it is also true that their hopes and expectations for the future are perhaps only slightly less significant. Parents have their own fantasies and wishes for their child. An understanding of the nature and content of these may aid in an understanding of parental actions and attitudes. Armed with such an understanding, the clinician is in an excellent position to assist in evaluating the appropriateness of these hopes and providing suitable guidance.

Evaluation of the preschool child and the therapeutic plan which may emerge from it requires a careful study of the complexities of the development of the child in his environment. But it requires an equally careful assessment of his symptom patterns, their relationship to his growth processes, and the reactions they evoke in others. It is often difficult to separate transient symptoms arising from usual developmental stresses from more fixed symptoms, but it is essential to make this distinction. Attention is often focused on the concepts of arrest and regression as an explanation for symptoms or behavioral deviations. Too often omitted from such consideration is the fact that developmental arrest or regression is for all practical purposes never complete, and that when such phenomena do occur, they affect only certain areas of progress. While other aspects of progress may be affected, development does continue. Even where there are severe problems in statural growth which are likely to affect many aspects of development, there may be considerable cognitive growth and continuing behavioral adaptation. Early infantile autism is probably the most extreme form of

"arrest" in the development of object relationships. And yet these children, too, continue to develop in other ways—they grow and they develop motorically. At times, the progressive development in other areas can be viewed with hope. Compensations can and do occur. On an experiental basis, this would seem to be particularly likely if there is a constitutional or biological problem which interfers with the overall sequence of development. Children with difficulties in fine motor movement may avoid some activities and find satisfaction in others which make fewer demands for these skills. At other times, developmental progress in areas not directly related to primary symptoms may add to the difficulties. Thus, the care of the child with severe brain damage may be further complicated by growth in height and weight. The ability of parents to control and protect the child with early infantile autism may be compounded by the development of locomotion and by growth itself. In addition, progress in some areas of development may alter the feelings, tolerances, and attitudes of the parents. Deficits in one area may become more obvious and increase parental anxieties and concerns. Progress may also increase the expectation that the primary symptoms will abate spontaneously, or increase the frustration if they do not.

It is clear that, directly or indirectly, a symptom can affect other aspects of development. Yet, withal, development does proceed, and whatever progress is achieved may have a positive or negative effect on the functioning of the child. It also seems clear that the symptom alone, even a rather limited one, may affect the people near to the child and thereby influence his developmental progress and adaptation. Thumb-sucking may be the only symptom in the preschool child. Yet to some parents, it may be of such concern that inordinate attention is drawn to it, affecting all other family interaction. Thus, the meaning of symptoms to the parents and to the child becomes critical in the evaluation of the preschool child.[1]

Initial Clinical Contact

In the evaluation and treatment of a preschooler, certain aspects of development take on particular importance. These aspects often require flexibility and special adaptations of technique. The preschool child is never brought to the child psychiatrist on his own initiative. That decision always rests with parents or other caretakers.

As consultant to a day-care center or a pre-school program, the child psychiatrist may be asked to discuss and perhaps observe the child prior to direct involvement with parents. This poses special problems at both a clinical level and an ethical level. It might be wiser for a child psychiatrist acting in such a capacity to avoid any direct contact with a child unless this is done with the explicit knowledge and consent of the parents. If consultative discussions with the staff lead to a decision that it would be helpful for him to see the child, he should encourage the staff to bring the parents into the process. Teachers, day-care workers, and family physicians are often in a position to refer the parents of a preschool child to a child psychiatrist. Unfortunately, at the outset, the parents often share the child's confusion. Because the decision is not made by the child, he usually does not understand why he is seeing a child psychiatrist, what the problem is, why the child psychiatrist is the person to see, and what to expect. Parents may comply with the suggestion of the "expert" with an almost equal lack of understanding. The parents may approach the situation with fear, bewilderment, guilt, or resentment. The clinician must be prepared to deal with both child and parents on the assumption that they do not know why they are there or what to expect. With the parents, this may be because they know little about child development or about the functions of a child psychiatrist. It may also be because of their view of the nature of the symptoms. Basically, however, it stems from their values and/or their own emotional status and defense mechanisms. In addition to the similarities between the attitudes of parents and young child, there are differences as well which must be recognized. Many a preschool child who comes to evaluation or therapy does not experience distress; it is rather the parents who do. It is they, and not the child, who are willing to make sacrifices for treatment.[31] Once the work is under way, the expectations of parent and child may well be quite different. Parents may expect therapy to change the child, while the child, even the one who does experience distress, may expect the external environment to change and thus relieve his discomfort.[24]

Such differences in expectations may reflect fundamental issues in the development of the child and in the psychodynamics of parents. Mothers often seem to view the child under five years essentially as an extension of themselves. Thus, if the child has problems, the mother may feel she is responsible, or that she herself also has "problems." Such feelings may produce considerable anxiety and guilt along with varying degrees of denial, projection, or repression. Many of the conflicts in the preoedipal child are between the child's instinctual drives and the environment rather than between the drives and the superego.[18] The parents, particularly the mother or other primary caregiver, form a crucial part of that environment. On the other hand, a combination of the preschool child's dependency, belief in parental omnipotence, and limited capacity for insight is likely to lead the child to the conclusion that the disturbances are external rather than internal.

While there are certain differences in approach among clinicians, with preschool children it is usual to meet with parents before the child is seen. During this meeting, there must be some exploration of the appropriateness of the referral as well as some delineation of the issues. A crucial goal for these initial meetings with the parents is to lay the foundations for a therapeutic alliance. It may be very difficult to establish an alliance with so young a child; unless there is a real commitment to the treatment plan by the parents, little productive work may be accomplished.

It is essential that parents have significant understanding and agreement in order to prepare their child optimally for his first meeting with the clinician. It is often necessary for the child psychiatrist to give parents direct aid in planning how to prepare their child. Even young preschool children who have acquired only the simplest use of language can understand that parents are concerned and are seeking help. The child and the parents need to know what to expect, and what not to. The preparation should be simple, open, and designed in keeping with the child's level of cognitive functions. Nevertheless, for all practical purposes, the issues which have prompted the need for the consultation are well known to everyone in the family. Usually they have been the focus of considerable interaction between child and parents or others involved with the child.

Aside from the specific content, the manner in which the parents communicate their intentions is critical. If they are uncertain or ambivalent, such feelings will inevitably be conveyed to the child. Under such circumstances, the child's first meeting with the child psychiatrist may be fraught with difficulty. This difficulty, in turn, may be enough to tip the parents' ambivalence away from an investment in the evaluation. All preschool children are fearful during the initial sessions. Some show aggressive behavior in direct proportion to their level of anxiety. Others are extremely inhibited;

they may have great difficulty in entering the office or playroom. Inadequate or ambivalent preparation is likely to intensify such reactions. Parents should be forewarned and prepared for these possibilities. They must be reassured that the clinician will not hold them responsible for such behavior.

Developmental Considerations in Promoting a Therapeutic Alliance

The cognitive functioning of the child requires special consideration. The two-year-old views the parents (and to a lesser extent, other adults) as omnipotent. Fraiberg[6] relates a delightful story of a two-year-old girl who watched the sun set and said to her father: "Do it again, Daddy." The child's belief in such incredible power must be viewed with respect, not with amusement. The therapist must recognize this and avoid using the child's fantasy destructively. At this age, children feel their own thoughts and wishes have the power of action. Since such thinking does not abide by the laws of logic, time, place, and causality, the child's view of the world may be very different from the therapist's. The therapist must strive continually to aid the child in distinguishing reality and recognizing the limits of thought, fantasy, and wish. Yet, such efforts cannot be based on rationality, for the child cannot be expected to think rationally.

Clear, brief declarative statements are far more effective than lengthy, logical explanations. In addition to the cognitive processes themselves, the language used to convey what the child intends to say may have quite a different meaning to the child than it does to the therapist.[24] To the young preschool child, words have a highly concrete value. The therapist must learn to understand the child's language and to express himself in a way that the child will understand. In any process of verbal communication, the therapist must recognize that the capacity for auditory memory and the ability to process auditory information are also developmental phenomena which progress slowly during the preschool years. As a result, the language of the therapist should be brief, direct, and simple.

Infantile omnipotence also creates a special vulnerability. Fears and anger, frightening fantasies, and hostile wishes have the value of danger. These may be very difficult for the young child to express directly; he feels that if these thoughts are spoken, they will come true or there may be some ominous retaliation. He is likely to be far better able to deal with these through play or story-telling. Such fears, fantasies, and wishes are important to the child and will probably be repeated; with work the therapist may aid in clarification. The therapist needs to be cautious about encouraging too much expression of these feelings and impulses, however. Often, these thoughts and the associated behavior have led to parental rebuke or punishment. There is the risk that the therapist may be viewed as seductive, or as a person who spoils the child's techniques for avoiding punishment. The overzealous encouragement of expression, or the interpretation of these feelings or impulses, may prompt a child to protect himself from the therapist.[13, 29]

Furthermore, the permissive, nonjudgmental stance of the therapist may be confusing and anxiety-provoking. The young preschool child depends on external controls. Should the child sense that those controls are absent, the fear of loss of mastery over his impulses may be intensified. The child needs to perceive the therapist as someone on whom he can rely and who is not threatened by these impulses. While clarification of reality is important, the therapist may also aid by assuring external controls and helping the child use play and verbal expression as a means of mastery and tension reduction. At the same time, the therapist must not convey disrespect. Clearly, it is not therapeutic to suggest that a child not only lacks omnipotence but is in fact powerless.

The child may continue to maintain a degree of what Piaget[26] calls ego-centrism. This means that the child believes his point of view is the only one possible. During the third year of life, the child develops a more mature capacity to think about his action and its consequences and thereby is no longer wholly dependent upon action itself. The evaluation or treatment of a child with these thought processes requires a high level of tolerance and acceptance. The opportunity for repetitive mental and physical learning through trial and error is important; hence, a nonjudgmental, yet reality-based, response to a child's pronouncements is essential. The child's propensity to repeat actions, play themes, or stories often requires a fine sense of discrimination on the part of the therapist. It must be determined whether this behavior is, indeed, helping the child. It may be aiding him to master an experience by turning a passive state into an active one, or it may be a compulsion or the acting out of an impulse. Play ceases to be useful if it becomes compulsive and the child loses control over it. At two or two and one-half years, play is not of great value for symbolic communication or conflict resolution, yet it may aid in clarifying and developing a sense of mastery and autonomy.

By age three, there are attempts at verbal reasoning and symbolic activity in play. Play takes on a truly interactional quality so that others can participate, and often there are real-life themes, with the participants assuming rather well-defined roles. Play now begins to have a significantly expanded potential for mastery, communication, and conflict resolution.[35] Not only may more information and understanding be derived from observation of play, but the therapist now has a far greater opportunity for direct personal involvement and, thereby, for assisting the child directly in his coping.

Gradually, but steadily, the child moves toward greater accommodation with reality. Piaget[27] refers to the latter portion of the preoperational stage as the "intuitive" stage. Yet, there continues to be a propensity to follow a particular line of thought which is the child's own and to engage in relatively little verbal exchange of information. Another characteristic of this period is the child's belief that punishment automatically and inevitably follows wrong-doing. The importance of this cannot be underestimated. It determines how one deals not only with the actual transgressions of the preschool child, but also with the fantasies. But punishment also seems to relieve a sense of having been "bad," and some children seem to seek punishment. As the child moves closer to the end of the preschool period, the capacity to deal verbally with issues increases, and the central need for play as a means of communicating and coping diminishes somewhat.

Parental Involvement

The child's relationship with others and the impact of this on the child's concept of himself may require special attention. As indicated previously, at about two years, the child is still struggling with the process of separation and individuation. For some, being away from parents may be anxiety-provoking. Not infrequently, at the time of the initial visits, this may be manifest by a child's reluctance to leave the parents and accompany the clinician. Due recognition of this as a significant developmental task allows the therapist to invite the parents to join the child in the session. The possibility that such an invitation might be extended is often suspected on the basis of historical information provided by the parents prior to the child's first visit. The parents should be instructed to deal with this in a matter-of-fact and supportive way and to remain unintrusive in the session itself unless the therapist elects to use it as an opportunity to intervene directly in parent-child interactional issues. Later in the course of therapy this same anxiety may manifest itself as a resistance to coming for treatment at all. It is often appropriate to continue to allow the parent(s) to be present during therapeutic sessions.

Frequently, young children believe that they are brought for treatment because they have done things of which the parents did not approve. Almost inevitably, there is a fear that the parents do not love the child and that they want to get rid of him. The presence of the mother may reduce some of this anxiety. Additionally, it may aid the child to trust the therapist without feeling disloyal, and it may help the mother understand, recognize, and model other methods of dealing with the child. Such an approach is often useful. and the mother may be willing and indeed eager to participate in the child's treatment. At the same time, both therapist and mother must recognize that there may come a time when the mother's presence is no longer needed and appropriate. She should be prepared for the possibility that her child may need to have the therapist all to himself. Some parents find it difficult to accept that others may have techniques of relating to their child which seem more effective than their own. Therapists must be prepared to deal with these feelings; if they are ignored, the parents' response may be destructive to further therapy.

Regardless of the presence or absence of the parent in the therapy session, the child will view the therapist as a potential agent or ally of the parent. The clinician must make it clear that he is not the "agent" of the parents nor their ally; at the same time he is not in opposition to them. Despite the differences in his behavior and that of the parents with respect to the child, he shares the parents' concerns. Because of the child's perceptions of parental power, his needs for security and for their love, there is a unique kind of "loyalty" which may draw the child toward even quite malevolent parents. Such an attachment may make it exceedingly difficult for the troubled preschooler to be fully open about his feelings or to create new relationships, which even if more positive, nonetheless threaten the ties to the parents. Emotionally healthy youngsters are more likely to be frank and to accept others than those who are in greater need.

Transference, as it is experienced in therapy of adults, adolescents, and older children, probably does not occur with preschool children. The interactions with parents are ongoing, and the vulnerability of the young child to those interactions and to fantasies about them are of such degree that the true transference relationship does not develop. The child's defenses are extremely limited, less well established, and untested. Even if a child could detach his feelings sufficiently from the real parent to invest in the therapist, dealing with a real parent and a transference parent simultaneously might be overwhelming. Nonetheless, attachments to therapists do develop, and these are often remarkably like the attachments that have gone before. Indeed, they may have the character of displacement. The study of the child's object relationships helps illuminate the nature of his relationship with the therapist. As therapy progresses, the child may come to view the therapist almost like a not-well-defined member of the family rather than as a replacement for one or the other parent. Such a relationship may continue to be important even after relief of symptoms has occurred.

Because of the child's dependence on his home and the critical quality of the interactions at home, it is of the utmost importance that the family be involved in his therapy. At the very least, parents need a reasonable and understandable explanation of the nature of the problem and some ideas about how their interactions can be helpful. They must feel like partners in the effort to assist their child. They further need an understanding of the goals of treatment.

The issue of confidentiality can be as important in work with a preschool child as with an older child or adolescent. However, the rules may be somewhat different. As mentioned, the young preschool child tends to think his ideas are the only ones possible, and if others have ideas, they are surely the same. The older preschooler may not only recognize that there are differences but may also feel that some of his thoughts and feelings are quite unacceptable to his parents. Nonetheless, from the outset, the child needs to know that everyone agrees that the subject of the therapy is the child, his feelings, his development, behavior, and relationship to others. He further needs to know that his parents will be involved in discussions about him with the therapist, that

there will be a mutual exchange of information. "Secrets" shared with the therapist can be treated as such, and the child should be given assurances that his confidence will be respected provided it is not counter to his best interests to do so. The therapeutic interpretations of the therapist and his other efforts are more likely to be accepted if the child recognizes that the parents endorse therapy. In some cases, this requires parental presence.

Some parents require more than periodic information sharing. There are differences of opinion regarding whether the child's therapist should actually treat the parents. There are those who maintain that the model established in the traditional child guidance clinic is still the most appropriate. In that setting, the child's therapist did not work with the parents. Others believe that with the preschool child particularly, it is more important for only one therapist to be involved. At some level, many preschool children seem to expect their therapist, perhaps like their baby-sitter or preschool teacher, to interact with their parents. It is safe to say that both approaches have been useful. Perhaps the judgment should be based not so much on abstract rules as on the specific needs of the child and the parents, the nature of the therapy, and on certain practical considerations.

As mentioned, at times it is appropriate for the parent(s) to be present during the therapeutic sessions. Such sessions may involve the individual work with a child, or they may be part of an ongoing program in a therapeutic nursery. Aside from such involvement, parents may be included in the therapeutic process in other ways. For example, after evaluation, the therapy of the preschool child may be conducted by way of the parents without direct contact with the child. Because of the unique closeness which exists between a preschool child and the mother, during this period a mother may be able to understand and influence her child better than anyone else. There are three general methods employed. The first of these is based on education in parenting. In such an effort, the work is focused on the process of development with attention directed to the specific needs of the child and to alternative means of responding to those needs. This approach is useful in assisting parents who are well-integrated personalities and whose child is simply having difficulties with the usual stresses and conflicts of development. At another level, the parent(s) may be involved in their own individual or couples' therapy aimed at resolving internal or interpersonal conflicts. The expectation here is that improvement in the relationships with the child will result. Finally, parent(s) may be involved in a supportive-educative therapy with the intent of helping their understanding of and direct intervention with the child. Such indirect approaches are most appropriate when the child's conflicts are not yet internalized.

While all parents may, of course, profit from learning to help their child, many are not capable of being the primary therapist. Those who are psychotic, those with infantile personalities, those who are pseudomasochistic with their children, those who feel the child does not need help, those with defenses or symptoms similar to those of their child, and those for whom their child's symptoms unconsciously represent something about themselves are not appropriate candidates for this indirect approach.[10] (A more detailed discussion of these indirect approaches is available in chapters 8 and 9.) At other times, parents, because of their own difficulties, may require therapy aimed at their own problems.

Decisions regarding therapeutic approaches must be based on the specific needs of both child and parents and on their strengths and assets. Approaches cannot be determined on the basis of diagnostic labels. Schopler and Reichler[30] have demonstrated substantive improvement in severely disturbed children with parents carrying a primary responsibility for intervention. While there are few rules, with all else being equal, it does seem apparent that the younger the child the greater the potential for an indirect approach. The parent(s) would then be the primary therapist, and the child psychiatrist would serve as "consultant," "supervisor," or even therapist for the parent(s). There are situations in which parental psychopathology is such that it may interfere with the treatment of the child, or when they are resistant to therapy, or to changes in their own behavior. If the child's symptoms seem to have arisen from trauma or conflicts with which the parents have had considerable difficulty in the past, it is best that the child be treatred directly.

Therapeutic Focus

The focus of therapeutic work with a preschool child obviously depends on the nature of the disturbance. It is also a function of the specific needs and the strengths of the individual child and the family. Often it appears likely that significant change and benefit will derive from the therapeutic process. Conflicts are not fully internalized and defenses are less rigid. The preoedipal child is in the process of ego development; he needs help with integrative efforts, defense development, and adaptation. The young phallic child needs assistance in handling his excitement, wishes, and fantasies, and the oedipal child needs aid in internalizing the superego formation.[20] At various times and to varying degrees, the therapy involves uncovering, education and alternative seeking, clarification, support, and reassurance. The child needs the opportunity to experience a more satisfactory interpersonal experience, and the therapist can aid in this by relating to the child as a real object and encouraging the child to relate similarly to the therapist. Therapy should not provide a means by which the pathologic reaction from the past can be undone and integrated in current ego functioning. It should also be oriented toward the future to a far more significant degree than is work with older children or adolescents. Therapy should pave the way for future development of new psychic functions.[24]

There has been considerable controversy and discussion about the role of interpretation in therapeutic work with the preschool child. While rather extreme positions have been taken in the past, currently it would appear that brief, clear, ego-oriented interpretations can have an important function. If interpretations address experiences which were inadequately understood, they may well relieve anxiety. If, however, they focus on the impulses, attitudes, or behaviors which are associated with rebuke or punishment, they may intensify anxiety.

Despite the young child's potential for change, the environment, and the parents in particular, may impose limits on what can be done. For some parents, their own capacity for change is great, and such change may greatly facilitate more healthy development by the child. With others, little change may be possible. Therapy may assist the child to reach a more optimal adaptation to his environment and a somewhat diminished vulnerability; nonetheless, the goal of healthy emotional and interpersonal development may not be reached. The maintenance of a positive relationship between therapist and parents during therapy and, particularly, at termination provides a foundation which will allow the parents to seek further help if needed in the future.[24] If the positive relationship with the therapist can be maintained beyond the point of symptom relief, the child, too, may be more willing to accept future help. Furthermore, sustaining the relationship permits greater independence to occur through the natural course of development and for other social relationships to blossom, thus limiting noxious influences in the home environment.

Physical Setting and Equipment

The setting and structure of therapy with a preschool child may be quite different from that with an older child. The room in which the work takes place should have characteristics with which the child is comfortable. It should not appear fragile or formal, nor convey the message that it is a place for adults in which children are simply guests. Everything about it should proclaim that it is a room for young children. Again, there are differences of opinion. Some child psychiatrists accommodate young children by setting up their own offices with a play area and some toys readily visible. Others maintain that work with preschool children requires a playroom that is separate and distinct, with all necessary equipment and materials available within it. Most child psychiatrists agree that psychotherapeutic work is best conducted in a specific room and not while strolling in the park, jumping rope, or playing catch—though these may be valuable adjuncts. The room itself should be big enough to allow a little child some distance, if he feels such a need. Crowded quarters may increase anxiety in the active preschooler.

Toys and other equipment used in the therapy differ greatly. To some extent, the number and variety of "things" available for the child to manipulate seems to diminish with the experience of the therapist. Some therapists favor a very well-equipped playroom, often with a rather standardized inventory. This includes a sink with running water. a sandbox, building blocks, dolls, trucks, weapons, eating utensils, a dollhouse and doll family, games, paints, crayons and paper, and others. Other therapists will function with much less: perhaps only some crayons and paper, modeling clay, and possibly a doll. Perhaps the most important factor is the needs of a particular child and making available the toys or other equipment which will facilitate the specific therapeutic effort. It must be remembered that for some children an abundance of toys may be distracting and confusing. This applies particularly to those who are very disturbed, often with some difficulty in reality testing, and to those who appear hyperactive. There should be an opportunity for children to keep in some safe place something special from one appointment to the next.

Timing of Sessions

The frequency and spacing of appointments call for some thought. The younger child may have considerable difficulty with time durations and with carrying a theme in therapy. If there is too much time in between, material which arose during one session may be lost by the next. On the other hand, if a toy or a drawing of some importance in one session can be kept and made available for the next, a young child's memory and ability to pick up where he left off may be quite amazing. Frequency should not be regulated on the basis of administrative need; considerable individualized flexibility is required. Some preschool children do much better when seen more than once weekly, while for others, it seems to make little difference.

The time of day of appointments can also be important. A child's natural pattern of activities, and, for some, rest periods, should be considered. Seeing a preschool child during the time he would usually be resting is often unproductive; occasionally it is downright devastating. The duration of the sessions themselves also needs thought. Even for the young child, psychotherapy can be an intense experience, and the sessions may need to be shortened to accommodate for fatigue.

While there is a need for flexibility in dealing with a preschool child, there is at least as much need for predictability. The child should know what to expect. Patterns should not be changed without the child's knowledge.

Treating the Preschool Child
in Groups

The preschool child may gain a great deal from treatment of children in groups. Interactions with other preschool children can be immensely reassuring. In this way children hospitalized with medical problems may obtain some measure of relief from the anxiety related to the hospital and to medical procedures. The form of such groups (which are discussed in chapters 10 and 35) is often similar to that found in nursery schools.

At times, it may be appropriate for the child psychiatrist to recommend an ordinary nursery school experience for certain of his young patients. This exposure may provide the youngster with an opportunity for a positive interaction with healthier peers and a potentially more supportive and understanding interaction with adults. It may also give the parents a much needed respite. Also available are therapeutic nursery schools, which are specifically designed to address the needs of emotionally disturbed preschool children. Their programs vary rather widely in terms of interventional strategies and procedures. Various roles and tasks are assigned to therapists and teachers, who may interact directly with the children both in groups and individually. The amount of time devoted to each during the school day is determined by the needs of the child. The personnel may teach, support, clarify, provide structure and limits, and encourage affective expression through play and verbalization.

In some programs, parents, particularly mothers, are directly involved in the activities of the school and work with the children. In these settings, teachers and therapists assist and guide the interactions of the mothers and the children and also serve as role models. This approach offers the advantages of somewhat expanded time for therapeutic activities, a setting which is more usual and "normal," and the opportunity for the children to share in peer interactions. Mothers gain a great deal from their interactions with the staff. They may develop greater sensitivity to their child's needs, new ways of interacting with him, and assurance that comes with bearing some of the responsibilities. At times, they may find comfort in the realization that a child is difficult even for the "professional." In addition to any direct involvement with the children, therapeutic nursery schools may provide either group or individual therapy for the parents. This work may be conducted by those who work directly with the children or by staff who are unrelated to the children's activities.

Some children have been helped by group therapy itself. It has been particularly useful for youngsters who have difficulties in interactions with peers, either because of withdrawal or aggressiveness. The groups have involved only the preschoolers and not their parents. They are formed around play activities and provide an opportunity for supervised free play, in the course of which some sensitive environmental controls can be imposed by the therapist. (Group therapy is discussed further in chapter 10.)

Aside from the benefits of the various group approaches that have already been mentioned, such groups of children and groups of parents and children provide a superb opportunity for a broad range of observations regarding the child's functioning and progress. Many believe that for most preschool children, peer-group interaction is virtually essential to the overall therapeutic effort. Whether this takes place in a nursery school, a therapeutic nursery school, or a therapeutic play group depends on the child's needs, his tolerances, and the available services.

Other Therapeutic Measures

The question of pharmacotherapy for the preschool child raises strongly held, but often divergent, opinions among child psychiatrists. It is vigorously requested by some parents and equally vigorously resisted by others. The preschool child is developing neurophysiologically as well as emotionally and intellectually. Drug actions and drug doses for the very young child are frequently less well understood than for the older child and adolescent. At the least, medication should be considered only as part of an overall therapeutic plan and should be used with specific indications and goals. Frequently evaluation of effectiveness and of potential side effects is essential. If the drug seems ineffective, or if signs of important side effects or toxicity appear, it should be discontinued promptly and appropriately. No child should be maintained on a drug longer than is absolutely necessary. (This is discussed in detail in chapter 23.)

Almost inevitably, when the problems of preschool children are discussed, the removal of the child from the home is examined as a possible solution. It may be inappropriate, and, in some cases, unrealistic to view this literally as a "last resort." At the same time, it does require very careful consideration and great caution. The importance of parents, even less than ideal parents, cannot and must not be dismissed. It may be possible to create a positive rationale for removing a child from the home. It is essential, however, that the negative consequences and the realistic possibilities of an improved situation must also be weighed in the decision-making process. There may be negative consequences to leaving a child in the home; but there are also negatives in removing him. The actual safety of the child must be considered and balanced against the psychological consequences of either choice. This is perhaps the most serious decision to be made; it demands complete information and understanding (see chapters 15 and 18).

The attractiveness of the concept of early intervention, the plasticity of the preschool child, and the effectivness of environmental change make the treatment of the preschool child an appealing and worthwhile venture. But effective intervention requres understanding of the uniqueness of this developmental period. It also requires that there be modifications of therapeutic approaches, modifications based on an understanding of development, symptom formation, and family interactions.

REFERENCES

1. ANTHONY, E. J., "The Significance of Jean Piaget for Child Psychiatry," *British Journal of Medical Psychology,* 29:20–34, 1956.

2. AXLINE, V., *Play Therapy,* Riverside Press Cambridge, Mass., 1942.

3. ERIKSON, E., "Identity and the Life Cycle," *Psychological Issues,* vol. no. 1, International Universities Press, New York, 1959.

4. FISH, B., "Drug Therapy in Child Psychiatry: Pharmacological Aspects," *Comprehensive Psychiatry, 1:*212–227, 1960.

5. ———, "Drug Therapy in Child Psychiatry: Psychological Aspects," *Comprehensive Psychiatry, 1:*55–61, 1960.

6. FRAIBERG, S., *The Magic Years,* Scribner's, New York, 1959.

7. FREUD, A., *Normality and Pathology in Childhood,* International Universities Press, New York, 1965.

8. ———, *The Psychoanalytic Treatment of Children,* Imago, London, 1946.

9. FREUD, S., "Analysis of a Phobia in a Five-Year-Old Boy," in Jones, E. (Ed.), *Collected Papers,* vol. 3, Hogarth Press, London, 1953.

10. FURMAN, E., "Treatment of Under-Fives by Way of Their Parents," in Eissler, R. S., et al., (Eds.), *The Psychoanalytic Study of the Child,* vol. 12, pp. 250–262, International Universities Press, New York, 1957.

11. FURMAN, R. A., and KATAN, A. (Eds.), *The Therapeutic Nursery School: A Contribution to the Study and Treatment of Emotional Disturbances in Young Children,* International Universities Press, New York, 1969.

12. GARDNER, R. A., *Therapeutic Communication with Children,* Science House, New York, 1971.

13. GERARD, M. S., "Direct Treatment of the Preschool Child," *American Journal of Orthopsychiatry, 12:*50–55, 1942.

14. GINOTT, H. G., *Group Psychotherapy with Children,* McGraw-Hill, New York, 1961.

15. GOULD, R., *Child Studies Through Fantasy: Cognitive-Affective Patterns in Development,* Quadrangle Books, New York, 1972.

16. HAWROTH, M., *Child Psychotherapy,* Basic Books, New York, 1964.

17. ISAACS, S., *The Nursery Years,* Schocken Books, New York, 1968.

18. JACOBS, L., "Methods Used in the Education of Mothers," in Eissler, R. S., et al. (Eds.), *The Psychoanalytic Study of the Child,* vol. 3/4, pp. 409–422, International Universities Press, New York, 1949.

19. KATAN, A., "Some Thoughts About the Role of Verbalization in Early Childhood," in Eissler, R. S., et al. (Eds.), *The Psychoanalytic Study of the Child,* vol. 16, pp. 184–188, International Universities Press, New York, 1961.

20. KESTENBERG, J. S., "Problems of Technique of Child Analysis in Relation to the Various Developmental Stages: Prelatency," in Eissler, R. S., et al. (Eds.), *The Psychoanalytic Study of the Child,* vol. 24, pp. 358–383, International Universities Press, New York, 1969.

21. KLEIN, M., *The Psychoanalysis of Children,* Hogarth Press, London, 1932.

22. KRIS, E., "Notes on the Development and on Some Current Problems of Psychoanalytic Child Psychology," in Eissler, R. S., et al. (Eds.), *The Psychoanalytic Study of the Child,* vol. 5, pp. 24–46, International Universities Press, New York, 1950.

23. LEWIS, M. M., *Language, Thought and Personality in Infancy and Childhood,* Basic Books, New York, 1963.

24. NEUBAUER, P. B., "Psychoanalysis of the Preschool Child," in Wolman, B. B. (Ed.), *Handbook of Child Psychoanalysis—Research, Theory and Practice,* pp. 221–252, Van Nostrand Reinhold, New York, 1972.

25. PELLER, L. E., "Libidinal Phases, Ego Development, and Play," in Eissler, R. S., et al. (Eds.), *The Psychoanalytic Study of the Child,* vol. 9, pp. 179–198, International Universities Press, New York, 1954.

26. PIAGET, J., *The Construction of Reality in the Child,* Basic Books, New York, 1954.

27. ———, *The Language and Thought of the Child,* Harcourt, Brace and World, New York, 1926.

28. RANK, B., "Adaptation of the Psychoanalytic Technique for the Treatment of Young Children with Atypical Development," *American Journal of Orthopsychiatry, 19:*130–139, 1949.

29. ———, "Discussion," *American Journal of Orthopsychiatry, 12:*63–67, 1942.

30. SCHOPLER, E., and REICHLER, R. J., "Parents as Cotherapists in the Treatment of Psychotic Children," *Journal of Autism and Childhood Schizophrenia, 1:*87–102, 1971.

31. SCHWARTZ, H., "The Mother in the Consulting Room: Notes on the Psychoanalytic Treatment of Two Young Children," in Eissler, R. S., et al. (Eds.), *The Psychoanalytic Study of the Child,* vol. 5, pp. 343–357, International Universities Press, New York, 1950.

32. SCOTT, W. C. M., "Differences Between the Playroom Used in Child Psychiatric Treatment and Child Analysis," *Canadian Psychiatric Association Journal, 6:* 281–285, 1961.

33. SHRIES, D. K., and LORMAN, S., "Psychiatric Consultation at a Day Care Center," *American Journal of Orthopsychiatry, 43:*394–420, 1973.

34. SPEARS, R. W., and LANSING, C., *Group Therapy in Childhood Psychosis,* University of North Carolina Press, Chapel Hill, 1965.

35. WAELDER, R., "The Psychoanalytic Theory of Play," *Psychoanalytic Quarterly, 2:*208–224, 1933.

30 / Latency and Prepubertal Children

Suzanne T. van Amerongen

General Developmental Considerations

Latency is a uniquely human experience. No species but man goes through such a period of life, an epoch in which the pace of physical growth and sexual maturation slows down while mental capacities expand and accelerate.

It is in the areas of language development and abstract thought, of social and physical skills, and of the capacity for affective experience that these changes appear. During the years between six and thirteen, a sequence of events takes place which will in many ways determine the course of the future adult's life.

The latency/prepuberty child presents a number of paradoxes.[4, 6] Outwardly such a youngster is neither as charming, creative, imaginative, nor confiding as he was at four or five. Nor is he as provocative and puzzling as he will be at fourteen. He is likely to appear prosaic, secretive, and preoccupied with what adults perceive as rather uninteresting, concrete, ritualistic games and activities. He is interested in mundane everyday occurrences. His tastes in food, dress, and recreation are limited and strictly determined by those of his peers. He wants to know "facts" and, particularly in the presence of adults, scorns flights of fancy and imagination. When he is asked where he is going, his answer is "out" and when he returns home, he reports that he did "nothing much."

Those children seem outwardly self-sufficient and often appear independent, but it is a pseudo independence they display.[8] From the time child guidance clinics first opened, this age group has provided the majority of their patients. Where are the sources of stress for these boys and girls? American society makes heavy demands upon the latency child. He no longer goes to school in order to learn to play; he has to learn. Moreover, he must learn how to make friends and acquire a new set of social skills. Acceptance by peers will, in large measure, depend upon his ability to share their hobbies, to compete successfully in sports, and to perform competently in the classroom.

The skills and knowledge a boy or girl acquires during his latency years are far more impressive than adults are apt to acknowledge; and his inner anxieties, self-doubts, and fears of failure and rejection are far more intense than the youngster's nonchalant, outward attitude would lead adults to suspect.

If all goes well, latency children make relatively few demands upon the adults in their environment. When not pressured to satisfy parental aspirations, curiosity, or parents' need for more than a peripheral involvement in the child's life, and when friends are amply accessible to the child, these youngsters are predictable and easy to get along with. Competent and dedicated teachers can usually succeed in satisfying the school-age child's quest for knowledge and in whetting his appetite for increased intellectual mastery and independent learning. Under such circumstances, the youngsters tend to find school attendance and learning a major source of satisfaction.[2]

However, in view of the complexity of the intellectual, emotional, and social growth processes which take place during latency, many children, not surprisingly, at some time or other will require a helping hand. The intricate interweaving of the child's inner developmental processes and societal demands produces its own tensions; as a result diagnostic assessment and therapeutic interventions have to be carefully attuned to the latency child's maturational rate, his personal style, and the developmental tempo of a number of his ego functions. There are children with superior intellectual endowment who may be rapid learners but slow in adapting socially. Others make friends easily but have trouble concentrating upon intellectual tasks. Some youngsters have a winning way with adults and easily become teacher' pets, while others rejoice in peer popularity but remain at odds with their teachers.[2, 6, 9]

During latency, behaviors and symptoms may change rapidly for better or for worse.[7] These changes can be due to the child's developmental progress. As he catches up, troublesome symptoms may disappear overnight. In other instances, similar symptoms and behaviors may bring to the fore previously unrecognized psychopathological processes or cognitive difficulties. For instance: when a latency child displays rituals and obsessive symptoms; it is not unusual to discover that these were preceded in his earlier years by prolonged temper tantrums, sleeping disturbances, or hypochondriacal concerns. As he "outgrew" these symptoms, new ones took their place. "Normal events," as for instance, the birth of a sibling or a change of domicile, can sometimes create an acute crisis for a latency boy or girl. Changes in family composition, or in the child's living quarters, the loss of the old neighborhood, of a familiar school or of friends may precipitate an acute disruption in a child's behavior and performance.

While most children will be able to recover from such temporary regressions spontaneously and come out ahead, some will need assistance to regain their former composure and forward thrust. More serious loss of a parent through divorce or sudden death can precipitate an incapacitating school phobia or inability to learn. Preoccupied as the child is with the loss of one family member, he may fear that in his absence the other parent will desert him as well. To be away from home for a school day raises the specter of a return to a parentless home. It is not surprising either if a child's obnoxious behavior is motivated not so much by a wish to be "kicked out of school" as by the desire to return home as soon as possible. His inability to learn may not necessarily be due to neurotic inhibitions or learning difficulties, but to preoccupations and worries which leave him no energy to concentrate on schoolwork or enjoy peer relationships.

Such possibilities make it imperative for the clinician to proceed with care.[1, 9, 11] A complete and comprehensive diagnostic workup, followed by careful therapeutic planning, should be accompanied by the proper timing of intervention and a continuous monitoring of its effect upon the child and his surroundings. To intervene too quickly may interfere with the child's natural capacity to resolve normal developmental crises on his own. To postpone interventions unduly, hoping that the youngster will outgrow his difficulties, may cause the patient and those who care for him needless suffering, frustration, and increasing loss of confidence and self-esteem. Such a response may seriously hamper and interfere with the normal unfolding of age-appropriate ego functions. When he enters the first grade or changes from grade to junior high school, it is especially important for the child to be able to meet the challenge of these periods of transition with confident anticipation. Failure to get along with teachers or classmates may set the stage for social isolation, scapegoating, or defensively provocative behavior that will continue for years to come. These unfortunate stances can have a decisive effect upon a child's attitude toward teachers and peers in general and upon their responses to him.

Unless they are recognized early, perceptual handicaps and learning blocks may cause a child to detest school and learning. If they are allowed to persist during the early school years, these attitudes are not easily reversed. Therapeutic recommendations must evolve from the clinician's integration of his general knowledge of normal and pathological child development and his specific understanding of that particular child and his unique life history. The choice of therapeutic intervention will be based upon what is best for the child, and, given his current life situation, what is feasible.[2]

With due allowance for individual variation, the average child will begin to show prepubertal changes somewhere between ten and fourteen; this occurs earlier in girls than in boys. It is a period which commonly coincides with a transfer from grade school to junior high. If this transition coincides with other major environmental changes and with the impact of physical growth and the development of secondary sexual characteristics, the youngster's sense of security and self-confidence can be severely tested. A temporary imbalance in hormonal regulation may give rise to bouts of mild abdominal distress in girls or breast formation in boys. Weight gain in youngsters of both sexes tends to add insult to injury. The evident disparity between the growth rate of boys and girls at this age commonly contributes to a defensive alienation of the opposite sex. For that matter, youngsters with marked precocious or retarded development may find themselves at odds with members of their own sex as well. A flight into frantic, hypomanic activity or a retreat into excessive passivity may mask anxiety and depression.[3] It may be an indication that the youngster needs a helping hand in this period of transition from latency to adolescence.

To summarize: The early latency child emerges from his infantile dependency, the supremacy of his instinctual drives, and his struggles with aggressive impulses and oedipal competition; the prepuberty boy or girl prepares himself for the onslaught of a renewed battle with these old, familiar, forgotten themes, transposed into a new key and with the as yet unfamiliar force of sexual maturation. In the intermediate period, the stage is set for a major thrust in ego development, the consolidation of superego formation, and the acquisition of new object ties.[7]

As clinicians have become better acquainted

with children of all races from poverty and ghetto areas, they have been struck by the frequency with which the latency and prepubertal development among these children deviates from the range of "classical" norms. In some areas of development, these youngsters often show marked precocity accompanied by considerable retardation in others.[16] There are not yet sufficient data to determine whether the customary criteria of normality and pathology should be modified in the assessment of such children, and if so, in what ways. From very early on, those child-rearing practices which shape the child's personality are influenced by cultural differences and values and by parental attitudes toward dependency, aggression, and sexuality. It seems likely that developmental deviations of poverty- and ghetto-area children are not due to inherent genetic, social, or cultural differences but instead result from the child and family's struggle for survival, their problems with acculturation and discrimination, and from their attempts to adapt to the stress of chronic socioeconomic deprivation.

Strengths and weaknesses of such latency and prepuberty youngsters have to be carefully appraised. When they must fend for themselves in a life-endangering urban environment where theft, murder, and rape are common, the interface between normality and pathology becomes blurred. Professional workers often face a dilemma as to how best to help these children. The youngsters may need therapeutic intervention desperately, but pose a difficult judgment: one needs to sort out whether, for instance, a girl's fear of attack is due to a neurotic phobia or to justified fears or to a combination of the two. Aggressive behavior by latency boys can be an adaptive way of keeping neighborhood bullies at bay. It also may represent a counterphobic identification with the aggressor. Ghetto children need defenses and coping devices that do not necessarily foster their optimal emotional and intellectual development.

In cities where for the sake of integration children are "bused" away from their familiar neighborhoods to schools in unfamiliar, and often hostile, surroundings, a number of children react to this stress with crippling anxiety and with intractable aggressive behavior. Bright black children bused from the city into suburban white schools often find themselves ostracized by their neighborhood friends and remain isolated from their suburban peers as well.

Early puberty girls are particularly prone to display provocative and aggressive behavior in junior high school. The situation tends to become aggravated if the girls are skilled at manipulating their teachers, who may overidentify with the girls' rebellion. Unfortunately, they often succeed in provoking expulsion from school. They seem to explode under the weight of developmental and environmental stresses as well as cultural and intrapsychic tensions.

It is common for schools to place the total burden of the responsibility for this behavior upon these youngsters. They are promptly referred to a child psychiatric clinic or mental health center for "psychiatric treatment."

A morose, stubbornly silent, thirteen-year-old girl or her angry, verbally abusive counterpart is likely to give an on-the-spot demonstration of the defensive stance these girls adopt to cover up their shaky self-esteem and feelings of loneliness. They are exquisitely attuned to even subtle expressions of ambivalence and past masters at bringing about the self-fulfilling prophecy that they are unwanted and doomed to failure.[16]

General Therapeutic Considerations

Therapeutic considerations with children during these years of latency and prepuberty have to take into account the degree to which a child's development is progressing harmoniously.[1, 4, 6] The goal of therapeutic intervention is to correct physical, intellectual, and psychosocial lags and to remedy handicaps which threaten to deflect growth or have already interfered with it. The effort to help him requires an assessment of the child's native endowment, his developmental and family history, his cultural heritage, the environmental setting within which he grows, and the degree of his psychopathology. During latency in particular, therapeutic interventions present a major opportunity to foster a child's progressive momentum at a key transitional point in his development and to address specifically those roadblocks or impediments he had not been able to overcome. Treatment seeks to bolster the child's self-esteem and to increase his opportunity for personality expansion and ego growth.

Frequently, symptoms and maladaptive behaviors tend to appear during the crucial transition phases of the preschool to the latency years, and again from latency to puberty. At such points, it is the task of the diagnostician to create order out of an array of severe, often multiple and varied, complaints. More than that, he must also be alert to the essential meaning of what may sound like rather harmless and casual observations described by sensitive parents or teachers. These may suggest to him the presence of important deficiencies of psychopathological deviations in the child's character formation. Symptoms and behavior difficulties can have many meanings. They can be the current manifestation of longstanding intrapsychic and interpersonal problems, or they may be signs of more recent neurotic disturbances, of clashes with a new environment, or of acute traumatic experiences. In each instance, the appropriate therapeutic measures will be different.

Tensions can arise from a disparity between a child's physical maturational rate and the pace of his intellectual and emotional progression, from previously undetected intellectual handicaps, from major or chronic upheavals in his family life, or in connection with a move from a familiar environment into strange surroundings. The external expressions of these inner struggles may manifest themselves in similar ways, but they will call for quite different therapeutic strategies.[2, 6]

From a six-year-old who looks more like an eight-year-old, parents and teachers may be inclined to expect an undue degree of self-discipline and concentration; on the other hand, the low self-esteem of a puny seven-year-old will be reinforced if he is needlessly indulged or treated as if he were but five rather than as a small seven-year-old. A precociously mature, prepuberty girl will attract the attention of older boys well before she is emotionally ready to deal with this interest and to respond appropriately to their advances.

Youngsters who suffer from undetected dyslexic difficulties are often considered "dumb." The label may seriously affect their self-concept and the opinions of their unsophisticated teachers and ruthless peers. The behavior of many children referred for chronically obnoxious school behavior is less a reflection of primary developmental or psychological deviations than it is an expression of their anxiety and discontent about a disorganized, strife-ridden, and rudderless family life.

In general, the most effective interventions will be those which capitalize on the child's assets and enlist the support of his family, teachers, and peers. There should be as little interference as possible with his opportunity for learning and socialization. The young latency child's continued need for physical and emotional nurture from a secure family milieu and a supportive environment must be given great attention. Thus, the younger the child, the more essential is the cooperation and collaboration of parents and teachers in the therapeutic regimen.

However, the best laid plans will fail unless the prospective patient perceives the therapeutic recommendations as helpful. Latency and prepubertal children are seldom self-referred; they are brought to the clinic or private practitioner for reasons they do not always understand or may not acknowledge. What brings most children to treatment is the concern of the pediatrician, parent, or teacher about mysterious symptoms, "bad behavior," or school failure. The young patient who has escaped prior extensive, often frightening, physical checkups and tests is lucky, almost as rare as the older child who prior to his referral has not been subjected to punitive disciplinary measures or repeated humiliating failures, bribes, and threats. The prospect of yet another doctor, and "a shrink" to boot, will confirm a child's growing suspicion that something is very wrong with him, that he is "mental," or crazy, bad, stupid, and, in any case, hopeless.

Despite the reassurances of well-meaning adults, the fear the child feels that this time he will be kept at the clinic or be sent away from home can be intense. Often this represents a secretly harbored component of an ambivalent wish. This secret part is seldom meant to come true, however, and the fear can be allayed only if it is possible to enlist the necessary cooperation of parents and teachers. It is up to the clinician to determine how much and what kind of collaboration is essential for which type of intervention. Whatever a child's prior history or symptomatology, the treatment plan designed for him will depend a great deal upon his current life situation. For instance (as discussed in chapters 2 and 3), intensive psychotherapy or psychoanalysis is eminently appropriate for children whose neurotic difficulties and inhibitions can be traced back to early childhood.[12, 13] However, it is practical only if the patient lives in a relatively stable and supportive family setting and if geographic and socioeconomic conditions allow for such a major investment. Furthermore, the patient has to be at least partially willing to communicate his conflicts and distress.[13]

An unhappy, regressed six-year-old girl who responds to her doctor's invitation for a return visit the following week with an eager "Tomorrow?" clearly conveys her wish for a therapeutic relationship; while a second-grader who wonders if the diagnostician can help him to learn to read is a willing candidate for the type of intervention likely to achieve precisely that.

The younger the child, the greater the therapist's need for regular meetings with his parents, and very likely, their need for some concomitant therapeutic work for themselves (see chapter 8). When disturbed latency children are living in chaotic conditions, a prerequisite for outpatient treatment is some measure of stabilization of the environment. If this is not feasible, removal from home into a foster home or residential placement will become necessary (see chapters 15 and 18). These measures, however, have to be used sparingly. Removal from home represents a severe disruption of the child's total life situation, while foster home placement can mark the beginning of a series of subsequent separations which will act to compound the original loss. Residential placement is at best a temporary measure. Sooner or later the child will either have to return home or to find out that there is no longer a home to which to return. When it is possible to improve their home life, even if only a little, many such children will profit greatly from a continuing therapeutic relationship. The therapist provides them with a model for identification, a corrective human experience and steady ego support. Given such help, they can then turn with greater confidence and faith to other parent substitutes for continued emotional and intellectual input. The deprived child's positive therapeutic experience can provide a foundation upon which teachers, boy or girl scout leaders, recreational and community workers, and "big sisters" or "big brothers" can build. In time, they will be able to take over the bulk of the supportive and educational functions.

Early Latency

Whatever the nature of the six- or seven-year-old's difficulties, it is important always to remember that he is still a child who, despite his wish to be a "big" boy or girl, yearns at times to be "little" again. From many points of view, he still depends upon caring adults, a fact the therapist must recognize and respect. To remain on good terms with the patient's caretakers and to provide them directly or indirectly with appropriate assistance (as described in chapter 8) is as important as helping the child directly. At times, it is even more important.

One-to-one psychotherapy or individual therapeutic tutoring is frequently the appropriate modality for child in this age group. These modalities have the advantage of giving the youngster an opportunity for special attention and intimacy, a chance "to let his hair down" in the presence of an understanding and knowledgeable adult, and the freedom to do so without exposing himself to ridicule, censure, or retaliation. Sometimes, despite the clinician's best efforts to involve the parents in their child's rehabilitative process, they refuse to collaborate or continue to oppose the child's individual treatment. In such instances, the therapist may have to resort to those interventions on the child's behalf which the parents can accept. It is intolerable for young and dependent children to be thrust into a situation in which parents and therapist are in opposition and compete for the child's loyalty. In such cases, then, the therapeutic goals can be approached by referring the child to a therapeutic day-care or after-school program, to a special school placement with psychologically minded teachers, or to a special class which can offer him a good deal of individual attention and help (see chapters 17, 18, 19, 20).

If individual psychotherapy is both indicated and feasible, treatment generally focuses on those defenses which prevent the child from dealing effectively with his drives, hamper his intellectual, social, and emotional growth, and bring about pathological deviations.[5] Young latency children readily use play materials to express their fantasies and concerns. Dollhouse play often vividly reveals family relationships and interactions. Toy animals such as zebras and panda bears provide an opportunity to discuss black-white racial issues, especially when child and therapist are of different races or when youngsters are the product of racially mixed marriages. A young child can communicate his wishes, anxieties, and guilt feelings in a safe and displaced fashion via drawings and stories. (For further details, see chapter 25.)

A limited period of well-focused psychotherapy (as described in chapter 4) is often more beneficial than a long, diffuse, drawn-out, pseudo therapeutic relationship that goes on for many years and involves multiple transfers from one therapist to another (see also chapter 3). Clinicians tend to overtreat children; the fact is often ignored that to prolong a child's therapy can interfere with his natural resilience and foster excessive dependence. When specific goals have been accomplished, termination of treatment will allow a child to try to manage on his own. It is best to end on a positive note with the assurance to the child and his parents that if the child reaches a stalemate or regresses, he and they can obtain more help at a later time. This makes it clear to both that therapy is not a replacement for normal living. In teaching clinics, changes in staff and trainees are a common occurrence. The necessary transfer of patients from one therapist to another has many drawbacks. Indeed, such transfer to another therapist should be avoided unless the indications are urgent; prolonged treatment accentuates the child's and parent's feelings of inadequcy and helplessness. It also devalues the importance of the therapeutic experience and may support unrealistic fantasies that replacement is what counts rather than mastering the grief over the loss of an important relationship which had a specific and limited therapeutic goal. It is often surprising to observe how much can be accomplished, even with seriously disturbed children, by the use of carefully planned and well-executed psychotherapy. Termination of treatment allows for a consolidation of more appropriate defenses and ways of coping at the same time that the loss of the therapist fosters identification with him or her.

Certain kinds of youngsters, such as the seriously emotionally deprived, those with limited ego strength, and those lacking the capacity for age-appropriate object relations, will need to be provided with an appropriate "support system" in addition to intermittent psychotherapeutic assistance. Rather than encourage an exclusive attachment, the clinician is more useful if he presents himself as the representative of a helping institution which will continue to give help even though he personally may leave. From the beginning, such a youngster must be helped to face the painful reality that the doctor cannot replace his inadequate, sick, or absent parents. Other supportive adults and settings must be found to help him carry on his daily life. Consultation and collaboration between the therapist and the child's supporters are in and of themselves therapeutic for him. Many of these children have never had the benefit of dealing with a number of adults working together on his behalf, each of whom has something special to offer him and all of whom respect and complement each other.

It was noted in chapter 1 that family therapy, which is described in detail in chapter 7, has rarely been the treatment of choice for disturbed young latency children. More frequently, individual therapy is punctuated by occasional joint family sessions to help the child and his family take stock and integrate changes which have occurred over time or as a result of therapeutic intervention. In these joint family sessions, it should be remembered that a discrpancy exists between the child's ways of comprehending and expressing worries and the adult's. It is hard for the child to understand the difficulties adults face as compared to his own immediate concerns. Family sessions can thus add to his confusion, his sense of guilt and inadequacy, and his increasing anxiety. Often the patient feels left out because the adults monopolize the session and their conversation may be way over his head. (Different problems arise with older latency children, as will be discussed later in this chapter.)

Those disturbances in young latency children which require strictly psychotherapeutic intervention are usually caused by unresolved conflicts of early developmental periods. As a result, group therapy (discussed in detail in chapter 10), has generally been considered less beneficial than one-to-one treatment. However, for children who feel threatened by a one-to-one relationship, who lack sufficient trust of adults, and who feel safer in the presence of peers, a small, therapeutically low-keyed activity group may well be the treatment of choice.[15] Much will depend on the leader's skill in making the activity group into a meaningful therapeutic experience. Activity groups can give the child his first chance to gain pleasure from organized, constructive play, to develop inner controls by internalizing the outer controls enforced by the group leader, and to learn how to win and keep friends through mutual give and take.[14, 15]

The use of psychopharmacological agents in the treatment of latency children is still much debated. It has been discussed extensively in chapter 23 and will not be elaborated here. It suffices to say that hyperkinetic, epileptic, and acutely psychotic children can benefit greatly from appropriate medication. If medication is provided in an outpatient setting, the patient must be closely supervised. The clinician has to be sure that the caretakers can and do take responsibility for its proper administration. As discussed in chapter 1, pharmacological treatment does not preclude supportive psychotherapeutic help. On the contrary, as the child quiets down and the drugs take effect, such help provides an excellent opportunity to aid him to acquire a greater tolerance for stress, to teach him basic skills which enhance his self-confidence, and to strengthen his capacity to learn and to concentrate. In the course of supportive treatment medication can often be reduced, and in time discontinued. Careful monitoring of drug therapy is always necessary. The effects of medication do change as a child grows older, and undesirable side effects can occur if the treatment is unnecessarily prolonged.

Children with multiple physical, cognitive, and emotional handicaps should be treated with a variety of corrective and rehabilitative measures[10] (which are discussed in chapters 19, 20, 37, 38, 39, 40, 41, and 42).

Middle Latency

The moment of truth very often arrives after the child has entered the third grade. By this time, learning inhibitions are no longer so easily ignored, and it is difficult to dismiss persistent behavior problems as passing spells the child will outgrow. Among the symptoms frequently precipitating a referral of a mid-latency child to a child psychiatric clinic or practitioner are: habitual lying and stealing; aggressive destructive behavior; chronic school failure; lack of friends; persistent enuresis or encopresis; self-destructive behaviors; rituals; and compulsions often accompanied by self-devaluation, depressive moods, and withdrawal from people.[9]

While on the one hand a child in middle latency is now better able to speak for himself and is often more keenly aware of his own suffering, the discrepancy between his needs and wishes and those provided by his environment may be increased. The older the child, the more his immediate dependency upon his parents diminishes and the more his cooperation in treatment becomes a prerequisite for effective intervention. The youngster referred by his concernd parents or teachers who denies having any difficulties or who maintains a bland, indifferent, and often stubbornly silent facade can present a formidable challenge to the clinician's diagnostic and treatment skills.

The responsibility for precribing the treatment of choice rests ultimately with the clinician. Its successful implementation, however, will in large measure depend upon the child's conviction that it is for his benefit and is not just another attempt to mold him to conform to the wishes and expectations of his parents or teachers.

Although their verbal, or at least tacit, consent for his therapy remains necessary, parents' participation in older latency children's treatment may not be imperative. Parents with a genuine concern for the child's difficulties are likely to want to be included in one way or another, while those who contribute in fundamental ways to his problems should be. However, with an older latency child who is keenly aware of his distress and wants help, psychotherapy or psychoanalysis can be carried out successfully with minimal parental involvement.[12] Such a child is also able to tell his therapist when he is ready to terminate treatment, as did a ten-year-old boy who had been in psychoanalysis for an obsessive-compulsion neurosis. He announced his willingness and readiness to terminate treatment by remarking to his therapist that he was no longer so interested in exploring his dreams and fantasies. Instead, he would like to do things and to explore the outside world! While his fears and rituals had subsided, he also had entered the late latency phase of development in which outward directedness and repression of instinctual drives and wishes are common phenomena.

Middle latency children will still use play materials as an important medium for therapeutic communication. Card and checker games with the therapist often open up problems of competition and low self-esteem. Gender conflicts are revealed when a girl insists on playing only with boys' toys, while boys gravitate, albeit reluctantly, toward dollhouse play.[2, 5]

Where the acute symptoms are caused by a revival of early traumatic experiences, time-limited, focused psychotherapy is a particularly suitable modality for middle latency children. For instance, the loss of a beloved teacher may revive the still unassimilated feelings about a prior loss of a parent or other significant relative. If the child and therapist can together recognize the source of the difficulties and agree upon a fixed number of visits to help master this current and past traumatic event, time-limited therapy will bring out a repetition of past feelings and fantasies around the impending loss of the therapist. Intense transference feelings will permit a reworking of past events, put the child's guilt feelings and fantasies into their proper perspective, and help-him find more successful ways of dealing with grief (see chapter 4 for more details of brief therapy).

Self-sufficiency, self-respect, and acceptance by his peer group are the psychological mainstays of the older latency child.[4, 6] Therapeutic interventions will accordingly aim to disrupt the vicious cycle of poor school performance, loss of self-confidence and self-esteem, devaluation by more successful peers, and a growing pattern of seeking attention and approval by self-destructive behavior. Delinquent acts are frequently the child's way of drawing attention to his desperate plight; even though his "now" group consists of boys and girls who get him into even deeper trouble, he is still driven to do everything possible to win their respect and approval.

Although symptomatic behavior may be the entry ticket to a clinic or private office, it is rarely the topic of choice in the therapeutic encounter. On the other hand, the feelings which caused these manifestations certainly do find expression.

Privacy and confidentiality are highly prized by latency children. Treatment is most welcome when it is on their terms and refrains from intruding into their real and fantasy lives.[5] Adults are only slowly and gradually permitted to enter a child's private world; those who facilitate his independence, however, and who show an interest in whatever he is willing to reveal about himself, his interests, his friends, or his activities will often be rewarded by glowing reports of his remarkable improvement from parents and teachers.

For some older latency children, group therapy is an effective mode of intervention. In group sessions it is easier to see at first hand and to bring to a youngster's attention how he provokes others to make him a scapegoat or acts to bully and to antagonize those who reach out to him. This modality is also more palatable to children who defend themselves strongly against becoming involved in a one-to-one relationship.[15]

A ten-year-old boy referred for his passive negativistic stance with adults may languish in his diagnostic session with an older woman clinician. Mention of the possibility of a therapeutic boys' group where boys his age share their mutual concerns with a young male leader interested in children may cause him to liven up. This suggests that group therapy may be the most promising therapeutic approach for him at this time.

Older latency children will often make good use of family sessions. These help particularly to assess and clarify who or what is the real problem in the family. A latency child who can find no way to communicate the reason for his disturbed behavior to an experienced clinician, or who ascribes his difficulties repeatedly and consistently to his family members, very often serves as a family symptom. It is only after the family secret is brought into the open that it becomes possible to determine whether it is the identified patient who needs help or whether the rehabilitative efforts have to be directed primarily elsewhere.

Older children with marked perceptual handicaps will need expert tutorial help, and the sooner the better.[10] The more longstanding a child's school failure, the less likely the chance that he will recapture an enthusiasm for learning, despite major psychotherapeutic and educative efforts. For instance, consider the diagnositic assessment of an eleven-year-old with chronic learning difficulties. If he is still willing to perform tests which he well knows will reveal his level of achievmeent and also of failure, then he has clearly not yet given up, is still reaching out for help, and could be an excellent and willing candidate for expert psychoeducational assistance of the sort detailed in chapters 19 and 20. One way of reawakening an interest in learning in some of these youngsters is to provide them with an opportunity to teach younger children. To teach what he has learned, or to learn so he can teach others, can be an effective incentive for a late latency child to become involved in his own treatment.

Puberty

As puberty approaches, it is not unusual to see a resurgence of earlier difficutlies which had gone underground in the intervening latency years. As was mentioned earlier, bodily changes and the transition from grade to junior high school can elicit acute anxieties about growing up, about change in general, and about separation in particular.[3]

The difference in rate of growth and maturation between girls and boys can alienate the sexes or precipitate girls into premature sexual experimentation with older boys. The prepuberty youngster often feels caught in a web of demands and expectations by his parents, teachers, or peers, along with his own strivings for comfort and his own aspirations. An eleven-year-old girl who looks as if she were fifteen, or an eleven- or twelve-year-old boy whose size and general appearance are more commensurate with those of a nine- or ten-year-old, may suffer from the discrepancy between his physical and his emotional maturity. Whether he responds to his discomfort with regressive, pseudomature, or acting-out behavior, with transient psychosomatic complaints, or with withdrawal and depressive moods will depend upon a youngster's character structure and his defensive and coping styles. It is a delicate matter to determine whether he needs help, and if he does, how best to provide it. Again this requires an assessment of his earlier development and current conflicts. The patient must share in the decision about the type of intervention most suited to give him the necessary emotional support without injury to his self-esteem. Whether individual, family, or group therapy is the preferred modality will depend upon an understanding of his nuclear conflict and personal preferences.

Prepuberty youngsters often respond quite well to group therapy. Here they can share their sexual concerns with peers and have an opportunity to receive appropriate enlightenment and factual information from the adult group leader. They are often reassured to discover that their fears and fantasies are by no means unique.[15]

In family sessions, the therapist can interpret some of the youngster's feelings to family members. This may be a description of his resentment because he is treated "as if he were a baby," or the anxiety he feels because they do not give him enough structure, guidance, and supervision. In any case, it can clear the air and reestablish mutual communication within the family.

For children whose developmental course has been erratic, delayed, or fraught with ups and downs, prepuberty is an especially favorable time for individual psychotherapeutic intervention. Such help may prevent a more ominous breakdown or arrest of development during adolescence. Concerns about masturbation (which serves as a release for physical and emotional tensions), worries about body integrity, and fears about the upsurge of primitive sado-masochistic fantasies are more easily confessed and discussed in the private atmosphere of one-to-one therapy sessions.

At times, placebos or mild tranquilizers are useful temporary therapeutic adjuncts that help allay overwhelming anxiety and transient sleep disturbances. These have to be used sparingly and should be closely supervised, however, particularly today when drug use and alcoholism among young teenagers are on the upswing. Drug use and drinking are often attempts at self-medication for depressive moods and poorly tolerated anxiety. The adult's concern about the youngster's involvement with "pot and liquor" should not deflect attention from the serious precipitating factors. Once it has become a habitual and multipurpose pattern for relief of various kinds of inner turmoil, what started out as an experiment can become a practice not easily renounced. Habitual drug use can easily become a way to give vent to fierce resentment toward adult society, to gain acceptance from questionable friends, and to suppress poorly tolerated dystonic affects.

Conclusion

Although experienced child therapists have always tailored the treatment of patients to their developmental stage, it is only recently that the developmental viewpoint has come vividly to the forefront. Anne Freud's[7] developmental profile has helped assess the various psychological aspects of each developmental phase with greater precision and in finer detail than before. The present-day interest in Piaget's[17] careful analysis of children's cognitive development has helped gear remedial work more precisely to those areas of cognition which require specialized therapeutic intervention.

The family has come to be recognized as a dynamic system of interpersonal relationships, subject to its own progressive and regressive fluctuations. This has led to the use of family therapy as an important therapeutic modality, suited to rehabilitate the individual child as well as the psychological unit of which he is an integral part.

As clinicians came to realize more and more the vital importance to the growing youngster of peer acceptance and support, group therapy for children evolved.

The satisfactory resolution of infantile dependency and libidinal incestuous attachments is the key to a successful transition from preschool to the latency period, and from puberty and adolescence to adulthood.

Therapeutic considerations must be geared on the one hand to helping the child free himself from the regressive pull of his early childhood attachments, and on the other, to enhance his age-appropriate developmental progressive potential. Today, therapeutic considerations seem to be determined less by nosological labels than was true in the past. In prescribing therapeutic interventions, greater attention is currently given to the child's prior developmental achievements and his adaptive propensities than to his developmental failures and pathological deviations. Undoubtedly, the pendulum will swing again in the opposite direction as more accurate and specific knowledge is acquired about the many factors which cause or contribute to various forms of disturbance in school-age children. Such understanding will no doubt give rise to more focused and specialized therapeutic measures and techniques especially suited for the treatment of children's syndromes.

REFERENCES

1. ALLEN, F. H., "Therapeutic Work with Children: Statement of a Point of View," *American Journal of Orthopsychiatry, 4*:193, 1934.
2. ALPERT, A., "The Latency Period: Re-examination in Educational Setting," *American Journal of Orthopsychiatry, 11*:126, 1941.
3. BLOS, P., "The Initial Stage of Male Adolescence," in Eissler, R. S., et al. (Eds.), *The Psychoanalytic Study of the Child,* vol. 20, p. 145, International Universities Press, New York, 1965.
4. BORNSTEIN, B., "On Latency," in Eissler, R. S., et al. (Eds.), *The Psychoanalytic Study of the Child,* vol. 6, p. 279, International Universities Press, New York, 1951.
5. BUXBAUM, E., "Technique of Child Therapy: A Critical Evaluation," in Eissler, R. S., et al. (Eds.), *Psychoanalytic Study of the Child,* vol. 9, p. 297, International Universities Press, New York, 1954.
6. ———, "A Contribution to the Psychoanalytic Knowledge of the Latency Period," *American Journal of Orthopsychiatry, 21*:182, 1951.
7. FREUD, A., *Normality and Pathology in Childhood,* Hogarth Press, London, 1966.
8. FURFEY, P. H., "Case Studies in Developmental Age," *American Journal of Orthopsychiatry, 1*:292, 1930.
9. KAPLAN, S., "The Latency Period (A Panel Report)," *Journal of the American Psychoanalytic Association, 5*: 525, 1957.
10. LEVE, R., GRAFFAGNINO, P., and AVALLONE, S., "An Attempt to Combine Clinical and Educational Resources: A Report on the First Years' Experience of a Therapeutic School," *American Journal of Orthopsychiatry, 10*:108, 1971.
11. LOWERY, L. G., "Treatment of Behavior Problems: I. Some Illustrations of Variations in Treatment Approach," *American Journal of Orthopsychiatry, 4*:120, 1934.
12. MAENCHEN, A., "On the Technique of Child Analysis in Relation to States of Development," Eissler, R. S., et al. (Eds.), *The Psychoanalytic Study of the Child,* vol. 25, p. 175, International Universities Press, New York, 1970.
13. NOVICK, J., "The Vicissitudes of the Working Alliance in the Analysis of a Latency Girl," in Eissler, R. S., et al. (Eds.), *The Psychoanalytic Study of the Child,* vol. 25, p. 231, International Universities Press, New York, 1970.
14. SEIDLINGER, S., "Experiential Group Treatment of Severely Deprived Latency Children," *American Journal of Orthopsychiatry, 30*:356, 1960.
15. SUGER, M., "Interpretive Group Psychotherapy with Latency Children," *Journal of the American Academy of Child Psychiatry, 13*:648, 1974.
16. VOSK, J. S., "Study of Negro Children with Learning Difficulties at Onset of School Career," *American Journal of Orthopsychiatry, 36*:32, 1966.
17. WOLFF, P. H., *The Developmental Psychologies of Jean Piaget,* International Universities Press, New York, 1960.

31 / Adolescents

Bertram Slaff

A thorough knowledge of the dynamic process of growth and development is the *sine qua non* of effective treatment of the adolescent.

The therapist must comprehend the developmental challenges to the teenager: to negotiate the onset of puberty in the face of major changes in body configuration and intensification of sexual drives; to relinquish some of the dependency of childhood; to derive increasing security from his own growing mastery; to tolerate the losing of confidence in his parents and teachers as the repositories of wisdom; to develop his own skeptical and critical powers and to learn more and more how to think in independent terms; to cultivate the growth of his social skills; to learn how to deal with strong emotional states; to begin to be aware of the necessity of thinking ahead and considering his own future; to weigh increasingly important educational and career goals in a realistic fashion; to deal with sexual strivings and to conceive of love, marriage, and parenthood; ,and finally, to strive for complete independence. The totality of this development is known as separation and individuation; when it is successfully negotiated, it results in the establishment of an independent adult personality.

All therapeutic interventions with teenagers share a fundamental principle, that they *promote growth.* The therapist must strive to ascertain when blockages to growth exist and must work with his patient toward the removal of these interferences. When the individual is free to resume growth, the goal of therapeutic intervention is likely to have been reached.

CASE ILLUSTRATION

Eleven-year-old Marjorie suddenly developed a terror of going to school and absolutely refused to go. She was particularly alarmed about arithmetic, declaring she was stupid and couldn't understand anything at all about what was going on. Further questioning revealed that it was "addition" in arithmetic about which she felt particularly insecure.

What especially confused her parents was that previously Marjorie had been a reasonably bright student (although her grades were not as good as her fourteen-year-old sister's), and that arithmetic had been one of her better subjects.

She was referred to a therapist, who determined that she had developed a school phobia of a nature that contraindicated employing those "first aid" supportive measures that might facilitate a rapid return to school. He recommended that she be withdrawn from school on a medical leave of absence and that she enter psychotherapy.

Marjorie reacted with great relief. She thanked the therapist for rescuing her and, with great joy, began to work as her father's assistant in the studio where he painted in oils.

The feeling of relief and gratitude ended swiftly when the therapist insisted that the anxieties about school be confronted and discussed. Marjorie then perceived him as an enemy, pushing her to face pain. She felt that she ought to leave psychotherapy, as it was making her feel worse. Nevertheless, she stayed in treatment.

One day Marjorie declared vehemently that she had heard psychiatrists were always looking for a sexual meaning in everything. She wanted it clearly understood that sex had nothing to do with her problem. In fact, she found the whole subject unattractive. Her periods had not started yet, and she was happy about this. She thought from the way her sister talked about them that they were a "messy business." All she wanted to do was to stay a little girl, be at home with her parents, help her father in his studio, and have fun. She denied fearing growing up; rather she declared herself not especially interested in it. She was reacting as though she had the choice of whether or not to permit growing up.

Gradually it became apparent to Marjorie that she was fighting off the acknowledgment of the imminent beginning of her periods. She likened the expectation of having periods to the child's game "Pin the Tail on the Donkey." She elaborated on this by saying it was like having something added to oneself that made one feel different, no longer like oneself.

It was pointed out to her that she had compared the anticipation of her period to having something "added" to her. Suddenly she broke into tears and rushed out of the therapist's office crying, "I hate you!"

Although a period of resistance followed, an important clue had been elicited that contributed to the understanding of her school phobia. Marjorie was terrified of her expected periods, which she feared would be something "added" to her, changing her into something else, not herself. This included fear of the "addition" of breasts. Her defense was to try to go backward, to return to the security remembered from earlier years, to renounce school and learning, to stop time. Nevertheless, implicit in this apparent renunciation of adolescent sexuality was an unconscious return to oedipal sexuality in which, as a little

girl, she could spend time assisting her beloved father in his studio, while her older sister was compelled to attend school.

As it became clearer to Marjorie that she was trying to do the impossible, to stop time and growth, she gradually began to prepare to accept the imminent pubertal changes. She agreed to cooperate with home instruction classes for the balance of the term and did return to school when the new term began. The therapeutic goal had been accomplished.

Normative Crises

In everyone's life experience new steps in growth and development are often periods of extraordinary stress; these are called "normative crises." An obvious example of this would be a child's going off to school for the first time. Marjorie was attempting to cope with such a normative crisis, the imminence of puberty.

CASE ILLUSTRATION

Dwight, a seventeen-year-old high school senior who wanted to go away to college, was facing the normative crisis of leaving home. He had a childhood history of allergies which had caused much parental and medical concern. During early adolescence his sensitivities had lessened, and he now seemed to be a healthy youth.

In considering colleges to attend, he became concerned by the worrisome thought, "What happens if I get sick?" He was reluctant to tell anyone how terrified he was to be away from his mother.

The family of a close friend invited Dwight to accompany them on a vacation trip. Dwight agonized about what he would do if he became ill. He might throw up, he might sneeze all night, he might suffocate. Determined to keep his anxieties private, he declined the invitation.

However, he really wanted to go on the trip. It seemed a hopeless dilemma. His appetite declined, he slept poorly. Soon his parents realized that he was severely troubled and arranged for a psychiatric consultation.

In the course of the ensuing psychotherapy, it became abundantly clear that Dwight's inner picture of himself was that of a severely allergic youngster, perilously vulnerable to sneezing, choking, and life-threatening attacks of nausea and vomiting.

That he had been essentially well for over five years, that he had matured, and that he could now take adequate care of himself had not been comprehended by the anxious child within.

Dwight was encouraged to open up to the reality of his having outgrown his allergic sensitivities and having become a healthy youth. He was asked to anticipate possible allergic difficulties in the light of his new competence to handle them. He was strongly encouraged to take the proposed trip.

The vacation journey turned out to be successful, though in the final few days Dwight became anxious, thinking his good luck could not continue.

Gradually over the following months Dwight's anxieties faded and his self-confidence grew; he was able to embark on a college career away from home.

The cases of Marjorie and Dwight illustrate a major requirement for the therapist who deals with teenagers, the ability to help his patient comprehend and negotiate successfully the normative crises of youth. The natural tendency toward growth facilitates these efforts, so therapeutic goals are often reached in relatively brief periods of time.

The Diagnostic Evaluation

As a rule, it is the parents of the distressed teenager who seek out the therapist for consultation. Unless the youth objects strongly, his parents are likely to be seen first, to provide their views of the current problem, to offer a detailed developmental history, and to be observed in their own functioning. Plans are then made for the young person to meet with the therapist.

Diagnostic evaluation of a teenager must be part of a family and environmental study. Some youngsters get into difficulties in unconscious compliance with the needs of a parent. A youth's behavior may be in response to a parent's unconscious fostering as a result of a "superego lacuna" within the parent, as described by Adelaide Johnson.[25] A parent may demonstrate superego defects in his own behavior. Or, he may subtly incite his child to behave in a particular way by negative suggestion.

CASE ILLUSTRATION

Thirteen-year-old Ned stole a substantial sum of money from the church collection in a manner which suggested that unconsciously he expected to be caught. And he was.

Ned's father was a claims investigator for an insurance company, with the responsibility for ferreting out instances of possible fraud. He had nagged his son incessantly about the importance of being strictly honest.

The father had chosen a career of uncovering fraud, the antithesis of stealing. However, such an occupation exists on the premise that frauds are being perpetrated. It is possible that the son was responding to an unconsciously given suggestion by the father. The monotonously repeated "Don't steal!" may have come across to Ned as "How interested I am in theft!" In his behavior, he may have provided his father with the opportunity to practice his profession of opposing criminality. The father may have chosen his occupation as an undoing of an unconscious wish to steal. It may have been this wish that his son was vicariously living out.

An alternative possibility, that Ned was rebelling against his father's "Don't steal!" was considered to be unlikely because of Ned's basically conforming, eager-to-please personality and his almost open invitation to others to identify him as the culprit.

A particular individual may be "selected" to "scapegoat" for a family; by loading him with the blame for family disharmony, the other family members are enabled to avoid confronting their own contributions to the situation.

CASE ILLUSTRATION

Fourteen-year-old Debra was the only child of a lawyer-father who lived in Chicago and a painter-mother who kept her own apartment in New York, for professed career reasons. The parents would spend a month or so together in each location; in the course of these periods together, there would routinely be a major battle over Debra's behavior, and the parents would then separate again. Debra would stay with one parent or the other, until a toleration point had been reached; she then would be sent back to the other. Her well-off parents had even established her in private schools of comparable status in the two cities, so that as she was batted about, ping-pong style, school facilities were always available for her.

Both parents had established a "line"; it was Debra's impossible ways that prevented them from being able to stay together. Debra herself had never questioned the validity of this. She believed that she was the serpent who had wrecked the Eden of her parents' lives.

It is very probable that Debra's parents needed her as a scapegoat, a front behind which they could conceal their basic incompatibilities. It is quite likely that Debra misbehaved in unconscious acquiescence to her parents' needs.

An adolescent whose behavior is destructive may be acting at the direction of another family member.

CASE ILLUSTRATION

A thirteen-year-old youth was described by his parents as severely disturbed. He and his fifteen-year-old brother were angry young people who called both parents "fuzz" and "fascist oppressors." The behavior of the younger boy, Roger, included throwing dishes and threatening to destroy the household. Derek, the older brother, ridiculed the idea of seeing a psychiatrist and refused to consider it. Roger was willing to do so.

In early conversations with the therapist, Roger appeared friendly, lucid, intelligent, and talked with equanimity about what his parents had described as the "state of siege" at home. He laughed, saying his parents had "no sense of humor at all." He admitted that he had thrown dishes several times, when his parents were being "too uptight." Yes, he had threatened to destroy the household, but he really hadn't meant that. "My parents are alarmists; it's not nearly that bad." Speaking for himself and his brother, he admitted, "We tease them a lot."

After some time, the mystery of how Roger could be seen so differently by his parents and by his psychiatrist was opened for discussion. At Roger's appointment one afternoon, Derek, too, showed up, announcing that he wished to report on what was happening at home. He spoke about the persecuting behavior of both parents, occasionally demanding confirmation from Roger, who echoed him without question. He spoke condescendingly about the stupidity of both parents and remarked that it was sometimes necessary for him to get Roger to throw dishes off the table to get through to them.

During this meeting, it had become apparent that, when they were together and within the family, Roger functioned as a younger brother satellite to Derek. When not with Derek, Roger was a mischievous adolescent, but not paranoid. In Derek's company, however, he submitted to his brother's paranoid attitude and was available to act out whatever Derek wanted.

Diagnostic evaluation of a teenager must include a review of the adaptive successes and failures of the individual throughout development.

A youth cannot be adequately understood from the study of recent and present behavior alone; a lifetime developmental survey is the essential frame of reference for comprehension of this behavior.

CASE ILLUSTRATION

Sixteen-year-old Jeremy came to the attention of the student health office at his college after his philosophy instructor expressed concern about him. He was reading far more than anyone else in the class, often seemed preoccupied and withdrawn, and had ideas which seemed to his teacher to be extraordinarily original, possibly highly creative or, on the other hand, bizarre, or both. A careful review of Jeremy's life history revealed that as early as nursery school, he had been noticed as "different." His teacher had reported that he was always sweet and amiable but seemed to lack some quality of personal responsiveness, as though he didn't really care

very much whether or not anyone paid any attention to him. Some years later, he was observed in school to be highly gifted in learning and particularly adept at self-instruction. He was consistently ahead of his class in all his subjects. He cheerfully carried out additional assignments that his devoted teachers prepared for him alone.

At age nine, Jeremy regarded his classmates as childish and told them so. He identified completely with the adult world. Not surprisingly, the other children hated Jeremy and teased him unmercifully. Jeremy seemed not to care very much; by the third grade, he was already teaching himself Italian, botany, and astronomy.

During his childhood, Jeremy received much love and support from his parents, who understood and respected his right to be different. If they had fought him on this and pressed him to be more like other children, it is likely that they would have alienated him and that he would then have been even more isolated than he was.

As a young child, Jeremy freely admitted that he was different, saying in his characteristic way, "That is I."

In the course of the evaluation, his "atypical" behavior at college was felt to be consistent with his earlier character development and was not regarded as cause for concern. It was judged that Jeremy would probably continue to be an atypical person throughout his life, and that he would be likely to continue to gain major gratifications from exercising his intellectual capacities. If at some future time he became upset because of interpersonal difficulties, he might then seek help. Then, too, his "atypicality" would have to be respected.

Indications for Treatment of the Adolescent

Severe prolonged anxiety is a strong signal of the need for therapeutic intervention. The various neuroses which to some extent protect the youth from awareness of his anxieties are indications for treatment. These neuroses include the phobias, obsessive-compulsive reactions, conversions, and depressions.

CASE ILLUSTRATION

Seventeen-year-old David was an outstanding student at his large metropolitan high school. He had been elected president of the student body, was captain of the basketball team, and graduated third in his class.

Shortly after learning that he had been awarded an all-expense scholarship to the outstanding college which was his first choice, David underwent a major change in mood. He lost his appetite, slept with difficulty, withdrew socially, questioned his abilities, and began to express serious doubts about whether he should accept the scholarship and attend college. It was recognized that he had become depressed, and psychiatric help was sought.

David had for a long time been a "golden lad," generously endowed with health, intelligence, looks, physical and athletic skills, and a relaxed warmth and interest in others.

His parents, fearful that he might become conceited, had for many years reminded him of his good fortune in having inherited superior genes, which permitted him his successes. He was not to claim that he was better than others; he was merely luckier. And, *noblesse oblige*, certainly more would be expected of him because of his good fortune.

At the unconscious level, David experienced his considerable talents as an affliction. His latest success was viewed as an unbearable burden. In their efforts to protect David from becoming too self-assured, his parents had contributed to his developing a severely lowered self-esteem. Future successes seemed to augur further burdens, with the danger of his being expected to perform beyond even his exceptional capacities, and with gratifications apparently not permitted.

In the course of his therapy, David was able to recover from his depression only after he confronted the impasse he had gotten into with his parents. As he studied the meaning of his successes, he perceived that his parents' position was fundamentally unfair to him. He uncovered and allowed himself to experience the rage he felt at them for this and gradually began to permit himself a sense of achievement for what he, not his genes, was accomplishing.

David had only partially internalized his parents' point of view about his successes; his conflicts were partly interior and partly interpersonal. He was in a growth phase in which familiar attitudes frequently undergo major changes; he recovered from his depression fairly rapidly and went on to the college of his choice.

Many teenagers avoid anxiety and the symptoms of neurosis by developing their character in such a way that anxiety-stimulating perceptions are regularly avoided. Usually this leads to some warping and distortion of personality. The individual is likely to feel comfortable with this state of affairs since he lacks awareness of any alternative and feels: "That's me." Such youngsters make up the character problems that must be dealt with by the psychiatrist.

CASE ILLUSTRATION

Vanessa, a bright college student, had emotional relationships which followed an identifiable pattern; she was attracted to determined, forceful persons, whom she thought of as "strong." When difficulties arose within these friendships, it was mutually agreed that the fault had been Vanessa's. She would then make efforts to "improve"; often these attempts were unsuccessful. She and her friends would attribute this to her basic "selfishness," "inability to relate," and "immaturity." Vanessa was much given to brooding about these qualities.

A friend, Todd, lived several hundred miles away from Vanessa, and they could not see each other more often than one or two weekends per month. He asked her to transfer to a school in his area so that they could be together more often. Vanessa agreed and arranged to take a summer course near Todd. To her surprise and consternation during that summer, she found that Todd was so busy because of his professional responsibilities that he could see her only on weekends. Indeed, on several weekends, he was called out of state. When she remarked that she was not seeing more of him than before she had moved near him, he complained of her possessiveness and her apparent need to dominate. Later she reflected about these tendencies to possess and to dominate, and resolved to make a serious attempt to correct these characteristics.

Behaviorally, Vanessa led an active sexual life; inwardly she was obsessed with guilt over being sexual. She was taking birth control pills; nevertheless, she often felt certain that she had become pregnant. She worried constantly that she had developed venereal disease. She was aware of the irrationality of these worries and occasionally described them as representing some insane side of herself.

Vanessa's father had been the dominant figure in her family. A man of fervently expressed convictions, he could tolerate no disagreement. His favorite adjectives included "childish," "stupid," and "irresponsible," when his children expressed views different from his own. In particular, he opposed the trend toward greater sexual freedom for the young, and for many years had inveighed to Vanessa about the risk of unwanted pregnancy and venereal disease. To maintain peace in the family, Vanessa's mother would often comment, "After all, Father knows best."

Recently, a new young man named Victor had called to take Vanessa out. Shortly after being introduced to him, Vanessa's father offered comments about the rising rate of venereal disease among the young. Later, Victor commented that he thought it odd for that topic to have been raised. Vanessa replied that her father had always been "health-conscious." Victor pursued the discussion, asking Vanessa if she did not find something peculiar in this. When she heard herself saying, "Father knows best," she began to be aware that she actively refrained from ever allowing herself to be critical of her father.

Gradually, she began to see that she did this in other relationships, refusing to perceive possible flaws in the other person. Instead, she uncritically identified with the other person's point of view and saw faults only within herself. In this way, she avoided all important confrontations. The other person was always right; she was always wrong.

Through this maneuver, Vanessa had bought peace but at the enormous cost of feeling constantly in the wrong, always vulnerable, and never able to use her critical faculties. She had developed a character structure in which these painful feelings were not felt as symptoms of a disturbance, but as part of her true self. Her constant premonitions of sexual disaster (for example, pregnancy, venereal disease) were, it became apparent, the internalized expressions of her father, who had clearly warned her in just those terms.

Vanessa's developmental task now became clearer. She had to recognize and then abandon the "security blanket" of "Father knows best," drawing her new sense of confidence out of her actual achievements of growing up and becoming a perceiving individual. Reliance on self had to replace the earlier state of reliance on parents and parent figures.

The psychotic reactions in adolescence demand the most intense therapeutic attention. It may be a "last chance" opportunity for intervention to head off a lifelong pattern of mental illness.

CASE ILLUSTRATION

Andrea, a bright, creative, verbal, deeply troubled sixteen-year-old, was to an extraordinary degree similar to Deborah, whose psychotherapy and recovery were described by Hannah Green in *I Never Promised You a Rose Garden*.[18] The presenting behavioral disturbance in both situations was wrist cutting. Andrea, however, was less susceptible to prolonged, severely regressed states.

Andrea reported that she did not have any friends and was highly sensitive as a child. She began to make up names and then invent people to go with them. Increasingly, she believed in the reality of her inventions. At fifteen, she had an intense relationship with a boy which ultimately foundered when she was unable to accede to his sexual advances. "I was living inside then with my madeup people and my madeup things. This depressed me. I wanted to become regular, to be able to talk to people. So I cut my wrists."

Andrea was hospitalized and phenothiazine medication was promptly prescribed. During the early months of her hospital stay, she usually appeared alert and appropriate in her behavior. However, she was susceptible to states of severe withdrawal ("wrapped in cotton"), depression, and apathy, during which she appeared to be seriously ill. Depersonalization, derealization, auditory and visual hallucinations, and paranoid ideation were present to a marked degree.

These episodes of severe disturbance never lasted longer than three to six days. Because of Andrea's propensity for cutting her wrists or for burning herself with cigarettes during these crises, she was of major concern to everyone who cared for her.

Andrea believed that many different figures inhabited her life space. Periodically, she felt displaced. At times, she expressed the wish to jump out of the window (of a fifteenth-floor apartment), hoping the impact would "put the pieces back together."

When her suffering was extreme during these states of "daymare," Andrea was sometimes treated with sleep therapy for several days. The plan was to get her to sleep off the "daymare," as one would try to help a person wake up from a nightmare.

It gradually became clear that, probably for over ten years, Andrea had been involved in a paranoid system of thought. She was aware that in some way others posed a threat to this inner world, which she continued to be loath to describe fully. She felt that she was capable of perceiving in a new dimension, and that others were in error in speaking of her private world as "fantasy" or "delusion."

For many months, Andrea believed that her therapist was trying to poison her. Nevertheless, she continued to see him without protest, since she felt she was getting what she deserved, and that he was a relatively kindly poisoner.

Now a young adult and living on her own, Andrea considers that she has grown stronger and is able to "juggle" more successfully between the competing demands of this world and her inner world.

In psychophysiologic disorders, a particular organ system of the body appears to be specially sensitive to emotional stress. Disturbed functioning in that organ system may all too readily ensue, which in turn may ultimately lead to serious structural changes. The psychophysiologically ill adolescent may not suffer from conscious emotional distress; his disturbed state may instead express itself entirely through physical symptoms.

CASE ILLUSTRATION

Elaine was eighteen and a sophomore at college when she met Otto, a twenty-six-year-old graduate student, who had recently been divorced. An intense relationship followed. Elaine felt that she was deeply in love and was certain that they would marry.

Two months later, Otto announced that he felt it was all a mistake and that they should stop seeing each other. He said that he had tried to work up enthusiasm for being in love again, but it had not worked. From Elaine's point of view, it was a brutal and totally unexpected "Sorry and so long."

She was devastated. She cried, she pleaded with Otto to give the relationship another chance, but to no avail. He refused to see her again.

For several weeks Elaine mourned her loss. Gradually, then, her mood began to lighten.

At the same time diarrhea developed and rapidly worsened. Blood was present in the stools. Elaine lost weight and became anemic. She required intensive medical care over many months to relieve her of the distress of her colitis.

No infectious basis was found to account for the development of the colitis. Her internist suspected that some emotional factor may have contributed to the illness. In the discussions that followed, Elaine told her doctor that indeed she had been trying to get Otto "out of my system." It was recognized that her mood improvement had occurred at the same time as the onset of the diarrhea. It seemed likely that the emotional experience had been "somatized," and that the colitis represented Elaine's continuing efforts to handle her profound disappointment.

An important goal in the therapy of the psychophysiologically ill youth is to assist in confronting his emotional stresses directly; it is hoped that this will reduce the propensity for "somatization."

Additional indications for treatment of the adolescent are delinquency; special symptom formation as in tics, enuresis, stuttering; school and work problems, including underachievement and overachievement; drug addiction; and extraordinary crises in teenage living, such as illness or the death of a parent, the breakup of the parents' marriage, an unwanted pregnancy.

The Aims of Treatment

The teenager is in a state of continuing growth, with defenses not yet fixed. It has, therefore, been argued that efforts to investigate these defenses and to relate them to earlier significant events in the individual's life are unlikely to be profitable. Indeed, it has been recommended that therapeutic efforts should rather concentrate on present functioning. Speaking from vast erxperience with college students, Farnsworth states, "The problems of adolescence usually cannot be treated by the development of deep insights. . . . Instead, work should be done on the present situation, on the ego strength."[13]

Another view is that the therapist who has an appropriate understanding of the developmental tasks of the teenager, and who is capable of discriminating between growth-interfering defenses which should be looked into and corrected dynamically and growth-fostering defenses which need little attention, is not really confronted with this implied "either-or" choice.

In practice, the decision is often made by the teenage patient himself and the material that arises in his sessions.

CASE ILLUSTRATION

A seventeen-year-old boy in psychotherapy developed an insistent and pervasive feeling that his therapist was trying to pull thoughts out of his head. He knew that people often talk about their "shrinks" attempting to read their minds or pull thoughts out of their heads, but insisted that his concern was literal rather than metaphorical. He also had a feeling that his therapist in some way was going to kill him in the supposed process of helping him. His critical judgment told him that this was "paranoid," and he insisted that he did not really believe this, but nevertheless, he continued to be oppressed by these extremely disturbing preoccupations.

Months later, during a psychotherapeutic session, he began to feel as though his therapist had his hands on his head and was trying to choke him. Panic ensued, accompanied by a terror of being suffocated. A feeling of "It's for your own good" accompanied this anguished abreaction.

What had returned to awareness was a long-repressed experience that had occurred at age two when he had suddenly developed a respiratory blockage as part of a severe diphtheritic infection of the throat. His parents had rushed their cyanotic child to a physician who lived next door; at once, the physician forcefully removed part of the obstructing membrane from the throat, causing hemorrhaging but permitting the resumption of breathing. This life-saving experience had been perceived from the child's point of view as an assault and a suffocation, with the parents incomprehensibly standing by, saying, "It's for your own good."

CASE ILLUSTRATION

A fourteen-year-old boy had been in psychotherapy for six months, when a one-month vacation interrupted. On the resumption of treatment, Clyde felt a profound change had taken place in his therapist, that he looked thinner, preoccupied, depressed, in some fundamental way different, not himself, not the same person. Not aware of any major change in himself, the therapist saw this reaction as a mystery to be studied.

Ultimately, understanding was achieved. When Clyde was three, his mother had fainted and then had been rushed to the hospital, where she delivered a premature baby. She had been critically ill for some days and then recovered. When she had returned home, she was still weak and worried about her new baby, who was to remain in the premature nursery for several months.

Clyde felt that this saddened woman was different from the mother he had known, that she was "not the same person," but some kind of replacement. With the certainty that is characteristic of three-year-olds, he dealt with this individual politely, as though she were a stranger, while he waited for his real mother to return. Afterward, the whole disturbing experience disappeared into unconsciousness.

This event was not remembered but was relived in the relationship with the therapist, during the "transference." Clyde's perception of his therapist as "not the same person" led to the reconstruction of the original experience with his mother.

It is a fundamental requirement of efforts to understand children, teenagers, and adults that the developmental point of view be kept in mind. Piaget[17, 24, 38, 39] has described how the primitive ("sensori-motor") thinking of infancy is gradually transformed at about eighteen months into the egocentric ("preoperational") thinking of early childhood; this is followed by the "concrete operational" thinking of the six- to eleven-year-old and the "abstract operational" thinking of the eleven- to fifteen-year-old which continues into adulthood.

It is hypothesized that derivatives of infantile, egocentric, and concrete operational thought continue to be influential during youth. These leave the young person highly vulnerable to illogical fears, primitively determined assumptions, and various conclusions which he may suspect are absurd and yet continue to feel as true. At the same time, the youth may be much too embarrassed to speak about such things.

In dealing with the troubled youth, it is certainly the therapist's responsibility to alert the youth to these possibilities and to stimulate curiosity and willingness to explore early development. Excessive zeal in this direction, however, is likely to be counterproductive. Some youngsters, especially those who are impatient to outgrow their dependency position, may find it offensive to review their earlier childhood experiences. If the teenage patient determines that present concerns are what are to be focused on, the therapist must be sufficiently flexible to work with the youth on the level that is acceptable.

Technical Aspects

The adolescent has veto power over most therapeutic interventions; meaningful treatment is not likely to result because of orders from parents or school, or by judicial fiat. Early efforts must be devoted to helping a troubled teenager become aware, from his own point of view, that he has difficulties and that exploring these in therapy might overcome them. When this has been

achieved, the youth may be said to have become "engaged" in treatment; a "therapeutic alliance" has been formed.

CASE ILLUSTRATION

Mark, fifteen, was referred for therapy after his father's therapist, hearing about this "perfect" son, suspected disturbance and recommended psychological testing. The protocol suggested "a struggle against catatonic schizophrenia in a fantasy-ridden individual." Mark himself had no complaints.

At his first visit this adolescent was seen as outwardly well-functioning and unusually formal and proper. Mark stated that he had no need to see a psychiatrist. Only when assured he would *not* have to come back was he able to begin to describe his complicated inner life, in which he was concerned with thoughts having to do with order, rights to be happy, and many other elaborate mental constructions. These were presented as manifestations of a person deeply involved with ethical considerations; there was no awareness of the obsessional nature of these preoccupations.

Asked how he fared in sports, Mark mentioned that he was on his high school baseball team, and that he had gotten as many hits "as I am permitted." To an inquiry about this, he replied that after getting a hit, he felt compelled to strike out the next time he was up at bat, lest he become vain and offend God.

The therapist felt that it was quite likely that a paranoid system was present in Mark's thinking. He told Mark that he felt that he was not free to play baseball to the best of his abilities, and suggested that he might take the opportunity to explore with the therapist how these restrictions had come into being. Mark agreed to return, and soon weekly therapy sessions were instituted.

Most teenagers require positive expressions of interest in them.

A neutral position, even a benevolent neutrality, is often perceived as indifference or unconcern. An attitude of partiality is advisable, together with a sense of strong commitment by the therapist to work in what he believes to be the patient's best interests.

Adolescents usually require that the therapist participate actively in the therapeutic process. Many youngsters cannot tolerate prolonged periods of silence during therapy sessions; if active assistance is not provided by the therapist, they are prone to abandon treatment.

All who work with teenagers recognize the necessity for flexibility and adaptability. Original challenges are frequent, testing is almost universal, and some interactions are predictably unpredictable.

With the younger adolescent, especially at the start of treatment, techniques akin to the play therapy used with children may be necessary. Earlier, the case of Marjorie, an eleven-year-old girl with a school phobia, was presented as an example of an individual facing the normative crisis of imminent puberty. In the first sessions Majorie was too terrified to speak. Knowing of her artistic talent and interests, the therapist offered her the opportunity to express herself with oil paints. She accepted and soon began a series of paintings of the therapist as a monster. Not long afterward, Marjorie was able to speak about her fear that the therapist would cruelly force her back to school. Gradually, thereafter, she became able to discuss other worries.

One day she brought a dead goldfish to her session. This opened up the area of curiosity about body structure and functions, and led to the idea of dissecting a mackerel. It was only after they had actually done this that Marjorie became able to allow psychotherapeutic exploration of her ideas about her own body, the expected "addition" of her menstrual periods and breasts, and her developing sexuality.

Pubertal youngsters are frequently difficult to involve in meaningful therapy. Though the crisis of puberty is fairly well understood, the young teenager is frequently too embarrassed to talk about his worries, too pained and too sure that what he is going through is much worse than anyone could possibly imagine.

The therapist must be willing to play, or not play, a parental surrogate role, in response to the youth's particular needs. The adolescent is an older child. Although he is likely to make claims of adult status in an insistent manner, the therapist must perceive this as a manifestation of adolescent development, and not as a statement of fact.

Most teenagers are striving to emancipate themselves from dependent relationships with their parents. Not infrequently, such relationships are interrupted or broken before the youth is truly ready for independent functioning. He may be behaving in a reckless and potentially dangerous manner. At such crisis points the help of a psychotherapist may be sought.

Confronting a situation of urgency, the therapist may find himself between Scylla and Charybdis. On the one hand, if he fails to act meaningfully, he is seen as remote, passive, and uncaring: on the other hand, if he takes action, he is likely to be perceived as parental, intrusive, and controlling.

In this difficult situation, the therapist must be guided by what in his considered judgment best promotes growth. Drawing on his knowledge of

growth and development, he must evaluate whether this particular youth is sturdy enough to expand his understanding and modify potentially perilous behavior, or whether external controls, such as hospitalization, may be indicated. If the latter recommendation stimulates charges of being "just like my parents," the therapist may have to point out that he cannot abdicate his function as a responsible caring adult.

CASE ILLUSTRATION

Fifteen-year-old Walter spent a year being "stoned" on absolutely anything he could get his hands on: "uppers," "downers," "speed," "pot," "hash." He also had sex indiscriminately with girls, boys, and in groups of both. He considered himself "liberated" from the "square" characteristics of his parents, for whom he had the deepest contempt. At sixteen, he broke off relations with them and moved into a communal "pad" with a number of other young people.

Not long afterward, Walter began to realize that he was having a severe case of adolescent "new experience" indigestion. He was trying to do so much, so fast, and with such little wisdom that he was becoming massively confused. He was exhausting himself running around in circles; it dawned on him that he was actually getting nowhere. He himself sought psychotherapy.

Not surprisingly, he projected on to the therapist the "control drugs" side of his conflict and lived out a state of even more florid drug use than before. The therapist, quite appropriately alarmed, now insisted that a period of hospitalization was essential. Though Walter bitterly fought this recommendation and charged that his therapist was just as bad as his parents, he finally yielded to it. Some months later, he was able to admit that the hospitalization had been necessary to interrupt his frenetic self-destructive course. No longer dominated by the drug involvement, he was able to examine the forces which had influenced him in that direction and make significant progress toward finding more satisfying alternative techniques for living.

Adolescence is a period of intense questioning and searching. The therapist's task is not to help the teenager resolve his doubts, but rather to help him respect his quest and to support his efforts to create his own synthesis of the many conflicting components of his growing self.

The therapist must have a keen sense of appreciation for the timing of teenage preoccupations. Intense stress on career goals at fourteen would seem inappropriate. Preoccupation with orgastic achievements at fifteen would be premature. Anxiety about the ability to have mature object relations would appear precocious at sixteen.

While striving to avoid the possibility of sounding old-fashioned, the therapist must point out that gradual growth is a desirable quality and must warn that attempts to speed up adolescence endangers normal growth.

CASE ILLUSTRATION

A thirteen-year-old girl decided she was now old enough to experience sexual intercourse. She persuaded a classmate to have sex with her. The event was drab and unsatisfying to both thirteen-year-olds.

The therapist who works with youth must be sensitive to "non-problems," that is, issues that are brought to his attention as psychiatric difficulties which are merely expressions of the uncertainties inherent in the adolescent growth experience.

CASE ILLUSTRATION

A fifteen-year-old girl read Radclyffe Hall's *The Well of Loneliness*.[20] She knew that she had had several crushes on woman teachers and wondered if she might be a lesbian. Careful inquiry elicited that this young woman was leading an active social life with young men and that her sexual fantasies were predominantly concerned with men.

It appeared that this girl's concern about homosexual tendencies was more expressive of a literary yearning toward nonconformity than of an actual sexual conflict. It was decided that she needed more time to mature before the presence or absence of a sexual problem could be determined.

There are some technical aspects which are particularly important in the psychotherapeutic approach to adolescent schizophrenia. Optimally, the therapist should have sufficient awareness of the irrational in himself so that he is not made anxious by the irrationality of his patient. It is essential that he conceive of the psychotic process and its evolution as part of the human condition, a phenomenon capable of being studied and treated.

It is hoped that therapy will include significant corrective emotional experiences which will provide many patients with novel opportunities. The therapist's availability and capacity for nurturance will here be tested.

Therapy will also include a great deal of guidance and teaching about interpersonal relationships. Some schizophrenic youngsters are uninformed and unaware that it is possible for people to relate to each other in gratifying and nondestructive ways.

It may be of crucial importance to teach reality thinking. Some children are raised by parents who give them "double-bind" instructions equivalent to "Go swimming, but don't get wet." They have no opportunity to learn alternative kinds of thinking. They may think and talk in terms which express the parents' thought and voice.

The recognition and understanding of the patient's nonverbal communications contribute to treatment in an important way.

Delusional material must be evaluated in terms of its defensive value to the personality. Direct critical confrontation should be avoided until a firm therapeutic alliance has been established, and then used only when there are clear indications for it.

The therapist must be modest about therapeutic goals. Schizophrenic youngsters should be helped to achieve their full potentials as persons; they should not be pushed toward the achievement of any arbitrary standard of "normality."

The Therapist's Relationship with the Parents and the Problem of Confidentiality

The adolescent is an older child who usually lives with his family, goes to school, and participates in his peer culture. As a rule, there is need for periodic communication between the parents and the therapist. At times it is necessary for him to be in touch with school authorities as well.

It is vital that the confidentiality of the young person be respected. Communication with the parents and the school should take place with the knowledge and consent of the adolescent, and he should be kept informed about what was discussed.

The therapist must *not* give a pledge of total confidentiality to the troubled youth. There may be instances of suicidal preoccupation or vulnerability to hallucinations which compel the youth to behave dangerously; coping with these emergency situations is a responsibility which must be shared with the parents. If this is done with frankness, so that the teenager is fully informed about what is taking place, the risks to the therapeutic relationship are likely to be reduced.

The therapist must resist efforts to involve him in intrafamilial intrigue. He must zealously protect his integrity and his capacity to function therapeutically.

Ron, fourteen, had been referred for psychotherapy because of increasing withdrawal and sleepiness in class, a marked falling off in his grades, and general irritability and discontent at home. Ron visited his therapist without enthusiasm ("I'm coming because I have to") and had not yet become "engaged" in treatment.

Two weeks after therapy had been instituted, Ron's father called the therapist, told him that he had bugged his son's private line, and discovered that Ron was dealing in drugs at his school. He said, "I want you to know this, but I forbid your mentioning the source of this information to my son." The father said he would not confront his son with his knowledge because he did not want him to know that he had tapped his phone. "It's now your responsibility, not mine," he told the therapist. He said he was "too busy" to meet with him to discuss the matter further.

Ron's father had placed the therapist in an untenable position, which precluded his further usefulness. Given important information but forbidden to reveal its source, the therapist found himself trapped in intrigue and blocked by the father's unwillingness to cooperate in resolving the dilemma. At this point Ron, perhaps picking up the "static" in the parent-therapist interaction, decided to end his sessions.

Vigorous efforts must be made by the therapist to avoid becoming caught in the cross-fire of parent-teenager squabbles. The therapist's task is to try to provide illumination; he should avoid the temptation, even when asked, to try to become "super-parent."

The relationship the youth forms with his therapist is likely to include some feelings transferred from his own parents, as well as feelings which are in response to the therapist's own behavior. Not infrequently polarization takes place, with the actual parents seen as "bad," and the therapist, as "good." This phenomenon usually takes place early in therapy, during the so-called "honeymoon" period. It is extremely distressing to parents who have heretofore borne the full burden of raising their child. The stranger seems to be enjoying all the gratifications of being the good parent while they are targets for all the brickbats hurled at the bad.

Parents can be prepared for this possibility in advance. Moreover, they can be told that this period is unlikely to last longer than the first time the young person makes a demand on the therapist as though he were actually the parent (for example, "May I borrow your car?") and is turned down.

Treatment Modalities

Treatment modalities include dynamic psychotherapy, behavior therapy, group therapy, family therapy, environmental changing, pharmaco-therapy, hospitalization, residential treatment, and halfway house placement.

The case vignettes that have been provided are drawn from a primarily dynamic psychotherapeutic practice and demonstrate the variety of teenage problems which are treatable in individual psychodynamically oriented therapy.

In behavior therapy, which is discussed in more detail in chapters 5 and 11, an attempt is made to help the individual to unlearn maladaptive patterns of behavior. The aim is to modify current symptoms. Enuresis, stammering, tics, and eating disturbances are among the dysfunctions for which behavior therapy may be recommended.

In the American Psychiatric Association Task Force Report, *Behavior Therapy in Psychiatry*,[1] distinguishing characteristics of behavior therapy are reviewed:

. . . the therapist looks for particular situations in which the behavior typically occurs or fails to occur, as well as for current maintaining conditions . . . ; emphasis is placed on modification of the principal presenting symptoms, rather than on analysis or understanding of the character structure or unconscious conflicts presumed to underlie the behavior pattern . . . ; the behavior therapy treatment program . . . focuses on systematic manipulation of the environmental and behavioral variables thought to be functionally related to the disturbing performance . . . ; the therapist tries, whenever possible, to assess treatment outcomes in the same objective, quantifiable terms that characterized both the initial problem analysis and the formulation of the treatment program.

Currently there is wide belief that behavioral reinforcement operates in all psychotherapy.

Berkovitz and Sugar[4] have reviewed the indications for group psychotherapy for adolescents (see also chapter 10). Some youngsters are so well defended against therapeutic relationships that only in a peer group or network group can there be significant confrontation, introspection, or interaction with therapist or peers. Among the benefits that adolescents may glean from work in groups, these authors include the gaining of assistance and confrontation from peers; the securing of a miniature real-life situation for the study and change of behavior; the stimulation for finding new ways of dealing with situations and developing new skills in human relations; the encouragement for finding new concepts of self and new models of identification; reduction in feelings of isolation; providing a feeling of protection from the adult while undergoing changes; providing a bond to therapy to help maintain continued self-examination; allowing the swings of rebellion or submission which encourage independence and identification with the leader; and permitting the uncovering of relationship problems which may not have become evident in individual therapy.

Contraindications are said to be few; they involve primarily the exclusion from the group of an adolescent who is too deviant from the rest of the members.

The APA Task Force Report, *Behavior Therapy in Psychiatry*,[1] states:

Group therapy, with its *in vivo* display of habitual maladaptive social behaviors, is an ideal medium in which to use therapist-mediated social reinforcement as an agent for behavioral change. In group therapy and family therapy, the therapist has the enormous practical advantage of seeing maladaptive behavioral patterns unfold and develop *in vivo*. As a result, he can shift his strategy from relatively weak techniques of attitude change through verbal conditioning, and of "corrective" extinction of emotional experiences, to a much more rapid and powerful method, and one which is especially appropriate for patients whose primary problems center around their relationships with others. Many patients have problems that involve habitual, subtle maladaptive interpersonal behaviors. Bringing them into a group or family setting where they actually experience problems with other people can be extraordinarily important and catalytic both diagnostically in terms of what the patients' actual maladaptive behaviors are and therapeutically, because these settings allow for the direct behavioral shaping of alternative modes of behavior.

Some therapists will prefer to emphasize the objective behavioral procedures used in such settings, stressing the use of contingent social reinforcement for increasingly appropriate behavior and other related behavioral intervention methods. Others will prefer to conceptualize the therapy in dual terms, feeling that training and experience in both dynamic psychiatry and behavior therapy are useful here. In this view the therapist can be more effective if he can understand and work with the phenomena of unconscious motivation, and if he also is skilled in behavioral techniques.

When family problems are predominant, the family may be seen as the subject for treatment and family therapy may be instituted (see chapter 7). Family therapy can be extremely effective with marital disorders and with disturbances involving the relationships among the various family members. It can be helpful in assisting the family to deal with such crises as serious disturbance in a family member. When a teenager is delinquent, family therapy may help clarify evidence that he may be responding to verbal and nonverbal cues from other members of the family. He may be expressing someone else's needs. Or, he may be serving as scapegoat, drawing attention to himself when actually the whole family needs attention.

Sometimes the core figure in a disturbed situation refuses treatment; the other family members may need a good deal of help to deal with this effectively.

CASE ILLUSTRATION

A serious crisis occurred between Alfred, who was not quite thirteen, and his father. The conscious issue here was power. An only child, Alfred had long been accustomed to playing an important role within his family constellation. His Bar Mitzvah was approaching, and it soon became apparent that he was taking literally the traditional "Today I am a man" aspect of the religious ceremony. He began giving orders at home and threatened to call off the approaching celebration if he did not get his own way. He announced, "From now on, I'm boss around here."

At first, his parents humored him and went along with his demands. When finally his father rebelled, Alfred ordered him out of the house. Amid much screaming and with concern for the neighbors in the apartment building, Alfred's father spent the night at his office. Later his mother begged Alfred to relent and let his father come home. The boy agreed.

Alfred was willing at first to see a psychiatrist to enlist his aid as an ally against his father whom he described as a "Hitler." When the therapist asked questions about this, Alfred promptly concluded that he was on his father's side and refused to see the therapist again.

Far from being a dictatorial individual, the father actually was a soft-spoken, rather gentle person, who had left most of the decision making about Alfred's care to his wife. When pressed very hard, he did indeed tend to raise his voice.

The mother was a "peace at any price" advocate. In earlier confrontations between her son and her husband, she had tended to prevail on her husband to yield. "You're bigger, you can afford to be the more generous one."

Alfred liked to do his homework and watch television simultaneously. He also liked to have his mother's assistance with his homework. His mother liked to sit in the living room. Alfred at such times found his father's presence irritating. Many evenings were spent with the father staying in his bedroom, while his wife and son shared the living room.

At bedtime Alfred had difficulty falling asleep. He insisted on having either his father or his mother lie down next to him, until he was asleep.

Both parents were seen in therapy. They were made aware of the implications of the apparent oedipal power struggle going on and the importance to Alfred's further development of his mastering what appeared to be the repetition of a psychological stage of childhood.

His mother then told him that it would soon be time that he learned to do without a parent lying next to him at bedtime. Alfred reacted to this with rage, rejected his mother forthwith, and announced that from now on he only wanted his father next to him at bedtime. When his father supported his wife in this matter, Alfred concluded that both parents hated him, and he would be forced to kill himself. His parents did not panic at this remark which proved, said Alfred, that they didn't love him.

After many months of struggling over power, Alfred came to the conclusion that he liked his friends better than he liked his parents, that he had been foolish to waste so much time in trying to educate them to behave as he thought they should, and that he was now giving up interest in them as a bad job. Henceforth, they would just be his parents, and that was all.

This actually represented a victory for Alfred's own growth and development. The loosening of his childhood ties to his parents facilitated his freedom to make adolescent attachments in the world outside of the family.

Family therapy is more likely to be the treatment of choice in situations involving the younger adolescent. Since the thrust of growth and development for the older adolescent is toward increasing separation from the family and greater autonomy, intrafamilial difficulties may be resolved by separation of the teenager from the disturbed family unit. Traditionally, when interpersonal tensions at home have become unbearable, boarding schools and residential treatment centers have been turned to as an alternative. Another possibility is a foster family. Many teenagers who are at war with their parents have exceedingly good relationships with other adults. And their parents may get along well with the friends of their children and with other adolescents.

CASE ILLUSTRATION

Ella was fourteen when her parents were divorced, and each soon remarried. Their household had been chaotic for many years. Ella was bitter at both parents. She thoroughly disliked her new stepparents. She refused to consider boarding school. At first she chose to live with her father and stepmother. There were major stresses, and she asked to move to her mother and stepfather's home. This too proved to be impossible.

A neighbor of her mother, hearing about the difficulties, said that Ella had impressed her as a lovely child and that perhaps things would be different in her house. She had two children away at college.

There was an empty bedroom, and she and her husband had begun to find the house somewhat unpleasantly quiet. Perhaps inviting Ella to live with them would lessen their loneliness.

One might have assumed the odds were against this working. A reasonable supposition would be that Ella would transfer her hostilities from her parents and stepparents to her foster parents, and that the warfare would continue unabated.

Actually the new arrangement worked exceedingly well. Ella felt that she was successfully expressing her rage at her parents by living elsewhere. Unconsciously, she redistributed her ambivalent feelings toward parents, assigning the hostile emotions to her parents and stepparents and the affectionate feelings to her foster parents.

As she began living in a substantially happier manner, she began to express warm feelings toward her parents and stepparents. Subsequently, ordinary hostilities did show up within the foster family.

It was wisely agreed that Ella should stay with her foster parents until she went off to college. In all likelihood, a permanent relationship had been established which was gratifying to all concerned.

This is an example of successful environmental changing, an important resource in the treatment of adolescents (see chapter 18).

Pharmacotherapy, which is discussed in detail in chapter 23, is an increasingly important therapeutic resource for distressed teenagers. Young people who are depressed or excited or both can be aided significantly by drugs. Similarly, medication can be helpful in relieving some of the stress of severe obsessional thinking. Incipient panic states too can be eased by medication. Impulsive teenagers can also be helped to achieve improved control with appropriately chosen drugs. Many young people with schizophrenia can continue to function adequately as long as they are satisfactorily maintained on antipsychotic medication.

For the suicidal and acutely psychotic youngster, hospitalization is often the treatment of choice, offering protection to the patient from the opportunity to act out self-destructive impulses and providing the opportunity for carefully supervised antidepressant and antipsychotic medication in a therapeutic milieu. This in itself is helpful in that often enough it offers relief from unbearable tensions caused by the home environment.

For the youth who has partially recovered from a serious disturbance and for the chronically psychiatrically ill, halfway houses and residential treatment centers provide a therapeutic milieu in which growth may continue to take place in a protective and nurturant environment (see chapter 15).

Summary

A thorough knowledge of the dynamic process of growth and development is the *sine qua non* of effective treatment of the adolescent.

All therapeutic interventions with teenagers share a fundamental principle, that they *promote growth*.

In the life experience of everyone, there are periods of extraordinary stress associated with new growth and development; these are called "normative crises." A major requirement for the therapist who deals with teenagers is the ability to help his patient comprehend and negotiate successfully the normative crises of youth. The natural tendency toward growth at this period facilitates these efforts.

Diagnostic evaluation of a teenager must be part of a family and environmental study. It must include a review of the adaptive successes and failures of the individual throughout his development.

Indications for treatment of the adolescent include anxiety states; neuroses; character problems; psychosis; psychosomatic disorders; special symptom formations such as tics, enuresis, stuttering; delinquency; school and work problems; drug addiction, and extraordinary crises in living.

Since the teenager is in a growth state with defenses not yet fixed, should his difficulties be related to earlier meaningful events in his life, or should therapeutic attention be focused on current problems? It is suggested that, if the therapist has an appropriate understanding of the developmental tasks of adolescence and if he is capable of discriminating between growth-interfering defenses which require dynamic exploration and correction and growth-fostering defenses which should not be worked with, the "either-or" choice is not the central issue. In practice, the decision is often determined by the patient himself and the material he presents.

It is fundamental to the understanding of children, teenagers, and adults that the developmental point of view be kept in mind. It is hypothesized that derivatives of infantile, egocentric, and concrete operational thought continue to influence the youth, leaving him highly vulnerable to illogical fears, primitively determined assumptions, and various conclusions which he may suspect are absurd and yet continue to feel are true.

Technical aspects in the psychotherapy of adolescents have been reviewed. These include the need for the teenager to become "engaged" in treatment, the need for the therapist to be partial, active, flexible, adaptable, and willing to play or not play a parental surrogate role, in response to a youth's particular needs. Confronting a situation of urgency, the therapist may find himself between the Scylla of failing to act meaningfully, so that he is seen as remote, passive, and uncaring, and the Charybdis of taking action, and accordingly being perceived as parental, intrusive, and controlling. In this difficult situation, the therapist must be guided by what in his considered judgment best promotes growth.

The therapist must support adolescent searching, must have a keen sense of appreciation for teenage preoccupations, must discourage the artificial acceleration of adolescent growth, and must be sensitive to "nonproblems."

In working with adolescent schizophrenics, the therapist should be sufficiently aware of the irrational in himself to avoid being made anxious by the irrationality of his patient. He should realize that the psychotic process and its evolution are part of the human condition, to be studied and treated. He should be available for nurturance and corrective emotional experiences. He must provide a great deal of guidance and teaching about interpersonal relationships and about reality. He must be highly sensitive to nonverbal communications. Delusional material must be evaluated in terms of its defensive value to the personality. Direct critical confrontation should be avoided until a firm therapeutic alliance has been established, and then utilized only when there are clear indications for it. There is need for modesty about therapeutic goals; schizophrenic youngsters should not be pushed toward the achievement of any arbitrary standard of "normality."

There is usually need for periodic communication between the parents and the therapist. It is vital that the confidentiality of the young person be respected. Communication should take place with the knowledge and consent of the adolescent, and he should be kept informed of what was discussed. The therapist must *not* grant a pledge of total confidentiality to the troubled youth. There may be instances of suicidal preoccupation or vulnerability to hallucinations that compel him to behave dangerously; coping with these emergency situations is a responsibility which must be shared with the parents. If this is done with frankness, so that the teenager is fully informed about what is taking place, the risks to the therapeutic relationship are usually reduced.

The therapist must resist efforts to involve him in intrafamilial intrigue; even when asked, he must be careful to avoid the temptation to try to become "super-parent."

The adolescent's relationship with the therapist will include "transference" elements as well as responses to the therapist's own behavior. Not infrequently polarization takes place with the parents seen as "bad" and the therapist seen as "good." This may be extremely distressing to parents, who can be prepared for this possibility in advance. This "honeymoon" period is not likely to last longer than the moment when the young person makes a demand on the therapist as though he were actually the parent, and is turned down.

Treatment modalities include dynamic psychotherapy, behavior therapy, group therapy, family therapy, environmental changing, pharmacotherapy, hospitalization, residential treatment, and halfway house placement.

REFERENCES

1. AMERICAN PSYCHIATRIC ASSOCIATION TASK FORCE REPORT no. 5, *Behavior Therapy in Psychiatry*, American Psychiatric Association, Washington, D.C., 1973.

2. BECKETT, P. G. S., *Adolescents Out of Step*, Wayne State University Press, Detroit, 1965.

3. BERKOVITZ, I. H., *Adolescents Grow in Groups*, Brunner/Mazel, New York, 1972.

4. ———, and SUGAR, M., "Indications and Contraindications for Adolescent Group Psychotherapy," in Sugar, M. (Ed.), *The Adolescent in Group and Family Therapy*, pp. 3–26, Brunner/Mazel, New York, 1975.

5. BLOS, P., *The Young Adolescent*, Free Press of Glencoe, New York, 1970.

6. ———, *On Adolescence*, Free Press of Glencoe, New York, 1962.

7. BURTON, A. (Ed.), *Psychotherapy of the Psychoses*, Basic Books, New York, 1961.

8. CAPLAN, G., and LEBOVICI, S. (Eds.), *Adolescence: Psychosocial Perspectives*, Basic Books, New York, 1969.

9. COPELAND, A. D., *Textbook of Adolescent Psychopathology and Treatment*, Charles C Thomas, Springfield, Ill., 1974.

10. EASSON, W. M., *The Severely Disturbed Adolescent*, International Universities Press, New York, 1969.

11. ERIKSON, E. H., *Childhood and Society*, W. W. Norton, New York, 1950.

12. ESMAN, A. H. (Ed.), *The Psychology of Adolescence: Essential Readings*, International Universities Press, New York, 1975.

13. FARNSWORTH, D. L., *Psychiatry, Education and the Young Adult*, Charles C Thomas, Springfield, Ill., 1966.

14. FEINSTEIN, S. C., and GIOVACCHINI, P. (Eds.), *Adolescent Psychiatry: Developmental and Clinical Studies*, vol. 3, Basic Books, New York, 1974.

15. ———, *Adolescent Psychiatry: Developmental and Clinical Studies*, vol. 2, Basic Books, New York, 1973.

16. ———, and MILLER, A. A. (Eds.), *Adolescent Psychiatry: Development and Clinical Studies*, vol. 1, Basic Books, New York, 1971.

17. FLAVELL, J. H., *The Developmental Psychology of Jean Piaget*, D. Van Nostrand, Princeton, 1963.

18. GREEN, H., *I Never Promised You a Rose Garden*, Holt, Rinehart & Winston, New York, 1964.

19. GROUP FOR THE ADVANCEMENT OF PSYCHIATRY, *Normal Adolescence*, Group for the Advancement of Psychiatry, vol. 6, no. 68, 1968.

20. HALL, R., *The Well of Loneliness*, Covici, London, 1928.

21. HOLMES, D. J., *The Adolescent in Psychotherapy*, Little, Brown & Co., Boston, 1964.

22. HOWELLS, J. G. (Ed.), *Modern Perspectives in Adolescent Psychiatry*, Brunner/Mazel, New York, 1971.

23. HUDGENS, R. W., *Psychiatric Disorders in Adolescents*, Williams & Wilkins, Baltimore, 1974.

24. INHELDER, B., and PIAGET, J., *The Growth of Logical Thinking from Childhood to Adolescence*, Basic Books, New York, 1959.

25. JOHNSON, A. M., "Sanctions for Superego Lacunae of Adolescents," in Eissler, K. R. (Ed.), *Searchlights on Delinquency*, pp. 225–245, International Universities Press, Inc., New York, 1949.

26. JOSSELYN, I. M., *Adolescence*, Harper & Row, New York, 1971.

27. KALOGERAKIS, M. G. (Ed.), *The Emotionally Troubled Adolescent and the Family Physician*, Charles C Thomas, Springfield, Ill., 1973.

28. KIELL, N., *The Adolescent Through Fiction*, International Universities Press, New York, 1959.

29. LEWIS, M., *Clinical Aspects of Child Development*, Lea & Febinger, Philadelphia, 1973.

30. LORAND, S., and SCHNEER, H. I. (Eds.), *Adolescents: Psychoanalytic Approach to Problems and Therapy*, Hoeber, New York, 1961.

31. MASTERSON, J. F., *Treatment of the Borderline Adolescent: A Developmental Approach*, Wiley-Interscience, New York, 1972.

32. ———, *The Psychiatric Dilemma of Adolescence*, Little, Brown & Co., Boston, 1967.

33. MEEKS, J. E., *The Fragile Alliance*, Williams & Wilkins, Baltimore, 1971.

34. MEYER, V., and CHESSER, E. S., *Behavior Therapy in Clinical Psychiatry*, Science House, New York, 1970.

35. MILLER, D., *Adolescence: Psychology, Psychopathology and Psychotherapy*, Jason Aronson, New York, 1974.

36. OFFER, D., *The Psychological World of the Teenager*, Basic Books, New York, 1969.

37. ———, and OFFER, J. B., *From Teenager to Young Manhood*, Basic Books, New York, 1975.

38. PIAGET, J., *Judgment and Reasoning in the Child*, Humanities Press, New York, 1962.

39. ———, *The Language and Thought of the Child*, Humanities Press, New York, 1959.

40. RIMM, D. C., and MASTERS, J. C., *Behavior Therapy*, Academic Press, New York, 1974.

41. SKLANSKY, M A., SILVERMAN, S. W., and RABICHOW, H. G., *The High School Adolescent*, Association Press, New York, 1969.

42. SUGAR, M. (Ed.), *The Adolescent in Group and Family Therapy*, Brunner/Mazel, New York, 1975.

43. WEINER, I. B., *Psychological Disturbance in Adolescence*, Wiley-Interscience, New York, 1970.

44. ZUBIN, J., and FREEDMAN, A. M., *The Psychopathology of Adolescence*, Grune & Stratton, New York, 1970.

32 / Emergency Intervention

Gilbert C. Morrison

Description of the Method

Emergency intervention with children and adolescents involves immediate diagnostic evaluation and therapeutic planning for the child, the parents, and their environment. The goal is to provide early psychiatric management of child and family emotional crises. The treatment format utilizes the combined tcehniques of brief psychotherapy and family therapy. An emergency psychiatric treatment program for children and their families can be viewed as focusing psychiatric attention upon early amelioration of emotional disorders. The following elements are essential to the planning for such crises: (1) the provision of sufficient flexibility of schedules so that professional staff is available for immediate evaluation and follow-up care for children and their families in emotional crisis; (2) an immediate psychiatric appraisal of the child and his family; (3) the use of psychiatric emergency treatment methods; (4) the establishment and maintenance of good working relationships with all community agencies, schools, clinics, and juvenile courts involved.

Psychiatric emergencies involving children, adolescents, and their families have been handled by child psychiatric clinics or social work intake services. Unfortunately, the realities of treatment waiting lists and heavy individual staff caseloads have made service received by families less than optimal. Trained professional personnel with flexibility in their schedules and the immediate availability of a twenty-four-hour emergency room with inpatient facilities are unusual resources; they are associated with very few child psychiatric clinics. Even where such services can be offered, many families needing urgent help are unable to wait even a week after their initial contact with a children's psychiatric service or psychiatric emergency unit. Immediate response and ongoing continuity of care are essential to such emergency intervention.

The treatment approach to these families can be planned along lines formulated on the basis of previous psychiatric and medical experiences with families in crisis. The family members often expect immediate treatment, preferring that something be done to or for them, not with them. Frequently, they insist on results from a single visit, or a few visits, to an emergency room or to a doctor's office. Previously, they have often sought and obtained assistance for medical and psychiatric problems in one or a few visits. As a rule, they have been referred for further diagnostic studies or treatment but rejected the recommendation. If they did get through a diagnostic evaluation, they failed to follow the recommended treatment. To be effective, treatment for psychiatric emergencies must be specific to the symptoms presented and to the limited time that the families will make available. Additionally, one can strive to direct the response toward establishing a relationship on which a longer-term treatment can be based.

An effective initial diagnostic-therapeutic procedure is a group interview. This should include the child or adolescent and all significant family members together with a child psychiatric clinical team. This opening family interview focuses on the presenting problem; there is a conscious attempt to formulate a definition or statement of the nature of the child's or family's problem. The first goal is to reach some understanding of the problem which is acceptable to the family members and the clinical team. During the interview, a number of methods are described which the family can try as a means of coping with the crisis. From this, the family is helped to arrive at a working plan or direction for the immediate handling of the acute situation. In order to reevaluate the situation and, if possible, to clarify the underlying problems which contributed to the crisis, it is advisable to see most families again as a group from two to ten days later, depending upon their need and the nature of the problem. The treatment team works with the families as long as necessary to alleviate the crisis. For some families, further therapeutic management includes referral for additional psychiatric treatment. This may take the form of outpatient collaborative individual psychotherapy for parent and child or inpatient treatment. Alternatively, physical diagnosis and medical management may be indicated.

There is a relatively limited group of people for whom intensive and long-term methods of psychotherapy appear to be suitable. This seems related to intellectual, cognitive, economic, and cultural issues. In general, such long-term therapeutic approaches have been employed most with the middle and upper classes of American society.[14] For families experiencing a psychiatric emergency, effective short-term or brief psychotherapy has intrinsic as well as pragmatic advantages.[15, 29]

It must be noted at the outset, however, that brief or short-term psychotherapy is adapted from the knowledge and experience of long-term, intensive clinical psychiatric work with children and their families. The clinician attempting emergency psychiatric intervention should possess the clinical judgment and skills necessary for intensive psychodynamic psychotherapy. The same depth of understanding of child development, the recognition of the deviations from normal maturation, the assessment of conflicts between the child and the parents' personalities, and the capacity to formulate a treatment plan are as essential to brief emergency therapy as to long-term, intensive therapy. Additionally, the therapist must be able to reach diagnostic conclusions, to make treatment decisions, and to present recommendations in the presence of the family in crisis in collaboration with his colleagues. Often enough, he must do this without an opportunity for private reflection and consultative discussion. The child psychiatrist and his interdisciplinary professional colleagues planning emergency psychiatric intervention with children, adolescents, and their families should be able to reach reliable, on-the-spot conclusions about the essential characteristics of the parent-child relationship. This is necessary if he is to intervene actively in the reorganization of the pathological family interaction. Basically, one cannot conceive of a dynamic approach for short-term psychotherapy, which is discussed in chapter 4, that is different from the approach for intensive prolonged psychotherapy.[15]

History of the Development of the Method

The development of emergency services for children, youths, and their families has its roots in the earliest services provided to emotionally disturbed and delinquent children and adolescents. The need for urgent intervention methods has always had a high priority for professionals attempting to help emotionally troubled children. Present treatment methods are derived from the practice of child psychiatrists in the past combined with the most recent developments in the practice of community psychiatry (the clinical understanding of families under stress and the development of family therapy and the study of the process of normal grief and mourning, as well as the study of the symptomatology associated with interrupted grief) and the development of methods for crisis intervention.

In "Mourning and Melancholia," Freud[12] identified the normal regression associated with loss, grief, and mourning. He called attention to the vulnerability of certain individuals to the experience of pathological mourning, and he associated this with an increased susceptibility to emotional disorders and depression. Lindemann[19] provided further theoretical and clinical underpinnings for crisis intervention and crisis therapy based on his careful study of the emotional responses of the survivors of the Coconut Grove fire in Boston. His description of the stages of normal grief and mourning and his demonstration of the need for early evaluation and the development of responsive services continue to stand as a monumental study. It is surely the most significant contribution to the development of clinical crisis intervention.

Several authors have attempted to apply the public health concept of prevention and early intervention to mental health and mental illness.[6, 7, 30, 32] They have distinguished primary preventive activities, directed toward the promotion and maintenance of good health; secondary prevention, using early intervention, diagnosis, and prompt treatment; and tertiary prevention, which is directed toward limitation of disability and to rehabilitation. In clinical practice, emergency services usually provide early intervention directed toward secondary and tertiary prevention. This often implies a triage role; the attempt is to determine the most effective level of response and to distinguish the optimum potential for the prevention of any further decompensation. Such a service contrasts with a busy general psychiatry clinic that tries to provide a prompt response to all appeals and ends up becoming increasingly entrapped by excessive demands and long waiting lists.

As elaborated in chapter 7, family therapy has many roots. Because of its collaborative individual psychotherapy for the child and parents, it stems in part from child psychiatry. But it also derives from various research and clinical group therapy methods and from research into child development, family behavior, and family interactions. In any case, it has provided another essential support for the development of treatment methods for crisis intervention. Many treatment approaches are used with the child in emotional crisis. These run the gamut from juvenile court intervention and detention, to group treatment homes that provide family respite and a cooling off period, to hospitalization for acute emotional illness. Ultimately, however, the disturbed child or adolescent must reenter the community of peers, parents, and other significant adults. Parents must eventually join their child in seeking a more satisfactory way of responding to his provocations or of changing their own overstimulating or disruptive behavior. Until recently, the psychiatric hospital or the juvenile court detention center was thought of as a primary resource for the acutely disturbed child or adolescent. Until three or four decades ago, separate services for children were provided only in the most enlightened communities. Even today, it is possible to find adult psychiatric wards and jails which house acutely emotionally disturbed or psychotic children and youths. These are youngsters who have committed no crime against society other than displaying their emotional disturbance.

During the first quarter of this century, psychiatrists, social workers, and the other health professionals of the juvenile courts and mental hygiene clinics were often confronted by children brought to their services in acute emotional distress. Many psychiatric outpatient and inpatient services had developed in the second quarter of the century. The common practice was to use any staff member who was available and all family members who would cooperate. Subsequently, child guidance clinics attempted to provide for urgent emotional problems by the use of the social worker assigned that day to the intake service. While providing telephone consultation, this worker would also meet with walk-in families and provide emergency interviews. If necessary, he would obtain consultative backup from the clinic psychiatrist. Such services were often effective. They were limited only by the skill and experience of the social worker assigned and by his success in catching a psychiatric consultant with time and ability to provide consultation.

In the third quarter of this century, though communities have varied widely in the development and the effectiveness of their treatment settings, there has been an obvious trend toward the development of separate and enlightened psychiatric services for children. Children's psychiatric inpatient services often have had the same problems as psychiatric hospitals for adults; these resulted from the trend toward the progressive separation of the patient from the community and the tendency toward custodial care. This separation would occur despite the need for a planned treatment program for the child and concomitant treatment and preparation of the parents for the return of the child to his home, neighborhood, and school. With the exception of a few community and university psychiatric hospitals for children and one or two enlightened state programs, the vast majority have provided primarily separation with custodial care. This resulted in the progressive deterioration of family ties and the breakdown of social skills. As the years have passed, children who were admitted to these psychiatric custodial institutions became adults in the same institutions. Meanwhile, the family proceeded to close ranks during the child's absence and reorganized itself without the child. Most professionals and many enlightened community authorities deplored the criminal detention or psychiatric custodial retention of children. Despite this, few communities offer alternatives for the severely disturbed child or the emotionally exhausted family.

Today, it has become possible to distinguish three types of psychiatric services for children who are severely emotionally disturbed. To begin with, children's psychiatric treatment centers can provide intensive, long-term hospitalization with both individual psychotherapy and a well-defined therapeutic milieu (see chapters 14 and 15). Second, brief psychiatric hospitalization, as discussed in chapter 16, can help in a number of ways. It provides an opportunity for the remission of the patient's symptoms, it gives protection to the patient and his family during periods of crisis and exacerbation, and it allows the child and the family a period of rest when they have reached a point of frustration and exhaustion. And third, following an acute stress or trauma, child psychiatry teams can meet with the members of these families, their usual counselors, and the representatives from other community organizations. Together, they can devise a treatment program that will provide for protection, support, and skilled psychiatric treatment without the use of hospitalization and without separating the child from his family. This process provides an opportunity for both the child and his parents to gain confidence in their ability to understand the nature of the emotional disturbance, to define the causes of the problem, to participate in the understanding of and the planning for the resolution, and to experience the important discovery that the family, rather than the child, may be the patient.

Theoretical Understanding

It is as important to understand those events in a child's or adolescent's life which constitute a psychiatric emergency as it is to recognize emergencies in general medical and psychiatric practice. In many ways, this understanding is more difficult, because the youngster disguises his problems by behavior instead of revealing them by talk. The ability to decode the crisis requires looking more deeply into the immediate behavioral problem that led to the child's referral. Most children seen as psychiatric emergencies are referred for specific behavioral problems, although there have been long-standing manifestations of emotional and developmental problems. Most children and youths referred as emergencies show urgent behavioral symptoms; these often arise in response to well-defined crises in their lives. At the same time, most are poorly prepared for the stresses of normal development.[24] In many instances, referring sources believe that the child is reacting primarily to some family crisis, unaware of the developmental and intrapsychic stress suffered by the child. Referral sources are often aware of the environment's tolerance of the child's difficulties. However, in order to stimulate rapid intervention, they overstate or dramatize the child's current behavior.[36]

In defining an emergency in child psychiatry, Morrison and Smith[26, 27] have focused their attention on the normal emotional dependence of the child. They believe that the emotional disturbance in the family and in individual family members creates crisis for the child and leads to distortions or blocks in his emotional growth. They have defined an emergency in child psychiatry as "that situation in which the significant adults around the child can no longer help him master his anxiety and can no longer provide temporary ego support and control."[23] Parental absence, anxiety, or helplessness may arise in the face of environmental and developmental events. They provoke a situation which is experienced by the child as desertion and isolation. The child's coping maneuvers include withdrawal (suicide attempts, school phobia, conversion, dissociation), projection (assaultive and delinquent behavior), or decompensation (panic and psychosis).

Theoretical work by Caplan,[6, 7] Erickson,[11] and Hill[13] has laid a foundation for the clinical study and testing[21] of the concepts of crisis intervention with children and their families. Much of the work, however, has yet to be given practical application or evaluation. Comprehensive studies of individual symptoms such as school refusal and phobia,[8, 9, 20] hysterical conversions,[31] suicide attempt and threat,[*] runaway,[33] assaultive behavior,[4] and delinquency[16] have been derived from typical clinical settings.

Child psychiatrists are particularly concerned with the role of adults in ego lending and ego support for the child during periods of developmental crisis. Recognizing the natural emotional dependence of children upon adults, one can anticipate the effect of an anxious, disorganized adult upon an anxious, dependent child who may be looking to the adult for support and security and as a model of conflict resolution. There are situations in which a significant adult is unable to foster ego growth, to provide ego controls, or to indicate ways of tension reduction. It may then be hypothesized that these threaten potentially serious impairment of the ego development of the child. Caplan,[6, 7] Lindemann,[19] and others have indicated that successful crisis resolution provides a small but significant emotional development for the individual. Potentially, it may enhance his capacity for meeting later stresses without necessarily effecting recognizable characterologic change. In defining a crisis or emergency in child psychiatry, it is essential to return to the concepts of crisis intervention and coping methods. Caplan[32] defined a crisis as "an upset in a steady state," emphasizing that an individual strives to maintain a state of equilibrium through a constant series of adaptive maneuvers. In discussing coping styles, Murphy[28] noted

Individual differences in coping resources and resilience within the child, as well as differences in support from the environment, help to determine which children can weather these stresses sufficiently to permit continued growth, and can develop increasing capacity to reach workable relationships with the environment. [p. 220]

Rubin Hill[13] wrote a study entitled *Families Under Stress*. In it, he defined crisis as "any sharp or decisive change for which old patterns are inadequate. . . . A crisis is a situation in which the usual behavior patterns are found to be unrewarding and new ones are called for immediately." It is evident that the zones of development can be blocked or distorted by disintegrative reactions to extreme stress or crisis. Erickson[11] stressed that those zones most seriously affected are apt to be the ones whose maturation is still incomplete, or those dynamically related to the most recently acquired function. During periods of relatively rapid ego growth, unresolved crises distort this develop-

* See references 18, 22, 25, 34, 35, and 38.

ment and lead to regression, withdrawal, or the utilization of maladaptive defense mechanisms.

In defining emergencies in child psychiatry, it is not enough to focus on the degree or kind of disturbance experienced by the child. One should also scrutinize the kind of anxiety, the degree of helplessness, and the level of disorganization of those adults who are most closely involved with the child in his immediate life situation. Ackerman[1] discussed the capacity of one or more family members to contain significant family psychopathology. In studying the total functioning of the child, his parents, and his siblings, it is essential to give heed to the role of significant extended family members as well as to the members of the nuclear family. The treatment method proposed involves immediate psychotherapeutic intervention with the child, his family, and important adults in his environment; it is based on this defined developmental model. Immediate diagnostic evaluation and treatment utilize the techniques of conjoint collaborative interviewing, brief psychotherapy, and family therapy (see chapters 4 and 7, and volume I). Psychiatric attention is directed toward prevention and the early alleviation of emotional disorders. The important aspects of such an approach include the immediate and concurrent appraisal of the child, his family, and his milieu; the reestablishment or development of communication within the family and the environment by the emergency treatment method chosen; the establishment and maintenance of good working relationships with various community agencies, schools, and clinics; and the provison of sufficient flexibility within the treatment program to afford the frequency and intensity of contact to achieve these purposes.

Indications for Emergency Intervention

The point a which "normal" developmental problems and the usual stresses of growth and maturation escalate into a serious family crisis cannot yet be predicted or be given status by means of "the educated guess." One cannot predict when a boy's running away will involve a stolen car rather than merely a short stay at a friend's house; when complaints of vague fears of school will be replaced by specific physiological symptoms or frank panic; when a previously unhappy fourteen-year-old girl will add the tragic problem of pregnancy to her troubles; or when the numerous suicidal ruminations, threats, gestures, and manipulations of a teenager will become a cold mortality statistic.

Burks and Hoekstra[5] reviewed emergency child psychiatric referrals at the University of Michigan Medical Center in 1961. They found that children who had attempted suicide, those developing a psychosis, and those with an acute school phobia presented *bona-fide emergency situations which required prompt clinic intervention*. They believed that referrals often resulted from family crises rather than from an intrapsychic crisis in the child. The crisis theory approach and the development of treatment methods to involve the entire family as a unit have stimulated a new look at these familiar problems.

Morrison[24] studied child psychiatric consultations in the emergency room of the Cincinnati General Hospital and "urgent" applications at the Central Psychiatric Clinic in Cincinnati. He was concerned with planning the development of a Child Psychiatry Emergency Service in 1964, and he sought to determine the types of problems presented, the kinds of families who applied, their situation, and their environment. His study revealed that the applications peaked from January through March, and again in August. Referrals included children with acute anxiety states, school phobia, truancy and school refusal, acute behavioral disorders, adolescent turmoil, hysterical conversions, depressions, suicidal attempts or threats, and acute emotional problems associated with mental retardation. More than 80 percent of the patients were between the ages of thirteen and seventeen, and twice as many girls were referred as boys.

Following the establishment of the Child Psychiatry Emergency Service, several hundred consecutive families were studied to determine the types of presenting difficulties that brought them to this type of attention. The findings confirmed previous studies of families who came to an emergency room or sought urgent help in an outpatient psychiatric clinic. Three girls were seen for every two boys. Seventy-five percent of the patients were in the thirteen-to-seventeen-year-old age range. Suicide attempts and threats and school refusal (school phobia, truancy, and so forth) predominated as the primary causes for referral; they constituted approximately half of the applicants. Other presenting symptoms are listed here in the order of their frequency: conversion reaction with paralysis; sexual promiscuity (frequently associated with pregnancy); runaway; toxic psychosis from several types of drugs and inhalants; firesetting; manifestations of acute anxiety; incest; killing of pets; and symptoms associated with acute psychosis.

Mattsson, and associates[21] reported on the results of a retrospective and follow-up study of 170 child psychiatric emergencies seen by the Child Psychiatry Service at University Hospitals in Cleveland. The reader is referred to this study because of the careful quality of its demographic and statistical work. The emergencies concentrated in the adolescent age range (83 percent were twelve to eighteen years) and girls were more commonly seen than boys on an emergency basis (60 percent versus 40 percent). Interestingly, this is exactly the same percentage reported by Morrison[24] in a different setting, but in a similar type of university teaching hospital. Mattsson found that the preponderance of girls among the emergencies was due to the marked increase in their referral from age fourteen onward, reaching a peak at ages sixteen to eighteen. In the preadolescent group, boys were referred almost three times as often as girls. A breakdown of acute symptoms responsible for the emergency referrals (with each emergency only represented in one category) revealed that suicidal behavior accounted for almost half of the sample, followed by assaultive and destructive behavior, marked anxiety with fears and physical complaints, bizarre and confused behavior, school refusal, truancy, and runaway.

Morrison's and Mattsson's reports were remarkably similar except for the greater number of school phobia and refusal emergencies in Morrison's series. That was probably an artifact associated with the source of the referrals; many cases came through a children's psychiatric clinic well known to the community schools as being quickly responsive to the acute emotional problems of schoolchildren.

Mattsson also noted that more than half of the emergencies were referred because of extremes in mood and behavior, such as depression, often with suicidal behavior. Another group were children who, for the most part, had maintained satisfactory control of impulsive behavior toward the environment and who now presented somatic complaints and fears that indicated internalized emotional conflicts. The remaining group manifested emotional disturbances that were more outwardly directed in an impulsive, often unmanageable, fashion in the form of assaultive, delinquent, and truanting behavior. Mattsson considered the following criteria necessary for an effective child psychiatry emergency service program: (1) prompt diagnostic evaluation of the child and his family in crisis; (2) clarification for the family of the fac-

tors that were significant in provoking the emergency behavior and in determining its nature; (3) active involvement of the parents in a treatment plan, with specific and practical direction for immediate alleviation of the child's distress, that is, giving him adequate protection, ego support, and external control; (4) access to a psychiatric inpatient unit for the relatively few children requiring such admission; (5) clinic facilities for continued study and short-term therapy for the child and his family; (6) optimal collaboration with community agencies, clinics, and schools throughout the emergency treatment period (this implies establishing which agency has the main responsibility for the long-term care of the family; (7) flexibility of schedules for psychiatric trainees, social workers, and supervisors in order to meet these program needs; and (8) recognition of emergency service experience as an integral part of the training programs for child psychiatrists and social workers.

In an extensive study of child psychiatric emergencies, Morrison and Smith[26] compared socioeconomic groups in public and private practice settings. They felt that the immediate crisis in the family was often precipitated by threatened separation, actual object loss, or the anniversary of such a loss. Moreover, they found that more than half of the children seen in emergency consultation had lost a parent or near relative through illness, hospitalization, marital separation, or death within three weeks of the onset of their symptoms. In addition, impending high school graduation or return to school, a family move to a new neighborhood or city, interruption of a close friendship, or hospitalization of a parent were also significant threats of separation. Threatened and actual separations, the death of a parent, and the loss of members in the extended family should always be considered, and questions about such losses or potential losses should always be raised in the course of diagnostic evaluation and treatment planning for emergency intervention with children and their families.

Complications, Disadvantages, and Side Effects

Most experienced child psychiatrists have noted several complications that become apparent in the course of intervening in emergencies. These rather minor but troublesome complications have led some clinicians to refer to the methods used in response to these occurrences by derogatory labels. Such names as "the Band-Aid approach" or the "mental health worker's panacea" reflect the frequent convergence of the family's wish for a quick solution and the emergency therapist's hope for a brief, rapid answer to difficult human problems. Even a moderate review of the work of Caplan,[6, 7] Lindemann,[19] Berlin,[3] Parad,[29] and Langsley[17] will demonstrate the complexity of the problems and the enormous skill needed to apply emergency measures effectively to family crises. The complications of this method can be considered in terms of three general areas.

A highly skilled and experienced staff is necessary. This means that each member of the treatment team must have a solid grounding in his discipline, with additional experience in collaborative psychotherapy and family and group therapy methods. This level of sophistication is essential to emergency psychotherapy. There is a need for a solid theoretical background combined with practical experience in order to achieve the most effective results. This is evident in the practice of medicine, social case work, therapeutic work by psychologists, skilled nursing, and the development of pedagogic skills. Psychiatric educational settings often expose the least experienced students to the most complicated clinical problems, because interns and beginning residents are often on call in emergency medical facilities. At the same time, carefully established lines of clinical responsibility and supervision are provided by experienced backup personnel and elaborate procedures. These accentuate the need for the availability of skill and experience.

A second area of concern is the strong desire of the symptomatic child or adolescent and the persistent hope of their parents for an easy and rapid solution to long-standing and difficult problems. Patients seen by emergency services invariably ask for medication that will provide a quick solution, for hospitalization, for support, for the attribution of blame, and often, for placement of the child outside of the home.

A third complication results from the difficulty in deciding on the appropriate administrative management and physical placement of emergency services. Although such services are appropriately viewed as short-term programs utilizing brief treatment methodologies, they do not fit easily into the scheme of either emergency medical or the usual mental health services. The medical emergency room's orientation toward immediate resolution or alleviation of medical problems, or "disposition" to a specialty service or ward, mitigates against the amount of time and attention necessary to arrive at an understanding of the emotional problems underlying a child psychiatric emergency. On the other hand, the psychiatric clinic has a well-established therapeutic approach and rhythm that effectively discourages or inadvertently rejects those families needing emergency psychiatric intervention.

When emergency services have successfully established themselves and become recognized for their effective therapeutic achievements, a related problem develops. Families who have received skilled therapeutic attention often wish to continue treatment for other problems in that same setting. They may indicate their desire by subtle means or by undisguised and guilt-producing insistence that the help provided was useful but "just not enough." This causes even experienced professionals to have doubts about the effectiveness of their interventions, and to entertain plans for ongoing long-term therapies. Community agencies will often respond to their recognition of the effectiveness of such services by overemphasizing the emergency aspect of a family's emotional problems when, in fact, the difficulties have been present for many years. Such situations are generally unresponsive to, or actually contraindicated for, a brief, family-oriented type of approach.

The result of these signs of "success," if not accurately assessed and effectively counteracted, is the destruction of the emergency service by conversion into one more long-term treatment facility. Since there is always a need for successful and effective mental health services (and, historically, many well-known mental health facilities had this beginning), this is not in itself a disaster. However, the community is nonetheless the loser, because the need for crisis intervention continues one way or another. Though the experienced staff recognizes this temptation, it is nevertheless most susceptible to it. Professionals who know how to meet and therapeutically resolve individual and family crises are always in demand; it is hardly surprising that the history of well-established clinical services can often be traced backward in time to the development of crisis services. It is ironic that in their later forms, one often finds that such settings no longer provide crisis services or that the crisis services are progressively relegated to the less experienced professionals. A vicious circle can become established as these less experienced personnel take up the more demanding work of crisis services. Since these therapists are often unfamiliar with the means of preventing future emotional crises, the psychiatric service finds that it is contributing to some of the problems that it is trying to solve.

Those responsible for the planning and development of a community's mental health services should appreciate the importance of three levels of psychiatric response to mental illness. The first serves as a site for a triage and is structured along the line of the medical emergency room or the social work intake service. It provides the first site of response to a "hot" situation. The second is an emergency or crisis service that is able to provide an urgent indepth child psychiatric evaluation in a brief therapy/family therapy format. The third is a long-term psychiatric treatment facility using individual collaborative psychotherapy with brief or long-term child psychiatric hospitalization. Rudolf Ekstein,[10] in a poetic and practical paper entitled "Brief Therapy Versus Intensive Therapy Or: Patient-Oriented Treatment Programs," has summed up these problems with impressive clarity:

An intensive care treatment center tries to deny neither emergency nor long-term needs. . . . Treatment techniques must be modified according to the specific needs of the patient. It is necessary to continue to reduce the ideological and political basis of our clinical activities and to strengthen the scientific by thorough diagnosis, careful training of staff, and appropriate application of the whole range of treatment possibilities.[23] [pp. 11–12]

Contraindications to the Use of Brief Family Therapy for Emergency Intervention

Contraindications are closely related to the experience and background of the professionals applying this method. Families with emotional crises often exhibit well-established family styles and defenses. Inexperienced personnel are often led into a morass of minute detail, extensive history taking, exploration to find or assign fault, and temptation to take sides in individual and family misunderstandings. Therapy with these families appears to be deceptively simple because they rigidly hold to the defensive styles that they have long used to avoid their tensions. Thus, the range of family behavior is extensive; nonetheless, in their response to therapeutic assistance and guidance, the kinds of families seen by emergency services fall into two general groups. Many families use the emergency service to assist them to resolve their crisis and then immediately discontinue contact, ignoring therapeutic recommendations for further diagnostic evaluation or continued psychotherapy. Such families are often quite willing to return during a future family crisis. The brief therapy approach fits well with such a family style, and the therapy often becomes one of intermittent, occasionally deep involvements consisting of one or two short contacts each year over a period of many years. One advantage of the brief therapy approach is that at the time of succeeding crises, these families often come to the intervention service at an earlier point in their turmoil. There is one drawback, or side effect, of this family style. This arises from the progressively increasing staff frustration which results from unsuccessful attempts to convince the family that there are underlying problems that need continuing exploration and treatment.

Conversely, a second group of families simply absorb the crisis therapist or crisis team into the family style. They readily agree to work indefinitely and quickly learn the jargon as a means of avoiding their underlying problems. Without realizing it, the treatment team then becomes a part of the family's resistive style of verbiage and volume; at the same time it also avoids sharing the feelings of individuals within the family. An experienced crisis service responds to this complication by utilizing alternating family and individual therapy, and by referring individual family members for long-term intensive therapy. Inexperienced staff often miss such a family's cohesive, centripetal,[37] defensive mode.

In evaluating contraindications for the brief family-oriented therapy method, one can draw an analogy to the treatment of acute grief reactions as compared to the therapeutic approach to an individual with unresolved grief and chronic depression. The stages of a normal grief reaction can be defined[19, 29] and the signs of acute grief recognized. One can then distinguish them from resolving grief or a prolonged and unresolved grief process. Symptomatically, one can observe the tears of acute grief and recognize the description of tightness in the throat, shortness of breath, a need for sighing, an empty feeling in the abdomen, muscular weakness, and feelings of numbness. One can distinguish these symptoms from the more chronic sleep and appetite changes, early morning wakening, preoccupation with guilt, and feelings of failure associated with chronic depression.

Experienced clinicians recognize the importance of reviewing the history of such families and seeking evidence of loss, separation, or threatened separation that may have contributed to a family's helplessness and emotional crisis. With early intervention these crises respond to the brief treatment approach with resolution. Conversely, when used with the chronically disordered family, such an approach bogs down in endless and meaningless disputes over descriptions, causes, details, and denials. Frustration and suffering are apparent. The number of problems can be defined and measured, but the quality of the response and the evidence of movement are lacking. Individual and family therapy is useful for families with chronic and pervasive problems, but the brief therapy approach is generally inappropriate for such deep and long-standing problems. Crisis therapy serves only to delay appropriate treatment for these families. More than that, it utilizes the limited time of the crisis team inappropriately by setting them off in an endless pursuit of problems that have long since been incorporated into the family's mode of functioning.

Another area that is difficult to define deserves continuing attention. This involves those individuals and families who utilize the interest and zeal of mental health services, especially crisis services, to avoid the rules and demands of society. These families turn to mental health services when they feel threatened by the strictures and restraints of a juvenile court, children's protection agency, or laws relating to child care and school attendance. The mental health services, especially emergency intervention services, are resorted to only when the family is under pressure from the community; the treatment agency is rapidly deserted as soon as these external pressures diminish. Crisis services for these families are contraindicated. The juvenile courts should be helped to enlist and to utilize child psychiatric consultation, and to develop child psychiatric services ancillary to the court and the probation services. Juvenile court judges and probation officers often welcome the development of crisis services. They view them as a means of rapid relief for overloaded courts and overwhelmed probation departments. Neither the juvenile court nor the emergency intervention service benefits from such "treatment attempts"; it is the problem families who gain the least from such community ping-pong or roundsmanship maneuvers. Once again, the intervention of skillful child psychiatric consultation at the point of entry, whether it be with the juvenile court, probation department, emergency room, or crisis service, can preclude delays in appropriate planning and professional help.

The Technique of Emergency Intervention

Many comprehensive studies have been made of children and families undergoing psychiatric emergencies. These studies have involved the diagnostic evaluation of individual symptoms; by and large they have been taken from typical clinical settings. The past decade has seen the emergence of specific therapeutic approaches toward families with children who have displayed serious symptoms. These symptoms include: suicide attempt and threat, school refusal and phobia, hysterical conversion, runaway, assaultive behavior and delinquency, drug abuse and toxicity, and precocious sexual misbehavior. Primary preventive treatment is also being undertaken for children who are survivors of parental suicide; children who live with acutely psychotic or chronically emotionally ill parents; families who are confronted by premature birth; children who display the manifestations of autism; children with evidence of childhood depression; adolescents who are pregnant; children who have a chronic debilitating disease such as juvenile diabetes or who have a physical or physiological handicap; and others who have come to be recognized as "children at risk." From time to time, emergency psychiatric services for children have been confronted urgently by all these, as well as by other threats to children. To cope with these threats, practical means have been developed for synthesizing the constructs of crisis theory, family interaction, and individual psychodynamics into effective methods of psychotherapeutic intervention.

Several decades ago, there was agreement that within the realm of child psychiatry, three situations represented true emergencies: (1) acute psychotic decompensation, (2) suicidal expression, and (3) acute school phobia. Because of their potential aggressive action aimed either at the self or at others, both psychotic decompensation and suicidal expression fell within the scope of conditions defined as medical emergencies, that is, those conditions which constituted a threat to biological integrity or to life. The recognition that acute school phobia was an emergency opened up the possibility for child psychiatry to find a different defintion of an emergency. Traditionally, child psychiatry had integrated an understanding of both physical and emotional factors in the child's development and maturation. That recognition brought with it a willingness to attend to any factors which interfered with emotional maturation. Concern then centered upon ego development in all of its manifestations, and clinical services were designed to begin meeting the needs of children at risk.

The most often used specific treatment technique is brief family therapy. Several excellent books have been written on the development and wide application of this therapeutic modality to a variety of situations in which children are at risk. Among them are: *The Treatment of Families in Crisis* by Langsley and Kaplan;[17] *Crisis Intervention: Selected Readings* by Parad;[29] *Children and Their Parents in Brief Treatment* by Barten and Barten;[2] and *Emergencies in Child Psychiatry: Emotional Crises in Children, Youth and Their Families* by Morrison.[23]

The application of brief family therapy to families in crisis has evolved from a number of sources. Among these were diagnostic and therapeutic studies of families seen initially in emergency child psychiatric consultation. These studies were made in the course of both the public and private practice of child psychiatry. Other cases came from child psychiatric clinics associated with juvenile courts and community children's services, and from emergency rooms of public and private hospitals. These families rarely see any similarity or connection between their current psychiatric crisis and other events that may have happened earlier, or even quite recently in their history. During their previous crises, many obtained help from both private and public resources, yet they tend to treat each occasion as separate and unrelated. A great many had been referred for more definitive diagnostic evaluation or for further professional treatment, but few had followed this advice, even with assistance from the referring source, or they had made a tentative or limited trial and then quickly discontinued treatment. Occasionally, some member of the family would express the wish to have further treatment or assistance. However, the other family members would refuse to participate and would often deride the one who sought to explore the family and individual problems in greater depth. When these families come in with a defined psychiatric crisis or a child at risk, treatment usually involves a team approach. This includes at least a child psychiatrist and a psychiatric social worker. Depending on the character of the clinical problem, this team is often expanded by the addition of a clinical psychologist, a visiting teacher, a welfare or an agency case worker, a public health nurse, and, occasionally, by the family's physician, attorney, and/or clergyman. In summary, many representatives of the child's and family's environment are invited to attend and participate in the meetings, if they have been involved in or can contribute to the resolution of the crisis or can foster the child's further development and maturation.

This treatment approach is based on the clinical assumption that the crisis involves not only the patient with the acute symptoms but also the entire family and the community (represented by appropriately selected participants). The goal of the first interview is to identify the internal stress or the external situation that has provoked or contributed to the crisis. In addition, the interview is designed to clarify the child's clinical symptoms and the family's susceptibility to emotional problems. An assessment is made of the style each family member uses in dealing with his tensions and fears. Presently, the therapist attempts to demonstrate how the behavior of each family member distorts or interferes with the communication required for minimal support of the symptomatic child or adolescent. Although different versions of the problem may emerge, a clearer picture of the immediate situation is gained from seeing the whole family and appropriate representatives of their community. Inevitably, in the story presented by any one member of the family, there will be distortions, incomplete presentations, and missing details. This, then, is responded to by other family members or participants present. There are invariably secrets and so-called skeletons in the closet which are usually revealed in the family sessions. Occasionally, however, separate individual counseling by a member of the treatment team, while the group session proceeds in an adjoining room, allows for the revelation of the long kept secret that has contributed extra stimulus to the family tension. It is difficult to overestimate the importance of poor family communication, individual and family secrets, and private family collusions in the exacerbation of symptomatic behavior and family crises. The family's problems and secrets often involve threatened and actual separations and losses. These secrets are experienced as restrictions and qualifications of attention, tenderness, and love.

The immediate focus is necessarily on the current crisis which has brought the family to treatment. The emphasis rapidly broadens, however, to include many other symptoms in the "labeled" patient as well as in other family members. By the end of the first interview, the diagnostic-treatment team should be able to formulate a definition of the child's and family's problem which is acceptable to the members of the family, representatives of the community, and the clinical team. The immediate goal of this work is to reduce the level of tension and lower the pitch of emotional disturbance which accompanies the emergence of an acute physical symptom or symptomatic behavior. For the most part, in the initial interview, the treatment is nonspecific and directed toward symptoms rather than etiology. The team seeks to arrest any further regression and to initiate some beginning stabilization.[17]

The initial interview and those that follow it are not limited to the usual "therapy hour." Indeed, they may vary in duration from less than a half-hour to many hours. In a reversal of the usual psychotherapeutic approach, the length of the family sessions is determined by the amount of time it takes to achieve the agreed-upon understanding and resolution. The main order of business for such crisis meetings, then, is to arrive at an agreement on the goals that the group will attempt to achieve in this first session.

During all this, it is important that the family comes to appreciate that the behavioral problem or emotional symptom leading to the crisis is not the cause of the family problem; it is merely its latest expression. The treatment team and the community representatives should feel free to make concrete suggestions to the parents as to how they can protect their child in a responsible and realistic fashion. As a step toward the resolution of the specific crisis, family tasks can be proposed, and the family should be assigned activities directed toward the resolution of the current crisis. Specific assignments of "homework" should be made to the parents and to the child or adolescent. They should be asked to work together toward their own solutions of the family's problems and to bring their difficulties to subsequent therapy sessions. Examples of such assignments should include the determination of which parent shall assist the school-phobic child. This involves preparing for school attendance, transporting, and remaining temporarily at the school with the child if required. The child does not have the prerogative of remaining home but can make requests and negotiate for tension-reducing assistance.

The suicidal child can participate in the planning for his own observation and for the appropriate disposal of the tempting drugs from the family's medicine cabinet. The runaway child can share in the planning for temporary living arrangements or for modifications in the stresses at home. The obvious goal is to include the child in all planning, so that the adults are not managing a recalcitrant child nor the child manipulating the adults by his symptomatic behavior, "the tail wagging the dog." With adolescents who are moving toward independence, the entire family should have the home assignment of working out age-appropriate rules for dating, driving, and working. It is understood that these plans must be consistent with peer privileges and activities. Family conferences should work out a reasonable distribution of household tasks and family responsibilities. The family should be expected to attend to tasks rather than symptoms. During the group meetings, the treatment team should be alert to unspoken family alliances and nonverbal communications. Such nonverbal communications and alliances are often extremely valuable clues to disruptive family secrets.

It is essential that the family come to appreciate that the behavioral problems or physical symptoms which led to the crisis treatment represent the presence of underlying family problems rather than their cause. Alternative means of communication, rather than symptomatic expression, are discussed with both the children and their parents. Again, in contrast to conventional clinic and practice approaches, subsequent family meetings are determined by the capacity of family members to grasp their problems and the confidence of the treatment team that they understand the sources of family tension. Subsequent meetings are sometimes scheduled the same day; occasionally, several interviews may occur within a week. The frequency is often determined by the confidence or doubts expressed by members of the family or the treatment team. Specific treatment goals, or behavioral changes, are defined as subsequent meetings are scheduled. In turn, future meetings may be determined by the achievement of treatment goals or by the presence of new problems unearthed in family conferences in the home.

Emergency intervention with family crises should not be limited to group meetings at the clinic or private office. Home and school visits, meetings at the offices of involved community agencies, and extensive use of phone calls contribute actively to the education of the family in the handling of their crisis. A benefit that must not be underestimated results from the willingness of the crisis team to meet with agency and school personnel in their own setting. Such meetings demonstrate the willingness of the child psychiatric crisis team to interact with community agency representatives on their own territory. More than that, however, they also serve as inservice training that many agencies faced with large case loads, waiting lists, and long-term commitments would otherwise be unable to obtain. The brief treatment approach demonstrates to the family and to the community representatives that there are effective ways of solving individual and family emotional problems other than by developing physiological symptoms, symptomatic behavioral problems, or extruding a family member by runaway or hospitalization. The family participates in active psychological treatment and education to develop the capacity for adaptive management of future crises.

Kaffman[15] has summarized the goals and purposes of brief family therapy by commenting that

It is not within the scope of a short service of family therapy to bring about basic and extensive alterations in character structure of family members. . . . The therapist's help to all the members of the family, in obtaining focused insight into the nature of conscious and preconscious conflicts, is likely to lead to a readjusted and healthier family interrelationship, to goal modification, and to full use of potential possibilities. [pp. 205–206]

He believes that no measures that might contribute to a healthy family adjustment should be neglected by the therapist. He considers therapeutic counseling to be indicated if the patient or the family is ready to follow advice. Additionally, he stresses the importance of assisting the family to reach an emotional equilibrium by calling attention to clinical symptoms and helping to relieve them.

Most experienced psychotherapists have had the opportunity to observe many changes in a patient and members of his family, by the time an area of emotional tension and conflict has been explored and relieved through psychotherapeutic means. The crisis therapist has many opportunities to offer such relief: The patient and his family are highly motivated to be rid of their symptoms; and the therapist is usually viewed as a source of help, someone who has demonstrated interest in the family's problem by prompt involvement. The patient's and his family's anxiety can be directed toward the immediate problems and the related family conflicts from the past; and the usual characterologic defenses of the family members have been modified and realigned by the immediacy of the crisis. All of the foregoing can provide powerful leverage for modification of the previously rigid and destructive family interactions. Kaffman has referred to this as the "snowball phenome-

non" which can lead to favorable modifications in the child-parent relationship.

Preparation of the Family in Crisis for Brief Family Therapy

Many kinds of service deliverers need the skills necessary for brief family treatment approaches to families in emotional crisis. These include: individual and group practitioners, social agencies, pastoral counselors, school counseling programs, and court probation departments. Additionally, they should use or recruit professional personnel skilled in crisis treatment methodology. For their own part, they should understand this treatment method sufficiently so that they can prepare families to utilize such psychiatric crisis treatment services.

Referring agencies can be of significant help to these families. They can encourage them to view the problem as an opportunity for clarification of understanding and for growth and maturation. They can depict the approach as an alternative to withdrawing from, isolating, or expelling from the family the troubled individual. The family's ability to participate can best be evaluated and often can best be facilitated by those who have worked with it most closely and who have demonstrated their capacity to provide assistance during previous times of concern or disturbance. The value of the participation of the total family should be stressed; and, when possible, some community member can offer to accompany the family and participate with them during the initial stages of the family therapy or throughout the treatment program. This can be an agency worker, a school or court representative, or the family physician or his representative.

A community agency will often use an individual or family crisis referral as an opportunity to evaluate a psychiatric crisis service. At the same time, it can utilize the occasion to introduce members of its own staff to the crisis treatment methodology. This allows the staff members to extend their clinical capacities and to be more selective in planning individual and family referral.

One area in the preparation of a family for referral for emergency intervention by a child psychiatric crisis service creates special difficulty. This is the expectation that all members of the family actively participate in understanding the problem, and that all contribute to its resolution. A brief review of the history of school phobia can help clarify this; it illustrates the kind of clinical and theoretical work that has gone into the recommendation that all members of the family participate in attempting to resolve the problem. Almost five decades ago, school phobia was first recognized and described as a specific clinical entity with debilitating consequences. Society had recognized the need for education for all children. Some parents had treated children as chattel, primarily for the parents' own needs. For their part, few children were able to appreciate the importance of education. As a result, compulsory attendance at school up to a given age had been mandated by legislation.

Initially, school phobia was considered only in terms of the child's anxiety about school attendance, and treatment was sought to remedy this. During the following two decades, there was increasing recognition of the phobic child's attachment to his mother and an ever-increasing awareness of the mother's covert or overt participation in and contribution to the child's anxiety. A shift in attention took place with the recognition of the mother's fear and anxiety. Emphasis began to be given to the mother-child dyad as contributing to school phobia. With increasing attention to the mother, there was the discovery of marriage problems, attention to the husband-wife dyad, and the recognition that the child's father also played a part in the child's phobic symptoms and school anxiety. While some clinicians gave attention to the pragmatic issues of returning the child to school as quickly as possible, others focused on the psychiatric treatment of the child's and family's problems at sites in or near the school setting. Still others recommended individual intensive psychotherapy for each member of the family. School phobia as an aspect of family neurosis came to prominence in the late 1950s, culminating in an elegant paper by Malmquist.[20] A similar history of clinical discoveries and understanding can be traced for most clinical symptoms; that understanding need not be rediscovered with each family seen for emergency intervention.

It has been the experience of crisis services that the clear request for participation by all family members, members of the extended family, and representatives of involved agencies in sufficient for their participation.[17, 23, 29] Most referring agencies and professionals with some grasp of the development of emotional problems can use that understanding in planning the referral of families for crisis services.

The Economic Implications of Emergency Intervention

When one considers the economics of brief family psychotherapy for children and adolescents with acute emotional problems, one must ask, What symptom is receiving therapeutic attention? How intact is the family? and What is the therapeutic alternative? Because of their very nature, emotional crises are recognized in one way or another, and they have been responded to by a variety of treatment resources provided by organized society. Socially, disruptive behaviors (runaway, firesetting, sexual promiscuity) have come to the attention of the juvenile and family courts. Assaultive and homicidal behaviors (including drug abuse) have come to the attention of the criminal court system. Educational problems (school phobia, truancy, school disruption) have been the responsibility of the educational institutions and their counseling services. Urgent medical problems (suicide attempt and threat, conversion reactions, psychophysiological symptoms, bizarre or psychotic behavior, and the victims of sexual assault) have been initially evaluated and treated in hospital emergency rooms and other medical facilities. Some behaviors viewed as indicative of serious individual and family disturbance (incest, killing of pets, survivors of parental suicide, and children experiencing acute grief) rarely come to psychiatric attention, but subsequent emotional and economic costs can be very high. Crisis services can demonstrate an immediate economic usefulness when they are successful in preventing or reducing the number of fires set by a child, by preventing suicide attempts that result in hospitalization, and by reducing the impact of drug abuse and intoxication by appropriate and timely attention to the causes.

In addition to the cost of providing custodial services, hospital treatment, juvenile courts, detention centers, and hospital emergency room services, there are the usually unrecognized costs associated with the need for home education, police services, and the costs incurred by malicious mischief and blatantly destructive behavior. There is additionally the long-term, immeasurable cost associated with the child who has missed educational opportunities with the ensuing concomitant personal and social disability.

Langsley and Kaplan,[17] in their important book *The Treatment of Families in Crisis*, made an attempt to assess the cost of crisis services when compared with hospitalization cost. They arrived at an estimate that hospitalization and custodial care costs are approximately six times more than the operation of their Family Treatment Unit. Additionally, the personnel on the project were charged with obtaining control cases and measuring the effeectiveness of the control against the experimental cases. The professionals on the project team were engaged also in teaching crisis techniques to other mental health workers.

Cost effectiveness studies have not been performed on child psychiatric emergency services. This would be a very complex computation because of the variety of resources, in addition to hospitalization, utilized by the children's services. Estimations of effectiveness, however, could be made based on what is known of the staffing needs for children's services. These could be compared with the staffing needs for a children's psychiatric hospital and the capital outlay for hospital construction. In fact, such a cost comparison would be inappropriate and destructive; there is much to suggest that hospitalization and psychiatric services for children cannot be readily compared to equivalent services for adults. Resources for hospitalization of children and adolescents are far from optimally developed; up to the present, they have certainly not been excessively or unnecessarily utilized. Occasionally, children and adolescents have been sent to custodial facilities; as a rule, however, that has been the result of a shortage of appropriate care facilities for children and especially for adolescents. Emergency psychiatric services for children and their families need the back up provided by skilled children's psychiatric hospitals as noted earlier in this chapter. Resources for the treatment of emotional problems of children often operate at peak capacity and may have waiting lists; crisis services can provide the necessary triage for optimum development and use of alternative resources. Throughout their relatively short existence, children's clinical services have usually been "running to catch up." Thus, compared to the kinds of service they supplement, children's crisis services are relatively economical. Full-time staffing should include a child psychiatrist, a psychiatric social worker, and a psychiatrically-trained public health nurse. The full-time or part-time services of a clinical psychologist, a liaison schoolteacher, and

a community social worker familiar with children's services would complete the professional team. Additional expenses would include two full-time clerical workers and office rental.

Record keeping and correspondence are kept at a minimum by diagnostic check lists. These should end with a summarizing paragraph describing the conclusions and alternatives that were considered in the family group interviews. Most of the necessary information can be shared with other agencies by telephone and short letters, since the personnel of the service participate actively and directly in all referral planning.

The most challenging area for the personnel on such services is flexibility of professional time. Crisis services are developed along lines similar to medical emergency rooms and social service intake divisions. They are modeled on these rather than on the usual psychiatric clinics and social service agencies from which they have developed. This identification with medical emergency rooms and social work intake services makes it possible for specific staff always to have time free for telephone consultation, for interviews with walk-in patients and clients, and for diagnostic and treatment sessions of indefinite length. Such a service would be able to treat five to seven new families each week. This is the approximate service demand of a community mental health catchment area serving 200,000 people.

Simultaneous Activities Essential to Emergency Intervention

The active participation and involvement of parents and other important adults are crucial to the treatment of a child experiencing a psychiatric emergency. To support the crisis treatment approach, however, effective therapeutic intervention needs other simultaneous activities. A few examples will demonstrate the nature of these activities and will serve to highlight the need for interrelated services for such troubled children and their families. Suicidal adolescents will often display several symptoms which represent their attempts at a solution to their depression as well as expressing their low self-esteem. In addition to an overt suicide attempt, there may be associated symptoms such as school refusal, runaway, sexual promiscuity (with possible pregnancy or venereal disease), drug abuse and toxicity, and the physical complications resulting from the suicide attempt itself. There is the need for emergency medical facilities, backed up by an adolescent inpatient treatment unit or foster home care, a detoxification unit, contraceptive counseling, abortion services if requested or maternity and prenatal health care, and the opportunity for continuing education or vocational training if appropriate. There may be debate about the merits and drawbacks of the best way to provide this wide variety of expensive services. In view of the high personal and financial costs when they are absent, however, the necessity for their existence seems apparent.

To be effective, the treatment of school phobia requires enlightened school personnel who are able to cooperate and actively participate in the work of the psychiatric emergency team. During the first days of renewed school attendance, the child and the parents are likely to exhibit a high level of anxiety. This often provides a severe test of the flexibility of the school personnel. For several weeks, each weekend break and intervening holiday usually reactivates the child's wish to avoid the separation from the home. It also inflames the parents' anxiety about the child leaving them. The treatment of truancy, on the other hand, often calls for a different kind of educational or vocational training setting, one that can catch and hold the adolescent's interest. The effort is to keep him involved in a flexible educational program combined with vocational training. Adolescents, their parents, and the community all benefit from a vocational educational program provided through vocational schools, continuation schools, and evening and night school programs, all combined with opportunities for vocational testing and counseling.

Emergency medical facilities are essential not only as backup medical resources for patients with suicidal behavior but also for those with conversion and dissociative reactions, acute psychophysiological symptoms, and drug intoxication. Child and adolescent emergency services must maintain an active liaison with juvenile courts, probation departments, and law enforcement agencies for children involved in truancy, runaway, assaultive and destructive behavior, and for the victims of incest or sexual assault.

Much of the foregoing is obvious and familiar to experienced psychiatric clinicians. Nonetheless, it is worth restating that children's emergency services must continually maintain the lines of communication with their colleagues and collaborators in public agencies and in private practice. These referral sources must be able to obtain im-

mediate access to the professional personnel providing emergency services; the reciprocal of such access occurs when the emergency team feels that the family is ready to return to their initial referring source, or when the emergency team seeks to assist the family to continue with a different or additional public or private service.

Follow-up Patterns

For children and families who have received emergency psychiatric services, follow-up and continuing care should be provided. This is consistent with the psychological, medical, and demographic understanding of those families that are most likely to use or be referred for emergency services. These families tend to follow predictable patterns in seeking medical services. Understanding those patterns is essential to the development of such services and the planning for follow-up programs. Crises are often used as an opportunity for communication within the family and as a method of obtaining service from the community. Morrison and Smith[26] have reported on the many similarities found in families that tend to relate through their emotional crises; and they have observed that regardless of their socioeconomic, ethnic, or cultural background, there are many similarities among these families. Some differences were noted in the degree of family intactness in terms both of the cohesiveness of the family and of the presence or absence of parental figures; other differences were observed in their use of medical as compared with juvenile court facilities. Despite these, however, the similarities were far more prominent. The families often wanted an immediate resolution of their problems, prompt reduction of their anxiety, and a solution through the use of medication or hospitalization.

These families had histories of long-standing neurotic and deviant behavior that literally cried for professional attention. This problem behavior was so severe that Smith and Morrison were impressed by the families' capacity to tolerate so much stress. Yet, these troubled people would demand prompt solutions to symptomatic behavior that threatened an already fragile family equilibrium. As described earlier, the usual stresses in life such as childbirth, school separation, and family illness often precipitated dramatic emotional symptoms; and major stresses, such as a death in the family, the illness of a parent, or the imminence of a family move often resulted in total family disorganization. In the lower socioeconomic group, aggressive behavior of youths often led to juvenile court and detention, while similar behavior in the higher socioeconomic groups would be handled through private psychiatric treatment or a visit to the medical emergency room. Similarly, school phobia was referred for medical and psychiatric attention by the parents in the middle and upper middle socioeconomic groups. In the lower socio-economic groups, it was more likely to be neglected unless pressure was exerted by the school authorities.

Most of the children referred as emergencies for specific behavior problems showed long-standing manifestations of developmental deviations. Despite urgent behavioral symptoms precipitating the psychiatric emergencies, most of the children seen were poorly prepared for the stresses of normal development. Virtually none of these children presented single symptoms. Not only did they come to the emergency consultation with a combination of symptoms, but their past histories also revealed previous crises evidenced by different symptom complexes. It was not possible to categorize the symptomatic behavior as either clearly autoplastic or alloplastic. For example, a number of suicidal acts contained elements of both reaction to an internal fantasy and an almost consciously directed gesture toward the environment. Similarly many instances of promiscuity and pregnancy demonstrated trial attempts at both kinds of adaptation. Regardless of its additional autoplastic implications, however, the alloplastic, or acting-out quality of the symptom or behavior, appeared to motivate the more urgent and more frequent requests for emergency psychiatric intervention. Those children who were reacting to serious family losses or separations showed autoplastic symptoms most clearly.

These families have been described as representing centrifugal and centripetal patterns of behavior.[37] As the terms imply, the families are either quite close, trusting only immediate family members while viewing those outside of the family with suspicion and distrust, or they are unusually disorganized and maintain a certain distance from each other and from their community, figuratively moving out in all directions. The latter families are often described as having borderline family functioning and sharing only their living quarters and mutual distrust. Both types of families turn to professional and community services only in times of severe emotional crisis; they will predictably avoid the obligations of a continuing treatment program. They are difficult to refer to other community agencies, and they often precipitously discontinue participation in the usual psychiatric clinic programs. Since they fail to keep appointments, neglect the usual treatment schedules of a community clinic, and often request services at night or over the weekends when a community agency is least able to respond, such separations often occur by mutual consent. Follow up with these families is quite challenging to most community psychiatric clinics; however, it is relatively easy for the emergency psychiatric services which provide psychiatric care in a manner similar to emergency medical services.

Skilled social service and/or psychiatric intake evaluation are essential in providing emergency psychiatric services. At the time of the first contact, it is necessary to obtain telephone numbers and addresses of the family, extended family members, neighbors, place of employment, and other involved agencies. Cross-references using social service exchange information, when available, can prove very beneficial since the time available to work with these families will be limited; involvement by representatives from agencies previously used will sometimes facilitate planning for continuing and follow-up care. Experience has demonstrated that many of these families will continue in a follow-up or continuing care program if the major initiative and activity come from the emergency service or the previously involved social agency. The lack of follow-up care is more often an aspect of the family's disorganization; this is evident in the family's frequent moves, disconnected telephones, and failure to provide changed addresses. When one reviews the social work intake and psychiatric diagnostic information pertaining to changes of residence and employment, and other signs of family disorganization, the need for telephone numbers and addresses of relatives and employers becomes apparent. Most families provide information willingly, give permission for contact with other agencies and family members, and express gratification that the psychiatric emergency service will take an active role in contacting them.

Periodic telephone calls help these families recognize the interest and commitment that the therapeutic service has in them; more than that, telephone calls provide opportunities for encouraging continuation with referral sources. Such follow-up care affords an opportunity for these families to report developing problems. These can then be treated during their incipient stages before an acute crisis or threat to life develops. Similar information can be obtained through mail questionnaires, but again, a knowledge of the family style is essential to such inquiries. A notation to forward the letter along with the inclusion of a stamped, addressed envelope significantly improve the responses to such inquiries. With most crisis families, these patterns of follow-up care should be continued indefinitely. Contact should be maintained every month or two during the first year, and one or two times yearly thereafter.

A frequent problem in planning follow-up care for these families has been the increasing tendency to carefully delimit psychiatric services within specific geographic boundaries and catchment areas. Crisis-prone families move across city, county, and state lines to follow employment opportunities, to maintain family ties, and to avoid legal and financial entanglements. The development of catchment areas has further complicated the task of maintaining lines of communication with these families. Psychiatric and medical services are often confined to sources of funding support and political divisions. Once again, this may interfere with active follow-up care for families who have moved only a few miles from their address at the time they first sought care.

The free clinics, with their ease of access, availability, and informality have been helpful in providing early intervention. At best, however, they are no substitute for continuing care and follow-up programs. Hopefully, the value of emergency psychiatric services and the special skills provided by a well-trained professional staff will counteract the tendency to draw rigid political and geographical boundary lines. This will aid in the development of services primarily for children and families in need, rather than for limited geographic districts.

Summary

Therapeutic results have been reported by Morrison,[23] Langsley and Kaplan,[17] Parad,[29] and Barten and Barten.[2] These authors have used similar types of modified individual and family psychotherapeutic modalities in treating crisis-prone families. All have emphasized the need for continuing resources and the planning for follow-up services. Such efforts form a concomitant part of the treatment and support of families who come to psychiatric services in a state of emotional crisis. Reports indicate that the majority of families treated consider the psychiatric treatment programs to be very helpful. That result has been reported by Kaffman[15] as measurable symptom relief. Langsley and Kaplan[17] have presented information reviewing the financial cost of such services; they have tabulated the results of a specific program in terms of hospital days needed and prevented through the use of family crisis therapy. Their data on families in crisis that contain an acutely psychotic adult are similar to information on families in crisis that contain an acutely disturbed child.

The resolution of family crises, the avoidance of hospitalization, the resolution of psychiatric symptoms, and the return to school are all important to the emotional development of the child. The short-term family therapeutic approach to children and families in crisis is a useful and constructive means of prompt alleviation of emotionally crippling symptoms and behaviors. It should be available to all families in need of acute psychiatric care for their children.

REFERENCES

1. ACKERMAN, N. W., "Toward an Integrative Therapy of the Family," *American Journal of Psychiatry, 114:*727–733, 1958.
2. BARTEN, H. H., and BARTEN, S. S., *Children and Their Parents in Brief Therapy,* Behavioral Publications, New York, 1973.
3. BERLIN, I. N., "Crisis Intervention and Short Term Therapy: An Approach in a Child Psychiatric Clinic," *Journal of the American Academy of Child Psychiatry, 9:*595–606, 1970.
4. BURKS, H. L., and HARRISON, S. I., "Aggressive Behavior as a Means of Avoiding Depression," *American Journal of Orthopsychiatry, 32:*418–422, 1962.
5. BURKS, H. L., and HOEKSTRA, M., "Psychiatric Emergencies in Children," *American Journal of Orthopsychiatry, 34:*134–137, 1964.
6. CAPLAN, G., *Principals of Preventive Psychiatry,* Basic Books, New York, 1964.
7. ———, *Prevention of Mental Disorders in Children,* Basic Books, New York, 1961.
8. COOLIDGE, J., et al., "Patterns of Aggression in

School Phobia," in Eissler, R. S., et al., (Eds.), *The Psychoanalytic Study of the Child,* vol. 17, pp. 319–333, International Universities Press, New York, 1962.
9. EISENBERG, L., "School Phobia: Diagnosis, Genesis, and Clinical Management," *Pediatric Clinics of North America, 5:*645–666, 1958.
10. EKSTEIN, R., "Brief Therapy Versus Intensive Therapy Or: Patient Oriented Treatment Programs," in Morrison, G. C. (Ed.), *Emergencies in Child Psychiatry,* pp. 5–12, Charles C Thomas, Springfield, Ill., 1975.
11. ERIKSON, E. H., *Childhood and Society,* 2nd ed., Norton, New York, 1963.
12. FREUD, S., "Mourning and Melancholia," in Strachey, J. (Ed.) *The Standard Edition of the Complete Psychological Works of Sigmund Freud,* vol. 14, pp. 237–260, Hogarth Press, London, 1957.
13. HILL, R., *Families Under Stress,* Harper and Brothers, New York, 1949.
14. HOLLINGSHEAD, A. B., and REDLICK, F. C., *Social Class and Mental Illness,* Wiley, New York, 1958.
15. KAFFMAN, M., "Short-Term Family Therapy," in

Parad, H. J. (Ed.), *Crisis Intervention: Selected Readings,* pp. 202–219, Family Service Association, New York, 1965.

16. KAUFMAN, I., and HEIMS, L., "The Body Image of the Juvenile Delinquent," *American Journal of Orthopsychiatry,* 28:146–159, 1958.

17. LANGSLEY, D. G., and KAPLAN, D. N., *The Treatment of Families in Crisis,* Grune & Stratton, New York, 1968.

18. LEVI, L. D., et al., "Separation and Attempted Suicide," *Archives of General Psychiatry,* 15:148–164, 1966.

19. LINDEMANN, E., "Symptomatology and Management of Acute Grief," in Parad, H. J. (Ed.), *Crisis Intervention: Selected Readings,* pp. 7–21, Family Service Association, New York, 1965.

20. MALMQUIST, C.P., "School Phobia: A Problem in Family Neurosis," *Journal of the American Academy of Child Psychiatry,* 4:293–319, 1965.

21. MATTSSON, A., HAWKINS, J. W., and SEESE, L., "Child Psychiatric Emergencies," *Archives of General Psychiatry,* 17:584–592, 1967.

22. MINTZ, R. S., "Some Practical Procedures in the Management of Suicidal Persons," *American Journal of Orthopsychiatry,* 36:896–903, 1966.

23. MORRISON, G. C., *Emergencies in Child Psychiatry: Emotional Crises of Children, Youth and Their Families,* Charles C Thomas, Springfield, Ill., 1975.

24. ———, "Therapeutic Intervention in a Child Psychiatry Emergency Service," *Journal of the American Academy of Child Psychiatry,* 8(3):542–558, 1969.

25. ———, and COLLIER, J. G., "Family Treatment Approaches to Suicidal Children and Adolescents," *Journal of the American Academy of Child Psychiatry,* 8(1):140–153, 1969.

26. MORRISON, G. C., and SMITH, W. R., "Child Psychiatric Emergencies: A Comparison of Two Clinic Settings and Socio-Economic Groups," in Morrison, G. C. (Ed.), *Emergencies in Child Psychiatry,* pp. 107–114, Charles C Thomas, Springfielf, Ill., 1975.

27. ———, "Emergencies in Child Psychiatry: A Definition," in Morrison, G. C. (Ed.), *Emergencies in Child*

Psychiatry, pp. 13–20, Charles C Thomas, Springfield, Ill., 1975.

28. MURPHY, L. B., "Preventive Implications of Development in the Preschool Years," in Caplan, G. (Ed.), *Prevention of Mental Disorders in Children,* pp. 218–243, Basic Books, New York, 1961.

29. PARAD, H. J., *Crisis Intervention: Selected Readings,* Family Service Association, New York, 1965.

30. ———, "Preventive Casework: Problems and Implications," in Parad, H. J. (Ed.), *Crisis Intervention: Selected Readings,* pp. 284–302, Family Service Association, New York, 1965.

31. PROCTOR, J. T., "Hysteria in Childhood," *American Journal of Orthopsychiatry,* 28:394–407, 1958.

32. RAPOPORT, L., "The State of Crisis: Some Theoretical Considerations," in Parad, H. J. (Ed.), *Crisis Intervention: Selected Readings,* pp. 22–31, Family Service Association, New York, 1965.

33. ROBEY, A., et al., "The Runaway Girl: A Reaction to Family Stress," *American Journal of Orthopsychiatry,* 34:762–767, 1964.

34. SHAW, C. R., and SCHELKUN, R. F., "Suicidal Behavior in Children," *Psychiatry,* 28:157–158, 1965.

35. SHNEIDMAN, E. S. and FARBEROW, N. L., "Statistical Comparisons Between Attempted and Committed Suicides," in Farberow, N. L., and Shneidman, E. S. (Eds.), *The Cry for Help,* pp. 19–47, McGraw-Hill, New York, 1961.

36. SMITH, W. R., and MORRISON, G. C., "Family Tolerance for Chronic, Severe, Neurotic, or Deviant Behavior in Children Referred for Child Psychiatry Emergency Consultation," in Morrison, G. C. (Ed.), *Emergencies in Child Psychiatry,* pp. 115–128, Charles C Thomas, Springfield, Ill., 1975.

37. STIERLIN, H., "A Family Prespective on Adolescent Runaways," *Archives of General Psychiatry,* 29:56–62, 1973.

38. TUCKMAN, J., and CONNON, H. E., "Attempted Suicide in Adolescents," *American Journal of Psychiatry,* 119:228–232, 1962.

---

33 / Antisocial Youth

Robert J. Marshall

In order to plan a treatment program for a youthful offender, the factors which produce the behavior must be known. Unfortunately, the area of diagnosis of antisocial children and juvenile delinquents is still in a fairly primitive, if not chaotic, state, especially when the goal is determination of etiology, treatment, and prognosis. The legal definitions are clearly insufficient, if not misleading. The behavioral-social definitions, while sharpening concepts, are of some use to clinicians. Inner feeling states, intrapsychic processes, defensive patterns, motivations, early childhood experiences, along with conscious and unconscious variables of

the parents, appear to be central to currently useful definitions. However, these types of variables have been traditionally difficult to pin down in any operational sense. It appears that factor analytic studies, which can incorporate environmental, organismic, and behavioral variables within a theoretical framework and which can predict behavior, are those which will most clarify the diagnostic picture.

Mindful of the ease with which one talks about "delinquency," for purposes of this chapter a distinction will be made among (1) "normal," social or gang delinquency; (2) neurotic delinquency;

(3) psychopathic delinquency; and (4) borderline to psychotic delinquency. Although the "modal" or psychopathic delinquent, who is clinically commonplace, poorly understood, and highly resistant to treatment, will be the focus of the discussion of treatment which follows, it should be noted that neurotic and borderline features often are present, as there is a continuum in the maturity and organization of the ego and object relations.

Individual Psychotherapy

Central to the theory of psychotherapy to be outlined here are those relevant developmental events and phenomena which precede puberty's recrudescence of earlier conflicts. Most significant among them are: the defenses against feelings of helplessness, depression, and anxiety which derive from the inconsistency and rejection of the mother during the separation-individuation phase and an immature vulnerable ego and quasi-symbiotic relationship with the mother—all of which takes place within the context of a physically or emotionally absent or delinquent father who provides an inadequate model for identification.

THE FIRST STAGE: CREATING THE

NARCISSISTIC TRANSFERENCE

Aichhorn[3] observed:

As a rule, the adolescent is not in the psychological state in which we would like to have him. He is negativistic, often hostile, insecure, irritable; he feels superior and pretends a still greater superiority; often he is not interested in what we can offer him and very rarely does he expect that the hours with us will serve a useful purpose. [p. 65]

Lippman[75] defined the therapeutic problem more succinctly.

One of the greatest obstacles to effective psychotherapy with seriously delinquent youngsters is the narcissistic defense which they have set up . . . [the difficulty in treatment] is so marked as to lend one to suspect that these narcissistic delinquents show some of the characteristics of the psychotic reaction. [p. 160]

Easson[32] also perceived the major treatment problem as that of the narcissistic character who is the "neighbor" of the schizophrenic, according to Bergler.[10]

Aichhorn[4] apparently was the first to mount an effective treatment approach to the narcissistic

character of the delinquent. What enabled him to do this? Perhaps Eissler,[35] in his biographical note about Aichhorn, provides a clue. Emphasizing Aichhorn's "supreme faculty of identifying with the patient and of knowing his needs," Eissler observes, "Despite his dedication to the treatment of delinquents he has never lost his capacity to enjoy the adventure of crime nor his understanding of how sweet to the criminal is the violating of a rule to which the community bows." Anna Freud,[49] in an obituary of Aichhorn, reveals that his talent was related to his narrowly missing being a delinquent himself. Aichhorn understood, liked, and respected delinquents and, in the initial stages of therapy, seemed never to challenge, analyze, or break down their defenses. For example, with penultimate patience and confidence he could suggest to a delinquent that he run away from the institution or allow for the playing out of destructive, alienating behavior. Aichhorn[3] states, "If, however, the educator remains reserved and identified with society, and feels protective of the laws which the wayward youth is violating, no meaningful contact can be established."

Eissler[35] echoes Aichhorn's approach when he asserted that the technique for achieving the reversal from an alloplastic adaptation (which endeavors to mold the external environment) to an autoplastic one (which refers to adapting oneself to the environment)

is founded on the principle of establishing a tight, fool-proof attachment between the psychoanalyst and the delinquent in the shortest period of time. Why this is necessary becomes clear. If the delinquent were not attached to the therapist, he would discontinue his treatment . . . the therapist of delinquents must become the delinquents' ideal if he wants to stand a chance of getting any hold on him . . . If the analyst can convince the delinquent of the shortcomings of the technique he had applied and impress on him that he, the analyst, knows efficient and less dangerous techniques, then the delinquent is bound to look up to him and to establish a relationship of benevolent interest as all of us do when meeting persons who represent one of our ideals. [p. 17]

Anticipating objection to this ploy, Eissler goes on to explain that the therapist does more than become the ego ideal. The therapist also holds himself up as a successful, law-abiding citizen. He seldom acts in the expected manner, for the delinquent has contempt for what he can comprehend and control. The therapist also does not use his knowledge to the delinquent's disadvantage. Holmes[60] feels that the delinquent "deserves a credible demonstration of reality." Aichhorn[4] stresses the necessity to shift therapeutic gears: "But while it is of prime importance that the educator identify with the wayward youth in the beginning phase of rehabilitation, it would be dangerous for him to persist in this attitude since it would mean becoming wayward himself."

Hoffer[59] describes his own approach in this way:

The therapist has therefore to add something to his technique in order to evoke in the imposter a positive response and an interest in the therapeutic work. Such an addition is alien to the classical psychoanalytic technique [Freud] which we use with the neuroses and allied states. The therapist must assume something at which the imposter has himself been aiming and which he then unconsciously recognizes in the therapist. Thus, the therapist becomes identified with the juvenile imposter's own ideal of himself. And this has to be achieved in such a way that the adolescent does not become aware of what is going on in his mind. The change in his attitude toward the therapist must come to him suddenly and as a surprise. It is "narcissistic relationship" in which the imposter "loves" the therapist as if he were part of his own self and not an object in the outer world from which he gains some advantage. The aim of the initial stage of treatment is, therefore, the establishment of a narcissistic transference. Temporarily, the adolescent wants to be like the therapist. [p. 152]

Fries[53] also suggests, "The relationship to the analyst is a narcissistic one rather than an object relationship. That is, he experiences the analyst as an individual cleverer than himself, who can outwit him and therefore accepts him as a leader."

In dealing with a highly resistant nine-year-old who was disruptive in class and then refused to go to school, and who also scorned any need for help except to get out of school, the therapist held himself out as "an expert in getting kids out of school." After a series of unbelieving comments, John dared the therapist to help him.

> T: I'll have to know more about you, like what you'd like to do if you didn't go to school.
> John: (immediately): I'd sit in my trailer and watch TV.
> T: What programs would you watch?

John explained in detail his TV appetite as well as his fantasy of being completely self-sufficient and self-indulgent. The therapist from time to time posed reality problems relative to getting food, handling waste products in the trailer, and so forth, which tended to stump John, but the therapist intervened with a plausible solution to these problems. Several sessions were spent with John unfolding his womb-like fantasy of existence until John told the therapist to shut up about the trailer because things weren't going so badly at school and home.

THE ROLE OF OMNIPOTENCE

When dealing with such immature narcissistic, basically helpless children, the therapist may sometimes make contact by presenting himself as an omnipotent, omniscient parental surrogate who can join and reflect the child's narcissistic defenses. Eissler[35] notes, "It has been my repeated experience that the delinquent patient will establish a workable emotional relationship with the analyst only after he has experienced the analyst as an omnipotent being." Szurek,[143] on the other hand, believes in telling the delinquent early in the beginning that he cannot prevent delinquent behavior, nor can he protect the delinquent.

STRENGTHENING THE SYMBIOTIC RELATIONSHIP, LIMITING ANXIETY AND USE OF JOINING TECHNIQUES

The establishment of the narcissistic transference sets up a symbiotic relationship which must be maintained for an appropriate period of time. This allows the child to mobilize and strengthen his defenses rather than have them damaged any further. Schmideberg[114] has counseled that one should never induce anxiety in the delinquent. Using Miller's concept of conflict, Marshall[80] has shown that joining and reflecting techniques tend to reduce anxiety. If Ruben[112] is correct, the delinquent constantly defends against the loss of objects and the establishment of an object transference. The process of joining, however, prevents the formation of these defense-resistances, because the therapist is the ego object and not an external object. In effect, there is either no object relationship or an inconsistent one (depending on the amount of regression). Over a period of time, the delinquent reluctantly and ever testingly builds up a sense of trust in the therapist. Conceptually, it is as though one were recreating the symbiotic stage. The mother had been very inconsistent and rejecting, and in his identification with her and also in his attempt to avoid being hurt again, the delinquent becomes ever more inconsistent and rejecting as he senses the transference growing. In this regard, Eissler[35] and Aichhorn[4] counsel us to mirror the child and do the unexpected (be inconsistent), to reject the child's improper behavior—*never rejecting his thoughts, feelings, and memories.* Holmes[60] takes issue with this notion, claiming that the adolescent is naturally surprised by the justice and realism of the therapist. Aichhorn,[3] however, is explicit: "A feeling of uncertainty must be induced in the patient at the first moment of meeting by the very manner of our reception. . . . From the beginning, we put ourselves in the spotlight, we aroused the boy's interest in our person and awakened his desire to try his strength with us." And again: "While the juvenile delinquent is still unprepared for whatever awaits him and finds himself in a quite uncertain state of mind, there follows the dramatic act of unmasking, but without that dreaded consequence which is the only one he could have imagined—punishment."

In the initial stages of treatment, especially when he is being coerced by parents or court to attend therapy sessions, a delinquent may be the most willing to accept a seemingly nontherapeutic situation.

A teen-age girl, who had functioned as the scapegoat of the family and had been diagnosed as sociopathic and untreatable, had been hospitalized because of her running away and her thoroughly defiant behavior. Released from the hospital with dire warnings about her need for treatment, as well as her untreatability, she appeared for her first interview under threat of rehospitalization. She stubbornly denied any need for treatment and indicated that her appearance for the interview was only to avoid hospitalization. She had no conception of the proper use of the session and said she might read and the therapist might do paperwork. He asked her whether she had any objections to just coming to the sessions on time and bringing the fee at the end of the month, but there would be no therapy. She laughed and insisted that he was crazy. He asked her if she had any objection to his being crazy, which brought more laughter. He told her that under his plan everyone would be happy: her parents, because she was coming to a psychotherapist; she, because she would not be incarcerated; and he, because he would collect his fee and could use the time to do his own work. She asked if she could smoke. He said that he did not allow his patients to smoke during therapy sessions, but since she was not in therapy, she could smoke. The upshot of this arrangement was that with virtually no exceptions, she was prompt in arriving for her sessions, arranged to bring the fee, spent her time talking about her life, and, during a whole year, functioned in an integrated and socially appropriate manner so that her parents felt she no longer needed psychotherapy.

In this situation, the therapist appeared to the patient to be as detached, manipulative, "crazy," and selfish as she. The "mirroring" by the therapist of the patient's character defenses induces the patient to unconsciously feel "If he is like me, he must like me." And so the narcissistic transference is established. Persons and Pepinsky[96] found that 67 percent of delinquents who improved in therapy became more like their therapists and that 80 percent of the nonimproved delinquents did not "converge" toward their therapists. Rosekrans[109] showed that normal children tended to imitate behavior of a model perceived to be similar to themselves more than when the model was different. Could there be a primate analog in Fossey's[45] report of gorillas calming down when their initial belligerent behavior was mirrored?

Another method of mirroring or joining the patient's defense-resistance is to ask the patient to tutor the therapist in the patient's character style. Fifteen-year-old Al, who had no compunctions about stealing, was discussing the boredom that beset him wherever he went. The therapist asked him to describe further the feelings of boredom. To Al, boredom was "doing nothing, feeling nothing, and thinking nothing." Al was asked if he would be willing to help the therapist even though he himself wanted no help, nor had the therapist given him any assistance. He vaguely nodded assent. He was told that the therapist would like Al to teach him how to do, feel, and think nothing. Al appeared incredulous but interested—as though this was the first adult who had not criticized him for his detachment but had actually shown a positive interest. Al inquired in a slow, begrudging, wary manner about the therapist's motivations. The therapist explained that he had a personal difficulty in that it usually took him three or four days to unwind from his work when he went on vacation. Moreover, he would find himself involved in all kinds of athletics, sports, touring, and other kinds of busy activity rather than comfortably relaxing. And to cap it all, he found himself worrying and fretting for two or three days prior to returning to work. And indeed, if he could take off only a week in the wintertime, surely he was in trouble for he wouldn't have time to relax and be able to enjoy himself. The more he talked, the more wide-eyed and incredulous Al appeared. At first, he could not believe that the therapist had any problems, and second, he could not believe that his help would be solicited. On the other hand, he was absolutely fascinated with the idea that anyone could be so active and interested in the world, and was quite willing to describe in historical detail how he developed the emotional counterpart to the three monkeys' "see no evil, hear no evil, speak no evil." As it turned out, Al had emotionally turned himself off to the misbehavior of his parents such as their sexual escapades, their drinking, and the father's dishonesty as a businessman.

In this situation, the therapist appeared to the patient not so much as a mirror image, but as someone who wanted to be like him characterologically. Aichhorn suggested this approach when he asked a delinquent to tutor him in the patient's vocation. Strean,[142] Spotnitz[138] and Marshall[81, 82, 83] provide other clinical examples. Hardman,[57] recognizing that delinquents do not need the "excess baggage" of an object transference, provides some effective initial approaches for the delinquent. Whiskin[159] describes how he "feels into" the initial contacts. Kaufman and Makkay[71] counsel, ". . . plunging immediately into critical material pushes the anxiety level up to a point where the patient either drops out of treatment or seeks relief in further delinquency." Josselyn[67] advises that in the first stage of therapy with predelinquents, the therapist should not touch the neurotic conflict. Fleischer[43] advocates therapist warmth as a primary feature, although he considers that "identification with the aggressor" may occur when the patient is truly helpless against the therapist or when the therapist can provide gratifications. He lists other features of the therapist and expands on the therapist's interaction[44] with "untreatable" delinquents. Katz[70] also believes that attempts to obtain closeness and warmth are required in order for the therapist to become the object of identification. Jenkins[62] advocates that the therapist, in meeting with a delinquent's hostility and rejection, should express warmth and acceptance.

Zavitzianos[164] anticipates little difficulty in applying classical psychoanalytic technique when describing the treatment of a young woman. One only wishes that "he said, she said" dialogue had been included.

Ochroch and associates[91] summarize a series of papers on special techniques to be utilized with delinquents. Practical issues such as confidentiality, differences in social class, countertransference, fear, and setting limits are discussed. Schwartz and Schwartz[120] present a case in which the therapist increasingly directed an adolescent's delinquent manipulations until a firm identification was established. Ekstein,[36] in describing the treatment of a delinquent, emphasizes the importance of acceptance of the patient's communications at the patient's level, which leads to an identification with the therapist. Anna Freud's[50] injunction to therapists to make themselves interesting to their young patients certainly is of special importance in approaching the delinquent.

THE SECOND STAGE: ESTABLISHING CONTROLS

Frank[46] indicates that early in treatment he introduces a series of prohibitions against destructiveness. The therapist can freely, at this time, give orders or set limits especially in regard to the patient's behavior in the office—the primary rule being that the patient talk. Other demands are that the patient come on time, leave on time, and pay on time. Chwast[23] has cautioned, "Permissiveness without appropriate limit setting can prove utterly inadequate." Rexford,[107] on the one hand, states, "In the initial phases of psychiatric treatment, which may last from one to two years, the therapist must be prepared to tolerate overt physical and verbal hostile outbursts which may be extreme and persistent and may recur later at times of rising anxiety." On the other hand, she declares, "The therapist must make it clear from the beginning that he does not approve of or side with the child's unacceptable behavior although he is not punitive or moralistic in his attitude."

One of the therapeutic effects of these demands is to allow the patient to utilize the therapist as an object of hostility. Since the delinquent's defenses against depression (repressed rage) are so tenuous and primitive, the therapist sets himself up as the target for the patient's rage. This is done not because the catharsis as such is necessarily curative but because it releases the rage underlying the depression. This in turn prevents self-attack and provides a model to the patient for accepting blame, criticism, insults, and other forms of hostility. That is, since ultimately the patient will have to handle aggression from himself and others, as early as possible the therapist communicates that he is able to accept all the emotional and verbal attacks the patient can mount. A further advantage of this ploy is to indicate to the patient that the therapist is stronger than the patient—that the therapist cannot be "killed off" by the patient's feelings and words.

In all of this, the patient must be carefully and consistently educated and trained to distinguish between words and actions. Delinquents, especially those with trauma occurring before or during the preverbal, preconceptual level, do not make this distinction. By no means should the therapist tolerate the use of physical aggression in the office. The therapist may point out to the patient that he is "out of control," and that if his behavior continues, he will be dismissed for the day. Sometimes it may be permissible to threaten the patient with being "locked up" because his behavior is so intolerable. If the patient persists in acting in a hostile manner, the chances are that there are countertransference operations at work of which the therapist is not aware, or that the therapist does not have the proper qualifications for treating the patient. Aichhorn[4] argues that the therapist must prove quickly by the use of surprise that he is in control of himself and the situation. Eissler[34] provides clinical support for the contention that a patient will consistently test the therapist's control and power until he is convinced that he cannot defeat the therapist. With children who have very limited ego control, the loss of control and the physical provocation of the therapist pose less of a problem and may still lead to therapeutic gains.

Tom, an eight-year-old who was given to emotional maelstroms and whose defiance and rebelliousness had been of grave concern to parents and school for some time, began to tease the therapist by throwing "Nerf" balls and pillows. Then, with mounting violence, books and toys were thrown. The ultimatum to stop was ignored, whereupon Tom was informed that he would be controlled by holding him. Tom kicked and struggled, crying that the therapist was hurting and killing him. Since the therapist had just been informed that Tom had recently developed fears of dying (a good prognostic sign), he told Tom that he was correct and that if he broke the rules one more time, the therapist would indeed hurt or kill him. Surprised, the boy duly promised to behave himself, but once freed, laughingly engaged in behavior calculated to induce holding once again. During several weekly sessions, the scene was repeated many times with much talk, especially while Tom was in the therapist's arms. The talk contained much fantasizing about a dying man's last meal, his last act, his will; about Tom torturing the therapist, what would happen to him when he died, and so forth. In each instance, the therapist maintained the role of the active, controlling agent. At some points, Tom could not be sure whether they were in the realm of reality or play, but this seemed to be exciting for him and was perhaps the effective aspect of this "game." However, he was able to "shift down" well at the end of the session. That is, perhaps five minutes before the end of the session, Tom might be shrieking his hatred and proclaiming how much he'd like to kill the therapist, but as time was called, he would collect himself, say good-bye, and indicate his willingness to return.

In cases where the child has evolved a concept of the mother as harmful or murderous, the child usually recreates with the therapist his perception of the traumatic events. For example, Jim, a seven-year-old "terror," had been completely defiant of the parents and passive-aggressive in the classroom, accompanied by some display of anxiety and bullying. Jim viewed the world as extremely hostile, damaging, and murderous. Jim's fears were expressed in pseudoomnipotence and omniscience and a steady resistance to direction. Actually, Jim's "no" was a characterological negative to any control which he interpreted as a murderous invasion. In essence, his "no" was his way of saying, "No, I don't want to be murdered." On the other hand, Jim could be very cruel to others. Highly resistant to the sessions for the first year, Jim eventually revealed by his play the dynamics of his disturbance. Slowly, a game evolved which led to an effective change in behavior. He had established the mother doll as the focus of his omnipotent torturing hostility. In particular, he enjoyed the therapist crying out in mock pain and helpless rage as Jim played the mother's role. When Jim seemed to look forward to sessions, the therapist reversed roles. Basing his actions on Jim's previous behavior, that is, the tyranny, the fury, the vindictiveness, and so forth, he became Jim's mirror and threatened punishment, using demeaning names Jim and his mother had used. (These were later confirmed by the mother.) Jim's facial expression of seriousness and yet pleasure, as well as his quiet insistence on repetition, indicated his involvement and the meaningfulness of the game to him. In essence, the game evolved to the point where he could "murder" the therapist at his leisure, while the therapist tried to "hurt and murder" him. However, he put the therapist at a disadvantage. The therapist was not allowed to see him but could hear him. He would make a noise and the therapist would variously throw a ball, strike out with a stick, or shoot in the direction of the noise. The harder the therapist struck and the closer he came, and the more frustrated and enraged he appeared, the more delighted Jim was.

Typically, delinquents are late to sessions or are irregular in attendance. When they express mock sorrow or offer excuses, the therapist can ask why they are telling him their story and indicate that he is glad they were late or absent, and that in the future he will look forward to more of their delinquent behavior. After their surprise, they will attack the therapist for his seeming uncaringness.

Inevitably, at some point, the therapist must insinuate himself as the patient's superego. This shift from the therapist being the ego ideal to being the superego creates some problems. The second stage overlaps a great deal with the first. In any case, unconscious liking for the therapist must precede the patient's willingness to accept the therapist as the superego.

The first place to start, as indicated previously, is in the session where the patient's task is to talk and the therapist's task is to get the patient to talk. The importance of a patient talking in therapy is discussed by Spotnitz[138] and Lay.[72, 73] Even talking into a tape recorder seems to have some therapeutic impact, as indicated by Stollak and Guerney.[141] However, they did note considerable transference and resistance within this relatively depersonalized context. Shore and Massimo,[129] in their successful work with delinquents, found that verbalization serves as a mechanism by which control over hostile behavior may be obtained. They make the analogy to the child who, in developing controls, will verbalize prohibitions in an attempt to stop himself, preliminary to internalization of controls.

Many children and adolescents talk a great deal but without meaning. The patient simply is superficially acquiescing. Such children appear to be the most resistant to treatment because of their skilled interpersonal radar. Inevitably, they refuse to talk, and concentrate on doing other things which usually turn out to be endless resistances which cannot be analyzed. Also, these resistances can be most intriguing to the therapist, for these children have a knack for fending off transferences in a charming fashion. In these cases, the parents usually have to be called in for joint conferences to talk for the child. The child then tries to convince the parents that he is highly cooperative and needs no treatment. And indeed, those children with a modicum of control can manage to mobilize themselves so that, over a period of time, their behavior becomes appropriate.

Depending on the relative integrity of the ego, the therapist may focus on the patient's unwillingness to talk. That is, with an intact ego, the transference-resistance analysis occurs. With weaker egos, ego supportive and maturational experiences must be provided along the way. For example, a fifteen-year-old borderline schizophrenic black, who was nearing his institutional discharge, could not deal with the rage he felt toward the therapist (whom he perceived as leaving him as his father had left him), and lapsed into silence. One day he walked in with a button that read "Bust a nigger —boost a black man." The therapist expressed considerable interest in the button, and Charles was able to explain that he wanted to maximize the "black man" in him and get rid of his "nigger." He contended in poetic, yet textbook, terms

that the "black man" was not only his idealized father but his own ego and superego and the "nigger" was his id and the despised father. The therapist considered himself to be too rigidly a superego-ego person (moral, hard working, controlled) and that he was interested in having more of the feelings of the "nigger" (the gambler, drinker, rapist, sadist). Charles seemed to be shocked and bewildered and told the therapist he would never be able to do that unless he was able to experience the terror and frustration of a black youth's experience in the black ghetto. The therapist was insistent that Charles share those experiences. He insisted as well that on weekends at home, Charles leave his "nigger" with the therapist so that he could both get to know him and control him. Eventually, upon his discharge, Charles "gave" the therapist his "nigger" and would occasionally ask his caseworker how the therapist was doing with his "nigger."

Bird[20] perceives acting out as part of the symbiotic relationship with the mother, particularly her id. In the early stages of therapy, the therapist attempts to replace the acting-out mother; then by steady interpretation of the narcissistic relationship, individuation occurs.

As Eissler[35] had indicated, virtually all delinquents request money from the therapist. Eissler counsels that the therapist should not yield to the delinquent, lest the delinquent feel he has controlled the therapist. Instead, Eissler suggests that the therapist give money to the delinquent at an unexpected moment.

Joining the delinquent in his mercenary and avaricious mood is another alternative. Dan asked his therapist for several dollars, offering several reasons for the need, none of which seemed to have merit. The therapist wanted to know what was in it for him. Somewhat taken aback, Dan answered vaguely that he would become his friend, that the therapist would feel gratified in helping him, and so forth. Basically, the therapist asked why he should have any interest in any of these goals when he was happy with the money Dan's parents were paying him. Dan accused the therapist of seeing him only because of the fee involved, told him he was greedy, and that he was using him and his parents—to all of which the therapist responded to in an affirmative, accepting manner, which was calculated to strengthen the narcissistic transference, yet demonstrated that he could not be controlled by the patient.

Several authors have described the beneficial effects of the delinquent voicing his hostility to the therapist. However, the expectation of these benefits must be tempered by Berkowitz's[11] well-argued caution about the limitations of catharsis. The patient must understand that *only* in the therapy session is it permissible to reveal his feelings openly and that he must not express them in other settings such as school, or at home and to peers.

As the positive transference develops, the therapist should have no compunctions about giving direction, advice, or structure so that the delinquent gains a clearer understanding of the sort of behavior which will be acceptable on the outside. Fries[53] explains that "The child stops his asocial behavior not out of insight derived from analytic procedure because that would take too long, but out of love towards the therapist to whom he has developed this extremely strong transference and whom he would not wish to disappoint." Bilmes[18, 19] contends also that the induction of shame and guilt to the delinquent is a necessary aspect of adequate functioning. Light scolding or disapproval of inappropriate social behavior has been found to be effective in controlling external behavior. This tends to work best in those instances where the parents, particularly the mother, did not provide appropriate sanctions, controls, and assistance when the child began to walk, run, and move away from her. In agreement with this point of view is Gottesfeld,[56] who gave a questionnaire to delinquents who sharply defined their need for more activity and direction on the part of their therapists. Schmideberg[116] finds that "progressive" parents frequently do not take responsibility of advising and planning, particularly with girls who prove to be "rootless" and promiscuous. She offers the following enlightening clinical anecdote: "I once lectured a patient, quite severely, when to my surprise she beamed at me, 'You like me, don't you?' 'What makes you think so?' 'You talk like my grandmother and I know she loved me.' "

In a recent article, Schmideberg[115] discusses the necessity of dealing with reality in work with delinquents, and contends that the use of suggestion in this context is not to be feared. Engel,[39] in a similar vein, advocates simple and "economic" solutions to delinquents' problems.

Frequently, the patient will threaten suicide if his demands are not met. This ploy can be handled by telling the patient that he is not allowed to kill himself until at least six months after treatment is terminated. This is usually met with howls about the uncaring, tyrannical nature of the therapist. If the patient persists in talking about killing himself, the therapist may inquire about the timing and the ways and means to be used. At this point, the therapist may offer himself as an "expert" in methods of suicide and indicate alternate and more efficient methods for committing suicide so that the patient feels he is having a greater impact on his "audience." Still another joining technique, which must be used judiciously, is for the therapist to offer to kill the patient himself. As in the ploy cited previously, the rationale for this approach is severalfold: (1) It validates the patient's omnipresent and underlying fear that the therapist, like everyone else, is out to kill him. Frequently the patient will say, "I always suspected that." (2) It further insinuates the therapist as the superego of the patient. (3) It revitalizes the original fear that the parents would kill him.

All these ploys should be put in the form of questions such as, "Suppose I were to kill you rather than your killing yourself?" Furthermore, the ploy must be employed in such a way that the patient is not sure whether such an event could or could not occur. That is, the patient begins to worry. In one startling instance, a tough fifteen-year-old broke into tears when the therapist asked him who would care if he killed himself or was murdered. He responded with, "That's the trouble —only you." Paradoxically, many patients announce that the therapist's seeming willingness to murder them means that the therapist really cares for them. As one patient put it, "If you would take the trouble to put me out of my misery, that means that you'd do anything for me." Frequently, the implied offer to murder the patient rouses considerable hostility and criticism. The therapist's stance of "What's wrong with my being a murderer?" usually causes the patient to attack, which is an externalization of intolerable self-hate and allows the patient to structure for himself the reasons for the therapist (and himself) to conduct themselves in a more civilized and socially appropriate manner.

Strean[142] also believes that rather than interpreting distortions about himself the therapist should temporarily absorb the accusations as part of his ego. "The youth is grateful to the adult for accepting these noxious elements and slowly questions how dangerous they really are." Lipton[76] summarizes the intent of therapy:

Psychotherapy is based on the principle of corrective emotional experience. The patient is exposed to the same kind of emotional conflicts in the therapeutic situation that were in life unsolvable. The therapist, however, reacts differently than did the parents. Psychotherapy gives the individual the opportunity to face again and again in increasing doses, formerly unbearable emotional situations and to deal with them in a different manner than in the past. The reexperiencing of the unsettled old conflict with a new ending is the secret of successful therapy. [p. 543]

It appears that Alexander's[5] old dictum about providing the patient with a "corrective emotional experience" may be applied to the treatment of delinquents.

The therapeutic approach espoused in this section has certain similarities to Marie Coleman Nelson's[89] paradigmatic therapy which focuses on recreating and living through with the patient the old conflicts with parents. Masterson's[86] treatment of the borderline adolescent is similar. He also cites Mahler's separation-individuation concept as central to his thinking. His approach, however, is more intrusive and catabolic of defenses in the initial stages. Moreover, he works in an institutional setting which is suited to handling the explosive rage and deep depressions of his adolescents.

In those cases where delinquency stems from guilt and the need for punishment, the therapist may temporarily take over the disturbed superego role. Friedlander[51] states, "If . . . the delinquent could be brought back to the dependence of the small child in an adult person, a process of re-education could perhaps undo the faulty character development."

At the point where the patient does become more dependent, there is usually a stiffening of defenses, yet an increase in affects. The therapist should never lose sight of the fact that the delinquent is not usually interested in establishing an object relationship and barely tolerates a narcissistic or symbiotic relationship. One form of resistance, which Redl[102] indicates, is that the behavior of the patient may become more normalized and "model" in the treatment situation, but unknown to the therapist, the patient engages in more flagrant antisocial behavior outside the treatment hour. The therapist, therefore, must have not only good communications with the family and school, but must be aware that the patient may lull him into complacency. In general, the patient's behavior should improve steadily, first in relationship to the community, then the school, then the family, and only then in the therapeutic sessions. The objective is for the patient to bring all his distress, conflict, fear, and pathology to the treatment hour and then function in a more integrated manner in his milieu. That is, the more stormy the treatment sessions, the less the likelihood of acting out in the community. Several authors[138, 142, 148] have indicated that it is not only normal but desirable to maintain the delinquent in a state of negative transference. The purpose is to maintain the projective defense and identification with the therapist so that the patient is less inclined to direct his hostility at himself.

THE SUPEREGO LACUNAE PROBLEM

Johnson and Szurek[64, 65] have advanced the superego lacunae theory which states that parents induce their children to act out unconscious parental wishes. When parents are available for treatment, the pathological need system can be analyzed, thus taking pressure off the child. When parents do not present themselves for treatment, other approaches must be taken to resolve the child's need to carry out the parents' wishes. The following examples illustrate one avenue.

As a fourteen-year-old boy, precocious in every way, reluctantly began to unfold the story of his lurid life, the therapist found himself more fascinated than usual. It developed that Sam was the center of attention in his dormitory because of his ability to spin "weird tales." In interviewing the seemingly highly moral mother, she was also found to be morbidly interested in Sam's asocial sexual life. Highly offended, disapproving, and seemingly disgusted with her son's perversities, she nonetheless conveyed a vicarious pleasure in reading detectives' reports, showing the therapist Sam's pornographic notes and pictures, and imagining what he would do next.

One day, when Sam was telling the therapist what a bore treatment was and otherwise expressing reluctance to continue, he was told that the therapist was enchanted with his escapades and wouldn't he please take some pains to do things that would be of interest and make the sessions less boring. Sam's response was an explosive negative reaction in which he conveyed that he was tired of doing things that pleased others and that, if anything, he would live a straight life to spite the therapist. He went on to reveal that he had found himself trying to outdo his father whom he hadn't seen for ten years and who, from all accounts, was a highly psychopathic, perverse character. In this situation, the therapist believed he had made overt the covert demand of the mother and that Sam, in turn, had made a more appropriate and conscious response to the recreated pathological situation.

In another situation, an eleven-year-old had as his model the highly publicized dare-devil, Evel Knievel, and would attempt to perform similar hazardous activities which seemed to him to be a vitalizing force in his parents' otherwise dull lives. In this situation, the therapist indicated that he looked forward to the sessions in an otherwise boring day and to the recounting of the boy's adventures. The boy's response was to assert that he had given up dangerous activities and instead to bring to therapy drawings of thrilling and exciting events that he imagined or had seen in movies.

Of course, there is a certain risk in identifying oneself as vicariously living through the patient. In the context of a positive transference, the child may comply, leading to dangerous situations. However, in the context of a negative or developing narcissistic transference, the patient either resists the therapist or reluctantly becomes more attracted to him. Correctly performed, this technique of making overt the covert message of the parents reduces the anxiety surrounding the double bind. When the therapist suspects that the child is providing unconscious gratification for the parents, family sessions, as described in chapter 7, are recommended because, within a short period of time, it is easy to point out to the family the pleasure and vitality that the child's behavior afford its members.

THE THIRD STAGE: "TRADITIONAL" PSYCHOTHERAPY

As the treatment progresses from narcissistic transference to object transference, from symbiosis to differentiation, and from ego weakness to greater superego and ego strength, the more standard methods of treating the patient become appropriate. However, the therapist must be ever ready to recognize regression and join the patient as he takes one step backward preparatory to taking two steps forward.

PSYCHOTHERAPY OF THE FEMALE OFFENDER

Although there are several good reports of psychotherapy with delinquent girls, the literature appears to be limited in differentiating and contrasting therapy with boys and girls. In discussing the "unfeminine" delinquent girl who engages in violence and assault, Felsenburg[40] proposes that these girls do not want to become women. In their treatment, dependence on the therapist is encouraged to replace the influence of the mother. At the same time, the girl is directed toward a more feminine role through interpretation of the past, insight, advice, and encouragement. St. John[113] describes the way to develop a therapeutic alliance with adolescent girls through activity and directness. Coolidge[29] gives an account of his treatment of a fifteen-year-old girl who identified herself

with her dead brother. Kaufman and Makkay[71] give an excellent exposition of the treatment of a fifteen-year-old delinquent girl whose core problem was depression. Jurjevich[68] recounts in detail his therapy with institutionalized girls.

THE PRIMARY TREATMENT PROBLEM: COUNTERTRANSFERENCE

The primary problem in individual treatment of the delinquent appears to be that of countertransference. Sullivan's notion of participant-observer, as well as Aichhorn's intuitive understanding and control of delinquents, is critical. Since the impulses and defenses of the delinquent are primitive and disturbing to the point of appearing like "neighbors" of the schizophrenic's, the impulses and defenses evoked in the therapist are clearly factors that need to be dealt with continually and effectively. Briefly, all that has been written about countertransference, especially by Searles,[124] Spotnitz,[138] and Wolstein,[162] should apply in the treatment of the delinquent. It is little wonder that schizophrenia and delinquency remain the two disorders which are peculiarly resistant to psychological approaches.

The problem is compounded by the fact that the therapist usually must establish working relationships with parents, the family, the school, and representatives of the law in a way that remains constructive to the patient. The multiple transferences and countertransferences in such complex situations may dismay or misdirect even the most well-meaning and devoted therapist.

In addition, as indicated by Friedlander,[51] the number of individual therapists who are able to develop the necessary skills is limited by economic considerations. It is unlikely that enough therapists could be prepared to treat the existing number of delinquents on an individual basis. However, it seems worthwhile to develop and maintain a cadre of therapists who are willing not only to treat delinquents, but who are willing to explore in depth the variables related to the early emotional experience of the delinquent. Projects such as those devised by Bettelheim[17] and Redl[101] would be exemplary in this regard.

TREATMENT OF PARENTS OF DELINQUENTS

If the parents can be involved in counseling or treatment, the therapy of the delinquent has a much better prognosis. Typically, however, the parents, particularly the fathers, are highly resistant to involvement. The parental resistance must be investigated very carefully and a treatment plan evolved. Frequently, the mothers are borderline characters, suffer from overt or covert depressions, or indicate that they are greatly in fear of losing objects. Like their children, they give much evidence of a poor resolution of the separation-individuation process. Therefore, in their treatment, these mothers must be provided a dependable, temporary object through the relationship with the therapist.

Considerable clinical judgment must be brought to bear in determining whether the mother should have the same or a different therapist from that of the child. When the mother's character structure is primitive and undifferentiated, she may rely heavily upon her child as a symbiotic object. When the child is similarly structured, it is well to see mother and child together or in family therapy so that the essential, albeit pathological, defenses can be maintained while other therapeutic activities occur. In slightly less pathological and symbiotic situations, the mother-child relationship may tolerate the same therapist, but meet with him in separate sessions. In cases where separation-individuation is almost complete in mother and child, separate therapists are indicated. The therapeutic approach to the mother is somewhat similar to that made to the child. That is, a narcissistic or symbiotic relationship is to be established through joining techniques. As the mother's ego gains in strength, more traditional modes of therapy may be used. When a husband is available for meetings, every effort is made to help him become an object suitable for the mother. This is usually done by helping him become a narcissistic object so that a symbiosis is created between husband and wife. This state of affairs usually produces more adequate control systems for the child, while freeing him of his emotional fetters and permitting real growth. Frequently, the character structures of the parents are so limited that, although the therapist works toward their becoming autonomous persons, he must be satisfied if they can achieve a cooperative symbiosis.

One of the more complete presentations of a theory and technique for treating character disorders in parents of delinquents is described by Reiner and Kaufman.[104] Keying the treatment to the psychosexual stage of the parents, the authors find four steps necessary in the process: (1) establishing a relationship; (2) achieving identification of the client with the therapist; (3) emotional separation of client and therapist; and (4) understanding and insight.

Rather than rely on a single modality for treat-

ment of the delinquent, be it individual, group, individual with parent counseling, family, and so forth, Marshall[80] has introduced the concept of "Sequence Therapy," which is a form of family therapy. This approach takes into consideration not only the resistances of the designated patient, but all of the resistances from all family members to his and the family's healthy functioning. The course of therapy for the family is dictated by interventions usually of a joining or supportive nature at the point of the most treatment-destructive or pathological defense system. The therapist must be ready at any point to provide treatment for any combination of family members.

Summary

In summary, the individual psychotherapeutic approach should be determined by a diagnostic and psychodynamic study of the child, his family, and his environment, especially by those of us who do not share Aichhorn's intuitive gifts. Although he eschewed knowledge of the child before the first contact, Aichhorn[4] nevertheless indicates at the close of one of his last papers, "The rehabilitation of the wayward will no longer be limited to the accidental success of gifted educators, but will be the predictable result of systematic scientific work." Armed with careful diagnostic and historical data and guided by theory and a personality suited for work with antisocial and delinquent children, the therapist stands a good chance of coping with the formidable therapeutic problems.

Probably the most crucial requirement of a given case is an evaluation of the fixation point or points in a child's development. In particular, the degree of narcissism, the degree of symbiosis, the level of object relationships, and the maturity of ego functioning are crucial in orienting oneself to the child. Since it is assumed that most delinquents function at a narcissistic level where separation-individuation is incomplete, techniques appropriate to the handling of defense-resistances must be employed. The development of a narcissistic transference appears to be the *sine qua non* of effective treatment. The process of forming this development, while sometimes seeming raucous and primitive, really must be delicately and lovingly approached, inquired into carefully and nurtured tenderly, just as one attends to a hurt, crying baby. Every intuitive flash and countertransference feeling must be filtered through the ego of the therapist in his effort to join the patient at his level of adaptation and defense-resistance. Free association and interpretation do not prove effective at this point. Mirroring and joining techniques, judiciously formulated by the therapist, appear to reach the delinquent. They allow for a respite against the usual attacks on the delinquent's defenses and permit the patient to regress and establish a relationship which does not produce the panic and pain he is so ill equipped to endure. The therapist and patient fuse in a relationship which threatens neither. The therapist must strive to remain ever conscious of the inclination to maintain this relationship and ever ready to return to it when the patient panics. However, when he sees evidence of the patient's respect, love, and dependence, the therapist can begin to make more formal therapeutic demands on the patient and to use traditional techniques more suitable for a neurotic level of organization. Sensitive treatment must be provided to the parents and family as well as to the child. Last, but not least, the therapist should maintain a constant awareness of the impact of macrovariables such as school, peers, and community and the resources therein.

Individual Treatment in Institutions

Psychotherapy as described in the previous section may be more effective when conducted in institutions. The advantages result largely from the complementary and positive relationships that the therapist maintains with staff and administration. This area has been well delineated in the classic work of Stanton and Schwartz,[139] among others. Important "simple" factors are the management of the patient around the issue of attendance at therapy sessions, and the ability of the institution to control the flight and acting out of the patient. This is described especially well by Masterson[86] and in the series of papers by Rinsley.[108] The therapeutic atmosphere created by the "other twenty-three-hour" staff in conjunction with the treatment plan of the therapist is another major advantage of conducting therapy in an institution.[82] Difficulties may arise from complex institutional relationships.

Anthony Davids[31] has criticized institutions and therapists who sanction a policy of conducting psychodynamic therapy in a vacuum, outside of the turbulent reality of the patient's life. He advocates a "unit system" which integrates the therapist with the life of the staff and patients. Wills[100] and others submit that in order to fully utilize the transference, the therapist's office should be off institutional grounds.

Jurjevich[68] provides a frank, detailed account of eclectic individual treatment of delinquent girls, but does not dwell on institutional-staff issues. His attempts to evaluate the results of his therapy with psychological tests are salutory.

Under the somewhat pretentious title, *A Cure of Delinquents*, Shields[127] sets forth a readable account of his therapeutic activities with his adolescents and staff. He finds several stages in the delinquent's progress: (1) benign behavior; (2) manifest symptoms; (3) playful physical contact; (4) aggressive irresponsible behavior; (5) marked depression or disorientation; and (6) working through and reorientation. Shields found that his experience paralleled Aichhorn's in that after a period of hostility, the children evidenced "a violent outburst of emotion, weeping, and loss of control."

Shaw,[126] whose psychoeducational model is McNeill's Summerhill, founded Red Hill School in 1934. Inspired by psychoanalysts and religious men who discovered ways of loving the unlovable, Shaw appears to deal with delinquents much as did Aichhorn. For example, with a thief, Shaw proposed to give the boy a shilling every time he stole and two shillings every time he stole without being found out. To another boy who was dishonest and who would not accept generosity, Shaw offered a watch just as the boy was planning to steal a watch.

Persons[95] found that forty-one institutionalized boys who were subjected to once-a-week psychotherapy and twice-a-week group therapy fared better in the community one year after discharge than did forty-one matched controls.

Tortorella[146] found that thirty-nine institutionalized girls who involved themselves in a milieu program and weekly psychotherapy scored significantly higher on a Wechsler Adult Intelligence Scale retest and more normally on a Minnesota Multiphasic Inventory retest than did thirty-two girls who failed to complete the program.

Perhaps the most elaborate, best described, and one of the more successful programs of individual treatment in an institution is reported by Shore and Massimo[128, 129, 130] and Shore and associates.[131, 132] The counselors took an active role in helping their charges with reality aspects of life, particularly in the vocational area. A ten-year follow up reveals continued improvement in the treatment cases and increasing deterioration in the matched controls.

Psychopharmacology

The reports of the effect of various medications such as perphenazine,[88] dextroamphetamine,[33, 77] and diphenylhydantoin[74] give no clear-cut evidence of beneficial results. It seems appropriate that the use of psychopharmacology should be directed toward known diagnostic target symptoms such as schizophrenic behavior, hyperkinesis, and depression, rather than to delinquent behavior per se. For example, imipramine (Tofranil) has been used to treat enuresis in delinquents.[158]

Family Therapy

Perhaps the most well-organized family therapy program for delinquents is provided by the Utah University group headed by Parsons and Alexander.[93] Claiming a behavioral base, relying heavily on systems theory, and using fairly rigorous experimental paradigms, this group is systematically studying important variables. Moreover, the results demand more than cursory inspection. For example, they found that in a no-treatment control, the recidivism rate was 50 percent, a client-centered family group rate was 47 percent, an eclectic psychodynamic family program rate was 73 percent, while the short-term family behavioral treatment yielded a recidivism rate of 26 percent. Techniques used are: (1) labeling—sharpening observational skills especially relative to sequence of events; (2) reciprocal contracting wherein family members agree to change their behavior; and (3) focus on the parents' marriage rather than on the delinquent. Alexander and associates[6] demonstrated that siblings of treated "delinquent families" had only a 20 percent court contact rate compared to 40 percent for no-treatment families, 59 percent for client-centered treatment, and 63 percent for psychodynamic treatment.

Although they assiduously avoid the concept of transference because they rely heavily on structuring skills, Alexander and associates[6] found "unanticipated and perplexing" results in that "relationship skills—primarily sensitivity" of the therapist accounted for 46 percent of outcome variance.

Much of the work in family therapy with delinquents appears in the literature *ad passim* when various aspects of family therapy are discussed. For example, Ackerman,[1] in illustrating the phenomenon of scapegoating, describes the treatment of a delinquent. Ferreira[41] and Coodley,[28] discussing the double bind of the delinquent in his family, believe that the delinquent is enmeshed in a "split bind." That is, the child receives a bipolar message from the mother and father. The child not only tends to leave the conflict field, but the parents tend to push him out.

Stierlin,[140] in a contrast study of schizophrenic, wayward, and running-away children, relates these behaviors to family pressures. The schizophrenic child is caught in the binding mode. The runaway is a product of the delegating mode, while the wayward child is spun out from his family life like a function of the expelling mode.

Family Dynamics and Female Sexual Delinquency, edited by Pollack and Friedman,[98] provides not only excellent psychodynamic and social studies of families of delinquent girls but offers several therapeutically oriented articles.

Behavior Therapy

An important trend in the treatment of youthful offenders is exemplified by the work conducted by behavior therapists in individual clinical research studies and in major programs. Recently an impressive number of dissertations based on learning theory have been devoted to delinquency. The behavioral focus is on individual treatment, group therapy, family therapy, and institutional programs.

Slack[133] and Schwitzgebel,[121, 122, 123] in their famous street corner encounters, lured delinquents into their offices and laboratories with monetary rewards and demonstrated that delinquents could be conditioned to keep their appointments, accept employment, talk to a tape recorder —all leading to a reduction in delinquent acts. Although the language of the studies is behavioral, and the setting is Boston, observers are reminded of Aichhorn's innovativeness, sympathy, and directness.

Wolf, Phillips, and Fixsen[161] and Phillips[97] utilize the "teaching family" in a program called Achievement Place. The teaching-parents, working with five to ten children in a family-style home, utilize a token economy to modify the behavior in the home and school.

Patterson, Reid, Jones, and Conger[94] base their straightforward manual on the management of "aggressive, out of control" children on the work of the Oregon Research Institute. The criteria for including children in their program would seem to limit the number of "modal delinquents." Throughout the behavioral literature, it is extremely difficult to evaluate the nature of the "delinquent" because of the paucity of clinical detail and history.

Stollak and Guerney,[141] in their use of tape recorders instead of therapists, noted transference and resistance to many aspects of an ostensibly dehumanized situation. Wetzel[158] employed a warm, motherly cook as a reinforcer in his treatment of a child prone to stealing. Welsh,[157] in treating a juvenile who set fires, forced the child to keep lighting matches until he was "satiated."

Ferster[42] perceives behavior therapy as an additional tool but not a replacement for other forms of treatment.

Group Therapy

The area of group psychotherapy for delinquents has become a sort of treatment jungle. There is a mass of clinical reports; there are programs with an admixture of individual, group, milieu, and/or family therapies; there are inpatient programs and outpatient programs; there are even a few well-detailed outcome studies. The most confusing aspect of this ambiguous mass is the lack of adequate definition of the "delinquent" samples treated.

One of the few exceptions to the preceding ambiguity is the work of Slavson,[134, 135, 136, 137] who provides not only a well-organized theory, but sparkling descriptions of the patients and painstaking descriptions and rationale of his therapeutic activities. The originator of Activity Group Therapy, Slavson had restricted its use to Primary Behavior Disorders and not applied it to children with "psychopathic" personalities because the method calls for a good deal of freedom and lack of overt controls. However, in *Reclaiming the Delinquent*, Slavson[134] demonstrated how the essential structure of Activity Group Therapy could be maintained with therapeutic effect. The chaotic and tumultuous acting out which emerged in the initial stages of treatment is reminiscent of Aichhorn's patients. The ultimate trust and acceptance of the boys achieved by Slavson's therapists is also reminiscent of principles set down by Aichhorn. In what is termed para-analytic group psychotherapy, Slavson[134] describes how he "inverts" the delinquents' preoccupation with the outside world to introspection, insight, control, and superego formation.

In a series of interlocking studies, Truax* focused on several aspects of group therapy with delinquents. For example, Truax and associates[150, 154] found that therapists with high empathy and nonpossessive warmth produced significant behavioral and self-concept changes in institutionalized girls. Alternate group sessions lead to a poorer outcome, while in yet another study by Truax and associates,[151] therapy pretraining and depth of self-exploration were irrelevant. Truax[148] also observed positive outcomes in groups who were in a state of negative transference. The programmatic nature of the work along with built-in outcome measures provide a model for future investigators. Rosenthal[110] and Black and Rosenthal[21] have provided practical guidelines and techniques for treating the resistances of male and female delinquents. Schulman,[117, 118, 119] in very substantial papers, has sought to evolve techniques suited to delinquents. Rachman[100] discusses his encounters with delinquents employing Erikson's "ego identity" as a touchstone.

Kasoff[69] and Adler and associates[2] advocate the use of dual therapists to facilitate therapy, while Allen[7] introduces the "silent observer" with good results. Gadpaille[54] notes the sequence of resistances to therapy directed first to the external world (alloplastic) and then to inner problems (autoplastic). Thomas[145] directs his charges in the use of logic. Hersko[58] shares his experience of three years working with institutionalized girls. Corsini[30] courageously describes two groups that failed in an institution where the modus operandi of the groups and the institution were not compatible.

Franklin and Nottage,[48] in a clinical report, conducted psychoanalytic group therapy with several disturbed delinquents five times a week with considerable success. In an institutional setting, Franklin[47] met with limited success. Taylor,[144] in a controlled study in New Zealand, observed most improvement in girls treated with psychoanalytic group therapy in a borstal as compared with a regular counseling group and a no-treatment group.

McCorkle and associates[78] describes the group program at Essexfields and Highfields, while Miller[87] describes a replication in the south of the Highfield experiment.

Yong[163] describes the use and advantages of group therapy in an institutional setting. Arnold and Stiles,[9] comparing the results of a nationwide survey of correctional institutions conducted in

* See references 148, 149, 150, 151, 152, 153, and 154.

1950, 1959, and 1966, note an increasing reliance on group modalities.

Residential and Milieu Therapy

Besides being a gifted individual therapist, Aichhorn revealed himself to be an administrator sensitive to the therapeutic potential of the milieu.

Redl and Wineman,[103] in the very first words of their preface to *Children Who Hate*, stated, "The original inspiration for the work we are reporting here comes, of course, from August Aichhorn." One cannot estimate the impact of Redl's nearly one hundred publications (some of which are collected in *When We Deal with Children*[101]) except to say that in his very personal, down-to-earth style he has greatly influenced all levels of staff—educator, therapist, administrator—wherever children are institutionalized.

Redl and Wineman[103] also acknowledge their indebtedness to the contributions of Bettelheim.* Working primarily with younger schizophrenic children, Bettelheim has had to cope with delinquent behavior. For example, his account of Harry[16] provides a rare understanding of the dynamics of the terror underlying the aggression and the slow assumption of controls.

Aichhorn's two-stage concept of individual therapy is applied by Maxwell Jones[66] in his milieu therapy for character disorders by assuming that the delinquent has respect only for one who can effectively manipulate his own environment. Since few therapists have the wherewithal to command the respect of the delinquent, Jones relies on the delinquents' peers to play this role. As the delinquent begins to identify with the more stable and less delinquent peer, controls are assimilated. Reiter,[105] in administering an institution in Denmark, seeks to "break down massive wicked [*sic*] defense mechanisms" and render the delinquent doubtful of his value system and self-sufficiency. In a helpless position, through the milieu program, particularly occupational and educational therapies, the delinquent forms a new image of himself.

Slavson[135] describes the evolution of the twenty-year transition of Hawthorne-Cedar Knolls School from the status of a training school into that of a high caliber treatment institution. A series of articles by Rosmarin,[111] Goldsmith,[55] and Amler and associates[8] describes this setting in greater detail.

* See references 12, 13, 14, 15, 16, and 17.

The British Borstal system is basically a work-training program for one-third of all those under twenty-one who have been sentenced to prison. Once hailed as the most progressive national movement in penology, the system, according to Warder and Wilson[156] is hardly distinguishable from the regular prison system. In 1967, according to Cockett,[24] who followed 770 boys for two years after release, there was a 40 percent success rate over seven treatment centers.

Marshall[80] has described the positive changes in a milieu therapy program and analyzed its dismantlement.

McCord and McCord[77] evaluated another famous treatment center for delinquents—Wiltwyck. Papanek[92] gives further details of the functional democracy and the principles of consequences, permissiveness, and responsibility.

Conceived as an extension of Redl's work, Trieschman and associates[147] delineate the major routines of the day and reveal their approach to such phenomena as temper tantrums, therapeutic relationships, and therapeutic use of games.

Polsky[99] describes in detail the social system of delinquent boys in residential treatment.

In a research manner rare to this area, Jesness[63] determined that parole violation rates were lower for boys who had lived in a twenty-bed unit as compared with boys who had lived in a fifty-bed unit.

Sociological Approach and Therapies

The Provo experiment, summarized by Empey and Erickson,[37] applied sociological theory to the treatment of delinquents. Conceptualizing delinquency as a group phenomenon, a social structure was provided which: (1) permitted the delinquents to examine the role of authority; (2) allowed for an examination of the utility of a conventional versus a delinquent life; (3) provided an opportunity to declare publicly that a change would be beneficial; and (4) provided a maximization of peer group control. Daily group work and discussions, reference group support, and community action to aid in finding jobs were the major thrusts of the program.

The Silverlake Experiment,[38] designed as a neighborhood alternative to institutionalization, permitted the delinquent boys to attend the local high school and conduct business in the community. Stress was placed on group decisions to help bring about attitudinal change.

Cohen and associates[27] and Cohen and Filipczak[26] describe the program at the Institute for Behavioral Research at the National Training School for Boys. Cohen[25] also tells of his research in behavior modification and "behavioral engineering" programs in an institution for delinquents, as well as a school curriculum for adolescents.

From a more macroscopic view of the problem of juvenile delinquency, many spokesmen have decried the inadequate definition of delinquency, the paucity and ineffectiveness of psychological and psychiatric treatment, as well as the deleterious effects of institutionalization. For example, the 1967 Task Force Report of the President's Commission on Law Enforcement and Administration of Justice[106] devotes but one page to treatment and is highly skeptical of psychotherapy and environmental therapy. Norman,[90] representing the National Council on Crime and Delinquency, advocates the development of local Youth Service Bureaus which would divert all possible cases from the juvenile court to community programs for "non-coercive intervention." Howlett[61] criticizes the concept of the Youth Service Bureau as being another zealous "child saving movement." Within the National Institute of Mental Health is the Center for Studies of Crime and Delinquency, which proclaims as one of its goals: "In the future, the Center plans to stress development of intervention models aimed at social systems (rather than at individuals) in order to assist these systems in becoming more socially effective." Shah[125] is one of the more articulate spokesmen for the merits of long-term social approaches to the problem of delinquency and the accountability of service delivery systems.

REFERENCES

1. ACKERMAN, N. W., *Treating the Troubled Family*, Basic Books, New York, 1958.

2. ADLER, J., BERMAN, J. R., and SLAVSON, S. R., "Residential Treatment of Delinquent Adolescents: V. Multiple Leadership in Group Treatment of Delinquent Adolescents," *International Journal of Group Psychotherapy, 10:* 213–226, 1960.

3. AICHHORN, A., *Delinquency and Child Guidance: Selected Papers*, edited by O. Fleischmann, P. Kramer, and H. Ross, International Universities Press, New York, 1964.

4. ———, *Wayward Youth*, Viking Press, New York, 1936.

5. ALEXANDER, F., *Psychoanalytic Therapy: Principles and Application*, Ronald Press, New York, 1946.

6. ALEXANDER, J. F., KLEIN, N., and PARSONS, B. V., *Impact of Family Systems Intervention on Recidivism and Sibling Delinquency: A Study of Primary Prevention*, Mimeograph Series, Salt Lake Community Mental Health, 1974.

7. ALLEN, J. E., "The Silent Observer: A New Approach to Group Therapy for Delinquents," *Crime and Delinquency, 16:*324–328, 1970.

8. AMLER, A. R., et al., "The Interprofessional Treatment of the Disturbed and Delinquent Adolescent," *Annals of the New York Academy of Science, 105:*348–420, 1963.

9. ARNOLD, W. R., and STILES, B., "A Summary of Increasing Use of "Group Methods" in Correctional Institutions," *International Journal of Group Psychotherapy, 22:*77–92, 1972.

10. BERGLER, E., "Psychopathic Personalities are Unconsciously Propelled by a Defense Against a Specific Type of Psychic Pasochism—Malignant Masochism," *Archives of Criminal Psychodynamics, 4:*416–434, 1961.

11. BERKOWITZ, L., "Experimental Investigations of Hostility Catharsis," *Journal of Consulting Clinical Psychology, 35:*1–7, 1970.

12. BETTELHEIM, B., *A Home for the Heart*, Bantam Books, New York, 1974.

13. ———, *The Children of the Dream*, Macmillan, New York, 1969.

14. ———, *The Empty Fortress*, The Free Press, New York, 1967.

15. ———, *The Informed Heart*, The Free Press, Glencoe, Ill., 1960.

16. ———, *Truants from Life*, The Free Press, New York, 1955.

17. ———, *Love Is Not Enough: The Treatment of Emotionally Disturbed Children*, The Free Press, Glencoe, Ill., 1950.

18. BILMES, M., "Shame and Delinquency," *Contemporary Psychoanalysis, 3(2):*113–133, 1967.

19. ———, "The Delinquent's Escape from Conscience," *American Journal of Psychotherapy, (19)4:*633–640, 1965.

20. BIRD, B., "A Specific Peculiarity of Acting Out," *Journal of the American Psychoanalytic Association, 5:*630–647, 1957.

21. BLACK, M., and ROSENTHAL, L., "Modifications in Therapeutic Techniques in the Group Treatment of Delinquent Boys," in Strean, H. S. (Ed.), *New Approaches in Child Guidance*, pp. 106–122, Scarecrow Press, Metuchen, N. J., 1970.

22. *Center for Studies of Crime and Delinquency*, National Institute for Mental Health, mimeographed, p. 7, n.d.

23. CHWAST, J., "The Significance of Control in the Treatment of the Antisocial Person," *Archives of Criminal Psychodynamics, 2:*816–825, 1957.

24. COCKETT, R., "Borstal Training: A Follow-up Study," *British Journal of Criminology, 7:*150–183, 1967.

25. COHEN, H. L., "Programming Alternatives to Punishment: The Design of Competence Through Consequences," in Bijou, S. W., and Ribes-Inesta, E. (Eds.), *Behavior Modification: Issues and Extensions*, pp. 64–84, Academic Press, New York, 1972.

26. ———, and FILIPCZAK, J. A., *A New Learning Environment*, Jossey-Bass, San Francisco, 1971.

27. COHEN, H. L., et al., *Case I: An Initial Study of Contingencies Applicable to Special Education*, I.B.R. Press, Silver Spring, Md., 1967.

28. COODLEY, A. E., "Current Aspects of Delinquency and Addiction," *Archives of General Psychiatry, 4:*632–640, 1961.

29. COOLIDGE, J. C., "Brother Identification in an Adolescent Girl," in Gardner, G. E. (Ed.), *Case Studies in Childhood Emotional Disabilities*, vol. 2, pp. 141–173, American Orthopsychiatric Association, New York, 1956.

30. CORSINI, R. J., "Two Therapeutic Groups that Failed," *Journal of Corrective Psychology, 1:*16–22, 1956.

31. Davids, A., "Therapeutic Approaches to Children in Residential Treatment: Changes from the mid-1950's to the mid-1970's," *American Psychologist, 30:*809–814, 1975.

32. Easson, W. M., "Projection as an Etiological Factor in Motiveless Delinquency," *Psychiatric Quarterly, 41(2):*228–232, 1967.

33. Eisenberg, L., et al., "A Psychopharmacologic Experiment in a Training School for Delinquent Boys: Methods, Problems, Findings," *American Journal of Orthopsychiatry, 33(3):*431–447, 1963.

34. Eissler, K. R., "Ego Psychological Complications of the Psychoanalytic Treatment of Delinquents," in Eissler, R. S., et al. (Eds.), *The Psychoanalytic Study of the Child,* vol. 5, pp. 97–121, International Universities Press, New York, 1950.

35. ——, "Some Problems of Delinquency," in Eissler, K. R. (Ed.), *Searchlights on Delinquency,* pp. 3–25, International Universities Press, New York, 1949.

36. Ekstein, R., and Friedman, S. W., "The Function of Acting Out, Play Action, and Play Acting in the Psychotherapeutic process," *Journal of the American Psychoanalytic Association, 5:*581–629, 1957.

37. Empey, L. T., and Erickson, M. L., *The Provo Experiment: Evaluating Community Control of Delinquency,* D. C. Heath & Co., Lexington, 1972.

38. Empey, L. T., and Lubeck, S. G., *The Silverlake Experiment: Testing Delinquency Theory and Community Intervention,* Aldine-Atherton Press, Chicago, 1971.

39. Engel, S. W., "Some Basic Principles of Offender Therapy," *Journal of Offender Therapy and Comparative Criminology, 19:*11–21, 1975.

40. Felsenburg, R., "Special Problems in Treating Female Offenders: Unfeminine Delinquent Girls," *International Journal of Offender Therapy, 11(1):*21–23, 1971.

41. Ferreira, A. J., "The Double Bind and Delinquent Behavior," *Archives of General Psychiatry, 3:*359–367, 1960.

42. Ferster, C. B., "An Experimental Analysis of Clinical Phenomena," *Psychological Record, 22:*161–167, 1972.

43. Fleischer, G., "Identification and Imitation in the Treatment of Juvenile Offenders," *Journal of Contemporary Psychotherapy, 7:*41–49, 1975.

44. ——, "Treatment of Unmotivated Adolescents and Juvenile Offenders," *Journal of Contemporary Psychotherapy, 5(1):*67–72, 1972.

45. Fossey, D., "More Years with Mountain Gorillas," *National Geographic, 140:*574–585, 1971.

46. Frank, J., "Treatment Approach to Acting-out Character Disorders," *Journal of Hillside Hospital, 8:*42–53, 1959.

47. Franklin, G. H., "Group Psychotherapy with Delinquent Boys in a Training School Setting," *International Journal of Group Psychotherapy, 9:*213–218, 1959.

48. ——, and Nottage, W., "Psychoanalytic Treatment of Severely Disturbed Juvenile Delinquents in a Therapy Group," *International Journal of Group Psychotherapy, 19:*165–175, 1969.

49. Freud, A., "Obituary: August Aichhorn," *International Journal of Psycho-Analysis, 32:*51–56, 1951.

50. ——, *The Psychoanalytic Treatment of Children,* Images Publishing Co., London, 1946.

51. Friedlander, K., "Latent Delinquency and Ego Development," in Eissler, K. R. (Ed.), *Searchlights on Delinquency,* pp. 205–215, International Universities Press, New York, 1949.

52. ——, *The Psychoanalytical Approach to Juvenile Delinquency,* International Universities Press, New York, 1947.

53. Fries, M. E., "Some Points in the Transformation of a Wayward Child to a Neurotic Child," in Eissler, K. R. (Ed.), *Searchlights on Delinquency,* pp. 216–224, International Universities Press, New York, 1949.

54. Gadpaille, W. J., "Observations on the Sequency of Resistances in Groups of Adolescent Delinquents," *International Journal of Group Psychotherapy, 9:*275–286, 1959.

55. Goldsmith, J. M., "Treatment Milieu: Interdisciplinary Approaches," *Annals of the New York Academy of Science, 105:*396–407, 1963.

56. Gottesfeld, H., "Professionals and Delinquents Evaluate Professional Methods with Delinquents," *Social Problems, 13(1):*45–59, 1965.

57. Hardman, G. L., "Utilizing Crises for Treatment," *International Journal of Offender Therapy and Comparative Criminology, 19:*42–52, 1975.

58. Hersko, M., "Group Psychotherapy with Delinquent Adolescent Girls," *American Journal of Orthopsychiatry, 32:*169–175, 1962.

59. Hoffer, W., "Deceiving the Deceiver," in Eissler, K. R. (Ed.), *Searchlights on Delinquency,* pp. 150–155, International Universities Press, New York, 1949.

60. Holmes, D. J., *The Adolescent in Psychotherapy,* Little, Brown & Co., Boston, 1964.

61. Howlett, F. W., "Is the YSB All It's Cracked up to Be?" *Crime and Delinquency, 19:*485–492, 1973.

62. Jenkins, R. L., "Motivation and Frustration in Delinquency," *American Journal of Orthopsychiatry, 27:*528–537, 1957.

63. Jesness, C. F., "Comparative Effectiveness of Two Institutional Programs for Delinquents," *Child Care Quarterly, 1:*119–130, 1971.

64. Johnson, A. M., "Sanctions for Super-ego Lacunae," in Eissler, K. R. (Ed.), *Searchlights on Delinquency,* pp. 225–245, International Universities Press, New York, 1949.

65. ——, and Szurek, S. A., "The Genesis of Antisocial Acting-out in Children and Adults," *Psychoanalytic Quarterly, 21:*323–343, 1952.

66. Jones, M., "The Treatment of Character Disorders," *British Journal of Criminology, 3:*276–282, 1963.

67. Josselyn, I. M., "A Type of Predelinquent Behavior," *American Journal of Orthopsychiatry, 28:*606–612, 1958.

68. Jurjevich, R. R., *No Water in My Cup: Experiences and a Controlled Study of Psychotherapy of Delinquent Girls,* Libra, New York, 1968.

69. Kassoff, A. L., "Advantages of Multiple Therapists in a Group of Severely Acting Out Adolescent Boys," *International Journal of Group Psychotherapy, 8:*70–75, 1958.

70. Katz, P., "Treatment of Juvenile Delinquency," *Corrective Psychiatry and Journal of Social Therapy, 18:*28–38, 1972.

71. Kaufman, I., and Makkay, E. S., "Treatment of the Adolescent Delinquent in Case Studies," in Gardiner, G. E. (Ed.), *Childhood Emotional Disabilities,* vol. 2, pp. 316–352, American Orthopsychiatric Association, New York, 1956.

72. Lay, T., "Language Facilitation Among Delinquent Boys: A Pilot Study," *Journal of Communication, 15(4):*216–225, 1965.

73. ——, "Stimulating Communication Among Nonverbal Boys," *Corrective Psychiatry and Journal of Social Therapy, 11(5):*261–268, 1965.

74. Lefkowitz, M. M., "Effects of Diphenylhydantoin on Disruptive Behavior: Study of Male Delinquents," *Archives of General Psychiatry, 20(6):*643–651, 1969.

75. Lippman, H. S., "Difficulties Encountered in the Psychiatric Treatment of Chronic Juvenile Delinquents," in Eissler, K. R. (Ed.), *Searchlights on Delinquency,* pp. 156–164, International Universities Press, New York, 1949.

76. Lipton, H. R., "The Psychopath," *Archives of Criminal Psychodynamics, 4:*542–549, 1961.

77. McCord, W., and McCord, J., *Psychopathy and Delinquency,* Grune & Stratton, New York, 1956.

78. McCorkle, F. W., et al., *The Highfields Story: An Experimental Treatment Project for Youthful Offenders,* Henry Holt, New York, 1958.

79. Maletzky, B. M., "D-Amphetamine and Delin-

quency: Hyperkinesis Persisting," *Diseases of the Nervous System*, 35:543–547, 1974.

80. MARSHALL, R. J., "Sequence Therapy: A Variant of Family Therapy, unpublished manuscript, 1976.

81. ――――, "Joining Techniques in the Treatment of Resistant Children and Adolescents: A Learning Theory Rationale," *American Journal of Psychotherapy*, 30(1): 73–84, 1976.

82. ――――, "Meeting the Resistances of Delinquents," *The Psychoanalytic Review*, 61:295–304, 1974.

83. ――――, "The Treatment of Resistances in Psychotherapy of Children and Adolescents," *Psychotherapy: Theory, Research and Practice*, 9:143–148, 1972.

84. ――――, "The Rise and Fall of a Milieu Therapy Program," *Residential and Community Child Care Administration*, forthcoming.

85. MASSIMO, J. L., and SHORE, M. F., "The Effectiveness of a Comprehensive, Vocationally Oriented Psychotherapeutic Program for Adolescent Delinquent Boys," *American Journal of Orthopsychiatry*, 33:634–642, 1963.

86. MASTERSON, J. F., *Treatment of the Borderline Adolescent: A Developmental Approach*, Wiley-Interscience, New York, 1972.

87. MILLER, L. C., "Southfields: Evaluation of a Short-term Inpatient Treatment Center for Delinquents," *Crime and Delinquency*, 16:305–316, 1970.

88. MOLLING, P. A., et al., "Committed Delinquent Boys: The Impact of Perphenazine and of Placebo," *Archives of General Psychiatry*, 7(7):70–76, 1962.

89. NELSON, M. C., *Roles and Paradigms in Psychotherapy*, Grune & Stratton, New York, 1968.

90. NORMAN, S., *The Youth Service Bureau, A Key to Delinquency Prevention*, National Council on Crime and Delinquency, Paramus, N. J., 1972.

91. OCHROCH, R., et al., "Special Techniques in Treating the Young Offender: The Tough Boy and the Headshrinker," *International Journal of Offender Therapy*, 15(2):93–105, 1971.

92. PAPANEK, E., "Re-education and Treatment of Juvenile Delinquents," *American Journal of Psychotherapy*, 12:269–296, 1958.

93. PARSONS, B. V., and ALEXANDER, J. F., "Short-term Family Intervention: A Therapy Outcome Study," *Journal of Consulting and Clinical Psychology*, 41:195–201, 1973.

94. PATTERSON, G. R., et al., *Families with Aggressive Children: A Social Learning Approach to Family Intervention*, vol. 1, Castalia Publishing Co., Eugene, Ore., 1975.

95. PERSONS, R. W., "Relationship Between Psychotherapy with Institutionalized Boys and Subsequent Community Adjustment," *Journal of Consulting Psychology*, 31:137–141, 1967.

96. ――――, and PEPINSKY, H. B., "Convergence in Psychotherapy with Delinquent Boys," *Journal of Counseling Psychology*, 13(3):329–334, 1966.

97. PHILLIPS, E. L., "Achievement Place: Token Reinforcement Procedures in a Home-style Rehabilitation Setting for Pre-delinquent Boys," *Journal of Applied Behavior Analysis*, 1:213–223, 1968.

98. POLLAK, O., and FRIEDMAN, A. S. (Eds.), *Family Dynamics and Female Sexual Delinquency*, Science and Behavior Books, Palo Alto, Calif., 1969.

99. POLSKY, H. W., *Cottage Six, The Social System of Delinquent Boys in Residential Treatment*, Russell Sage Foundation, New York, 1962.

100. RACHMAN, A. W., *Identity Group Psychotherapy with Adolescents*, Charles C Thomas, Springfield, Ill., 1975.

101. REDL, R., *When We Deal with Children*, The Free Press, New York, 1966.

102. ――――, "The Psychology of Gang Formation and the Treatment of Juvenile Delinquents," in Eissler, R. S., et al. (Eds.), *The Psychoanalytic Study of the Child*, vol. 1, pp. 367–377, International Universities Press, New York, 1945.

103. ――――, and WINEMAN, D., *The Aggressive Child*, The Free Press, Glencoe, Ill., 1957.

104. REINER, B. S., and KAUFMAN, I., *Character Disorders in Parents of Delinquents*, Family Service Association of America, New York, 1959.

105. REITER, P. J., "Treatment of Psychopathic Delinquents in Denmark," *Journal of Social Therapy*, 4:16–25, 1958.

106. *Report of the Task Force on Juvenile Delinquency and Youth Crime*, President's Commission on Law Enforcement and Administration of Justice, U. S. Government Printing Office, Washington, D. C., 1967.

107. REXFORD, E. U., "Antisocial Young Children and Their Families," in Haworth, M. R. (Ed.), *Child Psychotherapy*, pp. 58–63, Basic Books, New York, 1964.

108. RINSLEY, D. B., "Residential Treatment of Adolescents," in Arieti, S., (Ed.), *American Handbook of Psychiatry*, vol. 2, revised ed., pp. 353–366, Basic Books, New York, 1974.

109. ROSEKRANS, M. A., "Imitation in Children as a Function of Perceived Similarity to a Social Model and Vicarious Reinforcement," *Journal of Personality and Social Psychology*, 7:307–315, 1967.

110. ROSENTHAL, L., "Some Dynamics of Resistance and Therapeutic Management in Adolescent Group Therapy," *Psychoanalytic Review*, 28:353–366, 1971.

111. ROSMARIN, S., "Individual Psychotherapy in Residential Treatment at Hawthorne Cedar Knolls Schools," *Annals of the New York Academy of Science*, 105:408–416, 1963.

112. RUBEN, M., "Delinquency: A Defense Against Loss of Objects and Reality," in Eissler, R. S., et al. (Eds.), *The Psychoanalytic Study of the Child*, vol. 12, pp. 335–355, International Universities Press, New York, 1957.

113. ST. JOHN, R., "Developing a Therapeutic Working Alliance with the Adolescent Girl," *Journal of the American Academy of Child Psychiatry*, 7:68–78, 1968.

114. SCHMIDEBERG, M., "The Analytic Treatment of Major Criminals: Therapeutic Results and Technical Problems," in Eissler, K. R. (Ed.), *Searchlights on Delinquency*, pp. 174–189, International Universities Press, New York, 1949.

115. ――――, "Some Basic Principles of Offender Therapy, II," *International Journal of Therapy and Comprehensive Criminology*, 19:22–32, 1975.

116. ――――, "Special Problems in Treating Female Offenders: Promiscuous and Rootless Girls," *International Journal of Offender Therapy*, 15(1):28–33, 1971.

117. SCHULMAN, I., "Modifications in Group Psychotherapy with Antisocial Adolescents," *International Journal of Group Psychotherapy*, 7:310–317, 1957.

118. ――――, "Delinquents," in Slavson, S. R. (Ed.), *The Fields of Group Psychotherapy*, pp. 196–214, International Universities Press, New York, 1956.

119. ――――, "The Dynamics of Certain Reactions of Delinquents to Group Psychotherapy," *International Journal of Group Psychotherapy*, 2:334–343, 1952.

120. SCHWARTZ, R., and SCHWARTZ, L. J., "Psychotherapy with Patients with Acting-out Disorders," in Hammer, M. (Ed.), *The Theory and Practice of Psychotherapy with Specific Disorders*, pp. 247–272, Charles C Thomas, Springfield, Ill., 1972.

121. SCHWITZGEBEL, R., "Learning Theory Approaches to the Treatment of Criminal Behavior," *Seminars in Psychiatry*, 3:328–344, 1971.

122. ――――, "Short-term Operative Conditioning of Adolescent Offenders in Socially Relevant Variables," *Journal of Abnormal Psychology*, 72:134–142, 1967.

123. ――――, *Street-corner Research: An Experimental Approach to the Juvenile Delinquent*, Harvard University Press, Cambridge, 1964.

124. SEARLES, H. F., "Oedipal Love in the Countertransference," in Searles, H. F., *Collected Papers in Schiz-*

ophrenia and Related Subjects, pp. 284–303, International Universities Press, New York, 1965.

125. Shah, S. A., "Some Interactions of Law and Mental Health in the Handling of Social Deviance," *Catholic University Law Review,* 13:674–719, 1974.

126. Shaw, O. L., *Youth in Crisis: A Radical Approach to Delinquency,* Hart Publishing Co., New York, 1966.

127. Shields, R. W., *A Cure of Delinquents, The Treatment of Maladjustment,* International Universities Press, New York, 1971.

128. Shore, M. F., and Massimo, J. L., "After Ten Years: A Follow-up Study of Comprehensive Vocationally Oriented Psychotherapy," *American Journal of Orthopsychiatry,* 43:128–132, 1973.

129. ———, "Verbalization, Stimulus Relevance and Personality Change," *Journal of Consulting Psychology,* 31:423–424, 1967.

130. ———, "Comprehensive Vocationally Oriented Psychotherapy for Adolescent Delinquent Boys: A Follow-up Study," *American Journal of Orthopsychiatry,* 36:609–615, 1966.

131. Shore, M. F., et al., "Changes in the Perception of Interpersonal Relationships in Successfully Treated Adolescent Delinquent Boys," *Journal of Consulting Psychology,* 29:213–217, 1965.

132. Shore, M. F., et al., "A Factor Analytic Study of Psychotherapeutic Change in Delinquent Boys," *Journal of Clinical Psychology,* 21:208–212, 1965.

133. Slack, C. W., "Experimenter-Subject Psychotherapy: A New Method of Introducing Intensive Office Treatment of Unreachable Cases," *Mental Hygiene,* 44:238–256, 1960.

134. Slavson, S. R., *Reclaiming the Delinquent Through Para-Analytic Group Psychotherapy and the Inversion Technique,* The Free Press, New York, 1965.

135. ———, *Re-educating the Delinquent Through Group and Community Participation,* Harper, New York, 1954.

136. ———, *Child Psychotherapy,* Columbia University Press, New York, 1952.

137. ———, "Contra-indications of Group Therapy for Patients with Psychopathic Personalities," in Slavson, S. R., *The Practice of Group Therapy,* pp. 95–106, International Universities Press, New York, 1947.

138. Spotnitz, H., *Modern Psychoanalysis of the Schizophrenic Patient,* Grune & Stratton, New York, 1969.

139. Stanton, A., and Schwartz, M. S., *The Mental Hospital,* Basic Books, New York, 1954.

140. Stierlin, H., *Separating Parents and Adolescents: A Perspective on Running Away, Schizophrenia and Waywardness,* Quadrangle/New York Times Book, New York, 1974.

141. Stollak, G. E., and Guerney, B., "Exploration of Personal Problems by Juvenile Delinquents under Conditions of Minimal Reinforcement," *Journal of Clinical Psychology,* 20(2):279–283, 1964.

142. Strean, H. S., "Difficulties Met in the Treatment of Adolescents," *New Approaches in Child Guidance,* Scarecrow Press, Metuchen, N. J., 1970.

143. Szurek, S. A., "Principles of Psychotherapy," in Szurek, S. A., and Berlin, I. N. (Eds.), *Training in Therapeutic Work with Children,* pp. 91–116, Science and Behavior Books, Palo Alto, Calif., 1967.

144. Taylor, A. J. W., "An Evaluation of Group Psychotherapy in a Girls Borstal," *International Journal of Group Psychotherapy,* 17:168–177, 1967.

145. Thomas, A., "Deductive Group Psychotherapy with Adolescent Delinquents," *Journal of Social Therapy,* 3:89–96, 1957.

146. Tortorella, W. M., "Personality and Intellectual

Changes in Delinquent Girls Following Long-term Institutional Placement," *Journal of Community Psychology,* 1:288–291, 1973.

147. Trieschman, A. E., Wittaker, J. K., and Brendtro, C. K., *The Other 23 Hours,* Aldine-Atherton, Chicago, 1969.

148. Truax, C. B., "Perceived Therapeutic Conditions and Client Outcome," *Comparative Group Studies,* 2:301–310, 1971.

149. ———, "Degree of Negative Transference Occurring in Group Psychotherapy and Client Outcome in Juvenile Delinquents," *Journal of Clinical Psychology,* 27:132–136, 1971.

150. ———, and Wittmer, I., "The Degree of the Therapist's Focus in Defense Mechanisms and the Effect on the Therapeutic Outcome with Institutionalized Juvenile Delinquents," *Journal of Community Psychology,* 1:201–203, 1973.

151. Truax, C. B., et al., "Antecedents to Outcome in Group Counseling with Institutionalized Juvenile Delinquents: Effects of Therapeutic Conditions, Patient Self-exploration, Alternate Sessions and Vicarious Therapy Pretraining," *Journal of Abnormal Psychology,* 76:235–242, 1970.

152. Truax, C. B., et al., "Self-Ideal Concept Congruence and Improvement in Group Psychotherapy," *Journal of Consulting and Clinical Psychology,* 32:47–53, 1968.

153. Truax, C. B., et al., "Changes in Self-concepts During Group Psychotherapy as a Function of Alternate Sessions and Vicarious Therapy Pretraining in Institutionalized Mental Patients and Juvenile Delinquents," *Journal of Consulting Psychology,* 33:309–314, 1966.

154. Truax, C. B., et al., "Effects of Group Psychotherapy with High Accurate Empathy and Non-possessive Warmth Upon Female Institutionalized Delinquents," *Journal of Abnormal Psychology,* 71(4):267–274, 1966.

155. Waitzel, I. D., Gallagher, E. J., and Marshall, R. J., "Control of Enuresis in Disturbed Adolescent Boys," *Journal of National Medical Association,* 61:474–475, 1969.

156. Warder, J., and Wilson, R., "The British Borstal Training System," *Journal of Criminal Law and Criminology,* 44:118–127, 1973.

157. Welsh, R. S., "The Use of Stimulus Satiation in the Elimination of Juvenile Fire Setting Behavior," in Graziano, A. M. (Ed.), *Behavior Therapy with Children,* pp. 283–289, Aldine-Atherton, Chicago, 1971.

158. Wetzel, R., "Use of Behavioral Techniques in a Case of Compulsive Stealing," *Journal of Consulting Psychology,* 30:367–374, 1966.

159. Whiskin, F. E., "Treating Depressed Offenders in the Court Clinic," *International Journal of Offender Therapy and Comparative Criminology,* 18:136–152, 1974.

160. Wills, D. W., *The Hawkspur Experiment,* Allen and Unwin, London, 1941.

161. Wolf, M. M., Phillips, E. L., and Fixsen, D. L., "The Teaching Family: A New Model for the Treatment of Deviant Child Behavior in the Community," in Bijou, S. W., and Ribes-Iresta, E. (Eds.), *Behavior Modification: Issues and Extensions,* pp. 51–62, Academic Press, New York, 1972.

162. Wolstein, B., *Countertransference,* Grune & Stratton, New York, 1959.

163. Yong, J. N., "Advantages of Group Therapy in Relation to Individual Therapy for Juvenile Delinquents," *Corrective Psychiatry and Journal of Social Therapy,* 17:34–39, 1971.

164. Zavitzianos, G., "Problems of Technique in the Analysis of a Juvenile Delinquent," *International Journal of Psycho-Analysis,* 48(3):439–447, 1967.

34 / Childhood Psychosis

Mohammad Shafii

The complexity of childhood psychosis is reflected by the massive proliferation of literature on this topic. Goldfarb and Dorsen[51] published the first bibliography on childhood schizophrenia and related disorders covering the pertinent literature up to 1955. Tilton, DeMyer, and Lowe[123] annotated works on childhood schizophrenia from 1955 to 1964. For the years between 1964 and 1969, Bryson and Hingtgen[18] summarized more than 420 papers and books on early childhood psychosis. From 1969 to the end of 1975, it was possible to find more than 800 papers published on this topic. Approximately 200 of these are related to the issue of treatment.

The field is a new one—about thirty years old. Major steps into this unknown territory have been taken in the last twenty years by Kanner, Mahler, Eisenberg, Ekstein, Bettelheim, Goldfarb, Geleerd, DeMyer, Bender, Rimland, Lovaas, Ritvo, Ornitz, Rutter, and Wing, among others. Withal, it is evident that this is just a beginning.

Special Considerations

In treating psychotic children, special consideration should be given to four factors: the severity of the psychological impairment, the creation of a therapeutic relationship, the formulation of realistic expectations, and the maintenance of therapeutic agility.

SEVERITY OF PSYCHOLOGICAL IMPAIRMENT

The impairment of affective and cognitive ego functions in psychotic children is usually severe. Among the more common deficits are: the inability to control aggressive outbursts, the inability to separate reality from fantasy, regressive and infantile behavior, autistic withdrawal, repetitive behavior, mutism, echolalic language, and functional retardation.

Childhood psychosis, particularly childhood autism, is, without a doubt, one of the most severe forms of psychopathology known. The intensity and chronicity of the impairments deplete the family's emotional and economic resources, burden the community, and strain the therapist.

For psychotic children, human contacts and interpersonal relationships are fragmented, disorganized, and, at best, tenuous .In therapeutic work with these children, nothing can be taken for granted. Establishing even a "fragile alliance" requires consistency on the part of the therapist and a predictable therapeutic setting. In developing a therapeutic relationship, minute changes on the part of the therapist can produce a catastrophic reaction in the patient. When the therapist is not sensitive to the effects of such changes, he may be confused and bewildered by the patient's reaction. This is illustrated by the following case vignette.

CASE OF BOBBY

Bobby was a seven-year-old psychotic boy. At the beginning of a session, after three weeks of daily therapy, he suddenly became severely agitated. He moved frantically around the room without any obvious reason. Occasionally he would bring his face close to the therapist's and then would run to the opposite corner of the room flapping his arms and hands. A few minutes later, after some reassurance, he would return to the therapist and then repeat the behavior. The therapist was puzzled for the entire day. In talking with the family, he could not find evidence of changes in the child's or the family's routines. The next morning while shaving, the therapist realized that he had used a different aftershave lotion the day before. He took this lotion to his office and when Bobby was there, put it on his face, and reassured Bobby that he was the same person. Bobby brought his face close to the therapist's as though smelling him. Then Bobby became slightly agitated. The therapist repeated putting lotion on his face and also on Bobby's face. After one or two times, Bobby became calm and was able to continue the interrupted therapeutic work.

In brief, to treat psychotic children demands that one be acutely aware of the most subtle changes and nuances in the therapeutic situation. There is a constant call for ingenuity, patience, and perseverance.

All therapeutic work with children is a creative process. Therapy with psychotic children, however, requires something of the creativity of an artist, along with the intellectual outlook of an archeologist who seeks to decipher the cuneiform messages.

On many occasions, the therapist finds that small gains, achieved with much travail, can suddenly evaporate—as though one step forward means two steps back. One needs to deal constantly with one's own frustrations, disappointments, and disillusionments. Although therapeutic gains may seem elusive, on the whole, they tend to be cumulative.

If he works with psychotic children, every child therapist can experience the agony and joy of observing and sharing in human development in slow motion. And in this process, the therapist's own growth and therapeutic maturity will be significantly enhanced.

REALISTIC EXPECTATIONS

The therapist needs to be satisfied with limited gains. Momentary eye contact, a genuine smile, the touch of a finger, a bubbling noise, an imitative sound, a response to his name, a "hello" or a "good-bye" can represent therapeutic milestones. The final goal is not freedom from all sysmptoms; the therapist seeks rather to help the psychotic child become less frightened, less withdrawn, and better able to relate with others through language. Hopefully, the child can also be helped to live at home, attend a public school, and learn a skill. One hopes that ultimately the child will be able to become relatively independent in his adult life.

THERAPEUTIC AGILITY

In working with the psychotic child, it is particularly necessary for the therapist to be well acquainted with his own theoretical orientation—whether it be psychoanalytic, psychodynamic, behavior modification, milieu therapy, supportive therapy, or psychopharmacotherapy—and to be familiar as well with the use of other treatment modalities. Mastery of a therapeutic modality does not mean dogmatism, rigidity, or inflexibility. The therapist working with the psychotic child, more than any other therapist, needs to remain curious, adventurous, and flexible. Together, these comprise therapeutic agility.

The fundamental requirements for therapeutic agility are acute sensitivty to the psychotic child's behavior, awareness of the range of therapeutic modalities, and the ability to use them when necessary. For example, a therapist with a psychoanalytic orientation can become more effective if he is able to make use of behavior modification techniques as well. A behavior therapist needs to be sensitive to the child's feelings and use empathic and dynamic communications in an integrative and effective approach.

The greater the number and variety of therapeutic techniques at his command, the more effective the therapist will be in helping the patient achieve his developmental potential. This does not mean compromising one's standards of excellence or one's commitment to a particular therapeutic orientation. It means instead recognizing the necessity for a synthetic and integrative approach to the treatment of psychotic children and their families. Therefore, this chapter will discuss the major contributions made by various schools of thought with an emphasis on the modifications necessary for the treatment of the psychotic child. The literature describes many diverse approaches to such management. Rigid adherence to any one specific theoretical orientation will limit the therapist's choice of possibilities.

HISTORICAL PERSPECTIVE

Although the major developments in the treatment of childhood psychosis have taken place in the last thirty years, scattered case histories and discussions of treatment can be found in the literature as far back as 1,000 years ago. This author[117] reported the case of a young prince who was treated by Avicenna, the Persian philosopher and physician who lived between A.D. 980 and 1037. By his acute clinical sensitivity, Avicenna was able to create a therapeutic relationship with this psychotic patient by use of metaphor. This manner of communication helped the prince trust Avicenna—the fragile alliance was established. Avicenna then had the attending physicians and relatives follow the same pattern of communication and thus developed a therapeutic milieu.

Vaillant[124] believes that John Haslam was the first psychiatrist to describe a case which resembles childhood autism in his 1809 textbook, *Observations on Madness and Melancholy*. The patient he discusses was a five-year-old boy admitted to Bethlehem Asylum, England, in 1799 (the same year that the Wild Boy of Aveyron was discovered in the woods in France. Itard[66] carried on a monumental effort to treat this boy, whose diagnosis remains in question to this date).

Szurek and Berlin[121] in their book *Clinical Studies in Childhood Psychosis* republished Lightner Witmer's pioneer work[127] with a psychotic five-year-old youngster named Don, who would spend hours looking at and scratching a card, oblivious of others. He resisted any human interaction and would have a major temper tantrum when his quiescence was interrupted. He would scratch and hurt himself when he was angry. He was fond of music. He never used a word spontaneously, and he had only eight words in his vocabulary. He was far behind his chronological age—functioning more like a one-year-old child. Witmer was gifted with patience and psychotherapeutic optimism. He worked intensively with Don, utilizing a psycho-educational model but explicitly "without any preferred theory . . . 'The first task of teacher and parent is to gain and hold the child's attention by giving him something he *can* do, and after that, something he can't do.'" After one and one-half years of intensive work, Don had improved dramatically. He was able to talk, read, dress himself, and function in a small community school. At the same time he continued to have an intense preoccupation with moving objects, such as cars and sailboats, and would often repeat a question or a sentence. Witmer[127] conceptualized Donnie's problem as follows:

Donnie was at the start dominated by fear, which plays still an important role in his behavior. His concentration on the card was in the nature of a defensive reaction. He disliked to get out of bed because he was afraid to get out of bed. He disliked to walk and talk because he was afraid—perhaps of failure. [p. 61]

Witmer discussed two types of "feeble-mindedness," the one caused by congenital defects and the other by arrested development. He felt that this arrested development produced psychosis in childhood and insanity in adulthood, but could be treated successfuly if treatment was begun very early.

Therapeutic Modalities

The theoretical orientation of the therapist and the setting in which he works influence the approach toward the psychotic child and his family.

PSYCHOANALYTIC AND DYNAMIC PSYCHOTHERAPIES

The psychoanalytic and psychodynamic approaches are generally nondirective. Therapeutic emphasis is placed on exploration of developmental conflicts and earlier traumatic experiences. This is accomplished by means of an intensive, long-term one-to-one relationship. The theory asserts that the child's symptoms are due to develop-

mental arrest or regression to a more primitive phase of object relationship and psychosexual development. The basic goal of the work, then, is to help him master the disorganization of his inner space and to further the integration of his ego functions. To do this, it is necessary to unravel the intrapsychic conflicts and environmental stresses which have contributed to his extreme reaction.

Bettelheim;[*] Mahler;[90, 91, 92, 93] Szurek and Berlin;[121, 122] Ekstein and associates;[†] Weiland and Rudnik;[125] Maslow;[94] King;[71] Kemph, Harrison, and Finch;[70] Wolf and Ruttenberg;[129] Holter and Ruttenberg[64] are among the more significant contributors to the formulation of psychoanalytic and psychodynamic therapies for psychotic children based on ego psychological conceptualization and theories of object relationship. Such psychotherapy with a psychotic child requires considerable patience and sensitivity.

1. The therapist must examine carefully countertransference feelings, rescue fantasies, and the motivation for accepting such patients into therapy.
2. The therapist must assess the patient's ego functions, strengths, and weaknesses skillfully and begin treatment at the patient's level.
3. The therapist must decipher the patient's verbal and nonverbal primary process communication with total openness and receptivity. He should not dismiss any form of the patient's behavior as nonsensical, even though at that particular time the behavior may be incomprehensible.
4. The therapist follows the patient's fantasies, delusions, and distortions. He becomes a participant observer, in the way that a parent might observe and play with his child, but allow the child to assume the lead. This technique is used often in play therapy with young children. Initially the therapist need not challenge the patient's distortions or question the unreality of his perceptions. At appropriate times, the affective component of the play or fantasy of the child can be put into words, but the therapist should never force his own perception of reality on the child. Ekstein[34] referred to this technique as "interpretation within the regression" or "interpretation within the metaphor." He states:

Such interpretation rests upon the temporary willingness to assume that the patient's grossly distorted perceptions reflect outer reality, because they accurately reflect his inner psychological reality and the state of his ego, which has temporarily lost the capacity to differentiate between inner and outer reality. [pp. 120–121]

5. In order to establish communication, especially at the beginning, the therapist may imitate and echo the behavior of the child.
6. Psychotherapy with psychotic children is un-

* See references 11, 12, 13, 14, and 15.
† See references 33, 34, 35, 36, 37, 38, and 39.

usually demanding. The therapist must allow a part of himself, the experiencing ego, to suspend reality and to become a playmate of the child's. At the same time, the therapist's other part, the observing ego, continues to study and understand these two "children" at play. The goal and the hope of this therapeutic approach is to win the basic trust of the pathologically frightened and withdrawn child. The more such trust develops, and the more the child allows himself to be reached by the accepting therapist, the less will he be totally alone and drowned in his frightening world of fantasies and delusions.

Psychotherapy can be particularly useful with a relatively bright psychotic child who by the age of five has already developed some form of language for communciation.

BEHAVIOR MODIFICATION

In the last fifteen years, behavior modification has been a major development in the assessment and treatment of autistic and severely psychotic children.

A behavior therapist examines the child's behavioral repertoire and tries to select target behaviors which he then seeks to extinguish. This may include self-stimulating and echolalic behavior, or such destructive and maladaptive behaviors as self-mutilation, biting, kicking, and hurting others. At the same time, the therapist selects a range of positive and adaptive behaviors such as looking at the therapist's face, imitating the therapist's voice, actions, and eventually language. These the therapist seeks to reinforce. The behavior therapist is not concerned generally with the etiological factors in the patient's psychopathology. Psychodynamic formulations or any emphasis on intrapsychic or environmental conflicts are avoided. The laboratory methods of experimental psychology are applied to the recognition and modification of a particular undesirable behavior. The therapeutic approach borrows extensively from learning theory.

Ferster[44] was the first to describe special laboratory methods for understanding and documenting the behavior of the autistic child. He argues that the autistic child manifests "impoverished behavior" due to the lack of social stimulation reward. A year later, Ferster and DeMyer[45] described "a method for the experimental analysis of the behavior of autistic children." Since then, there has been a massive proliferation of literature on behavioral therapy of psychotic children. The prominent contributors are Ferster;[40, 41, 42, 43] Ferster and Simons;[46] Wolf, Risley and Mees;[130] Wolf and Risley;[128] Hewett;[55, 56, 57] Lovaas;[74, 75, 76, 77] Lovaas and associates;[*] Hingtgen and associates;[†] and Churchill.[24, 25]

Lovaas, one of the most prolific researchers in this field was coauthor of a succinct article in which the writers note that:

Using the concepts of learning theory, one can view a child's development as consisting of the acquisition of two events: (a) behaviors and (b) stimulus functions. If we look at the behavioral development of autistic children, perhaps, the most striking feature about them centers on their behavioral deficiency. They have little if any behavior which would help them function in society. If one was going to treat autistic children based on this perspective, then one would try to strengthen behaviors, such as appropriate play and speech, by reinforcing their occurrence. When their occurrence is initially absent, those behaviors should be gradually shaped by rewarding successive approximations to their eventual occurrence. Similarly, one might attempt to treat certain behaviors, such as tantrums and self-destruction, by either systematically withholding those reinforcers which may be maintaining these behaviors or by the systematic application of aversive stimuli contingent on their occurrence.[80] [pp. 113–114]

SPECIAL CONSIDERATIONS IN BEHAVIOR THERAPY

There are a number of special considerations pertaining to behavior therapy. First of all, it is important to observe the behavior of the child carefully and document the different behaviors in detail. The observation and notation of the behavior should be specific, concrete, and free from subjective interpretation.

Then the therapist needs to establish a priority list for extinguishing unwanted behaivor and for developing appropriate behaviors.

In order to record observations and assess therapeutic outcome, behaviors should be reduced to the simplest possible unit. For instance, instead of saying the child is aggressive toward others, one might say the child is biting, scratching, kicking, or spitting. The therapist may decide to start eliminating biting behavior. After achieving this, he may then work on kicking or scratching behavior. Frequently there is some generalization from one behavior to another.

A variety of techniques has been found useful for the reduction or extinction of undesirable behaviors. These include ignoring the behavior, the use of punishment or aversion therapy (for example, an electric shock, slapping, or spanking), and

* See references 78, 79, 80, 81, 82, 83, 84, 85, 86, 87, 88, and 89.
† See references 58, 59, 60, 61, and 62.

the use of negative reinforcement (the withdrawal of reinforcers such as smiles, body contact, attention, and praise).

Also, a variety of techniques has been used as a form of reward or positive reinforcement. This involves the encouragement of particularly desired behavior such as looking at the therapist's face, imitating the movement of the therapist's mouth, the vocalization of certain sounds, and, later on, words and sentences, manipulating various objects by hand, and developing more sophisticated cognitive and social skills. At first, the rewards are frequently primary reinforcers, such as food or candy. Accompanying (paired with) the primary reinforcers, social rewards are also given. These consist, for example, of verbal praise and touching the child's face gently. The ideal theraputic program is based on a gradual decrease (fading) of primary reinforcers so that the desirable behavior is maintained by the social and psychological rewards of human contact. These serve as secondary or conditioned reinforcers. According to many practicing behavior therapists, psychotic and autistic children are impoverished by the lack of secondary reinforcers.

Once a behavior program gets underway, the initial improvement in target behavior may be dramatic. Nonetheless, the major criticism of behavior therapy with psychotic children is the limited generalization of the acquired behavior. For instance, the autistic child might be able to use words or perform a task with a particular therapist in a specific setting. A few minutes later, in a different place, he might not be able to reproduce that acquired behavior either with the same therapist or with someone else. Learning occurs through successive generalization. It appears that many autistic children have limited ability to generalize their learning experience.

Another criticism is that the behavior is reversible. After discontinuation of therapy, the child regresses frequently to the old maladaptive behavior. Lovaas and associates[83] reported a follow-up study of twenty autistic children treated with behavior therapy who initially manifested apparent sensory deficit, severe affect isolation, self-stimulatory behavior, mutism (about half of the children), echolalic speech, diminution or absence of receptive speech, and absence or minimal presence of social and self-help behavior. A small number manifested self-destructive or self-mutilating behavior. While they were involved in treatment, the inappropriate behaviors of all of these children decreased. Appropriate behaviors such as speech, social nonverbal behavior, and play increased. After eight months of therapy, some of the children who were initially echolalic had begun to use spontaneous language. The IQ's of these children also improved.

Particularly noteworthy was the revelation in one to four years of follow up that those children who were institutionalized in a state hospital facility regressed and lost all of their gains. However, those who were treated on an outpatient basis and whose parents were helped to become primary therapists not only sustained their gains, but continued to improve.

SENSORY PERCEPTION: STIMULUS OVERSELECTIVITY

Recently, there has been increasing emphasis on the study of visual and auditory perception and sensory integration in psychotic children. Lovaas and associates[84] found " . . . when autistic children were confronted with a complex stimulus, they selectively responded to only one component of the complex one." In a further follow-up study[78] the authors reported that when

autistic and normal children were trained to respond to a complex stimulus involving an auditory component [white noise] and a visual component [red flood light], the normal children were able to respond to both stimuli but autistic children only responded to one stimulus and ignored the other one. [p. 305]

Autistic children demonstrated "stimulus overselectivity." The authors postulated that the difficulties of the autistic child in developing language and complex behavior might be related to stimulus overselectivity and problems in responding to different stimuli at the same time.

These findings suggest that therapeutic programs for autistic children should reassess the gradualness and selectiveness with which they introduce additional stimuli (for example, tactile or visual) in an effort to prevent overflooding of the child with multiple stimuli. Avoidance of animate objects and preoccupation with sameness might be related to stimulus overselectity.

VESTIBULAR STIMULATION

Ritvo, Ornitz, and La Franchi,[100] Ornitz and associates,[97] and Ornitz[96] have addressed autistic children's disturbance in sensorimotor integration. In an excellent review of clinical and experimental literature on childhood autism, Ornitz[95] states:

Many of the behaviors of autistic children also suggest that they are actively seeking out vestibular and proprioceptive stimulation. They whirl themselves around and around, repetitively rock and sway back and forth, or roll their heads from side to side. The repetitive hand flapping also provides proprioceptive input. [pp. 26–27]

There is a paradoxical situation in the sensory stimulation of autistic children. Frequently, they search frantically for tactile stimulation by, for example, touching the surface of the wall or the sharp edges of tables, or playing with cards and rulers, but at the same time they are panic-stricken by the sudden noise of a toilet flushing or a vacuum cleaner running. Unexpected light may cause the same reaction. It seems that unexpected stimuli, whether auditory, visual, tactile, or vestibular, may create an immediate avoidance reaction. For instance, the child may cover his ears, avoid looking (gaze aversion), or react with overwhelming anxiety or agitation.

It has been observed that autistic children generally prefer the use of proximal receptors such as touch, smell, and taste rather than distal receptors such as hearing and vision.[50, 52, 53, 113] Although autistic children might have a "normal or even advanced form of perception, they make poor use of visual discrimination in learning."[95] Recognizing these perceptual difficulties in autistic children, Schopler and associates[115] provided a structured therapeutic setting to compare the development of these children in a structured versus a nonstructured setting.

A structured session was defined as one in which the adult determined what material was to be worked with, for how long the child was to work with it, and the manner in which he was to work. The unstructured session, on the other hand, was defined as one in which the child selected material, decided how long to work with it, and the manner in which he would use it. [p. 416]

The findings confirmed that the children reacted "more favorably to structure than to unstructure. Individual differences showed that autistic children on a higher developmental level were better able to utilize relative unstructure than those functioning on a lower developmental level."

COGNITIVE AND LANGUAGE DISABILITY

Rutter's extensive studies* perceive autism as a special clinical entity totally different from childhood schizophrenia.

In schizophrenia the individual develops normally at first. It is only with the onset of illness that he loses touch with reality. The autistic child, on the other hand, shows abnormalities of development from early

* See references 3, 4, 5, 31, 103, 104, 105, 106, 107, 108, 109, 110, 111, and 112.

infancy. It is not that he loses touch with reality—he fails to gain it. About ⅘ of autistic children never show normal development and even in the ⅕ that do, the onset is before 30 months.[103] [p. 149]

Rutter is convinced that autism is not psychogenic but is related to some form of organic brain disorder. He believes that deficiency in cognition, especially language comprehension, contributes significantly to the development of autism. The repetitive and stereotyped behavior of autistic children is perceived as a reaction to this cognitive disorder and to their inability to understand speech. Bartak and Rutter,[3] and Bartak, Rutter, and Cox[5] propose special educational treatment for autistic children diagnosed before the age of three. Such treatment includes behavior modification programs with emphasis on language development, and techniques for enriching the language and cognitive repertoire of the child with short, simple sentences. Also emphasized is the involvement of a home-based program for " . . . aiding social and linguistic development and reducing the tendency to develop rigid stereotyped patterns."[104]

SOMATIC THERAPIES

For the last thirty years, Bender, Fish, Chess, and more recently, Campbell have proposed a variety of somatic psychopharmacological treatments for autistic and severely psychotic children. Bender[8] states:

Schizophrenia in childhood may otherwise be defined as a form of encephalopathy appearing at different points in the development pattern of the biological unit and the social personality in a characteristic way, and, because of frustration, causing anxiety to which the individual must react according to his own capacities. [p. 630]

She believes that a maturational lag of the nervous system in utero, a disturbance in vasovegetative functions, and an imbalance in physiological rhythms of daily life are etiological factors in the development of autism and childhood schizophrenia.

She used electroconvulsive therapy and LSD in an effort to stimulate maturational growth and improvement of some of the psychotic behavior of these children,[6, 7, 9, 10] practices that are no longer popular or accepted.

Campbell and associates[20] reported an acute, double-blind cross-over study of fifteen hospitalized children, of whom thirteen were schizophrenic, comparing a placebo, chlorpromazine (a sedative neuroleptic), trifluperidol (a stimulating neuroleptic), dextroamphetamine, and chloral hydrate. Chlorpromazine increased the hypoactivity and lethhargic behavior of the subjects, who appeared to be very sedated. Statistically, trifluperidol proved to be more effective than chlorpromazine or a placebo in producing symptom relief.

Campbell and associates[21, 22] studied the effect of the thyroid derivatives, triiodothyronine and liothyronine sodium, on a group of chronic schizophrenic children of preschool age, who were functionally retarded, withdrawn, hypoactive, dreamy, had a bland affect, and lacked energy. With the administration of chlorpromazine, they became very sedated. Eleven of the sixteen euthyroid children given triiodothyronine (T_3) in a daily dose ranging from 12.5 to 75 micrograms showed marked improvement as opposed to the poor responses to dextroamphetamine.[22] In fourteen psychotic preschool-aged children, liothyronine sodium was given without any regard to hypo- or hyperactivity. After a period of eleven to nineteen weeks, all of these children showed improvement. The authors speculated on the antipsychotic and stimulating properties of these drugs: "Perhaps the central nervous system of the schizophrenic child needs a greater amount of thyroid hormone to function optimally."[21]

There is considerable interest, especially in Europe, in the use of lithium in the treatment of childhood psychosis. The rationale for its use is based on the possiblty that an equivalent of manic depressive illness exists in children.[1, 32, 48, 116] According to Schou, the role of lithium in the treatment of severe childhood psychopathology is not clear. There are a few scattered reports on the use of lithium with depressed children. Campbell and associates[19] undertook a controlled cross-over study on the effect of lithium and chlorpromazine on ten severely disturbed children, six of whom were schizophrenic and one of whom was autistic. Lithium was found to be less effective than chlorpromazine,

. . . except in one child whose autoaggressiveness and explosiveness practically ceased on lithium. . . . lithium may prove of some value in treatment of severe psychiatric disorders in childhood involving aggressiveness, explosive affect and hyperactivity.[19] [p. 234]

A butyrophenone derivative (haloperidol) and a phenothiazine derivative (thioridazine) are both being used for the symptomatic treatment of agitation, anxiety, hyperactivity, restlessness, destructive behavior, hallucinations, and delusions in children, particularly when there is evidence of psychosis. Thioridazine is one of the most widely used antipsychotic agents in pediatric psychiatry.

The usual dose is 75 to 200 milligrams, daily, although on occasion as much as 600 mg. daily can be given. The dose should never exceed 800 mg. daily because of the possibility of developing opacity in the lens of the eye. Haloperidol is being used increasingly for the same purpose, usually in the dosage range of 0.5 mg., two to three times per day, which can be gradually increased to 10 to 20 mg. daily.

Claghorn[26] reported a double-blind comparison of the use of haloperidol and thioridazine in sixty-three children under the age of twelve. Although faster signs of improvement seemed to appear with haloperidol, there was no statistically significant evidence of the therapeutic superiority of one over the other.

Greenbaum[54] evaluated the effectiveness of massive doses of niacinamide (megavitamin therapy) in a double-blind study of fifty-seven schizophrenic children, aged four to twelve, and concluded that there were no appreciable differences in improvement between those who used niacinamide and those who did not.

Ritvo and associates[101] administered L-dopa to four autistic children aged three to thirteen years. Three other autistic children and one normal adult served as controls. L-dopa significantly lowered the blood serotonin concentration in three of the experimental subjects, particularly in one. But L-dopa did not have any major effect on the behavior of autistic children.

GROUP THERAPY

Group therapy has been successful in treating some psychotic children. The therapeutic outcome is more promising when the psychotic or autistic child is verbal rather than the nonverbal. Speers and Lansing[119, 120] conducted a four-year group therapy program with one autistic child and four symbiotic children, aged three to five, with concomitant group therapy for their parents. Initially, the autistic behavior of the children increased as they became more withdrawn and panic-stricken. Gradually, however, the children showed improvement and began to interact and communicate with each other. Their panicky behavior decreased significantly and they became more attentive to activities. The parental group was separated into mothers and fathers. The mothers' group showed much more progress than the fathers', whose members were resistive and tended to isolate themselves in an attempt to avoid contact within the family. Speers and Lansing also prescribed the use of full-time "nannies" to care for the children at home. Mothers were resistive to the presence of nannies at home, but the nannies' presence helped significantly to decrease the care-taking burden on the mothers, allowing them to attend to their own needs.

Smolen and Lifton[118] described a treatment program for psychotic children in a child guidance setting that entailed indiividual and group therapy sessions for both the children and the parents. The therapists played an active role in setting goals for change for all family members.

Coffey and Wiener[29] in their book *Group Treatment of Autistic Children* describe the establishment of a day treatment program employing the principles of psychoanalytic group therapy. In each therapy group, children with more ego strengths were included as members of the group to serve as catalysts for improving the level of interaction. The authors report relative success with this approach in that of the thirteen patients who attended this day treatment program, all but three were able to stay at home and attend public school.

Romanczyk and associates[102] describe the application of behavioral modification techniques to the group treatment of severely disturbed children. They reported that social play as represented by the manipulation of a toy simultaneously with another child, improved significantly in a group setting with the introduction of food as a primary reinforcer and praise as a social reinforcer. This group approach could be an alternative to a one-to-one behavioral therapy approach.

FAMILY THERAPY

In the last decade a variant of family therapy has served to introduce a refreshing new trend in treating autistic and psychotic children. Active participation of the parents and, at times, siblings as cotherapists or primary therapistss is now encouraged.

Schopler and Reichler[114] are the strongest advocates of this approach. They have developed a home-based therapeutic program as an alternative to residential treatment for severely disturbed children. The therapeutic goals are to seek improvement in the areas of human relatedness, competence motivation, cognitive functions, and perceptual motor functions. Children and their parents are seen together twice a week by a therapeutic consultant. Parents are given the primary therapist role and become more effective therapeutic agents than the professional therapist. Active parental participation in the treatment plan and in the implementation of therapy, especially by the mothers, enhances the improvement and recovery of these patients significantly.

Howlin and associates[65] report on a home-based approach to the management and treatment of autistic children. The emphasis in this program is on normal social and linguistic development and on the decrease of maladaptive behavior. Operant conditioning techniques are used in their approach.

Chazan[23] reports on a group family therapy approach to childhood psychosis in which the whole family constellation is treated as the patient. Expression of emotion is emphasized, and reactivation of interpersonal conflict is encouraged within the therapeutic setting.

Clancy[27, 28] describes a family holiday workshop for eleven families with autistic children. These families met together with a professional consultant and voluntary helpers. Clancy reports that bringing these divergent families together in a holiday workshop helped to relieve the parents' feelings of futility and isolation, and created a vehicle for sharing practical aspects of the special management of an autistic child.

RESIDENTIAL TREATMENT

In the treatment of an autistic or psychotic child there arises the question of whether the child should be separated from his family and placed in a residential setting or remain at home and be treated on an outpatient or a day treatment basis.

Bender[6, 7] and Bettelheim[11, 12, 15] are proponents of special residential placement for psychotic children. The decision for the long-term placement of a psychotic child in a residential setting should be weighed very carefully as it is costly and therapy often takes months or years. If, by any chance, the child can benefit from outpatient therapy or day treatment and can thus continue to live at home, residential treatment should not be recommended. With the increased nationwide availability of outpatient child psychiatric facilities, special classes for emotionally disturbed children, therapeutic nurseries, day treatment facilities, and special schools for autistic children, long-term residential treatment can often be avoided.

Bakwin[2] is one of the earliest advocates of the home-management of psychotic children. More recently, Schopler,[114, 115] Rutter and Bartak,[110] and Bartak and Rutter[4] have been among the more vocal advocates for home-based programs for psychotic children. Freedman[47] and LaVietes[73] recommend day hospitals for these patients as an alternative to institutionalization.

After Kanner's publications on early infantile autism in 1943 and 1944,[68, 69] there was a surge of interest in the description and recognition of infantile autism, symbiotic childhood psychosis,[92] the atypical child[98] childhoood schizophrenia,[8] and borderline psychosis.[49]

Among many theoretical proposals on the etiology of childhood autism and childhood psychosis, the role of the parents, especially the mother, has been regarded as significant. In the 1950s and early 1960s, the concept of a "schizophrenogenic mother" or "refrigerator mother" who had failed to provide a good mothering experience for the psychotic child became a prevalent and forceful dynamic consideration in the management and treatment of these children.

"Parentectomy," or separation of the psychotic child from his parents, accompanied by long-term residential treatment of children in a psychiatric setting away from home, has been recommended.[12, 15] It was not uncommon for children to stay away from home for five to ten years, with limited meetings with parents. Some of the parents were involved independently in psychotherapy or psychoanalysis. This therapeutic modality worked successfully in some unusual specially designed residential settings which have been difficult to duplicate, such as the Orthogenic School in Chicago which is described in detail in chapter 14. The level of success in the therapeutic outcome with psychotic children in this setting is impressive.[12] The therapy is based on a counselor or therapist providing total physical and emotional care around the clock for a small number of children. A substitute mother provides children with a second chance to develop "basic trust." Also, an intensive educational program, which emphasizes affective and cognitive development of these children, is an integrated part of the school.

Recreation, art, music, and dance therapies are used extensively to complement other therapeutic modalities.

Hollander and Juhrs[63] have used Orff-Schulwerk, an interesting technique developed originally by Carl Orff, a German composer and music educator, to teach music to German school-age children. The method uses materials designed to be appropriate to the child's perspective, for example, high-quality percussion instruments and a failure-proof pentatonic scale, which enable children to create their own music. It was adapted subsequently for mentally retarded children and then applied to emotionally disturbed children.[16] Since the Orff method emphasized the rhythm in speech and body movement, and autistic children tend to respond to music and nonverbal commands, Orff-Schulwerk, according to Hollander and Juhrs, has proved an effective form of treatment. Even the most severely disturbed autistic child can play these instruments and derive reinforcement from them.

Along with this music technique, nonverbal communication, such as American sign language for the deaf, was used. The authors noticed that sign language seemed to be relatively nonthreatening to these children and that it enhanced the children's ability to use words rather than replace them.

More recently, some scientists have applied cybernetic concepts to childhood psychosis.[67] Colby[30] has developed a computer-based treatment program to teach language to nonspeaking autistic children based on the hypothesis that nonspeaking autistic children's primary difficulty is their inability to process symbols (dissymbolia). Colby's treatment method consists of encouraging an autistic child in exploratory play with a keyboard controlled computer. This keyboard computer is similar to a typewriter with a television-type screen attached to it. When the child plays with the keyboard, pictures, symbols, and the sounds of human voices appear on the television screen. The child plays an active role in creating his own program. Usually, an adult "sitter" is present, but the adult is an observer only and does not interfere with the child's play. The program is described as failproof. According to Colby, thirteen of seventeen autistic children involved in this program improved so much that they began voluntarily to use speech for social communication. Computer-based programs have shown promise in the treatment of severely disturbed children as long as the computers complement rather than replace human contact.

Conclusion

There are inherent limitations in all present therapeutic techniques for psychotic children. The complexity of the etiology and the severity of the psychological impairments require the therapist to transcend the boundaries of any single theoretical orientation.

After careful assessment of the child's strengths and deficits, the therapist should choose the appropriate method or, more likely, combination of methods to alleviate the child's pain and suffering and to stimulate healing and growth. Therapeutic agility, the thirst for and curiosity about new approaches, and the synthesis and integration of the available techniques are essential for effective treatment.

Gains for the patient and rewards for the therapist are liklely to be neither immediate nor dramatic. Ingenuity, patience, and perseverance will help the therapist overcome frustrations and disillusionments. Sustained and untiring interest in childhood psychosis will further contribute to the understanding of the mysteries of human growth and development.

REFERENCES

1. ANNELL, A., "Manic Depressive Illness in Children and Effect of Treatment with Lithium Carbonate," *Acta Paedopsychiatrica, 36*:292–361, 1969.

2. BAKWIN, H., "The Home Management of Children with Schizophrenia," *Journal of Pediatrics, 47*:514–519, 1955.

3. BARTAK L., and RUTTER, M., "The Use of Personal Pronouns by Autistic Children," *Journal of Autism and Childhood Schizophrenia, 4(3)*:217–222, 1974.

4. ———, "Special Educational Treatment of Autistic Children: A Comparative Study, I. Design of Study and Characteristics of Units," *Journal of Child Psychology, 14(3)*:161–179, 1973.

5. ———, and COX, A., "A Comparative Study of Infantile Autism and Specific Developmental Receptive Language Disorder: I. The Children," *British Journal of Psychiatry, 126*:127–145, 1975.

6. BENDER, L., "Treatment of Juvenile Schizophrenia," *Research Publications of the Association for Research in Nervous and Mental Disease, 34*:462–477, 1955.

7. ———, "The Development of a Schizophrenic Child Treated with Electric Convulsions at Three Years of Age," in Caplan, G. (Ed.), *Emotional Problems of Early Childhood*, pp. 407–430, Basic Books, New York, 1955.

8. ———, "Childhood Schizophrenia," *American Journal of Orthopsychiatry, 17*:40–56, 1947; Reprinted in Harrison, S.I., and McDermott, J. (Eds.), *Childhood Psychopathology*, pp. 628–646, International Universities Press, New York, 1972.

9. ———, FARETRA, G., AND COBRINIK, L., "LSD and UML Treatment of Hospitalized Disturbed Children," *Recent Advances in Biological Psychiatry, 6*:84–92, 1963.

10. BENDER, L., GOLDSCHMIDT, L., and SANKAR, S. D. V., "Treatment of Autistic Schizophrenic Children with LSD-25 and UML-491," *Recent Advances in Biological Psychiatry, 4*:170–179, 1961.

11. BETTELHEIM, B., *A Home for the Heart*, Knopf, New York, 1974.

12. ———, *The Empty Fortress, Infantile Autism and the Birth of the Self*, Free Press, New York, 1967.

13. ———, "Childhood Schizophrenia as Reaction to Extreme Situations," *American Journal of Orthopsychiatry, 26*:507–518, 1956.

14. ———, *Love Is Not Enough—The Treatment of Emotionally Disturbed Children*, Free Press, New York, 1955.

15. ———, *The Special School for Emotionally Disturbed Children*, 47th Yearbook of the National Society for the Study of Education, Bloomington, Ill., 1948.

16. BITCON, C., and PANATH, L., "Behavioral Analysis of Orff-Schulwerk," *Journal of Music Therapy, 9(2)*:56–63, 1972.

17. BOS, P., "The Use of LSD in Child Psychiatry," *Ceskoslovenska Psychiatrie, 67(4)*:237–241, 1971.

18. BRYSON, C. Q., and HINGTGEN, J. N., *Early Childhood Psychosis: Infantile Autism, Childhood Schizophrenia and Related Disorders, An Annotated Bibliography, 1964 to 1969*, National Institute of Mental Health, Rockville, Md., 1971.

19. CAMPBELL, M., et al., "Lithium and Chlorpromazine: A Controlled Cross-over Study of Hyperactive Severely Disturbed Young Children," *Jounral of Autism and Childhood Schizophrenia, 2(3)*:234–263, 1972.

20. CAMPBELL, M., et al., "Acute Responses of Schizophrenic Children to a Sedative and a 'Stimulating' Neuroleptic: A Pharmacologic Yardstick," *Current Therapeutic Research, 14(12)*:759–766, 1972.

21. CAMPBELL, M., et al., "Liothyronine Treatment in Psychotic and Non-psychotic Children under 6 Years," *Archives of General Psychiatry, 29(5)*:602–608, 1973.

22. ———, "Response to Triiodothyronine and Dextroamphetamine: A Study of Preschool Schizophrenic Children," *Journal of Autism and Childhood Schizophrenia, 2(4)*:343–358, 1972.

23. CHAZAN, R., "A Group Family Therapy Approach to Schizophrenia," *Israel Annals of Psychiatry and Related Disciplines, 12(3)*:177–193, 1974.

24. CHURCHILL, D. W., "Effects of Success and Failure in Psychotic Children," *Archives of General Psychiatry, 25(3:)*208–214, 1971.

25. ———, "Psychotic Children and Behavior Modification," *American Journal of Psychiatry, 125*:1585–1590, 1969.

26. CLAGHORN, J. L., "A Double-blind Comparison of Haloperidol (Haldol) and Thioridazine (Mellaril) in Outpatient Children," *Current Therapeutic Research, 14(12)*:785–789, 1972.

27. CLANCY, H., "A Group Family Holiday: An Innovation in the Therapeutic Management of the Autistic Child," *Slow Learning Child: The Australian Journal of the Education of Backward Children, 17(3)*:149–162, 1970.

28. ———, and McBRIDE, G., "Therapy of Childhood Autism in the Family," *Current Psychiatric Therapies, 12*:1–8, 1972.

29. COFFEY, H. S., and WIENER, L. L., *Group Treatment of Autistic Children*, Prentice-Hall, Englewood Cliffs, N. J., 1967.

30. COLBY, K. M., "The Rationale for Computer-Based Treatment of Language Difficulties in Nonspeaking Autistic Children," *Journal of Autism and Childhood Schizophrenia, 3(3)*:254–260, 1973.

31. COX, A., et al., "A Comparative Study of Infantile Autism and Specific Developmental Receptive Language Disorder: II. Parental Characteristics," *British Journal of Psychiatry, 126*:146–159, 1975.

32. DYSON, W., and BARCAI, A., "Treatment of Children of Lithium Responding Parents," *Current Therapeutic Research, 12*:286–290, 1970.

33. EKSTEIN, R., "Special Training Problems in Psychotherapeutic Work with Psychotic and Borderline Children," *American Journal of Orthopsychiatry, 32*:569–583, 1962.

34. ——, *Children of Time and Space, of Action and Impulse,* Appleton-Century-Crofts, New York, 1966.

35. ——, "On the Acquisition of Speech in the Autistic Child," *Reiss-Davis Clinical Bulletin, 1:*63–80, 1964.

36. ——, and CARUTH, E., "Distancing and Distance Devices in Childhood Schizophrenic and Borderline States: Revised Concepts and New Directions in Research," *Psychological Reports, 20:*109–110, 1967.

37. ——, "The Working Alliance with Monster," *Bulletin of the Menninger Clinic, 29:*189–197, 1965.

38. EKSTEIN, R., and WALLERSTEIN, J., "Choice of Interpretation in the Treatment of Borderline and Psychotic Children," *Bulletin of the Menninger Clinic, 21:*199–207, 1957.

39. ——, and MANDELBAUM, A., "Countertransference in the Residential Treatment of Children: Treatment Failure in a Child with Symbiotic Psychosis," in Eissler, R. S., et al. (Eds.), *The Psychoanalytic Study of the Child,* vol. 14, pp. 186–218, International Universities Press, New York, 1959.

40. FERSTER, C. B., "Operant Reinforcement of Infantile Autism," in Lesse, S. (Ed.), *An Evaluation of the Results of the Psychotherapies,* pp. 221–236, Charles C Thomas, Springfield, Ill., 1968.

41. ——, "Arbitrary and Natural Reinforcement," *Psychological Record, 17:*341–47, 1967.

42. ——, "The Transition from the Animal Laboratory to the Clinic," *Psychological Record, 17:*145–150, 1967.

43. ——, "Psychotherapy by Machine Communication," *Disorder of Communication, 42:*317–333, 1964.

44. ——, "Positive Reinforcement and Behavioral Deficits of Autistic Children," *Child Development, 32:*437–456, 1961.

45. ——, and DeMYER, M. K., "A Method for the Experimental Analysis of the Behavior of Autistic Children," *American Journal of Orthopsychiatry, 32:*89–98, 1962.

46. FERSTER, C. B., and SIMMONS, J., "Behavior Therapy with Children," *Psychological Record, 16:*65–71, 1966.

47. FREEDMAN, A. M., "Day Hospitals for Severely Disturbed Schizophrenic Children," *American Journal of Psychiatry, 115(10):*893–899, 1959.

48. FROMMER, E., "Depressive Illness in Childhood," in Coffeir, A., and Walk, A. (Eds.), *Recent Developments in Affective Disorders. A Symposium, British Journal of Psychiatry,* Special Publication no. 2, pp. 117–136, 1968.

49. GELEERD, E. R., "A Contribution to the Problem of Psychosis in Children," in Eissler, R. S., et al. (Eds.), *The Psychoanalytic Study of the Child,* vol. 2, pp. 271–291, International University Press, New York, 1946.

50. GOLDFARB, W., "An Investigation of Childhood Schizophrenia: A Retrospective View," *Archives of General Psychiatry, 11:*620–634.

51. ——, and DORSEN, M., *Annotated Bibliography of Childhood Schizophrenia and Related Disorders,* Basic Books, New York, 1956.

52. GOLDFARB, W., LEVY, D. M., and MYERS, D. I., "The Mother Speaks to Her Schizophrenic Child: Language in Childhood Schizophrenia," *Psychiatry, 35(3):*217–226, 1972.

53. GOLDFARB, W., YUDKOVITZ, E., and GOLDFARB, N., "Verbal Symbols to Designate Objects: An Experimental Study of Communication in Mothers of Schizophrenic Children," *Journal of Autism and Childhood Schizophrenia, 3(4):*281–298, 1973.

54. GREENBAUM, G. H., "An Evaluation of Niacinamide in the Treatment of Childhood Schizophrenia," *American Journal of Psychiatry, 127(1):*89–92, 1970.

55. HEWETT, F. M., "The Autistic Child Learns to Read," *Slow Learning Child: The Australian Journal of the Education of Backward Children, 13:*107–121, 1966.

56. ——, "Teaching Speech to an Autistic Child Through Operant Conditioning," *American Journal of Orthopsychiatry, 35:*927–936, 1965.

57. ——, "Teaching Reading to an Autistic Boy Through Operant Conditioning," *The Reading Teacher, 17:*613–618, 1964.

58. HINGTGEN, J. N., and CHURCHILL, D. W., "Differential Effects of Behavior Modification in Four Mute Autistic Boys," in Churchill, D. W., Alpern, G. D., and DeMyer, M., (Eds.), *Infantile Autism: Proceedings of the Indiana University Colloquium,* pp. 185–199, Charles C Thomas, Springfield, Ill., 1970.

59. ——, "Identification of Perceptual Limitations in Mute Autistic Children: Identification by the Use of Behavior Modification," *Archives of General Psychiatry, 21:*68–71, 1969.

60. HINGTGEN, J., N., and TROST, F. C., "Shaping Cooperative Responses in Early Childhood Schizophrenics, II. Reinforcement of Mutual Physical Contact and Vocal Responses," in Ulrich, R., Stacknick, T., and Mabry, J. (Eds.), *Control of Human Behavior,* pp. 110–113, Scott, Forest & Company, Glenview, Ill., 1966.

61. HINGTGEN, J. N., COULTER, S. K., and CHURCHILL, D. W., "Intensive Reinforcement of Imitative Behavior in Mute Autistic Children," *Archives of General Psychiatry, 17:*36–43, 1967.

62. HINGTGEN, J. N., SANDERS, B. J., and DeMYER, M. K., "Shaping Cooperative Responses in Early Childhood Schizophrenics," in Ullman, J., and Krasner, L. (Eds.), *Case Studies in Behavior Modification,* pp. 130–138, Holt, Rinehart & Winston, New York, 1965.

63. HOLLANDER, F. M., and JUHRS, P. D., "Orff-Schulwerk: An Effective Treatment Tool with Autistic Children," *Journal of Music Therapy, 11(1):*1–12, 1974.

64. HOLTER, F. R., and RUTTENBERG, B. A., "Initial Interventions in Psychotherapeutic Treatment of Autistic Children," *Journal of Autism and Childhood Schizophrenia, 1(2):*206–214, 1971.

65. HOWLIN, P., et al., "A Home-based Approach to the Treatment of Autistic Children," *Journal of Autism and Childhood Schizophrenia, 3(4):*308–336, 1973.

66. ITARD, J. M. G., *The Wild Boy of Aveyron,* translated by G. and M. Humphrey, Appleton-Century-Crofts, New York, 1962.

67. KAHN, R., and ARBIB, M., "A Cybernetic Approach to Childhood Psychosis," *Journal of Autism and Childhood Schizophrenia, 3(3):*261–273, 1973.

68. KANNER, L., "Early Infantile Autism," *Journal of Pediatrics, 25:*211–217, 1944.

69. ——, "Autistic Disturbance of Affective Contact," *Nervous Child, 25:*217–250, 1943.

70. KEMPH, J. P., HARRISON, S. I., and FINCH, S. M., "Promoting the Development of Ego Functions in the Middle Phase of Treatment of Psychotic Children," *Journal of the American Academy of Child Psychiatry, 4:*401–412, 1965.

71. KING, P. D., "Theoretical Considerations of Psychotherapy with a Schizophrenic Child," *Journal of the American Academy of Child Psychiatry, 3:*638–649, 1964.

72. ——, and EKSTEIN, R., "The Search for Ego Controls: Progression of Play Activity in Psychotherapy with a Schizophrenic Child," *The Psychoanalytic Review, 54:*639–648, 1967.

73. LAVIETES, R. L., "Day Treatment," in Freedman, A. M., and Kaplan, H. I. (Eds.), *The Child: His Psychological and Cultural Developments II. The Major Psychological Disorders and their Treatment,* pp. 381–384, Atheneum, New York, 1972.

74. LOVAAS, O. I., "Consideations in the Development of a Behavioral Treatment Program for Psychotic Children," in Churchill, D. W., Alpern, G. D., and DeMyer, M. (Eds.), *Infantile Autism: Proceedings of the Indiana University Colloquium,* pp. 124–144, Charles C Thomas, Springfield, Ill., 1970.

75. ——, "A Behavior Therapy Approach to the Treatment of Childhood Schizophrenia," in Hill, J. P. (Ed.), *Minnesota Symposia on Child Psychology,* vol. 1,

pp. 108–159, University of Minnesota Press, Minneapolis, 1967.

76. ———, "A Program for the Establishment of Speech in Psychotic Children," in Wing, J. K. (Ed.), *Early Childhood Autism: Clinical, Educational, and Social Aspects*, pp. 115–144, Pergamon Press, London, 1966.

77. ———, *Learning Theory Approach to the Treatment of Childhood Schizophrenia*, Paper presented at the American Orthopsychiatric Association, San Francisco, April 13–16, 1966.

78. ———, and SCHREIBMAN, L., "Stimulus Overselectivity of Autistic Children in a Two Stimulus Situation," *Behavior Research and Therapy, 9(4):*305–310, 1971.

79. LOVAAS, O. I., LITROWNIK, A., and MANN, R., "Response Latencies to Auditory Stimuli in Autistic Children Engaged in Self-stimulatory Behavior," *Behavior Research and Therapy, 9(1):*39–49, 1971.

80. LOVAAS, O. I., SCHREIBMAN, L., and KOEGEL, R. L., "A Behavior Modification Approach to the Treatment of Autistic Children," *Journal of Autism and Childhood Schizophrenia, 4(2):*111–129, 1974.

81. LOVAAS, O. I., SCHAEFFER, B., and SIMMONS, J. Q., "Building Social Behavior in Autistic Children by Use of Electric Shock," in Lovaas, O. I., and Bucher, B. D. (Eds.), *Perspectives in Behavior Modification with Deviant Children*, pp. 107–122, Prentice-Hall, Englewood Cliffs, N. J., 1974.

82. ———, "Building Social Behavior in Autistic Children by Use of Electric Shock," *Journal of Experimental Research in Personality, 1:*99–109, 1965.

83. LOVAAS, O. I., et al., "Some Generalization and Follow-up Measures on Autistic Children in Behavior Therapy," *Journal of Applied Behavior Analysis, 6(1):*131–166, 1973.

84. LOVAAS, O. I., et al., "Selective Responding by Autistic Children to Multiple Sensory Input," *Journal of Abnormal Psychology, 77(3):*211–222, 1971.

85. LOVAAS, O. I., et al., "The Establishment of Imitation and Its Use for the Development of Complex Behavior in Schizophrenic Children," *Behavior Research and Therapy, 5:*171–181, 1967.

86. LOVAAS, O. I., et al., "Establishment of Social Reinforcers in Two Schizophrenic Children on the Basis of Food," *Journal of Experimenal Child Psychology, 4:*109–125, 1966.

87. LOVAAS, O. I., et al., "Acquisition of Imitative Speech by Schizophrenic Children," *Science, 151:*705–707, 1966.

88. LOVAAS, O. I., et al., "Experimental Studies in Childhood Schizophrenia: Analysis of Self-destructive Behavior," *Journal of Experimental Child Psychology, 2:*67–84, 1965.

89. LOVAAS, O. I., et al., "Recording Apparatus and Procedure for Observation of Behaviors of Children in Free Play Settings," *Journal of Experimental Child Psychology, 2:*108–120, 1965.

90. MAHLER, M., *On Human Symbiosis and the Vicissitudes of Individuation. I. Infantile Psychosis*, International Universities Press, New York, 1968.

91. ———, "On the Significance of Normal Separation-Individuation Phase: With Reference to Research in Symbiotic Childhood Psychosis," in Schur, M. (Ed.), *Drives, Affects, Behavior*, vol. 2, pp. 161–169, International Universities Press, New York, 1965.

92. ———, "On Childhood Psychosis and Schizophrenia: Autistic and Symbiotic Infantile Psychosis," in Eissler, R. S., et al. (Eds.), *The Psychoanalytic Study of the Child*, vol. 7, pp. 286–305, International Universities Press, New York, 1952.

93. ———, and FURER, M., "Child Psychosis: A Theoretical Statement and Its Implications," *Journal of Autism and Childhood Schizophrenia, 2(3):*213–218, 1972.

94. MASLOW, A. R., "A Concentrated Therapeutic Relationship with a Psychotic Child," *Journal of the American Academy of Child Psychiatry, 3:*140–150, 1964.

95. ORNITZ, E. M., "Childhood Autism, A Review of the Clinical and Experimental Literature (Medical Progress)," *California Medicine, 118(4):*21–47, 1973.

96. ———, "Childhood Autism, A Disorder of Sensorimotor Integration," in Rutter, M. (Ed.), *Infantile Autism: Concepts, Characteristics and Treatment*, pp. 50–68, Churchill Livingston, London, 1971.

97. ———, et al., "Environmental Modification of Autistic Behavior," *Archives of General Psychiatry, 22:*560–565, 1970.

98. RANK, B., "Adaption of the Psychoanalytic Technique for the Treatment of Young Children with Atypical Development," *American Journal of Orthopsychiatry, 19:*130–139, 1949.

99. RIMLAND, B., *Infantile Autism*, Appleton-Century-Crofts, New York, 1964.

100. RITVO, E. R., ORNITZ, E. M., and LaFRANCHI, S., "Frequency of Repetitive Behavior in Early Infantile Autism and Its Variant," *Archives of General Psychiatry, 19:*341–347, 1968.

101. RIVTO, E. R., et al., "Effects of L-dopa in Autistic Children," *Journal of Autism and Childhood Schizophrenia, 1(2):*190–205, 1972.

102. ROMANCZYK, R. G., et al., "Increasing Isolate and Social Play in Severely Disturbed Children: Intervention and Postintervention Effectiveness," *Journal of Autism and Childhood Schizophrenia, 5(1):*57–70, 1975.

103. RUTTER, M., "The Development of Infantile Autism," *Psychological Medicine, 4(2):*147–163, 1974.

104. ———, "The Assessment and Treatment of Preschool Autistic Children," *Early Child Development and Care, 3(1):*13–29, 1973.

105. ———, "Childhood Schizophrenia Reconsidered," *Journal of Autism and Childhood Schizophrenia, 2(4):*315–337, 1972.

106. ———, "Autistic Children: Infancy to Adulthood," *Seminars in Psychiatry, 2:*435–450, 1970.

107. ———, "Concepts of Autism: A Review of Research," *Journal of Child Psychology and Psychiatry, 9(1):*1–25, 1968.

108. ———, "Psychotic Disorders in Early Childhood," in Coppen, A., and Walk, A. (Eds.), Recent Developments in Schizophrenia, *British Journal of Psychiatry*, Special Publication no. 1. pp. 133–158, 1967.

109. ———, "Behavioral and Cognitive Characteristics of a Series of Psychotic Children," in Wing, J. K. (Ed.), *Early Childhood Autism*, pp. 51–81, Pergamon Press, Oxford, 1966.

110. ———, and BARTAK, L., "Special Educational Treatment of Autistic Children: A Comparative Study. II. Follow-up Findings and Implications for Services," *Journal of Child Psychology and Psychiatry and Allied Disciplines, 14(4):*241–270, 1973.

111. RUTTER, M., and SUSSENWEIN, F., "A Developmental and Behavioral Approach to the Treatment of Preschool Autistic Children," *Journal of Autism and Childhood Schizophrenia, 1(4):*376–397, 1971.

112. RUTTER, M., SHAFFER, D., and SHEPHERD, M., "An Evaluation of the Proposal for a Multi-axial Classification of Child Psychiatric Disorders," *Psychological Medicine, 3(2):*244–250, 1973.

113. SCHOPLER, E., "Early Infantile Autism and Receptor Processes," *Archives of General Psychiatry, 13:*327–335, 1965.

114. ———, and REICHLER, R. J., "Parents as Co-therapist in the Treatment of Psychotic Children," *Journal of Autism and Childhood Schizophrenia, 1(1):*87–102, 1971.

115. SCHOPLER, E., et al., "Effect of Treatment Structure on Development in Autistic Children," *Archives of General Psychiatry, 24:*415–421, 1971.

116. SCHOU, M., "Lithium in Psychiatric Therapy and Prophylaxis, A Review with Special Regards to Its Use in Children," in Annell, A. (Ed.), *Depressive States in Childhood and Adolescence*, pp. 479–487, Almquist and Wiksell, Stockholm, 1972.

117. SHAFII, M., "A Precedent for Modern Psychothera-peutic Techniques: One Thousand Years Ago," *American Journal of Psychiatry, 128(12):*1581–1582, 1972.

118. SMOLEN, E., and LIFTON, N., "A Special Treatment Program for Schizophrenic Children in a Child Guidance Clinic," *American Journal of Orthopsychiatry, 36:*736–742, 1966.

119. SPEERS, R. W., and LANSING, C., *Group Therapy in Childhood Psychosis,* University of North Carolina Press, Chapel Hill, N. C., 1965.

120. ————, "Group Psychotherapy with Preschool Psy-chotic Children and Collateral Group Therapy of Their Parents: A Preliminary Report of the First Two Years," *American Journal of Orthopsychiatry, 34:*659–666, 1964.

121. SZUREK, S. A., and BERLIN, I., *Clinical Studies in Childhood Psychoses,* Brunner/Mazel, New York, 1973.

122. ————, "Elements of Psychotherapy with the Schizophrenic Child and His Parents," *Psychiatry, 19(1):*1–9, 1956.

123. TILTON, J., DeMYER, M., and LOWE, L., *Anno-tated Bibliography on Childhood Schizophrenia: 1955–1964,* Grune & Stratton, New York, 1966.

124. VAILLANT, G. E., "John Haslam on Early Infantile Autism," *American Journal of Psychiatry, 119(4):*376, 1962.

125. WEILAND, I. H., and RUDNIK, R., "Considerations of the Development and Treatment of Autistic Childhood Psychosis," in Eissler, R. S., et al. (Eds.), *The Psychoan-alytic Study of the Child,* vol. 16, pp. 549–563, Interna-tional Universities Press, New York, 1961.

126. WING, L., and WING, J. K., "The Prescription of Services," in Wing, J. (Ed.), *Early Childhood Autism: Clinical, Educational, and Social Aspects,* pp. 279–298, Pergamon Press, London, 1966.

127. WITMER, L., "What I Did with Don," in Szurek, S. A., and Berlin, I. N. (Eds.), *Clinical Studies in Child-hood Psychosis,* pp. 48–64, Brunner/Mazel, New York, 1973.

128. WOLF, M., and RISLEY, T., "Application of Oper-ant Conditioning Procedures to the Behavior Problems of an Autistic Child: A Follow-up and Extension," *Behavior Research and Therapy, 5:*103–111, 1967.

129. WOLF, E. G., and RUTTENBERG, A., "Communica-tion Therapy for the Autistic Child," *Journal of Speech and Hearing Disorders, 32(4):*331–335, 1967.

130. WOLF, M., RISLEY, R., and MEES, H., "Application of Operant Conditioning Procedures to the Behavior Prob-lems of an Autistic Child," *Behavior Research and Ther-apy, 1:*305–312, 1964.

---

35 / The Hospitalized Child

Elva Orlow Poznanski

Historically some of the earliest psychological issues raised in connection with hospitalized chil-dren were the problems of separation from par-ents, (the main focus was on the effects of separa-tion of the child from the family for long periods of time). This was in fact a serious problem for the early pediatric hospitals. Tight restrictions on visiting were enforced prior to the late 1940s be-cause in the absence of antibiotics, there was real danger of cross-infection of patients on hospital wards. Since complete bed isolation of children had proved to be effective, all visiting was prohib-ited. In the late 1940s and the early 1950s, follow-ing the development of a host of effective antibiot-ics, the majority of pediatric hospitals gradually removed most or all restrictions on parental visits to the children's wards.[9] The psychiatric litera-ture reflects this change. Studies reported prior to the mid 1950s were done on children in hospi-tals who were rarely visited by their parents and had little opportunity for group activities.

Progress in the medical side of pediatrics often changes in a direct way the psychological aspects of the hospitalization of children. Particularly noteworthy have been the development of safer anesthetics for children and an overall reduction in the length of hospitalization. This is due to many factors, including antibiotics. In pediatric surgery a shift is occurring in two directions—one toward more and more outpatient surgery for routine procedures, and the other, toward more dramatic kinds of surgery for the inpatients (open heart surgery and kidney transplants). Again the psychiatric literature follows these new trends, and more papers are being written about the possible psychological effects of open heart surgery and renal transplantation. It is only natural that ad-vances in pediatrics reduce some anxieties, that is, the concern about dangers of infection, while si-multaneously opening new areas for consideration and exploration.

Relationships Between the Pediatrician and the Psychiatrist

Pediatric liaison psychiatry necessitates close working relationships with medical colleagues in pediatrics, surgery, radiation therapy, and so forth, which can be a most satisfying aspect of this work. Such relationships are minimally necessary in order to clarify the reason for the psychiatric referral. As all consultants know, the stated reason written on a referral request form rarely corresponds to the actual situation which motivated the referral. Psychiatry is no exception. For example, a referral note may read: "Johnny seems upset" or "Mary has some difficulties," or "Kim the child of Mr. and Mrs. P is too quiet and too good on the ward." What is really meant but rarely written would read: "Johnny refuses to take all his pills," or "Mary is hostile to everyone walking in the door," or "Mr. and Mrs. P are constantly harassing the surgeon to run more tests."

Another reason for close relationships with pediatric colleagues is to discuss with them the possible ways psychological issues may interrelate with physical illness. It is not unusual for a pediatrician to believe the symptomatology is functional and the psychiatrists to believe it is organic; such differences may be resolved in open discussion, resulting in new respect for one another.

Another practical reason for working closely with the pediatrician is that he may have information from years of experience with a particular family which is not recorded anywhere. In addition, he will often continue to see the child and family after the psychiatrist is no longer active in the case. Informal follow-up information of interest to the psychiatrist may be relayed by the pediatrician at a later date.

Another significant reason for maintaining rapport with pediatrics is that the relationship is often satisfying for both sides. Psychiatry can be a lonely and isolated practice, and it is stimulating to discuss cases with colleagues who have a different perspective and whose confidentiality can be trusted.

Almost any relationship has ambivalences, and the relationship between pediatrics and psychiatry is no exception. Aside from the individual differences between different psychiatrists and pediatricians, there are two areas which may cause friction. The regard which psychiatry is accorded by the majority of medicine is dubious, particularly in certain medical centers. Frequently, psychiatry is not viewed as a necessary or essential part of the medical scene. These prejudices may be expressed in many ways. It may be implicit in a referral which asserts that the patient can be discharged pending psychiatric consultation, or it may be revealed by needless interferences with the psychiatric interviewing on the medical wards. Problems such as these tend to diminish as per-

sonal relationships grow but are often major frustrations to a physician when he first begins liaison psychiatry. Another potential focus of conflict is in the different way pediatricians and psychiatrists schedule their time. Pediatricians have a certain number of patients to see, procedures to do, during any one time period. Psychiatrists typically fill their schedule with fixed time slots allotted for specific patients. Hence, frustrations arise when the psychiatrists can be on the wards only between 11:00 and 12:00 and the pediatrician is nowhere in sight. Often a simple explanation of the different manner in which psychiatrists and pediatricians schedule their time reduces friction.

Additional factors in the interrelationships between child psychiatry and pediatrics are discussed in greater detail in chapter 22.

Most of the basic therapeutic skills of a psychiatrist are as applicable in a pediatric hospital ward as they are in any other setting. For example, here as everywhere, the good clinician establishes rapport and explores problems with the patient. Depending on the patient's psychological stance, the therapist combines supportive and interpretative comments in appropriate proportions. While the basic treatment skills remain the same, however, there are some aspects of dealing with a hospitalized child that are critical and do need emphasis. These crucial issues are: (1) an awareness of the nature of the physical illness itself and its effects on behavior; (2) the nature of the hospital environment with its strange and different routines; (3) some special issues of concern in psychiatric treatment for the hospitalized child.

Physical Illness and Its Effect on Behavior

The treatment of a hospitalized child requires assessment, and frequently reassessment, of the child's medical condition. A sick child is usually withdrawn and apathetic, and this behavior should correlate directly with the degree of physical illness. When the degree of mood and behavior change does not correspond to the degree of physical illness, important psychological factors are likely to be involved.

There is a common situation in which the patient's mood is disproportionately poorer than the physical status. This occurs after an older child or an adolescent has just received some disheartening medical news about his prognosis. The youngster then experiences a reactive depression. All too often, a good many of the hospital personnel are not aware of the situation. Even if staff members know that the patient has recently been given some discouraging information, they tend to cling to the myth that such news can be emotionally digested in a day or two. At other times, mood changes may relate to an impending parental divorce or to a host of other social and psychological factors which may or may not be known to the hospital staff.

Changes in the physical status of a child are frequently accompanied by changes in mood and behavior. Parents commonly recognize the onset of illness in their offspring by such changes in the child's behavior behavior, such as increases in irritability. McDermott and Finch[13] write that in cases of ulcerative colitis, at the time of an exacerbation, the children tend to withdraw; in an emotional sense, they regress massively. It was also noted, however, that if the child's attitude improved, the physical condition would tend to improve as well. It is not the fact of regression alone that is important, but rather the extent of the regression in relation to the child's physical state. Ascertaining this involves an important clinical judgment. An example of the need for this type of correlation is demonstrated in the following clinical vignette:

DEPRESSION AND VASCULAR PNEUMONIA

Ginny, a fifteen-year-old girl, was referred for psychiatric evaluation from a children's hospital inpatient ward. She was being treated for pneumonia, but the pediatric house officer noted severe anxiety and hyperventilation. When the psychiatrist came to see her, the pediatrician said she was "too sick" to see a psychiatrist. Persisting, the psychiatrist went to Ginny's room where the nurses were attempting to sit her up in a wheelchair. Ginny could barely speak and appeared extremely apathetic. More important, she was visibly saddened and depressed. The psychiatrist explored Ginny's depressed feelings and discovered some suicidal ideation. After the first visit, Ginny changed abruptly. She became much more active, less anxious and fearful, and more talkative; simultaneously, her clinical picture improved dramatically. The chest X-rays also showed a dramatic shift in her pneumonia. From the onset of her illness Ginny's X-rays had become progressively worse. After the psychiatrist's visit, the chest X-ray revealed a rapid clearing of her pneumonia. Retrospectively, it was quite clear that the pneumonia was exacerbated by her depression, because the depression kept her in bed, inactive, and unwilling and/or unable to expectorate.

In the treatment of a hospitalized child, it is important to clarify as much as possible the medical prognosis of the child's illness. Occasionally, the diagnosis itself is unclear; the anxiety this engenders in the medical personnel can then readily be transmitted to the patient. It is important for the therapist to know as much as possible about the disease and its prognosis, for he frequently needs to help define the real situation for himself, for the child, and for the family, and the therapist may, in addition, need to correct the child's misconceptions about his illness.

As a rule, patients and families who receive a diagnosis which implies a fatal outcome or a lifetime of chronic illness, such as cancer or diabetes, do not immediately accept such news. Usually, confusion and shock along with denial mechanisms operate for a few days. Sometimes the denial persists for a lifetime. The majority of patients, however, begin to accept the new unpleasant reality within a couple of weeks. The ward staff, particularly if they are young, may need support in permitting the family time to cope psychologically with a new and painful reality. Great difficulties can arise if a family chronically utilizes denial in coping with illness; the denial can interfere with the medical management of the disease. In these instances, psychotherapy is indicated. The psychotherapy is often prolonged and difficult (as is true in any situation where denial is the primary mechanism of defense).

Parental reactions to a child's illness become visible on the hospital ward and are of particular importance in chronic illness. The usual parental response to illness is to become protective, even somewhat overprotective, toward the child. Such overprotectiveness that lasts only for a few days or weeks during an acute illness scarcely constitutes a problem. However, when the illness becomes chronic and the overprotection continues, difficulties can arise which are not easily reversed and may constitute a serious psychological overlay to the primary medical illness. Thus, a teenage diabetic may take no responsibility for his diabetic management, expecting his mother to continue caring for him, and throughout complaining vociferously about his parents. In contrast, a few parents react to an illness of their child by withdrawal instead of overprotection; they leave the ill child alone until he becomes well again. Such parental withdrawal from the child does not usually constitute a problem if it is only for a brief period. If it goes on for a long time however, it becomes an entirely different matter. Medically, it makes for a difficult situation for the physician; and psychologically is perceived by the child as a catastrophic rejection.

Some discussion of medical problems is logical in a pediatric hospital. However, many children commonly employ medical symptoms to divert attention from other areas which need to be discussed. This is a defense which may demand interpretation to allow the work to proceed. This type of defensive posture is often adopted by the chronically ill child and by the child whose basic problems are psychological. To the extent that he knows something about the medical condition of the patient, the therapist can distinguish real fears from anxieties displaced onto bodily symptoms. He is thus far better able to make appropriate interpretations in order to facilitate understanding of the child's problem.

Psychological Effects of Hospitalization

As implied in the beginning of this chapter, the simple assumption that hospitalization in itself is emotionally traumatic for most children no longer appears to be valid. Controlled studies (such as that of Davenport and Werry[7] of children undergoing a brief stay for tonsillectomy in a modern hospital did not show evidence of a post-hospitalization upset (as measured by a questionnaire sent to their mothers). Predictably, however, more subtle expressions of anxiety and stress during a hospital stay indicate that a hospitalized child is under varying degrees of stress. In one study[19] of hospitalized children, evidence of stress was measured by elevated temperature, pulse rate, and blood pressure, and postoperatively, by emesis, disturbed sleep, and extended recovery time. Putting this together, it means simply that the average child experiences stress with brief hospitalizations but can cope adequately when the physical discomfort is minimal. Thus, hospitalization per se cannot be equated with emotional trauma. At the same time, certain factors associated with hospitalization tend to increase the likelihood that such emotional trauma will occur. These factors include a vulnerable age when separation is more of an issue, the medical diagnosis (no studies have ever explored how leukemic children view hospitalization!), the degree of pain and discomfort endured by the child, and the length of hospitalization.

The crux of the matter is that for any particular child, hospitalization is an unusual experience and must be viewed by the therapist from that child's individual perspective. Two brief clinical vignettes will illustrate this point.

PSYCHOLOGICAL FACTORS IN ASTHMA

One eleven-year-old boy with asthma, who came from a large, poor family, was noted to have repeated hospitalizations for his disease within a short period of time. In the hospital, his asthma cleared rather rapidly. Psychiatric consultation was sought because of the possibility of emotional components affecting his disease. Without going into the details of the boy's psychodynamics, during the interviews it became clear that when his respiratory tract was vulnerable, the boy was able to voluntarily induce an asthma attack. Perhaps even more important was the fact that he enjoyed being in the hospital where for the first time in his life he had his own bed, had regular, plentiful meals, and where, in addition, there were lots of playmates and toys. When he was overheard talking to his roommate about exactly what date they would plan to meet in the emergency room, it was clear that in addition to enjoying the hospital environment generally, part of his motivation for hospitalization was to be with his friend.

This boy's view of his hospital stay would be quite different from the following child's experience.

ANAL DILATION AND EMOTIONAL TRAUMA

A four-year-old girl with congenital anal stenosis had a previous colostomy, and the mother had been instructed to dilate her anus digitally every day. It was not clear whether the instructions given to the mother were confusing or the mother had simply refused to comply with them. In any case, the mother failed to dilate the anus at home, and the young girl was brought into the hospital for more adequate dilatation to be followed by reconstructive surgery. The medical hierarchy assigned the daily dilatations to the surgery resident, and he did the procedure at the end of his day. Interestingly, the nurses were not given the responsibility of doing the dilations because "their fingers were too small." The dilatations were a traumatic experience for all. The four-year-old child, pale and frightened, would refuse to eat until after they were over. The mother and nurses were not present, and the screaming, kicking child was held down by several male residents while one of them performed the dilatation. Significantly, the surgical resident commented that he felt that he was "raping" her. The degree of this youngster's terror of dilatation was demonstrated when she was taken for a simple X-ray procedure. Despite reasoned explanation of the X-ray picture and the fact that it would cause her no discomfort, she continued to scream and was afraid she was going to be dilated. After two to three weeks, a surgical hook-up between her anus and colon was attempted and turned out to be unsuccessful. In contrast with the previous case, this youngster's view of hospitals is laden with anxiety. She will need help to work this out in a posthospitalization period of psychotherapy. However, unless the therapist has some understanding of what this child experienced during her hospitalization, it would be difficult to understand her and to aid her to come to grips with her anxieties.

Among the various events a child may experience during any hospital stay, some are more fear-provoking than others. Burling and Collip[6] focused on what moments were the most anxiety producing during a child's stay in the hospital. The children in this study were between fifteen months and ten years of age, and the data were gathered by monitoring their heart rate. The authors found that procedures with needles, especially bone marrow aspirations, venipunctures, and spinal taps were the most stressful. The next most stressful procedure was the pediatric resident's admission examination. Nurses' visits were generally not stressful unless they gave an injection. For certain procedures, it was clear that the fear was inherent in the nature of the procedure itself. On the other hand, it is equally evident from clinical experience that any one procedure may sometimes be a vehicle for all the fears and anxieties that accumulate for the hospitalized child. For example, one bright eleven-year-old boy was completely petrified at the prospect of a second bone marrow aspiration. The youngster was a good student, had many friends, and was not otherwise a problem on the ward. In talking to the young man, it became clear he had fears of death associated with this procedure. It became evident that his fear of the bone marrow aspiration related not only to the procedure as such, but also, and of even greater importance, to his underlying anxiety about his illness. The boy had recently been diagnosed as having leukemia. He had not been told the diagnosis, but at some level he correctly perceived the seriousness of his condition.

In the yesteryear days of restricted visiting, hospitalization and separation anxiety were almost synonymous. Today, enormous variation may be observed in the amount of time parents visit with their child on the hospital ward. Some parents, usually a mother, literally stay in the hospital for weeks at a time, particularly if rooming-in arrangements are available. While this may be desirable for a young hospitalized child, it may be less helpful for other members of the family group, particularly if there are young siblings at home. At the other extreme are the parents who abandon their child in the hospital, never to to be seen again. Whatever visiting pattern the parents adopt, the therapist needs to be aware of that pattern and of the impact it has on the child, on the hospital ward staff, and on the parents themselves.

Generally, the ward staff is critical of either extreme. Despite the commitment by the hospital to permit mothers to room-in, in practice, the mother who is constantly present on active medical wards tends to be viewed as "underfoot" or "in the way" by the hospital staff. The mothers may feel trapped and in doubt about leaving their child alone in the hospital, both because of the child's illness and of their ofttime agonizing uncertainty about what their proper parental role should be.[14] Often a single meeting with the ward personnel and/or mother can clarify the issues and ease tension.

If the therapist is discussing visiting, the following observations may be helpful. Most professionals would encourage the mother of a young child to stay in the hospital as much as is reasonably possible. Various studies of children in the hospital indicate that the child under five years is most at risk to suffer in the mother's absence.[6, 11]

One study[14] focused on whether the young child's response to hospitalization was purely anxiety about separation from the mother or whether it was in fact due to the lack of adequate substitute mother care while in the hospital. Groups of children fourteen to thirty-six months old were selected for study as an age especially vulnerable to separation anxiety. The group having either a mother present *or a mother substitute* did reasonably well in the hospital. They played more, cried less, interacted better with others than a comparison group of toddlers whose mothers were absent. The mother substitute did not "replace" the mother; the children clearly preferred their mother when she visited. This study demonstrated that a great deal of the distress observed in young children in hospitals can be related to the pattern of institutional care. There was, however, no post-hospital follow up to this study.

Fortunately, the concept of "bed rest" has been largely abandoned, and in most situations, the child is allowed to regulate his own activity. This in fact has a sound practical basis. One study[3] quantitatively measured the activity of hospitalized children placed on complete bed rest as compared with children granted full activity. It turned out that the amount of activity of both groups was equal.

Just as children at home manipulate to get something they want, so do they behave the same way in the hospital. The therapist should be aware of these activities. Examples of some of the more common behaviors are the following: a child who is placed on fluid restrictions frequently gets the urge to clean his teeth often or is suddenly eager to water the flowers. Children who are placed on diet restrictions have to be watched so that they do not eat food from other children's trays. Mischievous teenage diabetics may switch urine with one another. Taking medications orally is a problem for some children under seven to eight years. Acquiring the knack of swallowing pills—often huge numbers—is sometimes required in the hospital and is strongly resisted by some children. Nurses occasionally find a child who takes up to two hours to swallow a few pills. On the other hand, if the child is engaged in an activity such as school or something else he enjoys, the nurses find that the amount of time it takes to swallow medications is greatly reduced. Evidently there is a considerable motivational faction involved. Other children, such as the asthmatics, long familiar with IV apparatus, fiddle with the IV clamp. When they are tired of being confined by an IV, or when they want the nurse's attention, they either shut it off or turn it on full blast.

Sometimes manipulative ward behavior goes even further. One twelve-year-old boy was hospitalized in the Children's Hospital with a rejection episode following kidney transplantation. He delighted in going to the main hospital laboratory to find out his latest creatinine level before the lab slips were sent back to the ward. The fact that he could tell the pediatric resident his latest blood test before the resident saw the lab slip himself did little to improve their relationship. One year later, in another of his many hospitalizations, this same youngster stored up some of his medication and then deliberately took an overdose in an attempt at suicide. As one might anticipate, this boy presented many problems, both physical and emotional. Another example of extreme manipulative behavior was provided by an eight-year-old girl who postsurgery literally would not eat unless the ward staff stayed with her. Her excessive demands for attention caused many difficulties in routine hospital care. For example, if the nurses wanted an accurate intake-output chart they had to accompany her to the bathroom each time she went. This young girl was a deserted and deprived child. She had little ego strength on which to draw to help her adapt to hospitalization, and she needed more emotional support than the hospital environment is normally able to make available.

Special Stresses on Special Units

There are some special units within the pediatric hospital which must deal with extraordinary problems and stresses. Among others, these are the modern intensive care unit[5] for babies and children who are critically ill. Patients in these units require a high nurse/patient ratio, restricted visiting, and an environment which includes all kinds of tubes, apparatus, and equipment such as oxygen, heart monitors, and so forth. The child who lapses into a coma or unconsciousness and wakes up in an intensive care unit finds himself in very strange surroundings indeed. The family too finds the intensive care unit a frightening place, and their anxiety does not reassure a sick and frightened youngster. The nurses and doctors who work on such units day after are always dealing with people in crisis. Often enough they find the family's emotional reactions so draining that in sheer self-defense they tend to slight the humanitarian requirements of medicine and to concentrate on the technical aspects of care. Once the children are transferred to the general wards of the hospital, they tend not to discuss their feelings about what it was like in intensive care. The therapist who works with such a hospitalized child may have to do considerable therapeueic work with the child before he can tap the feelings produced in these unusual settings.

Isolation is another situation which almost invariably causes children a great deal of stress. Whether the child is put in isolation because of the infectious nature of his disease, or isolation is prescribed because of the vulnerability of the child to possible infection from others, the net result for the child is not only medical isolation but nearly complete social isolation as well. The child is in a room alone without a roommate, and every visit by hospital staff or family requires special gown and mask. The latter procedures drastically cut down the number of visits by hospital personnel. In addition, the child is denied access to the hospital corridor, the unofficial play area and living room of the pediatric patient. When their parents are able to spend a great deal of time with them, such children gain some relief from the loneliness and sensory deprivation of isolation. For the young children, especially those who do not have their parents with them almost constantly, a massive regression in their behavior often sets in within a few days or a weeks of isolation. In such circumstances, it is not unusual to find a child who previously showed no evidence of emotional disturbance becoming apathetic, withdrawing, beginning to soil, and sometimes even smearing feces. Fortunately, this regressed condition responds fairly rapidly to removal from isolation status. Hence, the therapist must be aware of the implications for a child of any extended period of isolation. It will influence both immediate behavior as well as the problems that may need to be worked through later in psychotherapy.

A situation fraught with considerable distress both for child and adult patients is the burn unit. If a separate unit does not exist, similar difficulties can be observed among burned children on the general hospital wards. So common is this observation that clinicians have wondered if emotionally disturbed children tend to get burned, or if severe burns tend to produce disturbed children. Woodward's[20] follow-up study tends to favor the latter explanation. In her study of several burned children (where the burn covered 10 percent or more of the body surface), the mothers reported evidence of emotional disturbance in 81 percent of their children as compared to 7 to 14 percent in two control groups of children without burns.

The high incidence of emotional disturbance following severe burns suggests that it would be useful to review briefly the more common experiences of the burned child in the hospital. On the whole, burned children tend to regress and be more difficult to care for than any other group of hospitalized children. One of the greatest stresses the burned child endures is the once- or twice-daily changing of dressings. Removing a dressing from a burned area is an exquisitely painful procedure. The anticipation of pain and then the pain itself arouse considerable anxiety. The bathing of a burned child typically causes intense, rapid, and extreme changes in affect.[8] During dressing changes, in addition to the pain itself, there is at least one other source of anxiety; the child has the opportunity to witness the extent of the damage to his body. Depending on the extent of the burn, holding and cuddling the child may be impossible. In order to emphasize the extent of pain suffered by a burned child, Nover[17] reported a case of a child whose burn was in the lower part of his body, which was anesthetic from a spinal cord anomaly at birth. This child tolerated hospitalization easily and, unlike other burned children, did not become irritable, depressed, hostile, or overtly aggressive toward the medical staff. The staff reaction remained positive toward this child in contrast to the majority of burned children whose negativism in turn prompts negativism by the staff.

In addition to the problems of dressing changes, burn cases need to be protected from infection, a fact which may require isolation with all the emotional implications of that regime. Hence it is understandable that with burned children, to some extent, regression in behavior tends to be the rule.

Dynamically, guilt is a common factor in the lives of many families of burned children. The guilt is frequently related to the accident, and both child and parents may feel varying degrees of responsibility for the injuries. The guilt may have some basis in reality. However, the degree of guilt felt by both child and parents seems to relate as much to their personalities as to the circumstances of the accident.

The following clinical vignette illustrates some of the common problems seen in burned children.

EMOTIONAL PROBLEMS WITH A BURNED CHILD

Jeff, an eleven-year-old boy had been in the burn unit at the University of Michigan Medical Center for treatment of burns of both legs. After two months, he was referred for psychiatric evaluation because of "regressive behavior." The "regressive behavior" was described as negative, protesting attitude toward all treatment procedures, frequent crying and whining, an excessive attachment to his mother, vomiting after meals, and occasional albeit infrequent incontinence of his bowels. In the interview with the mother, she described Jeff as a hard-working boy, helpful, and kind. He was very close to his younger brother and to her. Prior to his burn, mother did not feel she had had any difficulties with Jeff although he always tended to be stubborn and strong-willed, and liked to be in control of situations. She said that since his burns, he had become increasingly more possessive of her, worried about her, and repeatedly asked if everything is all right at home. He insisted on some favorite food from home, stating that he was tired of hospital food and wanted to see his brother and his dog in the hospital. In spite of her reassurance, he seemed to be preoccupied with fears that something hazardous would happen at home. He also worried a lot about his future, felt that he would never get out of the hospital and would probably never be able to walk. He did not like the fact that the classmates of his brother sent him "get well" cards, stating that his burns are his own problem and nobody should broadcast them.

In two psychiatric contacts with Jeff (one when he was in his bed and the other when he was in the "tub"), he came across as an angry boy who was sarcastic, made a mockery of all sympathetic remarks, and tended to justify his behavior, saying that the other adult patients are much worse than he was. He also insisted on being in control of the pain. For example, he tended to give directions on how his blood was to be drawn and how the dressings were to be removed. Some of his dressings he removed himself. One of the hardest things for Jeff to do was to talk about his home and family. He repeatedly avoided this topic, and would insist that he wanted to go back to sleep. When pressured into talking, he made angry remarks with tears in his eyes, saying that nobody could take his mom away from him. He also said repeatedly that he hated being in the hospital and would like to go home immediately, that the hospital had not helped him so far, and that his pain was worse now, more so than before.

Jeff responded well to brief psychotherapy (see chapter 4). In addition to seeing Jeff, the psychiatrist saw the ward personnel in a couple of group meetings. These facilitated their understanding of Jeff and helped them to put together a treatment approach which considered the psychological as well as the medical needs of this eleven-year-old boy. Within a week, Jeff stopped having bowel incontinence, reacted more positively to the ward staff, and was transferred off the burn unit to the regular pediatric floor where more age-appropriate companions were available.

Psychotherapy on the Hospital Ward

The initial contact with the patient is very much facilitated if the physician in charge discusses the reasons for referral to a psychotherapist. This is particularly important for the patient in a general medical hospital who does not have a demonstrable organic disease. In this situation, the parents are oriented toward physical illness and are frequently reluctant to accept a psychological explanation for their child's symptoms. A medical workup with appropriate tests should be followed by a general physician's explanation of what was done and the meaning of the results. This helps pave the way for psychiatric referral. For example, both the child with recurrent stomach pains and his parents need to have the results of examinations and tests explained before the family is able to consider psychiatric referral. Interestingly, where there is chronic organic disease, for example, diabetes, ulcerative colitis, or asthma, children and families tend to accept referral for psychiatric consultation more readily. Clinically, it would appear that an inverse proportion exists between a family's readiness to accept referral to psychiatry and the degree of psychopathology. Families who are intact, stable, and interested in their children seem to welcome psychiatric referral, while those families with the most psychopathology are sometimes the most difficult to refer for psychological help.

It is possible to describe some of the more general factors which influence the referral of a child or adolescent for psychiatric consultation from a medical or pediatric floor.[2] Psychiatric consultants who work in medical hospitals comment frequently on how many patients in need of psychiatric help are not referred. Age appears to be an important factor; adolescents are the group most frequently referred, followed by the school-age child. On the other hand, the child under five is the age group least frequently referred. The length of a hospitalization influences referral; a longer stay is more likely to result in a psychiatric referral than

a short hospital stay. The longer hospital stay of the referred children appears to be due to a variety of factors. These include the presence of chronic medical illness and the ambiguity in the medical diagnoses. Other possible elements are that a longer hospitalization also lets the staff interact more with the children and/or gives the staff more time to send in a referral slip. Finally, children can and do develop symptoms arising from their hospitalization, and these children would then fall into the long hospitalization group as well. Repeated hospitalizations also tend to increase the chances of psychiatric referral.

Psychiatric evaluation and therapy with the hospitalized child demand a certain flexibility on the part of the therapist. First of all, the interview site is more likely to be the child's room in the hospital rather than anyone's office or playroom. Furthermore, the physical activity of the child may be compromised by intravenous apparatus, various tubes, casts, and so forth, and by the apathy accompanying the illness itself. Intrusions from ward nurses, clerks, janitorial staff, and other hospital personnel are routine. Nonetheless, if the child is able to talk and, perhaps, draw and play as well, a very satisfactory interview can usually be achieved. Despite the inconveniences of doing psychotherapy on a medical ward, it is often an anxious time in the child or adolescent's life and hence a time of intense need. Indeed, the hospitalization may constitute a mini or major crisis in the life of that child and/or family. It can, therefore, be a most appropriate time for psychotherapeutic intervention. As in any other setting, the distinction between psychological evaluation and psychotherapy is more in the mind of the therapist than in the mind of the patient. For many patients, evaluation is therapy, and for the physician, therapy may contain elements of evaluation until the last visit.

Obviously, at some point during the initial interviews a pragmatic decision has to be made as to whether or not the patient has a psychological problem, and if he does, whether that problem is amenable to some type of treatment. The therapist may decide on short-term treatment while the patient is still in a medical hospital. That plan, then, needs to be discussed at the very least with the referring physician, the patient, and the parents. If the patient's behavior troubles the ward staff, a meeting with the staff may well bring about a better relationship between them. An issue which is sometimes left unclear is whether the therapist will continue seeing the patient after he is discharged from the hospital. As in any other treatment situation, if not clarified at the outset, confusion over the realistic limits to the patient-therapist relationship can be harmful in the long run. It can be particularly destructive and frustrating because discharges from a general hospital medical ward are sometimes made precipitiously. Medical emergencies may arise when there is a shortage of beds, and suddenly the recovering patient is out without a warning. Unless a commitment is secured in advance to keep the patient until the psychiatrist has finished his work, the value of psychological evaluation and therapy may be given a rather low priority by the harried medical administrator.

In some respects, therapy with the medically hospitalized child resembles work with the psychiatrically hospitalized child. In both instances the nurses' observations of the child's behavior in a variety of situations are extremely useful. Unlike many psychiatric hospitals, however, the pediatric nurses often do not chart this kind of information adequately. The therapist is well advised to spend a few minutes chatting with the hospital staff charged with care of the child. This may include the nurses, schoolteachers, physical therapists, and so forth. Moreover, the pediatrician or family doctor who originally hospitalized the patient may have had extensive experience with the family for a long period of time. His more significant impressions are rarely written in the patient's chart. The current physicians may know of unusual reactions of the child and/or family during the stress of the present hospitalization. Such data can be valuable for the therapist and again are rarely written in the patient's chart. Obviously, a prior ongoing working relationship with the hospital personnel is valuable.

In a medical setting, the therapist should conform to the prevailing rules and write a note in the patient's chart about each visit. Among other reasons for doing this, the physician in charge of the patient prefers to learn of the psychiatrist's visits from the chart rather than from the patient. In addition, if other medical personnel are aware of the psychiatrist's involvement in the case, they can seek him out and pass on information.

The actual techniques which can be used in the psychotherapy of the hospitalized child are as varied as those for therapy in general. The technique used in any particular case depends to some extent on the preference of the therapist, the acceptability to the patient and family, and any physical limitations of the child or adolescent.

If information gathering is the primary objective, the classic one-to-one approach to the child and parents probably yields the greatest amount of information in the least amount of time. Seeing the child individually and the parents individually may be practical if the family lives at some distance from the hospital and maximum data are needed. If the patient is an early adolescent whose sexual feelings and desires for autonomy are too anxiety-laden to share with anyone but the therapist, it may be necessary to have separate therapists for the adolescent and the parents. During psychotherapy, many familiar issues will arise. However, an issue of particular importance to the hospitalized child may be the cause of his illness. Children form theories about what happened to them, and why. These are not the scientific explanation of physicians. Instead, they are idiosyncratic, emotionally charged personal explanations of "how it happened." Such beliefs may be defensive in nature, they may give clues to other emotional problems, or they may in fact simply represent reality as the child sees it.

The following clinical vignette illustrates how a nine-year-old girl, Kim, struggled with the explanation of the illness of her seven-year-old sister, Tracy.

LEUKEMIA: EXTRAVAGANT FANTASIES OF THE FAMILY

Tracy had suffered from leukemia for three years and was in remission at the time of this conversation with her sister. When Kim was asked how Tracy got sick, she immediately explained that Tracy often walked around the block with their brother, Tom. On one of their walks, Tracy saw a "red thing." She then explained to me that the Smiths have a cherry tree and Tracy thought that the red thing was a cherry. She ate it and she started getting sick a few days afterward. When their parents wondered why Tracy kept getting sick, Tracy told them she ate that thing. Then the mother explained that it was not a cherry but rather "a little poison red thing" and Dr. B said that Tracy would have to go into the hospital for a few days. Then when Tracy was in the hospital she had to take the medicine and she got "real, real sick" Kim explained that Tracy didn't like the medicine because she thought that if she took it she would get sick. Here Kim interjected an example about an occasion when she herself had to take some medicine and was afraid that it would make her sick. However, she spontaneously commented that she did not get sick. Kim struggled with the notion about whether or not the medicine was to blame, thinking on the one hand that it was, and on the other hand implicitly recognizing that really it wasn't. She went on to tell how Tracy was moved to another hospital where they gave her medicine, pills, shots, and checked her eyes and heart.

Tracy's doctors had initially questioned the possibility of an aplastic anemia on a toxic basis, hence the origins of the little red berry theory. In some ways, Kim's response paralleled that of her father, who when asked the same question about causation immediately responded that the family doctor wondered if Tracy ate something like fertilizer or insecticide. When the father was directly asked if he felt her illness might be caused by something she ingested he replied, "I don't think so anymore—maybe it's just a virus" but that he had "just quit thinking about it—because it's done and can't be fixed or changed." In contrast, the mother wondered if Tracy's illness was in fact something she was born with and went on to pour out her guilt because she had wanted to get rid of the pregnancy and perhaps God was repaying her for having a child she didn't want.

One can see in the preceding clinical example how the child's and family's thoughts about causation of illness reflected fragments of medical reality but tended to follow a family theme. There were, of course, individual and independent variations depending on the family member.

As compared to the well child, another issue in the psychotherapy of the hospitalized child is more likely to be of frequent and pressing concern. This involves changes in body image. Kaufman[10] wrote about the changes in body image that adolescents experienced as a result of illness. He noted that these changes were idiosyncratic and tended to be described as vivid visual pictures portraying various kinds of damage. As would be expected, these images of body functioning were not logical or anatomical; instead they followed primitive, prelogical modes of thinking. At times, the adolescent's ideas about the causation of his illness intermixed with the mental representation of the damaged body image. Zamorski and associates[21] carried out a psychological investigation of the relationship between body image and amputation in children. The authors felt that there was a correlation between the integrity of body image and family stabililty, that is, young amputees from intact, stable homes were more likely to develop an integrated body image than children from disorganized, chaotic homes.

Behavior therapy techniques are applicable in a pediatric setting. However, any system of positive and negative reinforcement must be kept very simple. The need for simplicity arises from the fact that the majority of pediatric hospitals are staffed by a variety of people with highly diverse backgrounds who are not used to communicating with each other. Generally speaking, the staff is not as alert to manipulation by the patient as they would be in a psychiatric setting. Yet all these people may be involved with any one patient.

A good example of the use of behavior modification is the methodology developed for achieving weight gain in cases of anorexia nervosa.[1] In fact, a variety of behavior modification schemes have been suggested for this condition. The one that seems to work the best in a pediatric hospital, however, is in fact the simplest one. The stipulation is laid down that only if the patient has gained one-half pound or more weight in the morning is she allowed out of bed. Failure to gain one-half pound means confinement to bed for the day without bathroom privileges.

In anorexia nervosa or other psychosomatic problems, it is difficult to assess whether psychotherapy should be used alone or should be combined with a behavior modifiication program. Specialized therapists, (behavior modification practitioners, family therapists, and so forth) tend to advocate their own therapeutic approach. Usually results are reported without comparison or control groups of patients who have been treated with a different therapy. For example, Minuchin and his coworkers[16] prefer family therapy for children with psychosomatic illness. Minuchin feels that families of such children can be characterized by enmeshment, overprotectiveness, rigidity, and lack of conflict resolution. Under these conditions, in any given family, illness can become a mode of communication. Whether these characteristics are limited to families with children who have psychosomatic disorders or are simply characteristic of dysfunctional families in general is not known. However, clinically, Minuchin and coworkers have found family therapy a rational way to approach the superlabile diabetic, the steroid resistant asthmatic, and so forth. They believe they can obtain dramatic improvements in the psychosomatic picture. In a similar fashion, family therapists have been successful in the treatment of anorexia nervosa.[12]

Preventive Psychotherapy with the Hospitalized Child

Some attempts have been made to try group psychotherapy as a preventive measure with a routine group of hospitalized children, that is, children who ordinarily would not be referred for psychotherapy. Rie and associates[18] contrasted two types of intervention with a population of medically hospitalized children. He employed an educational approach and a psychotherapeutic approach. His sample was drawn from newly admitted rheumatic fever patients whose mean age was ten years. The educational group was headed by a pediatrician and the psychotherapeutic group by a child psychiatrist. Both groups met three times for thirty-five to forty-five minutes. In the tutorial meetings, the children were given facts about their illness, including its onset, treatment, and follow-up care. In the psychotherapy meetings, the children explored a variety of concerns and fantasies that arose about being hospitalized and ill. At times, the psychotherapy tended to be supportive and at times it was educational. In any case, however, it was never specifically educational about rheumatic fever. The outcome of this study was as follows: After three weeks the tutorial group showed a reduction of some components of anxiety. The psychotherapy group did not. At a one-to two-year follow up, the children were tested again. At this point, the anxiety reduction was no longer found. At this same follow up, however, the psychotherapy group tended to view their medical illness more realistically and with greater consistency and clarity than the educational group. Thus, the long-term result seemed to be that the psychotherapeutic group "learned" better than did the didactic group and could cope with their illness more realistically over a long period of time. It is of particular interest that this result persisted after a relatively brief intervention in the initial stages of hospitalization.

Another story of the effectiveness of brief psychiatric intervention on the pediatric medical ward was carried out by Minde and Maler.[15] In this study, a child psychiatrist saw the children individually for two visits of thirty to thirty-five minutes. From the author's description, this contact was fairly didactic (psychiatrists discussed with each of the children their particular illnesses). They explained the course, possible duration, types of investigation needed, and so forth. Instead, in this study, the psychiatrist's role appeared similar to that of the tutorial group of the previous study. Minde and Maler found that their brief psychiatric contact did decrease immediate anxiety. One month later, the mothers of both the experimental and control group described their children as essentially similar. Again, these results are remarkably similar to those of the previous study. Another intriguing but unexplained finding in Minde and Maler's study was that the children who had talked to a child psychiatrist left the hospital somewhat earlier than the control subjects.

Obviously, the whole area of preventive psychotherapy is still restricted mainly to research projects. Some hospitals have attempted to hold weekly or biweekly group meetings with the children and the nurses, with a social worker or child psychiatrist occasionally taking part. The purpose of such meetings is to reduce the anxieties of the children about hospitalization. In the future, such group meetings may well become standard practice in pediatric hospital wards.

Therapy with the hospitalized child takes the therapist into the medical arena—frightening for some, exciting for others, for a few, even reassuring. It is a world where psyche and soma are inevitably entwined in ways that are at times still mysterious and unfathomable—but always fascinating.

REFERENCES

1. AGRAS, W. S., et al., "Behavior Modification of Anorexia Nervosa," *Archives of General Psychiatry*, 30:279–286, 1974.

2. AWAD, G., and POZNANSKI, E., "A Study of Psychopathology in a Pediatric Hospital," *The American Journal of Psychiatry*, 132(9):915–918, 1975.

3. BASS, H. N., and SCHULMAN, J. L., "Quantitative Assessment of Children's Activity In and Out of Bed," *American Journal of Diseases of Children*, 113:242–244, 1967.

4. BRANSLATTER, E., "The Young Child's Response to Hospitalization: Separation Anxiety or Lack of Mothering Care?" *American Journal of Public Health*, 59:92–97, 1969.

5. BRUCE, T. J. R., "Very Ill Children," *Developmental Medicine and Child Neurology*, 16(5):675–677, 1974.

6. BURLING, K A., and COLLIP, P. J., "Emotional Responses of Hospitalized Children," *Clinical Pediatrics*, 8:641–646, 1969.

7. DAVENPORT, H. T., and WERRY, J. S., "The Effect of General Anesthesia, Surgery and Hospitalization," *American Journal of Orthopsychiatry*, 40(5):806–824, 1970.

8. GOLDSTON, R., "The Burning and the Healing of Children, *Psychiatry*, 35:57–66, 1972.

9. JACOBY, N. M., "Unrestricted Visiting in a Childrens' ward," *Lancet*, 2:584–586, 1969.

10. KAUFMAN, R., "Body Image Changes in Physically Ill Teenagers," *Journal of the American Academy of Child Psychiatry*, 11(1):157–170, 1972.

11. LEE, J. S., and GREENE, N. M., "Parental Presence and Emotional State of Children Prior to Surgery," *Clinical Pediatrics*, 8(3):126–130, 1969.

12. LIEBMAN, R., MINUCHIN, S., and BAKER, L., "The Role of the Family in the Treatment of Anorexia Nervosa, *Journal of the American Academy of Child Psychiatry*, 13(2):264–274, 1974.

13. McDERMOTT, J. F., and FINCH, S., "Ulcerative Colitis in Children: Reassessment of a Dilemma, *Journal of the American Academy of Child Psychiatry*, 6(3):512–525, 1967.

14. MEADOW, S. R., "The Captive Mother," *Archives of Disabled Children*, 44:362–367, 1969.

15. MINDE, K., and MALER, L., "Psychiatric Counselling on a Pediatric Medical Ward: A Controlled Evaluation, *The Journal of Pediatrics*, 72(4):452–460, 1968.

16. MINUCHIN, S., et al., "A Conceptual Model of Psychosomatic Illness in Children," *Archives of General Psychiatry*, 32:1031–1038, 1975.

17. NOVER, R. A., "Pain and the Burned Child," *Journal of the American Academy of Child Psychiatry*, *12(3)*:499–505, 1973.

18. RIE, H., et al., "Immediate and Long-term Effects of Intervention Early in Prolonged Hospitalization," *Pediatrics*, *41(4)*:755–764, 1968.

19. SKIPPER, J. K., and LEONARD, R. C., "Children, Stress, and Hospitalization: A Field Experiment, *Journal*

of Health and Social Behavior, *9(4)*:275–287, 1968.

20. WOODWARD, J., "Emotional Disturbances of Burned Children," *British Medical Journal*, *1*:1009–1013, 1959.

21. ZAMORSKI, E., FISCHHOFF, J., and CUNEO, R., "Body Image and Amputations: A Psychological Investigation of Children," *American Journal of Orthopsychiatry*, *39(2)*: 254, 1969.

---

36 / Psychophysiological Disorders

Dane G. Prugh and Lloyd O. Eckhardt

General Considerations

The basic approach to the treatment of psychophysiological disorders should be founded upon an adequate diagnostic evaluation and the subsequent weighing of the degree of operation of somatic and psychological factors. In biologically predisposed individuals, psychophysiological disorders may be precipitated, exacerbated, or perpetuated by a variety of stressful stimuli. These triggers can be of a physical, psychological, or social nature; from whatever source derived, they act on the child to bring about a derangement of his adaptive equilibrium and the appearance of a disorder at the physiological level. Such disorders ordinarily involve those organ systems that are innervated by the autonomic or involuntary portion of the central nervous system. The symptoms of disturbed functioning at the vegetative level are regarded as having physiological rather than psychological symbolic significance. It is important to distinguish these from conversion disorders which involve those organ systems innervated by the voluntary portion of the central nervous system; overall, the symptoms tend to have symbolic rather than physiological significance. In certain disorders, some measure of overlap can occur.

Structural changes can occur in psychophysiological disorders, continuing so far that they may become irreversible, and, in some cases, life-threatening. Such disorders, thus, do not seem to represent simple physiological concomitants of emotions, as may occur in psychoneurotic disorders with accompanying anxiety, in reactive or other disorders, and in healthy responses. As Mirsky[146] and others have stressed, psychophysiological disorders have multiple etiological contributors: (1) biological predisposing factors of genetic or inborn nature, probably involving latent biochemical deviations; (2) developmental psychosocial determinants, with a limited kind of specificity; and (3) current precipitating factors of an individually stressful significance.

Although conflict situations of particular types, together with some fairly consistent psychosocial patterns, may be consistently involved in the predisposition towards and precipitation of these disorders, few controlled studies have been made. No type-specific personality profile, parent-child relationship, or family pattern has as yet emerged which can be consistently associated with individual psychophysiological disorders. Many similar psychological or psychosocial characteristics may be found in children having other disorders without psychophysiological disturbances. Psychophysiological disorders may also involve more than one organ system in sequence, with the occasional occurrence of more than one disorder simultaneously. In some disorders with heavier biological "loading," psychological factors may be implicated to a minor degree, while in others where somatic factors are less prominent, psychosocial influences may play the major role. Certain psychophysiological disorders may be associated with chronic and/or severe personality disorders of varying types, some even bordering on psychosis; others may occur in conjunction with milder personality disorders or reactive disorders. Most of the cases reported have been studied in hospital settings, where patients with more serious physical and psychosocial disorders tend to be seen. Milder cases occur in patients who show less disturbance in personality functioning; they are often encountered in pediatric ambulatory practice. Developmental considerations are also involved, as in the more global, undifferentiated responses of young infants. In some psychophysiological disorders, along with other factors, racial and ethnic (hypertension), as well as sex differences (peptic ulcer), have been described.

Mechanisms Involved in Psychophysiological Interrelationships

The physiological effect of stressful stimuli of psychological or social nature appear to be mediated by reciprocal neural interconnections between the cerebral cortex and the hypothalamus, in which lie controls for the autonomic and endocrine systems ("neuroendocrine system"). The limbic cortex or "visceral brain" plays an important role in the integration and regulation of external and internal perceptions and in the experiencing of emotions, while the ascending reticular activating system seems to be significantly involved as an alerting center (and in other ways). The posterior pituitary is apparently influenced by the hypothalamus, largely through nervous interconnections, while the influence of the hypothalamus upon the anterior pituitary is mediated through neurohumoral mechanisms.

Autonomic interrelationships and the effects of the release of epinephrine from the adrenal are reasonably well understood, although work remains to be done. Work on the effects of psychosocial stimuli upon the trophic hormones of the anterior pituitary and upon posterior pituitary functions, as well as upon the pituitary-adrenal cortical axis, is more recent, and much more remains to be learned. Stimulation of the anterior part of the hypothalamus, with its rich interconnections, appears to result in the "defense alarm reaction," which involves widespread neuroendocrine responses. A highly developed system of psychological coping devices, including defense mechanisms, is characteristic of man. As a result of their functioning, higher centers can apparently inhibit as well as initiate the defense alarm response.

Therapeutic Approach

In dealing with potentially serious and life-threatening disorders, such as ulcerative colitis, or diabetes, psychotherapeutic measures should never be undertaken without concomitant medical treatment and follow up. In some more mildly disturbed children, the pediatrician may use a supportive psychotherapeutic approach with the child and parent, using child psychiatric consultation initially and subsequently, as needed. If the patient is hospitalized, seeing him for brief periods at the beginning and/or the end of each day may be more effective than an hour or two a week. This approach encourages the development of an initially dependent relationship upon the physician, that may call for gradual weaning later on.

If the psychophysiological disorder continues, it becomes a chronic illness; such a condition has a profound effect upon the child's growth and personality development, and upon the family as well. Again, the pediatrician sees some children and families in ambulatory practice who are able to cope surprisingly well with these disorders. Long-term follow up is thus indicated for children with chronic psychophysiological disorders, such as ulcerative colitis, bronchial asthma, and juveniile diabetes mellitus. Treatment must be provided for later exacerbations which may be precipitated by developmental stresses or psychosocial conflicts.

The Use of Psychotherapy

For children who have more serious psychological disturbances, intensive psychotherapy with the child and his parents by a child psychiatrist or other mental health professional may be required. This should take place concurrent with medical treatment. In treating most disorders of this type, especially ulcerative colitis and asthma, a more supportive psychological approach should be undertaken at the beginning, in order to avoid stirring up intense feelings which may lead to exacerbations or serious medical complications. Later, a more intensive and insight-promoting approach may be employed, including psychoanalysis in some cases.[206] In such disorders as asthma and other allergic problems, ulcerative colitis, anorexia nervosa, migraine, and skin disorders, formal psychotherapy accompanied by the appropriate medical measures have been reported to be effective. The effects of psychotherapy in other disorders, such as peptic ulcer, appear to be variable. In hypertension, rheumatoid arthritis, and hyperthyroidism, the results are more difficult to evaluate.[27] However, as part of a comprehensive therapeutic approach to all such disorders, a supportive psychotherapeutic approach with children and parents should be considered. The use of different modalities of psychotherapy—individual, family, or group—will be discussed in relation to the different disorders. Selective application of behavior therapy, biofeedback, and other specific treatment modalities will also be reviewed.

Collaboration and Coordination in the Approach to Treatment

The preceding considerations all call for the implementation of certain basic principles in the care of children with psychophysiological disorders. *Continuity* in the relationship between the child and his parents and a single physician, nurse, or other professional is vital; *communication* among such professionals to bring about true and respectful *collaboration* among disciplines and *consistency* in management is of great importance; *consultation* between the child psychiatrist, psychologist, social workers, and the medical and surgical specialists must be freely available and appropriately employed; and *coordination* of all such activities must be provided if a unified plan of therapy is to be realized, with an appropriate balance of physical, psychological, and social measures.

In many cases, the pediatrician is best equipped to act as the coordinator, using the team approach to the management and treatment of children with these disorders. This is easier to accomplish in the hospital, where professionals and paraprofessionals (such as foster grandparents or other parent substitutes) are freely available, and where a weekly or semiweekly *ward management conference* can achieve the implementation of the principles mentioned. The pediatrician in private practice, however, can also accomplish this in large measure with the help of social workers, nurses, health associates, and other members of the newly evolving health team. Psychiatric, psychological, and other specialty consultants can be used when needed.

In some instances, the child with a psychophysiological disorder may be so disturbed that psychiatric hospitalization is required. Under these circumstances, the psychiatrist typically acts as the coordinator, drawing upon the contributions of the pediatrician and other consultants for the medical or surgical aspects of the treatment.

In all such efforts, close and cooperative contact with the parents should be maintained in the context of a therapeutic alliance with the professional personnel involved. Competition for the exclusive care of the patient by any one service or among the professionals involved must be avoided. This will permit the patient to be dealt with as a human being and as a member of a family in need of help.

Clinical Findings

The following list of disorders is divided by organ systems, following the classification offered in 1966 by the Group for the Advancement of Psychiatry.[31]

PSYCHOPHYSIOLOGICAL SKIN DISORDERS

Atopic eczema is a disorder which may be seen as an infantile condition and also in a later, more chronic form.[12] It usually occurs in the children of families with an allergic diathesis.[62, 100] Children affected by the chronic form are generally rigid, tense, and sometimes compulsive. They have a tendency to express strong emotions, particularly resentment of father or mother. The resented parent is frequently overcontrolling and may have offered inadequate contact comforts in infancy.[147] Exacerbations during adolescence are usually caused by increased conflicts over independence and sexuality. Many become overly inhibited individuals with strong underlying narcissistic bodily concerns accompanied by unconsciously exhibitionistic trends (apparently denied by the disfiguring skin lesions which arouse disgust in other persons). They receive a goodly albeit unconscious measure of pleasure, akin to the sexual, as well as a great deal of gratification of self-punitive needs, from their persistent and self-injurious scratching.[233]

In *psoriasis*, a different biological predisposing factor must be involved; nonetheless, somewhat similar relationships between stressful life events and the severity of the condition have been demonstrated.[74, 233]

Neurodermatitis, without an allergic component, often begins with pruritis, arising in connection with emotional conflicts.[28, 132] Scratching makes the lesions worse. These disorders can be helped by intensive psychotherapy in conjunction with dermatological measures.

Recurrent *urticaria* appears to be closely related to dermatographia. The skin reactivity is often constitutionally derived and is frequently associated with positive scratch tests.[86] The clinical manifestations may be brought out by emotionally traumatic experiences[75] or intensified by conflicts over sexuality and independence.[233] Patients are often shy and easily embarrassed, with ready blushing. They are frequently passive, immature, withdrawn, or inhibited children, with feelings of inadequacy, unconscious exhibitionistic trends, and overdependence on the mother. In younger children, urticaria may be brought on by overexertion or overexcitement.

Angioneurotic edema may be seen in anxious infants or young children.[151] A supportive psychotherapeutic approach based on helping the parents and child with their underlying conflicts is often effective in the treatment of these conditions. Tranquilizers have been used, but the intensity and danger of side effects renders them of dubious value.

Alopecia areata can occur in relation to emotionally traumatic events, including actual or symbolic losses,[137] as may *alopecia totalis*.[105] Psychotherapy may be helpful in alopecia areata; it is not often beneficial in alopecia totalis, however, and cosmetic measures are important.

Acne, if severe, may be deeply troubling to adolescents and may continue into early adult life. Individuals who exhibit marked chronic acne are often shy and inhibited. They experience conflicts about sexuality, and they are concerned about growing up.[162] Stressful life events can result in exacerbations of their acne; it is possible that increased production of skin-surface free fatty acids, with secondary infection, may play a role.[110] The adolescent's oppositional behavior or negative identity may lead him to resist appropriate skin care; this combined with the biological factors can worsen the condition. Psychotherapy with dermatological measures is most helpful.

In addition to its basic functions such as protection and secretion, the skin is also an organ of emotional expression. This is evident in such phenomena as flushing, sweating, blushing, pallor, and so forth. As such, it receives central representation as a part of the body image. Certain conversion phenomena may thus somehow take place in the skin just as they do in the somatosensory apparatus;[194] this is true even though no voluntary innervation is involved. Hypnotic suggestion has long been known to produce changes in the skin, such as blisters from a suggested "burn." Some cases of dermatitis thus appear to involve conversion mechanisms,[7] admixed at times with psychophysiologic components; this may also help to explain the effects of suggestion on certain types of warts,[233] such as verruca vulgaris (where a virus is known to be involved in the etiology).

PSYCHOPHYSIOLOGICAL MUSCULOSKELETAL DISORDERS

Juvenile Rheumatoid Arthritis. Children with juvenile rheumatoid arthritis often exhibit conflicts over the handling of aggression and dependence; intense closeness to and dependence upon the mother are characteristically present.[17, 30] The arthritis itself may represent a type of autoimmune response, and psychophysiologic interrelationships are as yet unclear.[141] Exacerbations of this disorder may be clinically related to shifts in the family's interpersonal balance.[125] Such a shift often involves situations in which the child fears loss of a key relationship and, at the same time, experiences angry feelings that he is afraid to express. Muscle tension, related to inner conflicts, may help to intensify the inflammation around the joints involved. Psychotherapeutic measures designed to help the child deal with these feelings and to help the parents understand the child's conflicts, as well as their own, may add to the effectiveness of medical treatment.

"Tension" Headaches. These headaches involve a tightening of the scalp and neck muscles. They occur in tense, often compulsive individuals in association with emotional conflicts.[64, 236] Psychotherapeutic intervention can be most effective.[77] New techniques in the field of biofeedback have been symptomatically helpful with adults.[22]

PSYCHOPHYSIOLOGICAL RESPIRATORY DISORDERS

This category includes certain cases of bronchial asthma, allergic rhinitis, and chronic sinusitis. It does not encompass breathholding spells, which begin with a voluntary action. Hyperventilation syndromes and sighing respirations usually involve conversion mechanisms initially.[50]

Bronchial asthma is seen twice as frequently in boys as in girls. In families with an allergic diathesis, attacks may be triggered in children by fears of separation from the parent, open conflict between child and parent, marital battles, and other conflictual situations.[123, 160] Involuntary psychophysiological mechanisms may involve conditioned vagal responses producing reflex broncho-constriction and increased bronchial mucous; these overlap with symbolic or voluntary components in triggering off attacks. These trigger mechanisms may combine and vary with the intensity of the allergic stimuli.

During an asthma attack, the parent may fear that the child will die from suffocation. This frequently results in overanxious and overprotective parental behavior, leading in turn to overdependent child behavior. Certain parents will show resentment or ambivalence toward the child, who may then feel rejected. The child may respond to such parental feelings with denial of his illness or with oppositional or manipulative behavior. Struggles for control can develop, with the child manipulating the parent by hyperventilating and triggering off of an involuntary attack of asthma.

In a study by Block and her colleagues,[16] children scoring low on a scale of allergic potential (APS) showed greater psychopathology, with more conflict in family and parent-child relationships, than did those with higher allergic potential. Differences between "rapidly remitting" and "steroid-dependent" groups of children have been demonstrated by Purcell.[173]

For the less seriously disturbed children, the primary physician can offer supportive psychotherapy along with appropriate medical measures. The major psychological issues to be dealt with are separation anxiety, and guilt and anger toward the parents. Psychological support must be offered to the parents, especially the mother, to help them with their feelings of guilt, resentment, and inadequacy in aiding their child. Intensive psychotherapy for the child and parents may be necessary.[160, 205] This is most effective if serious structural change has not occurred. Hypnosis has helped certain patients to abort attacks and to realize that they have some control over the onset, as well as the severity of an attack. Behavior modification programs have also seemed helpful.[148] Group therapy for parents of asthmatic children has been effective in reducing parental guilt and anxiety. Self-care clubs for children offer opportunities for ventilation and group support.[188]

Long-term hospitalization or residential placement should be reserved only for children with severe and protracted asthma.[188] The change in the social milieu afforded by such placement accompanied by related medical and psychological approaches can help immunize the child against future family conflicts when he returns home.[107] Parental visiting and work with the family, even through an agency in their home town, can help bring about family change.[143] "Parentectomy" alone may make some very dependent children worse. Recreational group programs in summer camps offer another alternative; they have been useful when combined with individual support for the child and family.

The dangers of overmedication, the possibility of steroid side effects, including depression and toxic psychosis, and the possibility of psychological dependence on nebulizers and steroids are all important considerations in the medical management of this disorder.[218] Incipient changes in body image and growth lag secondary to prolonged steroid use must also be considered.

Allergic Rhinitis. Among adolescents and adults in settings of increased emotional conflict, allergic rhinitis in ragweed-sensitive subjects has been shown by Holmes and his colleagues[94] and others[175] to undergo exacerbation. Supportive psychotherapeutic measures may make medical measures more effective in reducing nasal hyperemia, hypersecretion, and other symptoms.

PSYCHOPHYSIOLOGICAL CARDIOVASCULAR DISORDERS

Some children show intense autonomic responses to emotional conflicts or stressful situations, which may trigger off attacks of *paroxysmal supraventricular tachycardia*, followed by syncopal attacks,[54, 181] as well as other arrhythmias.[174] Supportive psychotherapy may be of value in reducing such conflicts and, with appropriate medical treatment, may help to prevent such attacks. Children with *essential hypertension* have not been extensively studied from a psychophysiological base. It is now recognized, however, that the disorder does occur fairly often in childhood and adolescence.[133] Adults with this disorder have shown significant conflicts in dealing with feelings of anger and in managing conflicts over dependence.[154, 235]

Studies have revealed that in both normotensive and hypertensive subjects, discussion of conflictual topics is accompanied by rises in blood pressure.[127] Along with this, increased catecholamines and peripheral resistance, as well as renal artery constriction, are present.[158, 197] Hypertensives, however, show a much more intense and prolonged response. In patients with benign hypertension, an intensification of conflicts has been demonstrated to precipitate malignant hypertension, with encephalopathy and other changes.[176] Psychophysiologic responses to chronic emotional conflict are presumed, though not as yet proven, to lead to structural changes in the kidney and vascular bed, although cholesterol and other factors are also involved. The relationship of such responses to the renin-angiotensin-aldosterone system is not yet clear.[226]

Since parental hypertension is significantly more common in families of hypertensive children, a biological predisposition to the development of hypertension is probably involved.[176] Some infants show hyperresponsivity continuing into adolescence to cold pressor tests. Young adults who later develop hypertension show a premorbid tendency to marked fluctuation in blood pressure. Ethnic differences in heart rate and blood pressure exist,[85, 191] although experiential factors may play a role in these.

Supportive psychotherapeutic measures should be combined with medical treatment; hopefully, such an approach in childhood may prevent serious hypertension and complications of hypertensive disease in adult life. Training in yoga exercises[37] and transcendental meditation has been shown by physiologic monitoring to be effective in control of heart rate and blood pressure. Biofeedback also has promise in helping to control hypertension.[198]

Children with chronic or recurrent *orthostatic hypotension* appear to be tense, anxious, and emotionally restricted. Constitutionally labile autonomic responses also appear to be involved in the hypotensive response. A supportive psychotherapeutic approach combined with parent counseling can be helpful. At times, referral for intensive psychotherapy may be necessary.

Similar autonomic mechanisms seem to be active in children or adolescents with *vasodepressor syncope*.[46] This involves sudden relaxation of the visceral nervous system with associated bradycardia and fall in blood pressure. Such attacks may be brought on by a sudden fright while standing or sitting, by pain from a venipuncture, or by anticipation of pain from other sources. Total loss of consciousness does not occur, but dizziness, weakness, or fainting may appear. Children who frequently show this response are usually anxious and somewhat inhibited. They also have a tendency to fear punishment or bodily mutilation. Psychotherapeutic measures and desensitization techniques can be affective treatment modalities. *Carotid sinus syncope*, resulting from a hyperreactive carotid sinus reflex, is uncommon in children. It is usually associated with chronic anxiety.

The preceding types of syncope must be distinguished from conversion syncope.[46] This usually, but not always, occurs in girls with hysterical personalities. In conversion syncope, no vascular changes occur, and the degree of loss of consciousness is variable. Other conversion symptoms are frequently seen. This type of syncope is of central origin; it appears to represent a symbolic and unconscious attempt to block out a conflict-producing situation. None of these types of syncope appears to bear any relationship to epilepsy, and all are fairly easily distinguished from the Stokes-Adams syndrome.[78]

Migraine begins to appear during school age. Headaches of any type are seen infrequently in preschool children, who localize pain poorly. There seems to be some relationship betwen migraine and idiopathic epilepsy.[96] Both disorders occur in families and at times in the same individual. Attacks are paroxysmal, sometimes periodic, and often hemi-cranial; they are associated with focal electroencephalogram (EEG) changes and transient reflex changes. Other reflex-localized neurological disturbances are present which relate to initial vasoconstriction and later vasodilation of the cerebral blood vessels, mediated through the autonomic nervous system.

The presence of an aura is often difficult to determine in children, and nausea annd vomiting may be more prominent symptoms than headaches. Emotional crises or overfatigue often precipitate attacks. Migraine patients tend to be overcompliant, rigid, and perfectionistic individuals with difficulties in handling feelings of anger.[139] The parents are often tense and overcontrolling, and the patient may have a special conflict-producing role in the family. Migraine headaches should be distinguished particularly from tension headaches and conversion headaches. The latter are often based on unconscious identification with the parent of the same sex who also has headaches. Medical measures and supportive psychotherapy with parental counseling can be of help. Intensive psychotherapy is often necessary.[207] Ergotamine tartrate should be used cautiously in children. The side effects, such as numbness of the extremities, may be quite distressing, and ergotamine tartrate may produce nausea and vomiting. With adults, biofeedback techniques have been symptomatically helpful,[190] as have hypnotic and other relaxation approaches.

Raynaud's disease has not been well studied in children. In adults with Raynaud's disease, stressful circumstances have been shown to be associated with a rapid fall in skin temperature; this is followed by severe pain in the cyanosed fingers.[73] If no irreversible tissue pathology has occurred, this disorder responds well to psychotherapy.[144]

Coronary heart disease and myocardial infarction, which appear to involve psychophysiologic components in adults,[29, 65, 187] occur rarely in childhood.[150]

PSYCHOPHYSIOLOGIC HEMIC AND LYMPHATIC DISORDERS

Numerous physiological concomitants of anxiety or responses to stress are encountered in relation to this system. These include variations in the blood level of leukocytes; lymphocytes; eosinophils, glutathione values; relative blood viscosity; clotting time; hematocrit; and sedimentation rates.[44, 152, 166] Ordinarily, these are reversible, and they are important principally because they present diagnostic problems. Chronic or recurrent states of leukocytosis may occur, however, as may "stress" or "benign" polycythemia[138] (this involves a decrease in plasma volume with a normal red cell volume). Evidence exists that "spontaneous" bleeding, unrelated to injury, may occur in response to emotional stress in children with hemophilia; the exact mechanisms are as yet unclear.[136] In addition, transient rash and hematuria have been reported in relation to exercise and emotion.[99]

PSYCHOPHYSIOLOGICAL GASTROINTESTINAL DISORDERS

The gastrointestinal tract is extraordinarily responsive to emotional stimuli, and this category, therefore, includes a wide variety of disorders. Among the major disorders are nonaganglionic megacolon, peptic ulcer, ulcerative colitis, the irritable bowel syndrome, certain types of recurrent abdominal pain, cyclic vomiting, cardiospasm, socalled "idiopathic" celiac disease, regional enteritis, obesity, and anorexia nervosa. In addition to these, pylorospasm, persistent colic, pseudo-peptic ulcer syndrome, certain types of constipation and diarrhea, certain disorders in salivation, and some types of periodontal disease[168] may involve psychophysiologic factors to some degree.

Nonaganglionic megacolon of psychophysiological nature has its origin in the infant's withholding of the stool during coercive toilet training.[14, 159] Autonomic imbalance seems to contribute to the enlargement of the colon, and

some constitutional factors may be involved in the predispositions to this disorder.[166] In its treatment, initial cleaning out of the bowel with oil retention or other enemas, with an attempt to regularize bowel evacuation, may be helpful, but as a rule, psychotherapeutic measures are also necessary.[182]

Peptic ulcer and *ulcerative colitis* begin to appear with some frequency in the school-age period; both have been reported at birth and in the neonatal period. These early cases, however, probably represent a response by pituitary-adrenal mechanisms to stress or medication. This may be related to the higher gastric acidity and higher level of adrenocortical steroids which occur during the first few hours and days of life. Both disorders may of course occur later as complications of adrenal steroid or ACTH administration. Acute "stress" ulcers with massive bleeding may occur in response to intense physical exertion associated with emotional tension.[166]

In school-age children and adolescents, the symptoms of *peptic ulcer* are different from those in adults.[142, 163] A preponderance of duodenal ulcers is seen, and boys are predominantly affected. Abdominal pain is not well localized, and symptoms are not as clearly related to meals. Nausea and vomiting are more common. Anorexia, headaches, and early-morning pain are often seen. Acute peptic ulcers, sometimes healing spontaneously, are probably more frequent in children than has been believed and are more common than in adults.[166] There is a high incidence of peptic ulcer in family histories.[142]

Changes in emotional state can spread to the body through cerebral cortical-hypothalamic interconnections and vagal stimulation. Among other effects are alterations in gastric and duodenal motility and secretion, and mucosal engorgement. These changes may lead to minute petechial hemorrhages and small ulcerations.[166] The mechanisms which produce chronic discrete ulcers are not clearly understood. However, there seems to be a diminution in the mucosal protective mechanisms, which may be a result of food stasis, secondary to an increase in circulating adrenal cortical steroids or ACTH and an increase in gastric acidity. Septic, traumatic processes, or certain hormonal mechanisms may also be involved. Most individuals who develop peptic ulcers show an apparent biological predisposition, with the presence of high serum pepsinogen levels from infancy.[145] Such high levels of pepsinogen reflect tendencies toward gastric hypersecretion.

In a blind study by Weiner and associates,[227]

such heightened physiological pepsinogen levels plus high levels of conflict over dependence have made it possible to predict that certain young adults would develop peptic ulcer later in a stressful situation. Children and adults who develop peptic ulcers have difficulty in handling feelings of anger. They are generally tense and overcompliant and often passive and dependent. However, they are often demanding of affection. The mother is usually dominant and overprotective but may be cold in her handling of the child. The father frequently is distant and passive, though occasionally rigid and punitive.[31, 220] The ulcer often develops in a situation involving actual, threatened, or symbolic loss. This may take the form of divorce, death of a loved one, intensified marital conflict, or other sources of separation threat.[166] Some overlap exists with the school-phobic picture, with which an acute peptic ulcer may occasionally coexist.

Children with peptic ulcer often respond readily to bland diets, antacids, and antispasmodics.[142, 163] Such a medical regimen should be combined with a supportive psychotherapeutic approach. Intensive psychotherapy for child and parents may be necessary, especially if pain is prominent.[220] Surgery is rarely indicated, but for occasional complications such as perforation or massive bleeding,[92] it may be life-saving.

Ulcerative colitis is a potentially severe, life-threatening disorder. Children with ulcerative colitis are generally overdependent, passive, inhibited, and show some compulsive tendencies.[3, 126, 171] In some cases, considerable manipulation of the parents around the illness is exhibited. Some children show only mild to moderate reactive disorders; some are disturbed to borderline or psychotic proportions; a number show chronic personality disorders. Often a core of depression exists. Within broad limits, the more seriously disturbed show more stormy and difficult courses of illness.[171]

The initial onset in childhood involves bleeding more frequently than it does diarrhea.[171] The precipitation of a fulminating type of colitis usually takes place in a situation involving actual or threatened loss of emotional support from a key figure, usually a parent. On the other hand, the insidious type of onset is more likely to be associated with stressful forces which gradually build up to significant levels. An acute, mild onset may also occur, with bleeding for only a few days or weeks. In these less disturbed children, an apparently permanent remission will often occur. Exacerbations are frequently related to family crises or to other intensifications of emotional conflict.

Within the family, the mother is usually the dominant figure, with the father passive and retiring. Characteristically, these families exhibit problems in communication, especially around negative feelings.

The nonspecific inflammatory response, usually, though not always, begins in the lower colon; it may progress upward even into the terminal ileum. Predisposing factors probably include familial patterns of autonomic response to stress. In "bowel-oriented" families, this tends to involve the lower gastrointestinal tract; it is possible that frequently coercive toilet training leads to conditioning of the defecation reflex to emotional conflict. Maternal overprotection and overdomination in early childhood lead to a combination of overdependence and resentment as the child begins to strive for autonomy. In the colon of normal individuals, changes in motility, secretion, and vascularity leading to petechial hemorrhages and minute ulcerations have been shown to appear as a result of emotional conflict. Some as yet unidentified biological predisposing factor, however, seems to produce the abnormal mucosal response of bleeding in patients who develop ulcerative colitis. This may possibly be related to an abnormality in the inflammatory process. Autoimmunization may be involved in some of the other manifestations, such as arthritis. Such findings reinforce the impression that this is often a systemic process rather than one involving only the bowel.[171]

Treatment of this potentially life-threatening illness should always include both medical and psychotherapeutic measures. Several studies[113, 171] have demonstrated the contribution of psychotherapy to physiological improvement. However, other studies[3] suggest that only the patient's psychological adjustment is helped. In any case, in the early phases the psychotherapeutic approach should ordinarily be limited to supportive measures. Premature emotional insights can produce exacerbations in the more fragile, overly dependent patient. At a later phase in treatment, more insight-producing psychotherapeutic approaches can be valuable; Sperling[204] has employed psychoanalysis successfully.

In the case of the child who is depressed or hopeless, who is not responding to steroids, but who is too ill for surgery, psychotherapy may be life-saving. Children with milder physical and psychological disorders will often respond readily to a supportive approach; dependence upon the pediatrician may develop rather rapidly, and prompt cessation of symptoms may then follow. The more seriously disturbed overdependent or manipulative personalities require more intensive psychotherapy. This includes extensive work with the parents, who tend to respond overanxiously to the child's fears or demands. Marital conflicts are common. Teamwork among the medical, nursing, psychiatric, social work, and surgical staff is especially important.[126] The pediatrician should be the captain of the team.

Careful follow up is necessary. The course of ulcerative colitis may be of a remitting, a chronic intermittent, or a chronic continuous type.[39] Sigmoidoscopy can be a stressful experience for children and has been associated with exacerbations of the colitis. Ordinarily, it should not be repeated more than once every six months (preferably once yearly) and may be done under general anesthesia if the child is especially anxious. A significant percentage of children with early onset and with a chronic continuous course may later develop bowel carcinoma. This may occur even after many years of remission. However, if the symptoms are under control, surgery to prevent carcinoma does not seem warranted. If significant response to combined medical and psychological measures does not appear within at least two years, or if "silent" progression of structural bowel changes occurs in spite of psychological improvement, surgery should be considered.[171]

In addition to other indications for surgery, long-continued delay in the adolescent growth spurt (beyond fifteen years) should lead to consideration of surgical procedures.[11] Even after colectomy or colostomy, however, psychotherapeutic measures should be continued. Surgery may result in striking physical improvement, but psychosocial disorders, overdependency, manipulative behavior, or school phobia may continue. The child and his parents are often people with compulsive trends; they will frequently have much unrecognized difficulty in dealing with a colostomy and its implications. Recurrences in ileostomy stumps, breakdowns in incisions, anxiety over colostomy bags, and other postoperative complications are frequent. Ileostomy clubs can offer valuable group support to older adolescents.

Older children and adolescents with chronic nonspecific diarrhea ("spastic colitis," "mucous colitis," "irritable bowel" syndrome) have family backgrounds with many of the same psychosocial conflicts as do the patients with ulcerative colitis.[165, 229] They are generally less disturbed, however.[165] In these patients, bowel response to vagal stimulation, as a result of intensified emotional conflict, seems to be very active; indeed, the response is even stronger than is true for patients with ulcerative colitis.[38] Strong family tendencies exist in this direction, along with a frequent history of coercive bowel training and other predisposing factors. The biological predisposition toward abnormal tissue response and mucosal bleeding, however, seems to be absent. The most effective approach seems to be combined medical and supportive psychotherapeutic measures by the pediatrician in conjunction with the social worker and consulting psychiatrist. Intensive psychotherapy for child and parents may at times be necessary.[165, 211]

Recurrent abdominal pain is a frequent symptom, occurring in about 10 percent of boys and 13 percent of girls.[2] Although some do show 14- and 6-per-second positive spikes on the EEG, these are not diagnostic. Such spikes occur in many normal children in the early school-age period with no associated symptomatology.[166] So-called "abdominal migraine" or "abdominal epilepsy" involves paroxysmal attacks followed by sleep. It occurs in association with EEG changes and is very rare in childhood. Over 90 percent of children with recurrent abdominal pain show no physical basis for the pain.[2] Localization of pain is still poor in school-age children, and the majority of symptoms are of epigastric or periumbilical nature. School-phobic manifestations are present in some, as are other symptoms such as headaches, dizziness, sleep disturbances, diarrhea, and vomiting. The recurrent episodes of pain are usually related to some emotional crisis; they are likely to appear in tense, timid, apprehensive, inhibited, and often overly conscientious children, who have usually experienced parental overprotection.[79] Abdominal pain, headache, or "nervous tension" are frequently present in one of the parents or another close family member. There appears to be no relationship between the ingestion of milk and recurrent abdominal pain. Some children exhibit disturbances in colonic motility, with changes in secretion and engorgement, but without bleeding.[216] This apparently represents oversensitive autonomic responses on a constitutional, often familial basis. In others, conversion mechanisms may be involved in the pain, based on identification with a family member or on other determinants. A supportive approach by the pediatrician is often helpful, with reassurance to parents and patient regarding the absence of serious physical causes. School adjustment problems may be productively explored with the teachers. Drugs are of little help, except for possible placebo effects. In some cases, intensive psychotherapy for child and parents may be necessary.

Cyclic vomiting appears to bear no relationship to epilepsy.[97] It occurs usually in tense, anxious, easily overstimulated, and overdependent children. The parents have often been overanxious and overprotective, and children may respond with demands or manipulation.[5] Episodes may be touched off by infections, frightening new situations, marital discord, or other family crises.[14] A familial tendency is common.[98] Although conversion mechanisms may contribute to the vomiting, in many cases an overactive gag reflex and physiological concomitants of anxiety seem to be involved. The resultant dehydration and metabolic reverberations can be serious and even life-threatening, with great anxiety and guilt aroused in the parents. Chlorpromazine (Thorazine) and other antiemetics have been helpful in aborting an attack, but psychotherapeutic intervention for child and parents is usually necessary.[115]

Cases of *cardiospasm* have been described in adults, but the condition is rare in childhood. Under the press of emotional influences, alterations may take place in smooth muscle functioning, involving the lower two-thirds of the esophagus.[55, 228] These may affect the efficacy of the involuntary components of the act of swallowing.[132] The reflex activity of the cardiac sphincter of the stomach is related coordinately to the swallowing movements of the mouth and the esophagus. The exact psychophysiologic mechanisms producing the cardiospasm, however, are not clear. In one anxious, tense, early-adolescent male with an overprotective mother and an absent father, an intensive psychotherapeutic approach resulted in disappearance of the symptoms, and improvement was maintained at one year's follow up.

So-called *idiopathic celiac disease* characteristically has its onset between six and eighteen months of age. The child manifests disturbance in appetite, failure to gain weight, irritable behavior, and diarrhea alternating with constipation. These symptoms are followed by the gradual appearance of large, foul, pale stools, striking fluctuations in weight, abdominal distention, increasing wasting and growth retardation, marked muscular weakness, anorexia or capricious appetite, evidence of severe depression, and other features. Intestinal malabsorption is present, together with a pattern of abnormal gastrointestinal motility and histologic abnormalities of the mucosa of the jejunem. Clinical evidence of vitamin and mineral deficiencies, as well as anemia, and secondary infection may be associated with the chronic picture.[169] With modern methods of treatment, these latter can be dealt with successfully, thus doing away with the high mortality rate formerly observed. It is important to rule out other causes of the "celiac syndrome," such as infection, obstruction, and malrotation of the intestines. Celiac disease in childhood and nontropical sprue in adults appear to be different phases of the same syndrome, although the adult form is ordinarily not as severe.[164]

Recent investigations have indicated that these patients have difficulty in the metabolic handling of the gliadin fraction of wheat gluten in particular. This apparently represents an enzymatic defect and not a true allergy. The disorder has a familial character, supporting the impression that genetic factors play a role in such a defect. A latent form is often found in relatives who do not manifest the characteristic clinical picture.[164] A gluten-free diet has in many instances produced gradual remission. Today, the disorder seems to be less common than formerly.

A consistent, though nonspecific, picture of an anxious, rigid, moderately compulsive personality has been noted among the mothers of children with celiac disease; the fathers are often rather distant and passive. A basic disturbance in the mother-child relationship is ordinarily present, beginning around struggles for control over feeding in early infancy and usually related to family or marital problems connected to the pregnancy, delivery, or neonatal period for this particular child. The mother's (or occasionally the father's) anxiously controlling approach may be intensified as the result of the fear and guilt associated with the appearance of the disorder. Children and adolescents are frequently overdependent and outwardly passive and inhibited, with marked difficulties in handling angry or resentful feelings; they often show some passive-aggressive or negativistic behavior. Increased vulnerability to separation from the significant parent is common. The effect of chronic illness or frequent exacerbations undoubtedly contributes to this picture, although adults with nontropical sprue often show similar personality characteristics, even without an early history of celiac disease.[169]

In many instances, the onset of celiac disease has occurred in relation to precipitating events.[25, 164] These usually involve an actual, threatened, or fantasied loss of dependency gratifications from the mother or from some other key nurturant figure. Prior to the onset of the disease, maternal depression is commonly present. This is related to marital problems or other distressing current circumstances and leads the mother to handle the infant more anxiously and, often, to withdraw from him emotionally. An answering depression may occur on the part of the infant. This in turn is associated with regression in behavior and disturbance in feeding and bowel habits. This sequence has a chronologic relationship to the onset of prodromal symptoms. At times such interpersonal events are combined with respiratory infection or other physical illness that appears close to the onset of the disorder.

In older children and adults, exacerbations of the illness have been observed to occur in relation to emotional conflict.[164] This exacerbation is particularly likely to appear in the face of frustrated dependency needs, or where actual or symbolic separation from supportive figures has taken place, associated with feelings of helplessness. Such exacerbations may also be influenced by depression or by other emotions; these can lead to conscious or unconscious giving up of a gluten-free diet. Resolution of such conflicts may be associated with an apparently spontaneous remission of symptoms. Where gluten is present in the diet, steatorrhea may occur with exacerbations related to emotional conflict; in its absence, diarrhea alone may result. Gluten ingested during the absence of emotional conflict may not cause symptoms. Apparently, the presence of gluten in the diet is a "necessary but not sufficient" condition for the appearance of steatorrhea, with emotional conflict, or, at times, intercurrent infection being required as well.

Physiologic studies have indicated that the absorptive defect may be temporarily reversed by parasympathomimetic or sympathetic-blocking agents, as well as by the administration of cortisone.[169] These, together with other data, would seem to implicate the autonomic nervous system and the neuroendocrine system. Both are capable of influencing bowel activity and, perhaps, the development of histologic changes. Thus, they may each function as partial contributors toward the difficulty in absorption. Emotional influences upon absorption may be transmitted through both systems, with the mediation of the hypothalamic-pituitary-adrenal cortical axis. Psychophysiologic effects upon the metabolism of gluten are as yet unknown.

A variety of remedies for celiac disease have been recommended over the years, many of them successful only in the hands of their originators. Prior to gluten-free diets, diets containing only simple carbohydrates and low fat were employed with considerable success; more recently, cortisone

was noted to produce remissions in many patients with celiac disease and nontropical sprue. A psychotherapeutic approach, involving supportive work with the mother, has also proved effective in some cases within a short time, without any change in dietary regime or other method of treatment. At times, this has been associated with hospitalization of the infant and with the assignment of one nurse to feed and care for him.[169] In adults, supportive psychotherapeutic measures in the treatment of exacerbations of nontropical sprue have produced equivalent effects. Thus, the most essential ingredient in the favorable response, even to gluten-free diets, seems to be a positive doctor-patient-parent relationship, involving confidence and a supportive psychotherapeutic effect. In addition to the use of dietary measures and the correction of metabolic abnormalities or deficiency states, psychiatric consultation may be indicated in some cases. At times, the employment of more intensive psychotherapy for patient and family is indicated. Following remission, the underlying defect in metabolism remains; this is often associated with persistent histologic changes in the intestinal mucosa.[164] Hence, a continuing relationship with the physician can be of help in preventing subsequent exacerbations related to emotional conflict or other factors.

Early studies of children with *regional enteritis* showed principally the psychological effects of a chronic illness.[109] More recent investigations indicate that such children may exhibit many of the same psychosocial characteristics as children with ulcerative colitis.[179] However, they are generally less disturbed. Both groups tend to respond to similar treatment.[128, 179, 209] In the course of this disorder surgery is indicated rarely if at all; it may serve only to compound difficulties. It is possible that the predominant involvement of the ileum rather than the colon, for undetermined reasons, is responsible for the differences in the pathophysiological and clinical pictures.[72]

Obesity. The temporary prepubertal accumulation of subcutaneous fat by most girls and some boys is common and normal. Beyond this, however, obesity is becoming more common today in this country, possibly related to affluence and patterns of overeating.[167] Formerly, it was felt that endocrine factors or pituitary lesions were prominently involved in many cases of obesity; currently, however, it appears that such factors are only rarely influential. As Bruch[21] has shown, most cases result basically from an excess of intake over output of calories, as a result of hyperphagia, usually associated with inactivity.[21] Obesity tends to occur in families with tendencies toward overeating. Increased appetite is a psychological phenomenon, one with much greater force than the pressure of physiological hunger.

Metabolic or other biological predisposing factors may also play a role. Hypothalamic regulation of eating ("glucostatic mechanism") may be influenced by the amount of fat in the body, whether in the form of circulating metabolites or in fat deposits. The level of free fatty acids in the blood can apparently be affected by autonomic stimulation, while steroid mechanisms may influence the storage of fat.[167] Thus, in individuals with biological predisposition, the neuroendocrine interrelationships are such that in situations of conflict, the "dynamics of fat metabolism" may respond to changes in psychological dynamics. Some persons seem to be constitutionally predisposed to remain overweight. With certain ethnic variations, obesity has been shown to be more frequent in persons from lower socioeconomic groups.[102, 217]

Bruch[21] has shown that, from the psychosocial point of view, markedly obese children and adolescents fall into two major groups: the reactive type and the developmental type. The obesity of the *reactive* type is related to overeating and underactivity. It comes about in response to an emotionally traumatic experience, such as the death of a parent or sibling, the breakup of a family through divorce, or school failure. These children tend to use the emotional significance of food as a substitute for more basic emotional gratifications lost through the traumatic experience. Under such circumstances, rather sudden gains of forty to fifty pounds have been observed in children and adolescents. This gain is sometimes reversed following the provision of adequate parent-substitute relationships or the resolution of the conflict. With this group, supportive psychotherapeutic measures by the pediatrician, accompanied by occasional psychiatric consultation, are often helpful. However, some children from more disturbed families require intensive outpatient individual or family psychotherapy to relieve the more persistent psychosocial problem.

The *developmental* type of obesity usually has its origins in strong familial tendencies toward obesity and overeating. This represents a disturbed way of life ("family frame") involving the patient and the whole family. The mother usually dominates and overprotects the child, often having been emotionally deprived as a child herself; and the father is ordinarily passive and retiring. Both parents, however, may unconsciously use one particular child to satisfy vicariously their own emotional needs or compensatory tendencies. Often the child is overvalued by the parents; this may come about for many reasons, for example, because of the death of a previous child. Overfeeding may also represent an attempt to deal with guilt, or, as Bruch[19] has indicated, the mother may be able to respond only with feeding to any discomfort on the part of the infant. This is a pattern which the child later internalizes. The child is often large at birth, soon becomes obese with overfeeding, and continues to be markedly obese from early infancy on. After early demanding behavior, the child usually becomes passive and oversubmissive, overdependent, and immature. These children are often taller than average and actually have an increased lean body mass.[167] This is in contrast to the "reactive" type, in which fat alone accounts for the gain in weight.

Obese children often have feelings of helplessness, despair, and a tendency to withdraw from social interaction; this becomes associated with a tendency to overeat. As Hamburger[84] has indicated, eating may unconsciously be used to deal with anxiety or tension, or food may be solace that helps to ward off depression or feelings of hostility. Eating or chewing may acquire unconscious symbolic significance as a conversion symptom, or patterns of "addiction" to food may result. Although obesity is a social handicap, some children or adolescents may hide behind the "wall of weight" and ward off sexual conflicts by feeling that they are ugly or unattractive.[21] This leads to a disturbance in their body image, with a lack of awareness of satiety. In the pickwickian syndrome, alveolar hypoventilation, compensatory polycythemia, and drowsiness are associated with marked obesity.[23] Overrapid reduction in weight may produce a "dieting depression" or even a psychotic picture in some markedly obese and seriously disturbed adolescents.[167]

Children and adolescents from such families may be very hard to treat. The parents or the patient may not be able to see the problem as a serious one. If the patient and parents can be helped to positive steps toward working on their problems, one must choose carefully between individual psychotherapy, group, or family therapy. Long-term psychiatric hospitalization or residential treatment may be necessary.

For those patients who are severely depressed, diets and anorectic drugs by themselves are ordinarily of little use. The parents of such children are unable to help the child maintain motivation and may unconsciously sabotage treatment. Used alone, the anorectic drug approach may lead to more complications than benefits. The central nervous system stimulants may become habit forming and should not be used with children and adolescents.

The surgical approach to reduce intestinal absorption in very obese persons has not been carefully evaluated clinically by an interdisciplinary study. Some patients appear to respond without signs of psychotic or other decompensation, but paradoxical psychological difficulties may be encountered.[26]

Some seriously disturbed obese persons are probably better off psychologically without marked weight reduction, maintaining a "preferred weight." A supportive relationship with the physician may be the most important factor. Weight Watchers clubs, which invoke group support, have been more successful than most other measures with markedly obese persons. Behavior modification techniques have also been shown to be valuable.[157]

In Bruch's[19] recent approach, she concentrates on helping the obese adolescent of the developmental type to achieve an identity separate from that of his parents, with a heightening of awareness of his individual concerns and needs. Weight reduction is a secondary issue. She feels that prevention can be achieved by helping those mothers who overfeed their infants to develop a more selective set of responses to their children's needs.

Obesity appearing during adolescence generally has a better prognosis than when it has been present since early life. This ordinarily represents the "reactive" type.[21] Such adolescents, however, experience serious secondary conflicts related to society's approval of slimness and its critical attitude toward obesity. This is partly justified medically by the greater incidence of hypertension, diabetes, and heart disease in obese adults. If positive motivation for weight loss is present, the pediatrician can utilize a supportive approach with the adolescent, in combination with parental counseling and the judicious use of diets and mild exercise.[167] Overstrenuous dieting or overly strong pressure toward dieting or exercise should be avoided. Summer diet camps can be of significant help to some; adequate social satisfactions are provided by such programs, together with group discussions or individual therapy. Some obese adolescents have particular difficulties resolving issues connected with their sexual identity. This often reflects their parents' unresolved problems in this area; marital conflicts are frequently present. Zakus and Solomon[238] have shown that these adolescents may respond to more intensive psychotherapy; additional help is offered to the parents to alleviate their overconcern and overcontrolling tendencies.

Anorexia nervosa is a syndrome observed most frequently during adolescence or postadolescence. It may, however, appear during the late school-age or prepubertal phases. It should be differentiated from anorexia as a symptomatic response in depression or other disorders. In the true syndrome, the conflict over eating becomes internalized and chronic. Loss of psychological appetite; denial of physical hunger; aversion to food; severe weight loss; hyperproteinemia, with edema at times; emaciation and pallor; amenorrhea; lowered body temperature, pulse rate, and blood pressure; flat or occasionally diabetic blood sugar curves; dryness of the skin and brittleness of the nails, and intolerance to cold may be encountered in part or together and with varying severity. Even in the face of marked loss of body weight (denial of emaciation), activity is often strikingly maintained. Indeed, some patients may exercise unrealistically in order to lose weight. Patients often appear preoccupied or irritable and have difficulty talking about their feelings. Some of the symptoms appear to be the result of a psychophysiological disturbance involving the pituitary-adrenal-cortical axis. Others, such as amenorrhea, may be the result of starvation. Although "pituitary cachexia" or hypopituitarism must be ruled out, its occurrence is rare.

Anorexia nervosa occurs predominantly in girls but may occasionally be seen in boys.[203] The onset often occurs in relation to a strenuous attempt at dieting; the diet is then continued until it cannot be controlled. The mother (or occasionally the father) has usually been strongly overcontrolling toward the patient, with an ambivalent and hostile-dependent relationship existing between mother and daughter. There is often a history of early feeding problems. The parents may value slimness and physical attractiveness, and the relationship of the girl with her father may have an overtly seductive quality. Not infrequently, the parents, as well as some older adolescent patients, are engaged in occupations related to food preparation. This may provide a compensatory sublimation for a few early or mild chronic cases.

During preadolescence, the patients are often overconscientious, energetic, and highly achieving persons. They remain strongly dependent upon their parents; unconsciously, however, they resent the parental control. Problems in emancipation from the parents are also usually involved; these reflect underlying difficulties in separation-individuation.[19] Food intake then becomes the area in which patients can assert their control. Many girls have previously been chubby or obese or have had fears of becoming fat. Alternating periods of obesity and anorexia have been described in certain of these adolescents, as have periods of bulimia followed by self-induced vomiting.[19] During puberty, these patients show significant difficulties in heterosexual relationships and often avoid dates or other social interaction by their many activities, athletic preoccupations, or social isolation. The onset of the anorexia may be related to the menarche or to traumatic experiences, often in the sexual area.

Three main groups of patients are seen diagnostically, with some overlap:[118]

1. Those with psychoneurotic disorders, with mixed hysterical and phobic trends. For these patients, eating appears to have strong sexual implications, derived from earlier unresolved conflicts; highly symbolic meanings are attached to bodily weight and contours, often associated with unconscious pregnancy fantasies or fears.
2. Those with obsessive-compulsive personality disorders. They manifest rigid, overconscientious, driving, and sometimes secretive personality trends, and develop fears of contamination or dirt in food.
3. Those with schizophrenic or borderline psychotic states. Often enough, the thought disorder and massive projection lead to fears of poisoning.

In all three groups, self-destructive or unconsciously suicidal implications of the failure to eat may be involved in the inability to eat. A small group of patients show a severe reactive disorder with strong depressive trends, superimposed on an overly dependent or on some other mild personality disorder. Underlying the personality disturbance is often a distorted self-concept; the patient fails to be in touch with body sensations or functions.[19]

For the largest group of patients, the symptoms begin in puberty. These adolescents are often involved in developmental crises, and they tend to exhibit reactive disorders or hysterical phobic psychoneurotic pictures. They are less disturbed and usually have a good prognosis for response to treatment. Those showing obsessive-compulsive personality disorders are more rigid and are difficult to treat. When this syndrome develops in older adolescence or during postadolescence, the patients tend more frequently to be of the schizophrenic or borderline psychotic type, and the prognosis is much more guarded. If the weight loss falls to a level of half the original body weight, serious physical debility may occur and may even lead to death.

Although hospitalization has been almost universally employed in treating this condition in the past, recently a number of patients have been treated successfully on an outpatient basis,[180] with a combined medical and psychological approach. Sometimes this has followed brief hospitalization. The less disturbed psychoneurotic or reactive group can benefit from a supportive psychotherapeutic approach by a pediatrician. This can include the judicious use of psychiatric consultation and help for the parents in avoiding battles over food. Intensive psychotherapy for patients and parents may be necessary, however, and family therapy may be especially effective for this group. Behavior therapy, with positive rewards for weight gain, has been of help to some of these patients; if behavioral methods are used, follow up is important, and work with parents is essential.[15] For those patients who have a more rigid, obsessive-compulsive personality disorder, a psychiatrist or psychologist, working closely with the pediatrician, can often be effective. Individual outpatient psychotherapy can be combined with family therapy.[121] If necessary, a pediatric adolescent inpatient ward can serve as a temporary adjunct to outpatient treatment.[67]

Severely disturbed patients with schizophrenic, borderline, and severe reactive disorders can be handled most successfully with psychiatric hospitalization or residential treatment.[203] This is particularly indicated for those who are extremely manipulative and controlling toward the parents. In a hospital setting, the patient can be permitted to prepare her own food on the ward; this may help to deal with fears or suspicions about the food. The patient should not be pressured to eat, although the seriousness of the problem should be pointed out to the patient and parents. Bruch[20] points out that the primary psychotherapeutic problem is to aid the patient in the desperate struggle for a separate and self-respecting identity. The rigid regulation of food intake and low body weight is made necessary by her need to achieve and maintain some type of control and identity, however shaky, uncertain, and unhealthy. A more healthy identity can permit her to give up this pattern.

If the body weight falls toward half its original level, combined medical and psychiatric treatment, using tube feeding if necessary, should be employed. The patient can be helped to accept the tube feedings if she is told this is being done to protect her from doing herself harm by her diet. Patients usually respond favorably when the doctor "takes over" responsibility for their welfare during this critical time.

PSYCHOPHYSIOLOGICAL GENITOURINARY DISORDERS

Menstrual disturbances are common in early adolescence. In the first year or so after the appearance of the menses, irregularity is usually the rule. During this interval, menorrhagia, metrorrhagia, or temporary amenorrhea are not uncommon. These may be intensified or perpetuated by emotional "shock" and emotional conflicts, as can functional bleeding[88] and amenorrhea[49] in older adolescents and adult women. Although the hypothalamic-pituitary-ovarian axis seems to be involved, the exact psychophysiologic interrelationships are still unclear.[83, 196]

Dysmenorrhea (appearing usually after ovulation begins) occurs in as many as 12 percent of the high-school girls in this country and causes much absence from school.[42] Its incidence may be influenced by attitudes of secrecy, misunderstanding, inconvenience, and disgust toward this function which still are widespread in society.[87] If dysmenorrhea is long continued and severe, the girl is usually experiencing significant difficulty in accepting her feminine role and in assuming the responsibilities of womanhood.[66, 91] The psychophysiologic mechanisms are not as yet fully understood.

Premenstrual tension, involving fatigue, irritability, anxiety, and mild depression, is frequent in adolescent girls.[201] It is evidently associated in some fashion with the hormonal and electrolyte shifts and other physiological changes preceding menstruation.[101] Although subjective effects have been reported in emotionally healthy females, there appear to be no objective effects of the menstrual cycle on cognitive and perceptual-motor performance.[202]

In older adolescent girls and adult women, *sterility* may have a psychophysiologic basis. This is related to expulsive contractions of the uterus arising from anxiety over sexual activity; anovulation, tubal spasm, and changes in cervical mucus may also be involved.[8] *Habitual abortion* occurs in young women having significant conflicts over sexuality and motherhood[80, 103] in whom "uterine dynamics" (strong contractions) seem to parallel psychodynamics.[130] Although the psychophysiologic mechanisms are not as yet completely un-derstood, emotional stress can apparently result in an increase in posterior pituitary hormones, with oxytocin accounting for the augmented uterine activity.[129]

In many menstrual disorders, discussion of attitudes, fears, or conflicts in the context of a supportive relationship with the pediatrician, together with counseling for the parents, will bring about relief. Some adolescent girls experience marked premenstrual tension and severe dysmenorrhea or persistent amenorrhea without demonstrable physical cause. In these cases, the associated personality problems are marked. These patients often respond to intensive psychotherapy combined with parental counseling. Married adolescent females with sterility or who suffer from habitual abortion can benefit from psychotherapy and/or marital therapy.

Infertility in older adolescent and adult males may stem from impotence and problems in ejaculation.[155] In addition, there is some evidence suggesting that emotional stress may lead to oligospermia.[189] The hypothalamic-pituitary axis, which regulates gonadotropin excretion, is presumably involved, although the psychophysiologic interrelationships are not fully understood. It is possible that supportive psychological measures may be helpful.

Disorders of urination are not uncommon, especially in adolescents. Eneuresis, like encopresis, ordinarily involves conversion, regressive, or other mechanisms and is not considered a true psychophysiologic disorder. *Urinary retention* is seen most frequently in adolescent females, although it may occur in males. The unconscious equation of genital with urinary function is characteristic, with conflicts over sexuality deriving from experiences in childhood. Identification with relatives with urinary pathology may also be involved, as may some earlier pathology of the genitourinary system or accidents involving the pelvis and urinary functions.[223] The patient may be unable to void for days or weeks; catheterization removes the urine but does not affect the retention. Urethral spasm is ordinarily present and bladder hypofunction, sometimes amounting to vesical paralysis, may be associated with conversion mechanisms involving the external bladder sphincter. Measurement of bladder pressure in an experimental situation involving exposure to stressful topics during an interview has shown that hypofunction occurred in some patients in relation to emotional conflict. In the same situation, other patients exhibited hyperfunction related to urinary frequency.[184] Supportive therapy may be helpful in some cases of urinary retention; in others, more intensive psychotherapy is required. This is also true for some cases of urinary frequency, particularly if associated with symptoms of urgency.

Polyuria may result from increased water intake, with symbolic meaning, as in some cases of "psychogenic" polydipsia.[116] Supportive psychotherapy may again be helpful.

PSYCHOPHYSIOLOGICAL ENDOCRINE DISORDERS

Hyperinsulinism and cases of "idiopathic" or "spontaneous" hypoglycemia related to emotional tension have been reported in adolescents.[33] The psychophysiological mechanisms, presumably involving increased vagal activity,[161] are not clearly understood, nor are the predisposing factors. In certain cases, unrecognized depression may be more important than the physiological manifestations.[58] Psychiatric consultation can be helpful, and formal psychotherapy may be necessary.

Diabetes is known to involve a hereditary predisposition and is also significantly influenced by psychophysiological mechanisms. Metabolic changes undoubtedly antedate the onset of the manifest clinical disorder. This is shown by the high percentage of women, particularly obese ones, who give birth to babies over eleven pounds and later develop diabetes. Prediabetic persons often show elevated oral glucose tolerance curves without other signs or symptoms.[41] A controlled study revealed that adolescent diabetics had a significantly higher incidence of parental loss and severe family disturbance prior to the onset of the disorder than did a comparable group of adolescents with blood dyscrasias.[213] Other observations indicate that diabetes is often precipitated in a setting of increased conflict, most often involving a real or threatened loss of a key figure or relationship.[82, 120] Exacerbations, including diabetic coma in children and adolescents, are frequently triggered by family crises or by other stressful stimuli.[90, 212] In such exacerbations, an initial fall in blood sugar often occurs; this is associated with an increase in blood and urine ketone bodies and diuresis. These, in turn, precede the actual rise in blood sugar, ketosis, and other features leading to coma.[90]

In childhood diabetes, the onset is often more abrupt and the course more stormy than in the adult form. This is particularly true during adolescence.[53] In contrast to some of the other psychophysiologic disorders, diabetes becomes a permanent handicap, and children and parents must be able to accept the loss of certain expecta-

tions. This is necessary even though there are no visible signs of disability and the resultant changes in life style may not be great.

Adolescents may feel socially isolated because of their diabetes[219] and may worry about marriage and the effect of their illness on their children.[215] As a result of the impact of the disorder, different coping styles emerge involving varying responses.[221] Some young persons may try to control their diet rigidly and carefully regulate their insulin. Others may deny the disorder and refuse to take their insulin, precipitating hypoglycemia and acidosis. Insulin reactions, if severe and often repeated, can produce brain damage and deleterious effects upon academic and social functioning.

No specific type of personality picture appears with diabetes. However, some retrospective observations suggest that infants and young children who later develop this illness are more demanding in respect to food intake. This may be related to premonitory metabolic changes. Some patients are overanxious and dependent while others are overly (pseudo-) independent. Younger children may misinterpret the illness and its treatment as punishment. Parents may experience reactions ranging from overprotectiveness and overanxiousness to rigidity and occasionally rejection. Struggles for control between parents and child may result in stealing food or overeating. In a number of families, however, the parents encounter no serious difficulty in accepting the illness, and no significant personality disturbance appears in the child.

The use of a "flexible" diet can include appropriate snacks, covered by adequate insulin, with limitations only on concentrated sweets and second helpings of some desserts. This seems to help make life more normal for those children and adolescents with diabetes.[60] Such an approach does not seem to increase significantly the incidence of diabetic complications in adult life. This approach may also help to avoid daily battles over dietary control, stealing and hoarding of food, and related problems. A few adolescents, however, seem to want external controls and may do better with the structure offered by a basic diet, with permission for some deviations on special occasions. In patients with mild diabetic disorders, the value of oral preparations as substitutes for injected insulin remains unproved. For many children and parents, counseling by the pediatrician within a supportive relationship will often suffice. Group discussions have been helpful with older children and adolescents, and special summer camp programs for such young people have aided the development of their capacity for self-regulation.[225] Disturbed adolescents will often use their diabetes to control or rebel against their parents, or will exhibit unconsciously self-destructive behavior by overeating or refusing to take insulin. Such cases require a more intensive psychotherapeutic approach, involving close cooperation among psychiatrist, social worker, and pediatrician. Inpatient pediatric or psychiatric settings may be necessary for this more acting-out, disturbed group. Beta adrenergic blocking agents may have promise in preventing emotionally induced exacerbations. Their use, however, is still in the experimental stage.

Anxious parents may experience intense guilt; there are some in particular who blame their own heredity. Such adults may have great difficulty in injecting insulin into and "hurting" their child. Others, with overprotective inclinations, may not be able to permit the child to learn to inject his own insulin when he is ready to do so. Counseling and support, including group discussion, may suffice for some parents, but more intensive psychotherapy may be necessary for others. In some difficult situations, particularly with so-called "brittle" diabetic adolescents, family therapy has appeared to be indicated and, when undertaken has proven helpful.

Thyrotoxicosis. Children and adolescents who develop this disorder often experience the onset in the context of gradually intensifying stressful circumstances or under conditions of real or threatened loss of an important emotional relationship. They appear to have particular difficulty in handling dependent needs. Some exhibit openly dependent tendencies, while others attempt to deny and cover up such needs with an overly (pseudo-) independent facade. Some are chronically depressed. Unplanned pregnancies on the part of adolescents with diabetes, overcontrolling parents, parents with marital conflicts, emotional deprivation, and broken homes are frequent events in the histories of these children.[18] In adult studies, individuals with higher levels of tension, involving motor, autonomic, and verbal activity, show higher serum iodine levels (within the normal range) than do those with lower levels of tension.[57] The decay of radioactive iodine has been shown to be increased by stress interviews, and it has been possible to predict the rate of decay on the basis of personality configuration, derived from a cluster of personality traits.[41] A longitudinal study of thyroid "hot spots"—areas which are hyperavid for radioactive iodine—in euthyroid individuals indicated that their personalities were similar to persons who develop thyrotox-

icosis. In contrast to a normal control group, this subject group showed waxing and waning of hotspot activity in a predictable direction as a concomitant consequence of life stress.[222] Various data suggest that hot spots can progress into modular and diffuse hyperthyroidism under conditions of prolonged or severe stress. Stressful experiences affect the levels of discharge through limbic-hypothalamic interconnections; this results in heightened stimulation of anterior pituitary thyrotropic hormone, which in turn brings about increased thyroid secretion. Since an increased rate of decay of radioactive iodine has been found in persons with a family history of thyrotoxicosis, a relationship must exist among thyroid functioning, stress, and a constitutional factor.

The effectiveness and ease of medical treatment of thyrotoxicosis in childhood usually makes formal psychotherapy unnecessary for the disorder itself. Successful treatment by psychotherapy alone has been reported in adults by Cope and his colleagues.[34] However, problems around dependence ordinarily continue, and psychotherapy may be indicated for the child and his parents. Lability of mood with occasional intense projection may require at least brief psychotherapeutic intervention. Since surgery carries some risks, brief psychotherapy may again be of value in helping a disturbed or depressed child respond to medical measures or preparation for surgery, if it becomes necessary.

Growth Failure in its various forms seems to involve certain psychophysiological effects upon endocrine function. These have not yet been fully clarified, however, and much overlap exists with nutritional and other factors. Growth failure occurring in situations involving psychosocial disruption has long been recognized by pediatricians. "Environmental," "maternal," and "sensory" deprivation have been used as descriptive terms, as have "deprivation dwarfism"[199] and "masked" emotional deprivation (which may be involved in the production of a variety of disorders other than growth failure, as Prugh and Harlow[170] have indicated). "Failure to thrive" refers to a syndrome arising from environmental stress and without relevant somatic etiologic factors. It is a more broadly applicable term, which is now generally accepted as differentiating this from other forms of growth failure.

As Barbero and his colleagues[6] have pointed out, infants and very young children with failure to thrive characteristically show weight below the third percentile on standard scales. Although weight-growth failure is often present, delay in height gain is less ubiquitous than delay in weight. Delay in psychomotor development is frequently present, although developmental milestones may not show significant lags. In a few cases, only developmental delay is present, without evidence of weight-growth failure. Apathy or, at times, extreme irritability may be manifest; withdrawn behavior may predominate, or warding-off behavior with the hands may be seen.

Other symptoms, such as physical weakness, distended abdomen, vomiting, diarrhea, anemia, or recurrent respiratory infections may be associated with failure to thrive. These call for careful physical and laboratory studies. However, they are generally secondary to the basic problem of deprivation. In some cases, failure to thrive may be associated with a primary somatic disorder. This may not be sufficient to account for the growth failure, or it may have brought about family responses leading to the syndrome.

In most instances, during several weeks of pediatric hospitalization for diagnostic study, weight gain, acceleration in development, disappearance of associated symptoms, and behavioral improvement begin to take place. The most important factor for this recovery seems to be an environment which provides adequate care and nurturance.

Evans, Reinhart and Succop[52] studied forty families of infants and young children hospitalized for failure to thrive. Most of the families were in lower socioeconomic groups. They were from both rural and urban backgrounds and tended to be isolated socially, with a third of the fathers absent from the home. Three subgroups, each comprising about one-third of the total, were delineated.

In the first subgroup, adequate living conditions and good physical care of the child were noted. All of the mothers were described as extremely depressed; they verbalized fears that their children would die or perceived them as retarded. All these mothers made efforts to feed and cuddle their babies, though in a tense, unsure manner. All had experienced a severe loss, such as the death of a parent, within four months before their child's hospitalization; they traced the breakdown in mothering to this event. The mothers in this group visited daily, accepted help in feeding and handling their children, and could express feelings of depression and ambivalence. They were most responsive to follow-up contacts and exhibited improvements in the nurturance of their children and in the family functioning. On long-term follow up, the children were found to have maintained and increased initial gains in weight, height, and development, and were continuing to thrive.

In the second group, the families showed some similarities to the first. They seemed to have fewer strengths, however, and in a wide range of areas appeared to be unable to cope with crises or with long-standing problems. Most were in the lowest socioeconomic group. Living conditions were deprived, and the children had received poor physical care.

The affected babies were often the youngest in a large family. Most of the mothers showed severe depression, usually compounded by marked or chronic medical problems, and marital difficulties. They had received limited mothering in their own childhoods, had experienced chronic economic and cultural deprivation, and seemed helpless and uncertain in caring for their children. They spoke of them as very ill or retarded. Most of these mothers were unable to relate easily to hospital staff and needed much help with basic economic and other needs. All the children improved dramatically in the hospital. In spite of valiant efforts to help such families utilize support, however, in most instances the improvement was not maintained. Significant improvement occurred only with occasional dramatic changes in family functioning, such as when a mother left an alcoholic, abusive husband or if different parenting figures became involved. Where families could not mobilize sufficient strengths, even with continued help, removal of the child from the home had to be seriously considered. In these families, the failure to thrive seemed to be more than a product of a disturbed parent-child relationship; it was rather the result of severe socioeconomic deprivation, with its roots in the backgrounds of both parents.

In the third subgroup, living conditions were adequate and physical care of the child had generally been good. All of the mothers displayed feelings of extreme resentment and hostility, and were antagonistic and provocative toward the hospital staff. They were overtly angry and often punitive toward their children, perceiving them as "bad" rather than ill or retarded. They seemed to identify the child with the "bad" part of themselves and to project their anger onto the hospital staff, with denial of guilt and refusal to accept responsibility for their child's problems. These mothers themselves appeared to have experienced inadequate mothering and, indeed, seemed to have had difficulty in establishing any meaningful relationships. They could not accept help from the hospital staff, and follow-up contacts were generally rejected. In some of these families, other children showed failure to thrive, and considerable evidence of physical abuse was also present. The children remaining in their homes showed continued retardation of growth and social functioning. Immediate removal of the child from the home seemed indicated because of the gross nature of family pathology. Where this was done, the children improved dramatically.

In certain families, when children display failure to thrive, the prognosis is guarded. Other studies[69] have agreed with the frequent need for foster-home placement in such instances, and there is some overlap with child battering.[108] However, there appear to be indications for treatment within the home.[69, 117] Follow up must be active. Even when the physical response is positive, emotional and behavioral problems may still be present,[45] and continuing intellectual retardation has been reported.[69] A nonjudgmental approach to the parents by hospital professional staff is necessary to help foster a therapeutic alliance. Such parents commonly feel guilty over the child's improvement in the hands of other people, and these feelings must be recognized and dealt with positively. Failure to thrive often occurs in families from lower socioeconomic groups; in fact, however, it may occur at any socioeconomic level, with some overlap with battering and other types of child abuse.

Certain workers have perceived the cause of the failure to thrive as arising from nutritional deficiencies.[231] In some cases, this may be true, or lack of appetite may be a related mechanism. However, in most instances, the disturbed parent-child relationship, with inability to provide adequate warmth, nurturance, and appropriate stimulation seems basic.

In some cases, as with older children who exhibit "deprivation dwarfism" described by Silver and Finkelstein,[199] a voracious appetite is present. There, the growth hormone levels are low, normal, or borderline. A functional insufficiency in the effects of growth hormone is believed by Silver to be the significant psychophysiological mechanism. In another study, children with "deprivation dwarfism" were compared with controls suffering growth failure from other causes.[111] It turned out that half of the deprived children had elevated cortisol secretion rates. Increased biologic activity of cortisol can result from stimulation of pituitary-adrenal cortical functioning by emotional stress; this hormonal change could in turn produce relative growth failure[156] in spite of increased appetite. Further studies are needed, but the psychophysiological effects of chronic emotional conflict on endocrine functioning and interrelationship seem to be of central importance. Constitutional factors may help determine whether weight-growth failure or developmental delay predominate. Whether *delayed puberty* may result from psychophysiological influences (as certain data suggest) remains to be more fully investigated.

Pseudocyesis has been reported in school-age girls, the youngest being six years of age.[195] The enlargement of the abdomen may involve conversion mechanisms, although increases in fatty tissue, gas, or fecal material have also been thought to be involved.[63] The physiological changes of pregnancy which appear in most women with pseudocyesis, even to the point of improvement of diabetic symptoms, appear to derive from psychophysiological influences on endocrine functions.[76] Psychic factors seem to act upon the hypothalamic-pituitary axis, with a resultant shift in various hormonal levels.[214] In some cases, evidence of increased corpus luteum activity has been reported.[193] Full understanding of the psychophysiologic interrelationships is not yet available.

This disorder usually occurs in females with hysterical personality disorders. However, it may occur early in the marriage in some young women with milder developmental conflicts over feminine identity and the assumption of the responsibilities of motherhood.[149] Women with pseudocyesis generally have a conscious wish for a baby, but they often experience unconscious fears or negative feelings. Some disturbed adolescent girls repress knowledge of sexual matters because of serious conflict; in such instances, pseudocyesis may appear after the first experience of kissing or petting, or with any genital contact.[104] Although a supportive, reality-oriented approach may suffice to bring about cessation of the symptoms of pregnancy, intensive psychotherapy and/or marital therapy may be necessary to deal with the underlying personality problems.

Adolescent mothers may experience *disorders in lactation* such as cessation of milk flow in relation to acute emotional stress or intensified conflict.[112] A central inhibition of oxytocin has been demonstrated in such cases, presumably mediated through hypothalamic-posterior pituitary interconnections.[36] Supportive psychotherapy may lead to conflict resolution and the return of lactation.

PSYCHOPHYSIOLOGICAL NERVOUS SYSTEM DISORDERS

Children with so-called *idiopathic epilepsy* often show personality disturbance antedating the onset. The onset of the disorder itself frequently produces psychic trauma and still carries an unfortunate stigma. Parents are often understandably anxious about the child's safety during an attack, and frequently are unrealistically restrictive about his activity. They tend to blame themselves for the hereditary factor. However, this factor is not as significant as many of them believe. (At least 10 percent of the general population—and many more during the critical or "sensitive" period of neutral integration, between three to nine years of age—have abnormal EEG records without developing seizures).[140] Parents often unconsciously equate the child's seizures with death or "craziness" and may fear what he will do during a seizure.

Children with idiopathic epilepsy often experience feelings of inferiority. They are troubled by shyness and a sense of being different from others. Many epileptic children show inhibition of their aggression associated with an increase in seizure activity.[71] However, some may exhibit irritability, temper outbursts, or aggressive behavior, particularly before a seizure. Children tend to experience fears of death just before a seizure; afterward, during the amnesic period, they may fear they have said or done something "bad." They are often afraid to ask what happened. There is no type-specific epileptic personality. Most of the disturbances in behavior are the result of the reaction of children and parents to the illness.

With proper seizure control, few children with the idiopathic type of epilepsy "deteriorate," intellectually or otherwise. The impression that such deterioration occurred came from the earlier tendency to include in this group children with "symptomatic" epilepsy whose brain damage resulted from trauma or disease, the those whose (reversible) depressed mental activity was due to sedative drugs. This impression was also strengthened by children who lacked educational and social opportunities and were in the past kept out of school or away from normal social interaction. Children who suffer febrile seizures in the preschool period have a slightly greater likelihood of later developing idiopathic epilepsy than those who do not, This may represent a lowered convulsive threshold resulting from hereditary or other sources.

Seizures take place more frequently during periods of emotional conflict or crisis within the family, sometimes after a buildup of tension; frequently, they are first precipitated within such a context.[71] Experimental studies of adolescents and adults have investigated the response to the experiencing of different emotional states. They have demonstrated that such states can give rise to paroxysmal changes in electroencephalographic activity and the triggering of actual seizures.[13, 106]

Such emotional factors involve hypothalamic-cortical interconnections; they are regarded by some as the most frequent triggering factors. Fatigue, low blood sugar, head trauma, and other stresses may also precipitate seizures in individuals with a lowered convulsive threshold.

The aforementioned influences are especially prominent in children with *petit mal*. Petit mal seizures involve brief "absences," and are at times associated with minor motor or vegetative phenomena. Petit mal seizures appear most commonly during the school-age period. Frequent seizures may interfere with school performance; continuous seizures (petit mal status epilepticus) may be confused with functional psychosis. With adequate medical treatment, there is usually a good prognosis, and this type of seizure disorder usually disappears by late adolescence. Children with petit mal are often inhibited emotionally, and they exhibit considerable guilt and conflict over handling feelings of anger.

Scolding, anxiety, upsetting sights, or unacceptable anger may all trigger petit mal attacks,[210] or the child may have attacks only in the presence of a particular parent with whom some conflict exists. Some adolescents can inhibit seizures in a way which is poorly understood. Various types of sensory stimulation, often associated originally with a disturbing experience, may also serve to precipitate attacks ("auditory" or "musicogenic" and TV-like photosensitivity or "flicker fusion" effects). When confronted by conflictual situations, some disturbed children may even touch off such attacks themselves by moving the fingers rapidly in front of the eyes or in other ways; at times they will employ such attacks in a manipulative fashion.

Psychomotor equivalents are encountered in the school-age group.[185] These may involve episodes of bizarre, automatic, or stereotyped movements, associated with autonomic disturbances emanating from a temporal lobe focus. Some clouding of consciousness combined with partial or complete amnesia may occur. Chewing and smacking movements, incoherent or irrelevant speech, outbursts of rage, and confused or somnambulistic-like states may suddenly appear, and may last for a few minutes or for several hours. Such episodes often appear in relation to some emotional crisis. At times, the content of such seizures may have meaningful psychodynamic significance,[51] although the behavior is not organized or purposeful.

Other symptoms such as headache, abdominal pain, and bursts of destructive behavior have been said to represent "latent epilepsy" or "seizure equivalents." Attacks of paroxysmal pain, usually periumbilical in location and colicky in nature, have been described, associated with ictal discharge on the electroencephalogram and often followed by sleep; these have been referred to as "abdominal epilepsy,"[43] or, by some, as "abdominal migraine." Such attacks are quite rare, however, and are to be differentiated from the recurrent abdominal pain mentioned earlier, as well as from other types. Headaches associated with ictal discharges are extremely rare. Ictal behavior disturbances are even rarer, if they exist (children with epilepsy may of course exhibit associated reactive, neurotic, or other disorders). The tendency to make a diagnosis of "epileptic equivalent" on the basis of exaggerated fears, repeated tantrums, aggressive behavior, marked withdrawal, running away from home, or sleep-walking, combined with poorly defined abnormalities on the EEG, is far too widespread. Most of the children suspected of such equivalents show disturbances in behavior related to conflicts within the family, and "treatment of the EEG" with anticonvulsant medication is not indicated.

Grand mal seizures may also be precipitated by emotional conflicts, as well as by sensory stimulation, hyperventilation, lowered blood sugar, head trauma, or other stimuli. Voluntary arrest of grand mal seizures, through changes in mental or physical activity, has been reported in adolescents and adults. This often occurs in response to the warning by an aura. Such attacks must be differentiated from "hysterical" or conversion seizures involving symbolic psychological conversion mechanisms. Conversion symptoms are often mixed with those deriving from the epilepsy, and conversion "seizures" may continue after the epilepsy is controlled.

In the treatment of these disorders by counseling and support, the pediatrician can help parents to view the child's illness realistically; the physician can thus deal with parental guilt as well as their fears of death, mental illness, or retardation. He can help them to keep their anxiety from over-restricting the child (beyond such limits as those on climbing high trees, swimming alone, and so forth) and from blocking his every step toward independence; of equal importance, he can help the parents and child avoid oppositional struggles over drug therapy or other control issues. Group discussions have been helpful, both with parents and with children.[40] By a supportive relationship, the physician or health associate can be of help to the

child in dealing with his fears or social difficulties; he can also offer greater understanding of the child's problems to parents, teachers, or other adult figures. The prognosis for response to treatment is good, as is the child's chance to live an independent, constructive life with few restrictions.

A few parents openly reject or stigmatize the child with epilepsy because of guilt or other feelings. In such a situation, early referral for psychiatric help is indicated. For the more seriously disturbed children, psychotherapy for the child and his parents can help deal with basic emotional conflicts.[71, 210] This can cut down on anxiety involved in emotional trigger mechanisms and can render drug therapy more effective. Family therapy has been reported to be beneficial.[119] A few children may require psychiatric hospitalization or residential treatment. For some children with petit mal, hypnosis has been reported to be effective.[68] Conditioning techniques using desensitization have been tried with some success on patients in whom photosensitivity[186] or musicogenic[59] components have played a role in seizures.

If at all possible, the goal of therapy should be complete control of seizures. The threat of another seizure can be devastating to some children and their parents. Nevertheless, care should be taken to avoid using too much or too many antiepileptic drugs. This may result in children becoming "dopey" or even mildly delirious. In addition, the use of phenobarbital can result in paradoxical stimulation with resultant hyperactivity, especially in preschool children. As with other psychophysiological disorders or any chronic illness, in some families the child's invalidism has become a significant feature in the balance of interpersonal forces. Complete relief from symptoms may then pose a problem in readaptation for the children and indeed for everyone concerned.[56]

A variety of symptomatic patterns has frequently been thought to bear some relationship to idiopathic epilepsy. The association with migraine has already been mentioned, as has the lack of association with syncope, recurrent abdominal pain, and cyclic vomiting. Other disorders mentioned in this connection include narcolepsy.

Narcolepsy is a syndrome characterized by paroxysmal and recurrent attacks of irresistible sleep, often precipitated by a sudden alteration in emotional state related to conflictual situations.[114] The disorder is uncommon in childhood and is said to be more frequent in boys than in girls.[237] The attacks of overpowering sleep may come on suddenly, during various activities, from one or two to many times daily. They may be associated with cataplexy (sudden attacks of muscle weakness without loss of consciousness) and hypnagogic hallucinations,[200] between waking and sleeping. The sleep during attacks is light, and the patient is easily awakened. Nocturnal sleep is usually within normal limits.

Although some unknown biological predisposing factor may be involved, the major factors appear to be psychopathological, often related to conflicts over independence or the handling of feelings of anger.[9] EEG recordings show only signs of light sleep during attacks and are otherwise normal. Although the course is generally chronic, spontaneous improvement may occur. Narcolepsy is to be differentiated from the pickwickian syndrome, in which sudden attacks of somnolence occur in markedly obese children and so-called "hysterical trances" or dissociative states; it appears to bear no relationship to epilepsy. Stimulants, such as methylphenidate or the amphetamines, are of some help in treatment, but intensive psychotherapy is often necessary to deal with underlying conflicts.[131]

Motion sickness (including car sickness and sickness from riding on trains, elevators, and swings) is more common in children than adults; seasickness and air sickness are less frequent. Vestibular irritation, autonomic responses, and psychological factors are all probably involved to different degrees in different children. Most children with this symptom improve markedly by adolescence.[4] Tense, apprehensive children or children with psychoneurotic phobic features are most affected. Frequent initiators of the symptoms are family arguments while driving. Dimenhydrinate (Dramamine) is usually of value in treatment; for phobic children, however, psychotherapy may be necessary.

Fever of psychophysiologic origin may occur in certain children and adolescents who show excitement[177] or continued emotional tension[70] in the absence of physical overactivity. In infants with "hospitalism" or in school-age children who are chronically anxious, such fever may be encountered on a chronic low-grade basis. In the latter instance, the parents, especially the mother, are often overanxious and continue to take the child's temperature daily long after the subsidence of a mild respiratory or other infection. The fever (generally under 101 degrees) usually disappears upon discontinuance of the daily temperature measurements. The physician should discuss the parents' apprehensions induced by guilt or other feelings, rather than offer blanket reassurance. When an infant with such fever has no other signs of physical illness, his discharge from the hospital following such a discussion usually brings the temperature down to normal.[230]

Hyperactivity has been variously viewed by different professionals. Certain examples of hyperactivity certainly are part of a clinical picture shown by children with diffuse cerebral cortical brain damage; a number of such children do not show hyperactivity, however, but rather hypoactivity or withdrawal. Hyperactivity also may be the result of anxiety, conflict, or underlying depression, often in a child with a temperamental tendency toward a high activity level. Hyperactivity can represent a developmental deviation, based on constitutional characteristics; parental difficulties in handling such a child may arouse anxiety in him, thus increasing the hyperactivity. In the latter two groups, hyperactivity would be viewed as a symptom with psychophysiological components.[166] The hyperactivity should not be treated independently by stimulant drugs; such groups should be used only as part of a total treatment plan, based on careful evaluation of child and parents. Stimulants may be of help for some children with hyperactivity with psychophysiological components, as well as for some but not all with diffuse brain damage. When employed, their side effects and toxic propensities, including growth retardation, should be kept clearly in mind, and they should not be used for long periods of time.

PSYCHOPHYSIOLOGICAL DISORDERS OF
ORGANS OF SPECIAL SENSE

These include certain cases of glaucoma, keratitis, blepharospasm, Meniere's syndrome, certain types of tinnitus, and hyperacusis. Most of the studies suggesting psychophysiological components in the precipitation or intensification of these disorders have been carried out with adults.[32, 61, 95, 192] In patients with glaucoma, which rarely occurs before adulthood, increased severity of eye symptoms and elevation of intraocular pressure coincides with accentuation of previous frustrations or with threats to security.[239] In one study, these findings were replicable during interviews,[183] and in another, hypnosis produced significant lowering of intraocular pressure.[10] Other studies have indicated there is no specific personality picture associated with glaucoma.

REFERENCES

1. ANTHONY, E. J., and KOUPERNIK, C. (Eds.), *The Child in His Family*, John Wiley, New York, 1970.

2. APLEY, J., "The Child with Recurrent Abdominal Pain," *Pediatric Clinics of North America, 14:*63, 1967.

3. ARAJARVI, T., PENTTI, R., and AUKEE, M., "Ulcerative Colitis in Children: A Clinical, Psychological, and Social Follow-up Study," *Annales Paediatriae Fanniae, 7:*259, 1962.

4. BAKWIN, H., and BAKWIN, R. M., *Clinical Management of Behavior Disorders in Children*, 2nd ed., W. B. Saunders, Philadelphia, 1958.

5. BARBERO, G. J., "Cyclic Vomiting," *Pediatrics, 25:*740, 1960.

6. ———, and SHAHEEN, E., "Environmental Failure to Thrive: A Clinical View," *Journal of Pediatrics, 71:*639, 1967.

7. BARCHILON, J., and ENGEL, G. L., "Dermatitis: An Hysterical Conversion Symptom in a Young Woman: Psychosomatic Conference," *Psychosomatic Medicine, 14:*295, 1952.

8. BARDWICK, J. M., and BEHRMAN, S. J., "Investigation into the Effects of Anxiety, Sexual Arousal, and Menstrual Cycle Phase on Uterine Contractions," *Psychosomatic Medicine, 29:*468, 1967.

9. BARKER, W., "Studies in Epilepsy: Personality Patterns, Situational Stress, and the Symptoms of Narcolepsy," *Psychosomatic Medicine, 10:*193, 1948.

10. BERGER, A. S., and SIMEL, P. J., "Effect of Hypnosis on Intraocular Pressure in Normal and Glaucomatous Subjects," *Psychosomatic Medicine, 20:*321, 1958.

11. BERGER, M., GRIBETZ, D., and KORELITZ, B. I., "Growth Retardation in Children with Ulcerative Colitis: The Effect of Medical and Surgical Therapy," *Pediatrics, 55:*459, 1975.

12. BERGMAN, R., and ALDRICH, C. K., "The Natural History of Infantile Eczema," *Psychosomatic Medicine, 25:*495, 1963.

13. BERLIN, I. N., and YAEGER, C. L., "Correlation of Epileptic Seizures, Electroencephalograms, and Emotional State," *American Journal of Diseases of Children, 81:*664, 1951.

14. BERLIN, I. N., et al., "Intractable Episodic Vomiting in a 3-Year-Old Child," *Psychiatric Quarterly, 31:*1, 1957.

15. BLINDER, B. J., FREEMAN, D. M. A., and STUNKARD, A. J., "Behavior Therapy of Anorexia Nervosa," *American Journal of Psychiatry, 126:*1093, 1970.

16. BLOCK, J., et al., "Interaction Between Allergic Potential and Psychopathology in Childhood Asthma," *Psychosomatic Medicine, 26:*307, 1964.

17. BLOM, G., and NICHOLOS, G., "Emotional Factors in Children with Rheumatoid Arthritis," *American Journal of Orthopsychiatry, 24:*588, 1954.

18. BOSWELL, J. J., et al., "Hyperthyroid Children: Individual and Family Dynamics, A Study of 12 Cases," *Journal of the American Academy of Child Psychiatry, 6:*64, 1967.

19. BRUCH, H., *Eating Disorders: Obesity, Anorexia Nervosa, and the Person Within*, Basic Books, New York, 1973.

20. ———, "Psychotherapy in Primary Anorexia Nervosa," *Journal of Nervous and Mental Diseases, 150:*51, 1970.

21. ———, *The Importance of Overweight*, W. W. Norton, New York, 1957.

22. BUDZYNSKI, T. H., STOYVA, J. M., and ADLER, C. S., "Feedback-induced Muscle Relaxation: Application to Tension Headache," *Behavior Therapy and Experimental Psychiatry, 1:*205, 1970.

23. BURWELL, C. S., et al., "Extreme Obesity Associated with Alveolar Hypoventilation—A Pickwickian Syndrome," *American Journal of Medicine, 21:*819, 1956.

24. CALL, J. D., et al., "Psychogenic Megacolon in 3 Preschool Boys: A Study of Etiology Through Collabora-

tive Treatment of Child and Parents," *American Journal of Orthopsychiatry, 33:*923, 1963.

25. CAMPAGNE, W. V. L., "Ein Enquite Bij Coeliakpatienten," *Luctor et Emergo*, Drukkerij, Leiden, 1960.

26. CASTELNUOVO-TEDESCO, P., and SCHNABEL, D., "Studies of Superobesity: II. Psychiatric Appraisal of Jejuno-Ileal Bypass Surgery," *American Journal of Psychiatry, 133:*26, 1976.

27. CHALKE, F. C. R., "Effect of Psychotherapy for Psychosomatic Disorders," *Psychosomatics, 6:*125, 1965.

28. CLEVELAND, S. E., and FISHER, S., "Psychological Factors in Neurodermatoses," *Psychosomatic Medicine, 18:*209, 1956.

29. CLEVELAND, S. E., and JOHNSON, D. L., "Personality Patterns in Young Males with Coronary Disease," *Psychosomatic Medicine, 24:*600, 1962.

30. CLEVELAND, S. E., REITMANN, E. E., and BREWER, E. J., "Psychological Factors in Juvenile Rheumatoid Arthritis," *Arthritis and Rheumatism, 8:*1152, 1965.

31. CODDINGTON, R. D., "Peptic Ulcers in Children," *Psychosomatics, 9:*38, 1968.

32. COLEMAN, D., "Psychosomatic Aspects of Disease of the Ear, Nose and Throat," *Laryngoscope, 59:*709, 1949.

33. CONN, J. W., and SELTZER, H. S., "Spontaneous Hypoglycemia," *American Journal of Medicine, 19:*460, 1955.

34. COPE, O., *Man, Mind, and Medicine*, J. B. Lippincott, Philadelphia, 1968.

35. COSTELL, R. M., and LIEDERMAN, P. H., "Psychophysiological Concomitants of Social Stress: The Effects of Conformity Pressure," *Psychosomatic Medicine, 30:*298, 1968.

36. CROSS, B. A., "Neurohumoral Mechanisms in Emotional Imbalance of Milk Ejection," *Journal of Endocrinology, 12:*29, 1955.

37. DATEY, K. K., et al., " 'Shavasan': A Yogic Exercise in the Management of Hypertension," *Angiology, 20:*325, 1969.

38. DAVIDSON, M., and WASSERMAN, R., "The Irritable Colon of Childhood (Chronic Nonspecific Diarrhea Syndrome)," *Journal of Pediatrics, 69:*1027, 1966.

39. DAVIDSON, M., BLOOM, A. A., and KUGLER, M. M., "Chronic Ulcerative Colitis of Childhood: An Evaluative Review," *Journal of Pediatrics, 67:*47, 1965.

40. DEFRIES, Z., and BROWDER, S., "Group Therapy with Epileptic Children and Their Mothers," *Bulletin of the New York Academy of Medicine, 28:*235, 1952.

41. DONGIER, M., et al., "Psychophysiological Studies in Thyroid Function," *Psychosomatic Medicine, 18:*310, 1956.

42. DOSTER, M. E., et al., "Data on Incidence and Degree of Dysmenorrhea," *American Journal of Public Health, 51:*1845, 1961.

43. DOUGLAS, E. F., and WHITE, P. T., "Abdominal Epilepsy: A Reappraisal," *Journal of Pediatrics, 78:*59, 1971.

44. DREYFUS, F., "Coagulation Time of Blood, Level of Blood Eosinophils, and Thrombocytes under Emotional Stress," *Psychosomatic Medicine, 1:*252, 1956.

45. ELMER, E., GREGG, G. S., and ELLISON, P., "Late Results of 'Failure to Thrive Syndrome,' " *Clinical Pediatrics, 8:*584, 1969.

46. ENGEL, G. L., *Fainting: Physiological and Psychological Considerations*, 2nd ed., Charles C Thomas, Springfield, Ill., 1962.

47. ———, *Psychological Development in Health and Disease*, W. B. Saunders, Philadelphia, 1962.

48. ———,, "A Unified Concept of Health and Disease," *Perspectives in Biology and Medicine, 3:*459, 1960.

49. ENGELS, W. D., PATTEE, C. J., and WITTKOWER, E. D., "Emotional Settings of Functional Amenorrhea," *Psychosomatic Medicine, 26:*682, 1964.

50. ENZER, N. B., and WALKER, P. A., "Hyperventilation Syndrome in Childhood," *Journal of Pediatrics, 70:*521, 1967.

51. Epstein, A. W., and Ervin, F., "Psychodynamic Significance of Seizure Content in Psychomotor Epilepsy," *Psychosomatic Medicine, 18:*43, 1956.

52. Evans, S. L., Rheinhart, J. B., and Succop, R. A., "Failure to Thrive: A Study of 45 Children and Their Families," *Journal of the American Academy of Child Psychiatry, 11:*440, 1972.

53. Falstein, E. I., and Judas, I., "Juvenile Diabetes and Its Psychiatric Implications," *American Journal of Orthopsychiatry, 25:*330–342, 1955.

54. Falstein, E. J., and Rosenblum, A. H., "Juvenile Paroxysmal Supraventricular Tachycardia: Psychosomatic and Psychodynamic Aspects," *Journal of the American Academy of Child Psychiatry, 1:*246, 1962.

55. Faulkner, W. B., "Severe Aesophageal Spasm," *Psychosomatic Medicine, 2:*139, 1940.

56. Ferguson, S. M., and Rayport, M., "The Adjustment to Living Without Epilepsy," *Journal of Nervous and Mental Diseases, 140:*26, 1965.

57. Flagg, G. W., et al., "A Psychophysiological Investigation of Hyperthyroidism," *Psychosomatic Medicine, 27:*497, 1965.

58. Ford, C. V., Bray, G. A., and Swerdloff, R. S., "A Psychiatric Study of Patients Referred with a Diagnosis of Hypoglycemia," *American Journal of Psychiatry, 133:*290, 1976.

59. Forster, F. M., et al., "Modification of Musicogenic Epilepsy by Extinction Technique," *Procedures of the 8th International Congress of Neurology,* vol. 4, p. 269, Vienna, 1965.

60. Forsyth, C. C., and Payne, W. W., "Free Diets in the Treatment of Diabetic Children," *Archives of Disease in Childhood, 31:*245, 1956.

61. Fowler, E. P., and Zeckel, A., "Psychosomatic Aspects of Meniere's Disease," *Journal of the American Medical Association, 148:*1265, 1952.

62. Freeman, E. H., et al., "Psychological Variables in Allergic Disorders: A Review," *Psychosomatic Medicine, 26:*543, 1964.

63. Fried, P., et al., "Pseudocyesis: A Psychosomatic Study in Gynecology," *Journal of the American Medical Association, 145:*1329, 1951.

64. Friedman, A., and Harms, E., *Headaches in Children,* Charles C Thomas, Springfield, Ill. 1967.

65. Friedman, M., and Roseman, R. H., "Type A Behavior Pattern: Its Association with Coronary Heart Disease," *Annals of Clinical Research, 3:*300, 1971.

66. Frisk, M., Widholm, O., and Hortling, H., "Dysmenorrhea-Psyche and Soma in Teenagers," *Acta Obstetricia et Gynecologia Scandinavica, 44:*339, 1965.

67. Galdston, R., "Mind Over Matter: Observations on 50 Patients Hospitalized with Anorexia Nervosa," *Journal of the American Academy of Child Psychiatry, 13:*246, 1974.

68. Gardner, G. G., "Use of Hypnosis for Psychogenic Epilepsy in a Child," *American Journal of Hypnosis, 15:*166, 1973.

69. Glaser, H. H., et al., "Physical and Psychological Development of Children with Early Failure to Thrive," *Journal of Pediatrics, 73:*690, 1968.

70. Goodell, H., Graham, D. T., and Wolff, H. G., "Changes in Body Heat Regulation Associated with Varying Life Situations and Emotional States, in Wolff, H. G., Wolf, S. G., and Hare, C. C. (Eds.), *Life Stress and Bodily Disease,* Williams & Wilkins, Baltimore, 1950.

71. Gottschalk, L. A., "Effects of Intensive Psychotherapy on Epileptic Children," *Archives of Neurology and Psychiatry, 70:*361, 1953.

72. Grace, W. J., "Life Stress and Regional Enteritis," *Gastroenterology, 23:*542, 1953.

73. Graham, D. T., "Cutaneous Vascular Reactions in Raynaud's Disease and in States of Hostility, Anxiety, and Depression," *Psychosomatic Medicine, 17:*200, 1955.

74. ———, "The Relation of Psoriasis to Attitudes and to Vascular Reactions of the Human Skin," *Journal of Investigative Dermatology, 22:*379, 1954.

75. ———, "The Pathogenesis of Hives: Experimental Study of Life Situations, Emotions, and Cutaneous Vascular Reactions," in Wolff, H. G., Wolf, S. G., and Hare, C. G. (Eds.), *Life Stress and Bodily Disease,* Williams & Wilkins, Baltimore, 1950.

76. Greaves, D. C., Green, P. E., and West, L. J., "Psychodynamic and Psychophysiological Aspects of Pseudocyesis," *Psychosomatic Medicine, 22:*24, 1960.

77. Green, M., "Headaches," in Green, M., and Haggerty, R. (Eds.), *Ambulatory Pediatrics,* W. B. Saunders, Philadelphia, 1968.

78. ———, "Fainting," in Green, M., and Haggerty, R. J. (Eds.), *Ambulatory Pediatrics,* W. B. Saunders, Philadelphia, 1968.

79. ———, "Psychogenic Recurrent Abdominal Pain: Diagnosis and Treatment," *Pediatrics, 40:*84, 1967.

80. Grimm, E., "Psychological Investigations of Habitual Abortion," *Psychosomatic Medicine, 24:*369, 1962.

81. Group for the Advancement of Psychiatry, *Psychopathological Disorders in Childhood: Theoretical Considerations and a Proposed Classification,* vol. 6, no. 62, Group for the Advancement of Psychiatry, New York, 1966.

82. Ham, G. C., Alexander, F., and Carmichael, H. T., "A Psychosomatic Theory of Thyrotoxicosis," *Psychosomatic Medicine, 13:*18, 1951.

83. Hamburg, D. A., Moos, R. H., and Yalom, J. D., 'Studies of Distress in the Menstrual Cycle and the Postpartum Period," in Michael, R. (Ed.), *Endocrinology and Human Behavior,* Oxford University Press, 1968.

84. Hamburger, W. W., "Psychological Aspects of Obesity," *Bulletin of the New York Academy of Medicine, 33:*771, 1957.

85. Harburg, E., et al., "Socio-Ecological Stress, Suppressed Hostility, Skin Color, and Black-White Male Blood Pressure: Detroit," *Psychosomatic Medicine, 35:*276, 1973.

86. Harms, E. (Ed.), *Somatic and Psychiatric Aspects of Childhood Allergies,* vol. 1, International Series of Monographs on Child Psychiatry, Macmillan, New York, 1963.

87. Heald, F. P., et al., "Dysmenorrhea in Adolescence," *Pediatrics, 20:*121, 1957.

88. Heiman, M., "The Role of Stress Situations and Psychological Factors in Functional Uterine Bleeding," *Journal of Mt. Sinai Hospital, 23:*755, 1956.

89. Hill, O. (Eds.), *Modern Trends in Psychosomatic Medicine,* Butterworth, London, 1970.

90. Hinkle, L. E., and Wolf, S., "A Summary of Experimental Evidence Relating Life Stress to Diabetes Mellitus," *Journal of Mt. Sinai Hospital, 19:*537, 1952.

91. Hirt, M., et al., "The Relationship Between Dysmenorrhea and Selected Personality Variables," *Psychosomatics, 8:*350, 1967.

92. Hollender, M. H., Soults, F. B., and Ringold, A. L., "Emotional Antecedents of Bleeding from Peptic Ulcer," *Psychiatry in Medicine, 2:*199, 1971.

93. Holmes, T. H., and Wolff, H. G., "Life Situations, Emotions and Backache," *Psychosomatic Medicine, 14:*18, 1952.

94. Holmes, T. H., Treuting, T., and Wolff, H. G., "Life Situations, Emotions, and Nasal Disease: Evidence on Summative Effects Exhibited in Patients with 'Hay Fever,'" *Psychosomatic Medicine, 13:*71, 1951.

95. Holmes, T. H., et al., *The Nose: An Experimental Study of Reactions Within the Nose in Human Subjects During Varying Life Experiences,* Charles C Thomas, Springfield, Ill., 1948.

96. Holquin, J., and Fenichel, G., "Migraine," *Journal of Pediatrics, 70:*290, 1967.

97. Hoyt, C. S., and Stickler, G. G., "A Study of 44 Children with the Syndrome of Recurrent (Cyclic) Vomiting," *Pediatrics, 25:*775, 1960.

98. Illingworth, R. S., "Practical Observations and Reflections, II. Vomiting Without Organic Cause," *Clinical Pediatrics, 4:*865, 1965.

99. ———, and HOLT, K. S., "Transient Rash and Hematuria after Exercise and Emotion," *Archives of Disease in Childhood, 32:*254, 1957.

100. JACOBS, M. A., et al. "Interaction of Psychologic and Biologic Predisposing Factors in Allergic Disorders," *Psychosomatic Medicine, 29:*572, 1967.

101. JANOWSKY, D. S., BERENS, S. C., and DAVIS, J. M., "Correlations Between Mood, Weight, and Electrolytes During the Menstrual Cycle: A Renin-Angiotensin-Aldosterone Hypothesis of Premenstrual Tension," *Psychosomatic Medicine, 35:*143, 1973.

102. KAHN, E. J., "Obesity in Children: Identification of a Group at High Risk in a New York Ghetto," *Journal of Pediatrics, 77:*771, 1970.

103. KAIJ, L., et al., "Psychiatric Aspects of Spontaneous Abortion, II. The Importance of Bereavement, Attachment, and Neurosis in Early Life," *Journal of Psychosomatic Research, 13:*53, 1969.

104. KAPLAN, A. J., and SCHOPBACH, R. R., "Pseudocyesis: A Psychiatric Study," *Archives of Neurology and Psychiatry, 65:*121, 1951.

105. KAPLAN, H., and REISCH, M., "Universal Alopecia: A Psychosomatic Appraisal," *New York State Journal of Medicine, 52:*1144, 1952.

106. KEMPH, J. P., and FELDMAN, B. H., "A Case Study of Some Emotional Factors Affecting Paroxysmal Cerebral Activity During Interviews," *Journal of the American Academy of Child Psychiatry, 7:*663, 1968.

107. KLUGER, J. M., "Childhood Asthma and the Social Milieu," *Journal of the American Academy of Child Psychiatry, 8:*353, 1969.

108. KOEL, B. S., "Failure to Thrive and Fatal Injury as a Continuum," *American Journal of Diseases of Children, 118:*565, 1969.

109. KRAFT, I. A., and ARDALL, C., "A Psychiatric Study of Children with Diagnosis of Regional Ileitis," *Southern Medical Journal, 57:*799, 1964.

110. KRAUS, S. J., "Stress, Acne, and Skin Surface Free Fatty Acids," *Psychosomatic Medicine, 32:*503, 1970.

111. KRIEGER, I., and GOOD, M. H., "Adrenalcortiial and Thyroid Function in the Deprivation Syndrome: Comparison with Growth Failure Due to Undernutrition, Congenital Heart Disease or Prenatal Influences," *American Journal of Diseases of Children, 120:*95, 1970.

112. KROGER, W. S., and FREED, S. C., *Psychosomatic Gynecology,* Wilshire, Hollywood, Calif., 1962.

113. LANGFORD, W. S., "The Psychological Aspects of Ulcerative Colitis," *Clinical Proceedings of the Children's Hospital, Washington, D.C., 20:*89, 1964.

114. LANGWORTHY, O. R., and BETZ, B. J., "Narcolepsy as a Type of Response to Emotional Conflicts," *Psychosomatic Medicine, 6:*211, 1944.

115. LAYBOURNE, P. C., "Psychogenic Vomiting in Children," *American Journal of Disease in Childhood, 86:*726, 1953.

116. LEIKEN, S. J., and CAPLAN, H., "Psychogenic Polydipsia," *American Journal of Psychiatry, 123:*1563, 1967.

117. LEONARD, M. F., RHYMES, J. P., and SOLNIT, A. J., "Failure to Thrive in Infants: A Family Problem," *American Journal of Diseases of Children, 111:*600, 1966.

118. LESSER, L. J., et al., "Anorexia Nervosa in Children," *American Journal of Orthopsychiatry, 30:*572, 1960.

119. LIBO, S. S., PALMER, C., and ARCHIBALD, D., "Family Group Therapy for Children with Self-Induced Seizures," *American Journal of Orthopsychiatry, 41:*506, 1971.

120. LIDZ, T., and WHITEHORN, J. C., "Life Situations, Emotions, and Graves' Disease," *Psychosomatic Medicine, 12:*184, 1950.

121. LIEBMAN, R., MINUCHIN, S., and BAKER, L., "The Role of the Family in the Treatment of Anorexia Nervosa," *Journal of the American Academy of Child Psychiatry, 13:*264, 1974.

122. LIPTON, E. L., STEINSCHNEIDER, A., and ROCHMOND, J. B., "Psychophysiological Disorders in Children,"

in Hoffman, M., and Hoffman, L. (Eds.), *Review of Child Development Research,* vol. 2, Russell Sage Foundation, New York, 1966.

123. LONG, R. T., et al., "The Psychosomatic Study of Allergic and Emotional Factors in Children with Asthma," *American Journal of Psychiatry, 115:*114, 1958.

124. LOOF, D. H., "Psychophysiologic and Conversion Reactions in Children: Selective Incidence in Verbal and Nonverbal Families," *Journal of the American Academy of Child Psychiatry, 9:*318, 1970.

125. MCANARNEY, E. G., et al., "Psychological Problems of Children with Chronic Juvenile Arthritis," *Pediatrics, 53:*523, 1974.

126. MCDERMOTT, J. F., and FINCH, S. M., "Ulcerative Colitis in Children: Reassessment of a Dilemma," *Journal of the American Academy of Child Psychiatry, 6:*512, 1967.

127. MCKEGNEY, F. P., and WILLIAMS, R. B., "Psychological Aspects of Hypertension, II. The Differential Influence of Interview Variables on Blood Pressure," *American Journal of Psychiatry, 123:*1539, 1967.

128. MCKEGNEY, F. P., et al., "A Psychosomatic Comparison of Patients with Ulcerative Colitis and Crohn's Disease," *Psychosomatic Medicine, 32:*153, 1970.

129. MALMQUIST, A., et al., "Psychiatric Aspects of Spontaneous Abortion I. A Matched Control Study of Women with Living Children," *Journal of Psychosomatic Research, 13:*45, 1969.

130. MANN, E. C., "Habitual Abortion," *American Journal of Obstetrics and Gynecology, 77:*706, 1959.

131. MARKOWITZ, I., "Psychotherapy of Narcolepsy in an Adolescent Boy: Case Presentation," *Psychiatric Quarterly, 31:*41, 1957.

132. MARMOR, J., et al., "The Mother-Child Relationship in the Genesis of Neurodermatitis," *Archives of Dermatology, 74:*599, 1956.

133. MASLAND, R. P., HEALD, F. P., and GOODALE, W. T., "Hypertensive Vascular Disease in Adolescence," *New England Journal of Medicine, 255:*894, 1956.

134. MASON, J. W., "'Over-all' Hormonal Balance as a Key to Endocrine Organization," *Psychosomatic Medicine, 30:*791, 1968.

135. MATTSSON, A., "Long-term Physical Illness in Childhood: A Challenge to Psychosocial Adaptation," *Pediatrics, 50:*801, 1972.

136. ———, GROSS, S., and HALL, T. W., "Psychoendocrine Study of Adaptation in Young Hemophiliacs," *Psychosomatic Medicine, 33:*215, 1971.

137. MEHLMAN, R. D., and GRIESEMER, R. D., "Alopecia Areata in the Very Young," *American Journal of Psychiatry, 125:*605, 1968.

138. MENDELS, J., "Stress Polycythemia," *American Journal of Psychiatry, 123:*1570, 1967.

139. MENKES, M. M., "Personality Characteristics and Family Roles of Children with Migraine," *Pediatrics, 53:*560, 1974.

140. METCALF, D. R., and JORDAN K., "EEG Ontogenesis in Normal Children," in Smith, W. I., (Ed.), *Drugs, Development and Cerebral Function,* Charles C Thomas, Springfield, Ill., 1971.

141. MEYEROWITZ, S., "The Continuing Investigation of Psychosocial Variables in Rheumatoid Arthritis," in Hill, A. G. S. (Ed.), *Modern Trends in Rheumatology,* Butterworth, London, 1971.

142. MILLAR, T. P., "Peptic Ulcers in Children," in Howells, J. G. (Ed.), *Modern Perspectives in International Child Psychiatry,* Oliver and Boyd, Edinburgh, 1969.

143. MILLER, H., and BARUCH, D. W., "Psychotherapy of Parents of Allergic Children," *Annals of Allergy, 18:*990, 1960.

144. MILLET, J. A. P., LIEF, H., and MITTELMANN, B., "Raynaud's Disease: Psychogenic Factors and Psychotherapy," *Psychosomatic Medicine, 15:*61, 1953.

145. MIRSKY, I. A., "Physiologic, Psychologic, and So-

cial Determinants in the Etiology of Duodenal Ulcer," *American Journal of Digestive Diseases,* 3:285, 1958.

146. ——, "The Psychosomatic Approach to the Etiology of Clinical Disorders," *Psychosomatic Medicine,* 19:424, 1957.

147. MOHR, G. J., et al., "Studies of Eczema and Asthma in the Preschool Child," *Journal of the American Academy of Child Psychiatry,* 2:271, 1963.

148. MOORE, N., "Behavior Therapy in Bronchial Asthma: A Controlled Study," *Journal of Psychosomatic Research,* 9:257, 1965.

149. MOULTON, R., "The Psychosomatic Implications of Pseudocyesis," *Psychosomatic Medicine,* 4:376, 1942.

150. NORA, J. J., and NORA, A. H., "The Pediatric Roots of Coronary Heart Disease," *Chest,* 68:714, 1975.

151. OBERMAYER, M. E., *Psychocutaneous Medicine,* Charles C Thomas, Springfield, Ill., 1955.

152. OGSTON, D., MacDONALD, G. A., and FULLERTON, H. W., "The Influence of Anxiety in Tests of Blood Coaguality and Fibrinolytic Activity," *Lancet,* 2:521, 1962.

153. ORBACH, C., and TALLENT, N., "Modification of Perceived Body and of Body Concepts," *Archives of General Psychiatry,* 12:126, 1965.

154. OSTFELD, N. M., and LEBOWITS, B. Z., "Personality Factors and Pressor Mechanisms in Renal and Essential Hypertension," *Archives of Internal Medicine,* 104:43, 1959.

155. PALTI, Z., "Psychogenic Male Infertility," *Psychosomatic Medicine,* 31:326, 1969.

156. PATTON, R. G., and GARDNER, L. L., *Growth Failure in Maternal Deprivation,* Charles C Thomas, Springfield, Ill., 1963.

157. PENICK, S. B., et al., "Behavior Modification in the Treatment of Obesity,"*Psychosomatic Medicine,* 33:49, 1971.

158. PFEIFFER, J. B., and WOLFF, H. G., "Studies in Renal Circulation During Periods of Life Stress and Accompanying Emotional Reactions in Subjects With and Without Essential Hypertension: Observations on the Role of Neural Activity in Regulation of Renal Blood Flow," *Journal of Clinical Investigation,* 29:1227, 1950.

159. PINKERTON, P., "Psychogenic Megacolon in Children: The Implications of Bowel Negativism," *Archives of Disease in Childhood,* 33:371, 1958.

160. ——, and WEAVER, C. M., "Childhood Asthma," in Hill, O. (Ed.), *Modern Trends in Psychosomatic Medicine,* Butterworth, London, 1970.

7961 take 17 ref 7-8 times roman w ital x 17 Patti 9-7 refs. pp. 2000-21

161. PORTIS, S. A., "Life Situations, Emotions, and Hyperinsulinism," in Wolff, H. G., and Hare, C. G. (Eds.), *Life Stress and Bodily Disease,* vol. 29, Association for Research in Nervous and Mental Diseases, Williams & Wilkins, Baltimore, 1950.

162. POWERS, D., "Emotional Implications of Acne," *New York State Journal of Medicine,* 57:751, 1957.

163. PROUTY, M., "Peptic Ulcers in Childhood," *Pediatric Digest,* 9:35, 1967.

164. PRUGH, D. G., "Psychophysiological Aspects of Inborn Errors of Metabolism," in Lief, H. I., Lief, V. F., and Lief, N. R. (Eds.), *The Psychological Basis of Medical Practice,* Harper & Row, Hoeber Medical Division, New York, 1963.

165. ——, "Natural History of Children with Chronic Diarrhea," in *Psychosomatic Aspects of Gastrointestinal Illness in Childhood,* Report of the 44th Ross Conference on Pediatric Research, Ross Laboratories, Columbus, Ohio, 1963.

166. ——, "Toward the Understanding of the Psychosomatic Aspects of Illness in Childhood," in Solnit, A., and Provence, S. (Eds.), *Modern Perspectives in Child Development,* International Universities Press, New York, 1963.

167. ——, "Some Psychological Problems Concerned with the Problems of Overnutrition," *American Journal of Clinical Nutrition,* 9:538, 1961.

168. ——, "Psychological and Psychophysiological Aspects of Oral Activities in Childhood," *Pediatric Clinics of North America,* 3:1049, 1956.

169. ——, "A Preliminary Report on the Role of Emotional Factors in Idiopathic Celiac Disease," *Psychosomatic Medicine,* 13:200, 1951.

170. ——, and HARLOW, R. G., " 'Masked Deprivation' in Infants and Young Children," in *Deprivation of Maternal Care: A Reassessment of Its Effects,* Public Health Papers 14, World Health Organization, Geneva, 1962.

171. PRUGH, D. G., and JORDAN, K., "The Management of Ulcerative Colitis in Childhood," in Howells, J. G. (Ed.), *Modern Perspectives in International Child Psychiatry,* Oliver and Boyd, London, 1969.

172. PRUGH, D. G., and SCHWACHMAN, H., "Observations on 'Unexplained' Chronic Diarrhea in Early Childhood," Society Transactions, *American Journal of Diseases of Children,* 90:496, 1955.

173. PURCELL, K., "Critical Appraisal of Psychosomatic Studies of Asthma," *New York State Journal of Medicine,* 65:2103, 1965.

174. RAHE, R. H., and CHRIST, A. E., "An Unusual Cardiac (Ventricular) Arrhythmia in a Child, Psychiatric and Psychophysiologic Aspects," *Psychosomatic Medicine,* 28:181, 1966.

175. REES, L., "Physiogenic and Psychogenic Factors in Vasomotor Rhinitis," *Journal of Psychosomatic Research,* 8:101, 1964.

176. REISER, M. F., FERRIS, E. B., and LEVINE, M., "Cardiovascular Disorders, Heart Disease, and Hypertension," in Wittkower, E. D., and Cleghorn, R. A. (Eds.), *Recent Developments in Psychosomatic Medicine,* J. B. Lippincott, Philadelphia, 1957.

177. RENBOURN, E. T., "Body Temperature and Pulse Rate in Boys and Young Men Prior to Sporting Contests, A Study of Emotional Hyperthemia: With a Review of the Literature," *Journal of Psychosomatic Research,* 4:149, 1960.

178. RHEINHARDT, R. F., "Motion Sickness: A Psychophysiological Gastrointestinal Reaction," *Aerospace Medicine,* 30:802, 1959.

179. RHEINHART, J. B., and SUCCOP, R. A., "Regional Enteritis in Pediatric Patients: Psychiatric Aspects," *Journal of the American Academy of Child Psychiatry,* 7:252, 1968.

180. RHEINHART, J. B., KENNA, M. D., and SUCCOP, R. A., "Anorexia Nervosa in Children: Outpatient Management," *Journal of the American Academy of Child Psychiatry,* 11:114, 1972.

181. RICHMOND, J. B., "Discussion of Juvenile Paroxysmal Supraventricular Tachycardia: Psychosomatic and Psychodynamic Aspects," *Journal of the American Academy of Child Psychiatry,* 1:265, 1962.

182. ——, EDDY, E. J., and GARRARD, S. D., "The Syndrome of Fecal Soiling and Megacolon," *American Journal of Orthopsychiatry,* 24:391, 1954.

183. RIPLEY, H. S., and WOLFF, H. G., "Life Situations, Emotions, and Glaucoma," *Psychosomatic Medicine,* 12:215, 1950.

184. RIPLEY, H. S., et al., "Disturbances of Bladder Function Associated with Emotional States," *Journal of the American Medical Association,* 141:1139, 1949.

185. ROBERTIELLO, R. C., "Psychomotor Epilepsy in Children," *Diseases of the Nervous System,* 14:337, 1953.

186. ROBERTSON, E., "Photogenic Epilepsy: Self-Precipitated Attacks," *Brain,* 77:232, 1964.

187. ROSENMAN, R. H., et al., "Clinically Unrecognized Myocardial Infarction in the Western Collaborative Group Study," *American Journal of Cardiology,* 19:776, 1967.

188. SADLER, J. E., "The Long-Term Hospitalization of Asthmatic Children," *Pediatric Clinics of North America,* 22:173, 1975.

189. SANDLER, B., "Emotional Stress and Infertility," *Journal of Psychosomatic Research,* 12:51, 1968.

190. SARGENT, J. D., GREEN, E. E., and WALTERS, E. D., "Preliminary Report on the Use of Autogenic Feedback Training in the Treatment of Migraine and Tension Headaches," *Psychosomatic Medicine, 35:*129, 1973.

191. SCHACTER, J., et al., "Phasic Heart Rate Responses: Different Patterns in Black and White Newborns," *Psychosomatic Medicine, 37:*326, 1975.

192. SCHLAEGEL, T. F., and HOYT, M., *Psychosomatic Ophthalmology,* Williams & Wilkins, Baltimore, 1957.

193. SCHWARTZ, N. B., and ROTHCHILD, I., "Changes in Pituitary LH Concentration During Pseudopregnancy in the Rat," *Proceedings of the Society for Experimental Biology and Medicine, 116:*107, 1964.

194. SEITZ, P. F. D., "Psychological Aspects of Skin Diseases," in Wittkower, E., and Cleghorn, R. (Eds.), *Recent Developments in Psychosomatic Medicine,* J. B. Lippincott, Philadelphia, 1957.

195. SELZER, A. G., "Pseudocyesis in a 6 Year Old Girl," *Journal of the American Academy of Child Psychiatry, 7:*693, 1968.

196. SHANAN, J., et al., "Active Coping Behavior, Anxiety, and Cortical Steroid Excretion in the Prediction of Transient Amenorrhea," *Behavioral Science, 10:*461, 1965.

197. SHAPIRO, A. P., "Psychophysiologic Mechanisms in Hypertensive Vascular Disease," *Annals of Internal Medicine, 53:*64, 1960.

198. SHAPIRO, D., et al., "Effects of Feedback and Reinforcement on the Control of Human Systolic Blood Pressure," *Science, 63:*588, 1969.

199. SILVER, H. K., and FINKLESTEIN, M., "Deprivation Dwarfism," *Journal of Pediatrics, 70:*317, 1967.

200. SMIT, C. M., and HAMILTON, J., "Psychological Factors in the Narcolepsy-Cataplexy Syndrome," *Psychosomatic Medicine, 21:*40, 1959.

201. SMITH, S. L., and SANDER, C., "Food Cravings, Depression, and Premenstrual Problems," *Psychosomatic Medicine, 31:*281, 1969.

202. SOMMER, B., "The Effect of Menstruation on Cognitive and Perceptual-Motor Behavior: A Review," *Psychosomatic Medicine, 35:*515, 1973.

203. SOURS, J. A., "Clinical Studies of the Anorexia Nervosa Syndrome," *New York State Journal of Medicine, 68:*1363, 1968.

204. SPERLING, M., "Ulcerative Colitis in Children: Current Views and Therapies," *Journal of the American Academy of Child Psychiatry, 8:*336, 1969.

205. ———, "Asthma in Children: An Evaluation of Concepts and Therapies," *Journal of the American Academy of Child Psychiatry, 7:*44, 1968.

206. ———, "Transference Neurosis in Patients with Psychosomatic Disorders," *Psychoanalytic Quarterly, 36:*342, 1967.

207. ———, "Further Contributions to the Psychoanalytic Study of Migraine and Psychogenic Headaches," *International Journal of Psychoanalysis, 45:*549, 1964.

208. ———, "Psychosomatic Disorders," in Lorand, S., and Schneer, H. J. (Eds.), *Adolescents,* Hoeber, New York, 1961.

209. ———, "The Psychoanalytic Treatment of a Case of Chronic Regional Ileitis," *International Journal of Psychoanalysis, 4:*612, 1960.

210. ———, "Psychodynamics and Treatment of Petit Mal in Children," *International Journal of Psychoanalysis, 34:*248, 1953.

211. ———, "Observations from the Treatment of Children Suffering from Nonbloody Diarrhea or Mucous Colitis," *Journal of Hillside Hospital, 4:*25, 1955.

212. STARR, P. H., "Psychosomatic Consideration of Diabetes in Childhood," *Journal of Nervous and Mental Diseases, 121:*493, 1955.

213. STEIN, S. P., and CHARLES, E., "Emotional Factors in Juvenile Diabetes Mellitus: A Study of Early Life Experiences of Adolescent Diabetics," *American Journal of Psychiatry, 128:*56, 1971.

214. STEINBERG, A., et al., "Psychoendocrine Relationships in Psuedocyesis," *Psychosomatic Medicine, 8:*176, 1946.

215. STERKY, G., "Family Background and State of Mental Health in a Group of Diabetic School Children," *Acta Paediatrica, 52:*377, 1963.

216. STONE, R. T., and BARBERO, G. J., "Recurrent Abdominal Pain in Childhood," *Pediatrics, 45:*732, 1970.

217. STUNKARD, A., et al., "Influence of Social Class on Obesity and Thinness in Children," *Journal of the American Medical Association, 221:*579, 1972.

218. SULTZ, H. A., et al., "Asthma and Eczema," in Sultz, H. A., et al. (Eds.), *Long-term Childhood Illness,* University of Pittsburgh Press, Pittsburgh, 1972.

219. SWIFT, C. R., SEIDMAN, F., and STEIN, H., "Adjustment Problems in Juvenile Diabetics," *Psychosomatic Medicine, 29:*555, 1967.

220. TABOROFF, L. H., and BROWN, W. H., "A Study of the Personality Patterns of Children and Adolescents with the Peptic Ulcer Syndrome," *American Journal of Orthopsychiatry, 24:*602, 1954.

221. TIETZ, W., and VIDMAN, T., "The Impact of Coping Styles on the Control of Juvenile Diabetes," *Psychiatric Medicine, 3:*67, 1972.

222. VOTH, H. M., et al., "Thyroid 'Hot Spots': Their Relationship to Life Stress," *Psychosomatic Medicine, 32:*561, 1970.

223. WAHL, C. W., and GOLDEN, J. S., "Psychogenic Urinary Retention: Report of 6 Cases," *Psychosomatic Medicine, 25:*543, 1963.

224. WARSON, S. R., TURKEL, S., and SCHIELS, H. S., "Pseudopeptic Ulcer Syndromes in Children," *Journal of Pediatrics, 35:*215, 1949.

225. WEIL, W. B., et al., "Social Patterns and Diabetic Glycosuria," *American Journal of Diseases of Children, 113:*464, 1967.

226. WEINER, H., et al., "Cardiovascular Responses and Their Psychological Correlates," *Psychosomatic Medicine, 24:*477, 1962.

227. WEINER, H., et al., "Etiology of Duodenal Ulcer, I. Relation of Specific Psychological Characteristics to Rate of Gastric Secretion (Pepsinogen)," *Psychosomatic Medicine, 19:*1, 1957.

228. WEISS, E., "Cardiospasm, A Psychosomatic Disorder," *Psychosomatic Medicine, 6:*58, 1944.

229. WENDER, E. H., et al., "Behavioral Characteristics of Children with Chronic Nonspecific Diarrhea," *American Journal of Psychiatry, 133:*20, 1976.

230. WHITE, K. L., and LONG, W. N., "The Incidence of 'Psychogenic' Fever in a University Hospital," *Journal of Chronic Diseases, 8:*567, 1958.

231. WHITTEN, C. F., PETTIT, M. G., and FISCHOFF, J., "Evidence That Growth Failure from Maternal Deprivation Is Secondary to Undereating," *Journal of the American Medical Association, 209:*1675, 1969.

232. WINKELSTEIN, A., "Some General Observations on Cardiospasm," *Medical Clinics of North America, 28:*589, 1944.

233. WITTKOWER, E. D., and RUSSELL, B., *Emotional Factors and Skin Diseases,* Paul B. Hoeber, New York, 1963.

234. WOLF, S., *Children Under Stress,* Allen Lane, London, 1969.

235. ———, et al., *Life Stress and Essential Hypertension,* Williams & Wilkins, Baltimore, 1955.

236. WOLFF, H. G., *Headache and Other Head Pain,* Oxford University Press, New York, 1963.

237. YOSS, R. E., and DALY, D. D., "Narcolepsy in Children," *Pediatrics, 25:*1025, 1960.

238. ZAKUS, G., and SOLOMON, M., "The Family Situations of Obese Adolescent Girls," *Adolescence, 8:*33, 1973.

239. ZIMET, C. N., and BERGER, A. S., "Emotional Factors in Primary Glaucoma: An Evaluation of Psychological Test Data," *Psychosomatic Medicine, 22:*391, 1960.

37 / Children with Perceptual and Other Learning Problems

Larry B. Silver

Introduction

In all aspects of the child mental health field, it is essential to view the individual as a total person. This is especially true when conceptualizing the issues involved in designing a treatment intervention. To understand the clinical picture, a host of variables must be taken into account. This includes the constitutional and neurological substrate; intrapsychic and interpersonal dynamics; learned behaviors; and family and other significant system interactions. Nowhere is the holistic approach to the total child or adolescent more critical than with those who have perceptual and learning problems. Any evaluation which focuses on only one aspect of the child will be incomplete; and any therapeutic intervention that does not study the total child and his family may be less than successful.

It is difficult to discuss such a problem until one can agree on what it is about the child that is different. The literature and the many labels used to describe these cases are confusing. Learning disabilities can be in the processing of sensory inputs (perception), integration of these inputs (cognition), storage and retrieval of these data (memory), or in the output process (language or motor behavior). Thus, in their reports some clinicians will refer to learning disabilities or specific learning disabilities, whereas others focus on perceptual, cognitive, memory, language, or motor problems. These authors are not necessarily writing about different children; the difference is whether one refers to the total theme or to specific parts. So, too, individuals may focus on specific presenting problems rather than on the underlying disabilities. For example, one reads of the child with dyslexia (difficulty with reading), dyscalcula (difficulty with mathematics), or dysgraphia (difficulty with written language). In this chapter, we will use the overall descriptive term, *learning disabilities.*

The literature and labels used to describe these children and adolescents are confusing in another way. One reads a reference to children with learning disabilities and notes a description of hyperactivity, distractibility, or emotional problems. Articles on hyperactivity often refer to the high frequency of associated learning disabilities. In some literature, all of these characteristics are described under one rubric, the "minimal brain dysfunction syndrome." This handbook deals with many of these individual areas in addition to covering the broad syndrome (see volume 2, chapters 20, 21, 22; and volume 3, chapter 38).

What then is the total child with learning disabilities? This confusion was first addressed in 1963, when a committee was formed to develop a symposium on the child with minimal brain dysfunction. Clements chaired a task force of this committee which focused on the complex issues relating to the terminology and identification of this syndrome.[2] After reviewing the literature and the current understanding of these children, he attempted to define the syndrome as consisting of:

> Children of near average, average, or above average general intelligence with certain learning or behavioral disabilities ranging from mild to severe, which are associated with deviations of function of the central nervous system. These deviations may manifest themselves by various combinations of impairment in perception, conceptualization, language, memory, and control of attention, impulse, or motor function.

Since Clements's monograph, many studies have supported this concept of a multidimensional syndrome, a syndrome manifested by specific learning disabilities, hyperactivity and/or distractibility, and emotional problems.* Other investigators undertook to provide descriptions of particular aspects of the syndrome as the primary issue, focusing on the specific learning disabilities, the hyperactivity, or the attentional deficits. Others described the emotional difficulties of the child and family. All these studies resulted in a better understanding of the individual clinical problems. However, as observers evolved their views of this syndrome and presented their findings, new labels emerged along with apparently conflicting outlooks.

It is helpful to keep in mind that what is under discussion here is a syndrome, a cluster of symp-

* See references 3, 5, 8, 9, 10, 12, 13, 16, 18, 19, and 24.

toms frequently grouped together. As Clements[2] noted, an overall schema for understanding such children would include three major components: specific learning disabilities, hyperactivity and/or distractibility, and social and emotional problems. Thus, to discuss the total child requires discussing all these components. The author prefers the term minimal brain dysfunction syndrome to reflect this schema.

In addition to perceiving these children as having a multidimensional syndrome, one other basic element is required for a truly comprehensive understanding of their condition. These children do not have just a school disability; they have a *life disability*. Their specific learning disabilities plus possible hyperactivity and distractibility interfere with all aspects of life, not just school. Their handicaps create problems in the family, on the playground, at club meetings, at summer camp— everywhere they interact and perform. Thus, the primary focus of this chapter will be on methods of helping the child or adolescent with learning disabilities; however, the effects of the possible hyperactivity, distractibility, emotional and family problems will also be examined.

Therapeutic Intervention for the Learning Disabilities

As specific learning disabilities are discussed in other chapters, they will only be briefly reviewed here. A child might have difficulty with input, receiving information into the brain. These difficulties comprise the group of perceptual problems and might involve any of the five senses. Visual and auditory perceptual disabilities are the two most commonly found. A child with a visual perceptual disability may have difficulty organizing a percept in space; faced with a symbol, he may reverse it or transpose it. Or, he may have difficulty with spatial relationships, confusing left and right or position in space. Another variety of problems relates to difficulty in distinguishing the significant elements of a scene from the background. Depth perception may also be affected by visual perceptual problems.

A child with auditory perceptual problems may have difficulty distinguishing subtle differences in sounds; he may misunderstand what is being said and perhaps respond incorrectly. He may have difficulty with sound figure-ground or sound depth perception. Some children have difficulty processing sound as quickly as ordinary speech requires; this auditory lag causes them to miss part of what they hear.

In addition to input difficulties, the child may have problems relating to the integration of information after is has been perceived by the brain. He may assign incorrect sequence to the symbols or have difficulty inferring abstract meaning from the literal percepts. These sequencing and/or abstraction problems may relate to visual or auditory inputs, or both.

Once perceived and integrated, information must be stored, later to be retrieved. Some children have difficulty with memory. In certain cases, this disability involves only short-term memory; that is, memory that is retained only as long as one attends to the information. For others, the difficulty is with long-term memory—recalling information that has been stored. Again, these disabilities can relate to visual, auditory, or both forms of input.

A final area of possible disabilities affects the process of getting information out of the brain. This output disability may include difficulty in expressing oneself by words and by language output or in expressing oneself through muscle activity in terms of motor output. Language disabilities usually involve difficulty with demand language. That is, the child may have no difficulty initiating a conversation, but he finds it hard to organize his thoughts or find the correct words when language is demanded, such as when asked a question.

A child with motor output disability may have difficulty with gross or fine motor performance. Gross motor difficulty may cause him to be clumsy or to have difficulty walking, running, or riding a bike. The child or adolescent with fine motor disabilities will have trouble organizing combinations of muscles to work together, such as in performing tasks with his hands—writing, for example. In school, the most commonly noted fine motor disability is in the area of written language. The child may have a problem coordinating the many muscles involved in speech production or may speak with poor articulation (dysarthria).

Common to all varieties of the minimal brain dysfunction syndrome is the fact that the individual has one or more of these learning disabilities. It is not difficult to see how such disabilities interfere with school tasks. The children may have reading, math, and writing difficulties; or, to use the accepted jargon dyslexia, dyscalcula, or dysgraphia. They do poorly in most learning situations.

It is difficult to picture any life activity in which these disabilities would not interfere with normal performance. At home, the child may have problems doing chores, cutting and eating food, dressing, or listening and talking with family members. The same is true in his relationships with peers. Whether it be baseball, basketball, football, four-square, hopscotch, tag, jump rope, table games, or just talking with friends, learning disabilities interfere with mastery and success.

Special educational programs in school can seek to maximize the child's strengths while compensating for or correcting his disabilities. With such help, the child will make academic progress. However, when the help ends with school, the child continues to suffer learning disabilities in other aspects of his life.

The key to therapeutic intervention for this condition is to make sure that the parents and whole family know and understand the nature of the child's specific difficulties. The parents must be able to set up experiences and tasks which maximize the possibility of success rather than emphasize the areas of weakness. Without understanding their child's weaknesses and strengths, they can be of little help. Rather than protecting or expecting nothing from the child, with such understanding, they can select chores which capitalize on his capabilities. Thus, they can influence him toward possible success rather than toward probable failures. They can improve communication by finding out whether their child receives information best through his eyes or ears. With such knowledge, the parents can reach out to the community and develop potentially positive experiences for their child.

As an example, if the director of a local youth center knows the child's areas of strength and weakness, he can help the parents select appropriate programs. A child with fine motor problems might do poorly in arts and crafts activities which require such fine motor performances as drawing and cutting. But he might do well in a photography club where most of the activity requires only gross motor efforts. The same approach can lead to success in sports. If a child has fine motor, visual motor, or sequencing difficulties, he might do poorly in such sports as baseball, basketball, or football. However, the same child might do quite well in sports that require gross motor abilities— swimming, bowling, horseback riding, soccer, hockey, skiing, and golf.

Advance planning will be helpful in other areas. An informed scout leader can assign tasks the child can do rather than ones that lead to frustration, failure, dropping out, and another social disaster. For example, for a child with fine motor problems but gross motor abilities, a scout leader might ask the child to carry the flag rather than emphasizing knot tying. A school teacher who understands that a child has a demand language disability would let the child volunteer to speak rather than call on him to answer a question. If the child has good fine motor skills, the teacher might feel free to ask him to write something on the blackboard.

Thus, if a professional team wants to help the total child, the parents must be as knowledgeable about their child's specific learning disabilities as are the special educators. They require counseling in understanding their child's weaknesses and strengths and in how to apply this understanding to maximize success and minimize failure. A specific model for helping the family will be discussed later.

Therapeutic Intervention for Hyperactivity and Distractibility

There are at least two types of hyperactivity and distractibility: anxiety based and physiologically based. Overall, anxiety is the most common cause of hyperactivity and/or distractibility among children and adolescents. There are children who express their anxiety through an increase in motoric behavior or reflect this anxiety by difficulty in concentrating; usually they exhibit these behaviors only during specific life-space experiences. On the other hand, children with the minimal brain dysfunction learning disability syndrome have a physiologically based motor hyperactivity and/or a decrease in the ability to filter out less important sensory stimuli, resulting in distractibility. The history of such behavior is chronic; often it is first noted while the child is *in utero*. The hyperactivity and/or distractibility does not relate to any specific events; it is not limited to school hours, but occurs all of the time and any place.

It is important to differentiate between physiologically based hyperactivity and increased motor activity due to anxiety. The former often responds to the psychostimulants; the latter may respond to a minor tranquilizer but will not respond to a psychostimulant. A child whose aggressive or agitated behavior reflects an underlying depression may also respond to a psychostimulant; its mood-lifting property will bring about an improvement in behavior. Here, too, the history and description of the behavior offer clues to the differential diagnosis. For reasons not yet understood, the physiologically based hyperactivity and/or distractibility may disappear with puberty; children who have been on medication throughout latency may no longer need such medication after the age of thirteen to fifteen. However, this is not always true. Clinical observations suggest that as many as fifteen percent of these individuals need medication throughout adolescence and into young adulthood.*

The specific aspects of the use of medication for hyperactivity and distractibility have been discussed in chapter 23. Some of this material will be reviewed here within the context of treatment planning. Dextroamphetamine and methylphenidate are probably the most commonly used drugs. Pemoline, a new product, is also now in use.

If one suspects hyperactivity and/or distractibility and none of the psychostimulants have been successful, it is helpful to determine whether the medication has been administered as prescribed, or whether the child is taking the medication at all. Other possibilities are that the hyperactivity is anxiety based rather than physiologically based or that the family or school situation is so stressful that the medication may be improving the physiologically based hyperactivity but not lowering the anxiety-based component.

It must be emphasized again that the hyperactivity and/or distractibility are not only educational disabilities; they are life disabilities. Such behaviors interfere with family, peer, and social activities. Thus, if a child responds positively to such medication, he should be on medication all day everyday, *not just during school hours*. It is just as important for a child to sit calmly and attend at the dinner table or while playing with a friend as it is to function in class. This is an important point, for many physicians still feel that the child should be on medication only during school hours. But the hyperactive and/or distractible child who responds positively to medication needs his medicine to help him function better at all times. He needs it whenever he must relax, relate, and function—at dinner with the family, watching television with siblings, attending a Cub Scout meeting, or Sunday School.

Parents should be educated about the effects and duration of the medication. Dextroamphetamine and methylphenidate work for about four hours with minimal or no residual effects. In-

* See references 1, 4, 11, 15, and 17.

formed of this, a parent can add or subtract from the usual dosage pattern to fit the activity. The child may be scheduled to take his last pill in the middle of the afternoon; however, if company is coming or if some activity is anticipated, he may need an extra dose at 6:00 or 7:00 P.M. Parents should understand this concept and be given permission to alter the dosage pattern as needed. On the other hand, if the family plans to go swimming and the child can run and be active, the dosage for these hours might be reduced or dropped.

The idiosyncrasies and toxic effects of the psychostimulant drugs are described in the drug manufacturers' literature. There are a few common clinical side effects which can often be managed without stopping the medication.[22] The psychostimulants may produce a loss of appetite, which usually decreases or disappears within a month. The parents should be encouraged to continue the treatment program. If the anorexia persists and weight loss ensues, the drug should perhaps be discontinued. It is the loss of weight that is the critical issue, not the loss of appetite. The medication decreases the child's appetite so that he becomes more selective about what he eats. Thus, a given child may not eat his meals but will eat candy and other snacks. Controlling snacks might result in better meal intakes.

Some children will have difficulty falling asleep while on these drugs and may lie restlessly in bed for three or four hours. As in the case of anorexia, this insomnia may disappear during the first month. With some children, the sleeplessness is a legitimate result of the psychostimulant, and it is then necessary to discontinue the mid- or late-afternoon dose. With other children, the sleeplessness is due not to the medication but to the disinhibiting rebound effect of being off of the medication. That is, a child on a three-times-a-day schedule is under the effect of medication from morning until about four hours after the last dose. When the medication wears off, at 8:00 or 9:00 P.M., the child rebounds to his usual or higher level of activity. The result is increased hyperactivity and restlessness at bedtime. He is put to bed at 9:00 or 9:30, but can't unwind. For this child, an additional dose of stimulant at about 8:00 P.M. may eliminate the difficulty in sleeping. Stopping the afternoon dose helps in some cases; adding a bedtime dose helps in others. The two possible causes for insomnia are difficult to differentiate; often, a trial dose at bedtime is necessary to clarify the issue.

Parents may report that their child is clinically improved while on the medication but that he now talks constantly, or breaks into tears or explodes at the slightest frustration. It is not clear how much of this emotional lability is a result of the medication and how much is functional. Because the medication lessens motor activity, the child may be better able to interact and communicate; thus, a quiet child might become more verbal. It is also possible that, because the medication allows the child to sit still and be available for learning, he is now forced to deal with his learning problems and thus becomes frustrated and more anxious. The increased anxiety may explain the increase in verbiage or in emotional lability. If reassurance to the parents and special educational help for the child do not minimize the emotional lability, the drug dosage may be decreased. If this does not help, stopping the medication or changing to another type might have to be considered.

Some children or adolescents who are doing well on a psychostimulant may become more hyperactive and/or distractible when placed on antihistamines for other reasons. It appears that the sedative effect of the antihistamine neutralizes some of the stimulant effect of the amphetamine or amphetamine-like drugs. This particular child may need an increased dosage of the psychostimulant while on the antihistamines.

The suggested use of megavitamins, trace elements, or the elimination of specific food additives has been proposed as a treatment for hyperactivity.[19] These approaches to treatment are discussed in volume 2, chapter 20.

Therapeutic Intervention for the Social and Emotional Problems

The specific learning disabilities as well as the sometimes presence of hyperactivity and/or distractibility cause these children to become frustrated. They experience many failures and have difficulty coping in the family, neighborhood, and school. In time, they are all too likely to develop social and emotional problems.[7, 21] Very often the learning disabilities are not recognized or treated, and the child continues to experience repeated frustrations and failures. If the child withdraws from learning and stops trying, he is likely to be sent for tutoring or to a special class. If, however, the emotional stress takes the form of a behavioral disorder, he is likely to be referred for psychiatric evaluation. Such a child does not have a primary emotional difficulty or a characterologic problem; rather, his emotional reaction is secondary to the unrecognized underlying syndrome. To view this condition otherwise is to miss a significant etiological factor. The inevitable result will be an inadequate treatment approach.

These children have difficulty with all stages of psychosocial development. The learning disabilities, hyperactivity, or distractibility interfere with mastery of most, if not all, developmental tasks. The child's difficulties weigh heavily on the parents and other family members, who may in turn become frustrated, helpless, and dysfunctional.[6, 7, 14, 20] A detailed review of the emotional problems of the child and the difficulties of the family are discussed in volume 2, chapter 20.

The critical differential factor that must be assessed here is whether a primary emotional problem is making the child or adolescent inaccessible for learning or whether the emotional problems are the result of the frustration and failure caused by the learning problems.

Where the child's emotional problems are causing the academic difficulties, psychotherapy will help. Where the child's emotional problems are secondary to the academic difficulties, psychotherapy alone will not be successful. In fact, focusing only on the secondary emotional difficulties may add to the child's difficulties by giving credence to the belief that the school problems are emotionally based. If special educational programs and appropriate medication are not included in the treatment plan, it will be difficult to help the child.

Psychotherapy can help the child with such disabilities cope and will make him more available for learning. However, when a child is experiencing frustration and failure all week long at school, such help is likely to be minimal. It is difficult to help a child replace a poor self image when he experiences daily failures at school. Without an appropriate educational program, the effects of psychotherapy may be quickly negated.

As mentioned, because the disabilities interfere with mastery of many play and interactional activities, these children have problems with peers. They cannot do many of the things their age-group do, or they may have difficulty understanding or communicating. They fail at everyday tasks and are often teased. Not uncommonly, they become socially inappropriate and immature, have difficulty making and keeping friends, and are withdrawn. Some may choose a younger peer group, seeking out a play level they can handle. The social immaturity may also be reflected in an inability to pick up appropriate social cues.

The social problems become understandable when one sees the effect of such disabilities on the child. Often, insight-oriented group therapy is of no help. Special educational programs aid the child in mastering or compensating for his disabilities; with this improvement, social growth may be observed. Groups designed for modeling social skills as well as for individualized activity or sports-related training can be helpful.

Psychotherapeutic approaches to the psychogenic difficulties secondary to minimal brain dysfunction are discussed further in chapter 38.

Therapeutic Intervention for the Total Child and Family

Each aspect of this syndrome has been discussed separately, but the clinician must focus on the total child. It is apparent that any evaluation or intervention approach that focuses only on the learning disabilities and the classroom will not succeed. So, too, the physician who recognizes hyperactivity and prescribes medication alone will fail to address all aspects of the problem. From initial request for help to final implementation of a model of intervention, a multidisciplinary team is required.

The evaluation of such a child requires such a team effort. Because there are so many areas of potential difficulty, ideally this team should consist of a child psychiatrist, neurologist, psychologist, social worker, special educator, speech pathologist, and the family physician. Each contributes to the complete understanding of the total child.

Frequently the history obtained from the parents begins to suggest the minimal brain dysfunction syndrome. Descriptions of the child's behavior, inconsistencies in the child's performance, delays in motor or language development, or poor academic performance imply possible specific learning disabilities. Continuous increased motor activity suggests hyperactivity; a short attention span might connote distractibility. If behavioral problems associated with poor academic performance began in the first year of school, this raises the possibility that the emotional difficulties might be related to this syndrome.

Once the evaluation is complete, the findings must be shared with all involved. It is best to begin with the parents. They should be helped to understand all aspects of the syndrome and how these problems explain their child's difficulties. They must understand each phase of the treatment approach and collaborate in implementing the program. With such knowledge, their feelings of helplessness can change to helpfulness.

In working with the parents, it is important to be aware of their reactions to learning that their child has a disability.[10, 18, 23] These normal reactions are described in detail in volume 2, chapter 20. Briefly, the parents of these children may go through a grief reaction similar, albeit of lesser intensity, to that experienced with a loss by death. They must give up an image of their child, an ambition that may now never be fulfilled. They may indeed react in a manner that tends to alienate their physician. In particular, they may seek a quick cure or magic pill.

As with other grief reactions, denial is often the initial phase of this response. They insist it cannot be true. It must be a mistake; "I don't believe it!" A parent may doubt the professional's competence or castigate him. Frequently, another opinion is sought. Unfortunately, while consultation is often useful, doctor shopping for someone who will tell the parent what he wants to hear is not. Another form of denial may be the cover-up reaction. One parent, usually the mother, will want to protect the other parent by concealing the results of the studies or by minimizing the problems. Some parents successfully cover up special school programs for years. Sadly, the unknowing parent builds up unrealistic expectations or makes demands on his child that the child cannot fulfill. The child often sees through this cover up and perceives the true reason, that his parents cannot accept him and have to deny him as he is and pretend he is different. The child may react with anger or sadness; to the extent that he feels that the parents do not accept him, he will surely have difficulty accepting himself.

The parental denial stage may be followed by a period of anger. This angry reaction is not uncommon. It may be directed inward or projected outward. On learning of a child's disability, it is normal for parents to feel anger and to express (or think) such sentiments as "Why me?" or "How could God do this to me?" This initial reaction often reflects feelings of helplessness and frustration.

If the initial anger is turned inward, the attack is against the self, resulting in a feeling of depression. Along with this reaction, there is often a feeling of guilt, a belief that it is all "my own fault." A parent may berate himself, telling himself, "God is punishing me because I didn't follow my doctor's advice" or "I've been given this extra burden to prove my worthiness."

If the depression is allowed to continue, the parent might withdraw from the child or from the other parent just at the time that he is most needed. For some parents, the guilt feeling might be an attempt to establish control over a situation that is experienced as hopeless. By attributing the cause to himself, the parent puts into his own hands the power to understand the situation and to control it. The rationale is that if he is not again guilty of the transgression, the situation will not happen again.

If, on the other hand, the initial anger is displaced outward, the parent enters into a pattern of blaming or attributing the fault to someone else. Like the guilt reaction, it places responsibility in the hands of mankind and protects one against feelings of helplessness. The parent might blame the obstetrician because he did not get to the hospital fast enough or might recall that on one occasion the pediatrician did not see the child when he had a high fever and instead prescribed over the phone. This reaction might be generalized to all professionals, who are then considered bunglers, incompetents, and charlatans. The professional may never hear the parents' complaints, but the child may never be allowed to forget them. Such reactions may undermine the child's faith in or respect for the very people he must turn to for help and for hope.

Some parents may attempt to suppress their feelings of guilt by overprotecting the child. The natural thing to do when a child is hurt is to reach out and protect. This is necessary and helpful. But the goal is to protect him where he needs protecting and to encourage growth where he does not need protecting. Too wide a blanket of protection may cushion the weaknesses, but it also blunts the strengths. Not only does this behavior keep the child immature or delay areas of growth, it also makes the child feel inadequate. He knows what is happening. When everyone else has a chore to do and he does not, when everyone takes turns clearing the table but he never has to, he might conclude that his parents regard him as inadequate.

Most parents of such handicapped children go through this sequence of denial, anger, and guilt. They might go through a stage similar to the hypercathexis prior to decathexis seen in the mourning process. During this time, parents may need to review the clinical findings again or they may ask repeated questions about their child, as if they have to overinvest in the symptoms and treatment programs before they can accept them.

Parents must understand the learning disabilities and grasp the type of special educational programs needed. By focusing on the needs versus the realities of their specific school district, they learn whom to contact, what to request, and how to negotiate with the school system. They need to understand their child's areas of weakness and strength as these relate to home and neighborhood. As discussed earlier, they must learn how to maximize success by building on the strengths while helping their child to compensate for or avoid areas of weakness. They must learn how to run interference for their child in selecting activities outside of the home.

If medication is indicated, the parents should be taught why and how the medication works. They need to know all aspects of selecting and managing the dosage pattern and side effects. Only then can they become the educated, available caretakers the child needs. If the parents are resistant, the therapist can delay implementing parts of the program until they have been helped to deal with their resistance.

Next, the emphasis should fall on the social and emotional problems as well as on the family's difficulties. One should try to relate these to the frustrations and failures the child and family have experienced. Models of helping are introduced.

Once the parents have begun to comprehend the implications of the minimal brain dysfunction syndrome for the total life experiences of their child, the child's school system can be contacted. A collaborative effort should be undertaken both to develop the necessary educational programs and to establish the necessary lines of communication. Such communication is essential for acquiring data on which to base adjustments of the medication pattern.

After the initial session(s) with the parents, the child should be seen. He requires help in understanding all aspects of the problem as thoroughly as do the parents. The only variation with age is in the approach and level of language. For most children, this insight into their problems is usually received with relief. The child now has an answer: He is not bad or stupid or lazy. The full treatment plan is discussed in detail.

Once the child appears to have an initial understanding, a family session can be scheduled. Every member of the family needs to know and understand the problems and the treatment plans. The siblings need to know and deserve to have their questions answered. With understanding, the child's image and role in the family begins to shift. The siblings can become allies in helping.

At this point in the interpretive process, the parents need help in negotiating with the school and other agencies. Together, medication plans can be worked out. All of this may take three to five sessions. These preventive family counseling sessions are designed to help the family understand the information and to encourage them to explore alternative styles of relating and behaving. If needed, modeling or behavioral management skills can be introduced.

With this preventive counseling approach to the total child and family, many, if not most, of the children and families relax and make progress. Social, emotional, and family problems diminish as the stresses are lessened and as opportunities for positive relationships and successes are increased. For those who do not improve, individual or family therapy may be needed. The recommendation for such therapy might best be delayed until the effects of the counseling can be observed.

At some point in this process, the parents will ask for advice about the future. They should be informed that there is much about the minimal brain dysfunction syndrome that is still unknown. Predicting the future is difficult, and prediction is often to the child's disadvantage. It is too easy to over- or underestimate abilities. The family must learn to accept the need to plan six to twelve months at a time; more is not always possible.

The literature is not helpful in providing advice to families about their child's progress. Studies on the natural history of these children are often difficult to follow. As with other aspects of this syndrome, the confusion is caused by terminology and the definition of terms. If one focuses on one aspect of the syndrome, treating only a certain group of symptoms, then follow-up studies are inconclusive.

Some investigators who studied follow-up treatment of hyperactive children on psychostimulants have concluded that they do not improve academically. But the psychostimulants are not expected to treat the learning disabilities, only the hyperactivity or distractibility. Thus, the wrong outcome variable is being measured. This finding does not suggest that the psychostimulants are not effective in improving the hyperactivity, only that the psychostimulants do not treat the learning disabilities. Without special educational intervention, medication will not, of course, overcome the learning disabilities.

There are probably multiple determinants for this syndrome. Several different etiologic factors can result in the clinical findings. The outcome may be based on the etiologic factors as well as on the types of clinical interventions.

The specific learning disabilities are best helped with special educational intervention. Without help, they compound and as the child gets older, he falls further behind. When the learning disabilities are due to maturational lag, the children appear to need special educational help until about age eight; then, the disabilities often minimize or are no longer observed. However, when they are due to an inherited, dysfunctional central nervous system, the children need to develop alternative learning pathways and compensation skills. They often need special help for four to five years, and many need additional support for even longer. Some of these disabilities, especially the fine motor ones, may persist throughout life. When structural brain damage results in learning disabilities, special educational help may be needed throughout the child's education. Residual findings—such as learning disabilities, distractibility, hyperactivity, or emotional problems—often persist during adulthood.*

With adequate doses of psychostimulants, the hyperactivity and/or distractibility will usually improve. Most children will need such medication until puberty. However, as noted earlier, 15 to 20 percent will continue to need this medication throughout adolescence and young adulthood.

Without total treatment of the total child for the total minimal brain dysfunction syndrome, emotional problems resulting in major psychiatric difficulties may develop in adolescence and adulthood. No studies have yet documented the number of school drop-outs, delinquents, or adolescent psychiatric hospital admissions which are a result of unrecognized and untreated learning disabilities and/or hyperactivity. Clinical experience suggests that as many as 30 or 40 percent of such individuals might exhibit symptoms consistent with this syndrome.

Conclusion

The child with the minimal brain dysfunction syndrome does not have a school disability—he has a life disability. The same disturbances that interfere with the normal learning processes also impinge on self-concept, self-image, peer relation-

* See references 1, 4, 11, 15, and 17.

ships, family relationships, and social interactions. The same hyperactivity or distractibility that affects the child's abilities in the classroom interfere with his adaptation to home and neighborhood.

Often such a child does not develop normally, or begins to develop secondary social and/or emotional problems, and is referred to a mental health clinician for evaluation. In undertaking such an evaluation, it is important to be alert for clues that suggest this syndrome.[18] It is extremely important to differentiate between emotional problems that reflect the stresses caused by this syndrome and emotional problems that are a primary cause of the presenting symptoms.

If the emotional difficulties are secondary to the learning disabilities, psychotherapy alone will not succeed. Indeed, it may add to the child's burden by giving credence to the belief that the academic problems are emotionally based. If special educational programs and appropriate medication are not included along with the psychotherapeutic intervention, it is difficult for the child to overcome the problems.

Properly recognized, diagnosed, and treated, the child with the minimal brain dysfunction syndrome has the potential for a reasonably successful future. Without help, the disabilities may become incapacitating and function as a major handicap that will pervade the child's life.

All aspects of this condition must be considered in understanding the child, planning a treatment program, and advising the family and schools. Any therapeutic approach which does not view this syndrome as a serious life disability affecting both the total child and his family is not likely to be successful.

REFERENCES

1. ARNOLD, L. E., STROBEL, D., and WEISENBERG, A., "Hyperactive Adult: Study of the 'Paradoxical' Amphetamine Response," *Journal of the American Medical Association*, 222:693–694, 1972.

2. CLEMENTS, S., *Minimal Brain Dysfunction in Children*, National Institute of Neurological Diseases and Blindness, Monograph no. 3, Department of Health, Education, and Welfare, Washington, D. C., 1966.

3. CONNERS, C., "The Syndrome of Minimal Brain Dysfunction: Psychological Aspects," *Pediatric Clinics of North America*, 14:749–766, 1967.

4. HARTOCOLLIS, P., "The Syndrome of Minimal Brain Dysfunction in Young Adult Patients," *Bulletin of the Menninger Clinic*, 32:102–114, 1968.

5. GARDNER, R. A., *MBD: The Family Book About Minimal Brain Dysfunction*, Jason Aronson, New York, 1973.

6. ———, "The Guilt Reaction of Parents of Children with Severe Physical Disease," *American Journal of Psychiatry*, 126:636–644, 1969.

7. ———, "Psychological Problems of Brain-Injured Children and Their Parents," *Journal of the American Academy of Child Psychiatry*, 7:471–491, 1968.

8. LAUFER, M. W., "Cerebral Dysfunction and Behavioral Disorders of Adolescents," *American Journal of Orthopsychiatry*, 32:501–507, 1962.

9. ———, and DENHOFF, C., "Hyperkinetic Behavior Syndrome in Children," *Journal of Pediatrics*, 50:463–474, 1957.

10. MCCARTHY, J. J., and MCCARTHY, D. J., *Learning Disabilities*, Allyn and Bacon, Boston, 1969.

11. MANN, H. B., and GREENSPAN, S. I., "The Identification and Treatment of Adult Brain Dysfunction," *American Journal of Psychiatry*, 133:9–13, 1976.

12. O'MALLEY, J. E., and EISENBERG, L., "The Hyperkinetic Syndrome," in Walter, S., and Wolff, P. H. (Eds.), *Minimal Cerebral Dysfunction in Children*, Grune & Stratton, New York, 1973.

13. PINCUS, J. H., and GLASSER, G. H., "The Syndrome of 'Minimal Brain Damage' in Childhood," *New England Journal of Medicine*, 275:27–33, 1966.

14. POZNANSKI, E., "Psychiatric Difficulties in Siblings of Handicapped Children," *Clinical Pediatrics*, 8:232–234, 1969.

15. QUITKIN, F., and KLEIN, D. F., "Two Behavioral Syndromes in Young Adults Related to Possible Minimal Brain Dysfunction," *Journal of Psychiatric Research*, 7:131–142, 1969.

16. SCHAIN, R. J., *Neurology of Childhood Learning Disorders*, Williams & Wilkins, Baltimore, 1976.

17. SHELLEY, E. M., and RIESTER, A., "Syndrome of Minimal Brain Damage in Adults," *Diseases of the Nervous System*, 33:335–338, 1972.

18. SILVER, L. B., "Playroom Diagnostic Evaluation of Children with Neurologically Based Learning Disabilities," *Journal of the American Academy of Child Psychiatry*, 15:240–256, 1976.

19. ———, "Acceptable and Controversial Approaches to Treating the Child with Learning Disabilities," *Pediatrics*, 55:406–415, 1975.

20. ———, "Emotional and Social Problems of the Families with a Child who has Developmental Disabilities," in Weber, R. E. (Ed.), *Handbook on Learning Disabilities*, Prentice-Hall, Englewood Cliffs, N. J., 1974.

21. ———, "Emotional and Social Problems of Children with Developmental Disabilities," in Weber, R. E. (Ed.), *Handbook on Learning Disabilities*, Prentice-Hall, Englewood Cliffs, N. J., 1974.

22. ———, "The Neurological Learning Disability Syndrome," *American Family Physician*, 4:95–102, 1971.

23. SOLNIT, A. J., and STARK, M. H., "Mourning and the Birth of a Defective Child," in Eissler, R. S., et al. (Eds.), *The Psychoanalytic Study of the Child*, vol. 16, pp. 523–537, International Universities Press, New York, 1961.

24. SULZBACHER, S. I., "The Learning Disabled or Hyperactive Child: Diagnosis and Treatment," *Journal of the American Medical Association*, 234:938–941, 1975.

SUGGESTED READING

For the Professional:
CANTWELL, D. P. (Ed.), *The Hyperactive Child. Diagnosis, Management and Current Research*, Spectrum Publications, New York, 1975.
JOHNSON, D. J., and MYKLEBUST, H. R., *Learning Disabilities. Educational Principles and Practices*, Grune & Stratton, New York, 1964.
McCARTHY, J. J., and McCARTHY, D. J., *Learning Disabilities*, Allyn and Bacon, Boston, 1969.
RENSHAW, D. C., *The Hyperactive Child*, Nelson-Hall, Chicago, 1974.
ROSS, A. O., *The Exceptional Child in the Family*, Grune & Stratton, New York, 1964.
SAFER, D. J., and ALLEN, R. P., *Hyperactive Children. Diagnosis and Management*, University Park Press, Baltimore, 1976.
SAPIR, S. G., and NITZBURG, A. C., *Children with Learning Problems*, Brunner/Mazel, New York, 1973.

WENDER, P. H., *Minimal Brain Dysfunction in Children*, Wiley-Interscience, New York, 1971.

For Parents:
GARDNER, R. A., *MBD: The Family Book About Minimal Brain Dysfunction*, Jason Aronson, New York, 1973.
BRUTTEN, M., RICHARDSON, S. O., and MANGEL, C., *Something's Wrong with My Child*, Harcourt Brace Jovanovich, New York, 1973.
ROSNER, J., *Helping Children Overcome Learning Difficulties*, Walker, New York, 1975.
WEISS, H. G., and WEISS, M. S., *Home Is a Learning Place. A Parents' Guide to Learning Disabilities*, Little Brown, Boston, 1976.
WENDER, P. H., *The Hyperactive Child. A Handbook for Parents*, Crown, New York, 1973.

38 / Psychogenic Difficulties Secondary to MBD

Richard A. Gardner

Like most children with a handicap, children with minimal brain dysfunction (MBD) are generally aware that they are different from others and compare themselves unfavorably with those who are unimpaired. As fate decrees for all children who are "different," those with MBD often suffer taunts from peers and rejection by parents and others. As a result, feelings of inadequacy and other untoward emotional reactions are commonly engendered. These are likely to contribute to the formation of secondary, purely psychogenic symptoms. This outcome not only imposes on such children an additional burden, but may intensify the primary organic symptoms as well.[36, 42, 46] During the last fifteen to twenty years, a plethora of articles have appeared describing the organic manifestations of MBD. Unfortunately, there are few publications in the psychiatric and psychological literature devoted to the treatment of these secondary psychogenic difficulties. And this despite the fact that most (if not all) of these children suffer in this way to varying degrees. Bender's book,[2] which is recognized as a classic on the subject, generally restricts itself to those psychogenic symptoms that are most intimately related to the organic manifestations. It does not provide any extensive discussion of psychotherapeutic technique.

Perhaps the paucity of articles on this subject is related to the notion that organic disorders may be treated only by physical and pharmacological methods. The efficacy of medication in alleviating some of the primary organic manifestations (such as hyperactivity, distractibility, and learning impairments) contributes as well to the amelioration of some of the secondary symptoms (such as low self-esteem, withdrawal from peers, and low academic motivation). This comes about through the alleviation of stress and the enhancement of competence that medication provides. However, even in the most responsive cases, medication does not totally remove all symptoms, and in any case, most medicated children still exhibit various secondary psychogenic difficulties. Perhaps the combination of a focus on medication combined with the difficulty of engaging such children in traditional psychotherapy has discouraged many from attempting such treatment. Whatever the reasons, the paucity of articles is unfortunate, because most of these children can profit from psychotherapy, although certain modifications of and departures from traditional methods are often desirable.

Basic Therapeutic Considerations

THERAPEUTIC GOALS

It is vital for the therapist to have a clear idea from the outset which symptoms are manifestations of the organic deficits and which are of superimposed psychological origin. The primary neurological symptoms are examined in detail in volume 2, chapter 20, and excellent discussions of these symptoms are available elsewhere.[6, 8, 11, 48] This chapter will emphasize the more common secondary symptoms as well as the primary organic manifestations that are likely to be intensified by psychogenic factors. Without such clear differentiation the therapist may attempt to employ psychotherapeutic measures to alleviate symptoms that are not amenable to such an approach. The likely outcome will be frustration and disillusionment for the patient, the parents, and the therapist himself.[41]

In addition, the therapist does well to appreciate that all children have basic temperamental characteristics that contribute to their behavioral patterns. Birch, Chess, and Thomas[5, 7, 44] describe nine areas in which such patterns may exhibit themselves: activity level, rhythmicity, approach and withdrawal, adaptability, intensity of reaction, threshold of responsiveness, quality of mood, distractibility and attention span, and persistence. Last, the therapist may have to accept goals that are much more modest than those he might set for patients with purely psychogenic problems. The basic neurological problems may persist for years (even throughout life), and the person may be confronted with them continually. To ignore these considerations may result in futility and frustration; to recognize them enables the therapist to focus his attention most efficiently.

THE FOUR BASIC TREATMENT MODALITIES

The treatment of children with MBD involves four modalities: (1) medication, (2) education, (3) parental guidance, and (4) psychotherapy.[17] The therapist does best to try medication on all children with MBD who present with hyperactivity, distractibility, or neurological learning impairments. These symptoms have been those traditionally most responsive to chemotherapy, and their alleviation makes work in the other three areas much easier. (It is beyond the scope of this chapter to discuss the medication of children with MBD, which is discussed in detail in chapter 23, as well

as by Millichap[35] and Fish.[13] Once properly medicated (many children are undermedicated[48]), the child is more likely to profit from his educational experiences. If the child begins to learn more efficiently, he is likely to feel more competent; this, in turn, will reduce some of the factors contributing to his psychogenic difficulties. At this point too, the child will generally be more amenable to parental management. This can have an obvious salutary effect. Parental guidance is a vital part of the psychological treatment of children with MBD. Again, because the focus in this chapter is on specific psychotherapeutic techniques, this parental aspect of treatment will not be discussed. Information for therapists who advise parents of children with minimal brain dysfunction[25] as well as books written specifically to be read by such parents[22, 38, 39, 47] are available.

PARENTAL INVOLVEMENT IN THE CHILD'S THERAPY

Although a confidential relationship with the therapist is vital to the treatment of most adults and adolescents, many children do not require such a relationship. In one sense, there is little in their lives that is not already known to their parents.[16] Even Freud saw no necessity for a confidential relationship with Little Hans and there is no indication that Hans objected to the therapeutic disclosures. Many children below the age of ten with MBD do better in treatment when the parent who brings the child (usually the mother) observes and, at times, actively participates in the therapeutic sessions. Watching the therapist deal with the child provides the parent with firsthand information on how to act. The mother who receives advice about an approach to which she has not been witness is less likely to carry out the suggestions with conviction. Nor does the presence of the parent necessarily interfere with the therapist's establishment of a close relationship with the child. Indeed the parent's presence may facilitate such development. Moreover, being present during the treatment lessens the likelihood of the parents' developing a jealous and resentful attitude toward the therapist. When such an attitude is present, it is invariably sensed by the child and tends to compromise his relationship with the therapist. When the child is seen alone in sessions and there is strict secrecy from the parents, this may have a divisive effect on the family. The therapist and patient may become "we," and the parents "they." The participating parent may provide information useful in dream and story analysis, may add data that make verbal interchanges with the child more meaningful, and may fill in the child's memory gaps (this contribution is especially useful in the treatment of children with MBD). Assisting the therapist in the treatment process lessens the guilt that parents of children with MBD so often feel by enabling them to *do* something actively that contributes to the child's improvement. With so much to be gained by parental observation and intermittently active participation, it seems wasteful to have the mother sitting in the waiting room reading a magazine when, with no extra investment of time by the therapist (or money by the parents), a far richer therapeutic experience may be provided the child.

Obviously, there are situations in which the parents' active involvement is therapeutically contraindicated. In the case of an overdependent-child, overprotective-mother relationship, it would be important for the therapist to establish a separate relationship with the child. A psychotic parent who is too fragile to withstand some of the negative comments that children almost invariably make during therapy is best kept out of the room. In short, the therapist must determine in each case whether or not active parental participation is advisable.

INDICATIONS FOR PSYCHOTHERAPY

Before making a final decision about whether or not psychotherapy is indicated for a child with MBD, the therapist owes it to both the child and the family to determine how much can be gained by medication alone. Moreover, the therapist should try to accomplish as much as possible with parental guidance alone before instituting psychotherapy. Where indicated, an educational program (tutoring, special classes, and so forth), should be instituted as soon as is practical, and the therapist should appreciate that such a program can contribute in a major way to an alleviation of the child's psychogenic problems. Such special education programs may last for years, however, and one cannot wait until the child has received maximum educational benefit before deciding whether therapy is indicated. In brief, after every effort has been made to reduce the child's difficulties in the aforementioned ways, psychotherapy should then be considered—and even then, not all children may warrant it. At that point, the persistence of significant signs and symptoms (described later in "Psychotherapeutic Approaches to the Secondary Signs and Symptoms") should alert the clinician to the possibility that psychotherapy may be

warranted. Most of these signs and symptoms exist to some degree in many children with MBD. However, when they reach such degree that they interfere significantly with the child's functioning in school, at home, or with his peer relationships, then psychotherapy is indeed indicated.

One important determinant here is the child's motivation for or receptivity to psychotherapy. Many (if not most) children with MBD are exquisitely aware of their deficits and pained by their unfavorable comparisons with others. Nevertheless, few children directly profess an interest in or motivation for psychotherapy. With or without MBD, most children to whom psychotherapy is proposed do not see how it is going to help them, nor do they generally wish to forgo other activities for it. In such cases, it behooves the therapist to try to motivate the child to come, even if from the child's point of view it is only because he likes to talk and play games. Hopefully, the therapist will utilize verbal, play, and other techniques that have a high degree of therapeutic efficacy. Chapter 25 in this volume describes some of these methods; some that may be particularly useful in engaging and treating children with MBD will be discussed later in this chapter. If the child for whom psychotherapy is indicated can be so engaged, then a treatment program should be instituted. One should not expect the child to express a desire for psychotherapy; rather, one should be satisfied if the child willingly comes and involves himself in the various types of therapeutic experience.

Because of their cognitive difficulties, many children with MBD cannot profit from an interpretive type of therapy.[10, 34] Instead, allegorical communications at the primary-process level transmitted, for example, in stories that the therapist relates, corrective emotional experiences, appeal to conscious control, and desensitization are among the approaches that can bring about significant therapeutic change.[21, 23] Among the many difficulties from which these children suffer are problems in organizing and synthesizing perceptual and motor functions. These are clear examples of ego deficits.[27] Accordingly, educational approaches that attempt not only to rectify deficient areas but seek as well to strengthen intact areas can be useful in their treatment.[10] MBD children who are receptive to direct confrontation and discussion may be good candidates for treatment.

The child with MBD may, of course, develop the same difficulties that warrant treatment in children without this disorder, for example, phobias, compulsions, depression, and so forth. Indeed, the MBD child is probably even more likely to develop such difficulties. In many cases, there may be significant overlap between the two classes of symptoms, but both warrant therapy.

FREQUENCY OF SESSIONS

Although a variety of arrangements are feasible, two psychotherapy sessions per week are probably optimal. When the child is seen more frequently, there is a risk that he will become resentful of the travel time and of having to forgo more pleasurable activities. He may then become "soured" on treatment. One session per week is too "watered down" for optimum therapeutic benefit; but if circumstances permit only this degree of involvement, some benefit usually results.

STRUCTURE OF THE THERAPEUTIC SESSIONS

Completely permissive, open-type therapeutic sessions can be very useful for children with other kinds of difficulties. They have little place, however, in the treatment of children with MBD. Lacking controls from within, such youngsters need controls from without.[10, 12] To allow them free reign may only increase their confusion and disorganization. On the other hand, an organized, predictable, and well-structured session is in itself therapeutic. In effect, the element of structure is inherently helpful to such children. Totally structured sessions, however, may deprive the child of the freedom of expression that is likely to provide the most information about his underlying problems. Accordingly, the therapist should seek to provide opportunities for relatively free expression within certain limits. For example, setting prescribed times for talk, providing the child with specific alternatives as to which games he can choose, and telling him in advance about what will come next may all be useful in this form of therapy.

The therapist should appreciate that the MBD child's hyperactivity and distractibility may be less apparent in the treatment sessions than they are in school and at home. In the one-to-one relationship, such children are often quieter and more attentive. The individual attention apparently reduces some of the elements that may be contributing to their hyperactivity. Having to cope with only one person (or two, if the parent is present) reduces the number of stimuli that contribute to the child's distractibility. And if the therapist makes an effort to titrate the stimuli presented to the child at any given time, he will reduce the distractibility even further. For example, presenting the child with a communication containing multiple components is a hazardous undertaking. Improperly done, it is likely to confuse him so much that none of the messages will be understood. However, when each component part is presented alone, and time is taken to make sure that everything has been understood, the child may demonstrate his total ability to comprehend.

Although hyperactivity and distractibility are usually described as two separate signs, they generally appear together and reinforce one another. Bender[3] considers hyperactivity to be ". . . an effort continually to contact the physical-social environment to re-experience and integrate the perceptual experiences in a continual effort to gain some orientation in the world." Birch[4] also considers the MBD child's hyperactivity to be secondary to his inability to focus on a particular object. Rappaport[36] agrees with those who consider the MBD child to have a normal level of activity. The child appears hyperactive only because he cannot focus on a single goal. It is his flitting from goal to goal that indicates the hyperactive state. Strauss and Kephart[42] consider the inability to appreciate the differences between important and unimportant stimuli, and between foreground and background, to be contributing elements to the MBD child's distractibility. Although there are many other factors that play a role in the hyperactivity and distractibility (see volume 2, chapters 20 and 21), most agree that the two intensify one another and that structuring the session in the aforementioned manner can reduce such signs and make the child more receptive to his therapeutic experiences.

The child's rambling may also be understood as a form of distractibility. In this case, it is his response to internal more than external stimuli that causes the child to talk on, going from subject to subject, without concerning himself with whether the listener understands. He simply verbalizes each thought as it arises. He seems to have a need to respond to each internal prodding without differentiating between what is important and what is not. He does not pay much attention to the reactions of the listener—whether boredom, confusion, failure to understand, or others. The therapist does such a child a great favor by interrupting him, asking him to go back to the point where the therapist last understood what the child was saying, and urging him to keep his communications on a single track. Although at times these interruptions may become tedious for the therapist, they may provide such children with a valuable therapeutic experience. Generally, others (even parents) do not have the patience to do this. Rather, they find it easier to let the child ramble on while feigning comprehension. This only entrenches the child's communication problem and alienates him further.

Some hold that the child with MBD should not be seen for the traditional forty-five to fifty minute session because of his distractibility and hyperactivity.[31] Experience indicates, however, that such children can be engaged in meaningful therapeutic endeavors by utilization of techniques such as those here. It is true that the hyperactivity and distractibility are organic in etiology, but it is also true that environmental and psychological factors contribute significantly to the degree to which they manifest themselves.

MULTISENSORY STIMULATION

It behooves the therapist to determine the exact nature of the child's perceptual impairment so that he can provide therapeutic communications that are most likely to be received, comprehended, and retained. "Talking therapy" is not going to work very well when the child has auditory perceptual and auditory memory deficits. With such a child, the therapist does well to make significant use of visual stimuli (drawing, doll play, and so forth). One must still use auditory stimuli, however, not only because it is difficult to avoid doing so, but because one is trying to strengthen the defective sensory modality. Similarly, when treating a child with visual perceptual and visual memory problems, one should give primary emphasis to auditory communications but continue to carefully utilize the visual.

Everyone's learning can be improved with multisensory stimulation, but for the child with MBD, it may be indispensable. Verbal communication with such a child is far less effective than transmitting the message in the form of a little dramatic performance. This allows visual, tactile, kinesthetic, and even olfactory and gustatory stimuli to be added to the auditory.[16, 19] If a closed-circuit television system is available (a most valuable tool for the child therapist), playback can provide further multisensory expression of the therapeutic communications. Memory problems are common among these children, and they need much more reiteration of the therapeutic messages than do children without MBD. Making audiotape recordings of the sessions provide an opportunity for such repetition between sessions. More than that, the child's listening to the tapes between sessions enhances the therapeutic relationship.

Other techniques have been found useful in treating children with perceptual and memory deficits. After an important statement has been made to the child the therapist may say: "I'd like you to repeat what I've just said so that I'm sure you have understood it." Most children with MBD will not be offended by this. The child with MBD knows that he has trouble getting things to "stick in his mind" and welcomes assistance. Occasionally, he will suddenly be unable to follow through with his train of thought. He stops in the middle of what he has been saying and seems unable to "get back on the track." He becomes frustrated and may even bang his head with his hand in an effort to jar things loose and recall what he has been saying. This is rarely a manifestation of a petit mal episode (sometimes an electroencephalogram may be indicated when there is some doubt) or of psychological blocking because anxiety-provoking material threatens to erupt (there is generally no relationship between the content and the blocking). Instead it seems there has been some sudden short-circuiting of neurological pathways. To try to analyze the reasons for the block is likely to be antitherapeutic. Rather, the therapist does well to help the child recall what he has been saying and quickly put him back on the track so that he can continue his train of thought.

When a child reports some positive accomplishment, the therapist may pick up his notes and say: "I'm very glad to hear that, Robert. I'm going to write that down on your chart." The therapist may then bring the child over to sit next to him and then slowly and dramatically write a laudatory comment verbalizing emphatically while he writes, for example, "I am very happy to be able to write here in Robert's chart that he has not had one screaming fit in school all week. I am sure that he must be very proud of himself." For added emphasis and reinforcement, a thick red frame may be drawn around the written comment. Similarly, when the child has repeatedly exhibited dangerous behavior, he may be informed that regretfully the therapist is going to have to record it in his chart, and, with similar fanfare, the transgression is duly noted.

THE THERAPIST-PATIENT RELATIONSHIP

Meaningful psychotherapy obviously requires a good therapist-patient relationship. From the outset, then, the therapist should attempt to do everything possible to form such a relationship.[12, 16] Certain aspects of this relationship are particularly pertinent to the therapy of children with MBD.

Kernberg[30] has observed that such children form a positive relationship with the therapist more rapidly than do children with neuroses, psychoses, and character disorders. She attributes the reluctance to relate by children in the latter groups to their greater conflicts with important figures in their lives. Others share Kernberg's experience, but attribute it to the greater craving by children with MBD for affectionate relationships. They suffer such severe rejection from so many people (often, even from their parents) that they eagerly latch on to anyone who treats them with warmth and sensitivity. This problem is so severe that, simply by not ridiculing them, the therapist provides a corrective emotional experience. In this way, he enhances the likelihood that the child will be able to anticipate similar benevolence elsewhere.

Many parents embark on extensive searches to find a doctor who will deny that the child has MBD or to find a therapist who will provide a magic cure (or at least a degree of alleviation that others have been unable to offer). This interferes with the child's capacity to form a good relationship with a therapist. The parents' disillusionment with each successive therapist becomes the child's; he doesn't stay long with any one therapist, and his trust in each succeeding one becomes less.

SPECIAL TECHNIQUES USEFUL IN THE TREATMENT OF CHILDREN WITH MBD

The mutual storytelling technique[23] is valuable in the treatment of uncooperative resistant children. In this method, which is described in more detail in chapter 25, the child first tells a story he has "made up" himself and explains its lesson or moral (a valuable clue to the story's central psychodynamic theme). The therapist in turn makes up a story of his own, using the same characters in a similar setting, but introduces what he considers to be healthier adaptations than those used by the child in his story. The method is particularly useful for children who have little motivation for the development of insight but who, nevertheless, will engage in storytelling and in listening to the therapist's stories. Because children with MBD are generally unwilling to or incapable of gaining insight into their difficulties, the mutual storytelling technique may be useful in their treatment.[18, 23] However, for these children certain modifications of this method are necessary. Since they tend to tell disorganized stories, it behooves the therapist to interrupt when necessary to gain clarification and to keep the child from going off on too many tangents. Even then he may not get a story with one or two simple, clear themes. He does well in such cases to try to surmise some underlying theme from the child's "story" and use this as the nucleus for his own. Because the child with MBD often has difficulty appreciating concepts and abstractions, he may not be able to provide a meaningful moral or lesson for his story—thereby depriving the therapist of a potentially important source of information about the story's psychodynamics.

It is also possible to engage the child in a series of games[15, 16, 18] that enhance the likelihood of the child telling stories. This is done by adding a game structure and token rewards to the story-telling therapeutic method. "The Board of Objects Game," "The Bag of Toys Game," "The Bag of Things Game," "The Bag of Words Game," "Scrabble for Juniors," and the "Alphabet Soup Game," which are discussed in chapter 25, are generally attractive to children with MBD and are useful for getting them to reveal themselves in play.

The "Talking, Feeling, and Doing Game" has been particularly useful in the therapy of children with MBD. Chapter 25 contains a more detailed description of this technique, in which the patient and therapist alternately throw dice and move their playing pieces along a path of colored squares which direct the player to take a Talking Card, Feeling Card, or Doing Card. If the player can respond to the question or directions on the card, he gets a token reward chip. The cards are designed to elicit psychologically meaningful material from children who cannot or will not reveal themselves directly or through storytelling (although with children who are capable of such revelation, the game may be utilized as an additional therapeutic modality). The issues raised on the cards serve as points of departure for further therapeutic interchange. Many of the cards are particularly useful for the child with MBD. Some touch on the common social perceptual problems from which many of these children suffer ("How do you feel when you stand close to someone whose breath smells because he hasn't brushed his teeth?" "How do you feel when someone hits you?" "A girl was the only one in the class not invited to a birthday party. Why do you think she wasn't invited?") The game provides structure which is in itself therapeutic for these children. It is generally sufficiently interesting to hold their attention—which is difficult enough because of their distractibility. The questions are designed so that they do not require too much abstraction and conceptualization and are readily understood by most MBD children. And the Doing Cards provide opportunities for dramatization and multisensory stimulation, which is so helpful in the therapy of the child with MBD.

The child with MBD often has difficulty understanding the rules of traditional games or appreciating the concepts necessary for successful play. Moreover, he is impaired in visuo-spatial competence. As a consequence, he often has great difficulty playing traditional games with peers.[24] These therapeutic games do not generally expose such defects (with the exception of the MBD child's common problem of formulating a moral or lesson about his self-created story). The utilization of token reinforcement by many of the games suggests a behavioral modification approach.[40] Nonetheless, they are not designed specifically to modify behavior per se but to provide the therapist with information about the child's psychodynamics. These data may then be used in a variety of ways.

Psychotherapeutic Approaches to the Secondary Signs and Symptoms

DENIAL

Denial of the unpleasant is one of the simplest and most primitive defense mechanisms. Making believe that a painful reality just doesn't exist is particularly easy for children—hence the ubiquitousness of this mechanism in this age group. Parental denial of the child's difficulties often contributes to the child's utilization of this defense. It is especially common for parents to deny the existence of the problem when it first manifests itself. It may be that only when the child starts school do the difficulties become so apparent that denial is no longer possible. Even after the parents accept the fact of the child's illness, they may not tell the child what is wrong with him, believing that such disclosure would be psychologically deleterious. They may even be supported by professional authorities in this conspiracy of silence. Such withholding not only facilitates the child's denial of his difficulties but creates anxieties and distrusts that might not otherwise have arisen. The child knows that he is different and that something is wrong with him. When he is not given information, it only makes him think that things are worse

than they are and that he may have an incurable and/or fatal illness. In addition, he senses his parents' duplicity when they avoid responding honestly to his requests for information, and this creates distrust. In effect, it burdens the child with an additional problem that he certainly does not need. Accordingly, one of the first things that can help such children in therapy is for the parents and therapist to apprise the child at his level of comprehension, of the nature of his illness, and to encourage him to ask as many questions as he wishes.[22] Although such discussions may initially be anxiety provoking, they may result in the child's feeling more secure and more trusting of his parents. They may even contribute to the alleviation of secondary psychogenic symptoms designed to deal with and diminish anxiety.[21] Furthermore, once the child has accepted the fact that he has a problem, he is in a far better position to do those things that can best alleviate his difficulties.

Even after the child has been told about the nature of his deficits, he is still likely (like all children) to avoid confrontation with them. He may deny that he does sloppy work, loses assignments, is forgetful in class, and so forth.[46] He may claim that his teacher is lying when she reports such incidents to his parents. The child may make up stories in which the protagonists suffer no repercussions for their deficient performances. To such stories, the therapist may respond with tales in which there are untoward consequences to the protagonist's deficient performance and he ultimately comes to appreciate that the only way to avoid such undesirable effects is to rectify the deficiencies that are causing them.[18]

DISTORTIONS ABOUT AND
IGNORANCE OF REALITY

As mentioned, many of the problems of the MBD child can be viewed as ego deficits. Accordingly, educational approaches constitute an important part of the therapy of such children. The better the relationship between the therapist and the patient, the greater will be the child's receptivity to the therapist's instructions. In the early phases of treatment, the patient may have to be reassured that he isn't crazy because he is seeing a therapist. Many children with MBD believe that they are retarded and some are taunted by other children with terms such as "retard"—thereby confirming their suspicions. Careful explanations of the differences between MBD and intellectual retardation may dispel these concerns. Many children harbor magic cure fantasies, which are often revealed in their "made up" stories. In response, the therapist does well to provide both direct and allegorical communications that emphasize the impossibility of such change and encourage dedicated effort instead. The therapist who would be of help to MBD children must be deeply committed to the work ethic. It is hard for these children to learn, and they must apply themselves with great vigor to their learning tasks if they are to alleviate their difficulties. Hence, the therapist must be deeply convinced that such efforts are worthwhile. In addition, the child should be reassured that as he grows older, as his brain and nervous system mature, things will improve for him. However, he must be discouraged from sitting back and waiting for such maturity; dedicated effort is necessary for optimum progress.

It is important in the treatment of the MBD child to assure him that no one is perfect, that everyone has some defects. His assets as well as his liabilities should be emphasized. These children tend to generalize from their deficiencies and to consider themselves totally unworthy. The therapist should help such children circumscribe their defects, to see themselves basically as functioning normally but as having isolated areas of deficiency. These and other therapeutic messages may often be more effectively communicated when visual material accompanies the verbal discussion. Reading material which describes the MBD child's difficulties, written at the child's level of comprehension,[22] may complement such discussion. It provides the children with the kind of multisensory communication so helpful in their treatment.

SOCIAL-PERCEPTUAL PROBLEMS

Although much has been written about the visual- and auditory-perceptual problems of children with MBD, less attention has been given to their problems with social perception. Typically, parents make such statements as: "I know, Doctor, that somehow he'll get to read well enough to get by, but he just can't make it with other people. That's my biggest worry." Unlike other children, those with MBD do not readily learn the basic ways of relating in social situations. They seem always to be saying the wrong thing at the wrong time, to be insensitive to the most obvious social cues. Kurlander[31] holds that the MBD child is so involved in dealing with perceptual and motor problems that he does not give proper attention to his social growth. Kernberg[30] considers impairments in cognitive development and difficulties in differentiating inner from outer reality to be important contributing factors to these social deficits.

It behooves the therapist to provide such social training in the course of the therapeutic work.[36] This is most efficaciously done when the child exhibits his socially inept or naive behavior in the session. The therapist then has the best opportunity to focus on what has just transpired, at a time when it is fresh in the child's memory and when both the child and therapist have been direct observers of the maladaptive behavior. On occasion, such a confrontation may necessitate interrupting what has been going on. The therapist should not hesitate to make such interruptions, because they generally result in accentuating material of primary importance. If the interruption is offered benevolently, along with an explanation of why it was necessary, the child will generally not be offended. A less effective, but nevertheless useful, approach is for the therapist to discuss the reasons for the child's social difficulties in other situations (school, neighborhood, and home) and to try to advise him what his errors were and how they might be rectified. Sometimes it helps to play-act a social interchange. These social difficulties can arise from the children's inability to project themselves into the observer's situation. Thus, it can be helpful to have the child try to imagine how he looks to others, or to get him to appreciate what others think and feel about what he is doing and saying.

In the classroom and at home, the MBD child's socially inept behavior is often viewed as an unwelcome intrusion that interferes with the smooth flow of interaction. Teachers and parents often react irately; they punish, discipline, or reprimand the child and attempt to reestablish the desired social "set" as quickly as possible. If such correction is viewed as one of the primary aims of the child's education, the confrontations might then be more benevolent—much to the child's benefit. Similarly, the therapist should consider discussions of social-perceptual problems to be one of the primary purposes of the treatment.[21]

IMMATURITY

The immaturity that these children often exhibit has both neurological and psychological sources. The developmental lag is known to retard development of such milestones as walking, talking, and toilet training, and later to slow academic development. It may also contribute to behavioral immaturities, for example, baby talk, whining, silliness, clowning, clinging dependency, and balking at assuming age-appropriate responsibilities. On the other hand, psychogenic factors may also result in the perpetuation of immature behavioral patterns. In short, the lag in neurological development does not sufficiently explain the child's immaturity; under more favorable circumstances this might not have become visible in the same way. It is on these environmental factors that the psychotherapist does well to concentrate his efforts.

Expressions of excessive dependency are among the most common of the psychological problems exhibited by children with MBD.[3, 11, 34] This results from the confusion these children often experience and their difficulty in making sense of the world around them. This child may readily be compared with the blind man and his dependence on his Seeing Eye dog; the MBD child's dependence upon his parents (especially the mother) for continual guidance may very well be his central existential problem. All this may be compounded by an overprotective response on the part of the parents. The parents, for their part, may have special reasons for such an overprotective stance.[20] For example, by keeping the child at a more immature level, the parents can hide from themselves the defects that would be revealed if the child were encouraged to function at a higher level. The parents might "help" the child with homework to such an extent that the child actually does little on his own. Helping the child blind himself to his deficiencies is a dubious service indeed. It deprives him of the opportunity to rectify his errors and advance his knowledge, and it prevents him from acquiring the ego-enhancing mastery of which he might otherwise have been capable. It is extremely difficult, if not impossible, to help the dependent child of such parents without working with the parents as well. If the child in therapy continues to live in a home in which he is overindulged, the therapist's efforts are not likely to be effective. And the child will not be motivated to suffer the discomforts associated with breaking his overdependent tie. The parents have to be helped to differentiate between the specific kinds of care the MBD child requires, and the more diffuse kinds of overprotection.

In the sessions with the child, the therapist is likely to find that the child will tend to be overdependent on him as well. The wise therapist will refrain from gratifying such inappropriate demands and will provide the child instead with experiences which help him recognize that he is capable of more mature and independent behavior. Hopefully, the gratification that comes from such mature be-

havior, and the ego-enhancement this provides him, will serve to motivate the child for further independent action. The child needs to be told (verbally, nonverbally, in story—in accordance with his level of comprehension and tolerance) how socially unacceptable are the regressive elements of his behavior. Children with strong infantile leanings may not be aware how they appear to others; it behooves the therapist to help them gain such appreciation ("If you're going to act so silly, I'm not going to continue playing this game with you. You're taking all the fun out of it for me. I wonder if this isn't one of the reasons why other children won't play with you?") The child has to be helped to appreciate that involvement with others in the world outside his home will inevitably involve frustration and discomfort. However, many gratifications to be derived from such involvements may more than compensate for the hurts one may suffer. In addition, the child should be helped to appreciate that entering unfamiliar situations is anxiety-provoking to everyone, and that only by suffering such anxiety can he hope to derive the benefits and gratifications that the new situations can offer. Last, the patient has to be helped to appreciate that there will come a time when his parents will no longer be available to him and when others will not be nearly so indulgent. Only by acquiring competence on his own can he hope to overcome the anxieties associated with this inevitability.[18, 21]

IMPULSIVITY

Impulsivity is traditionally considered to be one of the cardinal signs of MBD children. These children appear to be impaired in their ability to "put the brakes" on their actions, to exercise the same degree of self-control as others their age. Goldstein[26] and Strauss and Lehtinen,[43] early investigators of the behavioral and cognitive manifestations of brain damage, described the "catastrophic reaction" that is often seen in those afflicted with an organic brain syndrome. Following a frustration (of which the observer is sometimes aware, sometimes not) the patient has a sudden outburst of rage which has a quality of despair and impotence. The child appears to be totally overwhelmed, frustrated, and incapable of rectifying the troublesome situation. This is just one example of the impulsivity of these children. Typically, they blurt out answers in the classroom, strike others at the slightest provocation (and sometimes even without it), have severe rage reactions to losing a game (they may destroy the equipment in the course of such an outburst), have seemingly endless temper tantrums when punished, and so forth.

Although the MBD child's impulsivity is a manifestation of neurological impairment, psychogenic factors contribute as well. The parents are likely to have been told that the impulsivity is one of the signs of MBD and that they should be sympathetic to, and very tolerant of, the child's impaired self-control. They may consider the child to be almost totally incapable of self-control, and he may come to view himself similarly. Such a concept of the impulsivity is erroneous; even the most impulsive child has some degree of self-control, and to define his impulsivity as boundless and irresistible can intensify it immeasurably. The child who views himself as helpless to inhibit or abort his outbursts, and who is similarly viewed by others, is not likely to exert whatever degree of control is in fact possible.[47] The therapist does well to impress upon such a child that he can handle his impulsivity better than he professes; indeed the therapist should take opportunities to help such a child "practice" control over his outbursts. For example, when playing checkers with a child one might say: "I'm going to make a move now that may get you upset. I want to see whether you can stop yourself from doing things that you'll be sorry for or embarrassed about later." If the child responds with efforts to control himself, he should be complimented enthusiastically.

Strauss and Kephart[42] consider an important source of the MBD child's impulsivity to be his impairment in perceiving the various options open to him for dealing with frustration. For example, a child may get angry at a peer who beats him in a race and abruptly strike the winner. He does not consider alternatives such as trying to do better himself so he'll be less angry, suppressing his resentment, or verbalizing rather than acting it out. The therapist then may ask such questions as: "Do you think there was anything else you could have done besides hitting that boy?" Children with MBD make excellent scapegoats. They are different from others and are thus often singled out as targets. When they respond to taunts with uncontrollable outbursts and tears, it only encourages others to pick on them. The child has to be helped to appreciate that his outbursts are just what his tormentors want most and that if he can control them, he is less likely to be picked upon. Provided with such motivation for self-control, he will be more likely to try to achieve it. He should be helped to acquire a repertoire of responses (again the introduction of previously unperceived alterna-tives) that may prove useful in responding to those who bully him.

Many children with MBD feel extremely embarrassed after their outbursts have subsided. They are overwhelmed with feelings of guilt, project their feelings of self-loathing onto others, and then believe others share their own views of themselves as abominable.[37] The therapist must help such children be less critical of themselves. However, the therapist should take care, when attempting such guilt assuagement, not to go too far and leave the child with the impression that since he has no control at all over his impulsivity, he has no reason to feel guilty. To do so would substitute one symptom for another—inappropriate guiltlessness for an exaggerated sense of guilt.

The child may hope there will be no repercussions for his impulsive behavior, and his "made up" stories may reflect such fantasies. Or he may reveal wishes for a magic cure for the problem. The therapist should respond to such stories with comments or stories of his own in which such wishes are not realized and where more appropriate and predictably effective measures to reduce impulsivity are utilized. Helping the child appreciate the value of dealing with problems early (before feelings build up to explosive intensity) can also be useful. In extreme cases, the therapist may have to use limiting and restrictive measures in order to help the child control himself. For example, a child who insists in interrupting conversations between the therapist and other(s) may be warned that "if you don't give us a chance to talk—just like we gave you your chance to talk—you will have to leave the room for a few minutes so that we can talk without interruption." And if the child still does not restrain himself, then a few minutes out of the room may "help him remember" to try to exert such self-restraint in the future. Such a corrective emotional experience,[1] which as a behavioral technique is designated "time out (from reinforcement)" (see chapter 11) may be useful; however, it is more likely to be successful in therapy if the child has previously established a good relationship with the therapist.

PERSEVERATION

Perseveration is also traditionally considered to be one of the signs of brain dysfunction that is a manifestation of the neurological impairment. Phenomenologically, it is a form of verbal impulsivity in which the child's productions have a broken-record quality. The child appears to "get hooked" onto a particular topic and cannot free himself. He may repeatedly ask his mother the same question. The mother soon becomes weary and exasperated, but the child tenaciously continues with little evidence that the mother's answers are "sinking in."

It is possible that psychogenic factors contribute to the organic child's perseveration. The child may gain attention by this means. If he were to accept the response to his question the first or second time it was answered, the conversation might then be discontinued. He might then have to suffer once more the loneliness and isolation that is so often his lot. In short, it serves as an excuse for the maintenance of human contact. Having a small repertoire of issues upon which to draw for conversational purposes, the child makes the most of his limited means.[42]

Again, the child may perseverate a response to a question in order to hide ignorance. For example, after responding correctly to a question, he may provide the same answer to the next question in the hope of once again gaining a compliment from the questioner. Or he may repeatedly tell the same joke or story and may continue laughing at a joke long after everyone else has stopped. Again, the perseverated response serves to maintain the child's involvement with others. Indeed, the perseveration may serve to provide structure to the child's environment. It is as if his world is so chaotic that he can only assimilate it piecemeal—and perseveration may be one manifestation of such an attempt.[37] At times, the child's memory impairment may contribute to the perseverative process: Not retaining that which has been communicated to him, he repeats the inquiry in the attempt to assimilate the response.

The therapist and parents should try to ascertain the specific psychological factors that are operating to intensify the perseverative tendency. They should not involve themselves in the process but should try instead to provide an experience that will lessen or obviate the need for the perseveration. For example, the child who perseverates to avoid rejection and loneliness must be engaged in alternative activities that are more likely to maintain the interest of others. The child who perseverates to hide ignorance must be taught, so that his repertoire of socially interesting knowledge is expanded.

Sometimes the perseverated content has particular psychological significance. The repetition then takes on qualities of the classical obsession. One child with MBD was preoccupied with the fear that the food he ate would make him sick. He repeatedly questioned his mother about everything he ingested—pleading for reassurance that he would not be harmed by the food. From therapeutic work with this child, it emerged that he considered himself loathesome and that by the introduction of foreign material into his body he ran the risk of harming himself even more. The therapeutic approach involved not only a correction of these distortions but a general attempt to raise his self-esteem. When these approaches achieved some success, he was able to give up the preoccupation.

LOW SELF-ESTEEM

Most, if not all, children with MBD suffer with profound feelings of low self-esteem. The low self-worth problem of these children is complex, and the approaches to its alleviation may comprise the major part of the therapeutic work.

These children are generally extremely aware of their deficits (attempts on the part of parents, teachers, and even professionals to hide their defects from them notwithstanding). It is this very capacity for self-awareness that contributes so much to their low sense of self-worth.[33] Such children tend to generalize from their isolated defects and consider themselves *totally* unworthy. Part of the therapeutic work, then, is to help them view their deficiencies as circumscribed and to view themselves more realistically. This can contribute materially to the enhancement of their self-esteem.[10] Many consider themselves to be crazy and/or retarded, and for them, referral to a therapist is a confirmation of such fears. It is important to deal with these issues, to show that these concerns are not valid, and to help them differentiate between themselves and those with psychosis and retardation.[22]

Feelings of self-worth must ultimately be based on real capacities and accomplishments. An enhanced sense of self-esteem based on fantasies or false praise is not genuine or lasting. Accordingly, the child with MBD must be helped to gain competence in those areas where he shows aptitude or potential. Deep commitment to the work ethic is required of the therapist if he is to help the child tolerate the frustrations attendant to the acquisition of such skills. The child has to be reminded continually that he may have to work harder to achieve the same competence as others.[17] In short, the child must be able to gain the greatest possible skill in areas where his organic deficiencies are least disturbing; and he must be helped to work hardest in those areas that are weak but in which it is necessary for him to gain some competence if he is to function effectively in life.[10, 45]

For example, the child with a reading disability should receive tutoring by someone specially trained in this area. In addition, if his coordination is good, he should be encouraged to take part in sports. The latter may not only provide a feeling of enhanced competence, but the physical activity can provide a healthy and socially acceptable outlet for tensions and hostility. The child who is weak in certain sports requiring a high level of coordination (such as baseball) might be helped by special teaching from a teenager or gym teacher hired for this purpose. In addition, he might do quite well in sports that do not require a different kind of motor skill (soccer, trampoline, and general acrobatics).

There are devices that can help the child circumvent his defects. The child with a poor handwriting might be taught to type. The child who cannot learn easily to tell time may do so readily with a digital clock.

Last, false compliments should be discouraged. Telling a child that he is a "fine boy" or she is a "nice girl" does not usually work. The child will often sense that the general compliment is given because the adult cannot find a real attribute to praise. The adult does better to withhold such patronizing and disingenuous compliments and wait until he can provide one that is real: "Good shot"; "What a beautiful model you built. You must be proud."

The child with MBD often suffers contempt and abuse from peers. It is inevitable that he will ultimately accept their disparagements as valid. His parents, too, are often extremely disappointed with him, which contributes to his self-loathing.[11] In response to such experiences, he may develop an exaggerated and often pathetic craving for acceptance by others.[9] It is a necessary and not an easy part of the work to help such children appreciate that they are not necessarily what others consider them to be. They need to be encouraged to develop greater self-awareness, especially with regard to their assets and liabilities. At the same time, they must learn to discriminate, not to accept as valid a criticism that has no relationship to themselves. They have to learn an even harder lesson, to appreciate that there is something wrong with a person who is contemptuous of them, even if the criticism is directed toward a real defect. In the course of such work, the therapist might help the child gain a repertoire of retorts for those who taunt him, for example, "It shows how dumb you are if you think I'm retarded"; "There must be something wrong with you if you laugh at someone just because he can't read very fast." And if a

parent exhibits inappropriate disappointment with the child (a certain amount of this is inevitable), the child must be helped to appreciate the fallacies in such a parent's thinking—for example, "Your father has a strange idea. He thinks that a person is totally no good if he isn't very good in sports. Most people don't think that way. They know that lots of people aren't very good athletes and that they can still be very worthwhile people."

Children with MBD often suffer great guilt over their behavior.[37] After an impulsive outburst, the child may experience deep feelings of embarrassment and he may denigrate himself mercilessly. Such children have to be helped to recognize that they have special problems with control over their impulses and must therefore work harder than others to achieve such control. Surely they must not be freed from the responsibility of impulse mastery. Otherwise, as noted previously, one will be substituting one symptom for another.

Children with MBD may exhibit any of the various neurotic, and even psychotic, forms of esteem-lowering that the nonorganic child may develop.[20, 21, 22] Most psychogenic symptoms are developed, in part, in an attempt to enhance feelings of self-worth; but the mechanisms selected to accomplish this are such that the individual ends up feeling even worse about himself than he did originally. For example, all forms of guilt (whatever their origins or mechanisms) have an intrinsic element of lowered self-esteem. The depressive derogates himself. The phobic cannot but compare himself unfavorably with those who can do the things that he cannot. The therapeutic approaches to such esteem-lowering symptoms for the MBD child are similar to those used with the nonorganic child. Certain modifications of techniques may be necessary however, because it is harder for these children to achieve insight.[16, 23]

FEAR OF AND WITHDRAWAL FROM OTHERS

The child with MBD is not only very sensitive to his deficiencies but is continually confronted with the fact that others are aware of his deficits as well. Withdrawal may serve to avoid such confrontations with others and enables the child momentarily to forget his painful impairments.[31] At school especially, the MBD child may be taunted. Accordingly, it is common for these children to fear attending class, or to refuse to go to school (often developing various somatic complaints to rationalize their staying home), or to sit in class and lose themselves in daydreams, thereby protecting themselves from distressing academic comparisons.[37] The child's disorganization may so impede his functioning that he may feel safe only in the protective environment of his home.[3] The child may find himself simply unable to deal with and to organize the barrage of stimuli that come in from the world at large. This may also contribute to his withdrawal.[41] If he is kept in ignorance about the nature of his disorder, this may produce additional generalized anxieties that contribute to his withdrawal. Parental overprotection tells the child, either subtly or overtly, that the world is a dangerous place from which only his parents can protect him. Or the child may identify with parents who withdraw from others in the attempt to hide their child's deficits. Last, the child's generalized self-devaluation may lead him to assume that he will prove inept in areas in which in fact he has definite competence. The avoidance of involvement in activities in which he could have been successful deprives him of the gratifications and ego-enhancing mastery that he might otherwise have enjoyed.

To help such withdrawn and fearful children, the therapist must ascertain which of these processes is at work and direct his attention there. However, it is not enough to reduce the factors that contribute to the avoidance. Like all people, the child will still be afraid to try things that once frightened him. He must be helped to tolerate such anxieties, desensitize himself to them, and have the living experience that what he fears may happen will most often not take place. The child's environment should be made more inviting so that he can be less fearful of going forth into it. In this regard, special classes and schools for children with MBD may often be helpful. Athletic and social clubs for such children, often sponsored by various community organizations, are becoming ever more common. Being with other children with similar deficits helps the MBD child feel less defective, and he is more likely to gain acceptance from those truly his peers than from those without MBD.

ANGER

Children with MBD have much to be angry about. The frustrations they experience because of their defects inevitably produce resentment—resentment that is continually increased because they cannot escape or readily remove the sources of their frustration. They are taunted and bullied by peers. Only by withdrawing into their homes can they escape ridicule and mockery. And the price they then must pay for such protection is extreme loneliness. Although their parents are usually not overtly rejecting, such children sense the disappointment at their deficiencies, and this cannot but add to their resentment. Others learn, others do, others behave, and they cannot. They have no choice but to make such unfavorable comparisons which only add to their frustration and anger.

Because of their impulse control problem, many of these children act out their anger directly, often in the most primitive fashion. It is common for such children, when observing others to be more competent, to lash out at the more successful—striking, cursing at them, and even choking them. On occasion, parents will sanction the MBD child's acting out, rationalizing that it is healthy play. In this way, they deny its pathological implications. Or the parents may unconsciously or consciously gain gratification from the child's aggressivity. Such behavior always allows for a vicarious release of pent-up adult hostilities, which cannot be allowed overt expression. This is a common contributing cause of the antisocial acting out of many children;[28, 29] however, because of his impaired impulse control and poor judgment, the child with MBD lends himself to such utilization by parents all too well.[33]

It is unreasonable for the therapist to suppose that he can reduce the anger of the MBD child without helping him alleviate and rectify the neurological deficits over which he is frustrated and resentful. Accordingly, medication, education, and fostering a commitment to the work ethic are crucial. Urging and reinforcing conscious control of impulsivity accompanied by setting limits on the acting out of such behavior are strongly indicated. All children want limits and restrictions benevolently imposed upon them. This is one of the ways in which they learn how to function in the world. The child with MBD, genuinely confused about the world around him, is even more in need of restrictions that help him find a place in his milieu and provide him with a sense of order in it. It is also useful to set limits on antisocial acting out during the therapeutic session. Sending the child out of the room for a few minutes (while the therapist spends time talking to the mother) may be sobering. Or removing the child temporarily from any group that is important to him may also serve to motivate self-control of the acting out.[36] Providing corrective emotional experiences[1] in which the child learns directly that his behavior has repercussions, that he alienates others, causes them to withdraw or disengage themselves from him can be effective. Last, one must go beyond the aforementioned approaches. One must ascertain the particular neurotic factors that may be contributing to the child's anger and attempt to help him work out these aspects of the problem as well.

Concluding Comments

As previously mentioned, it is important for the therapist to have modest goals for the treatment of these children's psychogenic problems because of the likelihood of long-term persistence of the underlying organic deficits. Having unrealistically high goals may result in frustration and disillusionment for the patient, his parents, and the therapist as well. And the therapist who denies the existence of the MBD syndrome and considers all the signs and symptoms a manifestation of psychogenic problems is bound to have even more unrealistic goals for treatment, and is likely to cause even greater frustration to all concerned.

The efficacy of psychotherapy for the psychogenic problems of the MBD child is difficult to determine. As mentioned, there is very little in the literature describing such treatment, and what there is describes experiences with isolated cases. Although such reports often describe improvement via the utilization of such approaches as those described herein, they do not demonstrate the efficacy of the psychotherapeutic approach conclusively. There is no question that even without treatment there would be partial alleviation of some of these children's psychogenic problems. The natural history of the disorder is such that many children outgrow some of their difficulties. Psychotherapy can assist the normal developmental improvement as well as alleviate problems *in statu nascendi*. In this way, it may serve to prevent their intensification and solidification into more permanent forms of psychogenic disorder. If the latter do develop, as is often the case with the MBD child, then deeper and more intensive forms of psychotherapy are warranted,[32] but these may only be possible after the child has grown old enough to utilize them. Last, the term *termination* has little applicability to the treatment of children with MBD. Every phase of life will confront them with new challenges, challenges that they may be less well equipped to handle than nonorganic children. Accordingly, the therapist should be prepared to follow such children over many years— through their life cycle, and his own.

REFERENCES

1. ALEXANDER, F., et al., "The Principle of Corrective Emotional Experience," in *Psychoanalytic Therapy: Principles and Application*, The Ronald Press, New York, 1946.

2. BENDER, L., *Psychopathology of Children with Organic Brain Disorders*, Charles C Thomas, Springfield, Ill., 1956.

3. ———, "Psychological Problems of Children with Organic Brain Disease," *American Journal of Orthopsychiatry, 19(3):* 1949.

4. BIRCH, H. G., *Brain Damage in Children: The Biological and Social Aspects*, Williams & Wilkins, Baltimore, 1964.

5. ———, THOMAS, A., and CHESS, S., "Behavioral Development in Brain-Damaged Children," *Archives of General Psychiatry, 11(6):596–603, 1964.

6. CANTWELL, D. P., *The Hyperactive Child*, Spectrum Publications, New York, 1975.

7. CHESS, S., et al., "Interaction of Temperament and Environment in the Production of Behavioral Disturbances in Children," *American Journal of Psychiatry, 120(2):142–148, 1963.

8. CLEMENTS, S. D., *Minimal Brain Dysfunction in Children*, Public Health Service Publication no. 1415, U.S. Government Printing Office, Washington, D.C., 1966.

9. CRUICKSHANK, W. M., "The Effect of Physical Disability on Personal Aspiration," *Quarterly Journal of Child Behavior, 3:142, 1951.

10. DORIS, J., and SOLNIT, A. J., "Treatment of Children with Brain Damage and Associated School Problems," *Journal of the American Academy of Child Psychiatry, 2(4):625–633, 1963.

11. EISENBERG, L., "Behavioral Manifestations of Cerebral Damage in Childhood," in Birch, H. G. (Ed.), *Brain Damage in Children: The Biological and Social Aspects*, Williams & Wilkins, Baltimore, 1964.

12. ———, "Psychiatric Implications of Brain Damage in Children," *The Psychiatric Quarterly, 31(1):98, 1957.

13. FISH, B., "Stimulant Drug Treatment of Hyperactive Children," in Cantwell, D. P. (Ed.), *The Hyperactive Child*, Spectrum Publications, New York, 1975.

14. GARDNER, R. A., "Techniques for Involving the Child with MBD in Meaningful Psychotherapy," *Journal of Learning Disabilities, 8(5):128, 1975.

15. ———, "Psychotherapy in Minimal Brain Dysfunction," in Masserman, J. H. (Ed.), *Current Psychiatric Therapies*, vol. 15, Grune & Stratton, New York, 1975.

16. ———, *Psychotherapeutic Approaches to the Resistant Child*, Jason Aronson, New York, 1975.

17. ———, "Psychotherapy of Minimal Brain Dysfunction," in Masserman, J. H. (Ed.), *Current Psychiatric Therapies*, vol. 14, Grune & Stratton, New York, 1974.

18. ———, "The Mutual Storytelling Technique in the Treatment of Psychogenic Problems Secondary to Minimal Brain Dysfunction," *Journal of Learning Disabilities, 7(3): , 1974.

19. ———, "Dramatized Storytelling Child Psychotherapy," *Acta Paedopsychiatrica, 41(3):110–116, 1974.

20. ———, *Understanding Children*, Jason Aronson, New York, 1973.

21. ———, "Psychotherapy of the Psychogenic Problems Secondary to Minimal Brain Dysfunction," *International Journal of Child Psychotherapy, 2(2):224–256, 1973.

22. ———, *MBD: The Family Book about Minimal Brain Dysfunction*, Jason Aronson, New York, 1973.

23. ———, *Therapeutic Communication with Children: The Mutual Storytelling Technique*, Jason Aronson, New York, 1971.

24. ———, "The Game of Checkers as a Diagnostic and Therapeutic Tool in Child Psychotherapy," *Acta Paedopsychiatrica*, 36(5):142, 1969.

25. ———, "Psychogenic Problems of Brain-Injured Children and Their Parents," *Journal of the American Academy of Child Psychiatry*, 7(3):471–491, 1968.

26. GOLDSTEIN, K., *The Organism*, American Book Co., New York, 1939.

27. HARTMANN, H., *Essays on Ego Psychology*, International Universities Press, New York, 1964.

28. JOHNSON, A. M., "Juvenile Delinquency," in Arieti, S. (Ed.), *American Handbook of Psychiatry*, vol. 1, pp. 840–856, Basic Books, New York, 1959.

29. ———, "Sanctions for Super-ego Lucanae of Adolescents," in Eissler, K. R. (Ed.), *Searchlights on Delinquency*, International Universities Press, New York, 1949.

30. KERNBERG, P. F., "The Problem of Organicity in the Child," *Journal of the American Academy of Child Psychiatry*, 8(3):411, 1969.

31. KURLANDER, L. F., and COLODNY, D., " 'Pseudoneurosis' in the Neurologically Handicapped Child," *American Journal of Orthopsychiatry*, 35(4):141, 1965.

32. LAUFER, M. W., "Psychiatric Diagnosis and Treatment of Children with Minimal Brain Dysfunction," in De La Cruz, F. F., et al. (Eds.), *Minimal Brain Dysfunction*, Annals of the New York Academy of Sciences, vol. 205, New York Academy of Sciences, New York, 1973.

33. ———, DENHOF, E., and SOLOMONS, G., "Hyperkinetic Impulse Disorder in Children's Behavior Problems," *Psychosomatic Medicine*, 19(1):135, 1957.

34. LEVENTHAL, D. S., "The Significance of Ego Psychology for the Concept of Minimal Brain Dysfunction in Children," *Journal of the American Academy of Child Psychiatry*, 7(2):114, 1968.

35. MILLICHAP, J. G., "Drugs in the Management of Minimal Brain Dysfunction," *International Journal of Child Psychotherapy*, 1(3):65–81, 1972.

36. RAPPAPORT, S. R., "Behavior Disorder and Ego Development in a Brain-Injured Child," in Eissler, R. S., et al. (Eds.), *The Psychoanalytic Study of the Child*, vol. 16 International Universities Press, New York, 1961.

37. SCHECHTER, M. D., "Psychiatric Aspects of Learning Disabilities," *Child Psychiatry and Human Development*, 5(2):411, 1974.

38. SIEGEL, E., *The Exceptional Child Grows Up*, Dutton, New York, 1974.

39. ———, *Helping the Brain-Injured Child*, New York Association for Brain-Injured Children, New York, 1961.

40. SIMMONS, J. Q., "Behavioral Management of the Hyperactive Child," in Cantwell, D. P. (Ed.), *The Hyperactive Child*, Spectrum Publications, New York, 1975.

41. STONE, F. H., "Psychodynamics of Brain-Injured Children: A Preliminary Report," *Journal of Child Psychiatry and Psychology*, 1(3):112, 1960.

42. STRAUSS, A. A., and KEPHART, N. C., *Psychopathology and Education of the Brain-Injured Child*, vol. 2, Grune & Stratton, New York, 1955.

43. STRASS, A. A., and LEHTINEN, L. E., *Psychopathology and Education of the Brain-Injured Child*, vol. 1, Grune & Stratton, New York, 1947.

44. THOMAS, A., et al., *Behavioral Individuality in Early Childhood*, New York University Press, New York, 1963.

45. WAGNER, R. F., "Games Dyslexics Play," *Academic Therapy*, 11(1):211, 1973.

46. ———, "Secondary Emotional Reactions in Children with Learning Disabilities," *Mental Hygiene*, 54(4): , 1970.

47. WENDER, P. H., *The Hyperactive Child*, Crown Publishers, New York, 1973.

48. ———, *Minimal Brain Dysfunction in Children*, Wiley-Interscience, New York, 1971.

39 / Mental Retardation

Norman R. Bernstein

Intervention with the Retarded
The Range of Therapeutic

An enormous number of activities with the mentally handicapped have been designated as "therapeutic." Art therapy, movement, and music therapy have been used to help the patient toward a better adjustment or to improve his comfort. The *Heilpaedagogik* (remedial education) of many workers with the retarded has been classified as therapeutic; currently, behavior therapies and behavior modification have been included by some

and not by others. It seems best to restrict the term *therapy* to the use of planned, regular, verbal, and nonverbal communications with a designated patient, in the setting of a relationship, for the purpose of improving personal functioning and interpersonal competence, and to remove symptoms. To qualify, the person performing this function must be assigned as a therapist with a formal repertoire.

Even in the case of nonverbal or severely retarded patients, the therapist may have conflict resolution as a goal. Psychiatric treatment of the retarded encompasses the whole armamentarium of the child psychiatrist; it is based on the assumption that even for the child with diminished cognitive powers, self-realization is an important part of the overall aim. Some question the utility of psychotherapy for the retarded because practitioners differ in their value judgments about which of the traditional strategies to employ.

History

Greek literature, the Bible, and the other ancient works recognize the existence of the retarded, and in these works are scattered references to treating them with kindness, intermixed with a variety of epithets referring to stupidity. Humanistic enlightenment in the eighteenth century led to studies of various handicapped, deaf, retarded, and mute individuals. In the nineteenth century, schools were opened to deal with this population of handicapped people, and the special education of the feebleminded began to attract attention. Howe began to treat a few retardates in 1848 at the Perkins School for the Blind. In subsequent years, the development of public school classes for the retarded and of psychological testing scales advanced concurrently with the differentiation of various syndromes of retardation. There was little involvement of psychiatrists at this point.

Kanner[21] reports that in 1930 his child psychiatry clinic at Johns Hopkins was the first to include feeble-minded children and their families in the scope of its activities. In 1931, Clark[6] showed a film depicting the psychoanalysis of a retarded child, an activity that Chidester and Menninger[5] described in print in 1936. In the 1940s and 1950s, more papers were published on various therapeutic efforts. Some reports on psychotherapy with slow children told of a lower success rate; others found that "dull" children did as well if not better than others. They noted that intelligence need not be high to permit the formulation and verbalization of problems, and to allow the comprehension of interpretations. In 1960, Tizard[32] made a survey of research of psychologic and social problems of mental defect in England and Wales; he was able to locate less than fifteen people doing this work. During the subsequent ten years in the United States, the number of people engaged in such activity increased enormously. In 1970, Jakab[18] reported that within a therapeutic relationship it was possible for the feebleminded to work through a previously damaged development.

The emergence of counseling and the various therapies (family, group, and individual) continues to be a small part of the general psychotherapeutic endeavor. Psychodynamic theorists devoted little time or effort to the area of mental deficiency; in general, they held to the view stated by Freud[13] in 1904 that treatment candidates required a good education. School attention was focused upon tests and curricula. However, in the 1950s and 1960s, there was an expansion of psychological studies of the personality characteristics of the retarded; and toward the latter part of this period, behavior modification techniques began to be widely employed. Vocational rehabilitation workers too began to stress the need for counseling, and studies indicated that the personality patterns and characteristics of the retardate seemed to be more important determinants of his future effectiveness than did his mental level. In the last decade, there have been some efforts to combine modes of therapy. These have stimulated psychiatrists and psychologists to attempt psychotherapy with the retarded; and a readiness to share information among different areas of study appears to be imminent. The community psychiatry movement of the 1960s brought with it a broadened social awareness and prompted more versatile approaches to a variety of culturally and educationally handicapped individuals. At the same time, controversies over the value of psychometric testing have led some therapists to avoid using tests to monitor progress. Many of the old polemics persist, but all of the more recent publications include psychotherapy as an appropriate mode to be employed with the intellectually handicapped.

Treatment Indications and Attitudes

Mental retardation does not exclude any psychiatric disease. These patients present a group at risk for the whole spectrum of pathology. The standard DSM-II merely classifies retardates in terms of the severity of cognitive defect, though investigators[3, 25] have demonstrated the feasibility of making standard diagnoses of retarded patients. Psychiatric syndromes are somewhat altered by innate defects, the special course of development, and the stigmatized life circumstances in which the retarded live. How much is intrinsic to retardation rather than an outcome of psychopathology is a subject of some debate among authorities.[3, 25, 33] It appears that much more retardation is related to experience than is generally believed, and that a greater degree of response to psychotherapy may be obtained than is usually recognized. Retarded people are often considered social detritus, and most psychiatrists have shown little interest in their therapy.[16, 18] Johnson[19] describes some of the reasons why psychotherapists traditionally have had little enthusiasm for working with the retarded.

1. The retarded are unaware of difficulties and show little motivation to be helped.
2. Low intelligence precludes understanding the need to change behavior.
3. Impulse control is too poor and ego weakness too extensive for development of self dependence.
4. The effort is too great for the limited results.
5. Psychotherapists have insufficient understanding of the personality of the retarded.
6. Value conflicts exist between therapist and the retarded.

However, a good deal of work indicates that most of these premises are false. This prejudice should be confronted. There is mounting confirmation that low IQ (in the moderately retarded range) permits excellent results from therapy; indeed, these cases often respond in less time than equivalent categories of disorder in children with normal intelligence. Because of his personal dedication to intellect and its nourishment, the mental health worker is imbued with the value of intelligence as a prognostic factor. As a result, he has difficulty addressing himself to less educated individuals, especially to those who are inarticulate as well. Traditionally, a "good" patient is smart. *Self-realization* is usually viewed as a valuable quality in Western psychotherapy; but in regard to the retarded, it is often ignored.

The child guidance patient is traditionally brought for treatment by mother, school, or court because of his failures to cope or for some pattern of disruptiveness. The stimulus that brings the retardate is usually some problem in management, such as a disruptive behavior pattern. Nonetheless, there is a psychodynamic problem to be assessed here as well—the need to improve function and maximize development. For the child of average intelligence, there is hope, however illusory, of getting him back on a normal path. With the retarded, the goal is to help him reach a *higher* path of development. The achievement of self-esteem and self-realization may not be impressive in academic terms. But with therapy, a phobic retardate may be able to go out of his dormitory, or a depressed retardate move from a training school to a sheltered workshop. In fact, these advances make an enormous difference in the cost to society, the efforts demanded of staff and family, the social competence of these patients, and their personal happiness. Lifting their level of adaptation changes their life course and status. Sometimes therapy does this by *raising the IQ* itself.[5, 20] This results in both the removal of dysphoric affects and of conflicts which impair their utilization of cognitive skills. On the other hand, the maturation of some intellectual functions can be achieved through stimulation, and a number of training and education programs are available for this purpose. In any case, IQ raising should not be *the* aim of psychotherapy. The chief objective continues to be the relief of suffering from symptoms and improved adaptation.

Bruch[4] declares that hopefulness and coping improve the patient's chances for happiness but do not guarantee it; nor is "happiness" a direct goal of therapy. By the same token, the retardate's position in life rarely permits conventional happiness. He can be *happier*. The happy moron is largely a myth. Children with Langdon-Downs syndrome are not homogenously joyful. Retarded people are trapped in a set of dismal expectancies. They may mask their pervasive dejection, but the continuous awareness of a personal defect allows them no joy. Reality sense and judgment may be painful. The mentally handicapped person needs to find his sense of worth from some source other than being clever. Other competencies are possible but usually on a modest level.

Cost Effectiveness in Treating Retardates

When he considers his relatively low budget and sparse manpower, the mental health worker wonders where to apply his restricted efforts. He needs to understand that a small amount of time put into the therapy of a retarded school-age child or adolescent can be of enormous use. The same doctor who will work diligently and intensively with a psychotic child for months, even when no improvement occurs, is generally loath to undertake therapy with a retardate who has much more potential for change and social functioning. At the same time, in any setting, be it special class, training school, home, or day care center, the upset and fury of the staff at the tumult and rebellion of a retardate often engender intense pressure for intervention. With such a youngster, the therapist may want *expression* of the hostility, while the teacher generally wants its *suppression*. Progress in treatment for most retardates usually means getting them to do more in their environment, while the caretakers commonly want them to do less. Docility is often desired by the caretakers; the potential therapist needs to balance what he hopes to achieve *against* social pressures for conformity. Similarly, the tolerance of the family must be considered when a "total-push" program is planned to take place in a home. Sometimes the siblings and parents objectively cannot do what is needed to achieve therapy progress for the child; the cost is too great in terms of their own lives. A profoundly retarded child may be kept at home, tended diligently, and worked with by a therapist. In time, he may indeed make some detectable improvement, such as eating with less help, but he will remain an enormous burden to the family. The balance must shift away from nihilism, but not to Pollyannism. Fundamentally, therapy is indicated for removing standard psychiatric symptoms. In the absence of conflict, training is indicated. When neurotic or psychotic conflict supervenes, conflict resolution and psychotherapy, combined with other approaches, can be eye-opening to patients, teachers, parents, and child psychiatrists.

The economic argument about treatment intervention in retardation can be made very simply in terms of how much it costs at each successive level of functioning. Institutional costs for a retardate are thousands of dollars per year greater than the cost of attending special classes. If therapy can shift a child to a higher level so he can live in the community, the savings are clear. Being in a sheltered workshop or holding a job contributes to the financial strength of the family and the community.

Preparation of the Child and
His Family

Parents and retardates have a variety of prejudices. Many would rather be considered "slow" than "mental"; on the other hand, there are some families which have responded to the promise of modern psychiatry and prefer believing that their child is disturbed and therefore, rather than suffering from mental retardation, has a reversible condition. The family and the child must be presented with a coherent reason for the therapy. Sometimes a recommendation for the therapy is slipped in among suggestions for other interventions such as speech and milieu therapies. This is a self-defeating approach; the concept of specific psychotherapy requires defining target symptoms and issues as much as possible. Therapy may be explained as helping to improve relationships, decrease fear, increase independence, and permit the playing out of hidden fears. It sould be understood as synergistic with the child's educational program.

A high proportion of retardates without organic findings come from the culture of poverty, sometimes called the "sociofamilial" types of retardation. Largely undereducated, their parents will need support and reassurance and often enough casework that parallels the child's therapy. For the patient, all the traditional guidance clinic issues are likely to be present, with the child attempting bleakly to deny that there is anything wrong and behaving as if he has been caught in a crime. The jokes about "shrinks" and "head doctors" are fed into institutions and special schools both by conscientious consultants, by TV, and by current humor. The retarded are often unsubtle and will frequently scream at each other—"He's crazy . . . nuts . . . goofy." Patients need to be reassured about privacy and the defined status of their therapy. They must be protected against humiliation. Psychotherapy can be presented as a research project. This makes it nonstigmatizing and therefore socially acceptable. Often enough the distinctions between house doctor, pediatrician, psychologist, and child psychiatrist are never clarified, nor for that matter need they receive much attention. A simple declaration, demonstration of the room and toys, the absence of a white coat, and the fact of nonthreatening behavior are the best introduction. Parents need to be shown definitively, usually in terms of a straight-forward problem, that there is some advantage in treating the child.

A particular issue to be borne in mind is that parents of the retarded are generally, and usually justifiably, dissatisfied with the professional help they have received.[34] They are also suffering from a continuing tragedy which will not go away, and they face the problems of dealing with the patient daily if he is at home, or during visits when he is in an institution. The staff should scrupulously avoid treating the parents as neurotics or as truculent visitors. For many retarded children, the best outcomes are found in families where the mothers are aggressive and fight to get the best help for their children and where they insist on warding off procedures and techniques that they believe to be dubious. In addition, a number of the parents are themselves retarded or of borderline intelligence. If they have themselves been domiciled in training schools at some point, they may well have a dread of authority, a hope of getting their children away, or, at least, a strong wish to protect them. It is also useful for parents to receive brief reviews of progress, verbally as well as in writing. In these cases, the commitment of the parents is even more decisive than with neurotic children. Nor can one lose sight of the fact that the parents of the retarded may also be neurotic or psychotic, and not merely beset.

Techniques

There are diagnostic factors in retardation which will influence the type of intervention that a child psychiatrist may institute. The profoundly retarded can utilize little direct psychotherapy. The psychiatrist is likely to be called upon to help with the symptoms of rocking, head banging, failure in bowel and bladder control, and the like. In such instances, he is unlikely to act as a therapist directly. He is more likely to function as a consultant and recommend environmental changes, drugs, and behavior modification techniques. The adult retardate should be mentioned in passing (even in a book devoted to child psychiatry) to emphasize that among the 6 million in the population who are estimated to be retarded, most are chronologically adults. These adults are frequently seen among the general psychiatric population. They are often misdiagnosed and not given appropriate psychological treatment. The therapy they require is much closer to the approaches to be described later in this chapter for children than to methods for treating borderlines, psychotic, or neurotic adults.

The definition of retardation used by the American Association for Mental Deficiency includes the presence of subaverage intellectual functioning during the developmental phase. One fundamental result of delayed learning in early life is the failure to resolve basic dependency. Whether or not basic trust has been established, a general characteristic to be dealt with in the psychotherapy of retardates at each age level is their more oral way of relating. This dependency will tinge the personality even when therapy is successfully concluded. It is by no means an entirely negative element; in fact, it provides the vehicle for a great deal of im-

provement. It permits a more rapid establishment of positive transference and enables one to end on a cordial note. As Zigler[36] notes, in any given learning situation normally intelligent children get their gratification from actual mastery of the tasks at hand, whereas the retarded are generally more eager to have the approval of an adult. In psychotherapy with the retarded, then, it is important to utilize this dependent relationship by showing clear approval when the child does the right thing. The ultimate goal is to enable him to be as self-sufficient as possible. This judgmental posture is important. Child therapists are not as concerned with being nonjudgmental as in times past, but they are still not sufficiently prepared to encourage and praise as is required in working with the retarded. The primitivity, rigidity, and fearfulness[16, 26] of the retardate's superego have been shown to be less a part of the innate condition than a function of the environment within which the retardate grows. As a result of the apprehension, grief, and bitterness his parents exhibit when they discipline him, the retardate is conditioned in rather more primitive ways than are his siblings. This legacy becomes a problem during therapy, and the child must learn that in this regard the therapist is different. In the clinic, the distinction between the neurotic child and the retardate is one of degree rather than kind. It is important to bear this in mind. Masserman[24] has stressed that in order to be psychologically comfortable, an individual requires some confidence in his bodily soundness, a sense that his life has significance, and the awareness that he can give and receive love. As a stigmatized deviant, the retardate has realistic limitations in relation to these qualities and needs to be taught that he is valuable as a person through the corrective relationship of the therapy.

Therapeutic Style

As each clinician develops his style, he learns to employ specific tactics with different types of patients; with the retarded, the style should lean toward a more actively friendly approach. From the outset, the patient needs to be told repeatedly about the nature of therapy. He probably has a limited tolerance for silences, and these should be avoided without, however, interfering with his slow spontaneous productions. Many retarded children have speech impediments (defined as any alteration of speech pattern other than a foreign accent which calls attention to the speech itself). Attention should be given to allowing the patient to articulate without either overwhelming him with encouragement or ignoring the language problem.

The first stage of therapy has the goal of forming a relationship. Jakab[18] states that in this stage the main task will have to be accomplished by the therapist using more or less "intrusive" methods. For the severely retarded and the hyperactive, the therapist may have to rely on physical holding and touching; for the psychotic or autistic retardate, the therapist will probably be able to work without physical contact. Adams[1] stresses that the therapist himself is the instrument of therapy; he emphasizes that no matter how humane and democratic the therapist's philosophy, it is he who conducts the therapy and has authority and power over the patient. The therapist has to make many decisions about planning for the interviews, how to structure them, how to order the work for the brain-damaged or autistic retardate, and which equipment is likely to survive the hyperkinetic child. Toys should not be so much in evidence or so many in number that they create a stimulus overload that might confuse and disorganize. The duration of the individual session may have to be modified. Some retarded children cannot concentrate well, and organically damaged children may become fatigued. Therapists also find some of these children particularly difficult, and communicate their annoyance through body language. This is likely to produce regressive withdrawal on the part of many well-conditioned retardates who have long ago been taught to be silent and to fear expressing aggression. The hyperkinetic or autistic child may promptly decompose and become unmanageable. Music can be both soothing or stimulating, or part of an expressive play pattern.

Gifts, food, and prizes may all be employed if they are clearly part of the treatment program; they function best as supports and rewards. Since retarded children suffer many emotional deprivations and fail to assimilate experiences as well as do normal children, they are much more eager to receive gifts. The gifts need be no more than a specially shaped paper clip or a drawing or candy, and need not become a ritualized part of the treatment situation.

One particularly important area in the therapy of retardates is an emphasis on talking. Retarded children need to be given every opportunity to verbalize their fantasies. In spite of speech defects, habits of hiding, and previous instruction to be si-

lent, as a rule they can communicate far more readily if the style and rhythm of the interview does not appear to test or force. Therapists must avoid the tendency to work only on toys; the best conversational approach is one that can lead naturally into singing, joking, and speaking spontaneously. The retarded child who is not altogether regressed and psychotic does have a self-concept, albeit a damaged one. He can be helped greatly if given a chance to say what he thinks. These children have been exposed to more TV than the average child; as a result some of their composite language acquisitions may be a surprising admixture of commercials and current slang; this should not be construed as bizarre. Relentless enthusiasm is a tool of some recreational therapists. It is decidedly not the style for the psychotherapist who needs to show that he wants these children to express their personal wishes and their hurt, angry, bitter feelings. In general, any verbalization or acting out of negative affects is particularly inhibited by the families of retardates. As a result, the children need to be shown and told many times that this is permissible before they can really believe that these feelings are acceptable.

In their 1935 report on the psychoanalysis of a retardate, Chidester and Menninger[5] noted how astonished they were to get so much fantasy material from a defective patient. While analysis is not generally feasible, many patients will become more articulate when they feel that despite all their defects of grammar and their curse words, their fantasies are in fact accepted. This acceptance may be what is needed to reopen disturbed communication, first with the therapist and then with family and peers. Even for an inarticulate person, catharsis and ventilation may be enormously useful.

Pace of Therapy and Sequence of Issues

In his primer of psychotherapy for children, Adams[1] states that the therapist should examine feelings before he examines defenses; this principle is certainly directly applicable to the group under discussion. He also establishes a general rule that anger should be expressed prior to examining sexual lust. In contrast to normal children, retarded children tend to be smaller, to look and act somewhat younger, and to evade facing the threats of adolescence. Their difficulties in handling issues of autonomy and independence make them generally fearful of their impulses; in particular, they fear the instinctual flooding that comes with puberty. Unfortunately, at every turn of their sex education, they are handled poorly. Even those parents who are able to discuss erotic feelings with their other children often recoil from facing this subject with the retardate. This fear reflects prevailing public attitudes about the alleged perverse sexual habits of the retarded; retarded girls are seen as prospective recruits for prostitution, and retarded boys are viewed as potential sex offenders. In fact, most male sex offenders appear to be of normal or above-average intelligence, and the modern prostitute tends to be a highly disturbed intelligent female who has pushed the retardate out of competition.

Retarded patients have been subjected to a great deal of mass media stimulation and a melange of advice. For example, they are often told that they should learn to socialize. Schools and institutions organize parties and are charmed by the "cute" latency-type relations that occur. Like all children who are overstimulated and denied consistent directives for behavior—indeed, like all children —the retarded, as they grow older, engage in unsophisticated homosexual and heterosexual groupings. At this point, there is much less tolerance for their behavior. They have heard that brothers and sisters do certain things that are forbidden, and they share the general giggliness about all manner of secrets. Some parents are still inclined to think that their retarded child is inherently "oversexed"; but they convey to their child only a vague awareness that there is some terrible threat overshadowing him.

In order to get to these troublesome issues, the therapist must first give *reassurance* and *support* to the child, but these should not be so shotgun or massive as to become merely inchoate noises. The discussion should be directed in a clear manner with the therapist telling the child what he has heard from family members, and how he thinks about these matters; he may have to separate his role from that of more Victorian matrons or teachers at the institution where the patient resides, but he should avoid polarization between himself as therapist and the resident staff. If the child can then begin to produce some of his own feelings about what is happening, the therapist can reflect back some of what he has said and clarify the experiences and fantasies. In the realm of sexuality, it seems clear that the basic mechanisms of learning by the mentally retarded are fundamentally the same for normal children of about the same *mental* age.[7] What is difficult for the retarded is the mixture of messages, advice, and threat that they receive. The institutionalized child, especially, who is still the most likely candidate for therapy, is often faced with differing directives about what can be said and done. There is obviously enormous variation between those staff members who ignore four-letter words, masturbation, and obscene gestures, and those who respond with anger and punishment. Homosexual and heterosexual underworlds exist in most institutions; the retarded generally are able to perceive which standards of sexual conduct apply to them. However, the background of tension and inconsistency about what to tell and what not to tell them is something that requires special decontamination in therapy. The therapist often has to give advice and to explain things that these patients have missed because of their innate difficulties. They manifest the common reaction phenomenon of becoming so anxious over sexual material that they do not hear what is being said to them.

Currently there is not sufficient comparable data to permit giving conclusive advice about how quickly to move with retardates; the experience of seasoned workers seems to be that with some issues the retarded can move *faster* because their conflicts are simpler and they rely more directly on the wisdom and guidance of the therapist. This means aiming for a different result, with the patient complying with the directives of his authority figures. Jakab[18] questions whether it is better to try to alleviate the symptom which is most painful to the patient, or the one which is socially the least acceptable. Sadly for the retardate, the answer is that the community is not tolerant of his misadventures, and this compels a decision for social compliance.

Projective Techniques

The same basic principles which hold for neurotic children are applicable to the retarded. Once the patient realizes that his therapist is genuinely interested in his dreams, he is usually ready to tell about them. They can then be investigated in terms of wish fulfillments, oedipal themes (usually heavily tinged with oral issues), and classical dream symbolism. Drawings can be used for projective testing, to develop play themes, and to elucidate fantasies. With this group of patients, however, they are particularly important, also, as a shared activity with the therapist.

Dream and drawing studies lead to consideration of ego defects and the redistribution of psychological forces that are part of the altered development of the retarded. Many of the cases treated in institutions show a much higher incidence of cerebral palsy, seizure disorders, or other central nervous system defects. The investment of libido in these problems will be enormous, and there is an active interplay between the many images of the self which come up in dreams and drawings. The body image of the retarded comprises an important part of his personality, clothes, and manners.

Within the institutional population are many children of aberrant appearance. In spite of considerable improvement, there continue to be many problems concerned with dressing inmates in more attractive ways, keeping their hair cut, and so forth. These matters of appearance are important to social adjustment and self-image. Many young people who work as nurses and aides in training centers wear blue jeans, beards, and long hair. Their elaborately casual uniform is, nonetheless, rarely confused with the similar blue jeans dress of inmates because of the differences in body language and action patterns. The "look" on the face of many institutionalized retardates is important in two ways.

It marks them as different and it distorts and impairs interpersonal communication. However, the majority of retardates are in the community and 75 percent of them look indistinguishable from the rest of the population. They are subjected to the same propaganda from the cosmetic industry that barrages the general public, and they must cope with the whole range of emotions about attractiveness and looks. These issues need to be examined, and children should be encouraged to discuss in their therapy what looks right and wrong, and how people can change their appearance. Therapists need to advise patients on clothes and cosmetics. In part, this is one way to urge development of an active form of coping. It leads into discussion of the whole area of facial and body communication, a second theme in the communication of feelings. The retarded person learns to mask his feelings and to remain relatively blank or silent. This is actively indoctrinated. It is evolved by the child in response to both formal and informal pressures from the family, friends, and schools. Ultimately, it results in either frozen smiles or perpetual blankness. The issue of which comes first, an innate unresponsiveness or the interactional

shaping of the behavior, does not alter the visible facade that can be changed if it is given some attention and that needs to be changed. This is best approached by engaging the patient's feelings about the derogatory and contemptuous things people say about his appearance. Needless to add, those who have more mobile faces, who dress well, and who can better manage their social anxieties function more successfully in their general adaptation.

Personality Differences

Because of their lack of experience in treating mental defectives, most child psychiatrists tend to fall back upon categorizing disease rather than people. It is important to examine the retardate's personality systematically. One of the most useful ways to do this is in terms of the categories developed by Thomas, Chess, and Birch:[30] activity, rhythmicity, adaptability, approach/withdrawal, threshold of response, intensity, mood, distractibility, and persistence. These are all considered to be part of the child's endowment which is, in time, influenced by environment. Some of their concepts have been applied to the retarded and continue to be fruitful in explicating their patterns of reaction. This does not exclude dynamic formulations; it supplements them.

Ending Treatment

It has been suggested that these children are more vulnerable to losses than are normal youngsters. Their intense attachments to therapists seem to express some of this vulnerability. In planning termination, it is necessary to understand why this impacts more strongly on them than on other children, although the fundamental issues are not dissimilar. In work with institutionalized patients, some psychotherapists have made it their practice to maintain communication afterward, by cards, follow-up visits, and parental messages. Sometimes, this results from the therapist's guilt at not having "rescued" the child. At the end of therapy, one still is not dealing with a normal child; it is therefore extremely important to plan with the family, the teachers, and others concerned with the continuing care of the child for further training and educational help. In general, therapists who became intensely involved with these "needy" children find that this problem of realistic goals can get very sticky indeed.

Working with Families

No one pattern is universally applicable. Some therapists work exclusively with the child, and some feel that they must deal with mother and child together; it always seems useful to meet with the whole family and to ascertain their actual way of interacting with the child. Sometimes it helps to have periodic family meetings during the course of individual treatment. When feasible, this is true for the institutionalized child as well; under both sets of circumstances, it is essential to find optimal ways of balancing the needs and tolerances of the family against those of the child. There are some families who exhaust themselves by clutching grimly and relentlessly at every opportunity to do something for their child. Sometimes they subject the child to a dizzying barrage of stimulation, and sometimes they make the child aware that resisting these "opportunities" may be an enormous manipulative device. One sixteen-year-old retarded girl with hysterical paralysis of her legs gradually began to feign this symptom consciously in order to evade responsibility. She was responding to the desperation with which her parents brought in a variety of clinicians to get her up and, hopefully, out of the home. She was in fact successful in preventing her parents from sending her off to school; the situation didn't change until they obtained counseling and were able to alter the interactional pattern and divert some of the wrath underlying their desperation.

Many mental health specialists have developed what Menolascino[25] has called "systems of exclusion" to get rid of burdensome retarded patients. These attitudes need to be changed to help parents of retarded children who need a place with which to keep in touch. After therapy has been terminated, it is usually helpful to see these parents intermittently and to remain an active resource for them by requesting regular progress reports twice each year. The stigma of mental retardation affects the family as well as the child. Many families drop out of the medical care system because they feel they receive no help and experience many rejections. Psychotherapists who show continuing interest can help guide such parents and reinforce the efforts of the social worker. This again empha-sizes the point that families of the retarded are often given excessive consultation by people who pass them along—pediatricians, neurologists and psychiatrists. They give an opinion but do not continue with the family, or merely confine themselves to narrow issues rather than addressing the overall problem. With his interest in family dynamics, the child psychiatrist may be an ideal person for continued, brief contacts over long periods.

The national and state organizations for the retarded should be resources; they can offer sites where families can meet in groups, share interests, lobby for better facilities, and educate themselves and the public. For many, these are the best forums for parental support; they can also be complementary to the activities of the child's former or current psychotherapist. Contact with other agencies is very much the same as in other child guidance activities, although services are generally less well funded than even the usually overstretched child psychiatry facilities.

Group Therapy

Group therapy has been undertaken in many settings with parents of the retarded, with their siblings, and with the patients themselves.[37] The adolescent retardate about to leave the institution is in a situation particularly appropriate for short-term focused group therapy. Homogenous focused groups have been useful in handling sexual problems.[28] There is a tendency toward overlap between planned formal therapy groups and all of the informal patient meetings, milieu therapy, experimental groups, and educational functions in classes. Many of these are important and useful but do not require a psychiatrist for their implementation. Teachers, nurses, social workers, and pediatricians should be involved along with rehabilitation counselors; the psychiatrist may deploy his skills most usefully as a consultant. He can participate in these activities for training purposes, but his main role should consist of treating in groups large numbers of disturbed and psychiatrically handicapped children. Activity group approaches may be helpful, and other disciplines can become involved; for the child psychiatrist, however, the aim of group psychotherapy in the field of retardation should focus clearly upon the need to comprehend and alter disordered personality functions. It should not be diluted by replicating educational or purely supportive functions, which would be confusing to patients, families, and institutions. At the same time, the group therapist is usually a more outgoing sort. He works with observable behavior and is involved in aiding retarded children with their conflicts and helping them augment each other's expressions of feeling. Gratification of affective and dependent needs in adult therapy is often inadvisable, but the reality needs of the retarded in group therapy require a more directive, caretaking, and caring manner. At times, this treatment makes for intense, even for bitter, competition among the children for the approval and affection of the therapist. They want to sit near him, touch him, and often try to detain him after the group sessions. Group discussion to clarify the rules of group therapy and the role of the group leader are necessary. But the deprivations and affect hunger of the institutionalized children make them unable to give up altogether trying to obtain special attentions of the therapist. On the other hand, this in itself is a good sign of their motivation for better adaptation. It becomes a crucial matter in working with adolescents who will be going out to public schools, sheltered workshops, or rehabilitation settings, to help them deal better with a variety of strangers. Systematic efforts must be made by trained therapists to modify and improve the emotional conflicts of the retarded. Character patterns, temperament, and social style are commonly more decisive than intellectual levels in the functioning of the retardate in school and society. (For a more detailed discussion of group therapy, see chapter 10.)

Genetic Counseling

Many of the professionals who advise families on the basis of statistical and scientific knowledge of genetics adopt an authoritarian style. One of the inherent problems, however, is the long tradition of unconsciously employing genetics, the eugenics movement, and psychological testing to contribute to the social indictment of the retarded. In spite of the rapid spread of genetic counseling as a professional technique, little attention seems to be given to the emotional impact of all the information about zygotes and recessive traits. A critical factor is that only a few conditions like Downs syndrome, phenylketonuria, and galactosemia are clearly enough defined genetically to provide clear directives for counseling families. In addition, the victims of those syndromes which produce profound retardation are usually sterile.

Outcome of Therapy

Gunzberg[15] has made the astute observation that there is a new generation of therapists now beginning treatment of the retarded who lack any broad clinical knowledge of methodology, of patient behavior, or of the developmental course of these patients. However, he feels that supplying retardates with people who give them special attention, who join them in thinking out their problems, and who counsel with them will in itself improve their outlook and behavior. On the other hand, he does not feel that exploratory psychotherapy has any advantage over warmth and affection. He regards the environment of the retardate as the crucial site for determining whether the work of the therapist is actually productive. To a large extent his efforts have focused upon group approaches, and his criticisms apply as well to the vagueness of the distinctions drawn between such types of group intervention as activity groups, play groups, and discussion groups. Tizard,[32] too, has reservations about the value of reports on psychotherapy with the retarded; he raises questions of objective standards of reporting, criteria and sample sizes. Szurek and Philips* and Jakab[18] are more positive about the usefulness of psychotherapy with this population. They see it as helpful in reducing conflict and improving adaptation; in their view, retarded children who are treated are more integrated in their responses, acquire more optimism about themselves, and act with more spontaneity. Cytryn and Lourie[8] feel that individual and group psychotherapy have value, but they stress that the treatment must be effectively integrated into a plan for the whole life of the child, including family, treatment center, or school.

Most individual therapists who have embarked on this work feel that they have achieved a measure of very real success. At the same time, they are aware that such therapy entails all the methodological problems that have long bedeviled the assessment of results of child therapy in general. In this connection, retardation offers untapped opportunities for systematic research. It involves numerous observers of behavior who can contribute to

* See S. A. Szurek and I. Philips, "Mental Retardation and Psychotherapy," in I. Philips (Ed.), *Prevention and Treatment of Mental Retardation*, pp. 221–246, Basic Books, New York, 1966.

collecting data and evaluate the results of specific types of psychotherapeutic intervention.

Drugs

It is much easier to provide warnings and disclaimers about the use of psychotropic agents than to make positive recommendations. It is important to make clear that the issues here refer to the management of behavioral problems (discussed in detail in chapter 23) and not the treatment with thyroid extracts of syndromes such as cretinism. No consideration will be given to drugs which are supposed to improve intellectual functioning; their usefulness has not been established. The treatment issues involved in managing minimal brain dysfunction and hyperkinesis are discussed in volume 2, chapters 20 and 21, and in this volume, chapter 38, although the same principles are involved. Almost every aspect of the assessment of drug effects in children is hemmed in by methodological problems, and there is endless controversy about results. There are allegations that the retarded respond differently to psychopharmacologic agents. Freeman[12] stresses that this has not been supported by objective data. Fish,[11] on the other hand, believes that retardates do respond differently. In any case, both agree that diagnostic categories are not very helpful in treating children with these agents and that the drugs should be employed to treat particular behavioral symptoms. Cytryn and Lourie[8] caution against the widespread misuse of these medications; they point to problems with patterns of administration, carelessness about indications, side effects, and the huge range and irregularity of administration of medications in general. Both massive overdoses and homeopathic minuscule doses are commonplace. If the child is to be considered for medication, it should be a significant element in a treatment plan and not something thrown in for good measure. The setting must be evaluated so that the child is not medicated instead of handling an obvious conflict between members of the staff who disagree about him, or as chemical restraints given punitively because mother is angry. It is important to know the child's and family's experience with medications and to make sure that punitive implications are as few as possible. The other physicians involved in the care of the child should be provided with the medication schedule, and schoolteachers and matrons should be alerted about what to watch for, in order both to gauge results and to be on the watch for evidence of overdosage or side effects.

Hollister[17] stresses the need to avoid polypharmacy, and to use one agent at a time. This is important if one is to avoid confusion about the many factors altering behavioral responses. The best practice is to adjust schedules of administration so that only one medication at a time is given in order to determine its effectiveness level. The rather low level of toxicity and of complications in administering psychotropic medications to children have perhaps contributed to the casual way they have been prescribed. In institutionalized retardates, obvious brain damage, cerebral palsy, seizure disorders, and the many metabolic syndromes causing retardation are all very likely to coexist with behavior problems. At the same time, the patients may be receiving other medications which change their reactions.

Sedatives and *hypnotics* for the retarded are useful in stress situations. Chloral hydrate remains a reliable agent, while far less use is made of barbiturates. If tranquilizers are indicated during the day, in an effort to keep the drug regimen simple, they can be used in larger dosages as sleep medication at night. Paraldehyde is seldom employed.

Antidepressants. Stigma, taunting, and deprivation are all intrinsic to the life style of an intellectually handicapped child, and unhappiness is all too likely to be the dominant affect in his experience. His frozen expression and staring gaze make it difficult to assess mood changes which distinguish sadness, misery, melancholia, or clinical depression from apathy. The description of indications for treating depression chemically are imprecise. On the other hand, the results of using antidepressants have been so equivocal that once the novelty effect has disappeared, they have turned out to be of little help.

Minor Tranquilizers. Clinically, chlordiazepoxide (Librium), diazepam (Valium), and meprobamate still appear to be the agents most widely used. The reports of their results with the retarded are based largely on anecdotal data. Meprobamate is favored by some because of its low toxicity, but others find that it offers little advantage over the barbiturates.

Major Tranquilizers. A number of adolescent retardates exhibit states of enormous tension which do not respond to the minor tranquilizers. At the same time the patients do not show signs of psychotic illness. Chlorpromazine, often in surprisingly high doses, is required to contain their agitation. For the difficult-to-diagnose and overlapping groups of organic brain syndrome, psychotic syndromes, and intrinsic problems of retardation, where uncontrollable agitation has supervened, haloperidol is recommended by some. However, chlorpromazine remains the most widely used agent.

Hyperkinesis

This presents its familiar picture in the retarded child. Earl[9] considered overactivity to be part of the intrinsic nature of mental retardation, without the presence of a true, hyperkinetic syndrome. Later hyperkinesis is said to shift to the psychomotor retardation seen in older retardates, particularly in institutions. However, it is likely that to a large extent this phenomenon is a consequence of environmental pressures. At first when exhibited by younger children, the activity meets with alarm responses; later, because of the pressure to inhibit responses and the internalization of aggressive impulses, apathy and slowing down appear. Neither group of responses are suited to drug control. Hyperkinesis in its usual sense, along with all the rest of the spectrum of cerebral dysfunction, obviously occurs in a high percentage of the children in training schools. It should be treated in the manner described in volume 2, chapters 20 and 21, and chapters 23 and 38 of this volume.

Behavior Modification

The most active and rapidly expanding approach to the psychological care of the retarded is the group of operant procedures based on the work of Skinner. Here the emphasis falls on the study of observable behavior rather than upon dynamic or theoretical constructs. A large number of reports is accumulating,[14, 22, 27, 35] and it appears that all over the country in special classes, training schools, a few hospital wards, and in many home settings, varied conditioning methods are being employed with great vigor. The overall concepts and techniques involved in these efforts are discussed in considerable detail in volume 2, chapter 5, and in this volume, chapters 5 and 11. Only the special aspects related to retardation will be noted here.

However, it should be pointed out that the field of retardation has been a peculiarly important one for behavior modification efforts. There are several reasons for this. One that has been painfully clear is the overall lack of interest by psychiatrists in the care of the retarded. In contrast to this, psychologists have focused on retardates and have been concerned with utilizing the behavior modification approach. Another is the lack of funds for the care of the mentally handicapped. This makes behavior modification more appealing because it can be applied by teachers, nurses, social workers, and pediatricians, by less expensive professionals, and even by nonprofessionals. It is also evident that the influx of these people has changed the atmosphere in many institutions, improved morale strikingly, and improved the lot of patients. It has provided new enthusiasm for attacking some of the perennial problems of the institutionalized retardate: stealing, untrained eating habits, rocking, assaultiveness, window breaking, soiling, head banging, and resistance to training and schooling.

In Canada, Latin America, and the United States, the focus on behavior modification has led a new generation of workers to discover the need to reorganize institutions, to repaint, rebuild, and replace them, and to do this under the aegis of a new "scientific" idealism.[31] Many of these practitioners and investigators are hostile to psychiatry and psychodynamics; a few are seeking ways of developing joint approaches. Unfortunately, in the training schools for the retarded, the clinical problems have been contaminated by struggles for power and for the control of the administration of the institutions. This in-fighting has raged back and forth between medical and psychiatric forces on the one hand, and psychological services on the other. In fact, the medical profession directs about half of the state schools, but the level of care varies in all of them. It is therefore difficult to see these political movements as fundamentally helpful in the development of procedures to help the patients. The increased interest of child psychiatrists in learning about and utilizing behavior modification approaches as part of their own therapeutic armamentarium promises a better amalgamation of experience and practice for the future. At present, there are vigorous efforts being directed toward translating psychodynamics into behavioral terms by one group, and translating operant conditioning into psychodynamics by the other.

A large part of the appeal of behavior modification is the clarity, simplicity, and replicability of the approach. It is less dependent on verbal and abstract communication and is thereby applicable to moderately and profoundly retarded children. Bachrach and Quigley[2] warn that the worthy social goals and the deceptive simplicity of the theory will attract many "psychotechnicians" whose amateurism may damage the learning therapies. This is an interesting contrast to the position of most behavior modification investigators; generally academics, they are proud of their "objective" and verifiable methodology. Essentially, their procedures are based in the use of environmental vectors to alter the patient's responses to stimuli. Skinner[31] pointed out that according to psychodynamic formulations, behavior is an observable symptom of a concealed neurosis, while in his behaviorist view, behavior is the direct object of inquiry which does not require "black box" hypotheses about psychodynamics.

Eysenk[10] echoes this by noting that learning theory simply assumes symptoms to be learned habits which can be eliminated as such, without considering unconscious phenomena.

Behavior modification centers on careful observation and definition of the particular behavior to be changed. It compares the individual patient with his own performance, and therefore offers an individualized, scientifically useful approach which helps counter the dehumanization of many institutions. The aim is to modify a teaching environment in order to allow learning to occur with maximum ease, to reinforce this learning in suitable ways, and finally to make those changes in the surroundings which help transfer or generalize the new learning to the larger living environment. Learning can be defined as a change in behavior resulting from reinforced practice or experience. Most of the behavioral responses employed in working with the retarded are called *operants*. These are behaviors which are related to their consequences in the environment. In contrast to classical conditioning, they seem goal directed, purposeful, and volitional. Skinner uses the term *operants* to refer to responses such as picking up a fork to eat that are emitted by the organism and seen as voluntary. The behaviors that the practitioner wants to maintain or to develop are reinforced by means of rewards of candies, food, privileges, token, and the like. The undesirable activities that he seeks to eliminate or extinguish receive negative reinforcements such as ignoring, having the child leave the group for a period or lose privileges. Lovaas[23] has reported that the advantage of punishment is the rapidity with which it is coupled to the undesired behavior; the desperate need to arrest self-destructive behaviors by psychotic retarded children leads to difficult legal and ethical confrontations when the more painful forms of negative reinforcement, such as electric shocks, are employed.

There is enough knowledge about the natural course of the lives of the retarded in institutions and within the byways of the community to make it clear that often it is better to do something of controversial nature than to do nothing at all. The latter course will lead the retardate only into decreased learning and further failure in adaptation.

REFERENCES

1. ADAMS, P., *A Primer of Child Psychotherapy*, Little, Brown, Boston, 1975.
2. BACHRACH, A., and QUIGLEY, W., "Direct Methods of Treatment," in Berg, I., and Pennington, (Eds.), *An Introduction to Clinical Psychology*, 3rd ed., pp. 482–560, Ronald Press, New York, 1966.
3. BERNSTEIN, N. R., and RICE, J. O., "Psychiatric Consultations in a School for the Retarded," *American Journal of Mental Deficiency*, 76(6):718–725, 1972.
4. BRUCH, H., *Learning Psychotherapy*, Harvard University Press, Cambridge, 1975.
5. CHIDESTER, L., and MENNINGER, K., "The Application of Psychoanalytic Methods to the Study of Mental Retardation," *American Journal of Orthopsychiatry*, 6:616–625, 1936.
6. CLARK, L., "Child Analysis: A Motion Picture Dramatization," *Procedures and Addresses of the American Association of Studies of the Feebleminded*, 36:111–115, 1931.
7. CRUZ, F., and LAVECK, B., *Human Sexuality and the Mentally Retarded*, Brunner/Mazel, New York, 1973.
8. CYTRYN, L., and LOURIE, R., "Mental Retardation," in Freedman, A., Kaplan, H., and Sadock, B. (Eds.), *Comprehensive Textbook of Psychiatry*, 2nd ed., vol. 1, pp. 1158–1197, Williams & Wilkins, Baltimore, 1975.
9. EARL, C. J. C., *Subnormal Personalities*, Balliere, Tyndall and Cox, London, 1961.

10. EYSENK, H. (Ed.), *Behavior Therapy and the Neuroses*, Pergamon Press, New York, 1960.
11. FISH, B., "Drug Use in Psychiatric Disorders of Children," *American Journal of Psychiatry*, 124(Suppl. 8): 31–36, 1968.
12. FREEMAN, R., "Use of Psychoactive Drugs for Intellectually Handicapped Children," in Bernstein, N. (Ed.), *Diminished People*, pp. 277–304, Little, Brown, Boston, 1970.
13. FREUD, S., "Analysis Terminable and Interminable," in *Collected Papers*, vol. 5, p. 316, Hogarth Press, London, 1950.
14. GARDNER, J., "Training Nonprofessionals in Behavior Modification," in Thompson, T., and Dockens, W. (Eds.), *Applications of Behavior Modification*, Academic Press, New York, 1975.
15. GUNZBERG, H. C., "Psychotherapy," in Clarke, A., and Clarke, A. (Eds.), *Mental Deficiency: The Changing Outlook*, 3rd ed., pp. 708–728, Free Press, New York, 1975.
16. HEBER, R., "Personality," In Stevens, Harvey and Heber, (Eds.), *Mental Retardation, A Review of Research*, pp. 143–174, University of Chicago Press, Chicago, 1964.
17. HOLLISTER, N., personal communication, Massachusetts Rehabilitation Hospital, 1975.

18. JAKAB, I., "Psychotherapy of the Mentally Retarded Child," in Bernstein, N. (Ed.), *Diminished People and Care of the Mentally Retarded*, Little, Brown, Boston, 1970.

19. JOHNSON, G., "Psychological Characteristics of the Mentally Retarded," in Cruickshank, W. (Ed.), *Psychology of Exceptional Children and Youth*, Prentice-Hall, Englewood Cliffs, N. J., 1971.

20. JORSWIECK, E., "Analysis of a 12 Year Old Child with Defective Intelligence," *Prax Kinderpsychol. Finderpsychiat.*, 7:251–254, 1958.

21. KANNER, L., *A History of the Care and Study of the Mentally Retarded*, Charles C Thomas, Springfield, Ill., 1964.

22. KIERNAN, C., "Behavior Modification," in Clarke, A., and Clarke, A. (Eds.), *Mental Deficiency: The Changing Outlook*, 3rd ed., pp. 729–806, Free Press, New York, 1974.

23. LOVAAS, O., and SIMMONS, J., "Manipulation of Self-Destructive Behavior in 3 Retarded Children," *Journal of Applied Behavioral Analysis*, 1:143–157, 1969.

24. MASSERMANN, J., *A Psychiatric Odyssey*, Science House, New York, 1971.

25. MENOLASCINO, F. (Ed.), *Psychiatric Approaches to Mental Retardation*, Basic Books, New York, 1970.

26. SARASON, S., and DORIS, J., *Psychological Problems in Mental Deficiency*, 4th ed., Harper & Row, 1969.

27. SASLOW, G., "Application of Behavior Therapy," in Usdin, G. (Ed.), *Overview of the Psychotherapies*, pp. 68–91, Brunner/Mazel, New York, 1975.

28. SLIVKIN, S., and BERNSTEIN, N., "Group Approaches to Treating the Retarded," in Menolascino, F. (Ed.), *Psychiatric Approaches to Mental Retardation*, pp. 435–454, Basic Books, New York, 1970.

29. STACEY, C., and DeMARTINO, M., *Counseling and Psychotherapy with the Mentally Retarded*, Free Press, Glencoe, Ill., 1957.

30. THOMAS, A., CHESS, S., and BIRCH, H., *Temperament and Behavior Disorders in Children*, New York University Press, New York, 1968.

31. THOMPSON, T., and GRABOWSKI, J., *Behavior Modification of the Mentally Retarded*, Oxford University Press, New York, 1972.

32. TIZARD, J., "Treatment of the Mentally Subnormal," in Richter, D. (Ed.), *Aspects of Psychiatric Research*, pp. 125–153, Oxford University Press, London, 1962.

33. WEBSTER, T., "Problems of Emotional Development in Young Retarded Children," *American Journal of Psychiatry*, 120:34–41, 1963.

34. WOLFENSBERGER, W., and KURTZ, R., *Management of the Family of the Mentally Retarded*, Follett Publishing Co., Chicago, 1969.

35. YAMAGUCHI, K., "Application of Operant Principles to Mentally Retarded Children," in Thompson, T., and Dockens, W. (Eds.), *Applications of Behavior Modification*, pp. 365–384, Academic Press, New York, 1975.

36. ZIGLER, E., "Research on Personality Structure in the Retardate," in Ellis, N. (Ed.), *International Review of Research in Mental Retardation*, vol. 1, pp. 77–108, Academic Press, New York, 1966.

37. ZISFEIN, L., and ROSEN, M., "Personal Adjustment Training: A Group Counseling Program for Institutionalized Mentally Retarded Persons," *Mental Retardation*, 11:16–20, 1973.

---

40 / Handicapped Children

Elva Orlow Poznanski

Psychotherapy with the handicapped is a relatively new phenomenon. In the past, such children were not considered suitable candidates for psychotherapy, with many reasons offered to justify this stance. Their unfortunate situation was in itself felt to be an insurmountable barrier. There was also a belief that severe physical illness or incapacity would "drain" motivation and energy for psychotherapy.[11] Gradually, these prejudices have disappeared and currently many pediatric hospitals, orthopedic hospitals, and various clinics for the handicapped have consulting psychologists and psychiatrists on their staffs and employ social workers. These professionals have found new challenges in working with the handicapped. Indeed, subjectively, one receives the impression that psychotherapy can be as gratifying with these patients as with any other group.

The emotional problems of being handicapped, regardless of the medical diagnosis, have more in common with one another than do the specific effects of individual diseases. This chapter will therefore deal with the problems of the handicapped in general and how they relate to psychiatric intervention.

Countertransference Problems

The first problem to be faced by the potential therapist of a handicapped child is the therapist's own attitudes and feelings. Our cultural background insidiously instills the attitude that physical beauty is highly prized, without our necessarily being consciously aware of how much this attitude influences behavior. Frequently therapists, too, unwittingly have this same bias and tend to avoid association with the handicapped, not properly recognizing their need for psychological as well as physical help. If therapists are able to recognize their own aversions to disability, then it is less likely that these feelings will influence their judgment. The potential therapists of the handicapped must constantly be aware of their own countertransference.[13]

Sometimes it appears that the initial reluctance of therapists to work with handicapped individuals is caused not only by the patient's physical appearance but by a feeling of helplessness induced by the patient's compromised physical state. The adult therapist of a handicapped child may find his own buried childhood feelings of helplessness surfacing in a most disturbing way. Even if there is no direct memory, there is sufficient emotional recall to make the therapist feel uncomfortable. As children, all of us actively tried to master feeling helpless. To varying degrees, all of us have been successful, but potentially we are still vulnerable to the affect or the memory of painful childhood feelings and experiences.

With the handicapped, the therapist experiences feelings of repulsion because of the physical appearance of the individual. Moreover, he is likely to be threatened by his own feelings of helplessness in the situation. As a result, the interviews with the patient can be distorted in several ways. One way this can happen is for the therapist, who is not in touch with his own feelings, to gloss over the degree and extent of the handicapping situation (the therapist does not clearly ascertain what the handicapped person is and is not able to do). In order to be effective, it is absolutely necessary for the therapist to recognize the environment and constraints that act upon the patient. Nonetheless, the handicapped patient often enters into a conspiracy of silence with the therapist by not volunteering practical information about the extent of the disability. Sometimes the patient does not provide clear and correct answers even when directly asked about his limitations. In such instances, additional information from physical therapists, parents, nurses, and physicians will be needed. Rather than avoiding discussion of the patient's disabilities, the therapist and patient may unconsciously focus on narrow, concrete, and somewhat isolated areas of the patient's ability to function while avoiding the central issues of total adaptation. This, too, serves a defensive function for both the patient and the therapist and helps avoid the anxiety associated with the handicap.

Developmental Perspectives Relevant to Psychiatric Therapy

In order to understand the handicapped child and enter into his world as a therapist, it is necessary to review the additional problems of development created by a disability.

THE BIRTH OF A HANDICAPPED CHILD

To parents, the birth of a handicapped child always comes as a shock. During pregnancy, mothers often worry about the possibility of having a defective child, yet these passing thoughts in no way prepare the mother for an actual event. Typically, both parents react to the birth of a handicapped child by feeling helpless, disappointed, angry, confused, and guilty. Parents tend to see their children as an extension of themselves; hence, to bear a defective child is experienced as a personal failure. Solnit and Stark[28] liken the response to the birth of a defective child to a mourning reaction. During pregnancy, the image of an expected child that most parents have in mind is a combination of the desirable traits of the father, the mother, the grandparents, and so on. When the child is born defective, all this anticipation based on these pleasant expectations is crushed. Solnit and Stark feel that the pain of dealing with the loss of the fantasied normal child is essentially a grief reaction. Klein and Lindemann[16] consider the birth of a defective child a family "crisis" because here, as in other crisis situations, disorganization follows the event. The way the family resolves the crisis will have an important bearing on how the family will function later on.

There are some indications that the parental response may vary with socioeconomic class. The mourning reaction is said to be more extreme in higher socioeconomic families and, hence, may be a culture-bound phenomenon.[14] Perhaps this behavior is related to the tendency of higher socioeconomic families to have higher expectations for their child. When the child cannot meet these demands, the parents grieve. Family size may also influence the impact of having a defective child. For example, in large families parental investment in any one child may be less, and this may help dull the pain. Perhaps it is most difficult when the defective child is the firstborn. The parents are then the least secure about themselves as parents. At best, all parents experience a tangle of emotions at the birth of a handicapped child. When confronted with such stress, it takes time for the most normal of families to make a realistic adaptation.

How much time is enough, or what are the normal limits of time necessary to make such an adjustment we do not know. Often the younger hospital staff expect instant acceptance. It is wrong to expect this; even six months may not be enough for the resolution of so traumatic an event. Perhaps all traumas require a long time for adaptation. In the case of the handicapped child, however, the trauma is in a sense ongoing. The physical presence of the child is a constant reminder of grief and loss, while growth and development constantly present new problems with which the parents must cope.

When a handicapping condition appears in an older child, parental reactions follow a course similar to that of the response to the birth of a defective child. The parents must relinquish the goals and fantasies they have woven around their healthy child and must relate to a sick child—with a different and, usually, a reduced set of expectations. The transition is not easy. There is, however, one major difference: When the child becomes handicapped later, the parents have usually formed a strong attachment to the child. The mother's emotional attachment to the newborn child, although by no means trivial, is still undeveloped and is more easily arrested or interfered with than the attachment to an older child.

After the initial shock, parents often attempt to deny that the handicap is permanent. They may insist that the child will "outgrow" it, that "a cure will be found," or that the child is a "blessing in disguise." This sort of denial and reaction formation is usually a stage in the parental adjustment; sometimes, however, it becomes a lifelong attitude. There are those who argue that some parental denial is necessary in order to assuage their chronic sorrow and that it may even be adaptive to a certain degree.[23] Experience indicates that in its more blatant forms, over a long period of time, denial tends to interfere with good medical management and to hinder psychological adaptation by both parents and child.

The therapist should be cognizant of this highly vulnerable relationship between mother and a newborn child. It is important to be as reassuring as possible when giving necessary medical information. Today, families usually prefer to be informed of all possible consequences of an illness; in the interest of the long-term development of the child, however, a certain sensible restraint is required. When a handicapped child requires specialized medical care that physically isolates the child from the mother, for example, when the baby is put in an isolette with tubes and equipment, the mother is deprived of the simple visceral satisfaction of holding her baby. Under such circumstances, the mother-child attachment can be seriously disrupted. The mothers of such infants often need encouragement from the medical staff simply to visit their baby.

Recent studies[15] suggest that a lack of early physical contact between mother and child may retard the attachment of a mother to her child. Mothers whose contact with their infants was delayed—as compared to mothers with early infant contact—showed less attachment behavior as early as one month after a baby was discharged from the hospital. There was less looking at the infant, smiling at the baby, and fondling him. It has been hypothesized that this lack of early physical contact is the reason why so many premature infants are later hospitalized for failure to thrive. Similarly, physically abused children are more likely to have been premature or to have suffered serious illness at birth.[17] Therefore, the isolation of a mother from her defective child can bring about a critical interference with the child's development.

One immediate response to the emotional impact of parenting a handicapped child is to withdraw from the child, or to reject him. Children with Apert's syndrome, for example, have often been placed in institutions for the retarded. Experts on birth defects[7] now express considerable doubt that these children are in fact organically retarded, but believe they may function that way because of massive parental rejection during the formative period. Based on the studies of Spitz,[20] Goldfarb,[10] and Yarrow,[33] this possibility agrees with the known effects of maternal deprivation. In the case of Apert's syndrome, the massive rejection may be due to the infant's ugly appearance. At some medical centers, plastic surgeons are undertaking early surgery to reconstruct the appearance of the baby's face and limbs, hoping in this way to encourage acceptance of the child by the family.

EARLY INTERVENTION ISSUES

One of the most effective times to intervene with the family of a handicapped child is probably soon after the birth of such a child. Boone and Hartman[2] assert that most psychological evaluations of handicapped children occur too late. They suggest indepth counseling of the parents in the first few months of the child's life as an accompaniment of the regular pediatric check-ups. Similarly, in a program aimed at preventing additional problems for blind infants, Fraiberg[9] has demonstrated the advantages of intervention in the first year of life. She has shown that without entering deeply into parental neuroses, a therapist can teach parents by example how by playing with their blind infants, they can increase the baby's repertoire of skills. For handicapped children, play is particularly important and much thought should be given to the special needs of the child. For example, parents of children with cerebral palsy should be taught the importance of putting toys where the young child can reach them himself[19] (an obvious point frequently ignored). Somehow the parents and therapist need to stand in the child's shoes and see what the world looks like to him; at the same time they must be objective enough to perceive what the child needs for his growth and development.

One of the difficulties in working with families during the child's infancy is to get the family to accept counseling at this juncture. If the family physician or pediatrician is not extremely tactful, the family may perceive the referral to a psychiatrist as yet another trauma added to the birth of their defective child.

Indeed, in the early months of the child's life, the family physician or pediatrician has the advantage of being least threatening to the parents and may be the best person to provide counseling to them. Whoever does the counseling, however, it is well to keep in mind that it is important to deal with the parents' conscious motives—usually love and compassion rather than the unconscious feelings of hostility and rage. Boone and Hartman[2] suggest transferring the negative feelings of the parents to society at large since the parents are merely acting in the manner dictated by society. It is impossible to say at this juncture whether the type of supportive therapy these authors suggest would serve for all or even for some of the families of handicapped children.

THE PRESCHOOL HANDICAPPED CHILD

As the handicapped child grows, new developmental issues emerge. Discipline can become a problem area.

The parents of a handicapped child find it diffi-

cult to express their anger directly to their child. This makes discipline a difficult problem, because discipline usually entails a measure of anger. To direct anger and aggression toward a handicapped person evokes tremendous feelings of guilt in everyone. We all tend to act peculiarly toward handicapped people and to cloak feelings of anger. In this sense, the parents of the handicapped child are not unusual—they simply experience the conflict more intensely. The therapist may be useful to the parents by helping them identify and understand their own anger.

All parents wish occasionally that their child did not exist. This is true whether the child is normal or handicapped. Such feelings can be dealt with when they are fleeting. But when the wish occurs frequently and with intensity, the parents are apt to suffer guilt. As handicapped children make more demands on their parents and offer fewer rewards, they can at times produce even angrier feelings than parents would normally feel. The parental resentment of all the extra burdens, their irritation with the child's relentless demands, the subsequent guilt they feel at their own anger and hostility toward the helpless child—all these can be devastating for family life. Often enough, the child senses the parents' resentment and guilt and uses it to pressure them into complying with still further demands. Thus, the stage is set for a vicious cycle of resentment, guilt, and then overprotection. More generally, parents adopt strong defenses to keep their anger in check.

For the preschool child, depending in part on the nature of his handicap, his intellectual development may be in jeopardy. In development during the early years, the innate urge for motor activity is dominant and does not decline until after age six.[20] According to Piaget,[8] sensation and direct action constitute the beginnings of intelligence. Any handicap which limits sensation and/or motor expression has at least the theoretic possibility of interfering with intellectual development. In fact, there are some practical data which suggests this can occur. Fraiberg's[9] careful longitudinal studies of blind infants and children have demonstrated that the majority of cogenitally blind children display great unevenness in their development, and their capacity for education is limited.

While there are similar studies with congenitally deaf children available, Lesser and Easser[18] and Williams[31] suggest that similar interferences take place with the development of blind children. Again, one might anticipate that children with motor types of handicaps would have developmental difficulties similar to those of the blind and deaf child. In fact, this probably does not hold true, at least to the same degree as with sensory problems, since motor handicapping is rarely total.

THE SCHOOL-AGE HANDICAPPED CHILD

When the handicapped child enters school, a host of new realities are thrust upon the child and his family. Minde and associates[21] described the development of a group of physically handicapped children who attended a special school for the handicapped. They found that about 40 percent of the children experienced a depressive reaction. This was probably triggered by the childrens' realization that their handicap would endure, since they saw children older than themselves in wheelchairs and with crutches. This reaction suggests that there existed a large measure of previous denial toward their handicap on the part of these children—a belief that was more than likely supported by the family system. In addition, the schoolage child is isolated from his normal peers, and this too may contribute to their depression. Finally, depression was noted more frequently in the nonretarded child than in the retarded, suggesting that the cognitive recognition of reality may have been an important factor as well.

There is a major issue in the field which currently constitutes the focus of considerable debate. Opinions are divided as to whether the handicapped child is better off in special schools or should be integrated into the regular classroom. The parallel question is asked, whether such a child should be placed in a special camp for the handicapped or in a regular camp. Since the therapist may be asked to participate in decisions regarding school and camp selection, it becomes an issue which is directly relevant to therapy. Segregation allows for special groupings, a more concerned environment, formation of programs suitable for children with limited abilities, and protection from negative social reactions. On the other hand, integration better prepares a child for normal life. Dibner and Dibner[5] feel that a disabled child's adjustment to an integrated camp depended on two things: the severity of the child's disability and his personality and previous social adjustment. In terms of personality, the authors noted that parents whose children were described as "shy," "needs encouragement," and "needs discipline" were those children who were more likely to end up with a poor adjustment in camp. Contrariwise, those mothers who described their disabled child

as "outgoing" or "enjoyed new experiences" were more likely to have a child who would make an excellent adjustment in camp. The conclusion of these authors was that depending on the child there is a place for both segregation and integration in varying combinations.

A very real problem for handicapped children and their families is not only the availability of a school situation suitable to the child's needs, but the practical matter of transportation to and from school. Among parents of handicapped children, transportation is a frequently discussed topic. At the same time, it is a subject which may be ignored or glossed over in conversation with a therapist. As in any therapy, common problems which are never mentioned tend to become the vehicles for affects displayed from other areas.

Peer relationships are an increasingly difficult problem for the handicapped child. In the preschool years, children normally play with toys on the floor. At that point, the disabled child is usually not compromised to a significant extent in his ability to play and interact with other children. As the children grow older and the games switch to baseball, football, hockey, and so forth, the handicapped child is at a distinct disadvantage. The school-aged handicapped child encounters barriers to achieving good peer relationships that are almost insurmountable. If he attends a special school, his school friends are not likely to live in the immediate neighborhood. In regular schools, he tends to be held in lower esteem by his peers simply because of his handicap—and is less likely to be chosen as a friend than a nonhandicapped child.[5] Carried over into the neighborhood, this same attitude combined with the limitations of the disability mean that the handicapped child is not likely to have a best friend next door or down the street. In addition to the problems in peer relationships, he has less opportunity for special trips and excursions, which would widen his social horizon. It is no wonder that as they grow, such children tend to be inept in establishing and maintaining human relationships. One of the neglected areas of development is the socialization of the handicapped—an area which has important implications for the future ability of many people to hold jobs and enter into marriages.

It has been suggested by Richardson[27] that one therapeutic method for breaking through the social barriers created by disabilities would be role playing of problem situations. Certainly this technique, accompanied by other social rehabilitation practices, should be considered in the therapy of a handicapped child, particularly one of school age or older.

THE ADOLESCENT HANDICAPPED CHILD

From a developmental perspective, adolescence is a phase when the teenager strives for autonomy from his parents. The adolescent also works toward establishing his own self-identity. These tasks normally cause some degree of familial strain. With the handicapped adolescent, a meaningful level of autonomy is frequently more difficult to achieve; developmentally, he may well have been overprotected above and beyond his physical needs. Realistically, the disabled adolescent depends more on his family and is less likely to have a strong peer group to lean on while he attempts to sort out his feelings toward his parents. Thus, the shift from childhood to adulthood is more difficult and hazardous for the handicapped; in some instances, in fact, it may be impossible.

Adolescence generally means bodily changes that force an awareness of sexuality on both parents and child. Even if the parents are of little help in the sexual turmoil of the adolescent, peer feedback and support have immense value. The handicapped adolescent, as noted, is too often socially isolated. In addition, the handicap of physical appearance poses barriers to interacting successfully with the opposite sex. Often these drawbacks are heightened by parental attitudes. During group discussions with mothers of children with cerebral palsy,[22] the mothers were quite negative about expressions of sexual feelings by their adolescents and ambivalent about eventual marriage. Here, the overprotective parental stance designed to keep the handicapped a "child," is meant to keep him essentially asexual as well. It is therefore interesting that in their own group discussions, the handicapped adolescents moved far more quickly to issues of sexuality than did the parents. It is commonplace that many parents of normal children are uncomfortable in discussing sexual matters; hence, it is not surprising that the parents of handicapped adolescents find the subject difficult. Questions about sex are rarely put directly but are alluded to in vague, amorphous terms. The therapist who is himself comfortable about discussing sexual matters can be of enormous help both in giving information to and in counseling the handicapped adolescent and his parents. The therapist who counsels the handicapped adolescent must have a broad knowledge of human sexuality, as the adolescent may need encouragement to experiment in areas which carry personal or societal

taboos.[6] It should not be assumed, however, that all handicapped adolescents have sexual problems; some are able to handle their sexual concerns quite well.

EMPLOYMENT AND MARRIAGE PROSPECTS FOR THE HANDICAPPED

Since every late adolescent should be thinking about how to become self-supporting, some discussion about the handicapped and jobs seems appropriate. Perhaps an area which needs more attention is the relationship between education and employment. The employment picture is brighter for individuals who have received special training following their general education. In the Brieland study,[3] the major complaint of the students in a special school for the orthopedically handicapped was the lack of independence and freedom. This may provide another argument for integration of the handicapped with regular students when it appears feasible for any particular child.

The ultimate goal in the total adjustment of the handicapped is as much freedom and independence as is physically possible. A closer look at the employment picture may therefore help to assess any individual's chances of employability. Brieland[3] reviews several follow-up studies of children who attended special schools for the handicapped. He found that the blind and the mentally retarded were more successful in obtaining jobs than the orthopedically handicapped. A particularly important factor in obtaining a job was intelligible speech—his own study confirmed both the importance of speech as well as independent ambulation. It is, therefore, logical that the cerebral-palsied group has the largest number of unemployed, and unemployable individuals. It is also logical, and in fact confirmed, that there is a correlation between disability and employability; the greater the handicap, the less the chance of being employed.

It is wise for therapists to be aware of the generally bleak statistics regarding the employability of the handicapped.[3] The overall employment rate varies from 20 to 50 percent, according to various studies.[22] Follow-up studies on handicapped children indicate that they tend to drop out of school early and have trouble finding jobs. When they do find work, even when employed in situations where objectively they are able to perform the work, they tend to lose jobs.[26] In the long run, the emotional impact of disability is probably more crippling than the physical handicap itself.

Similarly, the follow up of orthopedically handicapped high school students is bleak for marriage as well as jobs.[22] The marriage rate was under 20 percent. Interestingly, a handicapped person rarely married another handicapped individual.

There are probably several reasons for the poor employment and marriage picture of the handicapped. As we have seen, the handicapped child's course of development encounters numerous obstacles that are not met by physically normal children. These difficulties, along with the probability of limited socialization, make the handicapped individual less able to cope with the working world. Thus, the end result of the difficulties in growth and development is in part reflected in employment and marriage statistics.

FAMILY PERSPECTIVES

In dealing with the problems of the handicapped child, the therapist should not overlook the situation and feelings of the entire family. Ultimately, the adaptations of a disabled child is the result more of family stability than of the extent of his own handicap. In consequence, a family-oriented approach is often the most helpful, and the need for a family approach cannot be over-emphasized.

One approach is group therapy with parents of handicapped children with focus on the special needs of their children. Wilson[32] reported on his experiences in conducting this type of group on a time-limited basis of eight sessions. He felt the group was successful in providing its members with an emotional outlet, and that the members were supportive to one another. It was noteworthy that the group—all parents of handicapped children including the group leader—interacted freely except when a guest speaker was present. In contrast to this, new members, who were also parents of handicapped children, were accepted immediately. Wilson's experience with this group led him to suggest that astute parents of a handicapped child could be trained as group leaders of such parent therapy sessions at which such issues as schools, transportation, friends, and so forth, could be discussed.

Of the various parental postures, that of overprotecting the handicapped child is probably the most common. The handicapped child often gets more attention than his handicap warrants, and, as a rule, more attention than do his siblings. This particular attitude of parents creates a barrier to the physical and emotional rehabilitation of their children. The problems that result from overprotection are many and varied. For example, in rehabilitation centers, physicians and physical therapists sometimes find that a new level of motor functioning cannot be reached without hospitalizing the child and in effect doing a "parentectomy." The frequent description of the handicapped child as being excessively passive and immature seems to correlate with parental overprotection.

Precisely because overprotection is such an issue, it is important to understand what lies behind it. Most obviously, parents are helped to deny their feelings of anger, resentment, and guilt by covering these with intense experiences of just the opposite emotions. Parents also are spared the pain of watching a child struggle with his limited capabilities; they do things for him so automatically that they are able to adapt without being reminded that limitations exist. And finally, overprotection allows the parents to "make up" to the child for his disability—a need that springs in part from their sense of guilt at having "bequeathed" him a defective endowment. Thus, overprotection serves many purposes.

Families with a handicapped child tend to become isolated from the community. Parents of chronically ill children often retreat from relationships with their neighbors; they seldom take their children on vacations or outings and tend to discourage any socializing by the handicapped son or daughter. This compounds the problem, since the relative isolation of these families affords little opportunity for much needed dilution of ambivalent feelings. Directly restricting the handicapped child's access to social interchange further limits both child and family and provides the parents with yet another source of resentment that they must cloak.

Parents tend to be isolated within their own families. Linder,[19] who did group work with parents of handicapped children, found that virtually all women reported that the topic of the child's disability was not talked of at home! Nor does the silence stop there. Parents of a handicapped child are reluctant to discuss the defect with the grandparents. Yet, perhaps the most critical silence is that between husband and wife. Here the toll is made evident by the higher rate of disrupted marriages in families with handicapped children.[19] Where the marriage remains intact, there is a tendency for the fathers to isolate themselves from the home and for the mothers to seclude themselves with the children. Of course this pattern, although not unique to families with a handicapped child, must be an added strain on marital relationships already under stress.

SIBLING REACTIONS TO A HANDICAPPED CHILD

In some instances, the mother tends to withdraw from the family and devote herself almost exclusively to the handicapped child.[19] In other families, the mother is so beset and overworked that the rest of the children are left more or less on their own. Either of these family situations puts a heavy burden on the siblings. In fact, a private psychiatrist commented that she was asked more often to see the sibling of a handicapped child for psychotherapy than to help the handicapped child himself.[24] In Berggreen's[1] careful study of the siblings of multihandicapped children, it was found that the outlook for nonhandicapped siblings was worse in families where there were only two siblings, or where the other siblings were close in age to the handicapped child. Thus, it appears that the normal child has great difficulty in competing with the handicapped for parental time and attention.

In her study, Grossman[12] reported that some youngsters appeared to have benefitted from having a handicapped sibling. As college students, they seemed to be more tolerant, compassionate, and aware of prejudice than were other young adults in their age group. Some of these students chose to train for a helping profession. It is not clear whether their decision was simply a matter of maturity or compassion, or whether it might also represent overcompensation for pervasive feelings of guilt or hostility, or both. There were not enough data to document either conclusion. Other siblings of the handicapped in the Grossman study were reported to be emotionally damaged—were bitterly resentful of the family's situation, felt deprived in their own right, and were angry. In some families, the larger burden falls to the oldest daughter, who is required prematurely to accept many of her mother's responsibilities.

CASE HISTORY

The following case history illustrates some of the developmental problems previously described and underscores the difficulties that a handicapping condition creates within the family.

Jerry was seen initially at age twelve. The complaints were: "personality problems," poor grades despite a superior IQ, and arguments with his parents regarding schoolwork.

Jerry was third in a sibship of four. The two oldest children, a girl and boy, eight and eleven years older than Jerry, were from his mother's first marriage. Jerry was closest to his younger sibling—a sister, age eleven.

Jerry was born with a meningocele. At three months, he suffered spinal meningitis. At six months, he underwent surgery for an abscess of the myelomeningocele and partial excision of a tumor, a teratoma of the spinal cord, was performed. The surgery left Jerry with a neurogenic bladder and bowel incontinence. Jerry walked and talked by two years. Walking was probably impeded by orthopedic difficulties since he later required heel cord lengthening and corrective surgery on his feet.

Jerry was a thin, acned, bespectacled boy, rather small for his age, who walked with a crippled gait. In his initial interviews, he appeared distant and sad, describing with pain the teasing he took from his peers because of his physical disability. Jerry was currently in seventh grade. On the first day of junior high, his mother had forced him to come home at noon in order to take an enema, empty his bladder, have a quick lunch, and rush back to school.

Since he was two, his mother had been concerned with the care of his bladder and bowels. She gave him one to two enemas a day for fear that he might have an accident, and regularly helped him empty his bladder by applying suprapubic pressure. His father refused to have anything to do with this and was generally reluctant to be involved with his son.

The relationship between son and mother was highly ambivalent on both sides. Overprotection, anxiety, and submerged hostility with reaction formation were abundantly evident. Because of this, a period of residential treatment in a children's psychiatric hospital was recommended to the family and eventually agreed to.

Jerry remained in the hospital one year. After discharge, he and his parents were seen for another year in the outpatient department. In the hospital, Jerry learned to care for his own bowel and bladder needs. He had difficulty relating to other children, tending to be an isolate, and a scapegoat. His school performance improved. With casework, Jerry's parents were gradually able to allow him some independence.

He was seen at age twenty for a long-term follow up. At that time, he was living at home, attending a local community college. He wanted girlfriends but was too shy and hesitant about approaching them to be successful. He had tried living away from home to attend college, but that had lasted only six months. He remained a passive, dependent young man who did reasonably well in academic work but had difficulties with social relationships. He was still dependent on his mother, but not to the degree he had been at an earlier age.

COMMUNITY REACTIONS TO HANDICAPPING

It is impossible to ignore cultural pressures. As a result, the community's response to the handicapped child tends subtly to shape the reactions of the disabled child and his parents. A young child often reacts to the sight of a handicapped person by asking, "Why can't that boy walk?" or "Why does that girl look funny?" The average parent is uncomfortable with such queries and will usually tell his child to be quiet, perhaps adding, "It's not polite to ask such questions." In the face of this public scrutiny, the parents of the handicapped child often feel ashamed. Out of a tacit collusion with the adult community's reluctance to recognize handicapped people, they choose social withdrawal both for themselves and their child. The therapist who has good rapport with parents can help them resist this common tendency toward social withdrawal.

The importance of the visibility of a defect cannot be overstressed. This is particularly true in initial social contacts. The person who is visibly different is immediately marked. To label someone as handicapped has immediate emotional implications, which include stereotyping and fixed attitudes by almost everyone. An achondroplastic person's main handicap is his small stature. (Culturally, small stature is held in lower social esteem than is unusual height. Giants, though abnormal in the opposite direction, do not suffer as much social rejection as do midgets.) A visible handicap is harder to deny and thus harder to avoid reacting to emotionally. It is more apt to provoke public curiosity as well as withdrawal.

On the other hand, in social relationships of longer duration, the visibility of a defect does not seem to be as influential. One study[12] which checked the choice of friendships of handicapped children found that on the first day of camp, appearance did indeed influence judgments. After thirteen days, however, friendships were no longer related to the visibility of the defect; instead they were correlated with personality factors. Both handicapped and nonhandicapped attended the camp, with a ratio of one to one; therefore, the handicapped were not a minority group as is usually the case. Hence, care must be taken in the interpretation of this study.

Parental sensitivity to the way strangers react to a disabled child is illustrated by the following clinical vignette. One four-year-old child was hospitalized for intensive medical testing in a pediatric hospital. The child's appearance was unusually ugly, with a grossly deformed face including inverted eyelids and mandibular hypoplasia as well as a lobster claw deformity of the hands and feet. The hospital aides told the consulting psychiatrists that the mother refused to allow them to care for the child; instead, she insisted on caring for the child herself. The child's parents were warm and responsive to their offspring and played games and read her age-appropriate stories. The mother readily admitted her dread of having to place her child in kindergarten the coming fall. It was ob-

vious that the mother's refusal to allow the aides to care for her child was based on her perception of the average person's reaction to the child's deformities.

The community's reluctance to deal with the handicapped can be illustrated in yet another way. Realtors are more reluctant to house a handicapped individual than a nondisabled person.[27] On the other hand, they are even more resistant to housing welfare recipients, alcoholics, and drug addicts. Nevertheless, the fact that the disabled are relatively unacceptable to realtors means that finding housing is more difficult for them. Also, handicapped need special architectural considerations in order to function independently in their homes.

INSTITUTIONALIZING THE HANDICAPPED CHILD

In general, a child's development at home is generally better than in an institution. As a result, today, most physicians encourage mothers to care for their handicapped children at home, especially until a child is six years old. In fact, some states require the child to stay at home until age five or six. Often enough, even when this is not a requirement, a child is virtually forced to do so because the waiting list for the institution is five to six years long. For some families this creates severe hardship. If the question of institutionalization is not raised until the child has grown older, the parents must face not only their feelings about having a defective child, but all the myriad of emotions engendered in the raising of the child. It is not surprising that parental reactions to institutionalization are intense and complex. Old ambivalences are reawakened and threaten them with the fearful question, "Am I rejecting my child?" or more commonly, "How can I be so wicked as to put my child away?" Families often struggle for years with their guilt, fears, and anxieties before making a final decision.

If the family does decide to institutionalize the child, certain realities quite apart from these emotional factors tend to influence the timing of the placement. The degree of the handicap is important. Thus, the more severely damaged children tend to be placed in institutions earlier. A second factor is age. It is easier to give physical care to a young child than to an older, larger adolescent. In addition, though it is rarely talked about, one suspects that the adolescent's sexuality plays a role in the timing of institutionalization.

The current swing is away from total institutional care for the handicapped child (including the multihandicapped) in favor of keeping the child at home with community support. This, too, has its dangers, however, and may lead to another irrational extreme. It will profit no one to burden the communities with disabled people before they have developed adequate support structures, such as day care centers, associated residential space which can give short-term care during emergencies and vacations, and counseling services.

The task of coping with a handicapped child is highly complex. This makes it imperative that the entire family be aided in rearing such a child and in managing so inherently stressful a situation.

REFERENCES

1. Berggreen, S., "A Study of the Mental Health of the Near Relatives of Twenty Multihandicapped Children," *Acta Paediatrica Scandinavica,* Suppl. *215:5–24,* 1971.

2. Boone, D., and Hartman, B., "The Benevolent Over-Reaction," *Clinical Pediatrics, 11(5):268–271,* 1972.

3. Brieland, D., "A Follow-up Study of Orthopedically Handicapped High School Graduates," *Exceptional Children, 33:555–562,* 1967.

4. Colbert, J., Kalsh, R., and Chang, P., "Two Psychological Portals of Entry for Disadvantaged Groups," *Rehabilitation Literature, 34(7):194–202,* 1973.

5. Dibner, A., and Dibner, S., "Integration or Segregation of Deviants? The Physically Handicapped Child," *Community Mental Health Journal, 7(3):227–235,* 1971.

6. Diamond, M., "Sexuality and the Handicapped," *Rehabilitation Literature, 35:34–40,* 1974.

7. Fifth Conference of the Clinical Delineation of Birth Defects, Discussion, Baltimore, Md., June 12–16, 1972.

8. Flavel, J., *The Developmental Psychology of Jean Piaget,* ed. D. C. McClelland, D. Van Nostrand, Princeton, 1963.

9. Fraiberg, S., "Intervention of Infancy: A Program for Blind Infants," *Journal of the American Academy of Child Psychiatry, 10(3):381–405,* 1971.

10. Goldfarb, W., "Infant Rearing as a Factor in Foster Home Placement," *American Journal of Orthopsychiatry, 14(1):162–166,* 1944.

11. Greenson, R., *The Technique and Practice of Psychoanalysis,* International Universities Press, New York, 1967.

12. Grossman, F., *Brothers and Sisters of Retarded Children: An Exploratory Study,* Syracuse University Press, New York, 1972.

13. Hulicka, I., "Psychodiagnostic and Psychotherapeutic Approaches to the Physically Disabled," *American Corrective Therapy Journal, 26(1):6–12,* 1972.

14. Jordan, T., "Research on the Handicapped Child and the Family," *Merrill-Palmer Quarterly, 8(4):243–260,* 1962.

15. Klaus, M., and Kennell, J., "Mothers Separated from their Newborn Infants," *Pediatric Clinics of North America, 17(4):1015–1037,* 1970.

16. Klein, D., and Lindemann, E., "Preventive Intervention in Individual and Family Crises Situations," in Caplan, G. (Ed.), *Prevention of Mental Disorders in Children,* pp. 283–306, Basic Books, New York, 1961.

17. Klein, M., and Stern, L., "Low Birth Weight and the Battered Child Syndrome," *American Journal of Diseases of Children, 122(1):15–18,* 1971.

18. Lesser, S., and Easser, B., "Personality Differences in the Perceptually Handicapped," *Journal of the American Academy of Child Psychiatry, 11(3):458–466,* 1972.

19. Linder, R., "Mothers of Disabled Children—The Value of Weekly Goup Meetings," *Developmental Medicine and Child Neurology, 12(2):202–206,* 1970.

20. McDermott, J. F., and Akina, E., "Understanding and Improving the Personality Development of Children with Physical Handicaps," *Clinical Pediatrics, 11(3):130–134,* 1972.

21. Minde, K., et al., "How They Grow Up: 41 Physically Handicapped Children and Their Families," *American Journal of Psychiatry, 128(12):1554–1560,* 1972.

22. Mowatt, M., "Emotional Conflicts of Handicapped Young Adults and their Mothers," *Cerebral Palsy Journal, 26(4):6–8,* 1965.

23. Olshansky, S., "Chronic Sorrow: A Response to Having a Mentally Defective Child," *Social Casework, 43(4):190–193,* 1962.

24. Poznanski, E., "Psychiatric Difficulties in Siblings of Handicapped Children," *Clinical Pediatrics, 8(4):232–234,* 1969.

25. Richardson, S., "Children's Values and Friendships: A Study of Physical Disability," *Journal of Health and Social Behavior, 12(3):253–258,* 1971.

26. ———, "Patterns of Medical and Social Research in Pediatrics," *Acta Paediatrica Scandinavica, 59(3):265–272,* 1970.

27. ———, "Some Psychological Consequences of Handicapping," *Pediatrics, 32(2):291–297,* 1963.

28. Solnit, A., and Stark, M., "Mourning and the Birth of a Defective Child," in Eissler, R. S., et al. (Eds.), *The Psychoanalytic Study of the Child,* vol. 16, pp. 523–537, International Universities Press, New York, 1961.

29. Spitz, R., "Hospitalism: An Inquiry into the Genesis of Psychiatric Conditions in Early Childhood," in Eissler, R. S., et al. (Eds.), *The Psychoanalytic Study of the Child,* vol. 1, pp. 53–74, International Universities Press, New York, 1945.

30. Tew, B., Payne, H., and Laurence, K., "Must a Family with a Handicapped Child Be a Handicapped Family," *Developmental Medicine and Child Neurology, 16(6, Suppl. 32):95–98,* 1974.

31. Williams, C., "Some Psychiatric Observations on a Group of Maladjusted Deaf Children," *Journal of Child Psychology and Psychiatry, 11:1–18,* 1970.

32. Wilson, A., "Group Therapy for Parents of Handicapped Children," *Rehabilitation Literature, 32:332–335,* 1971.

33. Yarrow, L., "Maternal Deprivation: Toward an Empirical and Conceptual Re-Evaluation," *Psychological Bulletin, 58(6):459,* 1961.

41 / Sensory-Handicapped Children

Stanley R. Lesser

Influence of Visual and Hearing Handicap on Personality

Whether socially or individually, people respond to the blind and the deaf in a traumatic fashion. Most human beings are horrified at the prospect of their own sensory handicap, whether it be blindness or deafness. They equate loss of vision or hearing with helpless dependency, inability to orient themselves in the physical world, loss of individual potency, and inability to anticipate an attack from a nondelineated and therefore hostile world. The deaf suffer even further from their difficulties with receptive and expressive verbal communication. These communication difficulties cause the deaf to appear even more deviant socially. They are isolated by society and isolate themselves from society. Man identifies himself closely with his distance receptors, sight and hearing. They are integral to his self-concept, and he narcissistically excludes those who remind him of the vulnerability of his identity and self.

Perhaps in reaction to this wish to turn its back on the handicapped, from time to time society has projected upon them a certain special inner sight or transcendent creativity, viz: Homer, the blind poet, or Thiresias, the soothsayer in Greek legend. On occasion, they have been regarded as special children of God. For the most part, however, either by overt, role designation or by covert neglect, society has relegated them to the role of the blind begger and/or the untouchable deaf and dumb beast.

Over the past several centuries, the advent of humanism and rationalism has brought with it some attempts to change these attitudes. These attempts have achieved a measure of success with conscious attitudes and have led to scientific interventions into care and education of the blind and the deaf. At the same time, however, the unconscious fears of injury and unconscious identification with the physically deprived have limited empathic understanding, scientific study, objective conceptual formulations, and rational interventions. It has been difficult to accept that the blind and the deaf are human enough to have similar needs and motivations and to be subject to the kinds of emotional conflicts that afflict everyone.

No matter how well trained they may be, mental health personnel share these difficulties. This limits their objectivity in evaluation, in guidance, and, even more distinctly, in the treatment of the handicapped. People either overidentify with the handicapped, which leads to a denial of the extent of their emotional difficulties, or they avoid the perceptually handicapped, which makes it impossible to see their problems' resemblance to the familiar conflicts and psychopathologies of the normal.

To keep these children in perspective, one must view them as both subject to and responsive to the usual developmental, interpersonal, and social needs, motivations, and desires experienced by normal children. At the same time, it is important to realize that deficiencies in such major ego functions as hearing and sight result in serious developmental deviations. These require major rehabilitative environmental interventions.

Significant difficulties in interpersonal relationships are common in both the blind and the deaf.[70] These difficulties result in part from the parental reaction to the narcissistic blow of having produced a deformed child,[9, 10, 25] partly from parental perplexity as to the proper rearing of a child with a constitutional deviancy, and in part from the extensive difficulties the child experiences in his transactions with his "nonaverage expectable environment."[33]

While the diversity of personality, capacity, and range of adaptation of these children must be noted, they do tend to display certain characteristic personality traits and psychopathological syndromes.[44, 67, 70] Overall the blind child is overdependent; the deaf child is hyperindependent; the blind child suffers from insecurity; the deaf child has difficulties with tension and frustration tolerance caused by his problems with communication, conceptual organization, and emotional control. Thus, the blind child most closely resembles the phobic personality and psychopathologically is specially vulnerable to depression; the deaf child is more prone to behavior disorders, to impulse disorders, and paranoid psychoses.

DEVELOPMENTAL DEFECTS

Major perceptual deficiencies have certain limiting effects on autonomous ego developments and coping mechanisms that are obvious, and on some that are more subtle. Each severe early perceptual handicap creates its specific obstacles to development and has inherent its own tendency to personality malfunctioning. The blind[50] suffer primarily in the realm of failures in individuation; the deaf,[67] primarily in interpersonal relations. What they all have in common is that their disability affects all the developing ego systems and functions and disturbs the rate and tempo of the maturation and development of these functions.[63, 64] There is a general lag, and all the perceptually handicapped diverge from the normal sequence in the various developmental lines.[8, 9, 11]

Compensatory mechanisms, for example, sound and touch orientation in the blind[20, 21] and the visual permanence of objects,[63] are delayed and ultimately only achieved through detoured routes. Hence, the normal environmental interactions that ordinarily enhance the experiences of mastery and effective coping[79] present these children with serious obstacles and render them prone to perplexity, anxiety, and doubt.

The basic flaw in their sense of personal competence is profoundly affected by many variables in the child's education, in the mutual affective experience of parent and child, and in the degree of acceptance the child achieves to rewarding social attitudes and opportunities. There is another major axis, which determines both personality development and vulnerability to mental illness; it is defined by the severity of the perceptual defect and its time of onset. Even minimal function, such as the residual preservation of the capacity of the blind to discriminate light from dark or low-toned sound perception by the deaf, makes an enormous difference. It greatly increases the likelihood of orientational scanning and the organization of environmental stimuli, and it decreases the risks of aberrant development. The loss of hearing after speech has already been attained (circa two years) avoids many of the communication and conceptual difficulties so typical of the congenitally deaf.[56] The later loss of hearing, or sight, does, however, produce a severe narcissistic trauma and depression.

Other sensory modalities can, at least in part, compensate for the defect, for example, touch in the blind. Unfortunately, these compensatory mechanisms do not play a major adaptive role until other ego structures and cognitive schemata have already been developed.[8, 9, 10, 63] Many blind nursery school children are not inclined to handle objects and are even more loath to touch rough or sticky surfaces. This characteristic stems from the lack of perception of inanimate objects, which they cannot see and follow during the first year of life.[20, 22] They are therefore delayed in their active searching for surrounding objects; in this they differ radically from the sighted child during the second six months of life. Concepts of space, object constancy, and causality[22, 63] are poorly developed. The inhibition is later reinforced by painful or unexpected experiences, for example falling, touching a hot object, and parental overprotectiveness because of fears of injury to the child. The intense interest and pleasure the normal child manifests in handling, moving and trying new things do not emerge. Blind children can be said to have a developmental *"locus minoris resistentiae,"* which results in a primary touch phobia. Later, this primary phobia blends with the normal child's fears of touching based on reaction-formation to fecal interests and masturbation. As a rule, later experiences and education often overcome these early difficulties, and compensatory sensory channels mitigate these early problems. At the same time, ego and self attitudes based on developmental inhibitions may remain fixated. Uncertainty about being able to anticipate accurately, and doubt about one's perceptual and executive capacities, underlie an anxiety about effective mastery of the physical world.[79] Presently, this leads to a lack of assurance about one's gender and social roles. These anxieties give a special cast to the personalities of those so afflicted. This persists well after compensatory modes have, in large measure, overcome reality problems and conceptual understanding should have ameliorated role status difficulties. The difficulties with assertiveness and the overdependence on caretakers induce a fear of expressing aggression or defiance. After all, this might provoke retaliation and lead to a loss of the dependent object; this in turn would leave the handicapped child exposed to overwhelming anxiety.

BASIC EGO DEFECTS

The root difficulty in the blind is his uncertainty, doubt, and fear of the physical world. This difficulty then interferes with the normal processes of separation-individuation.[52, 53] It is during this period that the normal child tests out his separation from his mother, develops his sense of mastery over his world, and permits the internalized representation of the early relational figures to be retained even in their absence.[25] The blind child, lacking a critical aspect of engagement with his lifespace and fearful of venturing, is hampered in this flow of separation and rapprochement.[52, 53] Thus, oppositional behavior, an important stage in the development toward autonomy, is curtailed. Excessive clinging, passivity, inhibition of aggression and assertion, and phobic manifestations are often the rule. As might be suspected in the light of these early separation difficulties, the blind show a predominance of depressive, hypochondriacal, and hysterical character modalities.

The basic ego fault of the deaf child stems from his difficulty in acquiring a complete and organized maternal image and model. This leads to limited self-awareness, especially in the affective realm. The early child-mother relationship is hampered both by the child's perceptual difficulties and the mother's response to her deaf child. However, the primary difficulty lies in the signaling difficulties between a hearing mother and her deaf child. The emotional and intellectual development of the deaf child raised by deaf parents is superior to that of the deaf child reared by hearing parents.[70, 73, 74] In the later case, the signaling system is often distorted, miscued, and always incomplete. There are repeated frustrations in communicating needs or in understanding requests, and anger frequently ensues.

VERBAL COMMUNICATION WITHOUT
DIRECTIONAL CUES

A three-year-old deaf child was evaluated because of temper tantrums whenever he was given directions, for example, "Would you mind going into the dining room." Although the parents' impatience at the child's lack of an appropriate response to a simple direction was apparent to the child, the parents had ignored and denied the child's needs for nonverbal directional cues. Education of the child to a series of simplified verbal and nonverbal signals rapidly dissipated the defiance and tantrums.

Observations of the deaf provides a natural experiment which once again underlines the fact that man's greatest achievement is, perhaps, his creation of symbolic verbal communication. It also highlights the complex processes, the interaction, and integration that occur as the child develops his affective attachment to early parental figures. In time, this enables him to turn, with sensitivity, from his egocentric orientation, from his own needs and beliefs, toward the cathexis of his physical environment. He develops an attachment to others and a different level of awareness of himself. Freud[26] related a vignette in which a child repeatedly threw away a physical object and then recovered it in order to master his pain over separation from his mother. Waelder[76, 77] extended this concept and asserted that it was one of the bases of play, that is, the mastery of inner tension through play by reversing passive acceptance by active control. In this regard, the deaf child is doubly deprived. He is deficient both in his use of language in the construct of fantasy to serve as displacement from his primitive impulses and in the interconnections he is able to form between human and inanimate objects. He is accordingly limited in his use of thinking and play to help in the mastery of his tensions and affects.

These developmental difficulties probably arise from the parents' inability to anticipate and the child's inability to communicate his desires. The blending of the "illusory world of the child" into a gradual merging with reality is disrupted.[80]

In any case, the deaf child is action oriented. His self is closely connected with his physical achievements. Frustrations in these achievements and tensions in living are expressed by bodily activity: These provide a major source of both the explosiveness and the hyperactivity of the deaf child. Two other sources compound this difficulty in control and inhibition. Ultimately, without a verbal substructure, he has difficulty in forming abstract conceptualizations (see Furth[28] for an opposite viewpoint), and in labeling, formulating, and hence gaining inner control of his affects.[37]

Intervention

The basic tenets of the treatment of the blind and deaf lie in grasping the nature of the "basic fault"[2] of the defects in the ego capacities of these children. Constant stress in adapting to a seeing and hearing world joins with these basic faults and greatly exacerbates their effects.

The two areas that have received major theoretical and clinical emphases have been: (1) the reactions and treatment of parents on premises stemming from psychodynamic formulations,[10, 23, 50, 71] and (2) special education for the handicapped which stresses the child's achievements, his intellectual potential, and career training. Conceptually, this movement has been led by clinical and academic psychologists.[46, 72] There has been little integration of these conceptual models. As a rule, they have ignored each other; from time to time, however, rather acrimonious interdisciplinary friction has arisen between them.

The advent of advocacy for total communication in the education of the deaf (rather than a primary emphasis on oral methods) has received support from both the psychiatric[67] and psychological viewpoints.[70, 75] In addition, the growth of ego and relational psychology[1, 6, 17, 34] with its emphasis on ego functions and adaptational capacities among psychoanalysts, along with the emergence of social psychiatric concepts of self-help, communal support, and advocacy, has given rise to the possibility (by no means attained at this point) of an integrated holistic approach to the treatment of handicapped children.

The segments involved in this holistic approach are being implemented in the same sequence as that of the nonhandicapped emotionally disturbed child. To cite Kanner,[36] treatment about the child (parents, and so forth); treatment for the child (remedial education and training); and finally treatment directly with the child.

Primary, secondary, and tertiary prevention[12] must all be given equal weight.

PRIMARY PREVENTION

Although it is of utmost importance prevention of blindness and deafness itself will be dealt with summarily in this chapter. About 50 percent of all blindness and deafness results from genetic mishaps. A few disorders, especially those resulting from dominant genetic loading (about 16 percent in the deaf), can be avoided by genetic counseling. Although disorders based on recessive genetic factors have not been entirely clarified, both genetic counseling and elective abortion should, in the not too distant future, reduce the number of handicapped children.[60] The role of teratogenic factors, ototoxic, and optitoxic drugs such as the mycines, and diseases: rubella, cytomegala virus, and so forth, especially during the early months of gestation, have become widely recognized. They are potentially preventable with advances in public hygiene, immunization, and amniocentecis.

Renewed emphasis on care during parturition and during the neonatal period is furthering the primary prevention of blindness and deafness. A new technique of monitoring the oxygen blood level in the umbilical cord promises better regulation of either hyper- or hypooxygenation of the newborn in the future.

SECONDARY PREVENTION

The possibility of preventing emotional disorders and/or character distortion in the blind or deaf child is greatly enhanced by early detection. Deafness and blindness in the infant is usually suspected first by the parents, recognized by the primary care physician, and confirmed by specialists in these disorders. The failure of the deaf child to respond with head and eye movements to a loud sound, the beginning of his vocalization with its rapid cessation, and, during his second year, his failure to develop speech are basic indications of deafness. In the blind child, his failure to follow objects in his visual field and, later, his lack of interest in objects that fall away from his sight are concomitant indicators of blindness.

In order to study these often overlooked developmental deviations in greater depth, more objective measures have been developed.

Following the work of the Ewings in England, mass screenings of newborn hearing ability have been developed.[15] Unfortunately, audiometric behavior observation results in a high percentage of false positives, inflicting unnecessary trauma on parents. The uncertainty of diagnosis in the neonate has led to the abandonment of unrestricted mass screening except for those infants at high risk. Other devices, speech audiometry, physiological responses to sight and sound, electroencephalography with evoked cortical potentials, and, most recently, the measurement of retinal and cochlear potentials are being further refined. They promise not only the detection of deficits but the possibility of differentiating central from peripheral disorders. This will allow for differential diagnoses, for example, from infantile autism, and for pinpointing the exact locale and degree of the disorder.[49]

THE NEEDS OF PARENTS

The key to preventing emotional disorders in the perceptually handicapped lies in the proper education, guidance, and treatment of parents. The infant-mother interaction is the vital foundation for future ego development and for later interpersonal relationships. It is threatened by two interrelated forces. The first is the reaction of the mother to the fact that she produced a defective child. The second is her perplexity about how to conduct a relationship with a child who does not give the usual interactional cues or provide a relational feedback as intense as she would wish—and needs.

The birth of a normal child extends a woman's sense of bodily and psychological integrity. Conversely, the advent of a defective child threatens to reawaken her sense of insufficiency and incompleteness. Two powerful emotions emerge, each with its own defensive reactions: (1) projected aggression against the child with attendant detachment, withdrawal and denial of his needs, even of his existence, and (2) guilt, the counterpoise of the aggression, with the inevitable lowering of maternal self-esteem and the concomitant depressive reaction.

As a product of their reaction-formations, these mothers often become overanxious, oversolicitous, and overprotective. This increases the child's potential for overdependency and his difficulty with both psychological and physical autonomy. Both the unconscious rejective aggression and the guilty depression can result in a partial denial of the child's defect. It becomes minimized, and there is an expectation of miraculous cure. In extreme cases, the condition is totally denied.

DENIAL OF HANDICAP

Monica, a five-year-old blind girl, was extremely restless, provocative, and domineering at nursery school. Further investigation revealed she did not know she was blind, a fiction forced upon her by her parents. She would say, "See the red truck passing by"; "Stop smiling," and so forth. Her therapist's efforts to combat the denial were ineffective until he could induce the parents to accept her condition and reveal it to the child. With further therapeutic work, which allowed Monica to differentiate between her auditory and tactile senses and to differentiate herself from sighted people, her intense need to implement the family delusion receded. She was then able to reduce her constant vigilance and excitement, and was enabled to learn and enjoy play with her classmates.[13]

Another mother refused to accompany her three-year-old deaf child outside her house. She felt that she had caused the child's affliction and his visible hearing aid was a constant exposure of her own worthlessness. Psychotherapy with the mother unearthed murderous unconscious hostility toward a younger brother. The hostility toward her sibling had always been strongly defended against and had now been displaced to her deaf child. The ventilation of her sibling rivalry permitted her a more satisfactory relationship with her child, and she was then able to displace her assertive strivings into social and political activities for the rights of her child and of deaf children in general.

The handicapped child faces a double burden. He is in need of superior mothering to compensate for his deficiencies. But in many cases, his mother is suffering from her own emotional problems which incline her toward emotional withdrawal and reduce the effectiveness of her coping solutions. This problem is heightened by the current emphasis on community-based treatment facilities which thrust the mother into the prime roles of caretaker, remedial developmental educator, and advocate of the child's interests. The mother is at once, emotionally, the most closely involved with her child and, at the same time, the most affected, the most confused, and the most challenged by her child.[43] The narcissistic trauma and its derivatives may press some mothers of defective children to seek psychotherapy. Most such mothers, however, can be helped to help their children without intensive psychotherapy. Parental perplexity, confusion, isolation, and psychic injury can be reduced by participation in well-led parent-sharing groups. Here, mutual problems and mutual emotional reactions can be shared, and mutual support garnered.

When the mother receives guidance in understanding her child's developmental needs and idiosyncracies, she is helped to overcome her passive helplessness and convert it into active coping. It is of even greater assistance when the mother experiences a positive feedback from her child's accelerated development and greater affective closeness.

There is a group of behaviors called "blindisms." These include: limp hands, drooping head, head banging, rocking, and eye gouging. Since over 45 percent of all congenitally blind children show varying degrees of these symptoms, they were once thought to be normal accompaniments of congenital blindness. However, Fraiberg and her coworkers[21] have shown that active maternal promotion of the blind child's interests in his surrounding objects can eradicate these behaviors.

When a mother is helped to chart out her deaf child's apparently "senseless" temper tantrums, it enables her to understand them. She perceives that they occur as a reaction to separation from herself, to rivalry for her attentions and/or to frustrated communications. This gives her both an effective means of modifying her child's behavior and a renewed sense of personal worth. It also reduces her feelings of isolation from her deaf child and modifies her apprehensions that the child does not really care about her. In one mother's words, "I always thought I could talk and have fun with my child; then it seemed to me that he did not care what I did. Now I can see that he really does react to me and that I am important to him." As Omwake and Solnit[62] observed during their psychoanalysis of a very infantile, clinging blind child: "As Ann was able to improve, the mother could respond more positively to the child."

Fathers have as strong a reaction to their defective children as do mothers, although it is less usual for them to express it as directly. Fathers frequently relate the child's problems to their own (often unconscious) fears of dependency and passivity. Overtly, the father will express his dismay that the child will not be able to compete with others, will be abused by his peers, and will not be able to sustain himself in a career. During psychoanalysis, a father of such a child related his fantasies: "How would the child be able to survive a concentration camp should there be another Hitler?" Further analysis unearthed the identification of the child with his own passive homosexual fears. Men are more likely to project the blame on their wives, while women tend to turn the blame back on themselves. Although not invariably, fathers tend to appear stoical and detached as a means of masking their underlying depression. Sexual problems with their wives are frequent: the birth of a defective child commonly initiates an episode of extramarital acting out, and/or the father may become obsessively involved in his work. In more infantile and dependent men, jealousy of the extra attention paid to the child induces hypochrondriasis, drinking, and/or a variety of other regressive behaviors. One father would become surly with his wife whenever she suggested visiting their child at his boarding school; a drinking binge would either precede or succeed the visit. During conjoint marital therapy, he was able to describe his anger at his wife's detachment from him when she focused her full attention on the child. Once he was able to make this connection, the drinking behavior was eliminated.

Tragedy sometimes unites; more often, however, it alienates. Even when a family is united, it can be by a common hostility projected onto an external enemy. Therapists and educators are frequent targets. Eliciting and, when necessary, confronting the bereavement reactions of parents (as well as the reactions of the siblings) are a *sine qua non* of successful intervention. Marital and family therapy have been the most useful methods, with greater advantages accruing when the therapy was focused and structured. Parent-sharing and special advocacy groups play an important role in the emotional welfare of both the parents and the child.

DIFFERENTIAL DIAGNOSIS

The blind and the deaf have neither "an average expectable environment"[34] nor an "average constitutional endowment."[44] When applied to deaf and blind children (particularly those deaf and blind from birth), the limitations of the more established developmental theories must be recognized and their diagnostic categories revised, or at least reevaluated. There is continuing study of the role of the sensory organs in the emergence of such integrated psychological systems as those of self, identity, and the organization of affective responses. These are shedding new light on the understanding of personality development. It is most difficult for an investigator to put himself in the place of a developing infant, and even more difficult to empathize with those suffering from severe perceptual difficulties. One must at least start with the premise that such a child is a different psychic organism from the infant who possesses his full perceptual faculties.

Many deaf adults have been found to have the following personality characteristics:[67] egocentricity, rigidity, impulsivity without the usual accompaniment of anxiety or guilt, a paucity of empathy, and an inability to realize the effect of their behavior on others. Translating these findings into psychodynamic terminology, the deaf show a relative lack of subtlety in their self-observing ego; a conscience formation different from that of hearing persons; a difficulty in the use of abstract symbols for evaluating the environment and for self-introspection; and poor tolerance for tension. On the cognitive side, their major difficulty lies in the acquisition of words, symbolization, and abstraction. All this makes it difficult for the child to acquire the necessary level of secondary process in order to control his primary process thinking. Concomitantly, this delay in the ascendency of secondary process thinking eases the regression to primary process thinking.

Rainer and Altschuler[67] have observed that the incidence of schizophrenia in the deaf appears to occur at the same rate it does in the general population; however, retarded depressions, especially those characterized by guilt and delusions of personal culpability, are almost nonexistent. Agitated, hyperactive forms of depression are encountered more often,[81] and paranoid trends are at least as frequent, but not as systematized.

Conversely, in the blind there is a predominance of depressive, hypochondriacal, and hysterical modes.[54] Nonetheless, it is important to correct some common assumptions about the stability of some of these syndromes in the blind and the deaf and about their prognostic significance.

SYSTEMATIZED DELUSIONS

A sixteen-year-old girl, congenitally blind from birth due to retrolenticular-fibroplasia, was hospitalized because of her delusions that the moon was entering her body and causing her to have destructive and sexual thoughts. She was symbiotically dependent upon her mother and an aunt. These obsessive ideas made her extremely fearful that she would lose the support of those upon whom she was dependent. Although she had been trained in her personal physical care and was intellectually rather advanced, there had been neither sexual nor social education. She retained, consciously, very primitive ideas of conception and of childbirth. After a few weeks of milieu therapy, she became more comfortable with peer interaction. The imparting of sexual knowledge by a sympathetic nurse allowed her to garner some insight into the connection between her delusions and her sexual desires and fears. With this, both her symptoms and their accompanying fears and depressive affects abated. Follow up after five years revealed no recurrence of her symptoms. Moreover, she had achieved greater independence from her maternal figures and a good general adaptation.

A congenitally deaf boy of ten feared that he had killed a neighbor and would be apprehended and executed at any moment. He had been subject to behavioral disorders characterized by impulsive aggressivity. Over the preceding year he had been attempting to control his behavior and had become reactively meek and passive. Communicating via a mixture of play, signs, and verbalization, he was able to form a good working relationship with his therapist. He gradually gained insight into his murderous impulses and his fears of retaliation. More important, after a period of tension and accompanying threats of aggression, he was able to admit his unhappiness at being different from others, his fears of attack due to his "weakened state," and conflicts concerning his masculinity. For a long period, there was a shift in his therapy, from a hyperindependent and "devil-may-care" attitude to a fearful clinging relationship with his therapist. Rivalry with the therapist's other patients became prominent, and, for the first time, various infantile habits and mannerisms appeared.

He then developed an open and rather vicious rivalry with his father, reawakening, or perhaps, for the first time initiating oedipal strivings. Transference interpretations modified the behavior and, perhaps of even greater importance, permitted careful scrutiny and delimitation of his specific affects. He was thus able to clarify the difference between aggression and assertion, desires for dependent comfort and fear of passivity, and sexuality and pleasure versus sexuality and power.

Superficially, these disorders sound like typical psychotic reactions. They cannot, however, be equated with common psychiatric syndromes, without allowing for the atypical developmental, interpersonal, and social conditions of the perceptually handicapped. Many do not show the depth of interpersonal withdrawal and the autistic features seen when the child with normal perceptual endowment becomes ill. Once the specialized characteristics of these children are given consideration, the treatment of these conditions can be effected more easily.

Behavior disorders among deaf children and phobic disorders among blind children are almost universal. The behavior disorders of the deaf are often misdiagnosed as evidence of brain damage. Should they be accompanied by a not uncommon emotional withdrawal, they are apt to be regarded as autism or mental retardation.[44, 55] If the hearing or sight loss can be corrected, for example, when adequate hearing aids are provided or when the child develops adequate modes of communication, such as speech or sign language, these behavioral characteristics often show a dramatic reversal.

CORRECTION OF DEFECT—AMELIORATION OF SEVERE MALADAPTIVE BEHAVIOR

During attendance at a Head Start nursery, Pamela had great difficulty separating from her stepmother and was apparently autistically withdrawn. She was alternately diagnosed as emotionally deprived and/or autistic. The nature of her eye fixation and her ability to relate when in close proximity to others raised the question of her visual acuity. On examination, she was found to have a severe corneal distortion. Corrective contact lenses produced an immediate and dramatic change in her behavior.

Differentiation between central and peripheral perceptual disorders is often difficult. The pendulum has probably swung too far in the direction of emphasizing central integrative disturbances. Many clinicians are insufficiently acquainted with the extent and kinds of developmental difficulties suffered by the deaf and blind. They are thus not able to give due weight to these problems and are overly impressed with the probability of central nervous system damage. The issue is greatly complicated in cases with multiple damage involving both systems. More than that, the deaf and blind child may show a lack of development of central integrative systems secondary to inadequate stimulation during critical and/or sensitive developmental periods.

Another prevalent characteristic of the deaf is the admixture of uncertainty which coexists with rigidity and obstinacy. These traits, combined with the deaf person's relatively dampened emotional display and his characteristic ability at rote tasks, combine to present the picture of an obsessive-compulsive personality disorder. The major underlying dynamics of the obsessive-compulsive are generally ascribed to unconscious conflicts around aggression and sex. His obstinacy is related to his battle with authority; his doubts stem from the rapid swings between rage and fear; his ambivalence from his fluctuations between love and hate. The doubt of the deaf emerges from other sources; it stems from insecurity about what he perceives and the way others perceive him. It extends to doubt about what he feels, and what others feel, and, somewhat later, what others feel about him.[48] These doubts extend into all psychological areas. This doubting characteristic does not make him a "Doubting Thomas," skeptical of the world and of others. Instead, it is directed toward uncertainties about his own capacities. He relies on a "seeing ear" for the consensual validation of his perceptions. Often, however, he does not feel that he has either enough communicative scope or trust in others' responses to allow himself to feel secure in spontaneous expression of affect.

For example, a deaf pupil will "cheat" on examinations without guilt or fear because to him it is not equated with stealing, as it would be with a normal child. Looking at another's paper is merely an integral part of checking on his environment. These obsessive-like traits are reinforced by the usual rearing and educational practices encountered by the deaf.[28] Both parents and teachers find little time to promote creativity and joy in learning. Fear of the child's impulsivity and aggression often provokes the caretakers to employ a rigid and unimaginative kind of discipline. Careful scrutiny will often reveal essential differences between his character makeup and that of the obsessive-compulsive. In general, deaf children do not isolate affect from thought, are not particularly prone to reaction-formation, do not indulge in doing and undoing, and are not usually fearful of emotional outbursts. The deaf person's actions may be accompanied by doubting but rarely by anxious ruminations.

Analogously, in the blind child, much of the phobic symptomatology has different dynamic and developmental sources. As noted previously, their phobias are often superimposed on a fear of touching. This arises from their infantile unfamiliarity with and failure to integrate environmental objects cognitively and from their later fears about the dangers of traversing unfamiliar space. These anxieties are further exacerbated in the blind by their overdependency, which induces a fear of their own impulses.

DIRECT PSYCHOTHERAPY

Direct treatment of the child must be closely co-ordinated with guidance and treatment of parents, collaboration with educators, and management of the child's peer and other social relationships. Situations do arise in which the goals of others involved in the child's development are in direct opposition to those of the therapist; for example, the educators may insist on "pure" oral communication, while the therapist is attempting to promote a total communicative environment. There can be other disagreements about goals, for example, the formation of a peer identity among the handicapped versus integration with nonhandicapped children. These can also be mutually misunderstood and can result in attitudes fraught with dogmatic zeal on the part of those most closely concerned with the management of the child.

These differences in aim, whether strategic or tactical, can usually be resolved with the help of open discussion. This does demand a sensitive awareness of the numerous challenges and of the tasks to be faced by everyone involved with the child.

There is a factor which, in a subtle fashion, is even more destructive to any attempt at therapy or remediation. This is the hope, maintained by the child and his parents, and all too often by his educators and therapists, that some miraculous cure will eliminate his handicap. Rescue fantasies are one of the common countertransference difficulties experienced by psychotherapists; they are counterpoised for the child and his parents by an initial overidealization, followed by a subsequent bitter devaluation.

It is often very difficult to bring out the child's confusion and narcissistic fixation on his handicapped status. "Am I blind?"; "Are you blind?"; and "What does it mean to be blind?" are the questions that must emerge from a successful therapy. Moreover, the deep resentment that "it isn't fair"[62] represents the aggressive revenge and the inhibiting guilt that underlies (and often undermines) the devalued and fearful self in these children. The cornerstone of psychotherapeutic effectiveness is the ability to allow the emergence and formulation of these ego attitudes.

THE HANDICAPPED SELF—SELF AND OBJECTS

Dan, a six-year-old boy with a severe high-toned nerve deafness, kept destroying his hearing aids. Psychotherapeutic intervention was elected when attempts to train him in their use met with aggressive attacks on the audiometrist. These were often directed at the audiometrist's genital area.

Deaf from cochlear damage at birth, Dan had been rejected by his father, of whom he was very fearful, and had been overprotected by his mother, toward whom he was haughty and domineering. Generally, he was distractible, aggressive, and became threatening when his wishes were frustrated.

Early in psychotherapy, he was surly and detached but gradually accepted a doll, "Soldier Joe," to whom he could relate. Soldier Joe had many omnipotent aggressive adventures. At first invulnerable, Soldier Joe began to sustain mutilating injuries. When injured, Soldier Joe became an object of scorn and disgust. But slowly (partly because Soldier Joe could be "patched up" by the therapist) a note of consolation and solicitude became discernible.

After a period of slow work with mixed and varying affects, Dan one day abruptly sat on the therapist's lap, took the therapist's hands, and pounded them against his own ears. "I can hear through here, here, and here (pointing to various parts of his body). No one can take them away from me. No one wants me. I can do anything I like." When the hectoring declamations ceased, Dan, for the first time, broke into loud sobs.

The therapist reassured Dan that people could like and want him even though he had trouble hearing. During several sessions, the therapist further asserted that Dan's deafness did not mean he was or could be mutilated. Moreover, his use of the hearing aids would permit him to let people know what he wanted so that they could understand and help him.

Dan, then, indulged in regressive play, wanting to be treated as a baby. This was accompanied by a panoply of verbal and nonverbal communications. Significantly, he insisted on the use of his hearing aid during these interchanges. Much clarification of both the content and structure of communication was possible. "Did you get that?" "I am not sure I know what you are asking me to do." "When I shake my head it can mean yes or no. Daddy does that." After several months, Dan's speech and nonverbal communications became much more precise. He began to boast of his hearing aids, calling them "my new ears."

After this burst of euphoria, a friend teased him about his hearing aids, and he became somber and rather depressed. "When can I hear like you hear, like Jacques (his friend) hears" became the theme. The therapist then explained that he would never hear exactly the same way as the therapist heard, or as his friends heard, that he would always need mechanical help for his hearing, but that, with this help, he could talk, learn, and be a wanted person. Moreover, the therapist insisted, "Should you continue to feel not only different but worse than others, you will always feel pitiable, will try to hide your difficulty in hearing, and will not be able to learn as fast nor get along with people as well and as happily."

This confrontation, later worked through step by step, marked the turning point in Dan's reevaluations of his self-worth, his cooperation in the learning process, and his awareness that he could be "different but equal." Interestingly, through the mechanisms of reversal and sublimation of his residual feelings of narcissistic injury, Dan has become an audiometric engineer.

It is much more difficult, and even more important, to introduce a "third party object" (in Winnicott's[80] terminology, a transitional object) in the treatment of blind and deaf children. Play objects, dolls, furry animals are not as readily employed by the child as instruments with which to express his emotions, his mastery of the passive roles he must at times play, his self-awareness, awareness of others, and awareness of the world about him.

Both blind and deaf children have difficulties with their early object relationships, with balancing their self-awareness effectively between their human objects and the objects in the world. The body-self and feeling-self do not develop properly as mediators among impulses of the body, relations with other people, and mastery of the external world. Through concrete play and imaginative fantasies, toys and other "transitional objects" can help bridge these gaps. The sensorily deprived child is further handicapped by a truncation of his ability to scan his world;[56] he cannot anticipate and integrate the sensory stimuli which impinge upon him without undue vigilance. In Myklebust's opinion,[56] while the ears scan the general environment, the eyes can focus on the particulate within the environment. Levine[46] has observed how frequently the deaf child will be distracted from his play in order to shift his eyes in the direction of an approaching person.

These then are the difficulties of the blind and deaf child: the uncertainly individuated self, the tension and vigilance in adaptation to environmental stimuli, the problem with differentiation of self from others in the blind, and the struggle with naming and understanding impulses and affects in the deaf. Each becomes a major strategic target in psychotherapy.

The young blind child presents problems in periods of separation from the mother. A favorite toy often serves as a bridge in the gap between the home and the therapist's office; symbolically the child transfers his sense of security from the mother to the therapist. Artifacts are provided that come apart and rejoin, for example, a lock and key. The child plays with these first with the mother, then with the therapist. This facilitates his capacity to leave the mother. Hide and seek games using touch, or even better, mutual and consensual touching to identify objects, further enables the child to separate and to explore the therapeutic environment.

Later in therapy, the child's inhibition of play, or regression to infantile clinging, frequently denotes emerging aggression and anxiety. At this time, it becomes possible to make the interpretive connection between these inhibitions, the child's fear of his own murderous rage, and his fear of losing the security of his dependence. In most cases, working through these conflicts between dependence and independence, between rage and retaliation will ameliorate these excessive dependencies, separation anxieties, and phobic symptomatologies.

Older blind children show similar conflicts. However, these are often more difficult to discern because the child's pride in independence (often a pseudo independence) and shame at admitting residual dependency needs modify the clinical picture. Touching the therapist for recognitional and security purposes should be accepted, even encouraged. Conversely, the therapist's willingness to touch the patient becomes a nonverbal communication of acceptance and mutual relationship. Psychotherapists are often embarrassed by touching, fearing an overdependent or an oversexualized transference. Not infrequently, this is a defense against the therapist's own countertransference fears.

With the deaf child, difficulties arise in the formation of a therapeutic relationship. His distractibility, his darting behavior, and his proneness to ignore the therapist make it difficult to engage him. Frustration, feelings of hopelessness, and suppressed (occasionally overt) anger are aroused in the therapist. Mechanical toys, although sometimes necessary at the outset of therapy, increase the detachment. Patient introduction of a toy such as a stuffed animal can be used to start the relationship. Mutual exploration of the office space will increase the child's security and begin to stimulate his curiosity. Gradually, multiple systems of communication are mutually experimented with the explored. Eye contact promotes both relationship and communication.

Once relationship and useful communication have been established, the deaf child begins to show evidences, albeit often indirect, of a deepening attachment. He wants to linger; he is disturbed by other patients' productions; he becomes angry if he feels misunderstood by the therapist. The therapist formulates the child's combined desire and uncertainty about the relationship and interprets his feelings about it. Such offerings are usually, but by no means always, accepted.

Labeling his affects as they emerge integrates the child's sense of himself; this increases his feeling of mastery of his impulses and control of his behavior. Incrementally, it becomes feasible to discriminate affects more precisely and, still later, to denote their sources.

LABELING OF AFFECT

A ten-year-old deaf child noticed a woman who had inadvertently entered the men's restroom. He stared at her perplexed and said, "Why is her face red?" The explanation of her experiences and its accompanied affect of embarrassment was communicated to the child. Following this, feelings and body sensations experienced by the patient during incidents he had encountered in the past were explored. A discussion ensued about affective expression and their communication between people. After redramatizing the incident several times, the child then related many incidents about his own sensitivity, feelings, and reactions, as well as his difficulty in understanding the emotional expressions of others.

Insight into and the working through of the therapist's countertransference reactions can be difficult and complex. The therapist shares the social fear and avoidance of the different and the mutilated. The most frequent gross reactions include reactive overprotection toward the blind and repressed anger with detachment toward the deaf. Excessive therapeutic zeal and overdirectiveness are indications of countertransference problems— most often of underlying rescue fantasies. Passivity and anxiety can connote overidentification, repressed rage, and/or unresolved complexes about martyrdom.

Psychotherapy of the perceptually handicapped can be rewarding and effective once the barriers of strangeness, communication, and countertransference are overcome. Some special stratagems, as noted previously, are necessary, but overall the general principles of child psychotherapy are applicable.

BEHAVIOR THERAPY

As discussed in chapters 5 and 11, behavior approaches are effective in eliminating undesirable behaviors by means of operant conditioning and other measures. In specific phobic symptomatology, desenitizing maneuvers can shorten the therapy. Relational difficulties are so predominant among the blind and deaf that combinations of conditioning and relational therapies are generally indicated.

PHARMACOTHERAPIES

Currently, medication has a very limited scope in the total therapeutic armamentarium for use in treating the blind and the deaf. Stimulants such as amphetamines and methylphenidate (Ritalin) are used to ameliorate distractibility and hyperactivity. They tend to be more effective with perceptually handicapped children who present a mixed picture of peripheral and central neurological difficulties. Phenothiazines are indicated in cases of severe behavior disorder and to treat psychosis with ego disintegration. As already mentioned, these disorders do not necessarily carry the malignant prognoses assigned to comparable symptomatology in the perceptually intact. A more extensive discussion of psychopharmacology is available in chapter 23.

GROUP PSYCHOTHERAPY

During preadolescence and adolescence, group psychotherapy is an important and often necessary therapeutic adjuvant. It relieves social anxiety, dissipates feelings of estrangement and isolation, and helps to integrate personal identity as is detailed in chapter 10.

Summary

Psychiatric treatment of the blind and deaf child poses an inherent paradox. It involves understanding that the needs of perceptually deficient children are the same as those not so afflicted, while at the same time taking note of their developmental difficulties and special treatment requirements. Further developmental research promises to make future therapeutic interventions more precise than they can be at present.

In general, therapeutic techniques and principles already developed in child psychiatry and described in the rest of this volume are applicable to the perceptually deficient. Special problems arise in communication, in establishing a therapeutic relationship, and in the therapeutic work with parents. Uncoordinated diffusion of therapeutic efforts among parents, educators, and psychotherapists is probably the greatest obstacle to good therapeutic results. In the past, both therapists and educators have resisted undertaking the therapeutic tasks and facing the challenges involved. While this resistance has not as yet been extirpated, therapeutic efforts have become more extensive and are becoming increasingly common.

REFERENCES

1. ARLOW, J., and BRENNER, C., *Psychoanalytic Concepts and the Structural Theory*, International Universities Press, New York, 1964.
2. BALTIN, M., *The Basic Fault: Therapeutic Aspects of Regression*, Tavistock, London, 1968.
3. BENDER, R. E., *The Conquest of Deafness*, Western Reserve University Press, Cleveland, Ohio, 1960.
4. BIRDWHISTLE, R. L., *Introduction to Kinesics*, University of Louisville Press, Louisville, Ky., 1952.
5. BLANK, H. R., "Psychoanalysis and Blindness," *Psychoanalytic Quarterly*, 26:1–24, 1957.
6. BOWLBY, J., *Attachment and Loss*, vol. 1, Basic Books, New York, 1969.
7. BRILL, R. G., "The Superior I.Q.'s of Deaf Children of Deaf Parents," *California Palms*, December 1969.
8. BURLINGHAM, D. T., "Some Problems of Ego Development in the Blind Child," in Eissler, R. S., et al. (Eds.), *The Psychoanalytic Study of the Child*, Vol. 20, pp. 194–208, International Universities Press, New York, 1965.
9. ———, in Eissler, R. S., et al. (Eds.), "Hearing and Its Role in the Development of the Blind," in Eissler, R. S., et al. (Eds.), *The Psychoanalytic Study of the Child*, vol. 19, pp. 95–112, International Universities Press, New York, 1964.
10. ———, "Some Notes on the Development of the Blind," in Eissler, R. S., et al. (Eds.), *The Psychoanalytic Study of the Child*, vol. 16, pp. 121–145, International Universities Press, New York, 1961.
11. ———, and GOLDBERGER, A., "Re-education of a Retarded Blind Child," in Eissler, R. S., et al. (Eds.), *The Psychoanalytic Studies of the Child*, vol. 23, pp. 369–390, International Universities Press, New York, 1968.
12. CAPLAN, G., *An Approach to Community Mental Health*, Grune & Stratton, New York, 1961.
13. DAVIDMAN, H., Personal communication.
14. DENMARK, J., "Mental Illness and Early Profound Deafness," *British Journal of Medical Psychology*, 39:117–124, 1966.
15. DOWNS, M. D., and STERITT, G. M., "Identifactory Audiometry for Neonates: A Preliminary Report," *Journal of Auditory Research*, 4:69–80, 1964.
16. ERIKSON, E. H., *Childhood and Society*, W. W. Norton, New York, 1950.
17. FAIRBAIRN, W. R. D., *The Object-Relations Theory of Personality*, Basic Books, New York, 1954.
18. FERENCZI, S., "Stages in the Development of the Sense of Reality," in Ferenczi, S., *Sex in Psychoanalysis*, Basic Books, New York, 1916.
19. FLAVELL, J. H., *The Developmental Psychology of Jean Piaget*, D. Van Nostrand, Princeton, N. J., 1963.
20. FRAIBERG, S., "Parallel and Divergent Patterns in Blind and Sighted Infants," in Eissler, R. S., et al. (Eds.), *The Psychoanalytic Study of the Child*, vol. 23, pp. 264–300, International Universities Press, New York, 1968.
21. ———, and FREEDMAN, D. A., "Studies in the Ego Development of the Cogenitally Blind Child," in Eissler, R. S., et al. (Eds.), *The Psychoanalytic Study of the Child*, vol. 19, pp. 113–169, International Universities Press, New York, 1964.
22. FREEDMAN, D. A., "On the Limits of Effectiveness of Psychoanalysis, Early Ego and Somatic Disturbances," *International Journal of Psychoanalysis*, 53(Part 3):363–370, 1972.
23. FREUD, A., *Normality and Pathology in Childhood*, International Universities Press, New York, 1965.
24. ———, "The Role of Bodily Illness in the Mental Life of Children," in Eissler, R. S., et al. (Eds.), *The Psy-*

choanalytic Study of the Child, vol. 7, pp. 69–82, International Universities Press, New York, 1952.

25. ———, *Ego and Mechanisms of Defense,* International Universities Press, New York, 1946.

26. FREUD, S., "Beyond the Pleasure Principle," in Strachey, J. (Ed.), *The Standard Edition of the Complete Psychological Works of Sigmund Freud* (hereafter: *The Standard Edition*) pp. 3–64, Hogarth Press, London, 1957.

27. ———, "On Narcissism: An Introduction," in Strachey, J. (Ed.), *The Standard Edition,* pp. 67–102, Hogarth Press, London, 1957.

28. FURTH, H. G., *Thinking Without Language,* Free Press, New York, 1966.

29. GARRETSON, M. D., "Total Communication," *The Volta Review,* 78(4):88–95, 1976.

30. GESELL, A., *The First Five Years of Life,* Harper & Brothers, New York, 1940.

31. GOLDFARB, W., *Childhood Schizophrenia,* Harvard University Press, Cambridge, 1961.

32. GREENBERG, J., *In This Sign,* Holt, Rinehart & Winston, New York, 1970.

33. HARTMANN, H., *Ego Psychology and the Problem of Adaptation,* International Universities Press, New York, 1958.

34. ———, et al., "The Mutual Influences of the Development of Ego and Id," in Eissler, R. S., et al. (Eds.), *The Psychoanalytic Study of the Child,* vol. 7, pp. 9–30, International Universities Press, New York, 1952.

35. HODGSON, K. W., *The Deaf and Their Problems,* Philosophical Library, New York, 1954.

36. KANNER, L., *Child Psychiatry,* 4th ed., Charles C Thomas, Springfield, Ill. 1972.

37. KATAN, A., "Some Thoughts about the Role of Verbalization in Early Childhood," in Eissler, R. S., et al. (Eds.), *The Psychoanalytic Study of the Child,* vol. 16, pp. 184–188, International Universities Press, New York, 1961.

38. KATES, S. L., *Cognitive Structures in Deaf, Hearing and Psychotic Individuals,* The Clarke School for the Deaf, Northhampton, Mass., 1967.

39. KESSLER, J. W., *Psychopathology of Childhood,* Prentice-Hall, Englewood Cliffs, N. J., 1966.

40. KHAN, M. M. R., *The Privacy of the Self,* International Universities Press, New York, 1974.

41. KOHUT, H., "The Psychoanalytic Treatment of Narcissistic Personality Disorders," in Eissler, R. S., et al. (Eds.), *The Psychoanalytic Study of the Child,* vol. 23, pp. 86–113, International Universities Press, New York, 1968.

42. LESSER, S. R., "Psychoanalysis with Children," in Wolman, B. (Ed.), *Manual of Child Psychopathology,* pp. 726–741, McGraw-Hill, New York, 1972.

43. ———, and EASSER, B. R., "The Psychiatric Management of the Deaf Child," *Canadian Nurse,* 71(10):23–25, 1975.

44. ———, "Personality Differences in the Perceptually Handicapped," *The Journal of the American Academy of Child Psychiatry,* 11(3):458–466, 1972.

45. LEVINE, E. S., *The Volta Review,* 78(4):23–33, 1976.

46. ———, *Youth in a Soundless World,* International Universities Press, New York, 1956.

47. ———, and Naiman, D. (Eds.), "Seminar on Behavior Modification for Psychologist Working with the Deaf," *American Annals of the Deaf,* 115:455–491, 1970.

48. LIPTON, E., "A Study of the Psychological Effects of Strabismus," in Eissler, R. S., et al. (Eds.), *The Psychoanalytic Study of the Child,* vol. 25, pp. 146–175, International Universities Press, New York, 1970.

49. LLOYD, L. L., and DAHLE, A. J., "Detection and Diagnosis of a Hearing Impaired Child," *The Volta Review,* 78(4):16, 1976.

50. LUSTMAN, S. I., "Some Issues in Contemporary Psychoanalytic Research," in Eissler, R. S., et al. (Eds.), *The Psychoanalytic Study of the Child,* vol. 18, pp. 51–74, International Universities Press, New York, 1962.

51. MAHLER, M. S., "A Study of the Separation-Individuation Process, in Eissler, R. S., et al. (Eds.), *The Psychoanalytic Study of the Child,* vol. 26, pp. 403–425, International Universities Press, New York, 1971.

52. ———, "Thoughts about Development and Individuation," in Eissler, R. S., et al. (Eds.), *The Psychoanalytic Study of the Child,* vol. 18, pp. 307–324, International Universities Press, New York, 1963.

53. ———, PINES, F., and BERGMAN, A., *The Psychological Birth of the Human Infant,* Basic Books, New York, 1976.

54. MICHELS, V., Personal communication, 1968.

55. MINSKI, L, *Deafness, Mutism, and Mental Deficiency in Children,* Heinmann, London, 1957.

56. MYKLEBUST, H. R., *The Psychology of Deafness,* 2nd ed., Grune & Stratton, New York, 1964.

57. ———, *Auditory Disorders in Children,* Grune & Stratton, New York, 1954.

58. NAGERA, H., *Early Childhood Disturbances, The Infantile Neurosis and the Adult Disturbance,* International Universities Press, New York, 1966.

59. NANCE, W. E., *The Volta Review,* 78(4):6–11, 1976.

60. ———, and SWEENEY, A., "Genetic Factors in Deafness of Early Life," *Otology Clinics of North America,* 8:19–48, 1975.

61. NIEDERLAND, W. G., "Narcissistic Ego Impairment in Patients with Early Physical Malformations," in Eissler, R. S., et al. (Eds.), *The Psychoanalytic Study of the Child,* vol. 20, pp. 518–534, International Universities Press, New York, 1965.

62. OMWAKE, E. G., and SOLNIT, A. J., " 'It Isn't Fair': The Treatment of a Blind Child," in Eissler, R. S., et al. (Eds.), *The Psychoanalytic Study of the Child,* vol. 16, pp. 352–404, International Universities Press, New York, 1961.

63. PIAGET, J., *The Construction of Reality in the Child,* Basic Books, New York, 1954.

64. ———, *The Origins of the Intelligence in Children,* International Universities Press, New York, 1936.

65. ———, *The Language and Thought of the Child,* Routledge & Kegan Paul, London, 1932.

66. RADFORD, P., "Changing Techniques in the Analysis of a Deaf Child," in Eissler, R. S., et al. (Eds.), *The Psychoanalytic Study of the Child,* vol. 28, pp. 225–248, Yale University Press, New Haven, 1973.

67. RAINER, J. D., and ALTSCHULER, K. Z. (Eds.), *Psychiatry and the Deaf,* Department of Health, Education and Welfare, Washington, D. C., 1967.

68. RUESCH, J., "Nonverbal Language in Therapy," *Psychiatry,* 18:323, 1955.

69. ———, and KEES, W., *Nonverbal Communication,* University of California Press, Berkeley, 1956.

70. SCHLESINGER, H., and MEADOW, K., *Sound and Sign,* University of California Press, Berkeley, 1972.

71. SOLNIT, A. J., and STARK, M. H., "Mourning and the Birth of a Defective Child," in Eissler, R. S., et al. (Eds.), *The Psychoanalytic Study of the Child,* vol. 16, pp. 523–537, International Universities Press, New York, 1961.

72. STEVENSON, E. A., "A Study of the Educational Achievement of Deaf Children of Deaf Parents," *Maryland Bulletin,* 69(74):63–64, 1965.

73. VERNON, M., *Multiply Handicapped Children: Medical, Educational and Psychological Considerations,* Council on Exceptional Children, Washington, D. C., 1969.

74. ———, "Techniques of Screening of Mental Illness in Deaf Clients," *Journal of Rehabilitation of the Deaf,* 2:22–36, 1969.

75. ———, and KOH, S. D., "Effects of Oral Preschool Compared to Early Manual Communication on Education and Communication in Deaf Children," *American Annals of the Deaf,* 116:569–574, 1970.

76. WAELDER, R., "Trauma and the Variety of Extraordinary Challenges," in Furst, S. (Ed.), *Psychic Trauma,* pp. 221–234, Basic Books, New York, 1967.

77. ———, *The Basic Theory of Psychoanalysis*, International Universities Press, New York, 1960.

78. WEST, P., *Words for a Deaf Daughter*, Harper & Row, New York, 1970.

79. WHITE, R., "Ego and Reality in Psychoanalytic Theory," *Psychological Issues no. 11*, International Universities Press, New York, 1963.

80. WINNICOTT, D. W., *Collected Papers*, Basic Books, New York, 1958.

81. WRIGHT, D., *Deafness*, Stein & Day, New York, 1969.

82. WOOD, G., *The Handicapped Child*, Blakweel Scientific Publications, London, 1975.

83. ZIVKOVIE, M., "Influence of Deafness on the Structure of Personality," *Perceptual Motor Skills*, 33:863–866, 1971.

42 / Severely Brain-Injured Children

Irene Jakab

Introduction

Treatment of severely brain-injured children requires consideration of the total patient. One cannot address either the psychological problems or the organic pathology in isolation. Indeed, a rational therapeutic plan is possible only after careful diagnostic assessment of the physical, psychological, educational, and social components of the presenting symptomatology.

There is controversy regarding the general validity of psychological tests, their specific value in assessing brain damage,[45] and about the merit of testing and retesting with the same instruments.[34] The need for frequent reevaluations makes retesting inevitable in dealing with brain-damaged children. This very complication of validity assessment stemming from the child's ability to "learn" from previous testing represents an indication of the potential for trainability or educability. Unfortunately, Anthony's[2] call for building up a developmental psychopathology based on sound research, including experimental methods, has not yet been satisfactorily answered. Diller[10] quotes several opposing views regarding the importance of the diagnosis of brain damage, while Palmer[35] stresses the importance of "fitting the treatment ot the diagnosis." This view, which is closer to traditional medical thinking—that is, the best treatment method is the one that takes into consideration the causal factors as well as the presenting diagnostic symptoms of an illness—will be the guiding principle of this chapter.

Consequences of Brain Damage

Brain damage may cause arrest of cerebral development or destruction of already developed areas of the brain. In both instances, manifest alterations of function will be revealed by neurological and psychological symptoms. Generally, when damage is diffuse, the amount of brain substance lost or damaged will grossly parallel the degree of impairment of neuropsychological function. This is shown by observations both of animals[26] and of neurological patients.[19] Diffuse brain damage may or may not be associated with the destruction of vital centers. When the more differentiated centers suffer isolated anatomical destruction, this can lead to localized symptoms without necessarily affecting the general level of the patient's functioning. For example, a small lesion in the calcarine fissure will cause obvious visual impairment but will not effect intellectual or emotional development.

In diffuse organic damage, those brain functions which are phylogenetically and ontogenetically the most recently acquired are the most likely to be affected first. Thus, as a result of generalized injury, the most vulnerable targets are the higher psychological functions of speech, concept formation, abstraction, symbol understanding, and goal-directed motor activity. When such diffuse injury occurs at a very early age, those higher functions may never develop; the result is a low level of emotional and cognitive development. When brain-injured children score unevenly on subtests of intelligence, this suggests emotional disturbance or circumscribed cortical function deficits.[15, 22]

Brain-damaged children often show regression, retardation, and/or an alteration in the course of their developmental phases. This was noted by Corboz[9] in brain tumor cases. In those children, the egocentric personality was dominated by primitive instinctual drives. Tolerance for anxiety is lowered in traumatic brain damage; this can be aggravated by parental overprotection, excessive parental demands, or by insufficient contact with normal peers.[27]

The stories told by brain-damaged persons are characterized by concreteness and simplicity. Sarason[39] found that themes of aggression, loneliness, and a desire for affection prevailed in the stories of mentally retarded children. These themes seem to be secondary to environmental deprivation; they can also be found in brain-damaged children. Additional evidence of emotional instability is manifested by restlessness and a tendency to joke inappropriately. In addition, lack of initiative can lower intelligence scores below the actual capabilities of the patient.

Physical impairment might be associated with disturbance of sensory organ functioning, intellectual deficit, epilepsy, and a decrease in the range of emotional flexibility and emotional stability in adaptive functioning. Any combination of these lead to multiple handicaps.[4, 7, 12]

Interrelation of Interventions

It requires great care to adapt psychiatric treatment methods to the needs and to the level of functioning of the individual brain-damaged child. To make these adaptations, it is necessary at the outset to assess each specific deficit and, then, to plan carefully the combined use of several treatment methods. The essential details of planning are:

1. Rehabilitation focused on specific neurological symptomatology resulting from the nature and localization of the brain injury.
2. Social intervention, including family counseling.
3. Psychiatric treatment or prevention of concomitant emotional disturbance.

These plans must be judiciously combined in order to achieve maximal rehabilitation and to prevent secondary emotional problems.

Physical-neurological rehabilitation should be paired with psychological support and/or psychotherapy, to help the child cope both with the physical symptoms and with the social discrimination to which the handicapped are exposed. The handicapped child has to be assisted to adjust to the changed emotional climate due to the adaptation of the family, school, and the community to his handicap.

Social intervention encompasses details as disparate as the selection of appropriate housing or architectural remodeling;[6] specially adapted appliances to help the child become more independent; public transportation training; and so forth. Beyond these practical requirements, the most important aspect of the social intervention is counseling the family. The latter may have to deal with many problems stemming from the child's pathology.[23, 29, 41] Some instruction and guidance is almost always necessary to allow the family to provide the child with an optimal emotional climate.

The rehabilitation process requires a good deal of social engineering. The child has to learn to utilize group support and to gain strength from identifying with successful handicapped persons, whom he or she meets at rehabilitation facilities. Within the limits of the organic brain injury, the child should ultimately be able to obtain subjective emotional satisfaction and develop the capacity for enjoyable interpersonal relationships with peers and adults.

The available psychiatric treatment modalities have been described in earlier chapters. In many instances where severely brain-injured children have emotional problems, the methods will have to be modified and combined with other rehabilitative interventions in order to treat the total child. This is outlined schematically in table 42-1.

Psychiatric intervention may include any combination of medication, individual or group psychotherapy, behavior therapy, special education, parent counseling and/or therapy, family therapy, and so forth. In general it will address itself to the following issues:

1. Living with an unchangeable handicap.
2. Increasing the cognitive potential and level of functioning in the intellectual and emotional spheres.
3. Increasing motivation and sustaining it while working toward a realistic life goal.

In many instances, therapeutic education must become an integral part of the overall treatment, a fact emphasized by Payne and associates.[36] Within the school system, behavior therapy is one of the most frequently used interventions in coping with the emotional problems of severely brain-injured children. The behavioral approach can aid in establishing or reestablishing basic self-help skills, such as toilet training or appropriate eating habits, which lie within the child's physiological capacities. It can also facilitate a lengthening of the child's attention span in the classroom, as well as contribute toward the achievement of more constructive interactional patterns.

A carefully designed treatment program often includes complex drug management. A dilemma often arises in the course of the concomitant treatment of more than one syndrome: The condition may require the simultaneous use of drugs of op-

TABLE 42–1

Treatment of the Child with Severe Brain Damage

Time of Intervention	Parent	Newborn	Infant and Toddler	Older Child and Adolescent
PREVENTION OF EMOTIONAL DISTURBANCE	Parent (Individual or Group) Counseling	*Parent:* Counseling— Reality of Goal, Method, and Prognosis	*Parent* education and psychiatric support	Early *parent* counseling, as for younger children's parents. Brief supportive professional contact for the recently injured *child*.
ACUTE STATE	Child and Parent Counseling— jointly or total family counseling	*Child:* Survival— Vigorous treatment and prevention of extending damage, e.g., alleviation of increased intracranial pressure	*Child:* Survival. Enrich *or* decrease stimulus in hyperactivity Diet (PKU, etc.) Physical therapy Drug treatment Psychotherapy	*Parent and teacher education:* Not to overprotect; not to be too demanding; to stimulate; to provide gratifying emotional interaction with adults and children. *Child:* Teach to play; to learn to accept handicap; to compensate with physical and psychological assets. Resolve acute reactive depression (drugs, psychotherapy)
CHRONIC IMPROVING	Child and Parent Counseling— jointly or total family counseling		*Child:* Plastic surgery, if necessary Vigorous treatment and rehabilitation Psychotropic drug treatment as necessary Epilepsy control	*Child at Home:* Group therapy for *child* and *parents*; join associations for special child. *Child in Institute:* Staff counseling same as for parents. Individual relationship building with selected staff for the child; role modeling.
CHRONIC UNCHANGED	Child and Parent Counseling— total family counseling including sibs, etc.		*Child:* Learn to compensate for neurological deficit, for hearing, visual, motor deficits Increase use of remaining assets Drug treatment if necessary	*Child:* Treatment if necessary for depression, anxiety, and aggressive feelings due to apprehension about being different. Supportive, therapeutic, counseling for *child and parents*. Motivation to live with handicap.

posing effects. For example, the control of epileptic seizures may require phenobarbital, which will tend to increase the brain-damaged child's hyperactivity. As discussed in chapter 23, the use of major tranquilizers to alleviate psychotic states confronts the physician with the problems of severe side effects, such as akathisia and oculogyric crises or respiratory distress due to muscle spasms.

Even with small doses, the side effects tend to be more frequent in brain-damaged children than in others. Furthermore, therapeutic dosage of some tranquilizers carries the additional risk of activating seizures that are hard to control. On the other hand, chlorpromazine, for example, can produce hydantoin toxicity by decreasing the metabolic breakdown rate of hydantoin.

If diffuse hyperactivity is one of the consequences of organic brain injury, methylphenidate may be the drug of choice.[11] As Conners[8] has demonstrated through electroencephalogram (EEG) monitoring, the hyperactive state is actually a state of lowered arousal; cortical stimulants should therefore help to counteract it. It is important to distinguish the diffuse hyperactivity of organic etiology from the easily triggered aggressivity of some psychotic or character disordered children and from the hyperalert restlessness of the overanxious patient. The truly hyperactive child is a restless one who cannot sit still, who moves in his chair or around the room—his attention is constantly attracted by different objects in the environment, and his incessant motion appears aimless. By way of contrast, the behavior of children with thalamic or isolated frontal or temporal lobe lesions may be characterized by frequent aggressive acts, which are directed at specific targets.

The success or failure of the treatment of brain-injured hyperactive children may hinge on the correctness of the etiologic diagnostic assessment. The differential diagnosis of the hyperactive syndrome will determine the choice of medication and/or psychotherapeutic method. The combination of drug and milieu treatment carried out with consistent staffing patterns and uniform staff attitude is frequently suggested in the case of multiple handicapped brain-injured children.[12, 24, 25, 44] To date, individual psychotherapy by itself has not yielded optimal results. In some cases, only a small number of therapeutic sessions have been offered over a short period of time.[1] It is possible that this has been insuffiient treatment.[17]

It is known that much flexibility is required even in the use of traditional methods. As Harrison[18] has pointed out: "There is no standard initial approach to children in psychotherapy." The well-established child psychiatric methods should be implemented with modifications in the technique, as necessary to adapt them to the brain-damaged child. In some cases, various combinations and special adaptations of play therapy, art therapy, rhythm therapy, speech therapy, physical therapy, may be required.[38, 40]

Reactions to Brain Damage

It is easy to underestimate the degree to which the consequences of brain damage are aggravated by emotional problems. A child who is brain damaged is handicapped further if there is an associated emotional disturbance, such as reactive depression, regression, and emotional immaturity. The all-too-likely outcome is that he is not capable of using such learning capacity as he possesses, or lacks the motivation for rehabilitation to begin with. As Gallagher[13] pointed out, inadequate ego control and regressive defensive mechanisms contribute to mental retardation. Failure to treat the emotional disturbance may result in such children functioning on a retarded level.[5, 31, 37] The necessary treament itself may create emotional strain. The intensive physical rehabilitation involves such methods as patterning and the imposition of frequency unpleasant and even painful maneuvering by physical therapists. Essentialy, the therapeutic regimen controls the brain-damaged child's total motor life. The inevitable frustrations accompanying such a program can contribute to low self-esteem, anger at the environment, feelings of impotence, and a desire to rebel even when the child understands the necessity of what he is subjected to. It can be helpful to provide as much freedom of choice for the child as is possible within the limits of various prescribed therapies. Enhancing the child's self-esteem and feeling of autonomy may serve to alleviate symptoms of depression and aggressive rebellion. The mother-child interaction should be normalized, since even the hyperactive syndrome may be caused by disruption of the mother-child interaction.[30]

In some cases which show marked improvement with physical rehabilitative measures, the child's emotional needs for play and recreational activities may be markedly curtailed. In their struggle to survive and become physically functional and intellectually competent, such children may develop into emotionally starved, hard workers, carrying a burden of chronic depression and unable to enjoy age-appropriate play and peer interaction. Some develop into angry and aggressive teenagers, while the more severely depressed may become extremely withdrawn.

It should be emphasized also that not all children with severe brain injury experience the aforementioned reactions, nor do they all require psychiatric intervention. One cannot neglect the importance of social adaptation[16] and must provide the optimal framework for it. Many of the secondary emotional problems associated with the adjustment to a handicapped life may be avoided by appropriate counseling of the family and/or institutional caretakers. Moreover, even in cases of rather severe brain damage, other areas of the brain may take over the functions of the damaged areas: The younger the child, the greater the potential for developing compensatory functions. In some cases of neonatal or very early hemispherectomy, the functions of the missing hemisphere can be assumed by the remaining portion of the brain.

Goals of Treatment

The overall goal of treatment should be to alleviate the patient's personal suffering and difficulties in adapting to the social environment. Behavior modification, for example, must be carried out with the total environment of the child—including his family, school, and therapeutic institution. Otherwise, the method may lead to confusion, because the child's concrete thinking and difficulty in assessing the environment may make it difficult for him to decide when and where a specific behavior is appropriate, and when it will lead to the reward.

For such children, there is considerable need to compromise in setting goals. Individual goals, similar to those advocated for the retarded by Hoejenbos,[20] must be set for the brain-damaged child. The therapist, the family, social agencies, and school, as well as the patient, must come to grips with the primary handicap and the uncertainty of the long-term prognosis. If there is willingness to compromise for limited goals, treatment that is carried out consistently and intensively and which addresses itself to all facets of the handicap will always bring some results. In order to keep the entire treatment program in perspective and to be able to live with the disadvantage of limited goals, it is advisable to set intermediary goals repeatedly. This requires both a careful diagnostic assessment and repeated reassessment of the progress of a flexible treatment plan. Nor should one ever lose sight of the importance of collaboration by the different specialists working with the same child.

The diagnosis is based on a detailed functional description of the child's assets as well as the pathology or deficits in the following evaluations: (1) medical-neurological examination; (2) psychological testing; (3) psychiatric evaluation; (4) educational assessment; (5) social assessment of the family; and (6) a study of the child's total environment, including the neighborhood, school, agencies, institutions, and so forth.

Only such a meticulously comprehensive evaluation can lead to the formulation of a realistic prognosis based on the weighing of the child's and the family's assets and liabilities. The prognosis should be outlined in explicit detail in all areas covered by the foregoing diagnostic outline and should be categorized into three types of reachable goals: (1) short-term goals, (2) intermediary goals, (3) long-term goals.

There is an important aspect of goal setting that is all too easy to overlook. This arises from the fact that the emotionally disturbed child often does not understand the need for psychiatric treatment because of his youth and/or because of the brain damage. It is the parents, the school, or the hospital staff who call on the psychotherapist. The treatment goals are to a great extent defined by the referral source; the child is a passive participant in his assessment and in the process of therapeutic intervention. The social environment, be it a family, hospital, school, or community, requires it members to fit into a smoothly operating system. As a result, it is the social environment that most urgently indicates the need for behavioral changes in the child.

As the goal strongly influences the choice of the treatment method, it follows that all these referral sources have considerable power of decision over all aspects of the child's treatment, for example, the type of treatment selected and the decisions about whether it should be initiated, continued, or discontinued. For instance, if a referral comes from a school which has the power to request and/or finance treatment, the urgent desire for behavioral change tends to favor behavioral modification methods which promise to "make the child better adjusted" to the rules and regulations of his surroundings. The real objective may be to make the work of the caretakers easier—to alleviate the distress caused by the child's behavior.

By way of contrast, a self-referred adult patient, not committed by a court of law, is often motivated by personal pain and suffering; in this case the most frequent treatment modalities are psychopharmacological and psychotherapeutic.

For each type of intervention, the process of establishing goals should entail a detailed description of the methods to be used in the process of rehabilitation. The medical-surgical, orthopedic, physical-therapeutic, special educational, psychopharmacological, psychiatric and social interventions should each be considered separately; each has its own degree of effectiveness in decreasing pathology and increasing the child's capacities in each sphere. In other words, one should establish in detail the methods to be used for reaching each partial goal.

It is important to institute control points at set intervals for the reevaluation and reassessment of progress. It is at those points that action can be taken to change method(s). This can be facilitated by the use of a schematic chart, as illustrated in table 42-2, to outline the assets and pathology in several spheres of functioning and to record the goals, methods, and progress at sequential checkpoints throughout the course of treatment.

Parents and/or other caretakers must be involved in this process. Inevitably, they will participate actively in carrying out some of the rehabilitation procedure; their insight, understanding, and expectations will be an integral part of the work, and their efforts must be coordinated with those of the professionals treating the brain-damaged, handicapped child. A prerequisite for securing the cooperation of the parents and other caretakers is to provide them with detailed information derived from the diagnostic assessments. They should be informed of the prognosis, the outlined goals, and the treatment plans as these emerge during the initial evaluation and during the scheduled reassessment checkpoints. When treatment includes psychotherapy, for instance, nothing can replace the genuine interest and time spent by the therapist in occasional personal contacts with the family, even when another professional is responsible for the family's counseling. In other words, the therapeutic alliance with the child must extend to the family and collaborating treatment staff; lacking this, the psychotherapy stands in danger of being discontinued or becoming less efficient than it might otherwise be.

The therapeutic alliance with the child must be established at his own intellectual and emotional level. Initially, this can be fostered by methods similar to that employed in the alliance with the parents—by giving the child detailed information about his present state at his own level of comprehension and allowing him to participate jointly in setting goals. This provides the child with a way of perceiving progress since the last checkpoint, as well as giving him some achievement to look forward to at the time of the next checkpoint. Most important of all, it helps the child understand what is required of him.[33]

TABLE 42–2

Diagnostic Data and Treatment Chart

NAME: DOB:	Date: Assets	Pathology	Short-term Goals	Methods	Date: Results	Long-term Goals	Methods	Date: Results
Intellectual MA: IQ:								
Educational								
Social (Child & Family)								
Emotional (Psychiatric)								
Medical Neurological								

Technical Considerations in Psychotherapy with Brain-Damaged Children

There is an inherently frustrating element that causes mental health clinicians to defer consideration of psychotherapy for brain-injured youngsters. It is the anticipation that the "end product" is likely to remain defective.[21] This attitude coexists with an awareness that relieving the youngster's emotional problems will enable him to utilize more of his intellectual and emotional potential in adjusting to his handicapped state. The clinician is also made vulnerable by his own rescue fantasies; these may lead him to be too passive and overprotectively tolerant of aberrant behavior. On the other hand, it is all too easy to become frustrated when the child does not change appreciably within a short time. This can result in a tendency to become overly active and to impose excessive demands on the child during the therapy sessions. In each of these instances, the psychotherapist runs the risk of losing sight of the primary intrapsychic conflict in favor of trying to impose behavioral change.

As a general rule, psychotherapy with brain-damaged children must use concrete methods. Most such children have difficulties with abstract thinking and many have lost or are unable to acquire the concept of time. The consequent low frustration tolerance is especially typical of children with diffuse cortical damage and of those with parietal lobe involvement. Another frustrating element in the child's emotional adaptation to his environment is his lack of speech or a delay in its development. While gearing the appropriate psychotherapeutic technique to the child's mental age, the psychotherapist must also take into consideration specific intellectual and communication handicaps. Generally, the therapist's communications must be offered clearly, repeatedly, and concretely.

As stated earlier, the disturbances of time concept may contribute directly to low frustration tolerance—if there is no tomrrow, all wishes must be fulfilled now. Furthermore, if there are difficulties in verbal expression, the only response to frustration may be a generalized bodily expression such as a temper tantrum. This expression of low frustration tolerance may interfere with psychotherapy for a long time, so it is advisable to alleviate it as rapidly as possible. It can be treated by systematic training in how to grasp the concept of time. The present is known to the child. The lived-through past can be remembered and placed within the context of a time frame, for example, "you visited grandma yesterday"; "you got a prize in school yesterday" and so on. The future can be learned by action related to the immediate future paired with a description of the action to be lived through by the child, for example, "in one-half hour you'll get your breakfast"; "in ten minutes you will go for a ride with father"; and so on. The statements must be clear and concrete without "ifs" or other conditional phrases. Each statement should be repeated when the action actually does take place, for example, "remember, I told you 'in ten minutes'." Through this method, the child's time concept can be expanded slowly to "tomorrow" and eventually further into the future. Frustration tolerance increases if there *is* a tomorrow.

The therapist's office and/or playroom must be arranged to meet the child's specific needs and handicaps. For instance, some children with brain damage may need a stimulating environment, while those with hyperactive symptomatology will benefit more from a quiet, low-keyed interaction. Thus, the number of objects, toys, or games visible in the therapist's room must be adapted to the nature of the child's difficulty.

The length of the therapy session should depend on the child's tolerance. The severely brain-damaged child usually has a short attention span and a brief tolerance for confinement within a given space, whether for an individual or group psychotherapeutic situation. Some become overexcited after a while, while others become tired and withdrawn. The length of the sessions should, therefore, be adjusted to the individual's tolerance, ranging from a brief ten minutes to a full hour. It helps if the starting time of the session remains precisely the same; concrete thinking and the often-associated lack of verbal facility interfere with understanding the therapist's delayed arrival. If the session does not start when it is expected to, the child can suffer undue anxiety and lack of trust. If is while the session is in progress that the therapist may be flexible and tailor the length of the session to the child's tolerance in order to avoid assuming the role of "jailer" for a child who wants to escepe.

Brain-injured children are often deficient in sensory perception or in the integrative cortical functions necessary for the processing of sensory perceptions. As a result, they frequently have difficulty in assessing reality. Thus, for the child, the physical presence of the therapist may in itself constitute a threat. The therapist must take care to become identified by the child as a person on whom one can rely and in whom trust can be invested. Intruding too early into the private world of such a fearful child may neopardize the development of the therapeutic alliance.

One of the most frequent consequences of diffuse brain damage (or localized damage in the region of the angular gyrus or the transitional parieto-occipital area) is difficulty in space orientation and distorted assessment of object size. Thus, an unexpected stimulus, such as a toy or a ball tossed suddenly in the child's direction, may elicit a panic reaction comparable to that seen in adult cases of space agnosia. The therapist should avoid startling such a child with actions outside of the child's visual field. At the same time, after gaining the child's attention and after establishing a positive and active interaction, the therapist may be well advised to associate his concrete verbal messages with emphatic gestures. Sternlicht[42] has emphasized the importance of communication through means other than verbal. When the child's ability to understand verbal psychotherapeutic interpretations is limited, nonverbal behavior must be highly explicit and occasionally overdramatized.

There are specific ways in which the therapist can help to increase the child's ego strength and frustration tolerance. He can play games of increasing levels of difficulty that gradually introduce tasks that are both physically and intellectually more demanding. Differentiation between fantasy and reality can be fostered through role playing, interpretation, symbolic use of play materials, and actual modeling and demonstration. For brain-injured children functioning on a higher verbal level, symbolic play activity and verbal interpretation can be used. Interpretation and insight into the child's reactions to his own handicap may help develop new ways of coping with symptoms and with the demands of the environment. At first glance, many severely brain-injured children appear so grossly handicapped that they convey an "odd" impression. As a result, they are compelled to cope with social prejudice and rejection. In any case, the therapist must help the patient with his reality adaptation, including recognition of the extent of his own handicap.

Concomitant with helping a child accept his handicap is the tedious task of working to restore the concrete body image. This is particularly important for those children who have experienced amputation of a limb or have undergone some other major surgical alteration of their body configuration. The physical therapist and educator can be particularly helpful in aiding the child cope with the psychological consequences of body image confusion. The use of art media such as painting, clay modeling, and so forth can assist in expressing feelings in a nonverbal way. This can facilitate the abreaction of conflicts for which the child may not possess the appropriate vocabulary. Further, if it is an enjoyable experience, the act of creating something will help reestablish the child's self-esteem. This will contribute to the restoration of his self-confidence and self-reliance in spite of the handicap.

The aim is to help the child to become more skillful in adapting to environmental demands in spite of his anxieties—and often in spite of his anger at the "nonhandicapped environment." Through the resolution of transference, a child can learn to adapt to his environment on a more mature level, using the role models that developed and were understood in the transference relationship.

In certain cases, group psychotherapy may be the treatment of choice. In mixed groups of brain-damaged and non-brain-damaged children of the same mental age, peer interaction helps to achieve normalization and a feeling of "not being different," It can be of particular benefit to involve the child in therapeutic activities with handicapped children who have already achieved some measure of success and who can serve as role models. As in any group therapy, the techniques employed must be adapted to the child's level of tolerance.

One of the most difficult aspects of psychotherapy is assessing its results in a given case. Research on psychotherapy lacks measuring instruments.[28] It is advisable, therefore, to carefully set both intermediary and long-term goals for each individual case, and to assess regularly the amount of time required and the extent to which these goals are achieved.

Coordination Within the Team

The seriously handicapped child is often the object of the work of many experts operating simultaneously. One specialist braces the legs and provides physical exercises and mobilization training; another corrects the visual-motor coordination problems; another may prescribe medication to inhibit hyperactivity; still another may deal with the reactive depression caused by the prospects of a handicapped life. A particular specialist may engage in one of the most important mental health services by providing the nonverbal brain-damaged child with a system of communication. (This can take the form of speech therapy including sign language, if necessary, to help the child communicate.) If this is successful, it will prevent the frustration of isolation which may cause severe emotional disturbance and lead ultimately to negativism, withdrawal, or hyperactive-aggressive behavior. All of these in turn generate social pressure on the family, which may presently require help from a family counselor in coping with the child's pathology. In view of this complex play of interventions, it is vital to designate unambiguously one person who is responsible for the coordination of the various efforts. If these multiple treatment methods are not guided and carefully coordinated, despite the fact that each specialist may do his or her "part" effectively, the child may become emotionally fragmented in the course of rehabilitation. In short, while all the specialists deal with "their" target difficulties, somebody has to deal with the total child.

Working with the Family

Brain-damaged children exert a profound influence on their family, especially if they are also emotionally immature and/or disturbed.[43] Goldenberg and Levine[14] have demonstrated the mutual influence exerted on each other by the mentally subnormal and their families. The family may literally assign one or more members to fulfill the role of the damaged child's entire care. This person will deny his own needs, such as for undisturbed sleep, as he anxiously wakes up to "watch" the vulnerable child. Vacations may become a remembered luxury since babysitters for brain-damaged children may be impossible to find or may not be trusted by overanxious and/or guilty parents. In time, martyred family members become increasingly irritable and angry; they confront clinicians with "demands" for visible improvements (even of a miraculous kind) as their reward. A particularly frustrating demand may be their expectation of an expression of gratitude from the child, who may be the least able to offer it on those particular terms. Obviously, vicious cycles

may readily become established during the "heroic stage" of total devotion to the process of rehabilitation, for example patterning, speech retraining, and so on. Such vicious cycles must be prevented or interrupted by early family counseling.

Help can be provided by establishing well-founded, step-by-step goals; training the family in methods of achieving these goals; and helping the family accept their own legitimate needs for rest, recreation, and privacy. As a preventive mental hygiene measure for the parents, professional agencies can provide regularly scheduled temporary care for the child in the home or away from it. A normal life rhythm that includes recreation for the family will ultimately assure more efficient emotional support for the brain-damaged child.

The family's attitude toward the brain-damaged child will greatly influence the child's expectations of himself and of his environment. If the caretakers tend to be irritable, depressed, or anxious, the likelihood is great that the child will be increasingly angry, guilty, anxious, and ambivalent. The child who senses that his already greater than average dependency needs are in continuous danger of being rejected and frustrated lives in a state of anxiety. Awareness of the environment's sacrifices may produce undue guilt in relation to the youngster's natural wish to become independent, because the parents may equate this wish with rejection of their home. Being considered "ungrateful" may generate anger and rebellion or evasive daydreaming about a "better than normal" supermanlike self-image. Such a child will alternate between an unrealistically omnipotent conception of himself that denies any problems at all and a self-effacing, depressive self-image that exaggerates his defective level of functioning. The latter decreases motivation, while the former stimulates aspiration far beyond reasonable levels of competency. Ultimately this inhibits normal and realizable goals of adjustment and vocational training.[3] As indicated earlier, a realistic self-image will facilitate the child's emotional growth and adaptation to a more or less handicapped future life. This process is fostered by a meticulously evaluated status quo, judicious goal setting, and reassessment at regular intervals. Each such occasion should encompass an open discussion of step-by-step improvements with both the child and the family.

The ideal self-concept is culturally determined.[32] Inevitably, the child's aspirations and his self-image as a success or failure in rehabilitation will be greatly influenced by the value system of the family, school, and/or hospital staff. The psychotherapist should be an active participant in the child's total treatment. He must seek to understand the various treatment phases in terms of their behavioral correlates, their influence on the child's life in his own environment, and their contribution toward shaping his self-image. The psychotherapist should help the family plan their part in the overall treatment program and enlist everyone who forms part of the patient's human environment to become active participants in his rehabilitation. This can lead to the following effects on the family.

Unexpected personal pathology may surface in those family members who have been focusing on their own feelings. In the course of developing insight into their nontherapeutic handling of the child (for example, overprotecting or rejecting), some parents will develop increased guilt feelings —this makes them function even less effectively, and dealing with such feelings requires skillful counseling (see chapter 8). When the child's pathology is alleviated, other family problems may surface that had been neglected in the concentration on the child's handicap. If family problems have been ignored in giving attention to the child's difficulties, then when these are dealt with, the emphasis tends to fall once again on the underlying interpersonal problems. For instance, the handicapped child frequently displaces the father from the parental bedroom in order to be cared for by an overprotective mother—thus establishing a situation where the father sleeps in a separate room. Once the child's problems are solved it becomes evident that the parental relationship cannot be restored due to other interpersonal problems. Thus, the alleviation of the child's sickness, the alleged cause of the parents' separation, brings into focus problems which the parents prefer to avoid. This underscores the need for skillfully managed family counseling or family therapy (see chapters 7 and 8).

Follow-up Treatment

Ultimately, the bulk of the treatment will be delegated to family members and paraprofessional mental health workers. Under the supervision of the psychiatrist, these nonprofessionals will provide support based on an understanding of the psychological needs of the child. With the help of such supervision, the physical therapist, speech therapist, or the recreational and rehabilitational workers who attend to these children in a rehabilitation center, or even within the family setting, are able to carry out important preventive and maintenance psychological tasks.

In order to assess the patient's continuing status and/or need for further treatment or counseling, office visits at the rehabilitation center, home visits, and meetings with school or job placement personnel should all be included in the follow-up procedures. Home visits and communication with teachers provide continuity of support to the family, while simultaneously facilitating assessment of the family interactions and early intervention in any new or recurring pathology.

Follow-up plans should include arrangements to make available professionals for future counseling at various crossroads in the child's life, for example, puberty, the moment of vocational choice, and at times of unexpected stress within the family such as divorce, death, and so on. It is assumed that both the child and the family will relate more easily with previous therapists; they might well be inclined to postpone a search for help if they must locate new sources of assistance. Therefore, it is recommended that whenever possible, the previous therapist be available as an initial contact person. After assessing the problem, the therapist may proceed to treat or counsel the family or to refer them elsewhere. By his familiarity with both the kind of "case" in general and with the idiosyncrasies of that child or that family in particular, the former therapist is in the best position to pinpoint the most suitable agency or person for the necessary intervention.

Summary

An appropriate choice for intervention modality accompanied by an adaptation of the technique to the child's level of functioning will markedly enhance positive results. The outcome is likely to be still better if the psychotherapist extends the therapeutic alliance to the family, the caretaking staff, and the multitude of therapeutic specialists. He must enlist their help in providing a therapeutic environment for the brain-damaged child. Those psychotherapists who are willing to accept limited goals and are able to share with the family and the child their conviction as to the validity of limited goals are likely to achieve the best possible outcome.

REFERENCES

1. ALBINI, J. L., and DINITZ, S., "Psychotherapy with Disturbed and Defective Children: An Evaluation of Changes in Behavior and Attitudes," *American Journal of Mental Deficiency, 69*:560, 1965.

2. ANTHONY, E. J., "The Behavior Disorders of Childhood," in Mussen, P. H. (Ed.), *Carmichael's Manual of Child Psychology,* vol. 2, p. 667, John Wiley, New York. 1970.

3. BALTHAZAR, E. E., and STEVENS, H. A., *The Emotionally Disturbed Mentally Retarded,* Prentice-Hall, Englewood-Cliffs, N. J., 1975.

4. BENDER, L., "The Brain and Child Behavior," *Archives of General Psychiatry, 4*:531, 1961.

5. BERKO, F. G., "Special Education for the Cerebral Palsied," in Mechan, M. J., et al. (Eds.), *Communication Training in Childhood Brain Damage,* p. 261, Charles C Thomas, Springfield, Ill., 1972.

6. BRYCE, T., "Housing the Handicapped," *Rehabilitation World,* vol. 1, no. 1, pp. 7–10, Rehabilitation International, New York, July, 1975.

7. COBB, S., "Personality as Affected by Lesions of the Brain," in Hunt, J. McV. (Ed.), *Personality and the Behavior Disorders,* vol. 1, pp. 550–581, Ronald Press, New York, 1941.

8. CONNERS, C. K., *Clinical Use of Stimulant Drugs in Children,* American Elsevier, New York, 1974.

9. CORBOZ, R., *Die Psychiatrie der Hirntumoren bei Kindern und Jugendilichen,* Springer Verlag, Wien, 1958.

10. DILLER, L., "Cognitive and Motor Aspects of Handicapping Conditions in the Neurologically Impaired," in Neff, W. S. (Ed.), *Rehabilitation Psychology,* pp. 1–33, American Psychological Association, Washington, D.C., 1971.

11. EISENBERG, L., "The Management of the Hyperkinetic Child," *Developmental Medicine and Child Neurology, 8*:593–598, 1966.

12. ———, "Psychiatric Implications of Brain Damage in Children," *Psychiatric Quarterly, 31*:72, 1957.

13. GALLAGHER, J. J., "Measurement of Personality Development in Preadolescent Mentally Retarded Children," *American Journal of Mental Deficiency, 64*:296, 1959.

14. GOLDENBERG, I., and LEVINE, M., "The Development and Evolution of the Yale Psycho-Educational Clinic," *International Review of Applied Psychology, 18*:101, 1969.

15. GOLDSTEIN, K., and SHEERER, M., "Abstract and Concrete Behavior, An Experimental Study with Special Tests," *Psychological Monographs, 53(2)*:1–151, 1941.

16. GOTTWALD, H. L., "A Special Program for Educable-Emotionally Disturbed Retarded," *Mental Retardation, 2*:353, 1964.

17. GUNZBURG, H. C., "Psychotherapy with the Feeble-Minded," in Clarke, A. M., and Clarke, A. D. B. (Eds.), *Mental Deficiency: The Changing Outlook,* pp. 1–596, Menthuen, London, 1965.

18. HARRISON, S. I., "Psychiatric Treatment of Children," in Freedman, A. M., and Kaplan, H. I. (Eds.), *Comprehensive Textbook of Psychiatry,* p. 1453, Williams & Williams, Baltimore, 1967.

19. HECAEN, H., and ANGELERGUES, R., *La cécité Psychique,* Masson et Cie., Paris, 1963.

20. HOEJENBOS, E. A., "Play Therapy for Imbecile Children," in *Proceedings of the Second International Congress on Mental Retardation,* Excerpta Medica International Congress Series, no. 43. Excerpta Medica, Amsterdam. 1961.

21. JAKAB, I., "Psychotherapy of the Mentally Retarded Child," in Bernstein, N. R. (Ed.), *Diminished People,* pp. 223–261, Little Brown, Boston, 1970.

22. ———, "Role des tests psychologiques de l'intelligence en psychiatrie," *Annales Medico-Psychologiques, 108*:585–606, 1950.

23. KANNER, L., *Child Psychiatry,* pp. 1–735, Charles C Thomas, Springfield, Ill., 1972.

24. KLAPMAN, H., and BAKER, F. B., "The Task Force Treatment: Intensified Use of the Milieu for the Severely Disturbed Child," *American Journal of Occupational Therapy, 17*:239, 1963.

25. KNIGHT, D., "The Role of Varied Therapies in the Rehabilitation of the Retarded Child: Occupational Therapy," *American Journal of Mental Deficiency, 61*:508, 1957.

26. LASHLEY, K. S., *Brain Mechanisms and Intelligence. A Quantitative Study of Injuries to the Brain,* Hafner Publishing, New York, 1964.

27. LAUX, W., "Zur Genese der Angst nach Wirrtraumen bei Kindern," *Zeitschrift für Psychotherapie und Medico-Psychologie, 15(1)*:31–38, 1965.

28. LUBORSKY, L., "Research Problems in Psychotherapy: A Three-Year Follow-Up," in Strupp, H., and Luborsky, L. (Eds.), *Research in Psychotherapy, Proceedings of a Conference,* Chapel Hill, N.C., May 1961, Baltimore, French Bray, 1962.

29. LUTZ, J., and PROBST, H., "Uber Psychische Folgen des Schadelbruchs im Kindesalter," *Zeitschrift für Kinderpsychiatrie, 15*:173–192, 1949.

30. MALLARIVE, J., and BOUGEOIS, M., "L'enfant hyperkinetique. Aspects psychopathologiques," *Annales Medico-Psychologiques, 134*:107–119, 1976.

31. MANNONI, M., *The Backward Child and His Mother: A Psychoanalytic Study,* Random House, New York, 1972.

32. MERENDA, P. F., et al., "Cross-cultural Perceptions of the Ideal Self-concept," *International Review of Applied Psychology, 18*:129, 1969.

33. MONKMAN, M. M. *A Milieu Therapy Program for Behaviorally Disturbed Children,* Charles C Thomas, Springfield, Ill., 1972.

34. MURSTEIN, B. I., *Handbook of Projective Techniques,* Basic Books, New York, 1965.

35. PALMER, J. O., *The Psychological Assessment of Children,* John Wiley, New York, 1961.

36. PAYNE, J. S., MERCER, C. D., and EPSTEIN, M. H., *Education and Rehabilitation Techniques,* Behavioral Publications, New York, 1974.

37. PHILIPS, I., "Children, Mental Retardation and Emotional Disorder," in Philips, I. (Ed.), *Prevention and Treatment of Mental Retardation,* pp. 1–463, Basic Books, New York, 1966.

38. RUBIN, J. R., and KLINEMAN, J., "They Opened Our Eyes: The Story of an Exploratory Art Program for Visually Impaired Multiply-Handicapped Children," *Education of the Visually Handicapped, 6*:106–113, 1974.

39. SARASON, S., *Psychological Problems in Mental Deficiency,* Harper & Row, New York, 1959.

40. SCHIEFELBUSH, R. L., and LLOYD, L. L., *Language Perspectives—Acquisition, Retardation and Intervention,* University Park Press, Baltimore, 1974.

41. SOLNIT, A. J., and STARK, M. H., "Mourning and the Birth of a Defective Child," in Eissler, R. S., et al. (Eds.), *The Psychoanalytic Study of the Child,* vol. 16, p. 523, International Universities Press, New York, 1961.

42. STERNLICHT, M., "Psychotherapeutic Techniques Useful with the Mentally Retarded: A Review and Critique," *Psychiatric Quarterly, 39*:84, 1965.

43. STEWART, M., and OLDS, S. W., *Raising a Hyperactive Child,* Harper & Row, New York, 1973.

44. STOCK, D., "An Investigation into the Interrelations Between the Self-concept and Feelings Directed Toward Other Persons and Groups," *Journal of Consulting Psychology, 13*:176, 1949.

45. YATES, A. J., "The Validity of Some Psychological Tests," in Smith, W. L., and Philippus, M. J. (Eds.), *Neuropsychological Testing in Organic Brain Dysfunction,* pp. 1–337, Charles C Thomas, Springfield, Ill., 1969.

Jackson, D. D., 118, 119, 121, 132
Jacobs, L., 149
Jakab, I., 629, 633, 634, 637, 663–673
James, W., 484
Janet, P., 109
Jarrett, M. C., 301
Jelliffe, D. B., 464
Jelliffe, E. F. D., 464
Jenkins, R. L., 540
Jersild, A., 334, 336
Jesness, C. F., 550
Johnson, A. M., 506, 544
Johnson, C. A., 189
Johnson, G., 630
Johnston, M. S. H., 69, 197
Jolly, J., 477
Jones, 548-549
Jones, B. H., 145–146
Jones, M., 14, 219, 550
Jones, M. C., 13–14, 84, 100
Jones, R., 337
Josselyn, I. M., 37, 171, 540
Juhrs, P. D., 563
Jurjevich, R. R., 545, 547

Kaffman, M., 69, 530, 535
Kalinowsky, L. B., 410
Kanner, L., 300, 366, 409, 417, 418, 555, 562, 629, 654
Kaplan, D. M., 123, 134, 481
Kaplan, D. N., 528, 532, 535
Kaplan, L., 308–309
Kasoff, A. L., 549
Katan, A., 149, 485
Katkovsky, W., 69
Katz, P., 540
Katz, R. C., 189
Kaufman, I., 546
Kaufman, J., 540, 545
Kaufman, R., 576
Kaufman, S. H., 422
Kant, I., 72
Kazdin, A., 89
Keeney, A. H., 412
Kernberg, O. F., 275
Kernberg, P. F., 619, 621
Kellogg, R., 422
Kemph, J. P., 557
Kennell, J., 480
Kephart, N. C., 617, 623
Kessler, J. W., 5
Kestenberg, 145
Kety, S. S., 3, 377
Kier, A., 434, 442
Kimmel, E., 96
Kimmel, H. D., 96
King, P. D., 557
Kirsner, D. A., 336

Klagsbrun, S., 4
Klaus, M., 480
Kleeman, J. A., 461
Klein, D., 642
Klein, D. F., 9, 401
Klein, M., 14, 16, 23–24, 26, 31, 35, 418
Knesper, D. C., 275, 284
Knievel, E., 544
Knights, R. M., 393
Knobloch, H., 457, 479
Kohlberg, L., 345, 348
Kornreich, M., 55
Kraepelin, E., 376
Kraft, I. A., 159–180
Kramer, C. H., 8, 127–130
Krasner, L., 72, 182
Kratochwill, T. R., 181–192
Kris, E., 150
Kritzberg, N. I., 427, 428
Kurlander, L. F., 621

La Franchi, S., 559
Laing, R. D., 119
Lambert, N. M., 195
Lambo, T. A., 436
Lang, P. J., 83, 84, 93–94
Langford, W. S., 366, 367
Lansing, C., 165, 561–562
Langsley, D. G., 123, 134, 525, 528, 532, 535
Lazarus, A. A., 6, 72, 79, 85, 198
LaVietes, R. L., 298, 315, 562–563
Lay, T., 542
Lee, J., 234
Lehrer, P., 275
Lehtinen, L. E., 622
Leiderman, P. H., 481
LePierre, K., 127, 130
Lessem, L., 281
Lessing, E. E., 69
Lesser, S. R., 644, 651–663
Lester, E. P., 63
Levine, E. .S, 659
Levine, F. M., 104
Levine, M., 671
Levine, S. V., 201
Levitt, E. E., 9, 55, 200
Levy, D., 366
Levy, D. M., 36, 58, 420
Liddell, H. S., 74–75
Lidz, T., 119, 123
Liébeault, A.-A., 109
Lifton, N., 562
Lincoln, A., 376
Lindsley, O. R., 72
Lindemann, E., 520, 522, 525, 642
Linder, R., 647

Linton, R., 437
Lipman, R. S., 377n
Lippman, H. S., 36, 537
Lipton, H. R., 543
Locke, J., 72
London, P., 104, 105
Long, N. J., 195, 198
Long, N., 346
Looker, A., 396
Lorenz, K., 477
Lourie, R., 637, 638
Lovaas, O. I., 102, 103, 555, 558, 559, 640
Lowe, L., 555
Luborsky, L., 9, 17
Lucas, A. R., 409–413
Lindemann, E., 58
Luria, A. R., 80
Luthe, W., 91, 92

McAndrew, J. B., 388
McCord, A. A., 447
McCord, J., 550
McCord, W., 550
McCorkle, F. W., 549
McDermott, J. F., 6, 8, 13, 366, 569
McDermott, J. F., Jr., 433–444
McGee, J. P., 72–107
MacGregor, R., 119, 123
Machover, K., 422
McLaren, A., 466n
McRee, C., 164–165
Maddux, J. F., 354
Maher, B. A., 69
Mahler, M. A., 462, 468, 544, 555, 557
Makkay, E. S., 540, 545
Malan, D. H., 9, 56
Maler, L., 577
Malmquist, C. P., 531
Malone, C. A., 8
Mandell, A. J., 9
Marcus, I. D., 46
Marcus, I. M., 425
Marks, I. M., 6, 75
Marschak, M., 461
Marshall, R. J., 536–554
Maslow, A., 194, 195, 557
Mason, 366
Mason, E. A., 481
Masserman, J., 632
Massie, H., 478
Massimo, J. L., 542, 547
Masterson, J. F., 176, 275, 280, 544, 547
Mattsson, A., 524
Mattox, B. A., 345–346
May, R., 195
Mayer, M. F., 235
Mayhy, W. D., 187
Mead, M., 436, 437
Mednick, S., 93

Meeks, J. E., 47
Mees, H., 558
Meichenbaum, D. H., 101–102
Melamed, B. G., 83, 93–94
Meltzer, H. Y., 377
Meltzoff, J., 55
Melzack, R., 368
Menninger, K. A., 216, 629, 633
Menninger, W., 216
Menolascino, F., 636
Mesmer, F. A., 36, 109
Merlis, S., 386, 387
Meyer, A., 72–73
Meyr, R. G., 174–175
Mikkelson, E. J., 391
Millar, S., 418
Miller, D., 284
Miller, G., 335
Miller, L. C., 538, 549
Miller, N., 5
Miller, N. E., 72, 91, 92
Millichap, J. G., 615
Minde, K. K., 168, 577, 644
Minge, M. R., 88
Minuchin, S., 125, 129, 131–133, 334, 576
Mira, M., 189
Mirsky, I. A., 578
Mitchell, 119
Montalvo, B., 124
Moreno, J. C., 427
Morrison, G. C., 519–536
Morse, W. C., 195, 333–352
Moskowitz, J. A., 430
Moustakas, C. E., 194, 198
Mowrer, O. H., 5, 14, 95–98
Munger, R., 351
Murphy, L. B., 477, 522
Murphy, M. A., 260
Murphy, 457
Myklebust, H. R., 659

Nash, H., 399n
Nebl, N., 69
Neill, A. S., 547
Nelson, K., 474
Nelson, M. C., 544
Newman, M. R., 46
Newman, R. G., 195
Nielson, G. H., 164
Nir, Y., 313
Norman, S., 551
Noshpitz, J. D., 6, 229, 278
Nottage, W., 549
Nover, R. A., 573